CRIMINAL PROCEDURES:
PROSECUTION AND ADJUDICATION

Read collateral estoppel
Read 273

ASPEN PUBLISHERS

CRIMINAL PROCEDURES: PROSECUTION AND ADJUDICATION

Cases, Statutes, and Executive Materials

Third Edition

MARC L. MILLER
Ralph W. Bilby Professor of Law
The University of Arizona James E. Rogers College of Law

RONALD F. WRIGHT
Professor of Law
Wake Forest University School of Law

Wolters Kluwer
Law & Business

AUSTIN BOSTON CHICAGO NEW YORK THE NETHERLANDS

Aspen Publishers
Attn: Permissions Department
76 Ninth Avenue, 7th Floor
New York, NY 10011-5201

To contact Customer Care, e-mail customer.care@aspenpublishers.com,
call 1-800-234-1660, fax 1-800-901-9075, or mail correspondence to:

Aspen Publishers
Attn: Order Department
PO Box 990
Frederick, MD 21705

Printed in the United States of America.

1 2 3 4 5 6 7 8 9 0

ISBN 978-07355-6980-5

Library of Congress Cataloging-in-Publication Data

Miller, Marc (Marc Louis)
    Criminal procedures: prosecution and adjudication cases, statutes, and executive
    materials / Marc L. Miller, Ronald F. Wright. — 3rd ed.
        p. cm.
    Includes bibliographical references and index.
    ISBN 978-0-7355-6980-5
    1. Criminal procedure — United States — Cases. I. Wright, Ronald F., 1959- II. Title.

KF9618.M524 2007
345.73'05 — dc22

2007024166

About Wolters Kluwer Law & Business

Wolters Kluwer Law & Business is a leading provider of research information and workflow solutions in key specialty areas. The strengths of the individual brands of Aspen Publishers, CCH, Kluwer Law International and Loislaw are aligned within Wolters Kluwer Law & Business to provide comprehensive, in-depth solutions and expert-authored content for the legal, professional and education markets.

CCH was founded in 1913 and has served more than four generations of business professionals and their clients. The CCH products in the Wolters Kluwer Law & Business group are highly regarded electronic and print resources for legal, securities, antitrust and trade regulation, government contracting, banking, pensions, payroll, employment and labor, and healthcare reimbursement and compliance professionals.

Aspen Publishers is a leading information provider for attorneys, business professionals and law students. Written by preeminent authorities, Aspen products offer analytical and practical information in a range of specialty practice areas from securities law and intellectual property to mergers and acquisitions and pension/benefits. Aspen's trusted legal education resources provide professors and students with high-quality, up-to-date and effective resources for successful instruction and study in all areas of the law.

Kluwer Law International supplies the global business community with comprehensive English-language international legal information. Legal practitioners, corporate counsel and business executives around the world rely on the Kluwer Law International journals, loose-leafs, books and electronic products for authoritative information in many areas of international legal practice.

Loislaw is a premier provider of digitized legal content to small law firm practitioners of various specializations. Loislaw provides attorneys with the ability to quickly and efficiently find the necessary legal information they need, when and where they need it, by facilitating access to primary law as well as state-specific law, records, forms and treatises.

Wolters Kluwer Law & Business, a unit of Wolters Kluwer, is headquartered in New York and Riverwoods, Illinois. Wolters Kluwer is a leading multinational publisher and information services company.

For our fathers, Howard Miller and Ronald Wright.

Summary of Contents

Contents

PART TWO

■

RESOLVING GUILT AND INNOCENCE   279

PART THREE
■

MEASURING PUNISHMENT AND REASSESSING GUILT   627

Preface

The American criminal justice system is huge, complex, and varied. Federal, state, and local governments together spend around $200 billion each year on policing, prosecution, trial, and punishment. More than 1.5 million prisoners serve time in federal and state prisons, as measured by year-end counts. If prisoners in local jails, juvenile facilities, and certain other specialized settings are included in the total, well over 2.3 million persons are incarcerated in the United States at any one time. Another 5 million are on probation or parole.

There are more than 15,000 separate police agencies in the United States, with around 800,000 sworn officers. There are even more "private police" and security agents. In an average year, these officers and agents make more than 14 million arrests.

Criminal cases are prosecuted by more than 2,400 prosecutors' offices, employing about 35,000 attorneys and more than 50,000 additional staff. They obtain about 1 million felony convictions every year, and even more misdemeanor convictions. Thousands of attorneys work as public defenders or as defense counsel in private practice. Thousands of judges hear cases in trial and appellate courts. Lawyers often find their first jobs in the criminal justice system. Some stay for life.

Criminal procedure is the body of law governing this collection of systems. The law of criminal procedure directs — or at least attempts to direct — the actions of police officers, prosecutors, defense attorneys, judges, and other government officials. Criminal procedure limits the way the government may interact with citizens, suspects, defendants, convicted offenders, and victims.

The federal government, every state government, and many local governments operate criminal justice systems. They all spend time, effort, and money each year running and reshaping their respective systems. There is no one criminal procedure: Each system follows its own set of rules, controlled to different degrees by outside authorities. Procedural rules come from many sources, including constitutions, legislatures, courts, and executive branch agencies. Because the issues of criminal procedure are common and accessible—unlike, say, antitrust law—a wealth of less formal constraints, including community views and the media, also shape procedure. We have titled this casebook "Criminal Procedures" to reflect these multiple layers and sources of law.

The Approach in This Casebook

A criminal procedure casebook must impose some order on the morass of cases, rules, and practices that characterize criminal justice systems. One accepted way to make this material accessible for newcomers is to focus on the role of one important institution, the United States Supreme Court, and on one important source of law, the United States Constitution.

Since the days of the Warren Court, starting in 1953, the Supreme Court has influenced criminal justice systems in profound ways. It made the Bill of Rights in the federal Constitution a shaping force for every criminal justice system. The Warren Court made the story of criminal procedure, told from the point of view of the Supreme Court, compelling. Decisions of the Court created a basic framework for providing defendants with counsel and for conducting criminal trials. For years, the focus on the Supreme Court's constitutional rulings guided students through the questions that most concerned judges and lawyers.

But the story of this one institution has shown less explanatory power as time passes. Traditional issues on the Court's constitutional criminal procedure docket now occupy less of the attention of judges, attorneys, defendants, victims, and others concerned with criminal justice. Most criminal defendants do not go to trial. These defendants and their lawyers care about pretrial detention, the charges filed, the plea agreements they can reach with the prosecutor, and their sentences.

The central questions have shifted in light of changes in the workload, politics, funding, and structure of criminal justice institutions. For example, the question of *whether* indigent defendants will get counsel has become a question of *what* counsel they will get. For judges, sentencing questions in particular have attained higher priority: Determining the proper sentence in some systems now requires more time from court personnel than resolution of guilt or innocence.

The U.S. Supreme Court leaves important dimensions of most procedural issues unresolved and thus leaves other institutions free to innovate; they have done so. The issues of current importance in criminal procedure are being shaped in multiple institutions, including state courts, legislatures, and executive branch agencies.

This book adopts a panoramic view of criminal procedure, emphasizing the interaction among, and variety within, criminal justice systems. In our opinion, students in an upper-level course such as criminal procedure can and should move beyond the skills of case synthesis and beyond the ability to appreciate the role of only one institution. Our materials emphasize the following themes and objectives.

- *Procedural variety.* In each area we present competing rules from the federal and state systems. We also occasionally examine procedures from earlier times or from non-U.S. systems. Reviewing different possible procedural rules encourages critical analysis and helps identify the assumptions held and judgments made in the design of each criminal system.

- *Materials from multiple institutions.* In addition to leading U.S. Supreme Court cases, we make extensive use of state high court cases, statutes, rules of procedure, and police and prosecutorial policies, and we encourage readers to consider the interactions among multiple institutions. Examining the efforts of different institutions to achieve similar goals highlights the reality of procedural innovation and reform.

- *Real-world perspective.* We focus on procedures and issues of current importance to defendants, lawyers, courts, legislators, and the public. We devote the most attention to the issues arising in the largest number of cases.

- *Street-level federalism.* Federal law, typically in the form of constitutional decisions by the U.S. Supreme Court, still plays an important role in guiding the prosecution of high-volume street crimes. The impact of abstract constitutional doctrine on daily courtroom reality raises important theoretical questions about federal-state relations and interactions among jurisdictions and governmental institutions.

- *Political context.* Materials trace the political environment surrounding different institutions and issues. We explore the impact of public concerns such as terrorism, drug trafficking, domestic abuse, and treatment of crime victims on procedural rules. Funding decisions with regard to criminal justice systems also offer a window into the political setting.

- *Impact of procedures.* We consider the effects that different procedures have on lawyers, courts, communities, defendants, and victims. We emphasize primary materials but include social science studies as well, especially when they have been the basis for procedural reform. This perspective keeps in mind the managerial needs of criminal justice: Any legal rule must apply to multitudes of defendants in overcrowded systems.

By studying the various ways in which state and local systems have answered crucial procedural questions, students become aware of a broader range of policy alternatives. They form a more complete picture of the complex and interactive workings of the criminal justice system. Our goal in emphasizing the variety within criminal procedure is to produce lawyers who know both the current law and the way to shape better law down the road.

Conceptual Anchors

Our emphasis on variety does not mean that we will survey the practices of all 50 states on each issue; this casebook is not a treatise. Rather, the materials highlight the majority and minority views on each topic, as well as the federal view. The major positions on a topic are usually summarized in the first note following the principal materials. Truly distinctive answers to problems are mentioned occasionally as a point of comparison with the leading approach, but the uniqueness of the position is always highlighted.

The book addresses a wide range of U.S. Supreme Court precedents, including the recognized core of essential cases and many of the most recent important decisions. State supreme court decisions summarizing and critiquing a U.S.

Supreme Court decision, or a line of cases, represent effective teaching tools since the state cases tend to highlight the competing doctrinal positions. State supreme court opinions by and large reflect less interest in the positions of individual justices than do U.S. Supreme Court decisions and less attention to questions about consistency with past decisions. State supreme court opinions often provide provocative settings that show how principles operate in practice. They tend to present succinctly the textual and institutional arguments favoring a procedural requirement, the values furthered by the rules, and their likely effects on police, suspects, and communities. State courts vary by jurisdiction and issue in the extent to which they respect, reject, or sidestep federal constitutional doctrine.

Studying a variety of possible answers to important procedural questions has an unexpected effect: through criticism and contrast it provides students with a firmer grasp of the federal approach, including current federal constitutional criminal procedure, than does presentation of federal law alone. Students become better equipped to understand what is truly important about the current norms. Short "problems" throughout the book also enable readers to apply and integrate basic concepts.

The state cases appearing in this book take every conceivable position with respect to Supreme Court precedent, ranging from total agreement to complete rejection, and encompassing subtle variations in interpretation and emphasis. For a large number of state cases that focus on state constitutional or statutory questions, the position of the U.S. Supreme Court is simply irrelevant. The case selection does not favor decisions merely because they reject the U.S. Supreme Court view—the "new federalism" approach. These materials are not a battle cry for state court independence; they simply reflect the vibrancy of state supreme courts and state law.

The Third Edition

The third edition of this book is a response to changes in the field, incorporating emerging themes and major issues. Such themes and issues—the turning points in the law—result at least as often from dramatic events outside the courtroom as from blockbuster judicial decisions. Such dramatic and unexpected "drivers" of change in criminal procedure over the decade since the first edition of this book appeared include increasing attention to issues of race and the "innocence" projects that have revealed strings of wrongful convictions. The third edition continues to explore the legal echoes within domestic criminal procedure of the attacks on September 11, 2001, and the ongoing war on terrorism.

We have made changes in every chapter. Some of those changes reflect actual shifts in doctrine, while others are the result of suggestions by teachers and students about cases and materials that worked well in the classroom, and others that might be improved.

Our attention to developments in the states provides a large pool of new cases, statutes, and rules to draw from, keeping the discussion anchored to current reality in criminal justice. For example, many of the cases in this book were decided after 2000. The overall goal of these changes has been to produce a book that remains fresh and engaging.

The "Bail to Jail" Course

This volume surveys the laws and practices at work between the time a person is charged and the time the courts resolve the offender's conviction and sentence. The upper-level law school course devoted to these subjects is often titled "Advanced Criminal Procedure" or "Criminal Procedure II," and sometimes goes by the more revealing shorthand name "bail to jail."

On first glance this course focuses on the criminal process once lawyers enter the picture. One of the definitive features of the criminal process from the point when the police recommend charges is that lawyers — prosecutors, defense lawyers, and judges — operate the system. Lawyers may use rules to constrain one another in ways they cannot constrain nonlawyers.

On closer examination, most of the major themes in this volume revolve around prosecutors. (In contrast, the police are the principal institutional focus of most introductory criminal procedure courses.) We consider the broad power of line prosecutors in selecting and resolving criminal charges, the power of supervising prosecutors to structure the work of line prosecutors, and the centrality of plea bargaining rather than trials in resolving charges. Other topics in this volume that highlight the importance of prosecutors include the interconnections between plea bargaining and sentencing rules and the ongoing influence of racial differences in criminal adjudication.

These materials also devote attention to the capacity of *detailed* procedural rules to achieve justice (as opposed to the use of more generalized standards typical in situations involving the work of police). One of the striking themes of these materials is the interplay between the recognition of formal rules and rights, for example constitutional and statutory trial rights, and the realities of money and organizational life that leave so little room for these formal rules to operate in criminal justice systems.

The materials throughout this volume address interrelated themes; criminal procedure is a relatively coherent field. It is not necessary, however, to study the materials on police practices before those on adjudication. Within each course, the teacher can approach topics from a variety of perspectives and using a number of different doctrinal starting points. Students should not be surprised if their professor presents the chapters in an order different from the one we have used or adds chapters, cases, or other materials to the course.

Procedure, Politics, and Reform

This book reminds readers regularly about the political environment shaping the work of every institutional actor in criminal justice. The materials consider the changing political priorities that make enforcement especially urgent for certain criminal laws — those punishing drug trafficking, environmental crimes, and sexual assault, to name a few. Such high-priority enforcement efforts influence criminal procedure more generally. Terrorism is the newest and most tragic law enforcement priority, and we consider the potential impact of new approaches and doctrines aimed at terrorists on domestic criminal procedure and the implications for more typical crimes.

The theme of jurisdictional and institutional variation draws critical attention to the role of states, whose systems handle 94 percent of the felonies prosecuted in the United States. But while the federal and state systems are the most appropriate levels at which to consider constitutional and statutory constraints, the local level is the true locus of criminal justice power. It is also the place where criminal justice systems in the United States engage most citizens. There are roughly 3,000 counties in the United States, including 254 in Texas and 168 in Georgia.

The local foundations of discretionary power in U.S. criminal justice systems are reflected in the funding for those systems. Just over half of all criminal justice funding comes from the local level, just over 30 percent from the state level, and just under 20 percent from the federal level. But funding is not spread evenly across system components. Police services are primarily funded at the local level, prisons are funded at the state level, and the costs of prosecution and adjudication are funded primarily at both the local and state levels. While there has been much legal and public debate over the 30-year expansion in the federal prosecution of what traditionally would have been local drug offenses, the bulk of federal investigation and prosecution still targets a more limited class of crimes, including immigration offenses, bank robbery, and large-scale fraud.

Students who appreciate the handful of basic political struggles that time and again shape procedural debates will be better able to direct changes in the system and to influence decisions in close cases. The struggles center on questions such as these: What are the purposes of the criminal justice system? In particular, what is the relevance of criminal law and procedure to the social goals of crime control and prevention? How does the theory and practice of federalism inform criminal justice theory and practice? Can we trust the police? How vital is the adversary system and the role of defense counsel to the success of that system? Are we comfortable with the broad discretion exercised on a daily basis by police and prosecutors? How important is it to treat suspects similarly? Should we explicitly consider the costs of procedures?

The priorities inherent in this textbook suggest a return to the study of criminal procedure as a genuine procedure course, not a course in constitutional adjudication. The constitutional component remains an indispensable part of the course but is not the sum total of criminal procedure.

The return to a fuller conception of criminal procedure offers enormous opportunities to those who study the system and to those who will soon participate in its operation and evolution. When many institutions are able to shape a legal system, there are many opportunities for change. We hope each student will leave this course with a sense of the drama and the special challenges of each case and of the entire process. We hope each student will finish school ready to create procedures more sound than those that exist today.

Marc Miller
Ron Wright

Tucson, Arizona
Winston-Salem, North Carolina
May 2007

Acknowledgments

Creating a new edition of this book powerfully reminded us of how communities make work more fun and make final products better. Our debts extend to our friends and colleagues, our institutions, our students, our teachers, and our families.

Advice from colleagues around the country came at many stages. Special appreciation goes to Doug Berman, Steve Easton, Alan Michaels, Jim Jacobs, Sandra Guerra Thompson, and David Yellen, who offered periodic suggestions as they taught from the book. We have also learned from two extensive published reviews of this book. See Robert Weisberg, A New Legal Realism for Criminal Procedure, 49 Buff. L. Rev. 909 (2001), and Stephanos Bibas, The Real-World Shift in Criminal Procedure, J. Crim. L. & Criminology (Winter 2003).

Some of the teachers who use this book contact us on occasion to suggest improvements for future editions. They include Laura Appleman, Frank Bowman, Darryl Brown, Steve Chanenson, Jack Chin, Jennifer Collins, Nancy Gertner, Sam Kamin, Kay Levine, Dan Markel, Tracey Meares, Tommy Miller, Kenneth Nunn, Kami Simmons, Jonathan Simon, Shandrea Solomon, Kate Stith, Paul Stokstad, and Andrew Taslitz.

Scholars who provided wise counsel on earlier editions, which is still very evident in the revised volume, include Albert Alschuler, Akhil Amar, Barbara Babcock, Adolph Dean, Nora Demleitner, George Fisher, Dan Freed, Mark Hall, Mark Harris, Lenese Herbert, Andrew Kull, Gerard Lynch, William Mayton, David Orentlicher, Leonard Orland, Alan Palmiter, Anne Poulin, Aaron Rappaport, Sadiq Reza, Natsu Saito, Stephen Schulhofer, Charles Shanor, Rick Singer, Michael Smith, Charles Weisselberg, Bert Westbrook, and Deborah Young.

We have both been graced with great teachers, all of whom became friends. We can trace in these pages the influence of Norval Morris, Frank Zimring, Edward Levi, Richard Epstein, Philip Kurland, David Currie, James Boyd White, Owen Fiss,

Robert Burt, Peter Schuck, Steven Duke, and Judges Frank Johnson and John Godbold.

Over the years we have worked on this project with many fine students whose energy renewed our own. They include Liz Asplund, Amber Byers, Pablo Clarke, Don Donelson, Ben Durie, Heather Gaw, Jennifer Gibbons, Elizabeth Goodwin, Whitney Hendrix, Emily Parish, Russ Rotondi, and Rebecca Stahl. Exceptional research help on earlier editions came from Roger Abramson, Nathan Adams, Wes Camden, Sean Monaghan, Tyronia Morrison, Alice Shanlever, and Daniel Terner.

We have made heavy demands on our home institutions, our libraries and technology experts. We appreciate the continued support of our deans, Toni Massaro (at Arizona), Bob Walsh (who is retiring after 18 years at the helm of Wake Forest), and Blake Morant (who is leading Wake Forest into its next phase). We owe special thanks for the third edition to Sarah Gotschall. Bibliographic help with earlier editions came from Marcia Baker, Terry Gordon, Will Haines, Deborah Keene, Holliday Osborne, John Perkins, Lori Levy, William Morse, Stuart Myerberg, and Erika Wayne. Steve Turner, the director of the Wilsonville, Oregon, public library, helped us achieve greater clarity throughout the book. Kristie Gallardo, Barbara Lopez, Beverly Marshall, Radine Robinson, and Marissa White provided timely administrative support for this edition and earlier ones: It is a miracle they did not ask to work with faculty other than us.

We also have debts to many of the hard-working and visionary lawyers in the criminal justice system. A few who provided special assistance are Harry Connick and Tim McElroy of the District Attorney's office in New Orleans; Numa Bertel of the Orleans Indigent Defender Program; Judge Camille Buras of the District Court in New Orleans; Lawson Lamar and William Vose of the State Attorney's office in Orange County, Florida; and Patricia Jessamy of the State's Attorney's office in Baltimore, Maryland. We appreciate the willingness of police departments and prosecutorial and defender's offices to give us copies of their policies and manuals. We have also gained insight from our conversations with skilled reporters and criminal justice reformers, including Kevin Corcoran.

Family debts for so consuming a project are hard to recognize in print, and even harder to repay in life. Joanna Wright (age 17), ever the curious one, shows an interest in everything from exclusionary rules to font sizes. Andrew Wright (19) keeps reminding us that justice for real people must be the bottom line for any legal procedure. Owen Miller (4) is full of questions about everything, starting with the basics: "What is a bad guy?" and "Why do police officers carry guns?" Evelyn Miller (10 months) is still focused on questions of even a more fundamental nature. Conversations with our brothers Travis Wright, who is a police officer, and Craig Miller, who for years worked on justice reform projects and now teaches inner-city high school students history and government, helped us remember that criminal procedure rules guide the behavior of people in very different settings. Other family members (especially Alex Miller, Renata Miller, Katy Miller, Denis Wright, Kyung Ah Wright, and the Ohlingers and Mannings) read parts of the manuscript and forgave us for the piles of papers and disks at every family gathering.

Our parents have been our teachers, our friends, and our models. Ron's father, Ronald F. Wright, Sr., died when Ron was a law student, but his energy and optimism pervade this book. Marc's father, Howard, for many years a law professor, provided steady advice from beginning to end. Our mothers, Marian and Shirley, showed a confidence that helped us keep our destination in mind when work seemed nothing but roads.

This book sits between covers only because of the daily encouragement and advice of Amy Wright and Christina Cutshaw. Putting up with writing projects is not part of the wedding vows; perhaps it should be.

Albert Alschuler, Implementing the Criminal Defendant's Right to Trial: Alternatives to the Plea Bargaining System, 50 U. Chi. L. Rev. 931 (1983). Copyright © 1983 by the University of Chicago Law Review. Reprinted with permission.

Paul Butler, Racially Based Jury Nullification: Black Power in the Criminal Justice System, 105 Yale L.J. 677 (1995). Copyright © 1995 by The Yale Law Journal Company. Reprinted by permission of The Yale Law Journal Company and Fred B. Rothman & Company.

Frank Easterbrook, Plea Bargaining as Compromise, 101 Yale L.J. 1969 (1992). Copyright © 1992 by The Yale Law Journal Company. Reprinted by permission of The Yale Law Journal Company and Fred B. Rothman & Company.

Victor E. Flango, Habeas Corpus in State and Federal Courts (1994). Copyright © 1994 by the National Center for State Courts. Reprinted with permission.

Fully Informed Jury Association, Jurors Handbook: A Citizen's Guide to Jury Duty (last modified Feb. 2, 1997), http://www.fija.org/juror-handbook.htm. Reprinted by permission of die Fully Informed Jury Association.

John Kaplan, Defending Guilty People, 7 U. Bridgeport L. Rev. 223 (1986). Copyright © 1986 by the University of Bridgeport Law Review Association. Reprinted by permission of the Quinnipiac Law Review.

Dale Parent, Structuring Criminal Sentences: The Evolution of Minnesota's Sentencing Guidelines (1988). Copyright © 1988 by Butterworth Legal Publishers. Reprinted with permission from LEXIS Law Publishing, Charlottesville, VA (800) 446-3410. All Rights Reserved.

Reena Raggi, Local Concerns, Local Insights, 5 Fed. Sent'g Rep. 306 (1993). Copyright © 1993, Vera Institute of Justice. Reprinted with permission of the author.

Lawrence W. Sherman and Richard A. Berk, The Minneapolis Domestic Violence Experiment. Washington, D.C., Police Foundation, 1984. Reprinted with permission of the Police Foundation.

Walter Steele & Elizabeth Thornburgh, Jury Instructions: A Persistent Failure to Communicate, 67 N.C. L. Rev. 77 (1988). Copyright © 1988, North Carolina Law Review Association. Reprinted with permission.

Michael Tonry, The Sentencing Commission and Its Guidelines, in The Sentencing Commission and Its Guidelines by Andrew von Hirsch, Kay A. Knapp, and Michael Tonry. Copyright © 1987 by Andrew von Hirsch, Kay Knapp, and Michael Tonry. Reprinted with the permission of Northeastern University Press.

Barbara Underwood, Ending Race Discrimination in Jury Selection: Whose Right Is It, Anyway? 92 Colum. L. Rev. 725 (1992). Reprinted by permission of the author and the Columbia Law Review.

Vera Institute of Justice, Fair Treatment for the Indigent: The Manhattan Bail
    Project, in Ten-Year Report, 1961-1971. Reprinted by permission of Vera
    Institute of Justice, Inc.
Ronald Wright & Marc Miller, The Screening/Bargaining Tradeoff, 55 Stan. L. Rev.
    29 (2002). Copyright © 2002 by the Board of Trustees of the Leland Stanford
    Junior University. Reprinted with permission.

CRIMINAL PROCEDURES:
PROSECUTION AND ADJUDICATION

PART ONE

EVALUATING CHARGES

I

Defense Counsel

During the earliest phases of the criminal process, defense lawyers are rarely to be seen. But as the prosecution and police formulate and file charges against some suspects, and as the courts begin to process those charges, defense counsel become involved.

In this chapter, we introduce the various sources of law that make it possible for a criminal defendant to get a lawyer. We also consider the practical value of these legal entitlements to the ordinary criminal defendant. Does having an attorney really matter to defendants? What do defense lawyers do? Can you imagine a criminal justice system without them?

A. WHEN WILL COUNSEL BE PROVIDED?

Not every person charged with a crime consults a lawyer. The most common reason for a defendant to face charges alone, without a lawyer, is financial — defendants often cannot afford counsel. But our legal systems have not left matters there. The same government that pays the judge, the prosecutor, and the investigators will also (at least in some cases) pay for the defendant's lawyer.

The question that has persisted over many decades is when the state will pay for defense counsel and when it will not. Some cases involve charges that are not serious enough to require counsel; some proceedings are too early or late in the process to require counsel. This section reviews the law on (1) the types of charges necessary to invoke constitutional and statutory rights to counsel and (2) the points in criminal proceedings when a defendant can expect to consult with counsel.

1. Types of Charges

Constitutions have much to say about the availability of defense counsel. The Sixth Amendment to the federal constitution states that "In all criminal prosecutions, the accused shall enjoy the right . . . to have the assistance of counsel for his defence." Almost every state constitution has an equivalent provision.

The most important early decision regarding the Sixth Amendment right to counsel was Powell v. Alabama, 287 U.S. 45 (1932). The defendants were nine young black men who were accused of raping two young white women on a train near Scottsboro, Alabama. The case against the defendants attracted much local attention: Soldiers escorted the defendants to and from their proceedings to protect them from hostile mobs. None of the defendants was literate, and none was a resident of Alabama.

The defendants were divided into three groups for trial. The first trial began six days after indictment, and each of the three trials was completed within one day. Until the morning of the first trial, the court named no particular lawyer to represent the defendants. The trial judge instead appointed all the members of the Scottsboro bar "for the limited purpose of arraigning" the defendants. Some members of the bar consulted with the defendants in jail, but did nothing further. A colloquy on the morning of the trial left it unclear which attorney, if any, would represent the defendants at trial. An attorney sent from Tennessee by people concerned about the young men's situation was unprepared to serve as lead counsel, but members of the Scottsboro bar were quick to say they would "assist" the newly arrived lawyer. The juries found all the defendants guilty and imposed the death penalty upon each of them.

The Supreme Court concluded that appointment of a primary defense lawyer, at least under these circumstances, was a requirement of due process. The Court made some general observations about the value of legal counsel:

> The right to be heard would be, in many cases, of little avail if it did not comprehend the right to be heard by counsel. Even the intelligent and educated layman has small and sometimes no skill in the science of law. If charged with crime, he is incapable, generally, of determining for himself whether the indictment is good or bad. He is unfamiliar with the rules of evidence. Left without the aid of counsel he may be put on trial without a proper charge, and convicted upon incompetent evidence, or evidence irrelevant to the issue or otherwise inadmissible. He lacks both the skill and knowledge adequately to prepare his defense, even though he had a perfect one. He requires the guiding hand of counsel at every step in the proceedings against him. Without it, though he be not guilty, he faces the danger of conviction because he does not know how to establish his innocence.

287 U.S. at 68-69. The opinion also stressed some of the more compelling facts in the case:

> In the light . . . [of] the ignorance and illiteracy of the defendants, their youth, the circumstances of public hostility, the imprisonment and the close surveillance of the defendants by the military forces, the fact that their friends and families were all in other states and communication with them [was] necessarily difficult, and above all that they stood in deadly peril of their lives, . . . the necessity of counsel was so vital and imperative that the failure of the trial court to make an effective appointment of

counsel was . . . a denial of due process within the meaning of the Fourteenth Amendment. Whether this would be so in other criminal prosecutions, or under other circumstances, we need not determine. . . . In a case such as this, whatever may be the rule in other cases, the right to have counsel appointed, when necessary, is a logical corollary from the constitutional right to be heard by counsel.

287 U.S. at 71. The Scottsboro case became an international *cause célèbre*. A crusading New York lawyer, Samuel Leibowitz, participated in the defense during the second trial, which also ended in the conviction of all defendants by an all-white jury. After the later convictions were overturned on appeal in the state system, the government agreed to a plea agreement allowing for the release of four defendants and prison terms for the other five. See James Goodman, Stories of Scottsboro (1994); Michael J. Klarman, *Powell v. Alabama*: The Supreme Court Confronts "Legal Lynchings," in Criminal Procedure Stories (Carol Steiker ed., 2006).

After a series of later Supreme Court cases considering the right to appointed counsel at trial, Betts v. Brady, 316 U.S. 455 (1942), settled on the "special circumstances" test to govern the appointment of counsel; that is, counsel would be constitutionally required only under "special circumstances," and not in every criminal case. Betts was indicted for robbery. Due to lack of funds, he was unable to employ counsel, and asked the judge to appoint counsel for him. The judge refused because the local practice was to appoint counsel only in prosecutions for murder and rape. Betts then pleaded not guilty and elected to be tried without a jury. Witnesses were summoned in his behalf. He cross-examined the State's witnesses and examined his own alibi witnesses. Betts did not take the witness stand. The judge found him guilty and sentenced him to eight years in prison. The Court concluded that due process did not require the appointment of counsel under these circumstances.

In the following case, the Supreme Court returned to the question of appointed counsel, this time giving a different answer.

■ CLARENCE EARL GIDEON v. LOUIE WAINWRIGHT
372 U.S. 335 (1963)

BLACK, J.

Petitioner was charged in a Florida state court with having broken and entered a poolroom with intent to commit a misdemeanor. This offense is a felony under Florida law. Appearing in court without funds and without a lawyer, petitioner asked the court to appoint counsel for him. [When the Court denied his request, Gideon objected: "The United States Supreme Court says I am entitled to be represented by Counsel."]

Put to trial before a jury, Gideon conducted his defense about as well as could be expected from a layman. He made an opening statement to the jury, cross-examined the State's witnesses, presented witnesses in his own defense, declined to testify himself, and made a short argument "emphasizing his innocence to the charge contained in the Information filed in this case." The jury returned a verdict of guilty, and petitioner was sentenced to serve five years in the state prison. [The state Supreme Court later denied habeas corpus relief.] Since 1942, when Betts v. Brady, 316 U.S. 455, was decided by a divided Court, the problem of a defendant's federal constitutional right to counsel in a state court has been a continuing source of controversy and litigation in both state and federal courts. To give this problem another review here, we granted certiorari. . . .

The facts upon which Betts claimed that he had been unconstitutionally denied the right to have counsel appointed to assist him are strikingly like the facts upon which Gideon here bases his federal constitutional claim. Betts was indicted for robbery in a Maryland state court. On arraignment, . . . Betts was advised that it was not the practice in that county to appoint counsel for indigent defendants except in murder and rape cases. He then pleaded not guilty, had witnesses summoned, cross-examined the State's witnesses, examined his own, and chose not to testify himself. He was found guilty by the judge, sitting without a jury. [Upon review of the conviction, this Court] held that a refusal to appoint counsel for an indigent defendant charged with a felony did not necessarily violate the Due Process Clause of the Fourteenth Amendment. . . . The Court said: "Asserted denial [of due process] is to be tested by an appraisal of the totality of facts in a given case. That which may, in one setting, constitute a denial of fundamental fairness, shocking to the universal sense of justice, may, in other circumstances . . . fall short of such denial." [316 U.S. at 462.]

Treating due process as "a concept less rigid and more fluid than those envisaged in other specific and particular provisions of the Bill of Rights," the Court held that refusal to appoint counsel under the particular facts and circumstances in the Betts case was not so "offensive to the common and fundamental ideas of fairness" as to amount to a denial of due process. Since the facts and circumstances of the two cases are so nearly indistinguishable, we think the Betts v. Brady holding if left standing would require us to reject Gideon's claim that the Constitution guarantees him the assistance of counsel. Upon full reconsideration we conclude that Betts v. Brady should be overruled.

The Sixth Amendment provides, "In all criminal prosecutions, the accused shall enjoy the right . . . to have the Assistance of Counsel for his defence." We have construed this to mean that in federal courts counsel must be provided for defendants unable to employ counsel unless the right is competently and intelligently waived. [In Betts, the Court] set out and considered "relevant data on the subject . . . afforded by constitutional and statutory provisions subsisting in the colonies and the States prior to the inclusion of the Bill of Rights in the national Constitution, and in the constitutional, legislative, and judicial history of the States to the present date." On the basis of this historical data the Court concluded that appointment of counsel is not a fundamental right, essential to a fair trial, [and thus was not a due process requirement applicable to the States.]

We accept Betts v. Brady's assumption, based as it was on our prior cases, that a provision of the Bill of Rights which is "fundamental and essential to a fair trial" is made obligatory upon the States by the Fourteenth Amendment. We think the Court in Betts was wrong, however, in concluding that the Sixth Amendment's guarantee of counsel is not one of these fundamental rights. Ten years before Betts v. Brady, this Court, after full consideration of all the historical data examined in Betts, had unequivocally declared that "the right to the aid of counsel is of this fundamental character." Powell v. Alabama, 287 U.S. 45, 68 (1932). While the Court at the close of its Powell opinion did by its language, as this Court frequently does, limit its holding to the particular facts and circumstances of that case, its conclusions about the fundamental nature of the right to counsel are unmistakable. Several years later, in 1936, the Court reemphasized what it had said about the fundamental nature of the right to counsel in this language:

> We concluded that certain fundamental rights, safeguarded by the first eight amendments against federal action, were also safeguarded against state action by the due process of law clause of the Fourteenth Amendment, and among them the fundamental right of the accused to the aid of counsel in a criminal prosecution.

Grosjean v. American Press Co., 297 U.S. 233, 243-44 (1936). [Similar statements appear in several other decisions. In] deciding as it did — that "appointment of counsel is not a fundamental right, essential to a fair trial" — the Court in Betts v. Brady made an abrupt break with its own well-considered precedents. In returning to these old precedents, sounder we believe than the new, we but restore constitutional principles established to achieve a fair system of justice.

Not only these precedents but also reason and reflection require us to recognize that in our adversary system of criminal justice, any person haled into court, who is too poor to hire a lawyer, cannot be assured a fair trial unless counsel is provided for him. This seems to us to be an obvious truth. Governments, both state and federal, quite properly spend vast sums of money to establish machinery to try defendants accused of crime. Lawyers to prosecute are everywhere deemed essential to protect the public's interest in an orderly society. Similarly, there are few defendants charged with crime, few indeed, who fail to hire the best lawyers they can get to prepare and present their defenses. That government hires lawyers to prosecute and defendants who have the money hire lawyers to defend are the strongest indications of the widespread belief that lawyers in criminal courts are necessities, not luxuries. The right of one charged with crime to counsel may not be deemed fundamental and essential to fair trials in some countries, but it is in ours. From the very beginning, our state and national constitutions and laws have laid great emphasis on procedural and substantive safeguards designed to assure fair trials before impartial tribunals in which every defendant stands equal before the law. This noble ideal cannot be realized if the poor man charged with crime has to face his accusers without a lawyer to assist him. . . .

The Court in Betts v. Brady departed from the sound wisdom upon which the Court's holding in Powell v. Alabama rested. Florida, supported by two other States, has asked that Betts v. Brady be left intact. Twenty-two States, as friends of the Court, argue that *Betts* was "an anachronism when handed down" and that it should now be overruled. We agree. . . .

HARLAN, J., concurring.

I agree that Betts v. Brady should be overruled, but consider it entitled to a more respectful burial than has been accorded, at least on the part of those of us who were not on the Court when that case was decided. I cannot subscribe to the view that Betts v. Brady represented "an abrupt break with its own well-considered precedents." In 1932, in Powell v. Alabama, a capital case, this Court declared that under the particular facts there presented — "the ignorance and illiteracy of the defendants, their youth, the circumstances of public hostility . . . and above all that they stood in deadly peril of their lives" — the state court had a duty to assign counsel for the trial as a necessary requisite of due process of law. It is evident that these limiting facts were not added to the opinion as an afterthought; they were repeatedly emphasized, and were clearly regarded as important to the result.

Thus when this Court, a decade later, decided Betts v. Brady, it did no more than to admit of the possible existence of special circumstances in noncapital as well as capital trials, while at the same time insisting that such circumstances be shown in order to establish a denial of due process. The right to appointed counsel had been recognized as being considerably broader in federal prosecutions, but to have imposed these requirements on the States would indeed have been "an abrupt break" with the almost immediate past. . . .

The principles declared in *Powell* and in *Betts*, however, have had a troubled journey throughout the years that have followed first the one case and then the other. . . . In noncapital cases, the "special circumstances" rule has continued to exist in form while its substance has been substantially and steadily eroded. [Since 1950] there have been not a few cases in which special circumstances were found in little or nothing more than the "complexity" of the legal questions presented, although those questions were often of only routine difficulty. The Court has come to recognize, in other words, that the mere existence of a serious criminal charge constituted in itself special circumstances requiring the services of counsel at trial. In truth the Betts v. Brady rule is no longer a reality. This evolution, however, appears not to have been fully recognized by many state courts, in this instance charged with the front-line responsibility for the enforcement of constitutional rights. To continue a rule which is honored by this Court only with lip service is not a healthy thing and in the long run will do disservice to the federal system.

The special circumstances rule has been formally abandoned in capital cases, and the time has now come when it should be similarly abandoned in noncapital cases, at least as to offenses which, as the one involved here, carry the possibility of a substantial prison sentence. (Whether the rule should extend to all criminal cases need not now be decided.) This indeed does no more than to make explicit something that has long since been foreshadowed in our decisions. . . .

■ In re ADVISORY OPINION TO THE GOVERNOR (APPOINTED COUNSEL)
666 A.2d 813 (R.I. 1995)

Weisberger, C.J.

To His Excellency Lincoln Almond, Governor of the State of Rhode Island and Providence Plantations: We have received from Your Excellency a request seeking the advice of the justices of this Court in accordance with article X, section 3, of the Rhode Island Constitution on the following question of law:

> In view of the historical development of the law relating to the right of appointed counsel under the federal and state constitutions, and the more recent developments in federal case law, is the State of Rhode Island required by the Rhode Island Constitution to provide free counsel to indigents notwithstanding that the trial justice determines that no incarceration will be imposed?

[The governor submitted this question to the Court in preparation for proposing to the legislature an annual operating budget for the state.] In response, we issued an order inviting briefs from various specified parties and all other interested parties. . . .

The Sixth Amendment to the United States Constitution mandates that "in all criminal prosecutions, the accused shall enjoy the right . . . to have the assistance of counsel for his defense." In 1963, the United States Supreme Court made this requirement applicable to the states via the Fourteenth Amendment in Gideon v. Wainwright, 372 U.S. 335.

The *Gideon* decision, however, did not reveal the contours of the right to counsel inasmuch as that holding was limited to facts that involved a felony conviction. The issue of the right to counsel was revisited in Argersinger v. Hamlin, 407 U.S. 25 (1972), in which the Supreme Court was asked to rule on whether indigent defendants facing misdemeanor charges are entitled to appointed counsel. The *Argersinger* Court concluded that the rationale of the *Gideon* decision "has relevance to any criminal trial, where an accused is deprived of his liberty." *Argersinger* went on to hold that any criminal prosecution resulting in the actual deprivation of an indigent defendant's liberty must be accompanied by the appointment of counsel for that defendant.

Although *Argersinger* did not specifically address the question of whether counsel must be appointed when no imprisonment will result, the Supreme Court did reach this issue seven years later, in Scott v. Illinois, 440 U.S. 367 (1979). Scott, an indigent defendant, was convicted of shoplifting and fined $50 after a trial in which he was not assisted by appointed counsel. In an opinion by Justice Rehnquist, the Court held that the right to appointed counsel under the Sixth and Fourteenth Amendments of the United States Constitution requires "only that no indigent criminal defendant be sentenced to a term of imprisonment unless the State has afforded him the right to assistance of appointed counsel in his defense." . . .

The Rhode Island constitutional analogue to the Sixth Amendment guarantee of the right to counsel is found in article I, section 10, of the Rhode Island Constitution. This section protects a defendant's right to assistance of counsel in terms almost identical to those of its federal counterpart: "In all criminal prosecutions, accused persons shall . . . have the assistance of counsel in their defense." In 1971, prior to the Supreme Court's rulings in *Argersinger* and *Scott,* this provision was interpreted in State v. Holliday, 280 A.2d 333 (R.I. 1971). In *Holliday,* this Court . . . construed article I, section 10, broadly to require appointment of counsel for indigent defendants charged with misdemeanors that carry a potential prison sentence in excess of six months, even if no imprisonment is actually imposed. . . . In *Holliday* this Court had no means of ascertaining the direction that the Supreme Court would take, and it is clear that our prognostication in *Holliday* was inaccurate. . . .

Although certain *amici* have argued that the protections afforded by the Federal Constitution establish only a minimum level of protection for criminal defendants, the decision to depart from minimum standards and to increase the level of protection should be made guardedly and should be supported by a principled rationale. We are presented with no such rationale here.

[The] balance achieved by the Supreme Court of the United States is as favorable to the perceived rights of defendants as should rationally be applied in criminal cases. We are unwilling to interpret article I, section [10] of the Rhode Island Constitution in such fashion as further to subordinate societal interests in effective prosecution of the guilty. . . . Moreover, this Court has recognized the validity of considering budgetary limitations in determining the extent of state-funded benefits for indigents. . . .

Certain of the *amici* would have this Court provide heightened constitutional protection to indigent criminal defendants who, although they may face no threat of imprisonment, may suffer such consequences as denial of public housing and loss of professional licenses. It is well settled, however, that the full panoply of due-process protections attaches only when loss of a fundamental liberty results from state action. . . . Although loss of a license or permit and denial of public housing are grave occurrences, they do not rise to the level of deprivation characterized by incarceration. An automobile driver, for instance, is not entitled to confer with counsel when asked to submit to a breathalyzer test, even though submission to or refusal of that test may result in loss of that driver's license, because there is no fundamental constitutional right to operate a motor vehicle. Therefore, we disagree with *amici* that counsel must be provided in a criminal proceeding simply because an indigent defendant may subsequently lose a comparable property right. . . .

We conclude that it is (1) within the authority of the General Assembly to determine that the public interest would be served by increasing appropriations to provide counsel in situations not constitutionally required and (2) not the province of this Court to impose upon the state obligations that have no constitutional or statutory basis. We therefore advise Your Excellency that the United States Supreme Court's interpretation of the Sixth Amendment as a guarantee of a criminal defendant's right to counsel only when imprisonment is actually imposed represents the appropriate standard that should be applied under article I, section 10, of the Rhode Island Constitution. In conclusion, therefore, we respond to Your Excellency's question in the negative.

Murray, J., dissenting.

I respectfully dissent. [This] state has a proud history of affording its citizens the right to counsel and has specifically declined to follow the United States Supreme Court in limiting the provision of counsel to indigents. In 1941, long before Gideon v. Wainwright, 372 U.S. 335 (1963), Rhode Island established a public counsel system for accused felons. Thirty years later, before the United States Supreme Court decided Argersinger v. Hamlin, 407 U.S. 25 (1972), this court, in State v. Holliday, 280 A.2d 333 (R.I. 1971), extended the right to counsel for indigent defendants charged with serious misdemeanors which could subject them to an imposition of penalty in excess of six months' imprisonment. In 1987, after the Supreme Court decided Scott v. Illinois, 440 U.S. 367 (1979), we stated in State v. Moretti, 521 A.2d 1003 (R.I. 1987), and in State v. Medeiros, 535 A.2d 766 (R.I. 1987), that the Rhode Island Constitution provides a broader right to counsel than that provided under the Federal Constitution.

Specifically, we found in *Moretti* that "the confluence of the federal and the state guarantees is if an indigent Rhode Island criminal defendant faces a potential sentence of more than six months, Rhode Island constitutional law guarantees to a defendant appointed counsel, even if the trial justice predetermines that no prison sentence will be imposed. If the potential sentence is less than six months, federal constitutional law guarantees the defendant appointed counsel unless the trial justice predetermines that no prison sentence will be imposed." [Thus,] even after *Scott*, this court held that the Rhode Island Constitution afforded indigent defendants a higher degree of protection; that is, we have recognized the right of indigent persons to appointed counsel notwithstanding that the trial justice determines that no incarceration will be imposed.

As a final matter, it should be stressed that we should not attempt to peer into the minds of trial justices. By answering His Excellency's request in the negative, the majority's decision effectively reduces the range of discretion previously afforded to trial justices in misdemeanor cases. The majority would have each trial justice determine whether incarceration may be imposed at the initial stages of an action, regardless of any later developments that may require the trial justice to impose a sanction of imprisonment. It is noteworthy that the District Court judges have represented that such a result would profoundly affect the quality of justice which is administered in the trial courts. . . .

In 2002 the Supreme Court again considered the types of situations that trigger a right to appointed counsel for indigent defendants. The precise issue in the case—whether the state must provide counsel when the judge gives the defendant a suspended sentence and does not order a prison term—may seem minor on first glance. But as we saw in *Gideon* and prior cases, decisions requiring the provision of counsel can impose substantial direct and indirect costs on the states. Of course, such monetary and policy costs must be weighed against the benefits of fundamental principles such as the right to counsel. Consider the balance between federal constitutional principle and practical considerations in the following case.

■ ALABAMA v. LeREED SHELTON
534 U.S. 654 (2002)

GINSBURG, J.

This case concerns the Sixth Amendment right of an indigent defendant charged with a misdemeanor punishable by imprisonment, fine, or both, to the assistance of court-appointed counsel. Two prior decisions control the Court's judgment. First, in Argersinger v. Hamlin, 407 U.S. 25 (1972), this Court held that defense counsel must be appointed in any criminal prosecution, whether classified as petty, misdemeanor, or felony, "that actually leads to imprisonment even for a brief period." Later, in Scott v. Illinois, 440 U.S. 367 (1979), the Court drew the line at "actual imprisonment," holding that counsel need not be appointed when the defendant is fined for the charged crime, but is not sentenced to a term of imprisonment.

Defendant-respondent LeReed Shelton, convicted of third-degree assault, was sentenced to a jail term of 30 days, which the trial court immediately suspended, placing Shelton on probation for two years. The question presented is whether the Sixth Amendment right to appointed counsel, as delineated in *Argersinger* and *Scott,* applies to a defendant in Shelton's situation. We hold that a suspended sentence that may "end up in the actual deprivation of a person's liberty" may not be imposed unless the defendant was accorded "the guiding hand of counsel" in the prosecution for the crime charged.

After representing himself at a bench trial in the District Court of Etowah County, Alabama, Shelton was convicted of third-degree assault, a class A misdemeanor carrying a maximum punishment of one year imprisonment and a $2000 fine. He invoked his right to a new trial before a jury in Circuit Court where he again appeared without a lawyer and was again convicted. The court repeatedly warned Shelton about the problems self-representation entailed but at no time offered him assistance of counsel at state expense.

The Circuit Court sentenced Shelton to serve 30 days in the county prison. As authorized by Alabama law, however, the court suspended that sentence and placed Shelton on two years' unsupervised probation, conditioned on his payment of court costs, a $500 fine, reparations of $25, and restitution in the amount of $516.69. Shelton appealed his conviction and sentence on Sixth Amendment grounds. . . .

Three positions are before us in this case. . . . Shelton argues that an indigent defendant may not receive a suspended sentence unless he is offered or waives the assistance of state-appointed counsel. Alabama now concedes that the Sixth Amendment bars *activation* of a suspended sentence for an uncounseled conviction, but maintains that the Constitution does not prohibit *imposition* of such a sentence as a method of effectuating probationary punishment. To assure full airing of the question presented, we invited an *amicus curiae* to argue in support of a third position, one Alabama has abandoned: Failure to appoint counsel to an indigent defendant does not bar the imposition of a suspended or probationary sentence upon conviction of a misdemeanor, even though the defendant might be incarcerated in the event probation is revoked.

In Gideon v. Wainwright, 372 U.S. 335 (1963), we held that the Sixth Amendment's guarantee of the right to state-appointed counsel, firmly established in federal-court proceedings in Johnson v. Zerbst, 304 U.S. 458 (1938), applies to state criminal prosecutions through the Fourteenth Amendment. We clarified the scope of that right in *Argersinger,* holding that an indigent defendant must be offered counsel in any misdemeanor case "that actually leads to imprisonment." Seven Terms later, *Scott* confirmed *Argersinger*'s "delimitation." Although the governing statute in *Scott* authorized a jail sentence of up to one year, we held that the defendant had no right to state-appointed counsel because the sole sentence actually imposed on him was a $50 fine. . . .

Applying the "actual imprisonment" rule to the case before us, we take up first the question we asked *amicus* to address: Where the State provides no counsel to an indigent defendant, does the Sixth Amendment permit activation of a suspended sentence upon the defendant's violation of the terms of probation? We conclude that it does not. A suspended sentence is a prison term imposed for the offense of conviction. Once the prison term is triggered, the defendant is incarcerated not for the probation violation, but for the underlying offense. The uncounseled conviction at that point results in imprisonment; it "ends up in the actual deprivation of a person's liberty." This is precisely what the Sixth Amendment, as interpreted in *Argersinger* and *Scott,* does not allow.

Amicus resists this reasoning primarily on two grounds. First, he attempts to align this case with our decisions in Nichols v. United States, 511 U.S. 738 (1994), and Gagnon v. Scarpelli, 411 U.S. 778 (1973). We conclude that Shelton's case is not properly bracketed with those dispositions.

Nichols presented the question whether the Sixth Amendment barred consideration of a defendant's prior uncounseled misdemeanor conviction in determining his sentence for a subsequent felony offense. Nichols pleaded guilty to federal felony drug charges. Several years earlier, unrepresented by counsel, he was fined but not incarcerated for the state misdemeanor of driving under the influence (DUI). Including the DUI conviction in the federal Sentencing Guidelines calculation allowed the trial court to impose a sentence for the felony drug conviction 25 months longer than if the misdemeanor conviction had not been considered. We upheld this result, concluding that "an uncounseled misdemeanor conviction, valid under *Scott* because no prison term was imposed, is also valid when used to enhance punishment at a subsequent conviction." In *Gagnon*, the question was whether the defendant, who was placed on probation pursuant to a suspended sentence for armed robbery, had a due process right to representation by appointed counsel at a probation revocation hearing. We held that counsel was not invariably required in parole or probation revocation proceedings; we directed, instead, a "case-by-case approach" turning on the character of the issues involved.

Considered together, *amicus* contends, *Nichols* and *Gagnon* establish this principle: Sequential proceedings must be analyzed separately for Sixth Amendment purposes and only those proceedings resulting "in *immediate* actual imprisonment" trigger the right to state-appointed counsel. . . . *Gagnon* and *Nichols* do not stand for the broad proposition *amicus* would extract from them. The dispositive factor in those cases was not whether incarceration occurred immediately or only after some delay. Rather, the critical point was that the defendant had a recognized right to counsel when adjudicated guilty of the felony offense for which he was imprisoned. Unlike this case, in which revocation of probation would trigger a prison term imposed for a misdemeanor of which Shelton was found guilty without the aid of counsel, the sentences imposed in *Nichols* and *Gagnon* were for felony convictions—a federal drug conviction in *Nichols,* and a state armed robbery conviction in *Gagnon*—for which the right to counsel is unquestioned. Thus, neither *Nichols* nor *Gagnon* altered or diminished *Argersinger*'s command that "no person may be imprisoned *for any offense* . . . unless he was represented by counsel at his trial." . . .

Amicus also contends that "practical considerations clearly weigh against" the extension of the Sixth Amendment appointed-counsel right to a defendant in Shelton's situation. He cites figures suggesting that although conditional sentences are commonly imposed, they are rarely activated. . . . *Amicus* observes that probation is "now a critical tool of law enforcement in low level cases." Even so, it does not follow that preservation of that tool warrants the reduction of the Sixth Amendment's domain. . . . *Amicus* does not describe the contours of the hearing that, he suggests, might precede revocation of a term of probation imposed on an uncounseled defendant. In Alabama, however, the character of the probation revocation hearing currently afforded is not in doubt. The proceeding is an "informal" one at which the defendant has no right to counsel, and the court no obligation to observe customary rules of evidence. More significant, the sole issue at the hearing—apart from determinations about the necessity of confinement—is whether the defendant breached the terms of probation. The validity or reliability of the underlying conviction is beyond attack.

We think it plain that a hearing so timed and structured cannot compensate for the absence of trial counsel, for it does not even address the key Sixth Amendment inquiry: whether the adjudication of guilt corresponding to the prison sentence is sufficiently reliable to permit incarceration. Deprived of counsel when tried, convicted, and sentenced, and unable to challenge the original judgment at a subsequent probation revocation hearing, a defendant in Shelton's circumstances faces incarceration on a conviction that has never been subjected to "the crucible of meaningful adversarial testing." The Sixth Amendment does not countenance this result.

In a variation on *amicus'* position, the dissent would limit review in this case to the question whether the *imposition* of Shelton's suspended sentence required appointment of counsel. . . . The dissent imagines a set of safeguards Alabama might provide at the probation revocation stage sufficient to cure its failure to appoint counsel prior to sentencing, including, perhaps, complete retrial of the misdemeanor violation with assistance of counsel. But there is no cause for speculation about Alabama's procedures; they are established by Alabama statute and decisional law, and they bear no resemblance to those the dissent invents in its effort to sanction the prospect of Shelton's imprisonment on an uncounseled conviction. . . .

Nor do we agree with *amicus* or the dissent that our holding will substantially limit the states' ability to impose probation or encumber them with a large, new burden. Most jurisdictions already provide a state-law right to appointed counsel more generous than that afforded by the Federal Constitution. All but 16 States, for example, would provide counsel to a defendant in Shelton's circumstances, either because he received a substantial fine or because state law authorized incarceration for the charged offense or provided for a maximum prison term of one year. There is thus scant reason to believe that a rule conditioning imposition of a suspended sentence on provision of appointed counsel would affect existing practice in the large majority of the States. And given the current commitment of most jurisdictions to affording court-appointed counsel to indigent misdemeanants while simultaneously preserving the option of probationary punishment, we do not share *amicus'* concern that other States may lack the capacity and resources to do the same.

Moreover, even if *amicus* is correct that some courts and jurisdictions at least cannot bear the costs of the rule we confirm today, those States need not abandon probation or equivalent measures as viable forms of punishment. Although they may not attach probation to an imposed and suspended prison sentence, States unable or unwilling routinely to provide appointed counsel to misdemeanants in Shelton's situation are not without recourse to another option capable of yielding a similar result.

That option is pretrial probation, employed in some form by at least 23 States. Under such an arrangement, the prosecutor and defendant agree to the defendant's participation in a pretrial rehabilitation program,[11] which includes conditions typical of post-trial probation. The adjudication of guilt and imposition of sentence for the underlying offense then occur only if and when the defendant breaches those conditions.

Like the regime urged by *amicus*, this system reserves the appointed-counsel requirement for the "small percentage" of cases in which incarceration proves

---

11. Because this device is conditioned on the defendant's consent, it does not raise the question whether imposition of probation alone so restrains a defendant's liberty as to require provision of appointed counsel.

necessary thus allowing a State to "supervise a course of rehabilitation" without providing a lawyer every time it wishes to pursue such a course. Unlike *amicus'* position, however, pretrial probation also respects the constitutional imperative that "no person may be imprisoned for any offense . . . unless he was represented by counsel at his trial." . . .

SCALIA, J., dissenting.

In Argersinger v. Hamlin we held that "absent a knowing and intelligent waiver, *no person may be imprisoned* for any offense . . . unless he was represented by counsel at his trial." Although, we said, the "run of misdemeanors will not be affected" by this rule, "in those *that end up in the actual deprivation of a person's liberty,* the accused will receive the benefit" of appointed counsel (emphasis added). We affirmed this rule in Scott v. Illinois, drawing a bright line between imprisonment and the mere threat of imprisonment: "[T]he central premise of *Argersinger*—that actual imprisonment is a penalty different in kind from fines *or the mere threat of imprisonment*—is eminently sound and warrants adoption of *actual imprisonment* as the line defining the constitutional right to appointment of counsel" [emphasis added]. We have repeatedly emphasized actual imprisonment as the touchstone of entitlement to appointed counsel.

Today's decision ignores this long and consistent jurisprudence, extending the misdemeanor right to counsel to cases bearing the mere threat of imprisonment. Respondent's 30-day suspended sentence, and the accompanying 2-year term of probation, are invalidated for lack of appointed counsel even though respondent has not suffered, and may never suffer, a deprivation of liberty. The Court holds that the suspended sentence violates respondent's Sixth Amendment right to counsel because it "*may* end up in the actual deprivation of [respondent's] liberty," *if* he someday violates the terms of probation, *if* a court determines that the violation merits revocation of probation, and *if* the court determines that no other punishment will "adequately protect the community from further criminal activity" or "avoid depreciating the seriousness of the violation." And to all of these contingencies there must yet be added, before the Court's decision makes sense, an element of rank speculation. Should all these contingencies occur, the Court speculates, the Alabama Supreme Court would mechanically apply its decisional law applicable to routine probation revocation (which establishes procedures that the Court finds inadequate) rather than adopt special procedures for situations that raise constitutional questions in light of *Argersinger* and *Scott.* The Court has miraculously divined how the Alabama justices would resolve a constitutional question. . . .

In the future, *if and when* the State of Alabama seeks to imprison respondent on the previously suspended sentence, we can ask whether the procedural safeguards attending the imposition of that sentence comply with the Constitution. But that question is *not* before us now. . . .

Our prior opinions placed considerable weight on the practical consequences of expanding the right to appointed counsel beyond cases of actual imprisonment. Today, the Court gives this consideration the back of its hand. Its observation that all but 16 States already appoint counsel for defendants like respondent is interesting but quite irrelevant, since today's holding is not confined to *defendants like respondent.* Appointed counsel must henceforth be offered before *any* defendant can be awarded a suspended sentence, no matter how short. Only 24 States have announced a rule of this scope.[4] Thus, the Court's decision imposes a large, new burden on a majority of the States, including some of the poorest (e.g., Alabama, Arkansas, and Mississippi). That burden consists not only of the cost of providing state-paid counsel in cases of such insignificance that even financially prosperous defendants sometimes forgo the expense of hired counsel; but also the cost of enabling courts and prosecutors to respond to the "over-lawyering" of minor cases. Nor should we discount the burden placed on the minority 24 States that currently provide counsel: that they keep their current disposition forever in place, however imprudent experience proves it to be.

Today's imposition upon the States finds justification neither in the text of the Constitution, nor in the settled practices of our people, nor in the prior jurisprudence of this Court. I respectfully dissent.

■ FLORIDA RULE OF CRIMINAL PROCEDURE 3.111

(a) A person entitled to appointment of counsel as provided herein shall have counsel appointed when the person is formally charged with an offense, or as soon as feasible after custodial restraint, or at the first appearance before a committing judge, whichever occurs earliest.

(b)(1) Counsel shall be provided to indigent persons in all prosecutions for offenses punishable by incarceration including appeals from the conviction thereof. In the discretion of the court, counsel does not have to be provided to an indigent person in a prosecution for a misdemeanor or violation of a municipal ordinance if the judge, at least 15 days prior to trial, files in the cause a written order of no incarceration certifying that the defendant will not be incarcerated in the case pending trial or probation violation hearing, or as part of a sentence after trial, guilty or nolo contendere plea, or probation revocation. This 15-day requirement may be waived by the defendant or defense counsel.

(A) If the court issues an order of no incarceration after counsel has been appointed to represent the defendant, the court may discharge appointed counsel unless the defendant is incarcerated or the defendant would be substantially disadvantaged by the discharge of appointed counsel. . . .

(C) If the court withdraws its order of no incarceration, it shall immediately appoint counsel if the defendant is otherwise eligible for the services of the public defender. The court may not withdraw its order of no incarceration once the defendant has been found guilty or pled nolo contendere.

(2) Counsel may be provided to indigent persons in all proceedings arising from the initiation of a criminal action against a defendant, including postconviction proceedings and appeals therefrom, extradition proceedings, mental competency proceedings, and other proceedings that are adversary in nature,

---

4. Ten of the 34 States cited by the Court do not offer appointed counsel in all cases where a misdemeanor defendant might suffer a suspended sentence. Six States guarantee counsel only when the authorized penalty is *at least* three or six months' imprisonment. South Dakota does not provide counsel where the maximum permissible sentence is 30 days' imprisonment if "the court has concluded that [the defendant] will not be deprived of his liberty if he is convicted." . . . Misdemeanors punishable by less than six months' imprisonment may be a narrow category, but it may well include the vast majority of cases in which (precisely *because* of the minor nature of the offense) a suspended sentence is imposed. There is simply nothing to support the Court's belief that few offenders are prosecuted for crimes in which counsel is not already provided. . . .

regardless of the designation of the court in which they occur or the classification of the proceedings as civil or criminal.

(3) Counsel may be provided to a partially indigent person on request, provided that the person shall defray that portion of the cost of representation and the reasonable costs of investigation as he or she is able without substantial hardship to the person or the person's family, as directed by the court.

(4) "Indigent" shall mean a person who is unable to pay for the services of an attorney, including costs of investigation, without substantial hardship to the person or the person's family; "partially indigent" shall mean a person unable to pay more than a portion of the fee charged by an attorney, including costs of investigation, without substantial hardship to the person or the person's family.

■ VERMONT STATUTES TIT. 13, §§5231, 5201

§5231

A needy person who is being detained by a law enforcement officer without charge or judicial process, or who is charged with having committed or is being detained under a conviction of a serious crime, is entitled:

(1) To be represented by an attorney to the same extent as a person having his own counsel; and

(2) To be provided with the necessary services and facilities of representation. Any such necessary services and facilities of representation that exceed $1,500 per item must receive prior approval from the court after a hearing involving the parties. . . . This obligation and requirement to obtain prior court approval shall also be imposed in like manner upon the Attorney General or a State's Attorney prosecuting a violation of the law. . . .

§5201

In this chapter, the term . . . "Serious crime" includes: (A) A felony; (B) A misdemeanor the maximum penalty for which is a fine of more than $1,000 or any period of imprisonment unless the judge, at the arraignment but before the entry of a plea, determines and states on the record that he will not sentence the defendant to a fine of more than $1,000 or period of imprisonment if the defendant is convicted of the misdemeanor. . . .

Notes

1. *Constitutional right to appointed defense counsel in minor cases: majority position.* The Rhode Island advisory opinion reflects the overwhelming majority view in this country: Provision of counsel is constitutionally required for any defendant charged with a felony and for any defendant charged with a misdemeanor that results in actual imprisonment, even if less than six months. The decision in Scott v. Illinois, 440 U.S. 367 (1979), declared that only misdemeanors resulting in "actual imprisonment" would require appointed counsel. Prior to the *Scott* decision, more than 20 states provided counsel (by statute or under the federal or state constitution) for

a broader range of misdemeanors, and not just those involving actual imprisonment. Today, fewer states go beyond the "actual imprisonment" rule as a matter of state constitutional law. See State v. Dowd, 478 A.2d 671 (Me. 1984) (accused receives counsel when facing charges that might result in prison term of more than six months or a fine of more than $500); Commonwealth v. Thomas, 507 A.2d 57 (Pa. 1986) (adopting actual imprisonment rule).

What explains this shift in constitutional rules over the years? Is it an example of the leading role the U.S. Supreme Court can play in constitutional interpretation? Does it exemplify what can happen when legal rules created in a system dealing with a relatively small number of cases are used in a system processing much larger numbers of cases? Is it significant that Rhode Island's governor requested an advisory opinion on the extent of the right to counsel when formulating the state budget?

What do the courts in *Gideon* and in the Rhode Island advisory opinion believe that lawyers do? Are attorneys indispensable to criminal justice, or an impediment to criminal justice, or both? Consider, in this connection, what happened to Clarence Gideon. After the Supreme Court reversed Gideon's conviction, an attorney defended Gideon at his retrial on the charges. He was acquitted. See Anthony Lewis, Gideon's Trumpet 223-38 (1964).

2. *Statutory right to appointed counsel in minor cases.* There is more variation among state statutes providing counsel than among state constitutional interpretations. Some states have statutes or rules that track the federal and state constitutional requirements. However, there is also a large group, represented by the Vermont statute above, that add to the list of crimes for which the state must provide counsel for indigent defendants. As the opinions in *Shelton* indicated, a number of state statutes provided counsel for defendants who receive a suspended sentence even before it became clear that the constitution requires defense lawyers in such cases. Some states also provide counsel for some cases involving large criminal fines.

Statutes providing for the appointment of defense counsel appeared early in the history of this country, and some covered a wide range of crimes. Many of the earliest statutes provided for appointed counsel in capital cases — which included a broader range of crimes at that time than it does today — but some (like a 1795 Act in New Jersey) required appointment in the case of any person tried upon an indictment. See Betts v. Brady, 316 U.S. 455, 470 n.28 (1942).

Perhaps the most important statutory provisions and rules on this subject are the ones (like the Florida rule above) giving a trial judge the *discretion* to appoint counsel in any criminal proceedings, regardless of the crime involved. The critical decisions here are funding decisions, which are often made at the local rather than state level. See Bureau of Justice Statistics, Indigent Defense Services in Large Counties, 1999 at 3 (Nov. 2000, NCJ 184932) (in largest 100 counties, 69 percent of funds for indigent defense comes from county or city government, 25 percent from state). Will a city provide enough money to fund attorneys for all those accused of violating its criminal ordinances? As a trial judge, can you identify any class of cases where you would not routinely appoint counsel even if the funds were available?

3. *Determination of indigence.* The trial court typically determines, in a hearing soon after charges are filed, whether or not the defendant qualifies as an indigent to receive state-provided counsel. The trial judge must consult factors listed in appellate opinions, statutes, or procedure rules, but those factors tend to be general

enough to leave the trial judge with much discretion in deciding which defendants qualify. The judge often must consider such factors as the seriousness of the crime, the amount of bail bond required, the defendant's assets and debts, and the defendant's employment status. See Tenn. Code §40-14-202(c). The state might provide counsel and later attempt to collect the attorneys'fees from defendants who have more resources than they originally appeared to have. In the end, the great majority of felony defendants are indigents who receive public defenders or appointed counsel. By some estimates, more than three-quarters of all defendants charged with eligible crimes are provided with counsel. Bureau of Justice Statistics, Defense Counsel in Criminal Cases (Nov. 2000, NCJ 179023) (82 percent of felony defendants in state court represented by publicly financed counsel).

Why bother to distinguish between indigent and non-indigent defendants? Would the criminal justice system improve if the state offered to pay for an attorney (at state-determined rates) for any criminal defendant charged with an eligible crime — no questions asked about the defendant's ability to pay? Would this make the provision of defense counsel more like Social Security benefits, an entitlement with broad political support because it benefits a broad group?

4. *Recoupment of fees.* State statutes typically allow the state to recoup some fees for the services of the defense attorney if the defendant is convicted and the court later finds that the defendant has the funds for at least a partial payment of the attorney's fees. In most jurisdictions, judges tell the defendant about these recoupment laws when asking whether the defendant wants to waive counsel. Exactly how would you word this notice to defendants if you were a trial judge?

5. *Distribution of offenses.* The decision about providing counsel to different classes of misdemeanants has serious consequences, not the least of them fiscal. If felonies rest at the top of a "pyramid" of criminal charges, the least serious misdemeanors are the charges at the broad bottom of the pyramid: In most systems, they are by far the most numerous charges. See Bureau of Justice Statistics, Prosecutors in State Courts, 2005 at 6 (July 2006, NCJ 213799) (prosecutors'offices close three times more misdemeanor cases than felony cases). As a result, choices about the appointment of counsel for the lowest-level charges will generally have the largest impact on the system for providing counsel. The federal system is atypical on this score, since only about a quarter of all charges filed in a given year are misdemeanors. Many states create special court systems to handle the lowest-level offenses, with names such as "misdemeanor court" or "district court."

6. *Constitutional sources of the right to counsel.* It is important to keep in mind the different constitutional sources for the right to counsel. In some settings (a "criminal prosecution"), the Sixth Amendment requires counsel to be present. When it comes to police station interrogations, the Fifth Amendment requires that a defendant be told about the right to have counsel present. In others (such as some postconviction proceedings), the due process clause requires counsel. In still other settings, the equal protection clause requires the state to provide counsel to all if it provides counsel to some. Recall also that most states have analogs to these federal constitutional provisions. What constitutional source was the basis for the *Gideon* decision?

What does the text of the Sixth Amendment suggest about the types of cases in which the state must provide counsel? On the one hand, the amendment does provide for a right to counsel "in *all* criminal prosecutions." Thus it would seem to cover any misdemeanor — even one not resulting in imprisonment. On the other hand, the Sixth Amendment was originally thought to address access to *retained* counsel, not defense counsel provided by the state. The Sixth Amendment right to counsel apparently was drafted as a repudiation of the common law of England, which prevented those accused of most felonies from relying upon retained counsel to conduct their defense at trial. Before the federal constitution was adopted, the constitutions of most states (including Maryland, Massachusetts, New Hampshire, New York, and Pennsylvania) granted the accused in criminal proceedings the right to retain counsel. When James Madison drafted the federal Bill of Rights, he drew upon existing provisions in various state constitutions. However, there is no extensive history to show the intentions of those who adopted the right to counsel embodied in the Sixth Amendment to the federal constitution.

7. *Incorporation.* Long before *Gideon,* the Supreme Court had declared that the Sixth Amendment required the government to appoint counsel for all criminal defendants in *federal* court. See Johnson v. Zerbst, 304 U.S. 458 (1938). The language of the Sixth Amendment and the rest of the Bill of Rights applied only to the federal government, not to the states. Thus, the *Gideon* Court had to resolve the larger question (given the relative sizes of the federal and state criminal systems) of whether the due process clause of the Fourteenth Amendment — which did apply to the states — "incorporated" the specific guarantees of the Bill of Rights.

The majority in *Gideon* argued that the *Betts* rule was an aberration and a departure from earlier cases dealing with the incorporation of the right to counsel; Justice John Marshall Harlan suggested instead that the *Betts* case was a plausible but impracticable extension of earlier cases. Who was right? Was the *Betts* approach simply not clear enough to provide predictable guidance, or was it faulty in some other respect?

The Supreme Court has decided that due process "selectively" incorporates some Bill of Rights guarantees. *Gideon* was an important development in this broader constitutional trend. While there has been debate over the years about the extent to which the framers and adopters of the Fourteenth Amendment intended to incorporate provisions of the Bill of Rights, the current consensus seems to be that the Court was substantially correct to incorporate most, if not all, of the provisions. See Michael Kent Curtis, No State Shall Abridge: The Fourteenth Amendment and the Bill of Rights (1986); Akhil Amar, The Bill of Rights and the Fourteenth Amendment, 101 Yale L.J. 1193 (1992).

8. *Actual imprisonment for later crimes.* A conviction for a misdemeanor that is not punished with a prison sentence might become relevant at a later time, during sentencing for some different crime. Can a sentencing judge use an earlier uncounseled misdemeanor conviction to lengthen the prison term imposed for the later offense? In Nichols v. United States, 511 U.S. 738 (1994), the Supreme Court decided that a sentencing court may consider a defendant's previous uncounseled misdemeanor conviction in sentencing him for a subsequent offense. The opinion argued that the later sentencing decision does not convert the punishment for the original crime into a prison term, and that sentencing judges often rely on past conduct not proven in a criminal trial as a part of sentencing. Should the state provide counsel for *any* crime if a conviction for that crime will affect a person's liberty, whether now or later? Compare Brisson v. State, 955 P.2d 888 (Wyo. 1998) (rejects *Nichols*; use of prior uncounseled misdemeanor conviction to enhance later sentence is violation of state right to counsel).

Problem 1-1. Lawyers and Experts

Paul Husske was charged with rape. Part of the government's case against him was a DNA analysis of tissue obtained from the rape victim. Several months before trial, the defendant filed a motion asserting his indigence and requesting that the trial court appoint an expert, at the government's expense, to help him challenge the DNA evidence that the prosecution intended to use. Husske asserted that because DNA evidence is "of a highly technical nature," it is "difficult for a lawyer to challenge DNA evidence without expert assistance." He expressed concern about the use of DNA evidence because the state's laboratory in the Division of Forensic Science had a "well-known record" for incompetent or biased testing. He also attached an affidavit from a local attorney who had read extensively on the subject of DNA and who also asserted the need for expert assistance to test the reliability of such evidence. Even though the trial court denied the defendant's motion, the court appointed the local attorney as co-counsel to assist the defendant, because he was "the most knowledgeable member of the local bar in the area of forensic DNA application."

A researcher from the Division of Forensic Science and a faculty member from a nearby state university testified at trial for the government as expert witnesses on the subject of DNA analysis. The experts each testified that the defendant's DNA profile matched the profile of the individual who had attacked the victim. They said that the DNA analysis did not exclude the defendant as a contributor of the genetic material that the assailant left on the victim's body and clothing. They also stated that the statistical probability of randomly selecting a person unrelated to the defendant in the Caucasian population with the same DNA profile was 1 in 700,000.

Was the trial judge obliged to appoint an expert to assist defense counsel? Compare Husske v. Commonwealth, 476 S.E.2d 920 (Va. 1996).

Note

In Ake v. Oklahoma, 470 U.S. 68 (1985), the Supreme Court held that the due process and equal protection clauses (but not the Sixth Amendment) require a state to provide an indigent defendant with access to a psychiatrist if the defendant makes a preliminary showing that his sanity will be a "significant issue" at trial. Later litigation focused on the question of when an appointed expert is one of the "raw materials integral to building an effective defense." See Caldwell v. Mississippi, 472 U.S. 320 (1985) (trial court properly denied an indigent defendant's requests for the appointment of a criminal investigator, a fingerprint expert, and a ballistics expert). Most courts that have considered the appointment of a non-psychiatric expert have held that state constitutions require the appointment of non-psychiatric experts to indigent defendants where they make a "particularized" showing of the need for the assistance. See Harrison v. State, 644 N.E.2d 1243 (Ind. 1995) (no appointment of DNA expert required because evidence involved "precise, physical measurements and chemical testing," and no showing that state's evidence was less than precise); Rey v. State, 897 S.W.2d 333 (Tex. Crim. App. 1995) (requiring appointment of pathologist to assist in cross-examination of state pathologist regarding autopsy).

2. Point in the Proceedings

When does the constitutional right to counsel take effect? For typical crimes, it would probably be unworkable to provide counsel (or even to give notice of the right to counsel) as soon as a person becomes a suspect or interacts with the police. Consider, in this regard, the great variety of interactions between citizens and police. The right to counsel more plausibly could attach whenever a person is arrested, though no jurisdiction has found a right to counsel based simply on the fact of arrest. Perhaps no right to counsel should attach until a person appears in court and is asked to plead guilty or not guilty, or at some other point in the standard criminal process.

Courts trying to determine when the right to counsel attaches have concluded that different constitutional provisions create obligations arising at different points in the process. There are at least two distinct counsel rights — one based on the Sixth Amendment and its state analogs, the other based on the Fifth Amendment privilege against self-incrimination.

The Fifth Amendment right to counsel — a right derived from the inherently compulsory nature of custodial interrogation and from the need to protect against compulsory self-incrimination — was recognized in Miranda v. Arizona, 384 U.S. 436 (1966). The Fifth Amendment right to counsel arises whenever the police conduct a custodial interrogation. Because interrogations usually occur before charging (since they are used to gather evidence), the Fifth Amendment right to counsel will often arise before any Sixth Amendment right to counsel.

The Sixth Amendment provides that "[i]n all criminal prosecutions, the accused shall . . . have the assistance of counsel for his defense." The language raises the question: What is a "criminal prosecution"? One aspect of the right to counsel is largely settled and uniform. All jurisdictions, led by the U.S. Supreme Court, agree that the right to counsel attaches by the time of arraignment — a hearing in which the defendant typically is informed of the charges that have been filed and is asked to plead "guilty" or "not guilty." See Hamilton v. Alabama, 368 U.S. 52 (1961). The legal test is also phrased in more general terms: the analysis of whether a Sixth Amendment right to counsel attaches turns on whether the procedure is considered a "critical stage" of the criminal process, taking place after the "initiation" of the adversarial judicial proceedings. The U.S. Supreme Court considers post-indictment lineups to be a "critical stage" of the criminal process. What is it that makes a police technique or judicial hearing a "critical stage"?

■ ALABAMA RULE OF CRIMINAL PROCEDURE 6.1(a)

A defendant shall be entitled to be represented by counsel in any criminal proceedings held pursuant to these rules and, if indigent, shall be entitled to have an attorney appointed to represent the defendant in all criminal proceedings in which representation by counsel is constitutionally required. The right to be represented shall include the right to consult in private with an attorney or the attorney's agent, as soon as feasible after a defendant is taken into custody, at reasonable times thereafter, and sufficiently in advance of a proceeding to allow adequate preparation therefor.

■ MISSOURI SUPREME COURT RULES 31.01, 31.02

31.01

Every person arrested and held in custody by any peace officer in any jail, police station or any other place, upon or without a warrant or other process for the alleged commission of a criminal offense, or upon suspicion thereof, shall promptly, upon request, be permitted to consult with counsel or other persons in his behalf, and, for such purpose, to use a telephone.

31.02

(a) In all criminal cases the defendant shall have the right to appear and defend in person and by counsel. If any person charged with an offense, the conviction of which would probably result in confinement, shall be without counsel upon his first appearance before a judge, it shall be the duty of the court to advise him of his right to counsel, and of the willingness of the court to appoint counsel to represent him if he is unable to employ counsel. Upon a showing of indigency, it shall be the duty of the court to appoint counsel to represent him. If after being informed as to his rights, the defendant requests to proceed without the benefit of counsel, and the court finds that he has intelligently waived his right to have counsel, the court shall have no duty to appoint counsel. . . .

■ STATE v. GREGORY PIERRE
890 A.2d 474 (Conn. 2006)

BORDEN, J.

[At about 1:30 A.M. on August 23, 1998, James Conner drove a light-colored Saab to Lucky's Cafe, a bar located in New London, in an effort to buy a small quantity of crack cocaine from Gregory Pierre. Pierre was there with his friends, Abin Britton and Jeffrey Smith. When Conner arrived at Lucky's, Pierre informed him that he did not have any drugs with him, but that he could get some from his home. Conner offered to drive Pierre to his home to obtain the cocaine and then drive him back to Lucky's once the transaction was complete. Pierre agreed to go.

In the parking lot at Pierre's apartment building, a witness saw Pierre and his friends pull Conner out of the Saab, punch and kick him for several minutes, then load him into the back seat of the car and drive away.]

On August 23, 1998, at approximately 6:30 A.M., Harrison Fortier, a sergeant with the Waterford police department, was called upon to investigate a Saab that was partially submerged in the town's duck pond. When Fortier arrived at the scene, the driver's side door of the car was open, the transmission was in neutral, the keys were missing, and the parking brake was disengaged. In addition, there were bloodstains throughout the interior of the vehicle. A search of motor vehicle records revealed that the Saab was registered to Donald Conner, the victim's father. Upon further examination of the vehicle, the police also discovered two palm prints, . . . later identified as matching Britton's palms. . . . Among the items found in the car was a card for Lucky's. . . .

On January 10, 1999, the badly decomposed remains of a body were found in Bates Woods, a recreation area in New London located across from Michael Road, where the defendant lived. Upon examining the skull found at the scene, Harold Wayne Carver, chief medical examiner for the state of Connecticut, identified the remains as belonging to the victim and classified the manner of death as a homicide. . . .

The office of the state's attorney first became involved in the investigation of the victim's death when the victim's skeletal remains were located in Bates Woods. . . . During the course of their investigation, between February 10, 1999, and March 8, 1999, the police obtained three written statements from the defendant. In each of these statements, the defendant minimized his role in the crime. On May 13, 1999, the Connecticut state police submitted an arrest warrant application with an attached information for the defendant, which was reviewed and signed by both an assistant state's attorney and a judge of the Superior Court. On June 14, 1999, law enforcement authorities from the Connecticut state police, New London police department, and the Garden City police department arrested the defendant in Garden City, New York, as a fugitive from the underlying Connecticut warrant.

Upon being arrested in New York, the defendant met with [Detectives James McGlynn and Anthony Buglione of the Connecticut state police] and provided an eleven page statement and three diagrams related to the victim's murder. This statement included reference to the fact that the defendant was with the victim when he was beaten in the parking lot of the defendant's apartment and taken to Bates Woods, as well as the fact that Britton had taken a metal pipe from the victim's car and had hit the victim about the face until he died. Additionally, the defendant provided oral statements to McGlynn and Buglione on June 24, 1999, while they were transporting the defendant back to Connecticut for arraignment. Specifically, after entering Connecticut from New York, the defendant . . . noted that his girlfriend in New York was pregnant and he became emotional about the prospect of not being able to see his child. The defendant also inquired about what was going to happen to him upon returning to Connecticut, and he stated that he was upset that Smith had not been arrested. McGlynn and Buglione suggested that it may be a good time for the defendant "to speak to the state's attorney and look for some type of deal." They also inquired as to whether the defendant would "take fifty years — fifty-five years," to which the defendant replied, "well, it's better than life, he would take it." The defendant subsequently was arraigned in Connecticut the following day . . . at which point the arrest warrant with the attached signed information also was filed with the court.

Prior to trial, the defendant moved to suppress his June 14, 1999, written statement as violating his sixth amendment right to counsel. The trial court denied the motion to suppress, holding that an arrest following the issuance of a warrant does not mark the commencement of formal legal proceedings against the defendant. Subsequent to this ruling, the defendant filed a supplemental motion to suppress, seeking the suppression of the oral statement the defendant made to McGlynn and Buglione on June 24, 1999. Following an evidentiary hearing, the trial court again denied the motion, referencing its earlier decision, and concluding once again that an arrest pursuant to a warrant does not signal the formal commencement of legal proceedings entitling a defendant to the protections of the sixth amendment. . . .

The sixth amendment guarantees that "[i]n all criminal prosecutions, the accused shall enjoy the right . . . to have the Assistance of Counsel for his defence." This right attaches only "at or after the initiation of adversary judicial criminal proceedings — whether by way of formal charge, preliminary hearing, indictment, information, or arraignment." Kirby v. Illinois, 406 U.S. 682, 689 (1972).

> The initiation of judicial criminal proceedings is far from a mere formalism. It is the starting point of our whole system of adversary criminal justice. For it is only then that the government has committed itself to prosecute, and only then that the adverse positions of [the] government and [the] defendant have solidified. It is then that a defendant finds himself faced with the prosecutorial forces of organized society, and immersed in the intricacies of substantive and procedural criminal law. It is this point, therefore, that marks the commencement of the criminal prosecutions to which alone the explicit guarantees of the Sixth Amendment are applicable.

Id. at 689-90. We also have noted that the time of the attachment of the right to counsel under the federal constitution is no different under article first, §8, of the constitution of Connecticut. See State v. Palmer, 536 A.2d 936 (Conn. 1988).

The United States Supreme Court has indicated that the sixth amendment's core purpose is to assure that in any criminal prosecution the accused shall not be left to his own devices in facing the prosecutorial forces of organized society. By its very terms, it becomes applicable only when the government's role shifts from investigation to accusation. For it is only then that the assistance of one versed in the intricacies of law is needed to assure that the prosecution's case encounters the crucible of meaningful adversarial testing. In this regard, we have consistently adopted the reasoning of the United States Supreme Court with respect to when the sixth amendment right to counsel attaches in a criminal proceeding, finding that no right to counsel attaches until prosecution has commenced.

For example, in State v. Falcon, 494 A.2d 1190 (Conn. 1985), we concluded that an extradition hearing does not represent the same type of critical confrontation between an accused and a prosecutor such as found in an arraignment where counsel is constitutionally required. Specifically, we noted: "At an arraignment, a defendant is advised of the charges against him and enters a plea. . . . By contrast, at an extradition hearing, a defendant is not asked to plead or to make any other decisions that could affect his right to a fair trial. . . . Most courts in other jurisdictions have held that even proceedings contesting extradition are not a critical stage in the prosecution requiring the presence of counsel."

Similarly, in State v. Vitale, 460 A.2d 961 (Conn. 1983), we concluded that an interrogation following an arrest, but prior to arraignment or indictment, regardless of whether accompanied by a warrant, does not call into play the sixth amendment right to counsel. In particular, in *Vitale* we noted that the defendant "seeks to analogize his situation . . . to that of a defendant who has been formally charged with a crime by indictment or information. From such a defendant the government may not elicit self-incriminating evidence in the absence of counsel." . . .

We recognize that, prior to the present case, we have not specifically addressed the question of whether the signing of an information in conjunction with obtaining an arrest warrant constitutes the commencement of adversarial judicial proceedings within the meaning of the sixth amendment. The defendant argues that once the state's attorney signed an information in conjunction with obtaining a warrant for his arrest, the state had committed itself to prosecute. We are not persuaded. To the contrary, we conclude that it is not simply the signing of the information document that triggers the protections of the sixth amendment. Rather, it is the state's decision to move forward with the prosecution of the crimes charged in the information document, by arraigning the suspect and filing the information with the court, that signifies the state's commitment to prosecute as well as the initiation of the adversary judicial proceedings that trigger a defendant's right to counsel under the sixth amendment. See State v. Falcon ("neither the request of a state's attorney, nor the action of a court in granting that request, converts an arrest warrant into an official accusation signaling the state's commitment to prosecute").

Additionally, as we noted in *Falcon,* if an arrest and extradition hearing have not been viewed as a commitment to prosecute or the initiation of an adversarial judicial proceeding triggering rights under the sixth amendment, the signing of an information attached to an arrest warrant application hardly can be considered definitively prosecutorial and adversarial in nature. Indeed, the arrest warrant and information are prepared largely without the defendant's knowledge and it is not until the defendant is formally charged in open court at arraignment that he enters a plea, is faced with an adversarial judicial process, and the prosecution begins.

Furthermore, we agree with the state that a review of the procedure for and contents of an arrest warrant and information, as set out in Practice Book §§36 and 37, is instructive. "The warrant shall be signed by the judicial authority and shall contain the name of the accused person, or if such name is unknown, any name or description by which the accused can be identified with reasonable certainty, and the conditions of release fixed, if any. It shall state the offense charged and direct any officer authorized to execute it to arrest the accused person and to bring him or her before a judicial authority without undue delay." Practice Book §36-3. The offenses charged are written on court form JD-CR-71, entitled "Information," and the "Title, Allegation and Counts" section of the form is filled out and signed by a state's attorney. A copy of the arrest warrant with the attached and signed information are then given to the accused upon being taken into custody. See Practice Book §36-5. Subsequently, once the information is filed and the defendant is brought before the court at arraignment, he is advised of his constitutional rights, including his right to the services of an attorney. See Practice Book §37-3.

The rules of practice also contain provisions for canceling or amending arrest warrants and informations as necessary. . . . These provisions of the rules of practice all indicate that the signing of an information does not necessarily represent a commitment by the state to prosecute the defendant. Instead, it may be more accurately considered a prelude to a criminal prosecution, subject to amendment or cancellation as necessary, rather than the initiation of an adversarial judicial proceeding in its own right. In short, as suggested by Practice Book §37-3, we conclude that the defendant's constitutional right to counsel did not attach upon the signing of the information, but when the information was acted upon by the state and filed at the defendant's arraignment. It is at this point in the process that the "prosecutorial forces of organized society" aligned against the defendant, and the defendant actually found himself "immersed in the intricacies of substantive and procedural criminal law," thus warranting protection under the sixth amendment. Kirby v. Illinois, 406 U.S. at 689.

[In] the present case the information was not filed at the time of signing on May 13, 1999, but more than one month later when the defendant was arraigned. Consequently, [we agree with the state that the Sixth Amendment right to counsel had not attached at the time of Pierre's June 14 and June 24 statements].

Problem 1-2. Psychiatric Examinations

Raymond Larsen was charged with murder in Illinois. He admitted that he killed the victim but relied on the affirmative defense of insanity at the time of the slaying. The state filed a written pretrial motion to require Larsen to submit to examination by a state-designated psychiatrist as provided by statute. The court appointed Dr. Robert Reifman, assistant director of the Psychiatric Institute of the Circuit Court of Cook County, to conduct an examination "on August 23, or on any date subsequent, necessary to complete such examination." The defendant's counsel did not receive notice of the location and time, or of the name of the psychiatrist, prior to the examination, which was conducted on August 24.

Based on the court-ordered psychiatric examination, Dr. Reifman testified for the state on rebuttal at trial. He opined that the defendant had an antisocial personality but did not suffer from a mental defect or disease and had substantial capacity to conform his conduct to the requirement of the law and to appreciate the criminality of his conduct. On appeal the defendant argues that the psychiatric examination was a "critical stage" of the proceedings and that he had the right to notice and presence of counsel. How would you rule? See People v. Larsen, 385 N.E.2d 679 (Ill. 1979).

Notes

1. *Critical stages before trial: majority position.* The federal constitutional right to counsel applies only when two preconditions are met. First, the right attaches only after the initiation of an "adversarial proceeding." Second, even after the initiation of adversarial proceedings, the government must allow a defense attorney to participate only during a "critical stage" of those proceedings. The right extends to preliminary hearings in which the government must demonstrate a prima facie case against the defendant, Coleman v. Alabama, 399 U.S. 1 (1970), because defense counsel at such a hearing can obtain discovery of the state's evidence, make a record for later impeachment of state witnesses at trial, and preserve defense witness testimony. However, the federal constitutional right to counsel does not begin with arrest, or even with a postarrest probable cause hearing required by Gerstein v. Pugh, 420 U.S. 103 (1975).

State constitutions are almost always interpreted to cover the same pretrial proceedings as the federal constitution. Typically, a state's rules of criminal procedure will track these constitutional boundaries and will provide for the appointment of legal counsel at the defendant's initial appearance before a magistrate, when the defendant is informed of the charges. The Missouri rule reprinted above is typical.

Some high state courts have read their state constitutions to provide for a right to counsel earlier than in the federal system. See Page v. State, 495 So. 2d 436 (Miss. 1986) (right to counsel attaches before arraignment, when proceedings reach "accusatory" stage); cf. McCarter v. State, 770 A.2d 195 (Md. 2001) (statute gives defendant right to counsel at initial appearance; not necessary to decide if initial appearance is "critical stage" for constitutional counsel right). A minority of states have concluded that a post-arrest identification lineup or photo identification can qualify as a "critical stage" that triggers the right to counsel. See, e.g., People v.

Jackson, 217 N.W.2d 22 (Mich. 1974) (photo lineup); Commonwealth v. Richman, 320 A.2d 351 (Pa. 1974) (lineup). Some states also conclude that it is a violation of the right to counsel to fail to inform a suspect during interrogation that his attorney is trying to make contact. See Haliburton v. State, 514 So. 2d 1088 (Fla. 1987).

2. *Defense counsel for initial bail determination.* Defense attorneys are usually not available when the judge makes the first determination of bail or pretrial detention at the initial appearance. See, e.g., Fenner v. State, 846 A.2d 1020 (Md. 2004). Roughly 20 states provide no counsel at the time of bail. About half the states, however, do provide counsel at the time of bail in urban centers, even though defense lawyers are not available elsewhere in the state. A study of the Baltimore courts compared defendants who were all charged with similar nonviolent offenses, some represented by counsel and others not. The presence of counsel made an enormous difference in outcomes: two and a half times as many represented defendants were released on recognizance as unrepresented defendants. More than twice as many represented defendants had their bail reduced to affordable amounts. See Douglas L. Colbert, Ray Paternoster & Shawn D. Bushway, Do Attorneys Really Matter? The Empirical and Legal Case for the Right of Counsel at Bail, 23 Cardozo L. Rev. 1719 (2002).

3. *Defense counsel for DWI examinations: majority position.* In most states, there is no constitutional or statutory right to counsel for DWI examinations if they precede formal charging. Roughly a dozen high state courts have granted a person arrested on DWI charges the right to consult with retained counsel before performing sobriety tests. See State v. Spencer, 750 P.2d 147 (Or. 1988). Does this position create a special rule for DWI defendants not applicable to most criminal defendants? Are DWI defendants as a class different from other criminal defendants? Will the lawyer be able to persuade a problem drinker to seek treatment?

4. *Handwriting and blood samples.* Under federal law, a defendant has no right to counsel when she produces a handwriting exemplar, even after issuance of a formal charge, because the taking of such an exemplar is not a "critical stage" of the proceedings. Gilbert v. California, 388 U.S. 263 (1967). Similarly, there is no federal constitutional right to consult with counsel before submitting to an order for the drawing of a blood sample. A few states disagree. See Roberts v. State, 458 P.2d 340 (Alaska 1969) (right to counsel during collection of handwriting samples).

5. *Are psychiatric examinations a "critical stage"?* Should there be a rule governing whether all psychiatric examinations are a critical stage in the proceedings, or should it depend on the use of the information gained by the examination? Courts in about a dozen states have concluded that there is a right to counsel during at least some psychiatric exams, and these opinions typically state that the examination might be a "critical stage" in some cases but not in others. More than 20 states have declared that there is no constitutional right to counsel during any psychiatric exams. Should competency examinations be treated differently from examinations used to undermine potential defenses? Those used at sentencing? Those used to establish aggravating factors for a capital sentence? In Estelle v. Smith, 451 U.S. 454 (1981), the Supreme Court held that use of a psychiatrist's testimony at a capital sentencing proceeding based on a pretrial psychiatric examination at which defendant had not been represented by counsel violated defendant's Fifth Amendment rights against compulsory self-incrimination. What would a lawyer do at a psychiatric examination? Would a lawyer have a right to review a psychiatrist's questions before the examination?

6. *Right to counsel at sentencing.* The Sixth Amendment and its state constitutional analogs apply to sentencing hearings; the government must provide the defendant with an attorney at these hearings. Mempa v. Rhay, 389 U.S. 128 (1967); State v. Alspach, 554 N.W.2d 882 (Iowa 1996) (right to counsel at postconviction hearing to challenge amount of restitution). However, counsel is not required if the trial court sentences a defendant to probation and the state later attempts to convince the judge to revoke the defendant's probation (and send the defendant to prison) because she has violated the conditions of probation. Gagnon v. Scarpelli, 411 U.S. 778 (1973). If the end result is the same for the offender (a prison term), what is the constitutional distinction between sentencing hearings and probation revocation hearings?

7. *Right to counsel on appeal.* The criminal prosecution ends with a conviction and sentence. If the defendant appeals the case, the government is defending the judgment rather than "prosecuting" the case. As a result, courts say, the Sixth Amendment right to counsel does not apply to criminal appeals. The federal constitutional right to counsel on the first appeal as of right is based instead on both due process and equal protection principles. See Douglas v. California, 372 U.S. 353 (1963). The federal constitutional right does not extend to discretionary appeals. Ross v. Moffitt, 417 U.S. 600 (1974). The government also has no federal constitutional obligation to supply counsel for postconviction proceedings such as habeas corpus. See Murray v. Giarratano, 492 U.S. 1 (1989). Once again, state courts have by and large followed the federal lead when interpreting their own constitutional provisions. Nevertheless, many states do appoint counsel for at least some defendants during these postconviction proceedings. See, e.g., Mont. Code Ann. §§46-8-103, 46-8-104 ("Any court of record may assign counsel to defend any defendant, petitioner, or appellant in any postconviction criminal action or proceeding if he desires counsel and is unable to employ counsel").

8. *Conditions of consultation.* For defendants held in custody, the government has great control over the physical setting where the defense lawyer and client meet and talk. Usually this occurs in special visitation areas in a jail, where the conversation between lawyer and client remains confidential and unmonitored.

After the terrorist attacks of September 2001, the U.S. Department of Justice announced a new policy allowing the government to monitor these conversations in exceptional cases. The monitoring will be conducted without a court order whenever the attorney general certifies that "reasonable suspicion exists to believe that an inmate may use communications with attorneys or their agents to further or facilitate acts of violence or terrorism." The department says that it will notify inmates and their attorneys about plans to listen in on the conversations; also, it will assign a special "taint team" to perform the monitoring, and the teams will not disclose what they hear to the prosecutors working on the case. 66 Fed. Reg. 55,062 (Oct. 31, 2001); George Lardner, Jr., "U.S. Will Monitor Calls to Lawyers; Rule on Detainees Called 'Terrifying,'" Washington Post, Nov. 9, 2001, at A1. How would a client react to news that a taint team from the Department of Justice will listen to conversations with the defense attorney? How would you construct an argument that this eavesdropping violates the right to counsel?

9. *What happens when funds dry up?* Economic downturns lead to reduced tax revenues, and ultimately to less public funding available for defense counsel. If the state does not pay for the defense lawyer in cases where the state has an obligation to furnish one, the case cannot go forward. Prosecutions must be postponed and

ultimately dismissed. As a prosecutor or trial judge facing such a quandary, which cases would you delay or dismiss? The least serious cases? All cases scheduled for Fridays? All cases on the calendar for November and December? For a survey of different responses to this dilemma, see Lisa Stansky, The Big Squeeze, Nat'l L.J., May 23, 2003 (Oregon prosecutors met budget shortfall by declining prosecutions for car theft, prostitutions, trespassing, shoplifting; judges closed courthouse on Fridays from March through June).

B. SELECTION AND REJECTION OF COUNSEL

Although the government may have an obligation to offer an attorney to most criminal defendants, not all defendants accept the offer. Some will insist on representing themselves, while others will be unhappy with the assigned lawyer and will ask for some other attorney. Which legal institutions must respond to these sorts of requests?

The U.S. Supreme Court, for one, has declared a general principle that the Sixth Amendment right to counsel includes a right to self-representation. In Faretta v. California, 422 U.S. 806 (1975), the Court pointed to historical practices giving the defendant power to waive counsel. The Sixth Amendment made the assistance of counsel "an aid to a willing defendant — not an organ of the State interposed between an unwilling defendant and his right to defend himself personally."

The right to self-representation, however, is far different from what most defendants might prefer: the right to select the attorney who will be appointed to represent them. Most defendants who choose to represent themselves do so after a frustrating experience with an attorney assigned to their case (or an attorney assigned to some earlier case). But it is clear that poor defendants do not have the legal right to select which attorney will represent them. Courts do not grant indigent defendants such a power, nor do most managers of public defender organizations. The decision about self-representation, then, is part of a broader negotiation between the defendant, the judge, the former attorney, and a prospective new attorney about who will represent the defendant. What interests will each of these parties bring to the negotiation?

■ STATE v. JOSEPH SPENCER
519 N.W.2d 357 (Iowa 1994)

McGiverin, C.J.

The question presented here is whether a criminal defendant suffered a violation of his sixth amendment right to self-representation when the district court appointed counsel for him over his objection. . . . On July 18, 1990, Monona County Sheriff Dennis Smith went to Joseph Spencer's rural home to investigate complaints that Spencer was discharging firearms on his property. Sheriff Smith [observed marijuana growing in Spencer's garden, obtained a search warrant, and seized marijuana plants, cocaine, and firearms from the house]. On August 20, trial informations were filed charging Spencer with possession of marijuana with intent to manufacture, unauthorized possession of firearms, possession of cocaine, and possession of marijuana. . . .

Defendant Spencer retained a private attorney, Richard Mock of Onawa, to represent him and pleaded not guilty. Attorney Mock filed a motion to suppress drugs and weapons seized during the execution of the search warrant. After an evidentiary hearing, the district court overruled the motion.

A trial date was set. On May 17, 1991, a few days before trial, attorney Mock moved to withdraw from his representation of defendant Spencer. During the hearing on that motion, the question arose as to who would represent defendant at trial. Defendant Spencer told the court he wished to represent himself but admitted he did not know legal procedures or how to object to improper evidence. After a lengthy colloquy, the district court stated, "As far as I'm concerned, although he indicates he wants to do it himself, I don't see that he's competent and qualified to do it himself." The district court then appointed attorney Richard McCoy of Sioux City to represent Spencer. The case was continued and went to trial about one year later. Attorney McCoy fully represented defendant prior to and during the trial. Spencer was found guilty by a jury and was sentenced on the four charges. Spencer appealed, contending through new counsel that the district court denied his right to self-representation. [He] contends that the district court forced counsel upon him, contrary to his rights under the sixth amendment of the federal constitution. . . .

The sixth amendment provides that an accused "shall enjoy the right . . . to have the assistance of counsel for his defence." The fourteenth amendment of the federal constitution extends this right to state prosecutions. In Faretta v. California, 422 U.S. 806 (1975), the Supreme Court held that the right to self-representation to make one's own defense is necessarily implied by the structure of the Sixth Amendment. However, the Supreme Court also recognized an important limitation on that right: Although the defendant may elect to represent himself (usually to his detriment), the trial court "may — even over objection by the accused — appoint a 'standby counsel' to aid the accused if and when the accused requests help, and to be available to represent the accused in the event that termination of the defendant's self-representation is necessary." Such an appointment serves "to relieve the judge of the need to explain and enforce basic rules of courtroom protocol or to assist the defendant in overcoming routine obstacles that stand in the way of the defendant's achievement of his own clearly indicated goals." McKaskle v. Wiggins, 465 U.S. 168 (1984). . . .

Moreover, a defendant waives his right to self-representation unless he asserts that right by "knowingly and intelligently forgoing his right to counsel." This waiver may occur despite the defendant's statement that he wishes to represent himself if he makes that statement merely out of brief frustration with the trial court's decision regarding counsel and not as a clear and unequivocal assertion of his constitutional rights. In addition, a waiver [of the right to self-representation] may be found if it reasonably appears to the court that defendant has abandoned his initial request to represent himself.

We believe that the trial court did not err in appointing an attorney for Spencer. The intent behind the appointment, from the comments of both the court and Mock, defendant's withdrawing attorney, was to provide Spencer with "standby counsel" as envisioned in *Faretta* and *McKaskle*. The following comments were made at the hearing on attorney Mock's application to withdraw:

The Court: Well, I don't think that you're [the defendant] in the position of being able to defend yourself. And the least I would do is have somebody appointed to sit and be available as your counsel. But, frankly, I'm not going to put the court in the position whereby you defend yourself and then it's reversed if there is a conviction, just because there was no attorney present. It's as simple as that. Now, do you have any other person in mind?

The Defendant: No, sir . . .

The Court: Well, what familiarity do you have with the legal system?

The Defendant: I don't have any, Your Honor. . . .

The Court: An ordinary citizen can defend himself, but frankly an ordinary citizen is going to have a little difficulty following the procedures, making the proper objections and defending his own interests, unless he's familiar with the procedure in court. That's the problem I have. If you think you can do that, that's one thing; otherwise, what will happen is, if there is a conviction, it will be appealed and they will say you should have had somebody here to protect your rights.

The court thus properly appointed attorney McCoy over defendant's objection. If defendant had wished to treat this appointed attorney as standby counsel, he could have done so. The record here, however, evinces Spencer's initial desire to be represented by counsel (in employing attorney Mock), leading us to conclude that even if he wished to proceed pro se at the time of the withdrawal hearing, he waived and abandoned that right by acquiescing to attorney McCoy's full representation of his case for the following year leading up to and during the jury trial. . . .

Spencer's request for self-representation came out of frustration rather than a distinct and unequivocal request for that constitutional right. When Spencer was first charged in August 1990, he hired a private attorney (Richard Mock). Spencer worked with him until his motion to suppress evidence was overruled. Then, in May 1991, Mock moved to withdraw. Defendant was exasperated and did not want to pay for another attorney. Yet he willingly accepted attorney McCoy's name and address from the court and clearly relied on McCoy's representation during the following year and throughout trial. Spencer never attempted to try the jury case himself with McCoy as standby counsel. He never again raised the self-representation issue in the trial court. . . . Finally, defendant Spencer has pointed to nothing that he would have done differently had he represented himself at trial, nor has he demonstrated any way in which attorney McCoy denied him "a fair chance to present his case in his own way." *McKaskle,* 465 U.S. at 177. . . .

We believe that the trial court's appointment of attorney McCoy to be available as standby counsel satisfied Spencer's request to represent himself but ensured that Spencer's other rights were protected as well. By his later acts Spencer waived and abandoned any right to self-representation that he may have had. . . .

LAVORATO, J., dissenting.

In a state criminal trial, a defendant has a Sixth and Fourteenth Amendment right under the federal Constitution to self-representation. Faretta v. California, 422 U.S. 806 (1975). Before the right attaches, the defendant must voluntarily elect to proceed without counsel by "knowingly and intelligently" waiving his Sixth Amendment right to counsel. In addition, the defendant's request to proceed without counsel must be "clear and unequivocal." Before a trial court accepts the request, the court must make the defendant aware of the dangers and disadvantages of self-representation, so that the record will establish that "he knows what he is doing and his choice is made with eyes open." *Faretta*, 422 U.S. at 835. A trial court may not bar a defendant from proceeding without counsel even though the defendant is not technically competent in the law. The defendant must only be competent to make the choice to proceed without counsel. . . .

I easily infer from the record that Spencer is above average in intelligence. He has college training in electronics and math. His work experience included several years in the Air Force. He also worked as an electronics technician at General Dynamics. . . .

Unlike the majority, I believe the following colloquy between the court and Spencer shows that (1) Spencer made a clear and unequivocal request—not once, but several times—to proceed without counsel, (2) his request was knowingly and intelligently made, and (3) the trial court understood Spencer was making a clear and unequivocal request to proceed without counsel: . . .

The Court: . . . Do you want to get another attorney or do you want to go to trial tomorrow with him?

The Defendant: I feel I would be better off defending myself, Your Honor. He doesn't want to listen to what I'm telling him. . . . I'll have to go pro—I'll have to defend myself.

The Court: Before I would let you do that, I would appoint somebody. If your status is as it appears to be, that you have property, those will be assessed—the fees of whoever is appointed will be assessed against that.

The Defendant: I don't see how you can force me to do that, Your Honor.

The Court: Well, I don't think that you're in the position of being able to defend yourself. And the least I would do is have somebody appointed to sit and be available as your counsel. But, frankly, I'm not going to put the court in the position whereby you defend yourself and then it's reversed if there is a conviction, just because there was no attorney present. It's as simple as that. [W]hat familiarity do you have with the legal system?

The Defendant: I don't have any, Your Honor. Shouldn't make the legal system that way where I can't defend myself. I'm the one that's familiar with the case. I'm the one that's arrested. I know what my best interest is.

The Court: Well, if I understand your complaint, [Mr. Mock] wanted to plead it and you wanted to fight it. Now, the question is, how are you going to fight it in the courtroom? My problem with it is that I don't want you to sit in the courtroom not being prepared for the procedures and end up with a verdict against you because you weren't familiar with the procedures. Do you understand what I'm saying?

The Defendant: I understand what you're saying, but I don't understand why you make them that way.

The Court: Why do we make what that way?

The Defendant: Court procedures that way. Ordinary citizen can't come in and defend himself. . . .

The Court: Okay. During the interim, the court has attempted to contact an attorney to represent the defendant in this case. I have contacted Richard McCoy in Sioux City. He practices in criminal court and he's . . . tried a lot of cases and I feel that he's a good attorney. He's indicated that he would be willing to take your case. . . . Does that meet with your approval?

The Defendant: Doesn't meet with my approval, Your Honor, but if you're going to force it on me, I'm going to have to take it. . . .

The Prosecutor: The appointment of Mr. McCoy is pursuant to [section] 815.10(2) then?

The Court: That's right. And I can appreciate that it says, ". . . if a person desires legal assistance and is not indigent." As far as I'm concerned, although he indicates he wants to do it himself, I don't see that he's competent and qualified to do it himself. There should be somebody there. And on that basis, [the] court interprets that section to apply. . . .

Spencer captured the essence of *Faretta* when he insisted that we "shouldn't make the legal system that way where I can't defend myself. I'm the one that's familiar with the case. I'm the one that's arrested. I know what my best interest is." On this point, *Faretta* eloquently says:

> . . . To force a lawyer on a defendant can only lead him to believe that the law contrives against him. Moreover, it is not inconceivable that in some rare instances, the defendant might in fact present his case more effectively by conducting his own defense. Personal liberties are not rooted in the law of averages. The right to defend is personal. [Although the defendant] may conduct his own defense ultimately to his own detriment, his choice must be honored out of "that respect for the individual which is the lifeblood of the law."

The majority . . . attempts to finesse the trial court's denial of Spencer's request to defend himself by simply characterizing the court's actions as appointment of standby counsel. [However, the] role of standby counsel is limited to assisting a pro se defendant when such defendant wants assistance. A pro se defendant has the right to control the case the defendant chooses to present to the jury. That means a trial court must permit the pro se defendant to control the organization and content of the defense, to make motions, to argue points of law, to participate in voir dire, to question witnesses, and to address the court and jury at appropriate points in the trial. . . . If the trial court permits standby counsel to participate in the defense over the defendant's objections, such participation effectively allows counsel to make or substantially interfere with any significant tactical decisions, or to control questioning of witnesses, or to speak instead of the defendant on any matter of importance. Such interference is a denial of the pro se defendant's right to self-representation. . . .

These stringent limitations were recently spelled out in McKaskle v. Wiggins, 465 U.S. 168 (1984), the first case in which the Supreme Court has described the role of standby counsel. Because the role of standby counsel is severely restricted, trial courts contemplating appointment of standby counsel should — at a minimum — explain the limitations I have sketched out above from *McKaskle*. The reason is obvious: if the right to self-representation is to mean anything, a defendant who is appointed standby counsel should know how far the defendant can go in defending himself or herself without interference.

Here the trial court should have granted Spencer's request to defend himself. If the court was still concerned, the court should have then explicitly told Spencer he was appointing standby counsel and should have explained the limitations on standby counsel's role. Although above average in intelligence, Spencer is still a layperson untrained in the intricacies of criminal law. . . . After the colloquy between the court and himself, Spencer could only have had one thought: appointed counsel was being forced upon him and he was not going to be allowed to defend himself. . . .

At English common law the insistence upon a right of self-representation was the rule, rather than the exception. It is ironic that in the long history of British criminal jurisprudence there was only one tribunal that ever adopted the practice of forcing counsel upon an unwilling criminal defendant. That tribunal was the Star Chamber, a tribunal that for centuries symbolized the disregard of basic human rights. And the insistence upon a right to self-representation was, if anything, more fervent in the American colonies than at English common law. As *Faretta* points out, [the] "value of state-appointed counsel was not unappreciated by the Founders, yet the notion of compulsory counsel was utterly foreign to them. And whatever else may be said of those who wrote the Bill of Rights, surely there can be no doubt that they understood the inestimable worth of free choice." In sum, I would hold that the trial court denied Spencer the right to represent himself. I would therefore reverse and remand for a new trial.

Notes

1. *Knowing and voluntary waiver of counsel: majority position.* Once the right to counsel has attached, the defendant can waive that right, but only if the choice is "knowing and voluntary." Johnson v. Zerbst, 304 U.S. 458 (1938). In Faretta v. California, 422 U.S. 806 (1975), the Supreme Court declared that the right to "assistance" of counsel logically implied a defendant's right to represent herself at trial without counsel. How does this square with the Court's observation in *Gideon* that a lawyer is a "necessity, not a luxury"?

As *Spencer* indicates, there is no simple answer to the question of how a trial court will determine that the defendant's request is a knowing and voluntary waiver of the right to counsel. Typically, courts say that the defendant can waive counsel and invoke the *Faretta* right to self-representation only if (1) the trial court informs the defendant about the dangers of such a strategy, or (2) it otherwise appears from the record that the defendant understood the dangers. See People v. Adkins, 551 N.W.2d 108 (Mich. 1996) (waiver of counsel requires an unequivocal request by defendant, offer by trial court to appoint counsel, explanation of dangers of self-representation and the punishment for the crime charged, and a finding that self-representation will not disrupt trial). Courts often say that a waiver hearing expressly addressing the disadvantages of a pro se defense is much preferred but not absolutely necessary. The ultimate test, they say, is not the trial court's express advice but the defendant's understanding.

Defendants who represent themselves sometimes claim after conviction that the trial judge did not adequately warn them about the perils of acting as their own counsel. What kinds of warnings should judges give? State v. Cornell, 878 P.2d 1352 (Ariz. 1994) (no reversible error where court did not warn defendant that self-representation would undermine his planned insanity defense). Should courts, legislatures, or drafters of procedural rules design the standard *Faretta* warnings? See Benchbook for United States District Judges, 1.02 (4th ed. 2000); People v. Arguello, 772 P.2d 87 (Colo. 1989) (model inquiry); Michigan Court Rules 6.005(D) and (E) (court must advise the defendant of the charge, the maximum possible prison sentence for the offense, any mandatory minimum sentence required by law, and the risk involved in self-representation).

2. *Reasons for waiver of counsel.* The old bromide says that "the man who represents himself has a fool for a client." Is the decision to waive an attorney indeed a foolish choice in most cases? It is difficult to answer such a question at the system level. A study of federal pro se defendants determined that very few of them showed

signs of mental illness, and the outcomes in their cases compared favorably with the outcomes for defendants represented by counsel. See Erica Hashimoto, Defending the Right of Self Representation: An Empirical Look at the Felony Pro Se Defendant, 85 N.C. L. Rev. (forthcoming 2007). Is it possible to conclude from this observation that defendants waive counsel in cases where the evidence is especially strong or especially weak? Or that defendants who waive have realistic concerns about the quality of the effort that busy defense lawyers can offer?

Another study, based on state court data, noted that defendants waive counsel far more often in misdemeanor cases (even those misdemeanors where the law requires the government to provide counsel upon request) than in felony cases. The study found no evidence to confirm the hypothesis that concerns about money—either an up-front "application fee" or later recoupment of a portion of the attorney's fees—influenced the waiver decision. Ronald F. Wright and Wayne A. Logan, The Political Economy of Application Fees for Indigent Criminal Defense, 47 Wm. & Mary L. Rev. 2045 (2006). How might an observer learn whether costs influence some defendants who waive counsel?

3. *Standby counsel.* Often a judge will respond to a request for self-representation by appointing "standby counsel." Even if the standby counsel gives the defendant unwelcome advice and direction, a conviction can be upheld. See McKaskle v. Wiggins, 465 U.S. 168 (1984) (appointment of standby counsel does not violate self-representation right unless counsel interferes with substantial tactical decisions of defendant); Partin v. Commonwealth, 168 S.W.3d 23 (Ky. 2005) (rights to self-representation and confrontation satisfied even though trial court prohibited defendant from personally cross-examining his wife during trial on domestic violence charges; cross-examination conducted by standby counsel). Is the obligation of the trial judge to warn the defendant about the dangers of self-representation lower when the defendant's lawyer accepts "standby counsel" status at the time defendant asks to represent herself? See State v. Layton, 432 S.E.2d 740 (W. Va. 1993) (allowing less extensive warning about self-representation when standby counsel played relatively active role at trial); Anne Bowen Poulin, The Role of Standby Counsel in Criminal Cases: In the Twilight Zone of the Criminal Justice System, 75 N.Y.U. L. Rev. 676 (2000).

The law in some states allows a defendant to partially waive the right to counsel; the defendant may rely on an appointed lawyer for some purposes, but also serve as co-counsel and examine some witnesses himself or herself. See Hill v. Commonwealth, 125 S.W.3d 221 (Ky. 2004) (judge must hold *Faretta* hearing before granting defendant's request to waive a portion of right to counsel and serve as co-counsel at trial).

4. *Imposing counsel.* In *Spencer,* what could the defendant have said to the trial judge to convince the appellate court that he had tried to exercise his right to represent himself? If trial judges can appoint counsel over requests like Spencer's, how vibrant is the right to self-representation? See State v. Colt, 843 P.2d 747 (Mont. 1992) (trial judge directs standby counsel to take over cross-examination after repeated courtroom errors by the defendant). Have state courts in effect overruled *Faretta?* Which constituency, if any, keeps *Faretta* rights alive? If you were a prosecutor, would you argue on behalf of defendants who want to represent themselves? If lawyers are essential to justice, shouldn't *Faretta* be reversed?

In Martinez v. Court of Appeal of California, 528 U.S. 152 (2000), the Supreme Court refused to extend the *Faretta* right of self-representation to a direct appeal. The appellate courts may properly appoint counsel for the appellant, even if the

appellant objects. Are trial judges better able than appellate jud
difficulties presented by defendants who represent themselves?
interests in self-representation stronger at trial than during an

5. *Competence to waive the right to counsel.* Some defendants a
make a "knowing and voluntary waiver" of the right to co
Moran, 509 U.S. 389 (1993), the Supreme Court held that t
does not require a higher standard to assess whether a defendant is
waive counsel or plead guilty than is used to assess competency to stand trial. See
State v. Day, 661 A.2d 539 (Conn. 1995). Is there any reason to employ different
standards for competence to stand trial and for waiver of counsel?

6. *Performance standards for pro se counsel.* In practice, trial courts appear to give
some leeway to lay lawyers, but appellate cases consistently hold that the ordinary
standards of practice and evidence are to be applied to defendants who appear pro se.
See Commonwealth v. Jackson, 647 N.E.2d 401 (Mass. 1995). Should judges assist
pro se litigants in questioning witnesses? Should judges give pro se litigants
miniature "lessons" in trial procedure and the rules of evidence?

7. *Selection of appointed counsel.* Defendants who retain their own lawyers may
retain any lawyer they can afford who will agree to take the case (assuming the
lawyer has no conflict of interest). This ability of the client to choose a particular
lawyer helps to create a cooperative relationship. The lawyer is urged to "establish a
relationship of trust and confidence with the accused." ABA Standards for Criminal
Justice 4-3.1 (1980). An indigent defendant, however, may not choose his appointed
counsel. In the homely phrase of the Nebraska trial judge in State v. Green, 471
N.W.2d 402 (Neb. 1991), "beggars can't be choosey." This is a fair, if blunt, assessment of the law in almost every jurisdiction. See Morris v. Slappy, 461 U.S. 1 (1983)
(upholds trial court's refusal to grant continuance necessary to allow original
counsel to represent defendant; trial proceeded with new appointed counsel).
Does this rule suggest we are committed to providing counsel only in the most
minimal sense to indigent defendants? If you were a supervisor in a public defender's office, would you institute a rule that allowed clients to take part in the choice
of their lawyers?

Should a judge appointing defense counsel place any weight on a defendant's
request to work with an attorney with specific qualities? Consider this possible conversation between a lawyer and client:

> "I want a Black lawyer to represent me." These are the first words you hear after you
> introduce yourself to your new client. . . . You are white. He is Black. You answer that
> you are an experienced criminal lawyer and will represent him to the best of your ability,
> regardless of his or your race. He responds that he too is experienced with the criminal
> justice system — a system that targets Black men, like himself, for prosecution far more
> than whites, that sentences Black men to prison more frequently and for a longer
> duration than whites, and that fails to acknowledge or address the role that race and
> racism play in the development, enforcement, and execution of the criminal laws estab-
> lished by "the system." . . . He explains that an African-American lawyer will be better
> able to understand and appreciate the circumstances that resulted in the bringing of
> these charges and that he, the client, can trust a Black lawyer more than a white one.

Kenneth P. Troccoli, "I Want a Black Lawyer to Represent Me": Addressing a Black
Defendant's Concerns with Being Assigned a White Court-Appointed Lawyer, 20
Law and Inequality: A Journal of Theory and Practice 1 (Winter 2002). See also

arcus T. Boccaccini and Stanley L. Brodsky, Characteristics of the Ideal Criminal Defense Attorney from the Client's Perspective: Empirical Findings and Implications for Legal Practice, 25 Law & Psychol. Rev. 81, 116 (2001) (client survey lists the following, in descending order, as most desired attorney characteristics: advocates for client's interest, works hard, keeps client informed, cares about the client, honest, gets favorable outcome, "would not do whatever prosecution says," listens to client, spends time with client before court date).

8. *Law students as counsel.* Almost every state allows some law students to participate in the defense of criminal cases. Statutes and court rules typically allow law students to represent indigent criminal defendants, so long as the defendant is informed that the representative is a law student and consents to the representation, and a licensed attorney supervises the student's efforts. See Fla. R. Crim. P. 11-1.2(b); Miss. Code Ann. §73-3-207. What would you say to a defendant to convince her to allow a law student to "practice" on her case?

C. ADEQUACY OF COUNSEL

Constitutions and other laws not only govern the availability of a lawyer; they also address the quality of the legal representation that the attorney must give the client. So long as lawyers make mistakes, courts and other legal institutions must decide whether the client will be the one who pays. The next case lays down a legal standard now followed almost uniformly by courts trying to determine whether an attorney has provided a client with the "effective assistance of counsel" necessary for a constitutionally acceptable criminal conviction.

■ CHARLES STRICKLAND v. DAVID WASHINGTON
466 U.S. 668 (1984)

O'CONNOR, J.

This case requires us to consider the proper standards for judging a criminal defendant's contention that the Constitution requires a conviction or death sentence to be set aside because counsel's assistance at the trial or sentencing was ineffective.

During a 10-day period in September 1976, respondent planned and committed three groups of crimes, which included three brutal stabbing murders, torture, kidnapping, severe assaults, attempted murders, attempted extortion, and theft. After his two accomplices were arrested, respondent surrendered to police and voluntarily gave a lengthy statement confessing to the third of the criminal episodes. The State of Florida indicted respondent for kidnapping and murder and appointed an experienced criminal lawyer to represent him.

Counsel actively pursued pretrial motions and discovery. He cut his efforts short, however, and he experienced a sense of hopelessness about the case, when he learned that, against his specific advice, respondent had also confessed to the first two murders. [Respondent also acted against counsel's advice in pleading guilty to all charges, and waiving the right to an advisory jury at his capital sentencing hearing.]

In preparing for the sentencing hearing, counsel spoke with respondent about his background. He also spoke on the telephone with respondent's wife and mother, though he did not follow up on the one unsuccessful effort to meet with them. He did not otherwise seek out character witnesses for respondent. Nor did he request a psychiatric examination, since his conversations with his client gave no indication that respondent had psychological problems. [To establish his claim of "emotional stress" as a "mitigating factor" against a death sentence, counsel decided to rely on the defendant's statements at the guilty plea colloquy about his emotional state, and not to introduce further evidence on the question. By foregoing the opportunity to present new evidence on these subjects, counsel prevented the State from cross-examining respondent on his claim and from putting on psychiatric evidence of its own.]

Counsel also excluded from the sentencing hearing other evidence he thought was potentially damaging. He successfully moved to exclude respondent's "rap sheet." Because he judged that a presentence report might prove more detrimental than helpful, as it would have included respondent's criminal history and thereby would have undermined the claim of no significant history of criminal activity, he did not request that one be prepared.

[Because the sentencing judge had a reputation as a person who thought it important for a convicted defendant to own up to his crime, counsel argued at sentencing that Washington's remorse and acceptance of responsibility justified sparing him from the death penalty. Counsel also argued that respondent had no history of criminal activity and that respondent committed the crimes under extreme mental or emotional disturbance, thus coming within the statutory list of mitigating circumstances. The trial judge found numerous aggravating circumstances and no significant mitigating circumstances, and sentenced respondent to death on each of the three counts of murder.]

Respondent subsequently sought collateral relief in state court on numerous grounds, among them that counsel had rendered ineffective assistance at the sentencing proceeding. Respondent challenged counsel's assistance in six respects. He asserted that counsel was ineffective because he failed to move for a continuance to prepare for sentencing, to request a psychiatric report, to investigate and present character witnesses, to seek a presentence investigation report, to present meaningful arguments to the sentencing judge, and to investigate the medical examiner's reports [about the condition of the victims' bodies] or cross-examine the medical experts. [The state trial court, the state appellate courts, and the federal district court all refused to find ineffective assistance of counsel, and therefore refused to grant postconviction relief. The federal appeals court announced a new legal standard for claims of ineffective assistance of counsel and remanded the case for further fact-finding under the new standards. This appeal followed.]

In a long line of cases that includes Powell v. Alabama, 287 U.S. 45 (1932) . . . and Gideon v. Wainwright, 372 U.S. 335 (1963), this Court has recognized that the Sixth Amendment right to counsel exists, and is needed, in order to protect the fundamental right to a fair trial [in the adversary system. It has also] recognized that the right to counsel is the right to the effective assistance of counsel. . . .

The Court has not elaborated on the meaning of the constitutional requirement of effective assistance in [cases] presenting claims of "actual ineffectiveness." In giving meaning to the requirement, however, we must take its purpose — to

ensure a fair trial — as the guide. The benchmark for judging any claim of ineffectiveness must be whether counsel's conduct so undermined the proper functioning
of the adversarial process that the trial cannot be relied on as having produced a just
result. . . .

A convicted defendant's claim that counsel's assistance was so defective as to
require reversal of a conviction or death sentence has two components. First, the
defendant must show that counsel's performance was deficient. This requires showing that counsel made errors so serious that counsel was not functioning as the
"counsel" guaranteed the defendant by the Sixth Amendment. Second, the
defendant must show that the deficient performance prejudiced the defense.
This requires showing that counsel's errors were so serious as to deprive the
defendant of a fair trial, a trial whose result is reliable. Unless a defendant makes
both showings, it cannot be said that the conviction or death sentence resulted from
a breakdown in the adversary process that renders the result unreliable. . . .

When a convicted defendant complains of the ineffectiveness of counsel's assistance, the defendant must show that counsel's representation fell below an objective
standard of reasonableness. More specific guidelines are not appropriate. The Sixth
Amendment refers simply to "counsel," not specifying particular requirements of
effective assistance. It relies instead on the legal profession's maintenance of standards sufficient to justify the law's presumption that counsel will fulfill the role in
the adversary process that the Amendment envisions. The proper measure of attorney performance remains simply reasonableness under prevailing professional
norms.

Representation of a criminal defendant entails certain basic duties. Counsel's
function is to assist the defendant, and hence counsel owes the client a duty of
loyalty, a duty to avoid conflicts of interest. Cuyler v. Sullivan, 446 U.S. 335
(1980). From counsel's function as assistant to the defendant derive the overarching
duty to advocate the defendant's cause and the more particular duties to consult
with the defendant on important decisions and to keep the defendant informed of
important developments in the course of the prosecution. Counsel also has a duty to
bring to bear such skill and knowledge as will render the trial a reliable adversarial
testing process.

These basic duties neither exhaustively define the obligations of counsel nor
form a checklist for judicial evaluation of attorney performance. In any case presenting an ineffectiveness claim, the performance inquiry must be whether counsel's assistance was reasonable considering all the circumstances. Prevailing norms
of practice as reflected in American Bar Association standards and the like, e.g., ABA
Standards for Criminal Justice 4-1.1 to 4-8.6 (2d ed. 1980), are guides to determining
what is reasonable, but they are only guides. No particular set of detailed rules for
counsel's conduct can satisfactorily take account of the variety of circumstances
faced by defense counsel or the range of legitimate decisions regarding how best
to represent a criminal defendant. Any such set of rules would interfere with the
constitutionally protected independence of counsel and restrict the wide latitude
counsel must have in making tactical decisions. Indeed, the existence of detailed
guidelines for representation could distract counsel from the overriding mission of
vigorous advocacy of the defendant's cause. Moreover, the purpose of the effective
assistance guarantee of the Sixth Amendment is not to improve the quality of legal
representation, although that is a goal of considerable importance to the legal
system. The purpose is simply to ensure that criminal defendants receive a fair trial.

Judicial scrutiny of counsel's performance must be highly deferential. It is all too tempting for a defendant to second-guess counsel's assistance after conviction or adverse sentence, and it is all too easy for a court, examining counsel's defense after it has proved unsuccessful, to conclude that a particular act or omission of counsel was unreasonable. A fair assessment of attorney performance requires that every effort be made to eliminate the distorting effects of hindsight, to reconstruct the circumstances of counsel's challenged conduct, and to evaluate the conduct from counsel's perspective at the time. Because of the difficulties inherent in making the evaluation, a court must indulge a strong presumption that counsel's conduct falls within the wide range of reasonable professional assistance; that is, the defendant must overcome the presumption that, under the circumstances, the challenged action might be considered sound trial strategy. There are countless ways to provide effective assistance in any given case. Even the best criminal defense attorneys would not defend a particular client in the same way.

The availability of intrusive post-trial inquiry into attorney performance or of detailed guidelines for its evaluation would encourage the proliferation of ineffectiveness challenges. Criminal trials resolved unfavorably to the defendant would increasingly come to be followed by a second trial, this one of counsel's unsuccessful defense. Counsel's performance and even willingness to serve could be adversely affected. . . .

An error by counsel, even if professionally unreasonable, does not warrant setting aside the judgment of a criminal proceeding if the error had no effect on the judgment. The purpose of the Sixth Amendment guarantee of counsel is to ensure that a defendant has the assistance necessary to justify reliance on the outcome of the proceeding. Accordingly, any deficiencies in counsel's performance must be prejudicial to the defense in order to constitute ineffective assistance under the Constitution.

In certain Sixth Amendment contexts, prejudice is presumed. Actual or constructive denial of the assistance of counsel altogether is legally presumed to result in prejudice. So are various kinds of state interference with counsel's assistance. Prejudice in these circumstances is so likely that case-by-case inquiry into prejudice is not worth the cost. Moreover, such circumstances involve impairments of the Sixth Amendment right that are easy to identify and, for that reason and because the prosecution is directly responsible, easy for the government to prevent.

One type of actual ineffectiveness claim warrants a similar, though more limited, presumption of prejudice. In Cuyler v. Sullivan, 446 U.S. 335 (1980), the Court held that prejudice is presumed when counsel is burdened by an actual conflict of interest. In those circumstances, counsel breaches the duty of loyalty, perhaps the most basic of counsel's duties. Moreover, it is difficult to measure the precise effect on the defense of representation corrupted by conflicting interests. Given the obligation of counsel to avoid conflicts of interest and the ability of trial courts to make early inquiry in certain situations likely to give rise to conflicts, it is reasonable for the criminal justice system to maintain a fairly rigid rule of presumed prejudice for conflicts of interest. . . .

Conflict of interest claims aside, actual ineffectiveness claims alleging a deficiency in attorney performance are subject to a general requirement that the defendant affirmatively prove prejudice . . . It is not enough for the defendant to show that the errors had some conceivable effect on the outcome of the proceeding. Virtually every act or omission of counsel would meet that test, and not every error that conceivably could have influenced the outcome undermines the reliability of the result of the proceeding. . . .

On the other hand, we believe that a defendant need not show that counsel's deficient conduct more likely than not altered the outcome in the case. [The "more likely than not altered the outcome" test, which is used to decide whether to grant a new trial based on new evidence,] is not an apt source from which to draw a prejudice standard for ineffectiveness claims. The high standard for newly discovered evidence claims presupposes that all the essential elements of a presumptively accurate and fair proceeding were present in the proceeding whose result is challenged. An ineffective assistance claim asserts the absence of one of the crucial assurances that the result of the proceeding is reliable, so finality concerns are somewhat weaker and the appropriate standard of prejudice should be somewhat lower. The result of a proceeding can be rendered unreliable, and hence the proceeding itself unfair, even if the errors of counsel cannot be shown by a preponderance of the evidence to have determined the outcome.

Accordingly, the appropriate test for prejudice finds its roots in the test for materiality of exculpatory information not disclosed to the defense by the prosecution, and in the test for materiality of testimony made unavailable to the defense by Government deportation of a witness. The defendant must show that there is a reasonable probability that, but for counsel's unprofessional errors, the result of the proceeding would have been different. A reasonable probability is a probability sufficient to undermine confidence in the outcome. . . .

Although we have discussed the performance component of an ineffectiveness claim prior to the prejudice component, there is no reason for a court deciding an ineffective assistance claim to approach the inquiry in the same order or even to address both components of the inquiry if the defendant makes an insufficient showing on one. In particular, a court need not determine whether counsel's performance was deficient before examining the prejudice suffered by the defendant as a result of the alleged deficiencies. The object of an ineffectiveness claim is not to grade counsel's performance. If it is easier to dispose of an ineffectiveness claim on the ground of lack of sufficient prejudice, which we expect will often be so, that course should be followed. . . .

Having articulated general standards for judging ineffectiveness claims, we think it useful to apply those standards to the facts of this case in order to illustrate the meaning of the general principles. . . . With respect to the performance component, the record shows that respondent's counsel made a strategic choice to argue for the extreme emotional distress mitigating circumstance and to rely as fully as possible on respondent's acceptance of responsibility for his crimes. . . . The trial judge's views on the importance of owning up to one's crimes were well known to counsel. The aggravating circumstances were utterly overwhelming. Trial counsel could reasonably surmise from his conversations with respondent that character and psychological evidence would be of little help. Respondent had already been able to mention at the plea colloquy the substance of what there was to know about his financial and emotional troubles. Restricting testimony on respondent's character to what had come in at the plea colloquy ensured that contrary character and psychological evidence and respondent's criminal history, which counsel had successfully moved to exclude, would not come in. On these facts, there can be little question, even without application of the presumption of adequate performance, that trial counsel's defense, though unsuccessful, was the result of reasonable professional judgment.

With respect to the prejudice component, the lack of merit of respondent's claim is even more stark. The evidence that respondent says his trial counsel should have offered at the sentencing hearing would barely have altered the sentencing profile presented to the sentencing judge. [At] most this evidence shows that numerous people who knew respondent thought he was generally a good person and that a psychiatrist and a psychologist believed he was under considerable emotional stress that did not rise to the level of extreme disturbance. Given the overwhelming aggravating factors, there is no reasonable probability that the omitted evidence would have changed the conclusion that the aggravating circumstances outweighed the mitigating circumstances and, hence, the sentence imposed. Indeed, admission of the evidence respondent now offers might even have been harmful to his case: his "rap sheet" would probably have been admitted into evidence, and the psychological reports would have directly contradicted respondent's claim that the mitigating circumstance of extreme emotional disturbance applied to his case.

[R]espondent has made no showing that the justice of his sentence was rendered unreliable by a breakdown in the adversary process caused by deficiencies in counsel's assistance. . . .

MARSHALL, J., dissenting.

[S]tate and lower federal courts have developed standards for distinguishing effective from inadequate assistance. Today, for the first time, this Court attempts to synthesize and clarify those standards. For the most part, the majority's efforts are unhelpful. . . .

My objection to the performance standard adopted by the Court is that it is so malleable that, in practice, it will either have no grip at all or will yield excessive variation in the manner in which the Sixth Amendment is interpreted and applied by different courts. To tell lawyers and the lower courts that counsel for a criminal defendant must behave "reasonably" . . . is to tell them almost nothing. In essence, the majority has instructed judges called upon to assess claims of ineffective assistance of counsel to advert to their own intuitions regarding what constitutes "professional" representation, and has discouraged them from trying to develop more detailed standards governing the performance of defense counsel. In my view, the Court has thereby not only abdicated its own responsibility to interpret the Constitution, but also impaired the ability of the lower courts to exercise theirs.

The debilitating ambiguity of an "objective standard of reasonableness" in this context is illustrated by the majority's failure to address important issues concerning the quality of representation mandated by the Constitution. . . . Is a "reasonably competent attorney" a reasonably competent adequately paid retained lawyer or a reasonably competent appointed attorney? It is also a fact that the quality of representation available to ordinary defendants in different parts of the country varies significantly. Should the standard of performance mandated by the Sixth Amendment vary by locale? The majority offers no clues as to the proper responses to these questions. . . .

I agree that counsel must be afforded wide latitude when making tactical decisions regarding trial strategy, but many aspects of the job of a criminal defense attorney are more amenable to judicial oversight. For example, much of the work involved in preparing for a trial, applying for bail, conferring with one's client, making timely objections to significant, arguably erroneous rulings of the trial judge, and filing a notice of appeal if there are colorable grounds therefor could profitably be made the subject of uniform standards.

I object to the prejudice standard adopted by the Court for two independent reasons. First, it is often very difficult to tell whether a defendant convicted after a trial in which he was ineffectively represented would have fared better if his lawyer had been competent. Seemingly impregnable cases can sometimes be dismantled by good defense counsel. On the basis of a cold record, it may be impossible for a reviewing court confidently to ascertain how the government's evidence and arguments would have stood up against rebuttal and cross-examination by a shrewd, well-prepared lawyer. The difficulties of estimating prejudice after the fact are exacerbated by the possibility that evidence of injury to the defendant may be missing from the record precisely because of the incompetence of defense counsel. . . .

Second and more fundamentally, the assumption on which the Court's holding rests is that the only purpose of the constitutional guarantee of effective assistance of counsel is to reduce the chance that innocent persons will be convicted. In my view, the guarantee also functions to ensure that convictions are obtained only through fundamentally fair procedures. The majority contends that the Sixth Amendment is not violated when a manifestly guilty defendant is convicted after a trial in which he was represented by a manifestly ineffective attorney. I cannot agree. Every defendant is entitled to a trial in which his interests are vigorously and conscientiously advocated by an able lawyer. [I would hold] that a showing that the performance of a defendant's lawyer departed from constitutionally prescribed standards requires a new trial regardless of whether the defendant suffered demonstrable prejudice thereby.

[I must also] dissent from the majority's disposition of the case before us. It is undisputed that respondent's trial counsel made virtually no investigation of the possibility of obtaining testimony from respondent's relatives, friends, or former employers pertaining to respondent's character or background. Had counsel done so, he would have found several persons willing and able to testify that, in their experience, respondent was a responsible, nonviolent man, devoted to his family, and active in the affairs of his church. . . . Had this evidence been admitted, respondent argues, his chances of obtaining a life sentence would have been significantly better. . . .

The State makes a colorable — though in my view not compelling — argument that defense counsel in this case might have made a reasonable "strategic" decision not to present such evidence at the sentencing hearing on the assumption that an unadorned acknowledgment of respondent's responsibility for his crimes would be more likely to appeal to the trial judge, who was reputed to respect persons who accepted responsibility for their actions. But however justifiable such a choice might have been after counsel had fairly assessed the potential strength of the mitigating evidence available to him, counsel's failure to make any significant effort to find out what evidence might be garnered from respondent's relatives and acquaintances surely cannot be described as "reasonable." . . . If counsel had investigated [and presented the available mitigating evidence], there is a significant chance that respondent would have been given a life sentence. . . .

Ineffective assistance of counsel claims are especially common in capital cases where the law is complex, and where errors can arise both at the guilt/innocence and sentencing stages of the trial. Typically, such claims arise on collateral review.

Sometimes ineffective assistance claims turn on a single act (or failure to act) by counsel, but often these claims take the form of a list, where the defendant claims that counsel's errors — individually and collectively — violated the standards of *Strickland.* Consider how the court in the following case assesses, for each of the defendant's multiple claims, whether the evidence shows unreasonable "performance" ("that counsel made errors so serious that counsel was not functioning as the 'counsel' guaranteed the defendant by the Sixth Amendment") or "prejudice" ("a reasonable probability that, but for counsel's unprofessional errors, the result of the proceeding would have been different").

■ MICHAEL BRUNO v. STATE
807 So. 2d 55 (Fla. 2001)

Per Curiam

Michael J. Bruno, under sentence of death, appeals the denial of relief following an evidentiary hearing on his first motion filed pursuant to Florida Rule of Criminal Procedure 3.850*.... For the reasons expressed below, we affirm the denial of relief....

On August 8, 1986, appellant Michael Bruno and his fifteen-year-old son, Michael Jr., were in the apartment of a friend, Lionel Merlano, when Bruno beat Merlano with a crowbar. Bruno then sent Michael Jr. elsewhere in the apartment to fetch a handgun and, when the boy returned with a gun, Bruno shot Merlano twice in the head. Bruno was arrested several days later and gave a taped statement wherein he at first denied any knowledge of the murder but then later admitted committing the crime, claiming it was self-defense. Michael Jr. also gave a full statement to police. Prior to being arrested, Bruno made numerous inculpatory statements to friends concerning both his plan to commit the murder and the commission of the crime itself. Police found the gun in a canal where a friend, Jody Spalding, saw Bruno throw it.

Bruno was charged with first-degree murder and robbery (he stole a stereo from the apartment after the murder) and his strategy at trial was to raise a reasonable doubt in jurors' minds by claiming that Jody Spalding was the killer. He was convicted as charged, and the judge followed the jury's eight-to-four vote and imposed a sentence of death based on three aggravating circumstances and no mitigating circumstances. This Court affirmed. Bruno filed the present rule 3.850 motion and the trial court conducted an evidentiary hearing at which Bruno presented six witnesses and the State presented one witness. The trial court denied the motion. Bruno appeals....

Bruno argues that the trial court erred in denying his postconviction claims concerning alleged ineffective assistance of counsel. The test to be applied by the trial court when evaluating an ineffectiveness claim is two-pronged: The defendant must show both that trial counsel's performance was deficient and that the defendant was prejudiced by the deficiency. The standard of review for a trial court's

---

*Fla. R. Crim. P. 3.850 is the statutory section providing for collateral review. — Eds.

ruling on an ineffectiveness claim also is two-pronged: The appellate court must defer to the trial court's findings on factual issues but must review the court's ultimate conclusions on the deficiency and prejudice prongs de novo.

In his brief before this Court, Bruno asserts several instances of ineffectiveness. . . . In subclaim two, Bruno contends that defense counsel was ineffective during the trial due to alcohol and drug impairments. Bruno points to the previous hospitalization of trial counsel for drug and alcohol use. Private counsel was retained in August 1986 to represent Bruno. Over the next few months, counsel developed a drinking problem and, when he was drinking, would occasionally use cocaine. He enrolled in Alcoholics Anonymous on October 15, 1986, and remained alcohol and drug free from then until March 1987, when he began drinking again but not using cocaine. He admitted himself into a hospital on March 15, 1987, for his drinking problem, remained hospitalized for twenty-eight days, and subsequently remained alcohol- and drug-free. After being released, counsel apprised both Bruno and the court of his problem and offered to withdraw, but Bruno asked him to continue as counsel. The trial, which originally had been set for March 30, 1987, was rescheduled for August 5, 1987, and began on that date. Counsel testified at the evidentiary hearing below that he never was under the influence of alcohol or drugs while working on this case. The trial court concluded that Bruno "failed to meet his burden of demonstrating how [counsel's] drug and alcohol usage prior to trial rendered ineffective his legal representation to the Defendant and how such conduct prejudiced the Defendant." We agree.

In subclaim three, . . . Bruno argues that defense counsel repeatedly divulged confidential and damaging information to the trial court. [One] example of the alleged conflict of interest relates to comments made by defense counsel during the penalty phase. The comments were made in response to Dr. Stillman's testimony that Bruno was insane at the time of the offense. Shortly after Dr. Stillman's testimony, defense counsel requested a side-bar conference and told the trial court that he was surprised by the testimony, as Dr. Stillman had previously informed defense counsel that Bruno was sane at the time of the offense. At the evidentiary hearing below, defense counsel explained that he conveyed his surprise to the court in order to justify his subsequent motion for an additional psychological examination. [The trial court found that the defense attorney's] "statements to the Trial Judge were made as a justification for his seeking leave of court to file a belated notice of intent to rely on an insanity defense. . . . The Defendant has failed to show that he was prejudiced by [defense counsel]'s statements to the trial judge." Ultimately, the trial court concluded that Bruno failed both prongs of the *Strickland* test. We agree.

In subclaim four, Bruno argues that counsel was ineffective because he failed to present a defense of voluntary intoxication. At the evidentiary hearing below, defense counsel testified that Bruno adamantly refused the presentation of a voluntary intoxication defense. In rejecting this claim, the trial court stated that "[t]he decision not to present the affirmative defense of 'voluntary intoxication' was based on a strategy decision which was motivated by the Defendant's conscious decision, rather than a result of [counsel's] legal incompetency." We agree with the trial court that Bruno has failed to satisfy the first prong of the *Strickland* test.

In subclaim five, Bruno asserts that counsel negligently failed to move to suppress Bruno's initial statement to the police. . . . Bruno was first interrogated by the police on August 12, 1986. Bruno alleges that he was not given *Miranda* warnings at this time. During the interrogation, Bruno told the police that he knew the victim and had previously consumed a few beers with the victim at the victim's apartment, which was located in the Candlewood apartment complex. Bruno told the police that, the weekend the crime was committed, he was working on Jody Spalding's car, with the exception of going to the Candlewood apartment complex to obtain a receipt for a refrigerator. . . . Bruno claims that this statement provided the police with additional evidence, as it contradicted the later statement in which Bruno claimed that he killed the victim in self-defense, it contradicted other testimony about his whereabouts in the days following the killing, and shows guilty knowledge. . . . The trial court concluded that Bruno failed to meet the second prong of the *Strickland* test. We agree. . . .

In subclaim ten, Bruno argues that counsel was ineffective in failing to investigate and present available mitigation. The trial court rejected this claim as follows:

> The testimony and exhibits presented at the evidentiary hearing reflect that the Defendant's mis-information to, and his failure to fully cooperate with [counsel] in the preparation of his defense, prevented [counsel] from initially obtaining information relating to the Defendant's previous hospitalization at Pilgrim State Hospital. . . . Dr. Stillman's trial testimony . . . acquainted the jury with the Defendant's extensive emotional and drug history, and drug use at the time of the murder. The Defendant's parents testified that Mr. Bruno had tried to commit suicide, and was briefly hospitalized until his sister had him released. The fact that there could have been a more detailed presentation of these circumstances does not establish that defense counsel's performance was deficient. Defense counsel cannot be faulted for failing to investigate background information, which he had no reason to suspect existed.

We agree. The trial court noted that Bruno's failure to cooperate with counsel prevented counsel from initially obtaining relevant information pertaining to the penalty phase. Despite this obstacle, counsel still presented evidence concerning several potential mitigating circumstances: Bruno's extensive emotional and drug history, Bruno's drug use at the time of the murder, Dr. Stillman's testimony that Bruno had organic brain damage as a result of his drug use, and testimony that Bruno had attempted suicide and was briefly hospitalized. . . . Counsel's performance in this case may not have been perfect, but it did not fall below the required standard. [Even] assuming that counsel's performance was deficient, we agree with the trial court that Bruno has failed to satisfy the second prong of the *Strickland* test. . . .

Bruno claims that counsel was ineffective in failing to provide Dr. Stillman with sufficient background information. Bruno argues that counsel's neglect prevented Dr. Stillman from sufficiently assessing Bruno's competence to stand trial and potential mitigating circumstances.

Prior to trial, Dr. Stillman was appointed to evaluate whether Bruno was insane at the time of the offense or incompetent to stand trial. The record reveals that Dr. Stillman informed defense counsel on two separate occasions that he did not believe that Bruno was either insane at the time of the offense or incompetent to stand trial. Subsequently, Dr. Stillman was called as a defense witness during the penalty phase. In preparing for this testimony, Dr. Stillman interviewed, for the first time, members of Bruno's family and a jail nurse who had contact with Bruno. These meetings occurred within two days of Dr. Stillman's testimony. During the State's cross-examination, Dr. Stillman opined that he believed that Bruno was insane at the time of the offense. Dr. Stillman testified that despite his previous determinations that Bruno was not insane, he still had a suspicion, and that this suspicion was confirmed upon meeting with members of Bruno's family and the nurse. . . . The trial court below rejected this claim as follows:

> Since Dr. Stillman is dead, there is no way for the court to ascertain what factors he considered, or did not consider, in the way of background material on the Defendant. . . . Dr. Stillman interviewed the defendant twice for a total of two and a half hours. He . . . spoke with the defendant's sister and parents, [and] was aware of the Defendant's extensive drug usage, and his stay at Pilgrim State hospital. . . . The fact that the defendant and his family withheld information from [counsel] does not render [counsel's] performance deficient.

We agree. As far as Dr. Stillman's penalty phase testimony, it is clear from the record that Dr. Stillman had been provided with all necessary information at the time of his testimony. In regards to whether Bruno was competent to stand trial or insane at the time of the offense, we find no negligence on the part of defense counsel. Defense counsel asked Dr. Stillman to evaluate Bruno prior to trial. Dr. Stillman rendered an opinion, on two separate occasions, that Bruno was neither incompetent to stand trial nor insane at the time of the offense. Bruno has not established that Dr. Stillman told defense counsel that he needed more information in order to form this opinion. [We] find no merit to this claim. . . .

Based on the foregoing, we affirm the trial court's denial of Bruno's motion for postconviction relief. . . .

ANSTEAD, J., concurring in part and dissenting in part.

. . . While I agree with the majority's analysis and rejection of claims of error as to eight of [the ineffective assistance] claims, it appears that two of Bruno's claims present valid instances of ineffectiveness. They include: (1) the improper and prejudicial disclosure of confidential information by counsel; and (2) counsel's critical failure to investigate and present mitigating evidence on behalf of the defendant to the sentencing jury and judge.

Bruno argues that his trial counsel substantially prejudiced the outcome of his penalty phase proceedings when trial counsel divulged confidential and damaging information to the trial court by informing the court during the penalty phase that he was completely surprised by Dr. Stillman's testimony that Bruno was "insane" at the time of the offense. After Stillman made the surprise disclosure that he believed Bruno was insane at the time of the crime, defense counsel approached both the court and the prosecutor and told them that Stillman had personally assured him many times just the opposite — that Bruno was "totally competent." Critically, the prosecutor later used this assurance during closing argument to completely impeach Stillman's testimony, and the sentencing court subsequently rejected Stillman's penalty phase testimony *in toto*. Bruno claims that his lawyer was ineffective because counsel's disclosures completely discredited Bruno's most important mitigation witness and his only expert witness, thereby conceding away virtually his entire case for mitigation. . . .

During direct examination, Stillman actually testified to the existence of some mitigation. According to Stillman, Bruno suffered from a passive-aggressive personality, and he also exhibited signs of a schizophrenic-type disorder when he was under the influence of drugs. . . . Stillman testified that Bruno started using L.S.D. and marijuana when he was married and that his drug abuse progressively worsened over the years. When his wife left him, he tried to kill himself by taking Quaaludes and by attempting to drown himself in the ocean. Further, Stillman testified that Bruno had been using an ounce of cocaine every day for weeks prior to the offense.

However, during cross-examination, Stillman proclaimed for the first time that he believed Bruno was insane at the time of the murder. . . .

In an apparent panic, trial counsel reacted to Stillman's revelation by immediately disclosing to the court two confidential letters to trial counsel in which Stillman had opined that Bruno was competent to stand trial and was not insane. Trial counsel told the court that he thought he was duty bound to bring this patent inconsistency in Stillman's evaluations to the trial court's attention.

At the evidentiary hearing in the 3.850 proceeding, trial counsel sought to justify his breach of confidence by claiming that he acted in order to justify his subsequent motion for an additional psychological examination. However, the record directly refutes this assertion. In the actual motion for psychiatric evaluation, which was filed after the jury's recommendation for death but prior to the trial court's sentencing, trial counsel made absolutely no reference to the fact that Stillman had changed his opinion concerning Bruno's sanity. Rather, the motion . . . alleges that trial counsel and Stillman were unaware of Bruno's psychological history until trial counsel talked with Bruno's sister and learned about Bruno's history of drug use, attempted suicide, and hospitalization for mental problems . . .

In Douglas v. Wainwright, 714 F.2d 1532 (11th Cir. 1983), the Eleventh Circuit noted that "the most egregious examples of ineffectiveness do not always arise because of what counsel did *not* do, but from what he *did* do — or say." . . . [I]n Blanco v. Singletary, 943 F.2d 1477 (11th Cir. 1991), the trial attorneys volunteered inappropriate information to the trial court concerning the fact that they did not have any mitigating evidence to present and that none of the defendant's friends or family members would agree to testify on his behalf. [T]he Eleventh Circuit held that counsel's errors did not fall within the range of competent performance expected in criminal cases.

Trial counsel in the instant case did present some mitigating evidence. . . . However, trial counsel's improper disclosure to the trial court that Stillman had earlier consistently opined that Bruno was sane highlighted a serious inconsistency in Stillman's professional opinion, which, when explored, completely undermined the expert's credibility to the jury and the court. . . .

Bruno further claims that counsel was manifestly ineffective in his more or less complete failure to investigate and present evidence of the abundant mitigating evidence that actually existed of Bruno's troubled history of mental problems and drug abuse. [T]he trial court allowed no break between the finding of guilt by the jury and the penalty phase of the trial; indeed, the penalty phase began the very next morning. Trial counsel acceded to this procedure.

[The defense attorney did call] Bruno's parents to testify. Bruno's mother described Bruno as he was as a young man, claiming that he was "good boy." However, she testified that after he left home and got married, he changed drastically. He started wearing his hair long (in a mohawk), tattooed his body, and started hanging around with a motorcycle group and bands. She testified that after his marriage ended he went "berserk," lost the desire to live and attempted to commit suicide by drowning himself and overdosing on drugs. . . .

Critically, however, at the end of her testimony, when trial counsel asked her whether she had anything to say to the jury about the possible punishment her son should receive, Bruno's mother declared: "All I can say is that I don't have much time, neither does my husband. But if that's your wish [i.e., the imposition of the punishment of death] and you think you are doing right, God bless you. But other than that I don't know what to say. I just feel sorry for my husband, but if a child does something wrong, he should be punished. That is my belief." [U]nlike Bruno's mother, Bruno's father testified that he did not believe that Bruno deserved the death penalty. . . .

On direct examination during the penalty phase, counsel did not elicit a single affirmative opinion from Stillman concerning the applicability of mitigators to this crime. Counsel was apparently unaware of his obligation to do so. Importantly, the record reflects that Dr. Stillman was appointed by the court *only* to assess Bruno's sanity and competency for guilt phase purposes, and not to evaluate Bruno and his background to determine the existence of mitigation for penalty phase purposes. . . . Counsel never sought a mental health evaluation of his client for mitigation purposes, an evaluation that is fundamental in defending against the death penalty.

Further, the record reflects that although trial counsel presented Bruno's parents and Dr. Stillman as witnesses at the penalty phase, counsel did nothing to prepare these witnesses for testifying and, most tellingly, was unaware of the content of their testimony beforehand, especially regarding the opinion of Bruno's mother that he must accept his punishment. . . . At the time of the penalty phase, counsel did not even know who comprised the members of Bruno's immediate family — he did not know of the existence of Bruno's younger sister, who held key mental health information concerning him. . . .

The postconviction record reveals that copious mitigation actually existed in this case. . . . Bruno has a life-long and extensive record of drug abuse beginning with sniffing glue and lacquer thinner at ages eleven to thirteen. At the postconviction evidentiary hearing, Bruno called . . . Dr. Dee, a neuropsychologist. . . . Dr. Dee testified that Bruno suffers from organic brain syndrome as a result of his continuous, heavy, chronic drug use, which included cocaine, LSD, and marijuana. The most significant injury to his brain is manifested by impaired memory, increased impulsivity, difficulty in impulse control, deteriorated work performance, and inability to hold a job. According to Dr. Dee, at the time of the murder, Bruno was under the influence of extreme mental or emotional disturbance due to cerebral damage and drug usage.

Dr. Dee testified that according to Bruno's son Michael, on the day of the murder, Bruno free-based cocaine mid-day and used it continuously throughout the day until he and his son left for the victim's apartment. Bruno had also taken three purple micro-dots of LSD and eight or nine Quaaludes. Dr. Dee also testified that Bruno's ability to appreciate the criminality of his conduct or conform his conduct to the requirements of the law was substantially impaired, also due to his cerebral impairment and intoxication. As for nonstatutory mitigation, Dr. Dee testified that Bruno and his siblings were physically beaten and abused by their mother as young children. This finding, based on accounts from Bruno's family members, differ significantly from Bruno's mother's testimony during the penalty phase proceedings that Bruno grew up in a happy home. . . .

Bruno has clearly demonstrated deficient performance by his counsel which prejudiced the outcome of the penalty phase of the proceedings. [T]he jury recommended death by a vote of eight to four, four votes for life even without the substantial mitigation we now know existed all the time. In the words of the United States Supreme Court in *Strickland,* it is apparent that confidence in the outcome of Bruno's penalty phase proceeding has been substantially undermined by counsel's neglect and lack of preparation.

Problem 1-3. *Cronic* Errors

Joe Elton Nixon was convicted of first-degree murder, kidnapping, robbery, and arson; the court sentenced him to death. Nixon's trial counsel made the following remarks during his opening statement in the guilt phase:

> In this case, there will be no question that Jeannie [sic] Bickner died a horrible, horrible death. In fact, that horrible tragedy will be proved to your satisfaction beyond any reasonable doubt. In this case, there won't be any question, none whatsoever, that my client, Joe Elton Nixon, caused Jeannie [sic] Bickner's death. This case is about the death of Joe Elton Nixon and whether it should occur within the next few years by electrocution or maybe its natural expiration after a lifetime of confinement.

During his closing argument, Nixon's counsel said:

> Ladies and gentlemen of the jury, I wish I could stand before you and argue that what happened wasn't caused by Mr. Nixon, but we all know better. I know what you will decide will be unanimous. You will decide that the State of Florida, through Mr. Hankinson and Mr. Guarisco, has proved beyond a reasonable doubt each and every element of the crimes charged, first-degree premeditated murder, kidnapping, robbery, and arson.

Nixon filed a motion for collateral review, claiming that his trial counsel was ineffective during the guilt phase of the trial. Nixon argues that these comments were the equivalent of a guilty plea by his attorney. He claims that he did not give his attorney consent to enter a guilty plea or to admit guilt as part of a trial strategy.

Nixon argues that his counsel's conduct in this case amounted to per se ineffective assistance of counsel and that the proper test for assessing counsel arises under United States v. Cronic, 466 U.S. 648 (1984), rather than Strickland v. Washington. In *Cronic,* decided the same day as *Strickland,* the Supreme Court created an exception to the *Strickland* standard for ineffective assistance of counsel and acknowledged that certain circumstances are so egregiously prejudicial that ineffective assistance of counsel will be presumed. In *Cronic,* the Supreme Court stated:

> [There are] circumstances that are so likely to prejudice the accused that the cost of litigating their effect in a particular case is unjustified. Most obvious, of course, is the complete denial of counsel. [A] trial is unfair if the accused is denied counsel at a critical stage of his trial. Similarly, if counsel entirely fails to subject the prosecution's case to meaningful adversarial testing, then there has been a denial of Sixth Amendment rights that makes the adversary process itself presumptively unreliable.

How would you rule on Nixon's motion? Compare Nixon v. Singletary, 758 So. 2d 618 (Fla. 2000); Florida v. Nixon, 543 U.S. 175 (2004).

Notes

1. *The test for ineffective assistance of counsel: majority position.* The *Strickland* opinion was the Supreme Court's first substantial effort to define the quality of representation required by the Sixth Amendment. In *Strickland,* the court announced its two-part standard: (1) counsel's performance must be "reasonably effective" and cannot fall below an "objective standard" of reasonableness, and (2) the defendant must show a "reasonable probability" that the outcome in the proceedings changed because of the attorney's deficient performance. The *Strickland* opinion has been enormously influential, with states overwhelmingly adopting its framework under state constitutions. Why did it take until 1984 (almost 200 years) to get a square decision from the U.S. Supreme Court on standards of attorney competence? Note that the Court did not explicitly require access to counsel as an element of due process in state criminal trials until Powell v. Alabama, 287 U.S. 45 (1932), and it was not until Gideon v. Wainwright, 372 U.S. 335 (1963), that state-provided attorneys became the rule rather than the exception. See David Cole, *Gideon v. Wainwright* and *Strickland v. Washington*: Broken Promises, in Criminal Procedure Stories (Carol Steiker ed., 2006). Why might these events be useful or necessary for the development of a constitutional standard for effective counsel?

State courts and lower federal courts were developing their own approaches to claims of ineffective assistance before the *Strickland* decision in 1984. The earliest standard declared that counsel would be ineffective in the constitutional sense only if the lawyer's performance converted the trial into a "farce and mockery" or a "sham trial." See Diggs v. Welch, 148 F.2d 667 (D.C. Cir. 1945); Anderson v. Peyton, 167 S.E.2d 111 (Va. 1969). By the late 1970s just under 20 states took this approach. See William Erickson, Standards of Competency for Defense Counsel in a Criminal Case, 17 Am. Crim. L. Rev. 233 (1979).

Before *Strickland,* another group of about 20 states used more general (and arguably more pro-defense) language to describe the standard for judging ineffective assistance. These courts spoke of the need for attorneys to demonstrate "reasonable competence" in light of the typical conduct of other attorneys faced with the same situation. See People v. Blalock, 592 P.2d 406 (Colo. 1979). Finally, a smaller group of states elaborated on this general "reasonable competence" by pointing to specific "checklists" of tasks for counsel. The checklists gave more precise meaning to the general phrases in certain settings. Very often, the ABA Defense Function Standards (approved between 1968 and 1973) were one source of these checklists, although some of the standards also developed in common law fashion. See People v. Pope, 590 P.2d 859 (Cal. 1979); Rodgers v. State, 567 S.W.2d 634 (Mo. 1978). State courts also differed from one another on the question of the level of prejudice that the defendant had to show. The possibilities ranged from a stringent "outcome determinative" test, or a "reasonable probability" that counsel's error affected the outcome, to an automatic reversal rule.

In *Strickland,* Justice O'Connor describes the effectiveness standard as an "objective" standard. What makes a standard "objective" or "subjective"? The majority also rules out strategic decisions as a basis for a finding of ineffectiveness. How should a court determine whether a decision is "strategic"? Is this an objective test? Why does the court create a "strong presumption" of sound lawyering? Is that an objective standard?

2. *Measuring prejudice.* The prejudice standard under *Strickland*, requiring a "reasonable probability" of a different outcome absent attorney error, calls for a counterfactual inquiry into what the outcome would have been in a hypothetical trial without attorney error. Is the prejudice standard too restrictive or too liberal? Should a court insist on reaching the difficult and counterfactual prejudice issue only after finding substandard attorney performance? The bulk of the appellate cases on ineffective assistance (and it is indeed a bulky body of cases) turn on prejudice rather than ineffectiveness. Although the *likelihood* of prejudice is central to this litigation, the *amount* of prejudice is not. See Glover v. United States, 531 U.S. 198 (2001) (increase in prison sentence due to inadequate performance by attorney does not have to meet any particular "significance" threshold to qualify as potential prejudice).

How should the standard for prejudice change when the defendant pleads guilty rather than going to trial? The majority of courts declare that a defendant can be prejudiced by an attorney's failure to explain a potential defense during consultations about a guilty plea, even if the defense would not have succeeded. See Grosvenor v. State, 874 So. 2d 1176 (Fla. 2004).

3. *Measuring performance.* The defendant has the burden of proving unreasonable performance, by a preponderance of the evidence. The most straightforward cases of substandard performance involve an attorney's failure to consult a client (or failure to follow client instructions) over the basic direction of the litigation, such as a decision whether to file a notice of appeal, or a decision to concede guilt and concentrate on the sentencing phase of a capital case. See Roe v. Flores-Ortega, 528 U.S. 470 (2000) (ineffectiveness often present but not presumed when counsel fails to consult client about appeal and misses deadline for filing).

The more common and more difficult claims about attorney performance involve questionable choices about trial preparation and presentation of evidence. The U.S. Supreme Court has applied the *Strickland* standard lately to emphasize the reasonableness of the investigation that precedes an attorney's trial choices, rather than focusing on the reasonableness of the trial decision itself. See Rompilla v. Beard, 545 U.S. 374 (2005) (unreasonable performance during pretrial investigation of prior related conviction that prosecution would emphasize as aggravating fact in capital case). Does the legal standard in *Strickland* prevent a finding of unreasonable performance in any case where the attorney (or an appellate court) can construct a *post hoc* justification for the choice? When a defendant complains about a large collection of attorney decisions, does the standard require a court to consider them one at a time, or can the court consider the collective impact of many borderline attorney choices?

With sad regularity, attorneys are accused of sleeping, being drunk or drugged, or otherwise being physically unable to present an effective defense. Courts sometimes hold that such impairments do not deny defendants effective counsel without specific proof about faulty legal decisions caused by the impairment. See, e.g., McFarland v. Texas, 928 S.W.2d 482 (Tex. Crim. App. 1996) (72-year-old lawyer who said he "customarily take[s] a short nap in the afternoon" held not to be ineffective assistance where napping might have been a "strategic" move to generate jury sympathy and where co-counsel remained awake). Are attorneys impaired if they do not know the most basic law governing the case? Should courts give experienced attorneys a stronger presumption of reasonable performance than newer attorneys?

4. *Structural ineffectiveness and presumed prejudice.* In a few settings, the trial might occur in a setting so likely to produce error that prejudice can be presumed; no attorney is likely to provide adequate defense in these settings. Examples of "structural" ineffectiveness appear in conflict of interest cases, in which an attorney represents multiple clients and runs the risk of harming one client while furthering the interests of the other. If defense counsel raises at trial the issue of potential conflict of interest, and the trial court fails to appoint new counsel or to hold a hearing to determine the risk of a conflict, prejudice is presumed. Holloway v. Arkansas, 435 U.S. 475 (1978); Lettley v. State, 746 A.2d 392 (Md. 2000) (presumed prejudice where attorney represented two clients, second client admitted guilt in crime for which first client was being tried); cf. People v. Morales, 808 N.E.2d 510 (Ill. 2004) (dual representation of defendant and potential witness does not establish per se conflict; retained counsel for defendant charged with first-degree murder in connection with drug-related shooting also represented defendant's boss in drug gang in a federal drug prosecution, and alleged murder victim was a courier sent by the boss to collect money from defendant). If the defendant raises the issue after trial, she must prove that there was an "actual conflict of interest" that "adversely affected" her lawyer's performance, but there is no need to prove that the adverse effects on lawyer performance changed the outcome at trial. See Cuyler v. Sullivan, 446 U.S. 335 (1980); but see Mickens v. Taylor, 535 U.S. 162 (2002) (defendant must show prejudice where defense lawyer had *potential* conflict of interest based on former representation of murder victim in juvenile proceedings).

Structural ineffectiveness (and the presumption of prejudice) is more difficult to establish in other settings. In United States v. Cronic, 466 U.S. 648 (1984), a companion case to *Strickland,* the Court rejected a presumption of ineffectiveness when an inexperienced lawyer was appointed shortly before a complex case. However, the court noted that such a presumption could be found "if the accused is denied counsel at a critical stage of his trial," or "if counsel entirely fails to subject the prosecution's case to meaningful adversarial testing." See, e.g., Florida v. Nixon, 543 U.S. 175 (2004) (attorney predicted that prosecution's evidence of guilt in murder trial would be virtually impossible to refute, and proposed to defendant a strategy of conceding guilt to focus on urging leniency at penalty phase, but defendant did not respond; no presumption of prejudice under *Cronic* for conceding guilt under these circumstances); Bell v. Cone, 535 U.S. 685 (2002) (*Cronic* presumption does not apply when client's complaint goes to specific aspects of counsel's performance — failing to present mitigating evidence and waiving closing argument); cf. Burdine v. Johnson, 262 F.3d 336 (5th Cir. 2001) (contrasting an intoxicated attorney with an attorney who was "repeatedly asleep, and hence unconscious, as witnesses adverse to Burdine were examined and other evidence against Burdine was introduced. This unconsciousness extended through a not insubstantial portion of the 12 hour and 51 minute trial. Unconscious counsel equates to no counsel at all.").

5. *Pervasiveness of ineffective counsel claims.* A claim of ineffective assistance of counsel may be one of the most common legal challenges to criminal convictions. Perhaps this is so because virtually any pretrial or trial error can be framed as ineffective assistance. If the lawyer failed to correct the error — even if the error itself is not of constitutional or otherwise sufficient magnitude — it is possible to question that lawyer's effectiveness on direct appeal or during a collateral attack on the conviction.

Is it common for defendants to obtain reversals of their convictions on effectiveness grounds? Richard Klein analyzed about 4,000 appellate decisions in state and federal court between 1970 and 1983 that raised ineffective assistance of counsel claims; he concluded that the court found ineffective assistance in about 3.9 percent of the cases. Richard Klein, The Emperor *Gideon* Has No Clothes: The Empty Promise of the Constitutional Right to Effective Assistance of Counsel, 13 Hastings Const. L.Q. 625 (1986). In an analysis of cases decided after 1984 (after *Strickland*), would you expect this "success" rate to go up or down?

6. *Public and private incompetence.* Should the judicial standards for ineffective assistance of counsel be the same for public defenders and private attorneys practicing criminal defense? There was a time when courts in some jurisdictions used different standards for publicly provided and privately retained defense counsel, applying a less demanding standard when reviewing the work of privately retained counsel because the work of such an attorney was not considered "state action." See People v. Stevens, 53 P.2d 133 (Cal. 1935). However, in Cuyler v. Sullivan, 446 U.S. 335, 344-45 (1980), the Supreme Court rejected the idea that private attorneys are to be judged by some lesser standard of constitutional scrutiny: "Since the State's conduct of a criminal trial itself implicates the State in the defendant's conviction, we see no basis for drawing a distinction between retained and appointed counsel that would deny equal justice to defendants who must choose their own lawyers." Although it is clear that retained attorneys cannot be scrutinized less carefully than appointed counsel, could they be scrutinized *more* carefully? On average, which type of attorney do you suppose would be more effective? Does your answer change for different types of criminal cases? See Bureau of Justice Statistics, Defense Counsel in Criminal Cases (Nov. 2000, NCJ 179023) (in both federal and state courts, conviction rates were the same for defendants represented by publicly and privately financed counsel; pretrial release less common for state court defendants with public counsel; state defendants with public counsel sentenced more often to prison or jail but for shorter terms than those with private lawyers).

7. *Does quality of counsel matter?* By focusing on the effectiveness of lawyers, do we lose sight of more important questions about the *contents* of procedural rules that the lawyers must use? If you are convinced that the law of criminal procedure is designed first and foremost to produce convictions efficiently, would you conclude that lawyers (regardless of their effectiveness) will rarely have any procedural claims available that could prevent a conviction from happening? Conversely, if you are convinced that the law of criminal procedure focuses more on police shortcomings than on a defendant's guilt or innocence, would you conclude that judges will find a way to review police conduct, whether or not a lawyer raises the claim in a timely and effective manner?

■ AMERICAN BAR ASSOCIATION, DEFENSE FUNCTION STANDARDS (3d ed. 1993)

STANDARD 4-3.6 PROMPT ACTION TO PROTECT THE ACCUSED

Many important rights of the accused can be protected and preserved only by prompt legal action. Defense counsel should inform the accused of his or her rights at the earliest opportunity and take all necessary action to vindicate those rights.

Defense counsel should consider all procedural steps which in good faith may be taken, including, for example, motions seeking pretrial release of the accused, obtaining psychiatric examination of the accused when a need appears, moving for change of venue or continuance, moving to suppress illegally obtained evidence, moving for severance from jointly charged defendants, and seeking dismissal of charges.

STANDARD 4-4.1 DUTY TO INVESTIGATE

(a) Defense counsel should conduct a prompt investigation of the circumstances of the case and explore all avenues leading to facts relevant to the merits of the case and the penalty in the event of conviction. The investigation should include efforts to secure information in the possession of the prosecution and law enforcement authorities. The duty to investigate exists regardless of the accused's admissions or statements to defense counsel of facts constituting guilt or the accused's stated desire to plead guilty. . . .

STANDARD 4-6.1 DUTY TO EXPLORE DISPOSITION WITHOUT TRIAL

(a) Whenever the law, nature, and circumstances of the case permit, defense counsel should explore the possibility of an early diversion from the criminal process through the use of other community agencies.

(b) Defense counsel may engage in plea discussions with the prosecutor. Under no circumstances should defense counsel recommend to a defendant acceptance of a plea unless appropriate investigation and study of the case has been completed, including an analysis of controlling law and the evidence likely to be introduced at trial.

■ RULE 33, COURT OF COMMON PLEAS, CUYAHOGA COUNTY, OHIO

No attorney will be assigned to defend any indigent person in a criminal case unless his or her name appears on the applicable list of approved trial counsel. . . . The approved trial counsel list shall remain in effect for a period of two years. . . . Counsel whose name appears on the approved trial counsel list shall file an application for renewal to serve as appointed counsel in order to remain on the approved trial counsel list. . . . The following experience qualifications shall be a prima facie basis for the inclusion of a lawyer on the lists designated below:

(A) Assigned counsel for murder cases (including charges of murder, aggravated murder and aggravated murder with specifications).

(1) Trial counsel in a prior murder trial; or

(2) Trial counsel in four first degree felony jury trials; or

(3) Trial counsel in any ten felony or civil jury trials;

(4) No lawyer may appear on the list for murder cases unless he is also listed as counsel for major felony cases described below.

(B) Assigned counsel for major felony cases (first, second and third degree felonies).

(1) Trial counsel in two previous major felony jury trials (first, second or third degree felonies); or

(2) Trial counsel in any four previous criminal jury trials; or

(3) Trial counsel in any previous six criminal or civil jury trials; or

(4) Trial counsel in any two criminal jury trials plus assistant trial counsel in any two criminal jury trials.

(C) Assigned counsel for fourth degree felony cases.

(1) Trial counsel in any previous criminal or civil jury trial; or

(2) Assistant counsel in any two civil or criminal jury trials. . . .

To assist attorneys in obtaining trial experience in criminal cases, and for the purposes of obtaining experience necessary for inclusion on one of the above lists, this Court will cooperate with programs organized by local bar associations in which interested attorneys may be assigned as assistant trial counsel on a non-fee basis in cooperation with regularly retained or assigned counsel in criminal case trials in this county, under the supervision of the trial judge. . . .

The office of the Cuyahoga County Public Defender shall be assigned no less than 35 percent defendants in each category of cases described above for which counsel are selected for indigent defendants. The assigned Public Defender, before being assigned to represent an indigent defendant, shall also meet the established criteria. . . .

Problem 1-4. More Objective Competence Standards

Assume that you are chief counsel to the senate rules committee in a state where the legislature promulgates rules of criminal procedure. The chair of the committee, with the support of the chief justice of the state supreme court, has asked you to draft specific competence standards for the pretrial process. In particular, you are directed to research and draft standards providing guidance on the following three questions:

- How soon must attorneys see a new client?
- How much time must attorneys have, at a minimum, to prepare for plea negotiations?
- What obligations, if any, should counsel have with respect to researching alibi or character witnesses?

How specific can such rules be without interfering with effective defense in some cases? Do nonbinding guidelines accomplish anything? Would you recommend ultimate adoption of these types of rules, or would you encourage the committee and the courts to rely on the *Strickland* standards without additional guidance?

Notes

1. *Rules and standards.* The majority in *Strickland* said that "specific guidelines are not appropriate." Was Justice O'Connor correct in concluding that courts should not specify what is adequate representation of a criminal defendant? What is the

significance of the fact that a few states had begun to announce specific expectations for defense counsel to meet? Is any institution other than the judiciary more capable of specifying the standards for effective assistance of counsel, or is lawyering an activity that simply cannot be reduced to enforceable standards?

2. *Performance standards versus experience standards.* The Cuyahoga County rules take a fairly typical approach to the problem of attorney competence: Like the court rules in many other local jurisdictions, these rules focus on the prior experience of attorneys rather than specifying the tasks a competent attorney should perform. Are the approaches embodied in the ABA Standards and the Cuyahoga County standards compatible? Were both standards drafted based on the same goals or assumptions? Should jurisdictions focus on the qualifications of counsel in the absence of clear performance standards? Do prospective standards for appointment prevent incompetent representation better than retrospective claims by disgruntled clients?

3. *Consequences for attorneys.* If substandard work by criminal defense counsel injures a client, can the client sue for malpractice? While malpractice suits in criminal cases are possible, they face more obstacles than civil malpractice claims. For suits against publicly financed attorneys, sovereign immunity and various official immunities block the suit unless state law waives those defenses. Often state law allows criminal defendants to bring malpractice suits only if they can prove they were actually innocent; it is not enough to claim that the attorney caused an overly severe sentence. See Meredith J. Duncan, The (So-Called) Liability of Criminal Defense Attorneys: A System in Need of Reform, 2002 BYU L. Rev. 1-52; Schreiber v. Rowe, 814 So. 2d 396 (Fla. 2002) (public defenders cannot assert judicial immunity in malpractice cases, but former defendant must prove actual innocence to maintain suit); In re Rantz, 109 P.3d 132 (Colo. 2005) (defendant does not have to obtain post-conviction relief before suing defense counsel for malpractice, but issue preclusion may prevent a defendant who lost an ineffective assistance of counsel claim in post-conviction proceeding from raising a civil malpractice claim; collects cases). Compare malpractice suits to an alternative form of accountability for attorneys, embodied in Rule 13 of the Rules of the Supreme Court of the State of Hawaii. Under Rule 13, after a conviction has been overturned because of ineffective assistance of counsel, the Supreme Court appoints a special master who can recommend "corrective action" against the attorney such as remedial education, suspension of the attorney's license to practice law, and referral to the state legal ethics authorities.

D. SYSTEMS FOR PROVIDING COUNSEL

We have surveyed the legal standards designed to ensure that individual defense counsel will provide effective assistance of counsel. The methods the government uses to fund and deliver legal services to the indigent also have a powerful effect on the performance of the defense counsel in individual cases. What institutions and sources of law shape entire systems for providing counsel?

The first method of providing defense counsel to indigent defendants in this country was the appointment of a private attorney to the case. The attorney might have handled the case as an unpaid volunteer or might have received some small compensation from the government. Early in the twentieth century, however, organizations of full-time defense attorneys began to spring up in major urban areas.

The first appeared in Los Angeles in 1914. Supporters of these "defender organizations" (public agencies and private charitable groups) hoped that they would provide criminal defense at less expense to the public and would avoid the distracting and needlessly confrontational style of the "shyster" lawyers who often accepted court appointments. As one prominent defense attorney put it, the publicly accountable defense attorney could join forces with the prosecutor to see that "no innocent man may suffer or guilty man escape." Mayer Goldman, The Need for a Public Defender, 8 J. Crim. L. & Criminology 273 (1917-1918).

These historical origins are still visible in our current systems for providing defense counsel to the indigent. Most places still use more than one method of providing defense counsel, but the "organizational" defenders have become the most important piece of the puzzle. Those who create and fund the defender organizations hope to control the costs of providing adequate criminal defense and to do so without compromising either the fairness or the efficiency of the criminal justice system. As you read the following materials, think about how to determine the proper goals of a system for delivering criminal defense services. Do the different systems provide defense counsel with different incentives to handle criminal cases in particular ways, such as choosing between plea bargains and trials?

■ STEVEN SMITH AND CAROL DEFRANCES, INDIGENT DEFENSE
(February 1996, NCJ 158909)

Court-appointed legal representation for indigent criminal defendants plays a critical role in the Nation's criminal justice system. In 1991 about three-quarters of State prison inmates and half of Federal prison inmates reported that they had a court-appointed lawyer to represent them for the offense for which they were serving time. In 1989, nearly 80 percent of local jail inmates indicated that they were assigned an attorney to represent them for the charges on which they were being held. . . .

TYPES OF DELIVERY SYSTEMS

Although the U.S. Supreme Court has mandated that the States must provide counsel for indigents accused of crime, the implementation of how such services are to be provided has not been specified. The States have devised various systems, rules for organizing, and funding mechanisms for indigent defense programs. As a consequence, each State has adopted its own approach for providing counsel for poor defendants. Three systems have emerged throughout the country as the primary means to provide defense services for indigent defendants.

Public defender programs are public or private nonprofit organizations with full- or part-time salaried staff. Local public defenders operate autonomously and do not have a central administrator. By contrast, under a statewide system, an individual appointed by the governor, a commission, council, or board is charged with developing and maintaining a system of representation for each county of the State. In 30 States a public defender system is the primary method used to provide indigent counsel for criminal defendants. . . .

Assigned counsel systems involve the appointment by the courts of private attorneys as needed from a list of available attorneys. Assigned counsel systems consist of two types. Ad hoc assigned counsel systems are those in which individual private attorneys are appointed by an individual judge to provide representation on a case-by-case basis. Coordinated assigned counsel systems employ an administrator to oversee the appointment of counsel and to develop a set of standards and guidelines for program administration.

Contract attorney systems involve governmental units that reach agreements with private attorneys, bar associations, or private law firms to provide indigent services for a specified dollar amount and for a specified time period. . . .

The Federal justice system provides indigent defense to eligible defendants through the Federal Defender Services, community defender organizations, and private attorneys as established by the Criminal Justice Act of 1964, as amended.

USE OF DIFFERENT TYPES OF COUNSEL FOR INDIGENT DEFENSE

Traditionally, assigned counsel systems and public defenders have been the primary means to provide legal representation to the poor. In 1992, 64% of State court prosecutors'offices nationwide reported a public defender program in their jurisdiction and 58% indicated an assigned counsel system. In 1992, 25% of prosecutors'offices indicated that their district contracted with law firms, private attorneys, or local bar associations to provide services to indigent offenders. . . . A majority of prosecutors'offices (59%) reported only one method was used in their jurisdiction to provide services to poor offenders.

Among all prosecutorial districts, a public defender program was used exclusively in 28%, an assigned counsel system in 23%, and a contract attorney system in 8%. Forty-one percent of the prosecutors'offices reported a combination of methods were used in their jurisdiction. The most prevalent was a combination of an assigned counsel system and a public defender program reported by 23% of the offices. In the Nation's 75 largest counties, 43% of the State court prosecutors'offices reported both an assigned counsel system and a public defender program operating in their jurisdiction. . . .

TYPE OF LEGAL REPRESENTATION REPORTED BY PRISON AND JAIL INMATES

Ninety-seven percent of inmates in State correctional facilities reported that they had an attorney to represent them for the offense for which they were incarcerated. Seventy-six percent of those who had an attorney were represented by a public defender or assigned counsel. Counsel assigned by the court may include legal representation provided by a public agency or by private attorneys whom the court pays.

Among those represented by counsel, 79% of black State prison inmates reported they had been represented by an assigned attorney. Among white State prison inmates, 73% said they had been represented by an assigned attorney. Among State prison inmates incarcerated for property offenses, 85% had an assigned counsel; for violent offenses, 74%; and for drug offenses, 70%.

Ninety-nine percent of Federal inmates reported that they were represented by counsel. Forty-three percent of those who had an attorney hired private counsel. Nearly 50% of white Federal inmates hired private counsel, as did 33% of black

Federal inmates. Almost two-thirds of black Federal inmates were assigned counsel by the court. Overall, among those Federal inmates serving time for violent offenses, 72% had court assigned counsel; for property offenses, 53%; and for drug offenses, 48%.

Eighty-three percent of jail inmates said they had a lawyer to represent them for the offense for which they were being held. Among those who had legal representation, about three-fourths had assigned counsel. About three-fourths of those in jail for a drug or violent offense relied on assigned counsel. Among those charged with property offenses, 85% had assigned counsel. About two-thirds of those jail inmates with hired counsel said they first met with their attorney either before admission or during the first week after admission.

■ STATE v. LEONARD PEART

621 So. 2d 780 (La. 1993)

CALOGERO, C.J.

. . . The legislature has [established] Louisiana's indigent defender system. LSA-R.S. 15:144 creates Indigent Defender Boards to oversee indigent defense operations in each judicial district. . . . LSA-R.S. 15:146 sets up a mechanism for local funding of individual districts' indigent defender systems. LSA-R.S. 15:304 is a general statute which requires all parishes and the city of New Orleans to pay "all expenses . . . whatever attending criminal proceedings. . . ."[2]

Leonard Peart was charged with armed robbery, aggravated rape, aggravated burglary, attempted armed robbery, and first degree murder. He is indigent.

In New Orleans, the Indigent Defender Board ("IDB") has created the Orleans Indigent Defender Program ("OIDP"). OIDP operates under a public defender model. The trial court appointed Rick Teissier, one of the two OIDP attorneys assigned to Section E, to defend Peart against all the above charges except first degree murder.

. . . At the time of his appointment, Teissier was handling 70 active felony cases. His clients are routinely incarcerated 30 to 70 days before he meets with them. In the period between January 1 and August 1, 1991, Teissier represented 418 defendants. Of these, he entered 130 guilty pleas at arraignment. He had at least one serious case set for trial for every trial date during that period. OIDP has only enough funds to hire three investigators. They are responsible for rendering assistance in more than 7,000 cases per year in the ten sections of Criminal District Court, plus cases in Juvenile Court, Traffic Court, and Magistrates' Court. In a routine case Teissier receives no investigative support at all. There are no funds for expert witnesses. OIDP's library is inadequate.

The court found that Teissier was not able to provide his clients with reasonably effective assistance of counsel because of the conditions affecting his work, primarily the large number of cases assigned to him. The court further ruled that "the system

---

2. [Indigent Defender Boards] choose between public defender, contract attorney, and assigned counsel models, or may use a combination of these models. LSA-R.S. 15:146 sets up a mechanism for local funding of individual districts' indigent defender systems. This provision, unique in the United States, creates a system whereby almost all of the funds for indigent defense come from criminal violation assessments [in] an amount ranging from $17.50 to $25.00 for each violation. Parking violations are excepted. . . .

of securing and compensating qualified counsel for indigents" in LSA-R.S. 15:145, 15:146 and 15:304 was "unconstitutional as applied in the City of New Orleans" because it does not provide adequate funding for indigent defense and because it places the burden of funding indigent defense on the city of New Orleans. The trial judge ordered short and long term relief. In the short term, he ordered Teissier's caseload reduced; ordered the legislature to provide funding for an improved library and for an investigator for Teissier; and announced his intention to appoint members of the bar to represent indigents in his court. For the long term, he ordered that the legislature provide funds to OIDP to pay additional attorneys, secretaries, paralegals, law clerks, investigators, and expert witnesses.

[While the State's appeal of this ruling was pending, Peart was tried and acquitted of armed robbery.] In a second trial, in which he was represented by other counsel, he was acquitted on the murder charge. He is awaiting trial on the aggravated rape charge. Teissier again represents him.[5] . . .

We begin with the proposition that because there is no precise definition of reasonably effective assistance of counsel, any inquiry into the effectiveness of counsel must necessarily be individualized and fact-driven. In different contexts, Louisiana courts have found a wide variety of attorneys' failings to constitute ineffective assistance. These courts [have determined] whether an individual defendant has been provided with reasonably effective assistance, and no general finding by the trial court regarding a given lawyer's handling of other cases, or workload generally, can answer that very specific question as to an individual defendant and the defense being furnished him.

[The] language of La. Const. art. 1 sec. 13 is unequivocal: "At each stage of the proceedings, every person is entitled to the assistance of counsel . . . appointed by the court if he is indigent and charged with a crime punishable by imprisonment." That assistance must be reasonably effective. Article 1 sec. 13 also provides that "the legislature shall provide for a uniform system for securing and compensating qualified counsel for indigents." As noted above, the legislature has enacted statutes responsive to these constitutional requirements.

However, we cannot say that the system these statutes have put in place invariably — or, in Section E, even regularly — affords indigent defendants reasonably effective assistance of counsel. We take reasonably effective assistance of counsel to mean that the lawyer not only possesses adequate skill and knowledge, but also that he has the time and resources to apply his skill and knowledge to the task of defending each of his individual clients.

[This] system has resulted in wide variations in levels of funding, both between different IDB's and within the same IDB over time. The general pattern has been one of chronic underfunding of indigent defense programs in most areas of the state. The system is so underfunded that [one recent study committee, appointed by the state judiciary, concluded that] there is a "desperate need to double the budget for indigent defense in Louisiana in the next two years." The unique system which

---

5. Ironically, the trial court judgment indicates that at the time of the judgment Peart himself was receiving the effective assistance of counsel guaranteed him by the constitution. As the trial judge wrote, "each of Mr. Teissier's clients is entitled to the same kind of defense Leonard Peart is receiving." That Peart himself could receive effective assistance, while Teissier's other clients do not, reflects the fact that indigent defenders must select certain clients to whom they give more attention than they give to others. . . . We therefore anticipate, although we do not decide, that the State may well be able to rebut the presumption of ineffectiveness in the pending rape case against Peart.

funds indigent defense through criminal violation assessments, mostly traffic tickets, is an unstable and unpredictable approach.[10] . . .

The conditions in Section E should be contrasted with the American Bar Association Standards for Criminal Justice (1991). These conditions routinely violate the standards on workload (Std. 4-1.3(e)) ("defense counsel should not carry a workload that, by reason of its excessive size, interferes with the rendering of quality representation"); initial provision of counsel (Std. 5-6.1) (counsel should be provided to the accused . . . at appearance before a committing magistrate, or when criminal charges are filed, whichever occurs earliest"); investigation (Std. 4-4.1) ("defense counsel should conduct a prompt investigation of the circumstances of the case and explore all avenues leading to facts relevant to the merits of the case"); and others. We know from experience that no attorney can prepare for one felony trial per day, especially if he has little or no investigative, paralegal, or clerical assistance. As the trial judge put it, "not even a lawyer with an S on his chest could effectively handle this docket." We agree. Many indigent defendants in Section E are provided with counsel who can perform only pro forma, especially at early stages of the proceedings. . . . In light of the unchallenged evidence in the record, we find that because of the excessive caseloads and the insufficient support with which their attorneys must work, indigent defendants in Section E are generally not provided with the effective assistance of counsel the constitution requires.

Having found that indigent defendants in Section E cannot all be receiving effective assistance of counsel, we must decide what remedy this Court should impose. Louisiana is not the only state to have faced a crisis in its indigent defense system. Over the last decade, numerous states have addressed problems like those Louisiana faces. In some states, legislatures have on their own initiative improved provision of indigent defense services. For example, in 1989 alone the legislatures of New Mexico, Missouri and Kentucky provided for large increases in the budgets of their statewide public defender offices; the Tennessee and Georgia legislatures established new statewide public defender offices. In other states, litigation challenging the adequacy of defense services has resulted in systemic changes. [The court cited cases from Arkansas, Florida, Kansas, New Hampshire, and Oklahoma.]

By virtue of this Court's constitutional position as the final arbiter of the meaning of the state constitution and laws, we have a duty to interpret and apply the constitution. In addition, the constitution endows this Court with general supervisory jurisdiction over all other courts. . . . Acting pursuant to the established sources of authority noted above, . . . we find that a rebuttable presumption arises that indigents in Section E are receiving assistance of counsel not sufficiently effective to meet constitutionally required standards. See State v. Smith, 681 P.2d 1374 (Ariz. 1984). This presumption is to apply prospectively only; it is to apply to those defendants who were represented by attorney Teissier when he filed the original "Motion for Relief" who have not yet gone to trial; and it will be applicable to all indigent defendants in Section E who have OIDP attorneys appointed to represent them hereafter, so long as there are no changes in the workload and other conditions under which OIDP assigned defense counsel provide legal services in Section E. If legislative action is not forthcoming and indigent defense reform does not take place, this Court, in the exercise of its constitutional and inherent power and

10. Examples of the approach's unpredictability abound. One particularly stark example: when the City of East Baton Rouge ran out of pre-printed traffic tickets in the first half of 1990, the indigent defender program's sole source of income was suspended while more tickets were being printed.

supervisory jurisdiction, may find it necessary to employ the more intrusive and specific measures it has thus far avoided to ensure that indigent defendants receive reasonably effective assistance of counsel. We decline at this time to undertake these more intrusive and specific measures because this Court should not lightly tread in the affairs of other branches of government and because the legislature ought to assess such measures in the first instance. . . .

We instruct the judge of Section E, when trying Leonard Peart's motion and any others which may be filed, to hold individual hearings for each such moving defendant and, in the absence of significant improvement in the provision of indigent defense services to defendants in Section E, to apply a rebuttable presumption that such indigents are not receiving assistance of counsel effective enough to meet constitutionally required standards. If the court, applying this presumption and weighing all evidence presented, finds that Leonard Peart or any other defendant in Section E is not receiving the reasonably effective assistance of counsel the constitution requires, and the court finds itself unable to order any other relief which would remedy the situation, then the court shall not permit the prosecution to go forward until the defendant is provided with reasonably effective assistance of counsel. . . . Reversed and remanded.

■ STATE v. ADRIAN CITIZEN
898 So. 2d 325 (La. 2005)

VICTORY, J.

These consolidated cases present the issue of funding for indigent defendants in criminal cases in the State of Louisiana. . . . The instant direct appeal arises out of two unrelated Calcasieu Parish killings. After a Calcasieu Parish grand jury returned a first-degree murder indictment on April 11, 2002, against Benjamin Tonguis, the trial court appointed the Chief Public Defender for the parish, Ronald Ware, to represent him. Ware informed the court of his prohibitive caseload, and the court removed him from the case and sought to appoint solo practitioner Phyllis E. Mann. On December 10, 2003, counsel filed a document captioned as a Motion to Determine Source of Funds to Provide Competent Defense. . . . On January 30, 2004, the trial court consolidated the *Tonguis* case with that of Adrian Shannondoah Citizen, another Calcasieu Parish first-degree murder defendant indicted on October 10, 2002, seeking to be represented by appointed counsel Phyllis Mann. Also on that date, the trial court held a hearing on the funding issues raised by Mann. At this hearing, counsel for the Calcasieu Parish Police Jury (the "CPPJ") filed a motion to dismiss his client as a party to Mann's motion, as in his view La. R.S. 15:304 [forbids] local funding for the representation of indigent defendants. The court then explored the possibility with prosecutors of amending the charges against each defendant to second-degree murder and, after receiving no favorable response, considered [testimony] regarding the financial status of the CPPJ, with an eye toward using it as a funding source.

[Counsel] for the CPPJ explained that the current system for maintaining the criminal justice system in Calcasieu Parish . . . evolved in 1985 after voters in the parish approved an *ad valorem* tax specifically dedicated to maintaining the Criminal Court Fund. [In] 2000, the tax, as supplemented by fines and forfeitures, put into the Criminal Court Fund $3,500,000, by far the largest portion of the total amount of $5,300,000, which also included funds from other sources such as grant programs. By agreement, 20% of the Fund portion generated by the *ad valorem* tax and fines and forfeitures goes into the witness and juror fee account, 60% to the D.A.'s office, and 40% to the district courts. Any surplus remaining in the witness and jury fee account at the end of the year does not revert to the general parish fund but is split on a 50/50 basis between the courts and the D.A.'s office. In 2000, that surplus amounted to some $440,000, an average figure over a seven year period. . . .

The parish attorney explained that . . . since voters in Calcasieu Parish had approved the *ad valorem* tax, by far the biggest component of the Criminal Court Fund, specifically for the purpose of maintaining the court system and the District Attorney's Office, the CPPJ had no obligation, or even the authority, to divert some of that tax money to criminal defense. Chief Public Defender Ware underscored the problem facing the court by stating that his office currently owed close to $47,000 for capital defense and expected to owe at least an additional $150,000 in upcoming cases which he had already committed to fund. He further informed the court that his office generated approximately $5,550 per month. Despite the apparent intransigence of the CPPJ, Prosecutor Wayne Frey suggested that the court pay defense counsel from the surplus monies contained in the CPPJ's Criminal Court Fund (provided the parties agreed upon a funding cap), and the court agreed to propose the idea to his fellow judges and to go before the CPPJ with a funding proposal. However, an increase in jury and witness fees had reduced the surplus in the Fund from a previous average of $450,000 to approximately $300,000. The court expressed its frustration with the continued lack of funding and the fact that it faces some version of the same funding dilemma in virtually every criminal case before it.

[After] meeting no success with the judges and district attorney, the court found that the CPPJ was the only possible source of adequate funding. The court went on to find [that La. R.S. 15:304 unconstitutionally deprives] the defendants of their right to a fair and speedy trial and their right to counsel. Finally, the court ordered the CPPJ to place $200,000 into the court registry to be distributed to the attorneys representing Tonguis and Citizen. In its ensuing written reasons, the court also ordered the CPPJ to place into an escrow account $75,000 for expert witness fees and case-related expenses. . . .

The current legislative system set out in an attempt to meet the constitutional command of La. Const. Art. I §13 to provide a uniform system for securing and compensating qualified counsel for indigents appears in La. R.S. 15:144 *et seq.* (Title XIV: Right to Counsel). These statutes require each judicial district to create an indigent defender board, which shall maintain lists of volunteer and non-volunteer attorneys licensed to practice law in Louisiana. Each board must then select the procedure for providing counsel to indigents, whether it be through court selection of volunteer attorneys (or non-volunteer attorneys if needed), through employment of a chief indigent defender and supporting assistants, through contracting with available attorneys, or through any combination of the above. . . . Finally, La. R.S. 15:151 *et seq.* establish a statewide Indigent Defense Assistance Board to provide for supplementary funds in certain cases, and to "cause counsel to be enrolled" to represent a defendant sentenced to death on direct appeal and in post-conviction proceedings.

[The trial court heard extensive testimony that the state, the local Indigent Defender's Office, and the Indigent Defense Assistance Board have no money to spare. In fact, the board's director, Edward Greenlee, testified that the state reduced his agency's funding by 25% after its first year of existence, then failed to restore funding to previous levels in the seven subsequent years. Additionally, Greenlee testified that the state prohibits the board from running a deficit. Accordingly, when the local parish police jury's justice fund runs an average surplus of several hundred thousand dollars per year, the trial court's decision to tap these funds proves tempting.]

In 1993, this Court addressed the issue of indigent defense funding in State v. Peart, 621 So. 2d 780, 785 (La. 1993). [The Court determined] that defendants assigned counsel in a particular section of Orleans Parish Criminal District Court received constitutionally deficient counsel, and thus found the existence of a rebuttable presumption of counsel's ineffectiveness in cases arising out of that section of court. . . .

Also in 1993, the Court decided State v. Wigley, 624 So. 2d 425, 426 (La. 1993), wherein we held that uncompensated representation of indigents, when reasonably imposed, is a professional obligation burdening the privilege of practicing law in this state and does not violate the constitutional rights of attorneys. However, we also held that "any assignment of counsel [from the private] bar to defend an indigent defendant must provide for reimbursement to the assigned attorney of properly incurred and reasonable out-of-pocket expenses and overhead costs."[8] . . . If the district judge determines that funds are not available to reimburse appointed counsel, he should not appoint members of the private bar to represent indigents. . . .

[In 1994], the legislature amended La. R.S. 15:304 to add a proviso that "nothing in this Section shall be construed to make the parishes or the city of New Orleans responsible for the expenses associated with the costs, expert fees, or attorney fees of a defendant in a criminal proceeding." . . . La. R.S. 15:304, as amended in 1994, now provides:

> All expenses incurred in the different parishes of the state or in the city of New Orleans by the arrest, confinement, and prosecution of persons accused or convicted of crimes, their removal to prison, the pay of witnesses specifically provided for by law, jurors and all prosecutorial expenses whatever attending criminal proceedings shall be paid by the respective parishes in which the offense charged may have been committed or by the city of New Orleans, as the case may be. . . . Nothing in this Section shall be construed to make the parishes or the city of New Orleans responsible for the expenses associated with the costs, expert fees, or attorney fees of a defendant in a criminal proceeding. . . .

[The defense attorney argued that this statute deprives her of] "her property interest in both her license to practice law and the financial interest of her law firm without due process of law in violation of the Fourth and Fourteenth Amendments to the United States Constitution and Article 1, Section 4 of the Louisiana Constitution of 1974 as amended." . . . The trial court rejected counsel's argument

---

8. In *Wigley*, we [found] that in order to be reasonable and not oppressive, any assignment of counsel to defend an indigent defendant must provide for reimbursement to the assigned attorney of properly incurred and reasonable out-of-pocket expenses and overhead costs. However, a fee for services need not be paid, as long as the time the attorney must devote to cases for which he does not receive a fee does not reach unreasonable levels. What is unreasonable in this context is to be determined by the trial judge in the exercise of his discretion. Such a system will strike a balance between the attorney's ethical duty to provide services *pro bono publico* and his or her practical need to continue to perform his or her other obligations. . . .

regarding counsel's own due process claim, but agreed with counsel's argument regarding the most recent changes to La. R.S. 15:304 . . . and their effect on the rights of the instant indigent defendants.

[The] trial court's ruling that La. R.S. 15:304 [violates] the defendants'rights of due process, right to counsel, and equal protection is erroneous. The constitution requires that indigent defendants are entitled to the assistance of counsel and that the legislature provide for a uniform system for securing and compensating qualified counsel. The statutes at issue clearly meet the constitutional requirements because they . . . specifically provide the medium in which to seek funding for indigent defense. The statutes do not declare that indigent defense costs will not be paid, they simply place this burden on the state. The fact that the legislature has not adequately funded the programs it has created to meet its constitutional mandate does not make the statutes themselves unconstitutional. Further, while the statutes prohibit the parishes from being required to pay for indigent defense, nothing in the statutes prohibits the parishes from paying these expenses if they so chose. . . .

The legislature has clearly determined through statutory enactments that the State, not the parishes, will pay for indigent defense pursuant to the constitutional mandate of La. Const. Art. I, §13. . . . Thus, we find that the trial court erred in ordering the CPPJ to place $200,000 in the court registry for the court-appointed attorneys and to place $75,000 in escrow for other case-related expenses. . . .

The legislature has taken steps to remedy the critical state of indigent criminal defense in Louisiana since our warnings in *Peart*. For instance, it created the statewide Indigent Defense Assistance Board in 1997. In 2003, the legislature, by separate but identical House and Senate Resolutions, created the Louisiana Task Force on Indigent Defense Services, effective January 12, 2004, to study the problem and make an initial report no later than March 1, 2004. The legislature has consti- tuted the Task Force as a blue ribbon committee whose members range from the Governor to the Chief Justice of this Court. It is not clear whether the 2003 Task Force ever made its report, but this year, by concurrent resolution, the legislature voted to continue the Task Force, directing it to report on its findings together with specific recommendations no later than April 1, 2005. We assume that, given the obvious deficiencies in funding from the State to satisfy its constitutional mandate in La. Const. Art. I, §13, this Task Force will work diligently to formulate specific recommendations on April 1, 2005, to address these problems and that the legis- lature will act quickly to promulgate these, or other, appropriate solutions.

However, even assuming that these steps will lead to sweeping reform of the system and to adequate funding for indigent defense, reform will not likely come in any reasonable time to help the present defendants. Until the legislature takes remedial action, this Court must address the immediate problems of the instant defendants in securing constitutionally adequate counsel (in a constitutionally and statutorily required timely manner) in their forthcoming capital prosecutions. We are very much cognizant of the lengths to which other state courts have gone to ensure that the indigents'constitutional rights are protected, in spite of legislative inaction.[12] This is particularly appropriate in cases involving indigent defense in our

---

12. For example, the Supreme Judicial Court of Massachusetts confronted a lack of legislative funding in Lavallee v. Justices in the Hampden Superior Court, 812 N.E.2d 895 (Mass. 2004). In that case, certain judicial districts lacked the funding to woo competent attorneys to represent the indigent. Additionally, the state agency charged with providing court-appointed counsel in most circumstances had no staff available to represent petitioners. [The court held that] "on a showing that no counsel is available

state courts, as this is an area over which the Court has supervisory jurisdiction and the duty to ensure that the criminal justice system is functioning in a constitutional manner.

In this case, Mr. Citizen, was indicted for first-degree murder on October 10, 2002, and he remains in jail with no funds available for the attorney appointed to represent him and, under current circumstances, may remain there indefinitely[13] unless funds are provided for his defense. Mr. Tonguis was indicted for the first-degree murder of his infant child on April 11, 2002, and though he is not incarcerated, no funds are available for the attorney appointed to represent him. Implicit in these defendants' constitutional right to assistance of counsel is the State's inability to proceed with their prosecution until it provides adequate funds for their defense. While La. R.S. 15:304 . . . cannot be construed to force the CPPJ to pay for the costs of these indigents' defenses, nothing . . . prohibits the CPPJ from paying these expenses, and these funds may come from the Criminal Court Fund upon agreement of the legal entities responsible for its administration under La. R.S. 15:571.11.

In order to assure timely representation, we now alter one of the rules previously laid down in *Wigley, supra.* A district judge should appoint counsel to represent an indigent defendant from the time of the indigent defendant's first appearance in court, even if the judge cannot then determine that funds sufficient to cover the anticipated expenses and overhead are likely to be available to reimburse counsel. The appointed attorney may then file a motion to determine funding, as was done in this case, and if the trial judge determines that adequate funding is not available, the defendant may then file, at his option, a motion to halt the prosecution of the case until adequate funding becomes available. The judge may thereafter prohibit the State from going forward with the prosecution until he or she determines that appropriate funding is likely to be available. . . .

---

to represent a particular indigent defendant despite good faith efforts, such a defendant may not be held more than seven days and the criminal case against such a defendant may not continue beyond forty-five days." The court . . . noted that several State courts have temporarily deferred in the first instance, and only temporarily, to legislative action to ensure that the system for compensation for indigent representation meets constitutional standards (citing *Peart*; State ex rel. Stephan v. Smith, 747 P.2d 816, 848-50 (Kan. 1987); Smith v. State, 394 A.2d 834, 839 (N.H. 1978)).

The *Lavallee* court also recognized that some state courts of last resort have granted preliminary relief in the form of increased compensation rates, but have simultaneously directed their Legislatures to amend permanently the compensation rates for indigent representation (citing State ex rel. Wolff v. Ruddy, 617 S.W.2d 64, 67-68 (Mo. 1981); State v. Lynch, 796 P.2d 1150, 1164 (Okla. 1990)). Along these lines, a New York trial court recently issued a permanent injunction directing that counsel be paid $90 per hour, and removed the statutory fee cap until the Legislature changed the rates and increased its appropriation for compensation for indigent representation. New York County Lawyers' Ass'n v. State, 196 Misc. 2d 761, 763 N.Y.S.2d 397 (N.Y. Sup. Ct. 2003). . . .

At least one indigent defender has prompted a trial court to take the extreme measure of threatening to hold a legislative body reluctant to release funds in contempt. When Kentucky cut the budget for his office, indigent defender Dan Goyette responded with a corresponding cut in services. Specifically, his office refused to provide attorneys for people facing involuntary mental hospitalization. The chief judge in Goyette's district reportedly ordered the official in charge of the state budget to restore Goyette's funding or face contempt. Other judges in the district ordered the release of four unrepresented persons hospitalized against their will.

13. There are time limitations imposed by the Code of Criminal Procedure for bringing indicted defendants to trial. There is no time limitation for the institution of prosecution for first-degree murder. However, no trial shall be commenced in a capital case after three years from the date of institution of the prosecution and in other felony cases after two years from the date of institution of the prosecution. La. C.Cr.P. art. 578. Additionally, all defendants have a right to a speedy trial. La. Const. Art. 1, §16; La. C.Cr.P. art. 701.

■ STATE v. DELBERT LYNCH
796 P.2d 1150 (Okla. 1990)

KAUGER, J.

In these cases of first impression, we are asked to decide whether the trial court erred in declaring 21 O.S. Supp. 1985 §701.14 unconstitutional because court appointed counsel were forced to represent indigent defendants without the assurance of receiving adequate, speedy, and certain compensation for such representation. We find that: 1) Although the statute is not facially unconstitutional, it is unconstitutional in application; 2) The present system presses lawyers into service without affording a post-appointment opportunity to show cause why they should not be forced to accept the appointment; and 3) The statute provides an arbitrary and unreasonable rate of compensation for lawyers which may result in an unconstitutional taking of private property depending on the facts of each case. While we recognize the responsibility of members of the Oklahoma bar to assist in the provision of legal representation to indigent defendants, we find that in some instances the arbitrary and unreasonable statutory scheme contravenes the due process clause of the Okla. Const. art. 2, §7. . . .

Two Seminole County lawyers, Jack Mattingly and Rob Pyron, were appointed by the district court to represent Delbert Lynch, an indigent who had been charged with first degree murder. Although the State had sought the death penalty, after a complicated trial, which began on August 21, 1989, and ended on August 31, 1989, the jury rendered a guilty verdict and gave Lynch a life sentence. Following Lynch's sentencing on September 6, 1989, the lawyers petitioned the court for fees and expenses.

At the hearing on counsel fees, Mattingly testified that he had spent 169 hours on the case, and incurred $173.03 in out of pocket expenses, requesting a $17,073.03 fee. Pyron's testimony was that he had expended 109.55 hours on Lynch's behalf, and he sought a $10,995.00 fee. Mattingly submitted a statement documenting his hourly overhead rate for 1986, 1987, 1988, which ranged from $45.80 to $53.53 — averaging $50.88. Pyron submitted his overhead figures for 1988, reflecting an average hourly rate of $48.00. Had the two lawyers split the maximum statutory fee of $3,200, Mattingly would have received $9.47 per hour, with Pyron receiving $14.61 per hour. Based on these computations, Mattingly would lose $41.41 and Pyron would lose $33.39 in overhead expenses for every hour that they worked on the defense. These figures do not reflect any compensation for the attorneys' services. The trial court approved the requested fees, finding that the $3,200 restriction on attorney fees was unconstitutional. . . .

The parties do not dispute that Oklahoma is required to provide attorneys for indigent defendants who are charged in Oklahoma courts with felonies, certain misdemeanors, competency to stand trial, contempt proceedings, and guardianship matters, or that the State of Oklahoma has attempted to provide such representation. The basic concern is not with the constitutional requirements of the Okla. Const. art. 2, §20, or the public policy which requires representation of indigent defendants; but, rather, with the practical application of the public policy and its impairment of constitutionally guaranteed private property rights. The State asserts that compensation should only exceed the statutory limit when extraordinary circumstances are shown as established in Bias v. State, 568 P.2d 1269 (Okla. 1977), and that an unconstitutional taking does not occur when a court-appointed attorney is required to represent indigent defendants.

The Okla. Const. art. 2, §7 provides that "No person shall be deprived of life, liberty, or property without due process of law." The lawyers contend that under this constitutional provision mandatory representation without just compensation is unconstitutional. The Oklahoma Constitution . . . also requires that competent counsel be provided for indigent defendants. [A] criminal defendant has a fundamental right to the reasonably effective assistance of counsel, regardless of whether counsel is appointed or retained. This means a lawyer must render the same obligations of loyalty, confidentiality, and competence to a court-appointed client as a retained client would receive. Oklahoma has fulfilled the constitutional requirement of competent counsel by utilizing public defenders' offices, voluntary pools, and court appointments. In order for the system to work, a balance must be maintained between the lawyer's [professional obligations], an indigent's fundamental right to counsel, and the avoidance of state action tantamount to confiscation of a lawyer's practice.

To achieve an appropriate balance of constitutional interests the rights of both the indigent defendant and the lawyer must be protected. Here, the constitutional right of the indigent to counsel is not at issue — the due process rights of appointed counsel for indigent defendants are. Although it is obvious that while Oklahoma's statutorily mandated cap may not be facially defective, and that in some instances payment of the statutory fee might even be an excessive rate of compensation, there is a substantial probability that it will be defective in application. Here, it is apparent that the maximum statutory fee is inadequate to compensate the lawyers who represented Lynch.[13]

In Bias v. State, a lawyer had been compelled both to subsidize indigent representation and to forsake his regular law practice during the representation of the indigent defendant. The *Bias* Court recognized that such circumstances may constitute a taking of private property without compensation. In order to harmonize conflicting interests, the Court authorized payment in excess of the statutorily prescribed norms for extraordinary expenditures of time and expense. . . .

Clearly, there is a substantial risk of the erroneous deprivation of property rights under the current appointment system. A lawyer's skills and services are his/her only means of livelihood. The taking thereof, without adequate compensation, is analogous to taking the goods of merchants or requiring free services of architects, engineers, accountants, physicians, nurses or of one of the 34 other occupations or professions in this state which require a person to be licensed before practicing the occupation or profession. None of the licensing statutes require that the members of those professions donate their skills and services to the public. We know that many of these professionals do so. We also know that it would be unusual for the various licensing boards to force their licensees to proffer their services to indigents or to offer cut-rate prices on haircuts, perms, embalming, dentures, or surgeries. . . .

Nevertheless, we also recognize that a lawyer's calling is different from that of other licensed professions. We are a government of laws and not of men and

---

13. The maximum statutory fee set by the legislature is: 1) in capital cases, $200 for services rendered before the preliminary hearing, $500 for services rendered during the preliminary hearing, $2,500 for services rendered from the time the defendant is bound over until final disposition in the trial court; 2) in other criminal cases, the fee is not to exceed $500; 3) in juvenile and guardianship cases, the fee is not to exceed $100 in a preliminary hearing, $500 if the cause goes to trial and $100 for post-disposition hearings. . . .

women. At the foundation of this republic is the respect for enforcement of the law in a neutral way. The services of competent counsel are necessary to insure that our system of justice functions smoothly, that justice is dispensed even handedly, and that the rights and interests of indigent defendants are safeguarded in a truly adversarial forum. A lawyer is weighted with responsibility which is uncommon to the ordinary professional, and as a member of the integrated bar, an Oklahoma lawyer has a duty to the oath of office, to the Courts, to his/her clients, and to the public at large to be more than a tradesperson.

Procedural due process of law requires adequate notice, a realistic opportunity to appear at a hearing, and the right to participate in a meaningful manner before one's rights are irretrievably altered. We find that in order to provide safeguards which will bring the system into compliance with due process, trial courts must proffer a post-appointment opportunity for the lawyer to appear and to show cause without penalty, why he/she should not be appointed to represent an indigent defendant. [This is] in accord with the Model Rules of Professional Conduct, 5 O.S. Supp. 1988 Ch.1, App. 3-A, Rule 6.2 and the committee comments thereto, which provide that a lawyer may refuse an appointment for the representation of an indigent upon a showing of good cause.

We find that good cause consists of, but is not limited to the following factors: 1) the lawyer is not qualified to provide competent representation; 2) the representation will result in a conflict of interest; and 3) the case is so repugnant to the lawyer that it would impair either the attorney-client relationship or the lawyer's ability to represent the client. Title 5 O.S. Supp. 1988 Ch. 1, App. 3-A, Rule 6.2. We also find that Rule 1.16 of the Model Rules of Professional Conduct, 5 O.S. Supp. 1988 Ch. 1, App. 3-A, is applicable to all client representation, and that it should be construed with the "good cause" factors. This rule provides that a lawyer may refuse to represent a client if: 1) the representation would violate the Rules of Professional Conduct or other law; 2) the lawyer's physical or mental condition materially impairs the lawyer's representation of the client; 3) the client persists in conduct involving the lawyer's service which the lawyer believes is criminal or fraudulent; 4) the client has used the lawyer's services to perpetrate a crime or fraud; or 5) the client discharges the lawyer. . . .

For all practical purposes [Oklahoma statutes] exempt attorneys in counties which have public defenders' offices from representing indigent defendants in state courts. Lawyers in these counties are subject to appointment only when a conflict of interest arises in the public defender's office. Currently, these attorneys are neither faced with impending financial disaster nor forced to ignore their practice in order to provide effective counsel for an indigent. Except in rare circumstances, these attorneys have been granted an "immunity" by the legislature. . . . Because lawyers who practice in certain counties are immunized from the representation of indigent defendants, not all Oklahoma lawyers are treated equally. [D]iscrimination between attorneys who may be forced to represent indigent defendants based solely on the population of the county in which they practice law is unconstitutional under any level of scrutiny. . . .

We applaud individual attorneys or associations of attorneys who volunteer to provide either pro bono legal representation or representation of indigent defendants at rates which may be drastically under the market value of the lawyers' skills and services. It reflects pride in the practice of law, and it exemplifies the best of many virtues found in the practicing bar. The provision of legal services to indigents is one of the responsibilities assumed by the legal profession, and personal involvement in the problems of the disadvantaged can be one of the most rewarding experiences in the life of a lawyer.

Every lawyer, regardless of professional prominence or professional workload, should find time to participate in or otherwise support the provision of legal services to the disadvantaged. We strongly urge the continuation of these services. We believe that attorneys would voluntarily donate their skills and services were they not unduly burdened with compulsory appointments. We also believe that Oklahoma lawyers will form local, county, district, and intrastate voluntary pools to assume this responsibility and to relieve lawyers who practice in counties with few lawyers from an unfair court-imposed case load. We also recognize that at this time voluntary services are insufficient to accommodate the right of indigent citizens to the effective assistance of counsel where that right is implicated.

[The State] has an obligation to pay appointed lawyers sums which will fairly compensate the lawyer, not at the top rate which a lawyer might charge, but at a rate which is not confiscatory, after considering overhead and expenses. The basis of the amount to be paid for services must not vary with each judge; rather there must be a statewide basis or scale for ascertaining a reasonable hourly rate in order to avoid the enactment of a proscribed special law.

Although we invite legislative attention to this problem, in the interim, we must establish guides which will apply uniformly without either violating due process rights or granting constitutional immunities. *Bias* provided some relief to Oklahoma lawyers; however, it did not address the constitutional infirmities which are squarely presented here. Therefore, in order to correct the defects which render the present statutory scheme unconstitutional, we must build on the foundation which was laid in *Bias*. We find that the most even handed approach in setting fees is to tie the hourly rate of the counsel appointed for the indigent defendant to the hourly rate of the prosecutor/district attorney and the public defenders.

[A]ll district attorneys receive the same salary — $56,180 per year or $29.26 per hour. We find that the trial court may award the attorney from $14.63 to $29.26 based on the attorney's qualifications. This range is tied to the salary range paid to assistant district attorneys and the district attorneys. (As a matter of course, when the district attorneys' and public defenders' salaries are raised by the Legislature so, too, would the hourly rate of compensation for defense counsel.) The overhead and the litigation expense of the district attorney are furnished by the state. In order to place the counsel for the defense on an equal footing with counsel for the prosecution, provision must be made for compensation of defense counsel's reasonable overhead and out of pocket expenses.

However, before the lawyer can be compensated for overhead, the percentage of reasonable hourly overhead rate directly attributable to the case in controversy, and the amount of out-of-pocket expenses incurred, must be presented to the trial court. . . . To receive payment for the reasonable overhead, attorney fees, and out of pocket expenses charged to the case, the lawyer must present accurate itemizations of overhead expenditures, time sheets, and invoices to support the number of hours reasonably spent on the defense.

Mattingly and Pyron have complied with the guidelines we are establishing. Were this not so, we would remand for further proceedings. We find that they are seasoned lawyers who should be paid an hourly rate of $29.26 per hour; that the average overhead rate and out of pocket expenses presented are reasonable; and that the lawyers spent the time alleged in the pursuit of Lynch's defense.

[T]he provision of counsel for indigent defendants, and the compensation of such counsel also lie within the Legislative sphere, and its consideration of the myriad problems presented is invited. This is an important area, which the Legislature should act to address. Nevertheless, until such time as the Legislature considers these matters . . . these guidelines shall become effective [immediately] in all cases in which the State of Oklahoma is required to provide assistance of counsel, insofar as the appointment of counsel and the implementation of post-appointment show cause hearings are concerned. [R]ecovery of attorney fees under the new guidelines will not be effective in non-capital cases until August 24, 1992, to allow the Legislature to address the problem, and to enact corrective legislation.

DOOLIN, J., dissenting.

The present traditional method of compensation and appointment of competent counsel to represent indigent defendants has worked well and existed in the British Colonial system when John Adams represented the British Troops who perpetrated the Boston Massacre, not to mention the example of Abe Fortas when he sounded *Gideon*'s trumpet in "Modern Times." I dissent.

SIMMS, J., dissenting.

Under our system of criminal jurisprudence, a licensed attorney finds himself in a very unique position. That lawyer is an officer of the court. And as such, is bound to render service when required by his or her appointment to represent an indigent defendant. However, he is not [an] "officer" within the ordinary meaning of that term. An attorney is not in the same category as marshals, bailiffs, court clerks or judges. A lawyer is engaged in a private profession, important though it be to our system of justice. [B]ecause of this unique relationship a lawyer enjoys with our system of criminal justice, fulfilling his legally recognized duty to render services when required by an appointment to represent an indigent defendant, cannot to me, be described in most instances in terms of a taking of his "property" without due process of law. . . .

We should direct the Legislature's attention to the Criminal Justice Act which the Congress of the United States enacted, titled "Adequate Representation of Defendants." . . . The federal act further provides for a uniform hourly rate for time expended in court or before a magistrate and a uniform hourly rate for time expended out of court. I would submit that enactment of a state statute closely paralleling [the federal act] might be a simple and direct answer to the problems raised by the majority opinion in this case. We should emphasize that the solutions to these problems are within the expertise and proper power of the Legislature and not this Court.

HODGES, J., concurring specially.

. . . I write separately to state that today's decision is merely a stopgap measure to remedy constitutional infirmities in the present system. The legislature is free to adopt any solution that is consistent with the Oklahoma and United States Constitutions. . . .

Dramatic changes have impaired the traditional method of compensation and appointment of counsel to represent indigent defendants. Recent years have witnessed increased complexity, specialization, and costs in criminal defense work. Added to this, the "War on Drugs" is fueling a dramatic increase in the number of criminal cases heaped upon an already heavily burdened system. These exacerbating factors have led to the emerging view that the responsibility to provide the Sixth Amendment right to counsel is a public responsibility that is not to be borne entirely by the private bar. . . . It is up to the Legislature to fulfill that obligation.

OPALA, V.C.J., concurring in part and dissenting in part.

. . . I join in concluding that the regime of assigning lawyers for criminal defense work in counties which are without public defender services is tainted by a constitutional infirmity. I recede from the court's interim institutional design that is to govern until the legislature overhauls the system. In my view, the whole scheme is affected by a fatal and incurable flaw. It saddles the judiciary with the responsibility of operating defense services in 75 counties — a function properly to be performed by the executive department. Until the legislature establishes a professionally independent statewide public defender system within the executive department, I would, merely as a stopgap measure, (1) develop guidelines that would equalize, on a statewide basis, the Bar's burden for providing defense services in those 75 counties and (2) call upon the Oklahoma Bar Association [hereafter called the Bar] to manage a statewide service pool of qualified lawyers for deployment in criminal as well as other mandated public-service work. . . .

The law must insulate from anyone's interference — judicial, legislative or executive — all aspects of a public defender's attorney/client relationship. The litigation-related strategy choices, as well as any other facet of professional decision-making in the conduct of a person's defense, must be beyond the pale of outsiders'-meddling. Nevertheless, the essence of the service to be provided is correctly characterized as extraneous to the judicial or legislative function and akin to that of the executive. It is the executive's responsibility to seek reversal-proof convictions in judicial tribunals properly constituted to administer that standard of adjudicative process which conforms to the dictates of our fundamental law. In short, in the aftermath of *Gideon* and its progeny, defense, as much as prosecution, is an essential component of government service for the enforcement of criminal laws. . . .

■ AMERICAN BAR ASSOCIATION, MODEL RULE OF PROFESSIONAL CONDUCT 1.5(d)

A lawyer shall not enter into an arrangement for, charge, or collect . . . a contingent fee for representing a defendant in a criminal case.

Problem 1-5. Flat Fees for Service

From 1967 to 1988, the Detroit Recorder's Court used an "event based" fee system to compensate counsel assigned to represent indigent criminal defendants. Under this system, a separate fee was paid for pre-preliminary examination jail visits, preliminary examinations, two post-preliminary examination jail visits, investigation and trial preparation, written motions filed and heard, calendar conferences, arraignments on the information, final conferences, evidentiary hearings, pleas, and forensic hearings. The system also provided compensation for each day of trial necessary to dispose of any particular case, and for counsel appearances in court for sentencing of the defendant.

In an effort to reduce jail overcrowding, a jail oversight committee studied the Recorder's Court and found a direct correlation between jail bed demand and the length of the criminal docket. The committee concluded that a substantial savings in jail bed demand could be recognized by reducing the time between a defendant's arrest and the ultimate disposition of the case. The committee was concerned that the event-based system gave assigned counsel an incentive to prolong final disposition of cases to earn a larger fee.

The committee asked the clerk of the Detroit Recorder's Court to devise a compensation system that would promote docket efficiency without reducing the overall level of compensation paid to assigned counsel. A statistical analysis revealed that attorneys tended to perform more "events" for clients who faced charges punishable by longer prison terms. The clerk grouped all assigned cases for the previous two years by potential maximum sentence and averaged the fees paid in each group of cases. The clerk then proposed a fee system that would pay attorneys a flat fee for representing a defendant, regardless of the number of "events" the attorney performed. Assigned counsel would be entitled to the full fee, regardless of whether the case is dismissed at the preliminary examination, the defendant pleads guilty at the arraignment on the information, or the case is ultimately disposed of after a jury trial. The flat fee would vary for different types of offenses and would reflect the average fees paid for defending such cases under the old system. The fixed rates would range from $475 for a 24-month maximum crime to $1,400 for a first-degree murder case.

The local court adopted the fixed fee system, and it succeeded in speeding up the docket. By shortening the time between arrest and disposition, the system alleviated some of the pressure for more jail space. A lawyer could earn $100 an hour for a guilty plea, typically three to four hours of work. If she went to trial the earnings could be $15 an hour or less. Prosecutors also noted a decrease in the number of "frivolous" defense motions and increased pressure from the defense bar for the prosecutor to dismiss weak cases at an earlier stage.

The fee system permits assigned counsel to petition the chief judge of the Recorder's Court for payment of extraordinary fees in cases requiring above-average effort. However, undercompensated attorneys have hesitated to petition for extraordinary fees, believing that such requests either would prove futile or perhaps even adversely affect their prospects of receiving future assignments. While more than 3,000 indigent criminal defense assignments were made in the Court during 1989, only 29 petitions were filed for extraordinary fees, of which 23 were granted, totaling $11,175. This is approximately 1.6 percent of the total indigent attorney fees paid for that year.

In Michigan, assigned counsel have a statutory right to compensation for providing criminal defense services to the indigent. The controlling statute provides that the chief judge "shall appoint" an attorney "to conduct the accused's examination and to conduct the accused's defense." The appointed attorney appointed "shall be entitled to receive from the county treasurer, on the certificate of the chief judge that the services have been rendered, the amount which the chief judge considers to be reasonable compensation for the services performed." Mich. Comp. Laws §775.16. Does the fixed fee system provide assigned counsel "reasonable compensation for the services performed"? Does it violate indigent defendants'right to effective assistance of counsel? Compare Recorder's Court Bar Ass'n. v. Wayne Circuit Court, 503 N.W.2d 885 (Mich. 1993).

Problem 1-6. The Neighborhood Defender

The Neighborhood Defender Service (NDS) of Harlem created a new method of organizing public defense resources. The differences between NDS and the more typical public defender's office were manifest in the outreach efforts of the office, the range of legal services offered to clients, and the assignment of staff to clients.

Rather than placing its offices in one location near the courthouse, NDS placed several offices around the community to make the organization more visible and available to its clients. The service also placed posters, business cards, and other outreach devices in the community so that people in the neighborhood would be familiar with the service before they or their family members needed legal representation in a criminal matter. NDS hoped that this would help attorneys establish a relationship with their clients earlier in the criminal process and would give clients more reason to trust and cooperate with their attorneys.

NDS also shifted its focus from trial to the early stages of cases (sometimes even before arrest), emphasizing investigation and early resolution of charges. Through mediation, attorneys in NDS could sometimes resolve conflicts between victims and defendants, leading the victim to ask the prosecutor to drop charges. The service also continued to advise clients after conviction, to avoid problems during probation or parole. On occasion, NDS would represent clients or their family members in civil matters closely connected to a criminal charge (for instance, possible eviction from public housing based on drug trafficking charges).

As for assignment of staff to the clients, NDS moved away from the typical arrangement of placing one attorney alone in charge of a proportional share of cases the office receives. Each NDS client is represented by a team, consisting of a lead attorney, secondary attorneys, community workers, an investigator, and an administrative assistant. Each NDS attorney is assigned to more total cases than he would handle alone under the traditional arrangement, but the attorneys share the workload on each of the cases. If a client ever has a second case, the same team handles the client's case again. The strategy is to assign more tasks to nonlawyers and to ensure continuity of representation over time and more widespread responsibility for making early progress on the cases.

Is this organizational model for public defender services likely to work in many different communities? If not, what are the conditions necessary for a neighborhood defender service to succeed? See National Inst. of Justice, Public Defenders in the Neighborhood: A Harlem Law Office Stresses Teamwork, Early Investigation (1997, NCJ 163061).

Notes

1. *Local variety in indigent defense systems.* As the materials above indicate, jurisdictions have created several different systems for providing defense counsel to indigent criminal defendants. Although public defender services are the exclusive

method of providing defense counsel in less than a third of all jurisdictions, they tend to be used in the largest jurisdictions, meaning that the majority of criminal defendants in this country receive their attorney through a public defender's office. Bureau of Justice Statistics, Indigent Defense Services in Large Counties, 1999 at Table 7 (Nov. 2000, NCJ 184932) (82 percent of cases in 100 largest counties handled through public defender programs). The federal system continues to rely on different systems from district to district. This local variation in the federal system is the legacy of one of the great justice reform reports in U.S. history, the Report of the Attorney General's Committee on Poverty and the Administration of Federal Criminal Justice (1963), known after its chair as the "Allen Report." The Allen Report led to the federal Criminal Justice Act of 1964, which provided a framework for funding indigent defense in the federal system.

In most states, local governments choose and finance systems of indigent defense. A growing group of states — currently over 20 of them — fund and operate statewide indigent defender services with full authority to provide legal services. See Mary Sue Backus & Paul Marcus, The Right to Counsel in Criminal Cases: A National Crisis, 57 Hastings L.J. 1031, 1046-53 (2006) (summarizing the work of the National Committee on the Right to Counsel). Other states create a statewide commission to provide uniform policies and training for public defenders but leave the choice and funding of systems to the local government. Still another group of 10 to 15 states use county and regional commissions to direct the work of local public defender programs within a single judicial district. See Robert Spangenberg & Marea Beeman, Indigent Defense Systems in the United States, 58 Law & Contemp. Probs. 31 (Winter 1995). There is more statewide uniformity for police practices and trial procedures (through state statutes, constitutional rulings, and procedural rules) than for the provision of defense counsel. Why have the local governments rather than the state governments become the focal point for choices about defense counsel?

2. *Legal challenges to public defender systems.* On those relatively rare occasions when defendants challenge the overall effectiveness of a public defender program, the caseload of the attorneys is always a key variable. See In re Order on Prosecution of Criminal Appeals by the Tenth Judicial Circuit Public Defender, 561 So. 2d 1130 (Fla. 1990) (backlog of appellate cases assigned to public defenders supports habeas corpus relief for indigent appellants unless new funds appropriated within 60 days); John Gibeaut, Defense Warnings, A.B.A. J., Dec. 2001, at 35 (describing litigation over caseloads for indigent defense in Quitman County, Mississippi; Pittsburgh; Connecticut; Coweta County, Georgia).

The ABA standards recommend annual caseloads of no more than 150 non-capital felonies per attorney, 400 misdemeanors, 200 juvenile cases, or 25 appeals. ABA Standards for Criminal Justice, Providing Defense Services §5-5.3 cmt. (3d ed. 1992). How do these standards compare with the workload of Rick Teissier, the defense attorney in *Peart?* Several states have statutes directing public defenders not to accept additional cases if the heavier caseload would prevent them from providing effective representation. A handful of states have statutes adopting specific annual caseload caps for public defender programs. See N.H. Rev. Stat. §604-B:6; Wash. Rev. Code §10.101.030; Wis. Stat. §977.08(5)(bn).

3. *Legal challenges to appointed counsel systems.* Almost all jurisdictions rely on volunteer attorneys to represent some indigent defendants. Sometimes these attorneys take cases when the public defender organization has a conflict of interest; in other places, the court appoints attorneys for all cases from a list of volunteers.

The amount of compensation varies. A volunteer attorney can ordinarily expect some compensation for "overhead" expenses and some reduced compensation for her time. But payment in some systems is discretionary, and the lawyers on the list do not have complete freedom to accept or refuse appointments from the court, depending on schedule and income needs. In a companion case to *Peart,* the Louisiana court in State v. Clark, 624 So. 2d 422 (La. 1993), upheld a contempt finding against an attorney who had refused to accept an appointment to represent a criminal defendant. The attorney, who had placed himself on the volunteer list, had been appointed to five felony cases over a four-month period; he refused to represent the fifth defendant because his private practice was suffering from neglect. The Louisiana court said that attorneys must represent indigents unless a court decides that the appointment is "unreasonable and oppressive," and that these circumstances were not enough to meet the standard.

Lawyers raising constitutional challenges to the adequacy of payments for their work as appointed or contract counsel in individual criminal cases have found modest but consistent success. Courts often recognize that lawyers can be asked to perform enough services for so little compensation that a due process or takings clause violation occurs. See Arnold v. Kemp, 813 S.W.2d 770 (Ark. 1991); Jewell v. Maynard, 383 S.E.2d 536 (W. Va. 1989) (when caseload attributable to court appointments occupies substantial amount of attorney's time, or when attorney's costs and out-of-pocket expenses from representing indigent persons charged with crime reduce substantially the attorney's net income from private practice, requirement of court-appointed service is confiscatory and unconstitutional). The challenge could also be based on a violation of the client's constitutional right to counsel or on violations of the ethical obligations of attorneys.

Broad-based challenges to appointment systems do not occur routinely. A few systemic lawsuits have produced more funding and better organization for appointed counsel systems, including recent litigation in New York City. See New York County Lawyer's Ass'n v. State, 763 N.Y.S.2d 397, 400 (N.Y. Sup. 2003); Susan Saulny, "Lawyers'Fees to Defend the Poor Will Increase," N.Y. Times, Nov. 13, 2003, at B1 (judge ordered increase in hourly rate from 40 to 90 dollars, plaintiffs then agreed to settlement based on legislation setting rate at 75 dollars). More often, however, courts conclude that the level of compensation at issue, while perhaps in need of an increase, does not create a constitutional problem. See Lewis v. Iowa District Court for Des Moines County, 555 N.W.2d 216 (Iowa 1996). What might explain the small amount of litigation over a subject as volatile as compensation for appointed attorneys? Do lawyers simply decline to participate in the appointment system (when the choice is theirs) rather than litigate over the adequacy of the compensation?

4. *Challenges to contract attorney systems: majority position.* In contract attorney programs, the government (typically at the county level) agrees with a private law firm, bar association, or nonprofit organization to provide indigent defense. The contract may cover all criminal cases or specific classes of cases (such as all juvenile cases or adult cases in which the public defender's office has a conflict of interest). These contracts become especially attractive in jurisdictions where the costs of appointed attorneys has increased. For instance, Oklahoma turned to lowest-bidder contract providers after the *Lynch* case was decided.

The method of pricing the services is the difficult issue. Some jurisdictions use a fixed price contract, in which the provider agrees to perform defense services at the stated price, regardless of the number of cases that actually arise. Although this method of setting the contract amount is relatively common, it has only rarely been challenged on constitutional grounds. In State v. Smith, 681 P.2d 1374 (Ariz. 1984), a defendant convicted of burglary argued that he was denied effective assistance of counsel because of his attorney's "shocking, staggering and unworkable" caseload, which was the product of a fixed price contract. The county had granted the contract to the lowest bidder, but the contract did not allow for support costs such as investigators, paralegals, and secretaries and did not consider the experience or competence of the attorney. Smith's attorney handled a "part time" caseload of 149 felonies, 160 misdemeanors, 21 juvenile cases, and 33 other cases in the year Smith was convicted, in addition to a private civil practice. The court therefore found that the bid system violated the rights of defendants to due process and the right to counsel. Would a government avoid these problems by entering a contract that pays a fixed fee per case?

The American Bar Association's Criminal Justice Standards discourage local governments from awarding an indigent-services contract based on a fixed price for a time period. The standards recommend that contracts include detailed information about minimum attorney qualifications, attorney workloads, use of support services, and so forth. ABA Standards for Criminal Justice, Providing Defense Services §5-3.3(b) (3d ed. 1992). The well-regarded system in Oregon asks potential contractors to submit information on caseloads, areas of coverage (including geographic limits and types of cases), level of services, staffing plans, and the applicants' experience and qualifications. Spangenberg Group, Contracting for Indigent Defense Services: A Special Report (2000, NCJ 181160). Will a contracting government be able to follow these standards and still obtain the predictability of legal expenses so necessary to government budgeting and administration?

5. *Remedies.* The most vexing question in much of the litigation challenging systems for providing defense counsel is the question of remedy. If an attorney is placed in a situation in which effective assistance is difficult or impossible for her to provide, what should the court do? Overturn individual convictions of those who challenge the effectiveness of their attorneys? Order the legislature to provide additional funding? Mandate a minimally acceptable caseload or fee schedule? After *Peart* was decided, the Louisiana legislature created the Louisiana Indigent Defender Board and gave it a $10 million budget to use for studying problems with indigent defense in the state and for granting operating funds in trouble areas, such as appointment of defense experts in particular cases. The legislature later cut the budget to $5 million, at a time when defense of capital cases was becoming a larger concern for the board. Does this aftermath of the *Peart* litigation tell you anything about the remedies a court should impose?

6. *Incentives for aggressive representation.* Which system — public defender organizations, appointed counsel, or contract attorneys — provides an acceptable defense for the least amount of money? The best defense for an acceptable amount of money? There is no single answer to these questions. Ontario, Canada, has an extremely well-funded public defender agency; it spent about $1,246 per matter in 1991. In Los Angeles, it costs an average of $683 for a public defender to defend a felony case, while it takes a court-appointed attorney an average of $2,914. See Am. Law., Jan.-Feb. 1993, at 64, 83. In the end, the cost of any of these systems will depend on what the public believes should be the "normal" method of defending a case. One often hears the assertion that defender organizations are funded at a level that

compels the attorneys to urge their clients to plead guilty in most cases. For instance, one public defender explained why some innocent defendants plead guilty: "[W]e don't have enough resources, and . . . the system is geared toward putting people away as efficiently as possible." Am. Law., Jan.-Feb. 1993, at 72. See Michael McConville & Chester Mirsky, Criminal Defense of the Poor in New York City, 15 N.Y.U. Rev. L. & Soc. Change 581 (1986-1987). Is it inevitable that defense attorneys who regularly accept money from the government will, in the long run, moderate their demands on prosecutors, police, and judges?

Some believe that "organizational" defenders are more cost-efficient because they represent many defendants at once and work in criminal justice full time. Thus, legislatures tend to create public defender programs because of potential cost savings. Are public defenders more efficient than appointed counsel, or do they choose certain cases and issues to pursue aggressively while allowing the other cases and clients to suffer from neglect? Is this what the public defender from Louisiana did in *Peart?* Would an appointed attorney be better able to represent each client more thoroughly, without trading off one client's needs against those of another? Are attorneys who spend all their time representing criminal defendants in the best position to bring systemwide challenges to the practices of police, prosecutors, or judges?

7. *Funding parity.* If popular support for prosecution of crimes is higher than the support for funding criminal defense, is the answer to require parity of funding between prosecution and defense? How would you accomplish this most effectively — through a constitutional ruling, a statute, or a local ordinance?

There is little doubt that the total resources available for the investigation and prosecution of crime are greater than those available for defending against criminal charges. See David Luban, Are Criminal Defenders Different? 91 Mich. L. Rev. 1729 (1993) (resources for prosecution versus public and private defense counsel may be at roughly comparable levels, but only when ignoring prosecutorial access to police and forensic expert support). The imbalance in resources has arguably become more pronounced over the past two decades, as governments have increased the size of police, prosecutorial, and judicial staffs without comparably increasing defense counsel funding. As prosecutions and convictions have risen faster than the number of defense attorneys, defense caseloads have risen faster than prosecution caseloads.

If it is true that prosecutors and police combined receive more resources than defense counsel, is that a problem? Perhaps one might respond that prosecutors have more funding because they perform a wider range of functions than defense counsel. For instance, they make screening decisions on cases that are never charged. Alternatively, one might ask whether the increased demands on defense counsel really translate into worse outcomes for clients. One study of nine jurisdictions, conducted in 1992 for the National Center for State Courts, concluded that publicly provided attorneys produced outcomes similar to privately retained defense counsel. Private and publicly funded attorneys produced no significant difference in rates of convictions or length of sentences. Privately retained counsel obtained slightly better results in avoiding incarceration for their clients. Roger Hanson, Brian Ostrom, William Hewitt & Christopher Lomvardias, Indigent Defenders Get the Job Done and Done Well (National Center for State Courts, 1992). Is there any basis for arguing that defense counsel should be funded on a level comparable to the prosecution if there is no demonstrable effect on the outcomes for defendants?

Apart from the question of funding for entire offices, is there any justification for paying individual prosecutors a higher salary than individual defense attorneys? See Ariz. Stat. §11-582 (public defender salary to be at least 70 percent of prosecutor salary); Tenn. Code §16-2-518 ("any increase in local funding for positions or office expense for the district attorney general shall be accompanied by an increase in funding of 75 percent of the increase in funding to the office of the public defender in such district"). For an effort to contrast the "ex post" evaluation of a lawyer's performance under *Strickland* with an "ex ante" evaluation of the resources available to prosecution and defense, see Donald Dripps, Ineffective Assistance of Counsel: The Case for an Ex Ante Parity Standard, 88 J. Crim. L. & Criminology 242-308 (1997); cf. Ronald F. Wright, Parity of Resources for Defense Counsel and the Reach of Public Choice Theory, 90 Iowa L. Rev. 219 (2004).

8. *Contingent fees.* Would private defense attorneys be more willing to represent criminal defendants if they could make contingent fee arrangements with their clients, calling for different levels of compensation depending on the outcome of the proceedings? The ABA standard reprinted above, barring the use of contingent fees in criminal cases, reflects the law of all the states. Why are contingent fees prohibited in criminal cases when they have been such an effective method (some might say too effective) for providing counsel to civil litigants? For further reading, see Pamela Karlan, Contingent Fees and Criminal Cases, 93 Colum. L. Rev. 595 (1993).

E. THE ETHICS OF DEFENDING CRIMINALS

If you are a defense lawyer, you may often hear the question, "how can you defend those people?" Should all lawyers be required to defend criminals, regardless of the crime of which the defendant is accused or the lawyer's view of the defendant's guilt? The following selections represent a range of time-honored answers to this question. As you read them, try to come up with a short phrase to describe the position suggested in each passage. Which of the positions reflects the current mainstream of thought among American lawyers? Among law students? What are the institutional and ethical implications of each position?

■ SPEECHES OF LORD ERSKINE
(James High ed., 1876)

In every place where business or pleasure collects the public together, day after day, my name and character have been the topics of injurious reflection.* And for what? Only for not having shrunk from the discharge of a duty which no personal advantage recommended, but which a thousand difficulties repelled. Little indeed did they know me, who thought that such calumnies would influence my conduct. I will forever, at all hazards assert the dignity, independence and integrity of the English Bar, without which impartial justice, the most valuable part of the English Constitution, can have no existence. From the moment that any advocate can be permitted to say that he will or will not stand between the Crown and the subject

---

*Lord Erskine was defense counsel for Thomas Paine, the influential pamphleteer. —Eds.

arraigned in the court where he daily sits to practice, from that moment the liberties of England are at an end. If the advocate refuses to defend, from what he may think of the charge or of the defense, he assumes the character of the judge; nay he assumes it before the hour of judgment; and in proportion to his rank and reputation puts the heavy influence of perhaps a mistaken opinion into the scale against the accused in whose favor the benevolent principles of English law makes all presumptions. . . .

■ JOHN DOS PASSOS, THE AMERICAN LAWYER
158 (1907)

I do not place the right of the lawyer to defend a client when he believes him to be guilty upon the ground that he cannot know that his client is guilty until his guilt has been officially and finally declared by a court and jury, because he often does know, in the sense that he has a moral conviction of the guilt of his client which he has derived through the ordinary channels of information. I place the right of the lawyer upon the ground that he is an officer of the law, and that it is his *duty* to see that the forms of law are carried out, quite irrespective of individual knowledge.

■ AMERICAN BAR ASSOCIATION AND ASSOCIATION OF AMERICAN LAW SCHOOLS, PROFESSIONAL RESPONSIBILITY: REPORT OF THE JOINT CONFERENCE (1958)

The Joint Conference on Professional Responsibility* was established in 1952 by the American Bar Association and the Association of American Law Schools. [T]hose who had attempted to teach ethical principles to law students found that the students were uneasy about the adversary system, some thinking of it as an unwholesome compromise with the combativeness of human nature, others vaguely approving of it but disturbed by their inability to articulate its proper limits. . . . Confronted by the layman's charge that he is nothing but a hired brain and voice, the lawyer often finds it difficult to convey an insight into the value of the adversary system. . . . Accordingly, it was decided that the first need was for a reasoned statement of the lawyer's responsibilities, set in the context of the adversary system. . . .

THE LAWYER'S ROLE AS ADVOCATE IN OPEN COURT

The lawyer appearing as an advocate before a tribunal presents, as persuasively as he can, the facts and the law of the case as seen from the standpoint of his client's interest. . . . In a very real sense it may be said that the integrity of the adjudicative process itself depends upon the participation of the advocate. This becomes apparent when we contemplate the nature of the task assumed by any arbiter who attempts to decide a dispute without the aid of partisan advocacy.

Such an arbiter must undertake, not only the role of judge, but that of representative for both of the litigants. Each of these roles must be played to the

*The conference was chaired by Lon Fuller and John Randall. — EDS.

full without being muted by qualifications derived from the others. When he is developing for each side the most effective statement of its case, the arbiter must put aside his neutrality and permit himself to be moved by a sympathetic identification. . . . When he resumes his neutral position, he must be able to view with distrust the fruits of this identification and be ready to reject the products of his own best mental efforts. The difficulties of this undertaking are obvious. If it is true that a man in his time must play many parts, it is scarcely given to him to play them all at once.

It is small wonder, then, that failure generally attends the attempt to dispense with the distinct roles traditionally implied in adjudication. What generally occurs in practice is that at some early point a familiar pattern will seem to emerge from the evidence; an accustomed label is waiting for the case and, without further proofs, this label is promptly assigned to it. [W]hat starts as a preliminary diagnosis designed to direct the inquiry tends, quickly and imperceptibly, to become a fixed conclusion, as all that confirms the diagnosis makes a strong imprint on the mind, while all that runs counter to it is received with diverted attention.

An adversary presentation seems the only effective means for combating this natural human tendency to judge too swiftly in terms of the familiar that which is not yet fully known. The arguments of counsel hold the case, as it were, in suspension between two opposing interpretations of it. While the proper classification of the case is thus kept unresolved, there is time to explore all of its peculiarities and nuances. . . .

Viewed in this light, the role of the lawyer as a partisan advocate appears not as a regrettable necessity, but as an indispensable part of a larger ordering of affairs. The institution of advocacy is not a concession to the frailties of human nature, but an expression of human insight in the design of a social framework within which man's capacity for impartial judgment can attain its fullest realization. . . .

THE REPRESENTATION OF UNPOPULAR CAUSES

One of the highest services the lawyer can render to society is to appear in court on behalf of clients whose causes are in disfavor with the general public. . . . Where a cause is in disfavor because of a misunderstanding by the public, the service of the lawyer representing it is obvious, since he helps to remove an obloquy unjustly attaching to his client's position. But the lawyer renders an equally important, though less readily understood, service where the unfavorable public opinion of the client's cause is in fact justified. It is essential for a sound and wholesome development of public opinion that the disfavored cause have its full day in court, which includes, of necessity, representation by competent counsel. Where this does not occur, a fear arises that perhaps more might have been said for the losing side and suspicion is cast on the decision reached. Thus, confidence in the fundamental processes of government is diminished.

The extent to which the individual lawyer should feel himself bound to undertake the representation of unpopular causes must remain a matter for individual conscience. The legal profession as a whole, however, has a clear moral obligation with respect to this problem. . . . No member of the Bar should indulge in public criticism of another lawyer because he has undertaken the representation of causes in general disfavor. Every member of the profession should, on the contrary, do what he can to promote a public understanding of the service rendered by the advocate in such situations. . . .

These are problems each lawyer must solve in his own way. But in solving them he will remember, with Whitehead, that moral education cannot be complete without the habitual vision of greatness. And he will recall the concluding words of a famous essay by Holmes:

> Happiness, I am sure from having known many successful men, cannot be won simply by being counsel for great corporations and having an income of fifty thousand dollars. An intellect great enough to win the prize needs other food besides success. The remoter and more general aspects of the law are those which give it universal interest. It is through them that you not only become a great master in your calling, but connect your subject with the universe and catch an echo of the infinite, a glimpse of its unfathomable process, a hint of the universal law.

■ JOHN KAPLAN,
DEFENDING GUILTY PEOPLE
7 U. Bridgeport L. Rev. 223 (1986)

I would like to address an often asked, many times answered, but still extremely complex question: Why would lawyers want to defend guilty people? I will try to do so by examining first a somewhat different issue: Why should society as a whole want guilty people to be represented by lawyers? . . . The first means of approach is to ask two related questions: "Why do we want lawyers to represent criminal defendants at all?" and, second, "How does this rationale change in the case when we know that the defendant is guilty?" . . .

The first of the questions seems simple, but there are three quite different reasons why we wish those accused of crimes to be defended by lawyers. The most obvious reason is that defense lawyers improve the accuracy of the fact-finding process in which they are engaged. Many people may dispute this, since over the years the adversary system has played, at best, to mixed reviews. . . . Often it was said that a system where each of the two sides was trying to put something over on the decision maker was a crazy method of deciding important questions. . . .

The second major reason why we want defendants in criminal cases to be defended by counsel is much more complex. [T]he basic idea is that one major characteristic of the due process model of criminal litigation is the use of the criminal process to check and regulate its own institutions. Thus, in a particular case, the defendant's lawyer will litigate much more than whether the defendant has violated a particular law with the appropriate state of mind. The lawyer also will be making sure that the arms of the state have complied with the many legal rules which bind them. . . .

The third major reason for providing an attorney for those accused of crimes involves the symbolic statement that it makes about us and our society; it is a multi-faceted statement. It says that we are a compassionate people and that in our society even the worst off (and it is hard to think of any who, as a class, are worse off than those accused of crimes) are entitled to have one person in their corner to help them. It underlines the value we place upon equality, because though lawyers vary considerably in their ability to manipulate our complex system of jury trials, their variation is far less than that among criminal defendants. [Our] trial system makes the statement that in our society the individual has rights against the state which can actually be enforced through the legal system. . . .

Next we move to the second question — which of these three reasons for having the defendant represented by an attorney no longer applies when we know that the defendant is guilty. [It] seems that only the first reason, improving the accuracy of the fact-finding process, loses its force. Of course, when the defendant is by hypothesis guilty, we need not worry about the accuracy of the process by which this is determined.

With respect to the second reason, checking the operation of the institutions of the criminal law, most of the checks are expected to apply where the accused is guilty of the crimes charged. . . . There is a thin line between arguing that a defendant is innocent — a matter that goes to fact-finding — and arguing that the police and prosecutors improperly brought the case on insufficient evidence — a matter involving the checking function.

The closeness of these two functions at this point is also seen when we adopt a dynamic, rather than a static, view of the criminal process. We must remember that when prosecutors and police do their jobs well, they do so in part because of the discipline imposed upon them by the fact that they will have to prove their case against a defendant represented by a lawyer. If that should cease, it may be impossible to guarantee that the police and prosecutors will continue at the same level of competence, energy, and integrity. The perhaps apocryphal example of a mountain village may be instructive: it is said that the town fathers took down the "dangerous curve ahead" sign because no one had gone off the road there. They had therefore concluded that the curve was no longer dangerous.

The fact that innocent defendants may benefit from some applications of the checking function, such as those related to the strength of the prosecution's case, might lead to the argument that at least as to these applications, the checking function should not be applied where the defendant is guilty. So far as the checking function is concerned, a defense lawyer is unnecessary in those cases where we know that the defendant is guilty. If enough innocent defendants went to trial so that we could perform the checking function adequately in their cases, why should a lawyer do so on behalf of one who is guilty? The problem . . . is that our criminal justice system is so heavily structured to produce guilty pleas that there may not be enough innocent defendants going to trial to raise the inadequacies of the police and prosecutorial screening in their cases. . . .

Similarly, the third major reason for having attorneys represent criminal defendants is not affected by whether the defendant is guilty. Indeed, the symbolic value of having an attorney represent a defendant may even be increased when we know the accused is guilty. The statement, then, becomes that much louder that the rights of those defendants whose guilt has not been officially and fairly determined are so fixed and important that, even if we knew they were guilty, these rights would remain. . . .

The last question we need to ask is, "Why would anyone want to make a living this way?" The answer to that question involves a very different kind of discourse, but my answer is simple. The question should not be asked. It is important to remember that, for one reason or another, criminal lawyers want to defend criminal defendants. Their taste may be as baffling to us as is the proctologist's, but we need both and should not try to dissuade either from pursuing his or her profession. Instead, we ought to encourage both because, whether they realize it or not — or even care — they are doing exactly what we want them to do.

■ AARON CUTLER,
IS A LAWYER BOUND TO SUPPORT
AN UNJUST CAUSE? A PROBLEM OF ETHICS
300-302 (1952)

The layman's question which has most tormented the lawyer over the years is: "How can you honestly stand up and defend a man you know to be guilty?" [A]dvocates enjoy reciting the following colloquy attributed to Samuel Johnson by his famous biographer, James Boswell:

Boswell: But what do you think of supporting a cause which you know to be bad?
Johnson: Sir, you do not know it to be good or bad till the Judge determines it. You are to state facts clearly; so that your thinking, or what you call knowing, a cause to be bad must be from reasoning, must be from supposing your arguments to be weak and inconclusive. But Sir, that is not enough. An argument which does not convince yourself may convince the judge to whom you urge it; and if it does convince him, why then, sir, you are wrong and he is right. . . .
Boswell: But, Sir, does not affecting a warmth when you have no warmth, and appearing to be clearly of one opinion when you are in reality of another opinion, does not such dissimulation impair one's honesty? Is there not some danger that a lawyer may put on the same mask in common life in the intercourse with his friends?
Johnson: Why, no, Sir. Everybody knows you are paid for affecting warmth for your client, and it is therefore properly no dissimulation: the moment you come from the Bar you resume your usual behaviour. Sir, a man will no more carry the artifice of the Bar into the common intercourse of society, than a man who is paid for tumbling upon his hands will continue to tumble on his hands when he should walk upon his feet. . . .

Such an attitude we submit entirely overlooks the bifurcated roles of a lawyer. The duty is not simply one which he owes his client. Just as important is the duty which the lawyer owes the court and society. Great as is his loyalty to the client, even greater is his sacred obligation as an officer of the court. He cannot ethically, and should not by preference, present to the court assertions he knows to be false. . . .

It is only when a lawyer really believes his client is innocent that he should undertake to defend him. All our democratic safeguards are thrown about a person accused of a crime so that no innocent man may suffer. Guilty defendants, though they are entitled to be defended sincerely and hopefully, should not be entitled to the presentation of false testimony and insincere statements by counsel.

It is too glibly said a lawyer should not judge his own client and that the court's province would thus be invaded. In more than 90 percent of all criminal cases a lawyer knows when his client is guilty or not guilty. The facts usually stand out with glaring and startling simplicity.

If a lawyer knows his client to be guilty, it is his duty in such case to set out the extenuating facts and plead for mercy in which the lawyer sincerely believes. In the infrequent number of cases where there is doubt of the client's guilt and the lawyer sincerely believes his client is innocent, he of course should plead his client's cause to the best of his ability.

In civil cases, the area of doubt is undoubtedly considerably greater. At a guess, only one-third [of] the cases presented to a lawyer are pure black or pure white. In only one-third of the cases does the lawyer indubitably know his client is wrong or right. In the other two-thirds gray is the predominant color. It is the duty of the advocate to appraise the client's cause in his favor, after giving due consideration to the facts on the other side. In such a case, it is of course the duty of the advocate to present his client's case to the best of his ability. . . .

A lawyer should worship truth and fact. He should unhesitatingly cast out the evil spirits of specious reasoning, of doubtful claims, of incredible or improbable premises. Truly, the best persuader is one who has first really persuaded himself after a careful analysis of the facts that he is on the right side. Some assert that lawyers must be actors. That is only partially true. An actor can portray abysmal grief or ecstatic happiness without having any such corresponding feeling in his own heart. A young actor can well portray the tragedy of King Lear, though his face is unwrinkled and unmarred after his make-up is removed. [But the] true lawyer can only be persuasive when he honestly believes he is right. . . .

Whatever the situation was in Johnson's day, there should be no artifice at the Bar. Nor should a man "resume his usual behaviour" the moment he comes from the Bar. The lawyer's usual behavior both in his office, and at the Bar and in Society, should be that of a man of probity, integrity and absolute dependability.

The argument that a lawyer should be a mouthpiece for his client, indelicate as that connotation may be, is specious and only logical to a limited extent. A lawyer should not be merely a mechanical apparatus reproducing the words and thoughts and alibis of his client, no matter how insincere or dishonest. Rather the lawyer should refuse to speak those words as a mouthpiece, unless the utterances of his client are filtered and purified by truth and sincerity. . . .

■ LETTER FROM WILLIAM TOWNSEND
4 N.Y. L. Rev. 173 (1926)

To William H. Townsend, of the Lexington, Kentucky, bar, writing for the February American Bar Association Journal, we are indebted for some interesting light upon Abraham Lincoln's views. . . . Mr. Townsend writes:

> Lincoln was regarded as a really formidable antagonist only when he was thoroughly convinced of the justice of his cause. He seemed utterly incapable of that professional partisanship that enlisted the best efforts of his colleagues at the bar, regardless of the side they were on. He would never argue a case before a jury when he believed he was wrong. His associate, Henry C. Whitney, says of him in this respect: "No man was stronger than he when on the right side, and no man weaker than he when on the opposite. A knowledge of this fact gave him additional strength before a court or a jury."
>
> Leonard Swett (one of Lincoln's closest friends) and Lincoln were once defending a man charged with murder, and, after all the evidence was in, Lincoln believed their man was guilty. "You speak to the jury," he said to Swett, "if I say a word they will see from my face that the man is guilty and convict him."
>
> In another murder case, the circumstantial evidence of guilt seemed almost conclusive and, when Lincoln, who had never wavered in his masterly defense, arose to address the jury, he frankly conceded that the testimony for the State was exceedingly strong. He said, in his slow, drawling way, that he had thought a great deal about the case and that the guilt of his client seemed probable. "But I am not sure," he said as his honest gray eyes looked the jury squarely in the face, "are you?" It was an application of the rule of reasonable doubt which secured an acquittal.

From the foregoing it would seem that Lincoln had no scruple against effort to acquit a guilty client, only that he preferred that associate counsel should do the summing up. In the other example Lincoln invoked the rule of reasonable doubt artfully and dramatically and the client whose guilt Lincoln conceded to be probable, was cleared of the crime.

Notes

1. *The line between obligation and excuse.* In England the question appears to be not whether lawyers should choose to represent those who are guilty but whether any advocate can or should ever refuse to represent a defendant. A barrister cannot refuse to take a case, whether to act as an advocate or to advise, "unless the barrister is professionally committed already, has not been offered a proper fee, is professionally embarrassed by a prior conflict of interest or lacks sufficient experience or competence to handle the matter." Anthony Thornton, Responsibility and Ethics of the English Bar, in Legal Ethics and Professional Responsibility 68 (Ross Cranston ed., 1995). In the United States, lawyers can choose whether to take a case and then are asked to defend this choice. Is the English practice the best way, in the end, to reduce public criticism of criminal defense work?

The ethics of defending criminals, the related question of the proper ethical boundaries in prosecuting criminals, presents questions that command the attention of attorneys in criminal practice, and not just legal ethicists. See Lisa J. McIntyre, The Public Defender: The Practice of Law in the Shadows of Repute 139-70 (1987) (based on interviews with public defenders in Cook County, Illinois). For some attorneys who represent criminal defendants, justifications based on the specialized roles of lawyers in an adversarial system do not adequately explain their decision to stay in this line of work. For some, no line of argument about the defense lawyer's role can counter the emotional costs of defending people accused of terrible crimes. See Susan A. Bandes, Repression and Denial in Criminal Lawyering, 9 Buff. Crim. L. Rev. 339 (2006). For others, a more heroic conception of the defense attorney supplements the traditional need to test factual and legal claims through an adversarial system. See Margareth Etienne, The Ethics of Cause Lawyering: An Empirical Examination of Criminal Defense Lawyers as Cause Lawyers, 95 J. Crim. L. & Criminology 101 (2005) (based on data from interviews with 40 criminal defense attorneys, concludes that many criminal defense attorneys consider themselves to be "cause lawyers" who are committed to individual clients but also to the cause of legal reform in criminal law).

2. *Asking the question.* Some of the justifications for representing potentially guilty defendants depend on the possibility (however slim) that a client could be innocent of the charges. If a defense lawyer learns that a particular client did indeed commit the crime as charged, what justifications remain for going forward with the case? Should a defense lawyer ever ask a client, "Are you guilty?" Experienced lawyers give different answers to this question. Some insist on asking their clients, because they believe they cannot prepare a good defense unless they know "the whole truth." Others do not ask, because they believe the answer would be irrelevant to the defense.

During the 1997 trial of Timothy McVeigh, who was ultimately convicted of bombing a federal courthouse in Oklahoma City and killing hundreds of people, reports circulated that McVeigh had confessed to his lawyers. The lead defense attorney, Stephen Jones, appeared on a nationally televised talk show to discuss the case with the viewers:

Oklahoma Caller: Yes, Mr. Jones, assuming McVeigh told you he was guilty, and assuming you got him off, how can you live with yourself morally the rest of your life?

Jones: Well, I think that's a fair question. . . . I'm not a judge. I'm a defense lawyer. I don't ask a client whether they're guilty. I ask them to tell me what happened. And then I compare what they tell me with what the evidence is. It's the prosecution's job to prosecute him, the jury's job to judge the facts, my job to represent him. . . . I don't have trouble sleeping at night. I have confidence in the system.

CNN Larry King Live, March 17, 1997 (Transcript #97031700V22). How might the Oklahoma caller respond to Jones's answer?

3. *Defense attorneys and crime control.* If one of the central functions of the criminal justice system is to deter crime and incapacitate dangerous criminals, what are the implications for the ethics of defending criminals? Consider whether the ethical dimension of a defense counsel's work looks different for those who emphasize other aspects of the system, such as rehabilitation or punishment for the crimes committed, leaving the job of crime prevention mostly to other government institutions. If defense attorneys were polled about crime control and other functions of criminal justice, what do you imagine they would say?

4. *Ethical deliberation for lawyers.* Even if a theory supporting the strong defense of criminal defendants, including those clients a lawyer believes to be guilty, provides general justification for an individual lawyer to defend criminals, these theories hardly answer the difficult questions that arise in actually defending clients. There are more than a few difficult questions of application. What ought a defense attorney to do if she believes her client is lying? What ought a defense attorney to do if she obtains possible relevant evidence (say, a gun)? Is it appropriate for a defense attorney to use procedural tactics or create scheduling conflicts to increase the chance that the state's case will weaken and that the memory of witnesses will fade? Some of these questions will receive further attention in later chapters. Each deserves considered reflection by a lawyer before the moment of decision. As Monroe Freedman explains: "In making a series of ethical decisions, we create a kind of moral profile of ourselves. You should be conscious, therefore, of how your own decisions on issues of lawyers' ethics establish your moral priorities and thereby define your own moral profile. In understanding lawyers' ethics, you may come to better understand your moral values, and yourself." Freedman, Understanding Lawyers' Ethics (1990); cf. Freedman, An Ethical Manifesto for Public Defenders, 39 Val. U. L. Rev. 911 (2005).

II

Pretrial Release and Detention

Not long after the police arrest a suspect, the government must decide what charges (if any) to file against the suspect. More or less contemporaneously with the preliminary charging decision, the court must decide whether to release the suspect from custody. Questions about charging and release arise, sometimes repeatedly, in a group of preliminary proceedings that differ in title and in detail from jurisdiction to jurisdiction. This chapter explores the decision whether to release or detain a suspect, and Chapter 3 considers the related decision of what charges to file.

For many suspects, the release decision is resolved at the police station, without any appearance before a judicial officer. Most jurisdictions allow "station-house bail" for minor crimes: An administrative official within the law enforcement agency (or perhaps an administrative employee of the courts) releases the suspect by following routine requirements. For instance, the suspect might make a written promise to appear at later proceedings or might pay a modest amount of money "bail" that would be forfeited upon a failure to appear.

Release decisions may also occur a few hours later, when the suspect appears before a judge or magistrate. This "initial appearance" before a judicial officer combines several functions: (1) a determination of whether the government had probable cause to support an arrest of the suspect, (2) an inquiry into whether it will be necessary to assign defense counsel to the case, and (3) the decision whether to release the suspect. The release decision might be the first determination of a bail amount (or other conditions of release), or it might involve an adjustment of a bail amount set earlier.

Finally, the release decision can occur at a later proceeding, when a judge reconsiders the bail amount or other conditions of release. The later proceeding might be a "preliminary hearing," when a judge also determines whether there is enough evidence to hold the defendant for trial; the later proceeding might also be a "bail hearing," devoted exclusively to the question of release or detention. Defense counsel could be involved at the earliest judicial determination of bail amounts, but usually counsel has little opportunity to become familiar with the defendant's circumstances and to make an effective argument at that point. Only when the court revisits the release decision (often several days after the arrest) can defense counsel develop and present relevant facts.

The release decision has changed dramatically over the past few generations, and it is still in flux. Section A below highlights the reform movement, begun more than 40 years ago and still a vibrant part of federal and state law, to make it easier for defendants to gain release from custody before trial. The section also describes the factors that influence the release decision and the institutions most responsible for making that choice. Section B then traces a more recent movement — in part a reaction to the first reform — to expand the state's power to detain some defendants until the time of trial in an effort to protect the public from further crimes the defendant might commit. Section C tracks the use of detentions without criminal trial in the related arena of terrorism investigations and prevention.

A. PRETRIAL RELEASE

1. *Method of Release*

Bail procedures have been the subject of extensive social science research. The researchers' interest in bail stems from the pervasiveness of bail determinations, the relative ease of quantifying bail determinations, and the moral problems raised by detaining those who have not yet been tried (and are, therefore, presumptively innocent) and releasing those who threaten additional harm. A classic illustration of the use of social science as an engine of reform is the Manhattan Bail Project conducted by the Vera Institute of Justice. In reading the following account of the bail experiment, consider the project's origin, implementation (including the essential role played by law students), and effects.

■ VERA INSTITUTE OF JUSTICE, FAIR TREATMENT FOR THE INDIGENT: THE MANHATTAN BAIL PROJECT
Ten-Year Report, 1961-1971 (May 1972)

There are many penalties imposed upon an accused person who is detained in jail because he is too poor to post bail. [The] detainee is more apt to be convicted than if he were free on bail; and, if convicted, he is more apt to receive a tougher sentence. [Detainees] lose income while they are away from their jobs, and suffer dislocation and sometimes even permanent rupture in their family lives. They frequently suffer social stigmatization and loss of self respect because of their confinement — even though they have not been convicted of anything and must be presumed innocent, and may eventually be acquitted. . . .

In a large city like New York, these people can also expect to be detained in jails where conditions are comparable to maximum security prisons. . . . Meanwhile, detained persons' defense preparations suffer as it is difficult or impossible for them to consult with attorneys, communicate with family or friends, locate witnesses, or gather evidence.

THE ORIGINS AND EVOLUTION OF BAIL

The concept of bail has a long history and deep roots in English and American law. In medieval England, the custom grew out of the need to free untried prisoners from disease-ridden jails while they were waiting for the delayed trials conducted by traveling justices. Prisoners were bailed, or delivered, to reputable third parties of their own choosing who accepted responsibility for assuring their appearance at trial. If the accused did not appear, the bailor would stand in his place.

Eventually it became the practice for property owners who accepted responsibility for accused persons to forfeit money when their charges failed to appear for trial. From this grew the modern practice of posting a money bond through a commercial bondsman who receives a cash premium for his service, and usually demands some collateral as well. In the event of non-appearance the bond is forfeited, after a grace period of a number of days during which the bondsman may produce the accused in court.

The Constitution of the United States did not specifically grant the right to bail, although the Eighth Amendment stipulated that "excessive bail shall not be required." The Judiciary Act of 1789 and subsequent statutes in all but seven of the states did require admission to bail, however, in all non-capital cases. . . .

The emergence of the bondsman as a commercial adjunct to the processes of American criminal justice brought with it certain advantages — he was added to the agencies seeking to enforce court appearance, for example — but it also brought serious drawbacks. Abuses tended to creep into the system, such as collusive ties some bondsmen developed with police, lawyers, court officials and also with organized crime. But more important, the central determinant in whether an accused person would go free on bail pending trial became the decision of a businessman who was interested not in the evenhanded application of justice, but in profit. . . .

VERA TAKES ACTION

[Vera instigators] felt that the best course might be to establish a bail fund, limited perhaps to helping youthful defendants between the ages of 16 and 21. It was thought that such a fund might pay the premiums on bail bonds for these young persons, and at the same time carry out research that would help identify who the good risks might be, and why; how a defendant behaves while his trial is pending; and how the cases were concluded. The fund might later be broadened to include older defendants.

[During discussions with city officials and legal experts, however,] the concept of a fund began to show serious defects. Successful operation of a bail fund would not change bail-setting procedures, and would promote the idea that an unfair system could somehow be made to function equitably with the help of private philanthropic support. It seemed clear that the whole system needed reform and should not be encouraged to rely upon private philanthropy. . . .

Real reform was indeed possible. . . . This was the idea of encouraging judges to release far more accused persons on their honor pending trial, and providing the

judges with verified information about the accused on which such releases could
be based. It was an obvious, but . . . daring idea: find out who can be trusted, and
trust them to appear for trial.

What was needed was a carefully designed project that would . . . develop information about defendants which would enable the courts to grant release to good
risks. . . . A project based on these concepts quickly took form:

1. Indigent defendants awaiting arraignment in Manhattan's criminal courts
    would be questioned by Vera staff interviewers to determine how deep their
    community roots were and thus whether they could be relied upon to return
    to court for trial if they were released without bail.
2. The test of indigency would be representation by a Legal Aid lawyer.
3. Questioners would develop information about the defendant's length of
    residence in the city, his family ties, and his employment situation.
4. Responses of the defendant would be verified immediately in personal or
    telephone interviews with family, friends, and employers.
5. When verified information indicated that an individual was trustworthy
    and could be depended on to return for trial, the Vera staff member
    would appear at arraignment and recommend to the judge that the accused
    be released on his own recognizance (R.O.R. or pretrial parole) pending trial.

A Demonstration Project Is Set Up

It was anticipated that such a simple but radical change in generally accepted
procedures would meet opposition from those accustomed to the old ways or fearful
of the new, and so the entire project was devised as a demonstration — an experiment to see whether people would return for trial if released without bail and, in
general, how their cases compared with the cases of those not granted release as well
as those released on bail. . . .

The experiment was scheduled to begin in the fall of 1961 in the arraignment
part of the Manhattan Magistrate's Felony Court. [Students] from the School of Law
at New York University were recruited as Vera staff interviewers and received a
period of training during which they learned how the arraignment court functioned. The Law School agreed to give the students credit for their Vera work in
conjunction with a University seminar on legal problems of the indigent. The entire
experience was thought to be an important introduction to the criminal justice
process for the aspiring young lawyer. . . .

On October 16, 1961 after months of detailed planning, the Manhattan Bail
Project began operations. Specifics attending the launching were carefully arranged:

1. No publicity was given the inauguration of the venture, on grounds that it
    would be most effective as a demonstration to the community if the results
    could later speak for themselves. . . .
2. The answers sought through the project were limited and precise: (a)
    Would judges release more defendants on their own recognizance if they
    were given verified information about the defendants than they would
    without such information? (b) Would released defendants return for trial
    at the same rate as those released on bail? (c) How would the cases of
    released defendants compare with a control group not recommended for
    release, both in convictions and in sentencing? . . .

3. All magistrates who would be sitting in court during the project were visited personally by Vera staff members prior to its initiation so that they would understand fully what was happening and why.

4. Since a primary function of the project was to demonstrate to the public and to those within the criminal justice system that pretrial parole was a device that could serve the public's interest as well as the defendant's, some offenders were excluded at the outset from the experiment. These were homicide, forcible rape, sodomy involving a minor, corrupting the morals of a child, and carnal abuse — crimes that were all thought to be too sensitive and controversial to be associated with a release program; narcotics offenses, because of special medical problems and . . . a greater risk of flight; and assault on a police officer, where intervention by Vera might, it was feared, arouse police hostility.

5. Comprehensive follow-up procedures were devised to be sure that released defendants knew when they were expected in court for further appearances in connection with their trials. These procedures included mailed reminders, telephone calls, visits at home or work, and special notifications in the defendant's language, if he did not speak English.

[The] law students began their interviews in the detention pens in the arraignment court. At first, they were asked to make subjective evaluations of the defendant's eligibility for pretrial parole after they had verified their community ties. It was discovered, however, that pressures were developing that caused some interviewers to withhold recommendations for release in cases where it was probably justified. To relieve the individual of these pressures and of the personal responsibility that, in part, created them, a weighted system of points was developed and the sole determinant as to whether or not a defendant would be recommended for release without bail was his achieving a point score of five or above. This development of a set of objective criteria on which to base release recommendations proved to be an important innovation. . . .

POINT SCORING SYSTEM
MANHATTAN BAIL PROJECT

To be recommended, defendant needs [a] New York area address where he can be reached and [a] total of five points from the following categories —

Prior Record

1   No convictions.

0   One misdemeanor conviction.

-1   Two misdemeanor or one felony conviction.

-2   Three or more misdemeanors or two or more felony convictions.

Family Ties (in New York Area)

3   Lives in established family home AND visits other family members (immediate family only).

2   Lives in established family home (immediate family).

1   Visits others of immediate family.

Employment or School

3   Present job one year or more, steadily.

2   Present job 4 months. . . .

1   Has present job which is still available, or Unemployed 3 months or less and 9 months or more steady prior job, or Unemployment Compensation, or Welfare.

3   Presently in school, attending regularly.

2   Out of school less than 6 months but employed or in training.

1   Out of school 3 months or less, unemployed and not in training.

Residence (in New York Area steadily)

3   One year at present residence.

2   One year at present [and] last prior residence or 6 months at present residence.

1   Six months at present and last prior residence or in New York City 5 years or more.

Discretion

+1   Positive, over 65, attending hospital, appeared on some previous case.

 0   Negative — intoxicated — intention to leave jurisdiction.

Comparing the Experimental and the Control Groups

. . . Vera was especially anxious to compare the experiences of those who had been recommended for release with the experiences of the control group, a statistically identical group for which recommendations had not been made to the judges. It found that 59 percent of its pretrial parole recommendations were followed by the court and that only 16 percent of the control group was released without bail by the judges acting on their own. Judges were clearly basing their actions on the availability of reliable information about the defendants. More significantly, 60 percent of those released pending trial during the first year eventually were acquitted or had their case dismissed, compared with only 23 percent of the control group. And only 16 percent of the released defendants who were convicted were sentenced to prison, where 96 percent of those convicted in the control group received prison sentences. Unquestionably, detention was resulting in a higher rate of convictions and in far more punitive dispositions. At the end of the second year, the control group was dropped. . . .

Modifications in Project Procedures

Further innovations came in the third year of the project. An important one was that the number of offenses that had been excluded for political reasons was sharply reduced to include only homicide and certain narcotics offenses. Also, the indigency requirement was dropped. It was felt that bail costs should not be imposed on a defendant merely because he had funds; the test for those with money, as well as for those without, should be the same: will the accused return to court for trial? . . .

Meanwhile, in 1963, two developments suggested that a large potential existed for applying new concepts of bail reform outside of New York City. One of these was the strong interest expressed by the United States Department of Justice in helping to sponsor a national conference on bail. The other was the speed with which civic leaders in Des Moines, Iowa, learned from the news media of the Vera experiment, decided to investigate the possibility of a bail project in Des Moines, then designed and adopted such a project.

[T]he Bail Reform Act of 1966 [was] signed into law by President Lyndon B. Johnson on June 22, 1966 — the first change in federal bail law since the Judiciary Act of 1789. [The] Act seemed a fitting climax to the effort begun just five years earlier. The Act stipulated that persons should not be detained needlessly in the federal courts to face trial, to testify, or to await an appeal; that release should be granted in non-capital cases where there is reasonable assurance the individual will reappear when required; that the courts should make use of a variety of release options, depending on the circumstances (for example, release in custody of a third party, or with cash deposit, or bail, or with restricted movements); and that information should be developed about the individual on which intelligent selection of alternatives could be based. The Act guaranteed the right to judicial review of release conditions, and also the right to appeal.

[In] the fall of 1964, the New York City Office of Probation took over the administration of the Vera project. . . . During the three years [of the Bail Project] 3,505 defendants had been released on their own recognizance following the recommendations of Vera staff members, out of a total of some 10,000 defendants who had been interviewed. Only 56 of these parolees, or 1.6 percent of the total, willfully failed to appear in court for trial. During the same period, 3 percent of those released on bail failed to appear, or nearly twice as many as had been released without bail. The figures strongly suggested that bail was not as effective a guarantee of court appearance as was release on verified information.

Over the thirty-five months, a little less than half — 48 percent — of those released through the Vera project were acquitted or had their cases dismissed, while the remaining 52 percent were found guilty. Of those found guilty, 70 percent received suspended sentences, 10 percent were given jail terms, and 20 percent were given the alternative of a fine or jail sentence.

During the Vera operation, staff recommendations became increasingly liberal as experience established that more and more persons could be released safely on their assurances that they would return for trial. Also judicial acceptance of the recommendations rose sharply. At the outset, Vera urged release for 28 percent of the defendants interviewed, while two and a half years later the figure was 65 percent. Judges were following Vera's advice 55 percent of the time in 1961, and 70 percent of the time in 1964. . . .

■ ALABAMA RULES OF CRIMINAL PROCEDURE 7.2, 7.3

RULE 7.2

(a) Before conviction. Any defendant charged with an offense bailable as a matter of right may be released pending or during trial on his or her personal recognizance or on an appearance bond unless the court or magistrate determines that such a release will not reasonably assure the defendant's appearance as required, or that the defendant's being at large will pose a real and present danger to others or to the public at large. If such a determination is made, the court may impose the least onerous condition or conditions contained in Rule 7.3

(b) that will reasonably assure the defendant's appearance or that will eliminate or minimize the risk of harm to others or to the public at large. In making such a determination, the court may take into account the following:

(1) The age, background and family ties, relationships and circumstances of the defendant.

(2) The defendant's reputation, character, and health.

(3) The defendant's prior criminal record, including prior releases on recognizance or on secured appearance bonds, and other pending cases.

(4) The identity of responsible members of the community who will vouch for the defendant's reliability.

(5) Violence or lack of violence in the alleged commission of the offense.

(6) The nature of the offense charged, the apparent probability of conviction, and the likely sentence, insofar as these factors are relevant to the risk of nonappearance. . . .

(11) Residence of the defendant, including consideration of real property ownership, and length of residence in his or her place of domicile.

(12) In cases where the defendant is charged with a drug offense, evidence of selling or pusher activity should indicate a substantial increase in the amount of bond.

(13) Consideration of the defendant's employment status and history, the location of defendant's employment, e.g., whether employed in the county where the alleged offense occurred, and the defendant's financial condition. . . .

RULE 7.3

(a) Mandatory conditions. Every order of release under this rule shall contain the conditions that the defendant:

(1) Appear to answer and to submit to the orders and process of the court having jurisdiction of the case;

(2) Refrain from committing any criminal offense;

(3) Not depart from the state without leave of court; and

(4) Promptly notify the court of any change of address.

(b) Additional conditions. An order of release may include any one or more of the following conditions reasonably necessary to secure a defendant's appearance:

(1) Execution of an appearance bond in an amount specified by the court, either with or without requiring that the defendant deposit with the clerk security in an amount as required by the court;

(2) Execution of a secured appearance bond;

(3) Placing the defendant in the custody of a designated person or organization agreeing to supervise the defendant;

(4) Restrictions on the defendant's travel, associations, or place of abode during the period of release;

(5) Return to custody after specified hours; or

(6) Any other conditions which the court deems reasonably necessary.

■ PRETRIAL RELEASE OF FELONY DEFENDANTS, 1992
BRIAN REAVES AND JACOB PEREZ
Bureau of Justice Statistics (November 1994, NCJ 148818)

An estimated 63 percent of the defendants who had State felony charges filed against them in the Nation's 75 most populous counties during May 1992 were released by the court prior to the disposition of their case. . . .

Nonfinancial Release. Among the 63 percent of felony defendants in the 75 largest counties who were released prior to case disposition, about 3 in 5 were released on nonfinancial terms that required no posting of bail. . . . Release on recognizance [ROR], granted to 24 percent of all defendants and to 38 percent of all released defendants, was the most common type of pretrial release. . . . Approximately 13 percent of all pretrial releases in the 75 largest counties (23 percent of nonfinancial releases) were on conditional release. About a fourth of conditional releases included an unsecured bail amount to be forfeited should the defendant fail to appear in court as scheduled. About two-thirds of conditional releases included an agreement by the defendant to maintain regular contact with a pretrial program through telephone calls and/or personal visits. Fifteen percent of conditional releases involved regular drug monitoring or treatment, and 6 percent included a third party custody agreement. . . .

Financial Release. Overall, about 2 in 5 defendants released before case disposition received that release through financial terms involving a surety, full cash, deposit, or property bond. Deposit, full cash, and property bonds are posted directly with the court, while surety bonds involve the services of a bail bond company. [To be released on full cash or property bond, defendants] must post the full bail amount in cash or collateral. . . . The cash or property is forfeited if the defendants do not appear in court as required. Typically, a defendant must provide 10 percent of the full bail amount to be released on deposit or surety bond. Either the defendant (deposit bond) or the bail bond company (surety bond) is liable to the court for the full bail amount if the defendant does not appear in court as required. Release on surety bond, the second most common type of pretrial release for felony defendants, was used in 54 percent of all financial releases and in 21 percent of all pretrial releases. . . .

FACTORS AFFECTING PROBABILITY OF RELEASE

Overall, 37 percent of the felony defendants included in the [sample] were detained until the court disposed of their case, roughly the same percentage as in [earlier] studies for 1988 (34 percent) and 1990 (35 percent). Five out of six detainees from the 1992 study had a bail amount set but did not post the money required to secure release. The remainder, representing 17 percent of detained defendants and 6 percent of all defendants, were ordered held without bail.

While denial of bail provides the court with an absolute assurance that a defendant will not be released prior to case disposition, the [data] also show that when a defendant is required to post bail, the probability of release decreases as bail amounts increase. When bail was set at $20,000 or more, 18 percent of the defendants were eventually released. When the bail amount was between $10,000 and $19,999, 38 percent of the defendants secured release; from $2,500 to $9,999, 52 percent of the defendants; and under $2,500, 66 percent. The effect of bail amount on the likelihood of a defendant's being released varied according to the type of arrest charge. For example, when the bail amount was set at $20,000 or more, drug defendants (29 percent) secured release more often than defendants charged with a public-order offense (18 percent), violent offense (17 percent), or property offense (11 percent). . . .

Seriousness of Offense. The [data] indicate that defendants charged with murder were the least likely of all felony defendants to be released prior to case disposition (24 percent). While about a fourth of murder defendants were released, about half of defendants charged with rape, robbery, or burglary were released, as were about two-thirds of assault, theft, or drug trafficking defendants. Murder defendants had the lowest release rate, mainly because they were the most likely to be denied bail or to have a high bail amount. Forty percent of murder defendants were denied bail, compared to 9 percent or less for other defendant. . . .

Criminal Justice Status. The [data] indicate that a defendant's criminal justice status at the time of arrest is also related to the probability of pretrial release. Among felony defendants without an active criminal justice status at the time of arrest, 72 percent were released before case disposition. In contrast, just 32 percent of defendants on parole and 44 percent of defendants on probation at the time of the current arrest were released. Among defendants who were already on pretrial release for a pending case when arrested, 56 percent were released pending disposition of the current charge. . . .

Court Appearance History. The court is also likely to consider a defendant's court appearance history when setting bail and the terms of release for the current felony charge. . . . Among defendants who made all scheduled court appearances related to prior arrests, 57 percent were released prior to disposition of the current case. The probability of release was somewhat lower for defendants who had failed to appear in court previously (51 percent). . . .

Prior Conviction Record. Defendants with more than one prior conviction or with a felony conviction record were less likely than other defendants to await disposition of their case outside jail. Just under half were released prior to case disposition. About 3 in 5 defendants with a single prior conviction or only misdemeanor convictions were able to obtain release, while 4 in 5 defendants with no prior convictions were released. About 10 percent of defendants who had a prior felony conviction were denied bail, compared to 3 percent of other defendants.

TIME FROM ARREST TO PRETRIAL RELEASE

Fifty-two percent of all pretrial releases occurred either on the day of arrest or on the following day, [77 percent occurred within 1 week,] and 91 percent occurred within 1 month of arrest. The time from arrest to release varied by factors that included the type of release conditions imposed, the bail amount set (if any), and the type of arrest charge. . . .

MISCONDUCT BY DEFENDANTS PLACED ON PRETRIAL RELEASE

Failure to Appear in Court. A primary goal of any pretrial release decision by the court is to ensure the defendant's appearance in court as scheduled. Among those felony defendants who were released prior to case disposition, 3 out of 4 made all scheduled court appearances. A bench warrant was issued for the arrest of the remaining 25 percent because they had missed one or more court dates. Two-thirds of these defendants had been returned to the court by the end of the 1-year study period [some of them voluntarily], while a third of them, 8 percent of all released defendants, remained fugitives. . . .

Rearrest for a New Offense. In addition to considering the likelihood that a released defendant may not return for scheduled court appearances, courts in most States also assess the risk of crimes being committed by a defendant who is not held in jail. Rearrest data collected during the 1-year study indicated that 14 percent of released defendants were rearrested for an offense allegedly committed while on pretrial release. . . . Released defendants with 10 or more prior convictions had a rearrest rate of 38 percent, 4 times that of defendants who had no prior convictions (9 percent). . . . For rearrested defendants, the median time from pretrial release to the alleged commission of a new offense was 48 days. . . .

Notes

1. Statutory fruits of 1960s bail reform: majority view. The thrust of efforts to change the bail system in the 1950s and 1960s was to increase the use of nonfinancial techniques such as release on recognizance (ROR) and to standardize the criteria used for release decisions as a way of preventing the wealth of defendants from dominating the release decision. See Daniel Freed & Patricia Wald, Bail in the United States (1964). The efforts bore fruit in the 1966 Federal Bail Reform Act, 18 U.S.C. §3146(b). Unlike the federal statute at work until that time, which gave essentially no guidance to the judge on release and bail decisions, the 1966 statute required courts to consider standard criteria in reaching their decisions. The statutory factors included "(1) the nature of the offense charged; (2) the weight of the evidence against the accused; (3) the accused's family ties; (4) employment; (5) financial resources; (6) character; (7) mental health; (8) the length of residence in the community; (9) a record of convictions; and (10) a record of failure to appear at court appearances or of flight to avoid prosecution." The ABA Standards on Criminal Justice, Pretrial Release (1968), also embodied many of the aspirations of critics of the money bail system. Both the 1966 Bail Reform Act and the ABA standards influenced state legislatures to revise their criteria for making release decisions, and most states have a similar (though not identical) list of factors. See, e.g., Cal. Penal Code §1275. Around 10 jurisdictions have statutes without lists of factors and leave the determination to the discretion of the judge or magistrate. See, e.g., Mass. Gen. L. ch. 276, §57. A similar number of states include only a very short list of factors. See, e.g., Fla. Stat. §903.03. State rules based on the ABA standards or the 1966 federal statute explicitly make ROR the presumptive outcome for defendants.

This era of federal and state legislation, together with changes in local practices, resulted in higher numbers of defendants being released before trial or guilty plea. While it was common earlier in the century for a state to release fewer than one-third of all defendants, it is now more common to release close to two-thirds of defendants. In large urban areas in 2002, 62 percent of felony defendants were released before disposition of their cases. Just under half of all released defendants faced no financial conditions such as bail. See Bureau of Justice Statistics, Felony Defendants in Large Urban Counties, 2002, at 16-22

(2006, NCJ 210818). Would this change in practice have occurred without changes in the federal and state statutes?

2. *Rates of failure to appear.* Of course, some of the defendants released before trial or the entry of a guilty plea fail to appear at their later court proceedings. How many? Statistics compiled every two years between 1990 and 2002 in large urban jurisdictions show consistent results: between 22 and 24 percent of the felony defendants who were released before case disposition failed to appear. Bureau of Justice Statistics, Felony Defendants in Large Urban Counties, 2002, at iii (2006, NCJ 210818); John Clark & D. Alan Henry, The Pretrial Release Decision, 81 Judicature 76, 77 (Sept.-Oct. 1997) (FTA rate of 25 percent, based on 1992 nationwide data). These statistics, however, include "technical defaults" where defendants miss the initial court date but come voluntarily at a later time for rescheduled hearings or trials. See Wayne Thomas, Bail Reform in America (1976). The FTA rate typically improves when a jurisdiction establishes a system of notification and supervision of those who are released before trial. Who should notify the defendant of the upcoming proceeding, and what form should the notice take?

3. *Bond dealers and bounty hunters.* In jurisdictions requiring payment of the full amount of money bail prior to release, many defendants rely on the services of bail bond dealers. Indeed, surety bonds remain the most common form of financial release. The bond dealer makes the required payment to the court in the form of a bond obligating the dealer to pay the amount of the bail if the defendant does not appear for court proceedings. The dealer charges the defendant a nonrefundable fee, often around 10 percent of the total bond amount, although it varies with the dealer's assessment of the risk that a particular defendant will flee. See State v. Leis, 835 N.E.2d 5 (Ohio 2005) (state constitution requires availability of bond rather than "cash bail" requiring defendant to deposit entire bail amount in cash).

About half of the states grant express authority to the dealer and their agents — often called "bounty hunters" — to arrest a defendant who tries to flee. See Ala. Code §15-13-117. Nineteenth-century authority confirms the substantial powers of bond dealers and bounty hunters, which in some respects exceeds that of government agents trying to recapture a fugitive. Reese v. United States, 76 U.S. 13 (1869); Taylor v. Taintor, 83 U.S. 366 (1872). This authority creates a potential for rough practices — and for adventures that have occasionally become the subject of front-page stories and the plot lines for movies, classic and otherwise.

4. *Abolition of surety bonds.* Critics of the surety bond system argue that it fosters violence and leaves defendants with no financial incentive to appear in court after their release. Jurisdictions have taken a number of steps to reduce the importance of bond dealers. A handful of states have directly outlawed the offering of surety bonds. Stephens v. Bonding Association of Kentucky, 538 S.W.2d 580 (Ky. 1976); Wis. Stat. §969.12. Around 20 states have made the surety bond less attractive to defendants by using "deposit" bonds, allowing defendants themselves to deposit a portion of their bail — usually 10 percent — comparable to the rates charged by sureties. See, e.g., Cal. Penal Code §1295; Ohio R. Crim. P. 46; Or. Rev. Stat. §135.265. Because the cash deposit to the state is refundable and the fee to the bond dealer is not, defendants have little reason to call on the dealer. The state can also profit from the use of cash bail because courts often do not collect bonds from sureties when the defendant fails to appear. Given all these advantages of cash bail, why does the surety bond system remain the most

common form of financial release? See also Commonwealth v. Ray, 755 N.E.2d 1259 (Mass. 2001) (under bail statute, judge may properly set alternative bails for pretrial release: surety company bond, or ten percent of that amount in cash, equivalent to maximum nonrefundable premium required to purchase surety bond).

Consider this alternative to bond dealers. Jails can now install an interactive kiosk allowing detainees to use a credit card to make bail. For relatively minor crimes with bails under $5,000, the necessary amount falls with the limit that many people carry on their credit cards. If the defendants do appear for their hearings, the county refunds the bail amount to the defendant's credit card account; the fees for the transaction are far lower than the 10 percent typically charged by bond dealers.

5. *Nonfinancial release conditions.* A defendant's pretrial release might be conditioned not on payment of bail but on performance of certain nonfinancial conditions. The most common nonfinancial release condition is a requirement that the defendant maintain regular contact with a pretrial program. It is also common for the judge to insist that the defendant avoid any contact with the victim of the alleged crime. An increasingly common condition of release is regular drug monitoring or treatment. See Kan. Stat. §22-2802 (drug testing limited to those charged with felonies); La. Code Crim. Proc. art. 336. Testing positive for some drugs (particularly cocaine) is a predictor, according to some studies, of a higher rate of nonappearance and arrests for crimes committed after release. Peggy Tobolowsky & James Quinn, Drug-Related Behavior as a Predictor of Defendant Pretrial Misconduct, 25 Tex. Tech L. Rev. 1019 (1994). If positive drug tests are not predictive of a failure to appear, should the tests still be administered? What is the rationale for requiring drug treatment? Another increasingly common nonfinancial condition of release is the use of electronic monitoring. An electronic device attached to the defendant's person (often a wrist or an ankle bracelet) allows the government to monitor his proximity to home or to some other location. Should electronic monitoring be used primarily for those who receive ROR or for those who would otherwise remain in jail?

6. *Racial and gender bias in release and bail decisions.* Evidence periodically surfaces to suggest that black and Hispanic defendants receive less favorable bail and release decisions than white defendants. One study of bail practices in Connecticut by Professors Ian Ayres and Joel Waldfogel revealed that bond dealers charged lower bond rates to black and Hispanic defendants than to white defendants, suggesting that judges set the bail amounts for black and Hispanic defendants higher than the real risk of flight. The "competitive market" — in the form of the bond dealers — thus was able to discount the rate for minority defendants and still make a profit. Ian Ayres, Pervasive Prejudice? Unconventional Evidence of Race and Gender Discrimination (2001). Studies have also consistently indicated that female defendants are more likely than male defendants to obtain pretrial release and to receive nonfinancial conditions of release. Why might a judge make more "lenient" release decisions for female defendants? See Ellen Steury and Nancy Frank, Gender Bias and Pretrial Release: More Pieces of the Puzzle, 18 J. Crim. Justice 417 (1990) (finding most of differential treatment for women explained by seriousness of offense and prior record).

7. *Effects of pretrial release on acquittal rates.* Bail researchers have long believed that a defendant's odds of acquittal at trial go down if the defendant fails to obtain

pretrial release. They reason that a defendant who remains in jail is less able to locate witnesses and otherwise prepare a defense. Caleb Foote's study of bail practices in Philadelphia in the 1950s observed that 67 percent of the defendants charged with violent crimes were acquitted if they were released before trial, while only 25 percent of jailed defendants were acquitted. Foote, Compelling Appearance in Court: Administration of Bail in Philadelphia, 102 U. Pa. L. Rev. 1031 (1954). A number of later studies found a causal relationship (and not just a statistical association) between pretrial release and acquittal rates. However, the trend (not uniform) among more recent studies is to conclude that pretrial release is correlated with — but does not necessarily cause — high acquittal rates. For instance, the seriousness of a charge is a factor both in making release less likely and in making conviction more likely because (among other reasons) prosecution witnesses are more likely to show up. See Gerald Wheeler & Carol Wheeler, Bail Reform in the 1980s: A Response to the Critics, 18 Crim. L. Bull. 228 (1982).

8. *Effects of pretrial release on sentences.* There is stronger evidence of a causal linkage between the pretrial release decision and the choice of punishment after a conviction. The best evidence indicates that defendants not released before their conviction are more likely to receive prison sentences than those who are released. For instance, one analysis of the New York City data produced in the Vera Institute study found that 64 percent of persons detained received prison sentences, compared to only 17 percent of those released before disposition of the charges. See Anne Rankin, The Effect of Pretrial Detention, 39 N.Y.U. L. Rev. 641 (1964). See also Stevens Clark, Jean Freeman & Gary Koch, Bail Risk: A Multivariate Analysis, 5 J. Legal Stud. 341 (1976) (study of Charlotte, North Carolina).

9. *Length of time before release.* Almost half of all defendants released are able to leave the jail within one day. Seventy-three percent of defendants who are released leave custody within one week; 90 percent leave within one month. Bureau of Justice Statistics, Felony Defendants in Large Urban Counties, 2002, at 19 (2006, NCJ 210818). What is likely to change between Day 2 and Day 31 of confinement that convinces so many judges to release more defendants?

2. Who Sets Bail?

We have seen examples of jurisdictions willing to reduce traditional bail amounts or to set nonfinancial conditions of release, and we have considered the multiple criteria that determine which conditions will be imposed. Which institution or decisionmaker is best positioned to choose among the expanded options for release in an individual case? To what degree should bail and release decisions be structured?

The earliest available point of release, "station-house bail," often occurs when officers use a "bail schedule," a listing of the presumptive amount of bail to require from various types of offenders. Most often, the presumptive bail is linked to the criminal charge a defendant is facing. For example, a recent Los Angeles County bail schedule made $60,000 the presumptive bail amount for voluntary manslaughter; for kidnapping for ransom, $500,000; and for bookmaking, $2,500. Along with the list of factors and rules reprinted above, Alabama provides a recommended set of bail ranges "as a general guide . . . in setting bail" and states that "courts should exercise discretion in setting bail above or below the scheduled amounts." Ala. R. Crim. P. 7.2. The recommended ranges in Alabama are as follows:

FELONIES

Capital felony	$10,000 to No Bail Allowed,
Murder	$5,000 to $50,000,
Class A felony	$3,000 to $30,000,
Class B felony	$2,000 to $20,000,
Class C felony	$1,000 to $10,000,
Drug trafficking	$3,000 to $1,000,000,

MISDEMEANORS (NOT INCLUDED ELSEWHERE IN THE SCHEDULE)

Class A misdemeanor	$300 to $3,000,
Class B misdemeanor	$100 to $1,000,
Class C misdemeanor	$50 to $500,
Violation	$50 to $500,

MUNICIPAL ORDINANCE VIOLATIONS

$100 to $1,000,

TRAFFIC-RELATED OFFENSES

DUI	$300 to $5,000,
Reckless driving	$100 to $300,
Speeding	$50 to $100,
Other traffic violations	$50 to $100,

The following case considers a trial court's efforts to reform bail practices by eliminating access to administrative bail for domestic violence offenders.

■ DONALD WESTERMAN v. CHRISTINE CARY
885 P.2d 827 (Wash. 1994)

MADSEN, J.

This case revolves around the Spokane County District Court's issuance of a general order providing that domestic violence offenders be detained in custody pending their first appearance in court. Under the previous bail schedule provision, such offenders would be eligible for release on bail preset by the court. . . .

On October 14, 1992, Spokane County's then-presiding District Court Judge, Christine Cary, issued a general order entitled "Domestic Violence Offense — Mandatory Court Appearance — No Bail." The Order provides: "Any person arrested for a crime classified under Section 10.99 of the Revised Code of Washington as Domestic Violence shall be held in jail without bail pending their first appearance. [This order] shall apply to all offenses listed under Section 10.99 . . . irrespective of their classification as a Felony, Gross Misdemeanor, or Misdemeanor." By requiring that bail be set at the first appearance, the District Court sought to amend the County's bail schedule and pretrial release procedures to conform with the Washington State Supreme Court's amendment of CrRLJ 3.2.* Under the previous procedure, jail personnel were allowed to determine bail according to a preset bail schedule and grant release prior to an individualized judicial determination or a preliminary court appearance. The District Court issued the Order as the first of a number of changes intended to bring the court's procedures into conformance with CrRLJ 3.2. The Order does not specify the length of detention; however, CrRLJ 3.2.1(d)(1) requires that an accused "detained in jail must be brought before a court of limited jurisdiction as soon as practicable after the detention is commenced, but in any event before the close of business on the next court day." An on-call judge was available under the Order to set bail prior to the preliminary appearance in appropriate cases.

On October 15, 1992, Prosecutor Brockett advised Sheriff Larry Erickson to disregard the Order because he believed it would violate arrestees' constitutional right to bail and would expose the County to liability. . . . The District Court then asked Prosecutor Brockett for a brief outlining his concerns with the legality of the Order. Brockett refused, suggesting instead that the District Court write a brief justifying its position to him. [T]he Spokane County public defender's office [supported by *amicus curiae*, the Washington Defender Association (WDA),] filed an emergency application for writ of review and for immediate stay of the Order in superior court. The public defender's office argued that the Order was unconstitutional and was not adopted in accordance with procedures required by the court's own local rules. *[A]micus curiae*, the Young Women's Christian Association (YWCA), filed a memorandum of authorities in support of the Order. [During the litigation], the new District Court Presiding Judge, Salvatore Cozza, issued General Bail Order [02-93] containing a new bail schedule . . . providing that misdemeanor domestic violence and harassment probable cause arrestees are to be held in jail pending their first court appearance absent a contrary judicial order. [The trial court ruled that the bail order was constitutional.]

Unlike the federal constitution, Washington's constitution has a specific provision creating a right to bail. Article 1, section 20 of the Washington Constitution provides that "all persons charged with crime shall be bailable by sufficient sureties, except for capital offenses when the proof is evident, or the presumption great." The issue presented in this case is the point at which the right to bail attaches. *Westerman* contends that the right attaches immediately following arrest. WDA argues that the right attaches within a reasonable time following the incidents of arrest. The District Court and the YWCA argue that the right does not attach until a judicial determination can be made. . . . *Westerman* argues that the "charged" language is determinative. While the provision uses the language "charged with crime," we find that this language was not intended to trigger the point at which the right attaches. Rather, the phrase "charged with crime" only modifies the word

---

*The current version of Rule 3.2(a) of the Criminal Rules for Courts of Limited Jurisdiction (CrRLJ) provides: "A court of limited jurisdiction may adopt a bail schedule for persons who have been arrested on probable cause but have not yet made a preliminary appearance before a judicial officer. With the exception of [certain traffic offenses], the adoption of such a schedule or whether to adopt a schedule, is in the discretion of each court of limited jurisdiction. . . ." — Eds.

"persons." This is evidenced by the fact that the drafters changed the language of the proposed section 20 which previously had said "all prisoners" to the current language of "all persons charged with crime." The reason for the substituted language was not articulated; however, it is significant that one was merely substituted for the other. Because the phrase "charged with crime" modifies "persons," we conclude that the framers [in 1889] chose this language to describe the status of persons entitled to bail rather than the time of entitlement. Furthermore, the time of charging makes little practical sense as the triggering point for the right given the context in which the question of bail arises. When an arrest is made pursuant to a warrant, charges will have been filed and the judge issuing the warrant will determine probable cause and set bail. However, when an arrest is made without a warrant, charges may or may not be filed prior to a preliminary court appearance which must be held by the next judicial day, or in any event, within 48 hours. CrRLJ 3.2.1; see also County of Riverside v. McLaughlin, 500 U.S. 44 (1991). Charges may not be filed for up to 72 hours (not including Saturdays, Sundays, or holidays) after the arrest. CrRLJ 3.2.1(f); CrR 3.2B(c). This may be hours after the accused's preliminary appearance where bail or release could have been determined.

While we reject the time of charging as the triggering point, the language of the provision alone provides no clear answer. We must then look to the context in which the provision arose to determine the drafters' intent. . . . At the time the constitution was adopted, the Code of 1881 provided that bail could be granted only by judges and the amount set on a case-by-case basis. Section 778 of the Code of 1881 is similar to the adopted version of Const. art. 1, §20 and reads:

> Every person charged with an offense except that of murder in the first degree, where the proof is evident or the presumption great, may be bailed by sufficient sureties . . . : Provided, That all persons accused of crime in any court of this Territory, whether by indictment or otherwise, shall be admitted to bail *by the court*, where the same is pending, . . . and the bail bond in such cases shall be reasonable and at the sound discretion of the court.

(Italics ours). . . . Today, bail and release remain judicial functions. Bail schedules have been recently developed by many counties to allow earlier release. However, these bail schedules are developed and maintained by each county's judiciary. In short, the fixing of bail and the release from custody traditionally has been, and we think is, a function of the judicial branch of government, unless otherwise directed and mandated by unequivocal constitutional provisions to the contrary.

This court has encouraged the giving of bail in proper instances because the State is relieved of the burden of keeping the accused and the innocent are set free. However, we have never mandated bail schedules; this is a choice best left to the counties. Moreover, we have established detailed procedures which require judicial determinations of bail or release to be made no later than the preliminary appearance stage. Even where bail or release has been actuated under a bail schedule, our rules provide that the individual case must be reviewed by a judge at this initial appearance. See CrR 3.2; CrRLJ 3.2. The primary purposes of the preliminary appearance are a judicial determination of probable cause and judicial review of the conditions of release. The preliminary appearance must be held "as soon as practicable after the detention is commenced, . . . but in any event before the close of business on the next judicial day." CrR 3.2B; CrRLJ 3.2.1. When combining a probable cause determination, this must be accomplished within 48 hours. County of Riverside v. McLaughlin, 500 U.S. 44 (1991).

Considering the history and case law regarding bail, as well as relevant court rules, we find that detention without bail pending a speedy judicial determination does not violate Const. art. 1, §20. Under the current system where bail must be determined at the preliminary appearance, the right is sufficiently protected. We decline to extend the right to bail beyond what it has traditionally been: the right to a judicial determination of reasonable bail or release. We conclude, however, that such a determination must be made as soon as possible, no later than the probable cause determination, and, as with probable cause, may be determined by a judge prior to the preliminary hearing. Our decision today is not intended to foreclose the use of bail schedules, but rather to leave the choice to counties, balancing the flexibility that the county courts need with the interests of those detained.

Our result is further supported by the results of other states who have upheld similar . . . provisions against challenge. [The court cited decisions from Rhode Island, California, Oklahoma, and Alaska]. We thus find the Order constitutional under Const. art. 1, §20 to the extent it conforms with this opinion. . . .

Westerman argues that the Order violates state and federal substantive due process. [An] individual's liberty interest is important and fundamental. A government action affecting this fundamental right is constitutional only if it furthers compelling state interests and is narrowly drawn to serve those interests.

The government has compelling interests in preventing crime and ensuring that those accused of crimes are available for trial and to serve their sentences if convicted. The Fourth Amendment permits limited restraint on the liberty of an arrestee. It is well recognized that a police officer may detain an individual without a warrant if the officer has probable cause to believe that the arrestee committed an offense. Gerstein v. Pugh, 420 U.S. 103 (1975). To justify further pretrial detention, a fair and reliable determination of probable cause must be made by a judicial officer promptly following the arrest. The Supreme Court later elaborated on *Gerstein* by requiring that the determination of probable cause must be made within 48 hours and cannot be delayed unreasonably. County of Riverside v. McLaughlin, 500 U.S. 44 (1991). [R]estrictions on liberty that comply with the Fourth Amendment and which do not constitute impermissible punishment do not violate substantive due process.

Given the limited nature of the detention and the legitimate reasons behind the Order, we do not find that the Order violates substantive due process. Under our ruling today, the Order imposes no more significant restraint on liberty than that allowed by the Fourth Amendment under *Gerstein* and *County of Riverside* because the probable cause and release hearing must be held within 48 hours of detention. After the preliminary appearance, release must be given to those arrestees. Furthermore, the District Court did not promulgate the Order for the purposes of punishing domestic violence arrestees. The District Court only sought to insure individualized judicial determinations of bail and conditions of release in domestic violence cases. . . .

Notes

1. Rules and discretion in bail: majority view. Most systems leave substantial discretion in the hands of judges in setting bail amounts. Many jurisdictions rely on bail schedules set at local levels, such as the Spokane bail schedule proposed in *Westerman* under general state rulemaking authority. See, e.g., Mont. Code §46-9-302 ("A judge may establish and post a schedule of bail for offenses over which the judge has original jurisdiction"). Tennessee allows magistrates substantial discretion but imposes statewide caps on bail amounts based on the nature of the offense. See Tenn. Code §40-11-105. A few states such as Alabama (printed above), Kentucky, and Utah have more specific statewide bail schedules.

The *Westerman* decision is not alone in revealing clashes between different actors over proper bail policies for domestic assault arrests. In Pelekai v. White, 861 P.2d 1205 (Haw. 1993), the senior judge of the Honolulu Family Court issued an order raising bail in domestic assault cases from the prior police department practice of $50 to between $500 and $900 depending on the prior record and threat posed by the accused. The Hawaii Supreme Court struck down the guidelines, holding that they eliminated the discretionary power given to judges or to the police department by Haw. Rev. Stat. §804-9, which provided that the "amount of bail rests in the discretion of the justice or judge or the officers [setting bail]; but should be so determined as not to suffer the wealthy to escape by the payment of a pecuniary penalty, nor to render the privilege useless to the poor." Nor is domestic assault the only crime for which judges have tried to alter bail practices. See City of Fargo v. Stutlien, 505 N.W.2d 738 (N.D. 1993) (rejecting district court rule providing minimum 12-hour detention for DUI arrestees who refuse blood-alcohol test). Bail decisions have become both more and less regulated with the use of bail schedules, and with the addition, often by statute, of new types of pretrial release terms such as lower bail amounts paid by the defendant directly to the court, supervised release, and electronic monitoring. Are specific bail guidelines useful? Who should develop guidelines?

2. Appellate court controls on bail. There are constitutional limits on the amount of bail a trial court can set. According to Stack v. Boyle, 342 U.S. 1 (1951), the "excessive bail" clause of the Eighth Amendment prevents a trial court from setting bail "higher than an amount reasonably calculated to fulfill the purpose" of ensuring the accused's presence at trial. A slight majority of states have an even stronger constitutional provision guaranteeing a right to bail. Do these constitutional provisions suggest that the appellate courts are the institution with the ultimate authority in setting bail? Should appellate courts actively review bail determinations? What impact would bail guidelines have on appellate review of individual cases?

3. Bail, race, and wealth. Would evidence of discriminatory bail practices support use of bail schedules? Recall that the 1994 study by Professors Ayres and Waldfogel offered evidence of such discrimination. Would factors in bail schedules need to be tested to make sure they did not incorporate a racial bias? If wealth is a significant predictor of likelihood of appearance, then which principle should govern: using accurate appearance rules or avoiding wealth-based discrimination?

4. Consultation with victims. All 50 states have passed statutes offering protections to victims during the criminal justice process, and about 30 have given some of these protections constitutional status. These provisions all require authorities to provide information to victims, such as explaining the possibility of pretrial release, notifying victims after a suspect is arrested, and notifying victims about the time and place of release hearings. See, e.g., Cal. Penal Code §4024.4 (granting power to local governments to contract for victim notification). About half of the states require that victims be notified of a suspect's release, and the terms of release, including the amount of any bail, though many states require the victim to make a written request for such information. See, e.g., Iowa Code §910A.6. Some states limit notice provisions to victims of specified crimes such as stalking, sex offenses, or domestic assault. See, e.g., Ga. Code §16-5-93 (stalking); Ky. Rev. Stat. §431.064 (assault, sexual offenses, and violations of protective orders). A few "victims' rights" provisions indicate that the judge should consider the concerns of the victim of the alleged crime when determining the conditions to place upon the defendant during pretrial release. Tenn. Code Ann. §40-11-150 (domestic assault); Texas Code Crim. Proc. art. 56.02 ("A victim, guardian of a victim, or close relative of a deceased victim is entitled to the following rights within the criminal justice system: . . . (2) the right to have the magistrate take the safety of the victim or his family into consideration as an element in fixing the amount of bail for the accused"). A few states allow the victim to have some input prior to the bail decision. See, e.g., Mo. Const. art. I, §32 (crime victims have the right "to be informed of and heard at . . . bail hearings, . . . unless in the determination of the court the interests of justice require otherwise"); Fla. Const. art. I, §16(b) (crime victims have "the right to be informed, to be present, and to be heard when relevant, at all crucial stages of criminal proceedings, to the extent that these rights do not interfere with the constitutional rights of the accused"). Are such provisions likely to change the release decisions that judges make? Are they consistent with the practice of station-house bail?

The implementation and effects of these laws have been uneven. According to a 1995 survey, over 60 percent of crime victims living in states with "strong" legal protections for victims were notified about the dates for bond hearings for the defendants, while about 40 percent of crime victims living in states with weaker legal provisions received this information. About 40 percent of victims in the strong states made a recommendation to the court at the bond hearing; about 25 percent in the weak states did. See Dean Kilpatrick et al., The Rights of Crime Victims — Does Legal Protection Make a Difference? (Research in Brief) (Dec. 1998, NCJ 173839).

5. Prosecutors and bail. Statutes and rules tell judges what they should consider in their bail and pretrial release decisions. What factors actually influence judges the most? Judges are less likely to release a defendant already on parole or probation at the time of the current charges; the same is true for defendants with prior arrests or convictions, and those currently charged with violent offenses. In particular, less than ten percent of murder defendants are released before trial. Bureau of Justice Statistics, Felony Defendants in Large Urban Counties, 2002, at 16-17 (2006, NCJ 210818).

Some observers of bail practices contend that the recommendation of the prosecutor is the single most influential variable as judges make bail and release decisions. A classic study of San Diego judges reached this conclusion. When researchers presented the judges with several hypothetical case files and asked them to set bail, the local ties of the defendant was the most important variable. However, when observers watched judges decide actual cases, the recommendation of the prosecutor became the most important variable in setting bail amounts — more important than severity of the crime, prior record, defense attorney recommendation, or local ties. The prosecutors, for their part, were most heavily influenced by the severity of the crime and (to a lesser extent) the defendant's local ties. See Ebbe Ebbeson and Vladimir Konecni, Decision Making and Information Integration in the Courts: The Setting of Bail, 32 J. Personality & Soc. Psychol. 805 (1975). Why did the researchers observe judges in the courtroom in addition to asking them about simulated case files?

B. PRETRIAL DETENTION

Until the 1980s, a substantial majority of state constitutions guaranteed a right to bail except in capital cases. Earlier in our history, the capital case exception applied to a large number of defendants because a wide range of crimes (from murder to burglary) were punishable by death. Once capital punishment became available only for a subset of murders, however, the state constitutional right to bail extended to a much larger group — indeed, to most criminal defendants.

These constitutional provisions never meant that all defendants were released before trial. A judge could, consistent with these constitutional provisions, deny bail altogether or set bail in prohibitively high amounts when necessary to ensure a defendant's appearance at trial or to prevent the defendant from threatening witnesses or otherwise undermining the integrity of the judicial process. These hard-to-identify practices blunted the practical impact of the constitutional provisions and statutes declaring in broad terms the "right to bail."

However, the success of the bail reform movement of the 1960s and 1970s in decreasing the use of money bail and increasing the number of defendants released before trial gave new visibility and urgency to an old question: What are the purposes of pretrial release and detention? Should systems refuse to release a defendant before trial only when necessary to preserve the integrity of the judicial process? Or could a judge deny bail altogether if necessary to serve different purposes, such as protecting the public from further wrongdoing by the defendant before trial?

In 1970, only four years after the 1966 Bail Reform Act, Congress passed a controversial pretrial detention law for the District of Columbia that allowed detention on the basis of the threat of additional criminal acts by the defendant before trial. In 1984 Congress declared, in a new Bail Reform Act, that prevention of future wrongdoing was indeed a proper basis for detaining a defendant in custody before trial. That declaration gave momentum to a movement that has now become the law in over half the states.

■ U.S. CONSTITUTION AMENDMENT VIII

Excessive bail shall not be required, nor excessive fines imposed, nor cruel and unusual punishments inflicted.

■ TENNESSEE CONSTITUTION ART. I, §§15, 16

15. That all prisoners shall be bailable by sufficient sureties, unless for capital offences, when the proof is evident or the presumption great. And the privilege of the writ of habeas corpus shall not be suspended, unless when in case of rebellion or invasion, the General Assembly shall declare the public safety requires it.

16. That excessive bail shall not be required, nor excessive fines imposed, nor cruel and unusual punishments inflicted.

■ 18 U.S.C. §3142(e), (f)

(e) If, after a hearing pursuant to the provisions of subsection (f) of this section, the judicial officer finds that no condition or combination of conditions will reasonably assure the appearance of the person as required and the safety of any other person and the community, such judicial officer shall order the detention of the person before trial. In a case described in subsection (f)(1) of this section, a rebuttable presumption arises that no condition or combination of conditions will reasonably assure the safety of any other person and the community if such judicial officer finds that—

(1) the person has been convicted of a Federal offense that is described in subsection (f)(1) of this section, or [a similar] State or local offense . . . ;

(2) the offense described in paragraph (1) of this subsection was committed while the person was on release pending trial for a Federal, State, or local offense; and

(3) a period of not more than five years has elapsed since the date of conviction, or the release of the person from imprisonment, for the offense described in paragraph (1) of this subsection, whichever is later.

Subject to rebuttal by the person, it shall be presumed that no condition or combination of conditions will reasonably assure the appearance of the person as required and the safety of the community if the judicial officer finds that there is probable cause to believe that the person committed an offense for which a maximum term of imprisonment of ten years or more is prescribed in the [federal laws proscribing drug trafficking, crimes of violence, and certain crimes with victims less than 18 years old].

(f) The judicial officer shall hold a hearing to determine whether any condition or combination of conditions . . . will reasonably assure the appearance of such person as required and the safety of any other person and the community—

(1) upon motion of the attorney for the Government, in a case that involves — (A) a crime of violence [or an offense involving specified forms of terrorism, for which a maximum term of imprisonment of 10 years or more is prescribed]; (B) an offense for which the maximum sentence is life imprisonment or death; (C) an offense for which a maximum term of imprisonment of ten years or more is prescribed in the [federal drug trafficking laws]; (D) any felony if such person has been convicted of two or more offenses described in subparagraphs (A) through (C) of this paragraph, or two or more [similar] State or local offenses . . . , or a combination of such offenses; or (E) any felony that is not otherwise a crime of violence that involves a minor victim or that involves the possession or use of a firearm or destructive device . . . or any other dangerous weapon, or involves a failure to register [as a sex offender]; or

(2) Upon motion of the attorney for the Government or upon the judicial officer's own motion, in a case that involves — (A) a serious risk that the person will flee; or (B) a serious risk that the person will obstruct or attempt to obstruct justice, or threaten, injure, or intimidate, or attempt to threaten, injure, or intimidate, a prospective witness or juror. . . .

The facts the judicial officer uses to support a finding pu
(e) that no condition or combination of conditions will reason
of any other person and the community shall be supported by
evidence. . . .

■ UNITED STATES v. ANTHONY SALERNO
481 U.S. 739 (1987)

REHNQUIST, C.J.

The Bail Reform Act of 1984 allows a federal court to detain an arrestee pending trial if the Government demonstrates by clear and convincing evidence after an adversary hearing that no release conditions "will reasonably assure . . . the safety of any other person and the community." . . . We hold that, as against the facial attack mounted by these respondents, the Act fully comports with constitutional requirements. . . .

Responding to "the alarming problem of crimes committed by persons on release," S. Rep. No. 98-225, p.3 (1983), Congress formulated the Bail Reform Act of 1984, 18 U.S.C. §3141 et seq., as the solution to a bail crisis in the federal courts. The Act represents the National Legislature's considered response to numerous perceived deficiencies in the federal bail process. By providing for sweeping changes in both the way federal courts consider bail applications and the circumstances under which bail is granted, Congress hoped to give the courts adequate authority to make release decisions that give appropriate recognition to the danger a person may pose to others if released.

To this end, §3141(a) of the Act requires a judicial officer to determine whether an arrestee shall be detained. Section 3142(e) provides that "if, after a hearing pursuant to the provisions of subsection (f), the judicial officer finds that no condition or combination of conditions will reasonably assure the appearance of the person as required and the safety of any other person and the community, he shall order the detention of the person prior to trial." . . . If the judicial officer finds that no conditions of pretrial release can reasonably assure the safety of other persons and the community, he must state his findings of fact in writing, §3142(i), and support his conclusion with "clear and convincing evidence," §3142(f).

The judicial officer is not given unbridled discretion in making the detention determination. Congress has specified the considerations relevant to that decision. These factors include the nature and seriousness of the charges, the substantiality of the Government's evidence against the arrestee, the arrestee's background and characteristics, and the nature and seriousness of the danger posed by the suspect's release. §3142(g). Should a judicial officer order detention, the detainee is entitled to expedited appellate review of the detention order. §§3145(b), (c).

Respondents Anthony Salerno and Vincent Cafaro were arrested on March 21, 1986, after being charged in a 29-count indictment alleging various Racketeer Influenced and Corrupt Organizations Act (RICO) violations, mail and wire fraud offenses, extortion, and various criminal gambling violations. The RICO counts alleged 35 acts of racketeering activity, including fraud, extortion, gambling, and conspiracy to commit murder. At respondents' arraignment, the Government moved to have Salerno and Cafaro detained pursuant to §3142(e), on the ground no condition of release would assure the safety of the community or any person. The District Court held a hearing at which the Government made a detailed proffer of evidence. The Government's case showed that Salerno was the "boss" of the Genovese crime family of La Cosa Nostra and that Cafaro was a "captain" in the Genovese family. According to the Government's proffer, based in large part on conversations intercepted by a court-ordered wiretap, the two respondents had participated in wide-ranging conspiracies to aid their illegitimate enterprises through violent means. The Government also offered the testimony of two of its trial witnesses, who would assert that Salerno personally participated in two murder conspiracies. Salerno opposed the motion for detention, challenging the credibility of the Government's witnesses. He offered the testimony of several character witnesses as well as a letter from his doctor stating that he was suffering from a serious medical condition. Cafaro presented no evidence at the hearing, but instead characterized the wiretap conversations as merely "tough talk."

The District Court granted the Government's detention motion, concluding that the Government had established by clear and convincing evidence that no condition or combination of conditions of release would ensure the safety of the community or any person. . . . Respondents appealed, contending that to the extent that the Bail Reform Act permits pretrial detention on the ground that the arrestee is likely to commit future crimes, it is unconstitutional on its face. . . . A facial challenge to a legislative Act is, of course, the most difficult challenge to mount successfully, since the challenger must establish that no set of circumstances exists under which the Act would be valid. . . . We think respondents have failed to shoulder their heavy burden to demonstrate that the Act is "facially" unconstitutional.

Respondents present two grounds for invalidating the Bail Reform Act's provisions permitting pretrial detention on the basis of future dangerousness. First, they [argue] that the Act exceeds the limitations placed upon the Federal Government by the Due Process Clause of the Fifth Amendment. Second, they contend that the Act contravenes the Eighth Amendment's proscription against excessive bail. We treat these contentions in turn.

The Due Process Clause of the Fifth Amendment provides that "No person shall . . . be deprived of life, liberty, or property, without due process of law. . . ." Respondents first argue that the Act violates substantive due process because the pretrial detention it authorizes constitutes impermissible punishment before trial. The Government, however, has never argued that pretrial detention could be upheld if it were "punishment." The Court of Appeals assumed that pretrial detention under the Bail Reform Act is regulatory, not penal, and we agree that it is. . . .

To determine whether a restriction on liberty constitutes impermissible punishment or permissible regulation, we first look to legislative intent. Unless Congress expressly intended to impose punitive restrictions, the punitive/regulatory distinction turns on whether an alternative purpose to which the restriction may rationally be connected is assignable for it, and whether it appears excessive in relation to the alternative purpose assigned to it.

We conclude that the detention imposed by the Act falls on the regulatory side of the dichotomy. The legislative history of the Bail Reform Act clearly indicates that Congress did not formulate the pretrial detention provisions as punishment for dangerous individuals. Congress instead perceived pretrial detention as a potential solution to a pressing societal problem. There is no doubt that preventing danger to the community is a legitimate regulatory goal.

Nor are the incidents of pretrial detention excessive in relation to the regulatory goal Congress sought to achieve. The Bail Reform Act carefully limits the circumstances under which detention may be sought to the most serious of crimes. See 18 U.S.C. §3142(f) (detention hearings available if case involves crimes of violence, offenses for which the sentence is life imprisonment or death, serious drug offenses, or certain repeat offenders). The arrestee is entitled to a prompt detention hearing, and the maximum length of pretrial detention is limited by the stringent time limitations of the Speedy Trial Act. Moreover, . . . the conditions of confinement envisioned by the Act appear to reflect the regulatory purposes relied upon by the Government. [T]he statute at issue here requires that detainees be housed in a facility "separate, to the extent practicable, from persons awaiting or serving sentences or being held in custody pending appeal." 18 U.S.C. §3142(i)(2). We conclude, therefore, that the pretrial detention contemplated by the Bail Reform Act is regulatory in nature, and does not constitute punishment before trial in violation of the Due Process Clause.

[T]he Government's regulatory interest in community safety can, in appropriate circumstances, outweigh an individual's liberty interest. For example, in times of war or insurrection, when society's interest is at its peak, the Government may detain individuals whom the Government believes to be dangerous. See Ludecke v. Watkins, 335 U.S. 160 (1948) (approving unreviewable executive power to detain enemy aliens in time of war); Moyer v. Peabody, 212 U.S. 78 (1909) (rejecting due process claim of individual jailed without probable cause by Governor in time of insurrection). Even outside the exigencies of war, we have found that sufficiently compelling governmental interests can justify detention of dangerous persons. Thus, we have found no absolute constitutional barrier to detention of potentially dangerous resident aliens pending deportation proceedings. Carlson v. Landon, 342 U.S. 524 (1952). We have also held that the government may detain mentally unstable individuals who present a danger to the public, Addington v. Texas, 441 U.S. 418 (1979), and dangerous defendants who become incompetent to stand trial, Jackson v. Indiana, 406 U.S. 715 (1972). We have approved of postarrest regulatory detention of juveniles when they present a continuing danger to the community. Schall v. Martin, 467 U.S. 253 (1984). Even competent adults may face substantial liberty restrictions as a result of the operation of our criminal justice system. If the police suspect an individual of a crime, they may arrest and hold him until a neutral magistrate determines whether probable cause exists. Gerstein v. Pugh, 420 U.S. 103 (1975). Finally, . . . an arrestee may be incarcerated until trial if he presents a risk of flight . . . or a danger to witnesses.

Respondents characterize all of these cases as exceptions to the "general rule" of substantive due process that the government may not detain a person prior to a judgment of guilt in a criminal trial. Such a "general rule" may freely be conceded, but we think that these cases show a sufficient number of exceptions to the rule that the congressional action challenged here can hardly be characterized as totally novel. Given the well-established authority of the government, in special circumstances, to restrain individuals' liberty prior to or even without criminal trial and conviction, we think that the present statute providing for pretrial detention on the basis of dangerousness must be evaluated in precisely the same manner that we evaluated the laws in the cases discussed above.

The government's interest in preventing crime by arrestees is both legitimate and compelling. In *Schall*, we recognized the strength of the State's interest in preventing juvenile crime. This general concern with crime prevention is no less compelling when the suspects are adults. . . . The Bail Reform Act of 1984 responds to an even more particularized governmental interest than the interest we sustained in *Schall*. The statute we upheld in *Schall* permitted pretrial detention of any juvenile arrested on any charge after a showing that the individual might commit some undefined further crimes. The Bail Reform Act, in contrast . . . operates only on individuals who have been arrested for a specific category of extremely serious offenses. Congress specifically found that these individuals are far more likely to be responsible for dangerous acts in the community after arrest. Nor is the Act by any means a scattershot attempt to incapacitate those who are merely suspected of these serious crimes. The Government must first of all demonstrate probable cause to believe that the charged crime has been committed by the arrestee, but that is not enough. In a full-blown adversary hearing, the Government must convince a neutral decisionmaker by clear and convincing evidence that no conditions of release can reasonably assure the safety of the community or any person. While the Government's general interest in preventing crime is compelling, even this interest is heightened when the Government musters convincing proof that the arrestee, already indicted or held to answer for a serious crime, presents a demonstrable danger to the community. Under these narrow circumstances, society's interest in crime prevention is at its greatest.

On the other side of the scale, of course, is the individual's strong interest in liberty. We do not minimize the importance and fundamental nature of this right. But, as our cases hold, this right may, in circumstances where the Government's interest is sufficiently weighty, be subordinated to the greater needs of society. We think that Congress' careful delineation of the circumstances under which detention will be permitted satisfies this standard. When the Government proves by clear and convincing evidence that an arrestee presents an identified and articulable threat to an individual or the community, we believe that, consistent with the Due Process Clause, a court may disable the arrestee from executing that threat. . . .

Respondents also contend that the Bail Reform Act violates the Excessive Bail Clause of the Eighth Amendment. . . . The Eighth Amendment addresses pretrial release by providing merely that "excessive bail shall not be required." This Clause, of course, says nothing about whether bail shall be available at all. Respondents nevertheless contend that this Clause grants them a right to bail calculated solely upon considerations of flight. They rely on Stack v. Boyle, 342 U.S. 1, 5 (1951), in which the Court stated that "bail set at a figure higher than an amount reasonably calculated [to ensure the defendant's presence at trial] is 'excessive' under the Eighth Amendment." In respondents' view, since the Bail Reform Act allows a court essentially to set bail at an infinite amount for reasons not related to the risk of flight, it violates the Excessive Bail Clause. Respondents concede that the right to bail they have discovered in the Eighth Amendment is not absolute. A court may, for example, refuse bail in capital cases. [A] court may [also] refuse bail when the defendant presents a threat to the judicial process by intimidating witnesses. Respondents characterize these exceptions as consistent with what they claim to be the sole purpose of bail — to ensure the integrity of the judicial process.

While we agree that a primary function of bail is to safeguard the courts' role in adjudicating the guilt or innocence of defendants, we reject the proposition that the Eighth Amendment categorically prohibits the government from pursuing other admittedly compelling interests through regulation of pretrial release. The above-quoted dictum in Stack v. Boyle is far too slender a reed on which to rest this argument. [T]he statute before the Court in that case in fact allowed the defendants to be bailed. Thus, the Court had to determine only whether bail, admittedly available in that case, was excessive if set at a sum greater than that necessary to ensure the arrestees' presence at trial.

The holding of *Stack* is illuminated by the Court's holding just four months later in Carlson v. Landon, 342 U.S. 524 (1952). In that case, remarkably similar to the present action, the detainees had been arrested and held without bail pending a determination of deportability. The Attorney General refused to release the individuals, "on the ground that there was reasonable cause to believe that [their] release would be prejudicial to the public interest and would endanger the welfare and safety of the United States." The detainees brought the same challenge that respondents bring to us today: the Eighth Amendment required them to be admitted to bail. The Court squarely rejected this proposition:

> The bail clause was lifted with slight changes from the English Bill of Rights Act. In England that clause has never been thought to accord a right to bail in all cases, but merely to provide that bail shall not be excessive in those cases where it is proper to grant bail. When this clause was carried over into our Bill of Rights, nothing was said that indicated any different concept. [342 U.S. at 545.]

Nothing in the text of the Bail Clause limits permissible Government considerations solely to questions of flight. The only arguable substantive limitation of the Bail Clause is that the Government's proposed conditions of release or detention not be "excessive" in light of the perceived evil. Of course, to determine whether the Government's response is excessive, we must compare that response against the interest the Government seeks to protect by means of that response. Thus, when the Government has admitted that its only interest is in preventing flight, bail must be set by a court at a sum designed to ensure that goal, and no more. We believe that when Congress has mandated detention on the basis of a compelling interest other than prevention of flight, as it has here, the Eighth Amendment does not require release on bail.

In our society liberty is the norm, and detention prior to trial or without trial is the carefully limited exception. We hold that the provisions for pretrial detention in the Bail Reform Act of 1984 fall within that carefully limited exception. The Act authorizes the detention prior to trial of arrestees charged with serious felonies who are found after an adversary hearing to pose a threat to the safety of individuals or to the community which no condition of release can dispel. The numerous procedural safeguards detailed above must attend this adversary hearing. We are unwilling to say that this congressional determination, based as it is upon that primary concern of every government — a concern for the safety and indeed the lives of its citizens — on its face violates either the Due Process Clause of the Fifth Amendment or the Excessive Bail Clause of the Eighth Amendment. The judgment of the Court of Appeals is therefore reversed.

MARSHALL, J., dissenting.

This case brings before the Court for the first time a statute in which Congress declares that a person innocent of any crime may be jailed indefinitely, pending the trial of allegations which are legally presumed to be untrue, if the Government shows to the satisfaction of a judge that the accused is likely to commit crimes, unrelated to the pending charges, at any time in the future. Such statutes, consistent with the usages of tyranny and the excesses of what bitter experience teaches us to call the police state, have long been thought incompatible with the fundamental human rights protected by our Constitution.

[In connection with the Due Process challenge,] the majority concludes that the Act is a regulatory rather than a punitive measure. The ease with which the conclusion is reached suggests the worthlessness of the achievement. . . . Let us apply the majority's reasoning to a similar, hypothetical case. After investigation, Congress determines (not unrealistically) that a large proportion of violent crime is perpetrated by persons who are unemployed. It also determines, equally reasonably, that much violent crime is committed at night. From amongst the panoply of "potential solutions," Congress chooses a statute which permits, after judicial proceedings, the imposition of a dusk-to-dawn curfew on anyone who is unemployed. Since this is not a measure enacted for the purpose of punishing the unemployed, and since the majority finds that preventing danger to the community is a legitimate regulatory goal, the curfew statute would, according to the majority's analysis, be a mere "regulatory" detention statute, entirely compatible with the substantive components of the Due Process Clause.

The absurdity of this conclusion arises, of course, from the majority's cramped concept of substantive due process. The majority proceeds as though the only substantive right protected by the Due Process Clause is a right to be free from punishment before conviction. The majority's technique for infringing this right is simple: merely redefine any measure which is claimed to be punishment as "regulation," and, magically, the Constitution no longer prohibits its imposition. Because . . . the Due Process Clause protects other substantive rights which are infringed by this legislation, the majority's argument is merely an exercise in obfuscation.

The logic of the majority's Eighth Amendment analysis is equally unsatisfactory. [The majority] declares, as if it were undeniable, that: "this Clause, of course, says nothing about whether bail shall be available at all." If excessive bail is imposed the defendant stays in jail. The same result is achieved if bail is denied altogether. Whether the magistrate sets bail at $1 billion or refuses to set bail at all, the consequences are indistinguishable. It would be mere sophistry to suggest that the Eighth Amendment protects against the former decision, and not the latter. Indeed, such a result would lead to the conclusion that there was no need for Congress to pass a preventive detention measure of any kind; every federal magistrate and district judge could simply refuse, despite the absence of any evidence of risk of flight or danger to the community, to set bail. . . .

The essence of this case may be found, ironically enough, in a provision of the Act to which the majority does not refer. Title 18 U.S.C. §3142(j) provides that "nothing in this section shall be construed as modifying or limiting the presumption of innocence." But the very pith and purpose of this statute is an abhorrent limitation of the presumption of innocence. . . .

The statute does not authorize the Government to imprison anyone it has evidence is dangerous; indictment is necessary. But let us suppose that a defendant is indicted and the Government shows by clear and convincing evidence that he is dangerous and should be detained pending a trial, at which trial the defendant is acquitted. May the Government continue to hold the defendant in detention based upon its showing that he is dangerous? The answer cannot be yes, for that would allow the Government to imprison someone for uncommitted crimes based upon "proof" not beyond a reasonable doubt. The result must therefore be that once the indictment has failed, detention cannot continue. But our fundamental principles of justice declare that the defendant is as innocent on the day before his trial as he is on the morning after his acquittal. Under this statute an untried indictment somehow acts to permit a detention, based on other charges, which after an acquittal would be unconstitutional. The conclusion is inescapable that the indictment has been turned into evidence, if not that the defendant is guilty of the crime charged, then that left to his own devices he will soon be guilty of something else. . . .

The finding of probable cause conveys power to try, and the power to try imports of necessity the power to assure that the processes of justice will not be evaded or obstructed. [Detention under] this statute bears no relation to the Government's power to try charges supported by a finding of probable cause, and thus the interests it serves are outside the scope of interests which may be considered in weighing the excessiveness of bail under the Eighth Amendment. . . .

Throughout the world today there are men, women, and children interned indefinitely, awaiting trials which may never come or which may be a mockery of the word, because their governments believe them to be "dangerous." Our Constitution, whose construction began two centuries ago, can shelter us forever from the evils of such unchecked power. Over 200 years it has slowly, through our efforts, grown more durable, more expansive, and more just. But it cannot protect us if we lack the courage, and the self-restraint, to protect ourselves. Today a majority of the Court applies itself to an ominous exercise in demolition. Theirs is truly a decision which will go forth without authority, and come back without respect. I dissent.

STEVENS, J., dissenting.

There may be times when the Government's interest in protecting the safety of the community will justify the brief detention of a person who has not committed any crime. [I]t is indeed difficult to accept the proposition that the Government is without power to detain a person when it is a virtual certainty that he or she would otherwise kill a group of innocent people in the immediate future. Similarly, I am unwilling to decide today that the police may never impose a limited curfew during a time of crisis. These questions are obviously not presented in this case, but they lurk in the background and preclude me from answering the question that is presented in as broad a manner as Justice Marshall has. Nonetheless, I firmly agree with Justice Marshall that the provision of the Bail Reform Act allowing pretrial detention on the basis of future dangerousness is unconstitutional. Whatever the answers are to the questions I have mentioned, it is clear to me that a pending indictment may not be given any weight in evaluating an individual's risk to the community or the need for immediate detention.

If the evidence of imminent danger is strong enough to warrant emergency detention, it should support that preventive measure regardless of whether the person has been charged, convicted, or acquitted of some other offense. In this case, for example, it is unrealistic to assume that the danger to the community that was present when respondents were at large did not justify their detention before they were indicted, but did require that measure the moment that the grand jury found probable cause to believe they had committed crimes in the past. It is equally unrealistic to assume that the danger will vanish if a jury happens to acquit them. . . .

■ NEW MEXICO CONSTITUTION ART. II, §13

All persons shall before conviction be bailable by sufficient sureties, except for capital offenses when the proof is evident or the presumption great and in situations in which bail is specifically prohibited by this section. Excessive bail shall not be required, nor excessive fines imposed, nor cruel and unusual punishment inflicted. Bail may be denied by the district court for a period of sixty days after the incarceration of the defendant by an order entered within seven days after the incarceration, in the following instances:

A. the defendant is accused of a felony and has previously been convicted of two or more felonies, within the state, which felonies did not arise from the same transaction or a common transaction with the case at bar;

B. the defendant is accused of a felony involving the use of a deadly weapon and has a prior felony conviction, within the state.

The period for incarceration without bail may be extended by any period of time by which trial is delayed by a motion for a continuance made by or on behalf of the defendant. . . .

■ VIRGINIA CODE §19.2-120

. . . A. A person who is held in custody pending trial or hearing for an offense, civil or criminal contempt, or otherwise shall be admitted to bail by a judicial officer, unless there is probable cause to believe that:

1. He will not appear for trial or hearing or at such other time and place as may be directed, or

2. His liberty will constitute an unreasonable danger to himself or the public.

B. The judicial officer shall presume, subject to rebuttal, that no condition or combination of conditions will reasonably assure the appearance of the person or the safety of the public if the person is currently charged with:

1. An act of violence as defined in [this code];

2. An offense for which the maximum sentence is life imprisonment or death;

3. A violation . . . involving a Schedule I or II controlled substance if (i) the maximum term of imprisonment is ten years or more and the person was previously convicted of a like offense or (ii) the person was previously convicted as a "drug kingpin" as defined in [this code];

4. A violation . . . which relates to a firearm and provides for a mandatory minimum sentence;

5. Any felony, if the person has been convicted of two or more offenses described in subdivision 1 or 2 . . . ;

6. Any felony committed while the person is on release pending trial for a prior felony under federal or state law or on release pending imposition or execution of sentence or appeal of sentence or conviction;

7. [Felony sexual assault] and the person had previously been convicted of [felony sexual assault] and the judicial officer finds probable cause to believe that the person who is currently charged with one of these offenses committed the offense charged;

8. A violation of [the statutes prohibiting the activities of criminal street gangs, acts of terrorism, or acts of bioterrorism against agricultural crops or animals]; or

9. A violation [involving driving while intoxicated] and the person has, within the past five years of the instant offense, been convicted three times on different dates of a violation of any combination of these Code sections, or any [similar ordinance or statute], and has been at liberty between each conviction.

C. The judicial officer shall presume, subject to rebuttal, that no condition or combination of conditions will reasonably assure the appearance of the person or the safety of the public if the person is being arrested pursuant to [the enforcement of federal immigration laws].

D. The court shall consider the following factors and such others as it deems appropriate in determining, for the purpose of rebuttal of the presumption against bail described in subsection B, whether there are conditions of release that will reasonably assure the appearance of the person as required and the safety of the public:

1. The nature and circumstances of the offense charged;

2. The history and characteristics of the person, including his character, physical and mental condition, family ties, employment, financial resources, length of residence in the community, community ties, past conduct, history relating to drug or alcohol abuse, criminal history, membership in a street gang . . . , and record concerning appearance at court proceedings; and

3. The nature and seriousness of the danger to any person or the community that would be posed by the person's release.

Notes

1. Preventive detention: majority position. Like the federal system, about half the states authorize courts to detain defendants before trial for the purpose of preventing the commission of new crimes ("preventive detention"). See, e.g., Mass. Gen. L. ch. 276, §58A. On the other hand, about 25 states have constitutional provisions that, like Tennessee, guarantee the right to bail except in capital cases. See People v. Purcell, 778 N.E.2d 695 (Ill. 2002) (strikes down law requiring defendant to show that guilt is not evident, because allocation of burden to accused is inconsistent with state constitution's presumption of bail). Detention based on risk of future crime is often distinguished from detention based on fear of flight or threat to witnesses. Do the categories of fear of flight or threat to witnesses overlap with risk of future crime?

Among states that authorize detention, the details of their statutes and constitutions vary substantially. A handful create a presumption against bail, but most allow detention in the discretion of the court. Some states limit preventive detention to "serious crimes"; others limit detention to offenders with specific combinations of prior record and sufficiently serious current charges. A handful of states have enacted limits on the maximum time a defendant may be detained to prevent crimes. See, e.g., Mass. Gen. L. ch. 276, §58A (90 days); Wis. Stat. §969.035 (60 days). Why have so many states continued to reject preventive detention laws over the more than 15 years since passage of the federal Bail Reform Act and the decision of the Supreme Court in *Salerno*? Are other states likely, over time, to make the statutory and constitutional changes necessary to allow preventive detention? Some state constitutional provisions that seemed to bar the use of preventive detention have either been amended by the voters (e.g., Ohio Const. art. I, §9 was amended in 1997) or read restrictively to avoid any inconsistency with a new preventive detention statute. See State v. Ayala, 610 A.2d 1162 (Conn. 1992); Mo. Rev. Stat. §544.457 (allowing preventive detention "notwithstanding" constitutional guarantee of bail).

2. *Presumption of innocence.* The justices in *Salerno* disagreed about the meaning of the presumption of innocence. See Daniel Richman, United States v. Salerno: The Constitutionality of Regulatory Detention, in Criminal Procedure Stories (Carol Steiker ed., 2006). A critic of the majority opinion might draw a comparison to the following passage from Lewis Carroll's *Through the Looking Glass*, where the Queen and Alice discuss the consequences of having a memory that works both ways:

> "I'm sure mine only works one way," Alice remarked. "I can't remember things before they happen."
>
> "It's a poor sort of memory that only works backward," the Queen remarked.
>
> "What sort of things do you remember best?" Alice ventured to ask.
>
> "Oh, things that happened the week after next," the Queen replied in a careless tone.
>
> "For instance, now," she went on, sticking a large piece of plaster on her finger as she spoke, "there's the King's Messenger. He's in prison now, being punished: and the trial doesn't even begin till next Wednesday: and of course the crime comes last of all."
>
> "Suppose he never commits the crime?" said Alice.
>
> "That would be all the better, wouldn't it?" the Queen said, as she bound the plaster round her finger with a bit of ribbon.
>
> Alice felt there was no denying that. "Of course it would be all the better," she said: "but it wouldn't be all the better his being punished."
>
> "You're wrong there, at any rate," said the Queen: "Were you ever punished?"
>
> "Only for faults," said Alice.
>
> "And you were all the better for it, I know!" the Queen said triumphantly.
>
> "Yes, but then I had done the things I was punished for," said Alice: "that makes all the difference."
>
> "But if you hadn't done them," the Queen said, "that would have been better still; better, and better, and better!" . . .
>
> Alice was just beginning to say, "There's a mistake somewhere—," when the Queen began screaming, so loud that she had to leave the sentence unfinished. "Oh, oh, oh!" shouted the Queen, shaking her hand about as if she wanted to shake it off. "My finger's bleeding! Oh, oh, oh, oh!" . . .
>
> "What is the matter?" she said, as soon as there was a chance of making herself heard.
>
> "Have you pricked your finger?"
>
> "I haven't pricked it yet," the Queen said, "but I soon shall—oh, oh, oh!"

Is this the message of the *Salerno* opinion? If not, in what sense can we say that *Salerno* respects the presumption of innocence?

3. Limitation to serious felonies and repeat offenders. Most of the states passing new statutory or constitutional provisions to allow preventive detention have limited its use to criminal defendants who are accused of committing a select group of serious or violent felonies. See Mendonza v. Commonwealth, 673 N.E.2d 22 (Mass. 1996) (upholding revised statute under federal and state constitutions; statute applies to felonies involving the use, or threatened use, of violence or abuse, or the violation of protective orders); Aime v. Commonwealth, 611 N.E.2d 204 (Mass. 1993) (striking down preventive detention law on federal grounds because of wide range of crimes covered; court distinguishes *Salerno*). Some, like the New Mexico constitutional provision above, apply only to those accused of a felony who have also been convicted of one or more felonies in the past. See also Colo. Const. art. II, §19 (new bail denied to those accused of committing violent crime while on prior bail, parole, or probation for previous charges of violent crime). Do both the "serious crime" and "repeat offender" limitations serve the same purpose? Another variety of selective detention statutes applies only to defendants accused of a particularly high-priority crime, such as stalking or domestic violence. See Alaska Stat. §12.30.025; Ill. Rev. Stat. ch. 725, para. 5/110-4. Do these provisions raise any concerns different from a provision focusing on all serious felonies?

4. Presumptions based on crime charged. Some of the preventive detention measures go further than authorizing the trial court to detain a defendant when necessary to protect the community: They instruct the judge that detention is presumed when a defendant is charged with committing designated crimes of drugs and violence. The Virginia statute above is an example. Are these statutes the modern equivalent of the old "capital punishment" exception in the typical constitutional bail provision? Or did the capital punishment exception serve more traditional purposes, such as preventing the defendant from fleeing upon his or her release?

5. How many defendants are detained? The number of defendants detained in the federal system is creeping upward. Among federal defendants in 1983 (the year before the passage of the Bail Reform Act), 24 percent remained in custody until their prosecutions were completed. In 1985 the figure rose to 29 percent (including those who failed to make bail and those who were ordered detained). In 2003 over 58 percent of federal defendants were not released before disposition of their cases. Bureau of Justice Statistics, Sourcebook of Criminal Justice Statistics, 1988, table 5.17 (1989); Bureau of Justice Statistics, Compendium of Federal Justice Statistics, 2003, table 3.3 (2005). As for the state systems, in large counties in 2002, 38 percent of defendants were detained until case disposition. These national average statistics obscure some real differences among jurisdictions.

What is the proper practical balance between the 1960s reform encouraging presumptive release and the 1980s reform encouraging open detention for those who threaten harm? Does detention until trial of almost one-third of those charged with felonies in the federal system seem too high? Does the federal system reflect the victory of candor? Is open preventive detention preferable to continued sub-rosa detention through unrealistically high bail requirements in states where there is no legal authority to detain defendants for the purpose of protecting the public from the commission of additional crimes?

6. Compensation for wrongful detention. Should the government compensate people who are detained under the Bail Reform Act or analogous state statutes and are later found at trial to be not guilty? See Masson v. Netherlands, 22 EHRR

491 (1996) (European Court of Human Rights reviewing domestic law that allows civil court, after a failure to convict a suspect in criminal proceedings, to grant compensation at expense of the state for damage suffered as a result of wrongful pretrial detention).

7. *Detention after completion of sentence.* States are now using post-sentence detention to extend their control over some persons convicted of sex offenses. Statutes passed since the mid-1990s authorize the government to request continued detention of convicted sex offenders after they have completed their sentences. These statutes typically require the government to demonstrate, on a year-to-year basis, that the offender remains "dangerous." The Supreme Court has upheld statutes against challenges based on the due process, ex post facto, and double jeopardy clause of the federal constitution. Kansas v. Hendricks, 521 U.S. 346 (1997). Employing the same distinction that it used in *Salerno,* the court said that this detention was "regulatory" rather than "punitive." See also Kansas v. Crane, 534 U.S. 407 (2002) (constitution does not require judicial finding of total or complete lack of control to support regulatory detention of sexual offender, but Constitution does require a showing that person does lack some control over his or her behavior).

8. *The revenge of social science.* Social science studies were the driving force behind legal changes to make pretrial release easier and less dependent on money bail. Similarly, social science figured prominently in the movement to expand the power of judges to detain defendants before trial. These studies focused on the number of defendants released before trial who were soon rearrested for committing additional crimes. In 2002, for example, 18 percent of released defendants were rearrested for a new offense allegedly committed while their original case was pending.

Over the past generation, we have reduced the number of people who are detained and have changed the acceptable reasons for detaining persons, allowing the detention of some defendants who at one time would have been released on bail. Do we now have it just about right? Are we now detaining the right people? Does this trend reflect a shift in the fundamental basis for the criminal law, punishing criminal propensities rather than criminal acts? See Paul H. Robinson, Punishing Dangerousness: Cloaking Preventive Detention as Criminal Justice, 114 Harv. L. Rev. 1429 (2001).

C. DETENTION OF EXCLUDABLE ALIENS AND ENEMY COMBATANTS

After the terrorist attacks of September 11, 2001, the federal government detained several groups of people as part of the effort to investigate the previous attacks and to prevent future terrorist crimes. First, the government detained a large number of noncitizens from Arab nations, present within the United States, on the basis of potential immigration violations such as expired student visas. Under the immigration laws, the government incarcerated these noncitizens for several months with limited access to counsel, while government agents investigated their potential immigration violations, along with their potential involvement in terrorist activities. The government has not released the precise number and identity of these detainees; estimates range from 1,200 to 2,000 persons. Many of these detainees were ultimately deported for their immigration violations, and a few were charged with crimes (although none were charged with crimes directly connected to terrorism). The government also declared that the immigration proceedings related to these people were closed to the public, and no individualized showing was needed to establish that secrecy was necessary in each particular case.

Second, the government detained dozens of people in the United States as "material witnesses" who might have information relating to the attacks. The traditional use of the federal material witness statute was to hold reluctant or fearful witnesses for a short time (typically a few days) to obtain their grand jury testimony. During this investigation, FBI agents obtained judicial approval for warrants allowing them to detain material witnesses, and then held them for several months; only about half the witnesses ever testified before a grand jury.

Third, the United States military captured men during the fighting in Afghanistan and transported several hundred of them to a military detention facility in Cuba. These men were held for questioning without criminal charges and without access to counsel. Problem 2-1 deals with the third category.

Problem 2-1. Traditions in Trying Times

During combat in Afghanistan in late 2001 and early 2002, U.S. military forces captured several hundred people on the battlefield. The military transported those captives to Guantanamo Bay in Cuba. The U.S. government designated those people as "enemy combatants" and detained them under the executive authority entrusted to the president as commander in chief of the armed forces.

The president issued a military order in November 2001 setting out procedures for the "[d]etention, treatment, and trial of certain non-citizens in the war against terrorism." The order stipulated that it applied to any individual who was not a citizen of the United States, after the president determined in writing that there was reason to believe (1) that such individual was a member of al-Qaeda or (2) that he was engaged in international terrorism, or (3) that it was in the interests of the United States that he should be subject to the order. The order provided that any such individual would be detained at an appropriate location and treated humanely. It stated that any individual "when tried" would be tried by a military tribunal, and it contained extensive provisions relating to such a trial. It further declared:

> With respect to any individual subject to this order . . . the individual shall not be privileged to seek any remedy or maintain any proceeding, directly or indirectly, or to have any such remedy or proceeding sought on the individual's behalf, in (i) any court of the United States, or any State thereof, (ii) any court of any foreign nation, or (iii) any international tribunal.

One of these enemy combatants, Feroz Ali Abbasi, was a British national. His family filed a lawsuit in the British courts, asking the judge to order the Foreign Office to "make representations" on behalf of Abbasi to the United States government. The British court refused to grant this relief to Abbasi's family. The judge, however, also observed that subjecting a person to indefinite detention without giving the person any opportunity to challenge the detention before a court or tribunal appeared to violate basic principles of Anglo-American justice:

> The United States executive is detaining Mr. Abbasi . . . in circumstances where Mr. Abbasi can make no challenge to his detention before any court or tribunal. How long this state of affairs continues is within the sole control of the United States executive. . . .
>
> The United Kingdom and the United States share a great legal tradition, founded in the English common law. One of the cornerstones of that tradition is the ancient writ of habeas corpus, recognised at least by the time of Edward I, and developed by the 17th Century into "the most efficient protection yet developed for the liberty of the subject". . . .
>
> The underlying principle, fundamental in English law, is that every imprisonment is prima facie unlawful, and that no member of the executive can interfere with the liberty . . . of a British subject except on the condition that he can support the legality of his action before a court of justice. This principle applies to every person, British citizen or not, who finds himself within the jurisdiction of the court. . . . It applies in war as in peace; in Lord Atkin's words (written in one of the darkest periods of the last war): "In this country, amid the clash of arms, the laws are not silent. They may be changed, but they speak the same language in war as in peace." . . . As one would expect, endorsement of this common tradition is no less strong in the United States. . . . The recognition of this basic protection in both English and American law long pre-dates the adoption of the same principle as a fundamental part of international human rights law. . . .

A similar evaluation appeared in a January 2002 statement from the United Nations High Commissioner for Human Rights:

> All persons detained in this context are entitled to the protection of international human rights law and humanitarian law, in particular the relevant provisions of the International Covenant on Civil and Political Rights (ICCPR) and the Geneva Conventions of 1949. The legal status of the detainees, and their entitlement to prisoner-of-war (POW) status, if disputed, must be determined by a competent tribunal, in accordance with the provisions of Article 5 of the Third Geneva Convention.

Imagine that you work as an attorney at the U.S. Department of State. The Senate has begun to consider various legislative proposals to regulate the detention of "enemy combatants" such as Abbasi. The Senate Judiciary Committee, with jurisdiction over these bills, wants you to testify and to evaluate in general terms the regulation of detainees suspected of being terrorists or enemy combatants. In particular, the senators hope that your testimony will focus on the potential impact of detention practices on the nation's international relationships. Can the United States reassure other nations that specialized rules for detention of suspected terrorists will be used only in that specialized context? Is it possible to maintain a distinction between detention for criminal purposes and detention for military purposes? As you think about this question, imagine that some additional terrorist atrocity is committed, perhaps by a group based in China. If investigators detained a large number of suspects of Chinese origin, what limits would apply to that detention? C.f. Feroz Abbasi v. Secretary of State, 2002 EWCA Civ. 1598 (Court of Appeal, Civil Division, 2002).

Notes

1. Detention of excludable aliens. In Zadvydas v. Davis, 533 U.S. 678 (2001), the Supreme Court invalidated a statute allowing an alien who is subject to a final order of removal to be detained beyond a 90-day statutory "removal period" at the discretion of the attorney general. The Court held that as a matter of due process aliens could not be detained indefinitely following a final order of removal and that the attorney general had to justify continued detention. Two years later, however, the Court in Demore v. Kim, 538 U.S. 510 (2003), upheld a statute requiring mandatory detention for deportable criminal aliens, as applied to a lawful permanent resident who entered the United States at age six and was convicted of burglary and "petty theft with priors." Is it significant that *Zadvydas* was decided shortly before September 11 and *Demore* a year and a half after September 11?

2. Detention of terrorism suspects. In April 2003, the inspector general of the Department of Justice issued a report reviewing the extended detention of excludable aliens rounded up in the days and months following September 11. The report both recognized the critical circumstances of terrorist threats to the United States and criticized the actions of federal officials in identifying suspects for detention and in extending the length of those detentions. Shortly thereafter, a Justice Department spokesperson defended the department's actions: "We make no apologies for finding every legal way possible to protect the American public from further terrorist attacks." Would you expect an internal executive branch report like the one by the inspector general to have an impact on law and policy?

3. Detention of material witnesses. Federal law empowers the government to detain "material witnesses" who might have information relating to the commission of a federal crime. The traditional use of the federal material witness statute was to hold reluctant or fearful witnesses for a short time (typically a few days) to secure their grand jury testimony. In terrorism investigations since 2001, FBI agents have obtained judicial approval for warrants allowing them to detain material witnesses, and then held them for several months; only about half of the witnesses ever testified before a grand jury. See Adam Liptak, "For Post-9/11 Material Witness, It Is a Terror of a Different Kind," N.Y. Times, Aug. 19, 2004 (recounts experience of former college football player arrested in March 2003 as a material witness in a terrorism investigation; held "in a small cell for hours and hours and hours buck naked"; federal judge ordered him to move in with his in-laws in Las Vegas; witness was never charged with a crime and never asked to testify as a witness; 16 months after his arrest, court said he was free to resume his life).

4. Migration of anti-terrorism practices to anti-crime efforts. To what extent do government practices that develop in response to threats from terrorists ultimately spread to more ordinary anti-crime contexts? Scholars sometimes try to answer this question historically, by studying government responses to various emergencies around the world over the years. For instance, some criminologists characterize the government response to violence in Northern Ireland as a "contagion." According to this thesis, Northern Ireland served as a testing ground for repressive police practices that would later spread elsewhere to extend the authority of the state. See Aogàn Mulcahy, The "Other" Lessons from Ireland? Policing, Political Violence and Policy Transfer, 2 Eur. J. Criminology 185 (2005) (based on qualitative interview data about impact of Northern Ireland conflict, assessing both the contagion thesis and more positive lessons other jurisdictions learned from the conflict); Oren Gross, Chaos and Rules: Should Responses to Violent Crises Always Be Constitutional? 112 Yale L.J. 1011 (2003) (collecting studies of impact of conflict in Northern Ireland and other prolonged "emergency" settings).

III

Charging

Soon after arrest, suspects learn why they have been detained. Most often, this occurs when the arresting officer files a form (sometimes called a complaint, sometimes an investigation report) indicating the charges to be filed against the arrestee. Those charges are subject to change at many points later in the process. A prosecutor ordinarily decides whether to accept the police officer's proposed charge and files that charge or another at an initial appearance before a judicial officer, a hearing that is given various names in different jurisdictions. This hearing takes place within a short period (typically 48 hours, or some other time defined by rule or statute). The charges can also change at a later hearing, sometimes known as a preliminary examination, or at an arraignment, when the defendant indicates how he will plead. Charges can also be dismissed later in the process.

You might think of the charging process as a set of screens following investigation: Various government institutions help decide which persons in custody will become criminal defendants and which charges they will face. The arresting police officer and the officer's supervisor have some input into the charging decision. Prosecuting attorneys usually have the most important voice in determining whether to charge and what charges to select; criminal codes commonly give the prosecutor more than one legally viable option in a particular case. The prosecutor might follow personal criteria, policies and principles established for the office, or (less frequently) statutes dictating the charging decision. Courts are usually less involved in the charging decision than in most other procedural choices. Much of the time, courts review charging decisions only to confirm that there is a minimal amount of evidence supporting the charge, enough to justify "binding over" the case for trial. Grand juries are another special institution designed in part to determine whether there is probable cause to charge defendants, especially in more serious cases.

Because the prosecutor's choices dominate the charging phase, we concentrate in this chapter on unfamiliar sources of law. As you survey the charging process, ask whether the various executive branch guidelines and practices at work here are comparable in any way—in origins, function, evolution, and so on—to the way legislatures and courts craft rules.

A. POLICE SCREENING

Should police officers make an independent judgment about whether to file charges for every crime that might be charged? Should police departments set up internal mechanisms to review arrests before submitting a file or report to prosecutors? On what grounds might a police supervisor reject a charge when the facts appear to satisfy the elements of the crime?

Police screening of charges is largely hidden in the modern, big-city criminal process. Hints about the extent of police screening can be seen in occasional studies of "clearance rates" and case "attrition." Clearance rates refer to the percentage of complaints made to police that are solved in some fashion. Attrition is the term describing how initial complaints drop out of the criminal process and why only a relatively small percentage of complaints end with convictions.

The amount of case attrition in a system depends on the interaction between police and prosecutors. Where the police and prosecutors have different ideas about which cases are worthwhile, many cases that the police assemble will fall out of the system, some sooner and some later. Police screening represents an effort to anticipate how the prosecutor will evaluate the case.

In practice, the types of interaction between police and prosecutors during the screening of cases can vary a great deal. According to one influential study attempting to measure the quality of prosecutors' offices, the arrangement between police and prosecutors depends as much on legal culture as on the legal authority to make charging decisions:

> In Buffalo, New York . . . the police arrest the defendant, take him before the committing magistrate where his bond is set, the complaint filed, defense counsel appointed, if necessary, and the case set for preliminary hearing. It is only prior to the preliminary hearing that the prosecutor is made aware of the case and the files are sent to him. Thus, the preliminary hearing provides the first opportunity for case review and witness interviews. The result is to place the prosecutor in a reactive position since he does not exercise the charging function which controls the intake into the system. . . .
>
> It is sometimes difficult to change the external conditions that create a transfer [of control to some other institution]. For example, in Buffalo, police arrestees are processed at the precinct level, not at a centrally located facility. This fragmentation coupled with a strong tradition of police filing charges has supported the transfer [of initial charging authority to police]. In other cities, such as Philadelphia, attempts have been made to overcome the absence of centralized booking. In one experiment, assistant prosecutors were stationed at the police precincts. But the problems resulting from irregularly occurring work, isolation from the main office and the attorney's

subsequent role identification with the police function, all worked against its success. [As] long as arrests are booked at scattered precincts, the opportunity for the prosecutor to intervene before the charge is filed in court is severely diminished.

Joan Jacoby, Basic Issues in Prosecution and Public Defender Performance 25-30 (1982). In the following police department rules, what differences do you see in the working relationships between police and prosecutors leading to a charging decision?

■ PHILADELPHIA POLICE DEPARTMENT DIRECTIVE 50 SUBJECT: INVESTIGATION AND CHARGING PROCEDURE

I. POLICY

A. All adults arrested for a felony or misdemeanor offense will be investigated, processed and charged in accordance with the procedures outlined in this directive. . . .

C. The Complaint Fact Sheet (CFS) will serve as the police report for the District Attorney's Charging Unit (DACU). Prior to slating a defendant, the DACU should receive the CFS from the investigating unit to clarify certain facts or to supply needed information. . . .

E. The Criminal Complaint will be prepared and delivered to the Arraignment Court by the DACU.

II. INVESTIGATING UNIT PROCEDURE

A. The assigned investigator will prepare the following forms:
1. Arrest Report
2. Hearing Sheet
3. Investigator's Aid to Interview
4. Complaint Fact Sheet. . . .
5. Investigation Report
B. The assigned investigator will ensure that:
1. When charging a suspect with a misdemeanor or felony offense, appropriate summary offenses are included in the Arrest Reports and Complaint Fact Sheet. Substantiated facts and testimony will be included in these reports to support all charges listed. . . .
3. The CFS is promptly submitted to the unit supervisor for review. . . .
4. In division/units electronically equipped with a facsimile transceiver, the CFS will be transmitted to the DACU immediately after review and approval by the supervisor. . . .
C. The investigating unit supervisor will ensure that:
1. The Complaint Fact Sheet is properly prepared and the charges are appropriate for the facts and testimony as listed on the CFS.
2. Review and approve CFS.
3. The CFS is promptly transmitted to the DACU if electronically equipped to do so. . . .

6. When any charges are modified or disapproved by the DACU, attach the Record of Declination form (when received) to the CFS . . . , and submit to the commanding officer for review. . . .

   D. Commanding Director of the Investigating Unit will [review] all modified and disapproved CFS and compare with submitted [CFS] for consistency [and forward] a memorandum through the chain of command describing any case where modification or disapproval appears to be totally unjustified or inconsistent with previous DACU decisions and policies.

■ HOUSTON POLICE DEPARTMENT GENERAL ORDER 500-7

Effective law enforcement requires cooperation between police officers and members of the district attorney's office. It is the purpose of this General Order to establish procedural guidelines for officers to use when consulting with the district attorney's office regarding the filing of charges.

1. CONSULTATION WITH AN ASSISTANT DISTRICT ATTORNEY

Before using the computer terminal to file any charges with the district attorney's office, the officer filing the charges must speak with an assistant district attorney to ensure that the charges will be accepted. During the consultation, the officer shall provide the elements of the offense, sufficient details to show that probable cause existed to arrest the person and evidence that the person being charged did in fact commit the offense. These probable cause details should be included in the charges filed via the [computer]. It is important that an adequate probable-cause statement be contained in the warrant because this is sometimes the only information available to the assistant district attorney when the defendant is arraigned before a magistrate during a probable-cause hearing.

An assistant district attorney also will be consulted before the simultaneous filing of both county *and* municipal charges against *one* suspect if these charges are based on the same set of circumstances or the same criminal action. This consultation eliminates the possibility of a case being dismissed because of noncompliance with the Speedy Trial Act or because of violations of legal restraints against placing a defendant in double jeopardy.

Whenever an officer is unsure of the elements of a particular case, he shall discuss the matter with his immediate supervisor or contact the district attorney's office. Under no circumstances will a lesser charge be filed merely as a matter of convenience. For example, a charge of public intoxication will not be filed if the actual offense was driving while intoxicated. Appropriate charges shall be filed according to the elements of the offense.

2. REJECTION OF CHARGES BY ASSISTANT DISTRICT ATTORNEYS

If an officer tries to file charges through the district attorney's intake office and these charges are rejected, he will include the following information in his original or supplemental offense report: a) Time and date the officer spoke with the assistant district attorney about filing charges in the case; b) Name of the assistant district attorney who rejected the charges; [and] c) Reasons given by the assistant district attorney for rejecting the charges.

If the charges are rejected because of alleged mishandling by an officer, the officer will refer the case to his supervisor for review. If the supervisor does find mishandling on the part of the officer, he shall instruct the officer on policy and proper procedures, to avert recurrences. . . .

Notes

1. *Police screening.* Police departments have many different approaches to screening cases. Many departments do not openly acknowledge that officers screen cases *after* arrest, even though almost all police officials recognize the substantial discretion of police officers in making arrest decisions. Some departments train officers to select certain kinds of charges from among different possible charges. Other departments institute a formal screening process, either at the scene of an arrest or as part of the booking process at jail. This screening can take the form of review by a supervisor or by an officer trained to examine the facts of cases and the charges filed. Many departments establish methods of pretransfer review by prosecutors. Under the Philadelphia and Houston police department policies reprinted above, how early do prosecutors review the charges? Which system gives the police greater control over the selection of initial charges?

2. *Police courts.* For most of this century many larger cities utilized what were known as "police courts." These courts of limited jurisdiction heard charges brought by police for violations and sometimes for more serious offenses. Police courts were sometimes located at police headquarters. Officers would act not only as witnesses but also, in effect, as the prosecutor, making police decisions the only charging "screen." In Atlanta, the police court was not abolished until the mid-1970s, when prosecutors and then public defense appeared on the scene. The Atlanta Municipal Court—the successor to the police court—did not physically leave Atlanta police headquarters until the early 1990s. Very few states still have police courts, and where they do still exist, they are mainly a product of city charter and not state statute. See Andrew Horwitz, Taking the Cop Out of Copping a Plea: Eradicating Police Prosecution of Criminal Cases, 40 Ariz. L. Rev. 1305 (1998).

Police courts offered a highly tempered form of justice. They resolved cases quickly, but they collapsed in the face of new requirements for counsel and enforcement of rights to a trial by jury. Some hint of how police courts operated—and some suggestion of why they have largely disappeared—comes from reading the brief U.S. Supreme Court decision in Thompson v. Louisville, 362 U.S. 199 (1960). Sam Thompson, who committed the grave offense of dancing by himself one evening in a café after eating macaroni and drinking beer, was convicted in the Louisville police court of disorderly conduct and loitering and fined $10 on each charge. The Supreme Court reversed the conviction, in an opinion by Justice Black, noting that "although the fines here are small, the due process questions presented are substantial." The court observed that there was "no semblance of evidence" supporting either charge, and found it a "violation of due process to convict and punish a man without evidence of his guilt." What kind of court could convict a person on the basis of no evidence at all? What are the minimum procedural elements of a just criminal justice system?

3. *Police cautions in England.* Because the police in England make the initial decision whether to prosecute a criminal case, a practice has grown up (without a statutory basis) known as a "police caution." The caution is a warning to an arrested person, delivered by a senior police officer. If the person accepts the caution, the police agree not to refer the case to the Crown Prosecution Service. The caution becomes part of the offender's prior record. The Home Secretary has issued "National Standards for Cautioning" to guide police decisions in this area. See Home Office Circular 18/1994, The Cautioning of Offenders; Andrew Ashworth, The Criminal Process (2d ed. 1998). Does the consent of the suspect (when he accepts a caution) make the caution fundamentally different from a conviction in police court?

4. *Screening and "the tank."* Police departments exercising a screening function may release a person under arrest before the time for an initial appearance. In the meantime, arrestees can spend one or two nights in the local jail or holding facility before release. What circumstances might properly lead a police department to arrest and then release a person without filing formal charges? Are the police effectively given the power to punish citizens for short periods of time without prosecutorial or judicial supervision? Should prosecutors review all arrests, even when the police department does not believe charges should be pursued?

B. PROSECUTORIAL SCREENING

Prosecutors (who go by various names, such as "district attorneys," "county attorneys," "state's attorneys," or simply "prosecuting attorneys") have the most to say about whether to file charges against a suspect and which charges to select. Granted, they react to an initial charge proposed by the police, and they may have to convince a judge or a grand jury that there is enough evidence to justify going forward with a prosecution. But in the end, the prosecutor can overrule police charging decisions without interference, and judges and grand juries only rarely refuse to go forward with the prosecutor's charging decisions.

The prosecutor's broad charging discretion has a long history in the common law, both in England and in the United States. Judges today explain their reluctance to become involved in charging decisions on three grounds: (1) under the separation of powers doctrine, the executive branch has the responsibility to enforce the criminal law; (2) judges are poorly situated to make judgments about allocation of limited prosecutorial resources; and (3) overbroad provisions in criminal codes require selection from among the possible charges that could be filed.

The charging decision is subject to some limits. The constraining rules come primarily from prosecutorial office policies, but they also appear at times in statutes and in a few judicial decisions. Even when charging decisions are not subject to such limits, external influences make them somewhat patterned and predictable. What considerations — both legal and otherwise — direct this prosecutorial decision?

1. Encouraging or Mandating Criminal Charges

Should prosecutors pursue every crime brought to them? Could they? Are there instances in which the substantial discretion typically granted to prosecutors in the United States should be limited or removed?

Many jurisdictions have restricted the power of prosecutors to decline or divert domestic assault cases, because these cases present distinctive challenges for prosecutors. "No-drop" prosecutorial policies combine with other system-wide policy initiatives regarding domestic assaults, including mandatory arrest policies, detention policies, and sentencing policies.

Many courts in the United States have appointed groups of lawyers to explore these specialized issues. One such group, the Missouri Task Force on Gender and Justice (1993), noted that domestic violence is surprisingly widespread: "Domestic violence is found at all socio-economic levels, in all racial and age groups, and among people with all degrees of education. National statistics show that three million to four million American women are battered each year by their husbands or partners." Victims of abuse are often reluctant to testify in criminal cases against their partners, preferring that prosecutors drop the charges. The Missouri Task Force describes the following psychological pattern that applies to many victims of domestic violence:

> [An] abusive relationship is characterized by a cycle of violence containing three phases. During Stage One, tension builds; although the victim is compliant and on good behavior, the batterer exercises increased tension, threats, and control. When the tension reaches a plateau, the relationship enters Stage Two. The batterer becomes unpredictable, highly abusive, and claims a loss of control. The victim feels helpless and trapped and is highly traumatized. After an acute episode of battering comes the remorsefulness of Stage Three, when the batterer is apologetic and attentive, promises to change, and manipulates the victim, causing her to feel guilty and responsible for the behavior of the batterer, yet making her want to believe his insistence that he will change. When tension begins again, the relationship reenters Stage One. Over time, the tension building stages occur more frequently, the battering becomes more acute, and the contrition stage shortens.

Victim advocates report that an abused woman will return to her partner an average of six times before she leaves permanently. A battered spouse is often isolated, having few friends or sources of support. She also might find the criminal process to be daunting and frustrating, particularly if the prosecutor fails to file serious charges in the case or delays its progress. A prosecutor's office can address some of these problems by adopting a "no-drop" policy, mandating prosecution for all domestic violence cases filed. Such a policy takes the victim "off the hook" and insulates her from pressure to drop the case coming from her partner, family, and friends. These policies also emphasize that society at large has an interest in deterring domestic violence. Domestic violence can lead to murder or to injuries that require medical treatment. Children growing up in violent families are more likely to suffer from alcohol or drug abuse, and are more likely to commit violent crimes themselves later in life.

The materials that follow offer several different responses to the special problems of domestic violence. The provisions from Italy, Germany, and West Virginia that close this unit place the issue of mandatory prosecution in a more general context.

■ FLORIDA STATUTES §741.2901

(1) Each state attorney shall develop special units or assign prosecutors to specialize in the prosecution of domestic violence cases, but such specialization need not be an exclusive area of duty assignment. These prosecutors, specializing in domestic violence cases, and their support staff shall receive training in domestic violence issues.

(2) It is the intent of the Legislature that domestic violence be treated as a criminal act rather than a private matter. . . . The state attorney in each circuit shall adopt a pro-prosecution policy for acts of domestic violence. . . . The filing, nonfiling, or diversion of criminal charges, and the prosecution of violations of injunctions for protection against domestic violence by the state attorney, shall be determined by these specialized prosecutors over the objection of the victim, if necessary. . . .

■ WISCONSIN STATUTES §968.075

(7) Each district attorney's office shall develop, adopt and implement written policies encouraging the prosecution of domestic abuse offenses. The policies shall include, but not be limited to, the following:

(a) A policy indicating that a prosecutor's decision not to prosecute a domestic abuse incident should not be based:

1. Solely upon the absence of visible indications of injury or impairment;

2. Upon the victim's consent to any subsequent prosecution of the other person involved in the incident; or

3. Upon the relationship of the persons involved in the incident.

(b) A policy indicating that when any domestic abuse incident is reported to the district attorney's office, including a report [which police officers are required by law to submit after responding to a domestic abuse incident], a charging decision by the district attorney should, absent extraordinary circumstances, be made not later than two weeks after the district attorney has received notice of the incident. . . .

(9) Each district attorney shall submit an annual report to the department of justice listing [t]he number of arrests for domestic abuse incidents in his or her county as compiled and furnished by the law enforcement agencies within the county [and the] number of subsequent prosecutions and convictions of the persons arrested for domestic abuse incidents. . . .

■ PROSECUTION GUIDELINES FOR DULUTH, MINNESOTA

The prosecution guidelines of the Duluth City Attorney's Office were first conceived in 1982. The current guidelines are a result of revisions made in 1989. The guidelines were developed through extensive meetings and discussions between prosecutors in the criminal division of the City Attorney's Office and staff persons of the Domestic Abuse Intervention Project (DAIP). The guidelines are used consistently by prosecutors in Duluth in the prosecution of domestic abuse cases.

These guidelines provide a framework upon which to base decisions. They do not make up a specific set of absolute procedures to fit the myriad possibilities these cases present. The prosecution goals stated below sometimes come into conflict and need to be balanced, based on the circumstances of each case. Because of the complex nature of victims' reluctance to testify against abusers, the prosecutor should not be motivated by a desire to punish the victim in effectuating the goals of this policy.

The goals of prosecution in domestic abuse cases are: 1) to protect the victim from additional acts of violence committed by the defendant, 2) to deter the defendant from committing continued acts of violence against others in the community, [and] 3) to create a general deterrence to battering in the community. In the prosecution of cases, the prosecutor will assist in maximizing the ability of the court to place controls on the abuser and in deterring continued use of violence by following these guidelines:

1) The prosecutor will seek to obtain convictions as an optimum result and will avoid entering into conditional deferrals, except where supported by statute, ordinance, case law, the Minnesota Rules of Criminal Procedure, and rules of conduct for prosecutors.

2) The prosecutor will attempt to proceed with these cases with as few continuances as possible to increase the likelihood of a conviction and to decrease the abuser's opportunity to pressure the victim and to continue to commit violent acts against her/him.

3) Whenever possible, the prosecutor and law enforcement officials will sign the complaint.

4) The prosecutor will subpoena the victim to shield her/him from pressure from the abuser or other parties who do not want the victim to participate in the case as a witness.

5) The prosecutor will approach plea agreements with the intent of expediting the goals of the prosecution, especially that of protecting the victim. Plea agreements will not be used to reduce the prosecutor's case load or the court's calendar. . . .

6) To ensure that victims have access to advocacy, the prosecutor will make a reasonable effort to provide information to the shelter . . . regarding cases charged in which no arrest procedure occurred. . . .

7) The prosecutor will review police investigation reports submitted by the police department in cases which did not result in an arrest but in which police officers believe that prosecution is warranted. . . .

8) The prosecutor shall make available to the shelter and the DAIP information regarding the disposition of all cases and actions taken on police investigation reports. . . .

■ ITALIAN CONSTITUTION ART. 112

The public prosecutor has the duty to exercise criminal proceedings.

■ GERMAN CODE OF CRIMINAL PROCEDURE 152(2)

[The public prosecutor] is required . . . to take action against all judicially punishable . . . acts, to the extent that there is a sufficient factual basis. [Translator: John Langbein]

■ WEST VIRGINIA CODE §7-4-1

It shall be the duty of the prosecuting attorney to attend to the criminal business of the State in the county in which he is elected and qualified, and when he has information of the violation of any penal law committed within such county, he shall institute and prosecute all necessary and proper proceedings against the offender, and may in such case issue or cause to be issued a summons for any witness he may deem material. . . .

Notes

1. *Discretion in filing charges: majority position.* At common law, each local prosecutor had complete discretion to refuse to file charges or to dismiss charges after they had been filed. See Wilson v. Renfroe, 91 So. 2d 857 (Fla. 1956). This remains the dominant position for most crimes in almost all jurisdictions, but there are three exceptions to this general rule. First, for some crimes (including domestic assault and weapons charges) some jurisdictions have implemented mandatory prosecution policies. See Daniel C. Richman, "Project Exile" and the Allocation of Federal Law Enforcement Authority, 43 Ariz. L. Rev. 369 (2001). Second, a few jurisdictions have statutes suggesting that prosecutors have an obligation to prosecute crimes for which they believe probable cause exists. See, e.g., Ala. Code §12-17-184. Third, some jurisdictions provide the state attorney general with varying degrees of supervisory power over all local prosecutors. See Conn. Gen. Stat. §§51-275 to 51-277; Del. Code Ann. tit. 29, §2502.

2. *No-drop policies for domestic abuse cases.* A number of jurisdictions have adopted policies limiting the discretion of prosecutors to decline or dismiss domestic assault and abuse cases, as illustrated by the Duluth, Minnesota, policy. It is difficult to count such provisions because, like most executive branch policies, they are often unpublished and are difficult to obtain. In addition to Florida and Wisconsin, the Minnesota and Utah legislatures have enacted laws encouraging or requiring the development of plans and policies to increase prosecutions and convictions in domestic abuse cases. Many jurisdictions, however, have implemented written or unwritten guidelines about domestic abuse cases in the absence of specific legislative guidance. A growing group of state attorneys general (for instance, in New Jersey and North Carolina) have adopted statewide policies discouraging local prosecutors from dropping domestic violence charges. Policies like the one set out in the Florida statute, encouraging the prosecutor to proceed over the victim's objections, are known as "hard no-drop" policies; the more common policies, focusing on victim support and encouragement, are known as "soft no-drop" policies. Other approaches require the prosecutor to consult with the victim or with other individuals or agencies before dismissing a prosecution. Should the decision be left to the police, or should it depend on the victim's willingness to make an initial complaint?

3. *Assessing no-drop policies: costs, benefits, and options.* Advocates of no-drop policies for domestic violence cases start with the observation that the rate of prosecution for domestic violence complaints remains lower than the rate of

prosecution for other types of complaints. In some communities, less than 10 percent of the misdemeanor complaints are prosecuted. See Jeffrey Fagan, Cessation from Family Violence: Deterrence and Dissuasion, in 11 Crime and Justice: An Annual Review of Research 377 (Lloyd Ohlin & Michael Tonry eds., 1989). Research indicates that no-drop policies do reduce the number of domestic abuse cases dismissed or diverted, although the most comprehensive studies on this question indicate that the effect is rather small. See Robert C. Davis, Barbara E. Smith & Bruce Taylor, Increasing the Proportion of Domestic Violence Arrests That Are Prosecuted: A Natural Experiment in Milwaukee, 2 Criminology & Pub. Pol'y 263 (2003). A study of the Duluth policies set out above showed a substantial reduction in dismissals in domestic abuse cases. Mary Asmus, Tineke Ritmeester & Ellen Pence, Prosecuting Domestic Abuse Cases in Duluth: Developing Effective Prosecution Strategies from Understanding the Dynamics of Abusive Relationships, 15 Hamline L. Rev. 115 (1991).

The impact of no-drop policies on public behavior has not been well established, but partial evidence has emerged. Hard no-drop policies appear to have had a substantial impact on domestic homicides in San Diego. Casey Gwinn & Anne O'Dell, Stopping the Violence: The Role of the Police Officer and the Prosecutor, 20 W. St. U. L. Rev. 297 (1993). What is the impact of no-drop policies on the victim? Is the victim "re-victimized" if she is forced, under threat of jail or other sanctions, to testify? Will no-drop policies encourage more women who have been abused to call police or prosecutors, or will they discourage calls for fear that the victim will again lose control of her situation? See Meg Obenauf, The Isolation Abyss: A Case Against Mandatory Prosecution, 9 UCLA Women's L.J. 263 (1999).

The relationship between no-drop policies and shall-arrest policies is not yet well understood. According to one analysis of arrest and prosecution records in domestic violence cases in Ann Arbor and Ypsilanti, Michigan, a shall-arrest policy leads to more frequent dismissal of charges and to more frequent acquittals after trial. Andrea Lyon, Be Careful What You Wish For: An Examination of Arrest and Prosecution Patterns of Domestic Violence Cases in Two Cities in Michigan, 5 Mich. J. Gender & L. 253 (1999). The same study found that the police arrested women in 12 percent of the cases. If the police had been called to a given residence before, they were more likely to arrest a woman — possibly a form of retaliation against women for staying in an abusive situation.

4. *Prosecutorial ethics and defendants.* No-drop statutes and rules emphasize the fact that prosecutors represent not only the victim but society as well. Prosecutors also have obligations to defendants, including a duty to clear quickly any defendants who are falsely accused. See National District Attorneys Association, National Prosecution Standards §§42, 43 (2d ed. 1991). Do no-drop policies conflict with the prosecutor's ethical obligations to defendants?

5. *Case "attrition."* Arguments for no-drop prosecution policies have been bolstered by statistics suggesting that the substantial majority of domestic abuse cases — perhaps in the range of 50 to 80 percent — are dismissed. The phenomenon of cases "falling out" of the criminal justice process is commonly referred to as case "attrition." One possible reaction to the level of case attrition is to claim that police and prosecutors are failing in their obligation to protect the public. What are other

possible implications of case attritions? A famous study conducted in the 1970s closely examined case attrition for felony cases in New York City. Vera Institute of Justice, Felony Arrests: Their Prosecution and Disposition in New York City's Courts (Malcolm Feeley ed., rev. ed. 1980). It found an unexpectedly high level of prior relationships throughout felony crime categories, and it attributed the bulk of case attrition to the relationships between the parties involved.

> [Criminal] conduct is often the explosive spillover from ruptured personal relations among neighbors, friends and former spouses. Cases in which the victim and defendant were known to each other constituted 83 percent of rape arrests, 69 percent of assault arrests, 36 percent of robbery arrests, and 39 percent of burglary arrests. The reluctance of the complainants in these cases to pursue prosecution (often because they were reconciled with the defendants or in some cases because they feared the defendants) accounted for a larger portion of the high dismissal rate than any other factor.

Does this study suggest that the problems with domestic abuse victims as reliable complainants are also commonplace for other crimes? Does this study suggest reasons to hesitate in implementing a no-drop policy for domestic abuse cases, or does it offer a reason to consider no-drop policies for at least some other crimes? From another perspective, is there a proper ratio of convictions to complaints (or arrests) for most types of crimes?

6. *Specialized units in prosecutors' offices.* Although the criminal code might give prosecutors huge amounts of discretion over whether to file criminal charges, the legislature or the chief prosecutor might structure the prosecutor's office in ways that will encourage the filing of some criminal charges and discourage the filing of others. For instance, the office might have specialized units whose work is easy to monitor. Line items in budgets offer strong incentives to pursue certain charges. Some investigative techniques or charging decisions require special authorization from those high in the prosecutorial hierarchy. As Professor Daniel Richman points out, these office structures establish predictable limits on the reach of substantive criminal laws, even when those criminal laws are drafted very broadly and delegate nominally large powers to the prosecutor. Richman, Federal Criminal Law, Congressional Delegation, and Enforcement Discretion, 46 UCLA L. Rev. 757 (1999).

7. *Discretion in charging in civil law systems.* The civil law tradition that prevails in most legal systems of the world nominally denies the prosecutor discretion in charging. Studies of such systems — especially the Italian, German, and French systems, which have received relatively close examination — suggest that prosecutors, in fact, exercise a substantial degree of discretion in charging. See, e.g., Marco Fabri, Theory Versus Practice of Italian Criminal Justice Reform, 77 Judicature 211 (Jan.-Feb. 1994); Abraham Goldstein & Martin Marcus, The Myth of Judicial Supervision in Three "Inquisitorial" Systems: France, Italy and Germany, 87 Yale L.J. 240 (1977); cf. John Langbein & Lloyd Weinreb, Continental Criminal Procedure: "Myth" and Reality, 87 Yale L.J. 1549 (1978). See also Mark West, Prosecution Review Commissions: Japan's Answer to the Problem of Prosecutorial Discretion, 92 Colum. L. Rev. 684 (1992) (finding that Japanese prosecutors have conviction rates of close to 100 percent because of selectivity in bringing charges).

8. *Mandatory charging statutes in the United States.* The West Virginia Code creates what seems to be a nondiscretionary charging obligation, in sync with the provisions from Italy and Germany. However, prosecutors retain substantial discretion in West Virginia despite the mandatory language of the statute. See State ex rel. Bailey v. Facemire, 413 S.E.2d 183 (W. Va. 1991). The Colorado Criminal Code permits a person to challenge the district attorney's decision not to charge, but the Colorado Supreme Court has warned that the statute does not permit a judge to substitute her judgment for that of the prosecutor. Colo. Rev. Stat. §16-5-209. The court must find that the "district attorney's decision was arbitrary or capricious and without reasonable excuse" before it will step in. Landis v. Farish, 674 P.2d 957, 958 (Colo. 1984). Why are courts so hesitant in both civil and common law systems to review and enforce mandatory charging provisions? Do the realities of justice systems or human nature make mandatory charging provisions unlikely to succeed?

2. Declination and Diversion

The initial question that a prosecutor faces is whether to file criminal charges at all. Many times when the police believe a person has committed a crime, the prosecutor "declines" to file charges. Prosecutors can also "divert" charges from the criminal process by suspending any decision about filing criminal charges while the potential defendant completes some agreed-upon rehabilitative or restitution program. If the person carries out the agreement, the prosecutor declines to file charges (or drops existing charges). If the defendant does not meet the conditions, the prosecutor goes forward with the charges. Are the legal and practical controls on declination and diversion decisions likely to be the same?

a. Declination Policies

Declinations are typically based on a prosecutor's ad hoc discretionary decision that the pursuit of criminal charges is not a good use of the limited resources of the office or is not a proper use of the criminal sanction. Sometimes, however, these discretionary decisions will develop into a pattern which may become formalized in internal office policies or rules. Chief prosecutors will at times create declination policies to control the decisions of the attorneys in the office. On rare occasions, statutes or judicial rulings require the creation of general policies to govern declinations.

The Justice Department produced the first two documents reprinted below in response to two critical reports from the General Accounting Office, a research arm of Congress. The most controversial of those reports was titled "U.S. Attorneys Do Not Prosecute Many Suspected Violators of Federal Law" (February 27, 1978). The third document contains guidelines for charging corporate defendants. The Department revised these guidelines in 2003 and again in 2006, responding to the national focus on corporate crime spawned by the securities and accounting frauds that preceded the downfall of the Enron Corporation.

■ U.S. DEPARTMENT OF JUSTICE,
UNITED STATES ATTORNEYS' WRITTEN GUIDELINES
FOR THE DECLINATION OF ALLEGED VIOLATIONS
OF FEDERAL CRIMINAL LAWS
A Report to the United States Congress (November 1979)

This report examines the written guidelines issued by various United States Attorneys concerning the types of alleged violations of federal criminal laws they will normally decline to prosecute. . . . They are promulgated by United States Attorneys, with the Department's knowledge and encouragement, as a means of formalizing and crystallizing prosecutorial priorities, thereby increasing the effectiveness of limited prosecutorial and investigative resources. Written guidelines represent United States Attorneys' attempts to respond to local demands and circumstances within the context of national law enforcement priorities. They are typically formulated after consideration of Department policies and consultation with federal investigative agencies. . . .

Although written declination guidelines are sometimes referred to as "blanket" declinations, they are, either explicitly or implicitly, made subject to the caveat that unusual or aggravating circumstances should always be considered before any complaint is declined. Decisions to decline cases pursuant to written guidelines are also typically subject to reconsideration, for example, if matters are referred to state and local prosecutors and declined or not pursued by them. In addition, alleged offenses that would otherwise be subject to the guidelines may be prosecuted in clusters at a later date if enough similar offenses accumulate and prosecution would have a significant deterrent impact.

Written declination guidelines are applied with varying degrees of frequency to different categories of federal criminal offenses. [They] are usually expressed in terms of the amount of money or value of property involved, whether the offense appears to be connected with other criminal activity, or other similar factors. The ranges and distributions of declination "cut-off points" vary across districts. For some offenses, the declination cut-off points of the various districts congregate around similar values and factors, while for others, the declination guidelines show considerable variation among districts. . . . Of the 94 United States Attorneys' offices, 83 reported written declination guidelines in some form. The remaining 11 offices reported that they did not have written guidelines, but instead made all declination decisions on a case-by-case basis.

[D]eclination policies are a crucial part of the investigative and prosecutorial system. Investigators and prosecutors alike rely upon such policies to help channel limited law enforcement resources toward their most productive uses. Indeed, since law enforcement resources are limited, it is clearly impossible to investigate and prosecute every alleged criminal violation. Some priorities are required to reduce wastage and to increase the effective deployment of scarce investigative and prosecutorial time and effort. . . .

WRITTEN DECLINATION GUIDELINES CURRENTLY IN USE BY
UNITED STATES ATTORNEYS

The specific written declination guidelines supplied by U.S. Attorneys were applicable to 42 categories of criminal offenses. [F]or a number of categories of offenses, only a few districts have written declination guidelines. For other types of offenses, written guidelines are very frequently in force. The following 11 categories of offenses are the ones most frequently made subject to written guidelines by U.S. Attorneys:

CATEGORIES OF CRIMINAL OFFENSES MOST FREQUENTLY SUBJECT TO
WRITTEN DECLINATION GUIDELINES

Category of Offense	Number of Districts with Written Declination Policies
1. Theft from Interstate Shipment	61
2. Interstate Transportation of Stolen Property	51
3. Bank Fraud and Embezzlement	51
4. Forgery of U.S. Treasury Checks	51
5. Theft of Government Property	48
6. Dyer Act: Interstate Transportation of a Stolen Vehicle	45
7. Crimes on Government Reservations	36
8. Bank Robbery and Related Offenses	33
9. Fraud Against the Government	28
10. Drug Offenses	24
11. Immigration and Naturalization — Illegal Aliens	24

A review of the written declination policies for various offenses indicates a number of general characteristics:

- Written guidelines are typically categorized by the type of criminal offense or the statutory provisions involved. . . .
- Written guidelines are more prevalent for non-violent criminal offenses, though some exist for violent crimes.
- Written guidelines are usually expressed in terms of the gravity of the alleged offense, the history and circumstances of the defendant involved, and the connection of the alleged offense to a pattern of illegal activity.
- Other frequently mentioned declination determining factors include the sufficiency and strength of the Government's evidence and the availability of alternatives to federal prosecution.

The most frequently used measurement of the gravity of the offense is the value of property or loss involved. Using Theft from Interstate Shipment as an example, the value of property involved is used by 52 of 61 districts as a declination-determining factor. . . . Written declination guidelines [use varying] ranges and distributions of declination cut-off points (e.g., monetary value, quantity of drugs) from district to district and from offense to offense. The variation among districts is illustrated again by the policies with respect to Theft from Interstate Shipment. [T]he range of declination cut-off points goes from $100 to $5,000 in property value, with many districts clustered around $500 (15 districts), $1,000 (11 districts), and $5,000 (10 districts). The declination cut-off points for other offenses are differently distributed across ranges of differing size. . . .

■ STATEMENT OF ASSISTANT ATTORNEY GENERAL
PHILIP HEYMANN
Before the Committee on the Judiciary of the United States Senate
(April 23, 1980)

Winning convictions is only half of a prosecutor's job. Equally vital is to sort out
which cases to prosecute and which to decline.

Declinations are the rule, not the exception. Of 171,000 criminal matters
referred to federal prosecutors in Fiscal Year 1976, 108,000 were declined — a declination rate of 63 percent. Many other uncounted declinations are made by the
investigative agencies, in accord with guidelines agreed on with federal prosecutors.

Cases are declined for a variety of reasons. The first is scarcity of resources; the
federal system cannot handle every allegation of a federal criminal violation generated in a country of 200 million people. We try to make our resources have the most
effect by selecting areas where deterrence is especially important, where the federal
interest is the greatest, cases of the greatest culpability and cases where we have a
good chance of winning. To conserve resources, we will often defer to state and local
prosecution, or in appropriate cases of lesser culpability, to administrative discipline
by a suspect's employer or professional association.

The more important reason for declining is lack of merit in the prosecution.
Often, upon investigation, we discover that there simply is no evidence supporting
the initial allegation. In other cases the available evidence turns out to be weak;
there is a vast difference between making an allegation and mustering sufficient
proof to convince 12 jurors beyond a reasonable doubt. Declining a weak case is part
of the prosecutor's duty of fairness, for the burdens of indictment and trial were
never intended to be a form of curbstone punishment to be used without a reasonable chance of securing a conviction. Declining weak cases is also important because
too many losses at trial would seriously weaken the credibility of the Department's
future prosecutions. . . .

Judging what is a weak case is partly a technical evaluation of the evidence —
what witnesses are likely to be available, what they will testify to and with what
credibility. It is also a matter of gauging whether the jury is likely to be impressed
by the wrongfulness of the defendant's conduct. The phenomenon of jury nullification is not unknown in the federal system and elements of a crime such as
"corrupt intent" provide another way for jurors to act on their assessment of the
wrongfulness of conduct. . . .

It is important to have public support and understanding of this part of the job of
prosecutors and investigators. . . . Without pubic understanding of the declination
function, the temptation always will be to prolong investigations that deserve to be
closed, to reveal information that should be kept a confidential part of the investigative
process, even to charge and prosecute where no indictment deserves to be brought.

[T]here are a number of common reasons why the declination function may
have been misunderstood. First, that declinations are so common an occurrence in
law enforcement is a fact frankly unfamiliar to many citizens, legislators and writers.
For instance, when GAO published a study two years ago describing the 63 percent
declination rate common to federal prosecutors, several Committees in the House
and Senate issued a request for a study of "recommendations for improving the
percentage of such [criminal] complaints which are prosecuted by the Department."

Second, it can be hard to keep in clear view the difference between scandalous
behavior and criminal behavior, and the difference between suspecting criminal
behavior and proving it — particularly when a matter is being discussed in the non-

technical confines of a journal or newspaper. When we pursue an investigation, often we find that the suspect behaved badly, may even have acted like a scoundrel, and yet has not committed a federal criminal violation. . . . Sometimes we end up at the conclusion of an investigation strongly suspecting that a person is guilty of a criminal offense, but unable to assemble adequate admissible evidence. Keeping these distinctions in mind is essential in understanding that a declination does not amount to approval or condoning of the examined behavior.

Another cause of potential misunderstanding is that we can't talk very much about our declinations. Investigative information is generally to be presented in court or not at all. By law we can't make grand jury information public, and by ethical practice, to protect privacy, we generally refrain from disclosing other investigative information except in the confines of an indictment and trial or in response to oversight requests from the Congress on closed cases. Certainly, as an agency following the rule of law, we have no business broadcasting our "suspicions" or "hunches" about guilt. So the public is often not given any detailed information on the reason for a declination; they simply learn that an investigation of an obvious scoundrel has been closed. This may contribute to suspicion that the real reason for the declination is political. . . .

I do not make light of the public's responsibility for scrutinizing the actions of law enforcement and prosecutorial agencies. That is a very strong long-term safeguard against abuse. But at the same time, we must avoid creating a system in which the only incentive is to prosecute, no matter how weak or nonexistent the case. . . . When we decline to prosecute unmeritorious cases, it is as much a part of a system of justice as when we prosecute the guilty.

■ FEDERAL PROSECUTION OF BUSINESS ORGANIZATIONS
United States Attorney Manual §9-162 (2006)

II. CHARGING A CORPORATION: GENERAL

A. *General Principle*. Corporations should not be treated leniently because of their artificial nature nor should they be subject to harsher treatment. Vigorous enforcement of the criminal laws against corporate wrongdoers, where appropriate, results in great benefits for law enforcement and the public, particularly in the area of white collar crime. Indicting corporations for wrongdoing enables the government to address and be a force for positive change of corporate culture, alter corporate behavior, and prevent, discover, and punish white collar crime.

B. *Comment*. [Corporations] are likely to take immediate remedial steps when one is indicted for criminal conduct that is pervasive throughout a particular industry, and thus an indictment often provides a unique opportunity for deterrence on a massive scale. . . . Charging a corporation, however, does not mean that individual directors, officers, employees, or shareholders should not also be charged. Prosecution of a corporation is not a substitute for the prosecution of criminally culpable individuals within or without the corporation. . . .

II. CHARGING A CORPORATION: FACTORS TO BE CONSIDERED

A. *General Principle*. Generally, prosecutors apply the same factors in determining whether to charge a corporation as they do with respect to individuals. See

United States Attorneys' Manual §9-27.220, et seq. Thus, the prosecutor must weigh all of the factors normally considered in the sound exercise of prosecutorial judgment: the sufficiency of the evidence; the likelihood of success at trial; the probable deterrent, rehabilitative, and other consequences of conviction; and the adequacy of noncriminal approaches. However, due to the nature of the corporate "person," some additional factors are present. In conducting an investigation, determining whether to bring charges, and negotiating plea agreements, prosecutors should consider the following factors in reaching a decision as to the proper treatment of a corporate target:

1. the nature and seriousness of the offense, including the risk of harm to the public, and applicable policies and priorities, if any, governing the prosecution of corporations for particular categories of crime;
2. the pervasiveness of wrongdoing within the corporation, including the complicity in, or condonation of, the wrongdoing by corporate management;
3. the corporation's history of similar conduct, including prior criminal, civil, and regulatory enforcement actions against it;
4. the corporation's timely and voluntary disclosure of wrongdoing and its willingness to cooperate in the investigation of its agents;
5. the existence and adequacy of the corporation's pre-existing compliance program;
6. the corporation's remedial actions, including any efforts to implement an effective corporate compliance program or to improve an existing one, to replace responsible management, to discipline or terminate wrongdoers, to pay restitution, and to cooperate with the relevant government agencies;
7. collateral consequences, including disproportionate harm to shareholders, pension holders, and employees not proven personally culpable and impact on the public arising from the prosecution;
8. the adequacy of the prosecution of individuals responsible for the corporation's malfeasance; and
9. the adequacy of remedies such as civil or regulatory enforcement actions. . . .

B. *Comment:* In determining whether to charge a corporation, the foregoing factors must be considered. The factors listed in this section are intended to be illustrative of those that should be considered and not a complete or exhaustive list. Some or all of these factors may or may not apply to specific cases, and in some cases one factor may override all others. For example, the nature and seriousness of the offense may be such as to warrant prosecution regardless of the other factors. In most cases, however, no single factor will be dispositive. Further, national law enforcement policies in various enforcement areas may require that more or less weight be given to certain of these factors than to others. Of course, prosecutors must exercise their judgment in applying and balancing these factors and this process does not mandate a particular result. . . .

VII. CHARGING A CORPORATION: THE VALUE OF COOPERATION

A. *General Principle:* In determining whether to charge a corporation, that corporation's timely and voluntary disclosure of wrongdoing and its cooperation with the government's investigation may be relevant factors. In gauging the extent of the corporation's cooperation, the prosecutor may consider, among other things, whether the corporation made a voluntary and timely disclosure, and the corporation's willingness to provide relevant evidence and to identify the culprits within the corporation, including senior executives.

B. *Comment*: In investigating wrongdoing by or within a corporation, a prosecutor is likely to encounter several obstacles resulting from the nature of the corporation itself. It will often be difficult to determine which individual took which action on behalf of the corporation. Lines of authority and responsibility may be shared among operating divisions or departments, and records and personnel may be spread throughout the United States or even among several countries. Where the criminal conduct continued over an extended period of time, the culpable or knowledgeable personnel may have been promoted, transferred, or fired, or they may have quit or retired. Accordingly, a corporation's cooperation may be critical in identifying the culprits and locating relevant evidence. . . .

In some circumstances, granting a corporation immunity or amnesty or pretrial diversion may be considered in the course of the government's investigation. In such circumstances, prosecutors should refer to the principles governing non-prosecution agreements generally. See United States Attorneys Manual §§9-27.600-650. These principles permit a non-prosecution agreement in exchange for cooperation when a corporation's "timely cooperation appears to be necessary to the public interest and other means of obtaining the desired cooperation are unavailable or would not be effective." . . .

Waiver of attorney-client and work product protections is not a prerequisite to a finding that a company has cooperated in the government's investigation. However, a company's disclosure of privileged information may permit the government to expedite its investigation. In addition, the disclosure of privileged information may be critical in enabling the government to evaluate the accuracy and completeness of the company's voluntary disclosure.

Prosecutors may only request waiver of attorney-client or work product protections when there is a legitimate need for the privileged information to fulfill their law enforcement obligations. A legitimate need for the information is not established by concluding it is merely desirable or convenient to obtain privileged information. . . . Whether there is a legitimate need depends upon: (1) the likelihood and degree to which the privileged information will benefit the government's investigation; (2) whether the information sought can be obtained in a timely and complete fashion by using alternative means that do not require waiver; (3) the completeness of the voluntary disclosure already provided; and (4) the collateral consequences to a corporation of a waiver.

If a legitimate need exists, prosecutors should seek the least intrusive waiver necessary to conduct a complete and thorough investigation, and should follow a step-by-step approach to requesting information. Prosecutors should first request purely factual information, which may or may not be privileged, relating to the underlying misconduct ("Category I"). Examples of Category I information could include, without limitation, copies of key documents, witness statements, or purely factual interview memoranda regarding the underlying misconduct, organization charts created by company counsel, factual chronologies, factual summaries, or reports (or portions thereof) containing investigative facts documented by counsel. Before requesting that a corporation waive the attorney-client or work product protections for Category I information, prosecutors must obtain written authorization from the United States Attorney who must provide a copy of the request to, and consult with, the Assistant Attorney General for the Criminal Division before granting or denying the request. . . .

Only if the purely factual information provides an incomplete basis to conduct a thorough investigation should prosecutors then request that the corporation provide attorney-client communications or non-factual attorney work product ("Category II"). This information includes legal advice given to the corporation before, during, and after the underlying misconduct occurred. This category of privileged information might include the production of attorney notes, memoranda or reports (or portions thereof) containing counsel's mental impressions and conclusions, legal determinations reached as a result of an internal investigation, or legal advice given to the corporation.

Prosecutors are cautioned that Category II information should only be sought in rare circumstances. Before requesting that a corporation waive the attorney-client or work product protections for Category II information, the United States Attorney must obtain written authorization from the Deputy Attorney General. . . .

If a corporation declines to provide a waiver for Category II information after a written request from the United States Attorney, prosecutors must not consider this declination against the corporation in making a charging decision. Prosecutors may always favorably consider a corporation's acquiescence to the government's waiver request in determining whether a corporation has cooperated in the government's investigation. . . .

Another factor to be weighed by the prosecutor is whether the corporation appears to be protecting its culpable employees and agents. Thus, while cases will differ depending on the circumstances, a corporation's promise of support to culpable employees and agents, e.g., through retaining the employees without sanction for their misconduct or through providing information to the employees about the government's investigation pursuant to a joint defense agreement, may be considered by the prosecutor in weighing the extent and value of a corporation's cooperation.

Prosecutors generally should not take into account whether a corporation is advancing attorneys' fees to employees or agents under investigation and indictment. Many state indemnification statutes grant corporations the power to advance the legal fees of officers under investigation prior to a formal determination of guilt. As a consequence, many corporations enter into contractual obligations to advance attorneys' fees. . . .

Another factor to be weighed by the prosecutor is whether the corporation, while purporting to cooperate, has engaged in conduct intended to impede the investigation (whether or not rising to the level of criminal obstruction). Examples of such conduct include: overly broad assertions of corporate representation of employees or former employees; overly broad or frivolous assertions of privilege to withhold the disclosure of relevant, non-privileged documents; inappropriate directions to employees or their counsel, such as directions not to cooperate openly and fully with the investigation including, for example, the direction to decline to be interviewed; making presentations or submissions that contain misleading assertions or omissions; incomplete or delayed production of records; and failure to promptly disclose illegal conduct known to the corporation.

Finally, a corporation's offer of cooperation does not automatically entitle it to immunity from prosecution. A corporation should not be able to escape liability merely by offering up its directors, officers, employees, or agents as in lieu of its own prosecution. . . .

IX. CHARGING A CORPORATION: RESTITUTION AND REMEDIATION

A. *General Principle.* Although neither a corporation nor an individual target may avoid prosecution merely by paying a sum of money, a prosecutor may consider the corporation's willingness to make restitution and steps already taken to do so. A prosecutor may also consider other remedial actions, such as implementing an effective corporate compliance program, improving an existing compliance program, and disciplining wrongdoers, in determining whether to charge the corporation.

B. *Comment*: . . . A corporation's response to misconduct says much about its willingness to ensure that such misconduct does not recur. Thus, corporations that fully recognize the seriousness of their misconduct and accept responsibility for it should be taking steps to implement the personnel, operational, and organizational changes necessary to establish an awareness among employees that criminal conduct will not be tolerated. Among the factors prosecutors should consider and weigh are whether the corporation appropriately disciplined the wrongdoers and disclosed information concerning their illegal conduct to the government. . . .

■ REVISED CODE OF WASHINGTON §9.94A.411(1)

STANDARD

A prosecuting attorney may decline to prosecute, even though technically sufficient evidence to prosecute exists, in situations where prosecution would serve no public purpose, would defeat the underlying purpose of the law in question or would result in decreased respect for the law.

GUIDELINE/COMMENTARY

. . . The following are examples of reasons not to prosecute which could satisfy the standard.

(a) Contrary to Legislative Intent — It may be proper to decline to charge where the application of criminal sanctions would be clearly contrary to the intent of the legislature in enacting the particular statute.

(b) Antiquated Statute — It may be proper to decline to charge where the statute in question is antiquated in that: (i) it has not been enforced for many years; and (ii) most members of society act as if it were no longer in existence; and (iii) it serves no deterrent or protective purpose in today's society; and (iv) the statute has not been recently reconsidered by the legislature. This reason is not to be construed as the basis for declining cases because the law in question is unpopular or because it is difficult to enforce.

(c) De Minimus Violation — It may be proper to decline to charge where the violation of law is only technical or insubstantial and where no public interest or deterrent purpose would be served by prosecution.

(d) Confinement on Other Charges — It may be proper to decline to charge because the accused has been sentenced on another charge to a lengthy period of confinement; and (i) conviction of the new offense would not merit any additional direct or collateral punishment; (ii) the new offense is either a misdemeanor or a felony which is not particularly aggravated; and (iii) conviction of the new offense would not serve any significant deterrent purpose.

(e) Pending Conviction on Another Charge — It may be proper to decline to charge because the accused is facing a pending prosecution in the same or another county; and (i) conviction of the new offense would not merit any additional direct or collateral punishment; (ii) conviction in the pending prosecution is imminent; (iii) the new offense is either a misdemeanor or a felony which is not particularly aggravated; and (iv) conviction of the new offense would not serve any significant deterrent purpose.

(f) High Disproportionate Cost of Prosecution — It may be proper to decline to charge where the cost of locating or transporting, or the burden on, prosecution witnesses is highly disproportionate to the importance of prosecuting the offense in question. This reason should be limited to minor cases and should not be relied upon in serious cases.

(g) Improper Motives of Complainant — It may be proper to decline charges because the motives of the complainant are improper and prosecution would serve no public purpose, would defeat the underlying purpose of the law in question or would result in decreased respect for the law.

(h) Immunity — It may be proper to decline to charge where immunity is to be given to an accused in order to prosecute another where the accused's information or testimony will reasonably lead to the conviction of others who are responsible for more serious criminal conduct or who represent a greater danger to the public interest.

(i) Victim Request — It may be proper to decline to charge because the victim requests that no criminal charges be filed and the case involves the following crimes or situations: (i) assault cases where the victim has suffered little or no injury; (ii) crimes against property, not involving violence, where no major loss was suffered; (iii) where doing so would not jeopardize the safety of society. Care should be taken to insure that the victim's request is freely made and is not the product of threats or pressure by the accused. . . . The prosecutor is encouraged to notify the victim, when practical, and the law enforcement personnel, of the decision not to prosecute.

Notes

1. *Number of declinations.* The precise number of criminal matters that are declined for prosecution each year is hard to pin down. In the federal system, where the best data are available, U.S. Attorneys' offices decline to prosecute a large proportion of criminal matters they receive. In 2003, federal prosecutors filed charges in district court in 62 percent of the "criminal matters" referred to them for investigation or prosecution. They declined to prosecute 26 percent of the matters and referred 12 percent of the suspects to federal magistrates (who handle misdemeanors and charges that are ultimately dismissed and prosecuted instead in state court). Bureau of Justice Statistics, Compendium of Federal Justice Statistics, 2003, table 2.2 (2005). This estimate of the number of declinations did not include minor matters which occupied less than one hour of a prosecutor's time. If these were included in the overall base of cases, the percentage of declinations would rise sharply. For instance, in a classic 1980 study of declinations in the federal system, Richard Frase calculated that U.S. Attorneys nationwide filed criminal cases in 20 percent to 23.4 percent of the "criminal matters received" during 1974-1978. The district Frase studied most closely, the Northern District of Illinois, prosecuted about 17 percent of all matters received and 21 percent of all suspects. See Richard Frase, The Decision to File Federal

Criminal Charges: A Quantitative Study of Prosecutorial Discretion, 47 U. Chi. L. Rev. 246 (1980).

The level of declinations varies a good deal depending on the offense involved. In 2003, federal prosecutors declined to file charges in 21 percent of the robbery cases they received, 18 percent of the drug cases received, 41 percent of the fraud cases, 6 percent of the immigration cases, and 92 percent of the civil rights cases.

The number of declinations in the typical state system also makes up a significant proportion of the criminal matters that a prosecutor's office handles. Among felony defendants in large urban counties in 2002, charges were dismissed for 24 percent of all defendants initially charged with a felony. Bureau of Justice Statistics, Felony Defendants in Large Urban Counties, 2002, table 23 (February 2006, NCJ 210818). Of course, the dismissal rate does not capture the total number of *arrests* declined for prosecution. Earlier studies have estimated that more than 40 percent of all felony arrests are declined for prosecution, while a similarly large group of felony arrestees are ultimately charged with misdemeanors. See Vera Institute of Justice, Felony Arrests: Their Prosecution and Disposition in New York City's Courts (Malcolm Feeley ed., rev. ed. 1980). See also Donald McIntyre & David Lippmann, Prosecutors and Early Disposition of Felony Cases, 56 A.B.A. J. 1154 (1970) (estimating a declination rate of 50 percent of felony arrests for Los Angeles; 30 percent in Detroit; 25 percent in Houston; and virtually no declinations reported in Chicago, Brooklyn, or Baltimore, but prosecutors in each of these cities screen out large proportions of arrests at preliminary judicial hearing).

2. *Reasons for declinations.* The reasons individual prosecutors decline to file charges are even more elusive than the number of declinations they make. Over the years, several scholars, commissions, and associations have described some common reasons for individual prosecutors to choose not to file criminal charges in a particular case. Frank Miller offered one such typology of reasons prosecutors decline charges, listing attitude of the victim, cost to the system, undue harm to the suspect, adequacy of alternative procedures, and willingness of the suspect to cooperate in achieving other enforcement goals. See Miller, Prosecution: The Decision to Charge a Suspect with a Crime (1969). The National District Attorneys Association, in its National Prosecution Standards, §42.3 (2d ed. 1991), lists several possible grounds for a prosecutor to decline a criminal case, including "doubt as to the accused's guilt," "possible improper motives of a victim or witness," "undue hardship caused to the accused," "the expressed desire of an accused to release potential civil claims against victims, witnesses, law enforcement agencies and their personnel, and the prosecutor and his personnel," and "any mitigating circumstances." How do these reasons compare to those in the Washington statute reprinted above?

How often do prosecutors actually rely on these plausible reasons for declination? In 2003, federal prosecutors gave the following reasons for their declinations: no crime committed (22 percent of the declinations), matter handled in other prosecutions (21 percent), pretrial diversion (1.6 percent), weak evidence (22 percent), minimal federal interest (3.6 percent), U.S. Attorney policy (2.7 percent), lack of resources (5.7 percent), and several others. What trends would you expect to find over time in the mix of reasons that federal prosecutors give for their declinations? See Michael Edmund O'Neill, Understanding Federal Prosecutorial Declinations: An Empirical Analysis of Predicative Factors, 41 Am. Crim. L. Rev. 1439 (2004).

Once again, data for state systems are sketchier. One older study pointed to insufficient evidence connecting the suspect to the alleged crime as the leading reason for rejections of felony charges in Los Angeles County. Peter Greenwood et al., Prosecution of Adult Felony Defendants in Los Angeles County: A Policy Perspective 66-68 (1973) (overall rejection rate of 45 percent of complaints).

3. *Declination policies versus ad hoc judgments.* Although most declination decisions fall within the discretion of the individual prosecutor, many offices develop written policies to govern the declination decision for at least some types of cases. For example, federal prosecutors in Southern California have determined, in evaluating possible immigration crimes, that "criminal charges shall not be filed in cases where the defendant makes an unaggravated illegal entry and has no prior criminal record." What do you suppose would be the purpose of such a policy? Why would the U.S. Department of Justice create written guidelines to govern the charging of corporate entities in particular?

The National District Attorneys Association, in its National Prosecution Standards (2d ed. 1991), declares, "The decision to initiate or pursue criminal charges should be within the discretion of the prosecutor . . . and whether the screening takes place before or after formal charging, it should be pursuant to the prosecutor's established guidelines." In speaking of "discretion" and "guidelines," is this standard sending an inconsistent message? The Washington statute reprinted above is one of the few legislative efforts to establish criteria for declination decisions. Is a legislature likely to produce declination guidelines that look different from guidelines that a prosecutor's office develops for its own use? What do you imagine is the attitude of Washington prosecutors about the declination statute? The same Washington statute provides that "crimes against persons will be filed if sufficient admissible evidence exists, which, when considered with the most plausible, reasonably foreseeable defense that could be raised under the evidence, would justify conviction by a reasonable and objective fact-finder." See Wash. Rev. Stat. 9.94A.411(2). How can this provision be reconciled with the declination provision printed in the text?

4. *Judicial review of declinations and decisions to file charges.* Judges might overturn a prosecutor's decision to file charges or not to file charges, but only in rare circumstances. See State v. Foss, 556 N.W.2d 540 (Minn. 1996) (acknowledging power of trial court to stay adjudication of guilt over prosecutor's objection in "special circumstances"; such circumstances existed in earlier case involving consensual sex with 14-year-old when victim and her mother did not desire criminal prosecution, but no special circumstances exist in typical misdemeanor assault case). Although a strong minority of states have statutes explicitly authorizing a judge to order a prosecutor to file and prosecute criminal charges, judges have interpreted these statutes to allow judicial review only under very deferential standards of review. See Colo. Rev. Stat. §16-5-209 (judge may order prosecution if refusal to prosecute was "arbitrary or capricious and without reasonable excuse"); Tooley v. District Court, 549 P.2d 772 (Colo. 1976) (court may not reverse prosecutor's decision absent "clear and convincing evidence" that the decision was arbitrary or capricious). Legislatures have been more willing to give judges power to review a prosecutor's *refusal* to prosecute than a prosecutor's decision to *file* charges. Why?

If an individual prosecutor appears to be violating a known office policy by filing criminal charges when the policy calls for declination, can the defendant convince a court to enforce the policy? See United States v. Caceres, 440 U.S. 741 (1979) (defendant may not enforce internal rules of law enforcement agency, such as IRS rule requiring internal approval before eavesdropping). Would the result depend on whether the policy includes an explicit disclaimer that it does not create any enforceable rights? On whether it is written? Are written policies a meaningful limit on prosecutorial choices if defendants cannot enforce them? See Kenneth Culp Davis, Discretionary Justice (1969); Gerard E. Lynch, Our Administrative System of Criminal Justice, 66 Fordham L. Rev. 2117 (1998).

5. *Public reasons.* Most larger prosecutors' offices require the prosecutor who declines to file charges to give reasons in some written form in the case file. What purposes might the requirement of written reasons serve? If, as chief prosecutor, you supervised an office that had an explicit declination policy, would you reveal to the public the terms of your policy? A few states (but a growing number) have statutes requiring a prosecutor to explain in writing each refusal to prosecute a case. See Mich. Stat. §767.41; Neb. Rev. Stat. §29-1606.

6. *Consultation before charging.* A declination policy is only one method of discouraging the use of criminal charges for specific types of cases. Prosecutors' offices will sometimes adopt policies requiring the "line" prosecutors to consult with supervisors or others in the office with special expertise before filing criminal charges under certain statutes. See U.S. Attorneys' Manual §9-2.400 (requiring line prosecutor to consult with supervisors before filing charges against member of news media or for desecration of flag, draft evasion, obscenity, RICO, and other offenses). Is it possible to predict which offenses are most likely to be singled out for a prior consultation requirement?

7. *Dismissals after charges are filed.* At English common law, the power of the prosecutor to dismiss a charge — to enter a plea of *nolle prosequi*—was every bit as broad as the discretion to file charges initially. An illustration of this power appears in the following conversation between an advocate, Lacy, and Chief Justice John Holt in seventeenth-century England. Lacy asked the chief justice to dismiss seditious libel charges against other members of his religious sect:

Lacy: I come to you, a prophet from the Lord God, who has sent me to thee, and would have thee grant a nolle prosequi for John Atkins, His servant, whom thou hast cast into prison.

Chief Justice Holt: Thou art a false prophet, and a lying knave. If the Lord God had sent thee, it would have been to the attorney general, for He knows that it belongeth not to the Chief Justice to grant a nolle prosequi; but I, as Chief Justice, can grant a warrant to commit thee to bear him company.

See 2 Francis Wharton, A Treatise on Criminal Procedure §1310 (10th ed. 1918). This common-law rule on dismissals took hold in the United States and was especially useful in systems that allowed private prosecutors to file charges without consulting the public prosecutor. Today, however, a strong majority of jurisdictions (more than 30) give prosecutors less control over dismissals than over the initial decision whether to charge. They require the prosecutor to state reasons and obtain the leave of the court before dismissing charges. See Mich. Comp. Laws §767.29; Fed. R. Crim. P. 48(a) (indictment, information or complaint can be dismissed "with leave of court"). For reasons you can well imagine, judges rarely deny a prosecutor's motion to dismiss charges.

8. *Prosecutorial policy and office size.* The size and structure of the prosecutor's office determines to some extent whether explicit declination policies will be in place and what topics the policies will address. As of 2001, the chief prosecutors in 47 of the 50 states were elected locally, most for four-year terms. Full-time prosecutors' offices in jurisdictions with large populations (one million persons or more) had a median of 151 assistant prosecutors; nationwide, the median prosecutor's office employed eight assistant prosecutors. Bureau of Justice Statistics, Prosecutors in State Courts, 2001 (May 2002, NCJ 193441). Prosecutors in the state system are decentralized to a great extent. In a few states, however, the state attorney general has some supervisory control over local prosecutorial decisions. See Conn. Gen. Stat. Ann. §§51-275 to 51-277. What effects will a decentralized structure have on the declination policies to be adopted or followed in prosecutors' offices?

9. *Corporations and declinations.* In the 2006 Department of Justice policy excerpted above, known as the "McNulty Memo," the leadership of the Department instructed line prosecutors around the country about the decision whether to charge a corporate entity with a crime. Do the relevant factors discussed in the DOJ policy on corporations differ from the factors relevant for deciding whether to charge an individual? Public debate about the corporate charging guidelines centered on the impact of those guidelines on the attorney-client relationship for the corporations and individuals under investigation. Earlier versions of this DOJ policy placed more explicit value on the waiver of attorney-client privilege by the corporation. Business leaders and the bar associations lobbied successfully for changes to the policy, making it less costly for corporations to assert their privileges or to retain counsel for their employees. Could individual defendants outside the corporate or white-collar context make similar arguments about the impact of cooperation on the prosecutor's charging decision?

b. Diversion of Defendants

Prosecutors file charges in some cases and decline to charge in others, but they have other options as well. The prosecutor may, for example, "divert" the suspect from the criminal justice system into an alternative program for rehabilitation and restitution. Diversion occurs in some states before charges are ever filed: The prosecutor agrees to withhold any criminal charges, provided the suspect successfully completes the designated program or other conditions that the prosecutor specifies. Diversion can also take place after charges are filed, in which case the prosecution is suspended while the defendant completes the diversion program. If the defendant succeeds, the prosecutor dismisses the criminal charges. The archetypal "diversion" case involves a first-time offender who has committed a nonviolent crime. Some diversion programs explicitly focus on classes of offenders, such as nonviolent drug offenders.

As you read the following materials, consider whether the prosecutor is properly situated to identify "good" cases for diversion and to set the proper conditions for a successful diversion program. Will a prosecutor systematically place requirements on a defendant that a judge at sentencing would not? Will defendants respond differently to diversion programs than they would to requirements imposed at sentencing after a conviction?

■ MONTANA CODE §46-16-130

(1) (a) Prior to the filing of a charge, the prosecutor and a defendant who has counsel or who has voluntarily waived counsel may agree to the deferral of a prosecution for a specified period of time based on one or more of the following conditions:

(i) that the defendant may not commit any offense;

(ii) that the defendant may not engage in specified activities, conduct, and associations bearing a relationship to the conduct upon which the charge against the defendant is based;

(iii) that the defendant shall participate in a supervised rehabilitation program, which may include treatment, counseling, training, or education;

(iv) that the defendant shall make restitution in a specified manner for harm or loss caused by the offense; or

(v) any other reasonable conditions.

(b) The agreement must be in writing, must be signed by the parties, and must state that the defendant waives the right to speedy trial for the period of deferral. The agreement may include stipulations concerning the admissibility of evidence, specified testimony, or dispositions if the deferral of the prosecution is terminated and there is a trial on the charge.

(c) The prosecution must be deferred for the period specified in the agreement unless there has been a violation of its terms.

(d) The agreement must be terminated and the prosecution automatically dismissed with prejudice upon expiration and compliance with the terms of the agreement. . . .

(3) After a charge has been filed, a deferral of prosecution may be entered into only with the approval of the court.

(4) A prosecution for a violation of [laws that prohibit driving while impaired] may not be deferred.

MONTANA COMMISSION ON CRIMINAL PROCEDURE: COMMENTS

A provision regulating pretrial diversion, sometimes called deferred prosecution, is new to Montana, although the practice has been statutorily recognized since at least 1979. The Commission believed a pretrial diversion provision was necessary because prosecutors have long employed diversion on an informal, individual basis by deferring prosecution if, for example, the accused agreed to undergo rehabilitative treatment. Since the President's Commission on Law Enforcement and Administration of Justice recommended such programs in its 1967 report, many states have formalized diversion by statute or court rule. Pretrial diversionary programs are premised on the belief that it is not always necessary and, in fact, may often be detrimental to pursue formal courtroom prosecution for every criminal violation. In most situations, the criminal prosecution is suspended subject to the defendant's consent to treatment, rehabilitation, restitution, or other noncriminal or nonpunitive alternatives.

The statute contemplates that the decision to divert lies with the prosecutor in an exercise of his powers and is not ordinarily subject to judicial review. This conforms with existing practice in that several Montana County Attorneys conduct formal diversion programs, yet no Montana case has been found that discusses the practice. However, some litigation has occurred in other jurisdictions. . . .

■ STATE v. WALLACE BAYNES
690 A.2d 594 (N.J. 1997)

GARIBALDI, J.

The Court again addresses whether a trial court correctly reversed a prosecutor's rejection of a defendant's admission into a Pretrial Intervention (PTI) Program. In particular, we must determine whether the Monmouth County prosecutor's decision, based on his stated policy of denying admission into PTI to any defendant charged with possession of a controlled dangerous substance within 1,000 feet of a school zone, constitutes a "patent and gross abuse of discretion."

The facts of this case are undisputed. On September 28, 1994, at approximately 5:30 P.M., defendant, Wallace Baynes, purchased .44 grams of heroin from Jose Morales. The purchase was made outside of the Rainbow Liquor Store, [which was under police surveillance at the time.] The location of the purchase occurred approximately 900 feet from the Garfield Primary School. Baynes was arrested and subsequently indicted [for possession of heroin within 1,000 feet of a school zone]. Drug possession is a third-degree crime.

Defendant claims that he purchased the heroin because he was having difficulty dealing with the serious illness of his mother, who has since passed away. At the time of his application for admission into the Monmouth County Pretrial Intervention Program, defendant was a 43-year-old gainfully employed father of one, residing with and supporting his elderly mother and his 17-year-old son. He had completed two years of college. According to defendant, he had been employed by the same employer for the previous nine years. . . .

The Director of the PTI program accepted Baynes's application for admission. Further, the head of the narcotics team that arrested Baynes did not object to Baynes's diversion. The prosecutor, however, advised Baynes in an April 27, 1995, memorandum that his PTI application was rejected because of that prosecutor's acknowledged policy to deny PTI admission to defendants charged with "school zone offenses," including those involving possession of controlled dangerous substances (CDS) for personal use.

On June 23, 1995, a hearing was held before the trial court for reconsideration of the prosecutor's decision. In reversing the prosecutor's decision and referring the matter back to the prosecutor for reconsideration, the court observed that "the prosecutor [had failed] to consider all the relevant factors" in this case. The decision to refer the matter back to the prosecutor follows our past decisions, finding remand to the prosecutor useful where "the prosecutorial decision was based upon a consideration of inappropriate factors or not premised upon a consideration of all relevant factors. . . ." State v. Bender, 402 A.2d 217 (N.J. 1979).

In a letter to the trial court, the prosecutor advised the court that he had reviewed all the information again and continued to oppose defendant's diversion into PTI. After a second hearing appealing that decision, the trial court ordered Baynes's admission into the PTI program over the prosecutor's objection, stating that [the prosecutor's decision was] "so clearly unreasonable that it shocks the judicial conscience, subverts the goals of PTI, and constitutes a clear error of judgment because it could not have reasonably been made upon a fair weighing of all relevant factors." . . .

PTI is a diversionary program through which certain offenders are able to avoid criminal prosecution by receiving early rehabilitative services expected to deter future criminal behavior. [The Supreme Court initially established PTI by Rule 3:28 in 1970, creating] the vocational-service pretrial intervention program operated by the Newark Defendants Employment Project. By October 1976, the Court had approved programs for 12 counties. In 1979, the Legislature authorized a state-wide PTI program as part of the Criminal Code of Justice. The Code provisions generally mirrored the procedures and guidelines previously established under Rule 3:28.

Admission into PTI is based on a recommendation by the criminal division manager, as Director of the PTI Program, with the consent of the prosecutor. The Court has provided criteria for making PTI decisions in its Guidelines for Operation of Pretrial Intervention. Guidelines 1, 2, 3, and 8 are particularly relevant to this case. Guideline 1 sets forth the purposes of PTI:

(1) to enable defendants to avoid ordinary prosecution by receiving early rehabilitative services expected to deter future criminal behavior; (2) to provide defendants who might be harmed by the imposition of criminal sanctions with an alternative to prosecution expected to deter criminal conduct; (3) to avoid burdensome prosecutions for "victimless" offenses; (4) to relieve overburdened criminal calendars so that resources can be expended on more serious criminal matters; and (5) to deter future criminal behavior of PTI participants.

Guideline 2 provides that "[a]ny defendant accused of crime shall be eligible for admission into a PTI program." Thus, . . . PTI decisions are primarily individualistic in nature and a prosecutor must consider an individual defendant's features that bear on his or her amenability to rehabilitation.

Guideline 3 refers to and supplements N.J.S.A. 2C:43-12(e), which presents 17 criteria that prosecutors and criminal division managers are to consider in formulating their PTI recommendation. Guideline 3(i) clarifies how "the nature of the offense" is to be used in assessing a defendant's PTI eligibility. That guideline explains that although all defendants are eligible for enrollment in a PTI program, the nature of the crime is only one factor to be considered. Moreover, Guideline 3(i) states that there is a presumption against acceptance into a program when "the crime was (1) part of organized criminal activity; or (2) part of a continuing criminal business or enterprise; or (3) deliberately committed with violence or threat of violence against another person; or (4) a breach of the public trust." A presumption against acceptance into a PTI program also exists when the defendant is "charged with a first or second degree offense or sale or dispensing of Schedule I or II narcotic drugs [and is] not drug dependent." Finally, Guideline 8 requires a judge, prosecutor, or criminal division manager, making a PTI decision, to provide the defendant with a statement of reasons justifying the decision, as well as demonstrating that all of the facts have been considered. That statement may not simply parrot the language of relevant statutes, rules, and guidelines. Additionally, the statement cannot be vague; it must be sufficiently specific to provide the defendant with an opportunity to demonstrate that the reasons are unfounded.

The decision to divert a defendant from criminal prosecution implicates both judicial and prosecutorial functions. . . . Judicial review of the prosecutor's PTI decision is strictly limited, but necessary because "PTI involves far more than merely an exercise of the charging function." State v. Leonardis, 375 A.2d 607 (N.J. 1977). "It is one thing not to charge and let the accused go totally free, but it may be quite another to withhold a charge, and hence not to invoke the jurisdiction of the court system, on condition that an uncharged, untried, unconvicted person submit to a correctional program."

[Our expectation is] that a prosecutor's decision to reject a PTI applicant will rarely be overturned. A prosecutor's decision is to be afforded great deference. In fact, the level of deference which is required is so high that it has been categorized as "enhanced deference" or "extra deference." Absent evidence to the contrary, a reviewing court must assume that all relevant factors were considered by the prosecutor's office. That presumption makes it difficult to reverse a prosecutor's decision. A reviewing court may order a defendant into PTI over the prosecutor's objection, only if the defendant can clearly and convincingly establish that the prosecutor's refusal to sanction admission into the program was based on a patent and gross abuse of discretion. In State v. Bender, 402 A.2d 217, 222 (N.J. 1979), the Court defined the "patent and gross abuse of discretion" standard:

> Ordinarily, an abuse of discretion will be manifest if defendant can show that a prosecutorial veto (a) was not premised upon a consideration of all relevant factors, (b) was based upon a consideration of irrelevant or inappropriate factors, or (c) amounted to a clear error in judgment. In order for such an abuse of discretion to rise to the level of "patent and gross," it must further be shown that the prosecutorial error complained of will clearly subvert the goals underlying Pretrial Intervention. . . .

In this case, the prosecutor's rejection of Baynes's PTI application falls under categories (a) and (c), as set forth in *Bender*. First, the prosecutor's rejection in this case was not based on all of the relevant factors. After the initial remand for reconsideration by the trial court, the prosecutor claimed to have considered all of the relevant factors. We do not doubt his veracity, in the sense that he re-read the application and the police report. He could not, however, have considered all relevant factors, because the per se rule under which he made his decision had effectively denied Baynes's application from the moment Baynes was charged with possession of CDS in a school zone.

By their nature, per se rules require prosecutors to disregard relevant factors, contrary to the guidelines, and when a defendant demonstrates that a prosecutor has relied on such a rule, the presumption that the prosecutor has considered all relevant facts is overcome. As a result, the June 23, 1995, memorandum denying Baynes's application was merely an impermissible "parrot-like" recitation of the language of relevant statutes, rules, and guidelines.

The State correctly points out that prosecutors may rely on the nature of the offense, in "appropriate circumstances," as the sole basis for making PTI decisions. Although caselaw supports the proposition that certain offensive conduct can outweigh all other factors considered, no court has indicated that possession of CDS for personal use is an "appropriate circumstance" that alone can justify denying PTI.

Where courts have found a prosecutor's reliance on the nature of the offense charged to be an appropriate basis for a PTI decision, the crime was of a more serious nature than possession of CDS for personal use. In State v. Wallace, 684 A.2d 1355 (N.J. 1996), for example, . . . Wallace had entered his former girlfriend's house with a loaded gun and threatened to kill her. He was charged with second-degree possession of a firearm for an unlawful purpose and third-degree making of terroristic threats. In supporting her decision, . . . the prosecutor primarily relied on a prosecutorial guideline that discourages PTI for those defendants charged with either first- or second-degree offenses [or criminal acts committed with violence].

Under the caselaw of this jurisdiction, it is, therefore, appropriate for prosecutors to base their rejections solely on the nature of an offense for which the Guidelines express a presumption against admission. . . . Our prior opinions indicate that possession of CDS for personal consumption does not fall into [this category].

In addition to satisfying the first category of abuse of discretion set forth in *Bender*, the prosecutor's veto also fulfills the third, i.e., it was a "clear error in judgment." A prosecutor will be found to have made a "clear error in judgment," when the decision was premised on appropriate factors and rationally explained but is contrary to the predominate views of others responsible for the administration of justice. Although a reviewing court cannot substitute its own judgment for that of the prosecutor, others responsible for the administration of justice in New Jersey hold contrary views of how first-time offenders charged with possession of drugs for personal use should, as a class, be treated.

The 1987 Comprehensive Drug Reform Act simply does not indicate the intent prescribed to it by the Monmouth County prosecutor. [T]he Legislature created a new crime, covering possession with intent to distribute or actual distribution of drugs in a school zone. Under that section, proof that the offensive conduct occurred within a school zone is an element of the offense, and if the defendant is found guilty a jail term must be imposed as well as a minimum term. The penalty structure for this type of offense is similar to that for second-degree offenses for which admission to PTI is presumptively unavailable.

Possession of CDS in a school zone, on the other hand, is not a separate crime. Rather, it is a sentencing factor that requires the court to impose 100 hours of community service as a condition of probation if the defendant is not given a prison term. . . .

The Monmouth County Prosecutor's Office is the only prosecutor's office in the State to have adopted the policy that a simple possession offense makes a defendant ineligible for admission into PTI. Nor has the Attorney General adopted such a policy. [A 1997 Directive from the Attorney General] prohibits a prosecutor from consenting to PTI for a person charged with simple possession of drugs within 1,000 feet of school property unless, as a condition of PTI, the defendant serves not less than 100 hours of community service and pays a Drug Enforcement and Demand Reduction penalty. . . . Clearly, that policy is inconsistent with the Monmouth County prosecutor's policy of excluding from PTI all defendants charged with simple possession of drugs in a school zone. In fact, early diversion programs were begun in many jurisdictions in order to cope with both the non-addict first offender and the drug-dependent defendant.

As a first-time offender charged with a non-violent, third-degree offense, Baynes is eligible for diversion into the PTI program. By abandoning his discretion in favor of a per se rule, the prosecutor made a decision unsupported by the legislative purpose behind both the PTI Statute and the Comprehensive Drug Reform Act, by the Guidelines, and by caselaw. Thus, the rejection of Baynes's PTI application was an abuse of discretion under two of the three categories of the *Bender* test. . . .

■ OFFICE OF THE DISTRICT ATTORNEY, ORLEANS PARISH, LOUISIANA DIVERSIONARY PROGRAM

The Orleans Parish District Attorney's Office first began a Diversionary Program in 1973 for first-time, non-violent offenders. . . . The program offers a constructive alternative to prosecution. The DA defers prosecution of eligible persons shortly after arrest. Upon successful completion of program conditions, the charge is dismissed. It permits the accused to voluntarily enter a course of treatment that will address the individual factors producing the criminal behavior. This option is offered prior to the acceptance of any formal charges. However, only cases which would be accepted for prosecution are eligible. Arresting officers and victims are contacted to discuss the program referral.

Individuals arrested for simple possession of a controlled substance comprise the majority of the caseload. Others, however, are in the program due to arrests for general crimes, such as theft. In all cases, the participant is harmfully involved in the use of alcohol or other mood-altering drugs.

The program seeks to enhance public safety, reduce criminal recidivism, reduce the demand for drugs, alleviate overburdened court dockets, and provide close case monitoring including drug testing and individually-tailored treatment plans. These benefits are achieved through smaller caseloads than normal probation services as well as collaboration with community resources for a comprehensive approach. This includes substance abuse, mental health, and educational assistance. The social and health care costs directly related to criminal activity are reduced through this intervention. The Diversionary Program is cost effective by freeing up scarce resources for the more dangerous offender and utilizing the cost benefits of treatment. It is designed to reduce the risk of continued progression into a criminal lifestyle and steer individuals toward more productive goals. The benefits directly affect not only program participants but their families and the community at large.

ELIGIBILITY CRITERIA

The program is offered to individuals who:

- are first-time arrestees of state misdemeanor or felony statutes (no prior convictions and no significant arrest history including any prior acts of violence).
- have not been arrested for a violent crime, drug distribution, illegal carrying or use of a weapon, or heroin possession.
- abuse substances (alcohol, illicit drugs, or prescription medications).
- are willing to accept professional treatment recommendations.
- are a resident of the greater New Orleans area.
- are aged 17 or older.
- acknowledge their wrongdoing.

PROGRAM REQUIREMENTS

- Regular meetings with Diversionary Program Case Managers-Counselors.
- Abstinence from all mood-altering substances (unless prescribed by a physician).

- Periodic hair tests for illicit drugs; daily telephone contacts for random urine testing.
- Family involvement.
- Compliance to treatment recommendations from local substance abuse treatment providers (such as drug education, out-patient, in-patient, or longer-term residential treatment).
- Attendance at 12-step groups, if appropriate.
- Referrals to other support services for educational and vocational needs, mental health care, medical services, housing, etc.
- Payment of a sliding scale program fee and drug testing costs.
- Payment of restitution in full to victims for property crimes.
- Minimum program length of 3 months for misdemeanor charges and 6 months for felony charges.

Initial violations of program conditions result in a program extension and intensified treatment. Continued violations or re-arrest result in unsuccessful termination. Prosecution of the deferred charges occurs when a person violates out of the program. . . .

Notes

1. *Prevalence of diversion.* Diversion of arrestees is not as common as the outright rejection of criminal charges or the filing of felony charges. Prosecutors are most likely to offer diversion to suspects who face misdemeanor charges. Less than 7 percent of all felony arrestees in the largest urban counties in 2002 took part in diversion or "deferred adjudication" programs. Bureau of Justice Statistics, Felony Defendants in Large Urban Counties, 2002 (February 2006, NCJ 210818). Federal diversion programs are small: About 1,100 suspects were handled through pretrial diversion in 2003 (compared with more than 80,000 defendants prosecuted and 33,000 defendants whose cases were declined).

2. *Authority for diversion.* Prosecutors do not always have clear legal authority to take part in diversion programs. In some states, programs have statewide statutory authority (illustrated by the Montana statute reprinted above). Elsewhere, judges establish and supervise diversion programs (as in the New Jersey program described in *Baynes*). In a few jurisdictions, prosecutors send offenders into diversion programs without any explicit statutory authority to do so. Combinations of these situations are also possible: A statute might authorize diversion of offenders only after the filing of charges, yet the prosecutor may decide unilaterally to send some offenders into diversion programs before filing charges. Did the origins of the New Jersey program in the judicial branch influence the outcome or analysis in *Baynes*? Would the source of authority affect the level of funding for the program or the prosecutor's control over the conditions that program participants must meet?

3. *Who decides who enters the program?* State statutes dealing with pretrial diversion programs most often empower judges to approve of prosecutorial recommendations of individual offenders. Yet, as the New Jersey court in *Baynes* recognized, in practice prosecutors decide which defendants or suspects will enter a pretrial diversion program, and a court will give great deference to the prosecutor's decision. Indeed, in many states courts refuse to review the prosecutor's decision on whether

to offer diversion to a suspect unless the prosecutor relies on unconstitutional grounds such as race. Flynt v. Commonwealth, 105 S.W.3d 415 (Ky. 2003) (court must have prosecutor's approval to admit defendant into diversion program; separation-of-powers doctrine requires this reading of statute). Statutes in about a dozen states give prosecutors complete control over who may enter pretrial diversion programs. Prosecutors' offices sometimes create policies to govern eligibility for diversion, at least for some types of cases.

Legislatures also create some preconditions for defendants or suspects to participate in pretrial diversion programs. See, e.g., Ind. Code §33-39-1-8 (prosecutor "may" withhold prosecution against a person charged with a misdemeanor if person agrees to listed conditions of pretrial diversion program); Utah Code §77-36-2.7 (court may not approve diversion for domestic violence defendants but may hold guilty plea in abeyance during treatment program). If the prosecutor and the suspect disagree about the proper interpretation of the statute defining eligibility requirements, can a court review the prosecutor's decision based on its independent interpretation of the statute? Or must it defer to the prosecutor's reading of the statute?

4. *Who decides whether the defendant has completed the program?* Suppose a defendant believes she has fulfilled all the conditions of the diversion program but the prosecutor disagrees and files criminal charges. Will a court review the prosecutor's conclusion that the defendant failed to complete the program? Is there any reason to treat this question differently from the question of who will enter a diversion program? Among states with statutes addressing this question, the majority require court approval for a decision to remove an offender from a diversion program, but some (fewer than 10) have statutes granting this decision exclusively to the prosecutor. See Fla. Stat. §948.08. Compare State ex rel. Harmon v. Blanding, 644 P.2d 1082 (Or. 1982) (criminal defendant is not entitled to full hearing on issue of whether he had violated his diversion agreement but only to limited hearing on issue of whether reasonable basis existed for district attorney's finding) with State v. Hancich, 513 A.2d 638 (Conn. 1986) (once defendant was admitted to pretrial alcohol-education program following her first arrest for driving under the influence, she could not be removed unless court made independent determination that she had lost her eligibility or that she had not completed program successfully). What circumstances might enable a court to make an independent judgment about the defendant's success or failure in the program?

5. *Statement of reasons.* A few diversion programs require the prosecutor to provide an applicant to the program with written notice of rejection, along with the reasons for the rejection. The statement of reasons facilitates judicial review of the prosecutor's decision and is thought to help the courts identify arbitrary and abusive denials by the prosecutor. See State v. Herron, 767 S.W.2d 151 (Tenn. 1989). However, fewer than 10 states have a statewide legal requirement that the prosecutor give written reasons. Why do most states refuse to require a statement of reasons from the prosecutor? Have they concluded that such statements are pointless?

6. *Suspended charges vs. suspended sentences vs. probationary sentences.* Cases considered for diversion might be handled in various ways, including holding charges in abeyance during treatment, suspending an imposed sentence, or mandating probation. In each case, the primary goal may be treatment of the person rather than punishment. For example, voters in California in 2000 passed Proposition 36, which places all convicted nonviolent drug offenders in treatment, but which repealed a

deferred entry of judgment program for narcotics and drug abuse statutes. See 2000 California Op. Atty. Gen. 207. Other emerging reform efforts include creation of entirely distinct courts with "therapeutic" purposes. See, e.g., Teresa W. Carns, Michael G. Hotchkin & Elaine M. Andrews, Therapeutic Justice in Alaska's Courts, 19 Alaska L. Rev. 1 (2002) (discussing the concept and use of "wellness court," drug courts, mental health court, and therapeutic justice courts); Peggy F. Hora, William G. Schma & John T. A. Rosenthal, Therapeutic Jurisprudence and the Drug Treatment Court Movement: Revolutionizing the Criminal Justice System's Response to Drug Abuse and Crime in America, 74 Notre Dame L. Rev. 439 (1999). What are the legal, institutional and policy advantages to diverting a person out of the criminal justice system rather than using the power and control over citizens that the criminal justice system authorizes?

Problem 3-1. Youth Court

There are approximately 500 "youth courts" in the United States. These courts are intended to provide prosecutors, police, and schools with an alternative to juvenile courts. Often the "judges" in youth courts are not lawyers; sometimes they are not even adults, but rather the offender's peers. Does the creation of diversion courts (as opposed to diversion programs) exacerbate, undermine, or sidestep concerns about prosecutorial power and discretion? Consider the Utah statutes reprinted below, which provide for the creation and operation of youth courts; youth courts had been created on an ad hoc basis prior to the statute's enactment. Youth court jurisdiction in Utah extends to "status offenses" (offenses that would not be a crime if committed by an adult), lesser misdemeanors, infractions, and violations of municipal and county ordinances. Youth court jurisdiction in Utah does not extend to felonies, class A misdemeanors, possession of controlled substances, offenses committed as part of gang activity, or any offense where a dangerous weapon is used. Youth courts can be established by nonprofit entities.

If you were a district attorney, would you encourage the development and use of youth courts in your state? What other kinds of offenders or offenses might be handled with similar group diversion models?

■ UTAH CODE ANN. §78-57-103

(1) Youth Court is a diversion program which provides an alternative disposition for cases involving juvenile offenders in which youth participants, under the supervision of an adult coordinator, may serve in various capacities within the courtroom, acting in the role of jurors, lawyers, bailiffs, clerks, and judges.

(a) Youth who appear before youth courts have been identified by law enforcement personnel, school officials, a prosecuting attorney, or the juvenile court as having committed acts which indicate a need for intervention to prevent further development toward juvenile delinquency, but which appear to be acts that can be appropriately addressed outside the juvenile court process.

(b) Youth Courts may only hear cases as provided for in this chapter.

(c) Youth Court is a diversion program and not a court established under the Utah Constitution. . . .

(2) Any person may refer youth to a Youth Court for minor offenses. Once a referral is made, the case shall be screened by an adult coordinator to determine whether it qualifies as a Youth Court case.

(3) Youth Courts have authority over youth:

(a) referred for a minor offense or offenses, or who are granted permission for referral under this chapter;

(b) who, along with a parent, guardian, or legal custodian, voluntarily and in writing, request Youth Court involvement;

(c) who admit having committed the referred offense;

(d) who, along with a parent, guardian, or legal custodian, waive any privilege against self-incrimination and right to a speedy trial; and

(e) who, along with their parent, guardian, or legal custodian, agree to follow the Youth Court disposition of the case. . . .

(5) Youth Courts may exercise authority over youth described in Subsection (4), and over any other offense with the permission of the juvenile court and the prosecuting attorney in the county or district that would have jurisdiction if the matter were referred to juvenile court. . . .

(7) Youth Courts may decline to accept a youth for Youth Court disposition for any reason and may terminate a youth from Youth Court participation at any time.

(8) A youth or the youth's parent, guardian, or custodian may withdraw from the Youth Court process at any time. The Youth Court shall immediately notify the referring source of the withdrawal.

(9) The Youth Court may transfer a case back to the referring source for alternative handling at any time.

(10) Referral of a case of Youth Court may not prohibit the subsequent referral of the case to any court.

■ UTAH CODE ANN. §78-57-105

(1) Youth Court dispositional options include:

(a) community service;

(b) participation in law-related educational classes, appropriate counseling, treatment, or other educational programs;

(c) providing periodic reports to the Youth Court;

(d) participating in mentoring programs;

(e) participation by the youth as a member of a Youth Court;

(f) letters of apology;

(g) essays; and

(h) any other disposition considered appropriate by the Youth Court and adult coordinator.

(2) Youth Courts may not impose a term of imprisonment or detention and may not impose fines.

(3) Youth Court dispositions shall be completed within 180 days from the date of referral.

(4) Youth Court dispositions shall be reduced to writing and signed by the youth and a parent, guardian, or legal custodian indicating their acceptance of the disposition terms.

(5) Youth Court shall notify the referring source if a participant fails to successfully complete the Youth Court disposition. The referring source may then take any action it considers appropriate.

3. *Private Prosecution*

If prosecutors won't prosecute, perhaps an aggrieved citizen will. Indeed, there is a long tradition of private rather than public prosecution. Public prosecutors— like many of the institutions of criminal justice, including police and public defense counsel—are a modern invention. An older tradition, which saw tort and crime more closely linked, required private parties to bring criminal actions against alleged wrongdoers. Throughout much of the eighteenth and nineteenth centuries, it was common for private citizens to bring complaints to a grand jury or a magistrate, *and* to hire private attorneys to assist the public prosecutor or to prosecute the criminal case alone. Only at the turn of the twentieth century did the public prosecutor become the primary method for initiating criminal charges.

Remnants of true private prosecution exist still in United States law. The "victim's rights" concept has strengthened the accountability of public prosecutors to victims of crime. Prosecutors also reflect the political priorities of the voters or the Executive who appoints them, and the Legislature which funds them.

As traditional and well recognized as interest group politics may be, the link between private preferences and public prosecution is not widely recognized. Consider the legal and policy dimensions of the modern forms of private prosecution described in the following statute, case, and problem.

■ WISCONSIN STATUTES §968.02

(1) Except as otherwise provided in this section, a complaint charging a person with an offense shall be issued only by a district attorney of the county where the crime is alleged to have been committed. A complaint is issued when it is approved for filing for the district attorney. . . .

(3) If a district attorney refuses or is unavailable to issue a complaint, a circuit judge may permit the filing of a complaint, if the judge finds there is probable cause to believe that the person to be charged has committed an offense after conducting a hearing. If the district attorney has refused to issue a complaint, he or she shall be informed of the hearing and may attend. The hearing shall be ex parte without the right of cross-examination.

■ STATE v. DONALD CULBREATH
30 S.W.3d 309 (Tenn. 2000)

Anderson, C.J.

We granted this appeal to determine whether the trial court abused its discretion by disqualifying a District Attorney General and his staff due to the use of a private attorney to assist the prosecution where the private attorney received substantial compensation from a private, special interest group. . . . We agree that the prosecution's appointment and use of a private attorney who received substantial compensation from a private, special interest group created a conflict of interest and an appearance of impropriety that required disqualification of the District Attorney General's office. [The] prosecutor's use of the private attorney under the circumstances of this case violated the defendants' right to due process under the Tennessee Constitution and required dismissal of the indictments. . . .

In December of 1995, Larry Parrish, an attorney in Memphis, Tennessee, was approached by the executive director of an organization known as the Citizens for Community Values, Inc., ("CCV"), who asked him to meet with two Shelby County assistant district attorneys, Amy Weirich and Jennifer Nichols, regarding the prosecution of obscenity cases. Parrish, a former Assistant United States Attorney, was experienced in the prosecution of obscenity cases.

Parrish met with Weirich and Nichols for three hours. When they asked for his help, Parrish replied, "I haven't been asked." On the following day, then-Shelby County District Attorney John Pierotti contacted Parrish and requested his assistance. Pierotti told Parrish that his office could not pay for Parrish's services but could reimburse expenses. When Parrish asked if he could be compensated by outside sources, Pierotti agreed. According to Parrish, "that's how it got started."

Thereafter, Parrish conducted an extensive investigation into sexually-oriented businesses in Shelby County, Tennessee, with the assistance of two assistant district attorneys, an investigator from the District Attorney General's office, and investigators from the Tennessee Bureau of Investigation and the Department of Revenue. Parrish met with these employees in his law firm office on a daily basis for several months. Beginning in January of 1996, the group's investigation consisted of conducting surveillance of sexually-oriented establishments and taking statements from a large number of witnesses. Although Parrish testified that it was "understood" that General Pierotti had the ultimate decision-making authority, there were no procedures or guidelines establishing Parrish's specific duties or Pierotti's oversight.

The initial agreement called for the District Attorney General's office to pay for expenses incurred during the investigation, but Parrish began to pay expenses from contributions by CCV and numerous members of the community. Parrish testified that CCV received a monthly statement itemizing his time and expenses, just as any other client. Parrish's expenses included the use of court reporters to take statements, a TV/VCR, copying and courier expenses, video monitors, special telephone lines, and various office supplies and equipment. The expenses were paid from CCV contributions. . . .

On July 11, 1996, Parrish was "appointed" as a "Special Assistant District Attorney" by General Pierotti and was administered an oath of office for the first time. On the same day, a civil nuisance suit seeking injunctive relief against several sexually-oriented businesses was filed in Shelby County Chancery Court. The civil complaint was signed by Parrish as "Special Assistant District Attorney General," District Attorney General Pierotti, and two assistant district attorneys. At Pierotti's request, Parrish was appointed as additional counsel in matters relating to the civil cases in chancery court by Governor Don Sundquist on August 30, 1996. The letter of appointment noted that Parrish would not be compensated by the State, that Parrish would disclose the amount and source of any compensation received, that such information was a matter of public record, and that Parrish was under the direct supervision of General Pierotti.

When Pierotti resigned, effective November 1, 1996, his successor, William Gibbons, continued to work with Parrish in the investigation and prosecution of sexually-oriented businesses. In addition to the civil nuisance suit already filed in chancery court, Gibbons sought criminal indictments from the grand jury. In December of 1996, the grand jury returned an 18-count indictment against the defendant, Donald L. Culbreath, [including ten counts of promoting prostitution, six counts of prostitution, and two counts of public indecency].

The trial court found that over a 19-month period, Parrish received $410,931.87 for his services from CCV and other private contributors between December of 1995 and July of 1997. Of this amount, Parrish's expenses exceeded $100,000. The trial court found that Parrish's substantial involvement in the prosecution of these cases and his "enormous" compensation from a private, special interest group created a conflict of interest that required Parrish's disqualification. . . .

In determining whether to disqualify a prosecutor in a criminal case, the trial court must determine whether there is an actual conflict of interest, which includes any circumstances in which an attorney cannot exercise his or her independent professional judgment free of "compromising interests and loyalties." See Tenn. R. Sup. Ct. 8, EC 5-1. If there is no actual conflict of interest, the court must nonetheless consider whether conduct has created an appearance of impropriety. See Tenn. R. Sup. Ct. 8, EC 9-1, 9-6. If disqualification is required under either theory, the trial court must also determine whether the conflict of interest or appearance of impropriety requires disqualification of the entire District Attorney General's office. The determination of whether to disqualify the office of the District Attorney General in a criminal case rests within the discretion of the trial court. . . .

A District Attorney General is an elected constitutional officer whose function is to prosecute criminal offenses in his or her circuit or district. Tenn. Const. art. VI, §5. The District Attorney General "[s]hall prosecute in the courts of the district all violations of the state criminal statutes and perform all prosecutorial functions attendant thereto. . . ." Tenn. Code Ann. §8-7-103(1). . . .

The proper role of the prosecutor in our criminal justice system has been addressed on numerous occasions by various courts and ethical rules. As early as 1816, the Tennessee Supreme Court said that a prosecutor

> is to judge between the people and the government; he is to be the safeguard of the one and the advocate of the rights of the other; he ought not to suffer the innocent to be oppressed or vexatiously harassed any more than those who deserve prosecution to escape; he is to pursue guilt; he is to protect innocence; he is to judge of circumstances, and, according to their true complexion, to combine the public welfare and the safety of the citizens, preserving both and not impairing either.

Foute v. State, 4 Tenn. (3 Haywood) 98 (1816). The United States Supreme Court has said that a prosecutor:

> is the representative not of an ordinary party to a controversy, but of a sovereignty whose obligation to govern impartially is as compelling as its obligation to govern at all; and whose interest, therefore, in a criminal prosecution is not that it shall win a case, but that justice shall be done. As such, he is in a peculiar and very definite sense the servant of the law the twofold aim of which is that guilt shall not escape or innocence suffer.

He may prosecute with earnestness and vigor — indeed, he should do so. But, while he may strike hard blows, he is not at liberty to strike foul ones.

Berger v. United States, 295 U.S. 78 (1935).

These principles are likewise embodied within the ethical considerations of the Model Code of Professional Responsibility governing the conduct of prosecutors:

> The responsibility of a public prosecutor differs from that of the usual advocate; his duty is to seek justice, not merely to convict. This special duty exists because: (1) the prosecutor represents the sovereign and therefore should use restraint in the discretionary exercise of governmental powers, such as in the selection of cases to prosecute; (2) during trial the prosecutor is not only an advocate but also may make decisions normally made by an individual client, and those affecting the public interest should be fair to all; and (3) in our system of criminal justice the accused is to be given the benefit of all reasonable doubts.

Tenn. R. Sup. Ct. 8, EC 7-13; see ABA Standards for Criminal Justice, Standard 3-1.1(c) (1979) ("[The] duty of the prosecutor is to seek justice, not merely to convict"). The Model Code also discusses the differences in the role of the prosecutor from that of the private attorney:

> With respect to evidence and witnesses, the prosecutor has responsibilities different from those of a lawyer in private practice; the prosecutor should make timely disclosure to the defense of available evidence, known to the prosecutor, that tends to negate the guilt of the accused, mitigate the degree of the offense, or reduce the punishment. Further, a prosecutor should not intentionally avoid pursuit of evidence merely because the prosecutor believes it will damage the prosecutor's case or aid the accused. [Tenn. R. Sup. Ct. 8, EC 7-13.]

In short, public prosecutors hold a unique office in our criminal justice system. [Prosecutors] are expected to be impartial in the sense that they must seek the truth and not merely obtain convictions. They are also to be impartial in the sense that charging decisions should be based upon the evidence, without discrimination or bias for or against any groups or individuals. Yet, at the same time, they are expected to prosecute criminal offenses with zeal and vigor within the bounds of the law and professional conduct.

Under English common law, the criminal justice system required the victim of a criminal offense, or the victim's family, to initiate and pursue criminal proceedings. Although the development and role of the public prosecutor in the United States over the past several centuries has largely supplanted the English common law in this regard, many jurisdictions still allow a private attorney to be retained or appointed to assist in the prosecution of a criminal case.

Numerous courts and commentators have recognized, however, that the use of a private attorney in the prosecution of a criminal case may present ethical dilemmas, including conflicts of interest. The private attorney must comply with the standards and ethical responsibilities for a public prosecutor — to not merely seek convictions but also to pursue justice. At the same time, however, the private attorney's ethical duty "both to client and to the legal system, is to represent the client zealously within the bounds of the law, which include Disciplinary Rules and enforceable professional regulations." Tenn. R. Sup. Ct. 8, EC 7-1.

In Tennessee, there are two statutes pertaining to the prosecutor's use of additional counsel. One, which the parties agree is not applicable in this case, permits the victim of a crime or the victim's family to retain an attorney to assist in the trial of a criminal case under the supervision of the District Attorney General. Tenn. Code Ann. §8-7-401. The second, which the parties contend is applicable here, provides for the employment of additional counsel:

> [Where] the interest of the state requires . . . additional counsel to the attorney general and reporter or district attorney general, the governor shall employ such counsel, who shall be paid such compensation for services as the governor, secretary of state, and attorney general and reporter may deem just, the same to be paid out of any money in the treasury not otherwise appropriated. [Tenn. Code Ann. §8-6-106.]

Although the statutory provisions in Tennessee, similar to the laws in other jurisdictions, purport to address the potential conflicts by requiring that the private attorney work under the supervision of the District Attorney or be compensated by the state, they do not foreclose the risk that a conflict of interest, or appearance of such a conflict, may exist under the circumstances of a particular case. For example, there is a conflict of interest whenever an attorney is retained to assist the prosecution and acquires a direct financial interest in the proceeding. Moreover, an actual conflict or an apparent conflict may exist anytime a lawyer cannot exercise his or her independent professional judgment free of "compromising influences and loyalties." Tenn. R. Sup. Ct. 8, EC 5-1. Accordingly, a court must review the facts and circumstances of each case with these standards in mind.

In this case, Parrish's involvement began without any formal appointment by the Governor and no oath of office, and it continued in this manner for eight months from December of 1995 to July 1996. Parrish was compensated for his services by a private, special interest group that he billed each month. During this time, Parrish spearheaded a comprehensive investigation with a "staff" that included two assistant district attorneys and three investigators. There was no specific agreement or arrangement as to Parrish's role, the extent of his participation, or the extent of District Attorney General Pierotti's supervision — for all practical purposes, there appeared to be little supervision or control by Pierotti. . . .

Although General Pierotti purportedly appointed Parrish as a special prosecutor on the same day the [civil nuisance] suit was filed, there was (and is) no constitutional or statutory authority for such an appointment to be made. Moreover, although Parrish was later appointed as additional counsel by the Governor, there was (and is) no legal authority allowing Parrish to be compensated on an hourly basis by a private, special interest group. . . .

Parrish had an actual conflict of interest under the circumstances of this case. He was privately compensated by a special interest group and thus owed a duty of loyalty to that group; at the same time, he was serving in the role of public prosecutor and owed the duty of loyalty attendant to that office. Moreover, because Parrish was compensated on an hourly basis, the reality is that he acquired a direct financial interest in the duration and scope of the ongoing prosecution. . . .

The State contends that there was no conflict of interest because Parrish and the prosecution had the same interest — eradicating sexually-oriented businesses. The prosecutor's discretion about whom to prosecute and to what extent they should be prosecuted, however, is vast and to a large degree, not subject to meaningful review. Moreover, as the United States Supreme Court has recognized, the prosecutor's discretion goes beyond initial charging decisions:

> A prosecutor exercises considerable discretion in matters such as the determination of which persons should be targets of investigation, what methods of investigation should be used, what information will be sought as evidence, which persons should be charged with what offenses, which persons should be utilized as witnesses, whether to enter into plea bargains and the terms on which they will be established, and whether any individuals should be granted immunity. . . .

Young v. United States ex rel. Vuitton et Fils S.A., 481 U.S. 787, 807 (1987). [T]he foundation for the exercise of the vast prosecutorial discretion is freedom from conflict of interest and fidelity to the public interest.

Finally, we agree that the trial court did not abuse its discretion in disqualifying the District Attorney General's staff based on the appearance of impropriety created by Parrish's conflict of interest. [T]he record supports the trial court's finding that Parrish played a substantial role in the prosecution. . . . Despite Parrish's extensive contact with the office of the District Attorney General, including daily working involvement with two assistant district attorneys and several investigators, there were no guidelines as to Parrish's duties and no efforts to screen Parrish from other members of the District Attorney General's office. Both [Pierotti and Gibbons] knew that Parrish was being compensated by a private, special interest group. Moreover, the trial court found that on one occasion, Pierotti, Gibbons, and Parrish attended a fund-raiser which "stressed the necessity to continue on with the prosecution of criminal activity in topless clubs and the need for continued donations to pursue these goals." . . .

Here, the private attorney's conflict of interest tainted the entire prosecution of the case well before the charges were presented to the grand jury. Accordingly, we conclude that the proceedings were inherently improper and that dismissal of the indictments is the appropriate remedy to redress the constitutional error. . . .

Problem 3-2. Private Money, Public Prosecutions

The Massachusetts legislature created the Insurance Fraud Bureau (IFB), to investigate charges of fraudulent insurance transactions and to refer any violation of law regarding insurance fraud to the appropriate prosecutor. The IFB is governed by a board of fifteen members, five each from the governing committees of two insurance rating bureaus (one for auto insurance and the other for workers' compensation insurance) and five public officials, including the Commissioner of Insurance and the Commissioner of the Department of Industrial Accidents.

According to the statute, every insurer "having reason to believe that an insurance transaction may be fraudulent" must report its suspicions to the IFB. The IFB must review each report and may investigate further. Whenever the IFB's executive director is satisfied that a material fraud or intentional misrepresentation has been committed in an insurance transaction, he must "refer the matter to the attorney general, the appropriate district attorney or the United States attorney, and to appropriate licensing agencies." A person convicted of any law concerning insurance fraud, following an IFB referral for prosecution, "shall be ordered to make restitution to the insurer for any financial loss sustained as a result of such violation."

The IFB receives reports of suspected insurance fraud from a variety of sources. During the IFB's first seven years, slightly more than half of these reports came from insurance companies. Other reports come from government agencies, professional organizations, and the public. Of the more than 12,800 reports received in those seven years, more than 5,000 were accepted for investigation, 64 percent of which were from insurance companies.

The Commissioner of Insurance must cover the IFB's investigation costs through annual assessments against the two insurance rating bureaus, which are themselves funded by insurance companies operating in the state. For fiscal year 1999, the appropriation from the general fund for the investigation and prosecution of automobile insurance fraud was $270,871, and the assessment against the auto insurance rating bureau was $250,000. In that same year, the legislative appropriation for the investigation and prosecution of workers' compensation fraud was $463,159 and the assessment against workers' compensation rating board was $250,000.

The commissioner must also collect from the rating bureaus enough money to cover funds spent for fringe benefits "attributable to personnel costs of the attorney general's office related to the purposes" of the program. Under this law, the Attorney General uses the assessments to hire 13 assistant attorneys general, six for automobile insurance fraud matters and seven for workers' compensation insurance fraud matters.

James Ellis and Nicholas Ellis were partners in a law firm that represented plaintiffs in workers' compensation and personal injury cases. Along with other associates, employees and clients, they were charged with insurance fraud and related offenses. Both defendants moved to dismiss the indictments based on the partiality of the attorneys prosecuting the cases. They challenged the constitutionality of the statutorily funding scheme.

The state argued in reply that routine cooperation from a victim of a crime is often necessary and should be encouraged. Victims of commercial or corporate crimes may assist the prosecution by collecting and organizing necessary information and may properly hire private investigators for external investigation of suspected crimes. In addition, the state noted that assessments are made industry-wide, rather than on one particular victim corporation, and are spent on investigation and prosecution of automobile and workers' compensation insurance fraud generally, rather than for the particular benefit of any one victim. How would you rule on the motion to dismiss? Compare Commonwealth v. Ellis, 708 N.E. 2d 644 (Mass. 1999).

Notes

1. *Private filing of complaints.* Is it possible to encourage the filing of criminal charges by giving the power to file a criminal complaint directly to an aggrieved citizen, allowing the citizen to bypass the public prosecutor? Most states give the public prosecutor exclusive authority to file criminal complaints. See Cal. Govt. Code §26500 ("The public prosecutor shall attend the courts, and within his or her discretion shall initiate and conduct on behalf of the people all prosecutions"). The same is true in the federal system. The court in Harman v. Frye, 425 S.E.2d 566

(W. Va. 1992), considered criminal complaints for battery that two participants in a fight filed against each other. The opinion summarized the reasons why most states have required the public prosecutor to approve of the filing of any criminal charges:

> [Problems] have resulted from allowing citizens to file criminal complaints before a magistrate without the approval of the prosecuting attorney or law enforcement officers. First, citizens can misuse the right to file a criminal complaint before a magistrate by exaggerating the facts or omitting relevant facts they disclose to the magistrate so as to transform a noncriminal dispute into a crime. The magistrate, who must remain neutral, is not in the same position as the prosecuting attorney or law enforcement officers to ascertain whether all of the relevant facts have been disclosed accurately. . . . When citizens file criminal complaints before the magistrate which later prove to be frivolous, retaliatory or unfounded, the prosecuting attorney is required to take the time to investigate the complaint before moving a nolle pros to dismiss. . . . - Moreover, additional time and expense are also incurred when either the public defender or an attorney-at-law must be appointed to represent indigent persons against whom frivolous, retaliatory or unfounded charges have been filed. . . . Finally, private citizens have not undergone the same professional training as prosecuting attorneys or law enforcement officers nor are they subject to the same rules of professional conduct and discipline which are imposed on prosecuting attorneys and law enforcement officers.

In a few states, statutes authorize citizens to file criminal complaints even when the prosecutor has declined to do so. Most of these statutes (like the Wisconsin statute reprinted above) allow the private complaint to occur only after the public prosecutor has affirmatively decided not to file charges, and they require the citizen to obtain approval for the charges from a judge or grand jury. A few of the statutes apply only to particular crimes, such as domestic violence or issuance of a worthless check. See W. Va. Code §§48-27-902, 61-3-39a. Can the public prosecutor prevent any abuses of private complaints simply by dismissing charges once they are filed? If the prosecutor retains the power to dismiss charges filed by a private citizen, has the mechanism accomplished anything other than creating more recordkeeping?

2. *The historical roots of private prosecution of criminal cases.* By the turn of the twentieth century the public prosecutor became the primary method for initiating criminal charges. Private prosecutions became the exception rather than the rule as public prosecutors became more professionalized and independent of the courts, professional police departments became more common in metropolitan areas, and acquittal rates rose for privately initiated complaints. See Allan Steinberg, The Transformation of Criminal Justice: Philadelphia, 1800-1880 (1989); Michael McConville & Chester Mirsky, The Rise of Guilty Pleas: New York, 1800-1865, 22 J.L. Soc'y 443 (1995). This transformation was part of a larger formalization of the entire criminal process, starting in the English courts for felony cases in the 1730s. See John Langbein, The Prosecutorial Origins of Defense Counsel in the Eighteenth Century: The Appearance of Solicitors, 58 Cambridge L.J. 314 (1999) (courts allowed participation of defense counsel to counter increasing influence of solicitors in investigating and preparing witnesses).

Traces of the older private prosecution system remain visible today, and are gaining renewed attention as a method of empowering the victims of crime. More than half the states still have statutes or constitutional provisions that allow private counsel, retained by a crime victim, to participate in criminal proceedings. In most jurisdictions, the private prosecutor may only assist the prosecutor, while in a few the private prosecutor has more authority to direct the criminal proceedings. See, e.g., Pa. Stat. tit. 16, §1409 (the court may "direct any private counsel employed by [a complainant] to conduct the entire proceeding"). Are private prosecutions of crime an effective way to supplement the limited resources of a public prosecutor, much as we rely on "private attorneys general" to help enforce some civil statutes? What if private prosecutions could only result in non-prison sentences?

3. *Private financial aid to public prosecution.* What is wrong with private parties funding public prosecutions so long as the public prosecutor makes the decisions? In Commonwealth v. Ellis, 708 N.E. 2d 644 (Mass. 1999), which provides the basis for Problem 3-2, the Massachusetts Supreme Court upheld the statutory industry funding scheme for insurance and fraud prosecutions, finding no appearance of conflict. The court observed:

> If we were confronted with a challenge to an arrangement between insurers and the Attorney General of the sort involved here that was not endorsed by statute, the appearance of the possibility of improper influence would be far clearer. Although statutory endorsement of an unconstitutional plan cannot make it constitutional, where the question is whether the appearance of an arrangement may support a determination of unconstitutionality, the fact that the Legislature has endorsed the plan, has supervisory authority over it, and appropriates funds for it substantially changes appearances.

Can you distinguish the outcomes in *Culbreath* and *Ellis*? See also Hambarian v. Superior Court, 44 P.3d 102 (Cal. 2002) (prosecutor's office need not be removed despite use of accountant paid by victim). Do *Culbreath* and *Ellis* suggest a resurgence of private prosecution? A prosecutor who is paid by a private interest but is working under the direction of a public prosecutor can be said to serve two (or more) clients. One client might be considered the private funding source. Who is the other client? Do these clients have conflicting interests?

4. *Victim notice and consultation regarding charges.* Crime legislation over the past generation has given victims of alleged crimes more input into prosecutorial decisions. Almost all states now have passed statutes or constitutional provisions that focus on the prosecutor's power to resolve criminal charges through plea agreements or other methods. Most, however, do not give the victim any right to "consult" with the prosecutor about the charges. They simply instruct the prosecutor to inform the victim about the charges to be filed or about the decision not to file charges. See Ariz. Stat. §13-4408 (prosecutor to give victim notice of the charge against defendant and concise statement of procedural steps in criminal prosecution, and to inform victim of decision to decline prosecution, with reasons for declination). Are these "notice" and "consultation" statutes an inevitable response to the abandonment of private prosecutions? Is the victim, in a functional if not literal sense, the client of the prosecuting attorney? Cf. Gina Cappello, "Women's Groups Can Oversee Sex Cases," N.Y. Times, March 21, 2000 (Philadelphia police allow women's organizations to help evaluate and classify sexual assault complaints; response to revelations that department mislabeled rapes as less violent offenses to make city seem safer).

5. *Special prosecutors.* Almost all states have statutes empowering a judge (or a prosecuting attorney) to appoint a "special prosecutor" to file and prosecute

criminal charges. The court appoints the special prosecutor when the district attorney "refuses to act" or "neglects" to perform a duty. See Ala. Code §12-17-186; Tenn. Const. art. 6, §5 ("In all cases where the Attorney for any district fails or refuses to attend and prosecute according to law, the Court shall have power to appoint an Attorney pro tempore"). Courts will also order the use of a special prosecutor when the prosecuting attorney has a conflict of interest regarding a suspect, a complainant, or some other person involved in a potential criminal case. See Young v. United States ex rel. Vuitton et Fils S.A., 481 U.S. 787 (1987) (district courts have authority under Rule 42(b) to appoint private attorney to prosecute contempt case, but should do so only after requesting public prosecutor to initiate case). If an independent official who decides whether to file criminal charges does not operate within a limited budget and does not compare the current case to all other potential criminal cases that an office might prosecute, will the quality of the prosecutorial decision improve? Are budget constraints a necessary evil, or are they the essence of prosecutorial accountability?

4. Selection of Charges and System

Up to this point, we have focused on prosecutorial choices that would place a suspect either "in" or "out" of the criminal justice system. But prosecutors also make important choices about each criminal defendant who will be charged. For one thing, the prosecutor selects among a range of criminal charges that could apply to the case. For another, prosecutors might select which judicial system (state or federal, juvenile or adult) will adjudicate the charges.

a. Selection Among Charges

■ U.S. DEPARTMENT OF JUSTICE, PRINCIPLES OF FEDERAL PROSECUTION
(1980)

SELECTING CHARGES

1. Except as hereafter provided, the attorney for the government should charge, or should recommend that the grand jury charge, the most serious offense that is consistent with the nature of the defendant's conduct, and that is likely to result in a sustainable conviction.

2. Except as hereafter provided, the attorney for the government should also charge, or recommend that the grand jury charge, other offenses only when, in his judgment, additional charges:

(a) are necessary to ensure that the information or indictment: (i) adequately reflects the nature and extent of the criminal conduct involved; and (ii) provides the basis for an appropriate sentence under all the circumstances of the case; or

(b) will significantly enhance the strength of the government's case against the defendant or a codefendant.

3. The attorney for the government may file or recommend a charge or charges without regard to the provisions of paragraphs 1 and 2, if such charge or charges are the subject of a pre-charge plea agreement. . . .

■ MINNESOTA STATUTES §388.051

(1) The county attorney shall [prosecute] felonies, including the drawing of indictments found by the grand jury, and, to the extent prescribed by law, gross misdemeanors, misdemeanors, petty misdemeanors, and violations of municipal ordinances, charter provisions and rules or regulations. . . .

(3) [E]ach county attorney shall adopt written guidelines governing the county attorney's charging . . . policies and practices. The guidelines shall address, but need not be limited to, the . . . factors that are considered in making charging decisions. . . .

■ PEOPLE v. JALEH WILKINSON
94 P.3d 551 (Cal. 2004)

George, C.J.

[In] the early morning hours of February 27, 1999, a motorist observed defendant driving erratically on a street in the City of Santa Monica. Defendant's vehicle crossed over the center divider, struck a parked car, and continued down the street, swerving between lanes. Defendant eventually stopped her car at a curb and placed her head on the front passenger seat. [Officers] tapped on the window of defendant's parked car, whereupon defendant looked at one of the officers and drove off. The police gave chase for three blocks before defendant stopped. Defendant, who smelled strongly of alcohol and exhibited slurred speech, indicated she had consumed some drinks but not many. She could not complete a field sobriety test and did not respond when told she was required to submit to a blood or breath test for alcohol.

Officers transported defendant to the police station. She was belligerent during booking and resisted a patsearch. At one point, defendant grabbed a custodial officer's arm with both hands, causing a visible welt. When taken to a holding cell, defendant charged at an officer and yelled, kicked, and banged at the door. After the police reminded defendant that she would have to submit to a blood or breath test, defendant covered her ears, stated "I can't hear you," and began running around inside the cell. An officer testified defendant appeared to be under the influence of alcohol but not of drugs.

Defendant testified in her own defense as follows. On the night in question, defendant, a bank vice-president, went to a bar, where she met a man who offered to buy her a drink. She accepted and eventually consumed two glasses of wine. The man invited defendant to dinner, and they agreed to meet at a Santa Monica restaurant. At the restaurant, defendant consumed three alcoholic beverages over the course of three hours while she waited for the man, but he never arrived. She left her drink several times to use the restroom and to smoke a cigarette outside. She eventually left the restaurant, driving away without feeling any signs of intoxication. The next thing she remembered was waking up in jail, with no recollection of her encounter with the officers. After her release from custody, defendant filed a police complaint alleging she had been drugged.

A toxicologist, testifying on behalf of the defense, expressed the opinion that on the night in question defendant was under the influence of alcohol and gamma hydroxy butyrate (hereafter GHB), commonly known as a "date rape" drug, basing his opinion on a review of the police report and a videotape of defendant's conduct in the holding cell. GHB depresses the nervous system, exaggerates the effects of alcohol, and may cause drowsiness and memory loss. Depending upon a person's personality, the drug may make a person more emotional and combative. . . .

The jury convicted defendant as charged, and the trial court placed defendant on formal probation for three years. . . .

Defendant was convicted of violating Penal Code section 243.1, which states in full: "When a battery is committed against the person of a custodial officer as defined in Section 831 of the Penal Code, and the person committing the offense knows or reasonably should know that the victim is a custodial officer engaged in the performance of his or her duties, and the custodial officer is engaged in the performance of his or her duties, the offense shall be punished by imprisonment in the state prison." Section 831, subdivision (a), in turn, defines a "custodial officer" as "a public officer, not a peace officer, employed by a law enforcement agency of a city or county who has the authority and responsibility for maintaining custody of prisoners and performs tasks related to the operation of a local detention facility used for the detention of persons usually pending arraignment or upon court order either for their own safekeeping or for the specific purpose of serving a sentence therein." Because section 243.1 provides for a punishment of imprisonment in state prison, but does not otherwise specify the term of imprisonment, under section 18 the offense is punishable "by imprisonment in any of the state prisons for 16 months, or two or three years. . . ."

At the time section 243.1 was enacted in 1976, section 243 prescribed the punishment (1) for simple battery (which section 243 made punishable as a misdemeanor), (2) for battery against a person who the defendant knew or should have known was a "peace officer or fireman engaged in the performance of his duties" (which section 243 made punishable as either a felony or a misdemeanor, commonly known as a "wobbler"), and (3) for battery resulting in the infliction of "serious bodily injury" (which section 243 also made punishable as a wobbler, prescribing a punishment of two, three, or four years' imprisonment for a felony violation).

In 1981, the Legislature divided section 243 into subdivisions, with subdivision (a) covering simple battery (punishable as a misdemeanor with a maximum jail sentence of six months), subdivision (b) covering battery on a person who the defendant knows or should know is a peace officer, firefighter, etc. (punishable as a misdemeanor with a maximum jail sentence of one year), subdivision (c) covering battery on a peace officer, firefighter, etc., that results in the infliction of injury (a wobbler with a possible state prison term of 16 months, two years, or three years), and subdivision (d) covering battery that results in serious bodily injury (a wobbler with a possible prison term of two, three, or four years). The following year, in 1982, the Legislature added a reference to custodial officers to subdivisions

(b) and (c) of section 243, defining custodial officers by reference to section 831. Thus, as amended in 1982, section 243, subdivision (b), provided that battery on a person who the defendant knows or reasonably should know is a custodial officer is punishable as a misdemeanor with a maximum imprisonment of one year in county jail, and section 243, subdivision (c), provided that when such a battery results in injury to the custodial officer, the offense is punishable as a wobbler with possible imprisonment in state prison for 16 months, two years, or three years. . . .

On appeal, defendant [contends] that the current statutory scheme pertaining to battery on a custodial officer is "irrational" and violates the federal and state guarantees of equal protection because one who commits the "lesser" offense of battery on a custodial officer without injury can receive felony punishment under section 243.1 while a person committing the "greater" offense of battery on a custodial officer with injury can be convicted of a wobbler offense under section 243, subdivision (c)(1) and can receive a misdemeanor sentence. . . .

We begin our discussion with an overview of relevant case authority. . . . In People v. Chenze, 97 Cal. App. 4th 521 (Cal. App. 2002), the defendant contended that he was improperly charged and convicted under section 243.1 because that provision had been "impliedly repealed" when the Legislature amended section 243 to include references to custodial officers. The defendant urged that the two statutes were in "irreconcilable conflict" since the older statute, section 243.1, provides that any battery against a custodial officer is a felony, whereas the more recent statute . . . permits felony treatment only if injury is inflicted.

The Court of Appeal in *Chenze* disagreed that the two statutes were in irreconcilable conflict and thus rejected the claim of implied repeal. The court cited an enrolled bill report . . . which explained the need for an amendment to section 243 to include references to custodial officers notwithstanding the existence of section 243.1: "According to the bill's sponsors, simple battery charges against custodial officers are rarely pursued by local prosecutors because the present law only provides for felony charges with imprisonment in a state prison. Thus, these violators are rarely, if ever, punished. By providing for the option of county jail and/ or fine for such violations, proponents hope that simple battery charges will be prosecuted more vigorously. Felony battery charges can still be pursued for the more serious cases." . . . Under section 243, the offense may be punished as a misdemeanor (§243(b)), or a misdemeanor or felony if injury is inflicted (§243(c)(1)). But the Legislature also apparently envisioned that there might be circumstances under which no or only slight injury was inflicted, but felony charges would nonetheless still be appropriate. . . .

The United States Supreme Court's decision in United States v. Batchelder, 442 U.S. 114 (1979), . . . concluded that the defendant properly could be sentenced under one federal firearms statute, although an almost identical statute prescribed a lesser punishment. In *Batchelder*, the court took note of legislative history indicating that Congress "intended to enact two independent gun control statutes, each fully enforceable on its own terms." The court in *Batchelder* then stated that . . . "when an act violates more than one criminal statute, the Government may prosecute under either so long as it does not discriminate against any class of defendants." The high court concluded that the statutory scheme at issue fell under this rule: "There is no appreciable difference between the discretion a prosecutor exercises when deciding whether to charge under one of two statutes with different elements and the discretion he exercises when choosing one of two statutes with identical elements. In the former situation, once he determines that the proof will support conviction under either statute, his decision is indistinguishable from the one he faces in the latter context. The prosecutor may be influenced by the penalties available upon conviction, but this fact, standing alone, does not give rise to a violation of the Equal Protection or Due Process Clause." . . .

Batchelder instructs us that neither the existence of two identical criminal statutes prescribing different levels of punishments, nor the exercise of a prosecutor's discretion in charging under one such statute and not the other, violates equal protection principles. Thus, defendant may not complain that she was charged with a felony violation under section 243.1 even though section 243, subdivision (b) is an identical statute prescribing a lesser punishment. [Numerous] factors properly may enter into a prosecutor's decision to charge under one statute and not another, such as a defendant's background and the severity of the crime, and so long as there is no showing that a defendant has been singled out deliberately for prosecution on the basis of some invidious criterion [such as race or religion], that is, one that is arbitrary and thus unjustified because it bears no rational relationship to legitimate law enforcement interests, the defendant cannot make out an equal protection violation. Defendant does not allege that her prosecution was motivated by improper considerations.

[Defendant's argument] is based upon the questionable premise that battery on a custodial officer without injury always is a less serious offense than battery with injury, so as to warrant inevitably a lesser punishment. [Consider, however,] whether a hypothetical defendant who, in the course of grabbing the arm of a correctional officer, inflicts a puncture wound with her fingernail that requires medical attention would be more culpable than a defendant who repeatedly hits and kicks the correctional officer, intending to cause serious injury but does not do so through no lack of effort. [The Legislature amended section 243] to allow misdemeanor prosecutions of batteries committed on custodial officers, and the Legislature did not repeal section 243.1 to allow felony prosecutions for more serious cases, even if no injury was inflicted. The Legislature's actions tend to demonstrate it contemplated that the ostensible "lesser" offense of battery without injury sometimes may constitute a more serious offense and merit greater punishment than the "greater" offense of battery accompanied by injury. . . .

The only difference between sections 243.1 and 243, subdivision (b) on the one hand, and section 243, subdivision (c)(1) on the other, is that, because section 243, subdivision (c)(1) is a wobbler, a trial court has discretion at sentencing either to impose misdemeanor punishment or grant probation and later, upon the defendant's successful completion of probation, declare the offense to be a misdemeanor. . . .

The circumstance that the Legislature did not grant to the trial court the same discretion in prosecutions under section 243.1 to reduce the charge to a misdemeanor as it did for prosecutions under section 243, subdivision (c) does not render the statutory scheme unconstitutional. A rational basis for these statutes exists; the Legislature reasonably could have concluded that reduction of the section 243.1 offense is not appropriate in cases of a battery on a custodial officer that is deemed serious enough by the prosecutor to warrant felony prosecution under the latter statute. . . . It is the prerogative, indeed the duty, of the Legislature to recognize degrees of culpability when drafting a Penal Code. . . . Because a rational basis exists for the statutory scheme pertaining to battery on a custodial officer, these statutes are not vulnerable to challenge under the equal protection clause.[7] . . .

KENNARD, J., dissenting.

[The] statutory scheme lacks any rational basis, in my view, and thereby violates the constitutional guarantee of equal protection of the laws. . . . The first prerequisite to a meritorious claim under the equal protection clause is a showing that the state has adopted a classification that affects two or more similarly situated groups in an unequal manner. In this case, persons who commit the same illegal act — a battery on a custodial officer causing injury — are in that respect similarly situated, but they are treated differently depending on whether they are charged under section 243.1, which does not require proof of injury, or under section 243(c), which does. . . .

[The] current scheme encourages arbitrary, irrational charging. In the case of a battery on a custodial officer that causes injury, there would be no incentive for the prosecutor to charge the defendant under section 243(c). . . . By ignoring the injury and charging the defendant under section 243.1 . . . , the prosecutor is spared the burden of proving the injury and the trial court is precluded from treating the offense as a misdemeanor, an option that would be available to the court if the defendant had been charged with, and convicted of a violation of section 243(c). . . .

Other consequences of the statutory scheme are even more perplexing, as illustrated by the problems involved in instructing a jury in the trial of a defendant charged with a violation of section 243(c). A trial court must instruct the jury on a lesser included offense when the evidence raises a question whether all of the elements of the charged crime are present, and the evidence would support a conviction of the lesser offense. . . . Because a defendant cannot commit battery on a custodial officer with injury (§243(c)) or battery on a custodial officer causing serious bodily injury (§243(d)) without committing all elements of battery in violation

7. In arguing that the existing statutory scheme is irrational and violates equal protection principles, the . . . dissenting opinion states that prosecutors would have no incentive to charge a defendant with a wobbler under section 243(c), because that provision requires proof of the additional element of injury and prescribes a "lesser" penalty than that provided for a violation of the straight felony of section 243.1. This point misjudges the significance of the United States Supreme Court's holding in *Batchelder* that the existence of two statutes covering the same criminal conduct but carrying different penalties does not violate either equal protection or due process principles, even though a prosecutor may be influenced by the different penalties available upon conviction in determining under which statute to charge a defendant. Defendant in the present case cannot point to any harm that she suffered by virtue of the circumstance that section 243(c) applies only to battery on a custodial officer with injury, inasmuch as she properly could have been charged under section 243.1 (even if section 243(c) applied to battery on a custodial officer without injury) and persons who commit battery on a custodial officer with injury may be charged and punished under section 243.1.

[Justice Kennard's] observation that the prosecutor in this case twice offered to dismiss the section 243.1 charge pursuant to a plea agreement does not call into question our conclusion that the Legislature properly can eliminate a trial court's discretion to reduce a charge in cases deemed by the prosecutor to warrant felony treatment. Such offers may reflect the prosecutor's judgment regarding the benefits of avoiding the administrative burden and expense of a trial rather than reflecting an assessment by the prosecutor regarding the seriousness of the offense. . . .

In addition, contrary to the suggestion in the . . . dissenting opinion, the present case does not involve any issue regarding necessarily included offenses, because there is no claim that section 243.1 is a necessarily included offense of section 243(c), so that a jury must be instructed on section 243.1 when a defendant is charged under section 243(c). Defendant was charged and the jury was instructed only under section 243.1. If a jury were to be instructed on a lesser necessarily included offense in a case in which the defendant is charged under the wobbler provision of section 243(c), it appears that the lesser necessarily included offense that the jury would be instructed upon would be the misdemeanor offense prescribed by section 243(b), rather than the felony offense prescribed by section 243.1.

of section 243.1 (battery on a custodial officer without injury), the latter is an offense necessarily included in the crimes of battery on a custodial officer with injury or with serious bodily injury. Consequently, when a defendant is charged with a battery on a custodial officer with injury or serious bodily injury, and there is a question whether the injury occurred, the trial court must instruct on the necessarily included offense of battery in violation of section 243.1 (battery on a custodial officer without injury). If the jury then found the defendant guilty as charged of a battery on a custodial officer causing injury (§243(c)), the court would have discretion to impose a misdemeanor sentence. But if the jury, because it entertained a reasonable doubt that the battery had caused an injury to the custodial officer, found the defendant guilty only of the necessarily included offense of battery on a custodial officer (§243.1), the trial court would be required to sentence the defendant as a felon.

I can perceive no rational basis for this rather startling statutory scheme. The majority . . . observes that if we compare two different batteries, it is possible that a particular battery without injury could be more heinous than another battery that did cause an injury. By the same reasoning, however, a particular petty theft could, depending on the circumstances, be more serious than a particular grand theft, and a particular grand theft could be more serious than a particular robbery, and so forth. Under this reasoning, the legal classification of crimes as inherently "greater" or "lesser" becomes meaningless and a rational ordering of crimes and punishment in the penal law becomes impossible. In deciding which of two crimes is the greater, the only meaningful comparison is between the elements of each crime, . . . not the particular circumstances of their commission. . . .

Here, after charging defendant with a felony battery under section 243.1, the prosecutor offered to dismiss the felony charge if defendant would plead guilty to a misdemeanor battery, which would be further reduced to an infraction if she successfully completed probation. Defense counsel refused the offer. The prosecutor then offered to dismiss the battery charge if defendant would plead guilty to the misdemeanor of driving under the influence of alcohol or drugs. Defense counsel rejected this offer as well. The case was then prosecuted as a felony. The trial court expressed dismay that the case had not been settled, and, after the jury found defendant guilty as charged, the court placed defendant on probation instead of sending her to prison for the felony conviction. . . .

This kind of injustice is the predictable result of the current irrational statutory scheme. . . .

———————————

In 1988, the Florida legislature revised the state's "habitual offender" statute. Under the new statute, a prosecutor's decision to charge an eligible defendant as a habitual offender translated into longer prison sentences. Within a few years, defendants and others began to complain that prosecutors were using their new charging power in an arbitrary and discriminatory manner. Legislative committees asked for a study of the use of the habitual offender statute. The study, completed in 1992, concluded as follows:

> [First, in] most circuits, and certainly on a statewide basis, the statute has not been limited to use against the very worst offenders but has been applied more frequently to the less serious offenders. . . . Second, the circuit in which an offender is prosecuted is

of enormous importance to the risk of habitualization. This means that for the roughly one third of all guilty adjudications who are eligible for habitualization, Florida does not have a single statewide system of reasonably uniform sentencing. For this group of offenders . . . there are effectively 20 separate sentencing systems that vary widely in their treatment of offenders eligible for habitualization.

Third, in all but two circuits [those encompassing Miami and Sarasota], the habitual offender sanctions are much more likely to be used against black offenders than non-black offenders, even after adjusting for prior record, the nature of the current offense and a variety of other factors that might have a bearing on the decision to habitualize. It was also found that, on a statewide basis, prosecutors were much more likely to use the statute against male offenders than similarly situated female offenders. . . .

After receiving this report, several state legislators called for revisions to the statute that would restrict or remove the prosecutor's power to decide when to charge an offender as a habitual felon. Consider the following statement that a group of prosecutors in the state made in this volatile context.

■ FLORIDA PROSECUTING ATTORNEYS' ASSOCIATION, STATEMENT CONCERNING IMPLEMENTING OF HABITUAL OFFENDER LAWS
(1993)

The Florida Prosecuting Attorneys' Association desires to provide continuing effective protection to the public from habitual offenders by discouraging the legislature from the total elimination of habitual offender laws and minimum mandatory sentence laws through the voluntary adoption by the State Attorneys of implementation criteria for use of habitual offender laws.

To fulfill this desire, the State Attorneys of the State of Florida adopt the criteria set forth below for the implementation of the habitual offender laws of Florida in their respective circuits to be utilized whenever such utilization would not result in the interference with the proper and fair administration of the duties of a State Attorney, as shall be determined by the respective State Attorney. Recognizing that there will be cases which would justify habitual offender treatment which will not meet these criteria, such cases shall have the reasons set forth in writing and signed by the designated Assistant State Attorney(s), and the State Attorneys filing such cases shall notify this Organization's President of such filings.

I. HABITUAL VIOLENT FELONY OFFENDERS

    A. Charged offense must be a second degree felony or higher . . . , AND
    B. Charged offense must be an enumerated violent felony, AND
    C. Defendant must have at least one prior conviction for an enumerated violent felony, AND
    D. The felony for which the defendant is to be sentenced was committed within five years of the date of the conviction for the last enumerated violent felony or within five years of the defendant's release, on parole or otherwise, from a

prison sentence or other commitment imposed as a result of the prior enumerated felony conviction.

II. HABITUAL FELONY OFFENDERS

A. *Violent Offenses:* Defendants charged with a second degree or higher enumerated violent felony . . . must have at least two prior felony convictions of
   any type.
B. *Second Degree Felonies (Excluding Sale or Purchase of or Trafficking in Controlled
   Substances and Burglary Cases):* Defendants charged with a non-violent,
   second degree or higher offense (excluding Sale or Purchase of or Trafficking in a Controlled Substance and Burglary) must have at least three prior
   felony convictions of any type, or two prior enumerated violent felony
   convictions.
C. *Second Degree Burglary:* Defendants charged with a second degree or higher
   Burglary must have at least two prior felony convictions of any type.
D. *Sale of or Trafficking in Controlled Substances:* Defendants charged with a
   second degree or higher sale of or trafficking in a Controlled Substance
   (including attempts and conspiracies of a second degree or higher) must
   have at least two prior felony convictions for sale of or trafficking in Controlled Substances (including attempts or conspiracies but not including
   Counterfeit Drugs); OR two prior enumerated violent felony convictions;
   OR one sale or trafficking in a Controlled Substance (including attempts
   and conspiracies but not including Counterfeit Drugs) conviction and one
   enumerated violent felony conviction.
E. *Third Degree Felonies:* Defendants charged with third degree felonies shall
   receive habitual offender sanctions only if they meet one of the following
   criteria:
   1. The defendant is charged with: Aggravated Assault, OR Aggravated Stalk-
      ing, OR Attempted Sexual Battery (victim 12 or older, no physical force),
      OR Battery on a Law Enforcement Officer, OR Child Abuse, OR Felony
      DUI, OR Resisting Arrest with Violence, OR . . . Vehicular Homicide,
      AND the defendant has at least four prior felony convictions of any
      type, or two prior enumerated violent convictions; OR
   2. The defendant is charged with Burglary of a Structure AND the
      defendant has at least two prior felony convictions, one of which is a
      Burglary of a Dwelling or Structure; OR
   3. The defendant is charged with Grand Theft of a Motor Vehicle AND the
      defendant has at least four prior felony convictions, three of which must
      be for Grand Theft of a Motor Vehicle. . . .

Problem 3-3. Available Charges

On the evening of January 9, Ida County deputy sheriff Randy Brown was on
patrol in Ida Grove. He observed three snowmobiles traveling on a downtown sidewalk and then on the streets in a careless and reckless manner. Once Brown began
pursuit, the trio split up. With the aid of another deputy, Brown eventually stopped
and arrested Mitch Peters.

At the time of arrest, Peters had a strong odor of alcohol on his breath. The deputies took him to the Ida County sheriff's office, where they administered sobriety tests. Peters failed the horizontal gaze nystagmus test and the preliminary breath test, registering above .10. Peters was charged with operating a motor vehicle while intoxicated, second offense, under Iowa Code §321J.2, which provides as follows:

> A person commits the offense of operating while intoxicated if the person operates a motor vehicle in this state [w]hile under the influence of an alcoholic beverage or other drug or a combination of such substances, [or while] having an alcohol concentration . . . of .10 or more.

Peters objects to the charge, claiming that he could be prosecuted only under section 321G.13(3), which provides as follows: "A person shall not drive or operate an all-terrain vehicle or snowmobile [w]hile under the influence of intoxicating liquor or narcotics or habit-forming drugs." This statute carries a lesser punishment than §321J.2. The trial court rejected Peters's claim. After conviction Peters appealed, claiming that §321J.2 did not apply to his conduct. How would you rule? Compare State v. Peters, 525 N.W.2d 854 (Iowa 1994); People v. Rogers, 475 N.W.2d 717 (Mich. 1991).

Notes

1. *Selection among charges: majority view.* According to judges in the United States, prosecutors may select among all applicable statutes in deciding what charges to bring, with no outside interference. The occasional claim by defendants that one crime better fits the offense and offender than another virtually always fails. In United States v. Batchelder, 442 U.S. 114 (1979), the Supreme Court considered two overlapping criminal statutes. Although both statutes prohibited convicted felons from possessing firearms, one provision imposed only a two-year maximum penalty while the second imposed a maximum penalty of five years. The Court held that Batchelder's conviction and sentence to the maximum term under the five-year statute did not violate the due process, equal protection, or separation of powers doctrine by granting the prosecutor charging discretion. While some courts reach this result as a matter of constitutional doctrine, others rely on statutory interpretation. These courts apply a technique of statutory interpretation or "rule of construction" referred to by its Latin name, *in pari materia,* which leads courts to presume that all related statutes make up a single, coherent statutory scheme, regardless of when they were enacted. Courts often work hard to treat statutes that at first appear to be general and specific instances of the same offense as separate crimes subject to the prosecutor's discretion.

Such a hands-off judicial attitude is easiest to explain when the two statutes involve a greater offense and a lesser included offense. It is more difficult to justify, however, when two statutes with different penalties require the prosecutor to prove precisely the same elements. A few courts create rules of statutory interpretation that apply the lesser penalty in a situation where two identical statutes impose different penalties, assuming that the legislature made an error. See State v. McAdam, 83 P.3d 161 (Kan. 2004).

2. *Structuring the charging discretion.* Does the absence of judicial regulation of selection among available charges create the need for detailed charging guidelines? What institutions could develop charging policies? Should legislatures draft policies or should they follow the Minnesota legislature's approach, simply directing that each prosecutor draft charging policies?

Consider again the Justice Department's Principles of Federal Prosecution. Do they give any surprising or meaningful direction to a prosecutor making a charging decision? The National District Attorneys Association lists the following among the appropriate factors for a prosecutor to consider in selecting charges: "the probability of conviction," "the willingness of the offender to cooperate with law enforcement," "possible improper motives of a victim or witness," "excessive cost of prosecution in relation to the seriousness of the offense," "recommendations of the involved law enforcement agency," and "any mitigating circumstances." National Prosecution Standards §43.6 (2d ed. 1991). Does this list differ in emphasis or in particulars from the federal standards? If prosecutors develop written charging policies on their own initiative, should the policies be made public? Should prosecutors be rewarded for obtaining convictions on whatever charges they initially file? See Tracey Meares, Rewards for Good Behavior: Influencing Prosecutorial Discretion and Conduct with Financial Incentives, 64 Fordham L. Rev. 851 (1995).

3. *Charges of overcharging.* Defense attorneys and many observers of the criminal justice system claim that prosecutors routinely "overcharge" cases in anticipation of plea bargain negotiations. Standard 3-3.9 of the ABA Standards for Criminal Justice (3d ed. 1993) advises prosecutors against bringing charges greater than necessary "to reflect the gravity of the offense" or charges where there is not "sufficient admissible evidence to support a conviction." How can we know when prosecutors are "overcharging" for strategic reasons? If it is difficult to prove that an abuse is taking place at all, is there any hope of reducing the amount of any abuse?

4. *Statutory limits on multiple convictions.* About a half-dozen states have statutes that approach the question of charge selection at the "back end" of convictions rather than the "front end" of charges. These statutes limit the number of convictions that can result from overlapping charges. Consider Mo. Ann. Stat. §556.041:

> When the same conduct of a person may establish the commission of more than one offense he may be prosecuted for each such offense. He may not, however, be convicted of more than one offense if [t]he offenses differ only in that one is defined to prohibit a designated kind of conduct generally and the other to prohibit a specific instance of such conduct. . . .

But cf. Ill. Ann. Stat. ch. 720, para. 5/3-3 ("When the same conduct of a defendant may establish the commission of more than one offense, the defendant may be prosecuted for each such offense"). Is a statute directed to the trial judge who enters final judgment more likely to produce consistent punishment for similar conduct than any effort to influence the charging decision more directly?

5. *Criminal code reform.* Would a well-drafted criminal code reduce concerns about consistent and fair charging? See Paul Robinson, Are Criminal Codes Irrelevant? 68 S. Cal. L. Rev. 159 (1994). Are there fewer overlaps and conflicts between statutes in states with a uniform criminal code? The majority of states revised their

criminal codes in the decades following the promulgation of the path-breaking Model Penal Code by the American Law Institute in 1962. Criminal codes before reform often include hundreds or, in some cases, thousands of separate crimes. The most prominent examples of jurisdictions that have failed to reform their codes — and in both cases the codes are complex and jumbled — are the federal system and California. See Ronald Gainer, Report to the Attorney General on Federal Criminal Code Reform, 1 Crim. L.F. 99 (1989). Whenever there is an apparent conflict between two statutory provisions, should the courts (or the lawyers) notify the appropriate legislative committees? Consider again the overlapping statutes in the *Wilkinson* case from California and the two statutes described in Problem 3-3. Why do you suppose the state legislatures passed these overlapping statutes? Was it an oversight that could be rationalized through criminal code reform?

b. Selection of System

The absolute number of juveniles arrested and prosecuted for criminal offenses has grown over the last generation. Most of the crimes committed by defendants under 18 years old are handled in specialized juvenile courts as "delinquency" cases. Juvenile courts handled more than 1.6 million delinquency cases in 2002 (up from 1.25 million in 1993); juveniles made up 16 percent of all arrestees in 2003. See *http://ojjdp.ncjrs.org/ojstatbb/* (statistical briefing book for juvenile justice).

Juvenile courts (which go by various names, such as "Family Court") operate differently from the adult criminal justice system. Their informal processes, which are considered civil rather than criminal proceedings, are designed to emphasize rehabilitation and avoid the stigma associated with adult criminal punishment. The juvenile justice system loses its authority over offenders when they reach age 18 or 21.

While most juvenile offenders have their cases adjudicated in the juvenile system, some are transferred to the adult criminal justice system. Less than 5 percent of all adjudicated juvenile cases transfer into the adult system. States have created a variety of mechanisms and presumptions to direct juvenile offenders into one system or the other. As with other charging decisions, the prosecutor is the key decisionmaker over this transfer decision, while the legislature also sets some important parameters. Do the limitations on the prosecutor's choice between systems differ from the limits on other prosecutorial charging decisions?

■ HOWARD N. SNYDER, MELISSA SICKMUND, AND EILEEN POE-YAMAGATA, JUVENILE TRANSFERS TO CRIMINAL COURT IN THE 1990'S: LESSONS LEARNED FROM FOUR STUDIES
National Center for Juvenile Justice (August 2000)

Juveniles may be prosecuted in criminal court under certain circumstances, and State law determines the conditions under which youth charged with a criminal law violation can be processed in the criminal, rather than the juvenile, justice system. The legal mechanisms for "transferring" juveniles from the juvenile to the criminal justice system differ from State to State. . . . These mechanisms, while having different labels across the States, fall into three general categories, according to who makes the transfer decision. The three mechanisms are judicial waiver, statutory exclusion, and concurrent jurisdiction; the decisionmakers are, respectively, the juvenile court judge, the legislature, and the prosecutor.

Judicial waiver (the juvenile court judge). In judicial waivers, a hearing is held in juvenile court, typically in response to the prosecutor's request that the juvenile court judge "waive" the juvenile court's jurisdiction over the matter and transfer the juvenile to criminal court for trial in the "adult" system. Most State statutes limit judicial waiver by age and offense criteria and by "lack of amenability to treatment" criteria. States often limit waiver to older youth or to youth who have committed certain serious offenses. Amenability determinations are typically based on a juvenile's offense history and previous dispositional outcomes but may also include psychological assessments. Under many State statutes, a court making an amenability determination must also consider the availability of dispositional alternatives for treating the juvenile, the time available for sanctions (for older juveniles), public safety, and the best interests of the child. Judicial waiver provisions vary in the degree of flexibility they allow the court in decisionmaking. Some provisions make the waiver decision entirely discretionary. Others establish a presumption in favor of waiver or specify circumstances under which waiver is mandatory.

Regardless of the degree of flexibility accorded to the court, the waiver process must adhere to certain constitutional principles of fairness. The U.S. Supreme Court, in Kent v. United States (1966), held that juvenile courts must provide "the essentials of due process" when transferring juveniles to criminal court. In 1996, approximately 10,000 cases—or 1.6 percent of all formally processed delinquency cases disposed in juvenile courts that year—were judicially waived to criminal court.

Statutory exclusion (the legislature). In a growing number of States, legislatures have statutorily excluded certain young offenders from juvenile court jurisdiction based on age and/or offense criteria. Perhaps the broadest such exclusion occurs in States that have defined the upper age of juvenile court jurisdiction as 15 or 16 and thus excluded large numbers of youth under age 18 from the juvenile justice system. NCJJ has estimated that (assuming such age-excluded youth are referred to criminal court at rates similar to those at which their juvenile counterparts are referred to juvenile court) as many as 218,000 cases involving youth under age 18 were tried in criminal court in 1996 as a result of State laws that defined them as adults solely on the basis of age. Whether juvenile and criminal court referral rates are in fact similar is not known. If they are not, or if the most minor incidents referred to juvenile court are never prosecuted in criminal court, the estimated number of age-excluded youth would be lower.

Many States also exclude certain individuals charged with serious offenses from juvenile court jurisdiction. Such exclusions are typically limited to older youth. The offenses most often targeted for exclusion are capital and other murders and violent offenses; however, an increasing number of States are excluding additional felony offenses. No national data exist on the number or characteristics of cases excluded by statute from juvenile court jurisdiction.

Concurrent jurisdiction (the prosecutor). Under this transfer option, State statutes give prosecutors the discretion to file certain cases in either juvenile or criminal court because original jurisdiction is shared by both courts. State concurrent jurisdiction provisions, like other transfer provisions, typically are limited by age and offense criteria.

Prosecutorial transfer, unlike judicial waiver, is not subject to judicial review and is not required to meet the due process requirements established in *Kent*. According to some State appellate courts, prosecutorial transfer is an "executive function" equivalent to routine charging decisions. Some States, however, have developed guidelines for prosecutors to follow in "direct filing" cases. No national data exist on the number or characteristics of the cases that prosecutors exclude or have the discretion to exclude from juvenile court jurisdiction.

State legislation delineates the conditions under which individuals charged with a violation of the law (and whose age places them under the original jurisdiction of the juvenile court) may or must be processed in the adult criminal system. Historically, the majority of States have relied on judicial waiver as the mechanism for transferring juveniles to criminal court. For many years, all States except Nebraska, New York, and, more recently, New Mexico have had statutory provisions that allow juvenile court judges to waive the juvenile court's jurisdiction over certain cases and transfer them to criminal court for prosecution. Statutory exclusion and concurrent jurisdiction provisions have been relatively less common, but the number of States in which these options exist is growing. Between the 1992 and 1997 legislative sessions, 45 States expanded their statutory provisions governing the transfer of juveniles to criminal court. Generally, States have done so by adding statutory exclusion provisions, lowering minimum ages, adding eligible offenses, or making judicial waiver presumptive. As of the end of 1997, legislatures in 28 States had statutorily excluded from juvenile court jurisdiction cases involving certain offenses and certain age youth, and, in 15 States, prosecutors had the discretion to file certain cases in criminal court.

Nearly all States rely on a combination of transfer provisions to move juveniles to the criminal system. As of the end of 1997, the most common combination (18 States) was judicial waiver together with statutory exclusion. Relying on judicial waiver alone was the second most common transfer arrangement (16 States). . . .

PRIOR RESEARCH ON TRANSFER

Research on transfers in the 1970's through the middle 1980's . . . found that although transfer to criminal court was intended for the most serious juvenile offenders, many transferred juveniles were not violent offenders, but repeat property offenders. In addition, studies found that transferred youth often were handled more leniently in criminal court than they would have been in juvenile court — arguably because they were appearing in criminal court for the first time at a relatively young age and with a relatively short offending history. . . .

Other studies, by contrast, have found that criminal courts were more likely than juvenile courts to incarcerate offenders. Fagan (1991), for example, compared juvenile and criminal court handling in 1981 and 1982 of 15- and 16-year-old felony offenders in similar counties in New York (where they are excluded from juvenile court) and New Jersey (where they are not). The study found that criminal court sanctions in New York were twice as likely to include incarceration as juvenile court sanctions in New Jersey. In a follow-up study of more recent cases (1986-87), however, Fagan (1995) found the reverse (at least for robbery cases). . . .

Recidivism rates of juveniles transferred to criminal court and juveniles retained in juvenile court have also been compared to assess the ultimate impact of transfer. For example, Fagan's 1991 analysis of felony burglary and robbery cases found that the likelihood of rearrest and reincarceration, as described earlier, did not differ among youth charged with burglary. Among juveniles charged with robbery, however, those handled in juvenile court in New Jersey were significantly less likely to be rearrested and reincarcerated than those handled in criminal court in New York. . . .

The difficulty with much of the research concerning the effect of transfer is that observed differences in case handling and outcomes may result from differences in the seriousness of the cases ultimately handled in juvenile and criminal courts. The underlying assumption is that transfer is reserved for the most serious cases. Because the very rationale for transfer is to allow courts to impose potentially harsher penalties on the most serious juvenile offenders, one would expect cases handled in criminal court to be more serious than those remaining in juvenile court. However, with numerous studies finding large proportions of relatively less serious cases (e.g., property cases) among transferred cases, it remains uncertain what case characteristics trigger a decision to transfer.

[Recent studies of juvenile justice in South Carolina, Utah, and Pennsylvania provide more current findings on these questions.]

FINDINGS: WHAT CRITERIA ARE USED IN THE TRANSFER DECISION?

Although there is a general sense that transfer should be reserved for the most serious juvenile cases, numerous studies have shown that a significant proportion of transfers seem to fall outside that category, calling into question the decisionmaking of the juvenile court judges and/or prosecutors who control transfer decisions. Other than the general seriousness of an offense, what characteristics make a case more likely to result in transfer? For example, does the likelihood of transfer vary with the seriousness of a victim's injury, the use of weapons (especially firearms), the presence of gang motivation in the underlying incident, or a juvenile's history of substance abuse or prior offending? Are there interactions between these characteristics?

Judges concurred with most waiver requests made by prosecutors (solicitors) in South Carolina and Utah. Two factors distinguished cases that were waived from those that were not: the extent of a juvenile's court history and the seriousness of his or her offense. . . . In South Carolina, offense seriousness was . . . a key determinant in the waiver decision. Regardless of a youth's court history, cases involving serious person offenses were more likely to be approved for waiver than other types of cases. Although the seriousness of the offense category alone was not as key in Utah as it was in South Carolina, the juvenile court in Utah was also quite consistent in its waiver decisionmaking. Characteristics of the crime incident were important in decisions to waive in Utah. Waiver was most likely to be granted in cases involving serious person offenders who used weapons and seriously injured someone, regardless of the offenders' court history. Even first-time offenders in Utah were waived if they seriously injured their victim. For other types of cases, the court looked to a youth's court history to decide whether to waive the matter to criminal court. In these cases, youth with long histories were more likely to be waived than those with shorter histories.

FINDINGS: DID THE NATURE OF TRANSFER DECISIONMAKING CHANGE DURING THE 1980'S AND 1990'S OVER AND ABOVE CHANGES IN LEGISLATION?

In the past several years, many States have passed legislation that makes it easier to transfer juveniles to criminal court. Has there been any change, however, in the nature of transferred cases and/or decision criteria in jurisdictions where transfer provisions did not change? In other words, did the transfer process change even where there was no change in State statutes?

A youth referred to juvenile court in Pennsylvania for a delinquency offense in 1994 was far more likely to be judicially waived to criminal court than a youth referred in 1986. The large increase in the likelihood of waiver does not appear to be related to a change in transfer legislation, the growth of the juvenile population, or a change in the overall number of juvenile arrests. Between 1986 and 1994, the 84-percent growth in judicial waivers was greater even than the 32-percent increase in juvenile arrests for violent crimes. . . .

The growth of waiver in Pennsylvania was greatly affected by the waiver of a much larger number of juveniles charged with drug offenses — in fact, about 40 percent of the overall increase in the number of waivers between 1986 and 1994 can be attributed to these youth. . . . Another important difference between the 1986 and the 1994 waiver groups was that juveniles waived in 1994 had less serious court histories than juveniles waived in 1986. . . .

FINDINGS: WHAT WAS THE IMPACT OF NEW LEGISLATION THAT EXCLUDES ADDITIONAL OFFENDERS FROM JUVENILE COURT JURISDICTION?

Of those States that have passed laws that make it easier to try juveniles in criminal court, the most common change was the enactment or expansion of statutory exclusion provisions. Legislatures responded to public outcry regarding "failures" of the juvenile justice system and proposed exclusion as at least a partial solution. The phrase "Do the adult crime, do the adult time" became a cliché. The efficacy of exclusion provisions, however, was not well established. Were more or different juveniles tried in the criminal system in jurisdictions that had enacted new statutory exclusion provisions? Did excluded juveniles receive harsher sanctions under new exclusion provisions than they would have received under prior judicial waiver provisions?

In many ways, implementation of Pennsylvania's 1996 exclusion law mimicked the State's judicial waiver process in previous years. Under the statute, when a case is not dismissed at the preliminary hearing, the criminal court judge's decision to keep the case in criminal court or to decertify it to juvenile court must be based on the same factors that a juvenile court judge uses to decide whether a youth should be waived to criminal court: the youth's age, prior referrals to juvenile court, and amenability to treatment.

The juvenile courts in the three Pennsylvania study counties judicially waived 277 youth in 1995. In the transition year of 1996, when the State's exclusion law took effect, the number of waivers dropped to 157 — a decrease of 120 youth. Of the 473 youth excluded from juvenile court jurisdiction in these counties in 1996, a total of 109 were convicted in criminal court. Assuming that cases still open in criminal court at the end of the study period resulted in the same proportion of convictions and dismissals, approximately 135 of the 473 excluded youth eventually would have been convicted in criminal court. The drop in the number of waived youth between 1995 and 1996 — 120 — is close to the number of excluded youth convicted in criminal court when all cases are closed — 135. These numbers suggest that the ultimate impact of Pennsylvania's 1996 exclusion legislation was to retain in criminal court those cases that the juvenile court would have judicially waived had it been given the opportunity. Consequently, regardless of the transfer path in Pennsylvania — judicial waiver or legislative exclusion — about the same number of youth were sentenced to an adult correctional facility.

Therefore, considering only case outcomes, the impact of Pennsylvania's new exclusion statute was negligible. The statute, however, increased the processing time for cases eventually handled within the juvenile justice system and placed an additional burden on local jails and the criminal courts. . . .

Findings from the project's four transfer studies can be summarized as follows:

Juvenile court judges largely concur with prosecutors as to which juveniles should be transferred to criminal court. These studies show that the juvenile court supports the prosecutor's request for transfer in approximately four out of five cases — indicating that these two key decisionmakers generally agree about who should be waived and who should not. Anecdotal evidence from the Utah study, in fact, indicates that in many cases in which a waiver petition was denied, the denial was based on a prosecutor's recommendation to withdraw the petition (following a plea bargaining agreement). It may be that the high proportion of judicial approval of waiver requests indicates that prosecutors are able to gauge which cases juvenile court judges will agree to waive and request waivers in only those cases. However, the study of exclusions in Pennsylvania implies that criminal court judges agree with juvenile court judges as to which youth should receive criminal court sanctions. . . .

Waiver decisions adjust to changing practice. The studies reveal that judges continued to waive those juveniles who failed in custody, even when custody occurred at an early stage in a youth's court career. It appears at first that between the mid-1980's and mid-1990's, waiver in Pennsylvania was modified by the public's concerns about a "new breed" of juvenile offender.

In response to these concerns, more and more youth with shorter juvenile court careers were waived. Unlike the earlier waiver group, a smaller proportion of the more recent waiver group in Pennsylvania had previously been placed on probation (51 percent of 1994 group versus 65 percent of 1986 group). However, approximately the same proportion (about 60 percent) of the youth waived in 1994 (who had shorter court careers) had been placed in custody at least once prior to the waiver incident. Thus, rather than changing the waiver decision criteria, the juvenile court [became] more likely to place juveniles in a facility without first trying probation. Recidivism after residential placement continued to be a key factor in the waiver decision.

The system adapts to large changes in structure. The structure of transfer decisions has changed in response to the public's concern over the increase in juvenile violence. Data in these studies confirm that the decisionmaking process will adapt to changing legal conditions and social pressure. For example, the study of the implementation of Pennsylvania's exclusion law found that even though the justice system adopted the State's new set of rules and followed new paths, case processing resulted in the same outcomes that would have occurred if the rules had not changed. There had been an expectation that the changed statutory exclusion provision would result in many, many more juveniles being tried in criminal court and in many of these youth ending up incarcerated in adult correctional facilities. However, Pennsylvania's exclusion legislation has had little overall impact on either the number of juveniles handled in criminal court or the proportion incarcerated in adult correctional facilities.

There was also an underlying assumption that transfer decisionmaking by juvenile court judges in Pennsylvania tended to favor juveniles and that decisionmaking by criminal court judges under the new provisions would be different. However, this study found that, in Pennsylvania, the decisionmaking process followed by criminal court judges regarding decertification was much the same as that followed by juvenile court judges regarding waiver. . . .

■ KRISTY MADDOX v. STATE
931 S.W.2d 438 (Ark. 1996)

Brown, J.

This is a juvenile-transfer case. On October 16, 1995, an information was filed charging appellant Kristy Maddox with criminal mischief in the first degree, a Class C felony. She was accused of intentionally throwing a Mountain Dew bottle from a moving vehicle and striking the victim's automobile, causing damage in excess of $500. Maddox, who was 17 years old at the time of the alleged incident, and who turned 18 on February 4, 1996, moved to have the charge transferred to juvenile court. Her motion was denied. She now appeals that denial.

Only two witnesses testified at the juvenile-transfer hearing. Pamela Maddox, the appellant's mother, related to the court that at the time of the hearing, Maddox was living with her and assisting around the house by doing chores and taking care of her younger siblings. She testified that Maddox was not currently in high school, but that she was working on her G.E.D. and planned to attend college in the Fall. She stated that she had a good relationship with her daughter, but that she did have to call the police on one occasion for an undisclosed "family disturbance." She and the prosecutor agreed that Maddox had no prior criminal history.

Sherry Lynn Kinnamon, the victim, was called as a witness by the prosecution. She testified that on April 20, 1995, she was driving her grandparents from Huntsville to the VA Hospital in Fayetteville when she noticed a red pick-up truck following very closely behind her. She stated that she tapped her brakes a few times to get the driver's attention and slowed so that the truck could pass, but that the driver would not do so. Even when given a straight stretch of road with no cars approaching, the driver of the truck would not pass her. She explained that the driver instead pulled alongside her car several times, and that the driver and two passengers would simply look at her, then drop back behind her car, where they made obscene gestures. She stated that she slowed her car to two miles an hour so that the truck would pass, but that it again would not. Finally, she accelerated, and the truck pulled alongside her car. Maddox hung out of the window on the passenger's side of the truck, held by her belt loops. She was holding a full glass bottle of Mountain Dew, and she and the other occupants of the truck were yelling obscenities at Kinnamon. Kinnamon testified that Maddox then intentionally threw the glass bottle at her car. It dented the front of the hood and cracked the windshield. Kinnamon said that after she regained her composure, she pursued the truck and got its license plate number. No one was injured, but she estimated that the damage to her car was about $800.

The trial court denied the motion to transfer after determining that Maddox's intentional throwing of the Mountain Dew bottle at Kinnamon's car was not only a serious act but a violent one. The court emphasized the harassing nature of the episode and referred to an incident in Oklahoma where a person was killed because an object had been thrown at his vehicle. The court noted that Maddox had no prior criminal record and mentioned that there had been no evidence introduced, one way or the other, with regard to her prospects for rehabilitation.

Maddox claims in her appeal that the trial court clearly erred in retaining jurisdiction of this matter. The Arkansas Juvenile Code provides that the circuit court shall consider the following factors in determining whether to retain jurisdiction or transfer a case to juvenile court: 1) The seriousness of the offense, and whether violence was employed by the juvenile in the commission of the offense; 2) Whether the offense is part of a repetitive pattern of adjudicated offenses which would lead to the determination that the juvenile is beyond rehabilitation under existing rehabilitation programs, as evidenced by past efforts to treat and rehabilitate the juvenile and the response to such efforts; and 3) The prior history, character traits, mental maturity, and any other factor which reflects upon the juvenile's prospects for rehabilitation. Ark. Code §9-27-318(e). The decision to retain jurisdiction must be supported by clear and convincing evidence. Ark. Code §9-27-318(f). In making its decision, the trial court need not give equal weight to each of the statutory factors. Furthermore, the trial court's denial of a motion to transfer will be reversed only if its ruling was clearly erroneous.

Maddox asserts a twofold challenge to the denial of her motion to transfer. She first urges that the trial court did not recognize the relevance of her mother's testimony and emphasizes that her mother presented sufficient evidence of her character traits to support a positive finding on the issue of her prospects for rehabilitation. She further argues that the charge of criminal mischief is a crime against property which the trial court improperly characterized as "violent" in order to keep the matter in circuit court.

The State responds that criminal mischief is a Class C felony that satisfies the seriousness criterion for purposes of section 9-27-318(e) and that violence was employed in the commission of this offense. The State also questions whether the mother's testimony was really relevant to the criterion of rehabilitation, when there was no showing that Maddox was remorseful or willing to accept responsibility for her actions. Finally, the State contends that the fact Maddox was 18 at the time of her hearing is sufficient, standing alone, to affirm the trial court's ruling.

In recent years, this court has fashioned the following rule in juvenile-transfer cases: The use of violence in the commission of a serious offense is a factor sufficient in and of itself for a circuit court to retain jurisdiction of a juvenile's case, but the commission of a serious offense without the use of violence is not sufficient grounds to deny the transfer. Sebastian v. State, 885 S.W.2d 882 (Ark. 1994). In Green v. State, 916 S.W.2d 756 (Ark. 1996), this court noted that manslaughter, a Class C felony, was a serious offense: "No doubt the offense charged is serious. Manslaughter is a Class C felony. If [the appellant] were convicted he would be sentenced to imprisonment for not less than three nor more than ten years." Criminal mischief in the first degree is also a Class C felony, and it satisfies the seriousness requirement.

The question we next address is whether the trial court was correct in its finding that Maddox committed a violent act. We agree with the trial court that she did. This is not a case where a juvenile merely committed a crime against property such as we had in Pennington v. State, 807 S.W.2d 660 (1991). In *Pennington,* two 17-year-olds broke about 30 tombstones in a cemetery and were charged with criminal mischief. The circuit court refused to transfer the cases to juvenile court, and we reversed on the basis that the trial court gave too much deference to the prosecutor, after the court acknowledged that violence was not embraced in the young men's actions.

In the instant case, the trial court noted that these facts would likely support an aggravated assault charge as well as a charge of criminal mischief. This court has observed that the crime of aggravated assault is not only serious, but that no violence beyond that necessary to commit aggravated assault is necessary to meet the requirement under Ark. Code §9-27-318(e)(1). We conclude that a violent act lies at the core of the alleged crime in the instant case — the willful throwing of a glass bottle at a moving vehicle containing three passengers, as testified to by Kinnamon. These facts are sufficient to sustain a refusal to transfer in our judgment.

There is, too, the fact that Maddox has now turned 18. Young people over age 18 can no longer be committed to the Division of Youth Services for rehabilitation unless they are already committed at the time they turn 18. The fact that Maddox cannot now be committed to the Division of Youth Services is highly relevant to her prospects for rehabilitation as a juvenile and is a factor that this court considers important in reviewing a trial court's denial of a motion to transfer. This circumstance lends additional support to an affirmance.

ROAF, A.J., dissenting.*

In 1989, the Arkansas General Assembly enacted . . . the Arkansas Juvenile Code of 1989. A declaration of purpose for this legislation is found at Ark. Code §9-27-302. It is important in the context of this appeal and warrants our reconsideration:

> This subchapter shall be liberally construed to the end that its purposes may be carried out:
>
> (1) To assure that all juveniles brought to the attention of the courts receive the guidance, care and control, preferably in each juvenile's own home, which will best serve the emotional, mental, and physical welfare of the juvenile and the best interests of the state;
>
> (2) To preserve and strengthen the juvenile's family ties whenever possible, removing him from the custody of his parents only when his welfare or the safety and protection of the public cannot adequately be safeguarded without such removal; . . .
>
> (3) To protect society more effectively by substituting for retributive punishment, whenever possible, methods of offender rehabilitation and rehabilitative restitution, recognizing that the application of sanctions which are consistent with the seriousness of the offense is appropriate in all cases;
>
> (4) To provide means through which the provisions of this subchapter are executed and enforced and in which the parties are assured a fair hearing and their constitutional and other legal rights recognized and enforced.

Since 1991, this court has been called upon numerous times to interpret the provisions of the juvenile code dealing with how we treat youth who are charged with criminal offenses. The General Assembly has in turn had the opportunity on several

---

*Associate Justice Roaf incorporated by reference here the dissenting opinion from another case, Butler v. State, 922 S.W.2d 685 (Ark. 1996). — EDS.

occasions to react to our holdings. I submit that this court and the General Assembly have so woefully failed to consider a significant portion of the stated purposes underpinning the juvenile code that this language has become meaningless.

We have neither liberally construed the statute to the benefit of the emotional, mental, and physical welfare of the juveniles, nor even for the best interests of the state. We have failed to insure that methods of rehabilitation and restitution are substituted wherever possible, for retributive punishment, and we have surely failed to provide that juveniles are assured fair hearings and that their constitutional and other rights provided by this statute are uniformly recognized and enforced. We share this responsibility equally with our elected state representatives.

Today, we once again affirm a trial court's refusal to transfer a criminal case involving a juvenile to juvenile court. The trial court's ruling, and our affirmance, were foregone conclusions because of the prior holdings of this court, because of the weight of stare decisis, and because of the legislature's failure to revisit this legislation in light of our holdings. Children between the ages of 14 and 17 years are paying the price for our failures. We cannot even take comfort in the notion that the best interests of the state are being served, for many of these juveniles will return to our midst as adults, and the opportunity to use our best efforts to rehabilitate, guide and care for them will have been lost.

The landmark case which has led us down this path is, of course, Walker v. State, 803 S.W.2d 502 (Ark. 1991). In *Walker,* by a 4 to 3 decision, this court reached several significant holdings which have been repeatedly reavowed and reaffirmed since *Walker*— that a juvenile movant has the burden of proof when seeking to transfer a case from circuit court to juvenile court — that the trial court need not give equal weight to the three factors that the statute directs it to consider in determining whether to transfer a case — that the prosecutor is not even required to introduce proof on each of the three factors that the trial court is directed to consider — that the criminal information alone can provide a sufficient basis for the denial of a transfer to juvenile court — that a trial court does not have to make findings of fact or provide a rationale for its decision in a juvenile transfer proceeding. We have also held that juveniles "ultimately" charged and tried in circuit court are subject to the procedures prescribed for adults, and are not afforded the protections provided by the juvenile code, such as the requirement of parental consent to a waiver of right to counsel.

I am not unmindful of the fact that since 1991, the general assembly has twice amended Ark. Code §9-27-318, which deals with waiver and transfer to circuit court, each time to the detriment of juvenile defendants. However, they have not seen fit to amend the stated purposes for the juvenile code. I suggest that they do so at the next opportunity. Until then, our decisions and their inaction are in direct conflict with these purposes. I dissent.

Notes

1. *Choice of system for juvenile offenders: majority position.* The choice between the adult and juvenile systems is cluttered with various starting presumptions, shifting burdens of proof or persuasion, and opportunities to reconsider the choice of systems. In the end, the statutes in almost every state (along with the federal juvenile system) initially assign the great majority of juveniles to the juvenile court, and then

allow a judge in the juvenile court to "waive" jurisdiction after an investigation, a hearing, and a statement of reasons by the court. See Kent v. United States, 383 U.S. 541 (1966). About 15 states give prosecutors the power in some cases to select between the adult and juvenile systems when there is "concurrent" jurisdiction (ordinarily for the most serious offenses and the oldest juveniles). Most states initially place into the adult system the oldest juveniles who commit the most serious crimes, and place into the juvenile system (at least initially) the youngest juveniles and those who commit the least serious crimes. Franklin Zimring's major study suggests that, despite major changes in the laws dealing with the assignment of juveniles to the adult criminal justice system, the legal changes have made little difference in the numbers of juvenile cases actually resolved in the adult system. See Zimring, American Youth Violence (1998).

Where the law gives the prosecutor the initial choice of systems, that decision is usually subject to judicial review, and the burden of proof usually falls on the party seeking to transfer the case (that is, the juvenile attempting to move into the juvenile court). In Arkansas, as we saw in the *Maddox* case, the trial court in the adult system may retain jurisdiction if there is "clear and convincing evidence" that the juvenile should be tried as an adult. In many other states, such as North Dakota, the trial court in the adult system retains jurisdiction if there are "reasonable grounds" (in essence, probable cause) to believe that the juvenile committed the crime as charged and would not be "amenable to rehabilitation" in the juvenile system. See In the Interest of A.E., 559 N.W.2d 215 (N.D. 1997). Does *Maddox* convince you that the statutory requirement of judicial review makes little difference in transfer cases?

In 2002, under 3 percent of all felony defendants in the nation's 75 largest counties were juveniles. Two-thirds of the juveniles transferred to criminal court were charged with a violent offense. The proportion of delinquency cases that were waived into the adult system was 1.4 percent in 1985; the proportion reached 1.5 percent in 1991 and then dropped to 0.8 percent by 2002. Howard N. Snyder & Melissa Sickmund, Juvenile Offenders and Victims: 2006 National Report 187 (2006).

2. *Constitutional challenges to charging of juveniles.* Juveniles in several states have challenged the constitutionality of statutes that mandate the choice of the adult system for some cases or that give prosecutors the discretion to file charges in the adult system. These challenges are based on many different clauses in state constitutions, most frequently due process and equal protection clauses. More often than not, the challenges have failed. See Manduley v. Superior Court, 41 P.3d 3 (Cal. 2002) (upholds constitutionality of system allowing prosecutor to choose juvenile versus adult system for certain defendants); but see State v. Mohi, 901 P.2d 991 (Utah 1995) (strikes down statute for excessive prosecutorial discretion; concludes that statutes in other states limit more severely the class of juveniles subject to transfer by prosecutor, or list criteria for eligible juveniles).

Juveniles have also found very limited success in challenging the procedures used at a judicial hearing to determine whether to transfer a case from one system to another, and in challenging the complete absence of such a judicial hearing. See In re Boot, 925 P.2d 964 (Wash. 1996) (statute giving exclusive original jurisdiction over juveniles charged with specified crimes to adult criminal court does not permit hearing on juvenile court jurisdiction; assignment to adult court without declination hearing does not violate procedural or substantive due process or equal protection); but see Hughes v. State, 653 A.2d 241 (Del. 1994) (statute's elimination of judicial investigation into factual basis of felony charge against child who reaches age of 18 while pending trial violates constitutional guarantees of due process and equal protection).

3. *Right to counsel in juvenile delinquency proceedings.* The right to retained counsel in delinquency proceedings was made a federal constitutional requirement in In re Gault, 387 U.S. 1 (1967). Because counsel is not appointed or is often waived, less than half of all juveniles are represented by legal counsel in their delinquency proceedings. Barry Feld, Criminalizing the American Juvenile Court 222 (1993). Statutes in many states have created systems for appointing counsel for at least some juvenile proceedings. Roughly 10 states have mandatory appointment statutes; about half the states make appointment of counsel discretionary. See Tory Caeti, Craig Hemmens & Velmer Burton, Jr., Juvenile Right to Counsel: A National Comparison of State Legal Codes, 23 Am. J. Crim. L. 611 (1996). Jury trials are not available in the juvenile system even when they would be required for comparable charges in the adult system. In situations where transfer into the adult criminal courts means that the state will appoint an attorney and provide a jury, will a juvenile welcome the transfer?

4. *Consequences at later sentencing.* In more than 40 states, adjudications in the juvenile system can be used years later to increase a sentence imposed in adult court for some later criminal offense. Adult criminal defendants have challenged this use of their juvenile adjudications, arguing that the lack of procedural safeguards in the juvenile system (such as absence of a jury trial or appointed counsel) should bar the use of the juvenile adjudication as a "prior conviction." Some courts have accepted this argument for cases in which the juvenile was not represented by counsel.

5. *Abolition of juvenile court?* The first juvenile court was created in Chicago after the Illinois legislature passed the Illinois Juvenile Court Act of 1899. By 1925, 46 states, 3 territories, and the District of Columbia had separate juvenile courts. See Robert E. Shepherd, The Juvenile Court at 100 Years: A Look Back, Juv. Just. Dec. 1999 at 13. About 20 states have created "family courts" with broader jurisdiction to handle the full range of criminal and civil issues involving children. Now, 100 years after their creation, juvenile courts are under attack. Are children who commit crimes better served by having a separate system for adjudicating their crimes and imposing sentences? Or would they be better off in a single criminal justice system, perhaps with special allowances made for their age? What conditions are necessary for a successful separate juvenile system?

6. *Disparate racial impact in juvenile justice.* A report funded by the U.S. Department of Justice and several private foundations documented some major disparities in the treatment of white and black defendants in the juvenile justice system. Some of the findings of the report are as follows:

> It is clear that minority youth are more likely than others to come into contact with the juvenile justice system. Research suggests that this disparity is most pronounced at the beginning stages of involvement with the juvenile justice system. When racial/ethnic differences are found, they tend to accumulate as youth are processed through the system. . . .
>
> • In 1998, African American youth were overrepresented as a proportion of arrests in 26 of 29 offense categories documented by the FBI.

- In 1997, the majority of cases referred to juvenile court involved White youth. Minority youth were overrepresented in the referral cohort. . . . While White youth comprised 66 percent of the juvenile court referral population they comprised 53 percent of the detained population. In contrast, African American youths made up 31 percent of the referral population and 44 percent of the detained population. . . .
- For offenses against persons, White youth were 57 percent of cases petitioned but only 45 percent of cases waived to adult court. African American youth charged with similar offenses were 40 percent of the cases petitioned but rose to 50 percent of cases waived to adult court. Similarly, in drug cases, White youth were 59 percent of cases petitioned but only 35 percent of cases waived to adult court. . . .
- In 1993, when controlling for current offense and prior admissions, incarceration rates to state public facilities were higher for African American and Latino youth than White youth. . . . African American youth were confined on average for 61 days more than White youth, and Latino youth were confined 112 days more than white youth.

Eileen Poe-Yamagata & Michael Jones, And Justice for Some (Building Blocks for Youth, 2000). The racial disparities described in the report are larger than disparities found in some studies of the adult criminal justice system. As a legislator, how would you respond to this study? Would you argue to transfer fewer juveniles into the adult system (even though the racial disparities in the adult system might be smaller overall)? To make the juvenile system less discretionary?

Another critical choice of system for many serious cases is between state and federal court, or between different state courts. For large classes of drug and firearm cases, for example, there is overlapping state and federal jurisdiction. Consider the following problem.

Problem 3-4. Federal Day

In Manhattan, federal prosecutors have developed a program known as "Federal Day." One day each week chosen at random, all drug arrests obtained by state and local police agencies are processed in federal court, where sentences for drug crimes are much higher than they are in the state courts. Prosecutors say that the program is designed to help the overwhelmed state courts and to deter criminal activity by imposing the stiffer sentences. Since 1983 there have been between 100 and 200 federal indictments per year in cases that the local police have developed. For instance, 231 cases went to federal district court under the Federal Day program between January 1984 and May 1986. During that same period, New York police made 5,837 felony narcotics arrests. Of the 5,606 cases sent to the state prosecutor in Manhattan, 1,172 resulted in state felony indictments. A total of 1,043 other cases were reduced to state misdemeanors.

A U.S. senator has heard about the Federal Day program and plans to introduce legislation requiring all U.S. Attorneys' offices to institute such programs. Would you advise the U.S. Attorney for Manhattan to continue the program? Under what conditions? Do you believe that those who support the Manhattan policy will also support the proposed legislation, and vice versa? What are the prospects for its passage? Compare Katherine Bishop, "Mandatory Sentences in Drug Cases: Is the Law Defeating Its Purpose?" N.Y. Times, June 8, 1990, at B16. See also Sara Sun Beale, Federalizing Hate Crimes: Symbolic Politics, Expressive Law, or Tool for Criminal Enforcement? 80 Boston U. L. Rev. 1227 (2000); Kathleen Brickey, Criminal Mischief: The Federalization of American Criminal Law, 46 Hastings L.J. 1135 (1995).

Notes

1. *The federalization trend.* It is often said that criminal justice remains primarily a state and local function, and in term of volume that remains true. The federal courts still produce less than 10 percent of the felony convictions in this country each year, and virtually all misdemeanor convictions come out of the state courts. But the areas of potential overlap between the federal and state criminal justice systems have been growing. The federal government has been exerting more authority and money on criminal matters during the last few decades than at any previous point in the nation's history. In particular, the federal presence in narcotics enforcement has grown enormously over the years. See Michael M. O'Hear, Federalism and Drug Control, 57 Vand. L. Rev. 783 (2004).

The 1999 report of the American Bar Association's Task Force on Federalization of Criminal Law documents various aspects of this growth. Federal crime legislation has become more common: "more than forty percent of the federal criminal provisions enacted since the Civil War have been enacted since 1970." The number of federal investigators and prosecutors has expanded along with the number of available federal crimes. The report lists some negative consequences of federalization: "diminution of the stature of the state courts in the perception of citizens" and "disparate results for the same conduct." What would be a legitimate basis for extending federal law to criminalize additional conduct? Would the same arguments support a new emphasis in enforcing existing federal laws? See Michael A. Simons, Prosecutorial Discretion and Prosecution Guidelines: A Case Study in Controlling Federalization, 75 N.Y.U. L. Rev. 893 (2000).

2. *Potential limits on the federalization of crime.* Some restraint on the growth of federal criminal law might come from various constitutional provisions, such as the commerce clause, that were designed to limit the authority of the federal government and to preserve essential areas of state authority. Those constitutional limits, however, have produced very few rulings that in fact limit congressional authority to create federal crimes. In United States v. Lopez, 514 U.S. 549 (1995), the Supreme Court held that possession of a gun near a school is not an economic activity that has a "substantial effect" on interstate commerce; thus, Congress went beyond its constitutional authority in passing a federal crime to cover this activity. More typical of recent cases, however, is Sabri v. United States, 541 U.S. 600 (2004), where the Court held that Congress had constitutional authority to make it a federal crime to bribe officials of a local organization or government that receives federal program funds, even when the bribe has nothing to do with the federal funds. Even a remote connection to federal funds makes such a law a valid exercise of Congress's authority under the Constitution's spending clause.

5. Selective Prosecution

For each of the prosecutorial charging decisions considered in this chapter, judges mostly refuse to second-guess the exercise of charging discretion. A prosecutor might make very different charging decisions in two similar cases and will not have to explain those choices. In all of these cases, however, judges asked to review the prosecutor's decision point out that if a prosecutor bases the charging decision on some constitutionally suspect grounds — such as the defendant's race or gender — the court stands willing to step in. Similarly, the prosecutor cannot file a charge as a way of punishing a defendant for taking constitutionally protected action, such as exercising free speech or insisting on a jury trial. Thus, a prosecutor can have many different reasons for a charging decision, but she cannot rely on a limited set of constitutionally improper reasons. How is a defendant to know the prosecutor's reason for a particular charging decision?

■ UNITED STATES v. CHRISTOPHER ARMSTRONG
517 U.S. 456 (1996)

REHNQUIST, C.J.

In this case, we consider the showing necessary for a defendant to be entitled to discovery on a claim that the prosecuting attorney singled him out for prosecution on the basis of his race. We conclude that respondents failed to satisfy the threshold showing: They failed to show that the Government declined to prosecute similarly situated suspects of other races.

In April 1992, respondents were indicted in the United States District Court for the Central District of California on charges of conspiring to possess with intent to distribute more than 50 grams of cocaine base (crack) and conspiring to distribute the same, [and federal firearms offenses]. In response to the indictment, respondents filed a motion for discovery or for dismissal of the indictment, alleging that they were selected for federal prosecution because they are black. In support of their motion, they offered only an affidavit by a "Paralegal Specialist," employed by the Office of the Federal Public Defender representing one of the respondents. The only allegation in the affidavit was that, in every one of the 24 [narcotics] cases closed by the office during 1991, the defendant was black. Accompanying the affidavit was a "study" listing the 24 defendants, their race, whether they were prosecuted for dealing cocaine as well as crack, and the status of each case.

The Government opposed the discovery motion, arguing, among other things, that there was no evidence or allegation "that the Government has acted unfairly or has prosecuted non-black defendants or failed to prosecute them." The District Court granted the motion. It ordered the Government (1) to provide a list of all cases from the last three years in which the Government charged both cocaine and firearms offenses, (2) to identify the race of the defendants in those cases, (3) to identify what levels of law enforcement were involved in the investigations of those cases, and (4) to explain its criteria for deciding to prosecute those defendants for federal cocaine offenses.

The Government moved for reconsideration of the District Court's discovery order. With this motion it submitted affidavits and other evidence to explain why it had chosen to prosecute respondents and why respondents' study did not support the inference that the Government was singling out blacks for cocaine prosecution. The federal and local agents participating in the case alleged in affidavits that race played no role in their investigation. An Assistant United States Attorney explained in an affidavit that the decision to prosecute met the general criteria for prosecution, because

> there was over 100 grams of cocaine base involved, over twice the threshold necessary for a ten year mandatory minimum sentence; there were multiple sales involving multiple defendants, thereby indicating a fairly substantial crack cocaine ring; . . . there were multiple federal firearms violations intertwined with the narcotics trafficking; the overall evidence in the case was extremely strong, including audio and videotapes of defendants; . . . and several of the defendants had criminal histories including narcotics and firearms violations.

The Government also submitted sections of a published 1989 Drug Enforcement Administration report which concluded that "[l]arge-scale, interstate trafficking networks controlled by Jamaicans, Haitians and Black street gangs dominate the manufacture and distribution of crack." In response, one of respondents' attorneys submitted an affidavit alleging that an intake coordinator at a drug treatment center had told her that there are "an equal number of caucasian users and dealers to minority users and dealers." Respondents also submitted an affidavit from a criminal defense attorney alleging that in his experience many nonblacks are prosecuted in state court for crack offenses. . . . The District Court denied the motion for reconsideration. When the Government indicated it would not comply with the court's discovery order, the court dismissed the case. [The Court of Appeals affirmed the order.]

A selective-prosecution claim is not a defense on the merits to the criminal charge itself, but an independent assertion that the prosecutor has brought the charge for reasons forbidden by the Constitution. Our cases delineating the necessary elements to prove a claim of selective prosecution have taken great pains to explain that the standard is a demanding one. These cases afford a "background presumption" that the showing necessary to obtain discovery should itself be a significant barrier to the litigation of insubstantial claims.

A selective-prosecution claim asks a court to exercise judicial power over a "special province" of the Executive. The Attorney General and United States Attorneys retain "broad discretion" to enforce the Nation's criminal laws. Wayte v. United States, 470 U.S. 598 (1985). They have this latitude because they are designated by statute as the President's delegates to help him discharge his constitutional responsibility to "take Care that the Laws be faithfully executed." U.S. Const., Art. II, §3. . . .

Of course, a prosecutor's discretion is subject to constitutional constraints. One of these constraints, imposed by the equal protection component of the Due Process Clause of the Fifth Amendment, is that the decision whether to prosecute may not be based on "an unjustifiable standard such as race, religion, or other arbitrary classification," Oyler v. Boles, 368 U.S. 448, 456 (1962). A defendant may demonstrate that the administration of a criminal law is "directed so exclusively against a particular class of persons . . . with a mind so unequal and oppressive" that the system of prosecution amounts to "a practical denial" of equal protection of the law. Yick Wo v. Hopkins, 118 U.S. 356, 373 (1886).

In order to dispel the presumption that a prosecutor has not violated equal protection, a criminal defendant must present clear evidence to the contrary. We explained in *Wayte* why courts are "properly hesitant to examine the decision whether to prosecute." Judicial deference to the decisions of these executive officers rests in part on an assessment of the relative competence of prosecutors and courts. "Such factors as the strength of the case, the prosecution's general deterrence value, the Government's enforcement priorities, and the case's relationship to the Government's overall enforcement plan are not readily susceptible to the kind of analysis the courts are competent to undertake." It also stems from a concern not to unnecessarily impair the performance of a core executive constitutional function. "Examining the basis of a prosecution delays the criminal proceeding, threatens to chill law enforcement by subjecting the prosecutor's motives and decisionmaking to outside inquiry, and may undermine prosecutorial effectiveness by revealing the Government's enforcement policy."

The requirements for a selective-prosecution claim draw on ordinary equal protection standards. The claimant must demonstrate that the federal prosecutorial policy had a discriminatory effect and that it was motivated by a discriminatory purpose. To establish a discriminatory effect in a race case, the claimant must show that similarly situated individuals of a different race were not prosecuted. This requirement has been established in our case law since Ah Sin v. Wittman, 198 U.S. 500 (1905). Ah Sin, a subject of China, petitioned a California state court for a writ of habeas corpus, seeking discharge from imprisonment under a San Francisco county ordinance prohibiting persons from setting up gambling tables in rooms barricaded to stop police from entering. He alleged in his habeas petition "that the ordinance is enforced solely and exclusively against persons of the Chinese race and not otherwise." We rejected his contention that this averment made out a claim under the Equal Protection Clause, because it did not allege "that the conditions and practices to which the ordinance was directed did not exist exclusively among the Chinese, or that there were other offenders against the ordinance than the Chinese as to whom it was not enforced."

The similarly situated requirement does not make a selective-prosecution claim impossible to prove. Twenty years before *Ah Sin*, we invalidated an ordinance, also adopted by San Francisco, that prohibited the operation of laundries in wooden buildings. *Yick Wo,* 118 U.S. at 374. The plaintiff in error successfully demonstrated that the ordinance was applied against Chinese nationals but not against other laundry-shop operators. The authorities had denied the applications of 200 Chinese subjects for permits to operate shops in wooden buildings, but granted the applications of 80 individuals who were not Chinese subjects to operate laundries in wooden buildings "under similar conditions." . . .

Having reviewed the requirements to prove a selective-prosecution claim, we turn to the showing necessary to obtain discovery in support of such a claim. If discovery is ordered, the Government must assemble from its own files documents which might corroborate or refute the defendant's claim. Discovery thus imposes many of the costs present when the Government must respond to a prima facie case of selective prosecution. It will divert prosecutors' resources and may disclose the Government's prosecutorial strategy. The justifications for a rigorous standard for the elements of a selective-prosecution claim thus require a correspondingly rigorous standard for discovery in aid of such a claim.

The parties [describe] the requisite showing to establish entitlement to discovery . . . with a variety of phrases, like "colorable basis," "substantial threshold showing," "substantial and concrete basis," or "reasonable likelihood." However, the many labels for this showing conceal the degree of consensus about the evidence necessary to meet it. The Courts of Appeals require some evidence tending to show the existence of the essential elements of the defense, discriminatory effect and discriminatory intent.

In this case we consider what evidence constitutes "some evidence tending to show the existence" of the discriminatory effect element. . . . The vast majority of the Courts of Appeals require the defendant to produce some evidence that similarly situated defendants of other races could have been prosecuted, but were not, and this requirement is consistent with our equal protection case law.[3]

The Court of Appeals [in this case] reached its decision in part because it started "with the presumption that people of all races commit all types of crimes — not with the premise that any type of crime is the exclusive province of any particular racial or ethnic group." It cited no authority for this proposition, which seems contradicted by the most recent statistics of the United States Sentencing Commission. Those statistics show that: More than 90 percent of the persons sentenced in 1994 for crack cocaine trafficking were black, 93.4 percent of convicted LSD dealers were white, and 91 percent of those convicted for pornography or prostitution were white. Presumptions at war with presumably reliable statistics have no proper place in the analysis of this issue.

The Court of Appeals also expressed concern about the "evidentiary obstacles defendants face." But . . . if the claim of selective prosecution were well founded, it should not have been an insuperable task to prove that persons of other races were being treated differently than respondents. For instance, respondents could have investigated whether similarly situated persons of other races were prosecuted by the State of California, were known to federal law enforcement officers, but were not prosecuted in federal court. We think the required threshold — a credible showing of different treatment of similarly situated persons — adequately balances the Government's interest in vigorous prosecution and the defendant's interest in avoiding selective prosecution.

In the case before us, respondents' "study" did not constitute some evidence tending to show the existence of the essential elements of a selective-prosecution claim. The study failed to identify individuals who were not black, could have been prosecuted for the offenses for which respondents were charged, but were not so prosecuted. This omission was not remedied by respondents' evidence in opposition to the Government's motion for reconsideration. . . . Respondents' affidavits, which recounted one attorney's conversation with a drug treatment center employee and the experience of another attorney defending drug prosecutions in state court, recounted hearsay and reported personal conclusions based on anecdotal evidence. The judgment of the Court of Appeals is therefore reversed, and the case is remanded for proceedings consistent with this opinion. It is so ordered.

STEVENS, J., dissenting.

Federal prosecutors are respected members of a respected profession. Despite an occasional misstep, the excellence of their work abundantly justifies the

---

3. We reserve the question whether a defendant must satisfy the similarly situated requirement in a case involving direct admissions by prosecutors of discriminatory purpose.

presumption that they have properly discharged their official duties. Nevertheless, the possibility that political or racial animosity may infect a decision to institute criminal proceedings cannot be ignored. For that reason, it has long been settled that the prosecutor's broad discretion to determine when criminal charges should be filed is not completely unbridled. . . .

The Court correctly concludes that in this case the facts presented to the District Court in support of respondents' claim that they had been singled out for prosecution because of their race were not sufficient to prove that defense. Moreover, I agree with the Court that their showing was not strong enough to give them a right to discovery, either under Rule 16 or under the District Court's inherent power to order discovery in appropriate circumstances. [H]owever, I am persuaded that the District Judge did not abuse her discretion when she concluded that the factual showing was sufficiently disturbing to require some response from the United States Attorney's Office. Perhaps the discovery order was broader than necessary, but I cannot agree with the Court's apparent conclusion that no inquiry was permissible.

The District Judge's order should be evaluated in light of three circumstances that underscore the need for judicial vigilance over certain types of drug prosecutions. First, the Anti-Drug Abuse Act of 1986 and subsequent legislation established a regime of extremely high penalties for the possession and distribution of so-called "crack" cocaine. Those provisions treat one gram of crack as the equivalent of 100 grams of powder cocaine. The distribution of 50 grams of crack is thus punishable by the same mandatory minimum sentence of 10 years in prison that applies to the distribution of 5,000 grams of powder cocaine. . . . Second, the disparity between the treatment of crack cocaine and powder cocaine is matched by the disparity between the severity of the punishment imposed by federal law and that imposed by state law for the same conduct. For a variety of reasons, often including the absence of mandatory minimums, the existence of parole, and lower baseline penalties, terms of imprisonment for drug offenses tend to be substantially lower in state systems than in the federal system. The difference is especially marked in the case of crack offenses. . . . Finally, it is undisputed that the brunt of the elevated federal penalties falls heavily on blacks. While 65 percent of the persons who have used crack are white, in 1993 they represented only 4 percent of the federal offenders convicted of trafficking in crack. Eighty-eight percent of such defendants were black. . . . Those figures represent a major threat to the integrity of federal sentencing reform, whose main purpose was the elimination of disparity (especially racial) in sentencing. . . .

The extraordinary severity of the imposed penalties and the troubling racial patterns of enforcement give rise to a special concern about the fairness of charging practices for crack offenses. Evidence tending to prove that black defendants charged with distribution of crack in the Central District of California are prosecuted in federal court, whereas members of other races charged with similar offenses are prosecuted in state court, warrants close scrutiny by the federal judges in that District. In my view, the District Judge, who has sat on both the federal and the state benches in Los Angeles, acted well within her discretion to call for the development of facts that would demonstrate what standards, if any, governed the choice of forum where similarly situated offenders are prosecuted. . . .

The majority discounts the probative value of the [defendant's] affidavits, claiming that they recounted "hearsay" and reported "personal conclusions based on anecdotal evidence." But [it] was certainly within the District Court's discretion to credit the affidavits of two members of the bar of that Court, at least one of whom had presumably acquired a reputation by his frequent appearances there, and both of whose statements were made on pains of perjury. The criticism that the affidavits were based on "anecdotal evidence" is also unpersuasive. I thought it was agreed that defendants do not need to prepare sophisticated statistical studies in order to receive mere discovery in cases like this one. . . .

Even if respondents failed to carry their burden of showing that there were individuals who were not black but who could have been prosecuted in federal court for the same offenses, it does not follow that the District Court abused its discretion in ordering discovery. There can be no doubt that such individuals exist, and indeed the Government has never denied the same. In those circumstances, I fail to see why the District Court was unable to take judicial notice of this obvious fact and demand information from the Government's files to support or refute respondents' evidence. The presumption that some whites are prosecuted in state court is not "contradicted" by the statistics the majority cites, which show only that high percentages of blacks are convicted of certain federal crimes, while high percentages of whites are convicted of other federal crimes. Those figures are entirely consistent with the allegation of selective prosecution. The relevant comparison, rather, would be with the percentages of blacks and whites who commit those crimes. But, as discussed above, in the case of crack far greater numbers of whites are believed guilty of using the substance. The District Court, therefore, was entitled to find the evidence before her significant and to require some explanation from the Government.[6] I therefore respectfully dissent. . . .

Notes

1. *Selective prosecution: majority position.* The U.S. Supreme Court has made it clear from time to time that it is possible, at least in theory, for a court to overturn a prosecutor's charging decision when it is based on a constitutionally impermissible ground such as race, religion, or sex. A defendant who makes such a claim must establish that (a) the prosecutor made different charging decisions for similarly situated suspects (a discriminatory effect), and (b) the prosecutor intentionally made the decision on the basis of an "arbitrary" classification (a discriminatory intent). Arbitrary classifications would include "suspect classes" under equal protection doctrine and those exercising their constitutional liberties such as freedom of speech or religion. See Oyler v. Boles, 368 U.S. 448 (1962); Wayte v. United States, 470 U.S. 598 (1985).

Although a selective prosecution claim remains theoretically available, the claim is very difficult for a defendant to win. The *Wayte* decision made it clear that the government must choose the defendant for prosecution "because of" and not "despite" the protected conduct or status of the defendant. In that case, the government had prosecuted for draft evasion a person who had publicly

---

6. Also telling was the Government's response to respondents' evidentiary showing. It submitted a list of more than 3,500 defendants who had been charged with federal narcotics violations over the previous 3 years. It also offered the names of 11 nonblack defendants whom it had prosecuted for crack offenses. All 11, however, were members of other racial or ethnic minorities. . . .

criticized the military draft. The government had chosen to prosecute the case under a "passive enforcement" policy, in which the government filed charges only when told about a person's refusal to register for the draft and only when the person refused to comply with the law after a specific request. The government carried out this policy in Wayte's case, despite (and not because of) his speech criticizing the draft. This basic federal framework for analyzing constitutional challenges to discriminatory charging policies has also been very influential in state courts. See, e.g., Salaiscooper v. Eighth Judicial District Court ex rel. County of Clark, 34 P.3d 509 (Nev. 2001) (disparate treatment of prostitutes and customers is not discrimination on basis of sex); State v. Muetze, 534 N.W.2d 55 (S.D. 1995) (no proof that non-Native Americans who were not charged were similarly situated).

2. *Discovery to support selective prosecution claims.* According to the opinion in *Armstrong*, a court hearing a claim of selective prosecution may grant discovery to the defendant if there is "some evidence" to support each of the elements of the claim. Do you agree with the court that the defendants in *Armstrong* failed to produce "some evidence"? See also United States v. Bass, 536 U.S. 862 (2002) (overturns trial court order for discovery concerning capital charging practices; defendant failed to show disparate treatment of similarly situated persons).

What sort of evidence is likely to be available to support a selective prosecution claim? To show disparate treatment, a defendant must prove that he is "similarly situated" to a pool of other suspects who were not prosecuted. Those who are similarly situated would have committed basically the same act as the defendant. Further, there could be no significant difference in the harm caused by these similar acts, and prosecution of one case could not be significantly less costly or difficult than the others. Where can a defendant get information about this pool of unprosecuted suspects?

Will it ever be possible to prove disparate impact in those prosecutorial offices (the overwhelming majority) in which the prosecuting attorneys keep no records of the cases they decline to charge or of the reasons for the declination? Very few courts have reversed convictions on selective prosecution grounds, and no Supreme Court opinions have done so on racial grounds except for Yick Wo v. Hopkins, 118 U.S. 356 (1886). Does this pattern prove anything? What did the claimants in *Yick Wo* do that claimants today might emulate?

3. *Racial patterns in charging.* It is clear that racial minorities are charged with crimes at a rate disproportionate to their numbers. But is the rate higher after accounting for different levels of participation in crime? Criminologists addressing this question have studied records of large numbers of cases using statistical techniques (especially "regression" analysis) to compare similar cases and sort out racial and nonracial influences over charging decisions. For instance, one study by Richard Berk analyzed the correlation between race and crack cocaine charging practices in Los Angeles between 1990 and 1992. The study indicates that the U.S. Attorney prosecuted black offenders at a higher rate than comparable white offenders. Richard Berk & Alec Campbell, Preliminary Data on Race and Crack Charging Practices in Los Angeles, 6 Fed. Sentencing Rep. 36 (1993). See also Cassia Spohn, John Gruhl & Susan Welch, The Impact of the Ethnicity and Gender of Defendants on the Decision to Reject or Dismiss Felony Charges, 25 Criminology 175 (1987) (study of 33,000 felony cases between 1977 and 1980 to determine whether racial bias influenced prosecutor's decisions to decline felony charges; declinations occur more frequently for white suspects after controlling for age, criminal record, and

seriousness of offense); Developments in the Law — Race and the Criminal Process, 101 Harv. L. Rev. 1520 (1988) (summarizing other studies). Does any of this analysis support the conclusion that selective prosecution doctrine fails to control biased prosecution? If racial discrimination in charging is indeed widespread, is it unrealistic to ask a defendant to make a prediscovery showing?

4. *Racial discrimination and written charging policies.* Do charging policies reduce the likelihood that individual prosecutors will consider race as a factor in charging decisions? As we saw earlier in this chapter, the state of Washington has passed a statute instructing prosecutors on the general factors to consider when making a charging decision. A 1994 study of King County, Washington (where written office policies supplement the state statutes) attempted to determine whether race influenced the charging decisions of prosecutors. See Larry Michael Fehr, Racial and Ethnic Disparities in Prosecution and Sentencing: Empirical Research of the Washington State Minority and Justice Commission, 32 Gonz. L. Rev. 577 (1996/97). The study found that white defendants were charged in 60 percent of the cases referred to prosecutors, while black defendants were charged in 65 percent. The researchers could explain only part of this difference based on legally relevant factors, such as the type of crime involved.

5. *Prosecutorial vindictiveness.* If all criminal defendants were to insist on exercising all of their constitutional and statutory procedural rights, they could make life difficult for a prosecutor. Can a prosecutor charge defendants more severely if they insist on a jury trial, an appeal, or some other procedural right? In Blackledge v. Perry, 417 U.S. 21 (1974), a defendant was initially charged in state district court with misdemeanor assault. After conviction, he requested a trial de novo on the charges in state superior court, and the prosecutor changed the charges to felony assault. The Supreme Court concluded that a prosecutor in such a situation would have an incentive to "retaliate" against the defendant for taking an action that the prosecutor finds inconvenient. Thus, the prosecutor would have to demonstrate on the record that the change in charges was based on some factor other than the defendant's exercise of procedural rights. The limit on "prosecutorial vindictiveness" set out in Blackledge v. Perry does not apply, however, to a prosecutor's *pretrial* decision to add or reduce charges based on a defendant's willingness to waive procedural rights. See United States v. Goodwin, 457 U.S. 368 (1982) (no presumption of vindictiveness where prosecutor changes misdemeanor charges to felony after defendant requests jury trial); Peter J. Henning, Prosecutorial Misconduct and Constitutional Remedies, 77 Wash. U. L.Q. 713 (1999). Is this distinction a meaningful one?

6. *Prosecution in the sunshine.* Would prosecutors benefit or lose more from the collection and publication of data on the race of every defendant and victim for every criminal matter the office encounters? If a chief prosecutor were to carry out this policy (either voluntarily or pursuant to a statute), would she want to show the data broken down by type of crime and by the action the office chose to pursue? If you believe prosecutors would resist the collection and publication of such data, what arguments might they raise against this proposal? What if the legislature were willing to provide funds for any extra personnel needed to collect and analyze the data? See Angela J. Davis, Prosecution and Race: The Power and Privilege of Discretion, 67 Fordham L. Rev. 13 (1998) (proposing a requirement that prosecutors publish "racial impact studies").

C. GRAND JURY AND JUDICIAL SCREENING

> The grand jury would indict a hamburger.
> —Traditional courthouse wisdom

Pretrial judicial hearings that go by names such as "initial appearance" and "preliminary examination" serve multiple functions. At the initial appearance, the magistrate informs the defendant about the nature of the charges, the right to remain silent, the right to appointed counsel, and other features of the criminal process. An initial appearance also gives the magistrate an occasion to assign counsel to indigent defendants (or at least to ascertain whether a defendant is eligible for appointed counsel) and to set bail or other conditions of pretrial release.

For our present purposes, we will focus on the ability of judges in these pretrial hearings to screen out charges without enough factual support. If the prosecutor, in the adversarial "preliminary examination," is not able to produce evidence showing probable cause to believe that the defendant committed the crime as charged, then the charges are dismissed and the defendant released. If probable cause is present, the magistrate will "bind over" the defendant for arraignment and trial in a court with jurisdiction to try the offense.

There are alternatives to the use of the preliminary judicial hearing as the initial filter in the accusatory process. The charges in most criminal cases are contained in a charging document known as an "information," which the prosecutor can file after judicial screening at the preliminary hearing, without consulting a grand jury. But in just under half of the states, a defendant can insist that the prosecutor seek the permission of a grand jury before filing felony charges. If the grand jury agrees with the prosecutor's request to charge an individual, the charges appear in a grand jury "indictment." The grand jury has a traditional role in investigating crimes — the grand jury as a "sword." Now we consider the grand jury's function as a "shield" against unfounded prosecutions, and the interaction between the grand jury and the judicial "preliminary examination" as screening devices.

The traditional image of the grand jury as a shield might be misleading. By all accounts, grand juries indict in virtually all cases when a prosecutor requests the indictment. There are several possible reasons for this, all built into the structure of the grand jury. See Andrew Leipold, Why Grand Juries Do Not (and Cannot) Protect the Accused, 80 Cornell L. Rev. 260 (1995). First, the grand jury's review standard is quite low: It must determine only whether there is probable cause to believe that the accused has committed the crime that the prosecutor has specified. Second, the grand jury proceedings are not adversarial. Only the prosecutor presents evidence to the grand jury, and he has no obligation (in most states) to present any exculpatory evidence. In most jurisdictions, no representatives of the grand jury witnesses or targets are even present in the grand jury room during testimony or deliberations.

■ NEW YORK CONSTITUTION ART. I, §6

No person shall be held to answer for a capital or otherwise infamous crime . . . unless on indictment of a grand jury, except that a person held for the action of a grand jury upon a charge for such an offense, other than one punishable by death or life imprisonment, with the consent of the district attorney, may waive indictment by a grand jury and consent to be prosecuted on an information filed by the district attorney; such waiver shall be evidenced by written instrument signed by the defendant in open court in the presence of his or her counsel. . . .

The power of grand juries to inquire into the wilful misconduct in office of public officers, and to find indictments or to direct the filing of informations in connection with such inquiries, shall never be suspended or impaired by law. . . .

■ ILLINOIS ANNOTATED STATUTES CH. 725, PARA. 5/111-2

(a) All prosecutions of felonies shall be by information or by indictment. No prosecution may be pursued by information unless a preliminary hearing has been held or waived . . . and at that hearing probable cause to believe the defendant committed an offense was found. . . .

(b) All other prosecutions may be by indictment, information or complaint. . . .

(f) Where the prosecution of a felony is by information or complaint after preliminary hearing, or after a waiver of preliminary hearing in accordance with paragraph (a) of this Section, such prosecution may be for all offenses, arising from the same transaction or conduct of a defendant even though the complaint or complaints filed at the preliminary hearing charged only one or some of the offenses arising from that transaction or conduct.

■ COMMONWEALTH v. KHARI WILCOX
767 N.E.2d 1061 (Mass. 2002)

GREANEY, J.

After hearing six days of evidence during a three-month period, a Suffolk County grand jury indicted the defendant on charges of armed robbery and home invasion. The defendant moved for discovery of the grand jury attendance records to ascertain whether at least twelve of the grand jurors who voted to indict him had heard "all of the evidence" presented against him. (Of particular concern to the defendant was whether fewer than the required minimum of twelve grand jurors voting to indict him had heard certain exculpatory evidence, including evidence suggesting that he had been erroneously identified.) A judge in the Superior Court allowed the defendant's motion, but stayed discovery to give the Commonwealth an opportunity to seek interlocutory review of her order. . . .

The grand jury as known to the common law always has been regarded as a bulwark of individual liberty and a fundamental protection against despotism and persecution. It is an institution preserved by our State Constitution, which asserts the "great principle . . . that no man shall be put to answer a criminal charge [for a capital or otherwise infamous offense] until the criminating evidence has been laid before a grand jury," Commonwealth v. Holley, 69 Mass. 458 (1855). See Mass. R. Crim. P. 3(b)(1), 378 Mass. 847 (1979) ("A defendant charged with an offense punishable by imprisonment in state prison shall have the right to be proceeded against by indictment except when the offense charged is within the concurrent

jurisdiction of the District and Superior Courts and the District Court retains jurisdiction"). For an indictment to stand, the grand jury must hear sufficient evidence
to establish the identity of the accused and probable cause to arrest him.

The defendant's discovery motion is predicated on the argument that the
requirement in Mass. R. Crim. P. 5(e), 378 Mass. 850 (1979), of a "concurrence"
of at least twelve grand jurors to return an indictment, mandates that a core of at
least twelve grand jurors heard all of the evidence and voted to indict. He asserts that
the word "concurrence" presumes that a grand juror has been present to hear all of
the evidence presented before joining in a decision to indict, and that such an
obligation is necessitated by the grand jurors' oath. The defendant urges us to follow
the "better-reasoned decisions from other jurisdictions" that "recognize that an
informed grand jury that truly concurs to indict, based on hearing all of the
evidence, ensures the integrity of the grand jury process." We decline to add
such a requirement to rule 5.

Rule 5(e) has its origins in the common law. By the common law, a grand
jury "may consist of not less than thirteen, nor more than twenty-three persons,"
Crimm v. Commonwealth, 119 Mass. 326 (1876), and a concurrence of at least
twelve was required to return an indictment. Both the maximum number of
grand jurors and the minimum number required to indict prescribed by the
common law [were] kept intact by statute and rule. See G.L. c. 277, §§1, 2A-2G
(twenty-three grand jurors shall be selected to serve); Mass. R. Crim. P. 5(a), 378
Mass. 850 (1979) ("the court shall select not more than twenty-three grand jurors to
serve"); Mass. R. Crim. P. 5(e) ("An indictment may be found only upon the concurrence of twelve or more jurors"). The common law quorum requirement of
thirteen remains in place, unaltered by statute or rule.

Rule 5 is modeled in large part on its Federal counterpart, Fed. R. Crim. P. 6.
The Federal rule requires that every grand jury session be attended by "not less than
16 nor more than 23 members," Fed. R. Crim. P. 6(a)(1), and, for an indictment to
be found, requires "the concurrence of 12 or more jurors," Fed. R. Crim. P. 6(f).
Federal courts have nearly uniformly rejected the argument raised by the defendant
that the grand jurors voting to indict be required to hear all of the evidence presented. See United States v. Byron, 994 F.2d 747, 748 (10th Cir. 1993); but see
United States v. Provenzano, 688 F.2d 194, 202-203 (3d Cir. 1982) (expressing
uneasiness with approach followed by other Federal courts and providing procedure whereby replacement and absentee grand jurors are given transcript of missed
proceedings as well as an opportunity to recall witnesses for questioning). Often
quoted and relied on in these Federal decisions is the reasoning stated by Judge
Learned Hand, writing for the court in United States ex rel. McCann v. Thompson,
144 F.2d 604, 607 (2d Cir. 1944):

> Since all the evidence adduced before a grand jury—certainly when the accused does
> not appear—is aimed at proving guilt, the absence of some jurors during some part of
> the hearings will ordinarily merely weaken the prosecution's case. If what the absentees
> actually hear is enough to satisfy them, there would seem to be no reason why they
> should not vote. Against this we can think of nothing except the possibility that some of
> the evidence adduced by the prosecution might conceivably turn out to be favorable to
> the accused; and that, if the absentees had heard it, they might have refused to vote a
> true bill. No one can be entirely sure that this can never occur; but it appears to us so
> remote a chance that it should be left to those instances in which it can be made to

appear that the evidence not heard was of that character, in spite of the extreme difficulty of ever proving what was the evidence before a grand jury. Indeed, the possibility that not all who vote will hear all the evidence, is a reasonable inference from the fact that sixteen is a quorum. Were the law as the relator argues, it would practically mean that all jurors present at the beginning of any case, must remain to the end, for it will always be impossible to tell in advance whether twelve will eventually vote a true bill, and if they do, who those twelve will be. The result of such a doctrine would therefore be that in a long case, or in a case where there are intervals in the taking of evidence, the privilege of absence would not exist. That would certainly be an innovation, for the contrary practice has, so far as we are aware, been universal; and it would be an onerous and unnecessary innovation.

We reject the defendant's contention that the reasoning stated in the *Thompson* case is "unpersuasive." In most instances, grand jurors hear only inculpatory evidence. Commonwealth v. O'Dell, 466 N.E.2d 828 (Mass. 1984) (stating that prosecutors are not required "to bring exculpatory evidence to the attention of grand juries"). It is only when the prosecutor possesses exculpatory evidence that would greatly undermine either the credibility of an important witness or evidence likely to affect the grand jury's decision, or withholds exculpatory evidence causing the presentation to be "so seriously tainted," that the prosecutor must present such evidence to the grand jury. See Commonwealth v. Vinnie, 698 N.E.2d 896 (Mass. 1998). . . . Provisions governing grand jurors, which we decline to change, take into account the lengthy terms for which many grand juries sit, usually a number of months. The provisions also, as acknowledged by the defendant, insure that the grand jury can continue functioning despite absent members. See 1 S.S. Beale, Grand Jury Law and Practice §4:8, at 4-35 (2d ed. 2001) ("It is not unusual for individual grand jurors to miss a number of the sessions, yet to participate in the ultimate decision whether to indict or not. In this respect, the grand jury process differs radically from the trial process, where it would be unthinkable for a juror to miss several days of evidence, yet be permitted to deliberate and vote on the defendant's guilt"). Adoption of the rule the defendant proposes may cause the prosecution to seek to indict an accused on the basis of whatever evidence it can present in one day. In such circumstances, the prosecution may not be able to present the direct testimony of several witnesses, relying instead on the hearsay statements of one witness. While proceedings conducted in this manner would not be impermissible, see Commonwealth v. O'Dell, 466 N.E.2d 828 (Mass. 1984) ("an indictment may be based solely on hearsay"), they would run contrary to our "preference for the use of direct testimony before grand juries," Commonwealth v. St. Pierre, 387 N.E.2d 1135 (Mass. 1979), which inures to the accused's benefit. The defendant's rule would also be disruptive of witnesses, police and their schedules, court sessions, and the daily encumbered lives of grand jurors and their families.

Although the defendant correctly identifies that other States, either by statute, rule, or decision, have adopted the requirement that the grand jurors voting to indict have heard all the evidence presented, see, e.g., Ariz. Rev. Stat. Ann. §21-406(B); Me. R. Crim. P. 6(j); N.D. Cent. Code §29-10.1-20; Or. Rev. Stat. §132.360; Commonwealth v. Levinson, 389 A.2d 1062 (Pa. 1978) (explaining when "a substantial percentage of the total membership of the jury is absent from a significant portion of the presentation of evidence, it can no longer be said with confidence that the deliberations were not affected"), some State courts have followed the Federal approach. See, e.g., People v. Martin-Trigona, 444 N.E.2d 527 (Ill. App. 1982); State v. Blyth, 226 N.W.2d 250 (Iowa 1975); Johnston v. State, 822 P.2d 1118 (Nev. 1991). We join this latter group of courts. We add that it is precisely the unique and limited function of the grand jury that permits their proceedings, including those rules pertaining to grand jurors, to vary from the rules governing trials and petit jurors. . . . The case is remanded to the county court for entry of an order vacating the order of the Superior Court judge allowing the defendant's motion for discovery of the grand jury attendance records, and directing the entry of an order denying the motion. . . .

Notes

1. *Which crimes require an indictment?* In almost half the states, a grand jury indictment rather than a prosecutor's information is necessary for at least some charges. In some of these jurisdictions, such as New York, the constitution requires a grand jury indictment; in other "indictment" states, the state constitution allows the legislature to decide which if any crimes must be charged through grand jury indictment. For the most part, the "indictment" states have retained the traditional requirement embodied in the Fifth Amendment to the federal constitution: Indictment must occur in all capital and "infamous" crimes — that is, felonies. A few require indictments only for crimes punishable by death or life imprisonment. The grand jury requirement is one of the few provisions of the federal Bill of Rights that has not been "incorporated" against the states through the due process clause of the Fourteenth Amendment. Hurtado v. California, 110 U.S. 516 (1884).

In most states and for most charges, the grand jury is optional. Prosecutors can decide whether to proceed under an information or a grand jury indictment (as in Illinois, under the statute reprinted above). Indictments have become one weapon in the prosecutor's arsenal of ways to investigate and charge crimes. Prosecutors often use grand juries to charge politically sensitive crimes (to share responsibility for the charging decision) or to charge crimes that come to light as the result of grand jury investigations.

2. *Grand jury versus preliminary examinations.* In cases where the prosecutor files an "information" rather than seeking an indictment from the grand jury, the factual and legal basis for the prosecutor's charge is usually tested before trial in a judicial proceeding, usually called a "preliminary examination" or "preliminary hearing." Some defendants might actually prefer a preliminary examination over a grand jury indictment, because the judge might evaluate the evidence more skeptically than the grand jury, given that the grand jurors only hear the prosecution's side of the case. Defendants also may attend the preliminary examination, giving them discovery opportunities that are not generally available from the grand jury. Although the use of a preliminary examination might give such practical advantages to the defendant, the government holds the power to choose between the grand jury and preliminary examination options. The majority view is that there is no constitutional right to a preliminary hearing once a prosecutor has decided to seek an indictment. See State v. Edmonson, 743 P.2d 459 (Idaho 1987); People v. Glass, 627 N.W.2d 261 (Mich. 2001) (overruling earlier case granting right to preliminary examination to all defendants, including indictees).

Further, there is no federal constitutional requirement that either a judge or a grand jury determine whether probable cause supports the criminal charges filed against a defendant. Lem Woon v. Oregon, 229 U.S. 586 (1913) (upholding statute providing for no preliminary examination after information). All states have statutes offering at least some defendants a determination of probable cause underlying the charges, whether the determination comes from a judge in a preliminary hearing or from a grand jury indictment. A few states provide, as an alternative charging method, for "direct filing" of charges by the prosecutor without testing in a preliminary hearing or indictment. These states usually allow the defendant to file a motion to dismiss the charges after discovery is complete.

The statutes and constitutions providing for adversary preliminary hearings typically apply only when the prosecutor has *chosen* to proceed by information rather than indictment. See Cal. Const. art. 1, §14.1. In the federal system, once a prosecutor obtains an indictment the defendant cannot insist on a preliminary hearing. 18 U.S.C. §3060. A few states do require an adversary preliminary hearing (even after a grand jury indicts the defendant) and a few others require some showing that the prosecutor had satisfactory reasons for choosing indictments in some cases and informations in others. State v. Freeland, 667 P.2d 509 (Or. 1983). The practical value of an adversarial preliminary hearing for a defendant is the chance to preview the prosecution's witnesses and evidence.

3. *Waiver of indictment.* In the jurisdictions requiring indictment for some crimes, defendants often waive their right to indictment and proceed without any grand jury or judicial screening of the charges. Are there times when the legal system might prevent defendants from waiving the right to indictment? See N.Y. Crim. Proc. Law §195.20(a) (waiver must be written, executed in open court in presence of counsel); N.C. Gen. Stat. §15A-642(b) (waiver allowed except for offenses punishable by death or cases in which defendant waives counsel).

4. *Nonadversarial proceedings.* Time and again, judicial opinions point out that grand jury proceedings are not adversarial and are not a "mini-trial." Truer words have never been spoken. To begin with, the grand jury's task is far different from that of a trial jury: The grand jury need only decide whether the prosecutor has demonstrated probable cause to believe that the defendant committed the crime charged. In most jurisdictions, only the prosecutor presents testimony and documents to the grand jury, and none of it is subject to cross-examination or the rules of evidence. Costello v. United States, 350 U.S. 359 (1956). In a strong minority of states, attorneys for some grand jury witnesses may observe the testimony of their clients, but the attorneys may not question the witness or make any statements to the grand jury. See, e.g., Ill. Ann. Stat. ch. 725, para. 5/112-4.1.

In most systems, the prosecutor has no obligation to present exculpatory evidence, United States v. Williams, 504 U.S. 36 (1992), although support for this traditional position is eroding. More than a dozen states have statutes or judicial rulings that require the prosecutor to present exculpatory evidence under some circumstances. See People v. Lancaster, 503 N.E.2d 990 (N.Y. 1986). Prosecutorial policies also sometimes recognize the obligation of a prosecutor to present exculpatory evidence that would lead the grand jury to refuse to indict. See U.S. Attorneys' Manual §9-11.233; see also ABA Standards for Criminal Justice, Prosecution Function Standard 3-3.6(b) ("No prosecutor should knowingly fail to disclose to the grand jury evidence which tends to negate guilt or mitigate the offense"). Sometimes the target of a grand jury investigation must have notice and an opportunity to testify before the grand jury can indict. See Sheriff of Humboldt County v. Marcum, 783 P.2d 1389 (Nev. 1989).

Most traditional nonadversarial practices trace their roots to the earliest English grand juries in the twelfth century. See Richard Younger, The People's Panel (1963). Does this nonadversarial process serve any useful purpose now? Does the high rate of guilty pleas in modern criminal justice systems make these practices more questionable than they once may have been?

5. *Judicial review of indictments.* As you might imagine based on the other materials in this chapter, judicial dismissal of charges contained in an indictment is a rare event. Only about 10 states even authorize courts to inquire into the sufficiency of the evidence to support an indictment. See, e.g., Colo. Rev. Stat. §16-5-204(4)(k). Challenges based on prosecutorial misconduct are only slightly more successful as a basis for dismissal of an indictment.

Assuming that a court is willing to review an indictment, will there be a record of the proceedings sufficient to allow judicial review? Statutes and rules of procedure in the federal system and in a majority of the states require recording of at least the testimony that a grand jury hears, and a strong minority also require recording of other statements made to the grand jury, such as the commentary of the prosecutor. Virtually nowhere are the deliberations and votes of the grand jury recorded.

6. *Timing of initial appearance and preliminary hearing.* The federal constitution requires that the initial determination of probable cause to support an *arrest* (but not to support the charges) occur within 48 hours of the arrest. County of Riverside v. McLaughlin, 500 U.S. 44 (1991) (delay longer than 48 hours presumptively unreasonable). Some states have rules calling for such a hearing in even less time, but most simply require a hearing within a "reasonable" time. As for the determination of whether there is probable cause to support the crimes charged, the hearing usually takes place within 10 to 20 days of the initial appearance if the defendant does not waive the hearing or if the grand jury does not return an indictment in the meantime.

7. *Attendance of the defendant.* Statutes and rules (not to mention due process principles) generally grant defendants the right to attend the initial appearance and the preliminary examination. This presents a logistical challenge in some jurisdictions, requiring the authorities to shuttle many detained defendants from the jail to the courthouse and back again. One response to this administrative burden has been the use of videoconference technology linking the courtroom with a designated hearing room in the jail. If you were representing a defendant, would you be more effective during a preliminary examination by remaining with your client at the jail, or by being present in the courtroom with the judge? See Anne Bowen Poulin, Criminal Justice and Videoconferencing Technology: The Remote Defendant, 78 Tulane L. Rev. 1089 (2004).

If traditional grand juries provide defendants little protection, are there changes to the institution that might make the grand jury a more independent screen against unreasonable prosecution? Consider the following Hawaiian reform.

Consider, too, the mechanism of reform. Express constitutional reform of the federal system has been relatively rare, and amendments have reflected fundamental social and political changes (e.g. the Thirteenth, Fourteenth, Fifteenth, and Eighteenth Amendments). This is not the story in the states, where a 1987 account found 5,198 amendments to state constitutions (5,083 approved by voters in 49 states, out of 8,279 amendments submitted to them). See Janice C. May, Constitutional Amendment and Revision Revisited, Publius: The Journal of Federalism, 153 (Winter 1987) (finding the average number of amendments adopted per state to be 103.9).

■ STATE v. GABRIEL KAHLBAUN

638 P.2d 309 (Haw. 1981)

OGATA, J.

[T]he indictment against defendant-appellee, Gabriel Kahlbaun, was dismissed for lack of independent grand jury counsel as provided for under Article I, Section 11 of the Hawaii State Constitution. The question presented for our consideration is whether Article I, Section 11 of the Hawaii Constitution requires the physical presence of the independent grand jury counsel throughout the grand jury proceeding. . . .

On June 6, 1980, the statutory provisions implementing Article I, Section 11 were enacted into law. David Fong and retired Judge Masato Doi were appointed by the chief justice as independent grand jury counsel on June 19, 1980. Thereafter, on June 25, 1980, the independent counsel were sworn in and introduced to the members of the Oahu Grand Jury. A supplemental charge was then given to the grand jurors by the supervising circuit court judge, informing them of the role of the independent grand jury counsel.[1] . . .

As a matter of practice, the grand jurors were also informed that if they needed to consult with the independent grand jury counsel, the grand jurors were to call the Criminal Assignments Office of the First Circuit Court. Then, in turn, the assignments office clerk would contact the independent counsel, on a beeper, to come and consult with the grand jury.

Appellee was indicted by the Oahu Grand Jury on August 20, 1980, for burglary in the first degree. . . . Independent counsel David Fong was responsible for advising the grand jury on this date. The record indicates that Fong informally noted his appearance to the grand jury prior to the start of the grand jury proceeding. However, Fong was not present during the presentation of evidence in the instant case. And in this particular case, the grand jurors did not direct any questions of law to the independent grand jury counsel. On October 20, 1980, appellee filed a motion to dismiss indictment alleging . . . that the absence of the grand jury counsel during the grand jury proceeding requires the dismissal of the instant indictment. . . .

---

1. The supplemental charge read in pertinent part: . . . "The grand jury counsel shall serve as independent legal counsel to the grand jury, to be at the disposal of the grand jury during its proceedings in obtaining appropriate advice on matters of law sought by the grand jury, conduct legal research, and provide appropriate answers. [Y]ou are not to seek or obtain advice on matters of law from the prosecution. . . ."

Article I, Section 11 of the Hawaii State Constitution reads:

> Whenever a grand jury is impaneled, there shall be an independent counsel as appointed by law to advise the members of the grand jury regarding matters brought before it. Independent counsel shall be selected from among those persons licensed to practice law by the supreme court of the State and shall not be a public employee. The term and compensation for independent counsel shall be as provided by law.

This provision is unique in American jurisprudence for there is no comparable provision in either the federal or other state constitutions. [In] State v. Hehr, 633 P.2d 545, 546-547 (Haw. 1981), we held that Article I, Section 11 did not create a substantive right for the accused. We stated:

> Although this constitutional provision provides indirect benefits to the accused, the independent counsel's role is not to serve as an advocate on the accused's behalf. Rather, Article I, Section 11 was established to ensure an independent grand jury and to relieve the prosecutor of the conflicting burdens of presenting evidence in support of the indictment and advising the grand jury on matters of law.

Given [this prior interpretation] of Article I, Section 11, we are also mindful of the rules of construction relating to constitutional provisions. The fundamental principle in construing a constitutional provision is to give effect to the intention of the framers and the people adopting it. This intent is to be found in the instrument itself. When the text of a constitutional provision is not ambiguous, the court, in construing it, is not at liberty to search for its meaning beyond the instrument. However, if the text is ambiguous, extrinsic aids may be examined to determine the intent of the framers and the people adopting the proposed amendment. . . .

The language of Article I, Section 11, does not clearly express the intent of the framers on the issue of whether the independent grand jury counsel must be physically present at all times during the grand jury proceeding. The Constitution only requires that the independent counsel advise the grand jury. The function of advising the grand jury on matters of law still can be accomplished without counsel having to be physically present throughout the grand jury proceeding. . . . Using this term in its ordinary sense, "advise" does not indicate or suggest that a physical presence is required. Advice can come in many forms, but physical presence is not a prerequisite. Given this ambiguity, it is necessary to examine extrinsic aids in order to ascertain the meaning of Article I, §11 of the Hawaii Constitution.

Another established rule of construction is that a court may look to the object sought to be accomplished and the evils sought to be remedied by the amendment, along with the history of the times and the state of being when the constitutional provision was adopted. In addition, we can also look to the understanding of the voters who adopted the constitutional provisions, and the legislative implementation of the constitutional amendment.

It is important to remember the role the grand jury plays in the criminal justice system. The grand jury functions as a barrier to reckless or unfounded charges and serves as a "shield against arbitrary or oppressive action, by insuring that serious criminal accusations will be brought only upon the considered judgment of a representative body of citizens acting under oath and under judicial instruction and guidance." United States v. Mandujano, 425 U.S. 564 (1976); State v. Pacific

Concrete and Rock Co., 560 P.2d 1309 (Haw. 1977). . . . The grand jury system provides additional benefits which were aptly stated in Standing Committee Report No. 69, at 673, 3d Hawaii Constitutional Convention (1978):

> [T]he grand jury does have some positive aspects. In certain cases, such as sex crimes or those involving a youthful victim, it protects the victim against being cross-examined at the preliminary hearing level and at trial. Fears were expressed that undergoing cross-examination twice would be hard on those witnesses and may discourage them from acting as witnesses. . . .

However, in recent years, the grand jury system has come under severe criticism. Rather than being a shield to unfounded charges as intended, critics charge that the grand jury has become a rubber stamp of the prosecuting attorney. These criticisms were not unfounded; thus, a substantial movement developed to abolish the grand jury in total. Instead of completely abolishing the grand jury system in Hawaii, the 1978 Constitutional Convention sought to cure some of the ills by proposing the concept of the independent grand jury counsel. This proposal sought to relieve the prosecutor of the conflicting roles of advising the grand jury and presenting sufficient evidence to sustain an indictment. Ultimately, this measure would ensure the independence of the grand jury from the domination of the prosecutor. . . .

Our examination of the convention debates, proceedings and committee reports reveals that the intent of the framers of the constitutional convention in adopting the independent grand jury counsel provision was to ensure an independent grand jury. The concern of the delegates was evidenced in Standing Committee Report No. 69, at 673, where it was expressed:

> . . . In order to counter the dominance of the prosecutor, the independent grand jury counsel was proposed to remedy the situation. The independent grand jury counsel's role was envisioned by some delegates as follows: The role of counsel will be to advise the grand jury and not the witness or the prosecutor. Until now the prosecutor has served as the legal adviser to the grand jury, but there seems to be a conflict between presenting evidence to a grand jury in the hope that they will return an indictment and being their legal adviser. Independent legal counsel will be available to advise the grand jury on any appropriate matter. Your Committee believes that the parameters of the role of the independent counsel will be determined by the grand jury, but if his role is to be effective counsel should advise the grand jury whenever it is appropriate rather than when asked.

In the above-cited passage from Standing Committee Report No. 69, it indicates that the framers of the amendment wanted the independent grand jury counsel to be available to advise the grand jury. By definition, *available* means "that is accessible or may be obtained." Webster's Third International Dictionary. Given this definition, physical presence is not a necessary condition to availability. Thus, it further appears that the framers did not intend for the independent grand jury counsel to be physically present throughout the grand jury proceeding.

We also find it necessary to look to the understanding of the voters who adopted the constitutional provision. The 1978 Constitutional Convention provided to each voter an informational booklet which summarized each proposed amendment. These summaries fairly and sufficiently advised voters of the substance and effect of the proposed amendment. The summary for Article I, Section 11 reads as follows: "If adopted, this amendment provides . . . an independent lawyer to advise the grand jury . . . and requires that the legislature set their pay and how long they shall work." In this clear expression of their intent, the framers did not specifically require nor did they intend for the independent grand jury counsel to be physically present throughout the grand jury proceeding. . . . The independent grand jury counsel was established to advise the grand jury.

The legislative construction of Article I, Section 11 rendered a similar conclusion. The legislature enacted HRS §612-57, to implement Article I, Section 11 of the Hawaii Constitution. . . . That statute reads in pertinent part:

> The grand jury counsel may be present during the grand jury proceeding but shall not participate in the questioning of witnesses or the prosecution. The grand jury counsel's function shall be to receive inquiries on matters of law sought by the grand jury, conduct legal research, and provide appropriate answers.

By using the non-mandatory language, "may be present," the legislature found that the physical presence of the independent grand jury counsel throughout the grand jury proceeding was unnecessary and was not the intent of the framers of the 1978 Constitutional Convention.

A legislative construction implementing a constitutional amendment cannot produce an absurd result or be inconsistent with the purposes and policies of the amendment. However, when a legislative construction of a constitutional amendment is reasonable, courts will normally follow the legislative construction. We think that the legislative construction of Article I, Section 11 does not produce an absurd result nor is inconsistent with the purposes underlying the amendment. Therefore, we find that the legislative construction of Article I, Section 11 is reasonable and choose to follow such a construction.

Moreover, . . . the amendment has improved the situation that existed in the grand jury prior to the enactment of the amendment. Being that the independent grand jury counsel advises the grand jury on matters of law, the absence of the counsel does not revert the grand jury proceeding to its pre-amendment status. The independent counsel must still be consulted with by the grand jury if they have questions of law. . . .

We have held that the absence of the independent grand jury counsel from the grand jury proceeding must be shown to be prejudicial to the accused in order to invalidate the indictment. . . . The bare allegation of the absence of the independent grand jury counsel from the grand jury proceeding, without more, is insufficient to establish prejudice. Moreover, the record reveals that for the instant case the grand jury did not seek the advice of the independent grand jury counsel. The record also shows that the independent counsel was available to render advice to the grand jury. Therefore, based on this record, we find that the absence of the independent grand jury counsel was not prejudicial.

Although we found that the constitution does not mandate the physical presence of the independent grand jury counsel throughout the grand jury proceeding, and that appellee was not prejudiced by such an absence, we find it appropriate to express further views on the independent grand jury counsel.

In addition to advising the grand jurors on questions of law when asked, at the outset of each grand jury session, the independent counsel, on the record, must note his/her presence and instruct the grand jurors on the procedures to summon the counsel for consultation. By this act, a record will be available which shows the court that the independent counsel was present before the grand jury; that the independent counsel was available to advise the grand jury; and that the grand jurors knew the procedures to consult with their counsel.

Additionally, the independent grand jury counsel should be in close proximity to the grand jury. We do not mean that the independent grand jury counsel may return to his/her law office while awaiting to be summoned by the grand jury. Preferably, the independent counsel should be in a separate room, next to the grand jury. But at the very least, the independent counsel should be in the same building that the grand jury meets. Of course, the independent grand jury counsel is not prohibited from being in the grand jury room if desired. We impose this proximity requirement so that the independent grand jury counsel will be readily available to the grand jury and that delays will be kept to a minimum.

With these additional requirements, we believe that the independent grand jury counsel will be effective in insuring an independent grand jury. . . .

Notes

1. *Staff for grand jury.* As *Kahlbaun* indicates, Hawaii is in the minority in providing independent legal counsel for the grand jury. Fewer than 10 states have statutes authorizing support staff for grand juries, such as legal counsel, accountants, or detectives. See Kan. Stat. §22-3006. More frequently, statutes authorize the prosecutor to attend the sessions of the grand jury (except during deliberations and voting), to examine witnesses, and to provide legal advice to the grand jury. Fla. Stat. §905.19. The supervising judge for the grand jury is also available to provide legal advice, although the grand jury rarely requests advice from the judge. But other sources of staff support for the grand jury have not developed in most places. When grand juries attempted at the turn of the century to analyze information about government operations — say, an audit of the county books — the courts routinely denied the grand juries any power to hire their own accountants or detectives. Stone v. Bell, 129 P. 458 (Nev. 1912). When the grand jury lost confidence in the district attorney and sought legal counsel elsewhere, the supervising courts blocked the effort. Woody v. Peairs, 170 P. 660 (Cal. Ct. App. 1917). While private prosecutors appeared before grand juries in the nineteenth century, at the turn of the century courts began to exclude them from the grand jury proceedings. Hartgraves v. State, 114 P. 343 (Okla. 1911).

Consider this lack of support staff against the background of a growing bureaucracy attached to virtually every other governmental institution early in the twentieth century. Grand jurors were no longer personally aware of crimes committed or conditions to investigate, as they once were. They were without the increasingly specialized auditing and management skills necessary to investigate crimes or to monitor government. Given the complexity of governance, what institution of government could survive without support staff? Could Congress or the president perform their duties without the benefit of their own counsel?

2. *State constitutional interpretation.* Do the methods used by the Hawaiian Supreme Court to interpret Art. I, §11 look the like methods typically used by the U.S. Supreme Court to interpret the federal constitution? In what ways does constitutional interpretation change when many of the drafters are enacters (here

voters) are still very much alive, and part of constitutional debate? Does a shorter time frame provide stronger arguments for "originalism" as the primary theory of constitutional interpretation? Does the ability to actually amend the constitution provide arguments for originalism or some other interpretative theory?

3. *Grand jury reports.* Just as prosecutors will decline to file charges in many cases, grand juries sometimes investigate crimes and then decide not to indict. These grand juries sometimes write "reports" criticizing the targets of the grand jury's investigation, even though the grand jury issued no indictment or "presentment" (criminal charges which the prosecutor did not request). Should "reports" be issued as standard practice whenever a grand jury conducts an investigation? Should reports be used to encourage or set prosecutorial policies for prosecutors as opposed to making judgments in particular cases?

Grand jury reports can serve many purposes. Some state statutes encourage the use of grand jury reports to examine issues of public health and welfare. See Nev. Rev. Stat. Ann. §172.267. In some jurisdictions the prosecutors ask grand juries to determine whether a class of offense or a type of offender should be prosecuted. For example, a grand jury might give guidance on the prosecution of those who rent pornographic videos or the searching of rental records. An instruction from the grand jury not to prosecute may help shield a local (and usually elected) prosecutor from criticism.

The critical issue, both in jurisdictions that encourage grand jury reports and those that discourage them, is whether the grand jury uses its report power to harm the reputation of individuals without going so far as to charge them with any crime. Some states guard against this danger by insisting that a grand jury issue a report only in conjunction with criminal charges; others hold that the report cannot name any private individuals, and a few prevent the report from naming even public officials. Ex parte Simpson, 664 S.W.2d 872, 873 (Ark. 1984) (person mentioned in grand jury report has no right to cross-examine accusers; report is a state publication that carries aura of approval by judge who accepted it, and press has no way to look behind it to determine its fairness or accuracy).

Grand jury reports offer a way for lay citizens to participate in the court system and in criminal justice. Should we preserve or expand the tradition of reports as a way to increase the influence of one of the few truly democratic institutions in American criminal justice?

IV

Jeopardy and Joinder

Chapter 3 addressed the legal forces at work when a prosecutor chooses whether to charge a suspect and which charges to select. We concentrate now on those cases in which the prosecutor could file multiple charges. When several related criminal incidents happen, a prosecutor might file a single count or multiple counts in a single prosecution against one or more defendants, or she might instead file separate criminal cases.

Several sources of law shape the prosecutor's grouping of multiple charges. First, the constitutional bar against "double jeopardy," embodied in the Fifth Amendment of the U.S. Constitution and in most state constitutions, puts some pressure on the prosecutor to include more charges and more conduct within a single prosecution, because double jeopardy might bar any later attempt to pursue the related charges. Section A considers double jeopardy issues.

Prosecutors must also consider statutes and procedural rules on the conceptually related concepts of "joinder" and "severance" of charges and defendants. These rules define both the maximum and minimum range of charges that a prosecutor can join together into a single proceeding. Under the joinder and severance rules, both the prosecutor and the trial court decide whether to include or exclude charges or defendants in a single proceeding. Section B explores these rules.

A. DOUBLE JEOPARDY

A prosecutor must plan for the future when filing charges. If she chooses not to combine related charges in an initial set of proceedings and instead files some of the charges later, there is a risk that the court will bar the later charges. As mentioned above, the legal basis for this decision is the double jeopardy clause of the federal constitution and of most state constitutions. The Fifth Amendment to the federal constitution provides: "No person shall . . . be subject for the same offence to be twice put in jeopardy of life or limb. . . ."

Double jeopardy, it is often said, protects criminal defendants from (1) a second prosecution after acquittal, (2) a second prosecution after conviction, and (3) multiple punishments for the same offense within the same proceeding. The materials in this part touch on some prominent double jeopardy issues that flow from the charging decision. First, we consider a controversial and revealing limitation on the operation of the double jeopardy principle — the "dual sovereignty" exception. Second, we consider which charges in a later proceeding amount to the "same offence" that was charged in a prior proceeding.

1. Multiple Sovereigns

Federal and state governments have overlapping responsibilities for enforcing criminal laws. Many economic and other activities cross state lines, and the criminal codes of most states and the federal government now reach much of the same conduct. Often a person who engages in criminal behavior could face charges in two states, or in both state and federal systems.

The overlap between the federal and state criminal laws is a recurring issue for double jeopardy purposes. In United States v. Lanza, 260 U.S. 377 (1922), several defendants were convicted under state law in Washington for manufacturing, transporting, and possessing liquor and were fined $750 each. When the federal government also brought criminal charges under the National Prohibition Act, Lanza raised a double jeopardy objection to the federal prosecution. He noted that the Eighteenth Amendment, prohibiting the manufacture, sale, or transportation of intoxicating liquors, gave both Congress and the states "concurrent power to enforce" the prohibition. According to Lanza, the state and the federal criminal statutes were punishing the "same offense" because they each derived from the same constitutional authority.

The Court rejected this argument and embraced instead the doctrine known as the "dual sovereign" exception to double jeopardy:

> We have here two sovereignties, deriving power from different sources, capable of dealing with the same subject-matter within the same territory. Each may, without interference by the other, enact laws to secure prohibition. . . . Each government in determining what shall be an offense against its peace and dignity is exercising its own sovereignty, not that of the other.

260 U.S. at 382.

The following materials trace the continuing vitality of the "dual sovereign" doctrine during a time when the overlap between federal and state criminal laws has grown larger.

■ ALFONSE BARTKUS v. ILLINOIS

359 U.S. 121 (1959)

FRANKFURTER, J.

Petitioner was tried in the Federal District Court for the Northern District of Illinois on December 18, 1953, for robbery of a federally insured savings and loan association, the General Savings and Loan Association of Cicero, Illinois, in violation of 18 U.S.C. §2113. The case was tried to a jury and resulted in an acquittal. On January 8, 1954, an Illinois grand jury indicted Bartkus. The facts recited in the Illinois indictment were substantially identical to those contained in the prior federal indictment. The Illinois indictment charged that these facts constituted a violation of [the Illinois robbery statute. Bartkus entered a plea of autrefois acquit, which the trial court rejected. Bartkus was tried, convicted, and sentenced to life imprisonment.]

The state and federal prosecutions were separately conducted. It is true that the agent of the Federal Bureau of Investigation who had conducted the investigation on behalf of the Federal Government turned over to the Illinois prosecuting officials all the evidence he had gathered against the petitioner. Concededly, some of that evidence had been gathered after acquittal in the federal court. The only other connection between the two trials is to be found in a suggestion that the federal sentencing of the accomplices who testified against petitioner in both trials was purposely continued by the federal court until after they testified in the state trial. The record establishes that the prosecution was undertaken by state prosecuting officials within their discretionary responsibility. . . . It establishes also that federal officials acted in cooperation with state authorities, as is the conventional practice between the two sets of prosecutors throughout the country. It does not support the claim that the State of Illinois in bringing its prosecution was merely a tool of the federal authorities, who thereby avoided the prohibition of the Fifth Amendment against a retrial of a federal prosecution after an acquittal. It does not sustain a conclusion that the state prosecution was a sham and a cover for a federal prosecution. . . . Since the new prosecution was by Illinois, and not by the Federal Government, the claim of unconstitutionality must rest upon the Due Process Clause of the Fourteenth Amendment. . . .

Time and again this Court has attempted by general phrases not to define but to indicate the purport of due process and to adumbrate the continuing adjudicatory process in its application. The statement by Mr. Justice Cardozo in Palko v. Connecticut, 302 U.S. 319, 324-325 (1937), has especially commended itself and been frequently cited in later opinions. Referring to specific situations, he wrote:

> In these and other situations immunities that are valid as against the federal government by force of the specific pledges of particular amendments have been found to be implicit in the concept of ordered liberty, and thus, through the Fourteenth Amendment, become valid as against the states.

[H]e suggested that [due process] prohibited to the States only those practices "repugnant to the conscience of mankind." In applying these phrases in *Palko*, the

Court ruled that, while at some point the cruelty of harassment by multiple prosecutions by a State would offend due process, the specific limitation imposed on the Federal Government by the Double Jeopardy Clause of the Fifth Amendment did not bind the States. [*Palko* sustained a first-degree murder conviction returned in a second trial after an appeal by the State from an acquittal of first-degree murder.]

The Fifth Amendment's proscription of double jeopardy has been invoked and rejected in over twenty cases of real or hypothetical successive state and federal prosecution cases before this Court. While United States v. Lanza, 260 U.S. 377 (1922), was the first case in which we squarely held valid a federal prosecution arising out of the same facts which had been the basis of a state conviction, the validity of such a prosecution by the Federal Government has not been questioned by this Court since the opinion in Fox v. Ohio, 46 U.S. 410 (1847), more than one hundred years ago.

In Fox v. Ohio, argument was made to the Supreme Court that an Ohio conviction for uttering counterfeit money was invalid. This assertion of invalidity was based in large part upon the argument that since Congress had imposed federal sanctions for the counterfeiting of money, a failure to find that the Supremacy Clause precluded the States from punishing related conduct would expose an individual to double punishment. Mr. Justice Daniel, writing for the Court (with Mr. Justice McLean dissenting), recognized as true that there was a possibility of double punishment, but denied that from this flowed a finding of pre-emption, concluding instead that both the Federal and State Governments retained the power to impose criminal sanctions, the United States because of its interest in protecting the purity of its currency, the States because of their interest in protecting their citizens against fraud. . . .

The experience of state courts in dealing with successive prosecutions by different governments is obviously also relevant in considering whether or not the Illinois prosecution of Bartkus violated due process of law. Of the twenty-eight States which have considered the validity of successive state and federal prosecutions as against a challenge of violation of either a state constitutional double-jeopardy provision or a common-law evidentiary rule of autrefois acquit and autrefois convict, twenty-seven have refused to rule that the second prosecution was or would be barred. These States were not bound to follow this Court and its interpretation of the Fifth Amendment. The rules, constitutional, statutory, or common law which bound them, drew upon the same experience as did the Fifth Amendment, but were and are of separate and independent authority. . . .

With this body of precedent as irrefutable evidence that state and federal courts have for years refused to bar a second trial even though there had been a prior trial by another government for a similar offense, it would be disregard of a long, unbroken, unquestioned course of impressive adjudication for the Court now to rule that due process compels such a bar. A practical justification for rejecting such a reading of due process also commends itself in aid of this interpretation of the Fourteenth Amendment. In Screws v. United States, 325 U.S. 91 (1945), defendants were tried and convicted in a federal court under federal statutes with maximum sentences of a year and two years respectively. But the state crime there involved was a capital offense. Were the federal prosecution of a comparatively minor offense to prevent state prosecution of so grave an infraction of state law, the result would be a shocking and untoward deprivation of the historic right and obligation of the States to maintain peace and order within their confines. It would be in derogation of our federal system to displace the reserved power of States over state offenses by reason of prosecution of minor federal offenses by federal authorities beyond the control of the States.[25] . . .

The entire history of litigation and contention over the question of the imposition of a bar to a second prosecution by a government other than the one first prosecuting is a manifestation of the evolutionary unfolding of law. Today a number of States have statutes which bar a second prosecution if the defendant has been once tried by another government for a similar offense. A study of the cases under the New York statute, which is typical of these laws, demonstrates that the task of determining when the federal and state statutes are so much alike that a prosecution under the former bars a prosecution under the latter is a difficult one. [E]xperience such as that of New York may give aid to Congress in its consideration of adoption of similar provisions in individual federal criminal statutes or in the federal criminal code.

Precedent, experience, and reason alike support the conclusion that Alfonse Bartkus has not been deprived of due process of law by the State of Illinois. Affirmed.

BLACK, J., dissenting.

. . . The Court's holding further limits our already weakened constitutional guarantees against double prosecutions. United States v. Lanza, decided in 1922, allowed federal conviction and punishment of a man who had been previously convicted and punished for the identical acts by one of our States. Today, for the first time in its history, this Court upholds the state conviction of a defendant who had been acquitted of the same offense in the federal courts. . . . Palko v. Connecticut, 302 U.S. 319 (1937), expressly left open the question of whether "the state [could be] permitted after a trial free from error to try the accused over again." That question is substantially before us today.

Fear and abhorrence of governmental power to try people twice for the same conduct is one of the oldest ideas found in western civilization. Its roots run deep into Greek and Roman times. Even in the Dark Ages, when so many other principles of justice were lost, the idea that one trial and one punishment were enough remained alive through the canon law and the teachings of the early Christian writers. By the thirteenth century it seems to have been firmly established in England, where it came to be considered as a "universal maxim of the common law." [S]ome writers have explained the opposition to double prosecutions by emphasizing the injustice inherent in two punishments for the same act, and others have stressed the dangers to the innocent from allowing the full power of the state to be brought against them in two trials. . . .

The Court apparently takes the position that a second trial for the same act is somehow less offensive if one of the trials is conducted by the Federal Government and the other by a State. Looked at from the standpoint of the individual who is being prosecuted, this notion is too subtle for me to grasp. If double punishment is what is feared, it hurts no less for two "Sovereigns" to inflict it than for one. If danger

---

25. Illinois had an additional and unique interest in Bartkus beyond the commission of this particular crime. If Bartkus was guilty of the crime charged he would be an habitual offender in Illinois and subject to life imprisonment. The Illinois court sentenced Bartkus to life imprisonment on this ground.

to the innocent is emphasized, that danger is surely no less when the power of State and Federal Governments is brought to bear on one man in two trials, than when one of these "Sovereigns" proceeds alone. In each case, inescapably, a man is forced to face danger twice for the same conduct.

The Court, without denying the almost universal abhorrence of such double prosecutions, nevertheless justifies the practice here in the name of "federalism." This, it seems to me, is a misuse and desecration of the concept. Our Federal Union was conceived and created "to establish Justice" and to "secure the Blessings of Liberty," not to destroy any of the bulwarks on which both freedom and justice depend. We should, therefore, be suspicious of any supposed "requirements" of "federalism" which result in obliterating ancient safeguards. I have been shown nothing in the history of our Union, in the writings of its Founders, or elsewhere, to indicate that individual rights deemed essential by both State and Nation were to be lost through the combined operations of the two governments. . . .

The Court's argument also ignores the fact that our Constitution allocates power between local and federal governments in such a way that the basic rights of each can be protected without double trials. The Federal Government is given power to act in limited areas only, but in matters properly within its scope it is supreme. It can retain exclusive control of such matters, or grant the States concurrent power on its own terms.

[T]his practice, which for some 150 years was considered so undesirable that the Court must strain to find examples, is now likely to become a commonplace. For, after today, who will be able to blame a conscientious prosecutor for failing to accept a jury verdict of acquittal when he believes a defendant guilty and knows that a second try is available in another jurisdiction and that such a second try is approved by the Highest Court in the Land? Inevitably, the victims of such double prosecutions will most often be the poor and the weak in our society, individuals without friends in high places who can influence prosecutors not to try them again. The power to try a second time will be used, as have all similar procedures, to make scapegoats of helpless, political, religious, or racial minorities and those who differ, who do not conform and who resist tyranny.

There are some countries that allow the dangerous practice of trying people twice. [Such practices] are not hard to find in lands torn by revolution or crushed by dictatorship. I had thought that our constitutional protections embodied in the Double Jeopardy and Due Process Clauses would have barred any such things happening here. Unfortunately, [today's decision causes] me to fear that in an important number of cases it can happen here. I would reverse.

BRENNAN, J., dissenting.

Bartkus was tried and acquitted in a Federal District Court of robbing a federally insured savings and loan association in Cicero, Illinois. He was indicted for the same robbery by the State of Illinois less than three weeks later, and subsequently convicted and sentenced to life imprisonment. The single issue in dispute at both trials was whether Bartkus was the third participant in the robbery along with two self-confessed perpetrators of the crime.

The Government's case against Bartkus on the federal trial rested primarily upon the testimony of two of the robbers, Joseph Cosentino and James Brindis, who confessed their part in the crime and testified that Bartkus was their confederate. The defense was that Bartkus was getting a haircut in a barber shop several miles away at the time the robbery was committed. The owner of the barber shop, his son and other witnesses placed Bartkus in the shop at the time. The federal jury in acquitting Bartkus apparently believed the alibi witnesses and not Cosentino and Brindis.

The federal authorities were highly displeased with the jury's resolution of the conflicting testimony, and the trial judge sharply upbraided the jury for its verdict. The federal authorities obviously decided immediately after the trial to make a second try at convicting Bartkus, and since the federal courthouse was barred to them by the Fifth Amendment, they turned to a state prosecution for that purpose. It is clear that federal officers solicited the state indictment, arranged to assure the attendance of key witnesses, unearthed additional evidence to discredit Bartkus and one of his alibi witnesses, and in general prepared and guided the state prosecution. . . .

I think that the record before us shows that the extent of participation of the federal authorities here [made] this state prosecution [into] a second federal prosecution of Bartkus. The federal jury acquitted Bartkus late in December 1953. Early in January 1954 the Assistant United States Attorney who prosecuted the federal case summoned Cosentino to his office. Present also were the FBI agent who had investigated the robbery and the Assistant State's Attorney for Cook County who later prosecuted the state case. The Assistant State's Attorney said to Cosentino, "Look, we are going to get an indictment in the state court against Bartkus, will you testify against him?" Cosentino agreed that he would. Later Brindis also agreed to testify. Although they pleaded guilty to the federal robbery charge in August 1953, the Federal District Court postponed their sentencing until after they testified against Bartkus at the state trial, which was not held until April 1954. . . . Both Cosentino and Brindis were also released on bail pending the state trial, Brindis on his own recognizance.

In January, also, an FBI agent who had been active in the federal prosecution purposefully set about strengthening the proofs which had not sufficed to convict Bartkus on the federal trial. . . . He uncovered a new witness against Bartkus, one Grant Pursel. . . . The first time that Pursel had any contact whatsoever with a state official connected with the case was the morning that he testified. . . .

Given the fact that there must always be state officials involved in a state prosecution, I cannot see how there can be more complete federal participation in a state prosecution than there was in this case. I see no escape from the conclusion that this particular state trial was in actuality a second federal prosecution—a second federal try at Bartkus in the guise of a state prosecution. If this state conviction is not overturned, then, as a practical matter, there will be no restraints on the use of state machinery by federal officers to bring what is in effect a second federal prosecution. . . .

Of course, cooperation between federal and state authorities in criminal law enforcement is to be desired and encouraged, for cooperative federalism in this field can indeed profit the Nation and the States in improving methods for carrying out the endless fight against crime. But the normal and healthy situation consists of state and federal officers cooperating to apprehend lawbreakers and present the strongest case against them at a single trial, be it state or federal. . . .

■ U.S. ATTORNEYS' MANUAL §9-2.031, DUAL PROSECUTION AND SUCCESSIVE PROSECUTION POLICY (*PETITE POLICY*)

A. Statement of Policy: This policy establishes guidelines for the exercise of discretion by appropriate officers of the Department of Justice in determining whether to bring a federal prosecution based on substantially the same act(s) or transactions involved in a prior state or federal proceeding. See Rinaldi v. United States, 434 U.S. 22, 27, (1977); Petite v. United States, 361 U.S. 529 (1960). Although there is no general statutory bar to a federal prosecution where the defendant's conduct already has formed the basis for a state prosecution, Congress expressly has provided that, as to certain offenses, a state judgment of conviction or acquittal on the merits shall be a bar to any subsequent federal prosecution for the same act or acts. See 18 U.S.C. §§659 [interstate or foreign shipments by carrier], 660 [embezzling carrier's funds derived from commerce], 2101 [travel in interstate commerce to incite a riot].

The purpose of this policy is to vindicate substantial federal interests through appropriate federal prosecutions, to protect persons charged with criminal conduct from the burdens associated with multiple prosecutions and punishments for substantially the same act(s) or transaction(s), to promote efficient utilization of Department resources, and to promote coordination and cooperation between federal and state prosecutors.

This policy precludes the initiation or continuation of a federal prosecution, following a prior state or federal prosecution based on substantially the same act(s) or transaction(s) unless three substantive prerequisites are satisfied: first, the matter must involve a substantial federal interest; second, the prior prosecution must have left that interest demonstrably unvindicated; and third, applying the same test that is applicable to all federal prosecutions, the government must believe that the defendant's conduct constitutes a federal offense, and that the admissible evidence probably will be sufficient to obtain and sustain a conviction by an unbiased trier of fact. In addition, there is a procedural prerequisite to be satisfied, that is, the prosecution must be approved by the appropriate Assistant Attorney General. . . .

In order to insure the most efficient use of law enforcement resources, whenever a matter involves overlapping federal and state jurisdiction, federal prosecutors should, as soon as possible, consult with their state counterparts to determine the most appropriate single forum in which to proceed to satisfy the substantial federal and state interests involved, and, if possible, to resolve all criminal liability for the acts in question.

B. Types of Prosecution to Which This Policy Applies: [T]his policy applies whenever the contemplated federal prosecution is based on substantially the same act(s) or transaction(s) involved in a prior state or federal prosecution. This policy constitutes an exercise of the Department's prosecutorial discretion, and applies even where a prior state prosecution would not legally bar a subsequent federal prosecution under the Double Jeopardy Clause because of the doctrine of dual sovereignty (see Abbate v. United States, 359 U.S. 187 (1959)), or a prior prosecution would not legally bar a subsequent state or federal prosecution under the Double Jeopardy Clause because each offense requires proof of an element not contained in the other. See United States v. Dixon, 509 U.S. 688 (1993); Blockburger v. United States, 284 U.S. 299 (1932).

This policy does not apply, and thus prior approval is not required, where the prior prosecution involved only a minor part of the contemplated federal charges. For example, a federal conspiracy or RICO prosecution may allege overt acts or predicate offenses previously prosecuted as long as those acts or offenses do not represent substantially the whole of the contemplated federal charge, and, in a RICO prosecution, as long as there are a sufficient number of predicate offenses to sustain the RICO charge if the previously prosecuted offenses were excluded. . . .

D. Substantive Prerequisites for Approval of a Prosecution Governed by This Policy: As previously stated there are three substantive prerequisites that must be met before approval will be granted for the initiation or a continuation of a prosecution governed by this policy.

The first substantive prerequisite is that the matter must involve a substantial federal interest. This determination will be made on a case-by-case basis, applying the considerations applicable to all federal prosecutions. See Principles of Federal Prosecution, USAM 9-27.230. Matters that come within the national investigative or prosecutorial priorities established by the Department are more likely than others to satisfy this requirement.

The second substantive prerequisite is that the prior prosecution must have left that substantial federal interest demonstrably unvindicated. In general, the Department will presume that a prior prosecution, regardless of result, has vindicated the relevant federal interest. That presumption, however, may be overcome when there are factors suggesting an unvindicated federal interest.

The presumption may be overcome when a conviction was not achieved because of the following sorts of factors: first, incompetence, corruption, intimidation, or undue influence; second, court or jury nullification in clear disregard of the evidence or the law; third, the unavailability of significant evidence, either because it was not timely discovered or known by the prosecution, or because it was kept from the trier of fact's consideration because of an erroneous interpretation of the law; fourth, the failure in a prior state prosecution to prove an element of a state offense that is not an element of the contemplated federal offense; and fifth, the exclusion of charges in a prior federal prosecution out of concern for fairness to other defendants, or for significant resource considerations that favored separate federal prosecutions.

The presumption may be overcome even when a conviction was achieved in the prior prosecution in the following circumstances: first, if the prior sentence was manifestly inadequate in light of the federal interest involved and a substantially enhanced sentence — including forfeiture and restitution as well as imprisonment and fines — is available through the contemplated federal prosecution, or second, if the choice of charges, or the determination of guilt, or the severity of sentence in the prior prosecution was affected by the sorts of factors listed in the previous paragraph. An example might be a case in which the charges in the initial prosecution trivialized the seriousness of the contemplated federal offense, for example, a state prosecution for assault and battery in a case involving the murder of a federal official.

The presumption also may be overcome, irrespective of the result in a prior state prosecution, in those rare cases where the following three conditions are met: first,

the alleged violation involves a compelling federal interest, particularly one impli-
cating an enduring national priority; second, the alleged violation involves egregious conduct, including that which threatens or causes loss of life, severe economic
or physical harm, or the impairment of the functioning of an agency of the federal
government or the due administration of justice; and third, the result in the prior
prosecution was manifestly inadequate in light of the federal interest involved.

The third substantive prerequisite is that the government must believe that the
defendant's conduct constitutes a federal offense, and that the admissible evidence
probably will be sufficient to obtain and sustain a conviction by an unbiased trier of
fact. This is the same test applied to all federal prosecutions. See Principles of
Federal Prosecution, USAM 9-27.200 et seq. . . .

E. Procedural Prerequisite for Bringing a Prosecution Governed by This Policy:
Whenever a substantial question arises as to whether this policy applies to a prosecution, the matter should be submitted to the appropriate Assistant Attorney
General for resolution. Prior approval from the appropriate Assistant Attorney
General must be obtained before bringing a prosecution governed by this policy.
The United States will move to dismiss any prosecution governed by this policy in
which prior approval was not obtained, unless the Assistant Attorney General retroactively approves it on the following grounds: first, that there unusual or overriding
circumstances justifying retroactive approval, and second, that the prosecution
would have been approved had approval been sought in a timely fashion. Appropriate administrative action may be initiated against prosecutors who violate this
policy.

F. . . . No Substantive or Procedural Rights Created: This policy has been promulgated solely for the purpose of internal Department of Justice guidance. It is not
intended to, does not, and may not be relied upon to create any rights, substantive
or procedural, that are enforceable at law by any party in any matter, civil or
criminal, nor does it place any limitations on otherwise lawful litigative prerogatives
of the Department of Justice.

■ NEW JERSEY STATUTES §2C:1-11

When conduct constitutes an offense within the concurrent jurisdiction of
this State and of the United States, a prosecution in the District Court of the
United States is a bar to a subsequent prosecution in this State under the following
circumstances:

a. The first prosecution resulted in an acquittal or in a conviction, or in an
improper termination . . . and the subsequent prosecution is based on the same
conduct, unless (1) the offense of which the defendant was formerly convicted or
acquitted and the offense for which he is subsequently prosecuted each requires
proof of a fact not required by the other and the law defining each of such
offenses is intended to prevent a substantially different harm or evil or (2) the
offense for which the defendant is subsequently prosecuted is intended to prevent
a substantially more serious harm or evil than the offense of which he was formerly
convicted or acquitted or (3) the second offense was not consummated when the
former trial began; or

b. The former prosecution was terminated, after the information was filed or the indictment found, by an acquittal or by a final order or judgment for the defendant which has not been set aside, reversed or vacated and which acquittal, final order or judgment necessarily required a determination inconsistent with a fact which must be established for conviction of the offense of which the defendant is subsequently prosecuted.

■ OHIO REVISED CODE §2925.50

If a violation of this chapter is a violation of the federal drug abuse control laws . . . a conviction or acquittal under the federal drug abuse control laws for the same act is a bar to prosecution in this state.

Problem 4-1. Rodney King's Attackers

Rodney King was driving while intoxicated on a major freeway in Los Angeles. California Highway Patrol officers spotted King driving more than 80 miles per hour and decided to follow him with red lights and sirens activated. They ordered him by loudspeaker to pull over, but he continued to drive. Los Angeles Police Department officers joined in the pursuit, including Officer Laurence Powell. King left the freeway and eventually stopped at an entrance to a recreation area. LAPD Sergeant Stacey Koon arrived at the scene and took charge.

The officers ordered King and his two passengers to exit the car and to lie face down on the pavement with legs spread and arms behind their backs. King's two friends complied. King got out of the car but put his hands on the hood of the car rather than lying down. The officers again ordered King to assume a prone position. King got on his hands and knees but did not lie down. Several officers tried to force King down and to handcuff him, but King resisted, so the officers retreated. Koon then fired taser darts (designed to stun a combative suspect) into King.

King rose from the ground and stepped toward Officer Powell. Powell used his baton to strike King on the side of his head. King fell to the ground. King attempted to rise, but Powell and another officer each struck him with their batons to prevent him from doing so. For about one minute after this point, several officers struck King more than 50 times with their batons and kicked or stepped on him. King remained on the ground. He was eventually hospitalized for facial fractures, a broken leg, and other injuries.

A bystander captured most of the events on videotape, and it was broadcast right away on the local and national media. Within one week of the beating, Los Angeles District Attorney Ira Reiner sought charges against the officers for excessive use of force. The Los Angeles County grand jury returned an indictment.

When the trial judge in Los Angeles County refused to grant the defendants' motion to change venue, they appealed and the ruling was overturned. The case was then reassigned to a different court, in suburban Ventura County. The district attorney's office did not appeal the intermediate appellate court's decision to transfer venue, nor did it challenge the selection of Ventura County as the new venue site. Trial commenced in Simi Valley before a predominantly white jury, containing no African American jurors; King was an African American. The prosecution's case at trial relied heavily on the videotape. The prosecution did not call an expert on the use of force by police until the rebuttal phase of the trial. The prosecutors also did not present any civilian witnesses to the beating. Rodney King did not testify in the case because of his prior criminal background and his inconsistent prior statements about the beating.

The state court jury acquitted all the officers of the excessive force and assault charges. Following the verdict, riots erupted in Los Angeles; at least 45 people were killed and more than 5,000 buildings were destroyed. Political and community leaders in Los Angeles asked for a federal prosecution of the officers. The President announced on television that he was surprised by the verdict and that the federal authorities would renew their investigation of the matter.

Federal prosecutors could charge the officers under 18 U.S.C. §242 with willfully violating the civil rights of Rodney King. Section 242 provides in pertinent part:

> Whoever, under color of any law . . . willfully subjects any inhabitant of any State . . . to the deprivation of any rights, privileges, or immunities secured or protected by the Constitution or laws of the United States [shall] if bodily injury results . . . be fined under this title or imprisoned not more than ten years, or both. . . .

A provision of the California constitution and a California statute both prohibit a state prosecution if the federal government has already prosecuted the defendant for the "same offense." Cal. Const. art I, §15; Cal. Penal Code §§656, 793-794. As U.S. Attorney for the Southern District of California, would you file charges against the officers? What legal considerations would be relevant to your choice? What other considerations? Compare Laurie Levenson, The Future of State and Federal Civil Rights Prosecutions: The Lessons of the Rodney King Trial, 41 UCLA L. Rev. 509 (1994); Powell v. Superior Court, 283 Cal. Rptr. 777 (Ct. App. 1991) (venue); United States v. Powell, 34 F.3d 1416 (9th Cir. 1994); Koon v. United States, 518 U.S. 81 (1996) (sentencing).

Notes

1. *Double jeopardy and dual sovereigns: majority position.* The Supreme Court has never repudiated its 1959 decision in *Bartkus*, despite all the changes in state-federal relations that it wrought through its incorporation decisions from that same era. See United States v. Lara, 541 U.S. 193 (2004) (dual sovereignty doctrine permits federal government to prosecute Native Americans for offenses after they have already been convicted of similar offenses in tribal courts). A substantial majority of states follow the U.S. Supreme Court and hold that the constitutional double jeopardy bar does not prohibit a second prosecution by a different sovereign, even for an offense defined by identical elements that would be considered the "same offence" within one jurisdiction. See State v. Franklin, 735 P.2d 34 (Utah 1987) (avowed racist killed two black men who were jogging in park with two white women; federal conviction for civil rights crime does not bar state murder trial under state statute or constitution). A few states have extended their constitutional double jeopardy provisions to bar a second prosecution for the same offense — or sometimes a similar offense — if it has been prosecuted in another jurisdiction. People v. Cooper, 247 N.W.2d 866 (Mich. 1976) (balancing test to determine whether subsequent prosecution allowed).

2. *Dual sovereign statutes.* In contrast to the narrow constitutional rulings, around fifteen states reject the dual sovereignty doctrine by statute. See, e.g., Cal. Penal Code §656 ("Whenever on the trial of an accused person it appears that upon a criminal prosecution under the laws of another State, Government, or country, founded upon the act or omission in respect to which he is on trial, he has been acquitted or convicted, it is a sufficient defense"). Most statutory limits on second prosecutions are limited to particular categories of offenses, such as the Ohio statute relating to drug offenses. Typically, these statutes are based on either the Uniform Narcotic Drug Act or the Uniform Controlled Substances Act. Unif. Narcotic Drug Act 21, 9B U.L.A. 284 (1958); Unif. Controlled Substances Act 418, 9 U.L.A. 596 (1990). See State v. Hansen, 627 N.W.2d 195 (Wis. 2001) (state statute applicable to controlled substance offenses bars prosecution of defendant by state officials for offenses arising out of the same conduct for which the defendant has been federally prosecuted). Why might legislatures restrict statutory double jeopardy provisions to specified types of crimes? The statutes are intended to pre-vent the unfairness of multiple prosecutions and to avoid the unnecessary use of state resources to prosecute cases already adequately prosecuted in federal courts. They often provide for exceptions when a reprosecution serves a different purpose or addresses a different evil from the earlier prosecution. See Ga. Code Ann. §16-1-8(c) (barring reprosecution except to prevent a "substantially more serious" or different harm or evil).

3. *Silver platters and dual sovereigns.* When more than one system can prosecute a criminal case, choice of law questions will crop up. For instance, which system's rules will be used to evaluate the work of the government agents who collected the evidence? Will the agents of one sovereign, acting in violation of the rules of their own government, be able to offer any evidence they obtain on a "silver platter" to prosecutors in another jurisdiction? When the federal constitution creates the obligations for the government agents, the answer is clear: No court (state or federal) may rely on evidence obtained by any state or federal agents in violation of the federal constitution. But what happens when the states have different rules from the federal government? If a state has its own rules (constitutional or statutory) to control government agents, and its agents violate those rules and offer the tainted evidence to federal prosecutors, the federal courts will admit the evidence. See United States v. Wright, 16 F.3d 1429 (6th Cir. 1994). State courts also accept evidence from government agents in another jurisdiction that violate the rules of that other jurisdiction. See Burge v. State, 443 S.W.2d 720 (Tex. Crim. App. 1969). Should a prosecutorial office policy dealing with prosecutions by multiple jurisdic-tions also address the use of evidence obtained in violation of law in another jurisdiction?

4. *Creation of the federal* Petite *policy.* Some jurisdictions that do not have constitutional or statutory limitations on filing cases already prosecuted in another jurisdiction nonetheless have *internal* prosecutorial rules or guidelines limiting successive prosecutions. The best-known illustration is the federal *Petite* policy. One week after the decision in *Bartkus,* which made it clear that the "dual sovereign" exception to the constitutional doctrine of double jeopardy would allow both state and federal prosecutions of the same crime, the Department of Justice issued a policy limiting federal prosecution after a state prosecution. The policy allows a federal prosecution following a state prosecution only when necessary to advance compelling interests of federal law enforcement. The policy later took its name from

Petite v. United States, 361 U.S. 529 (1960), in which the Court noted with approval the existence of the policy. It was designed to limit successive prosecutions for the same offense to situations involving distinct federal and state interests. In announcing the policy, Attorney General William Rogers stated:

> We should continue to make every effort to cooperate with state and local authorities to the end that the trial occur in the jurisdiction, whether it be state or federal, where the public interest is best served. If this be determined accurately, and is followed by efficient and intelligent cooperation of state and federal law enforcement authorities, then consideration of a second prosecution very seldom should arise.

Dept. of Justice Press Release, Apr. 6, 1959, at 3. The policy creates internal guidance only and does not create any rights that a defendant can enforce in court. See United States v. Snell, 592 F.2d 1083 (9th Cir. 1979). Are such policies properly considered "law"?

5. *Double jeopardy and international extradition.* The law in some other nations clearly rejects any dual sovereignty exception. As global legal regimes emerge, should double jeopardy principles bar multiple prosecutions by different countries? Is the principle barring double jeopardy an essential element of human rights? A partial answer to this question may be worked out on a bilateral basis as part of extradition treaties, for if a country cannot obtain control over the defendant, it is difficult to conduct a trial or to punish a person. A version of the double jeopardy principle also appears in Article 14(7) of the International Covenant on Civil and Political Rights: "No one shall be liable to be tried or punished again for an offence for which he has already been finally convicted or acquitted in accordance with the law and penal procedure of each country."

The European Union (EU) Convention implementing the Schengen Agreement of 1985 states in Article 54 that "[a] person who has been finally judged by a Contracting Party may not be prosecuted by another Contracting Party for the same offences provided that, where he is sentenced, the sentence has been served or is currently being served or can no longer be carried out under the sentencing laws of the Contracting Party." In two consolidated cases, the European Court of Justice held in 2003 that under this provision a person cannot be prosecuted in another member state even if (1) his case was discontinued by the prosecution after payment of a certain amount of money (based on a procedure of discontinuation) or (2) the case was settled out of court through a monetary payment (also based on national procedure). C-187/01 *Hüseyin Gözütok* and C-385/01 *Klaus Brügge* (Feb. 11, 2003). Article 54 sweeps far more broadly than internal United States double jeopardy barriers. The decision is noteworthy because it equates the discontinuation of procedures through a decision by the public prosecutor with a trial (or other judicial action).

6. *Double jeopardy and the Interstate Agreement on Detainers.* Even in the domestic U.S. context, one state's refusal to extradite a suspect could limit the capacity of another state to try that person regardless of the double jeopardy law in either jurisdiction. The possibility of such conflicts, however, has been reduced through the Interstate Agreement on Detainers, which provides a regular method of processing criminal charges filed by more than one state. The IAD is an interstate compact that most state legislatures have adopted. See Calif. Penal Code §1389. It allows

prosecutors to notify officials holding a criminal defendant in an out-of-state facility that the state wishes to pursue criminal charges against the defendant; such notice is called a "detainer." The IAD also allows the defendant to request that the state issuing the detainer dispose of the charges promptly.

2. *"Same Offence"*

The limitations on double jeopardy apply only when a person is placed twice in jeopardy for the "same offence." Determining whether a second offense is the "same" offense raises difficult challenges. First, many criminal codes include hundreds or even thousands of crimes with overlapping elements, aimed at punishing similar harms. The federal code, for example, includes more than 3,000 separate offenses. Because of the intricacy (to use a kind label) of most criminal codes, courts have conceded that charges need not be brought twice under precisely the same statute in order to conclude that the prosecution is for the same offense. How to determine whether charges under different code provisions should be considered the same offense is the topic of this subsection.

The Supreme Court has tried several approaches to the problem of distinguishing similar and different offenses. In Blockburger v. United States, 284 U.S. 299 (1932), the defendant was convicted of three counts of violating the Harrison Narcotics Act based on the sale of small amounts of morphine hydrochloride. One of the counts of conviction charged a sale of eight grains of the drug not from the original stamped package; another count alleged that the same sale was not made according to a written order of the purchaser, as required by the statute. The court sentenced Blockburger to five years in prison and imposed a fine of $2,000 upon each count, the terms of imprisonment to run consecutively. Blockburger asserted that these two counts constituted one offense for which only a single penalty could be imposed. The Court disagreed, holding that "where the same act or transaction constitutes a violation of two distinct statutory provisions, the test to be applied to determine whether there are two offenses or only one is whether each provision requires proof of an additional fact which the other does not." 284 U.S. at 304.

The *Blockburger* test was criticized because the government could so easily obtain multiple convictions based on the same conduct, but it remained the applicable standard in federal courts and in most state courts until 1990, when the Court decided Grady v. Corbin, 495 U.S. 508 (1990). Thomas Corbin drove his car across the center line while intoxicated, killing Brenda Dirago and injuring her husband, Daniel. Corbin was charged with two misdemeanors, driving while intoxicated and failing to keep right of the median. He pleaded guilty and was punished with a $350 fine, a $10 surcharge, and a six-month license revocation. Two months later a grand jury indicted Corbin for reckless manslaughter, second-degree vehicular manslaughter, and criminally negligent homicide for causing the death of Brenda Dirago, third-degree reckless assault for causing physical injury to Daniel Dirago, and driving while intoxicated. The bill of particulars supporting the indictment alleged that Corbin operated a motor vehicle on a public highway in an intoxicated condition, failed to keep right of the median, and drove approximately 45 to 50 miles per hour in heavy rain, "a speed too fast for the weather and road conditions then pending." Corbin challenged the indictment as a violation of double jeopardy. The Court agreed, and added a "same conduct" test on top of the *Blockburger* "same elements" test for those cases when the government pursues successive prosecutions:

> If *Blockburger* constituted the entire double jeopardy inquiry in the context of successive prosecutions, the State could try Corbin in four consecutive trials: for failure to keep right of the median, for driving while intoxicated, for assault, and for homicide. The State could improve its presentation of proof with each trial, assessing which witnesses gave the most persuasive testimony, which documents had the greatest impact, and which opening and closing arguments most persuaded the jurors. Corbin would be forced either to contest each of these trials or to plead guilty to avoid the harassment and expense.
>
> Thus, a subsequent prosecution must do more than merely survive the *Blockburger* test. [T]he Double Jeopardy Clause bars any subsequent prosecution in which the government, to establish an essential element of an offense charged in that prosecution, will prove conduct that constitutes an offense for which the defendant has already been prosecuted. This is not an "actual evidence" or "same evidence" test. The critical inquiry is what conduct the State will prove, not the evidence the State will use to prove that conduct. [T]he presentation of specific evidence in one trial does not forever prevent the government from introducing that same evidence in a subsequent proceeding. [495 U.S. at 520-521.]

Applying the new standard, the Court held that the double jeopardy clause barred the second prosecution because "the State has admitted that it will prove the entirety of the conduct for which Corbin was convicted — driving while intoxicated and failing to keep right of the median — to establish essential elements of the homicide and assault offenses."

Three years later, the Court overruled *Grady* and reinstated the "same elements" test as the basic way to identify double jeopardy violations in United States v. Dixon, 509 U.S. 688 (1993). The complex facts in *Dixon* concerned two cases in which contempt judgments — in one case for violation of a condition of release, and in the other for violation of civil protection orders — were entered before each defendant was prosecuted for the offenses underlying the contempt violation.

> We have concluded . . . that *Grady* must be overruled. Unlike *Blockburger* analysis, whose definition of what prevents two crimes from being the "same offence," has deep historical roots and has been accepted in numerous precedents of this Court, *Grady* lacks constitutional roots. The "same-conduct" rule it announced is wholly inconsistent with earlier Supreme Court precedent and with the clear common-law understanding of double jeopardy. . . . *Grady* was not only wrong in principle; it has already proved unstable in application. [W]e think it time to acknowledge what is now, three years after *Grady*, compellingly clear: the case was a mistake.

509 U.S. at 704, 709, 711. The first of the following two cases shows the *Blockburger* test at work. The second case discusses the choices among different tests for the "same offense" and illustrates the response of state courts to the leadership of the U.S. Supreme Court in this difficult area.

■ ROBERT TAYLOR v. COMMONWEALTH
995 S.W.2d 355 (Ky. 1999)

COOPER, J.

. . . On the afternoon of October 9, 1996, Appellant, then seventeen years of age, his girlfriend, Lucy Cotton, and Cotton's infant son had attended the Daniel Boone Festival and were traveling through rural Knox County in a 1985 Buick owned by Cotton's mother. They had with them a .22 rifle, a .38 Derringer handgun, and two shotguns. When the vehicle stalled, Appellant sought assistance from Herman McCreary, who lived nearby. McCreary agreed to help and drove his 1984 Ford pickup truck to the location of the stalled vehicle. Upon arrival, he observed Cotton sitting in the passenger seat of the Buick holding a child in her lap. Several attempts to jump-start the Buick failed. According to Cotton, Appellant told her, "If it don't start this time, I'm gonna take his truck," and armed himself with the .22 rifle and the .38 handgun. According to Appellant, Cotton pointed the .38 handgun at him and threatened to shoot him if he did not steal McCreary's truck.

When a final attempt to jump-start the Buick was unsuccessful, Appellant got out of the vehicle, pointed the .22 rifle at McCreary, and ordered him to lie on the ground. When McCreary complied, Appellant fired a round from the rifle into the ground near McCreary's head. According to Cotton, Appellant then struck McCreary in the head with the stock of the rifle. McCreary temporarily lost consciousness. Upon regaining consciousness, McCreary experienced dizziness and noticed blood coming from the left side of his head. Appellant then told McCreary to get into the ditch beside the road or he would "blow his head off." McCreary again complied, whereupon Appellant, Cotton and the child departed the scene in McCreary's truck. McCreary walked to a neighbor's house and called the police. [Taylor and Cotton were later apprehended and Taylor was convicted of assault in second degree, robbery in first degree, and possession of handgun by a minor. Taylor] asserts that his convictions violated the constitutional proscription against double jeopardy. U.S. Const. amend. V; Ky. Const. §13.

In Commonwealth v. Burge, 947 S.W.2d 805, 809-11 (1997), we reinstated the "*Blockburger* rule," Blockburger v. United States, 284 U.S. 299 (1932), as incorporated in KRS §505.020, as the sole basis for determining whether multiple convictions arising out of a single course of conduct constitutes double jeopardy. The test in this case is not whether all three convictions were premised upon the use or possession of a firearm, or whether both the assault and the robbery occurred in the course of a single transaction. "[W]here the same act or transaction constitutes a violation of two distinct statutory provisions, the test to be applied to determine whether there are two offenses or only one is whether each provision requires proof of an additional fact which the other does not." Blockburger v. United States, 284 U.S. 299, 304 (1932).

KRS §515.020(1) defines robbery in the first degree as follows:

> A person is guilty of robbery in the first degree when, in the course of committing a theft, he uses or threatens the immediate use of physical force upon another person with intent to accomplish the theft and when he:
>   (a) Causes physical injury to any person who is not a participant in the crime; or
>   (b) Is armed with a deadly weapon; or

(c) Uses or threatens the use of a dangerous instrument upon any person who is not a participant in the crime.

The first paragraph of the statute sets forth three elements which must be proven in any robbery case, viz: (1) In the course of committing a theft, (2) the defendant used or threatened the immediate use of physical force upon another person (3) with the intent to accomplish the theft. Subsections (a), (b), and (c) of the statute then describe three separate and distinct factual situations, any one of which could constitute the fourth element of the offense. The indictment of Appellant for robbery in the first degree in this case charged that he committed the offense "by being armed with a deadly weapon." The jury was instructed that it could convict Appellant of robbery in the first degree only if it believed beyond a reasonable doubt that "when he did so, he was armed with a .22 rifle." Thus, both the indictment and the instruction were predicated upon a violation of KRS 515.020(1)(b). Neither the indictment nor the instruction required Appellant to have caused a physical injury to McCreary or to have used or threatened the use of a dangerous instrument upon McCreary.

KRS 508.020(1) defines assault in the second degree as follows:

A person is guilty of assault in the second degree when:
(a) He intentionally causes serious physical injury to another person; or
(b) He intentionally causes physical injury to another person by means of a deadly weapon or a dangerous instrument; or
(c) He wantonly causes serious physical injury to another person by means of a deadly weapon or a dangerous instrument.

The statute sets forth three alternative factual situations by which the offense can be committed. Although the indictment charged Appellant with having committed the offense "by striking Herman McCreary with a pistol," the jury instruction conformed to the testimony of Lucy Cotton, who provided the only evidence with respect to this offense:

You will find the defendant guilty under this instruction if, and only if, you believe from the evidence beyond a reasonable doubt all of the following: (a) that in this county on or about October 9, 1996 and before the finding of the indictment herein, he inflicted an injury upon Herman McCreary by striking him with a .22 rifle, a deadly weapon; AND (b) that in so doing, the defendant intentionally caused physical injury to Herman McCreary.[1]

Thus, conviction of either the assault or the robbery of McCreary required proof of an element not required to prove the other. The conviction of robbery required proof of a theft, which was not required to convict of assault. The conviction of assault required proof of a physical injury to McCreary, whereas the conviction of robbery required proof only that Appellant used or threatened the use of physical force upon McCreary while armed with a .22 rifle. . . .

---

1. Appellant did not object to the variance of this instruction from the language of the indictment. The indictment described the weapon used to inflict the injury as a pistol, whereas the instruction described the weapon as a .22 rifle. Generally, instructions should be based on the evidence introduced at trial, and any variance between the language of the indictment and the language of the instruction is not deemed prejudicial unless the defendant was misled.

STUMBO, J., dissenting.

Respectfully, I must dissent. I believe Appellant's convictions for both assault and robbery violated the prohibition against double jeopardy. . . . As written, the indictment did not violate the double jeopardy prohibition. The indictment charged Appellant with "Assault in the Second Degree by striking Herman McCreary with a pistol" and "Robbery in the First Degree by being armed with a deadly weapon while in the course of committing a theft of Herman McCreary." Clearly, these offenses arise from two distinct statutes. As charged, each would have required proof of a fact which the other did not. For the assault, the prosecution would have had to prove that Appellant struck McCreary with the .38 pistol causing a physical injury. For the robbery, the prosecution would have had to prove Appellant used or threatened to use physical force on McCreary while armed with a deadly weapon (presumably the .22 rifle) during the course of the theft of his truck.

In the end, however, the prosecution was unable to maintain this logically sound but practically impossible distinction. By the time the jury was instructed, the assault had merged into the robbery so that one was clearly included within the other. This is so because the jury instruction on second-degree assault required the jury to find the offense was accomplished "by striking him with a .22 rifle, a deadly weapon." The jury instruction on first-degree robbery required the jury to find Appellant "used or threatened the immediate use of physical force upon Herman McCreary; AND (c) that when he did so, he was armed with a .22 rifle." This melding of the charges allowed the jury to consider any assault with the .22 rifle during the incident as an element of the robbery and thus made the assault charge a lesser included offense of the robbery charge. Appellant may be convicted of only one of these offenses without violating the prohibition against double jeopardy. Therefore, I would vacate the conviction on the lesser charge of assault in the second degree.

■ PEOPLE v. MELISSA NUTT
677 N.W.2d 1 (Mich. 2004)

YOUNG, J.

. . . On December 10, 1998, Darrold Smith's home in Lapeer County was burglarized. Four firearms and a bow and arrows were stolen from the home. Lapeer County police officers and those of adjacent Oakland County conducted a joint investigation concerning three Lapeer County burglaries, including the burglary of Smith's home. The officers obtained a search warrant for a cabin in Oakland County that was occupied by defendant and John Crosley. During the execution of the warrant on December 14, 1998, three of Smith's stolen firearms were found hidden underneath a mattress inside the cabin. Smith's bow and arrows and property stolen from another residence were also seized during the search.

Defendant confessed to a Lapeer County detective that she participated as a getaway driver during three burglaries that occurred the week of December 10, 1998, including the burglary of the Smith residence. Defendant admitted that three of the guns stolen from Smith were concealed underneath a mattress in the Oakland County cabin.

In January 1999, defendant was charged in Lapeer County with three counts of second-degree home invasion and three counts of larceny in a building. Meanwhile, on February 16, 1999, an arrest warrant was issued in Oakland County alleging that defendant had committed one offense of receiving and concealing a stolen firearm.

On February 22, 1999, defendant pleaded guilty in Lapeer County of one charge of second-degree home invasion in connection with the burglary of the Smith residence and the theft of the firearms. The remaining five charges were dismissed pursuant to a plea agreement. Defendant was sentenced to probation.

In July 1999, defendant was bound over for trial in Oakland County on the charge of receiving and concealing a stolen firearm. Defendant moved to dismiss the charge, contending that it constituted an improper successive prosecution in violation of the double jeopardy clauses of the federal and state constitutions. Defendant argued that pursuant to People v. White, 212 N.W.2d 222 (Mich. 1973), the state was required to join at one trial all charges arising from a continuous time sequence that demonstrated a single intent and goal. Thus, defendant maintained, she could not be tried in Oakland County for possession of the same firearms that she was alleged to have stolen during the home invasion for which she was convicted in Lapeer County. The trial court granted defendant's motion to dismiss. . . .

The United States and Michigan Constitutions protect a person from being twice placed in jeopardy for the same offense. The prohibition against double jeopardy provides three related protections: (1) it protects against a second prosecution for the same offense after acquittal; (2) it protects against a second prosecution for the same offense after conviction; and (3) it protects against multiple punishments for the same offense. The first two of these three protections concern the "successive prosecutions" strand of the Double Jeopardy Clause, which is implicated in the case before us. In particular, because our Double Jeopardy Clause is essentially identical to its federal counterpart, we must determine whether the term "same offense" in our Constitution was, in *White*, properly accorded a meaning that is different from the construction of that term in the federal Constitution. . . .

FEDERAL SUCCESSIVE PROSECUTIONS PROTECTION AND THE SAME-ELEMENTS TEST

Application of the same-elements test, commonly known as the "*Blockburger* test," is the well-established method of defining the Fifth Amendment term "same offence." The test, which has deep historical roots, focuses on the statutory elements of the offense. If each requires proof of a fact that the other does not, the *Blockburger* test is satisfied, notwithstanding a substantial overlap in the proof offered to establish the crimes.

The *Blockburger* analytical framework "reflected a venerable understanding" of the meaning of the term "same offence" as used in the Double Jeopardy Clause. The Clause was designed to embody the protection of the English common-law pleas of former jeopardy, "auterfoits acquit" (formerly acquitted) and "auterfoits convict" (formerly convicted), which applied only to prosecutions for the identical act and crime. An examination of the historical record reveals that the English practice, as understood in 1791, did not recognize auterfoits acquit and auterfoits convict as good pleas against successive prosecutions for crimes whose elements were distinct, even though based on the same act. . . .

Although Justice William Brennan was a persistent advocate of the same transaction test, see Werneth v. Idaho, 449 U.S. 1129 (1981) (Brennan, J., dissenting), the idea that crimes arising from the same criminal episode constitute the same offenses for double jeopardy purposes has been consistently rejected by the United States Supreme Court. Instead, the . . . *Blockburger* same-elements analysis was consistently applied by the Court . . . until the Court in Grady v. Corbin, 495 U.S. 508 (1990), adopted a "same-conduct" rule—a somewhat compromised version of Justice Brennan's "same transaction" test—as an additional step to be performed in addressing successive prosecutions claims. In an opinion authored by Justice William Brennan, the Court held that "the Double Jeopardy Clause bars a subsequent prosecution if, to establish an essential element of an offense charged in that prosecution, the government will prove conduct that constitutes an offense for which the defendant has already been prosecuted."

Justice Scalia dissented, noting that the majority's holding was wholly without historical foundation and that it created a procedural mandatory joinder rule: "In practice, [the majority's holding] will require prosecutors to observe a rule we have explicitly rejected in principle: that all charges arising out of a single occurrence must be joined in a single indictment." Looking to the text of the Double Jeopardy Clause and its origins in the common law, Justice Scalia opined that the *Blockburger* rule best gave effect to the plain language of the Clause, "which protects individuals from being twice put in jeopardy 'for the same offense,' not for the same conduct or actions."

The *Grady* same-conduct test was short-lived. In United States v. Dixon, 509 U.S. 688 (1993), the Court overruled *Grady* as wrongly decided for the reasons expressed in Justice Scalia's *Grady* dissent and returned to the *Blockburger* formulation of the test for both successive prosecutions and multiple punishments. . . .

MEANING OF "SAME OFFENSE" IN MICHIGAN'S DOUBLE JEOPARDY PROVISION

Until *White* was decided in 1973, this Court defined the scope of our Constitution's double jeopardy protection by reference to the scope of the protection provided by the Fifth Amendment. In accordance with the principle that our double jeopardy provision was intended to embody English common-law tenets of former jeopardy, this Court more than one hundred years ago rejected the "same transaction" approach and instead embraced the federal same-elements test as supplying the functional definition of "same offense" under our Constitution's Double Jeopardy Clause. In People v. Parrow, 45 N.W. 514 (Mich. 1890), this Court held that Const. 1850, art. 6, §29 did not preclude the defendant's prosecution for larceny of money stolen during an alleged burglary where the defendant had previously been acquitted of burglary. . . .

However, in People v. White, 212 N.W.2d 222 (Mich. 1973), the majority . . . adopted the same transaction test advocated unsuccessfully by Justice William Brennan—one even more expansive than the defunct compromise *Grady* test. The defendant in *White* followed the victim to her home in Inkster, forced her to get into his car, drove her to Detroit, and, while in Detroit, raped her. The defendant was first tried and convicted in Wayne Circuit Court on a kidnapping charge. Subsequently, the defendant was tried and convicted in Detroit Recorder's Court on charges of rape and felonious assault.

[The Court] held that the rape and felonious assault convictions were violative of art. 1, §15. We noted that several other states had adopted the same transaction test, either under their own constitutions or under statutes requiring mandatory

joinder, and that . . . the same transaction test was necessary to effectuate the intent
of the framers that the state not be allowed to make repeated attempts to convict a
defendant. Without reference to our Constitution, its text, or its ratification process,
the *White* Court opined that the same transaction test fostered sound policy:

> In a time of overcrowded criminal dockets, prosecutors and judges should attempt to
> bring to trial a defendant as expeditiously and economically as possible. A far more
> basic reason for adopting the same transaction test is to prevent harassment of a
> defendant. The joining of all charges arising out of the same criminal episode at
> one trial . . . will enable a defendant to consider the matter closed and save the
> costs of redundant litigation. It will also help . . . to equalize the adversary capabilities
> of grossly unequal litigants and prevent prosecutorial sentence shopping.

The *White* Court also noted that the equivalent of the same transaction test had
long been the standard applied to civil actions by the court rule governing joinder and
by the doctrines of collateral estoppel and res judicata. Finally, the Court concluded
that the three crimes committed by the defendant were all part of a single criminal
transaction because they "were committed in a continuous time sequence and displayed a single intent and goal — sexual intercourse with the complainant." . . .

In Crampton v. 54-A Dist. Judge, 245 N.W.2d 28 (Mich. 1976), this Court, recognizing the difficulty of applying the same transaction test, introduced a different
inflection on the *White* "single intent and goal" factor where some of the offenses at
issue did not involve criminal intent: . . . "where one or more of the offenses does
not involve criminal intent, the criterion is whether the offenses are part of the same
criminal episode, and whether the offenses involve laws intended to prevent the
same or similar harm or evil, not a substantially different, or a very different kind of,
harm or evil." . . .

In our 1963 Constitution the narrower language of the 1850 and 1908 double
jeopardy provisions was replaced with language similar to that of the original
Constitution of 1835 and the Fifth Amendment: "No person shall be subject for
the same offense to be twice put in jeopardy." Art. 1, §15.

It is immediately striking that the plain language of the provision provides
no support for the conclusion that the term "same offense" should be interpreted
by reference to whether a crime arises out of the "same transaction" as another.
Rather, we believe that the plain and obvious meaning of the term "offense" is
"crime" or "transgression." . . .

The ultimate inquiry, of course, is the meaning ascribed to the phrase "same
offense" by the ratifiers of our 1963 Constitution. Examination of the record of the
Constitutional Convention of 1961 provides the historical context and persuasive
support for our decision to return to the original meaning given to the Fifth Amendment — based double jeopardy language in art. 1, §15. . . .

Of . . . significance to our analysis is the Address to the People[26] accompanying
Const. 1963, art. 1, §15:

> This is a revision of Sec. 14, Article II, of the present constitution. The new language of
> the first sentence involves the substitution of the double jeopardy provision from the

26. The Address to the People, widely distributed to the public prior to the ratification vote in order
to explain the import of the sundry proposals, is a valuable tool in determining whether a possible
"common understanding" diverges from the plain meaning of the actual words of our Constitution.

U.S. Constitution in place of the present provision which merely prohibits "acquittal on the merits." This is more consistent with the actual practice of the courts in Michigan. Thus, the ratifiers were advised that (1) the double jeopardy protection conferred by our 1963 Constitution would parallel that of the federal constitution, and (2) . . . the proposal was meant to bring our double jeopardy provision into conformity with what this Court had already determined it to mean. . . .

In 1973, this Court disregarded decades of precedent and, without consideration of the will of the people of this state in ratifying the Double Jeopardy Clause in our 1963 Constitution, adopted Justice William Brennan's long-rejected "same transaction" test. In adopting this definition and equating the word "transaction" with the constitutional term "offense," the *White* Court accorded to that term a meaning quite at odds with its plain meaning or the common understanding. In the absence of any evidence that the term "offense" was understood by the people to comprise all criminal acts arising out of a single criminal episode, we are compelled to overrule *White*. [The] same-elements test best gives effect to the intent of the ratifiers of the 1963 Constitution.[28]

APPLICATION

Defendant's Oakland County prosecution for possession of stolen firearms, following her conviction for second-degree home invasion in Lapeer County, withstands constitutional scrutiny under the same-elements test. Defendant was convicted of home invasion pursuant to MCL 750.110a(3), which provided: "A person who breaks and enters a dwelling with intent to commit a felony or a larceny in the dwelling or a person who enters a dwelling without permission with intent to commit a felony or a larceny in the dwelling is guilty of home invasion in the second degree." Required for a conviction of this offense was proof that defendant (1) entered a dwelling, either by a breaking or without permission, (2) with the intent to commit a felony or a larceny in the dwelling.

Defendant now stands charged with receiving and concealing a stolen firearm in violation of MCL 750.535b(2), which provides: "A person who receives, conceals, stores, barters, sells, disposes of, pledges, or accepts as security for a loan a stolen firearm or stolen ammunition, knowing that the firearm or ammunition was stolen, is guilty of a felony. . . ." Thus, the Oakland County Prosecutor is required to prove that defendant (1) received, concealed, stored, bartered, sold, disposed of, pledged, or accepted as security for a loan (2) a stolen firearm or stolen ammunition (3) knowing that the firearm or ammunition was stolen.

Clearly, there is no identity of elements between these two offenses. Each offense requires proof of elements that the other does not. Because the two offenses are nowise the same offense under either the Fifth Amendment or art. 1, §15, we

---

28. [Principles] of collateral estoppel and properly adopted procedural joinder rules might well compel the dismissal of charges in certain circumstances. Nevertheless, collateral estoppel and joinder are discrete, nonconstitutional concepts that should not be conflated with the constitutional double jeopardy protection.

This Court has appointed a committee to review the Rules of Criminal Procedure and to determine whether any of these rules should be revised. In light of our decision here today that the Constitution does not require the prosecutor to join at one trial all the charges against a defendant arising out of the same transaction, we will be requesting the Committee on the Rules of Criminal Procedure to consider whether our permissive joinder rule, MCR 6.120(A), should be amended to impose mandatory joinder of all the charges against a defendant arising out of the same transaction. . . .

affirm the result reached by the Court of Appeals majority and hold that defendant is not entitled to the dismissal of the Oakland County charge.

RESPONSE TO THE DISSENT

[The dissent] asserts that we have given short shrift to the purpose of the double jeopardy provision's successive prosecutions strand, which is to prevent the state from making repeated attempts to obtain a conviction for an alleged offense. However, the instant case in fact illustrates that this venerable purpose is in no way served by the ill-conceived rule set forth in *White.* Defendant was not subjected to repeated attempts to convict her of "an alleged offense." Rather, she was subjected to prosecution for two independent offenses in two separate jurisdictions. Application of the *White* rule, rather than ensuring that the state would not get more than "one bite at the apple," would preclude the state from ever trying defendant for one of the charges against her. This is not at all consistent with the purpose of the double jeopardy protection. . . .

CAVANAGH, J., dissenting.

. . . This Court's decision to overrule *White* is grounded in the improper belief that the same elements test is the sole test used by the United States Supreme Court to protect citizens' constitutional rights under the United States Constitution. However, the same elements test, also referred to as the *Blockburger* test, is not as entrenched in federal jurisprudence as the majority claims. "The *Blockburger* test is not the only standard for determining whether successive prosecutions impermissibly involve the same offense." Brown v. Ohio, 432 U.S. 161, 166 n.6 (1977). It has long been understood that separate statutory crimes need not be identical — either in constituent elements or in actual proof — in order to be the same within the meaning of the constitutional prohibition.

In numerous cases, the United States Supreme Court has used other tests because it recognized that the same elements test is not an adequate safeguard to protect a citizen's constitutional right against double jeopardy. In Ashe v. Swenson, 397 U.S. 436 (1970), the United States Supreme Court held that the double jeopardy clause includes a collateral estoppel guarantee. . . . As stated in Albernaz v. United States, 450 U.S. 333, 340 (1981), "The *Blockburger* test is a rule of statutory construction, and because it serves as a means of discerning congressional purpose the rule should not be controlling where, for example, there is a clear indication of contrary legislative intent." Further, in In re Nielsen, 131 U.S. 176 (1889), a conviction for unlawful cohabitation precluded a subsequent charge of adultery because the incident occurred during the same two and a half year period as that for unlawful cohabitation. In Harris v. Oklahoma, 433 U.S. 682 (1977), the defendant was convicted of felony murder after a store clerk was killed during a robbery. After the defendant's conviction for felony murder, the defendant was tried and convicted of robbery with firearms. The United States Supreme Court held that when "conviction of a greater crime . . . cannot be had without conviction of the lesser crime, the Double Jeopardy Clause bars prosecution for the lesser crime after conviction of the greater one." And in Brown, double jeopardy barred a subsequent prosecution for a greater offense even though the greater offense required proof of an additional element.

[It] is worth stating clearly that the purpose of the constitutional protection against double jeopardy is to limit the state to having generally only one attempt at obtaining a conviction. Otherwise, the state could repeatedly prosecute persons for the same crime, transforming the trial process itself into a punishment and effectively punishing the accused without his having been adjudged guilty of an offense meriting punishment. . . .

Our Double Jeopardy Clause is meant to protect our citizens from government zeal and overreaching; yet, the same elements test permits multiple prosecutions stemming from a single incident. . . . Notably, a technical comparison of the elements is neither constitutionally sound nor easy to apply. . . . If our courts struggle with the basics of determining what elements constitute a crime, it is inevitable that these struggles will continue when courts attempt to determine whether two crimes contain the same elements.

In contrast to the same elements test, the same transaction test requires the government to join at one trial all the charges against a defendant arising out of a continuous time sequence, when the offenses shared a single intent and goal. Although a single transaction can give rise to distinct offenses, the charges must be joined at one trial. However, the same transaction test also offers flexibility for certain circumstances, such as when facts necessary to sustain a charge have not yet occurred or have not been discovered despite due diligence. . . .

In this case, defendant pleaded guilty of second-degree home invasion, MCL 750.110a(3). She was subsequently charged with receiving and concealing stolen firearms, MCL 750.535b. Notably, defendant was the driver in the home invasion during which the guns were stolen. She also admitted that the guns concealed were the ones stolen during the home invasion. Defendant's actions represent a single intent and goal, as well as the events being part of a continuous time sequence. . . . Without double jeopardy protections, our citizens are at risk of facing multiple prosecutions by the government, regardless of a prior acquittal. Further, because the state can devote its resources to improving the presentation of its case, the probability of a conviction may increase with each retrial. Accordingly, [after] pleading guilty of second-degree home invasion, defendant's subsequent prosecution for receiving and concealing stolen firearms violated her double jeopardy rights.

■ NEW YORK CRIMINAL PROCEDURE LAW §40.20

1. A person may not be twice prosecuted for the same offense.

2. A person may not be separately prosecuted for two offenses based upon the same act or criminal transaction unless:

(a) The offenses as defined have substantially different elements and the acts establishing one offense are in the main clearly distinguishable from those establishing the other; or

(b) Each of the offenses as defined contains an element which is not an element of the other, and the statutory provisions defining such offenses are designed to prevent very different kinds of harm or evil; or

(c) One of such offenses consists of criminal possession of contraband matter and the other offense is one involving the use of such contraband matter, other than a sale thereof; or

(d) One of the offenses is assault or some other offense resulting in physical injury to a person, and the other offense is one of homicide based upon the death of such person from the same physical injury, and such death occurs after a prosecution for the assault or other non-homicide offense; or

(e) Each offense involves death, injury, loss or other consequence to a different victim; or

(f) One of the offenses consists of a violation of a statutory provision of another jurisdiction, which offense has been prosecuted in such other jurisdiction and has there been terminated by a court order expressly founded upon insufficiency of evidence to establish some element of such offense which is not an element of the other offense, defined by the laws of this state; or

(g) The present prosecution is for a consummated result offense . . . which occurred in this state and the offense was the result of a conspiracy, facilitation or solicitation prosecuted in another state. . . .

Notes

1. *Determining whether two charges are for the "same offence": majority position.* The Supreme Court's decision in United States v. Dixon, 509 U.S. 688 (1993), reestablished the "same elements" test of Blockburger v. United States, 284 U.S. 299 (1932). Under this test, if the two offenses *each* have at least one distinct "element," they are not treated as the same offense. Hence, multiple trials or multiple punishments based on these offenses do not violate the protection against double jeopardy.

About 30 state courts follow *Dixon* and have adopted (or readopted) the *Block-burger* "same elements" test under state law. See, e.g., State v. Alvarez, 778 A.2d 938 (Conn. 2001); City of Fargo v. Hector, 534 N.W.2d 821 (N.D. 1995). About 10 jurisdictions have interpreted their state constitutions to employ the *Grady* "same conduct" test (or the closely related "same evidence" test) in addition to the *Blockburger* analysis as a limit on multiple prosecutions. See State v. Lessary, 865 P.2d 150 (Haw. 1994). A smaller group of states (about a half dozen) apply a test that places even stronger limits on government attempts to bring multiple prosecutions: the "same transaction" test (also called the "same episode" or "same incident" test) suggested by Justice Brennan in his concurring opinion in Ashe v. Swenson, 397 U.S. 436 (1970). See, e.g., State v. Farley, 725 P.2d 359 (Or. 1986). Around 15 states have adopted statutory tests for whether a second charge is for the "same offense"; some statutes mirror the *Blockburger* test, Fla. Stat. §775.021(4)(a), while others add a "same facts" or "same conduct" test.

There is no shortage of suggestions in the academic literature for reworking this doctrine from the ground up. See Akhil Amar, Double Jeopardy Law Made Simple, 106 Yale L.J. 1807 (1997) (suggests due process rather than double jeopardy as remedy for vexatious litigation); George Thomas, A Blameworthy Act Approach to the Double Jeopardy Same Offense Problem, 83 Cal. L. Rev. 1027, 1041-49 (1995) (looks to blameworthiness rather than *Blockburger* as best indicator of legislative intent as to multiple punishment and trials). Consider this critique of the doctrine by Justice Breyer: "[T]he simple-sounding *Blockburger* test has proved extraordinarily difficult to administer in practice. Judges, lawyers, and law professors often disagree about how to apply it. [The *Blockburger* test is] the criminal law equivalent of Milton's 'Serbonian Bog . . . Where Armies whole have sunk.' " *Texas v. Cobb*, 532 U.S. 162 (2001). Exactly how do the Kentucky justices in *Taylor* disagree on the application of *Blockburger*?

2. *Punishment for greater and lesser included offenses.* A lesser included offense is one that is necessarily included within the statutory elements of another offense. Thus, if Crime 1 has elements A and B, it is a lesser included offense for Crime 2, with elements A, B, and C. In a straightforward application of the *Blockburger* test, a prosecution for either Crime 1 or Crime 2 would prevent a later prosecution or punishment for the second crime. An exception to this bar would allow a prosecution for Crime 2 after a prosecution for Crime 1, if the additional element C had not yet occurred at the time of the Crime 1 prosecution (for instance, if an assault victim dies after the trial for assault goes forward). See *Brown v. Ohio*, 432 U.S. 161, 169 n.7 (1977).

But the courts have gone beyond this literal understanding of lesser included offenses. Both federal and state courts declare that double jeopardy limits for the "same offense" also apply to "a species of lesser included offense." In *Harris v. Oklahoma*, 433 U.S. 682 (1977), the court held that a conviction for felony murder barred a later trial of the defendant for the underlying robbery. Strictly speaking, the robbery and felony murder statutes pass the *Blockburger* test: Felony murder requires proof of a killing (robbery does not), and robbery requires proof of forcible taking of property (which felony murder does not necessarily require). But the court was willing to treat robbery and felony murder as the "same offense" because in the *case at hand,* the prosecution was relying on forcible taking of property to establish the predicate felony for felony murder. See also *United States v. Dixon*, 509 U.S. 688, 697-700 (1993) (criminal contempt of court for violation of judicial order not to commit "any criminal offense" and possession of cocaine with intent to distribute are the same offense); *People v. Wood*, 742 N.E.2d 114 (N.Y. 2000) (multiple contempt convictions in different courts for same acts violate double jeopardy; defendant made late-night hang-up calls, violated no-contact orders issued by criminal court and family court). On the other hand, the same logic does not seem to apply to conspiracy or "continuing criminal enterprise" crimes. See *United States v. Felix*, 503 U.S. 378, 387-92 (1992) (conspiracy to manufacture narcotics is not same offense as manufacturing narcotics); *Garrett v. United States*, 471 U.S. 773, 777-86 (1985) (distribution of marijuana is not same offense as conducting a continuing criminal enterprise to distribute marijuana).

3. *The "multiple punishment" prong of double jeopardy.* Unlike the relatively clear rule against multiple *prosecutions* for the same offense, there are looser limits when the prosecutor files multiple charges in a *single proceeding,* and the defendant claims that the charges are actually an attempt to impose multiple punishments for what is really a single offense. In this setting, the legislature sets the constraints on the prosecutor. In *Missouri v. Hunter*, 459 U.S. 359 (1983), the Supreme Court held that "the Double Jeopardy Clause does no more than prevent the sentencing court from prescribing greater punishment than the legislature intended."

Most states follow *Missouri v. Hunter* and hold that in the context of a single prosecution, the *Blockburger* test (or an alternative test) only helps determine whether the legislature intended to allow separate convictions and punishments for a single criminal episode or event. See, e.g., *State v. Adel*, 965 P.2d 1072 (Wash. 1998). The courts reason that the legislature can select from a wide range of punishments for any particular offense. Other states have rejected the majority rule and have applied state law to limit cumulative punishments regardless of the legislature's intent. See, e.g., Ingram v. Commonwealth, 801 S.W.2d 321 (Ky. 1990). In one especially difficult area, states are split on whether punishment is acceptable for both felony murder and the underlying felony when they are tried together. See, e.g., Todd v. State, 917 P.2d 674 (Alaska 1996) (allowing multiple punishment); cf. Boulies v. People, 770 P.2d 1274 (Colo. 1989) (state merger rule barring multiple punishment).

What reasons might justify the different treatment of "multiple proceedings" on the one hand, and "multiple punishment" for the same conduct in a single proceeding on the other hand? Does this distinction make sense? See Nancy King, Portioning Punishment: Constitutional Limits on Successive and Excessive Penalties, 144 U. Pa. L. Rev. 101 (1995) (points to illogic of cases allowing multiple punishments in a single trial but not in successive trials; argues for limiting Eighth Amendment to a remedy for excessive punishments imposed in multiple proceedings).

4. *When do double jeopardy claims arise?* Double jeopardy claims can arise at a variety of points in the criminal justice process. A defendant can raise double jeopardy claims as soon as she is charged with multiple counts in a single proceeding. A defendant might challenge even a single count, claiming that jeopardy already attached at an earlier proceeding. Double jeopardy "attaches" at an initial trial when the jury is sworn in (for jury trials) or when the first witness is sworn in (for a bench trial) or when the court accepts a guilty plea. The defendant might raise a double jeopardy challenge at the time of sentencing, claiming that the state has requested multiple punishments for the same offense. Double jeopardy challenges might also arise when the state attempts to impose some civil penalties before or after adjudicating the criminal charges.

It is important to recognize that double jeopardy influences the work of all three branches of government. Double jeopardy rules have a substantial impact on what kinds of charges the prosecution chooses to file. Principles of prior jeopardy may also shape the actions of judges at sentencing, when the judge can group together charges to produce a single sentence lower than what technically could be imposed for each separate conviction. Finally, legislators will have a powerful effect on the grouping of crimes when they define the elements of different crimes. Ultimately, are double jeopardy principles anything more than instructions to legislatures to draft cleanly?

5. *Double jeopardy after mistrial.* Typically mistrials do not bar a retrial, even though double jeopardy protections have attached, so long as the retrial was a "manifest necessity." To allow any mistrial to bar subsequent prosecution would invite a moral hazard on the part of attorneys if a case turns against them during trial: their own misconduct in the later stages of a trial could gain the attorneys a second chance in a trial that went badly for them in the early stages. A significant minority of state courts view federal constitutional limits on prosecutorial misbehavior as insufficient to protect defendants' double jeopardy rights. See Commonwealth v. Martorano, 741 A.2d 1221 (Pa. 1999) (expanding scope of double jeopardy in light of "Machiavellian" prosecutorial misconduct in a murder case). See generally George C. Thomas III, Solving the Double Jeopardy Mistrial Riddle, 69 S. Cal. L. Rev. 1551 (1996). While the "prosecutorial misconduct" exception to the "manifest necessity" exception to double jeopardy protections seems to amount to nothing more than angels searching for a pin to dance on, mistrials do happen

relatively often in complex cases, making the scope of double jeopardy protections in this setting especially significant.

6. *Jurisdictions without double jeopardy provisions.* Five states have no double jeopardy provisions in their constitutions. Each has incorporated double jeopardy principles but through different conceptual doorways. Connecticut imports double jeopardy though its due process clause. See, e.g., State v. Nixon, 651 A.2d 1264 (Conn. 1995). Maryland, Massachusetts, and North Carolina rely on the common law as the source for their double jeopardy rules. See, e.g., Berry v. Commonwealth, 473 N.E.2d 1115 (Mass. 1985). Vermont courts have simply adopted federal double jeopardy standards. See In re Dunkerley, 376 A.2d 43 (Vt. 1977). In the United Kingdom, legislation allows a second prosecution after an acquittal for specified serious charges, if the government can demonstrate that "new and compelling evidence" has appeared and that a second prosecution would serve "the interests of justice."

7. *Consistency and respect.* What principles of decision making underlie the Supreme Court's boomerang from *Grady* (1990) to *Dixon* (1993)? It is arguable that *Grady* and *Dixon* both reveal substantial departures from established rules (*Grady* from *Blockburger*, and *Dixon* from *Grady*). All courts offer words of respect for stare decisis. Should courts have a different stare decisis rule with respect to constitutional and nonconstitutional decisions? Should all constitutional decisions have a natural life span? Should readers discount all constitutional decisions by the age of the justices and the number of justices who decided the case who are still active — a kind of actuarial jurisprudence? Are constitutions nothing more than the sum of the personal views of those who interpret and enforce them?

Problem 4-2. Multiplicity

On December 11, 1989, Ronald Gardner, Cato Peterson, Amir Wilson, and Aaron Banks were traveling in a white Cougar automobile from Detroit to Muskegon. Muskegon County Sheriff Deputy Al VanHemert received a tip from a confidential informant that Aaron Banks and several other persons would be transporting crack cocaine to a Muskegon Heights neighborhood that afternoon. Two deputies executed a legal stop and search of the vehicle. They seized 222 grams of crack cocaine and arrested the occupants of the car.

Ronald Gardner, Cato Peterson, and Amir Wilson each made statements to the officers. Gardner said that Ricky Franklin paid him two hundred dollars to drive Peterson, Wilson, and Banks to the Muskegon Heights area. He admitted that he had previously transported sellers and drugs to that area. Gardner also stated he had picked up money at the home of "Miss Louise" in Muskegon and transported the cash back to Detroit. He stated that cocaine was sometimes transported in the spare tire in the trunk. Gardner called Franklin the head of the organization, while Banks was the boss of the Muskegon portion of the operation.

Peterson stated to the officers that he was traveling to Muskegon to sell crack cocaine, that this was his second trip to Muskegon, and that Franklin was the head of the organization.

Wilson also made a statement to the Muskegon authorities after his arrest. He stated that he sold crack cocaine for Ricky Franklin and that he had sold drugs on three previous trips to Muskegon. He stated that Banks would stay at Miss Louise's house and dispense the crack baggies to the sellers there. The cocaine was transported in the spare tire in the trunk. Robert Johnson was also involved in the sale of cocaine.

On June 6, 1990, Amir Wilson was convicted by a Muskegon County jury of possession with intent to deliver and conspiracy to deliver between 50 and 225 grams of cocaine. On July 3, 1990, Wilson was sentenced to two concurrent prison terms of eight to twenty years.

On July 5, 1990, police arrested Gerald Hill in Southfield (in Oakland County, near Muskegon County) for possession with intent to deliver between 225 and 649 grams of cocaine. Southfield police made the arrest after a routine traffic stop of the vehicle in which Hill and Ricky Franklin were passengers. The police allowed Hill to go into a store across the street from where the vehicle was stopped. After Hill left the area, store employees alerted police officers that they had found cocaine in a jacket behind the store. The Muskegon and Oakland County Sheriff Departments joined efforts to investigate the "Franklin organization."

In December 1990, an Oakland County grand jury indicted Wilson, Banks, Hill, Johnson, and another individual, Terrence Moore, on charges of conspiring from October 1988 to December 1990 to possess with intent to deliver over 650 grams of cocaine. Wilson moved to set aside the indictment on the basis of a violation of double jeopardy. Should the trial judge in Oakland County grant the motion? Compare People v. Wilson, 563 N.W.2d 44 (Mich. 1997).

Notes

1. *Multiplicity: majority view.* At what point does the commission of one offense end and the commission of a second offense begin? This can be a very difficult question with criminal acts that occur in several locations (such as drug sales), through multiple events (such as conspiracies based on a series of conversations), or over extended periods of time. All jurisdictions must face claims that multiple, identical charges are applied to what is only a single event. See State v. Leyda, 138 P.3d 610 (Wash. 2006) (when defendant obtained victim's credit card and used it to make four purchases, the "unit of prosecution" for crime of identity theft was the act of obtaining identification of another person with criminal intent, rather than each discrete use). In fact, in *Blockburger* itself the defendant claimed that two drug sales on successive days constituted one offense. Shortly after delivery of the drug that was the subject of the first sale, the purchaser paid for an additional quantity to be delivered the next day. The defendant argued that these two sales to the same purchaser, with no substantial interval of time between the delivery of the drug in the first transaction and the payment for the second quantity sold, constituted a single continuing offense. 284 U.S. at 301. The Court rejected the claim: "The Narcotic Act does not create the offense of engaging in the business of selling the forbidden drugs, but penalizes any sale made. . . . Each of several successive sales constitutes a distinct offense, however closely they may follow each other." 284 U.S. at 302.

Some courts refer to the issue of dividing one offender's behavior into distinct offenses as the problem of "multiplicity." See, e.g., State v. Smith, 864 P.2d 709 (Kan. 1993). Though not all jurisdictions use the term, the question of multiplicity is common to all jurisdictions. To what extent does application of the *Blockburger* test answer the question of how many different crimes can be charged? Beyond the scope of *Blockburger*, what principles should govern?

2. *The special problem of conspiracies.* The puzzle of determining how many separate charges are possible is especially difficult in the context of conspiracies—especially drug conspiracies—which tend to take place over time and space and to involve multiple participants. To determine whether criminal conduct amounted to one conspiracy or two, courts consult the "totality of the circumstances," with special emphasis on (1) the time of the conduct, (2) the persons acting as co-conspirators, (3) the overlap among the statutory offenses charged in the indictments, (4) the overt acts charged by the government or any other description of the offenses charged that indicate the nature and scope of the activity that the government sought to punish in each case, and (5) places where the events alleged as part of the conspiracy took place. The procedural difficulties regarding the parsing of conspiracies reflect the substantive battles over the scope of conspiracy law. See Paul Marcus, Criminal Conspiracy Law: Time to Turn Back from an Ever Expanding, Ever More Troubling Area, 1 Wm. & Mary Bill Rts. J. 1 (1992); William Theis, The Double Jeopardy Defense and Multiple Prosecutions for Conspiracy, 49 SMU L. Rev. 269 (1996).

3. Collateral Estoppel

The common-law doctrine of collateral estoppel raises a question related to double jeopardy: When has an issue or a fact been resolved in one proceeding in a way that will bind the parties in later disputes? The doctrine of collateral estoppel has reached constitutional status in the criminal context. Collateral estoppel is obviously a cousin to double jeopardy, but how closely is it related? In what ways are the doctrines different?

■ EX PARTE PHILIP TAYLOR
101 S.W.3d 434 (Tex. Crim. App. 2002)

COCHRAN, J.

Appellant lost control of his car on a rural road and collided with an oncoming car. Appellant's two passengers died in the accident. A jury acquitted appellant of intoxication manslaughter in causing the death of one passenger. The State had alleged that appellant was intoxicated by alcohol. The State now seeks to prosecute appellant for intoxication manslaughter in causing the death of his second passenger. This time, however, the State alleges that appellant was intoxicated by either alcohol and marijuana or by marijuana alone. We must determine whether the appellant's acquittal in the first trial, of intoxication manslaughter, prevents the State from attempting to prove, in another criminal proceeding, an alternate theory of intoxication for causing the death of his second passenger. . . .

I.

. . . The evidence showed that appellant was driving his Ford Thunderbird on a rural road in Brazos County late one afternoon. His fiancee, Kyla Blaisdell, sat in the front passenger seat and her best friend, Michelle James, sat in the back seat. It was not disputed that appellant was speeding, but witnesses' estimates of his actual speed varied widely. As appellant came out of a curve, the Thunderbird's right front wheel left the paved surface and veered onto a grassy, gravely area. According to the defense expert, appellant overcorrected as he attempted to bring his front wheel back onto the pavement. Consequently, he lost control of the car, which veered into the left lane and collided with Ms. Varner's oncoming Suburban. According to the State's expert, appellant lost control of the car as he entered the curve at a high speed. Because of his speeding through the curve, the car headed into a ditch on the right hand side, and appellant pulled the steering wheel too much to the left, sending the car into the left lane. Regardless of where appellant lost control of the car, Kyla Blaisdell and Michelle James died in the collision. Ms. Varner and appellant were both seriously injured.

At the hospital, medical technicians drew a sample of appellant's blood to determine its blood alcohol concentration ("BAC"). Their analysis resulted in a .137 BAC reading. The DPS twice reanalyzed this blood sample, using more sensitive equipment. Its analysis returned BAC readings of .124 and .119. DPS took another blood sample from appellant more than three hours after the first sample. This second sample indicated a BAC of .06. Appellant's blood also tested positive for the presence of marijuana, but there was no evidence that he had smoked marijuana on that particular day. The prosecutor, agreeing that traces of marijuana may linger in the body for days after its actual use, did not oppose appellant's motion in limine barring any mention of marijuana during the trial. Kyla Blaisdell tested negative for both alcohol and drugs; Michelle James tested negative for drugs, but .04 for alcohol; and Ms. Varner tested negative for both drugs and alcohol. Appellant's toxicology expert testified that, according to his calculations, appellant's BAC at the time of the accident must have been between .07 and .09.

Kelsey Blaisdell, Kyla's brother, testified that the trio spent most of the afternoon at his parent's home. He said that they came over to do laundry and to "hang out." They had some wine with them and were drinking from about 2:30 until 6:00 P.M. Kelsey testified that appellant did not seem drunk or otherwise intoxicated: appellant did not slur his speech or have poor balance. . . .

At the conclusion of all evidence, the trial judge charged the jury that, if it believed from the evidence, beyond a reasonable doubt, that appellant [operated a motor vehicle] "while intoxicated, either by not having the normal use of his mental or physical faculties by reason of the introduction of alcohol into his body or by having an alcohol concentration of .10 or more, and by reason of that intoxication, if any, by accident or mistake, caused the death of Michelle James, you will find [appellant] guilty of intoxication manslaughter." The jury was also instructed, as an alternate basis for a finding of guilt, that if it believed from the evidence, beyond a reasonable doubt, that appellant [recklessly caused the death of Michelle James] "by operating a motor vehicle at an excessive speed and by driving into a motor vehicle occupied by Patricia Varner, you will find [appellant] guilty of manslaughter." . . .

The jury acquitted appellant of all counts of intoxication manslaughter and reckless manslaughter of Michelle James. The State subsequently dismissed appellant's indictment for causing Kyla Blaisdell's death. But later the State learned that appellant, sometime after the trial, allegedly told Kyla Blaisdell's mother that he and the girls had been smoking marijuana cigarettes on the afternoon of the accident.

Based upon this newly discovered evidence, the State re-indicted appellant for intoxication manslaughter in causing the death of Kyla Blaisdell, alleging that he had lost the normal use of his mental and physical faculties by reason of the introduction of alcohol, marijuana, or a combination of alcohol and marijuana.

Appellant filed an application for a pretrial writ of habeas corpus, contending that the doctrine of collateral estoppel barred any further State efforts to prosecute him for causing this accident based upon his alleged intoxication. The trial court largely denied appellant relief, concluding that only the issue of intoxication by reason of alcohol had been litigated in the first trial, but not the distinct factual question of whether marijuana, either alone or in combination with alcohol, had rendered him intoxicated. Appellant then filed a pretrial appeal. . . .

II.

At issue in this appeal is the scope of the factual finding that the jury made when it acquitted appellant. The State assumes that the first jury concluded that appellant was not intoxicated because of alcohol. It contends that this finding does not preclude the State from prosecuting appellant for the death of a second accident victim, when the State alleged intoxication by alcohol and marijuana or by marijuana alone. . . .

The first prosecution was for killing Michelle James; the second, for killing Kyla Blaisdell. For double jeopardy purposes, the unlawful killing of each victim is a separate offense. In its seminal case on collateral estoppel, Ashe v. Swenson, 397 U.S. 436 (1970), the Supreme Court noted that the defendant's reprosecution was not barred by double jeopardy under the usual *Blockburger* test because the second prosecution was for a different offense, namely the robbery of a different victim attending the same poker party. Thus, the Supreme Court had to turn to the related doctrine of collateral estoppel, which prevents a party who lost a fact issue in the trial of one cause of action from relitigating the same fact issue in another cause of action against the same party. The situation is the same in this case. If the State had prosecuted appellant for the same offense (causing the death of Michelle James) on a different theory, we would not have to resort to collateral estoppel. Reprosecution would be barred by autrefois acquit under *Blockburger.*

In Ashe v. Swenson, the Supreme Court stated that collateral estoppel "means simply that when an issue of ultimate fact has once been determined by a valid and final judgment, that issue cannot again be litigated between the same parties in any future lawsuit." To determine whether collateral estoppel bars a subsequent prosecution (or permits prosecution but bars relitigation of certain specific facts) courts employ a two-step analysis. Courts must determine: (1) exactly what facts were "necessarily decided" in the first proceeding; and (2) whether those "necessarily decided" facts constitute essential elements of the offense in the second trial.

In each case, courts must review the entire trial record to determine — "with realism and rationality" — precisely what fact or combination of facts the jury necessarily decided and which will then bar their relitigation in a second criminal trial. In Ashe v. Swenson, the Supreme Court emphasized that:

> the rule of collateral estoppel is not to be applied with the hypertechnical and archaic approach of a 19th century pleading book, but with realism and rationality. . . .
> The inquiry "must be set in a practical frame and viewed with an eye to all the

circumstances of the proceedings." Any test more technically restrictive would, of
course, simply amount to a rejection of the rule of collateral estoppel in criminal
proceedings, at least in every case where the first judgment was based upon a general
verdict of acquittal.

Although Texas courts have rarely discussed the scope of a fact barred by
collateral estoppel, cases from other jurisdictions have held that collateral estoppel
operates only if the "very fact or point now in issue" was determined in the prior
proceeding. It must be "precisely" the same issue in both cases. Goodson v.
McDonough Power Equip., Inc., 443 N.E.2d 978, 983 (Ohio 1983). Thus, issue
preclusion is limited to cases where the legal and factual situations are identical. . . .
On the other hand, issue preclusion cannot be defeated simply by advancing new or
different evidence to support the same issue already litigated. Thus, a party who
neglects to submit the evidence that would support a legal theory that the party
withheld in a first proceeding, cannot later point to its own omission as justification
for pursuing a second proceeding.

In sum, there are no hard and fast rules concerning which factual issues
are legally identical and thus barred from relitigation in a second criminal proceeding. As Professor Wright concludes: "If an ordinary person would expostulate, 'But
that's a different issue,' probably it is." 18 Charles Alan Wright, Arthur R. Miller &
Edward N. Cooper, Federal Practice & Procedure §4417 at 440 (2d ed. 2000).

In each case, the entire record — including the evidence, pleadings, charge,
jury arguments, and any other pertinent material — must be examined to determine
precisely the scope of the jury's factual findings. In one case, for example, a jury's
acquittal might rest upon the proposition that the defendant was "not intoxicated,"
while in another, that same verdict might rest upon the narrower proposition that
the defendant was "not intoxicated" by a particular substance, but he might well
have been intoxicated by a different substance. Generally, then, the scope of the
facts that were actually litigated determines the scope of the factual finding covered
by collateral estoppel.

Given the pleadings, the jury charge, the disputed issues, and the evidence
presented by both the State and the defense at the trial, the jury in this particular
case necessarily concluded that, at the time of the accident: 1) Appellant had not
lost the normal use of his mental or physical faculties by reason of the introduction
of alcohol; 2) Appellant did not have an alcohol concentration of .10 or more; and
3) Appellant did not recklessly drive at an excessive speed into another vehicle.

Thus, these three facts have been established, and they cannot be relitigated in
any future criminal proceeding against appellant. But do these discrete factual
findings leave open the possibility that appellant was intoxicated, but by some substance other than alcohol?

Not here. The only witness who testified to appellant's possible loss of normal
use of mental or physical faculties was Kelsey Blaisdell, the brother of one of the
victims. He stated that appellant and the two girls had some wine that afternoon. . . . Because the trial court granted appellant's unopposed motion in limine,
there was no mention at trial of any other possible source of intoxication and no
other evidence that appellant had lost the normal use of his mental or physical
faculties.

The source of appellant's intoxication was not a disputed issue in the first trial.
It was only the more general issue of intoxication — was he or wasn't he — that was

disputed, and upon this issue, the appellant prevailed. Had appellant's defense been one of conceding the fact of intoxication, but contesting the manner in which he became intoxicated, the situation would, of course, be different. Thus, considering the question in a practical, common-sense manner, it is evident that there is no reasonable possibility that the jury in the first trial could have decided, based upon this evidence, that appellant was intoxicated but not because of alcohol. . . . [29]

The State argues that it now possesses more and different evidence — namely that appellant admitted to Mrs. Blaisdell, after his acquittal, that both he and the girls had smoked marijuana that day. But here, as in Harris v. Washington, 404 U.S. 55 (1971), when an ultimate issue has been decided, the constitutional guarantee of collateral estoppel applies "irrespective of whether the jury considered all relevant evidence, and irrespective of the good faith of the State in bringing successive prosecutions." [In Harris v. Washington, a jury acquitted the defendant of murder, finding that the defendant had not mailed the bomb which killed the victim and his infant son and seriously injured the victim's wife. The Supreme Court found that the State could not reprosecute the defendant for killing the infant based upon additional evidence, namely a threatening letter that the defendant had allegedly sent to the victim's family.]

The State also argues that, because it was required [under State v. Carter, 810 S.W.2d 197 (Tex. Crim. App. 1991) to allege in the charging instrument] which type of intoxicant appellant consumed, collateral estoppel applies only to that specific intoxicant. Accordingly, the State contends, resolving whether collateral estoppel applies depends entirely upon the precise indictment allegations, regardless of the actual evidence or the facts "necessarily" found by the jury. But application of collateral estoppel depends not merely upon the pleadings, but also upon the evidence, charge, jury argument, and any other relevant material. The State fails to point to any evidence, argument, or other material in this record which would support its theory that this jury could have concluded appellant was intoxicated, but not by alcohol. . . . Therefore, we affirm the court of appeals.

HERVEY, J., dissenting.

. . . After examining relevant portions of the record from the first criminal prosecution, I cannot conclude that the jury in that case necessarily found that appellant was not intoxicated by alcohol. The offenses submitted to the jury in that prosecution were intoxication manslaughter and manslaughter. The jury was instructed to find appellant guilty of intoxication manslaughter if it found that appellant's intoxication, if any, caused the victim's death. The only theories of intoxication presented to the jury were "either by not having the normal use of [appellant's] mental or physical faculties by reason of the introduction of alcohol

29. The dissent argues that the jury could have decided that appellant was, in fact, intoxicated but that "his intoxication was not a contributing factor to the accident." This is, of course, a possibility, but that factual finding would not prevent the application of collateral estoppel. Quite the reverse. . . . If that were the fact that the jury necessarily decided, then collateral estoppel would apply to causation, rather than intoxication. . . .

In United States v. Larkin, 605 F.2d 1360 (5th Cir. 1979), . . . the Fifth Circuit noted that the jury's acquittal could have been based on either fact A or fact B. But because the government was required to prove both fact A and fact B in a subsequent prosecution, collateral estoppel barred relitigation of either fact. In the present case, both intoxication and causation are necessary elements in the State's current intoxication manslaughter indictment. Thus, collateral estoppel necessarily applies to one or the other fact in a case in which the State must prove both facts. . . .

into his body" or "by having an alcohol concentration of .10 or more." The charge instructed the jury to convict appellant of intoxication manslaughter if it believed beyond a reasonable doubt that appellant [operated] a motor vehicle in a public place "while intoxicated, either by not having the normal use of his mental or physical faculties by reason of the introduction of alcohol into his body or by having an alcohol concentration of .10 or more, and by reason of that intoxication, if any, by accident or mistake, caused the death of [the victim]." . . .

The State's theory was that appellant's alcohol intoxication caused him to drive recklessly at an excessive rate of speed which caused the accident resulting in the victim's death. Appellant's theory was that he was not intoxicated by any of the two manner and means submitted to the jury but that, if he was, his intoxication was not a contributing factor to the accident. . . . Appellant's accident reconstructionist supported these assertions at trial [and] contradicted other aspects of the prosecution's theory of how the accident occurred such as when appellant began to lose control of his vehicle (before the curve at a lower speed limit or after the curve at a higher speed limit).

It was undisputed that appellant had been drinking wine before the fatal accident. Responding to the prosecution's evidence that appellant's BAC at the time of the accident was above .10, the best appellant's toxicology expert could do was to admit that appellant's BAC at the time of the accident was between .07 and .09. . . . Significantly, appellant's toxicology expert also admitted that a BAC of .07 to .09 would cause most people to lose "some of the normal use of their abilities." . . .

During closing jury arguments, the defense argued that . . . the prosecution failed to prove that appellant's intoxication, if any, caused the fatal accident. The last thing the defense told the jury was that it should still acquit appellant even if the jury found that he was intoxicated.

> They haven't proved that he had an alcohol content of above .10 at the time he was driving, and they haven't proved that [appellant] had an accident because . . . he was intoxicated. [What] could have caused this accident? . . . Could be that the Varner vehicle was towards the middle of the road. It could be inattentiveness. It could be an animal ran out. . . . We will never know what caused that accident. . . . This is a tragedy. A verdict of not guilty does not mean that it isn't tragic. A verdict of not guilty means the government has not proved these allegations . . . beyond a reasonable doubt. Even if you find he was intoxicated, if you don't find that intoxication beyond a reasonable doubt caused this accident, you must return a verdict of not guilty. . . .

These portions of the record demonstrate that the jury could have acquitted appellant . . . because it did not believe that this intoxication was a contributing factor to the accident which the record reflects was one of the theories appellant urged at the first trial. . . .

The Court's opinion concedes that it is "a possibility" that the jury did not necessarily find that appellant was not intoxicated by alcohol. This should be fatal to appellant's collateral estoppel claim. But, the Court still concludes that this prosecution is jeopardy-barred because, even if the jury found that appellant was intoxicated, it nevertheless could have found that the "intoxication itself was not a contributing factor to the accident" in which case "collateral estoppel would apply to causation, rather than intoxication."

But, in analyzing the collateral estoppel issue this way, the Court concludes that this prosecution is jeopardy-barred even though it is unable to decide what the jury necessarily found in the first trial. In other words, the Court apparently bases its decision on what the jury could have found without deciding what the jury necessarily found. My understanding of collateral estoppel law, however, is that for the collateral estoppel bar to apply, the Court must be able to decide what the jury necessarily found in the first trial, not what it could have found.

The Court's analysis involving what the jury could have found in appellant's first trial also fails to take into account that it is entirely possible that the jury did not speak with one voice in acquitting appellant. For example, it is possible that some of the jurors believed that appellant was not intoxicated, some of the jurors believed that he was intoxicated but his intoxication was not a contributing factor to the accident, and some of the jurors believed that appellant should have been acquitted for other reasons. Cf. Schad v. Arizona, 501 U.S. 624 (1991) (Scalia, J., concurring) (stating the general rule that "when a single crime can be committed in various ways, jurors need not agree upon the mode of commission"). Under these circumstances, it cannot be said that the jury necessarily found anything in the first trial except possibly that it had a reasonable doubt of appellant's guilt. . . .

Apparently the Court decides that federal constitutional collateral estoppel principles prevent the prosecution from litigating these two issues of intoxication in this proceeding because it was the more general issue of intoxication — was he or wasn't he — that was disputed in the first trial and because the prosecution could have but did not litigate these other two theories of intoxication in the first trial. But federal constitutional collateral estoppel principles only prohibit a party from relitigating an issue that was necessarily decided in the first trial, and it is clear that the only issue litigated (and that could possibly have been decided) in the first trial was whether appellant was intoxicated by alcohol.

In deciding that the prosecution cannot litigate the other two theories of intoxication (marijuana and combination of marijuana and alcohol) in this proceeding because the prosecution could have litigated them in the first trial, the Court adds a new element to the federal constitutional collateral estoppel doctrine that *Ashe* and other United States Supreme Court cases do not require. The Court's decision expands *Ashe* to preclude litigating in a second trial issues of ultimate fact that could have been decided in the first trial. But the federal constitutional collateral estoppel doctrine applies only to issues of ultimate fact that were actually decided in the first trial. I respectfully dissent.

Notes

1. *Collateral estoppel: majority position.* The U.S. Supreme Court declared in Ashe v. Swenson, 397 U.S. 436 (1970), that the federal guarantee against double jeopardy includes the concept of collateral estoppel: "when an issue of ultimate fact has once been determined by a valid and final judgment, that issue cannot again be litigated between the same parties in any future lawsuit." There are several limitations, however, that prevent collateral estoppel from having an impact in a wide range of cases. First, the doctrine typically does not apply to matters resolved by guilty plea. Federal and state courts agree that collateral estoppel applies only after an "adjudication on the merits after full trial." Ohio v. Johnson, 467 U.S. 493, 500 (1984).

Second, as *Ex parte Taylor* illustrates, it is often difficult, based on a jury's general verdict, to determine exactly what factual findings were the basis for a jury's acquittal. This problem is commonplace because defendants are prone to give the jury more than one possible theory for an acquittal. Would the use of special interrogatories to the jury (to be completed only after the jury has delivered its general verdict) make the collateral estoppel doctrine a more meaningful limitation on multiple criminal trials?

2. *Collateral estoppel against defendants.* Although collateral estoppel binds the government, most courts say that the doctrine is asymmetrical; that is, it does not bind defendants. If a fact finder determines some fact against a defendant in one criminal proceeding, the defendant may still ask a fact finder in some later criminal case to find that same fact in his favor. For instance, in State v. Scarbrough, 181 S.W.3d 650 (Tenn. 2005), the defendant was convicted during a first trial of aggravated burglary and felony murder. Appellate courts affirmed the robbery conviction, but overturned the felony murder conviction because of improper jury instructions. On retrial for felony murder, the government asked the trial court to prevent the defendant from relitigating the underlying charge of aggravated burglary. The Tennessee Supreme Court concluded that the use of collateral estoppel by the prosecution against the defendant to establish an essential element of felony murder violates the right to trial by jury. The court also observed, however, that the prosecution is permitted to introduce evidence of the prior conviction of aggravated burglary if the trial court determines that its probative value is not substantially outweighed by the risk of unfair prejudice to the defendant. See also Byrd v. People, 58 P.3d 50 (Colo. 2002) (issue preclusion does not prevent defendant from contesting in criminal trial a factual issue that was previously determined in the prosecution's favor in a probation revocation hearing).

However, there are also a few cases applying collateral estoppel against defendants. See Hernandez-Uribe v. United States, 515 F.2d 20 (8th Cir. 1975) (after conviction and deportation for illegal entry into United States, defendant reenters and is charged again; defendant's alien status is established by collateral estoppel); People v. Majado, 70 P.2d 1015 (Cal. 1937) (conviction for failure to support child; in later criminal charges for another period of failure to support child, previous conviction estops relitigation of issue of paternity). Can you reconcile cases like *Majado* and *Scarbrough*?

3. *Collateral estoppel and administrative findings.* Can a finding of fact made in an administrative or civil proceeding be the basis for collateral estoppel in a later criminal proceeding? For instance, if a defendant in license revocation proceedings convinces the factfinder that some critical factual element of drunken driving charges is missing, does that finding bar a later criminal prosecution for driving while impaired? See State v. Hughes, 863 A.2d 266 (Me. 2004) (State was not collaterally estopped from pursuing prosecution for assault after a petition in civil court for domestic violence protective order against defendant was denied); State v. Brunet, 806 A.2d 1007 (Vt. 2002) (collateral estoppel did not bar the State from prosecuting defendant for assault charge that formed the basis of probation violation allegations decided adversely to the State). Does it matter that the two proceedings operate under two different standards of proof (preponderance of the evidence in the administrative proceedings, and beyond a reasonable doubt in the criminal proceedings)? In State v. Miller, 459 S.E.2d 114 (W. Va. 1995), a state hospital nurse was convicted of battery after slapping a patient. The state

hospital also attempted to terminate her employment and defended its decision during administrative proceedings before a state employee grievance board. Because the hospital failed to demonstrate grounds for termination before the grievance board, Miller argued that the battery charges were collaterally estopped. The court held that collateral estoppel did not apply because there were several possible grounds for the grievance board decision not to terminate the defendant's employment and there was no "privity" between the state agency that sought to terminate her employment and the prosecutor's office.

In Dowling v. United States, 493 U.S. 342 (1990), the Court held that the defendant's acquittal on robbery charges did not bar later use of testimony from a key witness from the first trial in a second criminal trial for a similar robbery charge against the same defendant. The Court allowed the testimony because the standard for admissibility of evidence was whether the second jury "could reasonably conclude" that the defendant committed the first robbery — a standard lower than the one applied by the first jury that acquitted the defendant. Does *Dowling* eviscerate collateral estoppel?

4. *Collateral estoppel and dual sovereigns.* It is common to find the collateral estoppel principle embodied in state statutes barring or limiting multiple prosecutions. Around 10 states have statutes recognizing collateral estoppel based on adverse factual findings made in criminal proceedings in another jurisdiction. See Colo. Rev. Stat. §18-1-303(1)(b). Recall that the common-law doctrine of collateral estoppel required "mutuality of parties" — that is, the same two parties had to be involved in both the original proceedings and the later relitigation of the same factual issue. Is there any reason to insist on "mutuality of parties" when it comes to dual sovereigns prosecuting the same person for crimes based on the same factual premise? In other words, should one government's loss in a criminal trial prevent another government from relitigating the same factual issue? Now consider mutuality of parties when it comes to defendants. Should a government victory against one criminal defendant prevent another defendant at another criminal trial from relitigating the resolved factual question?

B. JOINDER

Constitutional and statutory double jeopardy rules require prosecutors to choose carefully when grouping together the potential charges to be brought against a defendant. We now look at some doctrinal cousins to double jeopardy: the statutory and court rules that govern "joinder" and "severance" of potentially related charges. As you read the following materials, consider to what extent the joinder and severance rules further interests different from the constitutional or statutory bar on double jeopardy.

The most common joinder rules (exemplified by Rule 8 of the Federal Rules of Criminal Procedure) are known as "permissive" joinder rules. They define the outer boundaries of the prosecutor's power to join charges together for a single trial, that is, the *maximum* range of charges that can be grouped together. These rules address both the joinder of separate offenses filed against a single defendant and joinder of multiple defendants in a single trial. Some states also have "compulsory" or "mandatory" joinder rules. These rules identify the *minimum* range of charges that the prosecutor must group together for a single trial. Like the doctrines of double jeopardy and collateral estoppel, these compulsory joinder rules require dismissal of charges if they should have been tried in an earlier proceeding dealing with related charges. Rules on "severance" address the power of the court to override a prosecutor's joinder decisions and order separate trials for charges that were otherwise properly joined.

The joinder rules may on first inspection seem dry and technical. But joinder and severance rules are enormously important to defendants and prosecutors because they define the scope of each trial and determine whether more than one trial may take place. Decisions on joinder and severance can give prosecutors or defendants enormous strategic advantage and are therefore often strongly argued. The issues appeal to lawyers who enjoy puzzles.

1. Discretionary Joinder and Severance of Offenses

When a prosecutor files multiple charges against a defendant, the charges usually fall within the minimum and maximum range of charges that a prosecutor has the power to group together in a single case. If the prosecutor fails to join the charges and the defendant wishes to resolve them in one trial, the court has the discretion to join the charges even though the prosecutor did not file them together. The parties can also urge the trial court to sever the joined charges as a discretionary matter to avoid prejudice. These cases call for the use of lawyerly skills, including close reading and attention to trial strategies. Review the federal rules and Vermont rules reprinted below, then read the following case. Would the outcome of the case change under the Vermont rules?

■ FEDERAL RULE OF CRIMINAL PROCEDURE 8(a)

The indictment or information may charge a defendant in separate counts with two or more offenses if the offenses charged — whether felonies or misdemeanors or both — are of the same or similar character, or are based on the same act or transaction, or are connected with or constitute parts of a common scheme or plan.

■ FEDERAL RULE OF CRIMINAL PROCEDURE 13

The court may order that separate cases be tried together as though brought in a single indictment or information if all offenses . . . could have been joined in a single indictment or information.

■ FEDERAL RULE OF CRIMINAL PROCEDURE 14

(a) Relief. If the joinder of offenses or defendants in an indictment, an information, or a consolidation for trial appears to prejudice a defendant or the government, the court may order separate trials of counts, sever the defendants' trials, or provide any other relief that justice requires.

(b) Defendant's Statements. Before ruling on a defendant's moti⟨
the court may order an attorney for the government to deliver to the ⟨
camera inspection any defendant's statement that the government inter⟨
evidence.

■ VERMONT RULE OF CRIMINAL PROCEDURE 8(a)

Two or more offenses may be joined in one information or indictment, with each offense stated in a separate count, when the offenses, whether felonies or misdemeanors or both,

(1) are of the same or similar character, even if not part of a single scheme or plan; or

(2) are based on the same conduct or on a series of acts connected together or constituting parts of a single scheme or plan.

■ VERMONT RULE OF CRIMINAL PROCEDURE 14

(a) The court may order a severance of offenses or defendants before trial if a severance could be obtained on motion of a defendant or the prosecution under subdivision (b) of this rule.

(b)(1) Severance of Offenses.

(A) Whenever two or more offenses have been joined for trial solely on the ground that they are of the same or similar character, the defendant shall have a right to a severance of the offenses.

(B) The court, on application of the prosecuting attorney, or on application of the defendant other than under subparagraph (A), shall grant a severance of offenses whenever,

(i) if before trial, it is deemed appropriate to promote a fair determination of the defendant's guilt or innocence of each offense; or

(ii) if during trial upon consent of the defendant, or upon a finding of manifest necessity, it is deemed necessary to achieve a fair determination of the defendant's guilt or innocence of each offense.

VERMONT REPORTER'S NOTES

[Rule 8] is taken from ABA Minimum Standards (Joinder and Severance) §§1.1, 1.2, and is similar to Federal Rule 8. Rule 8(a) permits joinder of offenses either because they are of similar character though factually unrelated or because they are factually related. Note that each offense must be pleaded in a separate count. . . . Under the federal rule the phrase "same character" adopted for Rule 8(a)(1) has been ordinarily held to mean the same crime committed against distinct objects upon distinct occasions. Although joinder of similar offenses has been criticized as tending to prejudice the defendant through its cumulative effect, the ABA recommends the provision, because it may actually work to the defendant's advantage in preventing multiple trials and facilitating concurrent sentencing. Prejudice will be avoided because under Rule 14(b)(1)(A) defendant has an absolute right to severance of such offenses for trial. ABA Minimum Standards §1.1(a), Commentary. . . .

Rule 8(a)(2) is, of course, a rule of permissive joinder. As a practical matter, if the same facts are centrally involved in two offenses, joinder is virtually compelled. Otherwise, acquittal of the defendant upon one offense will bar prosecution for the second offense by virtue of the Fifth Amendment's Double Jeopardy Clause, which includes the principles of collateral estoppel. Ashe v. Swenson, 397 U.S. 436 (1970).

[Rule 14] is based on ABA Minimum Standards (Joinder and Severance) §§2.1-2.4, 3.1, with variations reflecting Vermont practice. It is similar in effect to the more complicated provisions of Federal Rule 14. Note that Rule 14 is a grant of discretion to sever a joinder otherwise proper under Rule 8 in the interests of fairness or to avoid prejudice. If a joinder is improper under Rule 8, a severance must be granted or it is reversible error. Rule 14(a) is based on ABA Minimum Standards §3.1(b). A power in the court to sever on its own motion, like the comparable power to join under Rule 13(a), is necessary to allow the court to carry out its responsibilities for the orderly conduct of the trial. The federal courts have recognized a power in the court to act on its own motion under Federal Rule 14. . . . Rule 14(b)(1), dealing with severance of offenses, is taken from ABA Minimum Standards §2.2. Subparagraph (A), conferring an absolute right of severance where offenses have been joined solely by virtue of Rule 8(a)(1) because they are of the same or similar character, is a necessary protection for defendants against what would otherwise be potential prejudice in such joinders. That prejudice may consist in the defendant's fear of testifying in his own behalf on one count because of the effect of such testimony on the other count, or in the danger that proof of one count will have prejudicial effect on the other count as inadmissible evidence of another crime. In requiring severance in these circumstances the rule is stricter than Federal Rule 14, although individual decisions under the latter rule have allowed severance for similar purposes. The rule is stricter than prior Vermont practice, which gave the court discretion as to severance even where unrelated offenses were involved. See State v. Dopp, 255 A.2d 186 (Vt. 1969). Severance of offenses joined under Rule 8(a)(2) as arising from the same or connected conduct or a single scheme is available to either party under Rule 14(b)(1)(A) when necessary in the interests of fair trial. . . .

■ DAMIAN LONG v. UNITED STATES
687 A.2d 1331 (D.C. 1996)

Ferren, J.

A jury found appellant, Damian Long, guilty of assault with intent to rob three victims while armed on September 8, 1992, at about 10:30 P.M., at 12th and Orren Streets, N.E. He also was found guilty of attempted robbery while armed and felony murder while armed of another victim several minutes later on Trinidad Avenue, N.E., a block away from the first crime. Long contends . . . the trial court erroneously joined the Orren Street and Trinidad Avenue offenses for trial and then abused its discretion in denying the defense motion for severance. . . . We affirm in part, reverse in part, and remand for reconsideration of Long's severance motion.

[Around 5:30 to 6:00 P.M. on September 8], appellant Long left the apartment of Scholethia Monk, located at Holbrook Terrace, N.E., where he had been spending time with Ms. Monk, her brother (David), and Kimberly Bridgeford. Long was dressed in a black suede jacket with fringe, a black shirt, black jeans, black boots, and a black silk-stocking skull cap. The Holbrook Terrace apartment was only a few blocks from the area where the Orren Street and Trinidad Avenue incidents at issue here took place.

Several hours later, at about 10:30 P.M., a man dressed in a black fringed jacket, black pants, and black shoes — later identified as Damian Long — approached the three Orren Street victims, Sabrina Fox, Carla Davis, and Guy Foster, who were standing in the street on the driver's side of the car that was parked against the curb in front of Fox's home. They were attempting to open the door and window of the car with a coat hanger because they had inadvertently locked the keys inside. Long crossed over to them from the opposite side of the street, pointed a revolver at them, and said something to the two women that sounded like "get the fuck out of here." He then pressed the pistol against Foster's head and demanded his money. When Foster protested that he had none, Long put his hand in Foster's pants pockets and satisfied himself that this was true. Long then ordered Foster to crawl under the car, and Long walked away in the direction of Trinidad Avenue.

Fox and Davis had fled in the same direction. They feared that their assailant was following them, so they hid in an alleyway a few blocks away from where the car was parked. Fox and Davis then heard gunshots and unsuccessfully tried to flag down a passing police cruiser. They hailed a taxi and went to a nearby police precinct where they told their story and gave a description of the perpetrator.

In the meantime, Fox's mother, Penelope Boyd-Fox, who had witnessed the assault on the three from the porch of her home on Orren Street, had immediately telephoned "911" for help. While she was still on the phone to the police department emergency number, she heard gunshots nearby. At about the same time, Foster came out from under the car and fled to his home on Orren Street. He telephoned the police to report the crime. While on the phone with the police, he heard gunshots and reported that as well.

Deborah Alford . . . was sitting on her front porch [on Trinidad Avenue] with several family members at approximately 10:30 P.M. the same night. A few minutes earlier, she had seen [her neighbor Louis Johnson] park his Suzuki sports vehicle on the street and enter his home several doors away. Apparently returning home from work, Johnson had been wearing his Army uniform. Shortly thereafter, Alford saw Johnson walking from his home, dressed in his bathrobe, and returning to his Suzuki. At this moment, Alford saw a man dressed in a black jacket ("I didn't know it had suede fringes on it"), black pants, and a black skull cap walking in Trinidad Street alongside the parked cars. Alford saw the man in black, after he had passed by Johnson, take out a pistol from his jacket and turn back toward Johnson as Johnson put the keys into the car's doorlock. Alford next saw the man in black and her neighbor "tussling." Frightened by the sight of the pistol, she and the others fled into their home. A few seconds later, Alford heard a series of gunshots. Johnson was later pronounced dead of gunshot wounds.

Kimberly Bridgeford testified that at around 5:00 P.M. on September 8, 1992, she and her boyfriend, David Monk, had gone with Damian Long to David's sister's, Scholethia Monk's, apartment on Holbrook Terrace. After awhile, Long left the apartment and, shortly thereafter, Bridgeford and David Monk left to go to the store. On the way to the store, Bridgeford heard gunshots, saw an ambulance, and walked by the Trinidad Avenue murder scene where she saw Johnson lying on the street with blood all over him. Bridgeford and David Monk then returned to the Holbrook Terrace apartment and found Long on the front porch. Long told Bridgeford that he had "shot a man on Trinidad Avenue because the man tried to rob him with a knife."

Scholethia Monk testified that Long returned later to her Holbrook Terrace apartment on September 8, 1992, "panicking and sweating." Long had told Monk that "two dudes" had tried to rob him on Trinidad Avenue and that he had just shot one of them. There was blood on Long's face, he no longer wore a skull cap, and he was carrying a pistol. Long put the gun under a couch. Monk told Long to get his pistol out of her apartment. He then wrapped it in a plastic bag and took it outside. Ten days later, the police recovered a gun from under the seat of the car where Long's close friend, Monk's brother, had been sitting just before they found the gun. A ballistics expert was "positive" that a bullet recovered from the scene of the murder on Trinidad Avenue had been fired by that pistol.

Homicide detective Willie Toland investigated the Trinidad Avenue case. When he arrived at the scene, he noticed a black skull cap seven feet from the place where Johnson had been shot, and Johnson's keys were still in the Suzuki's passenger door lock. As Toland investigated the crime scene, Foster arrived and informed Toland of what had happened earlier on Orren Street. Toland spoke with Davis and Fox later the same night and a few days later conducted a video lineup in which they identified Long as their attacker. . . .

Long's argument, raised before trial and renewed at the end of the government's case, [is] that the Orren Street and Trinidad Avenue charges had been improperly joined for trial. Specifically, Long protested joinder because the offenses were "not similar offenses[, nor] offenses committed in a single act or transaction, nor a series of offenses that [we]re sufficiently connected to each other."

Super. Ct. Crim. R. 8(a) provides for joinder of offenses when the offenses charged "are of the same or similar character or are based on the same act or transaction or on two or more acts or transactions connected together or constituting parts of a common scheme or plan." We review the trial court's joinder decision de novo.

The government urges that joinder was proper because the Orren Street offenses had been "connected together" with the Trinidad Avenue offenses in the sense that proof of the Orren Street offenses "constitut[ed] a substantial portion of the proof" of the Trinidad Avenue offenses. The facts, however, do not support the government's argument. None of the witnesses to the Orren Street incident saw the Trinidad Avenue incident, and neither crime depended on the other for its furtherance or success.

The government also argues that the Orren Street and Trinidad Avenue offenses had been properly joined as part of a "common scheme or plan," because Long had been "walking the neighborhood in search of people to rob." We have previously rejected such an argument when considering joinder of defendants under Super. Ct. Crim. R. 8(b), and we reject the argument in this context as well. See Jackson v. United States, 623 A.2d 571 (D.C. 1993) ("The goal of obtaining property from others, here money and guns, was too general for joinder of offenses under Rule 8(b).").

The government contends, finally, that the Orren Street offenses were similar in character to the Trinidad Avenue offenses, and we agree. The "similarity of offenses [under Rule 8(a)] is determined by the content of the indictment"; it is not dependent on whether evidence of one crime would be admissible in the trial of the other. In this case . . . the two crimes, as charged, "both involved armed robberies which were closely related in time and place." Accordingly, it cannot plausibly be maintained that they are insufficiently similar to one another to warrant initial joinder under Rule 8(a). We must conclude that the two sets of offenses were properly joined.

Long contends the trial court erred nonetheless in denying his severance motion under Super. Ct. Crim. R. 14. He says the Orren Street offenses should have been severed from the Trinidad Avenue charges because the evidence of each would be inadmissible in a separate trial of the other. Long adds he was further prejudiced because he was "precluded from presenting separate defenses" to each group of charges.[4]

We have noted that

[e]ven when offenses are properly joined, it is within the trial court's discretion to sever counts and order separate trials if the defendant would be prejudiced by joinder. Our standard of review of such rulings is abuse of discretion, and appellant must make a showing of compelling prejudice to show such error. Of course, there is a potential for prejudice whenever similar, but unrelated offenses are charged. However, the requisite prejudicial effect for a severance will not be found where the evidence [1] can be kept separate and distinct at trial or [2] is mutually admissible at separate trials. [Cox v. United States, 498 A.2d 231, 235 (D.C. 1985).]

Because the incidents were not tried separately and distinctly,[5] resolution of the severance issue turns on mutual admissibility: whether the evidence of each joined offense would be admissible at a separate trial of the other. The first sentence of Super. Ct. Crim. R. 14 provides:

[If] it appears that a defendant or the government is prejudiced by a joinder of offenses or of defendants in an indictment or information or by such joinder for trial together, the Court may order an election or separate trials of counts, grant a severance of defendants or provide whatever other relief justice requires.

In response to Long's contention, the government argues that the severance motion was properly denied because evidence of each group of offenses would have been admissible in a separate trial of the other "to explain the immediate circumstances surrounding the offense charged." Technically speaking, such evidence "is not other crimes evidence because it is too intimately entangled with the charged

4. Long apparently wanted to present a misidentification defense as to Orren Street and to claim self-defense at Trinidad Avenue, but realistically separate defenses appeared to be possible only if the offenses were tried separately. . . .

5. The evidence as to each offense was not "kept separate and distinct such that it would not be amalgamated in the jury's mind into a single inculpatory mass." Although the prosecutor attempted to structure the trial to separate the incidents, calling first the Orren Street witnesses and then the Trinidad Avenue witnesses, the evidence of the two crimes was closely tied together by some of the witnesses whose testimony pertained to both crimes, e.g., Scholethia Monk, Kimberly Bridgeford, and the homicide investigator, Willie Toland. Moreover, the government's closing argument also brought together evidence of the two crimes. Finally, the strong identification evidence and intent-to-rob evidence from the Orren Street incident served to supply identification and motive evidence for the Trinidad Avenue incident, so there was a substantial likelihood that the jury would cumulate the evidence. Accordingly, we cannot uphold the denial of severance based on the "separate and distinct" — sometimes known as the "simple and distinct" — theory.

criminal conduct."[6] Alternatively, the government argues that the evidence of each incident would be admissible in a trial of the other as "other crimes" evidence tending to prove "identity."[7]

Commonly, the question is whether uncharged criminal conduct shall be admitted in a trial of the charged crime, but in this case the question is the admissibility of a charged crime in the trial of another charged crime. If each would be admissible in the other, then there would be no reason why the two should not be tried together; but, if one or both would not meet the test for admissibility in the other, then severance is required. . . .

In this case, Long presented a misidentification defense at trial. Thus, identity was a contested issue. . . . We therefore believe it appropriate to scrutinize the evidence of each incident, as it bears on proving identity of the assailant in the other. . . . The Orren Street evidence informed the jury that, at about 10:30 P.M., on September 8, 1992, a man identified as Damian Long, dressed entirely in black (including a fringe jacket and skull cap) and carrying a gun, had . . . attempted a robbery at gunpoint. After the assault, the witnesses saw Long headed toward nearby Trinidad Avenue. They heard gunshots soon thereafter.

As for Trinidad Avenue, earlier on the same day at about 5:30 to 6:00 P.M., Scholethia Monk and Kimberly Bridgeford saw Long, dressed entirely in black (including a fringe jacket and skull cap), leave Monk's apartment. Bridgeford saw Long depart in the direction of Trinidad Avenue. Later that evening shortly after 10:30 P.M., Deborah Alford, from her front porch on Trinidad Avenue, saw a man dressed in a black jacket (she did not notice fringe on it), black pants, and a black skull cap walk past her neighbor, Louis Johnson, who was standing next to his car. . . . Alford never identified the assailant. Both Monk and Bridgeford, however, witnessed Long's return to Monk's apartment "panicking and sweating," admitting he had "shot a man on Trinidad Avenue because the man tried to rob him with a knife." Long had blood on his face and was carrying a pistol. His skull cap was missing. The police later found a black skull cap seven feet from where Johnson had been shot. Monk's apartment on Holbrook Terrace was but a few blocks away from where the offenses occurred on Orren Street and Trinidad Avenue.

We believe that the testimony of the Orren Street witnesses, Davis and Fox (who identified Long as a would-be robber), that they saw Long heading in the direction of Trinidad Avenue nearby, and then heard gunshots—all around 10:30 P.M., on September 8, 1992—provided powerful evidence of the Trinidad Avenue assailant's identity. Indeed, this evidence was particularly significant for the Trinidad Avenue prosecution, when coupled with Monk's and Bridgeford's testimony about Long's admission that he had shot a man on Trinidad Avenue, because the only person who saw the assailant approach Johnson, Deborah Alford, was unable to identify Johnson's killer (although Alford provided a description consistent with

6. The trial court accepted the government's . . . theory in denying Long's renewed motion to sever: "[T]his matter is so inextricably intertwined each with each other that there is no way the Government can separate it all and make sense of the whole matter. They absolutely need for identification purposes, if for nothing else, they absolutely have to have these cases tried together, they should be tried together temporally. And by temporally, I mean both time and place they are as connected as can be." Recently our en banc court discerned three subcategories of evidence embraced by [the] "immediate circumstances" rationale: such evidence (1) is direct and substantial proof of the charged crime, (2) is closely intertwined with the evidence of the charged crime, or (3) is necessary to place the charged crime in an understandable context.

7. . . . "[O]ther crimes" evidence is admissible only if [it is introduced to show] motive, intent, absence of mistake or accident, common scheme or plan, or identity as reflected in Fed. R. Evid. 404(b).

Fox's, Davis's, Monk's, and Bridgeford's description of Long). The Orren Street evidence also revealed the assailant's possible motive for approaching Johnson on Trinidad Avenue (robbery).

We also recognize that the Trinidad Avenue evidence was probative of the identity of the Orren Street attacker. Alford's description of an unidentified, black-jacketed, gun-carrying assailant on Trinidad Avenue, combined with the Monk/Bridgeford testimony that Damian Long had come to Monk's apartment with a gun, "panicking and sweating," tended to identify Long as the Orren Street assailant dressed in black seen heading toward Trinidad Avenue just before shots were fired around 10:30 P.M. The fact that Monk testified that Long's skull cap was missing when he returned to her apartment, coupled with the police officer's finding a skull cap on Trinidad Avenue, adds to Long's connection with the Orren Street attack by a man wearing a black skull cap.

Accordingly, without regard to the required probative value/prejudicial impact analysis, we can say that the Orren Street and Trinidad Avenue offenses [would be mutually admissible] in separate trials (and thus would not be joined prejudicially if prosecuted in a joint trial).

We turn to the ruling on probative value/prejudicial impact. The motions judge said, "I don't see prejudice under [Super. Ct. Civ. R.] 14 that would justify severance." The trial judge, in considering the renewed severance motion at trial, referred to the motions judge's ruling and then added his own belief that [a joint trial was permissible] because the cases were "inextricably intertwined."

The trial judge, therefore, said not a word about probative value relative to prejudice. That was unfortunate. At least as to admissibility of Trinidad Avenue evidence in an Orren Street trial, we see a serious question whether probative value outweighs prejudicial impact. Monk and Bridgeford identified the man — Damian Long — whom Alford apparently had seen accosting Johnson: a man fitting the description of the person who had attempted the robbery only blocks away on Orren Street minutes earlier. This identification evidence from Trinidad Avenue, however, was cumulative of — and of far less probative value than — the direct eyewitness testimony from Fox and Davis . . . that Long was the would-be bandit on Orren Street. Furthermore, this weaker identification evidence includes the powerfully prejudicial testimony that Long had committed a murder, not merely an assault, on Trinidad Avenue.

The trial judge, after a pretrial severance motion has been denied, has a continuing obligation to grant a severance if undue prejudice arises as a result of joinder at any time during trial. The trial judge recognized this obligation: "the Court of Appeals seems to indicate that I have to listen [to severance motions] again and again and again and again." Here, however, in denying the renewed severance motion, the trial judge, for his prejudice analysis, merely referred to the ruling of the motions judge, who did not "see prejudice" from a pretrial perspective. . . .

The probative/prejudicial analysis is a discretionary evaluation which an appellate court cannot undertake itself when the trial court fails to do so unless it is clear from the record, as a matter of law, that the trial court had "but one option." In this case, admissibility of the Trinidad Avenue murder evidence in an Orren Street trial appears to be a more difficult discretionary call than admissibility of the Orren Street assault in a Trinidad Avenue trial, but as to either case we find no sound basis on the record for this court to take over the trial court's function by ruling on probative value/prejudicial impact.

We, therefore, must remand the case for the trial judge to make a probative/ prejudicial ruling for each case and thus to rule once again on the severance motion — including consideration of Long's contention that he was prejudiced by his inability, in a single trial, to present separate defenses (Orren Street, mis-identification; Trinidad Avenue, self-defense). The judge shall order a new trial of the Orren Street prosecution if he concludes that the murder evidence from Trinidad Avenue should have been omitted from the Orren Street trial. Otherwise, the Orren Street convictions . . . shall stand, without prejudice to Long's right to appeal the severance ruling on remand.[17] Similarly, the judge shall make a proba-tive/prejudice ruling on admissibility of Orren Street evidence in the Trinidad Avenue trial, and also shall rule on Long's claim of prejudice from his practical inability to claim self-defense for Trinidad Avenue at a joint trial. The judge shall order a new trial, or not, as indicated. Absent a new trial order, the Trinidad Avenue conviction shall stand, subject to Long's right of appeal of that severance ruling. . . .

Problem 4-3. Compulsory Joinder

Matthew Hensley was involved in a bar fight in Kanawha County, West Virginia on November 16, 1991. Ambulances arrived at the scene took several people from the bar to a local hospital. Hensley and four other people were arrested at the scene and were immediately charged in magistrate court with public intoxication and destruction of property, both misdemeanors. On November 21, one of the victims of the fight, Barbara Lane, provided a statement to a detective with the Sheriff's Department regarding injuries she suffered during the fight. Lane told the detective that Hensley threw a cue ball, hitting her in her left eye, causing bone fractures and resulting in plastic and reconstructive surgery. However, no additional charges were brought against Hensley prior to his trial in magistrate court on March 13, 1992. He was acquitted of both misdemeanors following the trial in magistrate court.

The Sheriff's Department did not tell the prosecutor's office about the nature of Lane's injuries until January 1994, over two years after the bar fight and nearly two years after the acquittal in magistrate court. Soon after learning about the severity of Lane's injuries, the prosecutor charged Hensley with malicious assault, a felony. Hensley moved to dismiss the indictment under Rule 8(a) of the West Virginia Rules

---

17. We have indicated that other crimes evidence on occasion should be tailored to minimize prejudice. Theoretically, it would be possible to sanitize the Trinidad Avenue evidence for a separate Orren Street trial. In such a trial, the Trinidad Avenue identification testimony would have to be trimmed to leave out reference to a murder, and Deborah Alford would be limited to testifying that an unidentifi-able man in black had accosted Johnson with a gun at about 10:30 P.M. Scholethia Monk and Kimberly Bridgeford would be limited to saying that Long — dressed in black — had returned to the apartment shortly after 10:30 P.M., admitting he had just assaulted someone on Trinidad Avenue. The police could then testify about finding a black skull cap on Trinidad Avenue nearby.

The trial court will have to decide, as part of the required probative value/prejudicial impact anal-ysis, (1) whether the preferred approach would be admission of sanitized Trinidad Avenue evidence in a separate Orren Street trial, in order to keep prejudicial homicide evidence from that jury, or (2) whether, because (a) the Fox/Davis identification evidence was strong, (b) the Monk/Bridgeford testimony could be limited to identification of Long as the man who returned "panicking and sweating" at about 10:30 P.M., (c) the murder evidence was highly prejudicial, and (d) because sanitizing the evidence would be complicated, the Trinidad Avenue murder evidence should be kept out of the Orren Street trial altogether, or (3) whether sanitizing the Trinidad Avenue evidence would not work, and the pro-bative value of that evidence outweighs prejudice. If either of the first two instances applies, the court should grant the severance motion; in the third, the court should deny it.

of Criminal Procedure based on the failure of the State to join the felony charge with the misdemeanor charges prior to the trial in magistrate court in March 1992.

Rule 8(a) of West Virginia Rules of Criminal Procedure provides:

> Joinder of Offenses. — Two or more offenses may be charged in the same indictment or information in a separate count for each offense if the offenses charged, whether felonies or misdemeanors or both, are of the same or similar character. All offenses based on the same act or transaction or on two or more acts or transactions connected together or constituting parts of a common scheme or plan shall be charged in the same indictment or information in a separate count for each offense, whether felonies or misdemeanors or both.

West Virginia courts have developed several exceptions to the application of the rule despite the absence of explicit language within the rule. The first exception is that all offenses, even though based on the same act or transaction or constituting parts of a common scheme or plan, must have occurred in the same jurisdiction before there is a compulsion to charge all offenses in the same charging documents. The second exception applies when the prosecuting attorney does not know and has no reason to know about all the offenses. The third exception happens when the prosecuting attorney had no opportunity to attend the proceeding where the first offense is presented. See Cline v. Murensky, 322 S.E.2d 702 (W. Va. 1984) (two people involved in bar fight were charged and pled guilty in magistrate court to misdemeanor offense of brandishing weapon, all within few hours of fight; both were later indicted in Circuit Court for carrying weapon without license, state not precluded because prosecutor did not have opportunity to attend magistrate court's hearing).

If you were the trial judge in Hensley's felony case, what issues would you ask the parties to address during the hearing on the motion to dismiss? How would you expect to rule? Would your ruling change if the felony charges were already pending in Circuit Court at the time of the acquittal in magistrate court? Would the outcome change if West Virginia had adopted a rule identical to Federal Rule of Criminal Procedure 8(a)? Compare State ex rel. Forbes v. Canady, 475 S.E.2d 37 (W.Va. 1996).

Problem 4-4. Protective Order

Aurelio Chenique-Puey and Susan Lane cohabited from 1983 until 1987, and they had a daughter in 1986. After their separation in 1987, Chenique-Puey harassed Lane by banging on the door and windows of her New Jersey home, and by threatening to kill her. Lane obtained a domestic violence restraining order, which prohibited Chenique-Puey from "returning to the scene of the domestic violence" and "from having any contact with the plaintiff or harassing plaintiff or plaintiff's relatives in any way." It also curtailed his child-visitation rights.

Chenique-Puey was convicted and imprisoned on unrelated charges, so Lane did not have any further contact with him until 1991. Five days after his release from prison, Chenique-Puey came to Lane's apartment to see his daughter. At the time, Lane was watching a football game on television with two of her children and her boyfriend, John Clifford. Lane refused to admit Chenique-Puey and told him to leave. The parties disagree about what happened at that point. According to Lane, Chenique-Puey taunted Clifford through an open rear window. He reached his arm through the window bars and waved a knife at them. After failing to provoke Clifford, Chenique-Puey threatened to return to the apartment with a shotgun and kill the couple.

Chenique-Puey claimed that he went to the open rear window with his companions, Pedro and Marisa Mondo, and looked inside the apartment. Lane told them that she would not let them in and that they should leave. Chenique-Puey then told Lane that he would return on another day and they left. He says that there was no knife and that he made no threats to Lane and Clifford.

When Chenique-Puey and his companions left the premises, Lane called the police and filed a criminal complaint against him. He was indicted on charges of third-degree terroristic threats and fourth-degree contempt of a judicial restraining order. At the start of trial, the defendant moved for a severance of the contempt charge. He argued that joinder of this offense would prejudice him because evidence of the restraining order would convince the jury that he had in fact made the alleged terroristic threats against Lane.

In New Jersey, joinder of offenses is governed by Rule 3:7-6, which provides that two or more offenses may be charged together if they are "of the same or similar character or are based on the same act or transaction or on two or more acts or transactions connected together or constituting parts of a common scheme or plan." Mandatory joinder under Rule 3:15-1(b) is required when multiple criminal offenses charged are "based on the same conduct or arise from the same episode." Rule 3:15-2(b) vests a trial court with discretion to order separate trials if a defendant or the State is "prejudiced" by permissive or mandatory joinder of offenses.

To convict a defendant of the fourth-degree crime of contempt of a domestic violence restraining order, the State must prove that (1) a restraining order was issued under the act, (2) the defendant violated the order, (3) the defendant acted purposely or knowingly, and (4) the conduct that constituted the violation also constituted a crime or disorderly persons offense. The crime of terroristic threats in the third degree occurs if a person "threatens to kill another with purpose to put him in imminent fear of death under circumstances reasonably causing the victim to believe the immediacy of the threat and the likelihood that it will be carried out."

As a trial court judge, would you grant the motion to sever the offenses? Would you grant other relief? As an appellate court judge, would you reverse a trial court that had refused to grant the severance? Compare State v. Chenique-Puey, 678 A.2d 694 (N.J. 1996).

Notes

1. *Permissive joinder of offenses: majority view.* The rules governing joinder and severance work together to define the permissible bounds for single prosecutions and the extent of allowable judicial discretion. A slight majority of states track the federal rule on permissive joinder and allow prosecutors or judges to join offenses for trial, whether they are "related" charges ("based on the same act or transaction or on two or more acts or transactions connected together or constituting parts of a common scheme or plan") or similar but "unrelated" charges (having the "same or

similar character"). A significant minority of states authorize joinder only for "related" offenses utilizing a variety of formulations. See, e.g., Fla. R. Crim. P. 3.150; Ill. Ann. Stat. ch. 725, para. 5/111-4; Pa. R. Crim. P. 228; State v. Ramos, 818 A.2d 1228 (N.H. 2003) (adopts ABA standards for joinder, because former, more permissive approach produced inconsistent results; when two or more unrelated offenses are joined for trial, both prosecution and defense have absolute right to severance). Given that "related" offenses can include two or more acts "connected together or constituting parts of a common scheme or plan," will the results of this rule be much different from the results of a rule allowing joinder of acts with the "same or similar character"?

2. *The effects of joinder.* What are the effects of joinder on the trial prospects of the defense and the prosecution? Joinder may offer some benefits for defendants, since an attorney can charge less money to represent a defendant at a single trial than at multiple trials. Generally speaking, however, the conventional wisdom is that joint trials provide more advantages to the prosecution. What particular advantages might the prosecutor gain by combining related charges into a single trial?

One careful study of joinder in the federal courts compared outcomes at trial for joined offenses and separately tried offenses. After controlling for the seriousness of the charges and other variables, the study concluded that trial defendants who face multiple counts are roughly 10 percent more likely to be convicted of the most serious charge than a defendant who stands trial on a single count. Andrew D. Leipold & Hossein A. Abbasi, The Impact of Joinder and Severance on Federal Criminal Cases: An Empirical Study, 59 Vand. L. Rev. 101 (2006). If you were studying the effects of joinder in a state felony court system, what variables other than the number of counts would you want to investigate?

3. *Severance of offenses: majority view.* A majority of states have separate provisions governing severance. A group of about seven states (represented by the Vermont rule reprinted above) follow the recommendations of the ABA Standards for Criminal Justice by giving the defendant the absolute right to sever "unrelated but similar" offenses. This approach bars the joinder of the unrelated but similar offenses unless the defendant consents. See, e.g., Mich. R. Crim. P. 6.121; Tenn. R. Crim. P. 8(b), 14. What reasons might lead a defendant to accept joinder of unrelated but similar offenses? Most states with severance provisions require severance upon a finding of prejudice, or if necessary to promote a "fair determination of innocence or guilt." A few authorize severance in the "interests of justice."

Under what circumstances might a single trial of properly joined offenses create prejudice for the government? The *Long* decision from the District of Columbia reviews the most important sources of prejudice to defendants. First, a defendant might want to pursue separate and inconsistent defenses to the different charges. Was Long asking for the opportunity to mislead two different juries? A second common source of prejudice to defendants from a joint trial of separate offenses involves "other crimes" evidence. The rules of evidence limit the prosecutor's ability to introduce evidence of one crime during the trial of another crime, because the jury might infer that a person who committed one crime is more likely to have committed a second crime. Joinder of offenses might allow a prosecutor to overcome this evidentiary rule; thus, severance is often granted when a court determines that the rules of evidence would exclude evidence of one charge in a separate trial of the other charge. Federal Rule of Evidence 404(b) governs such questions in the federal system. Evidence of "other crimes" is admissible to show a defendant's motive, intent, absence of mistake or accident, common scheme or plan, or identity, but not her propensity to commit a crime. Even when the rules of evidence might exclude evidence of one crime during a separate trial for the other crime, the charges can still be joined if the evidence remains "simple and distinct" at trial. See United States v. Lotsch, 102 F.2d 35 (2d Cir. 1939) (Hand, J.) ("Here we can see no prejudice from the joining of the three charges: The evidence to each was short and simple; there was no reasonable ground for thinking that the jury would not keep separate what was relevant to each"). "Simple and distinct" (or "separate and distinct") refers both to the content of the evidence and to the method the prosecution uses to present it. If witnesses for one crime are presented together, followed by a different set of witnesses for the other crime, the evidence is more likely to be considered "simple and distinct."

4. *Appellate review of joinder and severance decisions.* Appellate courts rarely overturn a trial court's joinder and severance decisions. The standard of review in virtually all jurisdictions is "abuse of discretion." Did the trial court in *Long* abuse its discretion? Given that most joinder and severance decisions are resolved before trial and are based on the charges in the indictment or information rather than testimony of witnesses at trial, are trial courts really better situated to resolve these claims than an appellate court?

5. *Per se severance rules.* Consider Problem 4-4. Is it possible or desirable to develop per se severance rules — that is, rules *requiring* a trial court to exercise its discretion under certain circumstances to sever charges that were properly joined? Are there any advantages to a per se rule in the context of severance decisions?

6. *Insufficient proof at trial.* Although challenges to compulsory joinder and misjoinder are generally resolved in a pretrial motion, sometimes the prosecution's evidence presented at trial will reveal that the offenses are not as closely related as they first appeared. Can the defendant obtain a declaration of misjoinder at the close of the prosecution's evidence? The Supreme Court in Schaffer v. United States, 362 U.S. 511 (1960), said that a defendant may not obtain a misjoinder during trial but must instead show that some specific prejudice required the judge to grant a discretionary severance of charges. Misjoinder, which does not depend on any showing of prejudice, must be determined only from the allegations in the indictment or information.

7. *Mandatory joinder: majority position.* About 10 states have adopted a "mandatory" or "compulsory" joinder requirement, either by statute, procedural rule, or judicial ruling. See Colo. R. Crim. P. 8(a); N.Y. Crim. Proc. Law §40.40 ("Where two or more offenses are joinable in a single accusatory instrument against a person by reason of being based upon the same criminal transaction . . . such person may not . . . be separately prosecuted for such offenses"); Pa. R. Crim. P. 105(b). A larger group of states, following the federal approach embodied in Fed. R. Crim. P. 8(a), maintain a "permissive" joinder rule, which defines the maximum range of charges that the prosecutor can bring together in the same trial but does not speak to any minimum range of charges that the prosecutor must join together. Note that in a permissive joinder jurisdiction, double jeopardy principles and the related doctrine of collateral estoppel still define a minimum range of charges that must be resolved in a single criminal proceeding. Thus, the mandatory joinder jurisdictions have supplemented double jeopardy and collateral estoppel principles.

8. *Misjoinder.* The converse of mandatory joinder is "misjoinder." When a defendant believes that a prosecutor has grouped together more charges than the permissive joinder rules will allow, she can request the trial court to declare misjoinder. The remedy is separate trials, not dismissal of the charges. Misjoinder can occur in any jurisdiction, whether it has a permissive or compulsory joinder rule, because all jurisdictions define the maximum range of charges that may be grouped together. But not all jurisdictions declare the same maximum. Some follow the model of Fed. R. Crim. P. 8(a), allowing joinder of offenses based on (1) acts that are of the same or similar character or (2) the "same act or transaction" or (3) two or more acts or transactions connected together or constituting parts of a common scheme or plan. Another group of states do not include the first ground for joinder, acts of the "same or similar character." Can you imagine a class of cases in which this first ground for joinder would make a difference in the outcome on a motion to declare misjoinder, or do you expect the different formulations to produce essentially the same results?

2. Joint Trials of Defendants

The joinder and severance questions we have considered thus far all deal with multiple offenses and an individual defendant. Related questions arise when prosecutors charge two or more defendants with committing essentially the same crime. Under what circumstances will the co-defendants receive separate trials?

The key phrases in procedural rules such as the ones reprinted below are framed generally and require further elaboration by courts presented with recurring factual situations. Cases have generally held that a defendant should obtain severance from a co-defendant when (1) evidence admitted against one defendant is facially incriminating to the other defendant, such as a prior statement of one co-defendant that incriminates the other co-defendant; (2) evidence admitted against one defendant influences the jury so strongly that it has a harmful "rub-off effect" on the other defendant; (3) there is a significant disparity in the amount of evidence introduced against each of the two defendants; or (4) co-defendants present defenses that are so antagonistic that they are mutually exclusive.

Only clear examples of these types of prejudice will convince an appellate court to reverse a trial court's decision to require a joint trial. For instance, to determine if a "rub off" problem exists, the court must ask whether the jury can keep separate the evidence that is relevant to each defendant and render a fair and impartial verdict as to each. Even in some cases where such prejudicial factors are strong enough to warrant a severance, courts sometimes decide that curative jury instructions can remove any risk of prejudice that might result from a joint trial.

■ FEDERAL RULE OF CRIMINAL PROCEDURE 8(b)

The indictment or information may charge two or more defendants if they are alleged to have participated in the same act or transaction, or in the same series of acts or transactions, constituting an offense or offenses. The defendants may be charged in one or more counts together or separately. All defendants need not be charged in each count.

■ VERMONT RULE OF CRIMINAL PROCEDURE 8(b)

Two or more defendants may be joined in the same information or indictment:

(1) when each of the defendants is charged with accountability for each offense included;

(2) when each of the defendants is charged with conspiracy and some of the defendants are also charged with one or more offenses alleged to be in furtherance of the conspiracy; or

(3) when, even if conspiracy is not charged and all of the defendants are not charged in each count, it is alleged that the several offenses charged

(A) were part of a common scheme or plan; or

(B) were so closely connected in respect to time, place, and occasion that it would be difficult to separate proof of one charge from proof of others.

■ VERMONT RULE OF CRIMINAL PROCEDURE 14(b)(2)

Whenever two or more defendants have been joined together in the same information or indictment,

(A) On motion of the prosecuting attorney or a defendant before trial, the court shall grant severance of one or more defendants if the court finds that they are not joinable under Rule 8(b)(2).

(B) On motion of the prosecuting attorney before trial, other than under subparagraph (A) of this paragraph, the court shall grant severance of one or more defendants if the court finds that there is no reasonable likelihood of prejudice to any defendant. On motion of the prosecuting attorney during trial, the court shall grant severance of one or more defendants only with the consent of the defendant or defendants to be severed or upon a finding of manifest necessity.

(C) On motion of a defendant for severance because an out-of-court statement of a codefendant makes reference to, but is not admissible against, the moving defendant, the court shall determine whether the prosecution intends to offer the statement in evidence as part of its case in chief. If so, the court shall require the prosecuting attorney to elect one of the following courses:

(i) a joint trial at which the statement is not admitted into evidence:

(ii) a joint trial at which the statement is admitted into evidence only after all references to the moving defendant have been deleted, provided that the court finds that the statement, with the references deleted, will not prejudice the moving defendant; or

(iii) severance of the moving defendant.

(D) On motion of a defendant other than under subparagraph (A) or (C) of this paragraph, the court shall grant severance of the moving defendant unless the court finds that there is no reasonable likelihood that that defendant would be prejudiced by a joint trial.

(E) In determining whether there is no reasonable likelihood that a defendant would be prejudiced, the court shall consider among other factors whether, in view of the number of offenses and defendants charged and the complexity of the evidence to be offered, the trier of fact will be able to distinguish the evidence and apply the law intelligently as to each offense and as to each defendant.

(F) The court may, at any time, grant severance of one or more defendants with the consent of the prosecution and the defendant or defendants to be severed.

VERMONT REPORTER'S NOTES — 1995 AMENDMENT

Rule 14(b)(2) is amended to eliminate the absolute right of severance for a defendant in a felony case and to provide guidelines under which a motion for severance of defendants is to be considered. Under the prior rule, in misdemeanor cases severance or whatever other relief justice required was to be granted when either a defendant or the State was prejudiced by joinder. The amended rule applies to both felonies and misdemeanors. The amendment is based on ABA Standard 13-3.2. The purposes of the amendment are to give the court flexibility and to strike a proper balance between avoidance of multiple trials for victims and the right of defendants to a fair trial. . . .

When two or more defendants have been joined, the first issue for determination is whether the joinder is proper under the terms of that rule. Amended Rule 14(b)(2)(A) requires the court to grant a pretrial request by either prosecution or defense for severance on grounds of misjoinder, regardless of whether there is prejudice. If a defect in joinder appears during trial, a severance on that ground is to be considered in accordance with the standards of subparagraphs (B) and (D).

Under Rule 14(b)(2)(B), even if joinder is proper pursuant to Rule 8(b), the prosecutor will be granted a severance on motion before trial if the court finds "no reasonable likelihood" that any defendant would be prejudiced by the severance. . . . On an appropriate motion by a defendant under Rule 14(b)(2)(C), the court must determine whether Bruton v. United States, 391 U.S. 123 (1968), affects the severance decision. Under *Bruton*, the trial court must protect the confrontation rights of a nonconfessing defendant where a codefendant has confessed and that confession is admissible only against the confessing defendant. Rule 14(b)(2)(C)(i)-(iii) set out the options which must be followed for compliance with *Bruton*. . . .

If a defendant moves for severance before trial on grounds other than misjoinder or the potential use of a codefendant's confession, the court under Rule 14(b)(2)(D) is to sever the moving defendant unless it finds that there is no reasonable likelihood of prejudice to that defendant from the joinder. The standard for determining prejudice is set forth in Rule 14(b)(2)(E). That standard departs from the formulation, "fair determination of guilt or innocence," found in ABA Standard 13-3.2(b)(i), (ii). In deciding the question, the court is to consider "prejudice" in terms of the impact of the challenged joinder on each defendant's right to a fair trial where the prosecution makes the motion and on the moving defendant's fair trial right where a defendant makes the motion. [T]here is a reasonable likelihood of prejudice where the jury might consider evidence against one defendant that is properly offered only against a codefendant, either on the merits or as to character or credibility. Where the evidence against both defendants is substantially similar, however, they may be tried jointly in the absence of other factors giving rise to a reasonable likelihood of prejudice. . . .

Problem 4-5. Antagonistic Brothers

Brothers Durid and Kafan Hana were arrested following a controlled narcotics purchase in January 1988 that took place at the Sterling Heights home in which the brothers lived with their parents and siblings. The drug transaction arose out of a conversation between James Hornburger and Raed Alsarih at the Sterling Heights High School where they were students. Hornburger approached Alsarih about obtaining twelve ounces of cocaine for Stephen Putnam, who happened to be an undercover narcotics police officer. Alsarih agreed to the transaction after contacting Kafan. Hornburger, Putnam, and Alsarih drove to Kafan's home. Alsarih went to the door and spoke with Durid, who contacted Kafan by beeper and reported that Kafan would be back in 15 minutes. When the purchasers returned to the house later that evening, they saw Kafan drive up and Alsarih and Kafan went into the house together.

According to Alsarih, testifying pursuant to a plea bargain, he went with Kafan to a back bedroom where Durid was sleeping. Durid awoke when Kafan turned on the light. While Kafan opened a safe, Durid asked Alsarih whether the person outside was a police officer and whether Alsarih had dealt with him before. Kafan removed a plastic bag from the safe, mixed it with the contents from some other bags and gave it to Alsarih. They returned to the front of the house, and Kafan watched while Alsarih went out to Putnam's car. Durid was watching from the living room window. Alsarih then got in the back seat and gave the bag of cocaine to Putnam. Putnam signaled to a surveillance team, which moved in and arrested Hornburger, Alsarih, Kafan, and Durid. A subsequent search of the home, pursuant to a search warrant, disclosed that the safe contained three kilograms of cocaine, miscellaneous jewelry and papers, a telephone recorder, and a telephone beeper. Both Kafan and Durid initially denied knowing the combination to the safe. However, Kafan later supplied the combination, and Durid admitted that the safe was his.

Both Durid and Kafan filed pretrial motions for separate trials. Michigan Court Rule 6.121 provides for permissive joinder and conditional severance:

(A) Permissive Joinder. An information or indictment may charge two or more defendants with the same offense. [T]wo or more informations or indictments against different defendants may be consolidated for a single trial whenever the defendants could be charged in the same information or indictment under this rule. . . .

(C) Right of Severance; Related Offenses. On a defendant's motion, the court must sever the trial of defendants on related offenses on a showing that severance is necessary to avoid prejudice to substantial rights of the defendants.

(D) Discretionary Severance. On the motion of any party, the court may sever the trial of defendants on the ground that severance is appropriate to promote fairness to the parties and a fair determination of the guilt or innocence of one or more of the defendants. Relevant factors include the timeliness of the motion, the drain on the parties' resources, the potential for confusion or prejudice stemming from either the number of defendants or the complexity or nature of the evidence, the convenience of the witnesses, and the parties' readiness for trial. . . .

In a supporting affidavit, Durid's counsel explained the results of a meeting with Kafan's attorneys:

At said meeting affiant was advised by both counsel that the defense theory of the above case was that evidence would show that the controlled substances seized from

3105 Metropolitan Parkway were the property of, or possessed by, Durid Bajhat Hana and not by Kafan Hana. Given the fact that Durid Bajhat Hana's theory of the case is that the controlled substances seized from 3105 Metropolitan Parkway were the property of, or possessed by, Kafan Hana, and not by Durid Bajhat Hana, Durid Bajhat Hana will be compelled to act, for all practical purpose, as an assistant prosecutor as to Kafan Hana.

The trial court heard argument on the motions. Durid's attorney argued that "the two defenses could not be more antagonistic. Two people are pointing the finger at each other and the case is clear that severance must be granted." The prosecutor argued that it took more than "a mere allegation of pointing fingers at one another" to warrant separate trials. The trial court denied the motion.

The brothers were tried jointly before a jury in February 1989. Durid was tried on an aiding and abetting theory. In his opening statement, Kafan's attorney told jurors that their deliberations necessarily pitted brother against brother. During closing argument, Durid's attorney similarly described the defense postures as "brother pitted against brother." In closing arguments, Kafan's attorney disputed the theory that his client had control over the three kilograms of cocaine seized from the safe:

We know he used the Cadillac, we know he used the house, we know he used the safe, but we know he didn't own the Cadillac and own the house and own the safe. Everybody who has ever shared a locker in school or anybody who's ever shared an apartment, everybody who's ever lived in a rooming house and had to share a bathroom knows that you can share special areas and have absolutely no right to control something that belongs to somebody else.

The prosecutor pointed out the conflict during rebuttal closing argument when she noted: "That's real convenient for these two boys to sit here and say that the drugs belonged to one another." This remark was stricken. The prosecutor later stated:

The position that Durid Hana and Kafan Hana took in this trial is saying that the drugs did not belong to them, but they were in their bedroom and they were in a safe that they both had access to, and if you believe both Durid Hana and Kafan Hana, the good fairy must have delivered the drugs and locked them in the safe. It's not reasonable to believe that they did not know that they were there. Someone put those drugs in that safe, and if you look at all of the evidence that occurred that night, it is reasonable to believe that both of them knew it. . . .

The prosecutor further explained in closing argument: "As to Durid Hana, it is the People's theory that Durid aided his brother in the delivery of cocaine in the sum of 225 to 649 grams of cocaine, that he provided support, advice and encouragement and took an active role in that delivery. It is further alleged that Durid Hana knew that the cocaine was being stored in that safe and that he had dominion and control over the contents of what was kept in that safe, as did his brother Kafan Hana." Neither Durid nor his brother testified. Durid and Kafan were both convicted of possession of more than 650 grams of cocaine and delivery of more than 225, but less than 650, grams of cocaine.

Durid appeals, alleging that the trial court erred in denying his motion for a separate trial given the antagonistic defenses of the two brothers. He argues that the events at trial support his claim of antagonistic defenses. How would you rule? Compare People v. Hana, 524 N.W.2d 682 (Mich. 1994).

Notes

1. *Joinder of defendants: majority view.* Joint trials account for almost one-third of all federal criminal trials, a rate much higher than in most state systems. As a result, the federal courts have dealt extensively with severance issues. See Richardson v. Marsh, 481 U.S. 200 (1987). In general, the federal courts have shown a strong preference for joint trials. This preference has become even more pronounced in recent years, and severance requests in the federal courts are now routinely denied. Interestingly, one empirical study of the joinder of federal defendants concluded that joining co-defendants in a single trial had virtually no impact on the likelihood of conviction. Andrew D. Leipold & Hossein A. Abbasi, The Impact of Joinder and Severance on Federal Criminal Cases: An Empirical Study, 59 Vand. L. Rev. 101 (2006).

A majority of states leave decisions on the joinder and severance of trials for multiple defendants to the discretion of the trial judge. Defendants in these jurisdictions find courts generally unreceptive when they request separate trials based on the special legal and practical difficulties of defending against conspiracy charges. As the reporter's notes to Vermont Rule 14(b)(2) indicate, Vermont had a mandatory severance rule but amended it in 1995, in line with the dominant view, allowing the trial judge some discretion over whether to order joint trials. See Kan. Stat. §22-3204. A significant minority of states, including Vermont, provide more detailed rules to guide courts in assessing out-of-court statements by co-defendants. See, e.g., Fla. R. Crim. P. 3.152(b).

2. *Remedies short of severance.* Courts take several approaches short of severing trials to deal with conflicts among co-defendants. The most common is simply to issue cautionary instructions to the jury before it retires to consider the case. Sometimes the judge also instructs the jury at the beginning of the trial or when particular evidence is presented. Occasionally courts will bar the use of evidence that would be admissible at a trial of a co-defendant tried separately. A more complex option, which has been tried in a number of states, is the use of "dual" juries to hear the same case. Each jury considers the charges against one defendant. The court will excuse one of the juries when evidence is presented against one defendant that could not be presented against the other. For a general discussion of "mega-trials" in the federal courts, see James Jacobs et al., Busting the Mob: United States v. Cosa Nostra (1994).

PART TWO

RESOLVING GUILT AND INNOCENCE

V

■

Discovery and Speedy Trial

Parties must prepare for trial if the process is to create justice. The most critical task for the attorney preparing for trial is to gather information about the events in question. Much of the best information is in the hands of the other party. The rules of discovery govern how and when the parties exchange information that may be relevant in resolving the charges, whether through trial or guilty plea. These rules are grounded in constitutions, statutes, court rules, and local policies and practices.

Adequate preparation takes time. But all the while, the defendant must live with the shame of accusation and the inconvenience and expense of preparing for trial. For defendants who are detained, the period before trial can destroy employment and personal relationships. Many defendants, and especially those in detention, want a "speedy" trial. In this chapter, we review the tools for discovering information and the many sources of law that give parties the ability, and the incentive, to speed up or slow down the trial date.

A. DISCOVERY

In all litigation, there are rules about exchanging information among the parties and gathering information from nonparties. What the parties learn during discovery determines in large part the evidence they will have at their disposal at trial. Even more important for most defendants, discovery allows them to estimate their chances of success at trial and to enter plea bargain negotiations with that information in mind.

Two sets of interrelated questions dominate the law of discovery in criminal cases. First, discovery rules must resolve whether shared information or independent information is the norm. The answer to this question reflects the expected relationship among prosecutors, judges, and defense attorneys. Less exchange of information reflects a more adversarial and independent model, where each side develops its own evidence; more exchange reflects a more cooperative model of litigation, with the court taking a stronger role in coordinating a collective search for truth. When describing the criminal discovery process on this score, it may be helpful to draw a comparison to discovery in civil litigation. It is commonplace to hear that criminal discovery is less extensive than civil discovery. Is this claim accurate today? If so, will it remain true in the future? As you read and discuss the materials in this section, try to draw comparisons to civil discovery techniques and to identify trends over time toward more or less extensive criminal discovery.

The second set of questions deals with the symmetry of discovery. Will prosecution and defense have an equal ability to obtain information from the opposing side? In a system with other asymmetries built into it (such as the "beyond a reasonable doubt" standard of proof, the privilege against self-incrimination, and the government's funding of prosecutors and investigators), are asymmetrical discovery rights necessary or desirable?

1. Prosecution Disclosures

A defense attorney with enough time, ingenuity, and resources could learn much about the government's evidence in a criminal case. Rules of procedure and statutes in most jurisdictions set out the obligations of the prosecution to disclose some of the incriminating evidence against the accused, but only after the defendant requests it. Local court rules sometimes supplement the statewide rules.

Despite these discovery rules, however, the defense attorney frequently knows much less than the prosecutor about the case at the time of plea bargaining or trial. Some of the functional limits on discovery are built into the rules themselves, and others are a function of the defense attorney's limited time and resources.

The criminal discovery rules show remarkable variety from jurisdiction to jurisdiction. Federal Rule of Criminal Procedure 16 and the South Carolina rule reprinted below are typical of the more restrictive rules, which give the defendant access to only a handful of documents and tangible objects before trial. Most states go beyond these limited categories to allow defense discovery of a wider range of prosecution information. The ABA Standards for Criminal Justice have been an influential model for those states moving in the direction of wider discovery. The New Jersey rule reprinted below illustrates the broader scope of documents and other information that some states consider essential to the preparation of a defense.

Use the following problem as a setting for applying the New Jersey and South Carolina rules. Under each of these approaches to criminal discovery, what information gets exchanged, and what types of evidence go unmentioned? How will a plea negotiation or a trial progress if the defense lawyer does not have access to such information before trial? Can defense counsel develop the same information through different avenues?

Problem 5-1. Exchanging Words

Two groups in a bar were arguing one night. One group, which included Wayne Galvan, left shortly before the bar closed, while the other group, which included Perry Sutton, waited inside a few minutes longer, hoping to avoid any contact outside with the other group. When Sutton and his friends went outside, Galvan and his friends appeared from around the corner and started taunting Sutton's group. Soon the two groups were involved in a heated argument. In the midst of the noise and confusion, Galvan drew a small handgun and fired two shots while standing less than five feet from Sutton. The second shot killed Sutton. Galvan ran away. Several of Sutton's friends knew Galvan by name and identified him to police officers. The officers later arrested Galvan at his cousin's home, where they also found a small handgun.

You have been appointed to represent Galvan. During his initial conversation with you, Galvan claimed that he meant to frighten Sutton and his friends by firing his handgun into the air, but that he did not intend to harm Sutton. Galvan said that he had discussed the incident with two other detainees in the county jail.

You have obtained from your client the names and addresses of some of his friends who were present that evening. During telephone conversations with two of those friends, you learn that one was interviewed within a week of the shooting by a police officer and an attorney from the district attorney's office, both of whom were taking notes. The second was interviewed by a police officer alone, and the officer did not take any notes. You learned from Galvan's friends the name of one of Sutton's friends who was present on the night of the shooting, but that person refuses to talk to you.

Galvan has authorized you to engage in plea negotiations. What sort of discovery will you request before plea negotiations begin? Consider each of the following categories of potentially useful information:

- Any statements that Galvan made to police officers, prosecutors, his friends, or members of the rival group. Does it matter whether the statements have been recorded in a document?
- Any statements that members of the rival group made to police or prosecutors about what they saw or heard that night. Can you insist that the police tell you what they know about the background and reliability of these witnesses?
- Any statements that members of Galvan's group made to the police or prosecutors. Can the prosecutors gain discovery of these statements? Is there anything you can or should do to prepare these potential defense witnesses for an interview with the police or cross-examination at trial by the prosecutor?
- Any ballistics or other scientific tests performed on the gun, along with any medical examinations performed on Sutton.

Anticipate how the prosecutors might respond if the relevant discovery rules are similar to those in South Carolina. Then compare the government's response if the rules look like those in New Jersey. Would any of the evidence you might obtain through requests under these discovery rules dramatically change the course of the plea negotiations?

Think also about the timing of discovery. Suppose you are assigned to the case at the arraignment, less than a month after the charges are filed. The median time it takes to process felony cases in the state is 80 days (roughly the national median time), although a few cases last a good deal longer. About 10 percent of the felony cases require more than a year to resolve.

Finally, consider the investigative resources at your disposal. You work full time as a defense attorney, and you represent about 150 felony defendants per year (the maximum workload prescribed in the ABA Standards on Criminal Justice, but lighter than the load many defense attorneys actually carry). Your office employs a former police detective as an investigator, but seven other criminal defense attorneys in your office share the services of this investigator. In light of these resource constraints and the legal rules described below, what would be your strategy for obtaining the types of information listed above?

■ SOUTH CAROLINA RULE OF CRIMINAL PROCEDURE 5(a)

(1) *Information Subject to Disclosure.*

(A) *Statement of Defendant.* Upon request by a defendant, the prosecution shall permit the defendant to inspect and copy or photograph: any relevant written or recorded statements made by the defendant, or copies thereof, within the possession, custody, or control of the prosecution, the existence of which is known, or by the exercise of due diligence may become known, to the attorney for the prosecution; the substance of any oral statement which the prosecution intends to offer in evidence at the trial made by the defendant whether before or after arrest in response to interrogation by any person then known to the defendant to be a prosecution agent.

(B) *Defendant's Prior Record.* Upon request of the defendant, the prosecution shall furnish to the defendant such copy of his prior criminal record, if any, as is within the possession, custody, or control of the prosecution, the existence of which is known, or by the exercise of due diligence may become known, to the attorney for the prosecution.

(C) *Documents and Tangible Objects.* Upon request of the defendant the prosecution shall permit the defendant to inspect and copy books, papers, documents, photographs, tangible objects, buildings, or places, or copies or portions thereof, which are within the possession, custody, or control of the prosecution, and which are material to the preparation of his defense or are intended for use by the prosecution as evidence in chief at the trial, or were obtained from or belong to the defendant.

(D) *Reports of Examinations and Tests.* Upon request of a defendant the prosecution shall permit the defendant to inspect and copy any results or reports of physical or mental examinations, and of scientific tests or experiments, or copies thereof, which are within the possession, custody, or control of the prosecution, the existence of which is known, or by the exercise of due diligence may become known, to the attorney for the prosecution, and which are material to the preparation of the defense or are intended for use by the prosecution as evidence in chief at the trial.

(2) *Information Not Subject to Disclosure.* Except as provided in paragraphs (A), (B), and (D) of subdivision (a)(1), this rule does not authorize the discovery or inspection of reports, memoranda, or other internal prosecution documents made by the attorney for the prosecution or other prosecution agents in connection with the investigation or prosecution of the case, or of statements made by prosecution witnesses or prospective prosecution witnesses provided that after a prosecution witness has testified on direct examination, the court shall, on motion of the defendant, order the prosecution to produce any statement of the witness in the possession of the prosecution which relates to the subject matter as to which the witness has testified; and provided further that the court may upon a sufficient showing require the production of any statement of any prospective witness prior to the time such witness testifies.

(3) *Time for Disclosure.* The prosecution shall respond to the defendant's request for disclosure no later then thirty days after the request is made, or within such other time as may be ordered by the court.

■ NEW JERSEY COURT RULE 3:13-3

(a) Where the prosecutor has made a pre-indictment plea offer, the prosecutor shall upon request permit defense counsel to inspect and copy or photograph any relevant material which would be discoverable following an indictment pursuant to section (b) or (c).

(b) A copy of the prosecutor's discovery shall be delivered to the criminal division manager's office, or shall be available at the prosecutor's office, within 14 days of the return or unsealing of the indictment. . . . A defendant who does not seek discovery from the State shall so notify the criminal division manager's office and the prosecutor, and the defendant need not provide discovery to the State [except as] otherwise required by law. . . .

(c) The prosecutor shall permit defendant to inspect and copy or photograph the following relevant material if not given as part of the discovery package under section (b):

(1) books, tangible objects, papers or documents obtained from or belonging to the defendant;

(2) records of statements or confessions, signed or unsigned, by the defendant or copies thereof, and a summary of any admissions or declarations against penal interest made by the defendant that are known to the prosecution but not recorded;

(3) results or reports of physical or mental examinations and of scientific tests or experiments made in connection with the matter or copies thereof, which are within the possession, custody or control of the prosecutor;

(4) reports or records of prior convictions of the defendant;

(5) books, papers, documents, or copies thereof, or tangible objects, buildings or places which are within the possession, custody or control of the prosecutor;

(6) names and addresses of any persons whom the prosecutor knows to have relevant evidence or information including a designation by the prosecutor as to which of those persons may be called as witnesses;

(7) record of statements, signed or unsigned, by such persons or by co-defendants which are within the possession, custody or control of the prosecutor and any relevant record of prior conviction of such persons;

(8) police reports which are within the possession, custody, or control of the prosecutor;

(9) names and addresses of each person whom the prosecutor expects to call to trial as an expert witness, the expert's qualifications, the subject matter on which the expert is expected to testify, a copy of the report, if any, of such expert witness, or if no report is prepared, a statement of the facts and opinions to which the expert is expected to testify and a summary of the grounds for each opinion. . . .

Notes

1. *Defendant and co-defendant statements.* Discovery rules in all jurisdictions allow defense counsel at least some access to the government's evidence regarding statements that the defendant made about the alleged crime. This does not mean, however, that the government must turn over all statements by a defendant. Under Fed. R. Crim. P. 16(a)(1)(A), the defense may obtain "written or recorded" statements of a defendant and written evidence of "oral statements" made by a defendant in response to interrogation by a known government agent. The ABA Standard for Criminal Justice, Discovery 11-2.1(a)(i) (3d ed. 1996) calls for the prosecutor to disclose "all written and oral statements of the defendant or any co-defendant," along with any documents "relating to the acquisition of such statements." See also Fla. R. Crim. P. 3.220(b)(1)(C). What sorts of statements does the ABA standard cover that the Federal Rule does not? Does a defense attorney really need to obtain such statements from the government when he could simply ask his client about any statements he made? How would he use documents "relating to the acquisition" of a defendant's statement?

Note that Rule 16 makes no provision for the discovery of co-defendant's statements. Cf. Fla. R. Crim. P. 3.220(b)(1)(D) (discovery of "any written or recorded statements and the substance of any oral statements made by a codefendant if the trial is to be a joint one"). When might defense counsel use such a statement? Does defense counsel have an alternative method of preparing for any co-defendant statements that might be used at trial?

2. *Prosecution expert witnesses.* Criminal discovery rules, like their civil counterparts, recognize the special challenges of preparing for the trial testimony of expert witnesses. Fed. R. Crim. P. 16(a)(1)(E) calls for disclosure of a "written summary of testimony the government intends to use" from experts in its case in chief, which includes the expert's opinions, the bases and the reasons for the opinions, and the expert's qualifications. Once again, many states give the defense more information, by including disclosure of the reports or statements of any experts (such as the results of tests) made "in connection with" a particular case, whether or not the government plans to call the expert at trial. Fla. R. Crim. P. 3.220(b)(1)(J). The rules typically impose on both parties the same obligations of disclosure about their experts.

3. *Nonexpert witnesses and potential witnesses.* Perhaps the greatest variety in discovery rules involves information about nonexpert witnesses and potential

witnesses. Federal Rule of Criminal Procedure 26.2 provides for disclosure *at trial* by both the prosecution and defense of written "statements" of any witnesses other than the defendant. Any disclosure of witness statements before trial (or before entry of a guilty plea) results from negotiations between the parties. See Ellen S. Podgor, The Ethics and Professionalism of Prosecutors in Discretionary Decisions, 68 Fordham L. Rev. 1511 (2000). Some states, such as Texas, are silent about pretrial discovery of witness statements. See Tex. Code Crim. Proc. art. 39.14. What impact would this timing question have on the course of plea negotiations?

What is the rationale for providing such limited discovery of potential witnesses? To some extent, such discovery rules endorse the classic adversarial model of justice. Rules that limit disclosure of prosecution witnesses also reflect worries that defendants will engage in witness tampering, bribery, and intimidation. To the extent that defendants can use broader discovery to fine-tune misleading or perjured defenses, broader discovery could undermine the basic truth-finding function of criminal adjudication.

Discovery rules in other jurisdictions treat information about potential witnesses as a matter that the defense cannot develop alone before trial. The rules commonly require the government to give the defense — before trial — the names and addresses of its witnesses and other persons who have knowledge of the events surrounding the alleged crime. See Fla. R. Crim. P. 3.220(b)(1)(A); National District Attorneys Association, National Prosecution Standards 53.2(a) (2d ed. 1991) (covering prosecution witnesses but not potential witnesses). The rules also oblige the government to provide the defense with potential impeachment material, such as the prior criminal record of any witnesses or the nature of any cooperation agreement between the government and the witness. The rules also typically extend to any written summaries of witness statements, even if the statements are not "adopted" or "verbatim." See ABA Standard 11-2.1(a)(ii); Fla. R. Crim. P. 3.220(b)(1)(B). Is all of this discovery about witnesses necessary? Once a defense attorney has the name and address of a potential witness, can she obtain statements from the witness on equal terms with the government?

4. *Open file policies.* A few jurisdictions (such as New Jersey, as indicated in the provisions reprinted above) have embraced "open file" discovery—rules that require the prosecutor to keep any written records about the case completely open to the defense attorney. While such a position is unusual to find in statewide statutes or rules, it is commonplace to find individual prosecutors' offices that have committed themselves to open file discovery. Why would prosecutors create discovery rules that go well beyond the requirements of the applicable law? Does it save them the trouble of sorting through documents to comply with discovery requests? Keep in mind that prosecutors adopting an open file policy still must identify material exculpatory evidence for defense attorneys and offer such information to the defense, even if there is no specific request for it. See State v. Adam, 896 P.2d 1022 (Kan. 1995). Does an open file policy best achieve the discovery objectives identified by the National District Attorneys Association: "to provide information for informed pleas, expedite trials, minimize surprise, afford the opportunity for effective cross-examination, meet the requirements of due process, and otherwise serve the interests of justice"? National Prosecution Standards 52.1 (2d ed. 1991). Can a prosecutor's office count on the limited time available to a defense attorney in most smaller cases to minimize the impact of an open file policy? Cf. ABA Standard 11-1.2 (discovery "may be more limited" in cases involving minor offenses).

5. *Writings already in existence.* Even with open file policies, the emphasis is on written materials rather than the knowledge of the people who provide or analyze the evidence. Is this why the federal system, with its first-class capacity for developing written evidence and keeping records, has more restrictive discovery rules than most jurisdictions? Note that most of the discovery provisions described above require the prosecution to hand over existing documents, but they do not oblige the prosecutor to create or compile information (which is more common under civil discovery rules). There are a few exceptions to this pattern: Some discovery rules call on the prosecutor to commit to writing any known oral statement of the defendant, and to summarize information about expert witnesses. Given that criminal justice systems rely so heavily on guilty pleas rather than development of the facts during a trial, should the systems move in the direction of forcing the parties to summarize evidence before trial?

6. *Depositions.* Depositions of witnesses and other third parties, the lifeblood of civil discovery, does not hold an important place in criminal discovery. In the federal system and in most states, depositions are available only to preserve the testimony of a witness who is unlikely to be available at trial. A few states, however, have begun to make it easier to obtain depositions and to use them in criminal proceedings. These are sometimes called "discovery" depositions, as opposed to depositions used to preserve testimony. See Fla. R. Crim. P. 3.220(h). Why have criminal discovery innovators focused their attention on the available documents rather than the deposition or written interrogatory?

Despite the rarity of criminal depositions in most jurisdictions, the parties do interview witnesses before trial. Does this voluntary system of gathering evidence give the parties equal access to information? See ABA Standard 11-6.3 (neither prosecutor nor defense should advise persons other than defendant to refrain from speaking with counsel for opposing side).

7. *Remedies.* Discovery rules typically leave courts with a great deal of discretion in selecting a remedy for a violation of the law. The most common remedies are continuances (to allow the party time to develop a response to the evidence) and exclusion of the evidence that the party should have disclosed (particularly where the aggrieved party can show some prejudice flowing from the discovery violation). Trial courts have also dismissed charges for more serious discovery violations by a prosecutor. State ex rel. Rusen v. Hill, 454 S.E.2d 427 (W. Va. 1994). If an appellate court decides that a discovery violation occurred, it can reverse the conviction if the defendant shows prejudice. Contempt citations against the attorney or later disciplinary proceedings by the state bar are also possibilities.

8. *Discovery by any other name.* The rules of pretrial discovery are not the defendant's only method of finding out about the government's evidence. The preliminary hearing, where the government establishes probable cause to support the charges in the case, often gives defense counsel a glimpse of the government's theory of the case. Defendants will also on occasion request a "bill of particulars," a document that supplements the indictment or information when necessary to give proper notice to the defendant of the charges he must defend against.

Under the criminal discovery rules, the defense lawyer must ask before receiving material from the government. But the prosecutor's duty sometimes goes beyond responding to valid defense requests for discovery. There are several types of information that the law requires the prosecution to disclose to the defense, even if the defense lawyer never asks for the information.

One disclosure duty that courts place on prosecutors involves perjured testimony of government witnesses. If the prosecutor knows or should know that government witnesses are presenting false testimony or evidence, due process requires the prosecutor to disclose this fact to the defendant and to the court. A conviction must be set aside if there is any reasonable likelihood that the false testimony could have affected the judgment of the jury. See Mooney v. Holohan, 294 U.S. 103 (1935); Napue v. Illinois, 360 U.S. 264 (1959).

A second constitutional duty to disclose derives from Brady v. Maryland, 373 U.S. 83 (1963). In that case, a defense attorney in a murder case asked to review all the extra-judicial statements of a coconspirator, but the prosecutor withheld a statement in which the coconspirator admitted to shooting the victim. The Supreme Court ruled that the constitution's due process clause requires the prosecution to disclose "evidence favorable to an accused" if that evidence is "material either to guilt or to punishment." The Court expanded this disclosure duty in United States v. Agurs, 427 U.S. 97 (1976). The obligation to disclose all *material* evidence favorable to the accused, the Court said, applies even when the defendant makes only a general request for exculpatory information or makes no discovery request at all. Such material evidence includes evidence that the defense might use to impeach prosecution witnesses, along with evidence that more directly points to the defendant's innocence. See United States v. Bagley, 473 U.S. 667 (1985). Failure to disclose *nonmaterial* evidence does not violate *Brady,* regardless of whether defense counsel requested disclosure.

Litigation over *Brady* issues remains quite common. Courts struggle to identify which prosecutorial failures to disclose are important enough to justify overturning a conviction. This difficult question necessarily calls for the court to speculate: What would have happened if the prosecutor had disclosed the material? How certain does the reviewing court have to be?

■ DELMA BANKS v. DOUG DRETKE
540 U.S. 668 (2004)

GINSBURG, J.

Petitioner Delma Banks, Jr., was convicted of capital murder and sentenced to death. Prior to trial, the State advised Banks's attorneys there would be no need to litigate discovery issues, representing: "We will, without the necessity of motions, provide you with all the discovery to which you are entitled." . . . Ultimately, [some] long-suppressed evidence came to light. [The federal District Court, in habeas corpus proceedings, granted Banks relief from the death penalty, and we agree that he is entitled to relief.] When police or prosecutors conceal significant exculpatory or impeaching material in the State's possession, it is ordinarily incumbent on the State to set the record straight.

I.

On April 14, 1980, police found the corpse of 16-year-old Richard Whitehead in Pocket Park, east of Nash, Texas, a town in the vicinity of Texarkana. A preliminary autopsy revealed that Whitehead had been shot three times. Bowie County Deputy

Sheriff Willie Huff, lead investigator of the death, learned from two witnesses that Whitehead had been in the company of petitioner, 21-year-old Delma Banks, Jr., late on the evening of April 11. On April 23, Huff received a call from a confidential informant reporting that "Banks was coming to Dallas to meet an individual and get a weapon." That evening, Huff and other officers followed Banks to South Dallas, where Banks visited a residence. Police stopped Banks's vehicle en route from Dallas, found a handgun in the car, and arrested the car's occupants. Returning to the Dallas residence Banks had visited, Huff encountered and interviewed Charles Cook and recovered a second gun, a weapon Cook said Banks had left with him several days earlier. Tests later identified the second gun as the Whitehead murder weapon.

In a May 21, 1980, pretrial hearing, Banks's counsel sought information from Huff concerning the confidential informant who told Huff that Banks would be driving to Dallas. Huff was unresponsive. Any information that might reveal the identity of the informant, the prosecution urged, was privileged. The trial court sustained the State's objection. Several weeks later, in a July 7, 1980, letter, the prosecution advised Banks's counsel that "[the State] will, without necessity of motions provide you with all discovery to which you are entitled."

The guilt phase of Banks's trial spanned two days in September 1980. Witnesses testified to seeing Banks and Whitehead together on April 11 in Whitehead's green Mustang, and to hearing gunshots in Pocket Park at 4 A.M. on April 12. Charles Cook testified that Banks arrived in Dallas in a green Mustang at about 8:15 A.M. on April 12, and stayed with Cook until April 14. Cook gave the following account of Banks's visit. On the morning of his arrival, Banks had blood on his leg and told Cook "he [had] got into it on the highway with a white boy." That night, Banks confessed to having "killed the white boy for the hell of it and taken his car and come to Dallas." During their ensuing conversation, Cook first noticed that Banks had a pistol. Two days later, Banks left Dallas by bus. The next day, Cook abandoned the Mustang in West Dallas and sold Banks's gun to a neighbor. Cook further testified that, shortly before the police arrived at his residence to question him, Banks had revisited him and requested the gun. . . .

In addition to Cook, Robert Farr was a key witness for the prosecution. Corroborating parts of Cook's account, Farr testified to traveling to Dallas with Banks to retrieve Banks's gun. On cross-examination, defense counsel asked Farr whether he had "ever taken any money from some police officers," or "given any police officers a statement." Farr answered no to both questions; he asserted emphatically that police officers had not promised him anything and that he had "talked to no one about this case" until a few days before trial. These answers were untrue, but the State did not correct them. Farr was the paid informant who told Deputy Sheriff Huff that Banks would travel to Dallas in search of a gun. In a 1999 affidavit, Farr explained:

> I assumed that if I did not help Huff with his investigation of Delma that he would have me arrested for drug charges. That's why I agreed to help Huff. I was afraid that if I didn't help him, I would be arrested. . . . Willie Huff asked me to help him find Delma's gun. I told Huff that he would have to pay me money right away for my help on the case. I think altogether he gave me about $200 for helping him. He paid me some of the money before I set Delma up. He paid me the rest after Delma was arrested and charged with murder. . . . In order to help Willie Huff, I had to set Delma up. I told Delma that I wanted to rob a pharmacy to get drugs and that I needed

his gun to do it. I did not really plan to commit a robbery but I told Delma this so that he would give me his gun. . . . I convinced Delma to drive to Dallas with me to get the gun.

The defense presented no evidence. Banks was convicted of murder committed in the course of a robbery [and the] penalty phase ran its course the next day. . . . The critical question at the penalty phase in Banks's case was: "Do you find from the evidence beyond a reasonable doubt that there is a probability that the defendant, Delma Banks, Jr., would commit criminal acts of violence that would constitute a continuing threat to society?"

On this question, the State offered two witnesses, Vetrano Jefferson and Robert Farr. Jefferson testified that, in early April 1980, Banks had struck him across the face with a gun and threatened to kill him. Farr's testimony focused once more on the trip to Dallas to fetch Banks's gun. The gun was needed, Farr asserted, because "we [Farr and Banks] were going to pull some robberies." According to Farr, Banks "said he would take care of it" if "there was any trouble during these burglaries." When the prosecution asked: "How did [Banks] say he would take care of it?", Farr responded: "[Banks] didn't go into any specifics, but he said it would be taken care of."

On cross-examination, defense counsel twice asked whether Farr had told Deputy Sheriff Huff of the Dallas trip. The State remained silent as Farr twice perjuriously testified: "No, I did not." Banks's counsel also inquired whether Farr had previously attempted to obtain prescription drugs by fraud, and, "up tight over that," would "testify to anything anybody wanted to hear." Farr first responded: "Can you prove it?" Instructed by the court to answer defense counsel's questions, Farr again said: "No, I did not."

Two defense witnesses impeached Farr, but were, in turn, impeached themselves. James Kelley testified to Farr's attempts to obtain drugs by fraud; the prosecution impeached Kelley by eliciting his close relationship to Banks's girlfriend. Later, Kelley admitted to being drunk while on the stand. Former Arkansas police officer Gary Owen testified that Farr, as a police informant in Arkansas, had given false information; the prosecution impeached Owen by bringing out his pending application for employment by defense counsel's private investigator. . . .

Urging Farr's credibility, the prosecution called the jury's attention to Farr's admission, at trial, that he used narcotics. Just as Farr had been truthful about his drug use, the prosecution suggested, he was also "open and honest with [the jury] in every way" in his penalty-phase testimony. Farr's testimony, the prosecution emphasized, was "of the utmost significance" because it showed "[Banks] is a danger to friends and strangers, alike." Banks's effort to impeach Farr was ineffective, the prosecution further urged, because defense witness "Kelley knew nothing about the murder," and defense witness Owen "wished to please his future employers."

The jury answered yes to the . . . special issues, and the judge sentenced Banks to death. The Texas Court of Criminal Appeals denied Banks's direct appeal. [In a postconviction motion in state court,] Banks alleged "upon information and belief" that "the prosecution knowingly failed to turn over exculpatory evidence as required by Brady v. Maryland, 373 U.S. 83 (1963); the withheld evidence, Banks asserted, "would have revealed Robert Farr as a police informant and Mr. Banks' arrest as a set-up." . . . [In its reply, the State represented that] "Nothing was kept secret from the defense." [The state postconviction court rejected Banks's claims. Banks then filed for federal habeas corpus relief, and asserted again] that the State had withheld material exculpatory evidence "revealing Robert Farr as a police informant and Mr. Banks' arrest as a set-up." . . .

[In federal court, Banks produced] affidavits from both Farr and Cook to back up his claims that, as to each of these two key witnesses, the prosecution had wrongly withheld crucial exculpatory and impeaching evidence. Farr's affidavit affirmed that Farr had "set Delma up" by proposing the drive to Dallas and informing Deputy Sheriff Huff of the trip. Accounting for his unavailability earlier, Farr stated that less than a year after the Banks trial, he had left Texarkana, first for Oklahoma, then for California, because his police-informant work endangered his life. Cook recalled that in preparation for his Banks trial testimony, he had participated in "three or four . . . practice sessions" at which prosecutors told him to testify "as they wanted him to, and that he would spend the rest of his life in prison if he did not." . . .

One item lodged in the District Attorney's files, turned over to Banks pursuant to the Magistrate Judge's disclosure order, was a 74-page transcript of a Cook interrogation. . . . The transcript revealed that the State's representatives had closely rehearsed Cook's testimony. . . . Testifying at the evidentiary hearing, Deputy Sheriff Huff acknowledged, for the first time, that Farr was an informant and that he had been paid $200 for his involvement in the case.

[The District Court granted] a writ of habeas corpus with respect to Banks's death sentence, but not his conviction. [The Court of Appeals for the Fifth Circuit reversed. Even though the prosecution had suppressed Farr's informant status and his part in the fateful trip to Dallas, the court determined that Banks was not appropriately diligent in pursuing his state-court application.] Banks should have at that time attempted to locate Farr and question him; similarly, he should have asked to interview Deputy Sheriff Huff and other officers involved in investigating the crime. . . .

II.

A.

. . . We set out in Strickler v. Greene, 527 U.S. 263 (1999), the three components or essential elements of a *Brady* prosecutorial misconduct claim: "The evidence at issue must be favorable to the accused, either because it is exculpatory, or because it is impeaching; that evidence must have been suppressed by the State, either willfully or inadvertently; and prejudice must have ensued." . . . As to the first *Brady* component (evidence favorable to the accused), beyond genuine debate, the suppressed evidence relevant here, Farr's paid informant status, qualifies as evidence advantageous to Banks. . . .

B.

Our determination as to "cause" for Banks's failure to develop the facts in state-court proceedings is informed by *Strickler.* In that case, Virginia prosecutors told the petitioner, prior to trial, that "the prosecutor's files were open to the petitioner's counsel," thus "there was no need for a formal *Brady* motion." The prosecution file given to the *Strickler* petitioner, however, did not include several documents prepared by an "important" prosecution witness, recounting the witness' initial difficulty recalling the events to which she testified at the petitioner's trial. Those absent-from-the-file documents could have been used to impeach the witness. . . .

This Court determined that in the federal habeas proceedings, the *Strickler* petitioner had shown cause for his failure to raise a *Brady* claim in state court. Three factors accounted for that determination:

> (a) the prosecution withheld exculpatory evidence; (b) petitioner reasonably relied on the prosecution's open file policy as fulfilling the prosecution's duty to disclose such evidence; and (c) the [State] confirmed petitioner's reliance on the open file policy by asserting during state habeas proceedings that petitioner had already received everything known to the government.

This case is congruent with *Strickler* in all three respects. First, the State knew of, but kept back, Farr's arrangement with Deputy Sheriff Huff. Second, the State asserted, on the eve of trial, that it would disclose all *Brady* material. As *Strickler* instructs, Banks cannot be faulted for relying on that representation. Third, in his January 1992 state habeas application, Banks asserted that Farr was a police informant and Banks's arrest, "a set-up." In its answer, the State denied Banks's assertion. The State thereby "confirmed" Banks's reliance on the prosecution's representation that it had fully disclosed all relevant information its file contained. In short, because the State persisted in hiding Farr's informant status and misleadingly represented that it had complied in full with its *Brady* disclosure obligations, Banks had cause for failing to investigate, in state postconviction proceedings, Farr's connections to Deputy Sheriff Huff. . . .

Banks's case is stronger than was the petitioner's in *Strickler* in a notable respect. As a prosecution witness in the guilt and penalty phases of Banks's trial, Farr repeatedly misrepresented his dealings with police; each time Farr responded untruthfully, the prosecution allowed his testimony to stand uncorrected. . . . It has long been established that the prosecution's "deliberate deception of a court and jurors by the presentation of known false evidence is incompatible with rudimentary demands of justice." Giglio v. United States, 405 U.S. 150 (1972). If it was reasonable for Banks to rely on the prosecution's full disclosure representation, it was also appropriate for Banks to assume that his prosecutors would not stoop to improper litigation conduct to advance prospects for gaining a conviction. . . .

[A rule] declaring "prosecutor may hide, defendant must seek," is not tenable in a system constitutionally bound to accord defendants due process. Ordinarily, we presume that public officials have properly discharged their official duties. We have several times underscored the special role played by the American prosecutor in the search for truth in criminal trials. . . .

C.

. . . Kyles v. Whitley, 514 U.S. 419 (1995), instructed that the materiality standard for *Brady* claims is met when "the favorable evidence could reasonably be taken to put the whole case in such a different light as to undermine confidence in the verdict." A defendant need not demonstrate that after discounting the inculpatory evidence in light of the undisclosed evidence, there would not have been enough left to convict. In short, Banks must show a "reasonable probability of a different result."

As the State acknowledged at oral argument, Farr was "paid for a critical role in the scenario that led to the indictment." Farr's declaration, presented to the federal habeas court, asserts that Farr, not Banks, initiated the proposal to obtain a gun to facilitate the commission of robberies. Had Farr not instigated, upon Deputy Sheriff Huff's request, the Dallas excursion to fetch Banks's gun, the prosecution would have had slim, if any, evidence that Banks planned to "continue" committing violent acts. Farr's admission of his instigating role, moreover, would have dampened the prosecution's zeal in urging the jury to bear in mind Banks's "planning and acquisition of a gun to commit robbery," or Banks's "planned violence."

Because Banks had no criminal record, Farr's testimony about Banks's propensity to commit violent acts was crucial to the prosecution. . . . The prosecution's penalty-phase summation, moreover, left no doubt about the importance the State attached to Farr's testimony. What Farr told the jury, the prosecution urged, was "of the utmost significance" to show "[Banks] is a danger to friends and strangers, alike." . . .

Had jurors known of Farr's continuing interest in obtaining Deputy Sheriff Huff's favor, in addition to his receipt of funds to "set Banks up," they might well have distrusted Farr's testimony, and, insofar as it was uncorroborated, disregarded it. . . .

At least as to the penalty phase, in sum, one can hardly be confident that Banks received a fair trial, given the jury's ignorance of Farr's true role in the investigation and trial of the case. On the record before us, one could not plausibly deny the existence of the requisite "reasonable probability of a different result" had the suppressed information been disclosed to the defense. Accordingly, as to the suppression of Farr's informant status and its bearing on the reliability of the jury's verdict regarding punishment, all three elements of a *Brady* claim are satisfied.

[The Court also held that the State's failure to disclose a transcript showing extensive pre-trial preparation of a prosecution witness (Cook) created another potential ground for habeas corpus relief that the Fifth Circuit improperly refused to consider.]

THOMAS, J., dissenting.

. . . Although I find it to be a very close question, I cannot conclude that the nondisclosure of Farr's informant status was prejudicial under Kyles v. Whitley and *Brady.*

To demonstrate prejudice, Banks must show that the favorable evidence could reasonably be taken to put the whole case in such a different light as to undermine confidence in the verdict. The undisclosed material consisted of evidence that Willie Huff asked Farr to help him find Banks' gun," and that Huff gave Farr about $200 for helping him. . . . I do not believe that there is a reasonable probability that the jury [after hearing this evidence] would have altered its finding. The jury was presented with . . . evidence showing that Banks, apparently on a whim, executed Whitehead simply to get his car. The jury was also presented with evidence, in the form of Banks' own testimony, that he was willing to abet another individual in obtaining a gun, with the full knowledge that this gun would aid future armed robberies. . . . The jury also heard testimony that Banks had violently pistol-whipped and threatened to kill his brother-in-law one week before the murder. . . . Even if the jury were to discredit entirely Farr's testimony that Banks was planning more robberies, in all likelihood the jury still would have found "beyond a reasonable doubt" that there was "a probability that Banks would commit criminal acts of violence that would constitute a continuing threat to society." The randomness and wantonness of the murder would perhaps, standing alone, mandate such a finding. Accordingly, I cannot find that the nondisclosure of the evidence was prejudicial. . . .

■ HAWAII PENAL PROCEDURE RULE 16

(b) Disclosure by the Prosecution.

(1) Disclosure of Matters Within Prosecution's Possession. The prosecutor shall disclose to the defendant or the defendant's attorney the following material and information within the prosecutor's possession or control: . . . (vii) any material or information which tends to negate the guilt of the defendant as to the offense charged or would tend to reduce the defendant's punishment therefor.

(2) Disclosure of Matters Not Within Prosecution's Possession. Upon written request of defense counsel and specific designation by defense counsel of material or information which would be discoverable if in the possession or control of the prosecutor and which is in the possession or control of other governmental personnel, the prosecutor shall use diligent good faith efforts to cause such material or information to be made available to defense counsel; and if the prosecutor's efforts are unsuccessful the court shall issue suitable subpoenas or orders to cause such material or information to be made available to defense counsel. . . .

(d) Discretionary Disclosure. Upon a showing of materiality and if the request is reasonable, the court in its discretion may require disclosure as provided for in this Rule 16 in cases other than those in which the defendant is charged with a felony, but not in cases involving violations.

(e) Regulation of Discovery.

(1) Performance of Obligations. Except for matters which are to be specifically designated in writing by defense counsel under this rule, the prosecution shall disclose all materials subject to disclosure pursuant to subsection (b)(1) of this rule to the defendant or the defendant's attorney within ten calendar days following arraignment and plea of the defendant. The parties may perform their obligations of disclosure in any manner mutually agreeable to the parties or by notifying the attorney for the other party that material and information, described in general terms, may be inspected, obtained, tested, copied or photographed at specified reasonable times and places.

(2) Continuing Duty of Disclose. If subsequent to compliance with these rules or orders entered pursuant to these rules, a party discovers additional material or information which would have been subject to disclosure pursuant to this Rule 16, that party shall promptly disclose the additional material or information, and if the additional material or information is discovered during trial, the court shall be notified.

■ UTAH CRIMINAL PROCEDURE RULE 16

(a) Except as otherwise provided, the prosecutor shall disclose to the defense upon request the following material or information of which he has knowledge: . . . (4) evidence known to the prosecutor that tends to negate the guilt of the accused, mitigate the guilt of the defendant, or mitigate the degree of the offense for reduced punishment. . . .

(b) The prosecutor shall make all disclosures as soon as practicable following the filing of charges and before the defendant is required to plead. The prosecutor has a continuing duty to make disclosure.

Notes

1. *Evidence favorable to the accused: majority position.* The Supreme Court decision in Brady v. Maryland, 373 U.S. 83 (1963), remains central to discovery practice in American criminal justice. Because the disclosure duty described in *Brady* is a requirement of federal due process, it applies in every criminal case unless the defendant expressly waives the disclosure. As illustrated by the Hawaii and Utah rules reprinted above, over 40 states have passed rules or statutes codifying the *Brady* disclosure requirement, although many of these rules and statutes (unlike the constitutional requirement) only take effect after a request from the defense. See Ohio R. Crim. P. 16(A) (disclosure upon defendant's request).

Defendants often win *Brady* claims that are appealed in the state courts, at least when those claims are the focus of the appeal (as opposed to one in a laundry list of claims, especially in capital cases). See, e.g., State v. Higgins, 788 So. 2d 238 (Fla. 2001) (prosecutors failed to turn over a statement by a minor witness that a prosecution witness might herself have been seen driving the victim's vehicle). But *Brady* claims appear to be appealed infrequently, so the relative success of defendants in this context says little if anything about the nature of *Brady* claims and discovery practice in the mine run of cases.

2. *Exculpatory or impeachment evidence in government hands.* The defendant who seeks dismissal of charges because of a *Brady* violation need not show bad faith by the prosecutor. The prosecutor does not even have to know about the evidence that must be disclosed: Evidence in the hands of government agents (such as criminal investigators) who regularly report to the prosecutor can be the basis for a *Brady* violation because the prosecutor has a duty to inquire about such information. See Kyles v. Whitley, 514 U.S. 419 (1995); Commonwealth v. Burke, 781 A.2d 1136 (Pa. 2001) (obligation extends to exculpatory evidence in files of police agencies of the same government bringing the prosecution); Stanley Z. Fisher, The Prosecutor's Ethical Duty to Seek Exculpatory Evidence in Police Hands: Lessons from England, 68 Fordham L. Rev. 1379 (2000) (police in England must comply with specific legislation requiring record keeping and regular notification of prosecutors about exculpatory evidence; prosecutors and police in U.S. left to make their own arrangements for tracking exculpatory evidence).

Does "exculpatory" material only include evidence that could be admitted at trial? Must the prosecutor disclose under *Brady* facts suggesting that a search was illegal? Compare People v. Jones, 375 N.E.2d 41 (N.Y. 1978) (*Brady* does not require disclosure of fact that prosecution witness died).

3. *Materiality of exculpatory evidence.* The major limit on the *Brady* disclosure duty is the requirement that the undisclosed evidence be "material" to the defense. Under federal law, all *Brady* violations share a uniform materiality standard: The defendant must show a "reasonable probability" that the verdict would have been different if the prosecution had disclosed the exculpatory evidence. It does not affect the standard one way or the other if the defendant requests the disclosure.

State courts have split over the proper materiality standard. About 30 states have adopted the federal "uniform" standard, but a strong minority have granted defendants a more favorable materiality standard in cases where the defense makes specific requests for the information. People v. Vilardi, 555 N.E.2d 915 (N.Y. 1990); Roberts v. State, 881 P.2d 1 (Nev. 1994) (collecting cases). Does a specific request for discovery from the defense change the legitimate expectations of both parties? Note also that many state rules of criminal procedure (like the Utah rule reprinted above), include something similar to the *Brady* disclosure duty without including any materiality requirement; most of these rules, however, depend on a request from the defense.

4. Brady *and plea bargaining*. While *Brady* information might affect the outcome at trial, it could also affect the negotiating strength of the defendant during plea bargaining. Given the dominance of guilty pleas and plea bargaining in American criminal justice, it is critical to know whether a defendant can challenge the validity of a guilty plea if she discovers later that the prosecutor failed to disclose *Brady* material. A few states have statutes or rules that explicitly link the prosecutor's disclosure obligation to a defendant's not-guilty plea at arraignment. See N.H. Super. Ct. R. 98 (prosecutor to disclose exculpatory material within 30 days from a not-guilty plea). The U.S. Supreme Court addressed one aspect of this question in United States v. Ruiz, 536 U.S. 622 (2002), stating that "the Constitution does not require the Government to disclose material impeachment evidence prior to entering a plea agreement with a criminal defendant." Ruiz was challenging a provision in a proposed plea agreement that required her to waive certain *Brady* rights as part of the arrangement, but the Court's statement appears broad enough to cover guilty pleas reached without any explicit waiver of *Brady* rights in a plea agreement. Note that the ruling extends to impeachment material but not to exculpatory material.

State courts are split over whether *Brady* violations by the prosecution invalidate a defendant's guilty plea. See Gibson v. State, 514 S.E.2d 320, 324 (S.C. 1999) (*Brady* violation automatically renders plea invalid); State v. Harris, 680 N.W.2d 737, 741 (Wis. 2004) (imposes disclosure at guilty plea stage as matter of state law); State v. Martin, 495 A.2d 1028 (Conn. 1985) (*Brady* claim barred by guilty plea). See generally Corinna Barrett Lain, Accuracy Where It Matters: Brady v. Maryland in the Plea Bargaining Context, 80 Wash. U. L.Q. 1 (2002); Kevin C. McMunigal, Disclosure and Accuracy in the Guilty Plea Process, 40 Hastings L.J. 957 (1989).

5. *Preservation of evidence*. It is often said that the duty to disclose evidence would be meaningless if the prosecutor were free to destroy evidence. Is this true? The Supreme Court has addressed the government's obligation, under the due process clause, to preserve some types of evidence. In California v. Trombetta, 467 U.S. 479 (1984), two defendants accused of drunken driving submitted to breath analysis tests, and the tests showed a blood-alcohol concentration high enough to presume intoxication. Each defendant tried to suppress the test results because the police (who were following their standard procedure) failed to preserve the breath samples. The Supreme Court rejected the defendants' arguments because the police discarded the samples "in good faith and in accord with normal practice." The *Trombetta* court also observed that the chances were slim that the defendants could have exposed inaccuracies in the breath analysis test, and a state's constitutional duty to preserve evidence can be applied

only to "evidence that might be expected to play a significant role in the suspect's case."

In Arizona v. Youngblood, 488 U.S. 51 (1988), the police failed to preserve semen samples from the victim's body and clothing. The defendant, accused of child molestation and sexual assault, argued that he could have performed tests on the samples that might have established his defense of mistaken identity. However, the Supreme Court noted that the state did not attempt to use the materials in its own case in chief, and it limited the government's duty to preserve evidence as follows:

> [R]equiring a defendant to show bad faith on the part of the police both limits the extent of the police's obligation to preserve evidence to reasonable bounds and confines it to that class of cases where the interests of justice most clearly require it, i.e., those cases in which the police themselves by their conduct indicate that the evidence could form a basis for exonerating the defendant. We therefore hold that unless a criminal defendant can show bad faith on the part of the police, failure to preserve potentially useful evidence does not constitute a denial of due process of law.

Years later, Youngblood was found to be innocent on the basis of other DNA evidence, and was released two days before completing his original sentence. See also Illinois v. Fisher, 540 U.S. 544 (2004) (distinguishing between exculpatory information and information that is merely useful to the defense; exculpatory information must be turned over the defense even without any showing of bad faith).

Once again, there is dissension among state courts on an important aspect of this discovery issue. Most states directly addressing the question have accepted the holding in *Youngblood*. About a dozen states, however, have declared that bad faith is not a necessary part of the defendant's showing because the destruction of evidence often reflects some negligence by the government and because the evidence could sometimes be crucial to the defense. In State v. Morales, 657 A.2d 585 (Conn. 1995), the court held that a trial judge, in determining what consequences should flow from the government's breach of its duty, should consider (1) the degree of negligence or bad faith involved, (2) the importance of the missing evidence in light of the remaining evidence, and (3) the sufficiency of the other evidence to sustain the conviction. See also State v. Ferguson, 2 S.W.3d 912 (Tenn. 1999). Why do state courts seem so willing to part ways with the Supreme Court on constitutional questions involving discovery? Do the state courts take more responsibility for their own litigation management, in light of the state's needs and practices?

The preservation of evidence has made a critical difference in more cases lately as DNA testing procedures become available. These tests make it possible to reevaluate the convictions of some defendants in cases (such as rape and murder cases) where blood or other biological material from the perpetrator is available at the crime scene or from the victim. The incentive to test this material and to match it to the convicted defendant is very strong in capital cases, and a few capital defendants have been released on the basis of DNA test information.

6. *Disclosing false testimony.* Over the years, the U.S. Supreme Court has said that prosecutors must correct any false testimony presented by prosecution witnesses at trial. See Alcorta v. Texas, 355 U.S. 28 (1957). This can include false statements about any lenient treatment the witness expects to receive from the government as a result of cooperating as a witness. See Giglio v. United States, 405 U.S. 150 (1972) (reversal required when witness denied any arrangement for lenient treatment;

promise came from another prosecutor, unknown to government attorney at trial). The test for materiality under *Giglio* is whether there is a "reasonable probability" that the false evidence may have affected the judgment of the jury. Even if the prosecution does not lie on the witness stand about any promise of leniency, the existence of such deals with witnesses typically qualifies as *Brady* material. See State v. Bowie, 813 So. 2d 377 (La. 2002).

7. *The extent of disclosure violations.* How often do prosecutors and defense attorneys fail to disclose the information that they should to the opposing party? Periodic newspaper reports on "prosecutorial misconduct" focus on discovery violations; they suggest (inconclusively) that discovery violations by prosecutors occur regularly. The *Chicago Tribune* conducted an ambitious analysis of nationwide court records in 1999. It found records of 381 reversals of homicide cases since 1963, due to prosecutors concealing exculpatory evidence or using false evidence at trial. While this was an extremely small percentage of the homicide convictions during this time, the report notes that such violations are difficult to document and rarely lead to reversals of a conviction. See Ken Armstrong & Maurice Possley, "The Verdict: Dishonor," Chicago Tribune, Jan. 8, 1999; see also Cris Carmody, The *Brady* Rule: Is It Working? Nat'l L.J., May 17, 1993, at 30.

Prosecutors' offices sometimes evaluate the performance of their own attorneys and create systems to sanction wrongdoers and to train less experienced attorneys to avoid discovery violations. One such mechanism is the Office for Professional Responsibility (OPR) within the U.S. Department of Justice.

How would you measure in a reliable way whether prosecutors are now committing more discovery violations than in the past? If such a trend were proven, could it be traced to the number of new prosecutors hired in a given time period?

8. *Remedies for prosecutorial disclosure violations.* As we have seen, courts might reverse criminal convictions if the prosecutor fails to disclose material information when required by law. Will the state bar authorities also sanction prosecutors who violate their legal obligations to disclose information, even when the evidence is not material? Examples of disciplinary proceedings against prosecutors for discovery violations do get reported from time to time. See Disciplinary Counsel v. Jones, 613 N.E. 2d 178 (Ohio 1993) (prosecutor's failure to turn over two exhibits tending to establish defendant's self-defense argument resulted in prosecutor's suspension from practice for six months). However, state bar authorities discipline criminal prosecutors far less often than they discipline private attorneys. One survey of state bar records revealed that criminal attorneys (both prosecutors and defense attorneys) are sanctioned far less often than attorneys in civil practice, and that discipline rarely occurs after a "first offense." See Fred C. Zacharias, The Professional Discipline of Prosecutors, 79 N.C. L. Rev. 721 (2001). What might explain the relatively infrequent disciplinary actions against criminal prosecutors?

Problem 5-2. Preserving Evidence

Kanju Osakalumi and several other residents of New York City traveled to the home of Allison Charlton in Bluefield, West Virginia, bringing with them an assortment of drugs and firearms. On the afternoon of June 14, one of the persons from New York City, Chandel Fleetwood, died from a single gunshot wound to the head, fired from his own revolver. Osakalumi and others who were present took the body to a wooded area approximately one mile away. They also disposed of the victim's revolver and a bloodied cushion from the couch where the victim had been sitting. The following day, Osakalumi and his friends returned to New York City.

Officers from the Bluefield Police Department soon began hearing rumors that someone had been shot at the Charlton home. About seven months after Fleetwood's death, two detectives visited the home. Upon observing a stained couch, the detectives took samples from it and from the carpet surrounding it. Approximately two months later, police officers returned to the Charlton home, and inspected the couch again. This time, they discovered a bullet hole in it. Detective Ted Jones inserted a writing pen into the bullet hole to determine the trajectory of the bullet. He extracted a badly deformed bullet as well as some hair and bone fragments. The officers confiscated the couch and stored it at the police department.

The couch gave off an unpleasant odor and was both a fire and health hazard. As a result, the police (with the consent of the prosecutor's office) soon disposed of the couch at the county landfill. The police did not measure either the proportions of the couch, the location of the bullet hole in the couch, or the trajectory of the bullet. Neither did they photograph the couch or the bullet hole.

Two years after Fleetwood's death, a passerby discovered his skeletal remains in the woods. After the Bluefield police completed their investigation, Osakalumi was arrested in New York. He claimed that Fleetwood was under the influence of marijuana when he loaded one round of ammunition into his own revolver, spun the cylinder, put it to his own head and shot himself. Osakalumi said that he and the others in the house panicked and disposed of the body and the revolver in a nearby wooded area.

The only evidence that Fleetwood had been murdered was the trial testimony of Dr. Irvin Sopher, medical examiner for the state of West Virginia. Dr. Sopher testified that approximately 9 months after Fleetwood's death (but approximately 14 months before his body was found), Detective Ted Jones delivered to him the bullet, blood samples, and bone fragments. In addition, Detective Jones drew for Dr. Sopher a diagram of the couch, along with the location of the bullet hole and the position of the bullet when officers found it.

Although Jones's diagram of the couch was lost, Dr. Sopher drew Detective Jones's couch diagram from memory at trial. Dr. Sopher testified that based upon examination of the skull and the purported right-to-left, straight-line trajectory of the bullet through the couch, the manner of Fleetwood's death was homicide. Dr. Sopher testified that he came to this conclusion when he lined up the trajectory of the bullet through the skull with the right-to-left path of the bullet through the couch, as drawn by Detective Jones. Dr. Sopher determined that Fleetwood was held down on the couch and was shot through the head, with the bullet traveling in a straight line.

The jury convicted Osakalumi of first-degree murder. On appeal he claims that the trial court erred when it allowed Dr. Sopher to testify based on the condition of the couch. As the appellate court judge, how do you rule? Compare State v. Osakalumi, 461 S.E.2d 504 (W. Va. 1995).

2. Defense Disclosures

The trend over the past several decades has been toward broader criminal discovery rights for both the defense and the prosecution. The most potent arguments against expanding discovery at each juncture have pointed to some necessary limits on defense disclosures. There may be constitutional difficulties in forcing a defendant to disclose certain information to the prosecution. Among other things, forced disclosure might be considered self-incrimination in violation of the constitutional privilege. Faced with this sort of barrier, prosecutors have resisted the general expansion of criminal discovery on the basis of litigation fairness. If the defendant does not have to disclose evidence, prosecutors argue, then neither should they.

In the end, the arguments for limiting criminal discovery have lost more often than they have won — in part because the constitutional problems with compelling the defendant to disclose evidence have turned out to be surprisingly small. Where the Constitution has created no barrier, both defense and prosecution disclosures have increased.

If the Constitution will stop only a few types of defense disclosures, what are other possible grounds for evaluating discovery innovations? Are there some types of information that the prosecution will not develop if the defendant does not provide it? What, if anything, do we gain from a truly adversarial system of developing and presenting evidence?

■ PENNSYLVANIA RULE OF CRIMINAL PROCEDURE 573(C)

(1) In all court cases, if the Commonwealth files a motion for pretrial discovery, upon a showing of materiality to the preparation of the Commonwealth's case and that the request is reasonable, the court may order the defendant, subject to the defendant's rights against compulsory self-incrimination, to allow the attorney for the Commonwealth to inspect and copy or photograph any of the following requested items:

(a) results or reports of physical or mental examinations, and of scientific tests or experiments made in connection with the particular case, or copies thereof, within the possession or control of the defendant, that the defendant intends to introduce as evidence in chief, or were prepared by a witness whom the defendant intends to call at the trial, when results or reports relate to the testimony of that witness, provided the defendant has requested and received discovery under paragraph (B)(1)(e); and

(b) the names and addresses of eyewitnesses whom the defendant intends to call in its case-in-chief, provided that the defendant has previously requested and received discovery under paragraph (B)(2)(a)(i).

(2) If an expert whom the defendant intends to call in any proceeding has not prepared a report of examination or tests, the court, upon motion, may order that the expert prepare and the defendant disclose a report stating the subject matter on which the expert is expected to testify; the substance of the facts to which the expert is expected to testify; and a summary of the expert's opinions and the grounds for each opinion.

■ PENNSYLVANIA RULE OF CRIMINAL PROCEDURE 567(A)

A defendant who intends to offer the defense of alibi at trial shall file with the clerk of courts not later than the time required for filing the omnibus pretrial motion provided in Rule 579 a notice specifying an intention to offer an alibi defense, and shall serve a copy of the notice and a certificate of service on the attorney for the Commonwealth.

(1) The notice and a certificate of service shall be signed by the attorney for the defendant, or the defendant if unrepresented.

(2) The notice shall contain specific information as to the place or places where the defendant claims to have been at the time of the alleged offense and the names and addresses of the witnesses whom the defendant intends to call in support of the claim.

■ STATE v. JOHN LUCIOUS
518 S.E.2d 677 (Ga. 1999)

HUNSTEIN, J.

The State is seeking imposition of the death penalty against John R. Lucious for the murder of Mohammad A. Aftab in Clayton County. Lucious was indicted on charges of malice murder, two counts of felony murder, possession of a firearm during the commission of a felony, and misdemeanor possession of marijuana in connection with the alleged 1996 murder and armed robbery. During pretrial proceedings, the State refused to open its file except to the extent mandated by the Georgia and United States Constitutions because Lucious elected not to participate in Georgia's Criminal Procedure Discovery Act, OCGA §17-16-1 et seq. Lucious filed an omnibus motion seeking an order of the trial court declaring the Act unconstitutional. The trial court denied the motion but granted Lucious the unilateral right to discover specific material, including the State's trial witness list, scientific reports, and scientific work product. [The] State filed an application to appeal asserting that Lucious was not entitled to the pretrial discovery information granted by the trial court because of his election not to participate in the Act.

Prior to passage of the Act, there was no comprehensive Georgia statute or rule of law which governed discovery in criminal cases. Enacted in 1994, the Act [provides] for the "comprehensive regulation of discovery and inspection in criminal cases [and repeals] conflicting laws." . . . Ga. L. 1994, pp.1895-1896. The Act, which applies only to those cases in which the defendant elects by written notice to have it apply, broadens discovery in felony cases by imposing corresponding discovery obligations upon both the defendant and the State. For example, the Act requires the State and the defendant to disclose, inter alia, the identities and addresses of all persons they intend to call as witnesses at trial, relevant written or recorded statements of all witnesses, and scientific reports, physical or mental reports, and other evidence intended for use at trial or evidence obtained from or that belongs to the defendant regardless of whether the State intends to use such evidence at trial. The Act also [provides] for discovery of a custodial statement and [requires] notice of an intent to offer an alibi defense and a list of witnesses to be offered to rebut the defense of alibi. These provisions reveal that the Act provides a comprehensive scheme of reciprocal discovery in criminal felony cases. . . .

Lucious contends the Act's discovery provisions violate his right to due process under the United States and Georgia Constitutions. We disagree. In Wardius v. Oregon, 412 U.S. 470 (1973), the Supreme Court held that under the due process clause a defendant cannot be compelled to disclose to the State evidence or witnesses to be offered in support of an alibi defense absent reciprocal discovery of the State's rebuttal witnesses. The Wardius Court reviewed its earlier decision in

Williams v. Florida, 399 U.S. 78 (1970), which upheld Florida's notice-of-alibi statute because such statute provided reciprocal discovery, and stated:

> [a]lthough the Due Process Clause has little to say regarding the amount of discovery which the parties must be afforded, it does speak to the balance of forces between the accused and his accuser. The Williams Court was therefore careful to note that "Florida law provides for liberal discovery by the defendant against the State, and [Florida's] notice-of-alibi rule is itself carefully hedged with reciprocal duties requiring state disclosure to the defendant." . . . We do not suggest that the Due Process Clause of its own force requires [a state] to adopt [reciprocal discovery] provisions. But we do hold that in the absence of a strong showing of state interests to the contrary, discovery must be a two-way street. [412 U.S. at 474-475.]

The Court in *Wardius* thus articulated a due process requirement of reciprocity in criminal discovery statutes in the absence of a strong state interest to the contrary. This same requirement has been held to apply under the due process clause of the Georgia Constitution. See Rower v. State, 443 S.E.2d 839 (Ga. 1994) (to satisfy due process, discovery practices in criminal cases must provide a balance of forces between the defendant and the State). Applying this due process standard to the Act, we find that the Act furthers legitimate State interests by establishing a closely symmetrical scheme of discovery in criminal cases that maximizes the presentation of reliable evidence, minimizes the risk that a judgment will be predicated on incomplete or misleading evidence, and fosters fairness and efficiency in criminal proceedings. Because the Act provides for reciprocal discovery in criminal felony cases with any imbalance favoring the defendant, the Act does not violate the due process clause of the United States or Georgia Constitutions.

Nor do the Act's discovery provisions violate Lucious's right to confrontation. The right to confrontation is a "trial right," guaranteeing a defendant the ability to confront and question adverse witnesses at trial. See Pennsylvania v. Ritchie, 480 U.S. 39, 52-53 (1987). As a trial right, it "does not include the power to require the pretrial disclosure of any and all information that might be useful in contradicting unfavorable testimony," id. at 53, and does not guarantee "cross-examination that is effective in whatever way, and to whatever extent, the defense might wish." Delaware v. Fensterer, 474 U.S. 15, 20 (1985). Because the confrontation clause guarantees only the right to confront and cross-examine those individuals called to testify against a defendant at trial and the pretrial discovery provisions of the Act do not implicate or infringe upon such right, we find no merit to this argument.

[Lucious argues further] that the Act's reciprocal discovery provisions violate his right to effective representation of counsel by denying him the benefit of defense counsel's judgment of whether and when to reveal aspects of his case to the State. The Act simply requires disclosure of witnesses and evidence a defendant intends to introduce at trial as part of a reciprocal discovery process. The United States Supreme Court has affirmed the right of states to experiment with systems of broad discovery designed to aid in the administration of justice and to enhance the fairness of the adversary system. That the Act provides for discovery before trial rather than after a witness has testified is of no constitutional significance. See United States v. Nobles, 422 U.S. 225, 241 (1975) ("[t]he Sixth Amendment does not confer the right to present testimony free from the legitimate demands of the adversarial system").

Because there is no general constitutional right to discovery in a criminal case, the election not to invoke the discovery provisions of the Act necessarily entitles a defendant to only that discovery specifically afforded by the Georgia and United States Constitutions, statutory exceptions to the Act, and non-conflicting rules of court. This panoply of discovery rights exists separately from the Act and provides abundant discovery opportunities for all criminal defendants, including death penalty defendants, who elect not to have the Act apply to their case. We therefore find that the trial court erred in granting Lucious those discovery rights identified below which are not guaranteed under the United States or Georgia Constitutions or otherwise provided for by statute or court rule.

Specifically, the trial court erred by holding that a defendant who chooses not to participate in the Act is entitled to discover all of the State's scientific reports. In a broadly-worded order the trial court directed the State to produce its Georgia Bureau of Investigation "Crime Lab reports and any and all other scientific reports." A defendant's right to discover scientific reports is a procedural right derived from former OCGA §17-7-211, a statute expressly repealed by passage of the Act. Procedural rights which flow from a repealed criminal discovery statute can be eliminated. In order to obtain discovery of scientific reports, therefore, a defendant must elect to proceed under the provisions of the Act.

For the same reasons, we find the trial court erred in holding that a defendant who chooses not to opt into the Act is entitled to discover all of the State's scientific work product. The trial court's order provides that the State must produce "any and all . . . memos, notes, graphs, computer print-outs, photographs, and other data that the State's experts will rely on to support their testimony during direct examination." To the extent such information may be discoverable in felony criminal cases, its production is now governed by the Act and a defendant is entitled to this information only if he invokes the Act. Because the right to subpoena work product was derived from former OCGA §17-7-211 and is not a substantive right apart from the discovery provisions of the Act, [defendants may not] unilaterally obtain evidence of scientific work product.

The trial court also erred in holding that Lucious was entitled to the witness list provided by Uniform Superior Court Rule 30.3. Rule 30.3 provides that upon request of defense counsel, the State shall furnish the addresses and telephone numbers of trial witnesses known to the State. The Legislature intended, in enacting the Act, to amend the criminal discovery procedures and to provide certain criminal defendants the opportunity to discover information well in excess of that mandated by either the United States or Georgia Constitutions, including the opportunity to receive from the State a continuing list of trial witnesses and related information. Under the Act, a defendant is entitled to a trial witness list and information concerning trial witnesses only if he chooses to have the Act apply, thereby agreeing to the reciprocal discovery provisions of the Act. Because Rule 30.3 conflicts with OCGA §§17-16-3 and 17-16-8 in that it requires the State to furnish a trial witness list without imposing reciprocal discovery obligations upon the defendant, we find the Rule to be unenforceable. Rule 30.3 must yield to the substantive law contained in these statutes.

Although Lucious did not choose to have the Act apply to his case and, therefore, is not entitled to a list of trial witnesses pursuant to Rule 30.3, Lucious remains entitled to a list of witnesses who appeared before the grand jury and upon whose testimony the charges against him are founded. See Ga. Const., Art. I, Sec. I, Par. XIV; Evans v. State, 150 S.E.2d 240 (Ga. 1966).

Finally, we find the Act is inapplicable to presentence hearings. Discovery in presentence hearings in both capital or non-capital cases remains governed by OCGA §17-10-2, which was not among the various discovery statutes related to felony cases specifically repealed or amended by the enactment of the Act.

FLETCHER, P.J., concurring in part and dissenting in part.

Because the majority opinion interprets the discovery act as repealing by implication the defendant's right to the state's trial witness lists, scientific reports, and scientific work product, I dissent [from that portion of the opinion].

The majority construes too narrowly the constitutional requirement that the defendant shall be furnished "a list of witnesses on whose testimony such charge is founded." In Sutton v. State, 228 S.E.2d 820 (Ga. 1976), we held that the constitutional right to be furnished a list of witnesses "is the right, on demand, to be furnished by the district attorney's office, prior to arraignment, with the list of witnesses who will testify for the state on the trial."

As a matter of due process and fundamental fairness, I would continue to interpret the constitutional provision as requiring the state to provide a list of its trial witnesses despite the repeal of the statute. The requirement enables the defendant to prepare a defense by interviewing potential trial witnesses; it aids judicial economy by requiring defense counsel to investigate and interview the witnesses before trial, thus avoiding the need for a continuance; and it places no undue burden on the prosecutor, as shown by the attorney general office's practice of furnishing a list of potential trial witnesses in all criminal cases.

Even in the absence of a constitutional right, the better policy and practice is for prosecutors to furnish a list of potential trial witnesses to avoid unfair surprise and make trials more efficient. The discovery act repealed former OCGA §17-7-110, which required disclosure of witness lists and the indictment, but reenacted that provision to apply in misdemeanor cases. Because persons charged with less serious offenses are entitled to the names of trial witnesses, persons charged with felonies should receive the same information from the state.

The due process clause of the United States Constitution guarantees a defendant the right to an independent examination of critical evidence. Depending on the case, this right may include the state's scientific reports and data on which its experts will rely at trial. Despite the majority's unsupported assertion, the repeal of OCGA §17-7-211 cannot eliminate the defendant's due process right to scientific reports and work product when they are critical evidence. Any doubts about the importance of the evidence should weigh in favor of disclosure towards the defendant.

Both the Georgia Attorney General and the Georgia Association of Criminal Defense Lawyers agree that a defendant preparing for trial is entitled to a significant amount of information under the United States Constitution and the Georgia Constitution, statutes, court rules, and court decisions. Specifically, they agree that a defendant is entitled to the following:

1. Exculpatory material as set forth in Brady v. Maryland, 373 U.S. 83 (1963).
2. Evidence of an understanding, agreement, or promise of leniency under Giglio v. United States, 405 U.S. 150 (1972), and Patillo v. State, 368 S.E.2d 493 (Ga. 1988).

3. Evidence in aggravation that the state intends to rely on at presentence hearings and victim impact evidence under OCGA §17-10-1.2 and Livingston v. State, 444 S.E.2d 748 (Ga. 1994).

4. Independent examination of critical evidence under the due process clause of the United States Constitution.

5. Materials used by a witness to refresh memory as set forth in Sterling v. State, 477 S.E.2d 807 (Ga. 1996), and Johnson v. State, 383 S.E.2d 118 (Ga. 1989).

6. Notice of state's intent to introduce evidence of similar transactions that do not involve prior difficulties between the defendant and victim under Uniform Superior Court Rule 31.3 and Wall v. State, 500 S.E.2d 904 (Ga. 1998).

7. Certain information from the Georgia Crime Information Center under OCGA §35-3-34.

8. Notice of the state's intention to rebut evidence of specific acts of violence by the victim against third persons under Chandler v. State, 405 S.E.2d 669 (Ga. 1991), and Uniform Superior Court Rule 31.6.

9. Pre-trial examination of known handwriting samples under OCGA §24-7-7.

10. Disclosure of the name of an informant in certain circumstances under Roviaro v. United States, 353 U.S. 53 (1957), and Wilson v. State, 433 S.E.2d 703 (Ga. App. 1993).

11. Examination of any report prepared under OCGA §17-4-20.1 about an act of family violence for which the defendant has been arrested.

12. Presentation of evidence at a court proceeding by way of a notice to produce, if the matter would be admissible and the defendant needs it for use as evidence on his own behalf.

13. Access to records under the Open Records Act, OCGA §50-18-70.

These rights remain available despite a defendant's decision not to have the criminal discovery statute apply. . . .

Notes

1. *Reciprocal discovery: majority position.* The trend in American jurisdictions is toward increasingly reciprocal discovery. These statutes usually survive constitutional challenges. See State v. Brown, 940 P.2d 546 (Wash. 1997). However, the full "two-way street" form of discovery is more rare. Some courts have struck down the most ambitious efforts to create reciprocal discovery, particularly those requiring the defendant to reveal information about potential witnesses that she does *not* plan to call at trial. See Binegar v. District Court, 915 P.2d 889 (Nev. 1996). The Georgia decision in *Lucious* is typical in focusing on whether the material that the defense must disclose under the statute would be disclosed later at trial. See also Izazaga v. Superior Court, 815 P.2d 304 (Cal. 1991) (upholding California's redrafted discovery provisions). The most common constitutional objections are based on the self-incrimination privilege, the right to cross-examination, the right to effective assistance of counsel, and due process. See Robert P. Mosteller, Discovery Against the Defense: Tilting the Adversarial Balance, 74 Cal. L. Rev. 1569 (1986).

Discovery rules in most state regulate specialized defenses such as alibis, self-defense, or insanity. The Supreme Court has upheld the constitutionality of such statutes in Williams v. Florida, 399 U.S. 78 (1970). The defenses must be reciprocal: The Supreme Court has struck down a statute that required the defense to provide notice of an alibi defense without requiring the prosecution to disclose its alibi-rebuttal witnesses. Wardius v. Oregon, 412 U.S. 470 (1973). Why are alibi, self-defense, and insanity the three types of defense evidence that appear most often in the statutes and rules regarding disclosure? At least two of these defenses (alibi and insanity) require the development of evidence unrelated to the events of the alleged crime. But why should the government obtain special notice about self-defense? And once the government knows that a defendant plans to pursue an insanity defense, why should the government have access to defense experts? Can't the prosecution hire its own experts?

2. *Consensual discovery.* Statutes in many states finesse the constitutional questions involved in compelling defendant disclosures by giving the defendant the choice of opting out of extensive discovery. Only if the defendant obtains full discovery rights against the government must she also comply with the disclosure duties. Note that the *Lucious* court mentioned the consent feature of the Georgia statute. Does a defendant "waive" objections to disclosure in the same sense that he or she can "waive" the right to trial or to an appointed attorney? Does consensual discovery protect a true adversarial option?

3. *Work-product doctrine in criminal cases.* Recall that discovery rules usually include a privilege, developed at common law, for the "work product" of attorneys and their agents. The privilege limits the disclosures of both defense and prosecution. The U.S. Supreme Court recognized the work-product doctrine in Hickman v. Taylor, 329 U.S. 495 (1947), establishing a qualified privilege for certain materials prepared by an attorney in anticipation of litigation. The Court explained the decision as follows:

> Historically, a lawyer is an officer of the court and is bound to work for the advancement of justice while faithfully protecting the rightful interests of his clients. In performing his various duties, however, it is essential that a lawyer work with a certain degree of privacy, free from unnecessary intrusion by opposing parties and their counsel. Proper preparation of a client's case demands that he assemble information, sift what he considers to be the relevant from the irrelevant facts, prepare his legal theories and plan his strategy without undue and needless interference. . . . This work is reflected, of course, in interviews, statements, memoranda, correspondence, briefs, mental impressions, personal beliefs, and countless other tangible and intangible ways — aptly though roughly termed . . . as the [w]ork product of the lawyer. Were such materials open to opposing counsel on mere demand, much of what is now put down in writing would remain unwritten. An attorney's thoughts, heretofore inviolate, would not be his own. Inefficiency, unfairness and sharp practices would inevitably develop in the giving of legal advice and in the preparation of cases for trial. The effect on the legal profession would be demoralizing. And the interests of the clients and the cause of justice would be poorly served.

329 U.S. at 510-11. There are two levels of "work-product" protections. An "absolute" privilege attaches to any mental impressions, conclusions, opinions or legal theories of an attorney; that is, any document containing such material must be redacted to remove it before disclosure to another party. On the other hand, a "qualified" privilege attaches to other materials created "in anticipation of litigation." An opposing party can obtain this material if there is a strong enough reason for the disclosure.

See State v. Chagnon, 662 A.2d 944 (N.H. 1995) (rejects traditional civil requirements of "substantial need" and "unavailability from other sources" as prerequisites for obtaining qualified work-product material; in criminal litigation, work product subject only to discretion of trial court). Is a state that has embraced broad defense disclosures likely to weaken the work-product doctrine? Is the work-product privilege based on a view of an independent and adversarial development of information that is incompatible with extensive discovery?

4. *Remedies for defense discovery violations.* When the defense attorney violates discovery obligations, what price should the client pay? It is possible for a trial judge to prevent the defendant from using a witness if the defense lawyer fails to disclose the required information about that witness to the prosecution. See Taylor v. Illinois, 484 U.S. 400 (1988) (defense counsel deliberately withheld name of witness from prosecutor; trial court may preclude that witness from testifying); Coleman v. State, 749 So. 2d 1003 (Miss. 1999) (exclusion of alibi witness was appropriate sanction for delay in notifying prosecution and failure to disclose address of witness). Should sanctions for these violations be left instead to disciplinary proceedings brought against the attorney?

5. *Effective advocacy and reciprocal discovery.* Which of the following sorts of information would an advocate most want to withhold from the other party before trial: information about fact witnesses, expert witnesses, or documents? Do the discovery rules in criminal cases provide the most protection to information that requires the most effort to develop? Or do they protect the information that will have the most impact at trial? Or is the objective instead to require disclosure of information precisely *because* it is likely to have an impact at trial or *because* it is difficult to develop? Discovery rules that restrict independent development of evidence to peripheral issues make a profound statement about the adversary system. For instance, in Germany, the judge and the defense attorney have full access to the prosecution file, but the defense has no corresponding duty to disclose its information to the court or the prosecution. Do our discovery rules now declare that an adversarial development of evidence is more likely to obscure truth than to further it? As you evaluate the rules of criminal discovery, try to anticipate how lawyers in the adversarial tradition will react to rules that attempt to shift that tradition toward reciprocal discovery.

3. Discovery Ethics

During discovery, defense attorneys could face one of the classic puzzles of legal ethics. If a client gives her lawyer incriminating physical evidence, what are the lawyer's obligations? Do the obligations change if the material comes from a third party? If the client or a third party tells the lawyer about the location of such material? Finally, does defense counsel have an affirmative ethical obligation to seek out incriminating evidence?

Problem 5-3. Defense Attorney as Repository

Michael Hitch was indicted for first-degree murder and is currently awaiting trial on that charge. In the course of their investigation, the police interviewed

Hitch's girlfriend, Diane Heaton, who told them that the victim was wearing a certain wristwatch shortly before his death. Later, an investigator for the Public Defender's Office contacted Ms. Heaton, and she informed the investigator that she had found a wristwatch in Hitch's suit jacket. She also stated that she did not want to turn the evidence over to the police. The investigator contacted the defendant's attorney, who told him to bring the watch to the attorney's office. The attorney indicated that he did this for two reasons. First, he wanted to examine the watch to determine whether it was the same one that Ms. Heaton had described to the police. Second, he was afraid that she might destroy or conceal the evidence. Shortly thereafter, Hitch informed the police that he had taken a watch from the victim. The police were, however, unaware of the location of that watch.

The defense attorney filed a petition with the Ethics Committee of the State Bar, requesting an opinion concerning his duties with respect to the wristwatch. You are a practicing attorney in the state and serve as a volunteer member of the Ethics Committee. After reviewing the California and North Carolina ethics opinions reprinted below, what guidance would you give to Hitch's attorney? If the attorney ignores the guidance from the committee, does that constitute grounds for discipline against him? Cf. Hitch v. Pima County Superior Court, 708 P.2d 72 (Ariz. 1985).

■ STANDING COMMITTEE ON PROFESSIONAL RESPONSIBILITY AND CONDUCT, STATE BAR OF CALIFORNIA, CALIFORNIA FORMAL ETHICS OPINION 1984-76

Issue: What are the ethical obligations of a criminal defense attorney during the course of a pending criminal matter when the client places upon the attorney's desk or informs the attorney of the location of the instrumentality, fruits, or other physical evidence of the crime? . . .

Fundamental to this discussion is Section 954 of the Evidence Code, which provides that a client "has a privilege to refuse to disclose, and to prevent another from disclosing, a confidential communication between client and lawyer. . . ." Likewise, Business and Professions Code Section 6068, subdivision (e) places upon the attorney the duty "to maintain inviolate the confidence, and at every peril to himself to preserve the secrets, of his client." The rationale behind the evidentiary privilege and the professional obligation of the attorney is to allow the client to make disclosures to the attorney "without fear that his attorney may be forced to reveal the information confided to him." People v. Meredith (1981) 29 Cal.3d 682, 690.

On the other hand, by the provisions of Section 135 of the Penal Code, it is a violation of the law for one knowingly to conceal or destroy any "instrument in writing or other matter or thing [that] is about to be produced in evidence upon any trial, inquiry or investigation whatever, authorized by law . . .", and it is clear that the attorney-client privilege does not grant to the client the power permanently to "sequester physical evidence such as a weapon or any other article used in the perpetration of a crime by delivering it to his attorney." People v. Lee (1970) 3 Cal.App. 3d 514, 526. Likewise, rule 7-107(A) of the California Rules of Professional

Conduct states: "A member of the State Bar shall not suppress any evidence that he or his client has a legal obligation to reveal or produce."

The California Supreme Court in People v. Meredith has determined that physical evidence of a crime over which the lawyer has exercised dominion and control, thus taking possession, is not protected by the attorney-client privilege. Other jurisdictions have imposed a clear legal and ethical duty upon the lawyer to turn that evidence over to the prosecution. State v. Olwell, 394 P.2d 681 (Wash. 1964); Anderson v. State 297 So. 2d 871 (Fla. App. 1974). . . .

In considering the attorney's legal obligations to his client under the Sixth Amendment to provide effective counsel, the attorney should advise the client of the attorney's ethical as well as legal obligation with respect to the duty to deliver physical evidence of the crime to the prosecution if the attorney takes possession of such physical evidence. It is at this stage of representation that the impact upon the attorney-client relationship is at its greatest. The client is informed of the duties the attorney may have in the search-for-truth aspect of the adversary system, even to the extent of a legal duty imposed upon the attorney to participate in the very case against his client by delivering material evidence of the crime to the prosecution.

Although the fact of the delivery of the physical evidence of a crime by the client to the attorney is within the protection of the attorney-client privilege, the physical evidence itself is not. As a corollary, however, although it was held in Anderson v. State that the attorney acted properly under the circumstances that confronted him by turning the stolen items over to the police, "in order for the attorney-client privilege to be meaningfully preserved, the state cannot introduce evidence that it received the items from the attorney's office."

It was also held in State v. Olwell [that the] "attorney should not be a depository for criminal evidence. . . . Such evidence given the attorney during legal consultation . . . and used by the attorney in preparing the defense of his client's case . . . could clearly be withheld for a reasonable period of time. It follows that the attorney after a reasonable period, should, as an officer of the court, on his own motion turn the same over to the prosecution." The prosecution, however, must take "extreme precautions" to make certain that the source of the evidence is not disclosed at trial. Thus, in its *Olwell* decision, the court was seeking the proper balance between truth seeking by the prosecution, and the attorney-client privilege of the defense. . . .

[The] criminal defense attorney, after holding for a reasonable time for the purpose of preparing his client's defense, the instrumentality, fruits, or other physical evidence of the crime placed upon his desk by the client, is thereafter both legally and ethically obligated on his own motion to turn such evidence over to the prosecution.

It is apparent, however, that there is a significant difference in the legal and ethical obligations of an attorney when given possession of the physical evidence of a crime, as opposed to merely being told by his client of the location of the physical evidence of the crime.

[In] the situation wherein the client informs the attorney of the location of the physical evidence of the crime, or the attorney merely observes it without taking possession, the attorney need not disclose to the prosecution either its location or his or his agent's physical observations of the same. When, however, the defense attorney removes the physical evidence from its original location or takes possession of it, the evidence must, after reasonable time for investigation, be delivered to the prosecution and the location of its discovery will be subject to disclosure.

A criminal defense attorney should give careful consideration to the consequences of his actions before accepting possession of physical evidence or revealing any oral or observation evidence to the prosecution in light of the client's Sixth Amendment right to effective counsel and Business and Professions Code Section 6068, subdivision (e), requiring confidentiality. [Case law suggests] that all investigation and examination by a criminal defense attorney (with the exception of possession of physical evidence) is within the self-incrimination privilege of the defendant. . . .

This opinion is . . . advisory only. It is not binding upon the courts, The State Bar of California, its Board of Governors, any persons or tribunals charged with regulatory responsibilities, or any member of the State Bar.

■ NORTH CAROLINA STATE BAR (1995), RECEIPT OF EVIDENCE OF CRIME BY LAWYER FOR DEFENDANT, ETHICS OPINION 221

Inquiry #1: Attorney A and Attorney B work for different law firms. They have been appointed to represent Defendant, who is charged with first-degree murder. Defendant's wife, W, was apparently present during the altercation that led to the victim's death. During Attorney A and Attorney B's investigation, Defendant implicated W in the matter and told the attorneys that he had knowledge of relevant physical evidence. The police detectives who investigated the death are in possession of a stick they believe Defendant used to commit the murder, but neither the police detectives nor the prosecutors are aware of the existence of other physical evidence.

Defendant brought the physical evidence to Attorney B's office. Attorney B took possession of the physical evidence for purposes of examination and consultation with Attorney A concerning the extent to which the physical evidence might incriminate or exculpate Defendant.

Attorney A and Attorney B interviewed W, who incriminated herself. The story W told Attorney A and Attorney B is different from the statement that she gave to the police officers during the initial investigation.

Must Attorney A or Attorney B notify the district attorney's office or the investigating law enforcement agency of the existence of the physical evidence?

Opinion #1: No. On the one hand, a lawyer has a duty to preserve the confidences of the client and to zealously represent the client within the bounds of the law. Rule 4 and Canon VII of the Rules of Professional Conduct. On the other hand, a lawyer is an officer of the court and should not engage in conduct that is prejudicial to the administration of justice. Rule 1.2(d). In the absence of a court order or a common law or statutory obligation to disclose the location or deliver an item of inculpatory physical evidence that is not contraband (the possession of which is in and of itself a crime, such as narcotics) to law enforcement authorities, a defense lawyer may take such evidence into his or her possession for the purpose of testing, examination, or inspection. The defense lawyer should return the evidence to the source from whom the lawyer received it. In returning the item to the source, the lawyer must advise the source of the legal consequences pertaining to the possession or destruction of the evidence by that person or others. This advice should include the advice to retain the evidence intact and not engage in conduct that might be a violation of criminal statutes relating to evidence. See generally ABA Standards for Criminal Justice: Prosecution Function and Defense Function (3rd ed.), Standard 4-4.6(a)-(c), "Physical Evidence," and Commentary. If a defense lawyer receives a subpoena for inculpatory physical evidence in his or her possession, the lawyer may take appropriate steps to contest the subpoena in order to protect the interests of the client. However, the lawyer must comply with a court order to produce the evidence.

Similarly, pursuant to N.C.G.S. §15A-905, a defense lawyer must comply with any order entered by the court to produce evidence the defendant intends to introduce at trial.

Inquiry #2: What specific information, if any, is Attorney A or Attorney B allowed to disclose to the district attorney or the law enforcement agency regarding the weapon or how it was obtained?

Opinion #2: See opinion #1 above.

Inquiry #3: W provided information to Attorney A and Attorney B that would assist Defendant in his defense. Since Attorney A and Attorney B might be witnesses for Defendant, do they have to withdraw from the representation of Defendant?

Opinion #3: No. Rule 5.2(b) requires a lawyer to withdraw from the representation of a client if, "after undertaking employment in contemplated or pending litigation, a lawyer learns or it is obvious that he or a lawyer in his firm ought to be called as a witness on behalf of his client." However, he may continue the representation and he or a lawyer in his firm may testify under the circumstances enumerated in Rule 5.2(a). It is not "obvious" that Attorney A or Attorney B "ought" to be called as a witness for their client. Any information gained by Attorney A and Attorney B during the professional relationship with Defendant, including information obtained from third parties such as W, is confidential information. Rule 4(a); see also N.C.G.S. §15A-906. Unless Defendant consents to disclosure of the information gained from W, the lawyers may not testify about what W told them. Even if Defendant consents to the use of this information, W may be called as a witness herself, thus avoiding the need for Attorney A or Attorney B to testify. A problem of this nature can be avoided by having a nonlawyer present at all interviews with prospective trial witnesses.

Inquiry #4: Defendant has consented to the disclosure by Attorney A and Attorney B of the substance of W's statements to them. At trial, W is called as a witness and testifies contrary to her earlier statements to Attorney A and Attorney B. If the testimony of Attorney A or Attorney B is necessary to rebut the testimony of W, must one or both of them withdraw from the representation?

Opinion #4: Withdrawal may not be required. It is possible that by aggressive cross-examination of W, the need for one of the lawyers to testify will be avoided. If Lawyer A or Lawyer B must testify in order to rebut the testimony of W, moreover, the lawyers might conclude that an exception in Rule 5.2(a)(4) applies which would allow the lawyer to testify without withdrawing from the representation. Rule 5.2(b). Rule 5.2(a)(4) allows a lawyer to continue the representation despite acting as a witness in the trial if withdrawal "would work a substantial hardship on the client because of the distinctive value of the lawyer ... as counsel in the particular case."

If it is necessary for one of the lawyers to testify, the lawyer who testifies may have to withdraw from the representation but the other lawyer may remain in the case. Rule 5.2(b) only requires the lawyer who testifies for his client and the other members of his firm to withdraw from the representation.

Notes

1. *Ethical obligations to turn over physical evidence.* The rules governing a defense lawyer's obligations to disclose physical evidence are largely uniform. If a defense lawyer receives incriminating *testimony* from a client, the attorney-client privilege and the self-incrimination clause combine to prevent the attorney from revealing that information to the government. But if the defense lawyer receives incriminating *physical* evidence, the outcome is different. Discovery rules do not address this question. Instead, Rule 3.4 of the Model Rules of Professional Conduct, adopted as law in many states, provides the starting point for analyzing the attorney's duties:

> A lawyer shall not . . . unlawfully obstruct another party's access to evidence or unlawfully alter, destroy or conceal a document or other material having potential evidentiary value. A lawyer shall not counsel or assist another person to do any such act.

Hence, the key question is whether a lawyer's act is an "unlawful" obstruction of access or tampering with evidence. Most states have statutes that prohibit obstruction of investigations or tampering with evidence. In some places, an investigation must be pending before the destruction or concealment of potential evidence becomes unlawful, while elsewhere the intent to prevent detection of a crime is the critical element, regardless of the timing of the destruction or concealment. The courts addressing these situations have held that the attorney who takes possession of contraband relevant to a criminal investigation against a client must ordinarily give the evidence to the government. The attorney can return the evidence to its original location only if the return of the evidence does not create a risk that the evidence will be concealed or altered. See Rubin v. State, 602 A.2d 677 (Md. 1992). The National Legal Aid and Defender Association recommends that a lawyer deliver physical evidence to the government only if delivery is required by law or court order, or if "the item received is contraband, or if in the lawyer's judgment the lawyer cannot retain the item in a way that does not pose an unreasonable risk of physical harm to anyone."

What are the practical effects on defense counsel of the current rules? What would you say to your client or a third party about incriminating physical evidence? On the other hand, if you decided to deliver the physical evidence to the government, exactly how would you proceed? Could you deliver the item to some third party (say, a member of the Ethics Committee of the state bar) and ask that person to deliver the evidence anonymously?

2. *Source and type of evidence.* Does it matter that the watch in Problem 5-3 was not contraband (that is, it was not illegal for anyone to possess the watch)? Does it matter that the attorney learned of the location of the wristwatch from a third party rather than from the client? Can the prosecutor reveal to the jury that defense counsel was the source of the watch when it comes into evidence at trial? See State v. Olwell, 394 P.2d 681 (Wash. 1964) (if client provides defense counsel with evidence that

must be given to government, attorney-client privilege prevents prosecutor from informing jury about source of evidence). Can the prosecutor call the defendant's *former* lawyer to testify about the source of the evidence? See State v. Green, 493 So. 2d 1178 (La. 1986).

3. *Ethics rules and prosecutorial disclosures.* Rules of ethics often recognize a distinctive set of duties for prosecuting attorneys. How might these rules be relevant during the discovery process? Consider the following passage from Rule 8 of the Supreme Court of Tennessee, EC 7-13:

> The responsibility of a public prosecutor differs from that of the usual advocate; the public prosecutor's duty is to seek justice, not merely to convict. . . . With respect to evidence and witnesses, the prosecutor has responsibilities different from those of a lawyer in private practice; the prosecutor should make timely disclosure to the defense of available evidence, known to the prosecutor, that tends to negate the guilt of the accused, mitigate the degree of the offense, or reduce the punishment. Further, a prosecutor should not intentionally avoid pursuit of evidence merely because the prosecutor believes it will damage the prosecutor's case or aid the accused.

B. SPEEDY TRIAL PREPARATION

An old bromide reminds us that "justice delayed is justice denied." This can be true both for the prosecution and the defense in criminal cases. If preparations for trial last too long, the evidence becomes less reliable for both sides. The uncertainty about the criminal charges may harm the defendant's reputation and can make it difficult for the defendants and the victims of the alleged crime to move ahead with their lives. The need for speedy resolution of criminal charges has been mentioned in some of the earliest documents in our legal tradition, including the Magna Carta of 1215, which states, "we will not deny or defer to any man either justice or right."

The right to a speedy trial appears in constitutional provisions, both state and federal. The Sixth Amendment guarantees a "speedy and public trial," and most states have similar provisions. The federal and state due process clauses prevent some extreme forms of delay. Recent constitutional amendments recognizing the rights of victims of crime have declared that victims, too, have a right to a speedy trial. Many state and federal statutes also hurry the criminal process along. These include statutes of limitation (requiring charges to be filed within a limited time from the events in question) and speedy trial acts (requiring the parties and the courts to bring the matter to trial within a specified period from the start of the process).

Despite all this emphasis on speed, another bromide reminds us that "haste makes waste." Both prosecution and defense have some reasons to slow down the process. Some of their reasons may be less than noble. If testimony is going to damage one side or another, a witness's fading memory may make the testimony less convincing and more susceptible to attack. If a defendant remains in custody before trial, a prosecutor may not be so anxious to risk an acquittal that would release the defendant from custody; a defendant not in custody may want to delay the day of reckoning. But other reasons for delay are surely necessary, even praiseworthy, including a desire to complete the discovery processes examined in the previous section.

1. Pre-accusation Delay

Once a crime occurs and an investigation begins, the matter typically becomes the basis for criminal charges or is declined for criminal charges within a matter of days. Among the handful of matters that take more time, a small proportion can remain active for many months or years after the events take place. This is the first delay in the criminal process that suspects, victims, witnesses, and the general public encounter. What legal principles and institutions are available to limit the amount of time that can pass between the commission of a crime and the filing of criminal charges? Once a state legislature has passed a statute of limitations, is any further limitation necessary to avoid delays that might create hardship or unreliable outcomes?

■ NEW YORK CRIMINAL PROCEDURE LAW §30.10

1. A criminal action must be commenced within the period of limitation prescribed in the ensuing subdivisions of this section.
2. Except as otherwise provided in subdivision three:
   (a) A prosecution for a class A felony or rape in the first degree . . . or criminal sexual act in the first degree . . . or course of sexual conduct against a child in the first degree . . . may be commenced at any time;
   (b) A prosecution for any other felony must be commenced within five years after the commission thereof;
   (c) A prosecution for a misdemeanor must be commenced within two years after the commission thereof;
   (d) A prosecution for a petty offense must be commenced within one year after the commission thereof.
3. Notwithstanding the provisions of subdivision two, the periods of limitation for the commencement of criminal actions are extended as follows in the indicated circumstances:
   (a) A prosecution for larceny committed by a person in violation of a fiduciary duty may be commenced within one year after the facts constituting such offense are discovered or, in the exercise of reasonable diligence, should have been discovered by the aggrieved party or by a person under a legal duty to represent him who is not himself implicated in the commission of the offense. . . .
   (f) For purposes of a prosecution involving a sexual offense . . . committed against a child less than 18 years of age [other than those delineated in paragraph (a)], the period of limitation shall not begin to run until the child has reached the age of 18 or the offense is reported to a law enforcement agency. . . .
4. In calculating the time limitation applicable to commencement of a criminal action, the following periods shall not be included:
   (a) Any period following the commission of the offense during which (i) the defendant was continuously outside this state or (ii) the whereabouts of the defendant were continuously unknown and continuously unascertainable by the exercise of reasonable diligence. However, in no event shall the period of limitation be extended by more than five years beyond the period otherwise applicable under subdivision two.

(b) When a prosecution for an offense is lawfully commenced within the prescribed period of limitation therefor, and when an accusatory instrument upon which such prosecution is based is subsequently dismissed by an authorized court under directions or circumstances permitting the lodging of another charge for the same offense or an offense based on the same conduct, the period extending from the commencement of the thus defeated prosecution to the dismissal of the accusatory instrument does not constitute a part of the period of limitation applicable to commencement of prosecution by a new charge.

■ COMMONWEALTH v. STEPHEN SCHER
803 A.2d 1204 (Pa. 2002)

NEWMAN, J.

. . . Martin Dillon died of a gunshot wound to the chest on June 2, 1976 at the Dillon family recreational property called "Gunsmoke" in Susquehanna County. Scher was the only other individual present when Dillon died. How Dillon died, and whether that death was an accident or an intentional act of murder, is a story that evolved in fits and starts in the intervening two decades, culminating in murder charges being filed against Scher in 1996 and his conviction for first degree murder following a six-week jury trial in 1997. . . .

THE SCENE

Andrew Russin, a neighbor whose house was approximately two miles from Gunsmoke, testified that, on the day Dillon died, Scher appeared at Russin's house with his hands and mouth covered in blood and asked Russin to call the authorities because Dillon had been shot. [The men drove separately to Gunsmoke, and walked] towards the skeet shooting area, where Russin saw Dillon's body. . . . Russin then watched as Scher picked up the gun that was lying near Dillon's body and smashed it against a tree, breaking the barrel from the stock.

Trooper William Hairston of the Pennsylvania State Police . . . arrived at Gunsmoke with John Conarton, the Susquehanna County Coroner, . . . and walked up the path that led to a clearing where Dillon's body lay on its back. A pair of hunting goggles and shooting "earmuffs" were on the ground nearby. Trooper Hairston observed that the earmuffs had blood on them. There was a puddle of blood to the left side of Dillon's body. . . .

In his June 2, 1976 statement, Scher told Trooper Hairston: (1) he and Dillon had come to Gunsmoke to skeet shoot; (2) after firing about twenty rounds, they decided to take a break and returned to the trailer for some beer and potato chips; (3) the two sat in the trailer discussing an upcoming murder trial in which Dillon, a lawyer, was representing the defendant; (4) they then went back to the trail towards the clearing where the skeet-shooting trap was set up and fired a few more rounds; (5) Dillon then wanted to go back to the trailer to get cigarettes, so Scher loaded his shotgun, a sixteen-gauge, to be ready for the next round of firing, while Dillon unloaded his twenty-gauge shotgun and placed it on a nearby stump; (6) Scher and Dillon then walked down the trail, and Scher placed his loaded shotgun on a metal gun stand, approximately 120 feet from the skeet-shooting area; (7) as they went further down the trail, Dillon turned around and saw something in the open field that he thought was a porcupine, ran back up the trail and grabbed Scher's gun from the stand; (8) Scher heard Dillon cock the gun and heard it fire, but he could not see Dillon; (9) Scher then walked up the trail and found Dillon lying on the ground, face down; (10) Scher, a physician, ran up to Dillon and turned him over, saw that Dillon was bleeding from the chest and tried to stop the bleeding, but knew that Dillon was dead; (11) Scher took the car keys from Dillon's pocket and drove to Russin's house; (12) Scher and Russin returned to the scene, and Scher noticed that the trigger of the sixteen-gauge shotgun had a twig in it; (13) Scher then smashed the shotgun against the tree, and stated, "I know I shouldn't have done that." This June 2, 1976 statement to Trooper Hairston, as Scher's trial testimony more than twenty years later admitted, was a lie. . . .

Trooper Francis Zanin of the Pennsylvania State Police . . . documented the scene on June 2, 1976. Trooper Zanin observed Dillon's body lying on its back with its arms outstretched. Dillon was wearing eight-inch high boots that had round eyelets for the laces to pass through except at the top, where the laces would pass through three hooks. Trooper Zanin noticed that although the laces at the top of the right-foot boot were untied, the rest of the laces remained pulled tightly against the leg. He also noticed that Dillon's pant leg was pulled up higher than the boot. There were blood droplets on Dillon's boots and face, on the shooting goggles and protective eyewear that lay nearby, and on the tree stump that was approximately five-and-a-half to six feet from Dillon's body. Trooper Zanin observed, however, that there were no blood droplets immediately around Dillon's eyes and ears where the goggles and earmuffs would have been had Dillon been wearing them when he was shot. The barrel of the shattered sixteen-gauge shotgun lay close to Dillon's body, but a subsequent examination of the outside and inside of the shotgun barrel showed no evidence of blood. Inside the chamber of the broken sixteen-gauge shotgun was a discharged number four load high brass magnum shell — a variety not commonly used in skeet shooting. Beneath Dillon's left hand were unbroken clay pigeons.

THE INITIAL INVESTIGATION

On June 4, 1976, at 11:30 A.M., two days after his statement to Trooper Hairston, Scher came to the District Attorney's Office at the Susquehanna County Courthouse in Montrose, at the request of the investigators, and gave a statement. . . . During this interrogation, Scher repeated essentially the same story that he had related in his June 2, 1976 statement to Trooper Hairston. . . . One noteworthy difference between this second statement and the June 2, 1976 statement was that Scher said that he had placed the sixteen-gauge shotgun against a tree, whereas his June 2, 1976 statement indicated that he had placed the loaded shotgun on the metal gun stand. When asked whether he and Dillon had any disagreements, Scher said, "No. We were talking about this rumor. I told him I was thinking of leaving town. It was rough on him. He sat and told me I was just a quitter and chicken — 'don't run away . . . it was just small people talking.' " After giving this answer, Scher became angry, terminated the interview, and left the room.

Edward Little, the District Attorney of Susquehanna County from 1968 to 1980, testified at pretrial hearings on Scher's Motion to Dismiss . . . and explained why no charges were filed during his tenure in office. Dr. James Grace, a general practitioner who conducted an autopsy of Dillon on June 3, 1976, had issued a report that . . . listed the cause of death as "gunshot wound of the chest," but made no determination whether the death was the result of a homicide. Coroner Conarton, who was present when Scher gave his June 2, 1976 statement to Trooper Hairston, had determined that Dillon's death was accidental and had listed this as the manner of death on Dillon's death certificate. Although Detective Collier had a strong belief that Dillon's death may have been a murder rather than an accident, and expressed this opinion in a June 9, 1976 report to Little, Scher was not arrested. Little explained that he, too, was not convinced that Dillon's death was an accident and requested that Coroner Conarton delay issuance of the death certificate in order to allow additional time to conduct the investigation. Little testified, however, that he never brought charges against Scher because he felt that there was insufficient evidence of murder to prosecute the case successfully.

Laurence Kelly succeeded Little as District Attorney of Susquehanna County in 1980, and held that office until 1988. Little testified that he had no discussions with Kelly regarding the investigation into Dillon's death. . . . For eight years, therefore, the investigation into the Dillon matter was dormant.

The Reactivated Investigation

Jeffrey Snyder was the District Attorney of Susquehanna County from 1988 until 1996. In 1989 [at the request of Martin Dillon's father, Lawrence Dillon], Snyder agreed to have the facts as developed by the investigation to that point presented to a panel of medical experts who were holding a conference at the University of Pennsylvania. . . . Dr. Isadore Mihalikis, a forensic pathologist, . . . presented the case to the conference attendees. Following this presentation, a significant majority of the conference members opined that a self-inflicted gunshot wound, either accidental or intentional, caused Dillon's death. Snyder viewed this vote as "an overwhelming defeat for the prosecution" and concluded that no successful prosecution could be mounted at that time.

[In 1994], again at the urging of the Dillon family, two Pennsylvania State Police officers who had no previous involvement in the case were brought in to reexamine the evidence, conduct interviews with witnesses, and, in Snyder's words, "winnow out the rumor, the innuendo, that in my opinion riddled much of the material that was already on file." The "rumor" referred to by Snyder was the report that Scher and Dillon's wife, Patricia, had been having an affair before Dillon's death. [Patricia Dillon married Scher in 1978.] These rumors were known to investigators at the time of the incident but, for reasons that do not appear in the record, were not pursued. [The officers put in charge of the case in 1994 developed evidence] that Scher and Patricia had been having an extramarital affair prior to Dillon's death. In 1995, the Commonwealth successfully petitioned, in spite of the objection of Patricia Scher, to have Dillon's body exhumed for a second autopsy. Following this second autopsy in April of 1995, the Commonwealth obtained support from its expert forensic pathologist, Dr. Mihalikis, for the position that the physical evidence of Dillon's gunshot wound was not consistent with an accidental discharge of a dropped shotgun. The Commonwealth concluded that it possessed sufficient evidence to prosecute murder charges successfully and charged Scher with first-degree murder in June of 1996.

SCHER'S TRIAL TESTIMONY

. . . Confronted with the Commonwealth's case, Scher took the stand and admitted that his previous statements to the investigators in June of 1976 were false. He proceeded to explain what happened that day at Gunsmoke.

> . . . He threw out ten birds for me, and then I threw off ten birds for him. He was still using the same gun, and I was still using the twenty gauge. Then my second round of ten, at the very end of the last shot, he turned to me, he said, Ann came to me and told me that you told her that you love Pat. . . .
>
> I put down the twenty gauge and I broke it in half and put it on the log. And I walked over to him to his side. . . . I said, Do you believe her?
>
> He said, I don't know. She's crazy. I don't know whether to believe her or not. But with all the rumors and talk and gossip in town and my father's breathing down my neck about this gossip, I really — I need to know. And he stopped and he looked down at the ground and it was like he — it was like he really didn't want to know, but, you know, but then he looked up. He looked right at me in the eye. He said, I have to know. Are you and Pat having an affair?
>
> And I just had — I had to tell him the truth. He was looking me in the eye. I could no longer keep it from him. I said, Yes, we're having, not a love affair, but a physical affair.
>
> And then he became very anxious and very, very upset. He was sitting there on the log and he had his hand over his ears and he was rocking down and asked me a whole bunch of questions. And I don't — I don't remember his exact words, how he phrased the questions. I don't even remember the order that he asked them, but he wanted to know from me, he wanted to know how did this start.
>
> I told him it just happened. Pat and I were close together all the time. It just happened. . . .
>
> I was embarrassed to talk to him this way, of course. I was looking at the ground. I said to him, You know, this is as much your fault as it is anybody's.
>
> Then I hear a scream, yell. And I look up and he has the sixteen gauge gun in his hand, reached around and I — I knew — I just knew I had to get that gun away. . . . I didn't know what he was going to do with it. I just knew with his state of mind at that time and my state of mind that it wasn't good to have a hold of a gun and I lunged. In a matter of that much time, I grabbed the gun and pulled away. We struggled and the gun went off.

Scher then explained why he decided to engage in a cover-up . . . and why he had lied to investigators, to the press, and to the public for the next twenty-one years.

> I was thinking, How can I tell anybody this accident happened like this and have anybody believe me in Montrose, what with all the rumors that were going on and me being a relative newcomer to the area and Marty's father is the mayor and I'm the only Jew in town, in the county? And I felt I couldn't tell anybody. . . .
>
> And I decided since it was an accident that I was going to make it into another accident. . . . So I made up that story and took the gun that I dropped right when it discharged and wiped off the barrel with a handkerchief and put it back into my pocket. I took the gun and I put it with the muzzle facing his head where he laid. Then I untied his shoelace to make it look like there was something he tripped over. . . .

The jury convicted Scher of first-degree murder and the trial court sentenced him to life imprisonment on October 22, 1997. On appeal to the Superior Court,

Scher [claimed] that the twenty-year delay in filing charges against him violated his right to due process of law as guaranteed by the United States and Pennsylvania Constitutions. The Superior Court reversed the Judgment of Sentence. . . .

THE DUE PROCESS STANDARD

. . . United States v. Marion, 404 U.S. 307 (1971), was the seminal case to address whether a defendant's federal constitutional rights are violated by an extensive delay between the occurrence of a crime and the indictment or arrest of a defendant for the crime. In *Marion*, the defendants were charged with having engaged in a fraudulent business scheme beginning in March of 1965 and ending in January of 1966. The federal prosecutor in *Marion* did not empanel a grand jury to investigate the scheme until September of 1969, and no indictment was returned until March of 1970. [The Supreme Court held that constitutional speedy trial claims do] not apply until "either a formal indictment or information or else the actual restraints imposed by arrest and holding to answer a criminal charge," which was not implicated in defendants' complaints of pre-arrest delay. Concerning the defendants' Fifth Amendment due process claims, the Court noted that the primary guarantee against the bringing of overly stale charges was whatever statute of limitations applied to the crime. The Court went on to note, however, "the statute of limitations does not fully define the appellees' rights with respect to the events occurring prior to indictment." The following passage from *Marion* is significant:

> Thus, the Government concedes that the Due Process Clause of the Fifth Amendment would require dismissal of the indictment if it were shown at trial that the pre-indictment delay in this case caused substantial prejudice to appellees' rights to a fair trial and that the delay was an intentional device to gain tactical advantage over the accused. Cf. Brady v. Maryland, 373 U.S. 83 (1963). However, we need not, and could not now, determine when and in what circumstances actual prejudice resulting from pre-accusation delays requires the dismissal of the prosecution. . . .

Six years after *Marion*, the United States Supreme Court revisited the due process implications of pre-arrest delay in United States v. Lovasco, 431 U.S. 783 (1977). Eugene Lovasco was indicted in March of 1975 for possessing firearms stolen from the mail beginning in July and ending in August of 1973. Lovasco moved to dismiss the indictment, claiming that the prosecutor's delay in bringing the indictment caused him prejudice through the deaths of two favorable witnesses and therefore violated his due process rights. [The Court stated that] the due process inquiry must consider the reasons for the delay as well as the prejudice to the accused. In [its] discussion of the "reasons for the delay," the Court stated, "in our view, investigative delay is unlike delay undertaken by the Government solely to gain a tactical advantage over the accused." . . .

All the federal circuits that have examined pre-arrest delay due process claims agree that the *Marion/Lovasco* standard requires that a defendant establish, as a threshold matter, that he or she suffered actual prejudice from the delay. All federal circuits also agree that *Marion* and *Lovasco* require another step for there to be a successful due process claim. There is a split of authority, however, as to what that next step involves. A majority of the circuits hold that a defendant bears the burden of proving both actual prejudice from the delay and that the delay was intentionally undertaken by the government for the purpose of gaining some tactical advantage over the accused in the contemplated prosecution or for some other impermissible, bad faith purpose. The Fourth and Seventh Circuits, on the other hand, read the second element of the *Marion/Lovasco* [standard to require] a "balancing test" once a defendant can show actual prejudice due to the delay. Pursuant to this scheme, once the defendant proves that he has suffered actual prejudice, the burden shifts to the state to "come forward and provide reasons for the delay." See United States v. Sowa, 34 F.3d 447 (7th Cir. 1994). . . .

Recently, we reviewed the standard for due process claims based on pre-arrest delay in Commonwealth v. Snyder, 713 A.2d 596 (Pa. 1998). Keith Snyder was charged in 1993 with the murder of his wife and child, who died during a fire at the Snyder home in 1982. The local and state police investigated the deaths for two years, and a special investigating grand jury was empanelled in 1984, but disbanded in 1986 without returning an indictment. In 1993, a new District Attorney reopened the case and charged Snyder with murder. [After Snyder's conviction, this court] concluded that Snyder had suffered actual prejudice from the pre-arrest delay. An autopsy of his wife's body showed that she had consumed a large amount of alcohol at the time of her death. Snyder argued that certain witnesses who had died by the time of his trial had heard statements from his wife that she was contemplating suicide. We determined that the death of witnesses who would have aided Snyder's defense theory that his wife actually set the fire as an act of suicidal depression prejudiced him.

[Under the second prong of the *Marion/Lovasco* test, the] Commonwealth argued that Snyder could prevail on his claim of deprivation of due process only if he demonstrated that the delay was an intentional ploy designed to give the Commonwealth an advantage at trial. We rejected this argument:

> . . . It appears that the prosecutors, in the exercise of their discretion, decided for reasons that do not appear in the record, that this case lacked prosecutorial merit. Nor is there any basis to conclude that [the current District Attorney] intentionally continued to defer this prosecution for inappropriate reasons. . . .
>
> Whether done intentionally or not, the Commonwealth gained a tremendous strategical advantage against the Appellant due to the passage of time and the loss of critical defense testimony through death and memory. . . . We hold that, based on all of the facts of this case, bringing this prosecution after more than eleven years caused actual prejudice to the Appellant and deprived him of due process of law unless there were proper reasons for the delay. . . .

In reviewing Scher's due process claim based on pre-arrest delay, the [intermediate appellate court held that in cases of excessive and prejudicial pre-arrest delay, a court] will not only inquire as to whether there has been any intentional delay by the prosecution to gain a tactical advantage over the accused, but [must] also consider whether the prosecution has been negligent by failing to pursue a reasonably diligent criminal investigation. . . .

We agree with the court below in its reading of *Marion* and *Lovasco* that delay intentionally undertaken by the prosecution to gain a tactical advantage over the defendant is one case, but not the only case, where pre-arrest delay would violate due process. However, in requiring, as we did in *Snyder*, an examination of the reasons for the delay, we did not intend to create an obligation on the Commonwealth to conduct all criminal investigations pursuant to a due diligence or negligence standard, measured from the moment when criminal charges are filed and the defendant raises his due process claim. Such a standard would be too onerous, requiring judicial oversight of decisions traditionally entrusted to the prosecutor. Furthermore, a due diligence or negligence standard would require an inquiry into the methods, resources, and techniques of law enforcement in conducting a criminal investigation that would amount to judicial second-guessing of how the Commonwealth must build its case. We are mindful of the Supreme Court's admonition in *Lovasco* against placing too stringent a responsibility on the prosecution to justify the delay in the face of these claims: "The Due Process Clause does not permit courts to abort criminal prosecutions simply because they disagree with a prosecutor's judgment as to when to seek an indictment."

[The] test that we believe is the correct one must take into consideration all of the facts and circumstances surrounding the case, including: the deference that courts must afford to the prosecutor's conclusions that a case is not ripe for prosecution; the limited resources available to law enforcement agencies when conducting a criminal investigation; the prosecutor's motives in delaying indictment; and the degree to which the defendant's own actions contributed to the delay. Therefore, to clarify the standard established in *Snyder*, we hold that in order to prevail on a due process claim based on pre-arrest delay, the defendant must first show that the delay caused him actual prejudice, that is, substantially impaired his or her ability to defend against the charges. The court must then examine all of the circumstances to determine the validity of the Commonwealth's reasons for the delay. Only in situations where the evidence shows that the delay was the product of intentional, bad faith, or reckless conduct by the prosecution, however, will we find a violation of due process. Negligence in the conduct of a criminal investigation, without more, will not be sufficient to prevail on a due process claim based on pre-arrest delay. With this clarification of the standard in mind, we turn to Scher's case.

Actual Prejudice

. . . In order for a defendant to show actual prejudice, he or she must show that he or she was meaningfully impaired in his or her ability to defend against the state's charges to such an extent that the disposition of the criminal proceedings was likely affected. This kind of prejudice is commonly demonstrated by the loss of documentary evidence or the unavailability of an essential witness. It is not sufficient for a defendant to make speculative or conclusory claims of possible prejudice as a result of the passage of time. Where a defendant claims prejudice through the absence of witnesses, he or she must show in what specific manner missing witnesses would have aided the defense. Furthermore, it is the defendant's burden to show that the lost testimony or information is not available through other means.

Scher claims that he suffered prejudice because certain witnesses died and important evidence was lost by the time of trial that would have aided his defense that the shooting of Dillon was accidental, not intentional. Specifically, he points to the deaths [of Dr. Grace and Coroner Conarton]. Scher also claims prejudice from the decomposition of Dillon's body that occurred during the twenty-year period, and from the Commonwealth's conduct of the second autopsy in 1995, which he claims interfered with his ability to present expert testimony in support of his position that Dillon's death was accidental. Further, Scher argues that the loss or destruction of other evidence, such as . . . the audio recording of the June 1976 autopsy; certain photographs taken of the scene; . . . and any bloodstains on the inside of the shotgun, impaired his ability to show that the shooting was accidental and not a premeditated act of murder.

In order to argue prejudice from the loss or destruction of evidence in these due process claims, the defendant must show that the loss or destruction of evidence related to the delay in filing charges. With respect to some of the items that Scher claims were lost or destroyed, the delay in filing charges clearly had no role in causing these items to be lost or destroyed. First, Scher contends that by the time charges were filed against him, the shotgun had been fired numerous times, thus eliminating any bloodstains that may have been inside the barrel, which would have tended to prove a close range of fire consistent with Scher's story that the shooting was an accident. However, one of Scher's experts, George Fassnacht, a forensic firearms consultant, testified that the repeated firing of the shotgun in 1976 by the police during testing of the weapon would have removed any bloodstains from inside the barrel. Accordingly, the loss of this evidence cannot be attributed to the delay in indicting Scher for murder. . . .

During the initial investigation of Dillon's death, Detective Collier apparently obtained Polaroid photographs of Dillon's body that were taken by the Pennsylvania game commissioner, who was one of the first individuals at the scene. [During the re-activated investigation, officers] were unable to locate the photographs and concluded that they had been destroyed. Scher now claims that the destruction of these photographs deprived him of potentially exculpatory evidence, and therefore prejudiced him. . . .

Here, the lost photographs were not the only photographs of Dillon's body as it appeared at Gunsmoke. Trooper Zanin had taken numerous photographs of Dillon's body at the scene, which were introduced at trial and had been reviewed by Scher's experts prior to their testimony. Scher fails to explain what would have appeared in the Polaroid photographs that could not be seen in the photographs taken by Trooper Zanin in his documentation of the scene. His claim of prejudice is entirely speculative and is without support in light of the other photographic evidence that was available to him.

Scher claims prejudice from the [death of Coroner Conarton. His claim is based on the assumption that because Conarton] never pressed for the filing of murder charges against Scher, [he] must have agreed that Dillon's death was an accident. . . . Scher notes that Dillon's death certificate, completed by Conarton, lists the cause of Dillon's death as accidental. Scher contends that he was prejudiced when he lost the opportunity to have Conarton explain why he believed Dillon's death was accidental. What Scher ignores, however, is that in the section of the death certificate that asks, "How did injury occur?" Coroner Conarton wrote, "Running with gun, fell, gun went off." As Scher admitted in his trial testimony, this is not how Dillon died, and his stories to Conarton, Collier, and the other investigating officers to this effect were lies. Conarton was present when Scher gave his statement to Trooper Hairston at the scene, which related the false story of how Dillon tripped while running with the shotgun. The record strongly suggests that Conarton formed his opinion as to the cause of Dillon's death based mainly on Scher's false statement and a cursory review of the scene where Dillon's body lay positioned in a manner, with shoelaces untied, that Scher deliberately set to make it appear that Dillon tripped and fell while carrying the shotgun. . . . Consequently, we cannot credit Scher's complaints of prejudice from the absence of Conarton's testimony . . . when it is apparent that Conarton accepted a version of the "accident" that Scher himself admitted was false and upon which he did not base his defense.

The most serious claim of prejudice raised by Scher concerns the death of Dr. Grace and the loss of audio recordings from the June 3, 1976 autopsy performed by Dr. Grace, as well as the alteration of Dillon's body during the second autopsy in 1995. The critical issue to Scher's defense was whether the physical evidence was consistent with an accidental discharge of the weapon during a struggle. Evidence of the angle of Dillon's chest wound, the presence or absence of "scalloping,"[23] the presence or absence of gunpowder around the wound, and the size of the wound were relevant to the determination of whether Dillon was shot from a close range, consistent with a struggle, or a more distant range that could not have been caused by an accidental discharge during a struggle.

In support of his defense theory, Scher presented a number of expert witnesses. John Shane, M.D., a pathologist, reviewed, among other evidentiary items: twenty-seven black and white photographs of the scene; the clothes worn by Dillon, the photographs taken during Dr. Grace's autopsy; photographs taken during the second autopsy in 1995; forty-three microscopic slides of tissue taken from Dillon's body; Dr. Grace's autopsy report; and the shot cup retrieved from Dillon's body. Dr. Shane observed that Dr. Grace did not note scalloping around the margins of Dillon's chest wound in his June 3, 1976 autopsy report, and that his own review of the photographs from that autopsy indicated no scalloping. Based on his review of the autopsy photographs and Dr. Grace's report, Dr. Shane opined, to a reasonable degree of medical certainty, that there was no scalloping around the margins of Dillon's chest wound and that this indicated a close range of discharge — within twelve inches. Dr. Shane also noted that the June 3, 1976 autopsy report showed "what was apparently powder burns" in the wound tract, and his examination of the slides from the 1995 autopsy indicated the presence of carbon that Dr. Shane identified as gunpowder residue. Dr. Shane testified that the presence of gunpowder residue in the wound tract signaled that the range of fire would have been within eighteen inches, due to the limited distance that gunpowder travels from the barrel when a firearm is discharged. [Scher also presented the testimony of two other expert witnesses who reviewed the available autopsy reports, photographs, clothing, and tissue samples; both concluded that the shot was fired from less than one foot from Dillon's body.]

The ability of Scher's experts to support his defense by offering opinions to a reasonable degree of medical certainty based on a review of the evidence available to them demonstrates why Scher's claims of prejudice fail. [There] was sufficient evidence, including photographs and Dr. Grace's report, for Scher's experts to offer specific opinions concerning the presence of gunpowder in the wound tract, the range of fire, and whether the physical evidence was consistent with a struggle. . . .

---

23. [Scalloping involves an impact pattern that falls into curved lines like that found on the shell of a scallop.] The presence of scalloping is useful in determining range of shotgun fire, according to [a trial expert], because "as the shotgun blast moves further back then the pellets are beginning to disburse a little bit. Then you will begin to get some irregular contouring of the edges of the wound."

REASONS FOR THE DELAY

[In] order for there to be a violation of due process, the Commonwealth's behavior must be more than merely negligent in causing the delay. Only where the Commonwealth has intentionally delayed in order to gain a tactical advantage or acted recklessly to such a degree as to shock one's conscience and offend one's sense of justice will we find a deprivation of due process. We do not find the Commonwealth's behavior in this case to be so outrageous as to meet that standard. There has been no allegation that the Commonwealth intentionally delayed indicting Scher in order to gain a tactical advantage over him, and the record contains credible denials from a succession of Susquehanna County District Attorneys that they ever intentionally employed delay tactics. Furthermore, we cannot accept the Superior Court's conclusion that the Commonwealth's actions were "grossly negligent." Astonishingly, the Superior Court's opinion makes no mention of the watershed moment in this case: when Scher admitted that he had lied to investigators about how Dillon's death occurred and that, for the past twenty years, he lied when he denied having had an affair with Patricia prior to the incident at Gunsmoke. [Scher] staged the scene and fabricated a story that gained some credence with investigators. Perhaps, as Scher argues, those investigators should have been more circumspect in accepting his tale and pursued their suspicions more thoroughly, but we cannot find the Commonwealth's actions towards Scher so egregious when, in a small town, in a rural part of Pennsylvania with a part-time District Attorney, those responsible for enforcing the law would find it difficult to disbelieve the word of a respected physician. Nor can we ignore the benefit that Scher gained by lying to authorities rather than remaining silent: he enjoyed his liberty for twenty years. In these circumstances, we cannot find that the Commonwealth's failure to charge Scher with murder sooner violated his right to due process of law. . . .

CASTILLE, J., concurring.

[The] lead opinion rejects the prevailing view in the federal Circuit Courts. That view would require the defendant to prove that the pre-arrest delay was intentionally undertaken by the government for the purpose of gaining a tactical advantage over the accused in the prosecution. Instead of this bad faith standard, which derives from the explicit language employed by the United States Supreme Court in its decisions in *Marion* and *Lovasco*, the lead opinion would adopt a subjective recklessness/conscience-shocking standard. It is here that I part ways with the lead opinion. . . .

I joined in the *Snyder* opinion, and I recognize that the lead opinion fairly characterizes it today. However, upon further careful consideration of this recurring federal question, and particularly in light of the difficulties in the Pennsylvania experience since *Snyder*, which necessitate the lead opinion's attempt to clarify the standard today, I am now firmly convinced that we should simply return to the standard actually articulated by the Supreme Court and followed by a majority of the Circuit Courts. Thus, I believe that a proper assessment of the reasons for the delay in initiating prosecution must be confined to the question of the prosecution's bad faith — i.e., whether the delay was intentionally undertaken by the prosecution to gain a tactical advantage over the defendant. . . .

Although the lead opinion recognizes that a negligence standard is unworkable, the recklessness standard it would approve amounts to nothing more than a heightened negligence standard. . . . A heightened negligence standard is no less impractical than a mere negligence standard, i.e., it would still require judicial oversight of decisions traditionally entrusted to the prosecutor. Consequently, the lead opinion's standard opens the door to the type of hindsight and second-guessing employed here by the Superior Court and eschewed by the Supreme Court. . . .

ZAPPALA, C.J., dissenting.

. . . The Commonwealth's inordinate and unexcused delay in filing charges against Dr. Scher resulted in actual prejudice to Dr. Scher's ability to defend himself against the charges. At trial, the pivotal issue was whether Mr. Dillon's death resulted from an accidental firing of the shotgun as he and Dr. Scher struggled with the shotgun or resulted from the intentional and deliberate firing of the shotgun by Dr. Scher at a distance of several feet away from Dillon. The Commonwealth premised its theory on the testimony of expert witnesses following an autopsy conducted 18 years after Dillon's death. The expert testimony sought to contradict the findings made by Dr. James Grace based upon the autopsy he conducted immediately after Dillon's death. During the trial, the competency of Dr. Grace to conduct the autopsy and the findings themselves were challenged by the Commonwealth.

The Commonwealth went to great lengths to disparage and criticize Dr. Grace's abilities and to undermine specific critical physical findings made by Dr. Grace regarding the condition of the wound. Dr. Grace's findings were contrary to the Commonwealth's theory of the case and undermined the testimony of Commonwealth experts who had not examined the body until it was exhumed eighteen years later. While Dr. Grace's observations of the body and the shotgun wound were of paramount importance in determining whether the shotgun fired accidentally, the Commonwealth's delay in bringing the prosecution resulted in the unavailability of Dr. Grace as a witness. . . .

While Dr. Grace lived for 19 years after the shooting incident, the Commonwealth lost the audio recording made during the 1976 autopsy performed by Dr. Grace and failed to subsequently preserve his recollection of the examination of crucial evidence. Other than the autopsy report prepared by Dr. Grace shortly after the incident, no efforts were made by the Commonwealth to interview Dr. Grace for the purpose of recording his personal observations of the physical condition of the body or the medical conclusions that were premised upon those observations. . . .

The resulting prejudice to Dr. Scher's defense due to the unavailability of this crucial witness was compounded by the Commonwealth's deliberate tactics at trial to disparage the findings made by Dr. Grace which were contrary to the prosecution's theory. In order to support its theory of the shooting, the Commonwealth attempted to flatly contradict Dr. Grace's observations by suggesting to the jury that as a physician he was incompetent to make even the simplest physical observations and claimed that the observations recorded by Dr. Grace in his autopsy report were not those that Dr. Grace actually intended to make.

[The] Commonwealth was willing to go to outrageous lengths to dispute the physical findings made by Dr. Grace when those findings contradicted the prosecution's theory. For example, the Commonwealth presented an expert witness to testify that when Dr. Grace referred to the area surrounding the shotgun wound as "somewhat darkened" in his autopsy report, Dr. Grace could have meant that the area surrounding the wound was not darkened at all. This reference to the darkened area surrounding the wound in Dr. Grace's autopsy report was extremely significant because the presence of carbonaceous material around the wound was inconsistent with the prosecution's theory that the shotgun was fired from a distance. . . .

[Throughout the twenty years that elapsed after the shooting, the Commonwealth possessed all] of the physical evidence that was collected after the shooting. This evidence included: the clothing worn by Dr. Scher and Mr. Dillon on the date of the shooting; Dr. Scher's 16-gauge shotgun, Mr. Dillon's 20-gauge shotgun, ammunition and shells found at the scene of the shooting, shooting glasses and ear protectors found at the scene, clay birds, bird thrower, and sections of a log. . . . District Attorney Snyder was critical of the investigation that had been done. He testified that the investigation was "not getting done; not properly." [Any of the witnesses interviewed by the troopers in the renewed investigation would have been available to be interviewed in 1976. The facilities and experts who conducted the testing were available to the Commonwealth when the investigation began. Any new tests performed by the Commonwealth and the Federal Bureau of Investigation failed to reveal any new and/or relevant information that could not have been discovered by testing procedures available to them in 1976.]

This record demonstrates that there was no ongoing investigation into the death of Mr. Dillon. The investigation was dormant for most of the 20 years of pre-arrest delay. Indeed, for 8 of those years, the "investigation" was non-existent. . . . There is no basis to conclude that the pre-arrest delay was required for further investigation. The record establishes that the Commonwealth did not have a proper reason for the inordinate delay. . . .

Problem 5-4. Child Victims

Gilbert Vernier is a 69-year-old grandfather. In July 1984, M.E., then 7 years old, supported by her sister, J.V., informed their mother, "Grandpa touched me in a bad way." The Wyoming Department of Family Services and the county sheriff's department investigated the claim. Two interviews of the victim and her sister were recorded on audiotape. A lieutenant in the sheriff's department who was present during the interview transcribed the second tape. No charges were filed at that time.

Ten years later, in 1994, another granddaughter, L.L., reported to the sheriff's department that in 1977 Vernier had molested her when she was 9 years old and was living with her grandparents. Two weeks after L.L. made this report, M.E. again informed the sheriff's department that Vernier had sexually assaulted her in 1984. J.V. corroborated M.E.'s statements, recalling that Vernier routinely took M.E. into a locked bedroom. During the same time frame in 1994, other evidence emerged about sexual abuse perpetrated by Vernier. D.H. and D.P., Vernier's daughters, recounted repeated sexual abuse and rape by their father when D.H. was between the ages of 12 and 16 and D.P. between the ages of 8 and 13.

Following the 1994 investigation, the state charged Vernier with two counts of indecent liberties and one count of second-degree sexual assault based on the alleged incidents in 1984. At his arraignment, Vernier entered a plea of not guilty and filed a motion to dismiss, claiming the state intentionally had delayed filing charges. Although Wyoming has no statute of limitations for prosecuting crimes, Vernier claimed that the delay violated his due process rights. He argued that the 10-year delay impaired his efforts to defend himself against the charges. During that

time, the government lost the two 1984 audiotapes of conversations between M.E.
and investigators. The transcript of the second tape still exists, however, along with
the deputy's notes reflecting her own observations about the interview. Vernier also
argued that in 1984 he might have recalled an alibi that would have been helpful.

The district court denied the motion. How would you rule on appeal? How
would you respond if Vernier asks your court to create a specific limitations period
for crimes in the absence of a statute of limitations, either as a matter of
constitutional law or as an exercise of the court's "supervisory" power over the
state's criminal justice system? Compare Vernier v. State, 909 P.2d 1344 (Wyo. 1996).

Notes

1. *Pre-accusation delay: majority position.* All state courts have interpreted the due
process provisions of their state constitutions to limit a few types of pre-accusation
delay, applying the test that the U.S. Supreme Court created in United States v.
Lovasco, 431 U.S. 783 (1977). A defendant raising a constitutional objection to a
delay between the date of an alleged crime and the time of the indictment or
information must show (1) the prejudice that the delay caused for the defense
and (2) the reason for the delay. There are two basic approaches in the state courts
on the burden of proving these elements. One group requires the defendant to
prove both prejudice and an intentional prosecutorial delay to achieve a tactical
advantage. See State v. Lacy, 929 P.2d 1288 (Ariz. 1996). A roughly equal number of
states give the defendant the initial burden of proving prejudice and then require
the government to prove a valid reason for the delay. See State v. Brazell, 480 S.E.2d
64 (S.C. 1997). In states that have passed statutes of limitations (as almost all states
have), does the *Lovasco* analysis enable the courts to identify correctly the "stale"
cases that the statute of limitations does not reach? Or does the constitutional
analysis merely make the law less predictable, without systematically improving
on the statutory limits?

2. *Reasons for delay.* The *Lovasco* Court declared categorically that there can be no
due process violation if "good-faith investigative delay" is responsible for the timing
of the charges. Courts also say that a delay created solely to gain a "tactical
advantage" for the prosecution does create a due process problem. The longer
the delay, the more willing courts are to find an improper reason for it.

A central question in the pre-accusation delay cases seems to be the good faith
of the prosecutor. Compare this interpretation of the requirements of due process
with the more general judicial reluctance to become involved in the prosecutor's
charging decision in ordinary cases. See Chapter 3. Will an inquiry into the prosecutor's state of mind regarding a delay lead to more judicial scrutiny of prosecutorial charging decisions than traditional doctrine has allowed? In other words, is
the test for pre-accusation delay more intrusive than the test for selective prosecution? Did the prosecutors in *Scher* and in Problem 5-4 delay charges for different
reasons, or did they each just change their minds about criminal charges?

Problem 5-4 illustrates one reason for delay: Crime victims in some cases —
notably for intrafamily sexual assaults on children — do not make allegations for
many years after the incidents. Should special constitutional rules apply to such
cases? See State v. Gray, 917 S.W.2d 668 (Tenn. 1996) (dismissal of charges of sexual
abuse brought 42 years after incident involving 9-year-old girl). Specialized statutes

of limitation in many states address this type of case (as does the New York statute above).

3. *Source of constitutional protections.* Although the federal constitution and most state constitutions provide specifically for a "speedy trial," these provisions do not apply to delays that occur before criminal charges are filed. The U.S. Supreme Court took the lead on this question in United States v. Marion, 404 U.S. 307 (1971). A review of the text and history of the Sixth Amendment's speedy trial clause (which speaks of a speedy trial for the "accused") convinced the Court that only "a formal indictment or information or else the actual restraints imposed by arrest and holding to answer a criminal charge" would trigger the protections of the speedy trial clause. See also United States v. MacDonald, 456 U.S. 1 (1982) (no speedy trial protection for period between dismissal of first charges and second indictment). As you read further materials in this chapter and encounter cases decided under the Sixth Amendment or analogous state constitutional clauses, consider whether the due process cases dealing with pre-accusation delay would be decided differently if they were analyzed under the more specific constitutional language requiring a "speedy trial."

4. *Statutes of limitation.* The Court in United States v. Marion noted that statutes of limitation provide "the primary guarantee against bringing overly stale criminal charges." The New York statute above is typical in several respects. First, it provides longer limitation periods for more serious crimes. Second, it creates special rules for marking the beginning of the limitation period for certain crimes unlikely to be detected or reported immediately. The statute leaves it for judges to answer the difficult question of when a continuing crime, such as conspiracy, is "committed" in the sense necessary to trigger the statute. Finally, the statute defines certain events that can "toll" (i.e., suspend) the statute after it has begun to run. Should the drafters of the New York statute have included a provision that would allow judges to create additional "tolling" rules "in the interest of justice"?

Should statutes of limitation influence a court ruling on a constitutional challenge to pre-accusation delay? More specifically, if a statute gives extra latitude to a prosecutor in some cases, should that lead a court to give prosecutors extra latitude for delay under the due process clause? Or should the due process protections be strongest when legislatures have provided less statutory protection against delay?

5. *Abolition of statutes of limitation.* Although most jurisdictions in the United States have statutes of limitations, they are not universal. Three states (South Carolina, Kentucky, and Wyoming) do not have a general statute of limitations; the same is true for many other nations, such as England. State legislatures in recent years have also proved willing to create exceptions to these time bars. Do statutes of limitations still serve a useful function? One purpose of a statute of limitations is to prevent the deterioration of reliable evidence over time (for instance, the memories of witnesses might become less reliable as time goes by). Some special cases (for instance, when the prosecution proves the case through scientific evidence such as the DNA found in biological material at the crime scene) do not deteriorate over time. In such cases, should prosecutors be able to suspend the statute of limitations by charging a defendant who is identified only by his or her DNA profile? Perhaps the rationale for a statute of limitations is based on something other than deterioration of evidence. Should we keep statutes of limitations because criminals tend to be more short-sighted than the general public, and the deterrent power of criminal

charges is lost if the case is not filed relatively quickly? See Yair Listokin, Efficient Time Bars: A New Rationale for the Existence of Statutes of Limitations in Criminal Law, 31 J. Legal Stud. 99 (2002) (because potential criminals tend to discount the future at higher rates than society, punishing crimes long after they are committed will have only a nominal deterrent effect, while they may cost society substantial sums).

2. Speedy Trial After Accusation

Once the prosecution obtains an indictment or files an information against a defendant, a wider array of legal provisions become available to move the process along. The Sixth Amendment grants to "the accused" the right to a "speedy and public trial." Analogous state constitutional clauses announce such rights in similarly general terms. The federal Speedy Trial Act creates a more specific obligation for the government to process all criminal trials within 70 days of the indictment or information, although it provides several ways to exclude days from the tally. Most states have statutes limiting the time between an accusation and the start of trial (or entry of a guilty plea). Statutes and judicial orders also allocate judicial resources to keep criminal dockets moving.

The deadlines become relevant in a great number of cases. In large urban jurisdictions in 2002, the median time it took to adjudicate a felony case was 98 days (up from 79 days in 1998). Just under half the cases were adjudicated within three months. Thirteen percent of the felony cases were still unresolved after a year had passed since the arrest. See Bureau of Justice Statistics, Felony Defendants in Large Urban Counties, 2002, at table 22 (2006, NCJ 210818).

As you read the materials in this section, pay particular attention to the interaction among the constitutions, statutes, and other legal provisions that relate to speedy preparation for trial. Do these provisions operate differently? If so, are they different because they are framed in different language (some general and some specific), or because they seek different objectives? Note that the constitutional provisions described above are framed in terms of the defendant's rights. But victims of crime and the public at large also are interested in prompt resolution of charges against criminal defendants. A few constitutional provisions and many statutes recognize the interests of crime victims and the public in requiring the parties to prepare quickly for trial. Whose interests triumph when the defendant's interest and the public's interest in timely resolution of cases conflict?

From its earliest opportunity, the U.S. Supreme Court has insisted that the constitutional guarantee of a "speedy" trial is a "necessarily relative" concept. See Beavers v. Haubert, 198 U.S. 77 (1905). The same length of time between accusation and resolution of criminal charges might be acceptable in one case and unacceptable in another, depending on the prosecutor's reasons, the harm that the defendant suffered, and other circumstances. In Barker v. Wingo, 407 U.S. 514 (1972), the Court settled on four circumstances that every court must consider when resolving a claim that the government has violated a defendant's constitutional right to a speedy trial. As you read the following exercise in applying the four-part *Barker* standard, consider how the four factors interact and ask whether some pertinent questions have now been placed out of view.

■ STATE v. DAVID MAGNUSEN
646 So. 2d 1275 (Miss. 1994)

SMITH, J.

David Eugene Magnusen, charged with rape, aggravated assault, two counts of robbery and two counts of burglary of an inhabited dwelling, was incarcerated in the Harrison County Jail for 15 months without being tried. The charges lodged against him were dismissed by the Circuit Court for the State's failure to grant a constitutionally guaranteed speedy trial. The State of Mississippi . . . requests that this Court find that the trial judge erred in dismissing all charges against Magnusen. . . . After careful consideration in a close case, we must reverse and remand and require Magnusen to stand trial.

On December 14, 1990, two indictments were returned against 19-year-old David Magnusen charging him in multiple counts with [committing burglaries, robberies, assaults, and a rape on May 11 and 19, 1990. Magnusen was arrested on May 30, 1990.] On June 12, 1990, Danny Holloway, a detective with the Gulfport Police Department, requested the performance of a rape protocol on 12 articles of evidence he delivered to the Mississippi Crime Laboratory (hereinafter "crime lab") in Gulfport. Fifteen months later, on August 22, 1991, only a hair comparison analysis had been completed by the crime lab. None of the serological work requested by Holloway had been performed. The results of the hair analysis linked Magnusen to the rape of Evelyn Verchinski, who had identified Magnusen as her assailant in a police showup conducted on May 30, 1990.

Holloway waited four months for the rest of the test results before submitting the files to the district attorney's office on October 8, 1990. The district attorney's office, in turn, waited another seven weeks until November 30, 1990, before presenting the cases to the Grand Jury. Indictments were finally returned on December 14, 1990, six and one-half months following the defendant's arrest. There was a delay in setting Magnusen's arraignment because of inadvertence in the court administrator's office. On the day the arraignment was set, Magnusen was without counsel, his lawyer having been permitted by the trial court to withdraw from the case the previous week.

[Debra Butler, a forensic serologist with the Mississippi Crime Laboratory,] was the only serologist for a 15 county area on the Mississippi Gulf Coast. The exhibits in question were received at the Gulfport office and sent to Jackson for hair and fiber comparison. The specimens were then returned to the Gulfport laboratory for a serological analysis. According to Butler, it would take 80 man hours to test the exhibits submitted in this case. There is no statutory provision for the state to contract with private laboratories to perform their work.

The State argues vigorously that the trial judge erred in finding as a fact and concluding as a matter of law that the State violated Magnusen's constitutional right, as opposed to his statutory right, to a speedy trial when a period of 449 days elapsed between his arrest [on May 30, 1990, and the August 22, 1991,] hearing adjudicating Magnusen's motion to dismiss the multiple charges. . . . Magnusen's constitutional right to a speedy trial attached [when] he was arrested. . . . In Noe v. State, 616 So. 2d 298 (Miss. 1993), we . . . stated:

> When a defendant's constitutional right to a speedy trial is at issue, the balancing test set out in Barker v. Wingo, 407 U.S. 514 (1972), is applicable. The factors to consider

are: (1) the length of the delay; (2) the reason for the delay; (3) whether the defendant has asserted his right to a speedy trial; and (4) whether the defendant was prejudiced by the delay.

This Court recognized in Beavers v. State, 498 So. 2d 788, 790 (Miss. 1986):

> No mathematical formula exists according to which the *Barker* weighing and balancing process must be performed. The weight to be given each factor necessarily turns on the quality of evidence available on each and, in the absence of evidence, identification of the party with the risk of nonpersuasion. In the end, no one factor is dispositive. The totality of the circumstances must be considered.

We are mindful indeed that no one factor is dispositive of the question. Nor is the balancing process restricted to the *Barker* factors to the exclusion of any other relevant circumstances. . . . We turn now to an analysis of the four *Barker* factors. The trial judge applied the correct legal standard in the form of the traditional four pronged balancing test but reached, in our opinion, an inappropriate result.

(1) LENGTH OF THE DELAY

The delay between arrest and trial was 449 days (approximately 15 months). The trial judge found that a delay of 449 days was sufficient to require the State to show that such delay necessitated a review of the remaining *Barker* factors. We agree.

In Smith v. State, 550 So. 2d 406 (Miss. 1989), this Court held "that any delay of eight months or longer is presumptively prejudicial." However, this factor, alone, is insufficient for reversal, but requires a close examination of the remaining factors. . . . "While such presumptive prejudice cannot alone carry a Sixth Amendment claim without regard to the other *Barker* criteria . . . it is part of the mix of relevant facts, and its importance increases with the length of the delay." Doggett v. United States, 505 U.S. 647 (1992).

The length of the delay not attributable to Magnusen or his lawyer or to the lower court is around 300 days . . . which, under the facts and circumstances in this case, is not an excessive or inordinate delay. In [five prior speedy trial cases decided in this court], each defendant, in the wake of a *Barker* analysis, was discharged following delays of 370, 423, 480, 298, and 566 days, respectively. We give Magnusen the benefit of any doubt. This factor favors the defendant, necessitating scrutiny of the case as to the remaining *Barker* factors.

(2) REASON FOR THE DELAY

The reason for delay included chronic congestion of trial docket; unavailability of evidence potentially material to the State's case as well as potentially exculpatory; heavy case load; understaffing and negligence of the crime laboratory; incarceration on other charges after bond was revoked; substitution of defense counsel; three continuances; unheard motions filed by the defense; and unavailability of judge at the time the trial was scheduled. This factor, viewed in its three part totality, favors the State, although slightly. At the very least, it weighs equally against the State and the defendant.

In the *Barker* case, the Supreme Court of the United States asserted:

[D]ifferent weights should be assigned to different reasons. A deliberate attempt to delay the trial in order to hamper the defense should be weighed heavily against the government. A more neutral reason such as negligence or overcrowded courts should be weighed less heavily but nevertheless should be considered since the ultimate responsibility for such circumstances must rest with the government rather than with the defendant. Finally, a valid reason, such as a missing witness, should serve to justify appropriate delay.

In the case at bar, 198 days or 6½ months elapsed between arrest and indictment, 104 days or 3½ months intervened between indictment and arraignment, and there were 147 days or 5 months intervening between arraignment and the hearing on the motion to dismiss the charges. . . .

The most critical period of delay is the 198 day preindictment delay between Magnusen's arrest on May 30 and his indictment on December 14, 1990. We weigh this portion of the delay against the State but not heavily. The trial judge found as a fact that both the Gulfport Police Department and the district attorney's office "had done their job." He found that the fault lay with the neglect of the crime lab, one of many tentacles of the State. It is unclear from the testimony of Debra Butler whether this neglect was excusable or without just cause. The delay certainly was not intentional. What is clear is that from June 14, 1990, to November 30, 1990, a period of approximately 5½ months, the district attorney's office awaited the results of the laboratory testing before presenting the case to the grand jury. [T]he results of the serology tests could have just as easily been exculpatory as not.

On the other side of the coin, a blood specimen taken from the victim in May of 1990 was allowed to putrefy before it was tested, thereby necessitating a requirement for a new specimen. Negligence causing delay should be weighed against the State but not heavily. An additional observation is that [Magnusen also faced charges of "unlawful touching for lustful purposes," based on events in February 1989, pre-dating the alleged offenses in this case. Although Magnusen was originally released on bond for the 1989 fondling charges, the bond was revoked on August 10, 1990. Thus, Magnusen would have been in jail on the "unlawful touching" charges during part of this period even if he had not been incarcerated on the charges at issue in this case]. It was not until December 21, 1990, a period of 133 days [from the time that bond was revoked], that the fondling indictments were dismissed because [the crime applied only to those at least 18 years old, and Magnusen was 17 at the time of the alleged offense].

In the final analysis, the official neglect of an understaffed and overworked crime lab gives this portion of the delay to the defendant but barely. . . .

We weigh [the 104 day delay from indictment to arraignment] equally because of [Magnusen's decision to substitute counsel in March 1991, a few weeks before the scheduled date of the arraignment]. Magnusen's two cases had not been set for arraignment any sooner because of inadvertence of the court administrator. More-over, the testimony reflects that a 3½ month delay from indictment to arraignment is not an unusual length of time. Finally, the State was under a continuing duty to disclose by virtue of the defendant's discovery request for crime lab results, filed February 1, 1991.

The bulk of [the 147 day delay between the March 28, 1991, arraignment and the motion to dismiss on August 22, 1991] is attributed to the defendant who was without counsel near the day of arraignment because his lawyer had been permitted to withdraw on April 1, 1991. A congested trial docket and three continuances also contributed to this portion of the delay which weighs heavily against Magnusen.

First, within the context of our [statutory] 270 day rule and the defendant's statutory right, as opposed to his constitutional right, to a speedy trial, docket congestion has been held to constitute good cause for delay. While a crowded docket will not automatically suffice to establish good cause, the specific facts of the case may give rise to good cause. The same rationale should apply when the defendant's constitutional right to a speedy trial, as opposed to his statutory right, is at issue.

Second, during the period from April 15, 1991, to August 16, 1991, a total of three continuances were granted on motion of either the court, the defendant, or both. The reasons for the continuances were, at least in part, a crowded docket, the unavailability of the circuit judge who was engaged in trial elsewhere, and the defendant's motion for an omnibus hearing filed on June 3, 1991, the day the case was set for trial. [The motion included a request for discovery of any lab reports and a request for a speedy trial.] The first continuance was granted on April 15, 1991, upon motion of the circuit judge who was engaged in trial elsewhere. The second continuance was granted on June 3, 1991, upon motion of both the court and the defendant because the defendant filed a motion for an omnibus hearing the day of trial. Trial was reset for August 12, 1991. The third continuance was granted August 16, 1991, upon motion of the circuit judge who again was engaged in trial elsewhere. Trial was reset for August 26, 1991. A delay of 129 days between April 15, 1991, and August 22, 1991 (the day the charges were dismissed), was a by-product of continuances granted because of (1) a congested trial docket and (2) the defendant's motion for an omnibus hearing.

Delays caused by overcrowded dockets are not to be weighed heavily against the State. Continuances granted to the defendant toll the running of our speedy trial statute and should not be counted against the State. Again, the same rationale should apply when a defendant's constitutional right . . . to a speedy trial is at issue. Accordingly, over 100 days during the period from April 15, 1991 to August 22, 1991 should be deducted from the total number of days sandwiched between Magnusen's arrest and trial. Thus, the length of the delay not attributable to either the defendant or his lawyer is approximately 300 days or ten months.

(3) Assertion of Right

Magnusen asserted his constitutional right to a speedy trial in a multi-faceted motion filed February 1, 1991, by attorney Davis; again in a multi-faceted motion filed August 7, 1991, by attorney Woods; and again on August 20, 1991, in the Motion to Dismiss charges filed by attorney Woods. . . . Buried in the midst of a four page, eleven paragraph document filed February 1, 1991, by attorney Davis and styled simply "Motions," is a three line statement found under paragraph VII in which Magnusen "asserts his right to a speedy, public trial by jury as guaranteed under the 6th Amendment. . . ."

The State, of course, bears the burden of bringing an accused to trial in a speedy manner. Although the defendant has neither a duty nor an obligation to bring himself to trial, points are placed on his side of the ledger when, as here, he has made a demand for a speedy trial.

This factor favors the defendant, but only slightly. This is because the bulk of the delay from February 1, 1991, when Magnusen first asserted his right to a speedy trial, to August 22, 1991, when the charges were dismissed, can reasonably be charged to the defendant while the reasons for other portions of the delay are, at best, neutral. Moreover, certain actions by defense counsel were in derogation of Magnusen's assertion of his right to a speedy trial.

Immediately after asserting his right to a speedy trial by and through attorney Davis [on February 1, 1991], Magnusen retained a new lawyer, Cecil Woods, Jr. [Woods himself withdrew from the case but was reappointed on April 8, the date the arraignment took place.] On April 15, 1991, the lower court, on its own motion, entered a continuance because the circuit judge was engaged in trial elsewhere. On June 3, 1991, the State was again prepared to go to trial without the crime laboratory results. Magnusen, by and through attorney Woods, filed a motion for an omnibus hearing which was set but never held due to a death in defense counsel's family. On a later date, due to the engagement of the circuit judge in a capital murder case, once again the omnibus hearing although set, was not conducted. In addition to this, Magnusen filed motions which he never set for hearing. The multi-faceted motions filed on February 1, 1991, and August 7, 1991, were never set for hearing by the defendant. Such, in our opinion, detracts from the assertion of his right to a speedy trial.

The record reflects the State was ready, willing and able to go to trial on four separate occasions, April 8, June 3, August 12, and August 16, 1991, but was prevented from doing so by circumstances clearly not the fault of the State. We weigh this *Barker* factor in favor of Magnusen, but barely.

(4) Prejudice to the Defendant

No actual prejudice to Magnusen was demonstrated by the delay. . . . The only prejudice articulated by the trial judge in his written order was that the defendant "lost his freedom" on the date of the arrest on charges which had gone untried for over a year. Although Magnusen testified at the evidentiary hearing, no claim of prejudice was made at that time. The only such inference appears in Magnusen's motion to dismiss filed on August 20, 1991. Therein, blatant allegations are made that witnesses may not be available and apparently the memories of those witnesses who are available have faded. . . . This prong of the *Barker* analysis was discussed as follows:

> A fourth factor is prejudice to the defendant. Prejudice of course, should be assessed in the light of the interests of defendants which the speedy trial right was designed to protect. This Court has identified three such interests: (i) to prevent oppressive pretrial incarceration; (ii) to minimize anxiety and concern of the accused; and (iii) to limit the possibility that the defense will be impaired. Of these, the most serious is the last, because the inability of a defendant adequately to prepare his case skews the fairness of the entire system. If witnesses die or disappear during a delay, the prejudice is obvious. There is also prejudice if defense witnesses are unable to recall accurately events of the distant past. Loss of memory, however, is not always reflected in the record because what has been forgotten can rarely be shown. [407 U.S. at 532.]

As for the first interest, Magnusen was incarcerated from May 30, 1990, until the charges were dismissed on August 22, 1991, a period of almost 450 days. A healthy number of days, however, should be weighed against the defendant. The 147 day time frame between March 28, 1991, and August 22, 1991, is weighed more heavily against Magnusen than against the State. The remaining ten month period of incarceration is the same period of incarceration found in the *Barker* case where the Supreme Court of the United States held that Barker was not denied his right to a speedy trial. . . .

No proof was offered by the defendant that his employment or family life was disrupted or his financial resources drained or his associations curtailed; to the contrary, . . . Magnusen was single and unemployed. Although Magnusen was incarcerated from the time of his arrest to dismissal of the charges, we cannot categorize his pretrial incarceration as particularly "oppressive."

The second interest protected by the constitutional right to a speedy trial is minimizing anxiety and concern. There was no proof during the hearing that Magnusen suffered an extraordinary, or even an ordinary, amount of anxiety and concern over this particular case. There were several serious charges pending against him, including two fondling charges. While Magnusen may have had a right to be anxious and concerned, not all of his woes and tribulations were a product of the charges . . . in this case.

The third interest protected by the constitutional right to a speedy trial is that of minimizing the possibility that the defense of the accused will be impaired. There has been no allegation that the defense was impaired because of a loss of witnesses or their memories. In short, there has been no demonstration of actual prejudice to Magnusen in preparing for the defense of his case. Although the delay in this case is presumptively prejudicial, we will not infer prejudice to the defense out of the "clear blue."

In the final analysis, where, as here, the delay is neither intentional nor egregiously protracted, and where, as here, there is an absence of prejudice, we find this factor favoring the State.

On balance, an analysis of the *Barker* factors, when considered together with other relevant circumstances, favors the State, but not heavily. . . . The trial court paid insufficient attention to the various distinct periods of delay in reaching its conclusion. Additionally, the trial court erroneously required that the delay be for "good and sufficient cause" rather than whether the reason weighed "heavily," "lightly" or "not at all." [The trial judge] placed too much weight on the negligence of the crime lab and failed to properly focus on the various distinct periods of delay in reaching his conclusion. The judgment of the trial court is reversed and the matter is remanded for Magnusen to stand trial on all charges.

SULLIVAN, J., dissenting.

. . . The majority opinion rests on the faulty premise that the trial court decided this issue using the wrong legal standard. . . . True, the trial court considered whether the state showed "good and sufficient cause" for the delay; however, the trial court did so in conjunction with its determination of how much weight to accord the justification offered. The trial court correctly relied on State v. Ferguson, 576 So. 2d 1252 (Miss. 1991), for the proposition that once the delay has been determined to be presumptively prejudicial, "the burden shifts to the prosecution to produce evidence justifying the delay and to persuade the trier of fact of the legitimacy of these reasons." This Court also stated in *Ferguson* that "where the accused has not caused the delay, and where the prosecution has failed to show good cause therefor, this factor [reason for the delay] weighs in favor of the accused." . . .

Justice Smith correctly acknowledges the fact that the length of delay in this case warrants examination of the remaining *Barker* factors. It is with Justice Smith's reasoning beginning with the second constitutional speedy trial factor, "reason for the delay," that I must disagree. The trial court found that the cause of the delay "certainly cannot be attributable to the defendant." We cannot find to the contrary short of concluding that the lower court was manifestly wrong in making this finding. Instead, the majority simply reexamines the record, splits the 455 day delay into different periods of delay, argues that the court applied the wrong legal standard, and somehow reaches the conclusion that the cause of delay weighs against Magnusen, or, "at the very least, it weighs equally against the State and the defendant." . . .

I furthermore disagree with Justice Smith's implication that docket congestion should be considered good cause to the extent that the constitutional speedy trial clock should be deemed to have stopped running during those periods of delay. The *Barker* Court stated: "Overcrowded courts should be weighed less heavily but nevertheless should be considered since the ultimate responsibility for such circumstances must rest with the government rather than with the defendant."

[Magnusen] made his first speedy trial demand on February 1, 1991, shortly after the indictment was returned against him, after a period of delay attributable to the state because of the negligence of the state crime lab. He did not knowingly delay in making his demand. . . . Today's decision does not, in my opinion, place the proper importance on Magnusen's assertion of his right. Moreover, the inference that the prosecution should not be held to have been aware of the speedy trial demand because it was buried in a lengthy motion is not persuasive. Magnusen clearly asserted his right. . . .

Because the first three factors weigh in Magnusen's favor, it is not necessary to examine the fourth *Barker* factor, prejudice to the defendant. Nonetheless, the trial court weighed this factor in Magnusen's favor. The court stated:

> I know of nothing that is more prejudicial to anyone than to be confined for a period of 447 days without the benefit of a trial. It's somewhat likened to getting the cart before the horse, because once again, the State does carry the burden of proving a person's guilt, not assuming the person's guilt.

First, when a presumption of prejudice has been established, as it was in this case, a defendant is not responsible for proving prejudice. That is, the prosecution is responsible for rebutting the presumption that the defendant has suffered prejudice as a result of the delay. . . .

The majority correctly points out the fact that in *Barker*, the Court found that the defendant did not suffer oppressive pretrial incarceration for a period of time similar in length to that Magnusen spent in jail prior to trial through no fault of his own. In *Barker*, however, the Court took specific notice of the fact that *Barker* did not want to be tried — he allowed the state to continue his case 16 times without objection. Here, as mentioned earlier, Magnusen filed his speedy trial demand approximately six weeks after he was indicted — Barker waited approximately three and one-half years. The *Barker* Court's reasoning regarding the defendant's desire to be tried, and how that desire relates to the question of whether the defendant suffered oppressive pretrial incarceration, favors Magnusen. . . .

I believe today's decision fails to give the proper deference to the findings and conclusions of the trial judge who served as a part of the proceedings against this defendant from their inception, and throughout, until the charges were dismissed against him. The majority admits that this is a close case, and as such, we should affirm the lower court's decision. The trial court applied the correct legal standard and reached the correct result. Because I believe we cannot reverse this case on the record before us, I respectfully dissent.

Notes

1. *Constitutional speedy trial rights: majority position.* The Supreme Court has incorporated the "speedy trial" clause of the Sixth Amendment as a component of the Fourteenth Amendment's due process clause that applies to the states. Klopfer v. North Carolina, 386 U.S. 213 (1967). In addition, virtually all states have used the four-part test from Barker v. Wingo, 407 U.S. 514 (1972), to determine the speedy trial rights of defendants under their state constitutions. As illustrated in the *Magnusen* case from Mississippi, the analysis of constitutional speedy trial claims often requires courts to answer a series of questions, assigning responsibility for each period of delay. The first *Barker* factor (the length of the delay) is a necessary threshold. Only when the delay becomes long enough will the court analyze the other factors. Although the exact length of time necessary is a question for common-law development, a delay of just under one year is usually sufficient to obtain a full review of the four factors. Once the full inquiry takes place, often the most important factor is whether the defendant has been prejudiced.

2. *Ranking reasons for delay.* Courts in most jurisdictions have followed the *Barker* Court's suggestion that a "deliberate attempt to delay the trial in order to hamper the defense" is weighed heavily against the government, while a "valid reason" such as a missing witness would justify some delay. Reasons such as prosecutorial negligence or lack of resources will count against the government, but not heavily. See State v. Spivey, 579 S.E.2d 251 (N.C. 2003) (delay of over four years in starting murder trial acceptable under *Barker;* reasons for delay included numerous homicide cases on docket, courthouse renovations). Does it make sense to make defendants bear the cost of inadequate court funding? Does a similar ranking system apply to a defendant's reasons for contributing to the delay? Will the defendant's actions only be weighed "heavily" against her claim if she has made a deliberate attempt to hamper the prosecution through delay? Did the *Magnusen* court place different weights on different actions of the defendant?

3. *Requests and waivers.* Before *Barker,* a number of states followed the "demand waiver" rule, which assumed that a defendant who did not request a speedy trial had waived the right. Even though a request for speedy trial is no longer strictly necessary to make a constitutional claim, a defendant can increase the chances of showing a violation if she asserts the right early in the process. Conversely, it is possible for a defendant to waive speedy trial rights explicitly. What if defense counsel waives speedy trial rights without consulting the client? Is this one of those rights (such as waiver of a jury trial) that a client should have to waive personally?

4. *Prejudice.* The *Barker* Court listed three types of prejudice that a speedy trial could avoid: (a) "oppressive pretrial incarceration"; (b) "anxiety and concern of the accused"; and (c) "the possibility that the defense will be impaired." Courts routinely say that the third type of prejudice, which can include disappearance of witnesses or loss of memory, is the most serious. If there is a statistical relationship between pretrial detention and conviction for the charged crime, is it plausible to argue that any prejudice of the first type (pretrial detention) also must count as prejudice of the third type (impairment of defense)? Does it matter what grounds the government has for holding the defendant? Speedy trial rights extend to persons imprisoned for other offenses. See Smith v. Hooey, 393 U.S. 374 (1969). Will incarceration for another offense weigh less heavily in favor of the defendant than incarceration only for the current charges? There are cases in which the other *Barker* factors create such a strong showing for the defendant that the court will presume prejudice. According to Doggett v. United States, 505 U.S. 647 (1992), the presumption of prejudice strengthens over time. The eight-year delay between indictment and arrest in *Doggett* was a product of the defendant's choice to leave the country (unaware that he was under indictment) and the government's negligence in pursuing him. The Court was willing to presume that such a lengthy delay would impair the defense. But see People v. Martinez, 996 P.2d 32 (Cal. 2000) (refuses to adopt federal rule that defendant need not show specific prejudice if delay is sufficiently long; defendant must always show prejudice under state law).

5. *Remedy.* What should a court do if it is convinced that the government has violated a defendant's constitutional speedy trial rights? According to Strunk v. United States, 412 U.S. 434 (1973), dismissal of the charges with prejudice is the only proper remedy for a violation of the Sixth Amendment speedy trial right. State courts by and large have interpreted their own constitutions the same way. Can you imagine any alternative remedies that would effectively prevent delay without losing convictions of guilty persons? How about a reduction of sentence to reflect the amount of improper delay? What about money damages for improper pretrial incarceration or prolonged anxiety? If these alternatives had been available to the Mississippi court in *Magnusen,* would it have been more willing to find a constitutional violation? See Anthony Amsterdam, Speedy Criminal Trial: Rights and Remedies, 27 Stan. L. Rev. 525 (1975). Should a court be able to select a nondismissal remedy only for particular kinds of prejudice (such as anxiety or loss of reputation) but not for others (such as impairment of defense)? See Akhil Amar, The Constitution and Criminal Procedure: First Principles 96-116 (1997).

6. *Victim's right to speedy trial.* Over the past generation, state constitutional amendments and statutes have recognized some of the interests and procedural rights of victims of alleged crimes. A majority of states now have statutory or constitutional provisions requiring the trial court to consider the interests of crime victims (especially youthful or elderly victims) when responding to requests for continuances. A few states declare more generally that victims have a right to a speedy trial. Take, for instance, Utah Code §77-38-7:

> (1) In determining a date for any criminal trial or other important criminal or juvenile justice hearing, the court shall consider the interests of the victim of a crime to a speedy resolution of the charges under the same standards that govern a defendant's or minor's right to a speedy trial. . . .

(3)(a) In ruling on any motion by a defendant or minor to continue a previously established trial or other important criminal or juvenile justice hearing, the court shall inquire into the circumstances requiring the delay and consider the interests of the victim of a crime to a speedy disposition of the case. . . .

What assurance does a crime victim have that a trial court will carry out these directives? Is the statute enforceable on appeal?

Almost all states now have statutes or procedural rules that oblige the government to complete criminal trials promptly. These "speedy trial acts" show some important differences from one another. First, these statutes and rules differ in how specifically they define the time period that may elapse between accusation and the start of trial. Most, like the federal Speedy Trial Act, give the state a specific number of days (70 days in the federal system) to process the case. Within the group of states that specify the time period, many allow more days to bring to trial a defendant who is not in custody than one who is in custody. See Ill. Ann. Stat. ch. 725, para. 5/103-5 (120 days for defendants in custody, 160 days for defendants released pretrial). A smaller group of states do not specify a number of days at all, but simply require the trial to take place within a "reasonable" time. Mich. R. Crim. P. 6.004 (provides that the "defendant and the people are entitled to a speedy trial and to a speedy resolution of all matters before the court," but states no specific time period for trial of charges against defendants not in custody).

Second, the statutes differ from one another in the methods available to extend the number of days the parties may use to prepare for trial. Some, like the federal statute, exhaustively list the events that can add time to the available days; a number of statutes allow the trial court to extend the time period for "good cause" (or on some other generally phrased grounds). Third, the statutes differ from one another in the remedies they provide for violations. The federal statute is typical of one group, giving the trial judge considerable discretion to choose whether to dismiss the charges with or without prejudice. Other statutes make it clear that one form of dismissal or the other is strongly preferred or required.

Can you identify a combination of features described above that is likely to have the most effect on the amount of time available to prepare a case for trial? The least effect? As you reflect on these statutes, keep a close eye on the interaction between rights and remedies. Is there a relationship between the clarity of the speedy trial obligations that the government faces and the stringency of the remedy for violations? Do these statutes "codify" the constitutional analysis or do they pursue different objectives, using different means?

■ 18 U.S.C. §3161

(c)(1) In any case in which a plea of not guilty is entered, the trial of a defendant charged in an information or indictment with the commission of an offense shall commence within 70 days from the filing date (and making public) of the information or indictment, or from the date the defendant has appeared before a judicial officer of the court in which such charge is pending, whichever date last occurs. . . .

(h) The following periods of delay shall be excluded in computing the time within which an information or an indictment must be filed, or in computing the time within which the trial of any such offense must commence:

(1) Any period of delay resulting from other proceedings concerning the defendant. . . .

(2) Any period of delay during which prosecution is deferred by the attorney for the Government pursuant to written agreement with the defendant, with the approval of the court, for the purpose of allowing the defendant to demonstrate his good conduct.

(3) . . . Any period of delay resulting from the absence or unavailability of the defendant or an essential witness. . . .

(6) If the information or indictment is dismissed upon motion of the attorney for the Government and thereafter a charge is filed against the defendant for the same offense, or any offense required to be joined with that offense, any period of delay from the date the charge was dismissed to the date the time limitation would commence to run as to the subsequent charge had there been no previous charge.

(7) A reasonable period of delay when the defendant is joined for trial with a codefendant as to whom the time for trial has not run and no motion for severance has been granted.

(8)(A) Any period of delay resulting from a continuance granted by any judge on his own motion or at the request of the defendant or his counsel or at the request of the attorney for the Government, if the judge granted such continuance on the basis of [findings on the record] that the ends of justice served by taking such action outweigh the best interest of the public and the defendant in a speedy trial. . . .

(B) The factors, among others, which a judge shall consider in determining whether to grant a continuance under subparagraph (A) of this paragraph in any case are as follows:

(i) Whether the failure to grant such a continuance in the proceeding would be likely to make a continuation of such proceeding impossible, or result in a miscarriage of justice.

(ii) Whether the case is so unusual or so complex, due to the number of defendants, the nature of the prosecution, or the existence of novel questions of fact or law, that it is unreasonable to expect adequate preparation for pretrial proceedings or for the trial itself within the time limits established by this section. . . .

(iv) Whether the failure to grant such a continuance in a case which, taken as a whole, is not so unusual or so complex as to fall within clause (ii), would deny the defendant reasonable time to obtain counsel, would unreasonably deny the defendant or the Government continuity of counsel, or would deny counsel for the defendant or the attorney for the Government the reasonable time necessary for effective preparation, taking into account the exercise of due diligence.

(C) No continuance under subparagraph (A) of this paragraph shall be granted because of general congestion of the court's calendar, or lack of diligent preparation or failure to obtain available witnesses on the part of the attorney for the Government. . . .

■ 18 U.S.C. §3162

(a)(2) If a defendant is not brought to trial within the time limit required by section 3161(c) as extended by section 3161(h), the information or indictment shall be dismissed on motion of the defendant. The defendant shall have the burden of proof of supporting such motion but the Government shall have the burden of going forward with the evidence in connection with any exclusion of time under subparagraph 3161(h)(3). In determining whether to dismiss the case with or without prejudice, the court shall consider, among others, each of the following factors: the seriousness of the offense; the facts and circumstances of the case which led to the dismissal; and the impact of a reprosecution on the administration of this chapter and on the administration of justice. . . .

■ CALIFORNIA PENAL CODE §1382

(a) The court, unless good cause to the contrary is shown, shall order the action to be dismissed in the following cases: . . .

(2) In a felony case, when a defendant is not brought to trial within 60 days of the defendant's arraignment on an indictment or information, or reinstatement of criminal proceedings. . . . However, an action shall not be dismissed under this paragraph if [the] defendant requests or consents to the setting of a trial date beyond the 60-day period. . . .

(c) If the defendant is not represented by counsel, the defendant shall not be deemed under this section to have consented to the date for the defendant's trial unless the court has explained to the defendant his or her rights under this section and the effect of his or her consent.

■ CALIFORNIA PENAL CODE §1387

(a) An order terminating an action pursuant to [section 1382] is a bar to any other prosecution for the same offense if it is a felony or if it is a misdemeanor charged together with a felony and the action has been previously terminated pursuant to [section 1382], or if it is a misdemeanor not charged together with a felony, except in those [cases in which] the judge or magistrate finds any of the following:

(1) That substantial new evidence has been discovered by the prosecution which would not have been known through the exercise of due diligence at, or prior to, the time of termination of the action.

(2) That the termination of the action was the result of the direct intimidation of a material witness, as shown by a preponderance of the evidence. . . .

(b) Notwithstanding subdivision (a), an order terminating an action pursuant to this chapter is not a bar to another prosecution for the same offense if it is . . . an offense based on an act of domestic violence, . . . and the termination of the action was the result of the failure to appear by the complaining witness, who had been personally subpoenaed. This subdivision shall apply only within six months of the original dismissal of the action, and may be invoked only once in each action. . . .

Problem 5-5. Whose Delay?

Michael Mayo was arrested in Illinois on February 3, 1998, and was charged the next day with two counts of aggravated criminal sexual assault. Mayo remained in custody and was never released on bond. On March 11, the trial court appointed a public defender to represent Mayo. The public defender entered a not-guilty plea on Mayo's behalf.

On July 1, Mayo's attorney demanded a trial; Mayo himself expressed his wish for the trial to begin quickly, but also said that he wanted to dismiss the public defender and to represent himself. The trial judge warned Mayo about the perils of self-representation, but allowed the public defender to withdraw and continued the case to July 9, on Mayo's request, so that he could answer the State's discovery motion.

On July 9, Mayo appeared in court without an answer to the State's discovery motion. He said that he needed some help and told the court and public defender that he could not represent himself. Based on Mayo's change of attitude, the trial judge reappointed the public defender. After a few status dates, Mayo appeared in court on November 30, this time with a different public defender assigned to the case. Mayo told the court that he wanted trial to be set. The public defender responded that if Mayo wanted to demand trial, he could try the case himself. The judge asked Mayo if he wanted to represent himself or have an attorney. Mayo said "I want an attorney." However, after the public defender and State's Attorney began to discuss a continuance date of December 21, 1998, Mayo interrupted the conversation as follows:

Mayo: I would like to take back my — I'm ready at this time. I don't need her help. She is not helping me.

Public Defender: I just got on the case. I'd like the record to reflect I got on the case two weeks ago and spoke to his wife.

The Court: Be back on December 21st. If you still want to represent yourself we'll go back at that time and you'll go to trial by yourself. I don't suggest it because I think it's —

Mayo: When this woman talked to my wife, she gave the impression that she is not working on my behalf. She told my wife she already finds no reason to be here. What is she doing for me if she is telling my wife that she shouldn't be here on my behalf?

Public Defender: I didn't tell her that.

Mayo: Ask my wife right there.

Public Defender: I don't want to get in the middle of this. If you want to get a private attorney or do this yourself you can.

Mayo appeared in court on December 21, with a different public defender than the one he had on November 30. Mayo informed the court that he wanted to go to trial and represent himself. The trial court did not dismiss the public defender. The judge stated that he was going to hold the case over until December 23, so that Mayo could discuss representing himself with the public defender who represented him on November 30. If Mayo continued in his wish to represent himself at that time, he could do so then. Mayo again stated that he had made his decision and that he wanted to represent himself. The trial court still held the matter over until December 23, 1998. The State's Attorney asked if Mayo was going to answer its discovery motion to which the trial court responded, "he will or he's not calling any witnesses."

On December 23, Mayo again demanded trial, stating his wish to represent himself. The trial court then dismissed the public defender and Mayo represented himself from that point forward. On February 18, 1999, Mayo moved to dismiss the charges on speedy-trial grounds. The court denied the motion on March 29. The trial commenced on April 12, and the jury found Mayo guilty of two counts of aggravated criminal sexual assault. The court sentenced defendant to eight years' imprisonment for each count of aggravated criminal sexual assault, to run consecutively.

On appeal, Mayo argues that his convictions should be reversed because the Speedy Trial Act was violated. The Illinois Speedy Trial Act, appearing at 725 ILCS 5/103-5(a), provides: "Every person in custody in this State for an alleged offense shall be tried by the court having jurisdiction within 120 days from the date he was taken into custody unless delay is occasioned by the defendant." The relevant period is 160 days from the date of arrest for defendants who were released from custody before trial.

In this case, over a year passed between Mayo's arrest and the start of his trial. Both parties agree, however, that at least 114 days of the delay should be attributed to the State. The parties only disagree about the responsibility for an additional 21 days of delay, falling between November 30 and December 21. According to case law in Illinois, each delay must be reviewed individually and attributed to the party who causes it. Any delay found to be occasioned by the defendant tolls the applicable statutory period. When a defense attorney requests a continuance on behalf of a defendant, any delay caused by that continuance will be attributed to the defendant. However, a defendant cannot be bound by his attorney's actions when he clearly and convincingly attempted to assert his right to discharge his attorney and proceed to an immediate trial.

Was there a violation of the Illinois Speedy Trial Act? If these proceedings had occurred in federal court, would the relevant 21-day period be counted against the 70-day limit of the federal statute? Do the Illinois and federal statutes turn on different factual inquiries? Compare People v. Mayo, 764 N.E.2d 525 (Ill. 2002).

Notes

1. *Speedy-trial statutes and the federal constitution.* Almost all states have statutes or court rules addressing speedy trial preparation. Some of these statutes are intended to implement the constitutional speedy-trial right, while others serve the additional purpose of clearing court dockets. Do these provisions add a new dimension to the constitutional analysis simply because they are more specific than a general right to a "speedy trial"? In the minority of states where statutes or rules use general language (such as a statutory bar against "unreasonable delay"), does the statute or rule add anything at all to the constitutional inquiry? Why would drafters of rules or statutes bother to pass a provision without specific time limits?

2. *Time allowed for preparation.* Speedy-trial statutes select many different time periods to allow the parties to prepare for trial. The federal statute's 70-day limit is one of the shorter periods; some state statutes allow periods longer than six months. Most have tighter time limits for defendants in custody than for those who have been released before trial. It is also customary for these statutes to provide longer time limits for felonies than for misdemeanors, and some create even finer distinctions between the more serious and less serious offenses. See Ohio Rev. Stat. §2945.71. The statutes list several events that can start the speedy-trial "clock." Under the federal statute, an arrest starts a time period that must end within 30 days in an indictment or information, while the indictment or information starts the 70-day countdown to the trial. Under most of the state statutes, an indictment or information starts the clock for felonies, and the filing of a complaint begins the period for misdemeanors. Trials that end in mistrials or in convictions reversed on appeal have their own specialized timing rules.

If you were drafting a speedy-trial statute, would you anticipate the ways that the parties might try to manipulate the time periods? For instance, would you address the defendant's ability to enter a plea agreement and withdraw it near the arrival of the statutorily designated number of days from the filing of the charge? How would you respond to the prosecutor's power to enter a nolle prosequi as the deadline nears and to refile charges when the case is ready to try?

3. *Speedy-trial rights for crime victims.* Generally speaking, the victims of alleged crimes prefer not to wait for trial to begin. What are the shortest preparation periods that a statute could grant to a defendant without being unconstitutional? Under the federal statute, a trial cannot commence "less than 30 days from the date on which the defendant first appears through counsel" unless the defendant consents to a quicker deadline. 18 U.S.C. §3161(c)(2). A minority of states have statutes setting a minimum time period for trial preparation. This question ordinarily arises as a constitutional challenge (based on due process or the right to counsel) to a trial court's refusal to grant a defense motion for a continuance; appellate courts almost always defer to the trial court's discretion on this question. See State v. Jones, 467 S.E.2d 12 (N.C. 1996).

A Florida statute allows the state attorney to file a demand for a speedy trial if the state has met its discovery obligations under the rules and the court has granted at least three continuances to the defense over the objection of prosecutors. Fla. Stat. §960.0015. A minimum of 125 days must pass from the day that felony charges were filed. After a prosecutor files a speedy trial demand, trial must begin no more than 45 days later, unless a "necessary" witness fails to show up or if "further extension may be required to prevent deprivation of the defendant's right to due process." Does a statute of this sort make the constitutional doctrine of Barker v. Wingo more important? Does it actually reshape the incentives built into the typical speedy-trial statute?

4. *Excluded time periods.* One major difference among speedy-trial statutes appears in the method of identifying "excluded" days, those that do not count toward the speedy-trial deadline. Most jurisdictions, represented by the federal statute reprinted above, list the particular events that can be excluded from the speedy-trial countdown. See Zedner v. United States, 126 S. Ct. 1976 (2006) (defendant may not prospectively waive the application of the federal Speedy Trial Act, and waiver does not prevent defendant from later requesting a continuance to serve the "ends of justice").

A minority of states, represented by the California statute above, do not specify the grounds for excluding days, instead allowing judges to determine in a particular case whether "good cause" exists to allow an exclusion. See Bulgin v. State, 912 So.2d 307 (Fla. 2005) (if state officials do not obtain express waiver of speedy trial rights, days that defendant spent cooperating with investigators must count against statutory limit of 175 days to begin trial). Some statutes, like the Illinois provision quoted above, state simply that any delay "caused" by the defendant is excluded from the countdown. Consult the federal statute again, giving particular attention to section 3161(h)(8). Does this provision convert the statute's itemized list into a less predictable standard? Is it inevitable that an itemized list of grounds for excluding days will include reasons such as these? How would a judge in California respond to a claim that "court congestion" is a "good cause" for a delay beyond the statutory limits? See People v. Johnson, 606 P.2d 738 (Cal. 1980) (ordinary congestion arising from inadequate resources is not good cause, but congestion arising from extraordinary and nonrecurring circumstances can be good cause).

5. *Sanctions for violations of statutes.* Another major difference among speedy-trial statutes is the remedy they require or encourage for statutory violations. As you saw in the federal statute reprinted above, dismissal without prejudice is the preferred remedy under some speedy-trial statutes. United States v. Taylor, 487 U.S. 326 (1988) (overturning trial court decision to dismiss with prejudice for Speedy Trial Act violation); State v. Clovis, 864 P.2d 687 (Kan. 1993) (government successfully showed a "necessity" for dismissing and refiling charges). Is dismissal without prejudice a toothless remedy? Consult again the New York statute of limitations reprinted at the beginning of this section and consider whether such provisions make the dismissal without prejudice remedy more effective. It is more common to find speedy-trial statutes or rules of procedure that make dismissal with prejudice the preferred remedy. See Neb. Stat. §29-1208. Does the California statute reprinted above make dismissal with prejudice the preferred remedy?

Is the dismissal remedy for speedy-trial violation similar to the exclusionary rule for unconstitutional searches and seizures because it rewards some guilty defendants out of proportion to the wrong that the state has committed? Would monetary damages be a better remedy, at least for defendants who make no showing that the delay impaired their defense? A Massachusetts statute offers compensation to some defendants whose cases are delayed beyond the statutory limits. See Commonwealth v. Bunting, 518 N.E.2d 1159 (Mass. 1988) (in action to recover damages for statutory speedy-trial delays, state can still litigate question of whether defendant consented to delays, even after dismissal of criminal charges on speedy-trial grounds).

6. *Prioritizing cases.* Speedy-trial statutes give priority to criminal matters over civil matters; among criminal matters, they give priority to felonies and cases involving defendants who are detained before trial. See Cal. Penal Code §1048. In a world where ordinary civil litigation must wait in line behind criminal cases, does this give every segment of society a concrete interest in speedy trials? Is this what courts mean when they speak of the "public's interest" in speedy trials?

VI

Pleas and Bargains

In criminal courts in this country, guilty pleas before trial occur far more often than verdicts after trial. In large urban counties in 2002, 9 of 10 felony defendants resolved their criminal charges through a guilty plea rather than a trial. Only murder charges produced trials in more than 10 percent of the cases; the rate of guilty pleas was even higher than 90 percent for misdemeanor charges. In the federal system in 2002, 96 percent of all convictions resulted from pleas of guilty or nolo contendere rather than trials. Most of the time, in most places in this country, the overwhelming majority of criminal charges are resolved through guilty pleas.

Why do we see so few criminal trials? Plea bargains are the short—and incomplete—answer. A large proportion of felony defendants enter pleas of guilty only after they have reached an agreement with the prosecutor, obliging the prosecutor to make some concessions. Perhaps the prosecutor will agree to dismiss some pending charges or to reduce the pending charge to something less serious (this is known as a "charge bargain"). Or perhaps the prosecutor will agree to recommend a particular sentence or to refrain from making certain recommendations (a "sentence" bargain). Other agreement terms are possible, such as a promise not to file charges against third parties.

But plea agreements are not the only explanation for guilty pleas. Some defendants plead guilty as charged without extracting any promises at all from the prosecutor (an "open" plea). These defendants (and their attorneys) know that judges tend to impose less severe sentences on offenders who plead guilty, compared to those who go to trial. This "plea discount" is a reality in virtually every court, but it is rare to find formal acknowledgment of the practice in case law, statutes, or procedural rules.

Anyone who wants to understand American criminal justice must study both guilty pleas and plea bargains. The numbers suggest that these topics are more fundamental than criminal trials. Of course, it may be that plea bargaining takes place in the "shadow" of criminal trials, so that the terms of any agreement reflect the parties' predictions about what *would* have happened at a trial. But it is also possible that some types of cases are resolved by guilty pleas so often that the rules of trial have little importance, while the trials that do occur represent some different universe of cases.

The materials in this chapter survey the boundaries that our legal institutions place on the practice of plea bargaining. We begin within those boundaries, examining some of the typical topics for bargaining and the ordinary motives of parties who enter plea agreements. We then move to the boundaries, looking at the types of bargains that the negotiating parties are willing to accept but the legal system as a whole rejects. Categorical constraints on plea bargains come from legislatures, the executive branch, and (less frequently) judges. As always, we will consider whether these different institutions create distinctive answers to the puzzle of what makes a fair plea bargain. Running throughout the chapter is a question about the controlling substantive principles: Does the common law of contracts provide the necessary guidance for determining which plea agreements are enforceable and which are not? The chapter closes with a discussion of the largest questions about plea bargaining: Is the practice inevitable, and is it desirable?

A. BARGAIN ABOUT WHAT?

Every defendant who pleads guilty gives up the right to a jury trial, and the concomitant rights to be represented by counsel, compel witnesses to testify, and confront adverse witnesses. Why would a defendant waive these key rights — essentially those guaranteed by the Fifth and Sixth Amendments to the federal constitution and their state analogs — along with the chance of an acquittal? And why would prosecutors be willing to bargain away the chance of a conviction in court, with the public affirmation of justice and the publicity that go along with it? The materials in this section explore the objectives of the prosecution and defense as they bargain over a possible plea of guilty. This section also pursues a second theme: Are there some terms that are implicit in every plea bargain? Are there some terms that our legal system will not allow the parties to negotiate?

■ FEDERAL RULE OF CRIMINAL PROCEDURE 11(a), (c)

(a)(1) A defendant may plead not guilty, guilty, or (with the court's consent) nolo contendere.

(2) With the consent of the court and the government, a defendant may enter a conditional plea of guilty or nolo contendere, reserving in writing the right to have an appellate court review an adverse determination of a specified pretrial motion. A defendant who prevails on appeal may then withdraw the plea.

(3) Before accepting a plea of nolo contendere, the court must consider the parties' views and the public interest in the effective administration of justice.

(4) If a defendant refuses to enter a plea or if a defendant organization fails to appear, the court must enter a plea of not guilty.

(c)(1) An attorney for the government and the defendant's attorney, or the defendant when proceeding pro se, may discuss and reach a plea agreement. The court must not participate in these discussions. If the defendant pleads guilty or nolo contendere to either a charged offense or a lesser or related offense, the plea agreement may specify that an attorney for the government will:

(A) not bring, or will move to dismiss, other charges;

(B) recommend, or agree not to oppose the defendant's request, that a particular sentence or sentencing range is appropriate or that a particular provision of the Sentencing Guidelines, or policy statement, or sentencing factor does or does not apply (such a recommendation or request does not bind the court); or

(C) agree that a specific sentence or sentencing range is the appropriate disposition of the case, or that a particular provision of the Sentencing Guidelines, or policy statement, or sentencing factor does or does not apply (such a recommendation or request binds the court once the court accepts the plea agreement).

(2) The parties must disclose the plea agreement in open court when the plea is offered, unless the court for good cause allows the parties to disclose the plea agreement in camera.

(3)(A) To the extent the plea agreement is of the type specified in Rule 11(c)(1)(A) or (C), the court may accept the agreement, reject it, or defer a decision until the court has reviewed the presentence report.

(B) To the extent the plea agreement is of the type specified in Rule 11(c)(1)(B), the court must advise the defendant that the defendant has no right to withdraw the plea if the court does not follow the recommendation or request.

■ PEOPLE v. GREGORY LUMZY
730 N.E.2d 20 (Ill. 2000)

HEIPLE, J.

. . . On June 10, 1997, defendant was charged with the offenses of aggravated battery and robbery. On June 23, 1997, defendant pled guilty to robbery in exchange for the State's dismissal of the aggravated battery charge. The circuit court of Lee County sentenced defendant to seven years in prison.

On August 1, 1997 defendant's attorney filed a motion to reconsider defendant's sentence. Defendant did not move to withdraw his guilty plea. The trial court denied defendant's motion and defendant filed a notice of appeal. . . .

The State argued that defendant's plea was a "negotiated plea" because the State had agreed to drop the aggravated battery charge in exchange for defendant's guilty plea. Accordingly, under the rationale of People v. Evans, 673 N.E.2d 244 (Ill. 1996), defendant could not ask the court to reconsider the length of his sentence without having first filed a motion to withdraw his guilty plea. The appellate court, with one justice dissenting, held that defendant could properly challenge the length of his sentence even though he had not filed a motion to withdraw his guilty plea. . . .

In *Evans,* this court held that . . . in a challenge to a sentence entered pursuant to a negotiated plea agreement, the defendant must (1) move to withdraw the guilty plea and vacate the judgment, and (2) show that the granting of the motion is necessary to correct a manifest injustice. While that terminology used in *Evans* was perfectly appropriate and adequate to dispose of the issue before the court in that case, it did not, nor did it purport to, address every conceivable type of plea agreement.

As Justice Freeman correctly observed in his special concurrence in People v. Linder, 708 N.E.2d 1169 (Ill. 1999), "not all 'negotiated' pleas are the same." Indeed, there are at least four distinct plea scenarios which can occur when a defendant decides to enter a plea of guilty. First, a defendant may simply enter a "blind," or "open," plea without any inducement from the State. In such a case, both the defendant and the State may argue for any sentence permitted by law. Likewise, the trial court in such a case exercises its full discretion and selects the defendant's sentence from the range provided by the relevant statute. . . .

At the other extreme, a defendant may enter a fully negotiated plea under which he agrees to plead guilty in exchange for a specific sentencing recommendation by the State. This was the fact pattern addressed in *Evans*. In that case, two defendants had each pled guilty pursuant to plea agreements under which the State agreed to drop other pending charges and to recommend a specific sentence. The trial courts accepted the plea agreements and entered judgment thereon. Subsequently, however, each defendant sought to reduce his respective sentence by filing a motion for sentence reconsideration. After those motions were denied, the defendants filed appeals arguing that their sentences were excessive.

Relying primarily on contract-law principles, this court in *Evans* rejected the defendants' attempts to reduce the sentences to which they had agreed as part of their plea bargains without first moving to withdraw their guilty pleas. This court recognized that a contrary rule would permit defendants to hold the State to its side of the bargain, by eliminating the possibility of convictions on the dropped charges or sentences in excess of the agreed-upon recommendation, while reneging on the agreement by trying to unilaterally reduce the sentences to which they had agreed.

This court considered a slightly different type of plea agreement in People v. Linder, 708 N.E.2d 1169 (Ill. 1999). In that case, we considered the consolidated appeals of two defendants who pled guilty pursuant to agreements under which the State agreed to drop other pending charges and to recommend a sentence not to exceed an agreed-upon cap. Under this third type of plea bargain, the State's ability to argue for the full range of penalties provided for in the Unified Code of Corrections was constrained by the terms of its agreements with the defendants. After the trial judges in *Linder* accepted the defendants' guilty pleas and imposed sentences within the caps, both defendants sought on appeal to challenge the sentences imposed upon them as excessive. Once again relying upon the contract-law principles described in *Evans,* this court held that such appeals were improper where the defendants had not moved to withdraw their guilty pleas. . . . Accordingly, this court held that it would be fundamentally unfair to permit defendants to unilaterally modify their sides of the plea bargains while simultaneously holding the State to its side of the bargain.

The instant case involves a fourth type of guilty plea which is fundamentally different from the pleas this court considered in *Evans* and *Linder*. Here, as in *Evans* and *Linder,* the State agreed to drop certain charges against defendant in exchange for defendant's plea of guilty to another charge. In stark contrast to the facts of *Evans* and *Linder,* however, the plea bargain in the instant case was utterly silent as to the sentence which defendant would receive. In this case, therefore, both the State and the defendant were free to argue for any sentence provided for in the Unified Code of Corrections. Likewise, the trial court was able to exercise its full discretion in selecting any sentence permitted by law.

Accordingly, where the record is clear that *absolutely no agreement existed* between the parties as to defendant's sentence, defendant manifestly cannot be breaching such a nonexistent agreement by arguing that the sentence which the court imposed was excessive. For the reasons stated above, the judgment of the appellate court . . . is affirmed.

FREEMAN, J., specially concurring.

[T]he State argues that, by reducing the charges, the State did make a sentencing concession because the sentence would have been greater had the aggravated battery charge not been dropped. I disagree. [A]n agreement by the State to reduce or dismiss charges against a defendant in exchange for the defendant's plea to the reduced or remaining charges, which has the effect of reducing the sentencing range or the number of sentences a defendant could face, does not constitute an implicit agreement as to sentence. By agreeing to drop a charge, the State has made only the concession of forgoing its right to establish defendant's guilt of that charge. To imply a sentencing concession on the part of the State in this circumstance would require this court to presume that defendant was, in fact, guilty of the charge. Such a presumption would, of course, fly in the face of the presumption of innocence that exists in our criminal justice system.

The rule enunciated in *Evans* focused on returning the parties to their status quo. When a defendant pleads guilty solely in return for the dismissal of charges, the State and defendant receive just what they bargained for, *i.e.*, a guilty plea in exchange for dismissing charges. The parties have not agreed as to the length of the sentence, which is left to the circuit court's full discretion. Thus, no part of the bargain would be undermined by allowing defendant to seek reconsideration of the sentence decided by the circuit court alone. [W]e should avoid a bright-line rule that places meaningless procedural obstacles in the path of an appeal. For these reasons and those expressed in the court's opinion, I concur in today's holding.

BILANDIC, J., dissenting.

. . . This court in People v. Evans, 673 N.E.2d 244 (Ill. 1996), interpreted Supreme Court Rule 604(d), which provides that a defendant may not appeal from a judgment entered upon a plea of guilty unless the defendant timely "files in the trial court a motion to reconsider the sentence, if only the sentence is being challenged, or, if the plea is being challenged, a motion to withdraw his plea of guilty and vacate the judgment." This court held that the motion-for-sentence-reconsideration provisions of Rule 604(d) apply only to "open," as opposed to "negotiated," guilty pleas. We defined an open guilty plea as one in which a defendant pleads guilty "without receiving *any* promises from the State in return." (Emphasis added.) Accordingly, we concluded that, following the entry of judgment on a negotiated guilty plea, a defendant must move to withdraw the guilty plea and vacate the judgment, even if the defendant wants to challenge only his sentence.

Evans explained that allowing a defendant to challenge only his sentence following the entry of judgment on a negotiated guilty plea would violate basic contract law principles. In such a circumstance, the defendant is attempting to hold the State to its part of the bargain while unilaterally reneging on or modifying the terms that the defendant had previously agreed to accept. For example, the defendants in *Evans* agreed to plead guilty and, in exchange, the State promised to dismiss other charges and recommend a specific sentence. . . .

Subsequently, in People v. Linder, 708 N.E.2d 1169 (Ill. 1999), this court determined that the holding in *Evans* applies to plea agreements in which the defendant agrees to plead guilty in exchange for the State's promises to dismiss other charges and to recommend a cap on the length of the defendant's sentence. We reasoned that, by agreeing to plead guilty in exchange for the sentencing cap, the defendant is effectively agreeing not to challenge a sentence imposed below the cap.

In this case, defendant was charged with robbery, a Class 2 felony, and aggravated battery, a Class 3 felony. At a hearing, the circuit court advised defendant of the charges against him and that he faced possible prison sentences of three to seven years for the robbery, and two to five years for the aggravated battery. The circuit court further advised defendant that he could receive extended prison terms and therefore be sentenced to prison terms of 14 and 10 years, respectively. Defendant and the State ultimately reached a plea agreement. Defendant agreed to plead guilty to robbery in exchange for the State's promise to dismiss the aggravated battery charge against defendant. The parties presented the plea agreement to the circuit court. The circuit court again advised defendant that he could be sentenced to a maximum of 14 years' imprisonment for the robbery. The circuit court accepted the plea agreement and, following defendant's guilty plea to robbery, sentenced defendant to seven years in prison.

Defendant's plea agreement is negotiated within the meaning of *Evans.* Defendant pled guilty in exchange for the State's promise to dismiss the aggravated battery charge against him. Because defendant obtained the State's promise to dismiss this charge, the prison sentence that defendant could have expected to receive was reduced from 12 years to 7 years if extended sentences were not imposed, and from 24 years to 14 years if extended sentences were imposed. The plea agreement that the parties negotiated, therefore, provided defendant the valuable benefit of a less severe sentence than he could have received had he been convicted of both robbery and aggravated battery.

Moreover, by pleading guilty to robbery in exchange for the State's promise to dismiss the aggravated battery charge, defendant, in effect, agreed that a sentence within the statutory range for robbery was appropriate. Defendant was in fact sentenced to seven years in prison for the robbery — a sentence within the statutory range.

Allowing defendant to modify unilaterally this plea agreement while holding the State to the terms of the agreement will discourage prosecutors from entering into plea agreements. . . . I therefore respectfully dissent.

Problem 6-1. Waiving the Right to Appeal a Sentence

The United States Attorney for your district adopted a policy to encourage defendants to waive the right to appeal. The new office policy states that any plea agreements with federal criminal defendants must include the following language:

> The defendant is aware that Title 18, United States Code, Section 3742 affords a defendant the right to appeal the sentence imposed. Acknowledging this, the

defendant knowingly waives the right to appeal any sentence within the maximum provided in the statute(s) of conviction (or the manner in which that sentence was determined) on the grounds set forth in Title 18, United States Code, Section 3742 or on any ground whatever, in exchange for the concessions made by the United States in this plea agreement. The defendant also waives his right to challenge his sentence or the manner in which it was determined in any collateral attack . . .

Any proposed plea agreements that do not include this language must receive approval from a supervisory committee, and the committee will grant these "exceptions" only under "extraordinary circumstances." The policy calls on prosecutors to negotiate for the government to retain its right to appeal any legal error in the application of the federal sentencing guidelines.

The policy recognizes that a sentencing appeal waiver provision does not waive all claims on appeal. The federal courts of appeals have held that appellate review of some claims cannot be waived, such as a defendant's claim that he was denied the effective assistance of counsel at sentencing, that he was sentenced on the basis of his race, or that his sentence exceeded the statutory maximum. The memo also warns that prosecutors must not use the appeal waiver provision "to promote circumvention of the sentencing guidelines."

You are the director of the office of the Federal Public Defender in this district. How will you respond to the new bargaining policy of the federal prosecutors? How do you predict this new policy will be received by the courts? Can you predict whether the policy will be difficult for the prosecutors to implement in particular types of cases? Develop some alternative bargaining strategies for the public defenders in your office to pursue. See United States v. Guevara, 941 F.2d 1299 (4th Cir. 1991); Memo from John Keeney, Acting Assistant Attorney General, October 4, 1995.

Problem 6-2. Dealing Away Double Jeopardy

The state of Florida charged Juan Novaton with multiple offenses arising from two separate incidents in the same year. Because he had two prior felony convictions, Novaton faced the possibility of being treated as a habitual violent felony offender and a probable sentence of life in prison without parole. Recognizing this possibility, Novaton entered into a plea bargain. The state agreed to give up the possibility of securing the usual sentence of life without parole for a habitual violent offender, while Novaton agreed to plead guilty to all of the charges and to accept concurrent sentences totaling 50 years, subject to a 15-year mandatory minimum requirement. As a result of this plea bargain, Novaton was adjudicated guilty and sentenced for burglary, robbery, and aggravated battery with a firearm and, in addition, was adjudicated guilty and sentenced for two separate crimes of possessing a firearm in the commission of the same felonies. Florida law would bar these latter two convictions and sentences under state double jeopardy principles. Can the court accept the plea agreement between Novaton and the prosecutor? Compare Novaton v. State, 634 So. 2d 607 (Fla. 1994); Daniel C. Richman, Bargaining About Future Jeopardy, 49 Vand. L. Rev. 1181 (1996).

Notes

1. *Common types of bargains.* Prosecutors and defendants are allowed to bargain over a wide variety of topics. What do prosecutors typically offer during plea negotiations? Under a "charge bargain" (see Federal Rule 11(c)(1)(A) above), the prosecutor agrees to reduce charges or to drop some counts entirely. The prosecutor might also agree not to file charges in the future against the defendant or some third party based on the events in question. Under a "sentence bargain" (see Rule 11(c)(1)(B) above), a prosecutor agrees to ask the sentencing judge for a certain outcome, or to refrain from asking for a certain outcome, or to make no sentencing recommendation at all. See ABA Standards for Criminal Justice: Prosecution Function 3-4.2(a) (prosecutor "should not make any promise or commitment assuring a defendant or defense counsel that a court will impose a specific sentence or a suspension of sentence; a prosecutor may properly advise the defense what position will be taken concerning disposition").

What does a defendant typically offer? The most important and obvious benefit the defendant can offer is to waive the trial and all its accompanying procedural protections, such as the right to confront witnesses. The waiver of a trial saves the government the expense of preparing and conducting a trial, along with the uncertainty about the outcome at trial. See Commonwealth v. Stagner, 3 S.W.3d 738 (Ky. 1999) (allowing defendant to plead guilty while jury is deliberating; some other jurisdictions prevent guilty pleas after the jury receives case because bargain no longer serves public function of clearing docket). A defendant can also offer to cooperate during investigations of other defendants and other crimes.

There are several ways for a defendant to give up some procedural options while preserving others. The "conditional plea" (see Rule 11(a) above) allows the defendant to plead guilty while reserving the right to appeal on a defined pretrial issue, such as the voluntariness of a confession. If the defendant succeeds on appeal, the guilty plea can be withdrawn. Although it is used less often than the conditional plea, the "slow plea" is another way for a defendant to preserve some options while waiving others. Under a slow plea, the defendant and the prosecution stipulate to the existence of some facts, and then go forward with an abbreviated bench trial to resolve the remaining factual and legal issues. See State v. Mierz, 901 P.2d 286 (Wash. 1995).

Finally, a defendant might offer a plea of nolo contendere rather than a plea of guilty. A plea of nolo contendere (meaning "I will not contest" the charges) allows the court to impose criminal sanctions, just as a guilty plea would, but the nolo plea cannot be used against the defendant in any later civil litigation as an admission of guilt. The court (and in some jurisdictions, the prosecutor) must agree before a defendant enters a nolo plea rather than a guilty plea.

2. *Why plead guilty? Plea discounts.* Defendants considering a guilty plea surely know the conventional wisdom that those who plead guilty receive less severe sentences than those who are convicted after a trial. The size of the so-called plea discount varies from place to place, and it is difficult to measure because where the plea discount is most effective (not necessarily where it is most generous) it results in very few trials as a point of comparison. One estimate placed the discount in the federal system at about 30 to 40 percent of the typical sentence imposed on those convicted after trial. See U.S. Sentencing Commission, Supplemental Report on the Initial Sentencing Guidelines and Policy Statements 48 (1987); David Brereton & Jonathan Casper, Does It Pay to Plead Guilty? Differential Sentencing

and the Functioning of Criminal Courts, 16 Law & Soc'y Rev. 45 (1981-1982). Many consider the fact of a plea bargain to be an illegitimate basis for sentencing some offenders less severely than others. See ABA Standards for Criminal Justice: Prosecution Function 14-1.8 (guilty plea alone is not sufficient grounds for leniency in sentence).

Would a legislature improve the certainty and honesty of criminal justice by specifying the proper size for a plea discount? The Italian criminal code offers an example of such an explicit plea discount. It provides for a one-third reduction in applicable sentence after guilty plea, provided that maximum sentence does not exceed two years and for an "abbreviated trial" with one-third reduction in applicable sentence upon conviction, available for more serious charges. See Codice di procedura penale art. 442, 444; Nicola Boari & Gianluca Fiorentini, An Economic Analysis of Plea Bargaining: The Incentives of the Parties in a Mixed Penal System, 21 Int'l Rev. L. & Econ. 213 (2001) (five years after 1989 revisions to Italian code, only 8 percent of cases are disposed of through new accusatorial proceedings).

3. *Presumed good faith in bargaining.* Courts in the United States, since at least the middle of the twentieth century, have generally presumed that plea bargaining is both an appropriate and necessary part of the criminal justice system. As the U.S. Supreme Court put it in Santobello v. New York, 404 U.S. 257 (1971), plea bargaining is "not only an essential part of the process but a highly desirable part for many reasons." The courts have also presumed, except in extraordinary cases, that a prosecutor who negotiates a plea bargain does so for proper reasons (such as faster disposition of cases and elimination of uncertainty) and not improper ones (such as obtaining convictions of innocent defendants). For instance, the Supreme Court has rejected claims that a prosecutor acted "vindictively" and contrary to due process by increasing the charges against a defendant who rejected an initial offer of a plea bargain. Bordenkircher v. Hayes, 434 U.S. 357 (1978). What sort of prosecutorial motives for entering plea negotiations might be improper ones? Is it possible for courts to identify such cases?

4. *Waiver of appeal.* Most state and federal courts have concluded that a defendant may explicitly waive the right to appeal a conviction as part of a plea agreement. See State v. Hinners, 471 N.W.2d 841 (Iowa 1991); People v. Seaberg, 541 N.E.2d 1022 (N.Y. 1989). A few courts maintain that public policy forbids prosecutors from insulating themselves from review by bargaining away a defendant's appeal rights. Cf. State v. Ethington, 592 P.2d 768 (Ariz. 1979) (defendant can appeal conviction, notwithstanding agreement not to appeal). Is it necessary for a defendant to waive the right to appeal explicitly, or does it go without saying that a defendant who pleads guilty will not attack the conviction on appeal? If a defendant wants to appeal some aspect of a conviction based on a guilty plea, should she explicitly condition the guilty plea on the outcome of the planned appeal? How might we decide what must be explicit in a plea agreement, and what will be implied? Does it depend on what the parties are likely to have contemplated, even if they did not address the issue in so many words? See Peter Westen, Away from Waiver: A Rationale for the Forfeiture of Constitutional Rights in Criminal Procedure, 75 Mich. L. Rev. 1214 (1977).

Consider the effect of this Michigan statute, enacted in 1999, on the decision to plead guilty:

> (1) Except as provided [below], a defendant who pleads guilty . . . shall not have appellate counsel appointed for review of the defendant's conviction or sentence.

(2) The trial court shall appoint appellate counsel for an indigent defendant who pleads guilty . . . if any of the following apply:

(a) The prosecuting attorney seeks leave to appeal.

(b) The defendant's sentence exceeds the upper limit of the minimum sentence range of the applicable sentencing guidelines.

(c) The court of appeals or the supreme court grants the defendant's application for leave to appeal.

(d) The defendant seeks leave to appeal a conditional plea. . . .

Mich. Comp. Laws §770.3a. How would a challenge to this statute differ from a challenge to a prosecutor's policy to seek waivers of appeal?

5. *Forfeiture of claims.* In some contexts, a guilty plea will lead a court to conclude that the defendant forfeited a legal challenge, even though the defendant did not knowingly and intelligently relinquish a known right. This "forfeiture" (as opposed to "waiver") of claims occurs most often when a defendant raises a claim in collateral proceedings such as habeas corpus, which take place after the direct appeal. A guilty plea will automatically bar most postconviction collateral challenges to the conviction based on events occurring before the entry of the plea. See United States v. Broce, 488 U.S. 563 (1989) (guilty plea bars later double jeopardy claim when further evidence is necessary to determine whether one conspiracy or two were present); Tollett v. Henderson, 411 U.S. 258 (1973) (forfeiture of claim of racial discrimination in grand jury selection); McMann v. Richardson, 397 U.S. 759 (1970) (forfeiture of claims regarding jury exposure to coerced confessions). For some exceptional claims, however, a defendant can raise the issue on collateral attack. See Menna v. New York, 423 U.S. 61 (1975) (allowing habeas petitioner to raise double jeopardy claim despite guilty plea); Blackledge v. Perry, 417 U.S. 21 (1974) (allowing petitioner for habeas corpus to raise claim of vindictive prosecutorial charging decision). The Supreme Court in *Blackledge* explained that these exceptional claims are not forfeited, despite the guilty plea, because they go to "the very power of the State" to charge the defendant. The claims that are forfeited after a guilty plea are those that would have been cured (absent the guilty plea) by recharging or retrying the case.

6. *Nonwaivable claims.* There are a few types of legal challenges to a conviction that some courts say a defendant may not waive, even if the waiver appears explicitly in a plea agreement. Courts have taken this position on constitutional speedy trial rights, People v. Callahan, 604 N.E.2d 108 (N.Y. 1992). Courts are split on whether the parties can agree to a sentence outside the statutorily authorized range of punishments; often they enforce illegal sentences falling below the authorized range of punishments but not illegal sentences set above the authorized range. Ex parte Johnson, 669 So. 2d 205 (Ala. 1995) (enforces prosecutor's agreement to two-year prison term, even though prosecutor failed to account for sentencing enhancements requiring additional minimum sentences); but see Patterson v. State, 660 So. 2d 966 (Miss. 1995) (holding plea bargain to life without possibility of parole invalid because no statute authorizes such a sentence for murder).

When defendants attempt to raise challenges that they waived in plea agreements, claiming that the agreement is unenforceable, it is far more common for courts to refuse to hear the challenge. Courts allow defendants to bargain away rights of all sorts. See United States v. Mezzanatto, 513 U.S. 196 (1995) (allowing defendant to waive protections of Rule 11(e)(6), which prevented later introduction into evidence of statements made during plea negotiations); People v. Stevens, 610

N.W.2d 881 (Mich. 2000) (statements made during plea negotiations are admissible in prosecution's case-in-chief); Cowan v. Superior Court, 926 P.2d 438 (Cal. 1996) (allowing waiver of statute of limitations); People v. Allen, 658 N.E.2d 1012 (N.Y. 1995) (allowing waiver of double jeopardy); Joseph A. Colquitt, Ad Hoc Plea Bargaining, 75 Tul. L. Rev. 695 (2001).

Is there any pattern that separates the waivable from the nonwaivable rights? Are the waivable rights the least important ones? See Nancy J. King, Priceless Process, 47 UCLA L. Rev. 113 (1999) (notes evolution of law in direction of more waiver allowed; argues for keeping as non-waivable rights only constitutional claims with impact on third parties, since legislature can decide whether to protect statutory rights from waiver). Should courts allow defendants to waive their right to effective assistance of counsel?

B. CATEGORICAL RESTRICTIONS ON BARGAINING

As we have seen, both the prosecution and the defense have reasons to make concessions during plea negotiations, leading to guilty pleas, and there are few categorical restrictions on topics for bargaining. But the parties do not act alone in reaching or enforcing agreements. Because the parties are negotiating about criminal punishments, many different people and institutions have an interest in the outcome. Increasingly, there are times when government officials will not approve the "deal" that the parties have reached. Officials may sometimes refuse to enforce the deal, or they may take measures to prevent similar deals in the future. In short, various actors remove terms from the bargaining table. In this section, we survey the limits that legislatures, prosecutorial supervisors, and judges have placed on the terms available to the negotiating parties during plea bargaining. As you read this material, note the precise subset of cases that these institutions target as unacceptable bargains. In what ways do the unacceptable bargains differ from the acceptable ones? Consider as well the ways that these institutions have developed distinctive approaches to plea bargaining limits.

1. Legislative Limits

Until recently, legislatures did not explicitly limit the power of the prosecution and defense to enter plea agreements. Even now, it is unusual to find a statute that addresses the topic of plea agreements directly, except to authorize the prosecuting attorney in general terms to enter such agreements. It is common to find statutes setting out the procedures necessary to ensure that a defendant enters a guilty plea knowingly and voluntarily, but these procedures apply both to negotiated pleas and non-negotiated (or "open") pleas.

Yet, in many jurisdictions, statutes have profound — even if indirect — effects on plea bargaining. Most states have at least some statutes that specify mandatory minimum penalties for certain crimes. The statutes do not require the prosecutor to charge the crime in question whenever there is sufficient evidence, and they do not stop the prosecutor from reducing or dismissing charges when this crime occurs. Nevertheless, these statutes do influence bargaining, for once the prosecutor obtains a conviction for the designated crime, the prosecutor has limited influence over the sentence and the judge has fewer sentencing options.

In addition to these sentencing statutes, some state legislatures have begun to address more directly the prosecutor's power to negotiate over charges and sentences. Three examples follow. In what ways do the statutes represent different strategies for limiting plea bargains? Which strategies are likely to have the most impact on actual charging and negotiating practices?

■ CALIFORNIA PENAL CODE §1192.7

(a) (1) It is the intent of the Legislature that district attorneys prosecute violent sex crimes under statutes that provide sentencing under a "one strike," "three strikes," or habitual sex offender statute instead of engaging in plea bargaining over those offenses.

(2) Plea bargaining in any case in which the indictment or information charges any serious felony, any felony in which it is alleged that a firearm was personally used by the defendant, or any offense of driving while under the influence of alcohol, drugs, narcotics, or any other intoxicating substance, or any combination thereof, is prohibited, unless there is insufficient evidence to prove the people's case, or testimony of a material witness cannot be obtained, or a reduction or dismissal would not result in a substantial change in sentence.

(3) If the indictment or information charges the defendant with a violent sex crime [such as rape, sexual penetration, sodomy, oral copulation, or continuous sexual abuse of a child], that could be prosecuted under [enhanced penalty provisions such as the "three strikes" habitual felon law], plea bargaining is prohibited unless there is insufficient evidence to prove the people's case, or testimony of a material witness cannot be obtained, or a reduction or dismissal would not result in a substantial change in sentence. At the time of presenting the agreement to the court, the district attorney shall state on the record why a sentence under one of those sections was not sought.

(b) As used in this section "plea bargaining" means any bargaining, negotiation, or discussion between a criminal defendant, or his or her counsel, and a prosecuting attorney or judge, whereby the defendant agrees to plead guilty or nolo contendere, in exchange for any promises, commitments, concessions, assurances, or consideration by the prosecuting attorney or judge relating to any charge against the defendant or to the sentencing of the defendant.

(c) As used in this section, "serious felony" means any of the following: (1) Murder or voluntary manslaughter; (2) mayhem; (3) rape; (4) sodomy by force, violence, duress, menace, threat of great bodily injury, or fear of immediate and unlawful bodily injury on the victim or another person; (5) oral copulation by force, violence, duress, menace, threat of great bodily injury, or fear of immediate and unlawful bodily injury on the victim or another person; (6) lewd or lascivious act on a child under 14 years of age; (7) any felony punishable by death or imprisonment in the state prison for life; (8) any felony in which the defendant personally inflicts great bodily injury on any person, other than an accomplice, or any felony in which the defendant personally uses a firearm; (9) attempted murder; (10) assault with intent to commit rape or robbery; (11) assault with a deadly weapon or instrument on a peace officer; (12) assault by a life prisoner on a non-inmate; (13) assault with a deadly weapon by an inmate; (14) arson; (15) exploding a destructive device or any explosive with intent to injure; (16) exploding a destructive device or any explosive causing bodily injury, great bodily injury, or mayhem; (17) exploding a destructive device or any explosive with intent to murder; (18) any burglary of the first degree; (19) robbery or bank robbery; (20) kidnapping; . . . (23) any felony in which the defendant personally used a dangerous or deadly weapon; (24) selling, furnishing, administering, giving, or offering to sell, furnish, administer, or give to a minor any heroin, cocaine, phencyclidine (PCP), or any methamphetamine-related drug, . . . (26) grand theft involving a firearm; (27) carjacking; . . . (31) assault with a deadly weapon, firearm, machinegun, assault weapon, or semiautomatic firearm or assault on a peace officer or firefighter . . . (32) assault with a deadly weapon against a public transit employee, custodial officer, or school employee . . . (33) discharge of a firearm at an inhabited dwelling, vehicle, or aircraft . . . (37) intimidation of victims or witnesses . . . (38) terrorist threats; . . . and (41) any conspiracy to commit an offense described in this subdivision.

■ NEW YORK CRIMINAL PROCEDURE LAW §220.10

The only kinds of pleas which may be entered to an indictment are those specified in this section:

1. The defendant may as a matter of right enter a plea of "not guilty" to the indictment.

2. Except as provided in subdivision five, the defendant may as a matter of right enter a plea of "guilty" to the entire indictment.

3. Except as provided in subdivision five, where the indictment charges but one crime, the defendant may, with both the permission of the court and the consent of the people, enter a plea of guilty of a lesser included offense.

4. Except as provided in subdivision five, where the indictment charges two or more offenses in separate counts, the defendant may, with both the permission of the court and the consent of the people, enter a plea of:

(a) Guilty of one or more but not all of the offenses charged; or

(b) Guilty of a lesser included offense with respect to any or all of the offenses charged; or

(c) Guilty of any combination of offenses charged and lesser offenses included within other offenses charged.

5. (a)(i) Where the indictment charges one of the class A felonies . . . or the attempt to commit any such class A felony, then any plea of guilty entered pursuant to subdivision three or four must be or must include at least a plea of guilty of class B felony. . . .

(iii) Where the indictment charges one of the class B felonies . . . then any plea of guilty entered pursuant to subdivision three or four must be or must include at least a plea of guilty of a class D felony.

■ REVISED CODE OF WASHINGTON §§9.94A.450, 9.94A.460

§9.94A.450

(1) Except as provided in subsection (2) of this section, a defendant will normally be expected to plead guilty to the charge or charges which adequately describe the nature of his or her criminal conduct or go to trial.

(2) In certain circumstances, a plea agreement with a defendant in exchange for a plea of guilty to a charge or charges that may not fully describe the nature of his or her criminal conduct may be necessary and in the public interest. Such situations may include the following:

(a) Evidentiary problems which make conviction on the original charges doubtful;

(b) The defendant's willingness to cooperate in the investigation or prosecution of others whose criminal conduct is more serious or represents a greater public threat;

(c) A request by the victim when it is not the result of pressure from the defendant;

(d) The discovery of facts which mitigate the seriousness of the defendant's conduct;

(e) The correction of errors in the initial charging decision;

(f) The defendant's history with respect to criminal activity;

(g) The nature and seriousness of the offense or offenses charged;

(h) The probable effect on witnesses.

§9.94A.460

The prosecutor may reach an agreement regarding sentence recommendations. The prosecutor shall not agree to withhold relevant information from the court concerning the plea agreement.

Notes

1. *Codifying plea considerations.* The Washington statute lists several considerations that prosecutors traditionally describe as reasons to reduce charges or to recommend a lesser sentence as part of a plea bargain. The National District Attorneys Association lists similar factors for a prosecutor to consider before negotiating a plea agreement, including the following: "the nature of the offense(s)"; "age, background, and criminal history of the defendant"; "sufficiency of admissible evidence to support a verdict"; "undue hardship caused to the defendant"; "possible deterrent value of prosecution"; "age of the case"; "willingness of the defendant to waive (release) his right to pursue potential civil causes of action arising from his arrest"; and "availability and willingness [of witnesses] to testify." National Prosecution Standards 68.1 (2d ed. 1991). A few other states have similar statutes. See Oregon Code §135.415 (nonexclusive list of criteria the prosecutor may consider in making plea agreements). Would the passage of such a statute alter any practices in a prosecutor's office? What would motivate a legislature to pass such a statute?

2. *Particular charges.* In recent years, it has become more common for legislatures to instruct prosecutors not to dismiss or reduce charges for specific crimes. As you might imagine, the crimes involved are usually those that have become high priorities for the public. See Nev. Rev. Stat. §§483.560, 484.3792 (prosecutor may not dismiss charges for driving with suspended or revoked license, or for drunk driving offenses, unless there is no probable cause to support charge). Cf. Miss. Stat. §43-21-555 (no plea bargaining in youth court).

3. *Size of discount.* The New York statute does not bar plea bargains for any particular crimes. Rather, it defines the maximum reduction in charges and authorized sentences that the prosecutor may offer. A statute specifying the size of the discounts a prosecutor can offer may create a very visible incentive to plead guilty. For instance, in Corbitt v. New Jersey, 439 U.S. 212 (1978), the Supreme Court upheld the constitutionality of a statute that required a mandatory term of life imprisonment for a conviction after trial; the same statute allowed either a life term or a 30-year term for a conviction under the statute based on a guilty or nolo plea. Compare United States v. Jackson, 390 U.S. 570 (1968) (overturning statute as undue burden on right to jury trial where death penalty is authorized only for defendants who go to trial); Shumpert v. Department of Highways, 409 S.E.2d 771 (S.C. 1991) (statute reducing period of driver's license suspension for those pleading guilty of drunk driving offenses is overturned as burden on trial rights).

4. *Exceptions under the California statute.* Section 1192.7 of the California Penal Code became law as a result of a voter referendum in 1982. Other provisions of the "victims' rights" referendum included greater admissibility of evidence of a defendant's prior convictions and increased penalties for repeat felony offenders. The statute has been amended often over the years, sometimes through ordinary legislation and at other times through voter initiatives (for instance, the "serious felonies" numbered higher than 27 were added as part of the 2000 Juvenile Crime Initiative). Subsection (a)(3) of the statute was not included in the original language. What does this portion of the statute change?

The plea bargain limitations for "serious felonies," however, never reduced the number of cases resolved through guilty pleas and plea negotiations in California. One study of California plea bargaining concluded that the statutory ban never reduced the use of guilty pleas because §1192.7 applied only to cases in superior court. Since virtually all serious felonies are charged initially in municipal court and transferred to superior court only after the preliminary examination, the prosecution and defense can negotiate a plea bargain in almost any case during the first few days after the filing of the charge, before any preliminary examination and before much discovery has taken place. See Candace McCoy, Politics and Plea Bargaining: Victims' Rights in California (1993). Even if the bar on plea negotiations were to apply to all court systems, how many dismissals and reductions of charges would it prevent? Consider the exceptions in subsections (a)(2) and (a)(3), allowing plea bargaining when there is "insufficient evidence" or when a material witness is not available, or when no substantial reduction in sentence would result. How many cases would fall within these subsections, and who would determine the breadth of coverage for this statutory language?

2. Judicial Rules

Judges are pulled in two directions when it comes to plea bargains. On the one hand, plea bargaining appears to be an extension of the prosecutor's charging decision, and judges are reluctant to become involved in charging decisions. See Chapter 3. On the other hand, plea bargaining is a key determinant in sentencing, and judges have customarily considered sentencing to be a judicial function. As a result, judges usually accept the practice of negotiated guilty pleas and allow prosecutors to dismiss or reduce charges. But they resist more strenuously when plea bargaining takes the form of a sentence bargain.

What form does judicial resistance to sentence bargains take? It is rare to find judges creating rules of criminal procedure or making other general pronouncements that place whole categories of agreements out of bounds. But they do frequently insist on the power, in individual cases, to make an independent judgment about any sentence that the parties might have selected under their agreement. This means that judges have been especially skeptical about agreements that give the judge only one sentencing option (the one that the prosecution and the defense have negotiated) and allow the defendant to withdraw the plea if the judge does not enter the sentence specified in the agreement. See Fed. R. Crim. P. 11(c)(1)(C) (parties may "agree that a specific sentence is the appropriate disposition of the case"). The following case indicates when judges are likely (or unlikely) to limit or scrutinize entire classes of plea bargains. Later in this chapter (in section C), we consider the role of the judge during plea negotiations in individual cases.

■ RAYMOND ESPINOZA v. HON. GREGORY MARTIN
894 P.2d 688 (Ariz. 1995)

CORCORAN, J.

Petitioner Raymond Espinoza, a criminal defendant in Maricopa County, challenges the policy adopted by a group of Maricopa County Superior Court judges of summarily rejecting all plea agreements containing stipulated sentences. . . .

The criminal divisions of the Maricopa County Superior Court are divided into four groups designated as quadrants A through D. Quadrant B [consists] of 5 judges. [T]he quadrant B judges issued a memorandum detailing a new plea agreement policy that was scheduled to take effect on January 25, 1993. The policy stated that quadrant B judges would no longer accept any plea agreements containing stipulated sentences because sentencing "is a judicial function which should not be subjected to limitations which are imposed by the parties, but are not required by law." . . . The relevant section of that policy reads as follows:

> 1. Plea agreements may stipulate to "probation," or "department of corrections" [DOC] for felonies, or "county jail" for misdemeanors. Agreements may not stipulate to any term of years (other than lifetime probation in dangerous crimes against children) or to any non-mandatory terms and conditions of probation. . . . , or to sentences running concurrently or consecutively. . . .

The only 2 exceptions to the quadrant B policy are as follows:

> 2. Exceptions will be made for legitimate cooperation agreements. If the state wishes to make stipulated sentencing concessions in exchange for information, testimony or cooperation from a defendant, that fact should be made known to the judge in an appropriate manner prior to the change of plea. . . .
> 4. Stipulations in capital murder cases to life imprisonment are viewed by the judges as charging concessions and not true sentencing stipulations. Therefore, such stipulations are unaffected by the policy.

On June 2, 1993, Espinoza was indicted on one count of offering to sell narcotic drugs and one count of misconduct involving weapons. At his arraignment, the case was assigned to respondent, quadrant B Judge Gregory Martin. On August 11, 1993, Espinoza appeared before Judge Martin in chambers to enter a plea of guilty to both counts pursuant to a plea agreement, which stipulated that the sentences would run concurrently with each other and with an unrelated probation revocation. Judge Martin summarily rejected Espinoza's plea agreement because the stipulation to concurrent sentences violated the quadrant B policy. . . .

Rule 17.4, Arizona Rules of Criminal Procedure, governs plea negotiations and agreements. This court has stated that "the rules [of criminal procedure] recognize that properly negotiated plea agreements . . . are an essential part of the criminal process and can enhance judicial economy, protect the resources of the State, and serve the ends of justice for the defendant, the State and the victim." State v. Superior Court, 611 P.2d 928 (Ariz. 1980).

This case turns on the meaning of rule 17.4(a), which reads as follows: "The parties may negotiate concerning, and reach an agreement on, any aspect of the disposition of the case. The court shall not participate in any such negotiation." The plain language of rule 17.4(a) gives the parties the right to negotiate and reach agreement on "any aspect of the disposition of the case." This means that the State and the defendant may bargain both as to the plea of guilty and as to the sentence to be imposed.

Although rule 17.4(a) allows the parties to negotiate plea agreements, including sentences, rule 17.4 also grants trial courts considerable discretion in deciding whether to accept or reject such agreements. Rule 17.4(d) provides in part:

> After making such determinations [of the accuracy of the agreement and the voluntariness and intelligence of the plea] and considering the victim's view, if provided, the court shall either accept or reject the tendered negotiated plea.*

Furthermore, even if a trial court accepts a plea agreement, it is not bound by negotiated provisions regarding the sentence or the terms of probation if a review of the presentence report reveals the inadequacy of those provisions.

In order to ensure that agreements negotiated pursuant to rule 17.4(a) have some meaningful effect, we interpret rule 17.4 as guaranteeing the parties the right to present their negotiated agreement to a judge, to have the judge consider the merits of that agreement in light of the circumstances of the case, and to have the judge exercise his or her discretion with regard to the agreement. Instead of hampering judicial sentencing discretion, the current version of rule 17.4, taken as a whole, contemplates the exercise of judicial discretion when determining whether to accept or reject each particular plea agreement. In exercising that discretion, the trial court must review the plea agreement to see if the ends of justice and the protection of the public are being served by such agreement. . . .

---

*Rule 17.4(d) continues as follows: "The court shall not be bound by any provision in the plea agreement regarding the sentence or the term and conditions of probation to be imposed, if, after accepting the agreement and reviewing a presentence report, it rejects the provision as inappropriate." Section (e) states as follows: "If an agreement or any provision thereof is rejected by the court, it shall give the defendant an opportunity to withdraw his or her plea, advising the defendant that if he or she permits the plea to stand, the disposition of the case may be less favorable to him or her than that contemplated by the agreement." — Eds.

After giving full consideration to the appropriateness of a plea agreement, the trial court has the discretion to either accept or reject the entire plea agreement, or to accept the agreement and later reject the sentencing provisions if deemed inappropriate after further inquiry. Therefore, there [is no need] to try to further enhance judicial sentencing discretion by approving a policy that limited the parties' right to negotiate. . . .

Espinoza agreed to plead guilty to two charges: attempting to knowingly sell a narcotic drug and knowingly possessing a deadly weapon during the commission of a felony. In exchange, the parties agreed that the sentences imposed on both charges would be served concurrently, and that those sentences would also be concurrent with a probation revocation. . . . Judge Martin did not consider the particular circumstances of the case and made no findings regarding the appropriateness of the negotiated sentence. Instead, the presence of a stipulated sentence in the agreement triggered the quadrant B policy and precluded any individualized exercise of discretion. Absent the quadrant B policy, Judge Martin could have weighed the merits of the plea agreement and accepted it, rejected it entirely, or rejected the sentencing provisions as inappropriate once he had reviewed the presentence report. This is the type of discretion contemplated by rule 17.4, and trial courts are obligated to exercise it.

[Groups] of judges may not implement policies to automatically reject all such plea agreements without considering whether a stipulated sentence is appropriate in light of the circumstances of the case. Our holding applies equally to the actions of individual judges. [A trial judge may not] automatically reject a plea agreement without individualized consideration because it contains a stipulated sentence. . . .

FELDMAN, C.J., specially concurring.

I fully concur in the majority opinion. Two comments in Justice Martone's dissent, however, require a response from the Chief Justice.

Because the dissent departs from the issue before us to castigate the court for failing to adopt the petition to amend Ariz. R. Crim. Proc. 17.4, it is appropriate to explain why we did not adopt that proposal. The dissent makes much of the number of comments favoring the petition, but, as is often the case, the numbers do not paint an accurate picture. Other than judges, only three writers, none of whom is a practicing lawyer, supported the rule change. The dissent fails to mention that, in fact, several judges opposed the change and that the comments of representatives of the lawyers who would have had to practice under the proposed rule were unanimously unfavorable. The prosecutors opposed it on the grounds that it was contrary to the interests of victims and the public, and the defense bar opposed it on the grounds that it would significantly hinder their attempts to obtain fair treatment for their clients under a mandatory sentencing regime. . . .

This debate is, of course, a non-issue in this case. Those readers who desire an in-depth review, however, should peruse the comment to the petition to amend Rule 17.4 filed by Judge Ronald Reinstein, Presiding Criminal Judge of the Maricopa County Superior Court. [I] quote here one paragraph of that comment:

> While some have argued that sentencing stipulations are regularly crafted by inexperienced young attorneys, and judges are best suited to determine in the first instance what an appropriate disposition in a case should be, the fact is that most of the more significant and sensitive cases in the justice system are handled by experienced

prosecutors and defense attorneys who have lived and breathed these cases for months. The sentencing judge on the other hand more than likely only reviews the presentence report the night before sentencing. Many of those judges, while perhaps experienced in life and the law, at least in the beginning of their judicial careers or their assignment to the criminal bench, have no experience at all in criminal sentencing. We are not all anointed with mystical and instant wisdom when we don our judicial robes.

Some may believe that we should damn the torpedoes and go forward with a rule opposed by all who would have to practice under it, but I disagree. Although we may empathize with the judges who seek to regain some of the discretion taken from them by mandatory sentencing, we must listen to those who would have had to practice under the changed rule. [I]t would be an abuse of power to impose the rule until it was first tried with a group willing to experiment. . . .

ZLAKET, J., dissenting.

The majority concedes that judges are empowered to reject plea agreements. I am of the additional opinion that they should be permitted to summarily reject those containing stipulated sentences for that reason alone, without having to go through the charade of considering each case individually. My hope is that most judges would not routinely follow such a course of action, at least until we can be sure it causes no damage to the plea-bargaining process that constitutes an integral part of our criminal justice system. Nevertheless, arriving at a general principle applicable to a class of plea agreements, after full consideration of the issue, seems to me more honest, more efficient, and every bit as thoughtful as pondering each agreement individually before rejecting it. . . .

I believe the court's ruling today not only threatens [judicial] candor but also reinforces the purely ministerial role about which [judges have] so vehemently and properly complained. Sentencing is, or at least should be, a judicial function. Regrettably, mandatory sentencing schemes have eliminated a great deal of judicial discretion in such matters. I prefer not to support a rule interpretation that potentially contributes to further erosion of this authority, especially where it is unnecessary to resolve the pending case.

MARTONE, J., dissenting.

I dissent. I would support the efforts of five trial judges to improve our criminal justice system. . . . The quadrant B policy was not in conflict with Rule 17.4. While Rule 17.4(a) allows the parties to agree on the disposition of a case, Rule 17.4(d) allows the court to "either accept or reject the tendered negotiated plea." Even after acceptance, the court may reject sentencing stipulations. Rule 17.4(d). If, after looking at the document, a judge is opposed to any part of the plea, he or she may summarily reject it. And that is precisely what Judge Martin did here. That he and other judges agreed to exercise their rights under Rule 17.4(d) does not make his decision conflict with the rule. Indeed, their agreement is collectively supportive of the rule. No one forced Judge Martin to participate in the policy. He was free to accept or reject it, altogether or in a specific case. He accepted it because he thought it was a good idea. The quadrant B policy was not binding on any judge who did not want to be bound by it.

[T]he Superior Court in Maricopa County has petitioned to amend Rule 17.4 to prohibit sentencing stipulations and the majority rejected it. See In re Rule 17.4,

Rules of Criminal Procedure, R-94-0007.* We are considering an experiment with the proposed amendment, but the majority rejected Maricopa County's request to participate in it.

I believe that this court should be in the business of rewarding creative efforts that arise elsewhere in the system. We have not been at the forefront of reform in the criminal justice system. . . . The trial judges are trying new ideas as we approach the next millennium. We should support them.

Problem 6-3. Bargaining Ban in a Lower Court

The trial courts in New Jersey include superior courts, which are the courts of general jurisdiction, and municipal courts, which are courts of limited jurisdiction to try lesser criminal offenses. In 1974, the New Jersey Supreme Court passed a rule prohibiting all plea bargaining in municipal courts in the state.

In passing this rule, the court expressed the concern that plea bargaining might be abused in municipal court because of the part-time nature of the personnel in many municipal courts and the informal nature of the proceedings. For instance, municipal courts are not required to maintain stenographic records or audio recordings of proceedings and most municipal courts do not have a prosecutor or a public defender assigned full time to the court. In the view of the Supreme Court, this structure left the municipal courts vulnerable to allegations of improper "back room deals."

For several years, the Supreme Court maintained its rule on plea bargaining and emphasized that the ban was particularly important in drunken-driving offenses. In 1983, Chief Justice Robert Wilentz issued a reminder to judges on assignment in municipal courts that "without in any way affecting the generality of the plea bargaining prohibition, I suggest that you emphasize the particular importance of not allowing plea bargaining in drunken driving cases."

In 1988, the Supreme Court Task Force on the Improvement of Municipal Courts recommended the authorization of plea bargaining in the municipal courts, giving the following reasons:

> The existence of a regulated plea agreement process is essential to serve both the ends of justice and the effective response to burgeoning municipal court caseloads. It will foster increases in the productivity and professionalism of the municipal court bench, administrators, clerks and staff. The process provides for the certainty and fairness of punishment to better protect the rights of the defendants, victims and the interests of society.
>
> The municipal courts have a volume of cases in excess of 6 million that must be processed and resolved in an expeditious and summary manner. The Committee has been advised and is of the opinion that unless plea agreements are permitted in the carefully defined fashion being proposed, they will certainly take place in an unregulated fashion. Certainly, in the absence of some form of expeditious disposition, these courts would not be able to cope with their heavy calendars given the part-time nature

---

* [This note is asterisked in the original dissenting opinion.] Of the approximately 60 comments received, over 40 were in favor of prohibiting sentencing agreements. . . . The majority is persuaded by the opposition of institutional bar groups. It is natural enough for lawyers to not want to surrender their sentencing power to judges. But if judges, and not lawyers, ought to possess the power to sentence, the reluctance of lawyers to transfer that power ought not carry the day. . . .

of the courts and the part-time nature of the judges, most of whom have full-time law practices.

The committee, while acknowledging the feasibility of plea bargaining in general in the municipal courts, determined that drunken-driving offenses posed special problems. It noted the extraordinary emotional and fiscal costs of drunken driving, and "the public's concern that the process of plea bargaining, as applied to alcohol and drug offenses, might undermine the deterrent thrust of New Jersey's tough laws in these areas." Accordingly, the committee's report recommended that while the ban on municipal court plea bargaining should be lifted, the prohibition on plea agreements in drunken-driving offenses should continue.

In 1990, the court instituted a regulated system of plea agreements in municipal courts. It allowed plea bargaining pursuant to New Jersey Court Rule 7:4-8. The guidelines that the court issued with the court rules specified that their purpose was "to allow for flexibility in the definitions and exclusions relating to the plea agreement process as that process evolves and certain offenses come to demand lesser or greater scrutiny." Guideline 4 adopted the recommendation of the committee that plea bargaining not be allowed in drunken-driving cases.

As a member of the New Jersey Supreme Court, how would you respond to the recommendations of the committee? What more would you like to know about the municipal courts and their caseloads before you decide? Compare State v. Hessen, 678 A.2d 1082 (N.J. 1996).

Notes

1. *Individualized rejection of plea agreements.* Statutes and rules give judges the opportunity to approve or disapprove plea agreements. The court must decide whether to accept or reject the defendant's plea of guilty; if the plea grows out of an objectionable plea agreement, the court can simply refuse to accept the guilty plea. Further, rules and statutes in more than 30 states require prosecutors to obtain the consent of the court to dismiss a charge. But does the court need any justification, or any particular type of justification, to reject a guilty plea based on a plea agreement or to refuse to dismiss a charge? Almost all appellate courts allow trial courts to reject guilty pleas or dismissals of charges without any serious review of the judge's reasons for refusing. A few cases, however, have held that a trial judge must state reasons for rejecting a guilty plea; the judge may refuse the guilty plea or the dismissal of charges only if the prosecutor has abused his discretion by failing to consider facts important to the public interest in the case. Sandy v. District Court, 935 P.2d 1148 (Nev. 1997); United States v. Ammidown, 497 F.2d 615 (D.C. Cir. 1973). Limits on the judicial power to reject guilty pleas are based on separation of powers concepts and on judges' limited knowledge both about the relative strengths of individual cases and about the most efficient allocation of prosecutorial resources. Would you expect such limits on judicial power to apply equally to charging agreements and sentencing agreements?

2. *Stipulated sentences.* As described in the *Espinoza* case from Arizona, the state supreme court had considered (and rejected) an amendment to the guilty plea rules dealing with "stipulated sentences," and the trial judges of quadrant B created their own rule about stipulated sentences. What exactly can a trial judge do when the

parties present a stipulated or "negotiated" sentence? The details vary from place to place. As with the federal rules, most jurisdictions allow the parties to choose the type of agreement they will present to the judge: They can agree either to recommend a sentence (leaving the judge free to accept or reject the recommendation) or to offer the judge only a stipulated sentence that the judge must simply accept or reject as a package with the guilty plea. A few states recognize only the "binding" form of sentencing agreements. See People v. Killebrew, 330 N.W.2d 834 (Mich. 1982) (when judge plans to impose sentence that exceeds sentence recommendation or agreement, defendant may withdraw guilty plea). Other states have statutes or rules to preserve the judge's power, in all cases, to accept a guilty plea but still depart from the sentence the parties recommend. See State v. Strecker, 883 P.2d 841 (Mont. 1994). English law permits plea bargaining but not negotiated sentences. See R. v. Turner (F.R.) [1970] 2 Q.B. 321, 54 Crim. App. 352 (guidelines for plea bargaining).

Even though most criminal procedure rules allow the parties to stipulate to a particular sentence, stipulated sentences are far less common in practice than charge bargains or nonbinding sentencing recommendations. Many judges declare that they will not accept "binding" sentence recommendations, even though the relevant rules of procedure authorize such agreements. Why does this pattern emerge in most places? Did the trial judges in Maricopa County need to create a common policy for the jurisdiction?

3. *Disfavored classes of agreements.* What was it about plea negotiations in the municipal courts (described in Problem 6-3) that made such practices a special concern to the New Jersey courts? See State v. Hessen, 678 A.2d 1082 (N.J. 1996). What features of drunken-driving cases created the need for special treatment? Were any of these features present in the types of plea bargains that the trial courts tried to ban in the *Espinoza* case from Arizona? Is there any explanation for the different outcomes in these cases, a ban on a category of plea bargains upheld in one case but not the other? Cf. State v. Hager, 630 N.W.2d 828 (Iowa 2001) (despite trial court rule forbidding plea bargains on day of trial, abuse of discretion not to consider plea entered on day of trial).

One type of agreement that courts have rejected categorically is known as the "consistency" agreement, in which a defendant receives charging concessions in exchange for an agreement to testify against another defendant and to testify consistently with past statements that the defendant has made. See State v. Rivera, 109 P.3d 83 (Ariz. 2005) (prosecutor may enter plea agreement that requires defendant to avow accuracy of prior statements to police and to provide truthful testimony in future, but may not enter agreement that requires defendant to testify in future consistently with prior statements). Why are judges in most jurisdictions willing to ban this type of agreement when they allow the parties to negotiate over so many other potential terms of agreement?

4. *Prosecutor's objection to guilty plea and sentence.* We have considered the situation in which the judge objects to a sentence that the parties have negotiated. Can a judge side with a defendant against a prosecutor and accept a guilty plea (and impose a sentence or dismiss a charge) over the prosecutor's objection? Most courts have given the prosecutor the power to block a guilty plea if the judge plans to dismiss charges or impose a sentence below what the plea agreement specifies. See State v. Vasquez-Aerreola, 940 S.W.2d 451 (Ark. 1997) (court may not dismiss charge of gang activity and accept guilty plea on other charges over prosecutor's objection);

People v. Siebert, 537 N.W.2d 891 (Mich. 1995) (court may not accept a plea bargain containing a sentence agreement but impose a lower sentence than that agreed to; in such a case, prosecutor must be given opportunity to withdraw from agreement). Nonetheless, a few courts insist, at least for sentence bargains, that the prosecutor cannot prevent the judge from selecting the sentence to impose. See State v. Warren, 558 A.2d 1312 (N.J. 1989) (prohibits use of plea agreements in which prosecutor reserves right to withdraw from plea agreement if court-imposed sentence is more lenient than one agreed to by parties or recommended to court by prosecutor).

3. Prosecutorial Guidelines

Decisions whether to offer or accept plea bargains, like decisions about charging a suspect, are often governed by executive branch policies. These policies vary in their level of detail; in many smaller offices, prosecutors follow consistent plea practices that may reflect unwritten (but explicit) guidelines, or they may simply reflect shared office culture and experience. Sometimes prosecutors develop formal plea review standards, describing substantively the types of bargains that are acceptable. Other times they create procedural review mechanisms, such as supervisory review or committee review of possible plea bargains. These guidelines or procedures might apply only for identified types of cases, such as those involving drugs or those likely to be controversial.

Federal prosecutors, under the central control of the attorney general, have developed a detailed set of written plea bargaining policies. In addition to the nationwide guidelines set out below, many of the U.S. Attorneys' offices in the 94 federal districts around the country have developed additional guidance to reflect the distinctive caseloads, resources, and other factors in each district.

The federal executive branch plea policies that follow were created against a background of major changes in sentencing law. At the time of the 1980 policy printed below, the federal system (and all but a handful of state systems) still had an "indeterminate" sentencing system. Under indeterminate sentencing systems the legislature defined most crimes to include a wide range of possible sentences, sometimes covering (for a single crime) everything from nonprison sanctions, such as fines or probation, to long prison terms. In theory, huge discretion was left to the sentencing judge to set terms within the statutorily authorized range. The actual sentence to be served was often determined through "back-end" review by parole boards once the offender had spent a minimum required portion of the judicially imposed term in prison. In such systems, the charge might have only a modest binding effect on the sentence a judge could impose or the time a defendant would actually serve. In practice, however, the processing of many cases by the same "working group" of attorneys and judges within the criminal court culture would lead to very firm expectations or "prices" for various crimes. See Milton Heumann, Plea Bargaining: The Experiences of Prosecutors, Judges, and Defense Attorneys (1978).

Remember as you read these policies that the Federal Rules of Criminal Procedure authorize three kinds of pleas: (1) agreements to enter a guilty plea to one or more charges in return for dismissal of other charges (a "charge" bargain under Rule 11(c)(1)(A)); (2) agreements to recommend a sentence in exchange for a guilty plea, subject to the judge's power to select the final sentence after accepting the guilty plea (a "sentence" bargain under Rule 11(c)(1)(B)); and (3) an agreement to a particular sentence in exchange for a guilty plea (a stipulated sentence plea under Rule 11(c)(1)(C)).

■ U.S. DEPARTMENT OF JUSTICE, PRINCIPLES OF FEDERAL PROSECUTION
(1980)

ENTERING INTO PLEA AGREEMENTS

1. The attorney for the government may, in an appropriate case, enter into an agreement with a defendant that, upon the defendant's plea of guilty or nolo contendere to a charged offense or to a lesser or related offense, he will move for dismissal of other charges, take a certain position with respect to the sentence to be imposed, or take other action.

2. In determining whether it would be appropriate to enter into a plea agreement, the attorney for the government should weigh all relevant considerations, including:

(a) the defendant's willingness to cooperate in the investigation or prosecution of others;

(b) the defendant's history with respect to criminal activity;

(c) the nature and seriousness of the offense or offenses charged;

(d) the defendant's remorse or contrition and his willingness to assume responsibility for his conduct;

(e) the desirability of prompt and certain disposition of the case;

(f) the likelihood of obtaining a conviction at trial;

(g) the probable effect on witnesses;

(h) the probable sentence or other consequences if the defendant is convicted;

(i) the public interest in having the case tried rather than disposed of by a guilty plea;

(j) the expense of trial and appeal; and

(k) the need to avoid delay in the disposition of other pending cases.

Comment: . . . The provision is not intended to suggest the desirability or lack of desirability of a plea agreement in any particular case or to be construed as a reflection on the merits of any plea agreement that actually may be reached; its purpose is solely to assist attorneys for the government in exercising their judgment as to whether some sort of plea agreement would be appropriate in a particular case. Government attorneys should consult the investigating agency involved in any case in which it would be helpful to have its views concerning the relevance of particular factors or the weight they deserve. . . .

A plea disposition in one case may facilitate the prompt disposition of other cases, including cases in which prosecution might otherwise be declined. This may occur simply because prosecutorial, judicial, or defense resources will become available for use in other cases, or because a plea by one of several defendants may have a "domino effect," leading to pleas by other defendants. In weighing the importance of these possible consequences, the attorney for the government should consider the state of the criminal docket and the speedy trial requirements in the district, the desirability of handling a larger volume of criminal cases, and the workloads of prosecutors, judges, and defense attorneys in the district.

3. If a prosecution is to be concluded pursuant to a plea agreement, the defendant should be required to plead to a charge or charges:

(a) that bears a reasonable relationship to the nature and extent of his criminal conduct;

(b) that has an adequate factual basis;

(c) that makes likely the imposition of an appropriate sentence under all the circumstances of the case; and

(d) that does not adversely affect the investigation or prosecution of others.

Comment: [T]he considerations that should be taken into account in selecting the charge or charges to which a defendant should be required to plead guilty . . . are essentially the same as those governing the selection of charges to be included in the original indictment or information.

(a) Relationship to criminal conduct — The charge or charges to which a defendant pleads guilty should bear a reasonable relationship to the defendant's criminal conduct, both in nature and in scope. . . . In many cases, this will probably require that the defendant plead to the most serious offense charged. . . . The requirement that a defendant plead to a charge that bears a reasonable relationship to the nature and extent of his criminal conduct is not inflexible. There may be situations involving cooperating defendants in which [lesser charges may be appropriate].

(b) Factual basis — The attorney for the government should also bear in mind the legal requirement that there be a factual basis for the charge or charges to which a guilty plea is entered. This requirement is intended to assure against conviction after a guilty plea of a person who is not in fact guilty. . . .

(c) Basis for sentencing — [T]he prosecutor should take care to avoid a "charge agreement" that would unduly restrict the court's sentencing authority. [I]f restitution is appropriate under the circumstances of the case, a sufficient number of counts should be retained under the agreement to provide a basis for an adequate restitution order. . . .

(d) Effect on other cases — . . . Among the possible adverse consequences to be avoided are the negative jury appeal that may result when relatively less culpable defendants are tried in the absence of a more culpable defendant or when a principal prosecution witness appears to be equally culpable as the defendants but has been permitted to plead to a significantly less serious offense. . . .

5. If a prosecution is to be terminated pursuant to a plea agreement, the attorney for the government should ensure that the case file contains a record of the agreed disposition, signed or initialed by the defendant or his attorney. . . .

Notes

1. *The shift away from discretionary sentencing.* Since the early 1980s the federal system and about half of the states have shifted to a more rule-bound sentencing process known as "guideline" or "structured" sentencing. The effect of such laws has been to take away some sentencing discretion from the judge. Sometimes the new laws also created more "determinate" systems that abolished or restricted the use of parole to adjust the sentence to be served. In such a system, the judge

announces the sentence that corresponds closely to the sentence that the offender will actually serve.

2. *Federal sentencing guidelines.* In the Sentencing Reform Act of 1984, Congress designed a radically new sentencing system. In place of the indeterminate sentencing system that allowed judges to choose sentences from a broad range of available outcomes, Congress created a new agency — the United States Sentencing Commission — to draft detailed sentencing guidelines. The U.S. Sentencing Commission, following general statutory guidance, produced a lengthy set of guidelines in 1987. The guidelines direct federal judges in most cases to impose sentences from a much narrower range than before.

Under the sentencing guidelines, the trial judge calculates an "offense level" (ranging on a scale from 1 to 43) to measure the seriousness of the offense, and a "criminal history category" (ranging on a scale from 1 to 6) to account for the offender's prior criminal convictions. To combine these scores, the guidelines create a grid, placing the offense levels on a vertical axis, and the criminal history categories on the horizontal axis. Each combination of the two scores corresponds to one of the 258 boxes in the grid, and each box contains a presumptive sentencing range (expressed as months of imprisonment, such as 51-63 months) for that particular offense level and criminal history score.

The guidelines begin with a "base offense level" for each crime and instruct the judge to adjust that number up or down, in specified amounts, based on specific characteristics of the case. These factors focus mostly on offense information, such as the amount of drugs sold, whether the offender used a gun, or whether the offender played a leading or minor role in a multi-person offense. Because these particular factual findings can have such a clear impact on the sentence, the guidelines have spawned a new kind of bargaining — "fact bargaining" — in which the parties agree to the presence or absence of these relevant sentencing facts in a given case.

The offense levels are based not only on the elements of the offenses charged but also on other activities of the defendant (called "relevant conduct") that are related to the charged offense. Relevant conduct can include uncharged behavior, behavior underlying dismissed charges, and even behavior underlying prior acquittals. For instance, the government might charge a defendant with participating in one sale of a small amount of narcotics, although there is evidence that he participated in larger, related sales. The sentencing judge can consider both the sale that formed the basis for the charge and the uncharged sales in setting the sentence for the crime of conviction. Thus, dismissing charges ("charge bargains") are less likely to have an impact on the ultimate sentence because the sentencing guidelines instruct the judge to consider the underlying conduct regardless of the charges.

Once the judge determines the designated sentencing range under the guidelines, she must also decide whether to "depart" up or down from the narrow range of sentences specified under the guidelines. A sentencing court departing from the guidelines can be overturned on appeal more easily if the ground for departure is not acceptable under the standard of 18 U.S.C. §3553(b) (part of the Sentencing Reform Act). Under that statute, departures may occur only in unusual cases, when "there exists an aggravating or mitigating circumstance of a kind, or to a degree, not adequately taken into consideration by the Sentencing Commission in formulating the guidelines."

3. *The federal guidelines and plea agreements.* What did the Sentencing Commission do about plea bargains, which account for roughly 90 percent of all convictions in the federal system, just as they do in most state systems? When the Sentencing Commission created its initial set of guidelines, it included a "policy statement" about plea agreements, reprinted below. At the time, it was generally assumed that policy statements had less binding effect than the guidelines themselves, although later events have all but erased this distinction. What was the commission trying to accomplish with regard to plea agreements?

4. *Guidance from Main Justice.* The U.S. Department of Justice realized that this new system of guideline sentencing was complicated. Thus, it issued special guidance to prosecutors that appeared simultaneously with the guidelines. Excerpts from the 1987 "Redbook" are reprinted below. Is this internal guidance to prosecutors consistent with the statute and with the policy statements? What changes does it make to the 1980 Principles of Federal Prosecution?

After the first few months of practice under the new sentencing and plea bargaining rules, officials in the Department of Justice believed that federal prosecutors in the field were not adhering closely enough to the department's plea bargaining policies. Consequently, the leadership of the Department (housed in "Main Justice" in Washington, D.C.) revised the 1987 Redbook by issuing the 1989 "Thornburgh Bluesheet," also reprinted below. The revision of the policy was aimed at increasing compliance with the plea practices that the leadership of the department wanted. What elements of the policy did the revisers focus on? What were the likely effects of the revisions?

5. *Change of administrations.* After the 1992 elections, the incoming Clinton administration appointed new leadership to the Department of Justice. The new Attorney General, Janet Reno, reviewed plea bargaining policies and issued a "Bluesheet" of her own. It is reprinted below. In most districts, this policy was carried out by newly appointed U.S. Attorneys, along with many career attorneys who had also served under the previous administration. What prior statements does the Reno Bluesheet hark back to? What, if anything, is new in the policy?

■ 28 U.S.C. §994(a)(2)(E)

The Commission . . . shall promulgate . . . general policy statements regarding application of the guidelines or any other aspect of sentencing or sentence implementation . . . including the appropriate use of . . . the authority granted under Rule 11(c)(2) of the Federal Rules of Criminal Procedure to accept or reject a plea agreement. . . .

■ U.S. SENTENCING GUIDELINES §§6B1.2, 6B1.4 (POLICY STATEMENTS)

§6B1.2

(a) In the case of a plea agreement that includes the dismissal of any charges or an agreement not to pursue potential charges [under Rule 11(c)(1)(A)], the court may accept the agreement if the court determines, for reasons stated on the record, that the remaining charges adequately reflect the seriousness of the actual offense behavior and that accepting the agreement will not undermine the statutory purposes of sentencing or the sentencing guidelines. Provided, that a plea agreement that includes the dismissal of a charge or a plea agreement not to pursue a potential charge shall not preclude the conduct underlying such charge from being considered under the provisions of §1B1.3 (Relevant Conduct) in connection with the count(s) of which the defendant is convicted.

(b) In the case of a plea agreement that includes a nonbinding recommendation [under Rule 11(c)(1)(B)], the court may accept the recommendation if the court is satisfied either that: (1) the recommended sentence is within the applicable guideline range; or (2) the recommended sentence departs from the applicable guideline range for justifiable reasons.

(c) In the case of a plea agreement that includes a specific sentence [under Rule 11(c)(1)(C)], the court may accept the agreement if the court is satisfied either that: (1) the agreed sentence is within the applicable guideline range; or (2) the agreed sentence departs from the applicable guideline range for justifiable reasons.

§6B1.4

(a) A plea agreement may be accompanied by a written stipulation of facts relevant to sentencing. [S]tipulations shall: (1) set forth the relevant facts and circumstances of the actual offense conduct and offender characteristics; (2) not contain misleading facts; and (3) set forth with meaningful specificity the reasons why the sentencing range resulting from the proposed agreement is appropriate.

(b) To the extent that the parties disagree about any facts relevant to sentencing, the stipulation shall identify the facts that are in dispute. . . .

(d) The court is not bound by the stipulation, but may with the aid of the presentence report, determine the facts relevant to sentencing.

■ PROSECUTORS' HANDBOOK ON SENTENCING GUIDELINES ("THE REDBOOK")
William Weld, Assistant Attorney General (1987)

[T]he validity and use of the Commission's policy statements by prosecutors should depend upon whether the agreement reflects charge bargaining or sentence bargaining under [Rule 11(c)].

SENTENCE BARGAINING

A significant problem with the Commission's policy statements on plea bargains which include a specific sentence under [Rule 11(c)(1)(B) and (C)], §6B1.2(b) and (c), is that the standard they set forth for acceptance or rejection of a sentence that departs from the guidelines appears to be of doubtful validity under the Sentencing Reform Act (SRA). The standard for departure from the guidelines is set forth in the Act and requires a finding that an aggravating or mitigating circumstance exists that was not adequately taken into consideration by the Commission in formulating the guidelines. Yet the Commission's policy statements relating to sentence bargains authorize departure "for justifiable reasons." We do not believe it is possible to argue that the Commission has not adequately taken into consideration the value of a plea agreement as a mitigating factor so as to support a departure. . . . We recognize, nonetheless, that many judges might be tempted to take a realistic approach; a sentence outside the guidelines in the context of a plea agreement is unlikely to result in an appeal of the sentence. Therefore, if urged to accept a plea agreement that departs from the guidelines, they will follow the policy statements despite their questionable basis.

Nevertheless, the Criminal Division has concluded that the apparent authority for a judge to depart from the guidelines pursuant to the Commission's policy statements, §6B1.2(b) and (c), for plea agreements involving a particular sentence under [Rule 11(c)(1)(B) and (C)] is at variance with the more restrictive departure language of [the statute] and that, consequently, these policy statements should not be used as a basis for recommending a sentence that departs from the guidelines. [P]rosecutors should not recommend or agree to a lower-than-guideline sentence merely on the basis of a plea agreement. They may, however, recommend or agree to a sentence at the low end of an applicable sentencing range [within the guidelines].

In addition to the above-described legitimate guideline reductions that may be used in sentence-type negotiations, a departure from the guidelines may be warranted and may be included in the recommended or agreed-upon sentence if the [statutory] standard . . . is met. That is, a mitigating circumstance must exist (other than the reaching of a plea agreement) that was not adequately taken into consideration by the Commission in formulating the guidelines and that should result in a sentence different from that described. Moreover, a departure from the guidelines may also be reflected in a plea agreement if the defendant provided substantial assistance in the investigation or prosecution of another person who has committed an offense. . . . Therefore, even though plea-bargained sentences must accord with the law and the guidelines, there is considerable room for negotiating.

The basic reason for rejecting the Commission's policy statements on sentence bargains and treating sentences which are the subject of a sentence bargain in the same manner as sentences which result from conviction after trial is that any other result could seriously thwart the purpose of the SRA to reduce unwarranted disparity in sentencing [among defendants with similar records who have been found guilty of similar criminal conduct]. Congress could not have expressed the concerns reflected in the SRA and the legislative history with unwarranted disparity and uncertainty in sentencing but have intended the reforms enacted to be limited to the small percentage of cases that go to trial. The legislative history of the SRA indeed indicates that Congress was concerned with the potential shift of discretion in sentencing from the court to the prosecutor through plea agreements and the unwarranted disparity that could result. . . .

CHARGE BARGAINING

The policy statement on charge bargaining addresses agreements that include the dismissal of any charges under [Rule 11(c)(1)(A)] or an agreement not to pursue potential charges. It authorizes the court to accept such an agreement if it determines, "for reasons stated on the record, that the remaining charges adequately reflect the seriousness of the actual offense behavior and that accepting the agreement will not undermine the statutory purposes of sentencing." §6B1.2(a). The requirement that the "remaining charges adequately reflect the seriousness of the actual offense behavior" in charge bargaining is important since the charge of conviction itself is the most significant factor in establishing the guideline sentence. . . .

Although Congress intended that courts exercise "meaningful" review of charge reduction plea agreements, it is our view that moderately greater flexibility legally can and does attach to charge bargains than to sentence bargains. While, as indicated previously, the Commission's quite liberal policy statements on sentence bargaining appear to be inconsistent with the controlling (and stricter) statutory departure standard, the statutory departure standard is not applicable in the charge-bargain context. . . .

Nevertheless, in order to fulfill the objectives of the Sentencing Reform Act prosecutors should conduct charge bargaining in a manner consistent with the direction in the applicable policy statement, §6B1.2(a), i.e., subject to the policy statement's instruction that the "remaining charges [should] adequately reflect the seriousness of the actual offense behavior" and that the agreement not undermine the statutory purposes of sentencing. In our view, this translates into a requirement that readily provable serious charges should not be bargained away. The sole legitimate ground for agreeing not to pursue a charge that is relevant under the guidelines to assure that the sentence will reflect the seriousness of the defendant's "offense behavior" is the existence of real doubt as to the ultimate provability of the charge.

Concomitantly, however, the prosecutor is in the best position to assess the strength of the government's case and enjoys broad discretion in making judgments as to which charges are most likely to result in conviction on the basis of the available evidence. For this reason, the prosecutor entering into a charge bargain may enjoy a degree of latitude that is not present when the plea bargain addresses only sentencing aspects. . . .

It is appropriate that the sentence for an offender who agrees to plead guilty to relatively few charges should be different from the sentence for an offender convicted of many charges since guilt has not been determined as to the dismissed charges. At the same time, however, sentence bargaining should not result in a vastly different sentence as compared to a sentence following trial. . . .

The overriding principle governing the conduct of plea negotiations is that plea agreements should not be used to circumvent the guidelines. This principle is in accordance with the policies set forth in the Principles of Federal Prosecution. . . . For example, charges should not be filed simply to exert leverage to induce a plea. Rather, the prosecutor should charge the most serious offense consistent with the defendant's provable conduct. . . .

A subsidiary but nonetheless important issue concerns so-called "fact" bargaining or stipulations. [The policy statement §6B1.4] attaches certain conditions to such stipulations. The most important condition, with which the Department concurs, is that stipulations shall "not contain misleading facts." Otherwise, the basic purpose of the SRA to reduce unwarranted sentence disparity will be undermined. Thus, if the defendant can clearly be proved to have used a weapon or committed an assault in the course of the offense, the prosecutor may not stipulate, as part of a plea agreement designed to produce a lower sentence, that no weapon was used or assault committed. If, on the other hand, certain facts surrounding the offense are not clear, e.g., the extent of the loss or injury resulting from the defendant's fraud, the prosecutor is at liberty to stipulate that no loss or injury beyond that clearly provable existed. Prosecutors may not, however, instruct investigators not to pursue leads, or make less than ordinary efforts to ascertain facts, simply to be in a position to say that they are unable clearly to prove a sentencing fact and thereby increase the latitude for bargaining. . . . Subject to the above constraints, however, the Department encourages the use of stipulations accompanying plea agreements to the extent practicable. . . .

■ PLEA POLICY FOR FEDERAL PROSECUTORS ("THORNBURGH BLUESHEET")
Richard Thornburgh, Attorney General (1989)

. . . Should a prosecutor determine in good faith after indictment that, as a result of a change in the evidence or for another reason (e.g., a need has arisen to protect the identity of a particular witness until he testifies against a more significant defendant), a charge is not readily provable or that an indictment exaggerates the seriousness of an offense or offenses, a plea bargain may reflect the prosecutor's reassessment. There should be a record, however, in a case in which charges originally brought are dropped. . . .

Department policy requires honesty in sentencing; federal prosecutors are expected to identify for U.S. District Courts departures when they agree to support them. For example, it would be improper for a prosecutor to agree that a departure is in order, but to conceal the agreement in a charge bargain that is presented to a court as a fait accompli so that there is neither a record of nor judicial review of the departure. . . .

The basic policy is that charges are not to be bargained away or dropped, unless the prosecutor has a good faith doubt as to the government's ability readily to prove a charge for legal or evidentiary reasons. It would serve no purpose here to seek to further define "readily provable." The policy is to bring cases that the government should win if there were a trial. There are, however, two exceptions.

First, if the applicable guideline range from which a sentence may be imposed would be unaffected, readily provable charges may be dismissed or dropped as part of a plea bargain. . . . Second, federal prosecutors may drop readily provable charges with the specific approval of the United States Attorney or designated supervisory level official for reasons set forth in the file of the case. This exception recognizes that the aims of the Sentencing Reform Act must be sought without ignoring other, critical aspects of the federal criminal justice system. For example, approval to drop charges in a particular case might be given because the United States Attorney's office is particularly overburdened, the case would be time-consuming to try, and proceeding to trial would significantly reduce the total number of cases disposed of by the office. . . .

The Department's policy is only to stipulate to facts that accurately represent the defendant's conduct. If a prosecutor wishes to support a departure from the guidelines, he or she should candidly do so and not stipulate to facts that are untrue. Stipulations to untrue facts are unethical. If a prosecutor has insufficient facts to contest a defendant's effort to seek a downward departure or to claim an adjustment, the prosecutor can say so. If the presentence report states facts that are inconsistent with a stipulation in which a prosecutor has joined, it is desirable for the prosecutor to object to the report or to add a statement explaining the prosecutor's understanding of the facts or the reason for the stipulation. . . .

■ CHARGING AND PLEA DECISIONS ("RENO BLUESHEET")
Janet Reno, Attorney General (1993)

As first stated in the preface to the original 1980 edition of the Principles of Federal Prosecution, "they have been cast in general terms with a view to providing guidance rather than to mandating results. The intent is to assure regularity without regimentation, to prevent unwarranted disparity without sacrificing flexibility."

It should be emphasized that charging decisions and plea agreements should reflect adherence to the Sentencing Guidelines. However, a faithful and honest application of the Sentencing Guidelines is not incompatible with selecting charges or entering into plea agreements on the basis of an individualized assessment of the extent to which particular charges fit the specific circumstances of the case, are consistent with the purposes of the federal criminal code, and maximize the impact of federal resources on crime. Thus, for example, in determining "the most serious offense that is consistent with the nature of the defendant's conduct, that is likely to result in a sustainable conviction," it is appropriate that the attorney for the government consider, inter alia, such factors as the sentencing guideline range yielded by the charge, whether the penalty yielded by such sentencing range (or potential mandatory minimum charge, if applicable) is proportional to the seriousness of the defendant's conduct, and whether the charge achieves such purposes of the criminal law as punishment, protection of the public, specific and general deterrence, and rehabilitation. Note that these factors may also be considered by the attorney for the government when entering into the plea agreements.

To ensure consistency and accountability, charging and plea agreement decisions must be made at an appropriate level of responsibility and documented with an appropriate record of the factors applied.

Notes

1. *The 1992 Terwilliger Bluesheet.* After a few years of experience with the new system, officials in the Department of Justice remained unsatisfied with the plea bargaining practices of its attorneys in the field. In a 1992 revision of the plea bargaining policy, known as the "Terwilliger Bluesheet," the department moved away from an emphasis on describing the types of bargains that are acceptable. Instead, the revised policy strengthened the procedural review process for plea agreements:

> All negotiated plea agreements to felonies or misdemeanors negotiated from felonies shall be in writing and filed with the court. . . . There shall be within each office a formal system for approval of negotiated pleas. The approval authority shall be vested in at least a supervisory criminal Assistant United States Attorney . . . who will have the responsibility of assessing the appropriateness of the plea agreement under the policies of the Department of Justice pertaining to pleas, including those set forth in the Thornburgh Memo.

The 1992 policy allowed for categorical review of certain plea bargains. Fact situations that "arise with great frequency and are given identical treatment" could be handled through a "written instruction" that "describes with particularity the standard plea procedure to be followed, so long as that procedure is otherwise within Departmental guidelines." The policy listed as an example "a border district which routinely deals with a high volume of illegal alien cases daily." What do you suppose were the effects of these 1992 policy changes?

2. *Prosecutorial discretion and control.* How would you describe these DOJ policies in terms of the degree of control each policy exerted over federal prosecutorial plea practices? Did all of these policies move toward increasing control over individual prosecutorial decisions? For further background on the creation of these federal policies, see David Robinson, The Decline and Potential Collapse of Federal Guideline Sentencing, 74 Wash. U. L.Q. 881 (1996). Are executive plea bargaining policies a good idea? What problems could they solve? What problems might they create?

3. *Policies and political accountability.* In response to the Reno Bluesheet, on January 13, 1994, Senator Orrin Hatch (R-Utah), the ranking minority member on the Judiciary Committee, sent Attorney General Janet Reno a letter strongly opposing her directive:

> The Department's new policy now permits prosecutors to make independent decisions about whether a prescribed guideline sentence or mandatory minimum charge is not "proportional to the seriousness of the defendant's conduct." In other words, this new policy increases the potential for the unwarranted softening of sentences for violent offenders. . . .
>
> I do not support the Department's announcement to drug traffickers and violent criminals that certain illegal conduct may not be charged because a Department employee may find the prescribed punishment too severe. If the Administration believes that existing sentences for drug cases and violent criminals are too severe, then it should seek to change the law or the relevant sentencing guidelines — not ignore them. I strongly urge you to reconsider your action in this matter.

Reno responded on March 8, 1994:

> Let me reiterate, as set forth in the clarifying bluesheet to which you allude, that it remains the directive of the Department of Justice that prosecutors charge the most serious offense that is consistent with the nature of the defendant's conduct, that is likely to result in a sustainable conviction; that prosecutors adhere to the Sentencing Guidelines; and that charging and plea agreements be made at an appropriate level of responsibility with appropriate documentation. In short, contrary to what you suggest, individual prosecutors are not free to follow their own lights or to ignore legislative directives. . . . We are steadfast in our opposition to unwarranted softening of sentences for violent offenders or drug traffickers. . . .

4. *Congress reasserts control over federal sentencing.* In 2003 Congress enacted the USA PROTECT Act, Public Law 108-21, 117 Stat. 650. Although the statute dealt primarily with crimes involving child abuse, it also changed several features of federal sentencing law more generally, making downward departures from the sentencing prescribed by the federal guidelines more difficult for judges to invoke. Congress also asked the attorney general to submit a report to the House and Senate Judiciary Committees, detailing the policies the Department would follow to discourage downward departures.

5. *The Ashcroft Memos.* The PROTECT Act requested a report from the Department of Justice within 90 days of the statute's passage. If such a report did not appear by that deadline, the law imposed a more onerous set of reporting requirements for the attorney general to follow. The statute was signed into law on April 30, 2003. On July 28, Attorney General John Ashcroft issued a set of policies concerning "sentencing recommendations and sentencing appeals." The policies emphasized "honesty in sentencing, both with respect to the facts and the law." A prosecutor's sentencing recommendations to the court "must honestly reflect the totality and seriousness of the defendant's conduct and must be fully consistent with the Guidelines," regardless of whether the individual prosecutor agrees with the policy embodied in the sentencing guidelines. Under the policy, prosecutors may not agree to "stand silent" while a defendant requests a downward adjustment to a sentence, "unless the prosecutor determines in good faith that the adjustment is supported by facts and the law."

Two months later, Attorney General Ashcroft issued a second policy statement, this one dealing with selection of charges and plea agreements. The policy is reprinted below. How does Ashcroft's policy compare with those of Reno, Terwilliger, Thornburgh, and Weld?

■ DEPARTMENT POLICY CONCERNING CHARGING CRIMINAL OFFENSES, DISPOSITION OF CHARGES, AND SENTENCING

John Ashcroft, Attorney General (September 22, 2003)

. . . The fairness Congress sought to achieve by the Sentencing Reform Act and the PROTECT Act can be attained only if there are fair and reasonably consistent policies with respect to the Department's decisions concerning what charges to bring and how cases should be disposed. Just as the sentence a defendant receives should not depend upon which particular judge presides over the case, so too the charges a defendant faces should not depend upon the particular prosecutor assigned to handle the case. . . .

I. DEPARTMENT POLICY CONCERNING CHARGING AND PROSECUTION OF CRIMINAL OFFENSES

A. GENERAL DUTY TO CHARGE AND TO PURSUE THE MOST SERIOUS, READILY PROVABLE OFFENSE IN ALL FEDERAL PROSECUTIONS

It is the policy of the Department of Justice that, in all federal criminal cases, federal prosecutors must charge and pursue the most serious, readily provable offense or offenses that are supported by the facts of the case, except as authorized by an Assistant Attorney General, United States Attorney, or designated supervisory attorney in the limited circumstances described below. The most serious offense or offenses are those that generate the most substantial sentence under the Sentencing Guidelines, unless a mandatory minimum sentence or count requiring a consecutive sentence would generate a longer sentence. A charge is not "readily provable" if the prosecutor has a good faith doubt, for legal or evidentiary reasons, as to the Government's ability readily to prove a charge at trial. Thus, charges should not be filed simply to exert leverage to induce a plea. Once filed, the most serious readily provable charges may not be dismissed except to the extent permitted in Section B.

B. LIMITED EXCEPTIONS

The basic policy set forth above requires federal prosecutors to charge and to pursue all charges that are determined to be readily provable and that, under the applicable statutes and Sentencing Guidelines, would yield the most substantial sentence. There are, however, certain limited exceptions to this requirement:

1. *Sentence would not be affected.* First, if the applicable guideline range from which a sentence may be imposed would be unaffected, prosecutors may decline to charge or to pursue readily provable charges. However, if the most serious readily provable charge involves a mandatory minimum sentence that exceeds the applicable guideline range, counts essential to establish a mandatory minimum sentence must be charged and may not be dismissed, except to the extent provided elsewhere below.

2. *"Fast-track" programs.* With the passage of the PROTECT Act, Congress recognized the importance of early disposition or "fast-track" programs [to handle the high volume of cases (particularly immigration cases) in some districts. As a matter of Department policy, Attorney General authorization is necessary for] any fast-track program that relies on "charge bargaining" — *i.e.*, an expedited disposition program whereby the Government agrees to charge less than the most serious, readily provable offense. Such programs are intended to be exceptional and will be authorized only when clearly warranted by local conditions within a district. . . .

3. *Post-indictment reassessment.* In cases where post-indictment circumstances cause a prosecutor to determine in good faith that the most serious offense is not readily provable, because of a change in the evidence or some other justifiable reason (*e.g.*, the unavailability of a witness or the need to protect the identity of a witness until he testifies against a more significant defendant), the prosecutor may dismiss the charge(s) with the written or otherwise documented approval of an Assistant Attorney General, United States Attorney, or designated supervisory attorney.

4. *Substantial assistance.* The preferred means to recognize a defendant's substantial assistance in the investigation or prosecution of another person is to charge the most serious readily provable offense and then to file an appropriate motion or motions under U.S.S.G. §5K1.1, 18 U.S.C. §3553(e), or Federal Rule of Criminal Rule of Procedure 35(b). However, in rare circumstances, where necessary to obtain substantial assistance in an important investigation or prosecution, and with the written or otherwise documented approval of an Assistant Attorney General, United States Attorney, or designated supervisory attorney, a federal prosecutor may decline to charge or to pursue a readily provable charge as part of plea agreement that properly reflects the substantial assistance provided by the defendant in the investigation or prosecution of another person.

5. *Statutory enhancements.* The use of statutory enhancements is strongly encouraged, and federal prosecutors must therefore take affirmative steps to ensure that the increased penalties resulting from specific statutory enhancements [such as use of a weapon] are sought in all appropriate cases. . . . In many cases, however, the filing of such enhancements will mean that the statutory sentence exceeds the applicable Sentencing Guidelines range, thereby ensuring that the defendant will not receive any credit for acceptance of responsibility and will have no incentive to plead guilty. Requiring the pursuit of such enhancements to trial in every case could

therefore have a significant effect on the allocation of prosecutorial resources within a given district. Accordingly, an Assistant Attorney General, United States Attorney, or designated supervisory attorney may authorize a prosecutor to forgo the filing of a statutory enhancement, but *only* in the context of a negotiated plea agreement. . . .

6. *Other Exceptional Circumstances.* Prosecutors may decline to pursue or may dismiss readily provable charges in other exceptional circumstances with the written or otherwise documented approval of an Assistant Attorney General, United States Attorney, or designated supervisory attorney. This exception recognizes that the aims of the Sentencing Reform Act must be sought without ignoring the practical limitations of the federal criminal justice system. For example, a case-specific approval to dismiss charges in a particular case might be given because the United States Attorney's Office is particularly over-burdened, the duration of the trial would be exceptionally long, and proceeding to trial would significantly reduce the total number of cases disposed of by the office. However, such case-by-case exceptions should be rare; otherwise the goals of fairness and equity will be jeopardized.

II. DEPARTMENT POLICY CONCERNING PLEA AGREEMENTS

[It] remains Department policy that the sentencing court should be informed if a plea agreement involves a "charge bargain." Accordingly, a negotiated plea that uses any of the options described in Section I(B)(2), (4), (5), or (6) must be made known to the court at the time of the plea hearing and at the time of sentencing, *i.e.*, the court must be informed that a more serious, readily provable offense was not charged or that an applicable statutory enhancement was not filed. . . . Charges may be declined or dismissed pursuant to a plea agreement only to the extent consistent with the principles set forth in Section I of this Memorandum.

[As for sentence bargains], prosecutors may enter into a plea agreement for a sentence that is within the specified guideline range. For example, when the Sentencing Guidelines range is 18-24 months, a prosecutor may agree to recommend a sentence of 18 or 20 months rather than to argue for a sentence at the top of the range. Similarly, a prosecutor may agree to recommend a downward adjustment for acceptance of responsibility under U.S.S.G. §3E1.1 if the prosecutor concludes in good faith that the defendant is entitled to the adjustment. . . .

In passing the PROTECT Act, Congress has made clear its view that there have been too many downward departures from the Sentencing Guidelines, and it has instructed the Commission to take measures "to ensure that the incidence of downward departures [is] substantially reduced." The Department has a duty to ensure that the circumstances in which it will request or accede to downward departures in the future are properly circumscribed.

Accordingly, federal prosecutors must not request or accede to a downward departure except in the limited circumstances specified in this memorandum and with authorization from an Assistant Attorney General, United States Attorney, or designated supervisory attorney. . . .

Federal criminal law and procedure apply equally throughout the United States. As the sole federal prosecuting entity, the Department of Justice has a unique obligation to ensure that all federal criminal cases are prosecuted according to the same standards. . . .

Notes

1. *Prosecutor plea policies and legislative oversight.* In what ways do the Ashcroft Memos reveal their intended function as responses to Congress's request to push sentencing practices in a particular direction? What do you make of the policy decision to equate the criteria for initial selection of charges (Section I of the Memos) and the criteria for evaluating charge bargains (Section II of the Memos)?

2. *Policies and practice.* Do "line" attorneys follow directives from their boss? The most complete studies of federal plea practices during the early implementation of the guidelines concluded that prosecutors manipulated the guidelines in 20-35 percent of all cases. Stephen Schulhofer & Ilene Nagel, A Tale of Three Cities: An Empirical Study of Charging and Bargaining Practice Under the Federal Sentencing Guidelines, 66 S. Cal. L. Rev. 501 (1992). Sentencing Commission studies found charge manipulation in 17 percent of all cases and 26 percent of drug cases. U.S. Sentencing Commission, The Federal Sentencing Guidelines: A Report on the Operation of the Guidelines System and Short-Term Impacts on Disparity in Sentencing, Use of Incarceration, and Prosecutorial Discretion and Plea Bargaining, Executive Summary 31-54 (December 1991). Why might line attorneys not follow plea guidelines? Why might different U.S. Attorneys' offices develop different patterns of plea bargaining?

3. *Written and unwritten guidance.* A striking feature of the plea bargaining policies in the federal system is the fact that they are written. Many other prosecutors' offices in state systems have pursued goals similar to those of the Department of Justice in creating its plea policies. They hope to maintain adequate control over prosecutors in the field and to send appropriate public signals about sentencing and plea bargaining. Nonetheless, within the state systems, such policies are rarely written, even when they are explicit. Why might a supervising prosecutor choose to keep such a critical office policy unwritten? See William Pizzi, Understanding Prosecutorial Discretion in the United States: The Limits of Comparative Criminal Procedure as an Instrument of Reform, 54 Ohio St. L.J. 1325 (1993) (discussing reasons that offices keep their plea bargaining policies informal and unwritten, including ill effects on deterrent value of criminal law, unfavorable public impressions of perceived lenient policies, need for flexibility in unusual cases, need to avoid judicial review of prosecutorial decisions); but compare Kim Banks Mayer, Applying Open Records Policy to Wisconsin District Attorneys: Can Charging Guidelines Promote Public Awareness? 1996 Wis. L. Rev. 295 (giving examples of prosecutorial charging and plea bargaining guidelines made public with no apparent ill effects; arguing generally for public availability of policies). Is there any reason not to create a written office policy, given that all plea agreements in individual cases will become a matter of public record?

4. *Sentencing guidelines and the shift to charge bargains.* A large number of states have changed their sentencing laws over the past few decades to reduce the discretion of judges in selecting a sentence and to restrict the discretion of corrections or parole officials in releasing offenders before the end of their announced sentences. These more "determinate" sentencing systems make the selection of the criminal charge more important than it was under more discretionary sentencing systems. Unlike the federal system, state guideline systems reject the use of uncharged conduct when setting a sentence. As a result, prosecutors and defendants in these jurisdictions have shifted away from sentence bargains toward charge bargains

and "fact" bargains. In Minnesota, which adopted a more determinate sentencing guideline system in 1980, studies focusing on the first few years of practice under the new laws revealed an increase in charge negotiations and a decrease in sentence negotiations. Terance Miethe, Charging and Plea Bargaining Practices Under Determinate Sentencing: An Investigation of the Hydraulic Displacement of Discretion, 78 J. Crim. L. & Criminology 155 (1987) (describing earlier studies).

5. *Uniformity within a jurisdiction.* The federal plea bargaining policies reprinted above apply to U.S. Attorneys' offices throughout the country. While these offices still have a great deal of independence, and vary from one another in their plea bargaining practices, they are still subject to more centralized control than the various prosecutors' offices located throughout a given state. Since prosecutors often create plea bargaining policies for their own offices, shouldn't there be great variety in plea bargaining practices among the different prosecutors within a state? Or are there institutions or incentives that produce similar prosecutorial plea policies throughout a state or even across different states? The following case addresses this topic.

■ STATE v. CHRISTOPHER BRIMAGE
706 A.2d 1096 (N.J. 1998)

GARIBALDI, J.

We are again presented with issues relating to Section 12 of the Comprehensive Drug Reform Act of 1987, N.J.S.A. 2C:35-1 to 36A-1 ("CDRA"). Under N.J.S.A. 2C:35-12 ("Section 12"), a prosecutor may, through a negotiated plea agreement or post-conviction agreement with a defendant, waive the mandatory minimum sentence specified for any offense under the CDRA. To satisfy the constitutional requirements of the separation of powers doctrine, N.J. Const. art. III, ¶ 1, this Court in State v. Vasquez, 609 A.2d 29 (N.J. 1992), held that prosecutorial discretion under Section 12 must be subject to judicial review for arbitrary and capricious action. To further that review, the Court held that prosecutors must adhere to written guidelines governing plea offers and state on the record their reasons for waiving or not waiving the parole disqualifier in any given case.

In response to that holding, the Attorney General promulgated plea agreement guidelines. . . . Although the Guidelines prescribe statewide minimum plea offers, they also direct each county prosecutor's office to adopt its own written plea agreement policy. . . . We must determine whether the Attorney General's Plea-Bargaining Guidelines are adequate to satisfy the separation of powers doctrine, as enunciated in *Vasquez*, and to meet the statutory goals of uniformity in sentencing.

I.

On May 12, 1995, the Franklin Township Police, armed with a search warrant, conducted a search of the Brimage residence. According to defendant's statements at the plea hearing, during the search defendant turned over to the police eighteen bags of cocaine totaling about six grams. . . . Defendant stated at the plea hearing that he had purchased the cocaine in New Brunswick and intended to resell it in Franklin Township. Defendant's residence was within 1000 feet of Franklin Township High School. In September 1995, defendant was indicted under the CDRA for possession of a controlled dangerous substance with intent to distribute . . . ; possession of a controlled dangerous substance with intent to distribute within 1000 feet of school property, contrary to N.J.S.A. 2C:35-7; and possession of a controlled dangerous substance, . . . all third degree offenses. . . .

According to the presentence report, defendant was twenty at the time of arrest and living in his grandparents' home with his grandparents, mother, and siblings. Defendant had not previously been arrested for an indictable offense, but he had three prior juvenile adjudications, the last when he was fourteen years old.

The Somerset County Prosecutor's Office offered, in exchange for defendant's guilty plea, to recommend the presumptive sentence for a third degree crime — four years incarceration — plus the mandatory three-year period of parole ineligibility specified in N.J.S.A. 2C:35-7 for the school zone offense. The prosecutor proffered the following reasons for not waiving the parole ineligibility term of N.J.S.A. 2C:35-7: the proofs available to sustain a conviction of defendant were very strong, including defendant's taped confession that he intended to sell cocaine for profit; defendant did not offer to cooperate in any other drug-related investigations; and the Somerset County Prosecutor's Office had sufficient resources to litigate this matter, unlike various other counties that were plagued with a lack of resources or with case management problems. . . .

Defendant then accepted the prosecutor's original plea agreement offer and pled guilty to all counts in the indictment, although he reserved the right to challenge the validity of the Guidelines and the applicability of the mandatory three-year parole disqualifier to his case. [At the hearing on his motion for waiver of the mandatory minimum sentence, Brimage] argued that the standard plea offer required by the Attorney General's Guidelines for a school zone offense was . . . probation conditioned on 364 days in county jail . . . and that the prosecutor acted arbitrarily and capriciously by not making that offer to defendant. . . . Finding that nonwaiver of the mandatory parole disqualifier was standard policy in Somerset County for school zone cases and that the Guidelines' lesser plea offer was only applicable when the prosecutor in his discretion decided to waive that disqualifier, the court denied defendant's motion. [The] court sentenced defendant to four years imprisonment with three years of parole ineligibility, in accordance with the prosecutor's recommendation. . . .

II.

. . . N.J.S.A. 2C:35-7 of the CDRA ("Section 7") requires a mandatory minimum custodial sentence between one-third and one-half of the sentence imposed, but no less than three years for those convicted of dispensing or possessing with the intent to distribute drugs within a school zone, and no less than one year for those convicted of the same offense with less than one ounce of marijuana. [The] Legislature's intention, as stated in its Declaration of Policy and Legislative Findings for the CDRA, [was] to "provide for the strict punishment, deterrence and incapacitation of the most culpable and dangerous drug offenders." N.J.S.A. 2C:35-1.1(c). To foster that policy, the Legislature included in the CDRA mandatory periods of parole ineligibility for various crimes. See, e.g., N.J.S.A. 2C:35-3 (providing twenty-five year parole bar for leaders of narcotics trafficking network).

Despite the nondiscretionary nature of N.J.S.A. 2C:35-7, that section, like other mandatory parole bar provisions in the CDRA, contemplates exceptions to its rule as provided by N.J.S.A. 2C:35-12 ("Section 12"). Section 12 allows a prosecutor to waive the period of parole ineligibility imposed under Section 7 as part of a plea or post-conviction agreement with a defendant. Because mandatory sentences usually do not permit judicial or prosecutorial discretion, the unique Section 7 and Section 12 sentencing scheme has been characterized as a hybrid, combining mandatory and discretionary features and delegating sentencing authority to both the courts and the prosecutors." *Vasquez,* 609 A.2d at 29.

The primary purpose of the Section 12 waiver provision is to provide an incentive for defendants, especially lower and middle level drug offenders, to cooperate with law enforcement agencies in the war against drugs. Assembly Judiciary Committee, Commentary to the Comprehensive Drug Reform Act, at 26 (Nov. 23, 1987). Another goal of N.J.S.A. 2C:35-12, as enunciated in the Department of Law and Public Safety's report on the CDRA, is to encourage plea bargaining so as not to plague the courts with too many defendants who, without any incentive to plead guilty, demand jury trials and thus overburden and backlog the system. That view of Section 12 is consistent with one of the Legislature's stated goals in enacting the CDRA, namely, the minimization of pretrial delay and the prompt disposition of criminal charges. N.J.S.A. 2C:35-1.1.

To achieve the Legislature's specific goal of encouraging cooperation and turning State's evidence and to prevent sentencing courts from undermining the effectiveness of prosecutors' strategies, N.J.S.A. 2C:35-12 requires the sentencing court to enforce all agreements reached by the prosecutor and a defendant under that section and prohibits the court from imposing a lesser term of imprisonment than that specified in the agreement. That shift in sentencing power from the judiciary to the prosecutor is uncommon. . . .

As a result of the atypical grant of sentencing power to the prosecutor in N.J.S.A. 2C:35-12, that statute has been the subject of various constitutional challenges on separation of powers grounds. We first considered the interaction of Section 7 and Section 12 in [State v. Vasquez.] In *Vasquez,* . . . we upheld the transfer of sentencing authority under Section 12, but stated that judicial oversight was "mandated to protect against arbitrary and capricious prosecutorial decisions." To enable judicial review, we required prosecutors to state on the record their reasons for waiving or not waiving the parole disqualifier in any given case and to promulgate written guidelines governing their exercise of discretion. The Court held that, if those conditions were met, the statute would withstand scrutiny under the separation of powers doctrine, and only those defendants who showed "clearly and convincingly that the exercise of discretion was arbitrary and capricious would be entitled to relief." . . .

In reaching our decision in *Vasquez,* we relied on our previous decision in State v. Lagares, 601 A.2d 698 (N.J. 1992). *Lagares* involved the constitutionality of the prosecutor's power to invoke the extended sentence requirement under N.J.S.A. 2C:43-6(f). Although N.J.S.A. 2C:43-6(f) requires a court to impose an extended term with a period of parole ineligibility for repeat drug offenders, the provision only takes effect upon the application of the prosecutor. Furthermore, once the prosecutor decides to apply for an extended sentence, the sentencing judge has no discretion to reject the application. [To] pass constitutional scrutiny, the Court required that prosecutorial decisions under Section 6f be subject to judicial review for arbitrariness, that prosecutors state on the record their reasons for seeking an extended sentence, and that "guidelines be adopted to assist prosecutorial decision-making."

Lagares based that decision, in turn, on previous decisions of this Court in State v. Leonardis, 363 A.2d 321 (N.J. 1976), and Monks v. New Jersey State Parole Board, 277 A.2d 193 (N.J. 1971). We held in *Leonardis* that prosecutorial discretion in dismissing charges against certain defendants and admitting them into pre-trial intervention (PTI) programs must be subject to uniform written guidelines and judicial review of the prosecutor's written statement of reasons. Similarly, we held in *Monks* that the parole board had to provide a statement of reasons to inmates who had been denied parole in order to meet the needs of simple fairness. . . . In summary, the *Vasquez/Lagares* line of cases held that judicial review of prosecutorial decisions through uniform written guidelines was necessary not only to meet the requirements of the separation of powers doctrine, but also to comport with the statutory goal of increasing uniformity in sentencing.

THE GUIDELINES

In response to this Court's ruling in *Vasquez*, on September 15, 1992 the Attorney General promulgated plea agreement guidelines for charges brought under the Comprehensive Drug Reform Act. Those original 1992 Guidelines governed at the time of defendant's plea. Recognizing the various goals of the Legislature in enacting the CDRA as well as the intentions of the Court in *Vasquez*, the Introduction to the 1992 Guidelines states: "In order to satisfy the principal goal of the Legislature to ensure a uniform, consistent and predictable sentence for a given offense, these decisions require that the prosecutorial decision-making process must be guided by uniform standards that channel the exercise of discretion and reduce the danger of uneven application." . . . The Introduction also emphasizes that the purpose of Section 12 is to provide incentives to defendants to cooperate with the State and recognizes that "swiftness" of punishment is also an important goal.

The Guidelines continue by asserting that the "specified mandatory term of imprisonment and minimum term of parole ineligibility" should be treated as norms and that prosecutors "should exercise caution and reluctance in deciding whether to waive the minimum sentence or parole ineligibility." §II.1. More specifically, in Section II.3 of those Guidelines, the Attorney General requires that all plea agreements for a CDRA offense impose on defendants a mandatory minimum term of incarceration, except where the agreement is or was necessary to obtain cooperation of "substantial value" to the State. That term must be a state prison term, except in the case of a school zone offense under N.J.S.A. 2C:35-7. The 1992 version of the Guidelines provides that the "minimum term of imprisonment for a school zone offense shall include the imposition of 364 days incarceration in a county jail as a condition of probation," unless the violation involves distributing, dispensing, or possessing with intent to distribute less than one ounce of marijuana in a school zone, in which case the prison term may be waived entirely. The 1992 Guidelines are also specific in their mandate of a three-year term of imprisonment without eligibility for parole for defendants who distribute, or possess with intent to distribute, a controlled dangerous substance while actually on school property, or one year in a case involving less than one ounce of marijuana, unless there are compelling reasons to justify a lesser term. §II.6. In Section II.9, the Guidelines specify various requirements for cooperation agreements. Finally, in Section II.5, the Guidelines outline criteria for deciding whether to approve or disapprove a plea agreement that incorporates an upward or downward departure from any plea agreement policy.

Despite those specific provisions in the Guidelines, Section II.4 directs each county prosecutor's office to adopt and implement its own written policy governing plea and post-conviction agreements, using the Guidelines as a model, and suggests that the counties may also promulgate their own "standardized plea offers for typical cases and offenders." The Guidelines state that the counties, in formulating those plea offers, may consider certain factors such as the nature and extent of the drug distribution and use problem, the number and type of drug arrests in the jurisdiction, and the backlog of drug and non-drug cases in the courts. They should also consider the seriousness of the offense, the role of the actor in the crime, the amount of time that has passed since the offense was committed, whether the defendant has previously been convicted of an offense, and the amount of resources already expended on the particular case. Finally, Section II.4 specifically states that "nothing contained in these guidelines shall preclude a prosecutor from adopting more stringent policies or standardized plea offers consistent with the needs, resources and enforcement priorities of each county." Thus, by its very language, Section II.4 of the Guidelines permits different counties to adopt disparate and varying plea offer policies. Not only does consideration of the numerous factors listed in Section II.4 assure different results in localities with differing conditions, but the Guidelines themselves direct each county to adopt their own individual standards and procedures.

Although the Introduction to the Guidelines recognizes the need to "guard against sentencing disparity," the Guidelines actually generated such disparity. The inter-county disparity created by the Guidelines is evidenced in the actual policies that have been adopted throughout the jurisdictions. . . . Although the standard plea offer in Gloucester and Hudson Counties [for a person in Brimage's situation] would have been probation with 364 days in jail, the pre-indictment offer in Mercer and Salem Counties was one year without parole. Meanwhile, the plea in Camden and Cumberland Counties would have been three years flat and three to five years flat, respectively. Even the counties that purported, at that time, to have adopted the Attorney General's Guidelines without modification differed in their potential offers. Ocean and Bergen Counties provided in 1996 for probation conditioned on 364 days in jail; Sussex in 1996 required three years imprisonment, one without parole; and Somerset, the county in this case, provided four years, three without parole.

THE SUPPLEMENTAL DIRECTIVE

Subsequent to Brimage's plea, the Attorney General issued additional guidelines in its 1997 Supplemental Directive; however, the Supplemental Directive fails to limit the discretion authorized by Section II.4 and thus maintains the resulting inter-county disparity. The Supplemental Directive was developed in response to Governor Christine Todd Whitman's Drug Enforcement, Education and Awareness Program, which required the Attorney General to issue new, revised guidelines concerning prosecutorial charging, case disposition, and plea bargaining policies to ensure that the CDRA is aggressively and uniformly enforced in court. The Supplemental Directive mandates, among other requirements, that each county reduce its plea policies to writing and review the policies at least once a year; that downward departures shall not be permitted except as provided in the Attorney General's Guidelines; that both downward and upward departures and all cooperation agreements shall be memorialized in writing; . . . and that offenders may be sentenced to treatment in lieu of imprisonment only if they meet a long list of explicit conditions. [While] the Directive states that the Guidelines are "intended and shall hereinafter be interpreted to establish drug prosecution policies that must be followed by every county prosecutor's office," the Directive nevertheless permits each county to adopt its own standards pursuant to Section II.4. . . .

THE UNIFORMITY DIRECTIVE

On January 15, 1998, the Attorney General issued its most recent amendments to the plea agreement Guidelines. Those amendments resulted from this Court's mandate in State v. Gerns, 678 A.2d 634 (N.J. 1996). In *Gerns*, this Court heard arguments on the issue of impermissible sentencing disparities under the Attorney General's Guidelines. Although specifically addressing the question of whether a defendant who signs a plea agreement calling for "cooperation" in state investigations can satisfy that agreement by good faith efforts that produce nothing of value to the State, the Court noted the significance of the defendant's disparity claims: "The arguments and the statistical data proffered in support of the claim of sentencing disparity are impressive." [The] Court . . . directed the Attorney General to undertake a review of statewide sentencing practices and experience under the Guidelines and to furnish the Court with the results of that review. The Attorney General promulgated the Uniformity Directive in response to that command.

The Uniformity Directive acknowledges that . . . in some counties, defendants charged with a third-degree school zone offense are routinely sentenced to an eighteen-month period of parole ineligibility, while in other counties, similarly situated individuals receive 364 days in county jail as a condition of probation. Furthermore, when parole laws and early release practices are taken into account, that latter sentence may be reduced to as little as ninety days of incarceration, which some counties even allow defendants to serve solely on nights or weekends.

The Uniformity Directive . . . also argues that, because of differences in resources and in the nature of the drug problem in different counties, it is "neither possible nor desirable to achieve absolute statewide uniformity in plea negotiation practices." As a result, the Uniformity Directive, unanimously approved by the County Prosecutors' Association, seeks to "restrict the range of permissible sentencing outcomes," but only by establishing a new base minimum plea offer.

The Directive provides that Section II.3 of the 1992 Guidelines is superseded to the extent that it conflicts with Section III of the current Directive. Whereas Section II.3 states that the minimum period of parole ineligibility for a school zone offense shall be probation conditioned on 364 days in jail, the new Section III requires that the minimum parole ineligibility term for an offense under N.J.S.A. 2C:35-7 shall be one year. Similarly, for violations involving less than one ounce of marijuana, Section II.3 of the 1992 Guidelines provides that a prison term may be waived entirely, while Section III of the Uniformity Directive states that the standardized plea offer may not be less than 364 days of incarceration as a condition of probation.

Although the Uniformity Directive succeeds in raising the base minimum plea offer for a school zone offense, the Directive does no more to promote uniformity in plea agreement policies. Section III clearly states: "Nothing in this Directive shall be construed to preclude a county prosecutor from establishing and implementing a plea policy that provides standardized offers . . . with a period of parole ineligibility greater than one year." Furthermore, the Directive maintains that "except as expressly provided, . . . all of the provisions of the previously issued Attorney General plea directives . . . shall remain in full force and effect." Therefore, despite the Directive's attempts to address disparity, Section II.4 of the 1992 Guidelines remains in effect and the Directive continues to allow for varying plea policies among the counties. . . .

III.

By permitting each county to adopt its own standard plea offers and policies, neither the former nor the current Guidelines serve as the universal, equitable prototype that the *Vasquez* line of cases had in mind. Although the guidelines adopted within each county may avoid arbitrariness with respect to decision-making among individual prosecutors, and while we concede that some disparity in sentencing is inevitable in the administration of criminal justice, the formalization of disparity from county to county is clearly impermissible. The inter-county disparity authorized by the Attorney General's Guidelines, both before and after their amendment, violates the goals of uniformity in sentencing and, thus, not only fails on statutory grounds, but also threatens the balance between prosecutorial and judicial discretion that is required under *Vasquez*. The Guidelines fail to appropriately channel prosecutorial discretion, thus leading to arbitrary and unreviewable differences between different localities. . . .

Accordingly, to meet the requirements of the *Vasquez* line of cases, the plea agreement guidelines for N.J.S.A. 2C:35-12 must be consistent throughout the State. To promote uniformity and provide a means for prosecutors to avoid arbitrary or abusive exercises of discretionary power under the extended sentencing provisions of N.J.S.A. 2C:43-6(f), the Court in *Lagares* ordered the Attorney General to adopt guidelines "for use throughout the state." . . . The same statewide application of the Attorney General's Guidelines is required here. Just as with the sentencing guidelines under the Code, which guide judicial sentencing discretion on a statewide basis, prosecutors must be guided by specific, universal standards in their waiver of mandatory minimum sentences under the CDRA.

Although the record does not indicate that the availability of county resources has been a significant factor in causing sentencing disparity between the counties, we recognize . . . the need for some flexibility among the different counties and some accommodation of local concerns and differences. The Declaration of Policy for the CDRA states that one of the goals of the Act is to "ensure the most efficient and effective dedication of limited investigative, prosecutorial, judicial and correctional resources," N.J.S.A. 2C:35-1.1. [Using] the waiver power to advance this legislative goal would not be an abuse of power. Consistent with that authority, we believe that differences in available county resources as well as varying backlog and caseload situations are legitimate factors that prosecutors may consider in deciding whether or not to waive a mandatory minimum sentence under N.J.S.A. 2C:35-12. See Uniformity Directive §I ("County prosecutors . . . must have some discretion in setting enforcement priorities and prosecution policies to reflect local concerns and enforcement opportunities"). However, before a prosecutor may take any such factors into account, those factors must be explicitly set forth in . . . the Attorney General's Guidelines, just as the requirements for cooperation agreements are precisely and distinctly enumerated. . . . Any flexibility on the basis of resources or local differences must be provided for and explicitly detailed within uniform, statewide guidelines. . . .

We therefore order the Attorney General to review and promulgate, within ninety days, new plea offer guidelines, which all counties must follow. [The Attorney General] must eliminate those provisions which specifically encourage inter-county disparity. The new guidelines should specify permissible ranges of plea offers for particular crimes and should be more explicit regarding permissible bases for upward and downward departures. The Attorney General may, if he chooses, provide for differences in treatment among various offenders based on specific factors of flexibility among the counties, such as resources or backlog, in certain circumstances. As in all plea offers, the individual characteristics of the crime and of the defendant, such as whether the defendant is a first or second time offender, must be considered. Finally, to permit effective judicial review, prosecutors must state on the record their reasons for choosing to waive or not to waive the mandatory minimum period of parole ineligibility specified in the statute. Additionally, for proper judicial review, if a prosecutor departs from the guidelines, the reasons for such departure must be clearly stated on the record.

The guidelines as amended will not only satisfy statutory and separation of powers concerns, but will also meet rational basis requirements for any equal protection challenge. Not only is there a clear rational basis for mandating uniform guidelines, as evidenced by the wealth of authority on this point, but there is also a rational basis for permitting a certain degree of flexibility within those guidelines, based on the differing resources and needs of the various counties, provided those factors are explicitly detailed by the Attorney General. . . .

In this case, defendant Brimage was sentenced in Somerset County, pursuant to a negotiated plea agreement, to four years in prison with a three-year parole disqualifier, the statutorily prescribed minimum period of parole for a school zone drug offense. N.J.S.A. 2C:35-7. [His] sentence should be vacated because of the impermissible inter-county disparity in plea offer policies. Defendant has the option of vacating his plea or renegotiating his plea. If he chooses the latter option, his plea shall be determined under the Attorney General's Guidelines as they stood at the time of his sentencing. If the State's plea offer is not in conformity with those Guidelines, the prosecutor must state on the record his or her reasons for departing from those Guidelines. [We] urge the prosecutor and the trial court to be particularly mindful of the disparity problem when reviewing defendant's plea agreement and sentence. . . .

Problem 6-4. Statewide Bargaining Guidelines

Soon after the New Jersey Supreme Court issued its decision in *Brimage*, the state attorney general issued a 64-page set of "*Brimage* Guidelines." The drafters patterned their prosecutor guidelines after judicial sentencing guidelines, including a grid laying out the offense seriousness on a vertical axis and the defendant's criminal history on a horizontal axis. Each box of the grid showed three different plea agreements a prosecutor might offer, with more favorable outcomes going to those defendants accepting offers earlier before the start of trial.

The immediate effect of the guidelines was probably an increase in the seriousness of drug charges that urban defendants faced. The more severe charging practices of the less urban counties became more standard across the state, and the guidelines left urban prosecutors less room to negotiate in the initial filing of charges or in the disposition of cases.

A few years later, a new state attorney general started to consider potential changes in the *Brimage* Guidelines. After consultations with county prosecutors, defense attorneys, and judges, the attorney general became concerned about the fairness of sentences in cases involving drug sales in school zones. The urban-suburban divide (and thus a racial divide) was stark for these crimes. In most urban areas, virtually all drug sales happened within 1,000 feet of a school; in less densely populated parts of the state, many more drug sales happened outside the 1,000-foot boundary.

The new attorney general is now considering revised guidelines that depend less on the crime of conviction. The plea agreements that prosecutors would be authorized to offer account for more specific offense characteristics (such as the amount of drugs and the presence of a weapon) and offender characteristics (such as gang membership or prior criminal record). The revisions also increase the minimum "authorized plea offers" available in cases involving defendants who carry or use weapons, while making more lenient offers possible for other drug defendants with prior records, or those who sold drugs near a school but presented no particular threat of violence. Prosecutors could also "depart" from the presumptive charge or disposition that is preferred under the guidelines if the evidence in the case is weak or if the defendant offers cooperation in other cases.

Suppose you are advising the attorney general. Who is likely to support or oppose this collection of policy changes? What arguments will they present? See *http://www.state.nj.us/lps/dcj/pdfs/agdir.pdf.*

Notes

1. *Uniformity in guidelines.* The New Jersey decision in *Brimage* is unusual; courts do not often order prosecutors to create statewide policies on questions of plea bargaining or requests for sentencing enhancements. Prosecutors themselves do not often create statewide guidelines for such matters, either. Instead, it is more common to find policies about plea bargaining and related matters set at the local office level. See Pamela Utz, Settling the Facts (1978) (comparing practices in California jurisdictions).

How are prosecutors likely to respond to a judicial requirement that they create statewide guidelines? Is there such a thing as too much uniformity from office to office? Within a single office? See State v. Pettitt, 609 P.2d 1364 (Wash. 1980) (striking down prosecutor's office policy mandating the filing of habitual criminal complaints against any defendant who had three or more prior felonies as abuse of discretion where policy resulted in mandatory life sentence for a defendant with three nonviolent property crimes).

The New Jersey court's opinion in *Brimage* did not explicitly require or prohibit any plea bargaining practices; it dealt instead with the prosecutor's decision whether to request a mandatory sentencing enhancement. However, the sentencing enhancement decision and negotiations for a plea agreement are linked. Many plea negotiations take place before the prosecutor has even filed charges, and the bargaining centers on the charges that the prosecutor will ultimately bring. Similarly, when the prosecutor has the power to request and receive an automatic sentencing enhancement, plea negotiations will include this topic. By requiring prosecutors statewide to create guidelines to govern the decision whether to request a sentencing enhancement, did the New Jersey court take any real plea bargaining discretion away from prosecutors in the field?

2. *Priority crimes.* Prosecutorial office policies on plea bargaining often restrict the power of the individual prosecutor to negotiate terms for a select group of high-priority crimes. While the line prosecutors remain free to reach plea agreements in less serious cases (which are by far the most numerous), the guidelines prohibit dismissal of charges or sentencing concessions in cases involving violent crimes such as murder, rape, or armed robbery. Alternatively, in such cases the guidelines may require special justifications for plea agreements or may limit the acceptable bargaining outcomes. See U.S. Department of Justice, Plea Bargaining: Critical Issues and Common Practices (1985). How do supervising prosecutors choose the priority crimes that will be subject to these special bargaining limitations? Do they take their cues from crime legislation and limit bargaining whenever the legislature has emphasized the importance of a crime by enhancing its penalty? See Milton Heumann & Colin Loftin, Mandatory Sentencing and the Abolition of Plea Bargaining: The Michigan Felony Firearm Statute, 13 Law & Soc'y Rev. 393 (1979) (evaluating mandatory-minimum-sentence statute for firearms cases, and contemporaneous county prosecutor's no-plea-bargaining policy for crimes charged under the statute).

3. *Internal review.* One common prosecutorial policy on plea bargaining is procedural rather than substantive. Instead of banning plea bargains for some crimes or limiting the outcomes that a prosecutor can accept in certain cases, these policies simply require the line prosecutor to obtain approval from a supervisor (or some committee of supervisors) before entering a plea agreement. See Richard Kuh, Plea Bargaining: Guidelines for the Manhattan District Attorney's Office, 11 Crim. L. Bull. 48 (1975) (supervisor review for proposed agreements reducing charges to extent greater than ordinarily allowed under office policy); Mario Merola, Modern Prosecutorial Techniques, 16 Crim. L. Bull. 232, 237-38, 251-55 (1980). What criteria will the reviewing attorneys use under such a policy?

4. Victim Consultation

Many prosecutors feel obliged to inform crime victims about their efforts to negotiate a guilty plea. But only recently have legal provisions and institutions reinforced this sense of obligation. Over the past 10-20 years, a majority of states have enacted statutes and constitutional provisions requiring prosecutors to inform or consult the victims of alleged crimes about any plea agreements in their case. These laws differ in the type of information the victim and the prosecutor must exchange and in the timing of the exchange. But they share the assumption that the involvement of a crime victim will change the outcomes in at least some plea negotiations. Is the effect of the victim's involvement in plea negotiations predictable? Will the timing of the victim's involvement make a difference in many plea negotiations?

■ MAINE REVISED STATUTES
TIT. 15, §812; TIT. 17-A, §§1172, 1173

TITLE 15, §812

1. The Legislature finds that there is citizen dissatisfaction with plea bargaining which has resulted in some criticism of the criminal justice process. The Legislature further finds that part of the dissatisfaction is caused because victims of crimes and law enforcement officers who respond to those crimes have no subsequent contact with the cases as they proceed through the courts for judicial disposition. Victims and law enforcement officers are many times not informed by prosecutors of plea agreements which are to be submitted to the court for approval or rejection. . . . It is the intent of this section to alleviate these expressions of citizen dissatisfaction and to promote greater understanding by prosecutors of citizens' valid concerns. This is most likely to be accomplished by citizens and law enforcement officers being informed of the results of plea negotiations before they are submitted to the courts. This notification will in no way affect the authority of the judge to accept, reject or modify the terms of the plea agreement.

2. Before submitting a negotiated plea to the court, the attorney for the State shall advise the relevant law enforcement officers of the details of the plea agreement reached in any prosecution where the defendant was originally charged with murder, a Class A, B or C crime or [an assault crime, sex offense, or kidnapping,] and shall advise victims of their rights under Title 17-A, Section 1173.

TITLE 17-A, §1172

1. When practicable, the attorney for the State shall make a good faith effort to inform each victim of a crime of the following: A) the details of a plea agreement before it is submitted to the court; B) the right to comment on the plea agreement pursuant to Section 1173; C) the time and place of the trial; D) the time and place of sentencing; and E) the right to participate at sentencing. . . .

TITLE 17-A, §1173

When a plea agreement is submitted to the court . . . , the attorney for the State shall disclose to the court any and all attempts made to notify each victim of the plea agreement and any objection to the plea agreement by a victim. A victim who is present in court at the submission of the plea may address the court at that time.

■ STATE v. PATRICK WILLIAM CASEY
44 P.3d 756 (Utah 2002)

DURRANT, J.

¶1 The central issue presented in this appeal is whether the district court deprived M.R., a victim of sexual abuse, of his constitutional and statutory right to be heard at defendant's change of plea hearing. . . .

¶3 On November 3, 1999, the Tooele County Attorney's Office charged defendant with aggravated sexual abuse of a child, a first degree felony. . . . Following a preliminary hearing in which both the victim, M.R., and his mother testified, the district court bound defendant over for trial.

¶4 A few weeks later the prosecutor handling defendant's case sent M.R.'s mother a letter explaining that defendant had requested a plea bargain. After receiving this letter, M.R.'s mother, according to her affidavit, met with the prosecutor and obtained an assurance that the first degree felony charge would not be reduced due to the strong evidence of guilt compiled against defendant.

¶5 Nevertheless, the prosecutor subsequently offered to reduce the first degree felony charge to lewdness involving a child, a class A misdemeanor, in return for a guilty plea. M.R.'s mother, upon learning of the State's extension of this offer and defendant's acceptance, contacted the prosecutor and expressed a desire to tell the district court how her family, including M.R., felt about the proposed plea. The prosecutor advised her to attend the change of plea hearing scheduled for October 24, 2000.

¶6 M.R. and his mother appeared at this change of plea hearing as directed. At a recess during this proceeding, M.R.'s mother approached the prosecutor, objected to the reduced charge, and reiterated M.R.'s, and her own, desire to make a statement. She later testified that she believed the prosecutor was going to inform the district court of her request. . . .

¶7 Notwithstanding his conversations with M.R.'s mother, the prosecutor did not inform the district court that M.R. and his mother had requested to be heard at the change of plea hearing. M.R. and his mother also failed to bring the issue to the court's attention. The court therefore proceeded with defendant's change of plea hearing unaware of M.R.'s request. Noting the "dramatic" reduction in the charge, the court refused to be limited to the four-month sentence recommended in the stipulated plea agreement. The State and defendant responded to the court's concern by agreeing to delete the stipulated sentence provision. The court then accepted defendant's guilty plea to the class A misdemeanor charge and set the matter for sentencing.

¶8 Subsequently, M.R.'s mother, acting on behalf of M.R., obtained legal assistance and filed two motions with the district court: a motion for a misplea and a motion to reject the plea bargain. In response, the prosecutor and defendant filed separate motions to strike M.R.'s pleadings, claiming that M.R. lacked standing to set aside the plea because he was not a party to the criminal proceeding.

¶9 Without ruling on whether M.R. had standing to challenge defendant's guilty plea, the district court held defendant's sentencing hearing on November 27, 2000. At the start of this hearing, M.R.'s counsel moved the court to set aside the accepted plea. . . .

¶10 M.R. and his mother testified that the court should have rejected the plea bargain. Specifically, M.R. declared, "I don't think it's right that defendant gets that less of a plea agreement because of what he's done. He's done it to me . . . and . . . he's hurt my whole family." M.R.'s mother testified that "the court should reject the plea bargain because a misdemeanor sentence did not truly reflect the seriousness of the offenses committed by defendant the same way that a felony conviction would." . . .

¶11 . . . M.R.'s counsel argued that the Victims' Rights Amendment of the Utah Constitution placed M.R. on equal footing with defendant and envisioned that M.R. could employ an attorney in exercising his legal rights. M.R.'s counsel then argued that (1) M.R. had the right to be heard before the court's acceptance of defendant's plea, (2) M.R.'s right to be heard had been violated, and (3) the court should grant a misplea and hear from M.R. before accepting any subsequent plea between the State and defendant. . . .

¶ 12 [The] court decided to "informally" reopen the plea hearing in order to accept the testimony that it had just heard from M.R. and his mother. Having accepted this testimony, the court "reaffirmed" defendant's plea at the class A level. The court then denied both of M.R.'s pending motions, sentenced defendant to eight months in jail on the class A misdemeanor charge, and fined him.

¶ 14 On appeal, M.R., by and through his legal guardian, contends that (1) he had the right to seek appellate review of the district court's adverse rulings on his two motions, (2) he had the right to be heard through counsel with respect to legal issues related to the constitutional and statutory rights afforded him as a victim, (3) he had a constitutional and statutory right to be heard regarding the appropriateness of the plea bargain, (4) he properly invoked his right to be heard at defendant's change of plea hearing by submitting a request to the prosecutor, and (5) the court, through the negligence of the prosecutor, denied him his right to be heard by accepting the plea bargain without hearing from him. . . .

¶ 18 In 1987, the Utah Legislature enacted the Victims' Rights Act. See Utah Code Ann. §§77-37-1 to -5. This statute included, among other things, a bill of rights for victims, and declared that these rights must be "protected in a manner no less vigorous than protections afforded criminal defendants." §77-37-1. The Utah Legislature then passed the Victims' Rights Amendment, which was ratified by Utah citizens. . . . Utah Const. art. I, §28. This constitutional amendment bestowed specific rights upon crime victims and gave the Utah Legislature the power to "enforce and define [its terms] by statute." Acting pursuant to this authority, the Utah Legislature subsequently enacted the Rights of Crime Victims Act. Utah Code Ann. §§77-38-1 to -14. This act elaborated upon the rights afforded crime victims under the Victims' Rights Amendment and defined several terms included in the amendment. . . .

¶ 21 Applying the principles outlined above, we first address whether M.R. had the right to appeal the district court's rulings regarding his right to be heard. The Victims' Rights Amendment does not address the question of M.R.'s right to appeal decisions impacting his right to be heard. The Rights of Crime Victims Act is on point, however, and we conclude that M.R. had the right to seek appellate review pursuant to the plain meaning of that statute.

¶ 22 We resolve this issue under a plain meaning analysis for two reasons. First, subsection 77-38-11(2)(b) explicitly provides that adverse rulings on a motion or request "brought by a victim of a crime . . . may be appealed under the rules governing appellate actions, provided that no appeal shall constitute grounds for delaying any criminal . . . proceeding." Second, subsection 77-38-11(2)(c) of the Utah Code declares that an appellate court "shall review all such properly presented issues, including issues that are capable of repetition but would otherwise evade review." . . .

¶ 23 We next address whether M.R. had the right to be heard at defendant's change of plea hearing. . . . In pertinent part, the Victims' Rights Amendment states as follows: "To preserve and protect victims' rights to justice and due process, victims of crimes have [the right, upon request, to be] heard at important criminal justice hearings related to the victim, either in person or through a lawful representative, once a criminal information or indictment charging a crime has been publicly filed in court." Utah Const. art. I, §28(1)(b). Using comparable language, section 77-38-4 of the Rights of Crime Victims Act similarly declares that the victim of a crime "shall have . . . the right to be heard at . . . important criminal . . . justice hearings."

¶25 [The] question that arises is what constitutes an "important criminal justice hearing" under the Victims' Rights Amendment and the Utah Code. Section 77-38-2 of the Rights of Crime Victims Act answers this question with respect to both the Utah Constitution and the Utah Code; it defines "important criminal justice hearings" involving the disposition of charges in this way: "For the purposes of this chapter and the Utah Constitution, important criminal justice hearings [means] any court proceeding involving the disposition of charges against a defendant [except for] unanticipated proceedings to take an admission or a plea of guilty as charged to all charges previously filed or any plea taken at an initial appearance." . . .

¶26 Here, the change of plea hearing conducted by the district court fell within the definition of an important criminal justice hearing because it disposed of a first degree felony charge filed against defendant in return for a guilty plea on a class A misdemeanor. . . .

¶27 While it is clear that the Utah Constitution and the Utah Code afforded M.R. the right to be heard upon request at defendant's change of plea hearing, neither the constitution nor the code mandates how M.R.'s request must be submitted. Relying on the Victims' Rights Act and the Rights of Crime Victims Act, M.R. argues that a request to be heard at a plea hearing suffices if it is submitted either to the district court or to the prosecutor. The State contends that the two statutes require a crime victim to petition the court directly. . . .

¶28 [T]he Victims' Rights Amendment . . . merely notes that the right to be heard is activated "upon request." Utah Const. art. I, §28(b). . . . The Victims' Rights Act states that victims have the "right to be informed and assisted as to their role in the criminal justice process," and all criminal justice agencies have "the duty to provide this information and assistance." Utah Code Ann. §77-37-3(1)(b). Additionally, the Victims' Rights Act declares that victims have a "right to clear explanations regarding relevant legal proceedings," and all "criminal justice agencies have the duty to provide these explanations." Id. §77-37-3(1)(c). Because prosecutors are a component of the criminal justice system and the Victims' Rights Act applies to "all criminal justice agencies," the aforementioned duties necessarily fall upon prosecutors. . . .

¶30 We further conclude that a prosecutor's obligation to provide "assistance" to the victim should mean, at a minimum, that a victim may submit a request to be heard at a plea hearing to a prosecutor and expect that the request will be forwarded to the court. Likewise, a prosecutor's obligation to provide a "clear explanation" of events occurring at a plea hearing should mean that a victim can rely on a prosecutor's statement indicating he or she will convey a request to be heard to the district court. . . .

¶32 In addition to having a duty to convey requests to be heard under the Victims' Rights Act and the Rights of Crime Victims Act, prosecutors also have a duty to convey requests to be heard as officers of the court. . . . The prosecutor "is the representative not of an ordinary party to a controversy, but of a sovereignty whose obligation to govern impartially is as compelling as its obligation to govern at all; and whose interest . . . in a criminal prosecution is not that it shall win . . . but that justice shall be done." State v. Emmett, 839 P.2d 781, 787 (Utah 1992). . . .

¶ 38 Based on the prosecutor's failure to relay M.R.'s request to be heard, the district court initially deprived M.R. of his right to speak at the change of plea hearing. At defendant's sentencing hearing, however, the court learned of M.R.'s earlier desire to be heard. The court then permitted M.R. and his mother to take the stand and testify regarding the appropriateness of defendant's plea bargain. The court also permitted extensive argument by M.R.'s counsel. Restricted in no respect by the court, all three individuals claimed that the plea bargain should have been rejected. After hearing this testimony and argument, the court "informally" reopened defendant's change of plea hearing and accepted the testimony that it had just heard from M.R. and his mother. The court then reaffirmed defendant's plea at the Class A level.

¶ 39 By taking these steps, the district court remedied its initial denial of M.R.'s right to be heard. . . . First, we note that the plea was subject to review up until the time of sentencing. Accordingly, in exercising its power to reopen the plea, the court permitted M.R. to be heard at a time when he could have persuaded the court to reject the proposed plea. Second, the record clearly demonstrates that the court reaffirmed the plea only after having accepted M.R.'s and his mother's testimony, and permitting argument by his counsel.

¶ 40 Thus, although M.R. was entitled to be heard at defendant's change of plea hearing, we conclude that he has enjoyed the fruits of the right he now claims he was denied. Accordingly, we hold that the district court, to its credit, cured the error initially committed at the change of plea hearing and honored M.R.'s right to be heard as soon as it discovered M.R. wished to be heard.[14] . . .

WILKINS, J., concurring: . . .

¶ 44 [When] the trial court was finally informed of M.R.'s desire to be heard, it was clearly insufficient for the trial court to "informally" reopen the change of plea hearing and "consider" M.R.'s concerns before summarily reaffirming the "accepted" plea. Doing so merely compounded the error invited by the prosecution in failing to promptly inform the court of M.R.'s initial request to be heard at the change of plea hearing. [The] defendant's plea had not yet been finally accepted at the time the trial court became aware of M.R.'s desire to be heard on the matter. The correct course would have been for the trial court to reopen the hearing, after notice to all concerned.

¶ 46 The constitutional provisions granting M.R. his right to be heard, however, also limit this right. Subsection (2) of the Victims' Rights Amendment, Article I, Section 28 of the Utah Constitution, specifically prohibits construing the rights afforded M.R. in such a way as to provide "relief from any criminal judgment." The defendant's plea, once accepted by the court and sentence imposed, is a criminal judgment. Consequently, once the trial court accepted defendant's plea and entered the judgment of sentence on the plea, M.R.'s rights as a victim could not result in the "misplea" M.R. sought. . . .

14. Because the district court upheld M.R.'s right to be heard in the present case, we decline to address what remedies are available for the hypothetical denial of a victim's right to be heard. We do note, however, that the Utah Legislature established a framework in which only three remedies were provided for the violation of a victim's right: injunctive relief, declaratory relief, and writ of mandamus. Utah Code Ann. §77-38-11(1)-(2)(i). Absent from this list is the right to obtain a declaration of a misplea. Moreover, even if the declaration of a misplea were assumed to be an available remedy, such a declaration would raise constitutional issues regarding the double jeopardy clauses of both the United States Constitution and the Utah Constitution.

¶47 A second difficulty is created by the provisions of the Rights of Crime Victims Act, Utah Code Ann. §77-38-11(2)(b), that authorize appellate review of an adverse ruling by the trial court on M.R.'s motions, but specifically provide that no such appeal "shall constitute grounds for delaying any criminal . . . proceeding." When juxtaposed with the rights of the criminal defendant to a speedy trial and the necessity to move forward with the criminal process despite an otherwise valid appeal by a victim, appellate relief for M.R. is a practical impossibility. Moreover, the same statute limits M.R.'s remedies to injunctive relief, declaratory relief, and writ of mandamus. If the criminal action proceeds, and if the victim is denied his or her constitutional right to address the court, the victim has little hope of a meaningful remedy. While the criminal proceeding moves forward, the victim denied rights may seek only an injunction or writ of mandamus that will preserve the right to speak if such an appeal can be filed, perfected, heard, and decided before entry of the criminal judgment. This will often not be the case. . . .

¶48 So, our hands are tied by the same constitutional and statutory provisions that gave M.R. his right to be heard in the first place. We cannot order the plea "undone" once the sentence and judgment have been entered by the trial court. We cannot impose any corrective action on the failure of the prosecutor to inform the court of the request to speak, or the failure of the trial court to fully reconsider the change of plea, with all due formality, thereby according M.R. his constitutional right to actually be heard.

¶49 As it works in practice, the right of a victim to be heard at a change of plea hearing is fragile at best, and may be made illusory by the intentional or unintentional mishandling of the situation by the prosecutor or the trial court, all without meaningful remedy. Perhaps the legislature may find it wise to reconsider the provisions of the statute addressing appellate review of the denial of a victim's request to assert the rights granted by the Victims' Rights Amendment. There may be other circumstances under which those rights may be just as easily and negligently denied as were M.R.'s in this case.

Notes

1. *Informing victims of plea agreements: majority position.* A majority of states now have statutes or constitutional provisions dealing with the rights of crime victims in the criminal process. Virtually all of these laws address plea bargains. The most common type of provision requires the prosecutor, when feasible, to inform a victim that the prosecutor plans to recommend that a court accept a guilty plea based on a plea agreement. The statutes also typically instruct the prosecutor to inform the victim of the time and place for the plea hearing. See U.S. Dept. of Justice, Victim Input into Plea Agreements (2002) (survey of state laws). Does a law requiring notice about a public document (the plea agreement) and a public hearing (the plea hearing) give crime victims anything of practical value? Would the notice requirement have a different effect if it were to apply before the prosecutor finalizes any plea negotiations? Does a notice requirement remain ineffective until the legislature authorizes funds to hire extra prosecutorial staff members to provide support to victims?

A smaller number of statutes require the prosecution to "consult" with the victim before recommending a plea agreement. See Ind. Code §35-335-3.5;

W. Va. Code §61-11A-6(a)(5)(C). A few laws also authorize the victim to make a statement to the court during the plea hearing or require the prosecutor to inform the court about the victim's views on any proposed plea agreement. R.I. Gen. Laws §§12-28-3 (14), 12-28-4.1. What might the victim say to the prosecutor or the judge that would provide new information relevant to the case?

2. *Responsiveness to victims.* Are prosecutors free to give controlling weight to the views of victims? The victims' rights laws described above all assume the validity of a prosecutor's partial reliance on the wishes of crime victims. When defendants raise constitutional and other legal challenges to prosecutorial decisions based partly on the views of victims, courts have upheld the decisions. See Commonwealth v. Latimore, 667 N.E.2d 818 (Mass. 1996) (district attorney's decision not to accept defendant's offer of guilty plea to lesser offense, based in part on victim's family's desire to pursue murder conviction, was not prosecutorial misconduct). Would you predict the same result if a statute explicitly provided the victim with controlling authority—a "veto" power over any proposed plea agreement? What if a prosecutor adopted such a policy in the absence of a statute? Does the legitimacy of the victim's input change if he has filed a civil suit to recover monetary damages from the defendant? See N.D. Cent. Code §§29-01-16 and 29-01-17 (provides for "compromise" of a misdemeanor; victim accepts civil settlement, and there is no criminal conviction).

3. *The impact of victims' rights laws.* All 50 states have some statutory protections for the rights of victims during the criminal process, and about 30 states have amended their constitutions to provide for such rights. But some states have stronger requirements than others. Does the type of law at work in a state influence the way that government officials deal with the victim of an alleged crime? Does a stronger law change the likely reaction of the victim? A 1998 survey suggests that stronger victim protection laws do translate into some noteworthy differences in practice. For instance, victims in "strong-protection states" are more likely to learn about sentencing or parole hearings than victims in "weak-protection states." However, the strength of the victim protection laws did *not* affect the number of victims who learned about plea negotiations or a decision to dismiss charges. See Dean Kilpatrick, David Beatty & Susan Smith Howley, The Rights of Crime Victims—Does Legal Protection Make a Difference? (Research in Brief) (Dec. 1998, NCJ 173839). What barriers might stand in the way of notifying victims about the progress of plea negotiations? Cf. Susan Bandes, Victim Standing, 1999 Utah L. Rev. 331 (the sorts of victim initiatives that have succeeded have been those that advance the prosecution's agenda, while preserving the prosecution's complete freedom from third party interference).

C. VALIDITY OF INDIVIDUAL PLEA BARGAINS

Most of the statutes and judicial opinions on the subject of guilty pleas do not address plea bargaining as an institution. Instead, they focus on the validity of the guilty plea in an individual case. There are three essential ingredients for a valid plea of guilty, whether the plea is "open" or "negotiated": The plea must reflect a knowing waiver of trial rights, the defendant must waive those rights voluntarily, and there must be an adequate "factual basis" to support the charges to which the defendant pleads guilty.

1. Lack of Knowledge

A defendant who pleads guilty must know about the nature of the charges and some of the consequences of waiving the right to trial and accepting a conviction. In essence, the defendant must see two future paths. Down one path, she must visualize the events likely to occur at a trial and after a possible conviction; down another path, she must picture the events likely to occur after a conviction based on a plea of guilty. But predicting the future is no easy task. Courts do not require that a defendant know every single consequence of pleading guilty; the challenge is to select *which* consequences a defendant must understand before entering a valid plea of guilty.

The rules of criminal procedure give the trial judge the primary responsibility for ensuring that defendants understand the consequences of waiving trial and pleading guilty. This judicial responsibility is also grounded in the federal constitution. In Boykin v. Alabama, 395 U.S. 238 (1969), the Supreme Court declared that guilty pleas will not be constitutionally valid unless the record affirmatively shows that defendants understand their privilege against self-incrimination, their right to trial by jury, and their right to confront their accusers. During a *Boykin* hearing, the judge asks the defendant a routine set of questions about these rights and other matters before the court will accept a plea of guilty or nolo contendere.

■ FEDERAL RULE OF CRIMINAL PROCEDURE 11(b)

(1) Before the court accepts a plea of guilty or nolo contendere, the defendant may be placed under oath, and the court must address the defendant personally in open court. During this address, the court must inform the defendant of, and determine that the defendant understands, the following:

(A) the government's right, in a prosecution for perjury or false statement, to use against the defendant any statement that the defendant gives under oath;

(B) the right to plead not guilty, or having already so pleaded, to persist in that plea;

(C) the right to a jury trial;

(D) the right to be represented by counsel — and if necessary have the court appoint counsel — at trial and at every other stage of the proceeding;

(E) the right at trial to confront and cross-examine adverse witnesses, to be protected from compelled self-incrimination, to testify and present evidence, and to compel the attendance of witnesses;

(F) the defendant's waiver of these trial rights if the court accepts a plea of guilty or nolo contendere;

(G) the nature of each charge to which the defendant is pleading;

(H) any maximum possible penalty, including imprisonment, fine, and term of supervised release;

(I) any mandatory minimum penalty;

(J) any applicable forfeiture;

(K) the court's authority to order restitution;

(L) the court's obligation to impose a special assessment;

(M) the court's obligation to apply the Sentencing Guidelines, and the court's discretion to depart from those guidelines under some circumstances; and

(N) the terms of any plea-agreement provision waiving the right to appeal or to collaterally attack the sentence.

■ UNITED STATES v. ANGELA RUIZ
536 U.S. 622 (2002)

BREYER, J.

In this case we primarily consider whether the Fifth and Sixth Amendments require federal prosecutors, before entering into a binding plea agreement with a criminal defendant, to disclose "impeachment information relating to any informants or other witnesses." We hold that the Constitution does not require that disclosure.

After immigration agents found 30 kilograms of marijuana in Angela Ruiz's luggage, federal prosecutors offered her what is known in the Southern District of California as a "fast track" plea bargain. That bargain—standard in that district—asks a defendant to waive indictment, trial, and an appeal. In return, the Government agrees to recommend to the sentencing judge a two-level departure downward from the otherwise applicable United States Sentencing Guidelines sentence. In Ruiz's case, a two-level departure downward would have shortened the ordinary Guidelines-specified 18-to-24-month sentencing range by 6 months, to 12-to-18 months.

The prosecutors' proposed plea agreement contains a set of detailed terms. Among other things, it specifies that "any [known] information establishing the factual innocence of the defendant" has been turned over to the defendant, and it acknowledges the Government's "continuing duty to provide such information." At the same time it requires that the defendant waive the right to receive "impeachment information relating to any informants or other witnesses" as well as the right to receive information supporting any affirmative defense the defendant raises if the case goes to trial. Because Ruiz would not agree to this last-mentioned waiver, the prosecutors withdrew their bargaining offer. The Government then indicted Ruiz for unlawful drug possession. And despite the absence of any agreement, Ruiz ultimately pleaded guilty.

At sentencing, Ruiz asked the judge to grant her the same two-level downward departure that the Government would have recommended had she accepted the "fast track" agreement. The Government opposed her request, and the District Court denied it, imposing a standard Guideline sentence instead. . . .

The Ninth Circuit vacated the District Court's sentencing determination. The Ninth Circuit pointed out that the Constitution requires prosecutors to make certain impeachment information available to a defendant before trial. It decided that this obligation entitles defendants to receive that same information before they enter into a plea agreement. The Ninth Circuit also decided that the Constitution prohibits defendants from waiving their right to that information. And it held that the prosecutors' standard "fast track" plea agreement was unlawful because it insisted upon that waiver. . . .

The constitutional question concerns a federal criminal defendant's waiver of the right to receive from prosecutors exculpatory impeachment material—a right that the Constitution provides as part of its basic "fair trial" guarantee. See U.S. Const., Amdts. 5, 6. See also Brady v. Maryland, 373 U.S. 83 (1963) (Due process requires prosecutors to avoid "an unfair trial" by making available "upon request" evidence "favorable to an accused" where the evidence is "material either to guilt or to punishment").

When a defendant pleads guilty he or she, of course, forgoes not only a fair trial, but also other accompanying constitutional guarantees. Boykin v. Alabama, 395 U.S. 238 (1969) (pleading guilty implicates the Fifth Amendment privilege against self-incrimination, the Sixth Amendment right to confront one's accusers, and the Sixth Amendment right to trial by jury). Given the seriousness of the matter, the Constitution insists, among other things, that the defendant enter a guilty plea that is "voluntary" and that the defendant must make related waivers knowingly, intelligently, and "with sufficient awareness of the relevant circumstances and likely consequences." *Brady,* at 742, 748. . . . We must decide whether the Constitution requires that preguilty plea disclosure of impeachment information. We conclude that it does not.

First, impeachment information is special in relation to the fairness of a trial, not in respect to whether a plea is voluntary ("knowing," "intelligent," and sufficiently "aware"). Of course, the more information the defendant has, the more aware he is of the likely consequences of a plea, waiver, or decision, and the wiser that decision will likely be. But the Constitution does not require the prosecutor to share all useful information with the defendant. Weatherford v. Bursey, 429 U.S. 545 (1977) ("There is no general constitutional right to discovery in a criminal case"). And the law ordinarily considers a waiver knowing, intelligent, and sufficiently aware if the defendant fully understands the nature of the right and how it would likely apply in general in the circumstances — even though the defendant may not know the specific detailed consequences of invoking it. A defendant, for example, may waive his right to remain silent, his right to a jury trial, or his right to counsel even if the defendant does not know the specific questions the authorities intend to ask, who will likely serve on the jury, or the particular lawyer the State might otherwise provide.

It is particularly difficult to characterize impeachment information as critical information of which the defendant must always be aware prior to pleading guilty given the random way in which such information may, or may not, help a particular defendant. The degree of help that impeachment information can provide will depend upon the defendant's own independent knowledge of the prosecution's potential case — a matter that the Constitution does not require prosecutors to disclose.

Second, . . . this Court has found that the Constitution, in respect to a defendant's awareness of relevant circumstances, does not require complete knowledge of the relevant circumstances, but permits a court to accept a guilty plea, with its accompanying waiver of various constitutional rights, despite various forms of misapprehension under which a defendant might labor. See Brady v. United States, 397 U.S., at 757 (defendant "misapprehended the quality of the State's case" [and] "the likely penalties"; defendant failed to "anticipate a change in the law regarding" relevant "punishments"); McMann v. Richardson, 397 U.S. 759, 770 (1970) (counsel "misjudged the admissibility" of a "confession"); United States v. Broce, 488 U.S. 563, 573 (1989) (counsel failed to point out a potential defense); Tollett v. Henderson, 411 U.S. 258 (1973) (counsel failed to find a potential constitutional infirmity in grand jury proceedings). It is difficult to distinguish, in terms of importance, (1) a defendant's ignorance of grounds for impeachment of potential witnesses at a possible future trial from (2) the varying forms of ignorance at issue in these cases.

Third, due process considerations, the very considerations that led this Court to find trial-related rights to exculpatory and impeachment information in *Brady* . . . argue against the existence of the "right" that the Ninth Circuit found here. This Court has said that due process considerations include not only (1) the nature of the private interest at stake, but also (2) the value of the additional safeguard, and (3) the adverse impact of the requirement upon the Government's interests. [A]s the proposed plea agreement at issue here specifies, the Government will provide "any information establishing the factual innocence of the defendant." . . . That fact, along with other guilty-plea safeguards, see Fed. Rule Crim. Proc. 11, diminishes the force of Ruiz's concern that, in the absence of impeachment information, innocent individuals, accused of crimes, will plead guilty.

At the same time, a constitutional obligation to provide impeachment information during plea bargaining, prior to entry of a guilty plea, could seriously interfere with the Government's interest in securing those guilty pleas that are factually justified, desired by defendants, and help to secure the efficient administration of justice. The Ninth Circuit's rule risks premature disclosure of Government witness information, which, the Government tells us, could "disrupt ongoing investigations" and expose prospective witnesses to serious harm. And the careful tailoring that characterizes most legal Government witness disclosure requirements suggests recognition by both Congress and the Federal Rules Committees that such concerns are valid. See, e.g., 18 U.S.C. §3432 (witness list disclosure required in capital cases three days before trial with exceptions); §3500 (Government witness statements ordinarily subject to discovery only after testimony given); Fed. Rule Crim. Proc. 16(a)(2) (embodies limitations of 18 U.S.C. §3500). Compare 156 F.R.D. 460 (1994) (congressional proposal to significantly broaden §3500) with 167 F.R.D. 221 (judicial conference opposing congressional proposal).

Consequently, the Ninth Circuit's requirement could force the Government to abandon its general practice of not disclosing to a defendant pleading guilty information that would reveal the identities of cooperating informants, undercover investigators, or other prospective witnesses. It could require the Government to devote substantially more resources to trial preparation prior to plea bargaining, thereby depriving the plea-bargaining process of its main resource-saving advantages. Or it could lead the Government instead to abandon its heavy reliance upon plea bargaining in a vast number — 90 percent or more — of federal criminal cases. We cannot say that the Constitution's due process requirement demands so radical a change in the criminal justice process in order to achieve so comparatively small a constitutional benefit.

These considerations, taken together, lead us to conclude that the Constitution does not require the Government to disclose material impeachment evidence prior to entering a plea agreement with a criminal defendant.

In addition, we note that the "fast track" plea agreement requires a defendant to waive her right to receive information the Government has regarding any "affirmative defense" she raises at trial. We do not believe the Constitution here requires provision of this information to the defendant prior to plea bargaining — for most (though not all) of the reasons previously stated. That is to say, in the context of this agreement, the need for this information is more closely related to the fairness of a trial than to the voluntariness of the plea; the value in terms of the defendant's added awareness of relevant circumstances is ordinarily limited; yet the added burden imposed upon the Government by requiring its provision well in advance of trial (often before trial preparation begins) can be serious, thereby significantly interfering with the administration of the plea bargaining process. . . .

THOMAS, J., concurring.

I agree with the Court that the Constitution does not require the Government to disclose either affirmative defense information or impeachment information relating to informants or other witnesses before entering into a binding plea agreement with a criminal defendant. The Court, however, suggests that the constitutional analysis turns in some part on the "degree of help" such information would provide to the defendant at the plea stage, a distinction that is neither necessary nor accurate. To the extent that the Court is implicitly drawing a line based on a flawed characterization about the usefulness of certain types of information, I can only concur in the judgment. The principle supporting *Brady* was "avoidance of an unfair trial to the accused." That concern is not implicated at the plea stage regardless.

■ IOWA v. FELIPE EDGARDO TOVAR
541 U.S. 77 (2004)

GINSBURG, J.

The Sixth Amendment safeguards to an accused who faces incarceration the right to counsel at all critical stages of the criminal process. The entry of a guilty plea, whether to a misdemeanor or a felony charge, ranks as a "critical stage" at which the right to counsel adheres. Waiver of the right to counsel, as of constitutional rights in the criminal process generally, must be a knowing, intelligent act done with sufficient awareness of the relevant circumstances. This case concerns the extent to which a trial judge, before accepting a guilty plea from an uncounseled defendant, must elaborate on the right to representation. . . .

On November 2, 1996, respondent Felipe Edgardo Tovar, then a 21-year-old college student, was arrested in Ames, Iowa, for operating a motor vehicle while under the influence of alcohol (OWI). An intoxilyzer test administered the night of Tovar's arrest showed he had a blood alcohol level of 0.194. The arresting officer informed Tovar of his rights under Miranda v. Arizona, 384 U.S. 436 (1966). Tovar signed a form stating that he waived those rights and agreed to answer questions.

Some hours after his arrest, Tovar appeared before a judge in the Iowa District Court for Story County. The judge indicated on the Initial Appearance form that Tovar appeared without counsel and waived application for court-appointed counsel. The judge also marked on the form's checklist that Tovar was "informed of the charge and his . . . rights and received a copy of the Complaint." . . .

At the November 18 arraignment,[2] the court's inquiries of Tovar began: "Mr. Tovar appears without counsel and I see, Mr. Tovar, that you waived application for a court appointed attorney. Did you want to represent yourself at today's hearing?" Tovar replied: "Yes, sir." The court soon after asked: "How did you wish

---

2. Tovar appeared in court along with four other individuals charged with misdemeanor offenses. The presiding judge proposed to conduct the plea proceeding for the five cases jointly, and each of the individuals indicated he did not object to that course of action.

to plead?" Tovar answered: "Guilty." Tovar affirmed that he had not been promised anything or threatened in any way to induce him to plead guilty.

Conducting the guilty plea colloquy required by the Iowa Rules of Criminal Procedure, the court explained that, if Tovar pleaded not guilty, he would be entitled to a speedy and public trial by jury, and would have the right to be represented at that trial by an attorney, who "could help [Tovar] select a jury, question and cross-examine the State's witnesses, present evidence, if any, in [his] behalf, and make arguments to the judge and jury on [his] behalf." By pleading guilty, the court cautioned, not only would Tovar give up his right to a trial of any kind on the charge against him, he would give up his right to be represented by an attorney at that trial. The court further advised Tovar that, if he entered a guilty plea, he would relinquish the right to remain silent at trial, the right to the presumption of innocence, and the right to subpoena witnesses and compel their testimony.

Turning to the particular offense with which Tovar had been charged, the court informed him that an OWI conviction carried a maximum penalty of a year in jail and a $1,000 fine, and a minimum penalty of two days in jail and a $500 fine. Tovar affirmed that he understood his exposure to those penalties. The court next explained that, before accepting a guilty plea, the court had to assure itself that Tovar was in fact guilty of the charged offense. To that end, the court informed Tovar that the OWI charge had only two elements: first, on the date in question, Tovar was operating a motor vehicle in the State of Iowa; second, when he did so, he was intoxicated. Tovar confirmed that he had been driving in Ames, Iowa, on the night he was apprehended and that he did not dispute the results of the intoxilyzer test administered by the police that night, which showed that his blood alcohol level exceeded the legal limit nearly twice over.

After the plea colloquy, the court asked Tovar if he still wished to plead guilty, and Tovar affirmed that he did. The court then accepted Tovar's plea, observing that there was "a factual basis" for it, and that Tovar had made the plea "voluntarily, with a full understanding of his rights, and . . . of the consequences" of pleading guilty.

On December 30, 1996, Tovar appeared for sentencing on the OWI charge and, simultaneously, for arraignment on a subsequent charge of driving with a suspended license.[5] Noting that Tovar was again in attendance without counsel, the court inquired: "Mr. Tovar, did you want to represent yourself at today's hearing or did you want to take some time to hire an attorney to represent you?"[6] Tovar replied that he would represent himself. The court then engaged in essentially the same plea colloquy on the suspension charge as it had on the OWI charge the previous month. After accepting Tovar's guilty plea on the suspension charge, the court sentenced him on both counts: For the OWI conviction, the court imposed the minimum sentence of two days in jail and a $500 fine, plus a surcharge and costs; for the suspension conviction, the court imposed a $250 fine, plus a surcharge and costs.

On March 16, 1998, Tovar was convicted of OWI for a second time. He was represented by counsel in that proceeding, in which he pleaded guilty. On

5. In order to appear at the OWI arraignment, Tovar drove to the courthouse despite the suspension of his license; he was apprehended en route home.

6. Prior to asking Tovar whether he wished to hire counsel, the court noted that Tovar had applied for a court-appointed attorney but that his application had been denied because he was financially dependent upon his parents. . . .

December 14, 2000, Tovar was again charged with OWI, this time as a third offense, and additionally with driving while license barred. Iowa law classifies first-offense OWI as a serious misdemeanor and second-offense OWI as an aggravated misdemeanor. Third-offense OWI, and any OWI offenses thereafter, rank as class "D" felonies. Represented by an attorney, Tovar pleaded not guilty to both December 2000 charges.

In March 2001, through counsel, Tovar filed a Motion for Adjudication of Law Points; the motion urged that Tovar's first OWI conviction, in 1996, could not be used to enhance the December 2000 OWI charge from a second-offense aggravated misdemeanor to a third-offense felony. Significantly, Tovar did not allege that he was unaware at the November 1996 arraignment of his right to counsel prior to pleading guilty and at the plea hearing. Instead, he maintained that his 1996 waiver of counsel was invalid — not "full knowing, intelligent, and voluntary" — because he "was never made aware by the court . . . of the dangers and disadvantages of self-representation." The court denied Tovar's motion. . . .

Tovar then waived his right to a jury trial and was found guilty by the court of both the OWI third-offense charge and driving while license barred. Four months after that adjudication, Tovar was sentenced. On the OWI third-offense charge, he received a 180-day jail term, with all but 30 days suspended, three years of probation, and a $2,500 fine plus surcharges and costs. For driving while license barred, Tovar received a 30-day jail term, to run concurrently with the OWI sentence, and a suspended $500 fine. . . .

Tovar contends that his waiver of counsel in November 1996, at his first OWI plea hearing, was insufficiently informed, and therefore constitutionally invalid. In particular, he asserts that the trial judge did not elaborate on the value, at that stage of the case, of an attorney's advice and the dangers of self-representation in entering a plea.

We have described a waiver of counsel as intelligent when the defendant "knows what he is doing and his choice is made with eyes open." We have not, however, prescribed any formula or script to be read to a defendant who states that he elects to proceed without counsel. The information a defendant must possess in order to make an intelligent election, our decisions indicate, will depend on a range of case-specific factors, including the defendant's education or sophistication, the complex or easily grasped nature of the charge, and the stage of the proceeding.

As to waiver of trial counsel, we have said that before a defendant may be allowed to proceed *pro se,* he must be warned specifically of the hazards ahead. The defendant in Faretta v. California, 422 U.S. 806 (1975), resisted counsel's aid, preferring to represent himself. The Court held that he had a constitutional right to self-representation. In recognizing that right, however, we cautioned: "Although a defendant need not himself have the skill and experience of a lawyer in order competently and intelligently to choose self-representation, he should be made aware of the dangers and disadvantages of self-representation, so that the record will establish that he knows what he is doing. . . ."

Later, in Patterson v. Illinois, 487 U.S. 285 (1988), we elaborated on "the dangers and disadvantages of self-representation" to which *Faretta* referred. "At trial," we observed, "counsel is required to help even the most gifted layman adhere to the rules of procedure and evidence, comprehend the subtleties of *voir dire,* examine and cross-examine witnesses effectively, . . . object to improper prosecution questions, and much more." Warnings of the pitfalls of proceeding to trial without counsel, we therefore said, must be "rigorously" conveyed. We clarified, however, that at earlier stages of the criminal process, a less searching or formal colloquy may suffice.

Patterson concerned postindictment questioning by police and prosecutor. At that stage of the case, we held, the warnings required by Miranda v. Arizona adequately informed the defendant not only of his Fifth Amendment rights, but of his Sixth Amendment right to counsel as well. *Miranda* warnings [convey to a defendant] the "ultimate adverse consequence" of making uncounseled admissions, *i.e.*, his statements may be used against him in any ensuing criminal proceeding. The *Miranda* warnings, we added, also [let the defendant] know "what a lawyer could do for him," namely, advise him to refrain from making statements that could prove damaging to his defense.

Patterson describes a "pragmatic approach to the waiver question," one that asks "what purposes a lawyer can serve at the particular stage of the proceedings in question, and what assistance he could provide to an accused at that stage. . . ." We require less rigorous warnings pretrial, *Patterson* explained, not because pretrial proceedings are less important than trial, but because, at that stage, "the full dangers and disadvantages of self-representation . . . are less substantial and more obvious to an accused than they are at trial." . . .

To resolve this case, we need not endorse the State's position that nothing more than the plea colloquy was needed to safeguard Tovar's right to counsel. Preliminarily, we note that there were some things more in this case. Tovar first indicated that he waived counsel at his Initial Appearance, affirmed that he wanted to represent himself at the plea hearing, and declined the court's offer of "time to hire an attorney" at sentencing, when it was still open to him to request withdrawal of his plea. Further, the State does not contest that a defendant must be alerted to his right to the assistance of counsel in entering a plea. . . . Accordingly, the State presents a narrower question: "Does the Sixth Amendment require a court to give a rigid and detailed admonishment to a *pro se* defendant pleading guilty of the usefulness of an attorney, that an attorney may provide an independent opinion whether it is wise to plead guilty and that without an attorney the defendant risks overlooking a defense?"

Training on that question, we turn to, and reiterate, the particular language the Iowa Supreme Court employed in announcing the warnings it thought the Sixth Amendment required: "The trial judge must advise the defendant generally that there are defenses to criminal charges that may not be known by laypersons and that the danger in waiving the assistance of counsel in deciding whether to plead guilty is the risk that a viable defense will be overlooked"; in addition, "the defendant should be admonished that by waiving his right to an attorney he will lose the opportunity to obtain an independent opinion on whether, under the facts and applicable law, it is wise to plead guilty." Tovar did not receive such advice, and the sole question before us is whether the Sixth Amendment compels the two admonitions here in controversy. We hold it does not.

This Court recently explained, in reversing a lower court determination that a guilty plea was not voluntary: "The law ordinarily considers a waiver knowing, intelligent, and sufficiently aware if the defendant fully understands the nature of the right and how it would likely apply *in general* in the circumstances — even though the defendant may not know the *specific detailed* consequences of invoking it." United States v. Ruiz, 536 U.S. 622, 629 (2002) (emphasis in original). . . . In prescribing scripted admonitions and holding them necessary in every guilty plea instance, we further note, the Iowa high court overlooked our observations that the information a defendant must have to waive counsel intelligently will "depend, in each case, upon the particular facts and circumstances surrounding that case," Johnson v. Zerbst, 304 U.S. 458, 464 (1938).

Moreover, as Tovar acknowledges, in a collateral attack on an uncounseled conviction, it is the defendant's burden to prove that he did not competently and intelligently waive his right to the assistance of counsel. In that light, we note that Tovar has never claimed that he did not fully understand the charge or the range of punishment for the crime prior to pleading guilty. Further, he has never articulated with precision the additional information counsel could have provided, given the simplicity of the charge. Nor does he assert that he was unaware of his right to be counseled prior to and at his arraignment. . . .

Given the particular facts and circumstances surrounding this case, it is far from clear that warnings of the kind required by the Iowa Supreme Court would have enlightened Tovar's decision whether to seek counsel or to represent himself. In a case so straightforward . . . the admonitions at issue might confuse or mislead a defendant more than they would inform him: The warnings the Iowa Supreme Court declared mandatory might be misconstrued as a veiled suggestion that a meritorious defense exists or that the defendant could plead to a lesser charge, when neither prospect is a realistic one. If a defendant delays his plea in the vain hope that counsel could uncover a tenable basis for contesting or reducing the criminal charge, the prompt disposition of the case will be impeded, and the resources of either the State (if the defendant is indigent) or the defendant himself (if he is financially ineligible for appointed counsel) will be wasted.

We note, finally, that States are free to adopt by statute, rule, or decision any guides to the acceptance of an uncounseled plea they deem useful. See, *e.g.,* Alaska Rule Crim. Proc. 39(a); Fla. Rule Crim. Proc. 3.111(d); Md. Ct. Rule 4-215; Minn. Rule Crim. Proc. 5.02; Pa. Rule Crim. Proc. 121, comment. We hold only that the two admonitions the Iowa Supreme Court ordered are not required by the Federal Constitution. . . .

Problem 6-5. Direct and Collateral Effects

Donald Ross pleaded guilty to three counts of second-degree child rape committed against his former stepdaughter. Those offenses carried a maximum sentence of 10 years and a $20,000 fine, a minimum sentence of 67 months, and a mandatory 12-month community placement. As part of the plea negotiations, the government agreed to recommend a prison term of 89 months. Ross did not receive an explicit warning of his mandatory one-year community placement term prior to entering his plea.

At the sentencing hearing, the judge imposed an 89-month sentence plus the mandatory one-year community placement. In addition to the standard community placement conditions, the court adopted special conditions recommended by the pre-sentence investigator: no contact with the victim; no contact with females under 16 years old; Department of Corrections approval of residence location and living arrangements; and urinalysis and polygraph at the will of his community corrections officer.

Ross then filed a motion to withdraw his guilty plea as involuntary. The state's rules of criminal procedure say this about knowing and intelligent pleas of guilt:

> The court shall not accept a plea of guilty, without first determining that it is made voluntarily, competently and with an understanding of the nature of the charge and the consequences of the plea. The court shall not enter a judgment upon a plea of guilty unless it is satisfied that there is a factual basis for the plea.

The trial court denied withdrawal, concluding that the omission of the mandatory 12-month community placement represented merely a "collateral" consequence of his plea. His lack of knowledge about this potential consequence, the court said, was not a sufficient basis for withdrawing the guilty plea.

Will an appellate court uphold the denial of the motion to withdraw the guilty plea? Appellate decisions in this state distinguish "direct" from "collateral" consequences by asking whether the component of the sentence represents "a definite, immediate and largely automatic effect on the range of the defendant's punishment." Cf. State v. Ross, 916 P.2d 405 (Wash. 1996).

Notes

1. *Knowledge of nature of charges and procedural rights.* The federal constitution requires a defendant to understand the nature of the charges before pleading guilty to them. Although defense counsel usually explains the elements of the offense to the client, the judge ordinarily confirms that the defendant understood what he was told. In Henderson v. Morgan, 426 U.S. 637 (1976), a defendant with below-average intelligence pleaded guilty to second-degree murder while insisting that he "meant no harm" to the victim. Because the judge during the plea colloquy did not explain to the defendant that intent was a "critical" element of the crime, the Court overturned the conviction, even though there was overwhelming evidence of the defendant's guilt. The *Henderson* decision, however, does not require the judge to explain every element of every crime to every defendant. The opinion addressed only "critical" elements of the offense. See Bradshaw v. Stumpf, 545 U.S. 175 (2005) (guilty plea is valid when "the record accurately reflects that the nature of the charge and the elements of the crime were explained to the defendant by his own, competent counsel").

Defendants must also understand the nature of trial rights they are waiving, such as confrontation of witnesses, representation by counsel, and jury factfinding. As with the nature of the charges, the judge need not describe every detail of the procedural rights that the defendant is waiving.

2. *Knowledge of direct penal consequences.* A valid plea of guilty does not require the defendant to understand each and every consequence of the sentence that could be imposed: the defendant must understand the "direct" consequences of the conviction but not the "collateral" consequences. A rich case law has developed in an effort to sort out direct from collateral consequences. Direct consequences include the maximum sentence authorized and some information about the prison term a defendant should expect. State v. Domian, 668 A.2d 1333 (Conn. 1996) (no need to inform defendant of 10-year mandatory minimum sentence when judge stated at plea hearing his intention to impose 10-year term). Most courts also conclude that

any substantial restitution payments would be a direct consequence. Possible deportation of a resident alien after completion of a prison term is usually treated as a collateral consequence that a defendant need not know before entering a valid guilty plea. People v. Ford, 657 N.E.2d 265 (N.Y. 1995). Eligibility for parole also tends to fall into the "collateral" category. The same is true for requirements that sex offenders register with law enforcement officers near their residence after the completion of any prison term. State v. Bellamy, 835 A.2d 1231 (N.J. 2003) (court must advise a guilty-pleading defendant of possible future civil commitment as a sexually violent predator); but cf. Mitschke v. State, 129 S.W.3d 130 (Tex. Crim. App. 2004) (sex offender registration is "direct consequence," but knowledge not required because it is also "nonpunitive").

3. *Guilty pleas and incompetent lawyers.* A defendant who pleads guilty must be represented by counsel or must waive the right to counsel. Moore v. Michigan, 355 U.S. 155 (1957). Furthermore, if a lawyer gives constitutionally inadequate representation that causes a defendant to enter a guilty plea, the defendant may later withdraw the plea. But this does not mean that any faulty legal advice will invalidate a plea. In Brady v. United States, 397 U.S. 742 (1970), counsel gave the defendant incorrect but competent advice about the constitutionality of the death penalty statute at issue in the case; the incorrect advice of counsel was not sufficient reason to invalidate the defendant's "knowing" waiver of trial rights. See In re Resendiz, 19 P.3d 1171 (Cal. 2001) (mistaken advice about immigration consequences can support claim of ineffective assistance); State v. Paredez, 101 P.3d 799 (N.M. 2004) (when guilty plea makes removal from country virtually certain for a non-citizen, defense counsel has duty to give client immigration advice more specific than an opinion that deportation is "possible"); Gabriel J. Chin & Richard W. Holmes, Jr., Effective Assistance of Counsel and the Consequences of Guilty Pleas, 87 Cornell L. Rev. 697 (2002) (failure to inform client of collateral matters should in some cases constitute ineffective assistance).

4. *Guilty pleas before discovery.* If defendants must know about the nature of the charges and the direct consequences of a guilty plea, must they also know about the basic facts the prosecutor could present against them at trial? The Supreme Court's decision in *Ruiz* is typical in its refusal to declare a per se rule against bargaining away discovery rights. A few courts, however, have concluded that in some cases, accepting a guilty plea based on a plea agreement that prevents the defendant from engaging in discovery violates due process. See State v. Draper, 784 P.2d 259 (Ariz. 1989) (due process and right to counsel sometimes may prohibit plea agreement conditioned on defendant not interviewing victim of alleged crime; remand to determine defendant's access to state's evidence through other witnesses). Can you identify circumstances in which a defendant could make a "knowing" waiver of the right to a jury trial without taking advantage of a discovery right? The *Ruiz* court found it significant that the condition relating to discovery was non-mandatory because the defendant could choose to go forward with discovery and forgo the plea agreement. Are there any terms that prosecutors simply may not offer because they prevent the defendant from making a knowing waiver?

5. *Professional obligations during plea negotiations.* Several sources of law address the information that attorneys for the prosecution and defense reveal to each other and to the defendant during plea negotiations. First, ethics rules and aspirational standards instruct a defense lawyer to inform the defendant about the terms of any proposed plea agreement because the client must decide what plea to enter.

See ABA Model Rule of Professional Conduct 4.1; ABA Standards for Criminal Justice: Defense Function 4-6.2(a), (b); see also People v. Whitfield, 239 N.E.2d 850 (Ill. 1968) (overturning conviction after trial because defense counsel failed to communicate plea bargain offer to client). These ethics rules and aspirational standards state that it is unprofessional conduct for an attorney (prosecution or defense) to knowingly make false statements during plea negotiations. ABA Model Rule 4.1 (lawyer shall not knowingly make a false statement of material fact or law to a third person); ABA Standards 3-4.1(c), 4-6.2. To what extent do discovery rules provide for disclosure of information before the entry of a guilty plea? Do professional obligations require greater or earlier disclosures than those required under the rules of discovery? See State v. Gibson, 514 S.E.2d 320 (S.C. 1999) (prosecutor's failure to disclose *Brady* information can undermine voluntariness of guilty plea).

6. *Hearing procedures.* The decision in Boykin v. Alabama, 395 U.S. 238 (1969), gave a constitutional foundation to some of the information a defendant must know before entering a guilty plea. The record must show the defendant's awareness of three major constitutional rights waived through entry of a guilty plea: the privilege against self-incrimination, the right to jury trial, and the right to confront adverse witnesses. In addition to these constitutional requirements, many rules of procedure have added requirements such as knowledge regarding the nature of the charges, the direct consequences of a conviction, and the factual basis for the charge. Trial courts engage in lengthy (and elaborately scripted) "plea colloquies" to create a record establishing that a defendant knows what is necessary before pleading guilty. What happens if the trial court fails to cover one of the necessary questions and thereby violates a rule of procedure? Fed. R. Crim. P. 11(h) allows a federal court to uphold a plea if the violation of the rule's requirements was "harmless error."

In United States v. Dominguez Benitez, 542 U.S. 74 (2004), the judge failed to warn the defendant, as required by Rule 11(c)(3)(B), that he could not withdraw his plea even if the judge did not accept the recommended sentence. The defendant did not object at the time of sentencing, but later sought to withdraw his guilty plea. Such a failure to warn, the Supreme Court said, is reversible error only if the defendant can show a reasonable probability that he would not have entered the plea after hearing a proper warning. The defendant here could not make such a showing because the government's evidence was strong and the plea agreement, with proper Rule 11 warnings, was read to him in his native Spanish.

2. Involuntary Pleas

Time and again, procedural rules and judicial opinions say that a plea of guilty or nolo contendere must be "voluntary." The question of voluntariness raises a familiar theme in criminal procedure: In what sense can we say that a defendant *chooses* to waive procedural advantages such as a right to jury trial? Surely a defendant is choosing among unpleasant options when she decides to plead guilty. Is it possible for the government to restrict the defendant's options in such a way that the defendant's decision to plead guilty is no longer a "choice" in any meaningful sense? In this section, we consider three settings in which defendants have repeatedly claimed that their decision to plead guilty was not truly voluntary.

a. *Alford* Pleas

A defendant who pleads guilty stands ready to accept punishment for the crime as charged. Is this decision coerced if the defendant insists that he did not commit the crime?

■ FEDERAL RULE OF CRIMINAL PROCEDURE 11(b)

(2) Before accepting a plea of guilty or nolo contendere, the court must address the defendant personally in open court and determine that the plea is voluntary and did not result from force, threats, or promises (other than promises in a plea agreement).

(3) Before entering judgment on a guilty plea, the court must determine that there is a factual basis for the plea.

■ NORTH CAROLINA v. HENRY ALFORD
400 U.S. 25 (1970)

WHITE, J.

On December 2, 1963, Alford was indicted for first-degree murder, a capital offense under North Carolina law. The court appointed an attorney to represent him, and this attorney questioned all but one of the various witnesses who appellee said would substantiate his claim of innocence. The witnesses, however, did not support Alford's story but gave statements that strongly indicated his guilt. Faced with strong evidence of guilt and no substantial evidentiary support for the claim of innocence, Alford's attorney recommended that he plead guilty, but left the ultimate decision to Alford himself. The prosecutor agreed to accept a plea of guilty to a charge of second-degree murder, and on December 10, 1963, Alford pleaded guilty to the reduced charge.

Before the plea was finally accepted by the trial court, the court heard the sworn testimony of a police officer who summarized the State's case. Two other witnesses besides Alford were also heard. Although there was no eyewitness to the crime, the testimony indicated that shortly before the killing Alford took his gun from his house, stated his intention to kill the victim, and returned home with the declaration that he had carried out the killing. After the summary presentation of the State's case, Alford took the stand and testified that he had not committed the murder but that he was pleading guilty because he faced the threat of the death penalty if he did not do so.[2] In response to the questions of his counsel, he acknowledged that his counsel had informed him of the difference between second- and first-degree murder and of his rights in case he chose to go to trial. The trial court then asked appellee if, in light of his denial of guilt, he still desired to plead guilty to

---

2. After giving his version of the events of the night of the murder, Alford stated: "I pleaded guilty on second degree murder because they said there is too much evidence, but I ain't shot no man, but I take the fault for the other man. We never had an argument in our life and I just pleaded guilty because they said if I didn't they would gas me for it, and that is all." [Alford later described his decision as follows:] "I'm still pleading that you all got me to plead guilty. I plead the other way, circumstantial evidence. . . . You told me to plead guilty, right. I don't—I'm not guilty but I plead guilty."

second-degree murder and appellee answered, "Yes, sir. I plead guilty on — from the circumstances that he [Alford's attorney] told me." After eliciting information about Alford's prior criminal record, which was a long one, the trial court sentenced him to 30 years' imprisonment, the maximum penalty for second-degree murder. [Alford sought postconviction relief, first in the state court, and later in federal habeas corpus proceedings.]

We held in Brady v. United States, 397 U.S. 742 (1970), that a plea of guilty which would not have been entered except for the defendant's desire to avoid a possible death penalty and to limit the maximum penalty to life imprisonment or a term of years was not for that reason compelled within the meaning of the Fifth Amendment. . . . The standard was and remains whether the plea represents a voluntary and intelligent choice among the alternative courses of action open to the defendant. That he would not have pleaded except for the opportunity to limit the possible penalty does not necessarily demonstrate that the plea of guilty was not the product of a free and rational choice, especially where the defendant was represented by competent counsel whose advice was that the plea would be to the defendant's advantage. . . .

Ordinarily, a judgment of conviction resting on a plea of guilty is justified by the defendant's admission that he committed the crime charged against him and his consent that judgment be entered without a trial of any kind. The plea usually subsumes both elements, and justifiably so, even though there is no separate, express admission by the defendant that he committed the particular acts claimed to constitute the crime charged in the indictment. Here Alford entered his plea but accompanied it with the statement that he had not shot the victim. If Alford's statements were to be credited as sincere assertions of his innocence, there obviously existed a factual and legal dispute between him and the State. Without more, it might be argued that the conviction entered on his guilty plea was invalid, since his assertion of innocence negatived any admission of guilt. . . .

In addition to Alford's statement, however, the court had heard an account of the events on the night of the murder, including information from Alford's acquaintances that he had departed from his home with his gun stating his intention to kill and that he had later declared that he had carried out his intention. Nor had Alford wavered in his desire to have the trial court determine his guilt without a jury trial. Although denying the charge against him, he nevertheless preferred the dispute between him and the State to be settled by the judge in the context of a guilty plea proceeding rather than by a formal trial. Thereupon, with the State's telling evidence and Alford's denial before it, the trial court proceeded to convict and sentence Alford for second-degree murder.

State and lower federal courts are divided upon whether a guilty plea can be accepted when it is accompanied by protestations of innocence and hence contains only a waiver of trial but no admission of guilt. Some courts, giving expression to the principle that "our law only authorizes a conviction where guilt is shown," Harris v. State, 172 S.W. 975 (Tex. 1915), require that trial judges reject such pleas. [The court cited cases from Michigan, New Jersey, New Mexico, and Washington along with lower federal court cases.] But others have concluded that they should not . . . force any defense on a defendant in a criminal case . . . particularly when advancement of the defense might "end in disaster. . . ." Tremblay v. Overholser, 199 F. Supp. 569 (D.D.C. 1961). They have argued that, since [guilt is at times uncertain, an accused who believes in his own innocence] might reasonably conclude a jury would be convinced of his guilt and that he would fare better in the sentence by pleading guilty. [The court cited cases from Idaho, Illinois, Iowa, Minnesota, Pennsylvania, and several lower federal courts.]

This Court has not confronted this precise issue, but prior decisions do yield relevant principles. . . . The issue in Hudson v. United States, 272 U.S. 451 (1926), was whether a federal court has power to impose a prison sentence after accepting a plea of nolo contendere, a plea by which a defendant does not expressly admit his guilt, but nonetheless waives his right to a trial and authorizes the court for purposes of the case to treat him as if he were guilty. The Court held that a trial court does have such power, and . . . the federal courts have uniformly followed this rule, even in cases involving moral turpitude. Implicit in the nolo contendere cases is a recognition that the Constitution does not bar imposition of a prison sentence upon an accused who is unwilling expressly to admit his guilt but who, faced with grim alternatives, is willing to waive his trial and accept the sentence. These cases would be directly in point if Alford had simply insisted on his plea but refused to admit the crime. The fact that his plea was denominated a plea of guilty rather than a plea of nolo contendere is of no constitutional significance with respect to the issue now before us, for the Constitution is concerned with the practical consequences, not the formal categorizations, of state law. . . .

Nor can we perceive any material difference between a plea that refuses to admit commission of the criminal act and a plea containing a protestation of innocence when, as in the instant case, a defendant intelligently concludes that his interests require entry of a guilty plea and the record before the judge contains strong evidence of actual guilt. Here the State had a strong case of first-degree murder against Alford. Whether he realized or disbelieved his guilt, he insisted on his plea because in his view he had absolutely nothing to gain by a trial and much to gain by pleading. . . . In view of the strong factual basis for the plea demonstrated by the State and Alford's clearly expressed desire to enter it despite his professed belief in his innocence, we hold that the trial judge did not commit constitutional error in accepting it.[11] . . .

Alford now argues in effect that the State should not have allowed him this choice but should have insisted on proving him guilty of murder in the first degree. The States in their wisdom may take this course by statute or otherwise and may prohibit the practice of accepting pleas to lesser included offenses under any circumstances. But this is not the mandate of the Fourteenth Amendment and the Bill of Rights. The prohibitions against involuntary or unintelligent pleas should not be relaxed, but neither should an exercise in arid logic render those constitutional guarantees counterproductive and put in jeopardy the very human values they were meant to preserve. . . .

Notes

1. *Guilty pleas by defendants claiming innocence: majority position.* Although there was once a real dispute among state courts about the constitutionality of accepting guilty

11. Our holding does not mean that a trial judge must accept every constitutionally valid guilty plea merely because a defendant wishes so to plead. A criminal defendant does not have an absolute right under the Constitution to have his guilty plea accepted by the court, although the States may by statute or otherwise confer such a right. . . .

pleas from defendants who maintained their innocence, that dispute is now largely resolved. A substantial majority of states follow the lead of the U.S. Supreme Court and allow a defendant to plead guilty, despite claims of innocence, so long as the prosecution establishes a strong factual basis to support the conviction. See People v. Canino, 508 P.2d 1273 (Colo. 1973). Fewer than a half-dozen states prevent trial judges from accepting *Alford* pleas. See Ross v. State, 456 N.E.2d 420 (Ind. 1983).

The live question in connection with *Alford* pleas is whether the trial judge has discretion to *reject* an *Alford* plea. The Supreme Court (in footnote 11) suggested that an individual trial judge, or a state court system as a whole through its rules of procedure, might refuse to accept such guilty pleas. Many individual judges do refuse to accept *Alford* pleas, and the majority of appellate courts uphold their discretion to do so. See Albert Alschuler, The Defense Attorney's Role in Plea Bargaining, 84 Yale L.J. 1179 (1975). If a state system decides not to prohibit *Alford* pleas, should it place controls on the power of the trial judge to refuse to accept such pleas? Would this step ensure the equal treatment of defendants and prevent litigants from shopping for judges? See ABA Standards for Criminal Justice: Pleas of Guilty 14-1.6 (defendant's offer to plead guilty should not be refused "solely" because defendant refuses to admit culpability). What reasons might a judge give to refuse an offer of an *Alford* plea in a specific case, apart from a general ban on such pleas?

2. Alford *pleas and free will.* If a defendant is *not* coerced when she pleads guilty while insisting that she is innocent, who *is* coerced into pleading guilty? Defendants who offer an *Alford* plea have a very limited set of options. We can presume that defendants prefer to have the option of entering an *Alford* plea rather than face the expense or publicity of a trial, along with the risk of a more severe sentence after trial. Are there reasons why the public should deny this option to the bargaining parties?

As you might expect, a defendant who enters any guilty plea must be mentally competent; otherwise, the court cannot consider the plea to be knowing and voluntary. See Godinez v. Moran, 509 U.S. 389 (1993) (same competence standard used for entry of guilty plea and capacity to stand trial); State v. Engelmann, 541 N.W.2d 96 (S.D. 1995) (allows withdrawal of *Alford* plea based on lack of mental competence at arraignment).

3. Alford *pleas and the truth.* If trials always uncovered the truth about the events surrounding alleged crimes, would there be any reason to allow *Alford* pleas? Is a system that accepts such pleas implicitly admitting that trials often fail to uncover the truth and that an innocent defendant might be justifiably concerned about an erroneous conviction after trial? Are *Alford* pleas even less reliable measures of truth than a criminal trial? The factual basis for an *Alford* plea must come from sources other than the statements of the defendant. Most courts say that it is not necessary that the factual basis establish guilt beyond a reasonable doubt. The Supreme Court's opinion in *Alford* called the factual basis in that case "strong" and "overwhelming"; state courts have suggested several formulations to describe the necessary level of proof. Clewley v. State, 288 A.2d 468 (Me. 1972) (not unreasonable to conclude guilt); Re Guilty Plea Cases, 235 N.W.2d 132, 145 (Mich. 1975) (might have been convicted at trial); State v. Hagemann, 326 N.W.2d 861 (N.D. 1982) ("strong" proof of guilt). Would the "beyond a reasonable doubt" standard seriously reduce the number of *Alford* pleas accepted? See Ala. Code §15-15-23

(adopting beyond-reasonable-doubt standard for acceptance of guilty pleas); Richard Uviller, Pleading Guilty: A Critique of Four Models, 41 Law & Contemp. Probs. 102 (1977) (clear and convincing evidence). It is also possible to view an *Alford* plea as the most honest route available in a system in which some defendants want to avoid a trial even though they believe in their own innocence. When a state bans *Alford* pleas, does it invite defendants to lie to their attorneys and to the court?

Problem 6-6. An Offer You Can't Refuse

Joan Capriccioso worked as a waitress at a diner in Staten Island, where she met Philip Fiumefreddo. After a two-month courtship, the two were married; she was then 39 and he was 68. Throughout four years of marriage to Philip, Joan often complained to acquaintances about him, saying that she wished him dead.

Eventually, Joan's father Salvatore Capriccioso withdrew $3,200 from the bank and gave it to Joseph Gurrieri, with the understanding that Gurrieri would arrange for the murder of Philip Fiumefreddo. Gurrieri hired Christopher Munroe to kill Fiumefreddo for $1,000. Munroe went to the Fiumefreddo residence at 6:30 A.M. Joan let him in. After offering to fix breakfast for him, she told Munroe to make the house look burglarized, gave him a pillow, and instructed him to use it to kill her husband, who was still sleeping. She then left for work. Munroe suffocated Philip with the pillow as he slept.

Becoming increasingly distressed about the murder, Gurrieri went to the police and confessed. Joan Fiumefreddo and her father were indicted for second-degree murder, second-degree conspiracy, and second-degree solicitation. On the same day, Munroe and Gurrieri were indicted for various crimes in connection with the killing; these latter two defendants soon pleaded guilty to the charges. On the day jury selection was scheduled to begin, Fiumefreddo and her attorney, John Collins, met for over an hour with the trial judge; her father; his attorney, Joseph Lamattina; and the prosecutor. Immediately following this discussion, Collins told the court: "My client is now prepared to plead with only one promise having been made by me. That promise is with her pleading to this top count that the Court would sentence her to 18 years to life." Lamattina stated that Salvatore Capriccioso was prepared to plead guilty to second-degree conspiracy in exchange for a sentence promise of one to three years.

Nine days after the plea colloquy, defendant made a motion pro se to withdraw her guilty plea. In the accompanying affidavit she stated that

> while I acknowledge that the Court advised me that I had certain rights, I nevertheless did not then, nor do I now realize the full consequences of my plea of guilty. I am not guilty of the offenses to which I pleaded guilty. I pleaded guilty with the promise that I would be sentenced to 18 to life and co-defendant's sentence would be lighter if the defendant pleads guilty to second degree murder.

The judge denied the motion to withdraw her plea, and sentenced her and her father to the agreed-upon terms of imprisonment. Was Fiumefreddo's guilty plea voluntary? Compare People v. Fiumefreddo, 626 N.E.2d 646 (N.Y. 1993).

Notes

1. *"Package" deals.* Can the prosecutor increase the cost of the trial by threatening to prosecute third parties, such as family members of the defendant? Courts have not announced any outright bans of "package deals" or "connected pleas," but they review them with some suspicion. What should a defendant emphasize to convince a court that her particular "package deal" produced an involuntary plea? How will the defendant obtain the evidence necessary to make this showing? Does the fact that a defendant's sentence is near the minimum available sentence help or hurt her claim that the plea was involuntary? See State v. Danh, 516 N.W.2d 539 (Minn. 1994) (requiring contingent terms of package-deal guilty plea to be explained on the record to trial court to allow assessment of voluntariness). Does the difficulty with package deals come from the defendant's reduced capacity to make decisions (because the package deal offers the defendant options that cannot be compared in a rational manner) or from the public's unease about using family or other intimate bonds to gain a litigation advantage?

2. *Coercive overcharging.* A prosecutor can make the decision to go to trial very costly, through a combination of serious charges and an attractive plea agreement. These decisions, however, will usually not provoke a court to rule that the defendant's guilty plea was involuntary. In Brady v. United States, 397 U.S. 742 (1970), the fact that the defendant believed that a decision to go to trial would expose him to a possible death penalty was not enough to invalidate the guilty plea. Nonetheless, some statutes and aspirational standards instruct the prosecutor not to "overcharge." Take, for instance, a North Carolina statute, N.C. Gen. Stat. §15A-1021(b), which forbids state agents from placing "improper pressure" on a defendant to plead guilty. According to the drafters' commentary, the statute (based on the American Law Institute's Model Code of Pre-Arraignment Procedure) was meant to prevent the prosecutor from filing charges not supported by provable facts or charges not ordinarily filed based on the conduct in question. See also ABA Standards for Criminal Justice, Prosecution Function 3-3.9(f) (prosecutor should not bring charges greater than "can reasonably be supported with evidence at trial" or greater than necessary to reflect gravity of offense).

3. *Civil consequences.* Do the prosecutor's proposed bargain terms become coercive when they move beyond matters of criminal charges and sentences to include civil consequences, matters that other legal institutions ordinarily decide? State courts have not expressed any special concern about such agreements. See Gustine v. State, 480 S.E.2d 444 (S.C. 1997) (prosecutor offers plea agreement on child sex-abuse charges contingent on defendant's giving up parental rights to stepdaughter; court does not declare parental rights term coercive as a matter of law but calls for case-by-case inquiry into knowing and voluntary nature of guilty plea). Is it wise to assume that criminal consequences are the most serious problems facing a defendant?

b. Judicial Overinvolvement

Earlier in this chapter we considered judicial efforts to place limits on the institution of plea bargaining, and the individual judge's responsibility during a plea hearing to confirm and document that the defendant is entering the guilty plea knowingly and voluntarily. But what is the individual judge's role prior to the guilty plea? Rules of procedure paint very different portraits of the judge's involvement in plea negotiations. Some rules, such as Pa. R. Crim. P. 319(b)(1), state that the trial judge "shall not participate in the plea negotiations preceding an agreement." See also Fed. R. Crim. P. 11(c)(1) ("The court shall not participate in any such discussions"). Others do not tell the judge what to do during the negotiations. Rules and statutes in a few states authorize the trial judge to take part in negotiations. See N.C. Gen. Stat. §15A-1021(a) ("The trial judge may participate in the discussions"). Do these rules reflect profound differences in practice, or do they reflect an ambiguity about what qualifies as judicial "participation" in the plea negotiations?

■ STATE v. LANDOUR BOUIE
817 So. 2d 48 (La. 2002)

CALOGERO, C.J.

We granted this writ application to determine whether the district court abused its discretion in not allowing the defendant to withdraw his plea of guilty, given that the trial judge had previously interjected his own opinions into the plea negotiations as to whether the defendant would be acquitted or found guilty. . . .

The state charged the defendant and his co-defendant, Cornelius Johnson, with attempted second degree murder. . . . The charge arose out of the shooting of Eddie Hughes, who had intervened in an attempt by [Bouie] and Johnson to secure the services of a prostitute doing business near Hughes's home. Using a rifle that [Johnson] retrieved from [Bouie's] house, where the two men had driven after the initial dispute with Hughes, Johnson confronted Hughes on the street outside his home and fired a bullet that struck the victim in the throat, severing his spinal column. The victim survived. . . .

From the outset, the defendant indicated that he wanted to go to trial, and throughout the discussions, he consistently indicated that he believed he was innocent of the charge of attempted second degree murder. . . . At the outset of the day set for trial, the defendant, represented by appointed counsel, stated that he understood that he was going to trial, and asserted that he *wanted* to go to trial. Immediately, the trial judge told the defendant that he was being tried for attempted second degree murder and that "if you go to trial, the penalty for that charge is fifty years at hard labor." The trial judge followed up by telling the defendant that, because he had been on probation at the time of the offense, he could be found guilty of being a second felony offender and receive a sentence of up to 100 years. But if he pleaded guilty, . . . and if the state filed a multiple offender bill, the trial judge would give the defendant the minimum twenty-five years at hard labor, or as low as ten years if the state did not file the multiple offender bill.

When the defendant was asked if this information helped him to make up his mind, the defendant responded affirmatively, but he also asserted, "Your Honor — uh — I'm just going you know, I haven't did anything." The trial judge quickly responded with his view on the certainty that the defendant would be convicted if he chose to go to trial: . . .

COURT: You may be able to be found not guilty. . . . But I can tell you this, all of the years that I've been either a prosecutor or a judge, I don't think I've ever seen more than one or two people who went to trial found not guilty. The D.A. knows what they're doing when they try somebody, generally, and the jury seems to believe them, generally. And the odds are not in your favor of going to trial and winning a case. Do you understand that? Do you?

BOUIE: Yes, sir.

COURT: And when I say all the years I've been doing that, that's been since 1981, so how long is that? Sixteen years I've been doing this, either a judge or an assistant district attorney and I think I've found two people found not guilty—uh—seen two people found not guilty in felony trials. Now, if you go to trial, I'm telling you the odds are against you winning. Do you understand that?

BOUIE: Yes, sir.

COURT: All right, then if you lose, then you're looking at the hundred years. . . . If you plead guilty, you're looking at no more than twenty-five and maybe as low as ten. Do you understand that?

BOUIE: Yes, sir.

At this point, the defendant was allowed to confer with his counsel and the matter of his co-defendant was taken up by the trial judge. Johnson, too, expressed indecision and questioned the state's version of the facts, but, after discussions with the trial judge, in which the judge offered the same deal and stated that a hundred-year sentence meant that Johnson would die in prison, Johnson eventually entered a plea of guilty as charged in return for a sentencing commitment by the court of twenty-five years imprisonment at hard labor, the minimum term for a second offender convicted of attempted murder and sentenced as a multiple offender. In its recitation of the case, the state indicated that Johnson had given a video-taped statement in which he stated that the defendant had encouraged him to retrieve the weapon and to shoot the victim. According to the state, Johnson said that, on the way back to the scene, the two men had struck a bargain in which the defendant agreed to drive the getaway car and Johnson vowed to shoot the victim. Johnson, in court, disagreed with the state's recitation, but he conceded that there had been a shooting and that what the state had said had basically happened "in so many ways."

After Johnson's plea was completed, the defendant returned to court. [The] defendant was asked what he thought he was facing and he replied, "Whew, um, I really don't know." Expressing some frustration, "All right, that's why I keep trying to explain it to you," the trial judge reiterated that the defendant was charged with attempted second degree murder, which carries a sentence of up to 50 years at hard labor, that a jury was waiting upstairs and would return a verdict in a few days if he elected to go to trial that day, that the defendant in fact had a prior felony conviction, and that the sentence would be up to 100 years at hard labor as a second felony offender if he went to trial, but only 25 years if he pleaded guilty. After conferring with his attorney, the defendant agreed to plead guilty, and the *Boykin* examination commenced. See Boykin v. Alabama, 395 U.S. 238 (1969).

During the colloquy, the trial judge gave a similar response anytime the defendant vacillated. When the defendant indicated that he thought he had been promised 10 years, the trial judge responded that it was only if the state chose not to file a multiple offender bill would he impose a sentence between 10 and 25 years at hard labor. The trial judge then asked if the defendant wanted to plead guilty. When he received no response, the trial judge stated that if not, "we've got the people waiting upstairs to get the trial started." The defendant responded, "I — whew, um — ." The trial judge again asked if the defendant wanted to finish the guilty plea and if he understood what was happening. The defendant said he did "in a way" and expressed doubt about the evidence against him. The trial judge then explained the law of principals, using the getaway driver of an armed robbery as an example. The trial judge [said that if the jury concluded that Bouie] provided a gun to Johnson, drove him back to the scene, and encouraged him to shoot the victim, then the defendant would be as guilty as if he had shot the victim.

The trial judge then had the state repeat its case against the defendant for the record. Unlike his co-defendant Johnson, the defendant expressed considerable doubt that he was guilty of any crime for transporting Johnson back and forth from the scene of the shooting. In his own statement to the police, the defendant had acknowledged only that he had been on the scene with Johnson to pick up a prostitute, that after the initial confrontation with the victim he had driven Johnson back to his (the defendant's) house where Johnson retrieved a rifle that he (Johnson) had hidden there earlier that evening, and that he (the defendant) had then returned with Johnson to the scene to "turn a trick" with the prostitute. The defendant had denied in his statement that he knew beforehand that Johnson would shoot the victim and he continued to insist in court that the two men had gone back "to see . . . where the trick was. [Johnson] got out the car and the only thing I heard was a shot. . . ." [After Bouie observed that "everything is pointing at me," the trial judge returned to the question of a guilty plea]:

COURT: Do you think it's in your best interest at this point to go ahead and accept a guilty plea and get the lesser years that you've been offered rather than running the risk of going to trial and getting the Habitual Act charged against you and getting, maybe, up to a hundred years?

BOUIE: (no answer)

COURT: Do you think this guilty plea today, right now, is better than doing that? In other words, this is in your best interest at this point.

BOUIE: It seems like, Your Honor.

The trial court then accepted the defendant's guilty plea.[2] However, after the state filed a multiple offender bill, but before sentencing, the defendant moved to withdraw his plea, alleging that he had been under "extreme emotional stress" when he entered the plea. At the hearing on the motion, the defendant testified that the court had, in effect, stampeded him into pleading guilty, not simply by the sentencing offer of 25 years imprisonment at hard labor but also by informing him, in effect, that "if I take you to trial, I was not going to win in your courtroom. You was going to give me fifty to a hundred years. So I feel as though I wasn't going to win no matter what." On the basis of that testimony, the attorney representing the defendant asked the court at the close of the hearing, "You saw [two acquittals] in nearly a twenty-year period. . . . How is he going to knowingly and intentionally plead guilty after he hears that, Your Honor?"

---

2. Notably, the trial judge never explained to the defendant that, to prove him guilty of attempted second degree murder, the state was required to prove that the defendant, even as a principal, had possessed the requisite specific intent to kill the victim. Consequently, whether a jury accepting the defendant's story as true could have rationally found the requisite specific intent proved beyond a reasonable doubt appears less certain than the trial judge advocated.

The trial judge denied the motion on grounds that it had spent over an hour and a half with the defendant in a painstaking effort to persuade him that a guilty plea was in his best interests "because he probably would have gotten convicted and been sentenced to fifty to a hundred years. [Instead] of doing that, I gave him twenty-five, and, certainly . . . that was in his best interest." The court . . . sentenced him to the promised term of 25 years imprisonment at hard labor. . . .

A trial judge has broad discretion in ruling on a defendant's motion to withdraw his guilty plea before sentencing. La. Code Crim. Proc. art. 559. When circumstances indicate that the plea was constitutionally invalid, the trial judge should allow the defendant to withdraw his plea. . . . However, as a general rule, an otherwise valid plea of guilty is not rendered involuntary merely because it was entered to limit the possible maximum penalty to less than that authorized by law for the crime charged.

[The] defendant contends that the nature and extent of the district court judge's participation in the plea agreement had a coercive effect on his decision to plead guilty. While this court has not directly addressed the issue of a judge's participation in negotiating a plea agreement, in State v. Chalaire, 375 So. 2d 107, fn.2 (La. 1979), albeit in dicta, we stated: "Although not objected to in this appeal, the judge's active participation in the plea negotiations evokes our concern. The ABA Standards recommend that the trial judge should not be involved with plea discussions before the parties have reached an agreement. ABA Standards, The Function of the Trial Judge §4.1 (Approved Draft 1972); accord, Fed. R. Crim. P. [11(c)(1)]." As we noted in *Chalaire,* the reasons for proscribing judicial participation in plea negotiations, according to the ABA Standards Commentary, are:

> (1) judicial participation in the discussions can create the impression in the mind of the defendant that he would not receive a fair trial were he to go to trial before this judge; (2) judicial participation in the discussions makes it difficult for the judge objectively to determine the voluntariness of the plea when it is offered; (3) judicial participation to the extent of promising a certain sentence is inconsistent with the theory behind the use of the presentence investigation report; and (4) the risk of not going along with the disposition apparently desired by the judge may seem so great to the defendant that he will be induced to plead guilty even if innocent. ABA Standards, Pleas of Guilty §3.3(a) Commentary 73 (Approved Draft 1968).

On the other hand, we also pointed out that . . . removal of the judge from the bargaining process usually places the sentencing prerogative in the district attorney's office. [We] concluded that . . . "any judge who directly participates in plea discussions should take extreme care to avoid the dangers described in the ABA commentary."

In our decision today, we do not adopt a rule absolutely prohibiting the participation of Louisiana trial judges in plea negotiations, such as that provided by the Federal Rules of Criminal Procedure [11(c)(1)] ("The court shall not participate in any such discussions"). Instead, we find that the interjection of the trial judge's personal knowledge and opinion in the plea discussions under the circumstances of this case did, or probably did, have a coercive effect on this particular defendant's decision that a guilty plea was in his best interest.

In the present case, the trial judge's explanations of the penalties the defendant faced if he went to trial and if he were convicted by a jury, and of the trial judge's discretion to impose greater penalties after conviction than offered in the course of plea negotiations, were not inherently coercive because the advice concerned information that an accused ought to possess to enter a knowing and intelligent guilty plea. Furthermore, the court's explanation of the law of principals under La. Rev. Stat. 14:24, which would form the basis of any verdict rendered by a jury, also served the same end.

However, when the trial judge coupled those lengthy explanations with his personal view that the result of a jury trial was all but a foregone conclusion, he went beyond simply facilitating the entry of a knowing and voluntary guilty plea. The trial judge's discussion of the chances of an acquittal at a jury trial conveyed the court's personal experience over the years in unrelated cases and its confidence in the soundness of the exercise of the charging discretion of the District Attorney's Office. No matter how benign the judge's intent, and no matter how solicitous of the defendant's interests, the trial judge clearly conveyed his opinion that this particular defendant had no realistic choice other than to plead guilty or face penalties ranging from two to four times as great as the court offered. Aside from the question of its reliability, such a message was inherently coercive because it came from the court, not from the prosecutor. . . . See Standley v. Warden, 990 P.2d 983, 985 (Nev. 1999) ("Appellant had good reason to fear offending the judge if he declined [the plea offer] because the same judge would have presided over the trial and, if the trial resulted in a conviction, the judge would have determined the appropriate sentence"). The defendant here voiced those concerns in his own words at the hearing on his motion to withdraw his guilty plea when he explained to the court that he took the sentencing offer because, "You told me, if I take you to trial, I'm not going to win in your courtroom."

We recognize that a defendant may enter a voluntary guilty plea even while he continues to protest his innocence. North Carolina v. Alford, 400 U.S. 25 (1970). . . . However, *Alford* presupposes that the defendant "must be permitted to judge for himself in this respect." Therefore, whether the offered plea agreement was in fact in the defendant's best interest was not for the court to decide, but for the defendant to determine with the advice of his counsel.

We concede that a fine line may at times separate a trial judge's attempts to insure that the defendant understands that a guilty plea might serve his best interest and the overbearing of a defendant's will to reach a result the court, with the best of intentions, deems appropriate. However, we find that the trial judge in this case, by stating his personal views on the virtual certainty that the defendant would be convicted by a jury, as well as on the prospect of a sentence much greater than that offered, when this judge would be determining the sentence to be imposed following the guilty verdict, overstepped his bounds and acted as more of an advocate than as a neutral arbiter of the criminal prosecution. We conclude that the defendant's guilty plea under these circumstances was not knowingly and voluntarily entered, such that the district court abused its discretion in not granting the defendant's motion to withdraw the guilty plea. . . .

WEIMER, J., dissenting.

. . . I do not believe the statements were sufficient to coerce the defendant or unreasonably persuade him to plead guilty. It has not been alleged that anything the trial court stated was inaccurate. . . . It should be noted that defendant's admitted behavior in the events surrounding the shooting subjected him to a risk of conviction. This risk of conviction was amplified when the statement of his co-defendant, which implicated the defendant, was considered. . . .

Certainly, the trial court can and must inform the defendant of the consequences of his plea. However, in doing so, the court must avoid the impression of coercing or persuading the defendant to plead guilty. Despite the defendant's allegations, I believe the court succeeded in avoiding that impression.

Notes

1. *Legal limits on judicial participation in plea negotiations.* States have addressed the role of the judge during plea negotiations through statutes, rules of criminal procedure, rules of judicial ethics, and in judicial opinions interpreting constitutional provisions. More than half of the states instruct the judge not to "participate" in the plea discussions, the position embodied in the Federal Rules of Criminal Procedure. See People v. Collins, 27 P.3d 726 (Cal. 2001) (judge's promise of "some benefit" for giving up jury trial right rendered guilty plea involuntary); State v. Wakefield, 925 P.2d 183 (Wash. 1996); Colo. Rev. Stat. §16-7-302; Ga. Unif. Super. Ct. R. 33.5(a); Mass. R. Crim. P. 12(b) (reporter's notes). Does this mean that the judges cannot even be present as an observer during such discussions?

Another group of states discourages judges from participating in plea negotiations but does not prohibit it. Judicial opinions in these states suggest that judicial participation in negotiations, while not the best practice, is not a reason to invalidate a conviction on constitutional or other grounds. State v. Niblack, 596 A.2d 407 (Conn. 1991); State v. Ditter, 441 N.W.2d 622 (Neb. 1989). A small but growing number of states (now over a dozen) have rules or statutes that do not discourage judicial participation, and some even authorize judges to take part. See Mont. Code §46-12-211; N.C. Gen. Stat. §15A-1021(a). Some of the laws authorizing judges to participate extend only to limited types of participation. For instance, some states allow judges to take part only when the parties extend an invitation. People v. Cobbs, 505 N.W.2d 208 (Mich. 1993). Others limit the judge to commenting on the acceptability of charges and sentences that the parties themselves propose. See Ill. Sup. Ct. R. 402(d); State v. Warner, 762 So. 2d 507, 514 (Fla. 2000) (once invited by parties, court may actively discuss potential sentences and comment on proposed plea agreements). Do these limits identify the judicial practices with the most potential for making a guilty plea involuntary?

The ABA Standards for Criminal Justice, Pleas of Guilty 14-3.3, have embodied over the years an ambivalence about judicial involvement in plea discussions. The original 1968 version of Standard 14-3.3 completely barred judicial participation in plea negotiations. The 1980 edition of the Standards established a more active role for judges as a participant in plea negotiations. The parties could request to meet with the judge to discuss a plea agreement, and the judge could "serve as a moderator in listening to their respective presentations" and could "indicate what charge or sentence concessions would be acceptable." On the other hand, "the judge should never through word or demeanor, either directly or indirectly, communicate to the defendant or defense counsel that a plea agreement should be accepted or that a guilty plea should be entered." The 1997 edition of the Standards set out a more limited role for the judge: "a judge may be presented with a proposed plea agreement negotiated by the parties and may indicate whether the court would accept the terms as proposed and, if relevant, indicate what sentence would be imposed."

2. *Judicial involvement in practice.* Judges do participate in plea negotiations. As the variety of legal rules on the subject suggests, the practice varies from place to place. One study from the late 1970s concluded that about a third of judges in felony and misdemeanor courts nationwide attended plea negotiations. Most of the judges attending the negotiations "reviewed" recommendations by the parties, while a few judges made their own recommendations to the parties. These nationwide figures concealed some variety among different jurisdictions. Judges in states with rules clearly barring their participation in plea bargaining were much less likely to attend the negotiations than judges in other states. John Paul Ryan & James Alfini, Trial Judges' Participation in Plea Bargaining: An Empirical Perspective, 13 Law & Soc'y Rev. 479 (1979). See also Allen Anderson, Judicial Participation in the Plea Negotiation Process: Some Frequencies and Disposing Factors, 10 Hamline J. Pub. L. & Pol'y 39 (1990).

3. *Judicial neutrality and plea negotiations.* Critics of judicial participation in plea negotiations have argued that a judge who proposes or ratifies the terms of a plea agreement cannot properly perform judicial duties later in the case. For instance, they say, such a judge cannot properly decide at the plea hearing whether the defendant is entering the guilty plea voluntarily. If the defendant rejects a proposed offer, it may be difficult for the negotiating judge to preside at the trial. The participating judge may also find it difficult at sentencing to give proper consideration to a presentence investigation that recommends some sentence different from the negotiated recommendation. See Richard Klein, Due Process Denied: Judicial Coercion in the Plea Bargaining Process, 32 Hofstra L. Rev. 1349 (2004). Are these concerns realistic? Are there ways to avoid these problems in systems that permit judges to participate in plea discussions? Should rules require different judges for the plea and the trial?

4. *Judicial coercion and plea negotiations.* The most common objection to judicial participation in plea discussions is that the judge will coerce the defendant into accepting a plea agreement. While the prosecutor does not hold ultimate authority to impose a sentence in most cases, the judge can say with certainty what sentence she will impose after trial or after a guilty plea. If the judge indicates that a particular outcome is a "good deal," does the defendant have much hope for a better outcome? One might conclude alternatively that judges who participate in plea discussions merely give the defendant more accurate and complete information about what will occur at sentencing. Their presence might prevent prosecutors from misrepresenting local sentencing practices or from proposing unreasonable outcomes. Albert Alschuler, The Trial Judge's Role in Plea Bargaining (pt. 1), 76 Colum. L. Rev. 1059 (1976). For reasons such as these, a law reform commission in Great Britain has called for a return to the practice of "sentence canvassing," in which a judge can tell a defendant in private the most severe sentence he might expect after a guilty plea. The courts in Great Britain have put a stop to this traditional practice. Report of the Royal Commission on Criminal Justice 112-13 (1993) (Runciman Commission).

How does judicial participation in plea negotiations compare to other sources of coercion to plead guilty? If a defendant can voluntarily plead guilty while claiming innocence, and can voluntarily plead guilty when the prosecutor plans to seek more severe sanctions against the defendant's family members unless they all enter guilty pleas, why object to a judge who tells the defendant the going rate for an offense?

D. MAKING AND BREAKING BARGAINS

The law of plea bargains is often described by analogy to the law of contract. Sometimes the reference is casual, since contracts and plea bargains both involve enforceable agreements. But sometimes the reference is more formal: In both areas courts must decide (for purposes of enforcing rights) when an agreement is made, what terms the agreement includes, whether a breach has occurred, and the appropriate remedies. This section considers the contractual dimensions of bargains.

One difference sometimes noted between contract law and plea bargain law is that a contract is said to be complete when two private parties reach an agreement supported by consideration, but a plea bargain is said to require the approval of a third party — the court — to become enforceable. Do plea bargains always require court certification to be enforceable?

The basic federal law for deciding when a bargain is made comes from the U.S. Supreme Court decisions in Santobello v. New York, 404 U.S. 257 (1971), and Mabry v. Johnson, 467 U.S. 504 (1984). In *Santobello,* the Supreme Court stated:

> When a defendant pleads guilty to a crime, he waives significant rights, including the right to a jury trial, the right to confront his accusers, the right to present witnesses in his defense, the right to remain silent, and the right to have the charges against him proved beyond a reasonable doubt. If the guilty plea is part of a plea bargain, the State is obligated to comply with any promises it makes: [W]hen a plea rests in any significant degree on a promise or agreement of the prosecutor, so that it can be said to be part of the inducement or consideration, such promise must be fulfilled.

404 U.S. at 262. The Court did not clearly identify the constitutional basis for this decision, which gave powerful support to a contractual view of plea bargains. In *Mabry,* the Court explained that the enforceability of bargains was guaranteed by the due process clause, but that a plea was not binding until it was entered and accepted by a court: Until that point the plea bargain was a "mere executory agreement" without "constitutional significance." In general, therefore, a prosecutor can withdraw an offer any time before the formal plea is accepted by the court. A majority of state courts have adopted this framework. A few states reject *Mabry* and hold the government to its bargains. In Ex parte Yarber, 437 So. 2d 1330, 1334 (Ala. 1983), the Supreme Court of Alabama explained:

> Employing contract law by way of analogy, we cannot conclude that a plea agreement is unenforceable merely because it is tentative in the sense that it is subject to the trial court's approval. The mere fact that a contract is subject, in effect, to the approval of a third-party, does not, by itself, render it unenforceable. For example, a contract for the purchase of realty is not rendered unenforceable because it is subject to the release and approval of the seller's contemplated mortgage. . . . If we allow the state to dishonor at will the agreements it enters into, the result could only serve to weaken the plea negotiating system. Such a result also is inconsistent with the "honesty and integrity" encouraged by [the] Alabama Code of Professional Responsibility.

What is the likely practical effect of making prosecutors stand by their bargains?

In most courts, a plea agreement may also be binding if, before entry of the formal guilty plea, the defendant acts in detrimental reliance on the bargain. It is often difficult, however, to determine whether there has been detrimental reliance. For example, in People v. Navarroli, 521 N.E.2d 891 (Ill. 1988), a state trial court had found that there had been an agreement between the defendant and the state and that the defendant had provided information to agents about other suspects. The Supreme Court of Illinois found that the defendant had not detrimentally relied on the bargain because he had provided information only about other people and not about himself (the latter might have implicated the privilege against self-incrimination or the right to counsel). Does detrimental reliance require some harm to the defendant, some benefit to the government, or both?

Once it becomes clear that the parties have indeed reached a binding plea agreement, breaches of that agreement have consequences. The principal case raises an important question: Are other state agents bound by a plea agreement between the prosecutor and the defendant? The problem following the case flags another difficult and central question: Who determines whether an agreement has been breached? The issue of proper remedies for breach is discussed in a second problem. For each of these critical questions about the nature of plea bargains, consider the extent to which contract law provides an analogy for the law of plea bargains. Where are there differences? Why do they exist?

■ STATE v. LIBRADO SANCHEZ
46 P.3d 774 (Wash. 2002)

BRIDGE, J.

We decide whether in each of these consolidated cases, the petitioner should be permitted to withdraw his plea of guilty because he entered it in exchange for a promise from the prosecutor to recommend a particular sentence to the sentencing judge. At the sentencing hearing, a person other than the prosecutor recommended a longer sentence than had been agreed to in the plea agreement. We hold that since neither of these people, Sanchez's investigating officer (IO) nor Harris's community corrections officer (CCO), was a party to the plea agreement, no breach of the plea agreement occurred. . . .

In 1991, Sanchez, who was 21 years old at the time, served as youth pastor to the church attended by 12-year-old CG and her family. In February or March of 1991, Sanchez kissed CG after they attended a movie together. For about eight months, the sexual contacts escalated, first to masturbation and oral sex, and eventually to two instances of penile-vaginal intercourse. The relationship terminated after CG's father saw Sanchez kissing her. CG disclosed the sexual contacts to her parents when she was 16, but did not report them to the police until October 10, 1997, when she was 19. In January 1998, Sanchez was arrested and ultimately charged. He then agreed to plead guilty to three counts of child molestation in the second degree and entered pleas accordingly. Pursuant to the plea agreement, the prosecutor agreed to make no sentencing recommendation at the sentencing hearing.

Prior to sentencing, Dr. Jerry Miller evaluated Sanchez for a Special Sex Offender Sentencing Alternative (SSOSA). Dr. Miller diagnosed Sanchez as suffering from sexual arousal to children, referring to a pattern of sexual contacts with younger children beginning when Sanchez was seven years old. Dr. Miller recommended that the judge impose a SSOSA sentence, stating his opinion that Sanchez would be amenable to treatment and was at a low risk to reoffend. Denise Hollenbeck, the CCO from the Department of Corrections, prepared a presentence report recommending a 75-month sentence, to be partially suspended under a SSOSA.

At the sentencing hearing, the prosecutor made no sentencing recommendation. He then advised the judge that CG, her parents, and Sergeant Dave Ruffin, the IO, wished to make statements to the court. The victim and her parents argued against a SSOSA on the grounds that the child had been severely traumatized, Sanchez had violated a position of trust to commit the crime, and indications of deceit in the report suggested a likelihood of reoffending. Sergeant Ruffin also argued against a SSOSA. In his opinion, Sanchez's acts "violated everything, the trust and what religion stood for," and were "as bad as if somebody drug someone in the bushes and violently raped them." Ruffin stated his belief that Sanchez had lied to Dr. Miller to get a SSOSA recommendation, and said that the judge should not give a SSOSA sentence. The judge then imposed a sentence, within the standard range, of 70 months in prison, stating that he did not believe a SSOSA was appropriate absent a perversion. . . .

Between October and December 1997, Mark Harris, who was in his mid-forties, performed oral sex on his 14-year-old nephew BJ on three or four different occasions. In December 1997, when BJ's parents became suspicious, they broke off the relationship between Mark and BJ. A year later, BJ informed his mother of what had happened. Harris was arrested on January 21, 1999. He was initially charged with third degree rape of a child. On May 13, 1999, as a result of a plea agreement, he entered a plea of guilty to an amended charge of communicating with a minor for immoral purposes. The prosecutor agreed to recommend a 29-month sentence, which was at the high end of the standard range. The standard range sentence was 22 to 29 months.

Pursuant to the plea agreement, the prosecutor recommended a 29-month sentence at the sentencing hearing. The CCO recommended an exceptional sentence of 60 months in his presentence report and spoke in support of that recommendation at the sentencing hearing. The court found the aggravating circumstances suggested by the CCO applicable, and sentenced Harris to 60 months. . . .

In each of these cases the prosecutor made the recommendation at sentencing to which he agreed in the plea agreement. The petitioners do not allege that the prosecutors breached the agreement by their own words or conduct. Rather, the issue presented is whether the recommendations made by others to the judge at the sentencing hearing breached the agreement. In effect, the petitioners claim that a plea agreement binds not only the individual prosecutor but also any other employee of the State of Washington or, indeed, in the case of the IO in Sanchez any government employee, even one in a separate department.

A plea agreement is like a contract and is analyzed according to contract principles. Petitioners point out that the caption in criminal cases is "State v. . . ." and they refer to courts' habit of using the terms "state" and "prosecutor" interchangeably. They also cite to RCW 36.27.005, which provides that prosecuting attorneys "appear for and *represent the state*" and RCW 36.27.020(4), stating that the prosecuting attorney shall prosecute "all criminal and civil actions in which *the state or the county may be a party*." (Emphasis added.) The petitioners assert that because a contract binds not only the party to the contract, but also the party he or she represents and that party's agents, the plea agreement binds all "agents" of the state.

The State responds that the duty is restricted to the prosecutor, and that plea agreements are made not between the "state" and the defendant, but between the prosecutor and the defense attorney (or defendant if acting pro se). Thus, the State asserts that the agreements did not bind either Sanchez's IO or Harris's CCO.

We have previously held that "the prosecutor and the defendant are the only parties to a plea agreement." State v. Wakefield, 925 P.2d 183 (Wash. 1996). The statutes governing the plea bargaining process are in accord with this holding. Former RCW 9.94A.080 ("The prosecutor and the attorney for the defendant, or the defendant when acting pro se, may engage in discussions with a view toward reaching [a plea] agreement"). . . . Conversely, when the police enter into an agreement with the defendant but do not make the prosecutor a party, the prosecutor is not bound by its terms. Because the prosecutor and the defendant are the only parties to a plea agreement, we find the agency analysis argued by the petitioners inappropriate. Instead, whether a government employee other than the prosecutor is bound by the agreement depends not on the employee's role vis-à-vis the prosecutor, but on the employee's role vis-à-vis the sentencing court. Thus, for example, the Court of Appeals has previously held that because juvenile court probation counselors are employees of the court, they are not bound by the terms of the plea agreement. State v. Poupart, 773 P.2d 893 (Wash. App. 1989). In contrast, a parole officer who has no statutory role in the sentencing hearing and whose input was not requested by the trial court is bound by the plea agreement because he or she is acting on behalf of the prosecutor rather than the court. State v. Sledge, 947 P.2d 1199 (Wash. 1997). . . .

Unlike the probation counselors in *Poupart,* neither Sanchez's IO nor Harris's CCO is an employee of the court. Unlike the parole officer in *Sledge,* both Sanchez's IO and Harris's CCO have a statutory role in sentencing. And unlike the parole officer in *Sledge,* the sentencing court in *Harris* requested the CCO's input. . . .

Florida alone has determined that a prosecutor's plea bargain binds all state agents. Lee v. State, 501 So. 2d 591 (Fla.1987). This is similar to the position of federal courts, which have held that absent an express limitation on the government's obligations, a plea agreement entered on behalf of the government by one assistant attorney general (AAG) binds another AAG because "the federal prosecutor's office is an entity and as such it is the spokesman for the Government." Giglio v. United States, 405 U.S. 150 (1972). Here, the petitioners go further and claim not that one prosecutor binds another prosecutor but that a prosecutor's agreement binds other persons, including at least one, Sanchez's IO, who [was employed by the Moses Lake Police Department, and is not] a state employee. We cannot agree.

The statutory role of Sanchez's IO is outlined in former RCW 9.94A.110. An IO is listed as a person whose arguments the court *must* allow: "The court *shall* . . . allow arguments from the prosecutor, the defense counsel, the offender, the victim, the survivor of the victim, or a representative of the victim or survivor, *and an investigative law enforcement officer* as to the sentence to be imposed." . . .

Sanchez asserts that when a prosecutor enters a plea bargain knowing that another government employee will present the sentencing judge with strong reasons to impose a harsher sentence, there is an appearance of unfairness. However, . . . the IO, an independent official, was not involved in the plea agreement. . . .

Furthermore, a prosecutor does not control the actions of an IO. Despite the dissent's contention that former RCW 9.94A.440 allows prosecutors to "direct the activities of law enforcement," former RCW 9.94A.440(2)(b) merely requires a prosecutor to ensure that the investigating officer's evidence is sufficient to support a decision to prosecute. Moreover, unlike a prosecutor's obligation to inform victims of a proposed plea agreement, a prosecutor need not even discuss the proposed plea agreement with an IO. . . . We therefore hold that Sanchez's IO did not have a duty to abide by Sanchez's plea agreement with the county prosecutor, and therefore, his plea agreement was not breached by Sergeant Ruffin's testimony at the sentencing hearing.

The statutory duty imposed on a CCO is to produce a presentence report pursuant to court order, though the statute does not specifically mention him/her as a person whose arguments must be allowed at the sentencing hearing: "[T]he court shall, at the time of plea or conviction, order the department to complete a presentence report before imposing a sentence upon a defendant who has been convicted of a felony sexual offense." . . . Former RCW 9.94A.110. [This statute specifies] a minimum amount of information which, if available and offered, must be considered in sentencing. [The] court may rely on any information in the presentence report, unless it is the subject of an objection. . . . By statute, the CCO has an independent duty of investigation and recommendation in these cases. The CCO is not part of the prosecution team. The CCO was not involved in the preparation of, nor the promises made in, the plea agreement. In these circumstances, we hold that a CCO cannot be bound by the plea agreement. . . .

CHAMBERS, J., concurring in part and dissenting in part.

. . . While the community corrections officer in *Harris* functioned as an agent of the *court*, the investigating officer in *Sanchez* functions as the investigating arm of the *prosecutor*. Under Washington law, the prosecutor has the duty and the power to ensure that a thorough factual investigation has been conducted before a decision to prosecute is made. This is for the pragmatic reason that a prosecuting attorney is dependent upon law enforcement agencies to conduct the necessary factual investigation which must precede the decision to prosecute. It is the prosecutor who is empowered to enter into plea agreements and to make sentence recommendations. Investigating officers are so integral to the prosecutorial effort that to permit the investigating officer to undercut a plea agreement would, in effect, countenance the State's breach of promise in violation of *Santobello*. The prosecutor is obligated to comply with plea bargain promises, and the prosecutor's investigating officers may not undercut those promises by making inconsistent recommendations. . . . A prosecutor may not undercut a plea agreement directly or by words or conduct. Nor may he do so by proxy. . . .

MADSEN, J., dissenting.

I agree with the majority that the Investigating Officer (IO) in Sanchez's case has a statutory role in a sentencing hearing. I disagree, however, with the majority's conclusion that Investigating Officers and Community Corrections Officers (CCO) are entitled to make sentencing recommendations which undermine a plea agreement negotiated by the defendant and the prosecutor as the representative of the State of Washington. Basic agency principles and simple fairness require that they be bound to a prosecutor's plea agreement. . . .

Because plea agreements are based in contract law, the pivotal issue is whether IOs and CCOs are agents of the state, or independent agents of the court. The majority declines to analyze the question of agency and instead resolves the question by looking only at the statutory role each plays in sentencing.[1] . . . The authority of a Washington prosecuting attorney to act as an agent of the state of Washington is well established. The language of our state constitution directs that "all prosecutions shall be conducted . . . by [the State of Washington's] authority." Constitution article IV, section 27. . . . Statutes also dictate that the prosecuting attorney represents the State as well as the county. RCW 36.27.005 provides that "[prosecuting] attorneys are attorneys authorized by law to appear for and represent the state and the counties thereof in actions and proceedings before the courts and judicial officers."

Based on the statutory duty placed on prosecutors by the Legislature to direct the activities of law enforcement, and the fact that the prosecuting attorney represents the State as well as the county, I would hold that the IO was bound by the plea agreement struck by the prosecuting attorney in *Sanchez*. Additionally, since case law establishes that the CCO is an agent of the State and the Constitution and state statutes dictate that the prosecuting attorney represents the State in criminal prosecutions, I would also hold that the CCO's recommendation undercutting the prosecutor's bargain requires reversal in *Harris*. . . .

Due process requires a prosecutor to adhere to the terms of the plea agreement. State v. Miller, 756 P.2d 122 (Wash. 1988) (holding that because a breach of plea agreement implicates fundamental principles of due process, the terms of a plea agreement override an otherwise contradictory statute). If a prosecutor cannot, per the plea agreement, make a contrary argument, it follows that IOs and CCOs are bound to the same due process limitations. . . .

To allow CCOs and IOs to present arguments to the sentencing judge, in any form, which contradict another state agency's contract not only appears unfair, but is unfair. It renders the prosecution's agreement meaningless, disintegrates the fabric of our criminal justice system, and will deter future plea agreements. In my view, IOs and CCOs are bound to prosecutorial plea agreements and, as a result, I respectfully dissent.

Problem 6-7. Breaking Bargains

On the afternoon of June 5, 1978, Floyd Jensen was robbed and murdered in his gasoline service station in Caledonia, Wisconsin. Shortly after the murder-robbery, Alan Rivest surrendered to police. Rivest, in a statement given to the police, admitted participating in the robbery of the gas station owner, but denied any involvement in his subsequent murder. Rivest indicated in his statement that Edward Rodriguez, his accomplice, repeatedly stabbed Jensen during the robbery; Rivest said that he did not participate in the murder and that he fled the gas station before Rodriguez but after the stabbing. Later that same evening, Rivest signed a sworn

---

1. The majority repeatedly makes the point that the only parties to the plea agreement are the prosecuting attorney and the defendant—that neither an investigating officer nor a community corrections officer is involved in the negotiations or a party to the agreement. The majority apparently thinks this renders the agency question irrelevant. However, the question who is a party to the contract simply does not answer the question of who is bound by the agreement under agency principles.

statement dictated to the police in which he repeated his earlier statement and denied any involvement in the stabbing of Floyd Jensen. Rivest, a minor, was initially charged with delinquency for the murder and armed robbery of Floyd Jensen in the juvenile court and was waived into adult court on August 1. Based on Rivest's prior statements and his investigation, Assistant District Attorney Finley charged Rivest only with the crime of armed robbery on August 3.

On September 25, Rivest took a private polygraph examination which showed that he was truthful in his denial of any participation in the stabbing of Floyd Jensen. Subsequent negotiations between Rivest, his attorney, and the Assistant District Attorney Finley produced a plea agreement. In the plea agreement, Rivest agreed to (1) plead guilty to a charge of robbery; (2) testify against Rodriguez whenever requested; and (3) pass a second polygraph examination conducted by a party chosen by the district attorney. The second polygraph examination indicated that Rivest was unaware that an assault was to be perpetrated on Jensen, and did not participate in stabbing Jensen. At a hearing on February 6, 1979, the plea agreement entered into between Rivest and the assistant district attorney was placed on the record and Rivest pled guilty to the crime of robbery, reduced from armed robbery. Rivest was sentenced to six years in prison.

On February 19, Rivest testified at the preliminary hearing of Edward Rodriguez. At the hearing, Rivest testified that he never got near Jensen nor did he come in physical contact with him. He also testified that he ran "straight out across the street" shortly after Rodriguez stabbed Jensen.

After Rivest's testimony at the preliminary hearing, the district attorney, Dennis Barry, while preparing the Rodriguez murder file, reviewed evidence that he believed directly contradicted both Rivest's initial statements to the police and his testimony at the preliminary hearing. This evidence established that there was a three to five minute delay between the time Jensen's body was discovered and the time that witnesses saw Rivest and Rodriguez flee the scene together. The evidence also proved that a "herringbone pattern" on the forehead of the victim matched the "herringbone pattern" on Rivest's shoes, but not Rodriguez's shoes. Finally, a State Crime Lab report indicated that the large bloodstains present on Rivest's pants and undershorts matched the blood type and factors of Floyd Jensen.

District Attorney Barry interviewed Rivest and confronted him with this evidence. At that interview, Rivest admitted leaving the gas station by a different door than the one he had originally testified about. However, Rivest offered no explanations for the presence of his shoe print on the deceased's head nor the presence of the deceased's blood on his clothing and he continued to repeat his original account of the stabbing. District Attorney Barry concluded after the interview that Rivest's account of the circumstances surrounding the stabbing was untrue, and that his prior testimony was false and thus, he breached the plea agreement. Based on this evidence, District Attorney Barry decided not to present Rivest's testimony at the Rodriguez trial.

The state filed first-degree murder charges against Rivest and then filed a motion before Judge Harvey to vacate the plea agreement and guilty plea. Judge Harvey entered an order setting aside the plea agreement and guilty plea and authorized the state to continue the prosecution of the murder complaint. The court held that Rivest had fraudulently induced the state to enter into the plea agreement through his false and misleading statements and had materially breached the agreement by giving false testimony at Rodriguez's preliminary hearing.

Rivest appeals, arguing that his inconsistent testimony did not provide evidence beyond a reasonable doubt that he had committed perjury, and that even if he did, his actions were not a sufficient (or "material") breach of the plea agreement that would justify vacation of the agreement. How would you rule? Compare State v. Rivest, 316 N.W.2d 395 (Wis. 1982).

Notes

1. *Who is bound by plea agreements: majority position.* As the court in *Sanchez* notes, a number of states have found that the plea agreement binds only the defendant and the prosecutor, but not other state agents. Florida clearly rejects this position:

> Under Florida Rule of Criminal Procedure 3.171, the prosecuting attorney represents the state in all plea negotiations. [Once] a plea bargain based on a prosecutor's promise that the state will recommend a certain sentence is struck, basic fairness mandates that no agent of the state make any utterance that would tend to compromise the effectiveness of the state's recommendation. [It] matters not whether the recommendation contrary to the agreement is made in open court or whether, as here, it is contained in a PSI report. The crucial factor is that a recommendation contrary to the state's agreement came to the sentencing court's attention. Regardless of how a recommendation counter to that bargained for is communicated to the trial court, once the court is apprised of this inconsistent position, the persuasive effect of the bargained for recommendation is lost.

Lee v. State, 501 So. 2d 591, 593 (Fla. 1987). Sometimes the question is not whether other government agents are bound by a plea agreement, but whether another agency is precluded from taking additional civil action against a defendant after plea. See, e.g., Dickerson v. Kansas Dept. of Revenue, 841 P.2d 466 (Kan. 1992) (plea agreement collaterally estopped state revenue collection of drug tax).

Federal courts also hold that a plea agreement by the United States Attorney binds other agents of the federal government. See Giglio v. United States, 405 U.S. 150, 154 (1972) ("A promise made by one [government] attorney must be attributed . . . to the Government"); Margali-Olvera v. I.N.S., 43 F.3d 345 (8th Cir. 1994) (plea agreement by U.S. Attorney bound I.N.S.). Is this because the federal system is a unitary system under the direction of the attorney general? Which way should that logic cut in the states? Within a particular county? Can one county's district attorney bind another county's district attorney? See Zebe v. State, 929 P.2d 927 (Nev. 1996) (holding that a second Nevada county was not bound by a plea to which it did not consent). Can the prosecutor of one state bind a prosecutor in another state (is this simply another way of asking whether double jeopardy or joinder rules apply)? Courts usually hold that one state cannot bind another. How can a defendant, as part of a plea bargain, protect against prosecution by multiple sovereigns?

2. *Assessing breach of plea bargains: majority position.* Plea bargains can be broken by the defendant, the prosecution, the court, or through an unanticipated change of circumstances that makes performance of the bargain impossible. The law regarding broken bargains might at first seem to be just a question of remedy; indeed, the question of available remedies will often shape a party's decision to breach a plea bargain. As with other kinds of contracts, if the cost of breaking the contract is lower than the cost of abiding by it, a person will often choose to breach.

Sometimes the parties disagree about whether the plea bargain has been breached at all. This often occurs when a defendant receives a stiff sentence and claims that the prosecution violated an agreement to recommend no sentence at all. When a prosecutor introduces elements of the defendant's prior record or otherwise implies that a higher sentence might be appropriate, the defendant may call this a breach of the agreement. Another common illustration occurs when the defendant agrees, as part of the plea bargain, to provide "complete" cooperation, or to testify against other parties, and the prosecution later alleges some inadequacy in the defendant's performance. Here, the defendant will claim performance, or substantial performance, and look to enforce the benefit of the bargain. What standard should a court apply to determine whether a party has fulfilled the terms of the agreement?

If the parties disagree about whether breach has occurred, the trial court will hold a hearing to determine relevant facts. Trial courts often treat the assessment of whether breach has occurred as a question of fact, without expressly reflecting on the standards to apply. When a party appeals the trial court's decision, however, an appellate court must decide whether breach is a question of fact, a question of law, or a mixed question of law and fact. State courts are divided on the proper standard to apply. Most treat the facts underlying the claim of breach as a factual matter for the trial judge, subject only to review for abuse of discretion. But some appellate courts have treated the question of whether particular facts are indeed breach or substantial compliance with a plea bargain as a question of law, subject to de novo appellate review. Courts more often find breach by defendants in failing to disclose all information than by prosecutors in failing to support a particular sentence recommendation. See, e.g., United States v. Benchimol, 471 U.S. 453 (1985) (prosecutor carried out agreement to recommend probation by saying agreement was accurate; there was no express agreement to be enthusiastic or to give reasons supporting probation); but see State v. Adams, 879 P.2d 513 (Haw. 1994) (government breached agreement to stand silent by providing probation officer with access to prosecution files).

Should prosecutors ever agree to support a particular sentence "with enthusiasm"? Could the prosecutor in Problem 6-7 have maintained full control over the plea by delaying Rivest's guilty plea hearing until after Rodriguez's preliminary hearing?

3. *Construing ambiguities.* How long would plea agreements become if they took account of all possible future events relevant to the bargain? All reasonably possible (if unlikely) events? Which side should get the benefit of ambiguous language? Should ambiguous terms be handled differently from events for which no term was drafted? See, e.g., State v. Wills, 765 P.2d 1114 (Kan. 1988) (ambiguity in agreement construed to favor defendant); State v. Bergman, 600 N.W.2d 311 (Iowa 1999) (prosecutor could not claim breach where defendant "did everything" under a cooperation agreement but was then charged before sentencing with possession of marijuana).

Often the parties will agree that a bargain has been broken, or the breach (such as defendant's failure to testify or the government's failure to dismiss charges) will be obvious. In such cases, the main issue is the appropriate remedy.

When one party breaches a contract, what remedies are available? A standard remedy for breach of a contract is money damages. Perhaps the state or the defendant should pay money damages for breaching a plea bargain, but this remedy has not been seriously considered. Instead, the typical remedies for breach of a plea bargain are either rescission or specific enforcement of the original bargain. Should the party against whom a breach has occurred get to choose the remedy?

Problem 6-8. Remedies for Broken Bargains

Following his arrest in 1999 in Billings, Montana, Daniel Munoz entered a pretrial agreement with the State. The State agreed to recommend that Munoz receive a three-year sentence in exchange for his voluntary plea of guilty to one count of sexual assault. On January 13, 2000, the court accepted Munoz's guilty plea and ordered a presentence investigation.

At a March 28 sentencing hearing, the prosecutor urged the court to adopt the five-year sentence recommended by Munoz's probation officer, who conducted the presentence investigation and issued a report. In addition to recommending the five-year sentence, the probation officer testified at the hearing that community supervision presented too much of a risk. Therefore, the officer recommended that all sex-offender treatment should be completed in prison.

The district court sentenced Munoz to the recommended five-year sentence. On April 27, Munoz filed a motion to withdraw his guilty plea and a motion for a new trial. The State conceded that it breached the plea agreement. However, the State also contended that the sentencing court, not the defendant, possesses the right to choose the appropriate remedy, and argued that under the circumstances here specific performance of the plea agreement would be appropriate: Munoz should receive a new sentencing hearing before a new judge and the State would then in good faith recommend the three-year sentence pursuant to the plea agreement.

The trial court ordered specific performance, and Munoz appealed, arguing that he was entitled to withdraw his guilty plea and proceed to trial due to the State's breach of the plea agreement. The Montana Supreme Court set the stage for its decision as follows:

> Generally, when the State breaches a plea bargain agreement, one of two equitable remedies is available to safeguard a defendant's due process rights. This notion of an equitable "remedy" for a "breach" is unquestionably guided by general principles of contract law. Even so where a defendant's due process rights are concerned a "strict contract characterization" of a plea bargain may give way to a "reasonable expectations" standard.
>
> The first equitable remedy identified by the court in Santobello v. New York, 404 U.S. 257 (1971), is "specific performance" by the government. To safeguard a defendant's due process rights, circumstances may require the State uphold its end of the bargain, and, before a new sentencing judge, comply with the terms and conditions of the plea agreement by recommending a specific sentence, moving for the dismissal of other charges, or simply not opposing the defendant's requested sentence.
>
> The second equitable remedy is "rescission." Circumstances may require that a defendant be allowed to withdraw his or her guilty plea and then face trial on the original charges as if the plea agreement had never been entered — which also means that the defendant's "performance" is returned; i.e., his or her constitutional rights that were waived by the guilty plea are thereafter reinstated.

The Court in *Santobello* left the choice of remedy "to the discretion of the state court." Three general positions have emerged in state and federal courts since *Santobello*. Some courts give the trial court authority to choose a remedy in each case. Other jurisdictions instruct trial judges to give deference to the defendant's choice of remedies, while some allow the defendant total discretion to choose between those remedies. What should Montana decide? See State v. Munoz, 23 P.3d 922 (Mont. 2001).

Notes

1. *Remedies for breach: majority position.* There are two standard remedies for breaches of plea agreements: rescission, in which the parties return to their positions before the agreement, and specific enforcement, in which the court orders government officials to carry out the terms of the agreement. State and federal courts split on whether the aggrieved party is allowed to select the remedy. In oft-quoted language, the U.S. Supreme Court in Santobello v. New York, 404 U.S. 257 (1971), stated that "when a plea rests in any significant degree on a promise or agreement of the prosecutor, so that it can be said to be part of the inducement or consideration, such promise must be fulfilled." Most courts have not interpreted this language to mean that defendants will always get specific enforcement of the bargain. The Court in *Santobello* left the choice of remedy to state courts, and most state courts follow what is commonly referred to as the "discretion of the court" rule. See State v. King, 576 N.W.2d 369 (Iowa 1998). Federal courts follow the "discretion of the court" rule, although some federal courts have expressed a preference for specific performance. See United States v. Clark, 55 F.3d 9 (1st Cir. 1995) (preference for specific performance before a different judge).

A second position in some state and federal courts is a twist on the "discretion of the court theme" where courts suggest that the defendant's views should receive some special deference. See Roye v. United States, 772 A.2d 837 (D.C. Ct. App. 2001). What difference do rules make that "encourage" deference within the framework of acknowledged discretion? A few states allow the defendant to select the remedy, absent special circumstances. See State v. Miller, 756 P.2d 122 (Wash. 1988) ("We hold now that the defendant's choice of remedy controls, unless there are compelling reasons not to allow that remedy"). Some states apply a multifactor test to select between rescission and specific enforcement. See Citti v. State, 807 P.2d 724, 726-27 (Nev. 1991):

> The goal in providing a remedy for breach of the [plea] bargain is to redress the harm caused by the violation without prejudicing either party or curtailing the normal sentencing discretion of the trial judge. The remedy chosen will vary depending on the circumstances of each case. Factors to be considered include who broke the bargain and whether the violation was deliberate or inadvertent, whether circumstances have changed between entry of the plea and the time of sentencing, and whether additional information has been obtained that, if not considered, would constrain the court to a disposition that it determines to be inappropriate. . . . Courts find withdrawal of the plea to be the appropriate remedy when specifically enforcing the bargain would have limited the judge's sentencing discretion in light of the development of additional information or changed circumstances between acceptance of the plea and sentencing. Specific enforcement is appropriate when it will implement the reasonable expectations of the parties without binding the trial judge to a disposition that he or she considers unsuitable under all the circumstances. [Quoting People v. Mancheno, 654 P.2d 211 (Cal. 1982).]

See generally Peter Westen & David Westin, A Constitutional Law of Remedies for Broken Plea Bargains, 66 Cal. L. Rev. 471 (1978). Is specific performance an available remedy when a *defendant* breaches a plea agreement? Does your answer to this question affect your view of the ordinary remedy when the government breaches? See State v. Mellon, 118 S.W.3d 340 (Tenn. 2003) (defendant could withdraw plea because he was not warned of consequences if he breached agreement; if agreement had been clear, state would be entitled to same remedies available to defendants, including rescission or specific performance).

2. *Planning for breach.* Plea agreements sometimes include terms that account for various kinds of possible breach or other barriers to completion of the plea agreement (e.g., an agreement about how another jurisdiction will act, even though the sentencing jurisdiction has no power to compel that result). Who should bear the "cost" of failing to anticipate any particular kind of development? Is the general rule that ambiguous statutes will be interpreted to favor the criminal defendant (the so-called rule of lenity) relevant to interpretation and enforcement of plea agreements? Would you advise prosecutors systematically to alter the terms of their plea agreements in the future to address various issues of breach and remedy, akin to a large commercial contract that specifies procedural and substantive terms in case of breach? If so, will plea agreements be hundreds of pages long?

E. THE FUTURE OF BARGAINING

Is plea bargaining bad or good? If courts and executive branch policies actually do "regulate" plea bargaining — as the materials in this chapter suggest — are those regulations effective at limiting the undesirable aspects of plea bargaining? Should we ban plea bargaining altogether?

1. Legitimacy of Bargaining

Many scholars, judges, and lawyers believe that plea bargaining is inevitable. They say that the use of other processes (especially trials) to decide guilt or innocence would at best be hugely expensive and at worst cause a meltdown of the justice system. But before we consider whether it is feasible to ban plea bargaining, we need to know whether an attempted ban would be worth the effort. Is plea bargaining legitimate? Would we keep it in an ideal world?

■ ALBERT ALSCHULER, IMPLEMENTING THE CRIMINAL DEFENDANT'S RIGHT TO TRIAL: ALTERNATIVES TO THE PLEA BARGAINING SYSTEM
50 U. Chi. L. Rev. 931 (1983)

. . . Plea bargaining makes a substantial part of an offender's sentence depend, not upon what he did or his personal characteristics, but upon a tactical decision irrelevant to any proper objective of criminal proceedings. In contested cases, it substitutes a regime of split-the-difference for a judicial determination of guilt or innocence and elevates a concept of partial guilt above the requirement that criminal responsibility be established beyond a reasonable doubt. This practice also deprecates the value of human liberty and the purposes of the criminal sanction by treating these things as commodities to be traded for economic savings — savings that, when measured against common social expenditures, usually seem minor.

Plea bargaining leads lawyers to view themselves as judges and administrators rather than as advocates; it subjects them to serious financial and other temptations to disregard their clients' interests; and it diminishes the confidence in attorney-client relationships that can give dignity and purpose to the legal profession and that is essential to the defendant's sense of fair treatment. In addition, this practice makes figureheads of court officials who typically prepare elaborate presentence reports only after the effective determination of sentence through prosecutorial negotiations. Indeed, it tends to make figureheads of judges, whose power over the administration of criminal justice has largely been transferred to people of less experience, who commonly lack the information that judges could secure, whose temperaments have been shaped by their partisan duties, and who have not been charged by the electorate with the important responsibilities that they have assumed. Moreover, plea bargaining perverts both the initial prosecutorial formulation of criminal charges and, as defendants plead guilty to crimes less serious than those that they apparently committed, the final judicial labeling of offenses.

The negotiation process encourages defendants to believe that they have, [in the words of a Chicago defense attorney], "sold a commodity and . . . , in a sense, gotten away with something." It sometimes promotes perceptions of corruption. It has led the Supreme Court to a hypocritical disregard of its usual standards of waiver in judging the most pervasive waiver that our criminal justice system permits. The practice of plea bargaining is inconsistent with the principle that a decent society should want to hear what an accused person might say in his defense — and with constitutional guarantees that embody this principle and other professed ideals for the resolution of criminal disputes. Moreover, plea bargaining has undercut the goals of legal doctrines as diverse as the fourth amendment exclusionary rule, the insanity defense, the right of confrontation, the defendant's right to attend criminal proceedings, and the recently announced right of the press and the public to observe the administration of criminal justice. This easy instrument of accommodation has frustrated both attempts at sentencing reform and some of the most important objectives of the due process revolution.

Plea bargaining provides extraordinary opportunities for lazy lawyers whose primary goal is to cut corners and to get on to the next case; it increases the likelihood of favoritism and personal influence; it conceals other abuses; it maximizes the dangers of representation by inexperienced attorneys who are not fully versed in an essentially secret system of justice; it promotes inequalities; it sometimes results in unwarranted leniency; it merges the tasks of adjudication, sentencing, and administration into a single amorphous judgment to the detriment of all three; it treats almost every legal right as a bargaining chip to be traded for a discount in sentence; and it almost certainly increases the number of innocent defendants who are convicted. In short, an effort to describe comprehensively the evils that plea bargaining has wrought requires an extensive tour of the criminal justice system. . . .

At the end of a long investigation of plea bargaining, I confess to some bafflement concerning the insistence of most lawyers and judges that plea bargaining is inevitable and desirable. Perhaps I am wrong in thinking that a few simple precepts of criminal justice should command the unqualified support of fair-minded people:

- that it is important to hear what someone may be able to say in his defense before convicting him of crime;
- that, when he denies his guilt, it is also important to try to determine on the basis of all the evidence whether he is guilty;
- that it is wrong to punish a person, not for what he did, but for asking that the evidence be heard (and wrong deliberately to turn his sentence in significant part on his strategies rather than on his crime);
- and, finally, that it is wrong to alibi departures from these precepts by saying that we do not have the time and money to listen, that most defendants are guilty anyway, that trials are not perfect, that it is all an inevitable product of organizational interaction among stable courtroom work groups, and that any effort to listen would merely drive our failure to listen underground.

From my viewpoint, it is difficult to understand why these precepts are controversial; what is more, I do not understand why the legal profession, far from according them special reverence, apparently values them less than the public in general does. Daniel Webster thought it a matter of definition that "law" would hear before it condemned, proceed upon inquiry, and render judgment only after trial. Apparently the legal profession has lost sight of Webster's kind of law. . . .

■ FRANK EASTERBROOK, PLEA BARGAINING AS COMPROMISE
101 Yale L.J. 1969 (1992)

Is plea bargaining good or bad? Should we keep it or kick it? . . .

The analogy between plea bargains and contracts is far from perfect. Courts use contract as an analogy when addressing claims for the enforcement of plea bargains, excuses for nonperformance, or remedies for their breach. But plea bargains do not fit comfortably all aspects of either the legal or the economic model. Courts refuse to enforce promises to plead guilty in the future, although the enforcement of executory contracts is a principal mission of contract law.

On the economic side, plea bargains do not represent Pareto improvements. Instead of engaging in trades that make at least one person better off and no one worse off, the parties dicker about how much worse off one side will be. In markets persons can borrow to take advantage of good deals or withdraw from the market, wait for a better offer, and lend their assets for a price in the interim. By contrast, both sides to a plea bargain operate under strict budget constraints, and they cannot bide their time. They bargain as bilateral monopolists (defendants can't shop in competitive markets for prosecutors) in the shadow of legal rules that work suspiciously like price controls. Judges, who do not join the bargaining, set the prices, increasingly by reference to a table of punishments that looks like something the Office of Price Administration would have promulgated. Plea bargaining is to the sentencing guidelines as black markets are to price controls.

Black markets are better than no markets. Plea bargains are preferable to mandatory litigation — not because the analogy to contract is overpowering, but because compromise is better than conflict. Settlements of civil cases make both sides better off; settlements of criminal cases do so too. Defendants have many procedural and substantive rights. By pleading guilty, they sell these rights to the prosecutor, receiving concessions they esteem more highly than the rights surrendered. Rights that may be sold are more valuable than rights that must be consumed, just as money (which may be used to buy housing, clothing, or food) is more valuable to a poor person than an opportunity to live in public housing.

Defendants can use or exchange their rights, whichever makes them better off. So plea bargaining helps defendants. Forcing them to use their rights at trial means compelling them to take the risk of conviction or acquittal; risk-averse persons prefer a certain but small punishment to a chancy but large one. Defendants also get the process over sooner, and solvent ones save the expense of trial. Compromise also benefits prosecutors and society at large. In purchasing procedural entitlements with lower sentences, prosecutors buy that most valuable commodity, Time. With time they can prosecute more criminals. When [eighty] percent of defendants plead guilty, a given prosecutorial staff obtains five times the number of convictions it could achieve if all went to trial. Even so, prosecutors must throw back the small fish. The ratio of prosecutions (and convictions) to crimes would be extremely low if compromises were forbidden. Sentences could not be raised high enough to maintain deterrence, especially not when both economics and principles of desert call for proportionality between crime and punishment.

True, defense lawyers and prosecutors are imperfect agents of their principals. Of what agents is this not true? Real estate agents? Corporate managers? Agency costs are endemic and do not justify abandoning consensual transactions. . . . Monitoring the performance of agents is difficult, and serious monitoring means substantially increasing the time and number of lawyers devoted to each case. Critics of plea bargaining commit the Nirvana Fallacy, comparing an imperfect reality to a perfection achievable only in imaginary systems. . . .

Why should we interfere with compromises of litigation? If the accused is entitled to a trial at which all his rights are honored and the sentence is appropriate to the crime, yet prefers compromise, who are we to disagree? . . . Why is liberty too important to be left to the defendant whose life is at stake? Should we not say instead that liberty is too important to deny effect to the defendant's choice?

Every day people choose where (if at all) to obtain an education, what occupation to pursue, whom to marry, whether to bear children, and how to raise them. Often they choose in ignorance — not simply because they do not know whether Yale offers a better education than the University of Southern Mississippi, but also because they do not know what the future holds. Technological changes or fluctuations in trade with foreign nations will make some educations obsolete and raise the value of others. People may, without the approval of regulators, climb mountains, plummet down slopes at eighty miles per hour on waxed boards, fail to exercise, eat fatty foods, smoke cigarettes, skip physical checkups, anesthetize their minds by watching television rather than reading books, and destroy their hearing by listening to rock music at high volumes. Sometimes courts say that the Constitution protects the right to make these choices, precisely because they are so important. . . .

Courts give effect not only to life-and-death choices actually made but also to elections by inaction. When a defendant's lawyer fails to make an important motion or omits an essential line of argument, we treat the omission as a forfeiture. How bizarre for a legal system that routinely puts persons in jail for twenty years following their agents' oversight to deny them the right to compromise the same dispute, advertently, for half as much loss of liberty. . . .

Curtailing the discount for pleading guilty has been justified in the name of equality. Yet the greatest disparity in sentencing is between those convicted at trial and those not prosecuted. A reduction in the number of convictions attributable to a decline in the number of pleas would dramatically increase the effective disparity in the treatment of persons suspected of crime. . . .

Plea bargains are compromises. Autonomy and efficiency support them. "Imperfections" in bargaining reflect the imperfections of an anticipated trial. To improve plea bargaining, improve the process for deciding cases on the merits. When we deem that process adequate, there will be no reason to prevent the person most affected by the criminal process from improving his situation through compromise.

Notes

1. *Plea bargains: contract or charade?* Some scholars have accepted the essentially contractual nature of plea bargaining, and have suggested that the problem with plea bargaining law is that it does not take the contracting analogy seriously enough. Robert Scott and William Stuntz, for example, focus on the risk of convicting an innocent defendant, arguing that "by following appropriate contract models, one can devise different rules that reduce the harm to innocent defendants and meanwhile reduce transaction costs and inefficiency for everyone else." Scott & Stuntz, Plea Bargaining as Contract, 101 Yale L.J. 1909 (1992). Critics of plea bargaining, such as Professor Stephen Schulhofer, have rejected the notion that plea bargains are fair simply because the defendant agreed to the terms and because the agreement puts the defendant in a better position than if the defendant went to trial. Schulhofer, Plea Bargaining as Disaster, 101 Yale L.J. 1979 (1992). Schulhofer and other critics focus on the public interest in criminal justice that the contract model obscures. Does plea bargaining undermine public confidence in the criminal justice system? Stanley Cohen & Anthony Doob, Public Attitudes to Plea Bargaining, 32 Crim. L.Q. 85 (1989-1990) (1988 survey found that more than two-thirds of Canadians disapprove of plea bargaining). What is Judge Easterbrook's attitude toward the use of contract law to explain plea bargaining? Does he take account of the public interest arguments? Does Professor Alschuler account for the contractarian argument that plea bargains are the fairest (most preferable) means for the defendant to address criminal charges, except in very limited circumstances? Would the fairness of plea bargaining be cast into doubt if there were no trials at all? See Malcolm Feeley, The Process Is the Punishment (1979) (of 1,640 misdemeanor cases, not one defendant requested jury trial). Is there such a thing as a "natural" rate of trials?

2. *The public interest in trials.* Judge Easterbrook treats plea bargains as the best way to honor the rights of the defendant, including the right to autonomy — to determine one's own destiny. But do not offenders forgo any such right when they commit a crime? Do criminal defendants have a constitutional right to bargain? Why should society care about giving free choice to a person who has acted in a way that denies rights (life, health, autonomy, ownership, and so forth) to others? Might the public have a greater interest in public trials than in more convictions? Might the public have an interest in convictions and sentences as close as possible to conceptions of what "really" happened, whether the conviction and sentence follow a trial or a nonbargained guilty plea?

3. *Bargaining and bribery.* Sometimes the government will enter a plea bargain with a defendant in exchange for the defendant's cooperation in other criminal investigations, including testimony against other criminal defendants. Does this sort of plea bargain amount to bribing a witness? Courts never took such an argument seriously until a panel of the U.S. Court of Appeals for the Tenth Circuit reversed a money laundering conviction on the ground that the government had bribed the cooperating witness. A few months later, the en banc court changed direction and upheld the conviction. The "anti-gratuity statute," 18 U.S.C. §201(c)(2), declares that whoever "directly or indirectly, gives, offers, or promises anything of value to any person, for or because of the testimony under oath or affirmation given or to be given by such person" has committed a crime. The en banc court read the word "whoever" to exclude prosecuting attorneys acting within the normal course of their authority. Any other result, the court said, would be a "a radical departure from the ingrained legal culture of our criminal justice system." United States v. Singleton, 165 F.3d 1297 (10th Cir. 1999) (en banc). What would be the effects if prosecutors stopped promising to enter lenient plea agreements with cooperative witnesses? Try to formulate alternatives that prosecutors might adopt to obtain cooperation from witnesses who were involved in alleged crimes.

2. Efforts to Ban Bargaining

Courts and commentators occasionally refer to plea bargaining as eternal and inevitable. It may be inevitable, though it is surely not eternal. Research suggests that plea bargaining was forbidden (at least formally) in the first two-thirds of the nineteenth century, and emerged in the last third of that century, becoming institutionalized and widespread in the twentieth century. See Lawrence Friedman, Plea Bargaining in Historical Perspective, 13 Law & Soc'y Rev. 247 (1979); Albert Alschuler, Plea Bargaining and Its History, 13 Law & Soc'y Rev. 211 (1979).

Professor George Fisher, through careful study of the origins of plea bargaining in nineteenth-century Massachusetts, revealed how plea bargaining first thrived for crimes that gave judges little choice over sentences (and therefore gave added importance to the prosecutor's choice of charges). Bargaining also became more attractive to prosecutors after the appearance of probation as a sentencing option. Judges became more amenable to plea bargaining after a flood of railroad tort suits created civil docket pressures. Fisher, Plea Bargaining's Triumph, 109 Yale L.J. 857 (2000).

Do the following cases indicate that plea bargaining was banned in fact, or do they instead imply a ban in law but a reality of underground bargains? As a historian, how would you determine which of the two stories — true bans, or de jure bans combined with de facto bargains — was closer to the truth?

■ COMMONWEALTH v. JOHN BATTIS
1 Mass. 95 (1804)

The Court will not direct an immediate entry of the plea of guilty to an indictment for a capital crime, but will give a reasonable time to the prisoner to consider the same, that he may, if he think proper, retract his plea.

The defendant, John Battis, a Negro of about twenty years of age, was indicted for the murder of one Salome Talbot, a white girl of the age of thirteen years, on the twenty-eighth day of June last. The indictment contained three counts. The 1st count charged the killing to have been with a stone, with which he beat and broke her skull, and etc. The 2d stated that the killing was by drowning; and the 3d charged the killing to have been by beating and breaking her skull with a stone, and throwing her body into the water, and suffocating and drowning. There was another indictment against the prisoner for committing a rape on the body of the said Salome, on the same day on which the murder was charged to have been committed.

On the second day of the term, in the forenoon, the prisoner was set to the bar, and had both indictments read to him, and pleaded guilty to each. The Court informed him of the consequence of his plea, and that he was under no legal or moral obligation to plead guilty; but that he had a right to deny the several charges, and put the government to the proof of them. He would not retract his pleas; whereupon the Court told him that they would allow him a reasonable time to consider of what had been said to him: and remanded him to prison. They directed the clerk not to record his pleas, at present.

In the afternoon of the same day, the prisoner was again set to the bar, and the indictment for murder was once more read to him; he again pleaded guilty. Upon which the Court examined, under oath, the sheriff, the jailer, and the justice (before whom the examination of the prisoner was had previous to his commitment) as to the sanity of the prisoner; and whether there had not been tampering with him, either by promises, persuasions, or hopes of pardon, if he would plead guilty. On a very full inquiry, nothing of that kind appearing, the prisoner was again remanded, and the clerk directed to record the plea on both indictments.

On the last day of the term, the prisoner was brought to the bar, and the Attorney-general (Sullivan) moved for sentence; which the chief justice delivered in solemn, affecting, and impressive address to the prisoner. The sentence was entered on the indictment for the rape. He has since been executed.

■ GEORGE EDWARDS v. PEOPLE
39 Mich. 760 (1878)

CAMPBELL, C.J.

Plaintiff in error was informed against on a charge of larceny, in the daytime, from a shop, of a gold watch of the value of twenty-five dollars. The information was sworn to on the 25th of June, averring the offense on the 11th. On the same 25th day of June the prisoner was arraigned, pleaded guilty and was sentenced to the Ionia house of correction for three years. . . . The error relied on to reverse the judgment is that the court did not make the proper investigation before proceeding to sentence the prisoner, to ascertain whether he ought not to have been put on trial.

It has always been customary, and is according to many authorities essential before sentence to inquire of the prisoner whether he has anything to say why sentence should not be pronounced against him; and that it is generally said should appear of record. . . .

The Legislature of 1875, having in some way had their attention called to serious abuses caused by procuring prisoners to plead guilty when a fair trial might show they were not guilty, or might show other facts important to be known, passed a very plain and significant statute designed for the protection of prisoners and of the public. It was thereby enacted as follows:

> That whenever any person shall plead guilty to an information filed against him in any circuit court, it shall be the duty of the judge of such court, before pronouncing judgment or sentence upon such plea, to become satisfied, after such investigation as he may deem necessary for that purpose, respecting the nature of the case, and the circumstances of such plea, that said plea was made freely, with full knowledge of the nature of the accusation, and without undue influence. And whenever said judge shall have reason to doubt the truth of such plea of guilty, it shall be his duty to vacate the same, direct a plea of not guilty to be entered, and order a trial of the issue thus formed. . . .

It is contrary to public policy to have any one imprisoned who is not clearly guilty of the precise crime charged against him, and thus equally contrary to policy and justice to punish any one without some regard to the circumstances of the case. By confining this statute to information and not extending it to indictments, it is easy to see that the Legislature thought there was danger that prosecuting attorneys, either to save themselves trouble, to save money to the county, or to serve some other improper purpose, would procure prisoners to plead guilty by assurances they have not power to make of influence in lowering the sentence, or by bringing some other unjust influence to bear on them. It is to be presumed they had evidence before them of serious abuses under the information system which in their judgment required checking by stringent measures.

Every one familiar with the course of criminal justice knows that those officers exercise very extensive and dangerous powers, that in the hands of an arbitrary or corrupt man are capable of great abuse. And unless the general impression is wrong, great abuses have been practiced by this very device of inveigling prisoners into confessions of guilt which could not be lawfully made out against them, and deceiving them concerning the precise character of the charges which they are led to confess. And it has also happened, as is generally believed, that by receiving a plea of guilty from a person whose offense is not aggravated, worse criminals who have used him for their purposes remain unpunished, because the facts which would convict them have not been brought out.

This statute not only requires the judge to examine carefully into the facts of the case, which can require no less than a search into the depositions if they have been returned or similar evidence if they have not been taken, but also compels him to examine the prisoner himself concerning the circumstances which induced him to plead guilty. It is evident that for this purpose it would be highly improper to take any thing on the statement of the prosecuting attorney, or to allow him to be present at the examination of the prisoner. . . . It could not have been contemplated that this should be done during the routine business of court and in presence of all the officers of justice and the prosecutor.

Without deciding that the absence from the record of a recital of such investigation must in all cases void the validity of a sentence on such plea, we have no hesitation in saying that the record ought to show the fact, and unless it does so, must show at least a reasonable delay between plea and sentence which may justify some presumption that this duty has been performed. . . .

Being of opinion that the record before us furnishes presumptive evidence at least that the statute was disregarded, we feel compelled to reverse the judgment.

It is to be hoped that some express provision of law will require the record to note what is done in these cases. The statute is a wholesome one, but in the evident want to care in carrying it out we do not feel warranted in holding that a failure to note the fact on the record is conclusive. It is too important a matter to be left without some more positive direction concerning its appearance on the court journals. Judgment must be reversed, and the prisoner discharged.

Plea bargaining bans are not only part of history. Bans have also appeared from time to time in modern criminal justice. The following article describes several bans on plea bargains, along with other efforts by prosecutors to limit their reliance on plea negotiations. Before reading this article, consider what you would expect to happen when legal systems try to ban plea bargaining. Does the account of New Orleans practices confirm or challenge your expectations?

■ RONALD WRIGHT AND MARC MILLER, THE SCREENING/BARGAINING TRADEOFF
55 Stanford L. Rev. 29 (2002)

When it comes to plea bargaining, we have created a false dilemma. . . . Scholars, judges, prosecutors, defense lawyers, and politicians have offered only two basic responses to the fact that guilt is mostly resolved through negotiated guilty pleas: They take it or they leave it.

Some take the system more or less as it is. They accept negotiated pleas in the ordinary course of events, either because such a system produces good results or because it is inevitable. They might identify some exceptional cases that create an intolerable risk of convicting innocent defendants, or unusual cases where there are special reasons to doubt the knowing and voluntary nature of the defendant's plea. These special cases might call for some regulation. But the mine run of cases, in this view, must be resolved with a heavy dose of plea bargains and a sprinkling of trials.

Then there are those who leave it, arguing that our system's reliance on negotiated guilty pleas is fundamentally mistaken. Some call for a complete ban on negotiated guilty pleas. Others, doubting that an outright ban is feasible, still encourage a clear shift to more short trials to resolve criminal charges. Restoring the criminal trial to its rightful place at the center of criminal justice might require major changes in public spending, and it might take a lifetime, but these critics say the monstrosity of the current system demands such a change.

This dilemma about plea bargaining — take it or leave it — is a false one. It is based on a false dichotomy. It errs in assuming that criminal trials are the only alternative to plea bargains. In this erroneous view, fewer plea bargains lead inexorably to more trials; indeed, the whole point in limiting plea bargains is to produce more trials.

This paper offers a different choice, and points to prosecutorial "screening" as the principal alternative to plea bargains. Of course all prosecutors "screen" when they make any charging decision. By prosecutorial screening we mean a far more structured and reasoned charge selection process than is typical in most prosecutors' offices in this country. The prosecutorial screening system we describe has four interrelated features, all internal to the prosecutor's office: early assessment, reasoned selection, barriers to bargains, and enforcement.

First, the prosecutor's office must make an early and careful assessment of each case, and demand that police and investigators provide sufficient information before the initial charge is filed. Second, the prosecutor's office must file only appropriate charges. Which charges are "appropriate" is determined by several factors. A prosecutor should only file charges that the office would generally want to result in a criminal conviction and sanction. In addition, appropriate charges must reflect reasonably accurately what actually occurred. They are charges that the prosecutor can very likely prove in court. Third, and critically, the office must severely restrict all plea bargaining, and most especially charge bargains. Prosecutors should also recognize explicitly that the screening process is the mechanism that makes such restrictions possible. Fourth, the kind of prosecutorial screening we advocate must include sufficient training, oversight, and other internal enforcement mechanisms to ensure reasonable uniformity in charging and relatively few changes to charges after they have been filed. If prosecutors treat hard screening decisions as the primary alternative to plea bargaining, they can produce changes in current criminal practice that would be fundamental, attractive, and viable. . . .

TRADITIONAL ALTERNATIVES TO PLEA BARGAINING

. . . For those who wish to establish that plea bargaining is an inevitable and irrepressible force in American criminal justice, Philadelphia is a problem. The city has long operated a system that relies more on short bench trials than on pleas of guilty. A number of scholars conducted case studies in Philadelphia (and a few other cities with high rates of bench trials) and concluded that the trials in those cities were not truly adversarial trials. Instead, they were "slow pleas" of guilt. The brief trials allowed the defendant to present evidence about the circumstances of the case, not to obtain an acquittal, but to influence the judge at sentencing.

Stephen Schulhofer visited the Philadelphia courts and took away a different impression. [He] observed a large number of bench trials in the city and concluded that they were genuinely adversarial proceedings where defendants retained many of the constitutional protections sacrificed during plea bargaining. Schulhofer called for other jurisdictions to follow Philadelphia's lead and to treat short trials as a viable alternative to plea bargaining. . . .

Explicit efforts to shorten trials have not been the preferred technique among American prosecutors who want to limit the reach of negotiated pleas. Instead, the handful of prosecutors who aspire to "ban" plea bargaining — either for targeted crimes or for the entire criminal docket — have issued strong ukases against bargaining, enforced by more rigorous screening and modest staffing increases, as their most workable solution. . . .

Among the most famous American plea bargaining bans occurred in Alaska during the 1970s and 1980s. In 1975, state Attorney General Avrum Gross declared that prosecutors would no longer engage in charge bargaining or sentence bargaining. Attorney General Gross hoped to restore public confidence in the system, increase the number of trials, improve the litigation skills of prosecutors, and return prosecutors to their traditional roles of evaluating evidence and trying cases instead of negotiating.

Major studies in 1978 and 1991 evaluated the impact of the Alaska plea ban. By all accounts, both charge bargaining and sentence bargaining became rare events during the first ten years of the policy. During the late 1980s, charge bargains reappeared, but prosecutors continued to avoid sentence bargains. For a few years, the trial rate increased modestly. Seven percent of charged cases went to trial before the ban, and the rate moved to 10% before returning to 7% by the end of the 1980s.

Since the cases were not ending in negotiated pleas or trials, what was happening to them? The answer was a combination of aggressive screening and open guilty pleas. Before the ban, prosecutors in Fairbanks refused to prosecute about 4% of the felonies referred to them by the police or other investigators. After the ban, the proportion of felonies that prosecutors declined to prosecute increased to about 44%. A large portion of the case load (about 23%) was disposed of through open pleas of guilt. This was part of the Attorney General's thinking when he created the plea ban. More careful selection of cases would make it possible to stick with the initial charges, even in front of a judge or jury.

The Alaska experience received lackluster academic reviews. Some implied that the failure to increase trials proved that unseen bargains were still driving the system, and explained the high number of open guilty pleas. Others pointed to the reappearance of charge bargaining after ten years, and suggested that it is futile to place controls on the quintessential prosecutorial decision of charge selection. Some implied that Alaska was too unusual a jurisdiction to offer any guidance to prosecutors in most major American cities. However, other jurisdictions scattered around the country have duplicated pieces of the Alaska experience over the years. Some prosecutors in other locales have picked out priority crimes like homicide and banned plea bargains for those cases.[53] Some of the bans target particular forms of bargaining rather than particular crimes.[54] The reaction to these experiences, like the reaction to the Alaska plea ban, has been subdued. If these prosecutors were not increasing their trial rates, the critics found the effort unimportant.

These experiences do not mean that any ban on charge reductions will produce small trial increases and large numbers of open guilty pleas. If prosecutors do not change their screening principles to insist on more declinations of cases referred to the office, the dispositions shift in other directions. In El Paso County, Texas during the 1980s, the chief prosecutor announced an end to all plea bargaining in burglary cases. There was no organized effort to change the screening of such cases, and the

53. In the 1970s, the prosecutor in Maricopa County (Phoenix), Arizona barred plea bargains in cases involving designated crimes such as drug sales, homicide, robbery, burglary, assault with a deadly weapon, and sexual misconduct. The policy did not increase trial rates for these crimes because more defendants pled guilty as charged. Moise Berger, *The Case Against Plea Bargaining*, 62 A.B.A. J. 621 (1976). Similar reports came after prosecutors in Multnomah County, Oregon and Black Hawk County, Iowa banned plea bargaining for selected crimes during the early 1970s. Note, The Elimination of Plea Bargaining in Black Hawk County: A Case Study, 60 Iowa L. Rev. 1053 (1975). . . .

54. In an example of one such effort to discourage some forms of bargaining, the District Attorney for Manhattan in the mid-1970s prohibited his attorneys from recommending sentences and established (and published!) a 1974 memorandum suggesting specific charge discounts to offer in exchange for guilty pleas. Richard H. Kuh, Plea Bargaining: Guidelines for the Manhattan District Attorney's Office, 11 Crim. L. Bull. 48 (1975). Thomas Church documented the efforts of a county in a Midwestern state during the early 1970s to eliminate charge bargaining in drug sale cases. Thomas Church, Jr., Plea Bargains, Concessions and the Courts: Analysis of a Quasi-Experiment, 10 Law & Soc'y Rev. 377 (1976). The prosecutor left sentence bargaining in place, and the proportion of the cases resolved through defendants pleading guilty as charged increased from 17 to 90% between 1972 and 1974. In Church's view, the county's experience demonstrated the inevitability of plea bargaining. But his interviewees believed that the concessions the defendants were promised after the ban were far less reliable and valuable than the concessions they negotiated before the ban.

number of trials increased enough to create a serious backlog of untried cases. Partial bans on plea bargaining appear regularly around the country. Most prosecutors today who plan to restrict plea negotiations focus on priority crimes, such as homicide or sex crimes. Some of the bans are limited to particular courts or phases of litigation, such as the statutory ban on plea bargains for most serious felonies in Superior Court in California, or the ban on plea bargaining in the Supreme Court in the Bronx in the mid-1990s.

When plea bans are limited to a particular court (such as the highest trial court), the effects are usually minimal because the bargainers simply move to a different (typically earlier) point in the process. Plea bans exist today, but we know little about their effects on case dispositions and sentences. The attention of academic observers has strayed to other areas, even as prosecutors keep innovating. . . . Thirty years of scholarship has missed a fundamental perspective on plea bargaining: there are in fact many alternative points of comparison when assessing the wisdom and necessity of plea bargains. . . .

THE SCREENING/BARGAINING TRADEOFF IN PRACTICE: NODA DATA

A chief prosecutor attempting to change plea practices faces both administrative and political hurdles. Will her proposed policy actually change the use of negotiated guilty pleas? If so, can the office sustain it over the long haul? We do not believe that plea bargaining is inevitable, but plea bargaining surely is pervasive and deeply entrenched. Any effort to limit plea bargaining must confront the habits and relationships of prosecutors and defense attorneys.

Reform efforts emerging voluntarily from within one criminal justice institution may have a greater chance to succeed than reforms imposed externally. A single institution can set up review and reward systems, allowing for more supervision — and, we believe, more consistency — than external constraints can provide. Among the many virtues we see in the screening/bargaining tradeoff described in this paper is the authority of a chief prosecutor, acting alone, to set this change in motion.

What should we expect to happen when a prosecutor decides to shift the screening/bargaining tradeoff in the direction of screening? As for changes in case processing, the most direct effect should be measurable: fewer plea bargains. The kinds of plea bargains that are easiest to track are charge reductions after cases are filed. A jurisdiction with hard screening practices should produce fewer and smaller charge reductions than jurisdictions with weaker screening practices.

[We can] test the plausibility of the screening/bargaining tradeoff using previously unstudied and unreported data about one major urban prosecutor's office: the New Orleans District Attorney's Office, or NODA. This data exists because the District Attorney for Orleans Parish, Harry Connick, has remained committed to principled screening throughout his long term in office. . . .

Harry Connick was elected as the District Attorney for Orleans Parish in 1974. He has remained in that office for the past twenty-eight years. Connick first ran for office in 1969 against incumbent Jim Garrison, the flamboyant District Attorney made famous in the film JFK. His first unsuccessful campaign did not focus on plea bargaining. He promised faster prosecution and better tracking of defendants who failed to appear for trial. His 1973 campaign began with a similar emphasis on swift prosecution. As the campaign wore on, however, Connick's speeches began to feature attacks on plea bargaining. . . .

Connick told voters that widespread plea bargaining was wrong; years later, he explained that victims were right to resent it when cases were bargained away simply because of a "lazy" prosecutor. He promised to eliminate "baseless" plea bargaining and to hire full-time prosecutors who would not use plea bargains just to move cases from the docket.

As in other American cities, the criminal courts in New Orleans deal with enormous volume. In the face of this large urban caseload, Connick needed a strategy to carry out his campaign statements about plea bargaining. During the weeks between his election victory and taking office, he started speaking publicly about a plan with two central components. First, Connick planned to devote expertise and resources to screening. He proposed a screening procedure that "would weed out those cases really not worthy of being on the criminal docket, so more courtroom emphasis can be devoted to the violent offender." Second, he instructed his prosecutors not to engage in plea bargaining — particularly charge bargaining — except under very limited circumstances. . . .

The distinctiveness of the screening process in the NODA office is apparent from a closer examination of the path each new case takes through the system. Police officers develop a case folder after they complete an investigation and file charges with the magistrate. The first stop for the case folder in the NODA office is the Magistrate Section, where the least experienced assistants work. They typically have logged six months or fewer on the job. The ADA from the Magistrate Section appears for the state at the first appearance and bail hearing before the magistrate. A public defender is also present for the first appearance, but the case is reassigned immediately after the hearing and there is typically no further defense presence or participation in the case until after the DA files an information or obtains an indictment.

After any proceedings in the Magistrate Division, the folder moves to the Screening Section of the NODA office. Connick devotes extraordinary resources to this operation. For instance, in the late 1990s, about fifteen of the eighty-five attorneys in the office worked in Screening. . . . All attorneys in the Screening Section served previously (usually a couple of years) in the Trial Section. This level of experience comes at a premium in New Orleans, where the turnover among prosecuting attorneys is quite high. The average tenure of an ADA in the NODA office is around two years.

Within the Screening Section, designated cases such as homicide or rape get assigned to screeners with special expertise. Drug cases and a few other high-volume cases go to a subgroup known as Expedited Screening. Ordinary cases go to the Screening Attorney on duty for that day. The screener reviews the investigation file, speaks to all the key witnesses and the victims (often by telephone, but sometimes in person), and generally gauges the strength of the case. If the police report neglects to mention a factual issue that is likely to arise at trial, the screening attorney will speak directly with the police officer to resolve it. There is a powerful office expectation that the Screening Attorney will make a decision within ten days of receiving the folder.

NODA instituted a variety of measures to ensure reasonable uniformity in screening decisions. Connick committed his screening principles to writing in an office policy manual. The general office policy is to charge the most serious crime the facts will support at trial. The policy does not, on its face, allow individual prosecutors to consider for themselves the equities in the case when selecting the charge.

By the same token, however, Connick insists that overcharging is unacceptable, because the charges chosen for the information will stay in place through the trial. If screening prosecutors overcharge cases too often, the Chief of the Trial Section might send the screening attorney back into the courtroom on at least one of those overcharged matters to "get his teeth kicked in."

Supervisors review all refusals to charge. Attorneys say they often compare notes, especially in early morning discussions, and this helps to educate and develop shared charging norms in the office. Office policy discourages refusal for select categories of crimes, notably domestic violence cases. For the most serious crimes, including rape and homicide, the office conducts "charge conferences" with senior prosecutors and police present to discuss the facts and potential charges.

Neither Connick nor any attorneys in his office claim to have abolished plea bargaining entirely from the New Orleans system. Prosecutors in the office acknowledge that sometimes new information appears and changes the value of a case. Witnesses leave town, victims decide not to testify, new witnesses appear, and investigators find new evidence. On occasion, the screening attorney makes a bad judgment and overcharges, and a plea could save the case.

Nevertheless, office policy tries to keep these changes in charges to a minimum. A supervisor must approve any decision to drop or change charges after the information is filed. The attorney requesting the change must complete a special form naming the screening and trial attorneys, and explaining the reason for the decision, drawing from a list of acceptable reasons. The ADAs believe there is a "stigma" involved in reducing charges, however strong the reasons for a reduction might be.

Attorneys from the NODA office believe that they decline to prosecute an exceptional number of cases. They view this as a necessary part of training police officers to investigate more thoroughly. The relatively high rate of declination also created a political challenge for Connick over the years. During each of his reelection campaigns — in 1978, 1984, 1990, and 1996 — Connick's challengers criticized the number of cases that the NODA office declined to prosecute. As his opponent Morris Reed put it in many public debates, "the PD arrests them and the DA turns them loose." Connick had several replies. Poor police work made declinations necessary. Further, he pointed to specific examples of how his office dealt severely with defendants once they were charged. Connick also explicitly linked his screening policies to his plea bargaining policies: Tough screening, he said, made it possible to keep plea bargaining at low levels.

Connick drew on case data to make specific claims about low rates of plea bargaining in the office: He asserted that plea bargaining in Jim Garrison's day reached 60 to 70%, but fell to 7 or 8% of all cases filed under his office policy. He also routinely mentioned the high number of trials in New Orleans compared to other Louisiana jurisdictions. In addition, Connick pointed to his routine use of the habitual felon law to enhance sentences. By the end of each of the four reelection campaigns, Connick convinced the voters that it was possible both to decline many cases and to run a tough prosecutor's office at the same time. . . .

The data mostly support District Attorney Harry Connick's claims to have implemented a screening/bargaining tradeoff over the last thirty years. Several kinds of information bolster that judgment, but the most substantial and useful by far is the data that Connick has kept to assist in his administration of the office. New Orleans shows that the screening/bargaining tradeoff does not necessarily lead to a disabling number of trials. The office also shows that a committed prosecutor can implement the screening/bargaining tradeoff even without the conscious support of other actors in the system. . . . Plea bargaining's triumph, and the cynical products of that triumph, are simply not as absolute as a century of practice and study suggest.

Notes

1. *The isolated popularity of bans.* Though a minor theme in current criminal justice debates, bans on plea bargaining occasionally become a topic of public concern, and they remain a subject of intense scholarly interest. Jurisdictions other than Alaska have experimented with formal plea bans, though none have been statewide; most are implemented by a single prosecutor with a particular vision for improving the criminal justice system. Other modern efforts to abolish plea bargaining include a ban in El Paso, Texas; a Detroit ban on bargaining in felony firearm cases; another effort in Michigan to abolish charge bargaining in drug trafficking cases; and a judge-imposed ban in Superior Court in New Hampshire. See Amy Fixsen, Plea Bargaining: The New Hampshire "Ban," 9 New Eng. J. on Crim. & Civ. Confinement 387 (1983); Robert Weninger, The Abolition of Plea Bargaining: A Case Study of El Paso County, Texas, 35 UCLA L. Rev. 265 (1987); see generally 13 Law & Soc'y Rev. (1979). A recent effort in the Bronx District Attorney's office banned bargains in felony cases after indictment. See Kenneth Jost, Critics Blast New York Plea Ban, 9 CQ Researcher No. 6, at 124 (Feb. 12, 1999). Which aspect of plea bargaining do these reforms target? Is selective restriction on bargaining preferable to a total ban?

2. *Alternatives to plea bargaining.* If bargains are banned, what takes their place? The Alaska and New Orleans experiences suggest that guilty plea rates may remain quite high even in the absence of bargains. Why might this be so? Professor Schulhofer and others have argued that it is possible to offer meaningful trials in place of bargains, including greater use of bench rather than jury trials. See Stephen Schulhofer, Is Plea Bargaining Inevitable? 97 Harv. L. Rev. 1037 (1984) (discussing use of short trials in Philadelphia). In an article excerpted at the beginning of this section, Professor Alschuler makes a particularly eloquent argument in favor of offering some kind of trial over any kind of bargain: "In providing elaborate trials to a minority of defendants while pressing all others to abandon their right to trial, our nation allocates its existing resources about as sensibly as a nation that attempted to solve its transportation problem by giving Cadillacs to ten percent of the population while requiring everyone else to travel by foot. . . . [L]ess would be more. . . ." Does the New Orleans District Attorney offer defendants, as a group, less procedural protection or less favorable outcomes than they might receive in a jurisdiction that negotiates more routinely for reduced charges?

3. *The inevitability of plea bargaining reconsidered.* The Alaska experience suggests that in some jurisdictions, at least, it is possible to have not only a formal plea ban, but one that causes substantial changes in the behavior of the key actors. But even in Alaska pressures led, over the course of a decade, to decay in the original stark vision of a land without bargains. Are bans likely to be effective only for a short time? Are plea bargains an inevitable answer to pressures within the justice system (whether

political, legal, social, or economic)? See generally Milton Heumann, Plea Bargaining: The Experiences of Prosecutors, Judges, and Defense Attorneys (1978). Can individual lawyers or judges "ban" bargaining? For a ban to work, does there need to be a more proportional and modest system of punishments? Is plea bargaining a necessity or virtue in highly punitive times? In other words, does a world with no plea bargaining require penalties that judges and prosecutors are actually comfortable enforcing?

VII

Decisionmakers at Trial

More than 90 percent of all criminal charges are resolved through plea bargains and guilty pleas, leaving less than 10 percent that go to trial. Looking at trials from this vantage point, however, obscures four important points. First, for some kinds of offenses and offenders, the trial rate is considerably higher. For example, in 2002 in state courts, over 45 percent of murder convictions were obtained through trial. Generally, trial rates for violent offenses against persons are higher than for property, drug, and weapons offenses.

Second, 10 percent of all charges may seem small compared with the proportion of charges settled through plea bargains, but there are still a large number of criminal trials in most U.S. jurisdictions. In 2002, for example, there were over 1,050,000 felony convictions in state courts. While 95 percent of the convictions were obtained through guilty pleas, there were still over 52,000 felony trials. A small change in the plea rate can have a major impact on the number of trials and the operation of court systems.

Third, there is not just one kind of trial. Public perception often seems to be shaped by long, high-profile trials. But in fact, most trials are short. In 2000, for example, of the 6,746 federal criminal trials, 48 percent were completed in a single day, 17 percent lasted two days, and 12 percent took three days. Thus, more than three-quarters of federal criminal trials were completed in three days or less. In contrast, 4 percent of the criminal trials lasted 10 days or longer. About half of state felony trials are handled by judges sitting without a jury. Judges try a much higher percentage of misdemeanor trials, though the rate varies enormously among the states and the proportion of the roughly 12 million misdemeanors each year that go to trial is difficult to determine.

Finally, plea bargaining practices do not develop in a vacuum: They reflect to some degree the availability, benefits, and costs of trials. For example, when sanctions imposed after trials start to resemble sanctions imposed after guilty pleas, more

454 VII ■ Decisionmakers at Trial

VII ■ Decisionmakers at Trial

defendants are likely to go to trial since there is always some chance that the government will fail to prove the case or that a jury or judge will find the defendant not guilty for some other reason.

A useful perspective for studying the U.S. trial system is to consider not only the substantial variety within the United States but the very different processes used in other countries. For example, the paradigm decisionmaker in U.S. criminal trials — the criminal jury — is virtually unknown in some other lands. Other countries employ institutions not familiar in the United States, such as multi-judge panels in criminal cases. In Germany lone judges try minor offenses, but more serious offenses are tried before panels made up of "professional" and "lay" judges.

The fact that other places conduct trials in other ways serves as a reminder that the U.S. justice system involves choices. One fundamental question about U.S. criminal trials is why they are relatively rare, compared with plea bargains, and whether that is a good or bad thing. If public criminal trials are preferred to private (and regulated) bargains, will different rules produce more trials?

This chapter examines different decisionmakers at trial. The first section examines the choice between jury and judge trials. The second and third sections study the procedures for selecting jurors and guiding juries as they perform their function. The final section considers the role of a decisionmaker in a larger sense — the public — in watching, reviewing, and judging criminal trials.

A. JUDGE OR JURY?

Perhaps the most distinctive feature of American criminal trials is the criminal jury. While studying these materials and the law related to juries, you should also sit as a judge, assessing the continuing vitality and relevance of this complicated and expensive institution. Consider whether the original assumptions and justifications for the criminal jury remain true today, or whether some other institution (perhaps judges) or some other form (perhaps smaller juries or juries that can convict on a majority vote) would be more appropriate.

1. Availability of Jury Trial

The Sixth Amendment provides in part: "In all criminal prosecutions, the accused shall enjoy the right to a speedy and public trial, by an impartial jury." The U.S. Supreme Court determined in Duncan v. Louisiana, 391 U.S. 145 (1968), that this fundamental right applies to the states through the due process clause of the Fourteenth Amendment. Despite the absolute language of the amendment ("*all* criminal prosecutions"), the right is not absolute; the constitutional guaranty of a jury trial does not cover "petty offenses." The *Duncan* Court explained that jury trials were not available historically for petty crimes and that non-jury trials are faster and less expensive than jury trials.

The question of which crimes qualify as "petty" crimes has enormous practical consequences because the largest number of cases in American criminal justice systems involve less serious (but not necessarily "petty") crimes. The Court in Baldwin v. New York, 399 U.S. 66 (1970), relied on the history of the Sixth Amendment in concluding that it was meant to protect jury trials only in cases that were triable by a jury at common law. In later cases, it has become clear that a "serious" offense covered by the federal right to jury trial must be punishable by a prison term of more than six months. In Blanton v. City of North Las Vegas, 489 U.S. 538, 541-42 (1989), the Court stated the test as follows:

> In determining whether a particular offense should be categorized as "petty," our early decisions focused on the nature of the offense and on whether it was triable by a jury at common law. In recent years, however, we have sought more objective indications of the seriousness with which society regards the offense. We have found the most relevant such criteria in the severity of the maximum authorized penalty. . . . In using the word "penalty," we do not refer solely to the maximum prison term authorized for a particular offense. A legislature's view of the seriousness of an offense also is reflected in the other penalties that it attaches to the offense. . . . Primary emphasis, however, must be placed on the maximum authorized period of incarceration.

The Court in *Blanton* held that a charge under Nevada's DUI statute, which had a maximum authorized prison term of six months as well as other possible penalties (including fines and wearing distinctive clothing to identify the offender as a convicted drunk driver), was not "constitutionally serious." In United States v. Nachtigal, 507 U.S. 1 (1993), the Court reiterated that "offenses for which the maximum period of incarceration is six months or less are presumptively 'petty.' . . . A defendant can overcome this presumption, and become entitled to a jury trial, only by showing that the additional mix of penalties, viewed together with the maximum prison term, are so severe that the legislature clearly determined that the offense is a 'serious' one." In *Nachtigal,* the Court held that a DUI charge with a maximum penalty of six months' imprisonment, a $5,000 fine, a five-year term of probation, and several other penalties, was not constitutionally serious.

Most state constitutions, like the federal constitution, protect the right to a jury trial. State courts interpreting these provisions have most often determined, like the U.S. Supreme Court, that the right to a jury trial applies only to "serious" offenses. However, most state courts have chosen a different line of demarcation between serious and petty offenses. State legislatures have also passed statutes guaranteeing a jury trial in a wider range of cases than the state or federal constitutions require. The majority and dissenting opinions in the following case offer two very different and archetypal approaches to the question of when a case is serious enough to warrant a jury trial.

■ STATE v. KENT BOWERS
498 N.W.2d 202 (S.D. 1993)

MILLER, C.J.

. . . On April 12, 1990, a large group of people, which included [Kent Bowers and four other appellants], gathered at the Women's Medical Clinic in Sioux Falls, South Dakota, to protest against abortions taking place there and to dissuade patients from entering the clinic to obtain an abortion. Prior to this protest, the organizers had met with police in hopes of keeping their protest peaceful. The protest consisted of praying, singing and reading the bible. The protesters congregated on the parking lot and lawn of the clinic and blocked the south and east doors into the clinic. Although the protesters made no threats and induced no violence, they obstructed at least one person's access to the clinic.

The police were called to the clinic. Anticipating a violent protest, they called in seventy-seven officers, including twenty-one off-duty officers. . . . An officer, using a bull horn to amplify his voice, read a statement to the protesters ordering them to leave the clinic's property. [P]rotesters crossed the police barrier to go back onto clinic property and to resume blocking the south and east doors of the clinic. The police then began to arrest protesters. . . . The arrested protesters were charged with one count of unlawful occupancy of property in violation of [a state misdemeanor statute] and one count of disorderly assembly in violation of [a Sioux Falls ordinance].

The protesters requested jury trials. . . . The magistrate judge denied the motions for jury trials, assuring the protesters that he would impose no jail sentences in the event they were found guilty. . . . The protesters were found guilty on both counts. The magistrate judge then imposed fines and jail sentences which included seven to fourteen days jail time which was suspended on the condition of no like offenses for one year. [On appeal, the] circuit judge affirmed the convictions but modified the sentences imposed by deleting the suspended jail time. This appeal followed.

The United States Constitution provides in part: "In all criminal prosecutions, the accused shall enjoy the right to a speedy and public trial, by an impartial jury of the State and district wherein the crime shall have been committed." U.S. Const. Amend. VI. This right, however, does not extend to crimes which carry a possible jail penalty of only six months' imprisonment. Baldwin v. New York, 399 U.S. 66 (1970).

The South Dakota Constitution provides in part: "In all criminal prosecutions the accused shall have the right to . . . a speedy public trial by an impartial jury of the county or district in which the offense is alleged to have been committed." S.D. Const. Art. VI, §7; SDCL 23A-16-3. In State v. Wikle, 291 N.W.2d 792 (S.D. 1980), this court explained that the right to a jury trial extends to a criminal prosecution for which there could be imposed "a direct penalty of incarceration for any period of time." In 1984, this court modified *Wikle* when we held "a court may deny a jury trial request in a criminal prosecution when the court assures the defendant at the time of request that no jail sentence will be imposed. This is, of course, limited to prosecution of offenses with maximum authorized jail sentences of less than six months." State v. Auen, 342 N.W.2d 236 (S.D. 1984). Appellants argue that the magistrate judge erred because the sentences imposed on them are beyond the scope of *Auen*.

Violators of either the state law, a Class 2 misdemeanor, or the municipal ordinance here at issue could, at the time of the alleged offenses, be punished by a maximum of thirty days in a county jail, a $100 fine, or both. When the magistrate judge was presented with the requests for jury trials, he noted that although he has granted jury trials in petty theft cases, he would not grant appellants jury trials. The magistrate judge assured appellants he would impose no jail sentences in the event they were found guilty. Nevertheless, after the trial the magistrate judge imposed suspended jail sentences as well as fines. The magistrate judge then placed appellants on probation for one year. . . .

On appeal, the circuit court noted that as the magistrate court "denied the jury trial upon this assurance [of no jail sentence], a final judgment entered imposing a suspended seven days in the county jail was contrary to the assurance of the court." The circuit court then modified the sentences imposed and deleted the portions of the judgments which imposed jail time. We agree with the circuit court judge that the magistrate judge improperly imposed a one-year probation with suspended jail sentences. . . . The circuit court's subsequent judgment cured the magistrate judge's improper sentencing.

We note further that appellants were not denied their Sixth Amendment right to a jury trial by being placed on probation for one year. No jail sentence remains which can be imposed on appellants even in the event that their suspended sentences are revoked. Of that part of the sentence which remained after the circuit court's judgment, not "one day of the defendant's freedom was involved . . . but only his pocketbook." *Wikle,* 291 N.W.2d at 795 (Henderson, J., concurring specially). Appellants were not improperly denied a jury trial. . . . Affirmed.

HENDERSON, J., concurring in part, dissenting in part.

. . . In the case before us, appellants were charged with disorderly assembly and unlawful occupancy of property. Whereas both offenses carry a maximum jail time of six months, the magistrate trial judge denied the request for a jury trial: "I'm not, first of all, going to open up the Pandora's box of giving trials to every Class 2 offense. I have done that in petty theft cases because no one wants to be a thief, but otherwise I'm not going to open up that box . . . so the request for a jury trial will be denied."

Attempting to follow *Auen,* the magistrate trial court assured the appellants that they would receive no jail sentence. Nevertheless, after the trial, the magistrate court imposed suspended sentences, community service, fines and probation. Although the circuit court eliminated the suspended sentences . . . , the one-year probation remained intact.

Both the magistrate court and circuit court erred in denying appellants a jury trial based upon the crime being a petty offense with no jail time. The first problem is defining "petty." Although the meaning and scope of petty crimes are not statutorily defined, the Court announced a formula in *Wikle* to distinguish the two. Courts must look to the maximum punishment and the nature of the offense, consider the common law background of the offense, determine if society views the offense with sufficient opprobrium, and consider the consequences of conviction.

Furthermore, Baldwin v. New York, 399 U.S. 66 (1970), does not hold that offenses which carry a maximum punishment of six months or less are automatically petty offenses. Rather, when deciding if an offense is "petty," the U.S. Supreme Court seeks out objective criteria reflecting the seriousness with which society regards the offense, and "we have found the most relevant such criteria in the severity of the maximum authorized penalty." Attempting to heed to that holding, this state broadly defines a "petty crime" as an offense that carries a maximum jail time of six months or less. *Auen.* What happened to our "eternal vigilance" here — as commanded by Thomas Jefferson, as being "the price of liberty"?

Under *Baldwin,* we are supposed to be looking at the maximum penalty, not simply jail time. Had appellants been charged with the state law version of disorderly assembly, rather than the city version, they would have violated a Class 1 misdemeanor with a maximum incarceration of one year. Thus, under state law, the court could not deny the appellants their mandatory and constitutionally guaranteed jury trial. Admittedly, these appellants were not charged with the state version. However, the inequity is obvious: Prosecutors can deftly deny a defendant a jury trial by simply charging him with the city version of a crime.

Granted, police and prosecutors may arrest and charge at their own discretion. But in Sioux Falls, a person can be denied a jury trial if the city officials believe the actions are petty, even though the state categorizes the actions as serious or when the judge decides not to "open up the Pandora's box," or when the prosecutor, as he stated during the motion hearing, does not want the appellants to use "the Court system as a forum by which to politicize their beliefs."

Despite the majority's labeling it as such, this protest was anything but petty. Before the protests began, organizers met with the police in hopes of keeping their assembly peaceful. Anticipating problems, the police, on the other hand, called in 21 off-duty officers, sent 77 officers to the protest, rented buses, brought video cameras, instituted new methods for arresting and identifying arrestees who might not be carrying identification. This was all set up in advance at an expense of nearly $5,000. Police Captain Gerald Kiesacker stated that he had anticipated more violence and more resistance than at previous similar demonstrations. Consider: The press was given its own observation area during the arrests. Petty? Baloney! . . .

Additionally, placing appellants on a one-year probation without benefit of a jury trial also denied them their Sixth Amendment rights. . . . Probation is an alternative to confinement where the defendant is under the control of the trial court in a manner designed to avoid incarceration. Public protection is provided through the ability of the trial court to revoke probation and impose a sentence should the defendant violate the terms of the probation. . . .

Thus, appellants were subject to a one-year punishment, a violation of which could subject them to jail time. Furthermore, though they may not be incarcerated, their actions are still under the disciplinary eye of the trial court. Appellants Dorr and Ellenbecker took jail time in lieu of the fine. . . . Today's holding permits a penalty beyond [the] six-month boundary. Probation, in itself, involves the freedom of a defendant. Even under the logic of *Baldwin* and *Auen,* the defendant escapes the grasp of the State within six months. Is not the purpose of the courts to protect, not chisel away, the rights of the accused? . . .

When the shadows are cast upon my judicial mantle, I am comforted with the conviction that I stood for jury trials and not against them. As Teddy Roosevelt once expressed: "I shall not join those weak and timid souls who know neither victory nor defeat." I have fought the good fight. Under the Statist's muskets, I have again fallen. So what. "Woe unto you, when all men shall speak well of you!" [Luke 6:26]. And so it may be said of these appellants.

■ MARYLAND COURTS AND JUDICIAL PROCEEDINGS CODE §12-401

(d) A defendant who has been found guilty of a municipal infraction . . . or a Code violation . . . may appeal from the final judgment entered in the District Court. . . .

(f) [In any criminal case, including a] case in which sentence has been imposed or suspended following a plea of nolo contendere or guilty, and an appeal in a municipal infraction or Code violation case, an appeal shall be tried de novo [in the trial court of original jurisdiction for felonies, the Circuit Court].

(g) In a criminal appeal that is tried de novo, there is no right to a jury trial unless the offense charged is subject to a penalty of imprisonment or unless there is a constitutional right to a jury trial for that offense.

Notes

1. *Jury trials and petty offenses under state constitutions: majority position.* Virtually all state constitutions guarantee the right to a jury trial, often by stating that the right "shall remain inviolate." Does this language suggest an effort to preserve a right in its limited historical form rather than an effort to declare a more extensive right based in natural law? Most state courts have concluded that the state constitution does not require a jury trial for all offenses, but only for "serious" (as opposed to "petty") offenses. However, most state courts disagree with the federal constitutional definition of a "petty" crime. The federal courts look primarily to the length of imprisonment imposed as an "objective" measure of a crime's seriousness for purposes of a jury trial. A crime whose punishment is more than six months' imprisonment is "presumptively" serious; any crime that is punished by a shorter term of imprisonment is very difficult to establish as "serious" under the Sixth Amendment, even when coupled with substantial fines and other penalties. Some state courts agree with this approach. See, e.g., State v. Smith, 672 P.2d 631 (Nev. 1983) (no jury trial for six-month prison term authorized for drunken-driving offense). A larger group of states adopt the federal methodology (focusing on the length of the prison term) but conclude that some shorter period of potential or actual imprisonment is enough to trigger the right to a jury trial. The majority opinion in *Bowers* offers an example of this approach. See also State v. Lindsey, 883 P.2d 83 (Haw. 1994) (30 days). Many states declare that any defendant facing the possibility of incarceration is entitled to a jury trial. See Opinion of the Justices (DWI Jury Trials), 608 A.2d 202 (N.H. 1992); State v. Dusina, 764 S.W.2d 766 (Tenn. 1989).

A substantial number of state courts reject the federal methodology for determining the scope of the right to a jury trial. Some of these courts continue to insist that jury trials are available only for the most serious crimes, but they give great weight to factors other than the length of potential or actual incarceration in deciding which crimes are serious. The dissenting opinion in *Bowers* illustrates this approach. See also Fisher v. State, 504 A.2d 626 (Md. 1986) (considers historical treatment of offense, "infamous" nature of offense, maximum authorized sentence, and place of incarceration). Other courts inquire about the "punitive" nature of the fines imposed. A number of courts turn to history to determine whether the offense is analogous to some crime that was tried by jury at the time the federal constitution was adopted. Medlock v. 1985 Ford F-150 Pick Up, 417 S.E.2d 85 (S.C. 1992). Are judicial decisions that look beyond the statutory length of authorized incarceration giving less authority to the legislature? State courts in more than 10 states have declared that the state constitution requires jury trials for all "offenses." The only exceptions involve crimes with trivial punishments or other characteristics that make them criminal offenses in name only. See Mitchell v. Superior Court, 783 P.2d 731 (Cal. 1989) (en banc) (jury trial for all misdemeanors and felonies and all infractions punishable by imprisonment); State v. Anton, 463 A.2d 703 (Me. 1983). If you were a state legislator hoping to draft a new criminal statute, would you prefer your state courts to use one of these constitutional approaches over the others?

2. *Statutory right to jury trials.* It is common to find state statutes that extend the right to a jury trial to a broader range of cases than the federal or state constitution requires. Some statutes provide a jury trial for a particular offense without declaring any general rule about the availability of jury trials. Others declare generally the minimum lengths of incarceration or minimum fine amounts that will create a right to a jury. See Neahring v. State, 804 P.2d 1142 (Okla. Crim. App. 1991) (jury trial for charge of running stop sign; statute provides jury trial for any offense punishable by $20 fine); Ohio Rev. Code §2945.17 (jury trial for any offense punishable by a fine exceeding $100); Ill. Ann. Stat. ch. 725, para. 103-6 (jury trial for "[e]very person accused of an offense"); see also ABA Standards for Criminal Justice, Trial by Jury 15-1.1(a) (3d ed. 1996) (jury trial should be available in prosecutions in which confinement in jail or prison may be imposed). Another type of statute grants a right to jury trial for less serious cases but places conditions on the exercise of the right, such as the payment of a fee. See Colo. Stat. §16-10-109 (granting jury trial for petty offenses, provided defendant pays $25 fee). A common form of this "conditional" statutory right to a jury trial appears in two-tiered court systems; the Maryland statute offers an example. These laws provide for jury trials in all cases falling within the jurisdiction of a felony-level trial court, and allow any defendant in a case initially charged and tried in the misdemeanor-level trial court to appeal the case for a trial de novo (before a jury) in the felony-level court. This system, in effect, gives even those charged with misdemeanors a statutory right to a jury trial, but only for those who persist in an appeal from the misdemeanor court. See, e.g., Ark. Code §16-17-703. Do such "conditional" systems effectively deny the right to a jury trial to those defendants without the resources or persistence to jump through the proper hoops before receiving a jury? See Ludwig v. Massachusetts, 427 U.S. 618 (1976) (upholding against due process challenge a two-tier system with de novo jury trial for those convicted of minor crimes in lower-level court).

3. *Combining petty offenses.* Will a defendant receive a jury trial if she faces several "petty" charges, where convictions on the multiple counts would authorize the judge to impose a sentence longer than six months? In Lewis v. United States, 518 U.S. 322 (1996), the Court held that a defendant who is prosecuted in a single proceeding for multiple petty offenses does not have a Sixth Amendment right to a jury trial. Lewis was charged with two counts of obstructing the mail, each charge carrying a maximum authorized prison sentence of six months. The Court concluded that Congress, by setting the maximum prison term at six months, had categorized the offense as petty. Congress's judgment, and not the punishment imposed in a particular case, determines the seriousness of an offense under the Sixth Amendment. See also People v. Foy, 673 N.E.2d 589 (N.Y. 1996). Criminal contempt charges have received a more complex treatment. Traditionally, state law empowers a judge to punish acts in contempt of court, without defining the maximum authorized punishment. According to Codispoti v. Pennsylvania, 418 U.S. 506 (1974), a jury trial is necessary in multiple contempt proceedings when the combined sentence for all acts of contempt exceeds six months. How might you reconcile *Codispoti* and *Lewis*?

4. *Trial at option of prosecutor or judge.* As the *Bowers* case from South Dakota illustrates, judges in most courts can avoid a jury trial for some crimes that authorize prison or jail sentences if they commit before the trial not to incarcerate the

defendants after conviction. The trial court in *Bowers* made such a promise but imposed a "suspended" prison term, which the offender does not serve unless he fails to complete the nonprison components of a sentence, such as payment of a fine. Should courts consider suspended sentences as incarceration for purposes of the right to a jury trial? Is it appropriate to allow trial judges to "override" the legislature's decision to make a crime eligible for jury trials?

Prosecutors also have much to say about the availability of a jury trial. The prosecutor can charge a defendant with multiple counts of a petty offense rather than a more serious one, or charge the lesser of two alternative offenses if the more serious offense triggers a jury trial. See City of Casper v. Fletcher, 916 P.2d 473 (Wyo. 1996) (prosecutor in battery case could choose between municipal ordinance, for which jury trial did not attach, and state statute that would qualify for jury trial). Is there any problem with the prosecutor initially filing the more serious charge, and revising the charge to some lesser crime (a non-jury trial offense) only for defendants who insist on a jury trial?

2. Waiver of Jury Trial

The seemingly simple question of how many trials are resolved by juries and how many by judges is surprisingly difficult to answer because of the lack of uniform records and lack of interest in low-level cases. In 1998, about 45 percent of the felony trials in state courts were bench trials rather than jury trials. But this overall rate of felony bench trials hides real differences among types of crimes and among jurisdictions. Juries are much more likely to try violent offenses, and judges are more likely to try drug offenses. In the federal system in 1999, about 25 percent of criminal trials were bench trials. Fewer than 10 percent of the felony trials are before the bench in some states (such as Alaska and New Jersey), while more than two-thirds of the trials are before the bench in other states (such as Virginia). See Sean Doran, John Jackson & Michael Seigel, Rethinking Adversariness in Nonjury Criminal Trials, 23 Am. J. Crim. L. 1 (1995). Note that these figures deal only with felony trials. A much smaller proportion of misdemeanor cases are tried before juries in most places. See Neil Vidmar, Sara Sun Beale, Mary Rose & Laura Donnelly, Should We Rush to Reform the Criminal Jury? Consider Conviction Rate Data, 80 Judicature 286 (1997) (2.6 percent of misdemeanor dispositions by jury trial in North Carolina superior courts).

The number of bench trials taking place each year is not simply a product of the legal rules that entitle some defendants and not others to a jury trial. Many defendants who could insist on a trial by jury instead waive the right and proceed to a bench trial with the judge as the sole factfinder. Sometimes the waiver of a jury trial will be welcome news to the government and to the public since jury trials are expensive and difficult to administer. Judges may even encourage some defendants to waive jury trials, perhaps by discounting the sentence in cases tried to the bench. However, there are times when the prosecutor or the judge will not share the defendant's desire to bypass the jury. In felony cases juries appear to convict at substantially higher rates than judges, though judges have a higher conviction rate for misdemeanors. See Kenneth Klein, Unpacking the Jury Box, 47 Hastings L.J. 1325 (1996). The defendant may believe the judge will better understand a complex defense or will react with more restraint to an abhorrent crime. What interests might lead a judge or a prosecutor to resist a defendant's waiver in such cases? Should defendants have a right to choose between jury and bench trials?

■ STATE v. ROBERT DUNNE
590 A.2d 1144 (N.J. 1991)

O'HERN, J.

A jury has convicted defendant of a bizarre murder that occurred in the South Mountain Reservation in 1986. The principal ground of appeal before us is that defendant was improperly denied the right to have the charges tried by a judge and not a jury. We hold that there is no unilateral right to a non-jury trial in such circumstances and that the trial court did not abuse its discretion in determining that the issues were properly to be decided by a jury.

[Dunne confessed to killing a stranger, who was sunbathing in a public area, by stabbing him in the chest.] Defendant anticipated raising an insanity defense at trial that would require testimony on the abnormal homosexual fantasies that may have moved defendant to attack the victim. Fearing adverse jury reaction to that defense, defendant made a pretrial motion for a non-jury trial. The trial court denied that motion. At trial, defendant raised the insanity defense, having indicated to his testifying physician that he had heard vague and indistinct voices telling him to "do it." The doctor testified that defendant suffered from paranoid schizophrenia. In the opinion of the doctor, defendant, on the morning of [the murder], became acutely psychotic and lost touch with reality. For unexplained reasons, defendant's persistent fantasies of homosexual gratification and aggression blended with reality, resulting in the attack. The doctor believed that defendant did not know that what he was doing was wrong.

The jury convicted defendant of murder. During deliberations the jury requested two read-backs of the psychiatric testimony offered by defendant, and asked the court for the legal definition of insanity. The jury also asked if it could return a verdict with a recommendation and if defendant would receive proper treatment and medication without regard to its verdict. Following the conviction, the court sentenced defendant to thirty years' imprisonment. . . .

As noted, the principal point raised in defendant's appeal is that the trial court erred in denying defendant's motion for a bench trial. . . . Defendant based his request for a non-jury trial on two grounds. First, defendant suggested that the jury would be prejudiced against him by the psychiatric testimony that was to be presented on the defense of insanity. He submitted that the jury "when encountering a really terrible killing which occurred in a public place for no apparent reason . . . may well feel that letting Mr. Dunne off on psychiatric grounds is not adequate, is dangerous, is risky, and goes against their moral beliefs." Second, he argued that because the defense would be presenting medical evidence that would reveal that defendant had violent and abnormal homosexual fantasies, the jury's evaluation of the testimony on the insanity defense would become tainted and biased against him.

Defendant argued that a jury waiver was appropriate because the court would be in a better position to evaluate the psychiatric testimony and the insanity defense without any of the anticipated biases of the jury. The trial court denied the motion to waive the jury, ruling that "this is the kind of case that is appropriate to have the community decide the case. . . . I see no compelling reasons why the case should go non-jury." The court further noted that the proposed jury voir dire would sufficiently screen out jurors who would be prejudiced against defendant.

We deal first with the question of whether defendant had a unilateral or absolute right to demand a non-jury trial, and then with the question of whether the trial court abused its discretion in not granting a non-jury trial.

Over sixty years ago, in Patton v. United States, 281 U.S. 276 (1930), Justice Sutherland set forth the guiding principles that dictate the disposition of this case. In *Patton,* a defendant in a prohibition bribery trial had consented in open court that his trial should continue with only eleven jurors, following the removal of one juror who had become seriously ill. The eleven remaining jurors found him guilty. [The Supreme Court, after a review of the history of Article III, §2, clause 3 and the Sixth Amendment of the federal constitution], concluded that "it is reasonable to conclude that the framers of the Constitution simply were intent upon preserving the right of trial by jury primarily for the protection of the accused." The Court [held] that "article III, §2, is not jurisdictional, but was meant to confer a right upon the accused which he may forego at his election. To deny his power to do so is to convert a privilege into an imperative requirement." [The opinion included these] principles that remain of enduring guidance.

> Not only must the right of the accused to a trial by a constitutional jury be jealously preserved, but the maintenance of the jury as a factfinding body in criminal cases is of such importance and has such a place in our traditions, that, before any waiver can become effective, the consent of government counsel and the sanction of the court must be had, in addition to the express and intelligent consent of the defendant. And the duty of the trial court in that regard is not to be discharged as a mere matter of rote, but with sound and advised discretion, with an eye to avoid unreasonable or undue departures from the mode of trial or from any of the essential elements thereof, and with a caution increasing in degree as the offenses dealt with increase in gravity. [281 U.S. at 312-313.]

Consistent with those principles, Rule 23(a) of the later enacted Federal Rules of Criminal Procedure provides that "[c]ases required to be tried by jury shall be so tried unless the defendant waives a jury trial in writing with the approval of the court and the consent of the government."

In Singer v. United States, 380 U.S. 24 (1965), the defendant challenged the constitutionality of Rule 23(a), arguing that the United States Constitution "gives a defendant in a federal criminal case the right to waive a jury trial whenever he believes such action to be in his best interest, regardless of whether the prosecution and the court are willing to acquiesce in the waiver." Singer was charged with mail fraud. He offered to waive a jury in order to shorten the trial. Even though the trial court was willing to approve the waiver, the prosecution refused to consent. After reviewing English and American history surrounding the waiver of a jury trial, the Supreme Court concluded:

> A defendant's only constitutional right concerning the method of trial is to an impartial trial by jury. We find no constitutional impediment to conditioning a waiver of this right on the consent of the prosecuting attorney and the trial judge when, if either refuses to consent, the result is simply that the defendant is subject to an impartial trial by jury — the very thing that the Constitution guarantees him. [380 U.S. at 36.]

Limiting its decision to the facts, however, the *Singer* Court suggested an exception to the rule by pointing out that because the petitioner had requested the waiver only to save court time, it need not determine "whether there might be some circumstances where a defendant's reasons for wanting to be tried by a judge alone are so compelling that the Government's insistence on trial by jury would result in the denial to a defendant of an impartial trial." Absent proof of such special circumstances, federal constitutional doctrine remains the same, that there is no federal constitutional right to trial by a judge alone.

The question arises, then, whether we should interpret our New Jersey constitutional provision for trial by jury in any significantly different manner. See N.J. Const. of 1947 art. I, §§9, 10. We are unable to find any significant constitutional preference in New Jersey's history or tradition for a different result. New Jersey's consistent tradition has been that every right and privilege secured by our State Constitution belongs to each citizen, "as a personal right." That tradition includes, specifically, the guarantee that "the accused shall have the right to a speedy and public trial by an impartial jury," N.J. Const. of 1947 art. I, §10, and "so far as [the] right to a trial by jury is concerned, [a defendant] may waive it." Our courts found, as did the United States Supreme Court, that there is no constitutional impediment to the exercise of jurisdiction to try criminal causes without a jury. In Edwards v. State, 45 N.J.L. 419 (1883), the [court held that the right to a jury trial was] personal to the defendant and could be waived. [Nothing] in New Jersey's history or tradition suggests any implied correlative right on the part of a defendant to demand trial by a judge and not by jury.

The remaining question is whether the trial court abused its discretion in denying defendant's request for a non-jury trial. Rule 1:8-1(a) is the provision in our Rules that deals with non-jury trials in criminal cases. Like the federal rule, our state Rule mandates that the defendant must first obtain the approval of the trial court in order to waive the right to a jury trial. Our Rule differs from the federal rule in that except in capital cases . . . our Rule does not require the approval of the prosecutor; it merely requires notice to the prosecutor that the defendant has waived the right. The 1969 Revision of our Rules changed criminal practice by eliminating the State's consent as a prerequisite to the defendant's waiver of a jury trial.

[T]he ability to waive a constitutional right does not ordinarily carry with it the right to insist on the opposite of that right. For example, although able to waive the right to a public trial, a defendant cannot compel a private trial. . . .

Thus, although we agree . . . that the denial of a request for a non-jury trial cannot be a reflexive reaction and must be based on "an exercise of discretion by the trial court based on its consideration of the circumstances of the case," neither the Constitution nor the Rules of the Court tilt in favor of a non-jury trial. Rather, we believe that the more serious the crime, the greater the "gravity" of the offense, the greater the burden on the defendant to show why there should be a non-jury trial.

[The trial] court must consider the competing factors that argue for or against jury trial. One of the most important factors to consider is the judiciary's obligation to legitimately preserve public confidence in the administration of justice. . . . Public confidence in a criminal verdict is best sustained by a jury finding. And when we speak of the appearance of justice, we are not trying to avoid judicial responsibility to ensure the actuality of justice. We always expect judges to be made of sterner stuff . . . and never to fear public clamor over any decision. . . .

A court must always ensure . . . that denying a defendant's request for non-jury trial never denies the defendant a fair trial. But the validity of a claim of unfairness is better shown after voir dire of prospective jurors. . . . In this case, the trial court formulated questionnaires, after consultation with counsel, to be submitted to the jury in the voir dire process. Jurors must have reassured the court that they could follow the law because defendant did not renew his motion for a non-jury trial after the jury-selection process. . . .

Other factors that will tip the scale will be the position of the State, the anticipated duration and complexity of the State's presentation of the evidence, the amenability of the issues to jury resolution, the existence of a highly-charged emotional atmosphere (this may work both ways . . .), the presence of particularly-technical matters that are interwoven with fact, and the anticipated need for numerous rulings on the admissibility or inadmissibility of evidence. The sources of principled decision-making will remain rooted in a statement of reasons that will accompany the decision. This statement of reasons will give structure to the trial court's discretionary judgment and will soundly guide appellate review. . . .

We would never deprive the defendant of a fair trial in order to maintain public confidence, and on those occasions when fairness requires a waiver, obviously it must be granted. Having said that, we must never forget, as we have stated so often, the importance of maintaining the public's confidence in our criminal-justice system. Trial by jury, for reasons rooted in our history and tradition, is one of the foundations of that confidence. It is a foundation not simply because of trust in the common man, trust in the verdict of one's peers, but because it has proven itself as the best vehicle for attaining justice. We surrender to no clamor when we protect trial by jury; we simply accept the wisdom of the ages and benefit from the experience of thousands of judges over hundreds of years who continue to marvel at the consistent soundness of jury verdicts. . . .

HANDLER, J., dissenting.

The defendant is a homosexual suffering from a serious psychosis, a symptom of which was a sexual fantasy in which he would stab or strangle a man and then sodomize the corpse. Tragically, defendant attempted to act out his psychotic fantasy. He was driving to work one morning when he saw a young man sunbathing. Defendant stopped his car, approached the man, and after a brief exchange of words, stabbed him in the chest. . . .

In State v. Belton, 286 A.2d 78 (N.J. 1972), this Court upheld Rule 1:8-1 against a constitutional challenge to the restriction conditioning defendant's waiver of a jury trial on court approval. The Court, now, however, construes the Rule so that a defendant cannot waive a trial by jury except in the most extraordinary circumstances, which the Court neither explains nor illustrates. . . .

One is hard pressed to find within the Court's opinion sound or persuasive considerations that support its determination to make it so hard for a criminal defendant to obtain a trial without a jury. The majority relies heavily on federal law. I believe it misperceives and misapplies that law. The Court, focusing on Patton v. United States, 281 U.S. 276 (1930), . . . seems oblivious to *Patton*'s holding that the constitutional right to a trial by jury "was meant to confer a right upon the accused which he may forgo at his election," that "the right of trial by jury [is] primarily for the protection of the accused," and that the framers did not intend to establish the jury in criminal trials as an "integral and inseparable part of the court." . . .

The approaches of the various states are so diverse they provide no clear direction. Some states require that a defendant's motion to waive jury trial be granted if the waiver is made knowingly and intelligently and for more than merely tactical reasons. E.g., State v. Duchin, 190 N.E.2d 17 (N.Y. 1963). Other states give the trial judge broad discretion in determining whether to grant a defendant's motion to waive a jury. E.g., State v. Bleyl, 435 A.2d 1349 (Me. 1981). Still other jurisdictions require approval of both the judge and the prosecution. E.g., Cal. Const. art. 1, §16; Mich. R. Crim. P. 6.401. Ten states, including New Jersey, provide either by constitutional provision, statute, or court rule that a criminal defendant may waive trial by jury with consent of the trial court. E.g., Mass. R. Crim. Proc. 19(a); N.Y. Const. art. 1, §2; Penn. R. Crim. Proc. 1101. . . . The supreme courts of two states have held that a criminal defendant may never waive trial by jury in a felony case. State v. Scalise, 309 P.2d 1010 (Mont. 1957); State v. Underwood, 195 S.E.2d 489 (N.C. 1973). Several states, the statutes of which do not explicitly condition waiver on the consent of the court or prosecutor, have interpreted those statutes to give criminal defendants an absolute right to waive a jury trial (provided the waiver is knowing and intelligent). E.g., Garcia v. People, 615 P.2d 698 (Colo. 1980); State v. Lawrence, 344 N.W.2d 227 (Iowa 1984). Most of the states that, like New Jersey, condition a defendant's waiver of a jury trial on consent of the trial court, give the trial courts wide latitude in determining whether to accept a defendant's request for waiver. [The dissent cites Minnesota and Missouri cases.]

Under the sixth amendment of the United States Constitution, trial by jury is a right specifically bestowed upon "the accused." Under our state constitution, trial by jury is provided for in article I, which enumerates the "Rights and Privileges" of citizens. Paragraph 10, entitled "Rights of persons accused of crime," specifies trial by jury as a right belonging to the "accused." . . .

Given that trial by jury is a right belonging to the defendant, the burden of the argument would seem to be on the proponents of limiting a defendant's ability to waive that right. Most of the arguments in favor of curtailing a defendant's ability to waive a jury trial, such as "community expectations," "equal treatment of prosecution and defendant," and "preservation of the role of the jury," are imprecise and insubstantial. . . .

Public expectations are often at odds with the procedural protections accorded criminal defendants. The community's criticism or disapproval, like the community's expectations, should not be used as a gauge for determining the protections available to criminal defendants. . . . Constitutional rights . . . are meant to protect the accused, not to promote relations between the judiciary and the public. . . .

Notes

1. *Waiver of jury trial: majority position.* Almost all jurisdictions allow a defendant to waive the right to a jury trial; more than 30 states, however, allow the judge to *deny* the defendant's request for a bench trial. N.Y. Crim. Proc. Law §320.10; Or. Rev. Stat. §136.001(2). About 10 states give the defendant the unilateral power to select a bench trial over a jury trial. See, e.g., Iowa R. Crim. P. 16(1). North Carolina stands alone in forbidding jury waiver through an explicit constitutional text. N.C. Const. art. I, §24 ("No person shall be convicted of any crime but by the unanimous verdict of a jury in open court"). About 25 states and the federal courts also empower the

prosecutor to block the defendant's choice of a bench trial. Fed. R. Crim. P. 23(a); Cal. Const. art. I, §6 ("consent of both parties"); Fla. R. Crim. P. 3.260; see also ABA Standards for Criminal Justice: Trial by Jury 15-1.2 (3d ed. 1996) (waiver must be "with the consent of the prosecutor"). Until the early twentieth century, very few states gave defendants facing felony charges the option to waive jury trial for bench trial; amendments to the rules allowing waiver of jury trial occurred at the same time that plea bargaining began to dominate criminal practice in the United States. Is there any connection between these developments? See George Fisher, Plea Bargaining's Triumph: A History of Plea Bargaining in America (2003).

Like the U.S. Supreme Court in Singer v. United States, 380 U.S. 24 (1965), most state courts have rejected constitutional challenges to rules and statutes that require the consent of the prosecution and the court before a waiver takes effect. People v. Kirby, 487 N.W.2d 404 (Mich. 1992); but see State v. Baker, 976 P.2d 1132 (Ore. 1999) (statute granting the prosecution right to insist on jury trial despite defendant's waiver violates the waiver provision of Oregon Constitution's jury trial guarantee). In jurisdictions that permit the court to deny a defendant's request for a bench trial, the rules (or the judicial opinions interpreting those rules) often say that a trial court has discretion to deny such a request, and an appellate court can review that decision for an abuse of discretion. What circumstances might amount to an abuse of discretion? What reasons did the trial court in *Dunne* give for denying the defense request? The New Jersey decision in *Dunne* discusses the interests of both the accused and the general public in trying a case before a jury. What is relevant in deciding exactly who has a right to a jury trial? Is the constitutional text dispositive?

2. *Written and informed waiver.* Procedural rules and statutes typically require a defendant to waive the right to a jury trial in writing; sometimes they also allow the waiver to take place on the record in open court. See Or. Rev. Stat. 136.001(2) (requires written waiver). What purpose does a written waiver serve? What information should a defendant have before making a choice about waiver? The same information that a defendant receives when pleading guilty?

3. *Law-trained judges.* Most state court systems have different levels of trial courts, with "limited jurisdiction" courts to try misdemeanors and other minor offenses in the first instance, and "general jurisdiction" courts to try all felonies and (sometimes) the cases of defendants who appeal a conviction from the limited jurisdiction court. Judges in the general jurisdiction courts virtually always have legal training. However, a number of judges in limited jurisdiction courts do not have legal training. Courts have usually turned aside due process challenges to this arrangement, but the opinions often rely on the fact that cases tried before a non-lawyer judge will ultimately receive meaningful review by a law-trained judge. See North v. Russell, 427 U.S. 328 (1976); Amrein v. State, 836 P.2d 862 (Wyo. 1992); but see Gordon v. Justice Court for Yuba, 525 P.2d 72 (Cal. 1974) (criminal trials before nonlawyer judges violate due process). What differences would you expect in the arguments that lawyers make to nonlawyer judges?

4. *Waiver of full-size jury.* Most states require a 12-person jury for felonies where the defendant gets a jury. They also, however, allow defendants to waive the right to a 12-person jury and be tried by a lesser number. Hatch v. State, 958 S.W.2d 813 (Tex. Crim. App. 1997). Standards for waiver of juries often include a requirement that the waiver be made personally by the defendant in open court, in writing, or both. See, e.g., In re Hansen, 881 P.2d 979 (Wash. 1994) (waiver of

12-person jury down to 10 must be in writing, personal waiver by defendant rather than by lawyer); but see Blair v. State, 698 So. 2d 1210 (Fla. 1997) (explanation to defendant from defense counsel during trial sufficient to support waiver of six-person jury down to five; no on-the-record inquiry from judge necessary).

5. *Other decisionmakers.* Many other countries involve citizens on panels resembling juries to decide criminal cases. See Neil Vidmar, World Jury Systems (2000). But the details vary in important ways. Some foreign legal systems utilize decisionmakers other than lone judges or juries. Consider, for example, the use of multimember panels in Germany to try serious offenses. The panels are made up of three "professional" and two "lay" judges. See William Pizzi & Walter Perron, Crime Victims in German Courtrooms: A Comparative Perspective on American Problems, 32 Stan. J. Int'l L. 37 (1996). Some parties in the United States hire a "private" judge — an arbitrator who mediates a settlement between the defendant and the crime victim, as part of a pretrial "diversion" program. What conditions would allow the use of alternative judges to flourish? History has given us judges and juries, but times and technologies change. What new forms of trial can you imagine?

B. SELECTION OF JURORS

Jury members are selected in two stages. The first stage involves the selection of the "venire" — the pool of potential jurors. Early in American history, only adult white males who owned a certain amount of property were eligible to serve on a jury. Over time, eligibility for service expanded in steps, first covering white males without property and eventually reaching all adults. As legal eligibility for jury service expanded, however, the actual methods for selecting the jury venire did not keep pace. Under the "key man" selection system used in many states, public officials or prominent citizens served as jury commissioners (the "key men") to nominate potential jurors. Not surprisingly, their nominations did not reflect a demographic cross section of the eligible jurors in the community.

The Supreme Court periodically has decided cases requiring the states to change their selection processes to produce venires that better represent the community. In the first case to deal with the question, Strauder v. West Virginia, 100 U.S. 303 (1880), the Court sustained an equal protection challenge to a statute excluding blacks from the jury venire. In Norris v. Alabama, 294 U.S. 587 (1935), the Court quashed an indictment because blacks were excluded *in fact* from serving on grand juries in the jurisdiction, even though they were legally eligible to participate. In later cases, the Court did not require the defendant to show complete exclusion of a racial group from jury service: A substantial disparity between the racial mix of the county's population and the racial mix of the venire, together with an explanation of how the jury selection process had created this outcome, would be enough to establish a prima facie case of discrimination. The government would then have to rebut the presumption of discrimination. See Turner v. Fouche, 396 U.S. 346 (1970) (underrepresentation of African Americans); Castaneda v. Partida, 430 U.S. 482 (1977) (underrepresentation of Mexican Americans).

The Supreme Court has also recognized a defendant's right to challenge the process of creating the venire in the Sixth Amendment's promise of an "impartial jury." In Taylor v. Louisiana, 419 U.S. 522 (1975), the Court held that a Louisiana law placing on the venire only those women who affirmatively requested jury duty violated the Sixth Amendment's requirement that the jury represent a "fair cross section" of the community. Duren v. Missouri, 439 U.S. 357 (1979), summarized the current test followed in both federal and state courts for challenging a venire under the Sixth Amendment and its analogs. The defendant must show that (1) the group allegedly excluded is a "distinctive" group in the community, (2) the representation of this group in venires is not reasonable in relation to the number of such persons in the community, and (3) this underrepresentation is a result of "systematic" exclusion of the group (not necessarily intentional discrimination) in the jury selection process. At that point, the burden of proof shifts to the government to show a "significant state interest" that justifies use of the method that systematically excludes a group. Courts have determined the distinctiveness of groups that are "cognizable" under the Sixth Amendment by looking to the shared attitudes and experiences of the group. By and large, this has meant that racial groups and gender are considered distinctive, while age groups (such as 18- to 24-year-olds) are not. See State v. Pelican, 580 A.2d 942 (Vt. 1990); Vikram Amar, Jury Service as Political Participation Akin to Voting, 80 Cornell L. Rev. 203 (1995) (arguing that "distinctive" groups for jury service should be defined by reference to constitutional grants of suffrage, including age groups).

1. *Voir Dire*

A second stage of juror selection takes place for each case. From among a large pool of prospective jurors at the courthouse on a given day, a random group will be called to a particular courtroom for a specific case. An initial group of jurors are seated in the jury box, and then the judge and lawyers determine which individuals will serve on the jury for that case. There are two ways to remove a potential juror from the box. First, there are removals "for cause": The judge removes from the panel any jurors who are not qualified to serve or are not capable of performing their duties. Second, the attorneys may remove a limited number of qualified jurors through "peremptory" challenges.

Each of these methods of removing potential jurors requires the judge and the attorneys to learn something about the attitudes and experiences of the individual jurors. Jurors are questioned in a process known as *voir dire* ("to speak the truth," or, more literally, "to see to say"). In most jurisdictions, statutes and rules of procedure allow both the judge and the attorneys to formulate the questions; often the judge asks questions proposed by counsel, but sometimes the attorneys query potential jurors directly. Fewer than 10 states allow the attorneys to conduct all the questioning. Some questions are directed to the jurors as a group, while follow-up questions with individual jurors are typical in most places. Regardless of the voir dire process described in statutes or procedure rules, the trial judge commonly retains discretion to alter the voir dire process in individual cases. The greatest authority of the trial judge relates to the content of the questions asked on voir dire. In the interest of saving time and preventing the attorneys from arguing their cases to the jury before the trial begins, judges will often prevent attorneys on both sides from asking some particular questions. Some of the most difficult challenges to judicial supervision of voir dire involve possible racial prejudice among the jurors.

■ ANDREW HILL v. STATE
661 A.2d 1164 (Md. 1995)

BELL, J.

This case requires that we revisit the issue of when, and define the circumstances under which, at the request of the defendant, voir dire in a criminal case must include a question regarding racial bias or prejudice. In line with what this Court consistently has held to be the overarching purpose of the voir dire examination — "to ascertain the existence of cause for disqualification . . ." — we shall hold that under the circumstances of the case sub judice, the trial court should have inquired, as requested, into the venire's racial bias. . . .

The State's only witness at trial was Barron Burch, a Baltimore City police officer. He testified that, while on armed robbery detail, he responded to the 2100 block of Booth Street, in answer to a call for a black male, wearing a black jacket and blue jeans, armed with a gun. When he arrived at that location, Officer Burch stated that he saw Andrew Hill, the petitioner. Observing that he matched the description he had been given, the officer approached the petitioner, placed him against the police cruiser Officer Burch was driving, and conducted a pat down search of the petitioner's clothing. He did not [discover a gun, but he did notice] that the petitioner was holding a box, inscribed with the word, "Dominoes." Despite the petitioner's express confirmation that the box did, indeed, contain Dominoes, Officer Burch took the box from the petitioner, opened it, and recovered 14 vials of cocaine.

The petitioner was charged with cocaine possession offenses. He elected to be tried by a jury. The petitioner being African-American and Officer Burch Caucasian, the petitioner requested the Circuit Court for Baltimore City to propound the following question during the voir dire examination of the venire:

> You have taken note, the defendant is African/American. Both sides to this case, and certainly the court want to make it abundantly clear to you that the racial background of the defendant is not to be considered against him in any way. It is imperative that the defendant be judged only upon the evidence or lack of evidence, without any regard whatever to whether he is African/American or white. If there is in your background any experience, or attitude, or predisposition, or bias, or prejudice, or thought that will make it more difficult for you to render a verdict in favor of this defendant because of his race, then I ask that you raise your hand.

The trial court refused to ask the question. It did ask, however, whether any member of the jury panel "knew of anything that would keep her or him from giving a fair and impartial verdict," and "whether any member knew of any reason why he or she should not serve on the jury." The jury having returned a guilty verdict as to both the possession and possession with intent to distribute cocaine charges, the petitioner, relying on the voir dire issue, among others, filed an appeal.

[In] Maryland, the principles governing jury voir dire are well settled. Of course, the nature and extent of the voir dire procedure, as well as the form of the questions propounded, are matters that lie initially within the discretion of the trial judge. [Informing] the trial court's exercise of discretion regarding the conduct of the voir dire, is a single, primary, and overriding principle or purpose: to ascertain the existence of cause for disqualification. This is consistent with the fundamental tenet underlying the trial by jury that each juror, as far as possible, be impartial and unbiased. Thus, the purpose of the voir dire examination is to exclude from the venire those potential jurors for whom there exists cause for disqualification, so that the jury that remains is capable of deciding the matter before it based solely upon the facts presented, uninfluenced by any extraneous considerations.

[Where] a defendant's proposed voir dire questions concern a specific cause for disqualification, he or she has "a right to have [those] questions propounded to prospective jurors. . . ." That "right" to examine prospective jurors to determine whether any cause exists for disqualification is guaranteed by Article 21 of the Maryland Declaration of Rights.* And the proper focus of the voir dire examination is the venireperson's state of mind and the existence of bias, prejudice, or preconception, i.e., "a mental state that gives rise to cause for disqualification. . . ."

In Davis v. State, 633 A.2d 867 (Md. 1993), we quite recently identified yet again areas of inquiry which, if reasonably related to the case at hand, are mandatory subjects of the voir dire examination. Because "[t]hese areas entail potential biases or predispositions that prospective jurors may hold which, if present, would hinder their ability to objectively resolve the matter before them," we concluded that the trial court must question the prospective jurors about them. Among the areas of inquiry is prospective jurors' possible racial bias. . . . Racial prejudice and bias has not been eradicated even as of today. And, as *Davis* recognized, a prospective juror who is prejudiced or biased based on race would be unable objectively to decide a matter in which a person of that race is a party.

In this case, the petitioner is an African-American on trial for a drug possession crime, whose guilt or innocence must be determined by the jury. We hold that he was entitled to have questions propounded to the venire on its voir dire concerning this possible prejudice or racial bias. The trial court's failure to propound such a question was an abuse of discretion.

We are aware, of course, that the Supreme Court of the United States has held that "there is no per se constitutional rule . . . requiring inquiry as to racial prejudice" based solely on an alleged criminal confrontation between an African-American assailant and a white victim. Ristaino v. Ross, 424 U.S. 589 (1976). That Court determined that the constitutional necessity to question prospective jurors concerning their racial or ethnic bias arises only when "special circumstances," of the kind reflected in Ham v. South Carolina, 409 U.S. 524 (1973), are present.

In *Ham,* the African-American civil rights activist, who was charged with a drug offense, defended on the basis that the police framed him in retaliation for his active, and widely known civil rights activities. Noting that "Ham's reputation as a civil rights activist and the defense he interposed were likely to intensify any prejudice that individual members of the jury might harbor," the *Ristaino* Court concluded that "racial issues . . . were inextricably bound up with the conduct of the trial" and that gave rise to the consequent need for voir dire "questioning specifically directed to racial prejudice" to assure the empanelling of an impartial jury.* In Rosales-Lopez

---

*Article 21 provides in relevant part: "[I]n all criminal prosecutions, every man hath a right . . . to a speedy trial by an impartial jury, without whose unanimous consent he ought not to be found guilty." — EDS.

*In Ristaino v. Ross, 424 U.S. 589 (1976), James Ross was tried in a Massachusetts court with two other black men for armed robbery and assault. The victim of the alleged crimes was a white man employed as a uniformed security guard. Under a state statute, the court was required during voir dire to inquire generally into prejudice. Ross asked the judge to question the prospective jurors specifically about racial prejudice. The judge refused to ask the more specific question. The Supreme Court held that a specific inquiry was not required in this case, based on the "mere fact that the victim of the crimes alleged was a white man and the defendants were Negroes." — EDS.

v. United States, 451 U.S. 182, 189 (1981), the Court explained the *Ristaino* holding as follows:

> Only when there are more substantial indications of the likelihood of racial or ethnic prejudice [than an interracial confrontation] affecting the jurors in a particular case does the trial court's denial of a defendant's request to examine the juror's ability to deal impartially with this subject amount to an unconstitutional abuse of discretion.

In [*Rosales-Lopez*], the Supreme Court characterized the racial discrimination issue as one involving a conflict affecting the appearance of justice. Acting pursuant to its supervisory authority over the federal courts, the Court acknowledged, as it previously had done in *Ristaino,* that "it is usually best to allow the defendant to resolve this conflict by making the determination of whether or not he would prefer to have the inquiry into racial or ethnic prejudice pursued." . . .

In Bowie v. State, 595 A.2d 448 (Md. 1991), we held that, where the defendant and the victim are of different races and the case involves the violent victimization of other persons, inquiry into juror racial bias is required. This is the first occasion that we have had to address the situation where voir dire into racial or ethnic bias was requested in a case which did not involve interracial violence. We agree with the Supreme Court that determining an appropriate nonconstitutional standard involves resolution of a conflict concerning the appearance of justice. Also like that Court, we agree that how the conflict is to be resolved ordinarily should be determined by the defendant. Unlike that Court, however, we strike a different balance when the trial court does not defer to the defendant's preferred resolution.

In Aldridge v. United States, 283 U.S. 308, 314-315 (1931),* in which an African-American was tried for the murder of a white police officer, the Court explained why it was proper for the venire to be questioned with regard to racial prejudice:

> The argument is advanced on behalf of the government that it would be detrimental to the administration of the law in the courts of the United States to allow questions to jurors as to racial or religious prejudices. We think that it would be far more injurious to permit it to be thought that persons entertaining a disqualifying prejudice were allowed to serve as jurors and that inquiries designed to elicit the fact of disqualification were barred. No surer way could be devised to bring the processes of justice into disrepute. . . .

While we have not heretofore embraced, in total, the *Aldridge* analysis, we do so now. We hold, as a matter of Maryland nonconstitutional criminal law, that the refusal to ask a voir dire question on racial or ethnic bias or prejudice under the circumstances of this case constituted reversible error. . . .

■ COMMONWEALTH v. BRIAN GLASPY
616 A.2d 1359 (Pa. 1992)

Nix, C.J.

Appellants Brian Glaspy and Victor Jackson were, at the time of the incident, black students enrolled in the Johnstown Campus of the University

---

* *Aldridge* involved a conviction under federal law and did not involve a constitutional requirement imposed on the states under the due process clause. — Eds.

of Pittsburgh. They have been found by a jury to be guilty of Rape [and related charges].

The factual matrix out of which this matter arises is as follows. Appellants attended a small party in one of the dormitory suites on the night of March 23, 1987. The victim was also a student at the time and was in attendance. On the night in question, the party was being held in a mutual friend's dormitory suite.

What happened next at the party is the basis of this appeal. The appellants have testified and continue to allege that what occurred that night was consensual sexual activity between Jackson and the victim, with Glaspy participating only to the extent of rubbing up against the victim while she danced and had sexual relations with Jackson. The victim's testimony was that Glaspy held her while Jackson removed her clothes and performed various sexual acts on her, and that Glaspy also penetrated her anally. The issue of the victim's consent was heatedly challenged at trial and various witnesses testified as to their own perceptions of her consent or lack thereof. The jury accepted the victim's allegations and convicted the appellants on all counts.

During the empanelling of the jury, defense counsel moved for individual voir dire to be conducted for all the jurors to explore any racial prejudices that the jurors may harbor. Defense counsel characterized this case as a "racially sensitive" case requiring heightened scrutiny of the jurors. The trial court denied the initial request for individual voir dire. During the questioning by the court, one prospective juror stated that he would not be able to render a fair verdict because of the race of the defendants. Defense counsel renewed the motion for individual voir dire and the trial judge again denied defense counsel's motion for individual voir dire. . . .

Appellants Glaspy and Jackson argue that the trial court incorrectly disallowed individual voir dire questioning about any particular racial prejudices. Appellants concede that it is within the trial court's discretion to conduct individual voir dire, but cite Commonwealth v. Christian, 389 A.2d 545 (Pa. 1978), as requiring individual voir dire when the court is faced with a racially sensitive case. Appellee responds that the only racial element in this case is that the co-defendants are black and the victim is white. Appellee relies on Commonwealth v. Richardson, 473 A.2d 1361 (Pa. 1984), to support its position that the bare fact that the victim is white and the assailants are black does not render this a racially sensitive case. For the reasons that follow, we agree with the appellants and hold that defense counsel should have been allowed to conduct individual voir dire. . . .

In Commonwealth v. Richardson, 473 A.2d 1361 (Pa. 1984), this Court reversed the Superior Court's order granting a new trial to a black defendant accused of raping a white victim and who was not allowed to question the jurors on potential racial bias. The majority of this Court stated that "[b]y posing such questions, however, the trial court would have risked creating racial issues in a case where such issues would not otherwise have existed." In this case, a prospective juror admitted during group voir dire that he could not render a fair verdict due to racial considerations. At that point the racial issue existed, and it was necessary for the trial court to allow counsel to examine the remaining jurors individually to ascertain whether any juror harbored any racial prejudices or biases that would affect that juror's ability to render a fair verdict. Thus, this case is distinguishable from *Richardson*.

We are not holding here that this jury was racially motivated. However, because the members of the jury were not examined individually, we cannot state that the jury was free of any prejudice that might have affected its judgment. As this writer stated previously, "[t]his type of situation requires that counsel be allowed to ascertain, of prospective jurors, whether personal deep seated biases would influence such a judgment. Often such predilections are consciously not evident even to the one possessing them and cannot be uncovered by the general question permitted in this case." *Richardson* (Nix, C.J., dissenting). In this case, counsel should have been allowed to question jurors individually in order to uncover any deep seated prejudices they might harbor. The failure of the trial judge to allow counsel to conduct individual voir dire was an abuse of his discretion. Therefore, unable to conclude that the voir dire in this case ensured the defendants a fair and impartial jury, we are constrained to grant a new trial to the defendants. The judgments of sentence are vacated and the appellants are granted a new trial.

CAPPY, J., concurring.

I join in the majority opinion and write separately to state that I would go further and specifically overrule Commonwealth v. Richardson as it applies to any case involving allegations of sexual misconduct where the parties are of different races — especially where the victim is white and the assailants are African-American. In my view, to conclude that allegations of rape or other sexual misconduct involving black males and white females is not racially sensitive per se, is to close your eyes to reality.

LARSEN, J., dissenting.

. . . The Rules of Criminal Procedure specifically provide that, in all non-capital cases, the trial judge shall select the method of voir dire — either individual voir dire or, in the alternative, group voir dire. Pa. R. Crim. P. 1106(e). In my view, group voir dire was sufficient to expose any racial inclinations or biases of the jury in the case herein. The fact that a prospective juror admitted during group voir dire that he was racially biased demonstrates that group voir dire was effective in ensuring a fair and impartial jury in this case. . . .

By holding that the trial court abused its discretion, the majority opinion creates an anomalous situation. In effect, the majority holds that, if group voir dire is effective in achieving its goal of ferreting out racial biases or inclinations, then group voir dire is not appropriate and the alternative method, individual voir dire, must be utilized. Whereas, if there is no evidence that group voir dire was effective (e.g., if none of the prospective jurors admitted racial bias), then group voir dire is proper.

The Rules of Criminal Procedure provide for alternative methods of voir dire at the discretion of the trial court. If the desired result is to remove that discretion from the trial judge and abolish group voir dire, the proper method to reach that result is to amend the Rules of Criminal Procedure — not to manipulate the facts in order to create situations, such as this, in which the trial court really has no choice. . . .

PAPADAKOS, J., dissenting.

I dissent since I perceive that the Chief Justice . . . seeks to establish a per se rule that, henceforth, in any racially mixed criminal proceeding, the trial judge is best advised to forgo discretion and conduct individual voir dire to ferret out any deep seated racial biases of the individual venirepersons. . . .

In Commonwealth v. Richardson we decided that individual voir dire in non-capital cases would be appropriate where the defense could demonstrate that "membership in a certain group or minority would be emphasized by the evidence presented at trial," thus making the case "race-sensitive." The essential facts in this case with respect to the potential bias of a jury are the same as in *Richardson*. The defendants are black and the victim is white and the defendants assert the defense of consensual intercourse. The Chief Justice attempts to embellish these essential facts by adding that one juror admitted during voir dire that he would be unable to render a fair verdict due to racial bias. [The Chief Justice does not explain why "at that point the racial issue existed" or why, if it did exist, it was not removed by the removal of that venireman from the panel and a request made to the remaining panel if anyone had the same problem.]

Would the Chief Justice require individual voir dire if a venireman stood up in a case involving an assault upon a police officer and said that I can not judge this case fairly because I don't trust policemen or I am partial to policemen? Would the Chief Justice require individual voir dire in any case in which a venireman stood up and professed a prejudice against any of the parties or the prosecutors, etc., etc., etc.?

The Chief Justice's concern for the avoidance of racial sensitivity in our criminal cases is laudable but misplaced in this case. Racial sensitivity is not created by the mere fact that a defendant is black, a victim is white, or that the defendant is charged with rape and the defense is that the intercourse was consensual. . . .

Problem 7-1. Defendant Bias and Voir Dire

In January 1992, the decomposed body of Delores Jackson, a black female, was found in a wooded area in Riceland County, South Carolina. The pathologist determined that she died from a blow to the head from a blunt instrument. After the media publicized the discovery of the body, several witnesses reported to the authorities that Charles Cason had admitted killing a black woman in October of the previous year. Further investigation led police to other witnesses, who said that Cason had been drinking on the day of the alleged murder. He was angry because his sister-in-law failed to pick him up at work as promised. Jackson jeered at Cason on the bus ride home and during their walk down Decker Boulevard towards their respective homes. Cason's neighbors told police that he had in his possession some of Jackson's personal effects after she disappeared, suggesting a robbery. Two witnesses said that Cason admitted several days later that he killed Jackson, using exceptionally crude language to describe the victim: "I killed a nigger bitch."

Prior to trial, defense counsel requested a specific voir dire to ascertain racial bias on the part of the jury. They requested the specific voir dire because two prosecution witnesses planned to testify at trial about Cason's description of the victim. The prosecutors objected to the voir dire question; they said that they planned to use Cason's pejorative words to show his state of mind and not to show that race was a motive for the crime.

The trial judge refused defense counsel's request for the specific voir dire question about race. Rather, the trial judge asked a general question as to bias or prejudice. The trial judge explained that a specific question related to race is required only when there are "special circumstances creating a constitutionally significant likelihood that, absent questioning about racial prejudice, the jurors would not be indifferent in the matter."

S.C. Code Ann. §14-7-1020 provides in pertinent part as follows:

> The court shall, on motion of either party in the suit, examine on oath any person who is called as a juror therein to know whether he . . . has any interest in the case, has expressed or formed any opinion or is sensible of any bias or prejudice therein. . . . If it appears to the court that the juror is not indifferent in the cause, he shall be placed aside as to the trial of that cause and another shall be called.

The jury convicted, and Cason appealed. How would you rule? Compare State v. Cason, 454 S.E.2d 888 (S.C. 1995).

Notes

1. *Racial bias questions on voir dire: majority position.* As the Maryland opinion in *Hill* indicates, the federal constitution requires the judge to ask specific voir dire questions about racial prejudice only when "special circumstances" in the case create a "reasonable possibility" that the jury will be influenced by racial prejudice. Virtually all state courts now agree on this general principle, saying that some "special circumstances" must be present before a trial court is obliged to ask racial prejudice questions on voir dire. See State v. Taylor, 423 A.2d 1174 (R.I. 1980). What did the *Hill* court hold about the necessary "circumstances"? Older decisions more often declared in general terms a defendant's right to insist on questions about racial prejudice. See Pinder v State, 8 So. 837 (Fla. 1891) (requiring questions on racial prejudice in murder case because such information is of "most vital import" to defendant); Spillers v. State, 436 P.2d 18 (Nev. 1968). While the state may not select an unrepresentative jury venire, the U.S. Supreme Court has repeatedly stressed that there is no right to a particular racial composition on a petit (trial) jury. See Virginia v. Rives, 100 U.S. 313 (1880). If an impartial jury requires a representative venire, why should it not also require a representative group of jurors actually chosen to serve at trial?

Most state courts say that special circumstances must amount to more than the fact that the defendant and the victim (or the arresting officer) are of different races. See Commonwealth v. Moffett, 418 N.E.2d 585 (Mass. 1981). But beyond this, there is little agreement about what qualifies as a "special" circumstance. State courts are split over whether charges of a "violent" crime are enough to invoke racial prejudice questions. Some conclude that a violent crime is enough, but others require some more specific showing. People v. Peeples, 616 N.E.2d 294 (Ill. 1993) (murder, no questions required); State v. Hightower, 680 A.2d 649 (N.J. 1996) (murder, questions required). Rape cases present some of the most compelling cases for questions about racial prejudice. In such cases, courts have concluded more often than not (like the Pennsylvania court in *Glaspy*) that racial prejudice questions were necessary in the case at hand, even if a blanket rule was not necessary. Commonwealth v. Sanders, 421 N.E.2d 436 (Mass. 1981) (questions required in interracial rape cases); but see State v. Jones, 233 S.E.2d 287 (S.C. 1977) (no specific questions required). Why have so few courts adopted a per se rule allowing the parties to insist on specific voir dire questioning about racial prejudice in any criminal case? Do such questions cause any harm? Do the questions create racial tensions or stereotyping where they would not otherwise appear? Do they allow a party to begin arguing a case before the evidence is introduced, by casting a case in racial terms? See Sheri Johnson, Racial Imagery in Criminal Cases, 67 Tul. L. Rev. 1739 (1993).

2. *Voir dire questions on other matters.* The trial court has substantial discretion over the content of voir dire questions regarding questions other than race. However, if the particular circumstances of a case make it reasonably likely that some potential jurors will not be able to render an impartial verdict, the court will inquire into those subjects if the parties request it. See State v. Thomas, 798 A.2d 566 (Md. 2002) (trial court may not refuse voir dire about attitudes toward crime charged; judge refused to ask venirepersons whether they had any "strong feelings regarding violations of the narcotics laws"). For instance, when a case has received media attention before trial, the judge asks specific questions about the juror's familiarity with the news coverage. Again, however, the trial court has broad discretion to decide how many questions to ask and whether to question jurors individually or as a group. See Mu'Min v. Virginia, 500 U.S. 415 (1991) (despite substantial publicity in the local news media about crime, trial judge properly denied motion for individual voir dire relating to content of news items that potential jurors might have seen or read; judge queried prospective jurors as a group, asking four separate questions about effect of pretrial publicity without asking about content of the publicity).

3. *Follow-up questions.* When a trial court allows specific questioning about juror prejudices—racial or otherwise—but limits it to one or two questions directed to the group of jurors as a whole, appellate courts are especially reluctant to rule that the trial court abused its discretion. See State v. Windsor, 316 N.W.2d 684 (Iowa 1982); but see State v. Tucker, 629 A.2d 1067 (Conn. 1993) (court should allow wide latitude to counsel in inquiring into possible prejudice of jurors whose preliminary responses to voir dire may indicate prejudice). If you were representing a defendant and the judge allowed only a single question about juror prejudice, would you use the question? How much success would counsel have in discovering racial prejudice through sharply limited questioning?

4. *Investigating venire members.* In the few cases in which the parties are able to spend lots of time and resources, they may decide to investigate the background of jury venire members prior to any voir dire questions. The parties also might hire jury consultants to assist in the selection of jurors. Part of the background investigation of the jurors involves a search for any record of prior criminal convictions or arrests. How might you argue as defense counsel that the government must share any information about prior criminal records of panel members? See State v. Bessenecker, 404 N.W.2d 134 (Iowa 1987) (prosecution must obtain court order before using arrest record of prospective juror, and defense counsel must have access to same report); Losavio v. Mayber, 496 P.2d 1032 (Colo. 1972) (granting public defender access to arrest records of prospective jurors when prosecution routinely obtained such information).

2. Dismissal for Cause

Recall that there are two methods to remove potential jurors from the panel: dismissal of any unqualified jurors "for cause," and dismissal of a limited number of qualified jurors based on "peremptory challenges" by the parties. We now consider the first of these methods of removal.

A potential juror might be unqualified to serve in any cases at all: For instance, the juror might be unable to understand English or might be a felon ineligible for jury duty. The juror might also be qualified to serve in some cases but not in others, as when a juror is closely related to the defendant or the alleged victim. More generally, the judge must dismiss a juror for cause whenever it appears that the juror cannot keep an open mind about the evidence and apply the relevant law. All these standards are straightforward, but they play out in a complex setting. Many jurors would prefer to avoid lengthy jury duty; the judge would prefer to seat the jury as quickly as possible without excusing many potential jurors; and the parties would prefer to convince the judge to remove unsympathetic jurors from the panel rather than using limited peremptory challenges. Everyone concerned must predict the jurors' future behavior based on brief answers to questions that are continually being rephrased. This subtle struggle calls for skills of perception and careful expression.

■ TEXAS CODE OF CRIMINAL PROCEDURE ART. 35.16

(a) A challenge for cause is an objection made to a particular juror, alleging some fact which renders him incapable or unfit to serve on the jury. A challenge for cause may be made by either the state or the defense for any one of the following reasons:

1. That he is not a qualified voter in the state and county under the Constitution and laws of the state; provided, however, the failure to register to vote shall not be a disqualification;

2. That he has been convicted of theft or any felony;

3. That he is under indictment or other legal accusation for theft or any felony;

4. That he is insane;

5. That he has such defect in the organs of feeling or hearing, or such bodily or mental defect or disease as to render him unfit for jury service . . . ;

6. That he is a witness in the case;

7. That he served on the grand jury which found the indictment;

8. That he served on a petit jury in a former trial of the same case;

9. That he has a bias or prejudice in favor of or against the defendant;

10. That from hearsay, or otherwise, there is established in the mind of the juror such a conclusion as to the guilt or innocence of the defendant as would influence him in his action in finding a verdict. To ascertain whether this cause of challenge exists, the juror shall first be asked whether, in his opinion, the conclusion so established will influence his verdict. If he answers in the affirmative, he shall be discharged without further interrogation by either party or the court. If he answers in the negative, he shall be further examined as to how his conclusion was formed, and the extent to which it will affect his action; and . . . if the juror states that he feels able, notwithstanding such opinion, to render an impartial verdict upon the law and the evidence, the court, if satisfied that he is impartial and will render such verdict, may, in its discretion, admit him as competent to

serve in such case. If the court, in its discretion, is not satisfied that he is impartial, the juror shall be discharged;

11. That he cannot read or write.

No juror shall be impaneled when it appears that he is subject to the second, third or fourth grounds of challenge for cause set forth above, although both parties may consent. All other grounds for challenge may be waived by the party or parties in whose favor such grounds of challenge exist. . . .

(b) A challenge for cause may be made by the State for any of the following reasons:

1. That the juror has conscientious scruples in regard to the infliction of the punishment of death for crime, in a capital case, where the State is seeking the death penalty;

2. That he is related within the third degree of consanguinity or affinity [to the defendant]; and

3. That he has a bias or prejudice against any phase of the law upon which the State is entitled to rely for conviction or punishment.

(c) A challenge for cause may be made by the defense for any of the following reasons:

1. That he is related within the third degree of consanguinity or affinity . . . to the person injured by the commission of the offense, or to any prosecutor in the case; and

2. That he has a bias or prejudice against any of the law applicable to the case upon which the defense is entitled to rely, either as a defense to some phase of the offense for which the defendant is being prosecuted or as a mitigation thereof or of the punishment therefor.

■ STATE v. RECHE SMITH
607 S.E.2d 607 (N.C. 2005)

Wainwright, J.

On 8 March 2002, defendant Reche Smith was convicted of first-degree murder and felony larceny. The jury found defendant guilty of first-degree murder on the basis of malice, premeditation, and deliberation and under the felony murder rule. Following a capital sentencing hearing, the jury recommended a sentence of death for the murder. The trial court accordingly imposed a sentence of death for the murder and further imposed a sentence of fifteen to eighteen months imprisonment for the felony larceny.

The evidence at trial showed the following: At 6:00 a.m. on 10 March 2001, the victim, Charles King, was at his home in Plymouth, North Carolina, when defendant knocked on his door. King, wearing a bathrobe and thermal shirt and pants, answered the door, and defendant asked him for a glass of water. King invited defendant into his home and headed toward his kitchen to get the water. However, before King reached the kitchen, defendant grabbed King around his neck and choked him until he became unconscious. Defendant then bound King's wrists with clear packaging tape, went to another room in King's house, found a clock, and used the clock's extension cord first to bind King's wrists and then his ankles. Next defendant covered King's entire face, including his nose and mouth, with clear packaging tape and pushed King under a hospital bed. Defendant left King under the bed to die of asphyxiation while he searched King's house for something to steal. As King lay suffocating under his bed, defendant took $250 from an envelope in King's bedroom, $20 from King's wallet, King's cell phone, bank card, and car keys. After thirty minutes of searching King's house and stealing these items, defendant took King's car, drove to Williamston, North Carolina, rented a room at a motel, and bought crack cocaine. . . .

Defendant first argues the trial court erred by denying his challenge for cause to prospective juror Charles Hassell. During voir dire, Hassell indicated he was strictly against drug use. Defense counsel then asked Hassell the following question: "Your position is such concerning drug use and abuse that in the event evidence came out in this trial that drug use was involved, it would affect or impair — substantially impair your ability to be fair and impartial; is that correct?" Hassell replied "yes" to this question. Defendant then challenged Hassell for cause. In response, the trial court engaged in the following colloquy with Hassell:

THE COURT: Well let me — Mr. Hassell, let me ask you . . . just a couple of questions if I could. I don't mean to embarrass you. There are no right or wrong answers, and I want to make sure I understand what you're saying, and I'm trying to frame the question in a way that — are you saying to me, sir, that your personal feelings about the use . . . of or possession of drugs is such that it would interfere or prevent you from following the law in this — as I would instruct you as it relates to this case?

MR. HASSELL: Well, I could follow the law.

THE COURT: All right. Now — and so I want to make sure what you're saying — you know, many people don't like drugs, don't approve of drugs, and I don't believe that's the question that [the defense attorney] was asking you, and that may have been how — that may have been what you are saying. I don't know one way or the other.

I'm not trying to put words in your mouth, but I — I'm just making sure I understand that's what you were saying or whether what you were saying is you didn't like drugs or are you saying to me that your feeling is such — I'm asking you as to whether or not your personal feelings about particular crimes or particular types of conduct are such that it would overwhelm your reason and common sense and your ability to follow the law as I would instruct you on should we reach some aspect of the case that may relate to the consumption or use or possession of drugs?

MR. HASSELL: No. It wouldn't do that.

THE COURT: You would be able and could and would follow the law as I would instruct you on regardless of what your own personal feelings would be as it relates to the use or possession of or consumption of drugs; is that correct?

MR. HASSELL: Yes.

THE COURT: Are you sure of that answer, sir?

MR. HASSELL: Yeah.

THE COURT: All right. The Challenge for cause is denied.

Defendant properly preserved error by exhausting the peremptory challenges available to him, renewing his challenge to prospective juror Hassell, and having his renewed challenge denied. N.C.G.S. §15A-1214(h). However, in addition to preserving error, defendant must show error by (1) demonstrating that the trial court abused its discretion in denying the challenge, and (2) showing defendant was prejudiced by this abuse of discretion.

Defendant contends the trial court improperly rehabilitated Hassell with leading questions, despite the prohibition against reducing determinations of juror bias "to question-and-answer sessions which obtain results in the manner of a catechism." Wainwright v. Witt, 469 U.S. 412, 424 (1985). However, we conclude that the trial court did not lead Hassell to answer that he would follow the law. Rather, the trial court questioned Hassell in an effort to determine whether, despite Hassell's feelings about drug use, he could follow the law.

We further conclude that the trial court did not abuse its discretion by denying defendant's challenge for cause. As the United States Supreme Court further stated in *Wainwright*:

> What common sense should have realized experience has proved: many veniremen simply cannot be asked enough questions to reach the point where their bias has been made "unmistakably clear"; these veniremen may not know how they will react when faced with imposing the death sentence, or may be unable to articulate, or may wish to hide their true feelings. Despite this lack of clarity in the printed record, however, there will be situations where the trial judge is left with the definite impression that a prospective juror would be unable to faithfully and impartially apply the law. . . . This is why deference must be paid to the trial judge who sees and hears the juror.

Thus, we must give substantial weight to the trial court's determination that Hassell was not biased. We defer to the trial court who could see and hear Hassell, and we conclude that the trial court did not abuse its discretion by denying defendant's challenge for cause. Defendant's assignment of error is overruled.

Next, defendant contends the trial court erred by failing to give him an additional peremptory challenge. Defendant claims he was entitled to an additional peremptory challenge because the trial court removed a seated juror for cause before the end of jury selection and after defendant had used all but one of his remaining peremptory challenges.

After both defendant and the prosecution accepted prospective juror Gloria Cox, Cox brought the trial court a note from her doctor recommending that she be excused from jury duty because serving as a juror would be too stressful for her. The trial court dismissed Cox for cause. Defendant then requested an additional peremptory challenge, stating that he had undergone a substantial portion of jury selection believing that Cox would be a juror. The trial court denied defendant's request.

Defendant contends the trial court erred by failing to use its inherent authority to restore a peremptory challenge to remedy a prejudicial development in jury selection. However, we disagree. Although a trial court must grant a defendant an additional peremptory challenge if, upon reconsideration of the defendant's previously denied challenge for cause, "the judge determines that the juror should have been excused for cause," N.C.G.S. §15A-1214(i), trial courts generally have no authority to grant additional peremptory challenges. In fact, trial courts are "precluded from authorizing any party to exercise more peremptory challenges than specified by statute." State v. Dickens, 484 S.E.2d 553, 561 (N.C. 1997) (holding that the trial court did not err by refusing to grant the defendant an additional peremptory challenge following the reexamination and excusal for cause of a juror). Because the trial court had no authority to provide defendant with additional peremptory challenges, defendant's argument is without merit and we overrule this assignment of error.

Next, defendant contends the trial court failed to comply with the N.C.G.S. §15A-1214(a) requirement for random jury selection when it placed a prospective juror in a specific seat after that juror was randomly called to fill another seat. Prospective juror Jonas Simpson, who had been summoned in the initial group of venire members to be examined for fitness to serve, was not present when the clerk called his name. The trial court called another prospective juror in Simpson's place. The trial court then examined this prospective juror and two other prospective jurors. Following a recess, Simpson arrived at the courtroom. The trial court placed him in panel A, seat twelve, the panel and seat for which he was originally called. After the trial court and the prosecutor questioned Simpson, the trial court allowed the prosecutor's request to challenge Simpson for cause, finding that Simpson was unequivocally opposed to the death penalty.

Defendant contends the trial court violated the §15A-1214(a) requirement for random jury selection when it placed Simpson in a specific seat. However, defendant has waived review of this issue . . . because he failed to follow the N.C.G.S. §15A-1211(c) procedure for challenging the randomness of jury selection. Subsection 15A-1211(c) states that all such challenges must be in writing, must "specify the facts constituting the ground of challenge," and must be "made and decided before any juror is examined." These challenges must be made at the trial court level. Defendant did not object to the trial court's placement of Simpson in a specific seat. Therefore, defendant has failed to preserve this issue for review, and we overrule his assignment of error. . . .

Notes

1. *Dismissals for cause: majority position.* The judge must confirm that each of the potential jurors meets the general requirements for service, such as residency and literacy requirements. At that point, the judge evaluates possible sources of bias against the defendant or against the government. The most common source of potential bias is a personal relationship between the juror and some person connected with the case, such as one of the attorneys. The judge also inquires into the prior experiences of the jurors; for instance, the judge might ask if a juror has been a victim of a crime. This ground leads to disqualification less often than do personal relationships. A juror who has learned before trial about the events that will be disputed at trial will receive special scrutiny. Although prior knowledge of the case alone does not disqualify a juror, a judge will sometimes conclude that the juror who has already learned about the events in question will be unable to keep an open mind and base a verdict only on the evidence presented at trial. Even if the judge allows the juror to remain on the panel, one of the parties will almost always remove the knowledgeable juror with a peremptory challenge. Does this special scrutiny of jurors who are aware of the relevant events systematically remove the most informed and intelligent candidates from the jury? Or is this a concern only in cases receiving unusual pretrial publicity?

2. *Excused for hardship.* The judge will at times "excuse" jurors who are qualified in general and who have no particular reason to favor one party or another. Statutes and procedural rules often specify that the judge may exempt jurors for "undue hardship" or "extreme inconvenience." Jurors themselves frequently raise this issue with the judge by describing the financial hardship of jury duty. See Sudler v. State,

611 A.2d 945 (Del. 1992) (trial court's excusal of five jurors based on their unavailability after holiday weekend violated defendant's right to jury trial). H. L. Mencken, the American journalist of the early twentieth century, defined a jury with this dynamic in mind: "Jury—A group of twelve men who, having lied to the judge about their hearing, health, and business engagements, have failed to fool him." What behavior might one expect from a juror who faces unusual hardships while serving on a jury? Would the juror predictably favor the prosecution or the defense?

The judge's decision about whether to excuse a juror for hardships interacts with rules about the length of service expected of jurors and the sanctions for citizens who do not appear for jury duty. How do you suppose a judge would react to a juror asking for a hardship excuse in a system requiring 10 days of service from jurors, and where only 5 percent of all citizens who are summoned actually appear for jury duty? Would the judge's response to the hardship request change in a "one day or one trial" system? Under the "one day or one trial" system, prospective jurors serve in a maximum of one trial and complete their service after one day if they are not chosen for a trial.

3. *Dismissals for cause in death penalty cases.* Special problems arise during voir dire in cases in which the prosecutor plans to seek the death penalty. Many jurors have pronounced views about the use of capital punishment, and those who strongly favor or oppose its use may still serve on the jury if they remain able to apply the law that dictates the cases eligible for the death penalty. However, if a juror declares that he would always vote to impose the death penalty, or to recommend against the death penalty, then he will be excluded for cause. See Witherspoon v. Illinois, 391 U.S. 510 (1968). If you were a prosecutor and a juror declares that she believes in the biblical injunction "an eye for an eye," what follow-up questions would you ask?

4. *Recusal of judges.* Just as jurors can be excluded when they are unable to find the facts impartially, a judge presiding at a trial may be removed from a case if she is not able to preside impartially. A party who questions the judge's impartiality may request that the judge "recuse" herself from the case. Statutes typically list some specific grounds for mandatory recusal, along with an instruction that the judge recuse herself whenever her "impartiality might reasonably be questioned." See 28 U.S.C. §455 (lists personal knowledge of disputed facts, family relationship with a party or attorney, and financial interest in outcome among the grounds for recusal). Another federal statute, 28 U.S.C. §144, allows a party to file an affidavit that the judge has a personal bias against him, supported by the reasons for that belief and a certificate that the affidavit is filed in good faith. Once the party has filed the affidavit, the judge must be removed from the case. A party can file only one such affidavit in any case. Is this affidavit a removal of the judge for cause, or is it the equivalent of a peremptory challenge? See Liteky v. United States, 510 U.S. 540 (1994) (recusal and removal statutes require "extrajudicial source" of bias; bias allegations cannot be sustained solely on rulings by judge or information judge received during judicial proceedings). These statutory standards give specific content to the constitutional requirement that judges be impartial. See Withrow v. Larkin, 421 U.S. 35 (1975) (judge may preside at trial despite ruling on pretrial matters such as warrant); Tumey v. Ohio, 273 U.S. 510 (1927) (due process requires recusal of judge who has direct pecuniary interest in outcome of case).

5. *Harmless error in denial of challenge for cause.* If the trial court refuses to excuse a juror for cause but the juror does not serve on the panel because the defendant uses a peremptory challenge to remove the juror, has any reversible error occurred?

e defendant had peremptory challenges to spare? Cf. United States v.
Salazar, 528 U.S. 304 (2000) (when judge fails to remove juror for
defendant must allow the juror on the panel to challenge the decision on
); Busby v. State, 894 So. 2d 88 (Fla. 2004) (defendant can challenge decision
emoval for cause even if juror excluded from panel based on peremptory; no
ual harm must be shown).

3. Peremptory Challenges

In addition to removal of jurors for cause, all states allow the parties to "strike"
additional jurors without any initial requirement of a reason or explanation. Such
strikes are called "peremptory challenges." The following Idaho statute sets out
the traditional definition: "A peremptory challenge . . . is an objection to a juror
for which no reason need be given, but upon which the court must exclude him."
Idaho Stat. §19-2015.

States usually allow a specific number of peremptory challenges, ranging from
2 to 20 or more. In some states, the parties have equal numbers of peremptories,
while elsewhere the defense may excuse more jurors than the prosecution.

The procedures for exercising peremptory challenges vary enormously. Statutes
and court rules describe the order in which peremptories must be exercised, often
establishing a back-and-forth pattern between defense and prosecution. Challenges
in some jurisdictions are made in the presence of jurors; in some jurisdictions
challenges must be made in writing. Generally, to preserve a challenge about jury
selection on appeal, a party must exhaust all peremptory challenges. The use of
objections for cause and peremptory challenges involves an intense mix of law and
trial strategy.

Why allow peremptory challenges? A number of theories have been advanced.
Consider the following explanation of the functions of peremptory challenges.

The peremptory challenge has traditionally served two principal functions. First, the
peremptory challenge provides a margin of protection for challenges for cause. [The]
difficulties of developing information about bias, together with the risk of error in
adjudicating claims of bias, combine to make the peremptory challenge an essential
fallback for use when a challenge for cause is rejected. . . . This device has the
advantage of saving the time of attorneys, jurors, and the court that would otherwise
be spent in probing the true extent, if any, of the bias of potential jurors. . . .

The second principal function of the peremptory challenge is to provide the
parties with an opportunity to participate in the construction of the decision-making
body, thereby enlisting their confidence in its decision. To fulfill this function, the
peremptory challenge gives the parties the power to exclude jurors who are indisput-
ably free of bias, merely because the parties would prefer to be judged by others instead.
(Indeed, the preference of the parties may well be not for unbiased jurors but for
favorably biased ones.) [This power] permits the parties to select jurors not only for
their freedom from bias, but also for such affirmative qualities as the parties may value.

This aspect of jury selection does not enhance the competence of the jury, because
by hypothesis it involves the exclusion of unbiased jurors, and therefore it does not
improve the accuracy of factfinding. Instead, it enhances the acceptability of the jury to
the parties, without in any way impairing the competence of the jury, and therefore it
enhances the acceptability of the verdict.

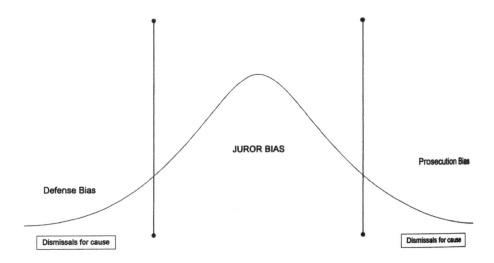

Barbara Underwood, Ending Race Discrimination in Jury Selection: Whose Right Is It, Anyway? 92 Colum. L. Rev. 725 (1992).

It may be helpful to think about a range of potential jurors, some of whom are biased for the prosecution, and others for the defense; indeed it may be helpful to picture the array of jurors along a bell curve (without making any necessary assumptions about the shape of the curve). Some of those biased jurors (and perhaps some unbiased jurors) will be dismissed by the court for "cause," either on the decision of the court or the motion of counsel. But some jurors in the middle of the bell curve will remain who the lawyers believe are likely to favor one side or the other. In theory, peremptory challenges allow the parties to shape a fair jury for their perspective, which may mean both avoiding antagonistic jurors and finding sympathetic ones.

Should peremptory challenges be allowed on any basis? Should lawyers ever be required to explain why they struck a particular juror? Until fairly recent times, these questions had relatively clear answers: peremptory strikes were just that, with no explanation required. Only if prosecutors engaged in a pattern of peremptory strikes across several cases that revealed racial discrimination would a review of those peremptory decisions be allowed. Strauder v. West Virginia, 100 U.S. 303 (1880); Swain v. Alabama, 380 U.S. 202 (1965). In 1978 California became the first state to prohibit race-based peremptory challenges in individual cases as a matter of state constitutional law, People v. Wheeler, 583 P.2d 748 (Cal. 1978). Massachusetts took a similar position in 1979, Commonwealth v. Soares, 387 N.E.2d 499 (Mass. 1979), as did Florida in 1984, State v. Neil, 457 So. 2d 481 (Fla. 1984). In 1986, the U.S. Supreme Court addressed the claim that the federal constitution prohibited race-based peremptory challenges in Batson v. Kentucky.

■ JAMES BATSON v. KENTUCKY
476 U.S. 79 (1986)

POWELL, J.

This case requires us to reexamine that portion of Swain v. Alabama, 380 U.S. 202 (1965), concerning the evidentiary burden placed on a criminal defendant who claims that he has been denied equal protection through the State's use of peremptory challenges to exclude members of his race from the petit jury.

Petitioner, a black man, was indicted in Kentucky on charges of second-degree burglary and receipt of stolen goods. On the first day of trial in Jefferson Circuit Court, the judge conducted voir dire examination of the venire, excused certain jurors for cause, and permitted the parties to exercise peremptory challenges. The prosecutor used his peremptory challenges to strike all four black persons on the venire, and a jury composed only of white persons was selected. Defense counsel moved to discharge the jury before it was sworn on the ground that the prosecutor's removal of the black veniremen violated petitioner's rights under the Sixth and Fourteenth Amendments to a jury drawn from a cross section of the community, and under the Fourteenth Amendment to equal protection of the laws. Counsel requested a hearing on his motion. Without expressly ruling on the request for a hearing, the trial judge observed that the parties were entitled to use their peremptory challenges to "strike anybody they want to." The judge then denied petitioner's motion, reasoning that the cross-section requirement applies only to selection of the venire and not to selection of the petit jury itself. The jury convicted petitioner on both counts. . . .

In Swain v. Alabama, this Court recognized that a "State's purposeful or deliberate denial to Negroes on account of race of participation as jurors in the administration of justice violates the Equal Protection Clause." This principle has been "consistently and repeatedly" reaffirmed, in numerous decisions of this Court both preceding and following *Swain*. We reaffirm the principle today.

More than a century ago, the Court decided that the State denies a black defendant equal protection of the laws when it puts him on trial before a jury from which members of his race have been purposefully excluded. Strauder v. West Virginia, 100 U.S. 303 (1880). That decision laid the foundation for the Court's unceasing efforts to eradicate racial discrimination in the procedures used to select the venire from which individual jurors are drawn.

[A] defendant has no right to a petit jury composed in whole or in part of persons of his own race. . . . But the defendant does have the right to be tried by a jury whose members are selected pursuant to nondiscriminatory criteria. The Equal Protection Clause guarantees the defendant that the State will not exclude members of his race from the jury venire on account of race, or on the false assumption that members of his race as a group are not qualified to serve as jurors.

Purposeful racial discrimination in selection of the venire violates a defendant's right to equal protection because it denies him the protection that a trial by jury is intended to secure. "The very idea of a jury is a body . . . composed of the peers or equals of the person whose rights it is selected or summoned to determine; that is, of his neighbors, fellows, associates, persons having the same legal status in society as that which he holds." *Strauder*. . . .

The harm from discriminatory jury selection extends beyond that inflicted on the defendant and the excluded juror to touch the entire community. Selection procedures that purposefully exclude black persons from juries undermine public confidence in the fairness of our system of justice. . . .

In *Strauder*, the Court invalidated a state statute that provided that only white men could serve as jurors. We can be confident that no State now has such a law. The Constitution requires, however, that we look beyond the face of the statute defining juror qualifications and also consider challenged selection practices to afford protection against action of the State through its administrative officers in effecting the prohibited discrimination. Thus, the Court has found a denial of equal protection where the procedures implementing a neutral statute operated to exclude persons from the venire on racial grounds, and has made clear that the Constitution prohibits all forms of purposeful racial discrimination in selection of jurors. . . .

Accordingly, the component of the jury selection process at issue here, the State's privilege to strike individual jurors through peremptory challenges, is subject to the commands of the Equal Protection Clause. Although a prosecutor ordinarily is entitled to exercise permitted peremptory challenges for any reason at all, as long as that reason is related to his view concerning the outcome of the case to be tried, the Equal Protection Clause forbids the prosecutor to challenge potential jurors solely on account of their race or on the assumption that black jurors as a group will be unable impartially to consider the State's case against a black defendant.

The principles announced in *Strauder* never have been questioned in any subsequent decision of this Court. Rather, the Court has been called upon repeatedly to review the application of those principles to particular facts. A recurring question in these cases, as in any case alleging a violation of the Equal Protection Clause, was whether the defendant had met his burden of proving purposeful discrimination on the part of the State. That question also was at the heart of the portion of Swain v. Alabama we reexamine today. . . .

The record in *Swain* showed that the prosecutor had used the State's peremptory challenges to strike the six black persons included on the petit jury venire. While rejecting the defendant's claim for failure to prove purposeful discrimination, the Court nonetheless indicated that the Equal Protection Clause placed some limits on the State's exercise of peremptory challenges.

The Court sought to accommodate the prosecutor's historical privilege of peremptory challenge free of judicial control, and the constitutional prohibition on exclusion of persons from jury service on account of race. While the Constitution does not confer a right to peremptory challenges, those challenges traditionally have been viewed as one means of assuring the selection of a qualified and unbiased jury. To preserve the peremptory nature of the prosecutor's challenge, the Court in *Swain* declined to scrutinize his actions in a particular case by relying on a presumption that he properly exercised the State's challenges.

[On the other hand, it] was impermissible for a prosecutor to use his challenges to exclude blacks from the jury "for reasons wholly unrelated to the outcome of the particular case on trial" or to deny to blacks "the same right and opportunity to participate in the administration of justice enjoyed by the white population." [A]n inference of purposeful discrimination would be raised on evidence that a prosecutor, "in case after case, whatever the circumstances, whatever the crime and whoever the defendant or the victim may be, is responsible for the removal of Negroes who have been selected as qualified jurors by the jury commissioners and who have survived challenges for cause, with the result that no Negroes ever serve on petit juries." Evidence offered by the defendant in *Swain* did not meet that standard. . . .

A number of lower courts following the teaching of *Swain* reasoned that proof of repeated striking of blacks over a number of cases was necessary to establish a violation of the Equal Protection Clause. Since this interpretation of *Swain* has placed on defendants a crippling burden of proof, prosecutors' peremptory challenges are now largely immune from constitutional scrutiny. For reasons that follow, we reject this evidentiary formulation as inconsistent with standards that have been developed since *Swain* for assessing a prima facie case under the Equal Protection Clause.

Since the decision in *Swain,* we have explained that [c]ircumstantial evidence of invidious intent may include proof of disproportionate impact. . . . Moreover, since *Swain,* we have recognized that . . . a defendant may make a prima facie showing of purposeful racial discrimination in selection of the venire by relying solely on the facts concerning its selection in his case. . . . A single invidiously discriminatory governmental act is not "immunized by the absence of such discrimination in the making of other comparable decisions." For evidentiary requirements to dictate that several must suffer discrimination before one could object would be inconsistent with the promise of equal protection to all.

[A] defendant may establish a prima facie case of purposeful discrimination in selection of the petit jury solely on evidence concerning the prosecutor's exercise of peremptory challenges at the defendant's trial. To establish such a case, the defendant first must show that he is a member of a cognizable racial group, and that the prosecutor has exercised peremptory challenges to remove from the venire members of the defendant's race. Second, the defendant is entitled to rely on the fact, as to which there can be no dispute, that peremptory challenges constitute a jury selection practice that permits those to discriminate who are of a mind to discriminate. Finally, the defendant must show that these facts and any other relevant circumstances raise an inference that the prosecutor used that practice to exclude the veniremen from the petit jury on account of their race. This combination of factors in the empanelling of the petit jury, as in the selection of the venire, raises the necessary inference of purposeful discrimination.

In deciding whether the defendant has made the requisite showing, the trial court should consider all relevant circumstances. For example, a "pattern" of strikes against black jurors included in the particular venire might give rise to an inference of discrimination. Similarly, the prosecutor's questions and statements during voir dire examination and in exercising his challenges may support or refute an inference of discriminatory purpose. These examples are merely illustrative. We have confidence that trial judges, experienced in supervising voir dire, will be able to decide if the circumstances concerning the prosecutor's use of peremptory challenges creates a prima facie case of discrimination against black jurors.

Once the defendant makes a prima facie showing, the burden shifts to the State to come forward with a neutral explanation for challenging black jurors. Though this requirement imposes a limitation in some cases on the full peremptory character of the historic challenge, we emphasize that the prosecutor's explanation need not rise to the level justifying exercise of a challenge for cause. But the prosecutor may not rebut the defendant's prima facie case of discrimination by stating merely that he challenged jurors of the defendant's race on the assumption — or his intuitive judgment — that they would be partial to the defendant because of their shared race. Just as the Equal Protection Clause forbids the States to exclude black persons from the venire on the assumption that blacks as a group are unqualified to serve as jurors, so it forbids the States to strike black veniremen on the assumption that they will be biased in a particular case simply because the defendant is black. The core guarantee of equal protection, ensuring citizens that their State will not discriminate on account of race, would be meaningless were we to approve the exclusion of jurors on the basis of such assumptions, which arise solely from the jurors' race. Nor may the prosecutor rebut the defendant's case merely by denying that he had a discriminatory motive or affirming his good faith in making individual selections. . . . The prosecutor therefore must articulate a neutral explanation related to the particular case to be tried. The trial court then will have the duty to determine if the defendant has established purposeful discrimination.

[We] do not agree that our decision today will undermine the contribution the challenge generally makes to the administration of justice. The reality of practice, amply reflected in many state- and federal-court opinions, shows that the challenge may be, and unfortunately at times has been, used to discriminate against black jurors. By requiring trial courts to be sensitive to the racially discriminatory use of peremptory challenges, our decision enforces the mandate of equal protection and furthers the ends of justice. In view of the heterogeneous population of our Nation, public respect for our criminal justice system and the rule of law will be strengthened if we ensure that no citizen is disqualified from jury service because of his race. . . .

MARSHALL, J., concurring.

I join Justice Powell's eloquent opinion for the Court, which takes a historic step toward eliminating the shameful practice of racial discrimination in the selection of juries. . . . I nonetheless write separately to express my views. The decision today will not end the racial discrimination that peremptories inject into the jury-selection process. That goal can be accomplished only by eliminating peremptory challenges entirely. . . .

Merely allowing defendants the opportunity to challenge the racially discriminatory use of peremptory challenges in individual cases will not end the illegitimate use of the peremptory challenge. . . . First, defendants cannot attack the discriminatory use of peremptory challenges at all unless the challenges are so flagrant as to establish a prima facie case. This means . . . that where only one or two black jurors survive the challenges for cause, the prosecutor need have no compunction about striking them from the jury because of their race. See Commonwealth v. Robinson, 415 N.E.2d 805 (Mass. 1981) (no prima facie case of discrimination where defendant is black, prospective jurors include three blacks and one Puerto Rican, and prosecutor excludes one for cause and strikes the remainder peremptorily, producing all-white jury). Prosecutors are left free to discriminate against blacks in jury selection provided that they hold that discrimination to an "acceptable" level.

Second, when a defendant can establish a prima facie case, trial courts face the difficult burden of assessing prosecutors' motives. Any prosecutor can easily assert facially neutral reasons for striking a juror, and trial courts are ill equipped to second-guess those reasons. How is the court to treat a prosecutor's statement that he struck a juror because the juror had a son about the same age as defendant, or seemed uncommunicative, or "never cracked a smile"? . . .

Nor is outright prevarication by prosecutors the only danger here. . . . A prosecutor's own conscious or unconscious racism may lead him easily to the conclusion that a prospective black juror is "sullen," or "distant," a characterization that would not have come to his mind if a white juror had acted identically. A judge's own conscious or unconscious racism may lead him to accept such an explanation as well supported. . . .

Some authors have suggested that the courts should ban prosecutors' peremptories entirely, but should zealously guard the defendant's peremptory as essential to the fairness of trial by jury. . . . I would not find that an acceptable solution. Our criminal justice system "requires not only freedom from any bias against the accused, but also from any prejudice against his prosecution. Between him and the state the scales are to be evenly held." Hayes v. Missouri, 120 U.S. 68 (1887). We can maintain that balance, not by permitting both prosecutor and defendant to engage in racial discrimination in jury selection, but by banning the use of peremptory challenges by prosecutors and by allowing the States to eliminate the defendant's peremptories as well. . . .

BURGER, C.J., dissenting.

Today the Court sets aside the peremptory challenge, a procedure which has been part of the common law for many centuries and part of our jury system for nearly 200 years. . . . The peremptory challenge has been in use without scrutiny into its basis for nearly as long as juries have existed. "It was in use amongst the Romans in criminal cases, and the Lex Servilia (B.C. 104) enacted that the accuser and the accused should severally propose one hundred judices, and that each might reject fifty from the list of the other, so that one hundred would remain to try the alleged crime." W. Forsyth, History of Trial by Jury 175 (1852). . . .

Permitting unexplained peremptories has long been regarded as a means to strengthen our jury system. . . . One commentator has recognized:

> The peremptory, made without giving any reason, avoids trafficking in the core of truth in most common stereotypes. . . . Common human experience, common sense, psychosociological studies, and public opinion polls tell us that it is likely that certain classes of people statistically have predispositions that would make them inappropriate jurors for particular kinds of cases. But to allow this knowledge to be expressed in the evaluative terms necessary for challenges for cause would undercut our desire for a society in which all people are judged as individuals and in which each is held reasonable and open to compromise. . . . Instead we have evolved in the peremptory challenge a system that allows the covert expression of what we dare not say but know is true more often than not.

Babcock, Voir Dire: Preserving "Its Wonderful Power," 27 Stan. L. Rev. 545 (1975). . . . A moment's reflection quickly reveals the vast differences between the racial exclusions involved in *Strauder* and the allegations before us today:

> [E]xcluding a particular cognizable group from all venire pools is stigmatizing and discriminatory in several interrelated ways that the peremptory challenge is not. The former singles out the excluded group, while individuals of all groups are equally subject to peremptory challenge on any basis, including their group affiliation. Further, venire-pool exclusion bespeaks a priori across-the-board total unfitness, while peremptory-strike exclusion merely suggests potential partiality in a particular isolated case. . . . To suggest that a particular race is unfit to judge in any case necessarily is racially insulting. To suggest that each race may have its own special concerns, or even may tend to favor its own, is not.

United States v. Leslie, 783 F.2d 541 (5th Cir. 1986) (en banc). Unwilling to rest solely on jury venire cases such as *Strauder*, the Court also invokes general equal protection principles in support of its holding. [However,] in making peremptory challenges, both the prosecutor and defense attorney necessarily act on only limited information or hunch. The process cannot be indicted on the sole basis that such decisions are made on the basis of assumption or intuitive judgment. As a result, unadulterated equal protection analysis is simply inapplicable to peremptory challenges exercised in any particular case. A clause that requires a minimum "rationality" in government actions has no application to "an arbitrary and capricious right." *Swain*.

[I]f conventional equal protection principles apply, then presumably defendants could object to exclusions on the basis of not only race, but also sex, age, religious or political affiliation, mental capacity, number of children, living arrangements, and employment in a particular industry or profession. In short, it is quite probable that every peremptory challenge could be objected to on the basis that, because it excluded a venireman who had some characteristic not shared by the remaining members of the venire, it constituted a "classification" subject to equal protection scrutiny. . . .

Our system permits two types of challenges: challenges for cause and peremptory challenges. Challenges for cause obviously have to be explained; by definition, peremptory challenges do not. . . . Analytically, there is no middle ground: A challenge either has to be explained or it does not. It is readily apparent, then, that to permit inquiry into the basis for a peremptory challenge would force the peremptory challenge to collapse into the challenge for cause. . . .

A "clear and reasonably specific" explanation of "legitimate reasons" for exercising the challenge will be difficult to distinguish from a challenge for cause. Anything short of a challenge for cause may well be seen as an "arbitrary and capricious" challenge, to use Blackstone's characterization of the peremptory. Apparently the Court envisions permissible challenges short of a challenge for cause that are just a little bit arbitrary—but not too much. While our trial judges are experienced in supervising voir dire, they have no experience in administering rules like this.

[One] painful paradox of the Court's holding is that it is likely to interject racial matters back into the jury selection process, contrary to the general thrust of a long line of Court decisions and the notion of our country as a "melting pot." . . . Today we mark the return of racial differentiation as the Court accepts a positive evil for a perceived one. Prosecutors and defense attorneys alike will build records in support of their claims that peremptory challenges have been exercised in a racially discriminatory fashion by asking jurors to state their racial background and national origin for the record, despite the fact that such questions may be offensive to some jurors and thus are not ordinarily asked on voir dire. . . .

REHNQUIST, J., dissenting.

. . . In my view, there is simply nothing "unequal" about the State's using its peremptory challenges to strike blacks from the jury in cases involving black defendants, so long as such challenges are also used to exclude whites in cases involving white defendants, Hispanics in cases involving Hispanic defendants, Asians in cases involving Asian defendants, and so on. This case-specific use of peremptory challenges by the State does not single out blacks, or members of any other race for that matter, for discriminatory treatment. Such use of peremptories is at best based upon seat-of-the-pants instincts, which are undoubtedly crudely stereotypical and may in many cases be hopelessly mistaken. But as long as they are applied across-the-board to jurors of all races and nationalities, I do not see — and the Court most certainly has not explained — how their use violates the Equal Protection Clause. [G]iven the need for reasonable limitations on the time devoted to voir dire, the use of such "proxies" by both the State and the defendant may be extremely useful in eliminating from the jury persons who might be biased in one way or another. . . .

■ RODNEY LINGO v. STATE
437 S.E.2d 463 (Ga. 1993)

HUNT, P.J.

Rodney Dwayne Lingo was convicted of murder, theft by taking of a motor vehicle, and armed robbery. He was indicted for but found not guilty of rape. The state unsuccessfully sought a death sentence. Lingo received a life sentence for murder, a consecutive life sentence for armed robbery, and a consecutive 20-year sentence for theft by taking.

At the time the victim, Tracy Plank, was killed, Lingo was living with a friend or acquaintance of the victim, Teresa Cooper. The evidence showed that on the evening of November 4, 1985, the victim and Lingo left the home of a mutual friend together in the victim's car. Several hours later, Lingo was seen driving the victim's car alone. The next day, Lingo was seen wearing the victim's jacket and trying to sell parts of the victim's car. The victim's body was found in a roadside wooded area about five days later. She had been shot twice in the head with a gun belonging to Lingo. In statements given to the police, Lingo claims that another friend, who was riding around with him and the victim, was the one who actually shot the victim. In subsequent statements, Lingo implicates two other, different people with pulling the trigger. . . .

Lingo, who is black, contests the trial court's ruling that the reasons given by the prosecutor for the exercise of his peremptory strikes were adequate under Batson v. Kentucky, 476 U.S. 79 (1986), and its progeny. We find that notwithstanding the prima facie inference of racial discrimination, the record supports the trial court's findings that the prosecutor's reasons for his strikes were racially neutral, and shows that the prosecutor was able to overcome the prima facie case.

The venire was made up of 50 qualified jurors, and the petit jury was selected from the first 47 jurors called. Of those 47 jurors, 34 were white and 13 were black. The state exercised its ten peremptory strikes against the first ten black venire members called. After the state had exhausted its peremptory strikes, two black jurors were added to the petit jury by the defense. The state then used its only peremptory strike for alternate jurors on the first black potential alternate juror to be called. The record does not indicate the race of the three qualified jurors who remained after the jury was empanelled. Therefore, at least 13 and no more than 16 of the 50 qualified jurors were black (26 percent to 32 percent), and 2 of the 12 jurors who served were black (16.7 percent). The prosecutor exercised 100 percent of his peremptory strikes to exclude black jurors and did not accept any of the black jurors called before he exhausted his strikes.

This overwhelming pattern of strikes establishes a prima facie inference of racial discrimination. Ford v. State, 423 S.E.2d 245 (Ga. 1992). To overcome this inference of discrimination, the prosecutor must present concrete, tangible, race-neutral and neutrally-applied reasons for the strikes exercised against black venire members. The greater the disparity between the percentage of black jurors in the venire and the percentage of strikes exercised by the state against black jurors, the more likely it becomes that racial bias underlies the exercise of the peremptory challenges, and the greater the scrutiny the trial court must apply to the prosecutor's proffered explanations. . . .

Thus, we must review the prosecutor's stated reasons for his strikes to determine whether they overcame the defendant's prima facie case of discrimination. In so doing, we must give the trial court's factual findings great deference. We may only disregard those findings if they are clearly erroneous. Of course, we may still disagree with the trial court's conclusions based on those findings and where there is a strong prima facie case, as here, we must carefully scrutinize those conclusions. We review each of the prosecutor's strikes as follows:

(1) The prosecutor gave as his reasons in support of his first strike, which was against a black woman, the fact that the woman was "indecisive" about the death penalty, and preferred a life sentence, and that she had a hearing problem. . . .

(2) The prosecutor's reasons for his second strike, against a black man, were that he was strongly opposed to the death penalty, and had a DUI conviction. . . .

(3) The prosecutor's reasons for his third strike, against a black woman, were that she was hesitant about the death penalty, and initially stated she would not stand up and affirm a verdict of death and the death penalty, and that she was familiar with the case and a witness in the case. . . .

(4) The prosecutor gave as his reasons for his fourth strike, against a black woman, the fact that she was opposed to the death penalty, and knew a witness in the case. . . .

(5) The prosecutor's reason in support of his fifth strike, against a black man, was that the juror made it very clear he did not want to serve, that the prosecutor was concerned the juror would be preoccupied with his financial problems, and that the prosecutor had difficulty in getting the juror to respond or pay attention to his questions. The trial court found these reasons to be race-neutral, specifically recalling that the juror could not keep still during the voir dire, and, itself, questioning whether "from his demeanor" this juror was "competent to handle this type of situation."

(6) The prosecutor's reasons in support of his sixth strike, also against a black man, were that the juror was opposed to the death penalty, and was familiar with the defendant and with a witness. . . .

(7) The prosecutor's reasons in support of his seventh strike, against a black woman, were that she was very opposed to the death penalty, and that if she served, the prosecutor was concerned she would be preoccupied with a sick child at home. The trial court . . . noted his recollection that the juror clearly did not want to be there, and someone had to be sent to get her for jury duty.

(8) The prosecutor's reasons for his eighth strike, against a black man, were that he was initially hostile in his responses, and this juror and the prosecutor "got

off on the wrong foot at the very start." The prosecutor also gave as reasons the fact that the juror's criminal justice degree might affect his objectivity, and that the juror had testified as a character witness on behalf of a defendant in a prior case. The trial court, in accepting the prosecutor's reasons as race-neutral, specifically recalled this juror's responses as belligerent.

(9) The prosecutor's reasons for his ninth strike, against a black woman, were that she knew a witness in the case, could not give her sentence if polled, and that she had a conviction for shoplifting. . . .

(10) The prosecutor gave as his reason for his tenth strike, against a black man, that the juror had a prior conviction, and had indicated on the jury questionnaire that he had a "bad check problem." . . .

(11) Finally, the prosecutor gave as his reasons for striking an alternate juror, a black woman, the fact that she was opposed to the death penalty, as well as the fact that she was a teacher and school was to start the following Monday. . . .

The record supports the trial court's findings that the reasons given by the prosecutor were not racially motivated, and demonstrates that the prosecutor was able to overcome the very strong prima facie inference of racial discrimination.

The dissent correctly cites Strozier v. Clark, 424 S.E.2d 368 (Ga. Ct. App. 1992), a recent Court of Appeals case, for the rule that where racially-neutral and neutrally-applied reasons are given for a strike, the simultaneous existence of any racially motivated explanation results in a *Batson* violation.[4] However, the dissent would misapply this rule by creating a presumption that any reason for striking a black juror, not also used against a white juror — regardless of other reasons for striking a black juror — is per se racially motivated. This is not what *Batson* or *Strozier* hold, or even imply. Rather, there is a *Batson* violation only where the prosecutor's explanation is determined to be racially motivated. Where there are multiple reasons for striking a juror, white or black, it cannot be presumed that a reason applied to one juror, of one race, but not applied to another juror, of another race, is racially motivated.

Of course we are required, in a strong prima facie case such as here, to carefully examine the prosecutor's remaining reasons, to determine if there is an underlying racial motive. And, where a reason is given against a black juror, not also used against a white juror, the reason is particularly suspect. However, we are not authorized to

4. . . . *Strozier* stands for the proposition that where it can be determined that the racially-neutral explanation is, in fact, pretextual since there is a racially motivated reason that can be independently determined, the jury selection process is invalid under *Batson. Strozier* does not hold that where one racially-neutral reason is given for striking a juror, any additional reason, not also used against a juror of another race, is per se racially motivated. The cases cited by *Strozier* illustrate that there must be some indication that the "additional reason" is, in fact, racially motivated. In Moore v. State, 811 S.W.2d 197 (Tex. Ct. App. 1991), the prosecutor stated that she struck one juror, in part, because that juror was a member of a minority club. Of course, this was not a racially-neutral reason, notwithstanding that the prosecutor also gave, as a reason for striking this juror, that the juror was hesitant to impose a life sentence. In State v. Tomlin, 384 S.E.2d 707 (S.C. 1989) the prosecutor gave the racially-neutral reason for striking a juror as the fact that the juror was unemployed, but also stated that the juror "shucked and jived." In *Strozier* itself, the prosecutor, in addition to stating the apparently neutral reason of the juror's age as his reason for striking her, also gave his completely unsupported opinion that the juror was dishonest in her answer to questions, an opinion he stated was based on an experience the prosecutor had previously, with other jurors, in an unrelated case. Thus, . . . it is apparent that the "additional reasons," in themselves, were racially motivated and, accordingly, rendered the selection process invalid under *Batson.*

create an inference of discrimination where none is apparent, and where none has been found by the trial court, to whose findings we must give great deference. . . . While we are required to carefully review the record in a case involving a *Batson* challenge, especially where a strong prima facie case is made, we are still required to give the trial court's findings "great deference," and we are not authorized to ignore them. Here, the trial court's findings are not clearly erroneous. . . . Judgment affirmed.

SEARS-COLLINS, J., dissenting.

When it comes to grappling with racial issues in the criminal justice system today, often white Americans find one reality while African-Americans see another. This perception gap is evident in the majority's affirmance of Rodney Dwayne Lingo's conviction. As I cannot ignore the race-based innuendo and subtle stereotyping used to exclude people of color from Lingo's jury, I must dissent.

The prosecutor exercised 100 percent of his peremptory strikes to exclude the first ten black jurors called from the venire. He was content with none of the African-American jurors called before he exhausted his strikes. This is an "overwhelming pattern" of strikes, as recognized by the majority, and establishes a powerful prima facie inference of racial discrimination. It is up to the prosecutor to present "concrete, tangible, race-neutral and neutrally-applied" reasons for the strikes exercised against black venire members. Ford v. State. In deciding whether the reasons given by the prosecutor were "neutrally applied," we consider whether the reasons given could apply equally to white jurors who were not struck by the prosecutor. "A prosecutor's failure to explain the apparently disparate treatment of similarly situated white and black jurors . . . diminishes the force of his explanation for striking a black juror." Ford v. State.

Even if racially-neutral and neutrally-applied reasons are given, the simultaneous existence of any racially motivated explanation "vitiates the legitimacy of the entire (jury selection) procedure." Strozier v. Clark, 424 S.E.2d 368 (Ga. Ct. App. 1992). . . .

The prosecutor explained that one potential black juror was struck because: he was "touchy" about one of the prosecutor's first questions and "hostile from there on"; he had previously testified in a trial as a character witness; and he had taken some criminal justice classes. The voir dire examination of this juror is set forth . . . as follows:

Q: Mr. Cothran, [this] is a potential death penalty case, and because of that I have to begin by asking you this question: Are you so conscientiously opposed to capital punishment that you would not vote for the death penalty under any circumstances?

A: No.

Q: Okay. . . . In a death penalty case, what happens is, and you may already be aware of this—you're a criminal justice major; you've taken some courses in criminal justice; is that right?

A: How was that revealed to you, sir? Was I supposed to answer that?

Q: Well, that's fine, but you put it on your questionnaire.

A: Oh, okay. I have forgot I put it down there, but I have taken some courses.

Q: So you already know this, . . . but in a death penalty case what happens is that trial is divided into two parts. The first part is called a guilt-innocence phase. [I]f and only if in phase one they find the defendant guilty of murder, then they move into phase two which we call the sentencing phase. . . . You understand that . . . the Court would authorize you to consider the death penalty as a sentence, but you'd also be obligated to consider life as a sentence? Now, would you be able to consider both of those options?

A: Yes.

Q: Okay. . . . if the Court charges you that proof beyond a reasonable doubt is not proof beyond all doubt, but is simply proof to a moral and a reasonable certainty, would you follow that charge?

A: If within myself, with the evidence that I have heard and able to reach an agreement within myself, then I would follow that.

Mr. Lukemire: Thank you.

With respect to this juror, the trial court stated:

> As far as Mr. Cothran was concerned, that one got very close to the line, but I do recall when he did make the response concerning the criminal justice degree that it definitely, just from an oral response, I was not looking at him, it caught my attention that he did seem to be belligerent, and I will be very candid about this, had there been no blacks on this jury, the court would have had real trouble with not possibly finding there might have been some type of pattern, just with [this juror].

Contrary to the trial court's statement, however, the fact that two black jurors were added to the jury after the prosecutor had exhausted his peremptory strikes is irrelevant to the inquiry of whether this juror was struck because of racial bias and does not eliminate the obvious racial discrimination in the prosecutor's strike against this juror. Moreover, the trial court's statement indicates that but for this irrelevancy it would have found racial bias in the striking of this juror. Furthermore, the above portion of the record reveals that other than being initially surprised by the prosecutor's knowledge of information the juror had provided on his juror questionnaire, the juror showed no indication of being "hostile" towards the prosecutor. Even giving great deference to the trial court, I still cannot believe that a white juror who gave exactly the same responses to the voir dire questions that this juror gave would have been labeled "hostile" and "belligerent." The hostility and belligerence found so readily by the prosecutor and the trial judge from this juror's one response evoke stereotypical images of the angry black man, who, at the slightest provocation and at even the faintest appearance of challenging the status quo will be tagged "hostile" or "belligerent."

The prosecutor further explained that he excluded this juror because he had served as a character witness in another proceeding. This reason was not neutrally applied, however, because the prosecutor accepted without complaint a white juror who had previously testified in a trial as a character witness. The prosecutor also explained that he did not want this juror on the panel because he had taken criminal justice classes. While a juror's legal background often justifies a strike, in this case the prosecutor asked the juror not one question as to whether the juror would be influenced by the classes he had taken, and when asked specifically whether he could follow the charge of the court the juror responded that he could do so.

To conclude, even assuming that the fact that the juror had taken some criminal justice classes was a non-racially motivated reason for striking this juror, both the prosecutor's application of the racial stereotype of the "hostile black male" and his failure to neutrally apply his other reason for striking this juror force me to conclude that improper racial motives played a role in the prosecutor's striking the juror.

The prosecutor explained that he struck one prospective juror, who was young, black, unemployed, and lived with his unemployed girlfriend and her three children, because he "made it very clear he did not want to be here" due to his financial problems, and might not be able to concentrate. When asked if he would have problems with service, this juror responded as follows: ". . . It's going to cause me a heap of problems. See, I've got a heap — I've got bills all the way up to my neck to pay. . . . I can't keep running down here and all because my girlfriend ain't working, and it's kind of hard on me. I can't go."

The record reveals that when asked, the juror stated that he would not have a problem focusing his attention on the trial. Moreover, the prosecutor accepted a white juror who was unemployed, and at least three other white jurors with whom the prosecutor was content stated specifically that jury service would be inconvenient or would pose a financial hardship for them. Compare the explanation given by one of the white jurors who expressed a problem with service on financial grounds:

> . . . I work for General Telephone, and if I don't work, I don't get paid, you know. I have no sick leave, no vacation leave, and I support my family, and it's, you know — you know, I know I have a civil duty to be here, but it's hard to make a living on . . . the money we receive.

While the white juror may have been better able to articulate his position, he made it no less clear that he did not want to be there. Yet the prosecutor accepted the white juror.

I would find on the basis of either of the above jurors alone that the prosecutor failed to overcome the powerful prima facie case of racial discrimination. In rebuffing the *Batson* challenge, the majority stresses the *Batson* edict that the trial court is to be afforded "great deference." I do not believe that "great deference" means ignoring blatant discrimination. . . .

With respect to seven of the black jurors struck by the prosecutor (including a prospective alternate juror), the prosecutor explained that the jurors had some aversion to the death penalty. The record reveals that one of the black jurors struck for this reason repeatedly indicated she was willing to impose a death sentence if warranted by the circumstances, and two others were hesitant about the death penalty, but said that they could consider it as a form of punishment after hearing the evidence. However, in ruling in the state's favor on the defendant's *Batson* motion, the trial court stated his recollection that while both black and white jurors expressed hesitancy about the death penalty, the black jurors struck for that reason were more adamant against the death penalty than were the white jurors. Even if we defer to the trial court's decision that this is a race-neutral reason, the fact remains that included among the prosecutor's reasons for striking those jurors were other reasons that were not well-founded in the record or were not neutrally applied among the black and white jurors. For example, the prosecutor reasoned that one potential juror would not be able to state her decision when polled in court. The record reveals, however, that the juror initially misunderstood the prosecutor's question; when it was clarified, she said that she would be able to give her decision when polled. Also, the prosecutor stated that one black prospective juror was struck because the juror had a hearing problem. While the prosecutor said that the juror had a hearing problem, the record indicates that the juror never claimed to have a hearing problem, and the state had no objection to a white juror who told the prosecutor twice during voir dire that he had a hearing problem.

The prosecutor stated that four black jurors were struck, among other reasons, because they knew witnesses. The record reveals that the state accepted six white jurors who also knew witnesses. Two of the four black jurors struck for this reason indicated they knew witnesses by sight but did not have personal relationships with those witnesses. Among the white jurors accepted by the state who knew witnesses, however, one played cards with two witnesses, while another had lived in the same neighborhood and belonged to the same church as a witness. . . .

The majority states that I would apply Strozier v. Clark to "create a presumption that any reason for striking a black juror, not also used against a white juror — regardless of other reasons for striking a black juror — is, per se racially motivated." That is not correct. To the contrary, as the majority itself notes, the inference of discrimination in this case is created by the prima facie case, which the prosecutor carries the burden of overcoming. I would apply to this case the rule established by this court that where there is a strong prima facie case, the prosecutor's reason for his strikes must be neutrally applied. Moreover, contrary to the implication in the majority, I do not say that any one non-neutrally applied reason renders the jury selection invalid, but that when inequity in application so permeates the process, the fact that a race-neutral reason was also given cannot . . . remedy the discrimination. The majority opinion does not refute the *Strozier* rule, but implies that it should not apply in this case because the "bad" reasons in *Strozier* were facially race-based or pretextual, whereas in this case it is necessary to look at all of the reasons given by the prosecutor to discern the overriding racial foundation for the strikes. I believe that this is a dangerous distinction without a difference, as subtle racial discrimination is just as damaging, if not more so, as overt racial discrimination.

We stand at the edge of the 21st century and many people of color in this country are still not free from insidious racial discrimination such as that manifested in this case. The constitutions of the United States and of Georgia demand the total, uncompromising racial neutrality of the jury selection process to ensure every American's right to fully participate, and Rodney Dwayne Lingo did not receive that neutrality. My candor in this dissent may lead some to believe that I am "hostile." I am not. I am, however, fully committed to the promise of the U.S. and Georgia Constitutions to afford their rights and privileges to all citizens.

Notes

1. *Number and theory of peremptory challenges: majority view.* States generally allow the most peremptory challenges in capital cases and the least in misdemeanor cases. In capital cases the number of challenges allowed varies between 4 (in

Virginia) and 25 (in Connecticut), with the majority of capital states allowing between 12 and 20. Some of these states grant the defense more challenges than the prosecution. For felonies, states allow between 3 (Hawaii and New Hampshire) and 20 (New Jersey) peremptory challenges, with about a third of states allowing 6 challenges. As with capital cases, a significant minority of states provide the prosecution with fewer possible challenges than the defense. For misdemeanor jury trials, the number of peremptory challenges allowed ranges between 2 (Missouri) and 10 (California and New Jersey), with almost half the states allowing 3 possible challenges. Bureau of Justice Statistics, State Court Organization 1998, at table 41 (June 2000, NCJ 178932). Peremptory challenges were allowed in the Judiciary Act of 1790 for treason and felonies punishable by death. In felony cases the federal system currently allows 10 strikes for the defense but only 6 for the prosecution. Fed. R. Crim. P. 24. In 1993, about 20 percent of all potential federal jurors were excluded through peremptory challenge. Under what theory are far greater numbers of challenges allowed in more serious cases? What differences explain the wide range in the numbers of peremptory challenges allowed in capital and serious felony cases?

In multi-defendant trials some states allow each defendant to exercise an individual allotment of peremptory challenges. See, e.g., Wyo. Stat. §711.103 ("The number of peremptory challenges allowed to the prosecution shall be multiplied by the number of defendants on trial in each case. Each defendant shall be allowed separate peremptory challenges"). Those states typically provide the prosecution with proportionately greater number of challenges as well. Some states limit the total number of peremptories in multi-defendant trials and require defendants to use fewer than if they were tried separately. See, e.g., Cal. Code Crim. Proc. §231(a) ("When two or more defendants are jointly tried, their challenges shall be exercised jointly, but each defendant shall also be entitled to five additional challenges which may be exercised separately, and the people shall also be entitled to additional challenges equal to the number of all the additional separate challenges allowed the defendants"). What theory of peremptory challenges supports limits on total peremptory challenges regardless of the number of defendants? What theory allows each defendant a separate allotment of peremptory challenges? Theories explaining peremptory challenges rely on often unstated assumptions. It is useful to articulate these assumptions and consider how you might test them. For example, if the goal of peremptories is thought to be the elimination of biased jurors, can jurors be tested for bias? See Hans Zeisel & Shari Diamond, The Effect of Peremptory Challenges on Jury and Verdict: An Experiment in a Federal District Court, 30 Stan. L. Rev. 491 (1978). If the goal of peremptories is to provide defendants with greater confidence in the fairness of the system, can this be tested? What other benefits might peremptories provide?

2. *Racial discrimination in peremptory challenges.* *Batson* has generated an enormous volume of state and federal case law as courts have wrestled with numerous claims of discrimination and pretext. *Batson* has also produced a large volume of commentary, with observers variously applauding the decision or criticizing it for not going far enough, for being unworkable, or for undermining an essential component of adversary trials. See, e.g., Barbara Underwood, Ending Race Discrimination in Jury Selection: Whose Right Is It, Anyway? 92 Colum. L. Rev. 725 (1992); Albert Alschuler, The Supreme Court and the Jury: Voir Dire, Peremptory Challenges, and

the Review of Jury Verdicts, 56 U. Chi. L. Rev. 153 (1989). Some state legislatures have tried to clarify the law by codified the right recognized in *Batson*. See, e.g., Tex. Code Crim. Proc. art. 35.261; La. Code Crim. Proc. art. 795.

3. *Stages of a* Batson *claim*. Many difficult legal and strategic questions arise under *Batson*. However, it is not legal but factual and strategic decisions that dominate day-to-day jury practice. The court in *Batson* sketched the basic procedure, which largely mirrors federal discrimination claims made under Title VII: First, the defendant must establish a prima facie case of intentional discrimination; second, the prosecutor must offer a neutral explanation for why it struck black jurors; finally, the trial court determines whether or not there has been "purposeful discrimination." In 1995 the Supreme Court, in the case of Purkett v. Elem, 514 U.S. 765 (1995), strengthened the analogy between *Batson* claims and claims made under Title VII when it held that the government's burden at the second stage is merely a burden of production that can be satisfied by virtually any race-neutral explanation (including a "silly" or "superstitious" explanation), and that it is the defendant who carries the burden of persuasion that purposeful discrimination has in fact occurred. See also Johnson v. California, 545 U.S. 162 (2005) (party trying to establish prima facie case under *Batson* need not show by preponderance of evidence that peremptory challenge was based on improper bias).

Trial courts are relatively amenable to hearing *Batson* challenges — in other words, recognizing that a prima facie case has been made — but find purposeful discrimination and grant relief much less often. See Kenneth Melilli, *Batson* in Practice: What We Have Learned About *Batson* and Peremptory Challenges, 71 Notre Dame L. Rev. 447 (1996). Professor Melilli studied all published *Batson* decisions in state and federal court between April 1986 and December 1993. He found that about 60 percent of prima facie claims were recognized by the court but that only about 20 percent of *Batson* claims resulted in a finding of discriminatory peremptory strikes.

4. *Pretext and truth*. The *Lingo* case illustrates both the established dynamic for *Batson* claims and the difficulty, for both trial and appellate courts, in assessing whether intentional discrimination has occurred. The key element of *Batson* battles are the explanations given by the prosecutor for striking one or more jurors. While courts hesitate to find a prima facie case when only a single juror strike is identified by the defendant as discriminatory, the decisions of trial and appellate courts often turn on the reasons given by the prosecutor for only one or two jurors, as in *Lingo*. Especially after Purkett v. Elem, prosecutors often find it easy to offer some race-neutral explanation for every juror: The difficult questions are whether the explanation, if honest, is sufficient and whether the explanation in each case is the "true" reason for a strike or is a pretext for striking a juror on the basis of race.

The *Lingo* case from Georgia provides several illustrations of the reasons that prosecutors offer for strikes, including opposition to the death penalty (especially in death penalty cases), prior criminal record on the part of the juror, relationship or acquaintance with a witness, and involvement in prior court proceedings. Are there particular kinds of explanations that should not be allowed because trial courts cannot easily assess whether they are the real reason? Which of the following reasons given by prosecutors for striking jurors seem most likely to be true, and which seem to be a pretext? Does the difficulty of this judgment reveal the flaws or virtues of the *Batson* approach?

- Appearance, e.g., shoulder-length, curly, unkempt hair, along with a mustache and a goatee-type beard (Purkett v. Elem); overweight; "a young, pretty woman" who might be "attracted to defendant or defense counsel"
- Unemployment, e.g., "unemployed people are less likely to be sympathetic to the prosecution"
- Age, e.g., "every juror below the age of 30 because . . . from my experience as a prosecutor and defense lawyer . . . older jurors are generally more likely to be prosecution minded or favorable to the prosecution"
- Place of residence, e.g., "high-crime area"
- Habits, e.g., "excessively verbal"; "loner"; "inattentive"
- Fortuitous links: juror has same last name as defense lawyer

Most courts reject simple "gut feelings" or "hunches" as a reason to strike a juror, though it is sometimes difficult to distinguish gut feelings from the reasons that are offered. See Commonwealth v. Maldonado, 788 N.E.2d 968 (Mass. 2003) (reasons based on subjective data such as juror's looks or gestures, or attorney's "gut" feeling should "rarely be accepted as adequate because such explanations can easily be used as pretexts for discrimination"). Is it possible to categorize explanations for strikes and to provide different standards of review to different types of explanations? If not, is the whole *Batson* scheme unworkable? Can't any bright lawyer with sufficient knowledge and planning always find a defensible reason to strike any juror? See Andrew D. Leipold, Constitutionalizing Jury Selection in Criminal Cases: A Critical Evaluation, 86 Geo. L.J. 945 (1998).

5. *Race-neutral reasons and appellate courts.* The trial court initially evaluates the reasons that a party gives for striking jurors and determines whether the race-neutral reason was a genuine explanation for the strikes. What sort of deference should this finding of the trial judge receive on appellate review? The Supreme Court offered some guidance on the proper role of appellate review in Miller-El v. Dretke, 545 U.S. 231 (2005). The court described several reasons to treat the prosecutor's race-neutral reason as a pretext:

> Out of 20 black members of the 108-person venire panel for Miller-El's trial, only 1 served. Although 9 were excused for cause or by agreement, 10 were peremptorily struck by the prosecution. The prosecutors used their peremptory strikes to exclude 91% of the eligible African-American venire members. Happenstance is unlikely to produce this disparity. More powerful than these bare statistics, however, are side-by-side comparisons of some black venire panelists who were struck and white panelists allowed to serve. If a prosecutor's proffered reason for striking a black panelist applies just as well to an otherwise-similar nonblack who is permitted to serve, that is evidence tending to prove purposeful discrimination. . . .

The opinion also reviewed the history of overt racial discrimination in the selection of jurors by prosecutors in the jurisdiction and noted systematic differences in the questions that prosecutors asked black and white jurors in this case. The Supreme Court then insisted that every judge evaluating a *Batson* claim — at both the trial and appellate levels — concentrate on the reason that the party gave at the time rather than strengthening the rationale later: "A *Batson* challenge does not call for a mere exercise in thinking up any rational basis. If the stated reason does not hold up, its pretextual significance does not fade because a trial judge, or an appeals court, can imagine a reason that might not have been shown up as false."

6. *Race and decision making.* Did the Court in *Batson* assume that the race of the juror will systematically lead to different judgments? Is such a belief necessary to justify the decision? Professor Sheri Lynn Johnson critiqued the available research in 1985 and reached the following conclusions:

> Laboratory findings concerning the influence of race on white subjects' perception of criminal defendants are quite consistent. More than a dozen mock jury studies provide support for the hypothesis that racial bias affects the determination of guilt. . . . Nine very recent experiments find that the race of the defendant significantly and directly affects the determination of guilt. White subjects in all of these studies were more likely to find a minority-race defendant guilty than they were to find an identically situated white defendant guilty. Four studies find a significant interaction between the race of the defendant, guilt attribution, and some third variable. The one study that did not find any differences based on the race of the defendant may be reconciled with these findings based upon a careful analysis of its methodology.

Johnson, Black Innocence and the White Jury, 83 Mich. L. Rev. 1611, 1625-26 (1985).

The *Batson* dissenters worried that allowing a discrimination claim for racial bias in peremptory challenges would require courts to recognize similar claims for peremptory challenges based on gender bias or other kinds of discrimination. The Supreme Court recognized the possibility of *Batson* claims on the basis of strikes against Latinos in Hernandez v. New York, 500 U.S. 352 (1991). In J.E.B. v. Alabama ex rel. T.B., 511 U.S. 127 (1994), the Court did extend *Batson* to cover peremptory challenges based on gender bias, holding that "gender, like race, is an unconstitutional proxy for juror competence and impartiality." State courts and lower federal courts have wrestled with the application of the *Batson* framework to claims of discrimination against other groups.

Problem 7-2. Extending *Batson*

Defendant Edward Lee Davis, an African American man, was charged with aggravated robbery. No jurors were struck for cause during the jury selection. The defense, however, exercised four of its five peremptory strikes, while the state used one of its three. When the state used the one peremptory to strike a black man from the jury panel, defense counsel objected and asked for a race-neutral explanation. The prosecutor, in response, stated for the record that the prospective juror would have been a very good juror for the state and that race had nothing to do with her decision to strike. She explained:

> However, it was highly significant to the State that the man was a Jehovah's Witness. I have a great deal of familiarity with the sect of Jehovah's Witness. I would never, if I had a peremptory challenge left, fail to strike a Jehovah's Witness from my jury. In my experience that faith is very integral to their daily life in many ways. At least three times a week he goes to church for separate meetings. The Jehovah's Witness faith is of a mind the higher powers will take care of all things necessary. In my experience

Jehovah's Witnesses are reluctant to exercise authority over their fellow human beings in this Court House.

The prosecutor concluded her statement by saying she did not feel it appropriate "to pry" into this matter with the juror because there was no need to do so when exercising a peremptory on race-neutral grounds. Defense counsel had nothing further to add, and the trial judge ruled the peremptory strike would stand.

The defendant concedes the state's peremptory was exercised for race-neutral reasons but contends that the race-neutral explanation offered by the state is constitutionally impermissible as religious discrimination. How would you rule on appeal? See State v. Davis, 504 N.W.2d 767 (Minn. 1993).

Notes

1. *Extending* Batson *claims to other groups: majority view.* The U.S. Supreme Court has extended the coverage of *Batson* in a line of cases. A prima facie case of racial discrimination arises when a party uses peremptory strikes to exclude Latinos from the jury. Hernandez v. New York, 500 U.S. 352 (1991); State v. Alen, 616 So. 2d 452 (Fla. 1993) (recognizing *Batson* claims for Hispanics). The Court applied the *Batson* framework to claims of gender discrimination in J.E.B. v. Alabama ex rel. T.B., 511 U.S. 127 (1994). State courts continue to wrestle with the application of *Batson* and analogous state decisions to nonracial challenges. For example, states are divided on whether to extend *Batson* to claims based on religious orientation. See Casarez v. State, 913 S.W.2d 468 (Tex. Crim. App. 1994) (allowing peremptory challenges based on religious orientation); State v. Hodge, 726 A.2d 531 (Conn. 1999). The battle over the extension of *Batson* does not extend only to groups subject to heightened standards of review under equal protection analysis. See, e.g., Commonwealth v. Carleton, 641 N.E.2d 1057 (Mass. 1994) (applying *Batson* to prosecutor's effort to strike all jurors with Irish-sounding names).

2. *Extending* Batson *to other proceedings and parties.* The federal and state courts have also extended the Batson limits on peremptory challenges to parties other than the prosecutor and to proceedings other than a criminal trial. In Powers v. Ohio, 499 U.S. 400 (1991), the Court held that any litigant, regardless of race, could raise a claim of racially discriminatory peremptory challenges. In Edmonson v. Leesville Concrete Co., Inc., 500 U.S. 614 (1991), the Court extended the prohibition against race-based strikes to civil trials. A year after *Edmonson,* the Court accepted challenges by prosecutors to race-based peremptory strikes by defendants in Georgia v. McCollum, 505 U.S. 42 (1992). While *Batson* claims can be made now in civil or criminal cases, and by defendants or prosecutors, criminal defendants made about 90 percent of *Batson* claims from 1991 to 1993 in state and federal courts. See Kenneth Melilli, *Batson* in Practice: What We Have Learned About *Batson* and Peremptory Challenges, 71 Notre Dame L. Rev. 447 (1996).

3. *Does* Batson *kill peremptories?* Some observers have argued that *Batson* and its progeny essentially eliminate the function of peremptory challenges. Barbara Underwood responds:

Critics of the rule against race-based peremptory challenges, both before and after it was announced by the Supreme Court, have suggested that under such a rule nothing — or nothing valuable — remains of the peremptory challenge. . . . The claim that the rule is in hopeless conflict with the challenge is frequently linked to the suggestion that the ban on jury discrimination must inevitably expand to prohibit not only jury selection based on race, but also jury selection based on religion, national origin, gender, language, disability, age, occupation, political party, and a host of other categories. The relationship between the two points is clear: the longer the list of prohibited categories, the less room there is for a lawful challenge other than a challenge for cause. . . .

If occupational groups are not protected by the *Batson* ban, then generalizations about people based on their occupations provide a rational nonracial reason for a challenge. The same can be said of generalizations based on membership in any other unprotected group. These generalizations might be supported by survey data or social science evidence of some kind, or they might be supported by the experiences of a particular attorney or group of attorneys. . . . The validity of this kind of challenge depends on what groups are protected by the ban on jury discrimination. For this kind of challenge involves precisely the same kind of generalization that *Batson* rightly outlaws when race is involved. . . .

Underwood, Ending Race Discrimination in Jury Selection: Whose Right Is It, Anyway? 92 Colum. L. Rev. 725 (1992). Peremptory challenges continue to play a central role in criminal trials, but should they be retained? A number of commentators have joined Justice Thurgood Marshall and advocated the abolition of peremptories, usually joined with a proposal for broader standards for removal of jurors for cause. See, e.g., Albert Alschuler, The Supreme Court and the Jury: Voir Dire, Peremptory Challenges, and the Review of Jury Verdicts, 56 U. Chi. L. Rev. 153 (1991); Raymond Broderick, Why the Peremptory Challenge Should Be Abolished, 65 Temple L. Rev. 369 (1992). Consider the observations of Justice Stephen Zappala of the Pennsylvania Supreme Court in Commonwealth v. Dinwiddie, 601 A.2d 1216, 1222-1223 (Pa. 1992):

[We] are headed for much contentious litigation over questions germane not to the guilt or innocence of the accused, but to the fairness, or apparent fairness, of the process by which guilt or innocence is determined. The questions, moreover, would seem to be inherently unanswerable; if the traditional purpose of peremptory challenges is to eliminate "irrational . . . suspicions and antagonisms," Swain v. Alabama, 380 U.S. at 224, how can the courts demand rational explanations for their use? Instead of pushing our courts into the morass of trying to judge between explanations for the irrational, perhaps the entire process would be better served by abandoning the use of peremptory challenges altogether, trying cases before the first group of twelve jurors randomly chosen from the venire, and allowing only challenges for cause.

4. *Remedies for* Batson *violations.* One of the many complicated questions courts have tried to answer in the wake of *Batson* is the question of the proper remedy. Should the judge start with a fresh venire, or reseat the improperly excluded jurors, or reseat all jurors excluded after the first improper peremptory strike? Some jurisdictions require trial courts, as a general rule, to disallow the strike and reseat the improperly stricken juror. A few states require the trial court to conduct jury selection from a newly convened venire. Most courts, however, have allowed the trial judge to choose among available remedies, without designating a preferred or required remedy. See Jefferson v. State, 595 So. 2d 38 (Fla. 1992); People v. Willis, 43 P.3d 130 (Cal. 2002). If the preferred remedy for a *Batson* violation is dismissal of

the initial panel and selection of the jury from a fresh venire, would the parties ever have an incentive to create a deliberate *Batson* violation? Which remedy is most consistent with the view that the jury is primarily a method of ensuring a fair trial? Which is most consistent with the view that the jury serves important functions for the jurors themselves and for the public at large? See Eric Muller, Solving the *Batson* Paradox: Harmless Error, Jury Representation, and the Sixth Amendment, 106 Yale L.J. 93 (1996). States have multifarious rules for the order of questioning and for the timing of the announcements about peremptory strikes. These rules have some bearing on the proper remedy for a *Batson* violation. Does it matter if the parties announce their peremptory decisions in the presence of some or all of the jurors or the remaining members of the venire pool?

5. *Peremptory challenges to judges.* What can be done if a party believes a judge is biased? Most jurisdictions typically allow parties to challenge judges for cause. In addition, about 20 states allow defendants to have one automatic strike — a kind of peremptory challenge — to the trial judge. See, e.g., Ill. Rev. Stat. ch. 38, para. 114-5(a); Minn. Stat. §487.40. Some statutes that appear to require evidence of bias in fact operate as essentially automatic challenge provisions; others, including several federal statutes, that appear to allow peremptory challenges to judges in fact require some evidence of bias. See, e.g., 28 U.S.C. §144. Is the presumption that judges are neutral stronger than for jurors? Do peremptory challenges to judges undermine public confidence in the judicial system? Should lawyers be required to provide a reason to a judicial review commission even if the effect of a motion to change judges is automatic? See Nancy J. King, *Batson* for the Bench? Regulating the Peremptory Challenge of Judges, 73 Chi.-Kent L. Rev. 509 (1998).

C. JURY DELIBERATIONS AND VERDICTS

Once the jury is seated, the trial begins. In a few jurisdictions, the judge delivers preliminary instructions regarding the task at hand, along with an outline of the procedures for the jury to follow at trial and during deliberation. More often, the jury hears right away the opening statements of the attorneys, followed by the government's case in chief. Assuming that the judge denies the customary defense motion to dismiss the charges at the close of the prosecution's case, the jury then hears the defense evidence, if indeed the defendant chooses to present a defense. After closing statements from the attorneys, the judge instructs the jury on the law relevant to the case, using a combination of standard jury instructions for criminal cases and a few customized instructions that the parties suggest. The case then rests in the hands of the jury. In this section, we consider the rules governing the jury's deliberations at the close of the case.

1. Instructions to Deadlocked Juries

Although most juries reach a unanimous verdict, many start out with divided views among the panel members about the proper outcome. Divisions among jurors may be easier to resolve when juries are presented with a range of offenses, including lesser included charges, that create room for negotiation. But courts are sometimes faced with deadlocked juries. What devices may the court use to encourage the jurors to reach a common decision?

■ NEW YORK CRIMINAL PROCEDURE LAW §310.30

At any time during its deliberation, the jury may request the court for further instruction or information with respect to the law, with respect to the content or substance of any trial evidence, or with respect to any other matter pertinent to the jury's consideration of the case. Upon such a request, the court must direct that the jury be returned to the courtroom and, after notice to both the people and counsel for the defendant, and in the presence of the defendant, must give such requested information or instruction as the court deems proper. With the consent of the parties and upon the request of the jury for further instruction with respect to a statute, the court may also give to the jury copies of the text of any statute which, in its discretion, the court deems proper.

■ DANIEL BAILEY v. STATE
669 N.E.2d 972 (Ind. 1996)

SULLIVAN, J.

We reaffirm that the proper procedure when the jury is apparently deadlocked is for the trial court to call the jury back into open court in the presence of all parties and their counsel and reread all instructions given to them prior to their deliberations, without emphasis on any of them and without further comment. Lewis v. State, 424 N.E.2d 107 (Ind. 1981).

During jury deliberations in defendant Daniel Bailey's trial for murder and [for] carrying a handgun without a license, the jury sent the trial court the following note: "What happens if we cannot come to a unanimous decision this evening?" Interpreting this note as an indication that the jury was deadlocked, the trial court called the jury back into open court and reread to the jury one, but only one, of the final instructions.[3] Defense counsel objected to the procedure, arguing "if one instruction's read to them, . . . they all need to be."

In 1896, the United States Supreme Court reviewed the murder conviction of 14-year-old Alexander Allen for the third time. Allen v. United States, 164 U.S.

---

3. The instruction reread by the court was as follows:

The Court further instructs you that all verdicts must be unanimous. While it is the duty of each juror to act upon that juror's own individual judgment and determine the issue of guilt or innocence of the defendant of the crime charged and that each juror must look solely to the law and the evidence in the cause in determining the guilt or innocence of the defendant, yet it is likewise the duty of each juror to consult honestly, freely and fairly with the other jurors and endeavor with them, by fair consideration of the law and the evidence in the cause to arrive at a just conclusion as to the guilt or innocence of the defendant. No juror, through carelessness or indifference should yield that juror's own judgment in this cause to the judgment of the other jurors. Neither should any juror allow mere pride or personal opinion to prevent deliberative and reasonable consultation with the other jurors in an honest and good faith effort to arrive at a just verdict in this cause.

492 (1896). Among the assignments of error addressed by the court was a challenge to a jury instruction which has come to be known as the "*Allen* charge." The court described the instruction as follows:

> These instructions were quite lengthy, and were, in substance, that in a large proportion of cases absolute certainty could not be expected; that although the verdict must be the verdict of each individual juror, . . . they should listen, with a disposition to be convinced, to each other's arguments; that, if much the larger number were for conviction, a dissenting juror should consider whether his doubt was a reasonable one which made no impression upon the minds of so many men, equally honest, equally intelligent with himself. If, upon the other hand, the majority was for acquittal, the minority ought to ask themselves whether they might not reasonably doubt the correctness of a judgment which was not concurred in by the majority. [164 U.S. at 501.]

The court found no error in these instructions. This unprepossessing leading authority spawned a host of appellate and scholarly commentary in the three quarters of a century following its pronouncement. One outgrowth of this discussion was the emergence of an approach recommended by the American Bar Association to be used by trial courts in criminal cases when the jury was deadlocked. This standard, adopted by many courts . . . , provided:

> (a) Before the jury retires for deliberation, the court may give an instruction which informs the jury:
> (i) that in order to return a verdict, each juror must agree thereto;
> (ii) that jurors have a duty to consult with one another and to deliberate with a view to reaching an agreement, if it can be done without violence to individual judgment;
> (iii) that each juror must decide the case for himself or herself but only after an impartial consideration of the evidence with the other jurors;
> (iv) that in the course of deliberations, a juror should not hesitate to reexamine his or her own views and change an opinion if the juror is convinced it is erroneous; and
> (v) that no juror should surrender his or her honest conviction as to the weight or effect of the evidence solely because of the opinion of other jurors, or for the mere purpose of returning a verdict.
> (b) If it appears to the court that the jury has been unable to agree, the court may require the jury to continue their deliberations and may give or repeat an instruction as provided in paragraph (a). . . .
> (c) The jury may be discharged without having agreed upon a verdict if it appears that there is no reasonable probability of agreement. [American Bar Assn., Project on Minimum Standards for Criminal Justice, Standards Relating to Trial by Jury §5.4, at 145-146 (1969 edition); Standard 15-4.4, at 133 (1980 edition).]

[In Lewis v. State, 424 N.E.2d 107 (Ind. 1981), our court disapproved of giving] any supplemental instructions to deadlocked juries other than rereading all of the original final instructions. [We expressed] concern that a trial judge's necessary discretion "not step over the bounds that limit him in the proper conduct of a trial. He must refrain from imposing himself and his opinions on the jury." We then [reiterated the established principle] that final instructions are not to be orally qualified, modified, or in any manner orally explained to the jury by the trial judge.

Ind. Code §35-1-35-1. With this background, we turned to . . . the use of the ABA standard. We said:

> It appears to us . . . that the procedure of paragraph (b) of the above [ABA] Standard in allowing the court to separate this instruction or parts of it from the other instructions and to re-give it to the jury after deliberations re-creates the problem of the *"Allen"* charge situation all over again in a different form. A better solution is . . . for the court to call the jury back into open court in the presence of all of the parties and their counsel, if they desire to be there, and to reread all instructions given to them prior to their deliberations, without emphasis on any of them and without further comment. . . . [424 N.E.2d at 111.]

[The] final instruction dealing with the manner of deliberations . . . is not a housekeeping instruction but an instruction that relates to the very office of the jury. That is, the considerations set forth in this instruction are no more or less important to the jury than the matters set forth in the other final instructions. A jury deadlock could be caused by, e.g., one or more juror's failure to consult "honestly, freely and fairly with the other jurors." But it could also be caused by one or more juror's failure to understand or remember the instruction on reasonable doubt, the instruction on the elements of an offense, or the instruction on the state's burden of proof. The trial court simply does not know whether juror intransigence or a genuine misunderstanding or memory lapse as to the substance of the final instructions has caused the deadlock. By rereading all of the instructions, the jury is taken back to the beginning of its assignment, reminded of all the instructions necessary to decide the case. Not knowing the source of the infection, rereading all the instructions provides a broad spectrum antibiotic for whatever has caused the deadlock. We consider it time well spent.

Despite the many cases and secondary materials addressing the *Allen* charge, our decision in *Lewis* was the first to address the *Allen* charge issue from the perspective that the charge constitutes an embellishment on final instructions and, therefore, can only be read if part of a rereading of all final instructions. We clearly rejected the notion advanced by many jurisdictions . . . that the wording of the ABA standard instruction differs in its impact on juries from the original *Allen* charge. And as the last of the five members of our court who unanimously decided *Lewis* retires, it is altogether fitting that we reaffirm this important principle of Indiana criminal jurisprudence. We reverse Bailey's convictions and remand to the trial court.

SHEPARD, C.J., concurring.

I join the Court's opinion because it reaffirms our precedent, prohibiting the use of *"Allen* charges" to break jury deadlocks and our rule that if one instruction is to be re-read they should all be re-read. The application of these rules appears awkward in this case because the jury's question to the court seems like a request for information and not a declaration that the jurors were deadlocked. The trial judge interpreted the question as an indication of deadlock, however, and it is possible that she was right. If so, as the Court's opinion indicates, the decision to give an *"Allen* charge" was error.

This appeal also suggests another question which will be ripe for examination when the appropriate case presents itself. Our declaration in Lewis v. State that a judge should re-read instructions to a deadlocked jury was written during an era when it was error to send instructions to the jury room. Now that we regularly give the jury the written instructions, this may be something left to trial court discretion.

Notes

1. *"Dynamite" charges: majority position.* The dynamite charge (or "hammer" charge) originated in Commonwealth v. Tuey, 62 Mass. 1 (1851), and came to national attention in Allen v. United States, 164 U.S. 492 (1896). The instruction produced verdicts, and its use spread rapidly. More recently, many courts have limited or abandoned the *Allen* instruction. About half the states have disapproved dynamite charges, in whole or in part. See People v. Gainer, 566 P.2d 997 (Cal. 1977); Paul Marcus, The *Allen* Instruction in Criminal Cases: Is the Dynamite Charge About to Be Permanently Defused? 43 Mo. L. Rev. 613 (1978). The case law on the subject is extensive. Some courts have limited the instruction through procedural devices, such as preventing judges from giving the instruction too early during the jury's deliberations or from giving it more than once. Along these lines, some courts say that an *Allen* charge is acceptable only if the judge delivered an identical charge to the jury at the start of its deliberations. Other courts focus on the content of the instructions. Appellate courts pay special attention to the balance between statements about the need for agreement and statements about the duty of individual jurors to stand by their own considered opinions. The alternative presented in the ABA standards (as discussed in *Bailey*) influences many courts. See State v. Weidul, 628 A.2d 135 (Me. 1993) (any departure from the ABA alternative will result in summary dismissal). Do you believe that the ABA alternative creates a different reaction among jurors than the traditional *Allen* charge? See also Lowenfield v. Phelps, 484 U.S. 231 (1988) (approving charge that does not instruct minority jurors to reconsider in light of majority views but does tell jurors not to hesitate to "reexamine" their views and to "change" their opinion if they are convinced that they are wrong). According to a study of federal appellate cases between 1964 and 1999, the *Allen* charge tends to hasten process of deliberation once it is given: Jury deliberations averaged about 13 hours before the charge and about 3 hours after the charge. About 4 percent of cases where a court delivered this charge resulted in mistrials. Appellate courts overwhelmingly affirm convictions appealed on the basis of such a charge. See Mark Lanier & Cloud Miller, The *Allen* Charge: Expedient Justice or Coercion? 25 Am. J. Crim. Just. 31 (June 2001).

2. *Numerical breakdowns.* When a jury sends out word that it is divided and cannot reach a consensus, two questions spring to mind: How many jurors are "holding out," and which side does the majority favor? Appellate courts usually express concern if a trial judge inquired about the numerical division of the jury, explaining that such inquiries might create undue pressure on the minority jurors to change their votes. However, courts are divided over whether such inquiries, standing alone, constitute legal error. The larger group, including the federal courts, say that a judge's inquiries about the jury's numerical division are per se error. See Brasfield v. United States, 272 U.S. 448 (1926); People v. Wilson, 213 N.W.2d 193 (Mich. 1973). In the other states, this type of inquiry becomes a ground for reversal when combined with other circumstances, such as the judge's further inquiry about whether the majority favors conviction, acquittal, or some other option. On the other hand, if

the jury *volunteers* information about its numerical division, the judge typically must inform the parties. Statutes and court rules typically state that the parties must be informed about any statement that the jury makes during its deliberations, and they must have an opportunity to argue to the judge about what she should say to the panel. What sorts of actions by a judge might influence a juror holding a minority view? See Eden v. State, 860 P.2d 169 (Nev. 1993) (no abuse of discretion for trial court to bring lone dissenting juror into chambers, in front of jury forewoman, and ask whether he had seen and heard the evidence and was willing to follow jury instructions). There is some social science evidence that jurors who cling most tenaciously to their views are also those who reach their views most quickly and are most likely to take a more absolutist view of the case. Deanna Kuhn, Michael Weinstock & Robin Flaton, How Well Do Jurors Reason? Competence Dimensions of Individual Variation in a Juror Reasoning Task, 5 Psychol. Sci. 289 (1994). If this description is generally true, should we give judges more opportunities to convince jurors with minority views to rethink their positions?

3. *The role of lesser included offenses.* Experimental data suggest that juries presented with alternatives for verdicts other than acquittal or the most serious available charge produce fewer acquittals and fewer hung juries. See Neil Vidmar, Effects of Decision Alternatives on the Verdicts and Social Perceptions of Simulated Jurors, 22 J. Personality & Soc. Psychol. 211 (1972) (in 54 percent of mock homicide trials, jury acquitted when choice of verdict was guilty of first-degree murder or not guilty; when jury had four options, jurors returned verdicts of first-degree murder in 8 percent of the cases, second-degree murder in 64 percent, manslaughter in 21 percent, and not guilty in 8 percent). Depending on the case, as a strategic matter the prosecution or the defense may favor or oppose the judge instructing the jury about lesser included offenses. The rules governing whether lesser included offenses must be charged are complex and varied among the states; they often turn on judicial assessments of the plausibility of fitting various "stories" to the facts. See Kyron Huigens, The Doctrine of Lesser Included Offenses, 16 U. Puget Sound L. Rev. 185 (1992).

In cases involving lesser included offenses or multiple charges, the judge may encourage agreement among jurors by providing instructions on the order for them to consider lesser included offenses. Two instructions are common. Under an "acquittal first" instruction, the judge tells the jury to reach a unanimous decision to acquit on the most serious charge before moving on to consider conviction for a lesser offense. See State v. Tate, 773 A.2d 308 (Conn. 2001) (if jury that has received "acquittal first" instruction asks for clarification about a lesser included offense and then reports itself deadlocked, trial court should first ask jury if it has reached a partial verdict before declaring mistrial). An alternative is the "unable to agree" or "reasonable efforts" instruction, which permits a jury to consider lesser included offenses if, after reasonable efforts, the jury cannot agree on a verdict on the more serious offense. The acquittal-first instruction was the more traditional of the two, but the reasonable efforts instruction is gaining a strong following among state courts. See State v. Thomas, 533 N.E.2d 286 (Ohio 1988). As defense counsel, which of these instructions would you ordinarily prefer? Under what circumstances might you prefer the other instruction?

4. *Sequestration of juries.* One powerful practical force working in favor of jury agreement is the fact that jurors are forced to remain together in a single room, at

least during working hours, until their task is complete. Indeed, for some cases involving an unusual amount of publicity that could taint the jurors, the court will "sequester" the jury and order them to remain together in a hotel during their meals, evenings, and off-days. See Tex. Code Crim. Proc. art 35.23. At one time, this process was much more explicitly designed to produce a verdict. Consider William Blackstone's description of the environment for jury deliberations: "the jury, . . . in order to avoid intemperance and causeless delay, are to be kept without meat, drink, fire, or candle, unless by permission of the judge, till they are all unanimously agreed." Blackstone, 3 Commentaries on the Laws of England 375 (1768).

5. *Alternate jurors.* Another device for producing jury verdicts becomes important when one or more of the sitting jurors cannot proceed with deliberations because of illness or for some other reason. In such a case, the court replaces the departing juror with an alternate juror who heard the evidence at trial and instructs the entire panel to begin its deliberations anew. Statutes and procedure rules authorize this procedure in virtually all jurisdictions, although alternate jurors are typically available only in the most serious or lengthy felony trials. But see Claudio v. State, 585 A.2d 1278 (Del. 1991) (state constitution prohibits use of alternate juror to replace jury member who became sick after one day's deliberations).

6. *Prevalence of hung juries.* In the popular imagination, the "hung jury" is a common occurrence. A study of juries in the 1960s found that hung juries occurred in 5.5 percent of the cases studied. Harry Kalven & Hans Zeisel, The American Jury 57 (1966). During the early 1990s, the Los Angeles County Public Defender collected data over an 18-month period suggesting that hung juries occurred in approximately 13-15 percent of felony trials. Among the hung juries, the numerical division was 11-1 in 21 percent of the cases (15 percent for guilty and 6 percent for not guilty), while another 21 percent hung 10-2 (16 percent for guilty and 5 percent for not guilty). Clark Kelso, Final Report of the Blue Ribbon Commission on Jury System Improvement, 47 Hastings L.J. 1433 (1996). A more recent study suggests that rates of hung juries in Los Angeles are higher than in other jurisdictions: 13 to 16 percent in Los Angeles, compared to 6.2 percent nationwide. In federal criminal trials, the rate of hung juries remains around 2 to 3 percent. See Paula L. Hannaford, Valerie P. Hans & G. Thomas Munsterman, How Much Justice Hangs in the Balance? 83 Judicature 59 (1999). Keep in mind that these rates reflect the number of juries that end their deliberations in deadlock; there are no data on the extent to which juries declare themselves deadlocked and ultimately reach a verdict. What outcomes would you expect during any later retrials of cases that initially produced a hung jury?

2. Changes to Jury Structure

The classic structure for a criminal jury calls for 12 members whose names are known to the parties. The jurors must agree unanimously on a verdict, based on their unaided memory of the testimony and other evidence. What effects might we anticipate from changes to this traditional structure?

■ GEORGIA CONSTITUTION ART. I, §I, PARA. XI

(a) The right to trial by jury shall remain inviolate. . . . In criminal cases, the defendant shall have a public and speedy trial by an impartial jury; and the jury shall be the judges of the law and the facts.

(b) A trial jury shall consist of 12 persons; but the General Assembly may prescribe any number, not less than six, to constitute a trial jury in courts of limited jurisdiction and in superior courts in misdemeanor cases. . . .

■ MONTANA CODE §46-16-110

(1) The parties in a felony case have a right to trial by a jury of 12 persons.

(2) The parties may agree in writing at any time before the verdict, with the approval of the court, that the jury shall consist of any number less than that to which they are entitled.

(3) Upon written consent of the parties, a trial by jury may be waived.

■ STATE v. SHERRIE TUCKER
657 N.W.2d 374 (Wis. 2003)

BABLITCH, J.

We are asked to decide under what circumstances a circuit court may restrict the disclosure of juror information in a criminal trial, and, if juror information is restricted, what precautions must be taken to avoid prejudice to the criminal defendant. . . .

In March 1998, law enforcement officers executed a search warrant at an apartment shared by Tucker and her boyfriend, Damien McCray (McCray). In the apartment, officers found cocaine in a bag marked "Shiree Tucker," a .38 caliber revolver, and bullets. Tucker made a statement to police after a *Miranda* warning was given, in which she admitted that the cocaine belonged to her and that she had been selling cocaine for about a month. Tucker was tried and convicted of possession of cocaine with intent to deliver within 1,000 feet of a school while armed with a dangerous weapon, which resulted in a seven year prison sentence. The circuit court judge stayed the prison sentence and instead ordered seven years of probation for Tucker.

Prior to jury selection for Tucker's trial, the circuit court judge told counsel off the record that "it has been my practice to use numbers and not names in this court. . . . What I'm prohibiting is the names of jurors being stated in the courtroom and for the record when other people may be sitting in the audience and using those names for any other reason." When defense counsel objected, the judge explained that the use of numbers is appropriate because this was a case "involving drugs and an allegation of drug dealing which I think raises the bar to some extent in terms of any danger to jurors." . . . During the trial, the judge corrected defense counsel when he referred to a juror by name, stating "it's my practice to refer to the jurors by number, so please follow the practice." There was no other statement made in front of the jury regarding the use of numbers instead of their names. . . .

Both parties had access to all the juror information, including the jurors' names. Furthermore, the public presumably could have obtained the jurors' names by inquiring at the clerk of courts' office. A jury is typically deemed "anonymous" when juror information is withheld from the public and the parties themselves. Therefore, the jury in this case was not a classic "anonymous" jury. Notwithstanding whether the jury in this case is characterized as an "anonymous" or a "numbers" jury, if restrictions are placed on juror identification or information, due process concerns are raised regarding a defendant's rights to an impartial jury and a presumption of innocence. Accordingly, although this case does not deal with the classic "anonymous" jury, the reasoning in cases involving anonymous juries is beneficial to our analysis.

The empanelling of an anonymous jury is a relatively recent phenomenon that was rarely utilized before the Second Circuit's opinion in United States v. Barnes, 604 F.2d 121 (2d Cir. 1979). The court in *Barnes* addressed juror anonymity with respect to its effect on the practice of voir dire. In *Barnes*, the district court ordered that the jurors' identities, addresses, religious affiliations, and ethnic backgrounds remain anonymous, even from the parties themselves. The court . . . examined each of the restrictions placed on juror information and concluded that the jurors' demeanors and responses to questions regarding their family, education and other matters would provide substantially the same information as the juror information that was restricted. Consequently, the court rejected the argument that the defendant was denied the ability to intelligently exercise peremptory challenges. . . . Although not explicit, the court essentially weighed the need to protect the jury, which was prompted by the defendant's ties to the mafia, against the rights of the defendant to an impartial jury.

A few years later, the Second Circuit addressed a different concern with the use of an anonymous jury in United States v. Thomas, 757 F.2d 1359 (2d Cir. 1985). In *Thomas*, the defendants argued that an anonymous jury is an unconstitutional infringement on a defendant's presumption of innocence because it gives jurors the impression that the defendant is dangerous and a threat to the jurors' safety. The court in *Thomas* acknowledged the fundamental tenet that a defendant is presumed innocent until proven guilty, but nevertheless determined that an anonymous jury might be permissible if jurors are in need of protection. Therefore, the court rejected a per se rule against empanelling an anonymous jury, but concluded that an anonymous jury is warranted only if there is a "strong reason" to believe that the jury needs protection and if the court takes "reasonable precautions" to minimize the impact of anonymity on the jurors' views of the defendant. The court noted that reasonable precautions were taken in that case, in part, because the judge gave the jury an "intelligent, reasonable and believable explanation for his actions that did not cast the defendants in an unfavorable light." In other words, the curative or precautionary instruction served to rebut any notion that the use of an anonymous jury was somehow a negative reflection on the defendant's guilt or character. The Second Circuit's approach in *Thomas* has been widely adopted by both federal and state courts. . . .

[We also find the reasoning in *Thomas* persuasive.] Therefore, before a circuit court restricts any juror information in an individual case, it should determine that the jurors are in need of protection and take reasonable precautions to avoid prejudice to the defendant. In this case, Tucker concedes that her opportunity for voir dire was not impeded since both parties had access to all the juror information. However, Tucker claims that her presumption of innocence was eroded by the circuit court's use of numbers without an individualized determination that the jury needed protection nor a precautionary statement made to the jury regarding the use of numbers instead of names.

Serious concerns regarding a defendant's presumption of innocence are raised when juror information is restricted, as in this case. [Accordingly, we] conclude that if a court withholds any juror information, it must both: (1) find that a jury needs protection; and (2) take reasonable precautions to avoid prejudicing the defendant. [We] hold that the circuit court erroneously exercised its discretion by failing to apply the correct standard of law. . . .

First, the circuit court did not make an individualized determination that the jurors needed protection based on the specific circumstances present in Tucker's case. Rather, the court informed counsel that "it has been my practice to use numbers and not names" in drug cases. The circuit court repeatedly referred to its "practice" of using numbers without specifically noting any particular factors that warranted the use of numbers in Tucker's case.

There are various factors that may be taken into account in making an individualized determination that a jury needs protection. Such factors may include, but are not limited to: (1) the defendant's involvement in organized crime; (2) the defendant's participation in a group with the capacity to harm jurors; (3) the defendant's past attempts to interfere with the judicial process; and (4) extensive publicity that could enhance the possibility that jurors' names would become public and expose them to intimidation or harassment.

Second, the circuit court did not take necessary precautions to minimize any prejudicial effect to Tucker. Although the circuit court explained the use of numbers instead of jurors' names to counsel off the record, the court did not make any statement to the jurors regarding its use of numbers. Rather, the jurors were just referred to by number instead of name. The only statement heard by the jurors regarding the use of numbers was when the circuit court corrected defense counsel by stating, "it's my practice to refer to the jurors by number, so please follow the practice." The circuit court did instruct the jury on Tucker's presumption of innocence and on the State's burden of proving guilt beyond a reasonable doubt. However, we conclude that this instruction, by itself, was insufficient. When jurors' names are withheld, as in this case, the circuit court, at a minimum, must make a precautionary statement to the jury that the use of numbers instead of names should in no way be interpreted as a reflection of the defendant's guilt or innocence. . . .

Any additional precautionary statements that are made to a jury when juror information is restricted should be based on factors and influences that may be present in a case, which could warrant withholding juror information. A precautionary statement must not mislead a jury, but must be based on factors and influences that are relevant in a particular case. . . .

Although the circuit court erred [in its use of numbered jurors in this case], the error in this case was harmless. An error is harmless if it is clear beyond a reasonable doubt that a rational jury would have found the defendant guilty absent the error. . . . In this case, Tucker admitted to police after she was given a *Miranda* warning that the cocaine belonged to her and that she had been selling cocaine for about a month. . . . In addition, the cocaine found in Tucker and McCray's apartment was in a plastic bag marked "Shiree Tucker." . . .

BRADLEY, J., concurring.

. . . If this were an anonymous jury, then I agree with the majority that the circuit court was required to make an individualized determination of the need for such a jury. I part ways with the majority because it fails to draw a distinction between a numbers jury, as here, and an anonymous jury. The result of this failure is that in concluding that harmless error applies in this "numbers only" situation, it incorrectly extends harmless error as a remedy in all truly anonymous jury cases. Such a widespread extension is contrary to precedent. . . .

Measures to shield juror information not only implicate the defendant's rights, but also contradict the presumption of openness that defines the American judicial system. The selection of jurors has always presumptively been a public process. . . .

A few years ago this court unanimously rejected a petition for an administrative rule governing juror confidentiality. The petition provided that jurors be referred to only by number and that no personal juror identifying information could be elicited during voir dire. . . . The breadth of such a proposal and its effect on our tradition of public trials were apparent to many who appeared in opposition to the proposal at the public hearing. The State Bar of Wisconsin was one of the groups that appeared in opposition to the petition. It cautioned that an anonymous jury should be used only in "an extremely rare circumstance."

A trial is a public event and a public trial lies at the foundation of our legal tradition. The public trial is rooted in the "principle that justice cannot survive behind walls of silence." Sheppard v. Maxwell, 384 U.S. 333 (1966).

The majority's failure to distinguish between a numbers jury and an anonymous jury serves to dilute the jurisprudence on anonymous juries. It compounds this problem by applying an across the board "no harm, no foul" analysis of the harmless error rule thus serving to make the use of anonymous juries more commonplace. [Instead, the use of an anonymous jury should be] the "last resort" and "a drastic measure." . . .

SYKES, J., concurring.

. . . The parties and the public had unrestricted access to all juror identifying information. As such, the anonymous jury case law does not apply. . . .

Voir dire by number does not implicate the presumption of innocence in the same way that the cases have assumed the use of an anonymous jury does. It has not been demonstrated—in this case or in the case law—that mere voir dire by number, without any restriction on access to juror information, has any serious adverse impact on the presumption of innocence. Any suggestion that it does is pure speculation. Indeed, the majority engages in no evaluation of this point at all, but merely extrapolates a presumption of innocence/due process violation from cases that involved true anonymous juries rather than the far more innocuous practice of voir dire by number.

Our courthouses today are equipped with various security precautions—metal detectors at courthouse entrances, security glass in individual courtrooms, armed deputy sheriffs in the courtroom and in the courthouse hallways—all of which suggest at least some level of risk to the people who work and visit there, including the jurors. . . . Certain special security precautions are sometimes taken in individual cases, such as posting extra deputies in the courtroom, without encumbering the presumption of innocence or requiring particularized due process justifications. Voir dire by number (if a circuit court chooses to use this technique) falls within this category of routine security measures, whether used as a general practice, in a certain class of cases, or case by case.

In my view, voir dire by number, without any other restriction on the scope of voir dire or the parties' or the public's access to juror identifying information, does not rise to the level of an encumbrance on the presumption of innocence so as to implicate the defendant's right to due process. . . .

Problem 7-3. Non-unanimous Verdicts

> A jury too frequently have at least one member, more ready to
> hang the panel than to hang the traitor.
>   —Abraham Lincoln to Erastus Corning, June 12, 1863

As in many states, prosecutors and citizens in California have expressed concern that too many trials result in hung juries and that a requirement of unanimity provides radical or irrational jurors with the power to block a just outcome. A 1996 Blue Ribbon Commission on Jury System Improvement in California recommended the following jury reform:

> The Legislature should propose a constitutional amendment which provides that, except for good cause when the interests of justice require a unanimous verdict, trial judges shall accept an 11-1 verdict after the jury has deliberated for a reasonable period of time (not less than six hours) in all felonies, except where the punishment may be death or life imprisonment, and in all misdemeanors where the jury consists of twelve persons. . . .

The commission explained that "eliminating the unanimity requirement is intended primarily to address the problem of an 11-1 or 10-2 hung jury where the hold-out jurors are refusing to deliberate, are engaging in nullification, or are simply [being] unreasonable (e.g., ignoring the evidence)." A slight majority of the commission preferred allowing only 11-1 and not 10-2 verdicts because "where two jurors share the same minority position, it seems less likely that the basis for the minority position is irrationality rather than a legitimate disagreement."

The commission's recommendation was a version of the "modified unanimity" approach — adopted in England and used in civil cases in several states — that gives judges the power to allow non-unanimous verdicts after a period of time (two hours in England). Opting for a time delay before allowing non-unanimous verdicts "forces the jury to begin its deliberations listening to all jurors and counting the votes of all jurors."

As a legislator in California, would you support a bill implementing the commission's recommendation? See Clark Kelso, Final Report of the Blue Ribbon Commission on Jury System Improvement, 47 Hastings L.J. 1433 (1996).

Notes

1. *Jury size: majority position.* Starting in 1970, the Supreme Court permitted experimentation with the size of criminal juries. In Williams v. Florida, 399 U.S. 78 (1970), the Court upheld the use of a 6-person jury in a criminal case; however, in Ballew v. Georgia, 435 U.S. 223 (1978), the Court struck down the use of a 5-person

jury as a violation of the Sixth Amendment. A handful of states took up this invitation and now allow felonies (other than capital cases) to be tried by juries of either 6 or 8 members, including Arizona (8-member juries except where sentences are 30 years or more), Utah (8-member juries), Connecticut (6-member juries), and Florida (6-member juries). Another small group of states, including Indiana and Massachusetts, allow 6-member juries for felony trials in limited jurisdiction courts but require full 12-member juries in general jurisdiction courts. In contrast, for misdemeanors, more than half of the states mandate that juries consist of 6 members, and another large group of states specify a jury size between 6 and 12 members. State Court Organization 1998 at table 42 (June 2000, NCJ 178932). Efforts in a few states to reduce the size of the criminal jury have been rejected on state constitutional grounds. See, e.g., Byrd v. State, 879 S.W.2d 435 (Ark. 1994); Advisory Opinion to the Senate of the State of Rhode Island, 278 A.2d 852 (R.I. 1971). Perhaps reducing the expense and difficulty of selecting and maintaining juries makes it possible to offer juries in a broader range of cases. Will a smaller jury function differently? In a predictable direction?

2. *Does jury size matter?* Social science played a role in the U.S. Supreme Court's decision in Ballew v. Georgia, 435 U.S. 223 (1978), which drew a constitutional line at a jury of six. The *Ballew* Court cited 19 studies on jury size conducted since 1970. An extensive discussion of these studies led the Court to conclude as follows:

> First, recent empirical data suggest that progressively smaller juries are less likely to foster effective group deliberation. . . . Second, the data now raise doubts about the accuracy of the results achieved by smaller and smaller panels. . . . Third, the data suggest that the verdicts of jury deliberation in criminal cases will vary as juries become smaller, and that the variance amounts to an imbalance to the detriment of one side, the defense. . . . Fourth, [smaller juries create] problems not only for jury decision-making, but also for the representation of minority groups in the community. . . . We readily admit that we do not pretend to discern a clear line between six members and five. But the assembled data raise substantial doubt about the reliability and appropriate representation of panels smaller than six. [435 U.S. at 232-39].

Does social science offer the best way to answer the question of the proper size of the criminal jury? If so, is study of internal jury dynamics the proper test? Few studies of the role of jury size on decision making in criminal cases have been conducted since the late 1970s. See Michael Saks, Michael J. Saks & Mollie Weighner Marti, A Meta-Analysis of the Effects of Jury Size, 21 Law & Hum. Behav. 451 (1997) (discussing recent studies, most pertaining to civil juries). For a survey of jury practice in other countries (including New Zealand, Canada, Scotland, Ireland, Spain, Russia, and Japan), see the symposium published at 62 Law & Contemp. Probs. 2 (Spring 1999).

3. *Non-unanimous verdicts.* In Apodaca v. Oregon, 406 U.S. 404 (1972), the Supreme Court reversed earlier cases and interpreted the Sixth Amendment right to jury trial to allow convictions based on 11-1 and 10-2 votes. A companion case, Johnson v. Louisiana, 406 U.S. 356 (1972), upheld a conviction based on a 9-3 vote. However, in Burch v. Louisiana, 441 U.S. 130 (1979), the Court concluded that a conviction based on a 5-1 vote violated the right to a jury trial. States have not rushed into this constitutional opening. Only Louisiana and Oregon currently allow juries to convict defendants of felonies on a non-unanimous vote, although this

reform is suggested fairly often, as the California proposal in Problem 7-3 illustrates. Some states have adopted non-unanimous verdict rules for misdemeanor trials, and a substantial number allow special exceptions to the unanimity requirement for verdicts, including consent of the parties.

The most famous study of non-unanimous juries is Reid Hastie, Steven D. Penrod & Nancy Pennington, Inside the Jury (1983). The study found several differences between behavior on unanimity-rule and majority-rule juries. Majority-rule juries reach a verdict more quickly; they tend to vote early and conduct discussions in a more adversarial manner; holdouts are more likely to remain at the conclusion of deliberations; members of small groups are less likely to speak; and large factions attract members more quickly. Is there a rational explanation for a constitutional doctrine that allows a 9-3 verdict but not a 5-1 verdict? Does democratic theory support any non-unanimous verdict that mimics what a simple majority of society at large would decide in a case? See George Thomas & Barry Pollack, Rethinking Guilt, Juries, and Jeopardy, 91 Mich. L. Rev. 1 (1992) (calculating statistical risk that different jury configurations would mistakenly vote for guilt when majority of society at large would vote for acquittal). If the jury is designed as a protector of individual liberty, would it be appropriate to allow non-unanimous acquittals while requiring unanimity for convictions? Ethan J. Leib, Supermajoritarianism and the American Criminal Jury, 33 Hastings Const. L.Q. 141 (2006). Non-U.S. legal systems without a long jury tradition have been more willing to allow non-unanimous verdicts. See EC Legal Systems: An Introductory Guide (Sheridan and Cameron eds., 1995) (discussing non-unanimous verdicts in Great Britain, Greece, Ireland, Italy, and Portugal).

4. *Different rationales for one verdict.* The unanimity requirement calls for each juror to agree to the group outcome, whether it be conviction or acquittal of each possible charge. Jurors may, however, take different routes to reach the same conclusion. For instance, a statute might list more than one method of committing a crime, and jurors may have differing views about which method the defendant used. In Schad v. Arizona, 501 U.S. 624 (1991), a defendant was indicted for first-degree murder, and the prosecutor argued both premeditated- and felony-murder theories. It was not clear whether the jurors all agreed on one theory when they returned a guilty verdict. The Court held that there was no due process violation because the state statute treated felony murder and premeditation as alternative *means* of establishing the single criminal element of mens rea. Thus, the key question is whether the statute makes a particular fact an element of the offense or instead an alternative means of establishing a crime element. State courts have also framed the question in these terms. See State v. Fortune, 909 P.2d 930 (Wash. 1996). However, it has proven difficult to determine which facts are the "means" (over which jurors may disagree) and which are the "elements" (on which jurors must agree). See State v. Boots, 780 P.2d 725 (Or. 1989) (Linde, J.); Richardson v. United States, 526 U.S. 813 (1999) (interpreting the federal Continuing Criminal Enterprise statute to require jury to agree unanimously on the "violations" that make up the "series of continuing violations" that define the enterprise; violations are elements of the offense, not merely the means of committing an element).

5. *Special verdicts: majority position.* Special verdicts require the jury to answer specific questions about its subsidiary findings of fact, and they instruct the jury about the sequence for proceeding from preliminary findings to final conclusions. Proponents of the special verdict argue that it gives the jury valuable information and allows judicial review of improper verdicts. See Larry Heuer & Steven Penrod,

Trial Complexity: A Field Investigation of Its Meaning and Its Effects, 18 Law & Hum. Behav. 29, 50 (1994) (survey of 160 actual trials; when special verdict forms were used, jurors reported feeling more informed, better satisfied, and more confident that their special verdict reflected proper understanding of judge's instructions). However, special verdicts are not often used in criminal cases, and some courts have struck down convictions based on special verdicts. See State v. Dilliner, 569 S.E.2d 211 (W. Va. 2002) (use of special interrogatories in criminal case in absence of statutory authorization is reversible error). According to the seminal case on this question, United States v. Spock, 416 F.2d 165 (1st Cir. 1969), special verdicts may coerce a jury into reaching a guilty verdict: "There is no easier way to reach, and perhaps force, a verdict of guilty than to approach it step by step. A juror, wishing to acquit, may be formally catechized." Could it also be argued that special verdicts might coerce a jury into a verdict of acquittal? Despite this general disinclination to use special verdicts, some state statutes or procedural rules provide for special verdicts in particular types of cases, such as those in which the defendant presents an insanity defense. Does the notion that the jury serves as a way to bring common sense into the process of factfinding suggest a wider reliance on special verdicts?

6. *Inconsistent verdicts.* When there are multiple defendants in a trial or multiple counts against a single defendant, the jury could reach inconsistent conclusions for the different defendants or charges. Yet because of the preference for general verdicts, there is no explanation available for how the jury reached its incongruent outcomes. Faced with this situation, the federal courts have decided that consistency among verdicts is not necessary when a defendant is convicted on one or more counts but acquitted on others. Dunn v. United States, 284 U.S. 390 (1932) (Holmes, J.). The incompatible results, these courts conclude, could be a product of jury lenity, but that does not invalidate the guilty verdict the jury did return. In the federal courts, the presumption that the inconsistent verdict was the product of jury lenity is not rebuttable. Under United States v. Powell, 469 U.S. 57 (1984), defendants cannot present evidence to show that the inconsistent verdict in their particular case resulted from a pro-government error rather than jury lenity. This approach, the Court said, is intended to prevent "speculation" about how the jury reached inconsistent verdicts. State courts have by and large followed the *Dunn* rule for inconsistent verdicts. People v. Caldwell, 681 P.2d 274 (Cal. 1984); Commonwealth v. Campbell, 651 A.2d 1096 (Pa. 1994). A small minority of state courts still hold that inconsistent verdicts require reversal. Many courts, however, recognize an exception for "logically" inconsistent verdicts (as opposed to "factually" inconsistent verdicts). When a jury has returned verdicts convicting a defendant of two or more crimes, and the existence of an element of one of the crimes negates the existence of a necessary element of the other crime, courts generally say that the verdicts should not be sustained. See United States v. Powell; State v. Hinton, 630 A.2d 593 (Conn. 1993). Why do courts hope to avoid inquiries into the reasons for inconsistent verdicts? If the primary objective is to avoid speculation about the basis for verdicts, would a presumption in favor of dismissing all inconsistent verdicts work just as well as the current majority rule? See Eric L. Muller, The Hobgoblin of Little Minds? Our Foolish Law of Inconsistent Verdicts, 111 Harv. L. Rev. 771 (1998).

7. *Jury reform: juror note-taking.* Traditionally jurors in criminal cases have been barred from taking notes during trial. However, the majority of states (around 35)

and the federal courts have begun to allow note-taking subject to judicial approval. See, e.g., Wash. Superior Ct. Crim. R. 6.8; Conn. R. Superior Ct., Crim. §845B; Mich. R. Crim. P. 6.414. Another group of states authorize note-taking without leaving the decision to the trial court in ordinary cases. See Minn. R. Crim. P. 26.03; Md. Crim. R. 4-326; see also ABA Standards for Criminal Justice: Trial by Jury 15-3.5 (3d ed. 1996). About five states still prohibit note-taking. See, e.g., Pa. R. Crim. P. 1113. In states where statutes and procedural rules do not address the question, courts often authorize note-taking. See, e.g., People v. Hues, 704 N.E.2d 546 (N.Y. 1998) (survey of cases). Research suggests higher juror satisfaction and no change in outcomes when jurors are allowed to take notes. See Larry Heuer & Steven Penrod, Increasing Juror Participation in Trials Through Note Taking and Question Asking, 79 Judicature 256 (1996). Even though the trend is toward letting the trial judge decide the issue, most rules and judicial opinions on the subject call for safeguards, such as the immediate destruction of the notes after the jury completes its deliberations and cautionary instructions to the jury not to rely too heavily on the notes or on other jurors who took notes. See State v. Waddell, 661 N.E.2d 1043 (Ohio 1996). Should note-taking require the consent of the parties? What explains the historical hostility toward note-taking? Do the same attitudes explain the "safeguards" that rules and court decisions impose on the use of notes?

8. *Jury reform: juror questions to witnesses.* Arizona allows jurors to submit written questions to witnesses. Ariz. Crim. P. R. 18.6(e) was amended in 1995 to provide as follows: "Jurors shall be instructed that they are permitted to submit to the court written questions directed to witnesses or to the court; and that opportunity will be given to counsel to object to such questions out of the presence of the jury. [F]or good cause the court may prohibit or limit the submission of questions to witnesses." Commentary to the rules explains what happens if the court refuses to ask a juror's question because it calls for inadmissible evidence: "If a juror's question is rejected, the jury should be told that trial rules do not permit some questions to be asked and that the jurors should not attach any significance to the failure of having their question asked." While it is hard to find other state rules or statutes that allow jurors to submit written questions for witnesses in criminal trials, the great majority of courts allow juror questioning in the sound discretion of the trial judge, even absent a rule or statute addressing the topic. See State v. Culkin, 35 P.3d 233 (Haw. 2001) (approves juror questioning of witnesses through trial judge); Slaughter v. Commonwealth, 744 S.W.2d 407 (Ky. 1987). Fewer than 10 state courts (but a majority of federal courts) have prohibited juror questioning of witnesses. Morrison v. State, 845 S.W.2d 882 (Tex. Crim. App. 1992). These courts have concluded that the power to question can create in the juror the mindset of an advocate. A nationwide survey of more than 500 trial judges indicated that 77 percent of them never allow jurors to ask witnesses questions. Larry Heuer & Steven D. Penrod, Some Suggestions for the Critical Appraisal of a More Active Jury, 85 Nw. U. L. Rev. 226, 229 (1990). The practice also creates a dilemma for attorneys. If they object to questions posed by the jurors, they risk alienating the jury. If they fail to object, they risk waiving errors that could form the basis of an appeal. Would you like jurors to have this power in a jurisdiction in which you were a prosecutor? A defense attorney?

9. *Non-unanimity in military criminal tribunals.* In the military justice system, a panel of military officers finds the facts to support a criminal conviction and sets the sentence. A three-fourths majority of the panel is necessary to select a sentence of more than 10 years. A set of regulations passed soon after the terrorist attacks

on September 11, 2001, created specialized courts-martial to try people accused of terrorism. On these panels, a unanimous verdict is required to impose a death penalty, but two-thirds of the panel is enough to find the accused guilty. 66 Fed. Reg. 57833 (Nov. 13, 2001). How might a panel of officers decide criminal matters differently than a panel of citizens on a criminal jury in the civilian system?

3. Jury Nullification

During its deliberations, the jury resolves factual disputes based on the evidence the parties present. It then applies the facts to the relevant legal principles that the judge provides in her instructions. But does the jury also have the power to interpret the law in light of its own values and priorities? Can the jury decide that the prosecution has proven a violation of the law but nevertheless choose to acquit because the jury believes that an injustice would otherwise result?

Judicial opinions on this subject widely recognize that the jurors have the "power" to ignore the law or to interpret the law themselves. This power has come to be known as "jury nullification." Nevertheless, judges usually consider jury nullification to be illegitimate. Hence, most courts refuse to instruct a jury that they have the power to "nullify" the law, and most do not allow defense counsel to make such an argument to the jury.

State constitutions and statutes fall into two camps on the issue of the jury's authority to decide questions of law (and thus to decide not to apply the law when an injustice would result). The state constitutions of Georgia (art. I, §1, para. 11, §A), Indiana (art. I, §19), Maryland (art. XXIII), and Oregon (art. I, §16) declare that the jury has authority over both the factual and legal aspects of each case. For example, the Indiana constitution provides: "In all criminal cases whatever, the jury shall have the right to determine the law and the facts." Ind. Const. art. 1, §19. Other state statutes take an opposite view. Cal. Penal Code §1126 ("In a trial for any offense, questions of law are to be decided by the court, and questions of fact by the jury. Although the jury has the power to find a general verdict, which includes questions of law as well as of fact, they are bound, nevertheless, to receive as law what is laid down as such by the court").

Consider the following pamphlet, widely distributed by a private organization that advocates broader use of the jury's power to nullify the criminal law as it applies in individual cases. To the extent that this pamphlet and others like it influence juror behavior, should it be considered a source of law?

■ JURORS' HANDBOOK: A CITIZEN'S GUIDE TO JURY DUTY, FULLY INFORMED JURY ASSOCIATION

Did you know that you qualify for another, much more powerful vote than the one which you cast on election day? This opportunity comes when you are selected for jury duty, a position of honor for over 700 years. . . .

JURY POWER IN THE SYSTEM OF CHECKS AND BALANCES

In a Constitutional system of justice, such as ours, there is a judicial body with more power than Congress, the President, or even the Supreme Court. Yes, the trial jury protected under our Constitution has more power than all these government officials. This is because it has the final veto power over all "acts of the legislature" that may come to be called "laws."

In fact, the power of jury nullification predates our Constitution. In November of 1734, a printer named John Peter Zenger was arrested for seditious libel against his Majesty's government. At that time, a law of the Colony of New York forbid any publication without prior government approval. Freedom of the press was not enjoyed by the early colonialists! Zenger, however, defied this censorship and published articles strongly critical of New York colonial rule. When brought to trial in August of 1735, Zenger admitted publishing the offending articles, but argued that the truth of the facts stated justified their publication. The judge instructed the jury that truth is not justification for libel. [S]ince the defendant had admitted to the "fact" of publication, only a question of "law" remained. Then, as now, the judge said the "issue of law" was for the court to determine, and he instructed the jury to find the defendant guilty. It took only ten minutes for the jury to disregard the judge's instructions on the law and find Zenger NOT GUILTY.

That is the power of the jury at work; the power to decide the issues of law under which the defendant is charged, as well as the facts. In our system of checks and balances, the jury is our final check, the people's last safeguard against unjust law and tyranny.

A JURY'S RIGHTS, POWERS, AND DUTIES

But does the jury's power to veto bad laws exist under our Constitution? It certainly does! . . . As recently as 1972, the U.S. Court of Appeals for the District of Columbia said that the jury has an "unreviewable and irreversible power . . . to acquit in disregard of the instructions on the law given by the trial judge" (U.S. v. Dougherty, 473 F.2d 1113 (1972)). Or as this same truth was stated in an earlier decision by the United States Court of Appeals for the District of Maryland: "We recognize, as appellants urge, the undisputed power of the jury to acquit, even if its verdict is contrary to the law as given by the judge, and contrary to the evidence. This is a power that must exist as long as we adhere to the general verdict in criminal cases, for the courts cannot search the minds of the jurors to find the basis upon which they judge. If the jury feels that the law under which the defendant is accused, is unjust, or that exigent circumstances justified the actions of the accused, or for any reason which appeals to their logic or passion, the jury has the power to acquit, and the courts must abide by that decision" (U.S. v. Moylan, 417 F.2d 1002 (1969)).

YOU, as a juror armed with the knowledge of the purpose of a jury trial, and the knowledge of what your Rights, powers, and duties really are, can with your single vote of not guilty nullify or invalidate any law involved in that case. Because a jury's guilty decision must be unanimous, it takes only one vote to effectively nullify a bad "act of the legislature." Your one vote can "hang" a jury; and although it won't be an acquittal, at least the defendant will not be convicted of violating an unjust or unconstitutional law. The government cannot deprive anyone of "Liberty," without your consent! . . .

JURORS MUST KNOW THEIR RIGHTS

You must know your rights! Because, once selected for jury duty, nobody will inform you of your power to judge both law and fact. In fact, the judge's instructions to the jury may be to the contrary. Another quote from U.S. v. Dougherty: "The fact that there is widespread existence of the jury's prerogative, and approval of its existence as a necessary counter to case-hardened judges and arbitrary prosecutors, does not establish as an imperative that the jury must be informed by the judge of that power."

Look at that quote again. The court ruled jurors have the power to decide the law, but they don't have to be told about it. It may sound hypocritical, but the *Dougherty* decision conforms to an 1895 Supreme Court decision that held the same thing. In Sparf v. U.S. (156 U.S. 51), the court ruled that although juries have the right to ignore a judge's instructions on the law, they don't have to be made aware of it by the court.

Is this Supreme Court ruling as unfair as it appears on the surface? It may be, but the logic behind such a decision is plain enough. In our Constitutional Republic (note I didn't say democracy) the people have granted certain limited powers to government, preserving and retaining their God-given inalienable rights. So, if it is indeed the juror's right to decide the law, then the citizens should know what their rights are. They need not be told by the courts. After all, the Constitution makes us the masters of the public servants. Should a servant have to tell a master what his rights are? Of course not, it's our responsibility to know what our rights are! . . .

America, the Constitution and your individual rights are under attack! Will you defend them? READ THE CONSTITUTION, KNOW YOUR RIGHTS! Remember, if you don't know what your Rights are, you haven't got any!

Problem 7-4. Juries and Social Justice

Defense counsel has asked the trial judge to instruct the jury as follows:

> The Court instructs the Jury that under the Constitution of the United States, the Jury has a paramount right to acquit an accused person for whatever reason and to find him not guilty, even though the evidence may support a conviction, and this is an important part of the jury trial system guaranteed by the Constitution.
>
> The Court further instructs the Jury that this principle of jury nullification is just as important to the constitutional process as any other instruction which the Court has given to this Jury, and that in the final analysis, you, the members of the Jury, are the sole judges of whether or not it is right and fair to convict the Accused or whether under the totality of the circumstances, the Accused should be found not guilty. In arriving at your verdict you are not compelled to answer to anyone or to the State, nor are you required at any time by the Court or any person or party to give a reason or to be brought to accountability for your decision and vote.

Alternatively, counsel has asked the court for permission to make such an argument to the jury in the closing statement. The prosecutor has objected to the proposed instruction and will object if defense counsel makes such an argument in the closing statement.

This issue has arisen in four cases. In State v. Adams, the defendant is charged with destruction of government property and criminal trespass because she scaled a fence at a military installation and spray-painted antinuclear slogans on military equipment used to maintain nuclear weaponry. In State v. Baker, the defendant is charged with criminal trespass for blocking the doorway to an abortion clinic. He was protesting the practices of the clinic and calling for an end to legal abortions.

In State v. Cunningham, the defendant is charged with robbery in the first degree. The prosecution will present evidence that the defendant took two 12-packs of beer at gunpoint from a convenience store. The minimum sentence for this crime is 10 years. The state has also charged the defendant with being a "persistent felony offender" in the second degree because of his prior felony convictions. If the jury finds him guilty on this charge, the judge will impose a 20-year mandatory minimum sentence.

In State v. Derby, the defendant is an African American man who is charged with distribution of crack cocaine. The government will present evidence that the defendant sold two ounces of crack to an undercover agent. Venue for the trial is set in a location where it is likely that a number of the jurors will be African Americans.

As trial judge in each of these cases, would you grant the motions? What particular circumstances that you do not yet know would influence your decision? Would it matter to you if there were a state constitutional provision stating that the "jury shall have the right to determine the law and the facts"? Compare Davis v. State, 520 So. 2d 493 (Miss. 1988); State v. Wentworth, 395 A.2d 858 (N.H. 1978); Medley v. Commonwealth, 704 S.W.2d 190 (Ky. 1985).

Notes

1. *Authority of jury to nullify: majority position.* There is widespread agreement among state and federal courts that juries have the technical power to "nullify" by issuing general verdicts, thus obscuring whether they have judged only the facts or the law as well. Yet courts in most places refuse to instruct juries about their power to judge the law or to "nullify" the charge, and attorneys are usually not allowed to inform the jury about this power. Typical is the following statement by the Rhode Island Supreme Court:

> While we concede that a jury may render a verdict that violates the law, when this is done, it is a violation of the legal responsibility of the jurors. Certainly, it would be erroneous and improper for a court to lend its approval to such lawless conduct, even if no sanction could be imposed for its exercise. The fact that a person or persons may ignore legal requirements with impunity does not make this failure a right. [State v. Champa, 494 A.2d 102 (R.I. 1985).]

See also Ramos v. State, 934 S.W.2d 358 (Tex. Crim. App. 1996); but see People v. Engelman, 49 P.3d 209 (Cal. 2002) (pattern instruction stated that jurors were required to conduct themselves as required by instructions, and other jurors had obligation to advise court if juror refused to deliberate or expressed intention to decide case on improper basis; instruction created inadvisable risk to proper functioning of jury deliberations and should not be given in future trials). Some states acknowledge the power of the jury to assess law and facts by the rather subtle shift from general jury instructions directing the jury that if it finds the facts to be true it "must" find the defendant guilty to language suggesting to the jury that it "should" or "may" find the defendant guilty. A handful of states allow the judge to instruct the jury more directly about its power. Some even allow attorneys to argue nullification directly to the jury if the trial judge allows it. See State v. Bonacorsi, 648 A.2d 469 (N.H. 1994). Limits on jury instructions and arguments about nullification generally apply even in states with constitutional "nullification" provisions. A larger number of states have constitutional provisions recognizing jury nullification powers specifically for libel and sedition cases, no doubt reflecting the tradition sparked by John Peter Zenger. See, e.g., Alabama Const. art. 1, §12; Maine Const. art. 1, §4; New Jersey Const. art. 1, para. 6.

For thorough examinations of the historical origins of jury nullification in the United States, see Clay S. Conrad, Jury Nullification: The Evolution of a Doctrine (1998); Stanton D. Krauss, An Inquiry Into the Right of Criminal Juries to Determine the Law in Colonial America, 89 J. Crim. L. & Criminology 111 (1998). It appears that many of the older cases affirming the power of the jury to "find the law" were intended to limit a judicial practice of directing the jury how to apply the law to particular facts.

2. *The continuing vitality of the nullification debate.* Despite the relatively uniform and restrictive law concerning nullification, the debate over its validity and use continues at a fever pitch. See, e.g., Darryl Brown, Jury Nullification Within the Rule of Law, 81 Minn. L. Rev. 1149 (1997); Andrew Leipold, Rethinking Jury Nullification, 82 Va. L. Rev. 253 (1996). In some cases, scholars have argued that a proper understanding of the power of criminal juries supports jury decision making on questions of law in particular contexts. See, e.g., Colleen Murphy, Integrating the Constitutional Authority of Civil and Criminal Juries, 61 Geo. Wash. L. Rev. 723 (1993); Jack Weinstein, Considering Jury Nullification: When May and Should a Jury Reject the Law to Do Justice, 30 Am. Crim. L. Rev. 239 (1993). Among the more controversial articles is one by Professor Paul Butler encouraging black jurors to refuse to convict some black defendants in an effort to challenge and change the criminal justice system:

> [F]or pragmatic and political reasons, the black community is better off when some nonviolent lawbreakers remain in the community rather than go to prison. The decision as to what kind of conduct by African-Americans ought to be punished is better made by African-Americans themselves, based on the costs and benefits to their community, than by the traditional criminal justice process, which is controlled by white lawmakers and white law enforcers. Legally, the doctrine of jury nullification gives the power to make this decision to African-American jurors who sit in judgment of African-American defendants. Considering the costs of law enforcement to the black community and the failure of white lawmakers to devise significant nonincarcerative responses to black antisocial conduct, it is the moral responsibility of black jurors to emancipate some guilty black outlaws. . . .
>
> Imagine a country in which more than half of the young male citizens are under the supervision of the criminal justice system, either awaiting trial, in prison, or on probation or parole. Imagine a country in which two-thirds of the men can anticipate being arrested before they reach age thirty. Imagine a country in which there are more young men in prison than in college. Now give the citizens of the country the key to the prison. Should they use it? . . .

In cases involving violent malum in se crimes like murder, rape, and assault, jurors should consider the case strictly on the evidence presented, and, if they have no reasonable doubt that the defendant is guilty, they should convict. For nonviolent malum in se crimes such as theft or perjury, nullification is an option that the juror should consider, although there should be no presumption in favor of it. A juror might vote for acquittal, for example, when a poor woman steals from Tiffany's, but not when the same woman steals from her next-door neighbor. Finally, in cases involving nonviolent, malum prohibitum offenses, including "victimless" crimes like narcotics offenses, there should be a presumption in favor of nullification.

Butler, Racially Based Jury Nullification: Black Power in the Criminal Justice System, 105 Yale L.J. 677, 679, 690, 714 (1995). See also Andrew Leipold, The Dangers of Race-Based Jury Nullification: A Response to Professor Butler, 44 UCLA L. Rev. 109 (1996). Jury nullification also becomes a forum for discussing controversial political and social issues other than race. Robert Schopp, Verdicts of Conscience: Nullification and Necessity as Jury Responses to Crimes of Conscience, 69 S. Cal. L. Rev. 2039 (1996). Would nullification instructions increase or undermine public respect for the justice system? Consider 1 Alexis de Tocqueville, Democracy in America 361 (Francis Bowen trans., 1862) (1835): "He who punishes the criminal is therefore the real master of society. Now, the institution of the jury raises the people itself, or at least a class of citizens, to the bench of judges. The institution of the jury consequently invests the people, or that class of citizens, with the direction of society."

Do the arguments for nullification change when a trial judge refuses to convict based on disagreement with the law as applied to a case? See United States v. Lynch, 952 F. Supp. 167 (S.D.N.Y. 1997) (acquittal of two abortion protesters of criminal contempt charges in bench trial; judge relies in part on "that exercise of the prerogative of leniency which a fact-finder has to refuse to convict a defendant, even if the circumstances would otherwise be sufficient to convict."); Pamela Karlan, Two Concepts of Judicial Independence, 72 S. Cal. L. Rev. 535 (1999) (discussing *Lynch*).

3. *Do nullification instructions and arguments affect jury decisions?* The battles over nullification instructions and arguments—and the efforts of jurors' rights groups—seem to assume that if juries knew they had the power to nullify, they would do so more often. Two studies cast doubt on this assumption. A 1985 study by a psychologist found that juries respond to judicial instructions about nullification only when those instructions are strongly worded; simply informing juries that they have the final authority to decide cases does not change outcomes. Irwin Horowitz, The Effects of Jury Nullification Instructions on Verdicts and Jury Functioning in Criminal Trials, 9 Law & Hum. Behav. 25 (1985). In a second study in 1988, Horowitz found that (1) juries responded to strong instructions about nullification whether those instructions came from the judge or lawyers, (2) strong instructions about the jury's power to "do justice" led both to more acquittals (for sympathetic defendants) and more convictions (for unsympathetic defendants), and (3) cautionary language to the jury from a second actor undermined the inflammatory impact of the instructions. Irwin Horowitz, The Impact of Judicial Instructions, Arguments, and Challenges on Jury Decision Making, 12 Law & Hum. Behav. 439 (1988). See also Keith E. Niedermeier, Irwin A. Horowitz & Norbert L. Kerr, Informing Jurors of Their Nullification Power: A Route to a Just Verdict or Judicial Chaos? 23 Law & Hum. Behav. 331 (1999); Jeffrey Kerwin & David Shaffer, The Effects of Jury Dogmatism on Reactions to Jury Nullification Instructions, 17 Personality & Soc. Psychol. Bull. 140 (1991).

4. *Jury information and jury tampering.* Suppose a nullification enthusiast tries to hand out a jurors' rights tract (like the one distributed by FIJA, reprinted above) or any other literature at a courthouse to those wearing a juror badge. What can a prosecutor or judge do? The legal lines become quite clear when any person tries to influence an active juror: such conduct is known as jury tampering, and the right to a free and fair trial overcomes any claim of a right to free speech. Convictions for jury tampering have been upheld against people who distribute FIJA literature or who publicize a FIJA "800" number within a courthouse to jurors with a button indicating their active service. See Turney v. State, 936 P.2d 533 (Alaska 1997). The legal lines are less clear, however, when people distribute literature outside the courthouse to all citizens, or only to those who are not specifically identified as jurors. Professor Nancy King has analyzed these tactics and concludes that they are constitutionally acceptable. King, Silencing Nullification Advocacy Inside the Jury Room and Outside the Courtroom 65 U. Chi. L. Rev. 433 (1998).

5. *Juror misbehavior.* Imagine that a juror lies during voir dire with the goal of exercising the "right" to nullify a conviction (or at least the power of a single juror to hang a jury). Or suppose a juror makes remarks during deliberations suggesting a racial motive in decision making (whether in favor of a guilty or not guilty verdict). What happens in these cases? If jurors violate direct instructions from the judge or lie during voir dire, and it comes to light before the jury starts deliberations, the jurors can be removed from the case and alternates put in their place. If their misbehavior comes to light after a verdict has been reached, depending on the nature and severity of the misbehavior, jurors may be prosecuted for jury tampering. Most states and the federal system place sharp limits on the introduction of information from or about jury deliberations in an effort to protect jury secrecy and maintain a focus on issues of guilt and innocence. In addition, a recent survey of judges suggests that serious misconduct is rare (although lesser misconduct, such as failing to be fully honest at voir dire and sleeping during trials, appears to be much more common). See Nancy King, Juror Delinquency in Criminal Trials in America, 1796-1996, 94 Mich. L. Rev. 2673 (1996) ("[O]ur present system enlists reluctant amateurs to perform a demanding and unfamiliar job, in secret, with little accountability. In such a scheme, some degree of misconduct is inevitable").

California now employs a jury instruction that requires jurors to inform the judge whenever a fellow member of the jury refuses to deliberate based on his or her disagreement with the law. People v. Williams, 21 P.3d 1209 (Cal. 2001) (upholding conviction after trial court replaced juror who was reported by fellow juror; replaced juror disagreed with statutory rape law as applied to 18-year-old male defendant and 16-year-old female victim). Do you expect to see this device spread eventually to many other states?

D. THE PUBLIC AS DECISIONMAKER

1. Public Access to Trials

The Sixth Amendment to the U.S. Constitution provides defendants with a right to a "speedy and public trial," as do analogous state constitutional provisions. A public trial might mean that any person could attend, including reporters. Or the right to a public trial might be a personal right of the defendant, giving the defendant a right *not* to have a public trial — the right to a closed trial — as well.

Courts have recognized both a private and a public interest in open trials. The presumption in favor of an open trial is not absolute, and the courts have wrestled with issues such as when the defense or prosecution has a right to a closed proceeding, and when the media has a right of access to proceedings even against the wishes of both parties. Questions regarding media coverage, particularly with cameras and microphones, have taken a higher profile with the creation of specialized television channels devoted to trials, and the increasing capacity through technology to create much wider access to trials. Consider whether the court in the following case properly balances the prosecutor's request to close the trial during the testimony of one key witness and the defendant's request that the trial remain open.

■ STATE v. BARRY GARCIA
561 N.W.2d 599 (N.D. 1997)

Meschke, J.

Barry Caesar Garcia appeals a jury verdict and a criminal judgment finding him guilty of murder and aggravated assault, and sentencing him to life imprisonment without parole. We affirm. . . .

During the evening of November 15, 1995, juveniles Jaime Guerrero, Juan Guerrero, Michael Charbonneau, Ray Martinez, Angel Esparza, and Garcia drove around Fargo-Moorhead in a brown, 1975, Minnesota-licensed, Ford sedan owned by Juan Guerrero's mother. The young men took along 10 to 15 red and green shotgun shells and a sawed-off shotgun owned by the Skyline Piru Bloods, a street gang whose members included Jaime Guerrero, Juan Guerrero and Martinez. While driving in a West Fargo residential area near 10 P.M., Garcia asked the driver to stop. Garcia and Charbonneau, who is much taller than Garcia, left the car. Garcia took the shotgun. Their car continued down the street and came to a stop, and Garcia and Charbonneau began walking around the neighborhood.

In the same neighborhood, Pat and Cheryl Tendeland were dropping off their friend, Connie Guler, who had accompanied them to a prayer service in Hillsboro. In the Tendeland car parked in Guler's driveway, while seated and talking, Guler saw a "taller boy . . . maybe six feet or taller" and a "shorter one . . . five feet or less tall" walking down the sidewalk toward them. Guler thought the shorter boy was carrying a gun, but Pat thought it was an umbrella. After the boys stood near Guler's driveway for awhile, they began walking back toward the brown Ford sedan. From their suspicious behavior, Pat decided to back up and follow the boys "to see where they [were] going."

As the Tendeland car slowly approached the Ford sedan, Guler saw the taller boy walking briskly toward the Ford and the shorter boy with the gun lagging behind. The Ford's lights were on, and it started to pull away. Cheryl read off the car's license number. Guler testified about the next thing she remembered:

> I caught out of the sight of my eye something, and I turned, and this shorter boy was coming down off my berm, and he was so close, he could have opened my car door. And the next — our eyes met, and all I remember was these cold, dark eyes. And that's all I

know. I don't have a face. And it just—he just raised it. I said, "My God, he's going to shoot," and it went off. I mean, it wasn't a matter of—it was just (indicating), like a click of the finger. It was so quick. . . .

Cherryl was shot in the forehead and shotgun pellets also struck Pat's face, knocking a lens from his glasses. Guler was not struck by the blast. Pat, who had difficulty seeing with blood running down his face and without the lost lens, decided to drive to a nearby police station. [Cherryl Tendeland died from the shotgun wounds.]

Jaime Guerrero, who had remained in the Ford, testified he did not see the gunshot, but he heard it. Guerrero said Charbonneau and Garcia got back in the car about 20 seconds after he heard the shotgun blast. According to Guerrero, Garcia, who was still carrying the shotgun, said "they got her," and "next time, don't look at me." [Based on descriptions of witnesses, the police located the Ford sedan that night.] Police recovered a sawed-off shotgun with a warm barrel from the backseat of the car along with several red and green shotgun shells. Shortly, the police chasing after Garcia captured him in an athletic field at Moorhead State University. When arrested, Garcia possessed one green and three red shotgun shells. . . .

The spent shotgun shell recovered at the scene had been fired from the sawed-off shotgun found in the brown Ford sedan. Neither Pat nor Guler could positively identify Garcia as the person who shot into the Tendeland car. No usable fingerprints were found on the shotgun. Atomic absorption tests on Garcia, Martinez, and Jaime and Juan Guerrero showed significant levels of antimony and barium on all four individuals, thus evidencing each of them could have recently fired a gun or handled a gun that had been recently fired. The pattern on the sole of Garcia's tennis shoes corresponded with shoeprints found at the scene of the shooting.

The Tendeland shooting brought on much publicity, and the trial court allowed expanded media coverage of Garcia's jury trial. See N.D. Admin. R. 21.* At the trial, the State called Jaime Guerrero as a witness. When asked his name, Guerrero replied, "I am not going to say nothing."

Away from the jury, the trial court learned Guerrero had not been granted immunity to testify, warned Guerrero he may be subject to contempt penalties,

*N.D. Admin. R. 21 provides in pertinent part as follows:

d. "Expanded media coverage" includes broadcasting, televising, electronic recording, or photographing of a judicial proceeding for the purpose of gathering and disseminating information to the public by media personnel. . . .
  Section 4. The court may permit expanded media coverage of a judicial proceeding in the courtroom while the judge is present, and in adjacent areas as the court may direct. Expanded media coverage provided for in this rule may be exercised only by media personnel. . . .
  b. The judge may deny expanded media coverage of any proceeding or portion of a proceeding in which the judge determines on the record, or by written findings:
    1. Expanded media coverage would materially interfere with a party's right to a fair trial;
    2. A witness or party has objected and shown good cause why expanded media coverage should not be permitted; . . .
    4. Expanded media coverage would include testimony of a juvenile victim or witness in a proceeding in which illegal sexual activity is an element of the evidence. . . .
  c. The judge may limit or end expanded media coverage at any time during a proceeding, if the judge determines on the record, or by written findings:
    1. The requirements of this rule or additional guidelines imposed by the judge have been violated; or
    2. The substantial rights of an individual participant, or rights to a fair trial will be prejudiced by the expanded media coverage if it is allowed to continue.

—EDS.

and also informed him of his Fifth Amendment rights to remain silent and to speak to a lawyer. Guerrero asked to speak with a lawyer, and the trial court appointed the same lawyer who was representing Guerrero in juvenile court to advise him. The court recessed, and Guerrero consulted his lawyer during the lunch hour.

When the trial court reconvened out of the presence of the jury [t]he State's attorney explained to the court:

> Mr. Guerrero has indicated some willingness to proceed and provide testimony to matters which he has already provided us information. I'm concerned—and it's been relayed to me—that there may be some concern about the media coverage, particularly the television camera, and also the number of viewers and spectators in the audience of the courtroom.
>
> It is—it's my request at this time that, for the testimony of Jaime Guerrero, that the Court terminate expanded media coverage, terminate the use of the television camera, terminate the feed to the television and/or radio just for that testimony, and that the Court also order that anybody other than the family of Barry Garcia or the family of Cherryl Tendeland be excused from the courtroom, to present—to present a more friendly environment, if you will, for the testimony of this child, who is only 15 years of age. I think there are good arguments to be made for the termination of the expanded coverage for a person only 15 years of age. There is some reason to believe that he is concerned about other persons' opinions and feelings and actions if he decides to go ahead and testify. . . .

Garcia's attorney resisted the State's request, arguing there was "no compelling reason to shut things down at this point." . . . The State's attorney explained he had promised to dismiss with prejudice the juvenile court charges against Guerrero if he testified truthfully in Garcia's trial. Guerrero's lawyer told the court Guerrero "is a juvenile, and he is intimidated by the audience and media coverage," and elaborated on Guerrero's reluctance to testify:

> I think he's intimidated by the whole spectacle of the trial, that he will be on television, he will be in the newspaper again. And it would put him at ease not to have to experience this. And he is a juvenile and does want his confidentiality preserved, if possible, but I guess that's . . . not really possible. But those are some of the factors that make him not want to testify. This would put him at ease if he didn't have to kind of run the gauntlet. . . .

Garcia's lawyer again objected to any closure of the trial. The State's attorney explained:

> I would like, just for the record, to note that in support of our request and our position, we are aware of another witness, not Mr. Guerrero, but another witness who has indicated a reluctance to provide testimony, who has been subpoenaed, because of actual repercussions that he's already experienced. So we are basing these requests on some real events, not just speculation. At least that's what I have been told. . . .

The court outlined its "initial thoughts," but recessed and deferred ruling until the media had an opportunity to be heard. After hearing argument from a media representative, the trial court ruled:

[It] is in the interests of justice to suspend the expanded media coverage order for this witness, and to suspend the rule as regards media coverage. Exercising the inherent powers of the Court to control the courtroom, I am going to order that the courtroom be cleared, that the feeds to the radio and the television be terminated, and that all persons, except for counsel, Mr. Garcia, and Detective Warren, and the immediate family of—was it—of Mr. Garcia, and the immediate family of Mrs. Tendeland. . . .

The cautionary instruction I intend to give . . . will read as follows: Ladies and gentlemen of the jury, as you are aware, Mr. Guerrero has indicated an unwillingness to testify. He has expressed a concern about all the media coverage, all of the people— and all the people in the courtroom. Taking into consideration the youth of Mr. Guerrero and his concerns, the Court has determined that in order to facilitate his testimony, the courtroom will be cleared of all persons. You are not to draw any conclusions or inferences from the clearance of the courtroom.

The court also allowed a single pool representative, chosen by the media, to remain in the courtroom. The court gave the jury the cautionary instruction, and Guerrero testified in the partially closed courtroom.

Garcia claims his constitutional rights to a public trial were violated when the trial court temporarily terminated expanded media coverage and excluded the general public from the courtroom for Guerrero's testimony.

The Sixth Amendment to the United States Constitution guarantees a criminal defendant "the right to a speedy and public trial. . . ." See also N.D. Const. Art. I, §12. Although the guarantee of a public trial was created for the benefit of criminal defendants, see In re Oliver, 333 U.S. 257 (1948), the right is also shared with the public; the common concern is to assure fairness. Press-Enterprise Co. v. Superior Court of Cal., 478 U.S. 1 (1986). "In addition to ensuring that judge and prosecutor carry out their duties responsibly, a public trial encourages witnesses to come forward and discourages perjury." Waller v. Georgia, 467 U.S. 39 (1984). The Supreme Court explained in Gannett Co., Inc. v. DePasquale, 443 U.S. 368 (1979): "Openness in court proceedings may improve the quality of testimony, induce unknown witnesses to come forward with relevant testimony, cause all trial participants to perform their duties more conscientiously, and generally give the public an opportunity to observe the judicial system." Precedents demonstrate, however, that the right to a public trial is not absolute and must give way in rare instances to other interests essential to the fair administration of justice.

The contours of a criminal defendant's right to a public trial in the context of total closure of an entire pretrial suppression hearing were confronted by the Supreme Court in *Waller*. The *Waller* Court ruled that defendant's public-trial guarantee had been violated, and explained:

[T]he party seeking to close the hearing must advance an overriding interest that is likely to be prejudiced, the closure must be no broader than necessary to protect that interest, the trial court must consider reasonable alternatives to closing the proceeding, and it must make findings adequate to support the closure. [467 U.S. at 48.]

The *Waller* Court made clear that a trial court's power to exclude the public from a criminal trial should be exercised sparingly and then only for the most unusual of circumstances.

We used the *Waller* standard to measure a trial court's temporary closure of a defendant's criminal trial on charges of gross sexual imposition during the testimony of the child victim, the defendant's adopted son. State v. Klem, 438 N.W.2d 798 (N.D. 1989). Klem's first trial had been entirely open to the public while the child victim testified, and had resulted in a hung jury. At the second trial, when the child witness was first seated to testify, the State's attorney abruptly requested closure of the trial for the child's testimony because the "sensitive nature" of the case "may be very distracting and very embarrassing for him in front of all these people and the people in the Courtroom may inhibit the testimony." After the defendant objected to the proposed closure, the court summarily ruled, "I think I will clear the Courtroom," and did so.

A majority of this Court concluded the trial court, in closing the trial to all but court personnel, parties, attorneys, jurors, and a public media representative during the child's testimony, deprived the accused of his right to a public trial. [The] majority concluded the trial court had failed to satisfactorily comply with the *Waller* requirements: "There was no hearing, no weighing of competing interests, and no findings to support closure." 438 N.W.2d at 801.

Garcia argues the trial court in this case, like the trial court in *Klem*, largely ignored the *Waller* requirements in ordering the partial closure of the courtroom, so that a reversal and a remand for a new trial are necessary. We disagree.

This case differs from *Klem* in several major ways. We pointed out in *Klem* that, ordinarily, a motion to close a trial to the public should be made before trial to avoid unfair surprise and to give the trial court the benefit of research and arguments, but the reasons for closure could not have been reasonably anticipated in this case. The mid-trial motion in *Klem* could have been made before trial, and the reasons for it were given in generalities as the child witness was seated to testify. The witness had in fact testified publicly in the first trial, so there was no apparent reason for either the closure motion or the order.

Here, Guerrero had given a sworn statement in exchange for the State's promise not to attempt to transfer his case from juvenile to adult court. Not until Guerrero was called as a witness for the State, refused to respond to any questions, and consulted with his attorney was the State's attorney or anyone else expecting Guerrero to decline to testify.

This trial court's actions show the careful consideration and weighing of competing interests so sorely lacking in *Klem*. In contrast to the summary ruling in *Klem*, this trial court held an in-chambers hearing, two open court hearings out of the jury's presence, and delayed ruling until the media could also be heard on the request for closure. Although this trial court did not hold a formal evidentiary hearing on the motion, an evidentiary hearing is not necessarily required unless requested.

The *Klem* trial court's exclusion of the general public, except for one media representative, more closely resembled a complete or total closure of the courtroom than what the trial court did here. This court allowed the Tendeland and Garcia family members to remain in the courtroom. This was only a partial closure, one that generally results in the exclusion of certain members of the public while other members of the public are permitted to remain in the courtroom. When a trial court orders a partial, rather than a total, closure of a court proceeding at the request of a party, a "substantial reason," less stringent than the *Waller* "overriding interest" requirement, can justify the closure. We believe this trial court had a substantial reason to partially and temporarily close Garcia's trial during Guerrero's testimony.

This trial court was aware of the widespread publicity generated by this case and the effect of the television camera in the courtroom. Allegations of street-gang activity dramatized this case. The State's attorney told the court about possible "repercussions" experienced by another subpoenaed witness. Guerrero's attorney explained his juvenile client's understandable intimidation from being seen testifying on television and publicized in newspapers that brought about his reluctance to testify. We would have much preferred the trial court to have gotten the explanation for Guerrero's reluctance to testify from Guerrero himself rather than filtered through the State's attorney and Guerrero's lawyer. But extensive interviews with the reluctant witness, while no doubt the better practice, are not constitutionally compelled. . . . Here, Guerrero's intimidation and hesitation to testify were amply demonstrated to the trial court by his opening refusal to even give his name.

A trial court can properly weigh an accused's right to a public trial against the interests of protecting a witness from intimidation to enable the witness to testify with more composure. A trial court may exclude members of the public from a trial if a witness will be inhibited or embarrassed to testify in the presence of an audience from his tender age or the nature of his testimony, from actual threats, or from the possibility of reprisals by others if the witness testifies. In this case, allegations of gang-related activities and possible "repercussions" like those experienced by another potential witness added to the weighing process. . . .

We disagree with Garcia that the trial court's partial closure order went further than necessary. . . . Garcia did not ask the court to allow other relatives or friends to remain in the courtroom during Guerrero's testimony, although he could have. If Garcia wanted others to remain, he should have pointed them out to the trial court and asked they be allowed to stay. The trial court's order for partial closure lasted only during Guerrero's testimony, and then those excluded were readmitted. . . .

A trial court must also consider reasonable alternatives to a partial closure. We recognize that "[c]losure of the courtroom to the public is not the only, nor necessarily the most effective, response to [witness] intimidation." We also recognize, however, that other alternatives sometimes provoke serious confrontation problems. This record is shallow on consideration of reasonable alternatives. The State's attorney, however, identified confrontation problems in possible alternatives in stating: "[W]e're not asking that Mr. Garcia in any way be deprived of any of his rights of confrontation, cross-examination, so forth. We're merely here to try and search for the truth through all the evidence that's available to us. . . ." The trial court considered variations for the partial closure order, at one point telling the attorneys:

> . . . My initial thoughts were — was to clear the courtroom of everyone except the immediate family of the Garcias. And my initial thought was to order the media not to publish in any fashion any of the testimony that's offered, but not necessarily exclude them from the courtroom. . . . Then, you know, as far as the jury is concerned, the only people that would be missing would be all the spectators.

Although this case poses a difficult question, we conclude the court properly considered reasonable alternatives, and found the partial closure to be the only adequate solution for the problem confronting the court. While it would have been helpful if the trial court had made more explicit findings about possible alternatives, we see no constitutional error here. . . .

We stress again that trial courts should not lightly close a criminal trial in any manner, and when dealing with a request for closure, a court must take pains to develop a complete record and make detailed findings about all the circumstances. More explicit findings would have facilitated review in this case. But, considering the circumstances with the findings the trial court did make, we conclude Garcia's constitutional rights to a public trial were not violated by the brief, narrowly tailored, and partial closure ordered for Guerrero's testimony. . . .

Notes

1. *"Public trial": majority view.* The defendant, prosecution, reporters, and the public may all have different interests with respect to whether a trial remains open. The public nature of criminal trials derives both from the express guarantee of the Sixth Amendment and its state analogs and from the First Amendment rights of both the defendant and the press. The presumption of open trials is usually tested when one party wants to close the proceedings and the other does not. A defendant might want to avoid publicity or retribution, exclude people who might provide new evidence, or reduce the risk of a biased jury. The government might want to protect the identity of an informant, undercover police officer, victim, or witness by limiting the number of people who watch the testimony. See, e.g., People v. Jones, 750 N.E.2d 524 (N.Y. 2001) (undercover officer). Courts are often most sympathetic to victim and witness concerns, especially in cases involving children and in cases of sexual assault and abuse. See generally Vivian Berger, Man's Trial, Woman's Tribulation: Rape Cases in the Courtroom, 77 Colum. L. Rev. 1 (1977); Carol Bohmer & Audrey Blumberg, Twice Traumatized: The Rape Victim and the Court, 58 Judicature 390 (1975). In which North Dakota case was the privacy interest of the witness greater — the child sexual victim in *Klem* or the gang member in *Garcia*? In which case did the state have a greater interest in closing the trial?

2. *Media access to the courtroom: majority view.* The press are members of the public and have the same initial rights as any other person to watch trials. In addition to recognizing the right to court access shared by all citizens, the U.S. Supreme Court has enumerated a qualified First Amendment right in the press to attend criminal trials. See Globe Newspaper Co. v. Superior Court for Norfolk County, 457 U.S. 596 (1982); Richmond Newspapers, Inc. v. Virginia, 448 U.S. 555, 572 (1980). But when the defendant or the government makes a strong claim for closure, the Sixth Amendment right to a fair trial and the less specific rights of the government or witnesses conflict with the First Amendment claims of the press. Federal and state law have created a framework governing press access that leaves substantial discretion in the hands of the trial judge, and newspapers and other media regularly sue for access to proceedings or materials. See, e.g., State ex rel. the Missoulian v. Judicial District, 933 P.2d 829 (Mont. 1997).

In addition to general claims for access, reporters often want to bring their cameras and microphones with them. Courts have largely rejected claims that the media have a constitutional right to bring cameras and microphones into the courtroom. However, 47 states currently allow cameras at trials (with various limitations on the placement and use of flash), and 35 states allow trials to be filmed — a dramatic shift since Florida first allowed cameras into its courtrooms in 1977. See Ruth Strickland & Richter Moore, Cameras in State Courts: A Historical Perspective,

78 Judicature (1994). As in North Dakota, state rules often leave the degree of access to the discretion of the trial judge. In contrast, the federal courts have experimented with but largely rejected the use of cameras in the courtroom. Will new technologies such as the Internet or satellite broadcasts that feature many more channels encourage far greater coverage of court proceedings? Will courts become more or less willing to allow video and audio coverage as requests for access expand to everyday proceedings?

3. *What parts of the trial process must be public?* The general requirement of public trials does not mean that all parts of all trials must be open to the public. The trial proceedings may include bench conferences or discussions between judge and counsel in chambers. Submissions will often be made in writing. Physical evidence may be difficult to view at a distance, or in the form presented in court. Does the defendant have a right to make these proceedings public? Pretrial proceedings often reveal information that, if reported, might influence the judgment of jurors at trial, and courts have been more willing to restrict access at this stage. See, e.g., State v. Archuleta, 857 P.2d 234 (Utah 1993); but see State v. Densmore, 624 A.2d 1138 (Vt. 1993) (allowing media access to psychosexual evaluation submitted by defendant for sentencing). Some information provided at pretrial proceedings, including detention and competency hearings, may be irrelevant to questions of guilt and innocence. Other proceedings, such as voir dire hearings, are closely linked to trial, and for these proceedings the rules governing media at trial apply. See Press-Enterprise Co. v. Superior Court of California, 464 U.S. 501 (1984).

4. *The public as jury.* The demands of the public may change as viewers become increasingly familiar with televised trials. Whether it is the daily fare of Court TV or the exceptional but widely viewed murder trial of O.J. Simpson, an expectation may develop that citizens have a right to see the justice system at work. Has Court TV increased U.S. citizens' respect for the legal system? As media coverage increases, will the pollution of jury pools and the corresponding risk of unfair trials increase?

5. *Televising appeals.* Is there a difference between televising trials and televising appellate arguments? Are trials or appellate proceedings likely to be of greater public interest? It is very difficult for most U.S. citizens to attend arguments in the U.S. Supreme Court, but the Court has fiercely resisted all efforts to film its arguments. Why? Should audio recordings of state and U.S. Supreme Court arguments be made more widely available?

6. *Press shield laws.* Reporters not only cover events in the courtroom, but also interview victims, witnesses and others outside the courtroom. Some states have "press shield" statutes that allow reporters to refuse to reveal their sources of information to criminal investigators. See Miller v. Superior Court, 986 P.2d 170 (Cal. 1999) (interpreting statute to protect reporter's interviews with offender; reporter cannot be jailed for refusing to turn over interview non-broadcast material to court under subpoena from prosecutor). Do these laws promote more active public scrutiny of the criminal justice system?

2. Community Courts

Does the criminal justice process require that decisionmakers be judges or juries? A legal realist might point out that the key decisionmakers in modern American criminal justice systems are often prosecutors rather than judges. But both judges and prosecutors are typically lawyers. Must key decisionmakers — those who choose which citizens to bring before a court and who adjudicate and sentence those convicted of offenses — be lawyers? If citizens are to have a voice in criminal justice decision making (beyond the role of complainant, victim or witness), does the long tradition of the American jury satisfy that need? Jurors are chosen for their lack of knowledge. Should they be chosen for their knowledge?

Two substantial movements are changing the forms of criminal adjudication in the United States. Both movements have deep historical roots.

One movement involves the creation of special "drug courts." There are now around 1,000 drug courts in the United States in action or in active planning. See U.S. Department of Justice, Bureau of Justice Assistance, Looking at a Decade of Drug Courts (1998, NCJ 171140). Drug courts address specific groups of offenders, typically drug offenders whose activities do not include violence. The offenders adjudicated in drug court must plead guilty, and must return to court often as they serve their sentences to update the court on their status. The first modern "drug court" was established in 1989. Drug courts provide a familiar kind of forum (a court) and a familiar decisionmaker (a judge), but with purposes distinct from general criminal courts. Drug courts reflect a rebirth of the goal of rehabilitation as a justification for punishment and social control, and a recognition that a general jurisdiction court handling serious cases of personal violence might have different purposes and priorities than an offense-specific court.

A second and even newer movement appears in the form of "community courts," which in their modern guise have close links to the idea of community policing and the philosophical aim of "restorative justice." The first modern community court opened in New York City in 1993; between 1998 and 2000, around a dozen other community courts were established, with additional courts planned, suggesting that the idea of community courts is spreading, just as the model of drug courts spread a few years ago. See Eric Lee, Community Courts: An Evolving Model (BJS 2000).

Unlike drug courts, community courts typically have a different forum (a conference room) and a different decisionmaker (community members). The goals of community court and the tools to achieve those goals also contrast with traditional criminal courts. Consider the case of four men cited for urinating in public in Manhattan, at different times and in different places. See Center for Court Innovation, "There Are No Victimless Crimes": Community Impact Panels at the Midtown Community Court (BJA 2000). About a month after they were charged, all four were summoned to a meeting with five other people — a "discussion facilitator" and a community panel made up of four people who live or work in the neighborhood: a man and woman in their 60s, a priest, and an out-of-uniform police officer.

The accused citizens are asked to explain what brought them to community court. Two are students from a local university, another is an immigrant cab driver. Each describes the time and place of his infraction. The cab driver explains that "The paper says 'public urination,' [but] it was not in public. It was dark. It was nine o'clock. No people, no vehicles, nothing. [I was] in front of Javits Center, on 38th Street. But there was no single person. Nothing!"

The community members then ask questions, such as "Everyone has to urinate; what do cabbies usually do?" and express their frustrations: "I'm on a community board and I've heard a number of complaints about cabbies who open their door and urinate on the street. It's very offensive, it bothers a lot of people, it's not hygienic. It helps to change the quality of a neighborhood. It's sort of like there's a pact people have in society. You behave in a certain way or you find yourself in a community that's known for breaking the laws."

All participants discuss the reasons for public urination by taxi drivers, students, and others. One of the students says, "I definitely would not want anybody in my doorway using it as a bathroom. But I understand it because I'm on this side. . . . There are a lot of clubs in the area, and a lot of people have the same problem. And it's not a problem that's going to go away by just talking about it; if you have to go and you're drunk, you're going to go."

After two hours of discussion, participants fill out post-meeting questionnaires. One of the offenders walks around the table to shake hands with each of the community representatives, who have been asked to remain in the room for a short post-meeting debriefing with the facilitator. Outside in the hallway a few moments later, the taxi driver reflects upon what he just experienced as he waits for the elevator. "It's very nice," he says. "We learned to keep the community clean." One of the students, standing nearby, steps forward. "It was nice," he says. "Well, not really 'nice,' but we got to experience the other side. We got to meet with the people, and that was good. We got a sense of the community."

Asked if the experience will influence his decision to urinate in public again, he pauses to think before answering. "I went in there knowing I did something wrong. I pissed in the street. Having to face these people made me feel worse. It gets to you more on a personal level than just having to pay a fine."

Consider what the creation of new kinds of courts says about our current criminal justice process. Should traditional courts be more like community courts? What percentage of the role of traditional criminal courts should be handled in community courts? What percentage of the work of community courts will reflect "net widening" — the assessment of matters that would not have been handled within the criminal justice system? Should participation in community courts be voluntary? Is there any problem with solving the community's problems in the community, with community members as decisionmakers?

■ JOHN FEINBLATT AND GREG BERMAN, RESPONDING TO THE COMMUNITY: PRINCIPLES FOR PLANNING AND CREATING A COMMUNITY COURT
(Feb. 2001, NCJ 185986)

For many years an important element has been missing from the criminal justice system. Although courts, police, and prosecutors have become increasingly modernized in recent years, they still often fail to meet the needs of the justice system's primary consumers: the neighborhoods that experience crime and its consequences every day. This problem was first recognized by advocates of community policing, who argued that police officers could address neighborhood crime and disorder more effectively if they established a close relationship with community residents and neighborhood groups. The idea of community justice has since spread to other branches of the justice system including courts, probation departments, prosecutors, and corrections offices. . . .

New York City's Midtown Community Court, which opened in October 1993, differs dramatically from the way that lower courts have operated in the city for many years. Nevertheless, it reflects a return to an old idea. In 1962, New York City closed a network of neighborhood magistrate's courts that handled intake for the city's court system. These courts arraigned defendants and disposed of low-level offenses that did not need to be forwarded to a higher tribunal. . . . While this change increased efficiency to an extent, its cost was remoteness — the new centralized courts were removed from the communities they served. As caseloads increased, felony cases naturally began to claim more and more attention. Fewer resources were devoted to quality-of-life misdemeanors like shoplifting, prostitution, and subway fare cheating, and judges were under tremendous pressure to dispose of such cases quickly. All too often defendants arrested for low-level offenses were released after being sentenced to either "time served" while awaiting their court appearance, a fine that might or might not be paid, or community service that might or might not be performed.

[T]he planners of the Midtown Community Court sought to recreate neighborhood-based intake and arraignment along the lines of the magistrate's courts, but with innovations to meet the needs of the 1990s. It was hoped that such a court could focus on quality-of-life crimes that erode a community's morale. This return to a concern about crimes that affect neighborhood life coincided with the New York City Police Department's new emphasis on community policing, as well as with a growing interest in community-oriented justice on the part of prosecutors, probation offices, and corrections agencies nationwide. . . .

With the help of the local community board — the smallest unit of government in New York City — planners found a location for the court near Times Square on the West Side of Manhattan, an area teeming with quality-of-life crimes. The 1896 building, which was once a magistrate's court, was renovated. . . . The court's location, architecture, and technology are part of a larger strategy to honor the idea of community by making justice restorative. Offenders are sentenced to make restitution to the community through work projects in the neighborhood: caring for trees lining the streets, removing graffiti, cleaning subway stations, and sorting cans and bottles for recycling. At the same time, the court uses its legal leverage to link offenders with drug treatment, health care, education, and other social services.

By the summer of 1996, Midtown had become one of the busiest arraignment courts in the city, arraigning an average of 65 cases per day for an annual total of more than 16,000 cases. Offenders sentenced by the court perform the equivalent of 175,000 dollars' worth of community service work per year. . . . Nearly 75 percent of offenders processed through Midtown complete their community service sentences as mandated, which is the highest rate in the city. . . .

Midtown Community Court's planning team pursued . . . goals they considered to be at the heart of community justice. [The goals included principles for restoring the community:]

- Recognize that communities are victims. Quality-of-life crimes damage communities. If unaddressed, low-level offenses erode communal order, leading to disinvestment and neighborhood decay and creating an atmosphere in which more serious crime can flourish. . . .
- Use punishment to pay back the community. Standard sentences that involve jail, fines, and probation may punish offenders, but they do little to make restitution for the damage caused by crime. A community court

requires offenders to compensate neighborhoods through community service.

- Combine punishment with help. By permanently altering the behavior of chronic offenders, social service programs can play an important role in crime control. Encouraging offenders to deal with their problems honors a community's ethical obligation to people who break its laws because they have lost control of their lives.
- Give the community a voice in shaping restorative sanctions. The most effective community courts open a dialog with neighbors, seeking their input in developing appropriate community service projects. A community advisory board can offer residents an institutionalized mechanism for interacting with the judge and court administrators. . . .

[Community courts also embody principles for bridging the gap between communities and courts:]

- Make justice visible. A community court puts offenders to work in places where neighbors can see what they are doing, outfitting them in ways that identify them as offenders performing community service. . . .
- Make justice accessible. A community court welcomes observers and visitors from the community, giving them an opportunity to see justice in action. Calendars and other information about activities in the courtroom are available to the public on computer terminals in the lobby. . . .
- Reach out to victims. A community court can be a safe haven for victims, offering them assistance and a voice in the criminal justice process. Because it is based in the neighborhood where victims live, a community court may be able to provide access to services more quickly and in a less intimidating setting than larger, centralized courts.

[These courts carry out] principles for knitting together a fractured criminal justice system, [and for helping offenders deal with problems that lead to crime:]

- Use the court's authority to link criminal justice agencies. Too often, criminal justice agencies work in isolation, moving cases from street to court to cell and back again without communicating or taking the time to solve problems. . . .
- Explore crossing jurisdictional lines. The problems citizens face often do not conform to the narrow jurisdictional boundaries imposed by modern court systems. A criminal defendant also may be involved in a landlord-tenant dispute or a small claims matter. Handling all of a defendant's cases in one place enhances the court's ability to address the defendant's underlying problems. . . .
- Use the court as a gateway to treatment. The trauma of arrest may prompt a defendant to seek help. A court can use its coercive power to reinforce that impulse.
- Remain involved beyond disposition of the immediate case. A judge in a community court can monitor offenders' experiences in treatment, using the court's authority to reward progress or impose new sanctions for failure.

[S]ome judges, attorneys, and police believe that greater involvement with the community compromises their objectivity. To maintain impartiality, judges traditionally have insulated themselves from the communities and victims affected by the issues they adjudicate, while prosecutors and police have restricted the discretion of frontline attorneys and officers on the beat. . . .

The underlying assumptions and guiding philosophies of law enforcement and social service differ in fundamental ways. Criminal justice professionals operate in a system of escalating sanctions in which defendants are punished more severely each time they fail; criminal courts are not comfortable giving offenders a second chance. Treatment professionals, however, expect relapses and believe that it is critical that clients remain in treatment when a relapse occurs. Addicts may need to hear the same message many times before the message finally sinks in. The community court's approach can work only if criminal justice and social service professionals are willing to adjust their outlooks and work together. . . .

Many quality-of-life problems in a community are not violations of the law and do not come to the attention of the police or the courts. The Midtown Community Court has sought to address these problems in [several] ways. First, the court established a mediation service to resolve neighborhood disputes (for example, the opening of an adult movie house or the operation of a noisy repair shop) before they escalate to legal battles. In addition to helping the community deal with such problems, the service conveys the court's commitment to the community and its quality of life. Second, the court set up a street outreach unit, staffed by police officers and caseworkers from the court, to enroll potential clients in court-based social service programs before they get into trouble with the law. Four mornings a week, outreach teams scour the neighborhood, encouraging likely clients-prostitutes, substance abusers, and homeless people-to come in for help voluntarily. . . .

Police and community groups lose heart in fighting low-level crime when they lack a reliable way to measure progress. To measure its impact on the community, a community court should deploy researchers, compile results, and publicize success. . . . Besides the traditional work of caseload and sentencing outcome analysis, research staff at the Midtown Community Court study problems raised by neighbors. The court's researchers monitor patterns of prostitution and drug dealing as well as street sanitation. To help community groups and police target resources, the researchers have developed neighborhood-specific computer software to map arrests, complaints, and other quality-of-life indicators. When the research confirms success, a community court should be ready to make this success known locally and to other communities that have established community courts. A court can create its own newsletter and Internet Web site and should promote media coverage to ensure feedback on successes to the community.

[T]o be effective a community court must address the needs of the court system's most important constituency: the people who live and work in neighborhoods affected by crime. To address these needs, a community court must ask a new set of questions. What can a court do to solve neighborhood problems? What can courts bring to the table beyond their coercive power and symbolic presence? And what roles can community residents, businesses, and service providers play in improving justice? . . .

Notes

1. *Special courts.* The dramatic emergence in the 1990s of special courts to handle drug offenders, the mentally ill, and now low-level community offenders have their roots in the many police and magistrate courts common throughout the United States until the middle of the twentieth century. Advocates of court unification in the early twentieth century, such as Harvard Law School Dean and jurisprude Roscoe Pound led the elimination of many special courts. Special juvenile courts and family courts remained in place in many jurisdictions through the twentieth century, the remnants of special courts. Other special courts include over 450 tribal forums.

Special courts have reemerged with a vengeance. Indeed some types, like drug courts, are proliferating at such a high rate that it is hard even to count them. From a single drug court in Florida in 1989, there are now around 1,000 drug courts operating in at least 48 states — most active, some in the final planning stages.

Now community courts have started their own dramatic upswing. Community courts move farther than drug courts in terms of changing the forum, the decision-makers, the sentences and the purposes of punishment and social control. By March 2000, community courts were operating in Connecticut, Florida, Georgia, Minnesota, New York, Oregon, Tennessee and Texas; more than dozen others have been proposed, including courts in California, Colorado, Delaware, Hawaii, Indiana, Maryland, and Pennsylvania. See Eric Lee, Bureau of Justice Assistance, Community Courts: An Evolving Model (BJS 2000, NCJ 183452).

2. *Do special courts work?* Special courts excite their supporters; whether they work is another question. For one early evaluation, see Denise C. Gottfredson, Stacy S. Najaka & Brook Kearley, Effectiveness of Drug Treatment Courts: Evidence from a Randomized Trial, 2 Criminology & Pub. Pol'y 171 (2003). Many supporters of special courts do not stop to define the measures of success, pointing instead to the failures of traditional criminal courts, the need to do something different, and to anecdotes of apparent success. Advocates of community courts chose the story about public urination to illuminate the idea and virtue of community courts: Is this a story of success?

Perhaps community courts are still too young for complete assessment. Given the huge number of citizens now passing through drug courts, and the proportion of such offenders who would have been handled through the traditional criminal justice system, there have been strong calls for more formal assessment. In April 2002, the General Accounting Office reported that data was not yet available to make a sound evaluation of drug court effectiveness, and called for a "methodo-logically sound national impact evaluation." See United States General Accounting Office, Report to Congressional Requesters, Drug Courts: Better DOJ Data Collection and Evaluation Efforts Needed to Measure Impact of Drug Court Programs (GAO-02-434) (April 2002). What should the measures of success for any special court be? Will it vary by the type of court?

3. *The limits of the criminal law.* Community courts, drug courts, family courts and other special courts appear to address problems related to, but beyond, the

traditional core of the criminal justice system. Among their common features are less legal process and fewer lawyers, but also less severe sanctions. What are the virtues and dangers and blurring the lines between criminal and civil justice systems? What are, and what should be, the limits of the criminal justice system to respond to the problems of society?

VIII

■

Witnesses and Proof

A complete understanding of felony trials requires a knowledge of substantive criminal law, the law of evidence, trial strategy, and procedural rules. Yet it is possible to boil down this wide-ranging material into a few core principles of procedure that define criminal trials. At a general level, these principles are familiar to lawyers and nonlawyers alike.

The first core principle is the presumption of innocence — the idea that a person is not guilty of a crime until the state proves to a factfinder that the person has committed a criminal act with the requisite mental state. The state must prove its case "beyond a reasonable doubt." This is now considered the mirror image of the presumption of innocence.

The second principle — the right to confront witnesses — is our central tool for squeezing truth from the evidence. It is not hard to imagine a system (however unpalatable) that does not presume innocence or that allows conviction on some standard lower than beyond a reasonable doubt, but it is difficult to imagine a system that does not allow a defendant the right to challenge and test witnesses and other evidence.

The defendant can confront any government witness, and the government can confront any defense witness. But can the government call any witness to prove a case? The third principle — the privilege against self-incrimination — recognizes the single great exception to the power of the government to call relevant witnesses. The principle recognizes that a defendant cannot be forced to testify, either by threat of prison or by calling the defendant's silence to the attention of the factfinder. This principle may preclude the government from calling the single person who may know most about the alleged offense.

This chapter explores these core principles. The first section examines the meaning and role of the reasonable doubt standard, since this concept sets up the hurdles that the prosecution must clear during its presentation of witnesses and other evidence. The second section considers the law of confrontation, looking primarily at the defendant's power to test the evidence that the government presents. The third section studies the implementation of the privilege against self-incrimination at trial. The fourth section highlights one of the most important ethical dilemmas in an adversary trial system devoted to finding the truth: What should a defense lawyer do if the lawyer believes the client or a witness is lying? What should a prosecutor do if the prosecutor believes a key witness is lying?

A. BURDEN OF PROOF

Some commentators are skeptical about the practical consequences of using various standards of proof in civil and criminal cases. Perhaps jurors would reach the same verdicts whether they were told to decide cases on preponderance-of-the-evidence, "clear and convincing" proof, or beyond-a-reasonable doubt standards. But the idea (if not the precise language) of the reasonable doubt standard has ancient roots, and the higher burden on the government to obtain a conviction in criminal cases is the cornerstone for principles and practices that appear throughout the criminal trial.

1. Reasonable Doubt

How should reasonable doubt be defined? How should juries be instructed to decide when the government has proven its case "beyond" that point? The very phrase "beyond a reasonable doubt" suggests a tension that makes the concept difficult to grasp: Doubt is a negative concept, but to go "beyond" a given amount of evidence is a positive concept. This tension — between a positive and a negative conception of reasonable doubt — is reflected in various definitions and rules that the states have adopted. Is there a single point at which reasonable doubt is passed, or do these positive and negative notions together define a range for juries to apply? Can this tension be resolved?

Some courts simply direct jurors to decide whether the government has proven all elements beyond a reasonable doubt, and allow no further explanation of the reasonable doubt concept. See Romano v. State, 909 P.2d 92 (Okla. Crim. App. 1995). A leading nineteenth-century treatise explains this position: "There are no words plainer than reasonable doubt and none so exact to the idea meant." 1 Joel Prentiss Bishop, New Criminal Procedure, §1094 (1895). Most jurisdictions either direct or allow judges to define reasonable doubt more precisely. Should judges be limited to a standard definition? If so, which one?

■ STEVE WINEGEART v. STATE
665 N.E. 2d 893 (Ind. 1996)

DICKSON, J.

How to instruct juries regarding reasonable doubt has long been a subject on which courts, individual judges, and lawyers have taken differing approaches. Today we seek not only to resolve conflicting opinions among different panels of the Court of Appeals but also to foster the improved wording of instructions so that we may achieve greater juror understanding and better application of the rudimentary principle of proof beyond a reasonable doubt.

Following a jury trial, defendant-appellant Steve Winegeart was convicted of the crime of burglary. . . . In his appeal from the conviction, the defendant contends that the trial court erred in instructing the jury regarding reasonable doubt. . . . The defendant asserts that the following instruction, which used the words "actual," "fair," and "moral certainty," permitted the jury to find guilt based upon a degree of proof below that required by the Due Process Clause of the Fourteenth Amendment to the United States Constitution. After stating that the burden is upon the State to prove guilt beyond a reasonable doubt, the challenged instruction explained:

> A reasonable doubt is such doubt as you may have in your mind when having fairly considered all of the evidence, you do not feel satisfied to a moral certainty of the guilt of the defendant. A reasonable doubt is a fair, actual and logical doubt that arises in the mind as an impartial consideration of all the evidence and the circumstances in the case. It is not every doubt, however, it is a reasonable one. You are not warranted in considering as reasonable those doubts that may be merely speculative or products of the imagination, and you may not act upon mere whim, guess or surmise or upon the mere possibility of guilt. A reasonable doubt arises, or exists in the mind, naturally, as a result of the evidence or the lack of evidence. There is nothing in this that is mysterious or fanciful. It does not contemplate absolute or mathematical certainty. Despite every precaution that may be taken to prevent it, there may be in all matters depending upon human testimony for proof, a mere possibility of error.
>
> If, after considering all of the evidence, you have reached such a firm belief in the guilt of the defendant that you would feel safe to act upon that belief, without hesitation, in a matter of the highest concern and importance to you, then you have reached that degree of certainty which excludes reasonable doubt and authorizes conviction. . . .

Winegeart contends that the giving of the reasonable-doubt instruction blatantly violated constitutional principles and deprived his jury trial of fairness. He asserts that in the reasonable-doubt instruction used in his jury trial, the words "actual" and "fair" expand the quantum of doubt needed to constitute "reasonable" doubt, and that the instruction refers to "moral certainty" instead of "evidentiary certainty," thus authorizing the jury to find guilt based on a degree of proof below that required by the Due Process Clause.

The Due Process Clause of the Fourteenth Amendment protects an accused "against conviction except upon proof beyond a reasonable doubt of every fact necessary to constitute the crime with which he is charged." In re Winship, 397 U.S. 358 (1970). Because of the transcending interest a criminal defendant has in his liberty, the risk of an erroneous conviction necessitates that a substantial burden of proof be placed upon the prosecution. The standard of proof beyond a reasonable doubt serves to impress upon the fact-finder "the need to reach a subjective state of near certitude of the guilt of the accused." Jackson v. Virginia, 443 U.S. 307 (1979). While the federal constitution requires that juries be instructed "on the necessity that the defendant's guilt be proven beyond a reasonable doubt," it does not require the use of "any particular form of words." Victor v. Nebraska, 511 U.S. 1 (1994). However, the jury instructions, taken as a whole, must correctly express the concept of reasonable doubt to the jury.

In Cage v. Louisiana, 498 U.S. 39 (1990) (per curiam), a reasonable-doubt instruction was determined to be constitutionally defective. In defining reasonable doubt, the instruction included language that equated reasonable doubt with "a grave uncertainty" and "an actual substantial doubt" and stated, "What is required is not an absolute or mathematical certainty, but a moral certainty." The Court found that the words "substantial" and "grave" suggested a "higher degree of doubt than is required for acquittal under the reasonable-doubt standard," and that these statements, together with the reference to "moral certainty," rather than "evidentiary certainty," permitted a finding of guilt based upon a degree of proof below that required by the Due Process Clause.

These principles were discussed and applied by the United States Supreme Court in the recent companion cases of Victor v. Nebraska and Sandoval v. California, 511 U.S. 1 (1994), which approved reasonable-doubt instructions that included phrases such as "to a moral certainty," and "actual and substantial doubt." In both of the instructions approved in *Victor* and *Sandoval*, the moral certainty language appeared in very similar sentences, which stated that reasonable doubt occurs when, after "consideration of all the evidence," the juror does not have "an abiding conviction, to a moral certainty" of the guilt of the accused. In this context, the Supreme Court explained that "the reference to moral certainty, in conjunction with the abiding conviction language," sufficiently emphasized "the need to reach a subjective state of near certitude of the guilt of the accused." The *Victor* court also distinguished its "moral certainty" instructions from the one in *Cage*, noting that "the problem in *Cage* was that the rest of the instruction provided insufficient context to lend meaning to the phrase." The Court noted, "Instructing the jurors that they must have an abiding conviction of the defendant's guilt does much to alleviate any concerns that the phrase moral certainty might be misunderstood in the abstract." Although clearly stating that the Justices "do not condone" and "do not countenance" the inclusion of the phrase moral certainty in a reasonable-doubt instruction, the Court found that in the context of the entire instruction, which explicitly directed the jurors to base their conclusion on the evidence of the case and not to engage in speculation or conjecture, the inclusion of the moral certainty language did not render the instruction unconstitutional. Similarly, while noting that equating reasonable doubt with substantial doubt is "somewhat problematic," the Court found that the context of the instruction, unlike that in *Cage*, contrasted substantial doubt with fanciful conjecture. It concluded that "taken as a whole, the instructions correctly conveyed the concept of reasonable doubt to the jury."

The challenged words and phrases in the reasonable-doubt instruction given to the *Winegeart* jury contain both significant differences from, and substantial similarities to, the instructions approved in *Victor*. The *Winegeart* instruction's reference to "moral certainty" lacks the "abiding conviction" language noted in *Victor*. On the other hand, the "actual and substantial doubt" wording in the Nebraska instruction in *Victor* is similar to the "fair, actual, and logical doubt" phrase used in Winegeart's trial. Moreover, the *Winegeart* jury was directed to base its decision on all the evidence; to disregard whim, guess, surmise, or mere possibility of guilt; and to consider the "hesitate to act" benchmark — all factors that the *Victor* court found significant. . . .

The proper constitutional inquiry "is not whether the instruction 'could have' been applied in an unconstitutional manner, but whether there is a reasonable likelihood that the jury did so apply it." *Victor*. [W]e conclude that there is not a reasonable likelihood that the jurors who determined the defendant's guilt applied the instruction in a way that violated the Due Process Clause. . . . However, we disapprove of the continued use of this instruction in the future.

The instruction uses 300 words in 11 sentences to explain reasonable doubt. This is not atypical for reasonable-doubt instructions, which often appear to be a conglomeration of phrases providing supplemental or alternative explication of reasonable doubt. Through the years, appellate decisions have held a wide variety of reasonable-doubt instructions to satisfy the minimal constitutional requirements. After a particular phrase has been thus tolerated by appellate courts, trial courts will often — usually in response to requests by counsel — incorporate such "approved" phrases into reasonable-doubt instructions. As a result, most reasonable-doubt instructions commonly in use in our courts today have not been crafted for the purpose of most effectively explaining the concept of reasonable doubt to jurors but rather are used primarily because the language therein is considered adequate to avoid appellate reversal.

As courts utilize such longer, more intricate explanations of reasonable doubt, juries are likely to draw an overall impression which may transcend the literal meaning of the substance of the words. Such lengthy and conceptually challenging instructions often present a drumbeat repetition, declaring that reasonable doubt is not every doubt, not whim, not guess, not surmise, not mere possibility, not fanciful, etc.; and that to qualify as reasonable doubt, such doubt must be fair, actual, logical, natural, etc. It is not surprising that jurors often have difficulty in synthesizing and comprehending reasonable doubt or that they may perceive that the instructing judge is minimizing the degree of doubt that will preclude a finding of guilt.

Although reluctant to find reversible error in instructions purporting to explain reasonable doubt, the United States Supreme Court has acknowledged: "Attempts to explain the term 'reasonable doubt' do not usually result in making it any clearer to the minds of the jury." Miles v. United States, 103 U.S. 304 (1881). The Seventh Circuit has declared:

> "Reasonable doubt" must speak for itself. Jurors know what is "reasonable" and are quite familiar with the meaning of "doubt." Judges' and lawyers' attempts to inject other amorphous catch-phrases into the "reasonable doubt" standard, such as "matter of the highest importance" only muddy the water. . . . It is, therefore, inappropriate for judges to give an instruction defining "reasonable doubt," and it is equally inappropriate for trial counsel to provide their own definition.

United States v. Glass, 846 F.2d 386, 386 (7th Cir. 1988). This view has found support in several other jurisdictions. [The court cited cases from Illinois, Kansas, Missouri, and the U.S. Court of Appeals for the Fourth Circuit.]

Professor Wigmore, noting that "various efforts have been made to define more in detail this elusive and undefinable state of mind," states: "In practice, these detailed amplifications of the doctrine have usually degenerated into a mere tool for counsel . . . to save a cause for a new trial. . . . The effort to [develop these elaborate unserviceable definitions] should be abandoned." 9 John Henry Wigmore, Evidence in Trials at Common Law §2497, 406-409 (James Chadbourn rev. 1981).

Substantial research by linguists, psychologists, and others suggests that many jurors have difficulty understanding jury instructions but much less difficulty understanding those that have been rewritten in light of psycholinguistic principles. See Peter Tiersma, Reforming the Language of Jury Instructions, 22 Hofstra L. Rev. 37 (1993). Researchers have provided valuable suggestions on how to write more comprehensible jury instructions, including the [elimination] of jargon and modifying clauses and the use of simpler language. Summarizing the suggestions of psycholinguists, Professor Tanford provides ten guidelines for the improvement of instructions.

1. Eliminate nominalizations (making nouns out of verbs) and substitute verb forms; e.g., changing "an offer of evidence" to "items were offered into evidence."
2. Replace the prepositional phrase "as to" with "about"; e.g., changing "you must not speculate as to what the answer might have been" to "you must not speculate about what the answer might have been."
3. Relocate prepositional phrases so they do not interrupt a sentence; e.g., avoiding sentences such as "proximate cause is a cause which, in a natural and continuous sequence, produces the injury."
4. Replace words that are difficult to understand with simple ones; e.g., changing "agent's negligence is imputed to plaintiff" to "agent's negligence transfers to plaintiff."
5. Avoid multiple negatives in a sentence; e.g., "innocent mis-recollection is not uncommon."
6. Use the active rather than passive voice; e.g., changing "no emphasis is intended by me" to "I do not intend to emphasize."
7. Avoid "whiz" deletions (omitting words "which is"); e.g., by changing "statements of counsel" to "statements which are made by counsel."
8. Reduce long lists of words with similar meanings to only one or two; e.g., shortening "knowledge, skill, experience, training, or education" to "training or experience."
9. Organize instructions into meaningful discourse structures that avoid connecting unrelated ideas in ways that make them seem related.
10. Avoid embedding subordinate clauses in sentences; e.g., "you must not speculate to be true any insinuation suggested by a question asked a witness."

J. Alexander Tanford, The Law and Psychology of Jury Instructions, 69 Neb. L. Rev. 71 (1990).

We agree in principle with the . . . jurisdictions that have concluded that the phrase "reasonable doubt" may suffice without further explication and that many attempts to provide effective additional explanation have fallen short. However, we are not convinced that the task is impossible in light of recent and ongoing research, and we thus prefer to endorse for use in Indiana courts a reasonable-doubt instruction that, to the maximum extent possible, reflects the wisdom of the various available resources.

There is an inherent challenge in devising a comprehensible and succinct instruction explaining to lay jurors the concept of reasonable doubt. They must be informed that their determination of guilt depends upon the absence of reasonable doubt. The existence of reasonable doubt precludes a finding of guilt. Viewed in this way, the reasonable-doubt instruction is necessarily an attempt to define a negative concept. When court instructions proceed to define this concept by stating what it is not, the resulting double negative concept diminishes juror comprehension even further. In addition, we perceive that instructions containing repeated statements narrowing the class of doubts eligible for consideration as reasonable doubt may have a cumulative effect of minimizing the value and importance of this bedrock principle of criminal justice.

Although not utilized by the trial court in the present case, one attempt to suggest an improved reasonable-doubt instruction is found in Indiana Pattern Jury Instruction 1.15:

> A reasonable doubt is a fair, actual and logical doubt that arises in your mind after an impartial consideration of all of the evidence and circumstances in the case. It should be a doubt based upon reason and common sense and not a doubt based upon imagination or speculation.
>
> To prove the defendant's guilt of the elements of the crime charged beyond a reasonable doubt, the evidence must be such that it would convince you of the truth of it, to such a degree of certainty that you would feel safe to act upon such conviction, without hesitation, in a matter of the highest concern and importance to you.

1 Indiana Pattern Jury Instructions—Criminal, instruct. 1.15 (2d ed. 1991). This instruction seeks to explain what reasonable doubt is and is not and then proceeds to equate "beyond a reasonable doubt" with the degree of probability a juror would require to act unhesitatingly "in a manner of highest concern and importance to" himself or herself. Such attempts to quantify the degree of probability have received mixed reviews.

The "hesitate to act" analogy is discussed in *Victor.* The *Victor* majority comments that "the hesitate to act standard gives a common-sense benchmark for just how substantial such a doubt must be." [However, a committee of distinguished federal judges, reporting to the Judicial Conference of the United States, has criticized this "hesitate to act" formulation."] The committee explained:

> [T]he analogy it uses seems misplaced. In the decisions people make in the most important of their own affairs, resolution of conflicts about past events does not usually play a major role. Indeed, decisions we make in the most important affairs of our lives—choosing a spouse, a job, a place to live, and the like—generally, involve a very heavy element of uncertainty and risk-taking. They are wholly unlike the decisions jurors ought to make in criminal cases.

Federal Judicial Center, Pattern Criminal Jury Instructions (1987). We find such reasoning persuasive and believe that, while the "hesitate to act" language may bolster an otherwise marginal instruction against constitutional challenge, use of this analogy is neither required nor particularly desirable in explaining the concept of reasonable doubt.

In contrast to the Indiana Pattern Jury Instruction and other common instructions that attempt to define the negative concept of reasonable doubt, a proposal from the Federal Judicial Center focuses upon the positive concept of proof beyond a reasonable doubt. It defines that term, succinctly, as proof "that leaves you firmly convinced," and explains that reasonable doubt is a greater degree of doubt than merely "possible doubt." It explains that a juror's choice between guilty and not guilty should be equated to the distinction between "firmly convinced" of guilt versus "a real possibility" that the defendant is not guilty. The instruction states:

> [T]he government has the burden of proving the defendant guilty beyond a reasonable doubt. Some of you may have served as jurors in civil cases, where you were told

that it is only necessary to prove that a fact is more likely true than not true. In criminal cases, the government's proof must be more powerful than that. It must be beyond a reasonable doubt.

Proof beyond a reasonable doubt is proof that leaves you firmly convinced of the defendant's guilt. There are very few things in this world that we know with absolute certainty, and in criminal cases the law does not require proof that overcomes every possible doubt. If, based on your consideration of the evidence, you are firmly convinced that the defendant is guilty of the crime charged, you [should] find [him/her] guilty. If on the other hand, you think there is a real possibility that [he/she] is not guilty, you [should] give [him/her] the benefit of the doubt and find [him/her] not guilty. [Federal Judicial Center, Pattern Criminal Jury Instructions (1987).]

In the exercise of our inherent and constitutional supervisory responsibilities, see Ind. Const. Art. VII, §4, we seek to assure that juries in criminal cases are equipped with instructions that will allow them to understand and apply correctly the concept of reasonable doubt. Informed by numerous studies and recommendations from academic and judicial authorities, we acknowledge the shortcomings in Indiana Pattern Jury Instruction 1.15, in the instruction at Winegeart's trial, and in the various other reasonable-doubt explanations commonly in use. A substantial improvement in effective communication may be achieved by utilization of the Federal Judicial Center's proposed instruction. We therefore authorize and recommend (but, acknowledging that two of the five members of this Court find the present Indiana Pattern Jury Instruction preferable, do not mandate) that Indiana trial courts henceforth instruct regarding reasonable doubt by giving the above-quoted Federal Judicial Center instruction, preferably with no supplementation or embellishment. We also request that this instruction be added to the next revision of the Indiana Pattern Jury Instructions — Criminal.

While the challenged instruction in the present case is less effective than we would prefer, it is not so deficient as to be constitutionally defective. We therefore reject the defendant's contention of reversible error regarding the trial court's reasonable-doubt instruction. . . .

DEBRULER, J., concurring in result.

I do not share the majority's perception of deep problems within this area, nor the belief that the Federal Judicial Center, Pattern Criminal Jury Instructions are the appropriate remedy. Specifically, I do not believe that "firmly convinced" equates to "beyond a reasonable doubt." Both objectively and subjectively, "firmly convinced" seems more similar to "clear and convincing" than to "beyond a reasonable doubt." I find the Indiana Pattern Jury Instruction more than adequate.

■ WALTER STEELE AND ELIZABETH THORNBURG, JURY INSTRUCTIONS: A PERSISTENT FAILURE TO COMMUNICATE
67 N.C. L. Rev. 77 (1988)

. . . Lawyers and judges have suspected for some time . . . that many jurors do not understand their instructions. These suspicions are confirmed by numerous reported cases in which jury confusion peeks through. Recent social science research has demonstrated empirically that juror comprehension of instructions is appallingly low. Some of that research further demonstrates that rewriting instructions with clarity as the goal can dramatically improve comprehensibility. Despite these findings, and despite the existence of books and articles explaining how to write instructions more clearly, lawyers and judges continue to produce jury instructions that are incomprehensible to juries. . . .

I. DOCUMENTED JURY CONFUSION

. . . Social scientists studying group behavior have conducted tests on juries to determine the uses jurors make of their instructions. Forston [performed empirical studies with jurors in the early 1970s. One such study attempted] to learn what percentage of the instructions individual jurors and deliberating jurors retain and comprehend. . . . His subjects this time were 114 experienced jurors in Polk County, Iowa. [The] jurors were divided into groups. Each group was given detailed background information about its case and read a set of instructions. Each individual juror was given a multiple choice retention-comprehension test. Then the jurors, in groups of six, were given the test as a deliberating group and told that they had to agree unanimously on the answers. The results again showed confusion and misunderstanding. While the deliberating juries scored 10 to 14 percent better than the mean of individual jurors, large numbers of the deliberating juries misunderstood important instructions. "Eighty-six percent of the criminal juries were unable to respond accurately to what constitutes proof of guilt." . . .

Other studies of jury behavior have noted both the influence of instructions and juror misunderstanding of those instructions. In one study, a videotaped reenactment of a murder trial was shown to people called for jury service in three Massachusetts counties. The researchers videotaped and analyzed the jury deliberations. When all the juries were analyzed, the researchers found that an average of 25 percent of the juror discussions referred to the judge's instructions. Analyzing one jury in detail, the researchers [found] that jurors made seven incorrect statements about the meaning of the judge's instructions, only one of which was corrected by other jurors. . . .

Probably the most thorough of the psycholinguistic studies of jury instructions was done by Robert and Veda Charrow in the late 1970s. While the earlier studies revealed that rewriting jury instructions could improve comprehension, they had not tested empirically the linguistic features that impeded comprehension. The Charrows set out to isolate the linguistic features that cause comprehension problems in jury instructions. Their study consisted of two major experiments, each conducted on people called for jury service in Prince Georges County, Maryland.

In the first experiment 35 jurors paraphrased each of 14 pattern jury instructions. In the second experiment the instructions were rewritten to eliminate the words and constructions that seemed to cause confusion in the first experiment. The rewritten instructions then were tested on 48 new jurors. The results showed dramatic improvement in juror comprehension. For example, comprehension of . . . an instruction about the use of evidence improved 52 percent. Overall comprehension improved 35 percent. This improvement occurred even in those instructions which were conceptually quite difficult, casting doubt on many practicing lawyers' argument that it is the conceptual complexity of a jury instruction that creates comprehension problems and that therefore rewriting instructions will not help. . . .

II. EMPIRICAL RESEARCH: CONFUSION AND CURE

The subjects for our test of juror comprehension of instructions were people called to jury service in Dallas County, Texas, who had not yet served on a jury. Thus, our experimental subjects were actual and potential jurors, demographically identical with the group we wanted to learn about. . . . We selected five pattern jury instructions for testing: (1) proximate cause; (2) new and independent cause; (3) negligence; (4) presumption of innocence; and (5) accomplice testimony. . . .

With two sets of instructions in hand — five pattern instructions and a corresponding set of five rewritten instructions — the next step was to test whether the "simplified" language in the rewritten set enhanced comprehension. To do this we created audio tapes to be played for the jurors. Each tape contained five instructions selected from the five pattern and five rewritten instruction sets. These five were selected in such a way that each tape had both pattern and rewritten instructions; however, to avoid any "learning effect" no tape contained both the pattern and the rewritten version of the same instruction. . . . We used a testing method known as a "paraphrase test": each subject was asked to explain the instructions in her own words. We played each taped instruction for the subject only once. After each instruction was played, we stopped the tape player and started a tape recorder into which the subject stated her understanding of the meaning of the instruction just played. That process was repeated until the subject had heard and paraphrased all five instructions.

In order to calculate the accuracy of each subject's responses, we developed a scoresheet for each instruction that listed the legally significant elements of that instruction. . . . We awarded a score of "1" on the score sheet for each element of the instruction correctly paraphrased by the test subject; "−1" on the score sheet for an incorrect paraphrase of an element; and "0" on the score sheet if the subject failed to mention an element of the instruction indicated on the score sheet. After we scored all responses, as outlined above, the percentages were calculated for each of the three possible responses. . . .

The figures we obtained, expressed in readily comprehensible percentages, confirmed that the jurors understood the rewritten instructions much better than the pattern instructions. Averaging the score sheet results for each set of five instructions revealed that only 12.85 percent of all of the paraphrases of the pattern instructions were correct, compared to 24.59 percent correct paraphrases of the rewritten set of instructions, an impressive 91 percent gain in understanding. [In the table below, the] percentage figures represent the percentage out of the total variables for each instruction. For example, if an instruction had 10 variables on the score sheet, and two of the ten were correctly paraphrased, the percentages would be 0 percent legally incorrect, 80 percent no paraphrase, and 20 percent legally correct. The results for multiple jurors were cumulated to get the results. . . .

Presumption of Innocence

	% of Legally Incorrect Paraphrases	% of No Paraphrases	% of Legally Correct Paraphrases
Pattern Charge	3.86 percent	78.77 percent	17.37 percent
Rewritten Charge	0.61 percent	76.06 percent	23.3 percent

To the uninitiated, the most telling statistic in our findings may be that the percentage of correct responses is very low in all of the charts. . . . This finding, which is consistent with the findings of other researchers, raises two important concerns. The first relates to the impact of jurors' difficulties in understanding on trial outcome: (1) Will a jury that misunderstands its instructions render the verdict it intends? (2) Will a jury that misunderstands its instructions render the same verdict that it would if it understood the instructions? The second concern relates to the vitality of the jury system regardless of effect on outcome. The use of incomprehensible instructions sends a message to jurors that the law is an undecipherable mystery and that juror understanding of the law is not important.

It seems reasonable to assume that juries render verdicts that are actually incorrect under the law because they do not understand the jury instructions as to that law. This assumption is supported by research and case law. Some of the social science research has demonstrated that the level of juror comprehension affects trial outcome in simulated trials. . . . Elwork and his associates showed identical videotaped trials to juries, half using pattern instructions and half using rewritten instructions. They found a statistically significant difference in the verdicts reached by the two groups. . . .

The integrity of jury verdicts is not the only reason why the clarity of jury instructions should be improved. The right to trial by jury has symbolic as well as actual importance to Americans. For most Americans, jury service is their only contact with the judicial system. Through our traditions and through the physical arrangement of our courtrooms we make clear to jurors that the judge represents the majesty of the law and that the instructions coming from the judge represent objectivity in the heat of battle. Incomprehensible instructions send jurors an undesirable message about the judicial system. . . .

Problem 8-1. A Doubt with a Reason

At 10:40 P.M. on October 29, Trooper Radford stopped Warren Manning on Highway 34 for a defective headlight. After writing Manning a warning ticket, Radford learned from his dispatcher that Manning was driving with a suspended license. Radford placed Manning under arrest and the two left the scene with Manning in the back seat of the patrol car.

Radford's patrol car was spotted early the next morning half-submerged in Reedy Creek Pond, about six and one-half miles from the McInnis residence. He had been shot twice through the head with his own revolver and severely pistol-whipped. The prosecutor charged Manning with murder.

The State's theory of the case was that Manning used his own .25 caliber pistol to threaten Radford. The prosecutor argued that Manning forced the trooper to drive to Reedy Creek Pond, where Manning murdered him and attempted to submerge the patrol car. Radford's revolver was found in a tobacco barn 75 yards behind Manning's home.

Manning testified on his own behalf that after he and Trooper Radford left in the patrol car, the trooper stopped another car traveling in front of them after a bag was thrown from its window. There were four people in the car. Radford approached the vehicle and while he was talking with the driver, Manning ran away from the patrol car unobserved. He walked to a friend's house and was driven back to his car.

After the close of evidence at trial, the judge gave the following charge on reasonable doubt:

> Beyond a reasonable doubt, in telling you that that is the degree of proof by which the State must prove, that phrase means exactly what it states in the English language, and that is a doubt for which you can give a real reason. That excludes a whimsical doubt, fanciful doubt. You could doubt any proposition if you wanted to. A reasonable doubt is a substantial doubt for which honest people, such as you, when searching for the truth can give a real reason. So it's to that degree of proof that the State is required to establish the elements of a charge.

Later in the charge, the judge added this thought about the meaning of reasonable doubt: "I instruct you to seek some reasonable explanation of the circumstances proven other than the guilt of the Defendant and if such a reasonable explanation can be found you should find the Defendant not guilty." As defense counsel, how would you argue that this charge was invalid? Compare State v. Manning, 409 S.E.2d 372 (S.C. 1991).

Notes

1. *Defining reasonable doubt: majority position.* As the Indiana court in *Winegeart* indicated, the federal constitution requires that the government prove all elements of an offense beyond a reasonable doubt, In re Winship, 397 U.S. 358 (1970), but it does not require that courts define reasonable doubt in a particular way. States have adopted a range of positions specifying both what is required and what is forbidden in defining reasonable doubt.

Several modern definitions trace their wording back to a famous decision by Chief Justice Lemuel Shaw, in Commonwealth v. Webster, 59 Mass. 295, 320 (1850):

> [W]hat is reasonable doubt? It is a term often used, probably pretty well understood, but not easily defined. It is not mere possible doubt; because every thing related to human affairs, and depending on moral evidence, is open to some possible or imaginary doubt. It is that state of the case, which, after the entire comparison and consideration of all the evidence, leaves the minds of the jurors in that condition that they cannot say they feel an abiding conviction, to a moral certainty, of the truth of the charge.

About 20 states emphasize the negative perspective, defining reasonable doubt as a doubt that would cause a reasonable person to "hesitate to act in their most important affairs." Another group of about 20 states requires the doubt to be "based on reason" or "a valid reason." Roughly 10 states refer to "actual and substantial doubt" or "serious and substantial doubt" or "fair and actual doubt." A handful require that the doubt be articulable, that it be "doubt for which a reason can be given," although some states forbid such formulations because they require jurors to be articulate and place the burden on the defendant to show reasonable doubt. See People v. Antommarchi, 604 N.E.2d 95 (N.Y. 1992). About a dozen states define reasonable doubt in positive terms, focusing on the "moral certainty of guilt" or saying the juror must be "firmly convinced of guilt." (Several states tolerate several different approaches, and thus the preceding categories total more than 50.)

See Craig Hemmens, Kathryn Scarborough & Rolando del Carmen, Grave Doubts About "Reasonable Doubt": Confusion in State and Federal Courts, 25 J. Crim. Just. 231 (1997); Steve Sheppard, The Metamorphoses of Reasonable Doubt: How Changes in the Burden of Proof Have Weakened the Presumption of Innocence, 78 Notre Dame L. Rev. 1165 (2003) (tracking twentieth-century shift to interpretation that emphasizes assignment of reasons as operational meaning of reasonableness).

State courts also diverge on the question whether to define reasonable doubt at all. About a dozen states allow the trial judge to avoid the issue by providing no definition to the jury, while two states forbid trial judges from giving definitions. Paulson v. State, 28 S.W.3d 570 (Tex. Crim. App. 2000) (best practice is not to define reasonable doubt for jury). Five states have statutory mandates to define reasonable doubt in all cases; 12 states have reached the same position through case law. A few states require a definition only if the defendant requests it, and another handful require a definition to be given only in complex cases.

One of the dangers of using a negative definition of "reasonable doubt" is that it seems to place a burden on the defendant to show reasonable doubt instead of placing the burden on the government to dispel reasonable doubt (or to offer proof "beyond" reasonable doubt). See Lawrence M. Solan, Refocusing the Burden of Proof in Criminal Cases: Some Doubt About Reasonable Doubt, 78 Tex. L. Rev. 105 (1999) (standard reasonable doubt instructions focus the jury on the defendant's ability to produce alternatives to the government's case, and thereby shift the burden of proof to the defendant). The positive formulation of the instruction — found in the Federal Judiciary Center version of the instruction, which requires a juror to be "firmly convinced that the defendant is guilty of the crime charged" — has gained legal momentum with the decision of the Indiana Supreme Court in *Winegeart* and a 1995 decision by the Arizona Supreme Court mandating the use of this instruction. State v. Portillo, 898 P.2d 970 (Ariz. 1995). The U.S. Supreme Court has refused to mandate a particular definition for all federal courts, and the circuits have adopted a range of positions parallel to those taken among the states. Leading commentators have called for the adoption of a more consistent standard in the federal system. See Jon Newman, Beyond Reasonable Doubt, 68 N.Y.U. L. Rev. 979 (1993).

2. *Do definitions help?* States that forbid trial courts from defining reasonable doubt, or those that leave the decision to the trial judge, echo the long-standing skepticism of observers like Joel Bishop and John Henry Wigmore. Definitions, they say, do not help jurors decide cases. But the difficulty of applying the concept suggests that if states or individual judges want to leave jurors to use their own conceptions of reasonable doubt, they may be saying more about their view of the jury's role than about reasonable doubt. Professor Richard Uviller has observed that "[m]ost people require considerable explanation, example, and parallel articulation to grasp the basic contours of [the concept of reasonable doubt]," and that a reasonable doubt instruction, unadorned by explanation, "is an invitation to clothe it by invention, its flexibility an opportunity to bend it to prefigured purposes." Richard Uviller, Acquitting the Guilty: Two Case Studies on Jury Misgivings and the Misunderstood Standard of Proof, 2 Crim. L.F. 1, 38 (1990). Would the criminal trial be fairer if courts adopted a uniform definition of reasonable doubt? Is such consistency a virtue, or is simply having *some* definition the real virtue? See Peter Tiersma, The Rocky Road to Legal Reform: Improving the Language of Jury Instructions, 66 Brook. L. Rev. 1081 (2001) (trial courts unlikely to improve jury

instructions; drafters of standardized jury instructions are more likely mechanism for reform).

Problem 8-2. Words and Numbers

Joseph McCullough was charged with possession of a controlled substance (marijuana) and possession of stolen property (a 1974 Chevrolet "Luv" pickup truck). During the voir dire examination of potential jurors, the district judge attempted to illustrate the concept of reasonable doubt with a numerical scale. On a scale of 0 to 10, the judge placed the preliminary hearing standard of probable cause at about 1 and the burden of persuasion in civil trials at just over 5. She then twice described reasonable doubt as about "seven and a half, if you had to put it on a scale." The judge did provide the jurors with the reasonable doubt standard described in Nev. Rev. Stat. §175.211, which provides as follows:

> A reasonable doubt is one based on reason. It is not mere possible doubt, but is such a doubt as would govern or control a person in the more weighty affairs of life. If the minds of the jurors, after the entire comparison and consideration of all the evidence, are in such a condition that they can say they feel an abiding conviction of the truth of the charge, there is not a reasonable doubt. Doubt to be reasonable must be actual and substantial, not mere possibility or speculation.

After introducing the jurors to the reasonable doubt standard provided by the Nevada statute, the judge again noted, "I have tried to give you that on a zero to ten scale." The jury convicted the defendant of both charges. He appeals, claiming that the judge's attempt to quantify reasonable doubt impermissibly lowered the prosecution's burden of proof and confused the jury rather than clarifying the reasonable doubt concept. How would you rule? See McCullough v. State, 657 P.2d 1157 (Nev. 1983).

Problem 8-3. Presumed Innocent or Not Guilty?

Jose Flores was tried and convicted of first-degree murder. The trial court instructed the jury by using a modified version of Oklahoma Uniform Jury Instruction — Criminal No. 903. The instruction read as follows:

> You are instructed that the defendant is presumed to be not guilty of the crime charged against him in the Information unless his guilt is established by evidence beyond a reasonable doubt and that presumption of being not guilty continues with the defendant unless every material allegation of the Information is proven by evidence beyond a reasonable doubt.

This jury instruction reflected the terms of Okla. Stat. tit. 22, §836, which provides that "[a] defendant in a criminal action is presumed to be innocent until the contrary is proved, and in case of a reasonable doubt as to whether his guilt is satisfactorily shown, he is entitled to be acquitted."

Flores now argues that the jury instruction diluted the presumption of innocence and diminished the State's burden of proving him guilty beyond a reasonable doubt. He argues the instruction also failed to advise the jury that the presumption of innocence remains in effect until the jury is convinced of guilt. Was the jury instruction erroneous? Is it more accurate to instruct the jury that a defendant is presumed innocent or presumed not guilty? Compare Flores v. State, 896 P.2d 558 (Okla. Crim. App. 1995); State v. Pierce, 927 P.2d 929 (Kan. 1996).

Notes

1. *Quantifying reasonable doubt.* Most state and federal courts discourage or prohibit trial judges from efforts to quantify the reasonable doubt standard. See State v. Cruz, 639 A.2d 534 (Conn. 1994). Can the preponderance standard for civil cases be quantified? Don't the preponderance, clear and convincing, and reasonable doubt standards all express degrees of proof? Wouldn't quantitative descriptions help the jury? Did the Nevada judge in Problem 8-2 just choose the wrong numbers? Some judges have used sports analogies rather than numerical descriptions. What if the judge said that the prosecution had to "take the ball way past the 50-yard line, but you don't have to go a hundred yards for a guilty finding"? See State v. DelVecchio, 464 A.2d 813 (Conn. 1983). Studies conducted in the 1970s found that jurors quantified reasonable doubt at around 86 percent certainty of guilt. See Saul Kassin & Lawrence Wrightsman, On the Requirements of Proof: The Timing of Judicial Instruction and Mock Juror Verdicts, 37 J. Personality & Soc. Psychol. 282 (1979). A more recent study suggests that jurors take a wide range of positions, associating the concept of "reasonable doubt" with anything from 50 to 100 percent certainty of guilt. See Terry Connolly, Decision Theory, Reasonable Doubt, and the Utility of Erroneous Acquittals, 11 Law & Hum. Behav. 101 (1987).

2. *Statistical proof of reasonable doubt.* What happens if an attorney wants to present statistical "proof" of an element of an offense or a defense? Courts have been generally critical of arguments that statistical evidence shows the likelihood of guilt or the existence of some element of the offense. They often find that such evidence is likely to confuse or mislead the jury. There is an extensive law of evidence related to the use at trial of individual scientific techniques, often limited to specific issues or types of cases. One important illustration is the use of DNA evidence in both criminal and civil cases. See, e.g., State v. Johnson, 922 P.2d 294 (Ariz. 1996) (approving the use of DNA probability evidence in sexual assault cases using restriction fragment length polymorphism (RFLP) protocol and modified ceiling method).

3. *Presumption of innocence and burden of proof.* Is the presumption of innocence anything more than another way to refer to the prosecution's burden of proof? In other words, when a defendant is said to be "presumed innocent," does that statement have legal ramifications beyond requiring the state to prove all elements of the offense beyond a reasonable doubt? Does it remind the jury not to place any evidentiary weight on the mere fact that the defendant has been charged with a crime? Most states declare that a separate instruction on presumption of innocence is not necessary in every case, while about 15 states do require a separate instruction. See, e.g., Ohio Rev. Stat. §2938.08 ("The presumption of innocence places upon the state (or the municipality) the burden of proving him guilty beyond a reasonable doubt. In charging a jury the trial court shall state the meaning of the presumption of innocence and of reasonable doubt in each case"). Does the presumption of

innocence tell the jury anything about how long the government bears its burden of proof? Consider this typical description from Horn v. Territory, 56 P. 846, 848 (Okla. 1899):

> A defendant's friends may forsake him, but the presumption of innocence, never. It is present throughout the entire trial; and, when the jury go to their room to deliberate, the "presumption of innocence" goes in with them, protesting against the defendant's guilt. And it is only after the jury has given all the evidence in the case a full, fair, and impartial consideration, and have been able to find beyond a reasonable doubt that the defendant is guilty as charged, that the presumption of innocence leaves him.

In Taylor v. Kentucky, 436 U.S. 478 (1978), the Supreme Court found a federal due process violation when a Kentucky judge refused to instruct the jury on the presumption of innocence. The Court cited Coffin v. United States, 156 U.S. 432 (1895), for the proposition that "[t]he principle that there is a presumption of innocence in favor of the accused is the undoubted law, axiomatic and elementary, and its enforcement lies at the foundation of the administration of our criminal law." A year later, however, the Court held that a presumption-of-innocence instruction was not a constitutional requirement in all cases. Kentucky v. Whorton, 441 U.S. 786 (1979). The instruction was necessary in *Taylor* only because of "skeletal" jury instructions and the prosecutor's repeated suggestions that the defendant's status as a person charged with a crime tended to establish his guilt.

4. *Guilty clothing.* The presumption of innocence can have an impact on the operation of the courtroom. For example, courts generally forbid the state from requiring the defendant to appear in prison garb or surrounded by armed guards. However, the defendant must object to the clothing or other circumstances. Estelle v. Williams, 425 U.S. 501 (1976). Federal and state courts allow the conspicuous use of security guards more readily than they will tolerate shackles or distinctive clothing on the defendant. See Holbrook v. Flynn, 475 U.S. 560 (1986) (upholding four uniformed state troopers sitting in the front spectator row during trial as security measure); Sterling v. State, 830 S.W.2d 114 (Tex. Crim. App. 1992) (seven uniformed deputies in courtroom).

2. Presumptions

Judges instruct juries, and lawyers argue to juries, about evidentiary presumptions — asserting either that the jurors should assume a fact to be true or that if one fact is found then another fact or conclusion is more likely to be true. These presumptions can undermine the requirement that crime elements be proven beyond a reasonable doubt. In Sandstrom v. Montana, 442 U.S. 510 (1979), the U.S. Supreme Court rejected an instruction in a deliberate homicide case where intent was an element of the offense. The instruction said, "the law presumes that a person intends the ordinary consequences of his voluntary acts." The defendant had confessed to the killing, making his mental state the key issue. The Court found that, from the standpoint of the reasonable juror, this instruction shifted the burden of proof from the state to the defendant.

In Francis v. Franklin, 471 U.S. 307 (1985), a Georgia prisoner attempting escape killed a man when he fired a gun through a door at the moment the victim slammed it. Again, the sole defense was lack of intent to kill. The trial court, using an instruction with a long pedigree, instructed the jury that "[t]he acts of a person of sound mind and discretion are presumed to be the product of the person's will, but the presumption may be rebutted. A person of sound mind and discretion is presumed to intend the natural and probable consequences of his acts but the presumption may be rebutted. A person will not be presumed to act with criminal intention but the trier of facts . . . may find criminal intention upon a consideration of the words, conduct, demeanor, motive and all of the circumstances connected with the act for which the accused is prosecuted." The jury was also instructed that the defendant was presumed innocent and that the State was required to prove every element of the offense beyond a reasonable doubt. The Supreme Court again rejected the instruction. Even though the trial court had stated that "the presumption may be rebutted," such qualifying language did not prevent a reasonable juror from believing that the defendant bore the burden of showing he did not intend to kill. The *Franklin* Court distinguished valid and invalid instructions involving evidentiary presumptions as follows:

> The court must determine whether the challenged portion of the instruction creates a mandatory presumption, or merely a permissive inference. A mandatory presumption instructs the jury that it must infer the presumed fact if the State proves certain predicate facts. A permissive inference suggests to the jury a possible conclusion to be drawn if the State proves predicate facts, but does not require the jury to draw that conclusion.

471 U.S. at 313. The following case from Washington analyzes jury instructions within this framework of mandatory presumptions and permissive inferences.

■ STATE v. JOHN DEAL
911 P.2d 996 (Wash. 1996)

ALEXANDER, J.

[John Deal was convicted on a charge of first degree burglary. He contends] that the Franklin County Superior Court erred in instructing the jury that it could infer that Deal acted with criminal intent to commit a crime against a person or property, unless he explained with satisfactory evidence why his unlawful entry or remaining in a building was done without criminal intent. Deal asserts that the jury instruction is flawed because it created a mandatory presumption which partially relieved the State of its duty to prove all of the elements of the charged crime and improperly shifted the burden of persuasion from the State to him. [We agree with Deal in part.]

In July 1992, Lori Deal separated from her husband, the Defendant John Deal. . . . In August 1992, [Gerald John Prins] came to Pasco [to help his friend] Jack Carr harvest his potato crop. While there, Prins stayed at Carr's guesthouse. On September 12, 1992, Prins and Lori Deal went out for dinner with some friends. After dinner, Prins and Lori Deal accompanied some members of their party to a club in Kennewick. . . . After Carr noticed that John Deal was also in the club, he suggested to Prins and Lori Deal that they should leave the establishment in order to avoid a "bad situation." Prins and Lori Deal took Carr's suggestion and returned to

Carr's guesthouse. Soon thereafter, John Deal appeared at the guesthouse and repeatedly kicked the door in an apparent effort to gain entry. Eventually, Deal picked up a wagon wheel and twice threw it against a window in the door. Deal then reached his arm through the now broken window, opened the door, and walked into the guesthouse where he assaulted Prins for approximately 15 to 20 minutes. He then left.

Deal was subsequently charged in Franklin County Superior Court with first degree burglary. At the ensuing jury trial, he admitted that he kicked the door of the guesthouse several times and that he broke the window in the door in order to gain entry to the residence. Deal also admitted that after entering the house, he remained there and assaulted Prins.

At the close of the trial, the trial court gave the jury the following jury instruction:

> A person who enters or remains unlawfully in a building may be inferred to have acted with intent to commit a crime against a person or property therein unless such entering or remaining shall be explained by evidence satisfactory to the jury to have been made without such criminal intent. This inference is not binding upon you and it is for you to determine what weight, if any, such inference is to be given.

Deal's trial counsel did not except to the giving of this instruction. The jury found Deal guilty of the charge and he was sentenced to serve 23 months in prison. [On appeal,] Deal assails the above jury instruction on several bases.[1] . . .

Deal argues first that the portion of the challenged instruction that precedes the word "unless" violates the due process clause of the Fourteenth Amendment of the United States Constitution, in that it allowed the jury to infer one element of first degree burglary (intent to commit a crime) from an unrelated element (unlawfully remaining in a building), thus, partially relieving the State of its obligation to prove all of the elements of the charged crime.

[B]ecause Deal was charged with first degree burglary, it was incumbent on the State to prove all of the elements of that offense. Those elements are set forth in RCW 9A.52.020(1), as follows:

> A person is guilty of burglary in the first degree if, with intent to commit a crime against a person or property therein, he enters or remains unlawfully in a dwelling and if, in entering or while in the dwelling or in immediate flight therefrom, the actor . . . assaults any person therein.

The State may use evidentiary devices, such as presumptions and inferences, to assist it in meeting its burden of proof. These devices generally fall into one of two categories: mandatory presumptions (the jury is required to find a presumed fact from a proven fact) and permissive inferences (the jury is permitted to find a presumed fact from a proven fact but is not required to do so). Mandatory presumptions potentially create due process problems. Indeed, they run afoul of a defendant's due process rights if they serve to relieve the State of its obligation to

---

1. The challenged instruction is identical to a pattern jury instruction. . . . The pattern instruction is based on Rev. Code Wash. §9A.52.040, which reads as follows: "In any prosecution for burglary, any person who enters or remains unlawfully in a building may be inferred to have acted with intent to commit a crime against a person or property therein, unless such entering or remaining shall be explained by evidence satisfactory to the trier of fact to have been made without such criminal intent."

prove all of the elements of the crime charged. Sandstrom v. Montana, 442 U.S. 510 (1979). Permissive inferences, on the other hand, do not necessarily relieve the State of its burden of persuasion because the State is still required to persuade the jury that the proposed inference should follow from the proven facts.

We must first determine if the portion of the instruction preceding the word "unless" creates a mandatory presumption or a permissive inference. Significantly, this court recently reviewed a jury instruction that was identical to that portion of the challenged jury instruction. In State v. Brunson, 905 P.2d 346 (Wash. 1995), we held that it was not error for the trial court to give such an instruction because it created a constitutionally valid permissive inference. We also held in *Brunson*, that when permissive inferences are only part of the State's proof supporting an element and not the "sole and sufficient" proof of such element, due process is not offended if the prosecution shows that the inference more likely than not flows from the proven fact.[4] We are not inclined to abandon that holding here.

Deal asserts that even under the lesser standard, the State failed to prove that a necessary element of the charged crime, Deal's intent to commit a crime against a person or property, more likely than not flowed from his unlawful presence at Prins's residence. We disagree, being satisfied that the more likely than not standard was met. We reach that conclusion because the permissive inference contained in the challenged jury instruction was not the sole and sufficient evidence of Deal's intent. As we have observed above, Deal testified at trial that he broke a window in order to enter the premises, and that once inside, repeatedly assaulted Prins. In our judgment, the acts which Deal admitted amply support a conclusion that it was more likely than not that Deal intended to commit a crime against Prins during the time he remained unlawfully on the premises.

Deal's next contention has considerably more merit. He argues that the portion of the challenged instruction that states "unless such entering or remaining shall be explained by evidence satisfactory to the jury to have been made without such criminal intent" created a mandatory presumption which improperly shifted the burden of persuasion to him. . . .

The standard for determining whether a jury instruction creates a mandatory or permissive presumption is whether a reasonable juror might interpret the presumption as mandatory. The constitutionality of mandatory presumptions is examined in light of the jury instructions read as a whole to make sure that the burden of the persuasion on any element of the crime does not shift to the defendant. The burden of persuasion is deemed to be shifted if the trier of fact is required to draw a certain inference upon the failure of the defendant to prove by some quantum of evidence that the inference should not be drawn.

The portion of the instruction we are focusing on in this part of the opinion has the vice identified in *Sandstrom*, in that it essentially requires the Defendant to either introduce evidence sufficient to rebut the inference that he remained on the premises with intent to commit a crime, or concede that element of the crime. In other words, a reasonable juror could have concluded that once Deal's presence on the premises was shown, a finding that he intended to commit a crime was compelled, absent a satisfactory explanation by Deal as to why he was on the premises. This had the effect of relieving the State of its burden of proving beyond a reasonable doubt

---

4. The United States Supreme Court has indicated that when an inference is the "sole and sufficient" proof of an element, the prosecution may be required to prove that the inferred fact flows from the proved fact beyond a reasonable doubt. County Court of Ulster County v. Allen, 442 U.S. 140 (1979).

the element of intent to commit a crime and, therefore, violated Deal's due process rights.

The problem discussed above is not, as the State suggests, mitigated by the last sentence of the jury instruction, which reads: "This inference is not binding upon you and it is for you to determine what weight, if any, such inference is to be given." In our judgment, that additional language does not eliminate the possibility that a reasonable juror could have concluded that a finding of intent to commit a crime was required unless Deal proved otherwise.

We are not unmindful of the fact that we have previously held that the clause following "unless" in the challenged instruction is a production-shifting presumption which, although "rarely necessary and usually ill advised," may be submitted to a jury when the defendant produces evidence on the issue of his or her intent in his or her case in chief. State v. Johnson, 674 P.2d 145 (Wash. 1983). The distinction between production-shifting and persuasion-shifting presumptions is not helpful in this case.[5] The "unless" clause in the instruction here did not require Deal to merely produce some evidence, but rather it required him to produce "evidence satisfactory to the jury" that he entered the premises without criminal intent. In our judgment, that language could have led a reasonable juror to understand that the burden of persuasion had shifted to Deal. That danger, in our view, did not disappear simply because Deal presented evidence that showed he did not have criminal intent.

Hearkening back to *Johnson*, we observe again that it is unnecessary to include this sort of language in such a jury instruction. Without the language, the instruction permits but does not require jurors to infer criminal intent from unlawful presence. The jury needs no further instruction on that issue because if a defendant is able to credibly explain his unlawful presence on premises, the jurors, as the instruction permits them to do, may simply reject the inferred conclusion of criminal intent.

Because the latter clause in the challenged jury instruction impermissibly shifted the burden of persuasion to Deal, it was error for the trial court to give it. The fact that the instruction is based on a statute, RCW 9A.52.040, does not lessen the violation of the Defendant's due process rights. [The court went on to conclude that the erroneous jury instruction was harmless beyond a reasonable doubt.]

PEKELIS, Justice Pro Tem, concurring.

[T]his court recently reviewed a jury instruction identical to the challenged instruction in this case, except that it did not contain the "unless" clause. In *Brunson*, we held that the inference of intent instruction created a permissive inference. . . . The question before the court in this case is whether the addition to the instruction of the "unless" clause transforms it such that it creates an unconstitutional mandatory inference.

---

5. In *Johnson*, we indicated that mandatory presumptions fall into two categories : "persuasion-shifting" presumptions that require a trier of fact to draw an inference unless a defendant by some quantum of evidence proves otherwise and "production-shifting" presumptions that require a trier of fact to draw an inference unless the defendant produces some evidence to the contrary. We cautioned, however, that any mandatory presumption could create constitutional concerns in that the State might be relieved of proving every element of the crime charged. We also observed that such a presumption "may also place undue pressure" on a defendant to relinquish his right to remain silent and when those constitutional concerns are operative, production-shifting presumptions are impermissible.

In State v. Johnson, 674 P.2d 145 (Wash. 1983), this court reviewed an instruction substantively identical to the challenged instruction in this case.[2] The *Johnson* court expressed concern that the "unless" clause "might well lead a reasonable juror to interpret the instruction as creating a mandatory production-shifting presumption." The *Johnson* court defined a "production-shifting presumption" as one that requires the trier of fact to draw a certain inference unless the defendant produces some evidence to the contrary. The court then held that, when operative, production-shifting presumptions are impermissible because when the defendant presents no evidence, the jury is required to find the existence of an element of the crime, effectively relieving the State of its burden of persuasion on that element.

The critical difference between *Johnson* and this case is that the defendant did not testify in *Johnson*. The *Johnson* court recognized that "[t]hese constitutional infirmities disappear, however, when the defendant in his own case produces sufficient evidence from which a reasonable juror could find he has met his burden." ... The issue of whether the jury might feel required to make the inference if the defendant were to produce no evidence simply does not exist when the defendant has in fact produced such evidence....

Problem 8-4. Presumption in the Fire

James Jubilee, an African American, moved with his family from California to Virginia Beach in April 1998. After a few weeks in the new neighborhood, he asked his new neighbor, Susan Elliott, about shots being fired from behind the Elliott home. Elliott explained to Jubilee that her son shot firearms as a hobby, and used the backyard as a firing range.

A few nights later, Elliott's son Richard drove a truck onto Jubilee's property, planted a cross, and set it on fire. He was trying to "get back" at Jubilee for complaining about the shooting in the backyard. Elliott was not affiliated with the Ku Klux Klan. The next morning, as Jubilee was pulling his car out of the driveway, he noticed the partially burned cross approximately 20 feet from his house. After seeing the cross, Jubilee was very nervous because "a cross burned in your yard tells you that it's just the first round." He worried about the violence that might follow.

Elsewhere in the state, a few months later, a separate cross burning incident took place. One August night, Barry Black led a Ku Klux Klan rally in Carroll County. Twenty-five to 30 people attended this gathering, which occurred on private property with the permission of the owner, who also attended the rally. When the sheriff of the county learned that a Klan rally was occurring in his jurisdiction, he went to observe it from the side of the road. Over the next hour or so, about 40 to 50 cars passed the site, and a few of the drivers stopped to ask the sheriff what was happening on the property.

Eight to 10 houses were located nearby. Rebecca Sechrist, who was related to the owner of the property where the rally took place, sat and watched to see what was going on from the lawn of her in-laws' home. She heard Klan members speak about what they believed in. As she put it, the speakers "talked real bad about the blacks

---

2. The challenged instruction in *Johnson* was as follows: "Any person who enters or remains unlawfully in a building may be inferred to have acted with intent to commit a crime against a person or property therein, unless such entering or remaining shall be explained by evidence satisfactory to you to have been made without criminal intent."

and the Mexicans." One speaker told the assembled gathering that "he would love to take a .30/.30 and just randomly shoot the blacks." The speakers also talked about "President Clinton and Hillary Clinton," and about how their tax money "goes to the black people." This language made Sechrist feel "very scared." At the conclusion of the rally, the crowd circled around a 25- to 30-foot cross, which was placed 325 yards away from the road. As the sheriff and others looked on, the cross went up in flame. The sheriff then went down the driveway, entered the rally, and asked who was responsible for burning the cross. Black responded, "I guess I am because I'm the head of the rally." The sheriff then told Black, "There's a law in the State of Virginia that you cannot burn a cross and I'll have to place you under arrest for this."

Barry Black and Richard Elliott were both charged with of violating Virginia's cross burning statute. Section 18.2-423 provides:

> It shall be unlawful for any person or persons, with the intent of intimidating any person or group of persons, to burn, or cause to be burned, a cross on the property of another, a highway or other public place. . . . Any such burning of a cross shall be prima facie evidence of an intent to intimidate a person or group of persons.

At Black's trial, the judge instructed the jury that "intent to intimidate means the motivation to intentionally put a person or a group of persons in fear of bodily harm. Such fear must arise from the willful conduct of the accused rather than from some mere temperamental timidity of the victim." The trial court also instructed the jury that "the burning of a cross by itself is sufficient evidence from which you may infer the required intent." The jury found Black guilty and fined him $2,500.

At Elliott's trial, the court instructed the jury that the Commonwealth must prove that "the defendant intended to commit cross burning," that he "did a direct act toward the commission of the cross burning," and that he "had the intent of intimidating any person or group of persons." The court did not instruct the jury on the meaning of the word "intimidate" or on the prima facie evidence provision of §18.2-423. The jury found Elliott guilty of attempted cross burning and sentenced him to 90 days in jail and a $2,500 fine.

Did either the statute or the judge's instructions in either of the two trials create an unconstitutional presumption of guilt? Cf. Virginia v. Black, 538 U.S. 343 (2003).

Notes

1. *Presumptions: majority position.* The *Deal* case from Washington illustrates the current law regarding burden-shifting presumptions. Both federal and state courts have followed the constitutional structure that the U.S. Supreme Court built in *Sandstrom* and *Franklin*. Federal and state courts differ, however, on the particular kinds of language that create an impermissible mandatory presumption. For instance, courts disagree on whether presumptions such as "a person generally intends the consequences of his acts" can be cured by additional language saying that such presumptions are rebuttable. *Sandstrom* claims apply as well to arguments made by the prosecutor in closing arguments. Should the same standards apply to review of judicial instructions and prosecutorial arguments?

Despite the best efforts of trial courts instructing juries, *Sandstrom* claims continue to arise. Should legislatures bar the use of all evidentiary presumptions?

Doesn't all circumstantial evidence require reliance on presumptions? Don't all findings about mens rea require jurors to rely on presumptions even if they are unstated?

2. *Reasonable doubt about what?* Every defendant benefits from the requirement that the state prove all elements of any criminal offense beyond a reasonable doubt. But what are "elements" of offenses, and what are "defenses" that the defendant must prove? Can states define crimes any way they want? The U.S. Supreme Court at times has wrestled with the idea that the federal constitution might place some controls on what the state can designate as an element of a crime or a defense to the charges. Current doctrine, however, reinforces the view that states have substantial discretion in defining crimes. In Patterson v. New York, 432 U.S. 197 (1977), the Supreme Court rejected a due process challenge to a New York law that made the defense of extreme emotional disturbance an affirmative defense that the defendant must prove by a preponderance of the evidence. The Court emphasized that "preventing and dealing with crime is much more the business of the States than it is of the Federal Government." The federal constitution limits the capacity of states to define crimes only to the extent that the state law "offends some principle of justice so rooted in the traditions and conscience of our people as to be ranked as fundamental." The court declined to adopt "as a constitutional imperative, operative countrywide, that a State must disprove beyond a reasonable doubt every fact constituting any and all affirmative defenses related to the culpability of an accused."

Thus, states appear to have substantial discretion within federal constitutional boundaries to define crimes and defenses and to allocate the burden of proving or disproving an element to either the prosecution or the defense. Sometimes the argument is not about whether the state *can* place a particular burden on the state or the defendant, but whether it has in fact done so.

3. *The burden on affirmative defenses: majority view.* States divide on the general issue of whether the prosecution carries the burden of proof on affirmative defenses. Roughly 35 states require the defendant to carry the burden of proof on all affirmative defenses, but they usually require only that the defendant prove the defense by a preponderance of the evidence. See, e.g., Ohio Rev. Code §2901.05 ("[T]he burden of proof for all elements of the offense is upon the prosecution. The burden of going forward with the evidence of an affirmative defense, and the burden of proof, by a preponderance of the evidence, for an affirmative defense, is upon the accused"). A handful of states require the state to carry the burden of proof on all affirmative defenses, though usually the defendant has the burden of going forward with facts sufficient to raise the defense. It is most common for states to require the prosecution to carry the burden on self-defense, while about half the states place the burden of proving insanity and related defenses on the defendant. See State v. Joyner, 625 A.2d 791 (Conn. 1993) (upholding statute placing burden of insanity defense on defendant).

4. *Elements and facts enhancing punishment.* Are facts that increase punishment — such as a finding that the defendant used a gun during the offense, or the amount of drugs involved — "elements" of the offense that the government must prove beyond a reasonable doubt? In McMillan v. Pennsylvania, 477 U.S. 79 (1986), the Supreme Court held that the reasonable doubt standard applied only to facts that "bear on the defendant's guilt," and upheld a statute enhancing the sentence if the prosecution proved by a preponderance of the evidence that the defendant "visibly

possessed a firearm." The majority of states also allow the government to prove sentencing facts, including facts related to the prior criminal history of the defendant, at standards lower than reasonable doubt. See People v. Wims, 895 P.2d 77 (Cal. 1995).

The Supreme Court has spoken again recently on the question of whether particular facts are "elements" of a crime (to be decided by a trial jury using the beyond a reasonable doubt standard) or are instead "sentencing enhancement" (to be decided after trial using a lower standard of proof). The decisions in Apprendi v. New Jersey, 530 U.S. 466 (2000), and Blakely v. Washington, 542 U.S. 296 (2004), are discussed in Chapter 9.

5. *Statutory definitions of sufficient evidence.* As we have seen, a legislature is free by and large to define the elements of crimes; it is more limited in its power to declare what inferences about crime elements that a jury must draw from the proven facts. However, the legislature may specify the type of evidence that is *not* sufficient to prove the elements. For instance, some statutes specify the minimum number of witnesses the prosecution must present to support a conviction for a particular crime (e.g., the traditional "two witness rule" for perjury convictions). In Carmell v. Texas, 529 U.S. 513 (2000), the Texas legislature amended its criminal statutes to authorize conviction of certain sexual offenses based on the victim's testimony alone; before that time, the statute required the victim's testimony plus other corroborating evidence to convict the offender. The Court held that when a legislature changes such rules dealing with the sufficiency of evidence, the change may only apply prospectively. Any retroactive application of such a law would amount to an ex post facto law.

Issues about the proper burden of proof and crime definitions draw from a mixture of substantive criminal law, constitutional law, criminal procedure, sentencing law, and evidence, and often from a blend of statutes, case law, and other kinds of legal authority. The mixed nature of questions about defining crimes means that a legislature might accomplish some goal with a rule of evidence that might be invalid as a crime definition. See Montana v. Egelhoff, 518 U.S. 37 (1996) (upholding state statute barring evidence of voluntary intoxication in determining the mental element of an offense); Ronald Allen, Foreword: *Montana v. Egelhoff*— Reflections on the Limits of Legislative Imagination and Judicial Authority, 87 J. Crim. L. & Criminology 633-91 (1997).

B. CONFRONTATION OF WITNESSES

An adversarial legal system, by its very nature, places great value on the testing of evidence. Cross-examination of witnesses presents the attorneys with their best opportunity to test the reliability of evidence. The cross-examination of a key witness creates high drama for any trial.

State and federal constitutions recognize the importance of this adversarial testing of evidence. Often, however, the constitutional provisions refer to "confrontation" of witnesses rather than to cross-examination. Consider the relevant clause from the Sixth Amendment to the federal constitution: "In all criminal prosecutions, the accused shall enjoy the right . . . to be confronted with the witnesses against him. . . ." In this section, we consider the devices available to test evidence.

1. The Value of Confrontation

Ordinarily the prosecution presents witnesses who testify at trial in the presence of the defendant, and the defense counsel cross-examines the witnesses with the defendant present. But does the presence of the defendant add anything? Is there some value in the "confrontation" of witnesses that goes beyond an effective cross-examination? See Richard D. Friedman, Confrontation: The Search for Basic Principles, 86 Geo. L.J. 1011 (1998). The Texas case reprinted below deals with an unusual trial setting in which the defendant is disguised during testimony. As you read it, reflect on what makes a cross-examination effective and what additional functions confrontation might serve. The second case, an opinion of the European Court of Human Rights, plays a variation on this theme: efforts by prosecutors in the Netherlands to use witnesses whose names remain unknown to the defendant. As you read the case, try to sort out which of the concepts discussed would be familiar to an American court and which would be unthinkable. What does this European decision tell us about criminal justice in the United States?

A word is in order about the European Court of Human Rights. More than 30 nations have signed a treaty known as the European Convention for the Protection of Human Rights and Fundamental Freedoms. The treaty was signed in 1950, after the revelation of outrageous human rights abuses during World War II and during a time when some European nations felt the need to distinguish their democratic forms of government from Communist legal systems during the Cold War.

Under the European Convention, an individual who is convicted in the criminal courts of a signatory nation can challenge that conviction if it was obtained in violation of the convention. The challenge first goes to the European Commission on Human Rights; either the defendant or the government may appeal the commission's decision to the European Court of Human Rights. The judges of the court are drawn from various signatory nations. They interpret the convention in light of broad principles of international and domestic law. The European Court of Human Rights both reflects and develops a consensus among nations about human rights, including the nature of a fair criminal trial.

■ Israel Romero v. State
173 S.W.3d 502 (Tex. 2005)

KELLER, P.J.

The question before us is whether the defendant's Sixth Amendment right to confront witnesses was violated when a witness testified in disguise. Although this is a very close issue, and one undecided by the United States Supreme Court, we answer that question "yes." . . .

Appellant was indicted for aggravated assault. On the morning of trial, Cesar Hiran Vasquez, one of the State's key witnesses, arrived at the courthouse but refused to enter the courtroom to testify. Vasquez, who had been subpoenaed by the State, notified the State that he "would rather go to jail than testify in this case" because of his fear of appellant. [Vasquez spoke little English, and all of his communications were through an interpreter.] The State informed the trial court of Vasquez's fear and his refusal to testify, and the trial court responded by threatening to fine Vasquez $500 for failing to obey the State's subpoena. Vasquez persisted in his refusal to testify, however, stating that, because he was worried for himself and his children, he "would prefer to pay" the fine rather than testify. The trial court then imposed the fine. Shortly thereafter, Vasquez entered the courtroom wearing dark sunglasses, a baseball cap pulled down over his forehead, and a long-sleeved jacket with its collar turned up and fastened so as to obscure Vasquez's mouth, jaw, and the lower half of his nose. The net effect and apparent purpose of Vasquez's "disguise" was to hide almost all of his face from view. The record reflects that, at the time of trial, appellant was aware of Vasquez's name and address.

Appellant objected to the "disguise" on the basis of his "right to confrontation" and, more generally, his right to a fair trial. The trial court overruled these objections.

The State then called Vasquez to the stand, outside the presence of the jury, to testify regarding appellant's motion to suppress Vasquez's in-court identification of appellant. Vasquez testified that he was operating a taxicab on May 10, 2002, at approximately 1:45 A.M., outside the Cosmos nightclub in Houston, when he saw appellant run toward the nightclub and, for no apparent reason, fire several shots in that direction. Given Vasquez's proximity to the nightclub's entrance, appellant's shots came fairly close to him. A security guard at the nightclub returned fire and hit appellant in the back. Appellant then retreated to a pickup truck and sped away, stopping once to fire again in the direction of the nightclub. Vasquez's testimony continued:

Q: [DEFENSE COUNSEL] If the Court were to order you not to wear your sunglasses, your hat, and your jacket with my client present in the courtroom, are you still going to testify. . . .
A: For my safety, I wouldn't do it. . . .
Q: [PROSECUTOR] Why are you afraid to testify against this defendant?
A: Because of the way that it could be seen that he was going to attack the security guard. It can be seen that he's a person who's dangerous on the street. . . .
Q: What are you afraid that he would do?
A: To take revenge. . . .
Q: [DEFENSE COUNSEL] Well, my client's never threatened you, has he?
A: No.
Q: All right. He's given you no reason to be afraid of him, right?
A: Didn't you see the way he's looking at me? . . .
Q: You just don't like the way he's looking at you, right, basically?
A: No.
Q: Then what is it?
A: The way I saw him attack with the gun. . . .

On direct appeal, appellant . . . argued that the trial court's ruling denied him his Sixth Amendment right to confrontation because Vasquez's "ball cap, large opaque sunglasses and mask [sic] prevented a face-to-face confrontation" and hindered the jury's ability to observe Vasquez's demeanor and assess his credibility. [The court of appeals] reversed the judgment of the trial court, and remanded the case to the trial court for further proceedings. . . .

The Sixth Amendment's Confrontation Clause ("In all criminal prosecutions, the accused shall enjoy the right . . . to be confronted with the witnesses against him") reflects a strong preference for face-to-face confrontation at trial. An encroachment upon face-to-face confrontation is permitted only when necessary to further an important public interest and when the reliability of the testimony is otherwise assured.

RELIABILITY

Whether the reliability of the testimony is otherwise assured turns upon the extent to which the proceedings respect the four elements of confrontation: physical presence, oath, cross-examination, and observation of demeanor by the trier of fact. In Maryland v. Craig, 497 U.S. 836 (1990), the Supreme Court found sufficient assurance of reliability in a procedure that denied one of these elements — physical presence — where the remaining three elements were unimpaired. In that case, a child witness testified in front of a one-way closed-circuit monitor that prevented her from seeing the defendant but permitted the judge, jury, and defendant to see the witness. Because the witness was under oath, subject to contemporaneous cross-examination, and her demeanor was on display before the trier of fact, the Supreme Court found that the procedure adequately ensured that the testimony was "both reliable and subject to rigorous adversarial testing in a manner functionally equivalent to that accorded live, in person testimony."

In this case, as with *Craig*, the presence element of confrontation was compromised. Although the physical presence element might appear, on a superficial level, to have been satisfied by Vasquez's taking the witness stand, it is clear that Vasquez believed the disguise would confer a degree of anonymity that would insulate him from the defendant. The physical presence element entails an accountability of the witness to the defendant. The Supreme Court has observed that the presence requirement is motivated by the idea that a witness cannot "hide behind the shadow" but will be compelled to look the defendant "in the eye" while giving accusatory testimony. Coy v. Iowa, 487 U.S. 1012 (1988). In the present case, accountability was compromised because the witness was permitted to hide behind his disguise.

But unlike *Craig*, the present case also involves a failure to respect a second element of confrontation: observation of the witness's demeanor. Although Vasquez's tone of voice was subject to evaluation and some body language might have been observable, the trier of fact was deprived of the ability to observe his eyes and his facial expressions. And while wearing a disguise may itself be an aspect of demeanor that jurors could consider in assessing credibility, that fact cannot by any stretch of the imagination be considered an adequate substitute for the jurors' ability to view a witness's face, the most expressive part of the body and something that is traditionally regarded as one of the most important factors in assessing credibility. To hold otherwise is to remove the "face" from "face-to-face confrontation."

IMPORTANT INTERESTS

While there may be circumstances sufficient to justify a procedure that overrides not just one but two elements of a defendant's right to confrontation, those circumstances should rise above the "important" interests referred to in *Craig* to interests that are truly compelling. But we do not see an important interest served in the present case, much less a compelling one.

One important, even compelling, interest might be to protect a witness from retaliation, but the disguise in this case did little to further such an interest because

Vasquez's name and address, but not his face, were already known to the defendant. Although Vasquez might reasonably fear that the defendant would be able to connect his facial features and appearance to his name and address, this connection could easily be made without any in-court appearance. A defendant seeking retaliation could simply knock on the door at the known address and ask for the named person. Moreover, this is not a case in which the defendant gave the victim or the authorities any concrete reason for suspecting retaliation, nor is this a case in which the defendant was shown to belong to a crime syndicate or a street gang from which retaliation might be anticipated.

At best, the disguise worked to allay the witness's subjective fear of retaliation. But some degree of trauma is to be expected in face-to-face confrontations. *Coy*, 487 U.S. at 1020 ("face-to-face presence may, unfortunately, upset the truthful rape victim or abused child; but by the same token it may confound and undo the false accuser, or reveal the child coached by a malevolent adult. It is a truism that constitutional protections have costs"). Calming an adult witness's fears is quite a different thing from protecting a child victim from serious emotional trauma. Adults are generally considered to be made of sterner stuff and capable of looking after their own psychological well-being. And the difference is especially great when the adult witness is not the victim, but merely a bystander who observed events, and when the basis of the witness's fear is simply that the defendant committed a violent crime and gave the witness a bad look. If those circumstances are sufficient to justify infringing on a defendant's right to face-to-face confrontation, then such infringement can be carried out against anyone accused of a violent crime. That outcome would violate the principle that face-to-face confrontation may be deprived only in exceptional situations. . . . We affirm the judgment of the Court of Appeals.

MEYERS, J., dissenting.

Mr. Israel G. Romero, this is your lucky day. You're going to get a new trial. The trial judge erred by allowing an eye witness to your crime to wear a ball cap, jacket, and sunglasses while testifying. . . .

The majority says that two elements of the confrontation clause were compromised — that being presence and demeanor. While I'm unsure what compromise means here, I'm fairly confident that the witness was there face-to-face to testify, was cross-examined, and that his demeanor showed that he was scared to death of the defendant. In Texas, is an accused entitled to more than this? Apparently so. Since Mr. Vasquez spoke through an interpreter, I really think this whole controversy is probably "lost in translation." . . .

The central concern of the Confrontation Clause is to ensure the reliability of the evidence against a criminal defendant by subjecting it to rigorous testing in the context of an adversary proceeding before the trier of fact. [As the Supreme Court noted in its earliest case interpreting the Confrontation Clause]:

> The primary object of the constitutional provision in question was to prevent depositions or ex parte affidavits, such as were sometimes admitted in civil cases, being used against the prisoner in lieu of a personal examination and cross-examination of the witness in which the accused has an opportunity, not only of testing the recollection and sifting the conscience of the witness, but of compelling him to stand face to face with the jury in order that they may look at him, and judge by his demeanor upon the stand and the manner in which he gives his testimony whether he is worthy of belief. Mattox v. United States, 156 U.S. 237, 242-243 (1895). . . .

But here's the catch, the defense basically neutralized the witness's disguise. Mr. Vasquez was the only one in the courtroom who thought he was The Phantom of the Opera. The only effect that wearing a hat and sunglasses had was to make Mr. Vasquez more comfortable on the stand and to limit the trauma he felt when testifying against someone whom he feared. This is similar to the cases cited by the parties, Coy v. Iowa, 487 U.S. 1012 (1988), and Maryland v. Craig, 497 U.S. 836 (1990), in which measures were used to prevent face-to-face contact between the defendant and the witness in order to prevent trauma to the victims. However, unlike the screen in *Coy* and the closed circuit television in *Craig*, in this case, the outfit worn by Mr. Vasquez did not prevent or encroach upon face-to-face contact between the defendant and the witness.

Attorneys often change the appearance of witnesses appearing in court. Drunks are sobered up, addicts are cleaned up, and the homeless are dressed up; prostitutes even appear in business suits. These modifications are intended to persuade the jury that the witness is reliable. Mr. Vasquez's additions were not intended to fool the jury. Rather it was simply a method to allay his fears about testifying. Nothing was compromised — just slightly camouflaged.

I agree with the trial court's decision to allow the witness to appear as secret agent man. Therefore, I respectfully dissent.

HOLCOMB, J., dissenting.
. . . After considering the record and the arguments of the parties, I conclude that an important state interest is implicated in this case. On this record, the trial court could have reasonably concluded that Vasquez's disguise was necessary to further the important state interest in protecting the physical well-being of witnesses who have a well-founded fear of retaliation on the part of the defendant. Vasquez testified that he witnessed appellant engage in an unprovoked, determined, and lethal attack on a nightclub in Houston. Vasquez also [remarked] about how appellant was looking at him in the courtroom, apparently in a threatening manner. On this record, the trial court could have reasonably concluded that Vasquez reasonably believed appellant was a dangerous person, possibly a sociopath, and that Vasquez had a well-founded fear of retaliation on appellant's part. The fact that the trial court made no such finding on the record is not determinative. . . .

Undoubtedly, the Sixth Amendment does not always require that the jurors have the ability to see the witness's eyes or see his mouth move as he talks. In some situations, for example, a witness may be blind and may wear sunglasses over his sightless eyes; in other situations, a witness may testify in sign language. In my view, the Sixth Amendment was satisfied in this case. . . .

■ DÉSIRÉ DOORSON v. NETHERLANDS
22 Eur. Ct. H.R. 330 (1996)

In August 1987 the prosecuting authorities decided to take action against the nuisance caused by drug trafficking in Amsterdam.[*] The police compiled photographs of persons suspected of being drug dealers, and showed the photos to about 150 drug addicts to collect statements from them. However, most of the witnesses

---

[*]Material in this opinion preceding paragraph 53 has been edited without indication. — EDS.

were only prepared to make statements on condition that their identity was not disclosed to the drug dealers they identified. Witnesses who had testified during a similar enforcement effort in 1986 had received threats.

In September 1987 the police received information from a drug addict that Doorson was engaged in drug trafficking. The police then included a 1985 photograph of Doorson in the collection of photographs they showed to other drug addicts. A number of addicts recognized Doorson from his photograph and told police that he had sold drugs. Six of these drug addicts remained anonymous; they were referred to by the police under the code names Y05, Y06, Y13, Y14, Y15 and Y16. The identity of two others was disclosed, namely R and N.

On 12 April 1988 Doorson was arrested on suspicion of having committed drug offenses. During the preliminary judicial investigation, Doorson's lawyer requested an examination of the witnesses referred to in the police report. The investigating judge ordered the police to bring these witnesses before him on 30 May 1988 between 09.30 and 16.00. Doorson's lawyer was notified and invited to attend the questioning of these witnesses before the investigating judge.

On 30 May 1988 Doorson's lawyer arrived at the investigating judge's chambers at 09.30. However, after an hour and a half had elapsed and none of the witnesses had appeared, he concluded that no questioning would take place. The attorney left for another appointment, after the judge promised him that if the witnesses should turn up later that day, they would not be heard but would be required to appear for questioning at a later date so that he would be able to attend. After the lawyer had left, two of the eight witnesses referred to in the police report turned up and were heard by the investigating judge in the absence of the lawyer, witness Y15 at about 11.15 and witness Y16 at about 15.00. Y15 and Y16 did not keep a promise to return for further questioning on 3 June.

In proceedings before the Regional Court, the named witness N appeared, but R did not. Both the prosecution and the defense were given the opportunity to put questions to N. Asked to identify Doorson, N stated that he did not recognize him. On being shown Doorson's photograph, he said that he recognized it as that of a man who had given him heroin when he was ill. However, towards the end of his examination he stated that he was no longer quite sure of recognizing the man in the photograph; it might be that the man who had given him the heroin only resembled that man. He also claimed that when shown the photographs by the police, he had only identified Doorson's photograph as that of a person from whom he had bought drugs because at the time he had felt very ill and had been afraid that the police might not give him back the drugs which they had found in his possession.

After the Regional Court convicted Doorson of drug trafficking and sentenced him to 15 months' imprisonment, he appealed to the Amsterdam Court of Appeal. Doorson's lawyer requested the procurator general of the Court of Appeal to summon the anonymous witnesses and the named witnesses N and R for questioning at that Court's hearing. The procurator general replied that he would summon N and R but not the anonymous witnesses, because he wished to preserve their anonymity.

The Court of Appeal decided to verify the necessity of maintaining the anonymity of the witnesses and referred the case back to the investigating judge for this purpose. The Court of Appeal also requested the investigating judge to examine the witnesses — after deciding whether their anonymity should be preserved or not — and to offer Doorson's lawyer the opportunity both to attend this examination and to put questions to the witnesses.

On 14 February 1990 the investigating judge heard the witnesses Y15 and Y16 in the presence of Doorson's lawyer. The lawyer was given the opportunity to put questions to the witnesses but was not informed of their identity. The identity of both witnesses was known to the investigating judge.

Both witnesses expressed the wish to remain anonymous and not to appear in court. Witness Y16 stated that he had in the past suffered injuries at the hands of another drug dealer after he had cooperated with the police, and he feared similar reprisals from Doorson. Witness Y15 stated that he had in the past been threatened by drug dealers if he were to talk. He also said that Doorson was aggressive. The investigating judge concluded that both witnesses had sufficient reason to wish to maintain their anonymity and not to appear in open court.

At its next hearing on the case, the Court of Appeal heard the witness N in Doorson's presence and his lawyer was given the opportunity to question the witness. N said that his statement to the police had been untrue and that he did not in fact know Doorson. The named witness R was initially present at these proceedings. Before he was heard, he asked the Court usher who was guarding him for permission to leave for a minute; he then disappeared and could not be found again.

The Court of Appeal decided to refer the case once again back to the investigating judge, requesting her to record her findings as to the reliability of the witnesses Y15 and Y16. On 19 November 1990 the investigating judge drew up a record of her findings regarding the reliability of the statements made to her by Y15 and Y16 on 14 February 1990. She stated in this document that she could not remember the faces of the two witnesses but, having re-read the records of the interrogations, could recall more or less what had happened. She had the impression that both witnesses knew whom they were talking about and had identified Doorson's photograph without hesitation. As far as she remembered, both witnesses had answered all questions readily and without hesitating, although they had made a "somewhat sleepy impression."

On 6 December 1990, the Court of Appeal found Doorson guilty of the deliberate sale of quantities of heroin and cocaine. As regards Doorson's complaint that the majority of the witnesses had not been heard in the presence of Doorson or his lawyer, the Court stated that it had based its conviction on evidence given by the witnesses N, R, Y15 and Y16. Doorson brought this appeal to the European Court of Human Rights.

53. The applicant alleged that the taking of, hearing of and reliance on evidence from certain witnesses during the criminal proceedings against him infringed the rights of the defence, in violation of Article 6(1) and (3)(d) of the Convention, which provide as follows:

> 1. In the determination . . . of any criminal charge against him, everyone is entitled to a fair . . . hearing [by an] impartial tribunal. . . .
> 3. Everyone charged with a criminal offence has the following minimum rights: . . . (d) to examine or have examined witnesses against him and to obtain the attendance and examination of witnesses on his behalf under the same conditions as witnesses against him. . . .

54. The applicant claimed in the first place that, in obtaining the statements of the anonymous witnesses Y15 and Y16, the rights of the defence had been infringed

to such an extent that the reliance on those statements by the Amsterdam Court of Appeal was incompatible with the standards of a "fair" trial. . . .

Although he conceded that in the course of the appeal proceedings Y15 and Y16 had been questioned by [the Investigating Judge] in the presence of his Counsel and had identified him from a photograph taken several years previously, that was not a proper substitute for a confrontation with him in person. Not knowing the identity of the persons concerned, he could not himself cross-examine them to test their credibility. Nor could the possibility of mistakes be ruled out. It would, in his submission, have been possible to examine the witnesses in his presence, protecting them, if need be, by the use of disguise, voice-distorting equipment or a two-way mirror.

In fact, he questioned the need for maintaining the anonymity of Y15 and Y16 at all. Both had stated before the investigating judge that they feared reprisals but there was nothing to suggest that they were ever subjected to, or for that matter threatened with, violence at the hands of the applicant. Moreover, the basis of the investigating judge's assessment of the need for anonymity was not made clear to the defence. . . .

55. In the second place, the applicant complained about the reliance on the evidence of the named witness R. Although R had been brought to the hearing of the Court of Appeal for questioning, he had — in the applicant's submission — been allowed to abscond under circumstances which engaged the Court of Appeal's responsibility. . . . Since he — the applicant — had not been able to cross-examine R, his statement to the police should not have been admitted as evidence. . . .

67. The Court of Appeal had been entitled to consider the reliability of the statements of Y15 and Y16 sufficiently corroborated by the findings of the investigating judge, as officially recorded on 19 November 1990, and by the statement in open court of the [investigating police officer] that the witnesses in the case had been under no constraint. In any case, the Court of Appeal had noted in its judgment that it had made use of the anonymous statements with "the necessary caution and circumspection." . . .

69. As the Court has held on previous occasions, the Convention does not preclude reliance, at the investigation stage, on sources such as anonymous informants. The subsequent use of their statements by the trial court to found a conviction is however capable of raising issues under the Convention. See Kostovski v. Netherlands, 12 Eur. Ct. H.R. 344 (1990).

[Under the *Kostovski* judgment, the use of statements by anonymous witnesses is acceptable when the statement is taken down by a judge who (a) is aware of the identity of the witness, (b) has expressed, in the official record of the hearing of such a witness, his reasoned opinion as to the reliability of the witness and as to the reasons for the witness's wish to remain anonymous, and (c) has provided the defence with some opportunity to put questions or have questions put to the witness. This rule is subject to exceptions; thus, according to the same judgment, the statement of an anonymous witness may be used in evidence despite the absence of the safeguards mentioned above if (a) the defence has not at any stage of the proceedings asked to be allowed to question the witness concerned, and (b) the conviction is based to a significant extent on other evidence not derived from anonymous sources, and (c) the trial court makes it clear that it has made use of the statement of the anonymous witness with caution and circumspection.]

70. It is true that Article 6 does not explicitly require the interests of witnesses in general, and those of victims called upon to testify in particular, to be taken into

consideration. However, their life, liberty or security of person may be at stake, as may interests coming generally within the ambit of Article 8 of the Convention.* Such interests of witnesses and victims are in principle protected by other, substantive provisions of the Convention, which imply that Contracting States should organise their criminal proceedings in such a way that those interests are not unjustifiably imperilled. Against this background, principles of fair trial also require that in appropriate cases the interests of the defence are balanced against those of witnesses or victims called upon to testify.

71. As the Amsterdam Court of Appeal made clear, its decision not to disclose the identity of Y15 and Y16 to the defence was inspired by the need, as assessed by it, to obtain evidence from them while at the same time protecting them against the possibility of reprisals by the applicant. . . .

Although, as the applicant has stated, there has been no suggestion that Y15 and Y16 were ever threatened by the applicant himself, the decision to maintain their anonymity cannot be regarded as unreasonable per se. Regard must be had to the fact, as established by the domestic courts and not contested by the applicant, that drug dealers frequently resorted to threats or actual violence against persons who gave evidence against them. Furthermore, the statements made by the witnesses concerned to the investigating judge show that one of them had apparently on a previous occasion suffered violence at the hands of a drug dealer against whom he had testified, while the other had been threatened. In sum, there was sufficient reason for maintaining the anonymity of Y15 and Y16. . . .

73. In the instant case the anonymous witnesses were questioned at the appeals stage in the presence of Counsel by an investigating judge who was aware of their identity, even if the defence was not. . . . In this respect the present case is to be distinguished from that of *Kostovski*. Counsel was not only present, but he was put in a position to ask the witnesses whatever questions he considered to be in the interests of the defence except in so far as they might lead to the disclosure of their identity, and these questions were all answered. . . .

74. While it would clearly have been preferable for the applicant to have attended the questioning of the witnesses, the Court considers, on balance, that the Amsterdam Court of Appeal was entitled to consider that the interests of the applicant were in this respect outweighed by the need to ensure the safety of the witnesses. More generally, the Convention does not preclude identification — for the purposes of Article 6(3)(d) — of an accused with his Counsel. . . .

76. Finally, it should be recalled that, even when "counterbalancing" procedures are found to compensate sufficiently the handicaps under which the defence labours, a conviction should not be based either solely or to a decisive extent on anonymous statements. That, however, is not the case here: it is sufficiently clear that the national court did not base its finding of guilt solely or to a decisive extent on the evidence of Y15 and Y16.

Furthermore, evidence obtained from witnesses under conditions in which the rights of the defence cannot be secured to the extent normally required by the Convention should be treated with extreme care. The Court is satisfied that this was done in the criminal proceedings leading to the applicant's conviction, as is

---

*Article 8 provides: "Everyone has the right to respect for his private and family life, his home and his correspondence." — EDS.

reflected in the express declaration by the Court of Appeal that it had treated the statements of Y15 and Y16 "with the necessary caution and circumspection." . . .

83. None of the alleged shortcomings considered on their own lead the Court to conclude that the applicant did not receive a fair trial. Moreover, it cannot find, even if the alleged shortcomings are considered together, that the proceedings as a whole were unfair. In arriving at this conclusion the Court has taken into account the fact that the domestic courts were entitled to consider the various items of evidence before them as corroborative of each other. . . . For these reasons, the Court holds, by seven votes to two, that there has been no violation of Article 6(1) taken together with Article 6(3)(d) of the Convention. . . .

RYSSDAL, J., dissenting.

It is not only in drug cases that problems may arise in relation to the safety of witnesses. It is not permissible to resolve such problems by departing from such a fundamental principle as the one that witness evidence challenged by the accused cannot be admitted against him if he has not had an opportunity to examine or have examined, in his presence, the witness in question.

In the instant case the applicant had this opportunity in respect of witness N, who withdrew his earlier statement. The applicant did not have such an opportunity in relation to witness R, who "disappeared," or witnesses Y15 and Y16, who were heard only in the presence of his lawyer. Moreover, Y15 and Y16 were anonymous witnesses whose identity was only known to the investigating judge but not to the applicant and his lawyer, nor to the Regional Court and the Court of Appeal.

Problem 8-5. Child Testimony

Teresa Brady was born in 1997. Her father and mother, Michael Brady and Carla Myers, were married at the time of her birth but were divorced in 1998. Under a court visitation order, Teresa spent a Friday night and a Saturday night in April 2001 with her father at the home of Michael's mother, Rosemary Brady. Michael returned Teresa to Carla's home on Sunday at 6:00 P.M. On Monday morning, one of Teresa's teachers discovered her hiding in the bathroom closet and complaining about genital pain. A physical examination produced evidence of sexual abuse. During the three months following the discovery of the child's injury, she made several statements to investigators that her father had hurt her. The state filed charges against Michael in July 2001.

In January 2002, the State asked the court to order that Teresa's testimony be videotaped for use at trial, using the statutory procedures for recording the testimony of children. In February, the trial court ruled that it was more likely than not that it would be traumatic for Teresa to testify in court and ordered that the videotape testimony be taken. In March, Teresa's videotape testimony was taken and was subsequently admitted at trial over appellant's objection and viewed by the jury. The tape had been taken at home in Teresa's kitchen and bedroom. The judge, prosecutor, defense attorney, investigator, Teresa's mother, and the operator of the video equipment were present during the videotaping. The videotape session lasted approximately two hours. Michael was situated in the garage of the house, and he was able to see and hear Teresa via closed-circuit television as she was questioned. Michael was also able to speak with defense counsel by a microphone hook-up.

Teresa was not able to see or hear appellant and was not aware of his presence. All of these arrangements carefully followed the statutory requirements.

Michael Brady maintains that this statute is unconstitutional on its face because it infringes upon his right to confront the witnesses against him as guaranteed by the Sixth Amendment of the United States Constitution and the analogous provision of the state constitution. The statute in question in this case is similar to the Maryland statute that the United States Supreme Court reviewed in Maryland v. Craig, 497 U.S. 836 (1990). The Supreme Court upheld the constitutionality of the Maryland statute as it found that the admission of the child victim's live testimony at the time of trial, transmitted to the courtroom and the trier of fact via one-way closed-circuit television, was consistent with the Confrontation Clause. The Supreme Court found it significant that Maryland's procedure preserves all of the elements of the confrontation right apart from the physical presence of the witness in the courtroom: "the child witness must be competent to testify and must testify under oath; the defendant retains full opportunity for contemporaneous cross-examination; and the judge, jury, and defendant are able to view (albeit by videotape monitor) the demeanor (and body) of the witness as he or she testifies."

The Supreme Court went on to state that in some cases the State's interest in protecting a child witness from serious emotional distress and trauma occasioned by testifying in the courtroom and in the presence of the defendant may outweigh a defendant's right to face his or her accusers in court. In such instances, the Supreme Court concluded that it was not necessary that the child witness be able to view, to hear, or otherwise perceive the presence of the defendant, who is viewing and listening in at the time.

The statute operating in this case resembles in some respects the Maryland statute at issue in *Craig*. The single significant dissimilarity in the two statutes appears to be that the statute here, unlike the Maryland statute, authorizes the use of videotaped pre-trial statements as well as the use of closed-circuit television during trial. How would you rule on Brady's claim? Cf. Brady v. State, 575 N.E.2d 981 (Ind. 1991).

Notes

1. *Anonymous witnesses: majority position.* In the United States, a witness is usually required to divulge both his name and address on cross-examination. This is said to allow the defendant to put the witness in a "proper setting" and to test the witness's credibility. See Alford v. United States, 282 U.S. 687 (1931); Smith v. Illinois, 390 U.S. 129 (1968). At the same time, the right to cross-examine prosecution witnesses about their identities or addresses is not considered absolute, and a trial court has discretion to restrict cross-examination on such topics if there is an adequate showing that the safety of the witness is at risk. Alvarado v. Superior Court, 5 P.3d 203 (Cal. 2000) (prosecution may not permanently withhold identities of key witnesses; although disclosure may be delayed until trial, safety concerns of prisoner-witnesses must be addressed by means less drastic than anonymous testimony if testimony is crucial to prosecution's case); State v. Vandebogart, 652 A.2d 671 (N.H. 1994) (witness allowed not to reveal address; she was victim of prior assault by defendant); Randolph N. Jonakait, Secret Testimony and Public Trials in New York, 42 N.Y.L. Sch. L. Rev. 407 (1998). Recall also that the government often may shield the identity of "confidential informants" during the investigation stage.

Courts in a number of nations have upheld convictions based on the testimony of "anonymous witnesses." Legislation in some nations (such as New Zealand) allows undercover police officers to testify without revealing their identities. The general trend has been to allow the use of anonymous witnesses only when accompanied by the sort of safeguards described in the *Doorson* opinion from the European Court of Human Rights. As European nations move toward more of a hybrid between common law and civil law processes (and thus a hybrid between adversarial and inquisitorial development of proof), will they become less likely to rely on devices such as anonymous witnesses?

2. *The value of comparative law.* The concept of confronting witnesses is a familiar one even in civil law legal systems, which are based on an "inquisitorial" model of factfinding (in which the judge takes responsibility for developing facts) rather than an "adversarial" model (in which the parties present their own facts and take responsibility for testing the factual claims of their adversaries). But the confrontation rights of defendants in civil law systems do not exactly track the confrontation rights of defendants in U.S. courts. Do the practices and values of European criminal justice systems have any relevance for American lawyers, legislators, or judges? See Diane Marie Amann, Harmonic Convergence? Constitutional Criminal Procedure in an International Context, 75 Ind. L.J. 809 (2000). Given the perceived differences between adversarial development of proof at trial (dominated by the attorneys) and inquisitorial methods of proof (dominated by the judge), is it fair to conclude that practices relating to confrontation of witnesses are less likely than other practices to interest those who operate within American criminal procedure rules?

3. *Confrontation of child witnesses: majority position.* Under the federal constitution, some witnesses may testify outside the courtroom and outside the presence of the defendant if the defendant is able to monitor the testimony and communicate with the defense attorney conducting the cross-examination. According to Maryland v. Craig, 497 U.S. 836 (1990), the trial court must make a case-specific finding that the witness would suffer from extreme emotional trauma during traditional testimony that would prevent the witness from reasonably communicating. The *Craig* Court distinguished Coy v. Iowa, 487 U.S. 1012 (1988), which struck down a statute protecting child witnesses without an individualized assessment of the potential trauma to the child.

Most high state courts to address this issue (more than 25) follow the federal position and allow prosecuting witnesses to testify outside the courtroom (and outside the defendant's physical presence) so long as the arrangement is "necessary to further an important public policy" and "the reliability of the testimony is otherwise assured." State v. Bray, 535 S.E.2d 636 (S.C. 2000) (lack of case-specific findings invalidated order for televised testimony). The cases often require that the defendant be able to monitor the cross-examination from a remote location or from a hidden or screened location in the room. Another group of high state courts (fewer than 10) have concluded that the defendant must be present (and visible to the witness) during the direct testimony and cross-examination, although some have concluded that it is enough if the defendant's electronic image is present during the testimony. Compare People v. Newbrough, 803 P.2d 155 (Colo. 1990) (approving use of videotaped deposition and questioning by court psychiatrist; defendant and defense counsel monitor questioning by one-way video and relay questions to psychiatrist) and People v. Cintron, 551 N.E.2d 561 (N.Y. 1990) (approving two-way closed-circuit testimony at trial) with People v. Fitzpatrick,

633 N.E.2d 685 (Ill. 1994) (striking down statute that allowed cross-examination on closed-circuit television).

The states departing from the federal position, by and large, are those with specific "face to face" provisions in their state constitutions. Almost 30 state constitutions track the language of the Sixth Amendment to the federal constitution and speak of the right of the accused to be "confronted" with adverse witnesses. About 20 state constitutions mention a defendant's right to meet adverse witnesses "face to face."

Which of the various elements of the classic courtroom confrontation create more reliable testimony? Does it matter that the testimony takes place during trial rather than during an earlier deposition? Does it matter whether the testimony takes place in a courtroom? Note that the statute described in Problem 8-5 required a video image of the defendant to be present during the testimony. Would a cardboard cutout image of the defendant suffice?

4. *Reliability of out-of-court statements by child witnesses.* As the opinions in *Brady* indicate, a strong majority of states have passed special statutes dealing with the testimony of child witnesses, including out-of-court statements. The statutes for shielded child testimony typically apply only in sex abuse crimes. In the absence of such a special statute, the rules of evidence (and in particular, rules about untested "hearsay" statements) might prevent the admission of an out-of-court statement. There are, however, exceptions to the hearsay rules that some courts have applied to child witnesses, even when a special child-testimony statute does not apply. In general, these exceptions try to identify out-of-court statements that seem reliable, despite the fact that the person made the statement outside the adversarial courtroom environment. Some courts have concluded that out-of-court statements by children were "excited utterances" or statements made to a professional offering medical diagnosis or treatment (both exceptions to the bar on hearsay).

Social science and psychology researchers have explored at great length the factors associated most strongly with reliable and unreliable child testimony. As one might expect, older children are more reliable witnesses than younger children. Young children depend more heavily than older children on "recognition memory" (responding to specific questions about an event rather than volunteering information in response to a general question). Suggestive questioning is more likely to influence younger children, and small differences in age can mean large differences in reliability. The number of times a child is questioned before trial also affects reliability. See Stephen Ceci & Maggie Bruck, Suggestibility of the Child Witness: A Historical Review and Synthesis, 113 Psychol. Bull. 403 (1993). Contrary to expectations, promptness in coming forward with an accusation or consistency in the details of a story is not a good indicator of a reliable child witness. If new research indicates that a factor listed in a statute is not a good indicator of reliability, how should the judge interpreting the statute respond?

5. *Defendant's presence during other proceedings.* Both federal and state courts have concluded that defendants have a right, both under confrontation clauses and due process clauses, to be present at "every stage" of the trial. The opinions also declare, however, that some trial or pretrial events do not require the defendant's presence. The defendant must be present only when "his presence has a relation, reasonably substantial, to the fullness of his opportunity to defend against the charge." Snyder v. Massachusetts, 291 U.S. 97 (1934) (Cardozo, J.). In Kentucky v. Stincer, 482 U.S. 730 (1987), the Court held that a defendant must be present for at least some

pretrial proceedings; however, there was no error when a trial court held a hearing on the competency of a witness to testify at trial, with the defense counsel present but not the defendant, because the questions asked did not relate to the alleged crime and did not interfere with any opportunity for cross-examination. See People v. Dokes, 595 N.E.2d 836 (N.Y. 1992) (presence required at pretrial conference to decide on prior convictions available for impeaching defendant's testimony).

6. *Waiver of presence.* Does a defendant waive the right to be present during the trial by engaging in disruptive behavior? See Illinois v. Allen, 397 U.S. 337 (1970) (no constitutional error to remove defendant from courtroom after repeated outbursts, if defendant is allowed to return to courtroom after promise of better behavior). By escaping from jail before trial? Crosby v. United States, 506 U.S. 255 (1993) (interpreting Fed. R. Crim. P. 43 to prevent trial in absentia of defendant who escapes jail before trial begins, but to allow such trials for defendants who escape after trial has begun). By failing to appear on the day set for trial after being released before trial? See People v. Johnston, 513 N.E.2d 528 (Ill. 1987) (failure to appear at trial, after appearing at pretrial hearing, is waiver of right to be present).

7. *Victims and sequestration of witnesses.* A traditional rule of evidence allows a party to insist that the judge exclude a witness from the courtroom until that witness has testified. This rule of "sequestration of witnesses" makes cross-examination more effective because it prevents the witness from changing her testimony to remain consistent with (or to rebut) the evidence presented up until that time. The judge's power to exclude witnesses existed at common law, and many states now have rules of evidence codifying this discretionary rule. Others, such as Fed. R. Evid. 615, give the parties an absolute right to exclude a witness; the judge has no discretion on the question for most witnesses.

The sequestration rule sometimes conflicts with the notion that the victim of an alleged crime has a special interest in attending a trial. Consider the following typical effort to reconcile these competing principles, contained in Utah R. Evid. 615(1):

> At the request of a party the court shall order witnesses excluded so that they cannot hear the testimony of other witnesses, and it may make the order on its own motion. This rule does not authorize exclusion of . . . a victim in a criminal trial or juvenile delinquency proceeding where the prosecutor agrees with the victim's presence.

Compare Mich. Comp. Laws §780.761(11) ("The victim has the right to be present throughout the entire trial of the defendant, unless the victim is going to be called as a witness. If the victim is going to be called as a witness, the court may, for good cause shown, order the victim to be sequestered until the victim first testifies"). Some states unequivocally grant the victim a right to attend the proceedings, while others grant the trial court discretion to allow the victim to attend. Under these rules and statutes, does the victim now have a right to presence at trial comparable to the defendant's right to be present? Does the presence of the victim in the courtroom influence other witnesses as they testify (creating a sort of "confrontation" right for a crime victim)? Do rules such as these convert the role of the victim from a component of the government's proof into a party in the litigation? See Paul Cassell, Balancing the Scales of Justice: The Case for and the Effects of Utah's Victim's Rights Amendment, 1994 Utah L. Rev. 1373; Robert Mosteller, Victims' Rights and the United States Constitution: An Effort to Recast the Battle in Criminal

Litigation, 85 Geo. L.J. 1691 (1997). If you were drafting rules dealing with victim attendance at trial, would you allow all victims to attend the trial from beginning to end? How about victims in assault cases, when the defendants claim that they acted in self-defense or were otherwise provoked by the alleged victim?

2. Unavailable Prosecution Witnesses

How can a defendant confront the person who accuses her if the accuser is not present in the courtroom? There may be many reasons for a witness or victim's absence from the courtroom. For the most part, the law of evidence dictates when statements made by unavailable witnesses will be admitted at trial. There is, however, a constitutional component to these questions as well. The two cases below deal with statements made to the police by a person other than the accused who was not available to testify at trial. Such statements raise the question whether the defendant is able to "confront" her accuser.

■ MICHAEL CRAWFORD v. WASHINGTON
541 U.S. 36 (2004)

SCALIA, J.

Petitioner Michael Crawford stabbed a man who allegedly tried to rape his wife, Sylvia. At his trial, the State played for the jury Sylvia's tape-recorded statement to the police describing the stabbing, even though he had no opportunity for cross-examination. The Washington Supreme Court upheld petitioner's conviction after determining that Sylvia's statement was reliable. The question presented is whether this procedure complied with the Sixth Amendment's guarantee that, "[i]n all criminal prosecutions, the accused shall enjoy the right . . . to be confronted with the witnesses against him."

I.

On August 5, 1999, Kenneth Lee was stabbed at his apartment. Police arrested petitioner later that night. After giving petitioner and his wife *Miranda* warnings, detectives interrogated each of them twice. Petitioner eventually confessed that he and Sylvia had gone in search of Lee because he was upset over an earlier incident in which Lee had tried to rape her. The two had found Lee at his apartment, and a fight ensued in which Lee was stabbed in the torso and petitioner's hand was cut. Petitioner gave the following account of the fight:

Q. Okay. Did you ever see anything in [Lee's] hands?
A. I think so, but I'm not positive.
Q. Okay, when you think so, what do you mean by that?
A. I coulda swore I seen him goin' for somethin' before, right before everything happened. He was like reachin', fiddlin' around down here and stuff . . . and I just . . . I don't know, I think, this is just a possibility, but I think, I think that he pulled somethin' out and I grabbed for it and that's how I got cut . . . but I'm not positive. . . .

Sylvia generally corroborated petitioner's story about the events leading up to the fight, but her account of the fight itself was arguably different—particularly with respect to whether Lee had drawn a weapon before petitioner assaulted him:

Q. Did Kenny do anything to fight back from this assault?

A. (pausing) I know he reached into his pocket . . . or somethin' . . . I don't know what.

Q. After he was stabbed? . . .

A. Okay, he lifted his hand over his head maybe to strike Michael's hand down or something and then he put his hands in his . . . put his right hand in his right pocket . . . took a step back . . . Michael proceeded to stab him . . . then his hands were like . . . how do you explain this . . . open arms . . . with his hands open and he fell down . . . and we ran (describing subject holding hands open, palms toward assailant).

Q. Okay, when he's standing there with his open hands, you're talking about Kenny, correct?

A. Yeah, after, after the fact, yes.

Q. Did you see anything in his hands at that point?

A. (pausing) um um (no).

The State charged petitioner with assault and attempted murder. At trial, he claimed self-defense. Sylvia did not testify because of the state marital privilege, which generally bars a spouse from testifying without the other spouse's consent. In Washington, this privilege does not extend to a spouse's out-of-court statements admissible under a hearsay exception, so the State sought to introduce Sylvia's tape-recorded statements to the police as evidence that the stabbing was not in self-defense. Noting that Sylvia had admitted she led petitioner to Lee's apartment and thus had facilitated the assault, the State invoked the hearsay exception for statements against penal interest, Wash. Rule Evid. 804(b)(3).

Petitioner countered that, state law notwithstanding, admitting the evidence would violate his federal constitutional right to be "confronted with the witnesses against him." According to our description of that right in Ohio v. Roberts, 448 U.S. 56 (1980), it does not bar admission of an unavailable witness's statement against a criminal defendant if the statement bears "adequate indicia of reliability." To meet that test, evidence must either fall within a "firmly rooted hearsay exception" or bear "particularized guarantees of trustworthiness." The trial court here admitted the statement on the latter ground, offering several reasons why it was trustworthy: Sylvia was not shifting blame but rather corroborating her husband's story that he acted in self-defense or "justified reprisal"; she had direct knowledge as an eyewitness; she was describing recent events; and she was being questioned by a "neutral" law enforcement officer. The prosecution played the tape for the jury and relied on it in closing, arguing that it was "damning evidence" that "completely refutes [petitioner's] claim of self-defense." The jury convicted petitioner of assault.

The Washington Court of Appeals reversed. It applied a nine-factor test to determine whether Sylvia's statement bore particularized guarantees of trustworthiness, and noted several reasons why it did not: The statement contradicted one she had previously given; it was made in response to specific questions; and at one point she admitted she had shut her eyes during the stabbing. . . . The Washington Supreme Court reinstated the conviction [and we] granted certiorari to determine whether the State's use of Sylvia's statement violated the Confrontation Clause.

II.

The Sixth Amendment's Confrontation Clause provides that, "[i]n all criminal prosecutions, the accused shall enjoy the right . . . to be confronted with the witnesses against him." . . . Petitioner argues that [the *Roberts*] test strays from the original meaning of the Confrontation Clause and urges us to reconsider it.

The Constitution's text does not alone resolve this case. One could plausibly read "witnesses against" a defendant to mean those who actually testify at trial, those whose statements are offered at trial, or something in-between. We must therefore turn to the historical background of the Clause to understand its meaning.

The right to confront one's accusers is a concept that dates back to Roman times. The founding generation's immediate source of the concept, however, was the common law. English common law has long differed from continental civil law in regard to the manner in which witnesses give testimony in criminal trials. The common-law tradition is one of live testimony in court subject to adversarial testing, while the civil law condones examination in private by judicial officers.

Nonetheless, England at times adopted elements of the civil-law practice. Justices of the peace or other officials examined suspects and witnesses before trial. These examinations were sometimes read in court in lieu of live testimony. . . . The most notorious instances of civil-law examination occurred in the great political trials of the 16th and 17th centuries. One such was the 1603 trial of Sir Walter Raleigh for treason. Lord Cobham, Raleigh's alleged accomplice, had implicated him in an examination before the Privy Council and in a letter. At Raleigh's trial, these were read to the jury. Raleigh argued that Cobham had lied to save himself: "Cobham is absolutely in the King's mercy; to excuse me cannot avail him; by accusing me he may hope for favour." 1 D. Jardine, Criminal Trials 435 (1832). Suspecting that Cobham would recant, Raleigh demanded that the judges call him to appear, arguing that "[the] Proof of the Common Law is by witness and jury: let Cobham be here, let him speak it. Call my accuser before my face. . . ." The judges refused, and, despite Raleigh's protestations that he was being tried "by the Spanish Inquisition," the jury convicted, and Raleigh was sentenced to death. . . .

Through a series of statutory and judicial reforms, English law developed a right of confrontation that limited these abuses. For example, treason statutes required witnesses to confront the accused "face to face" at his arraignment. Courts, meanwhile, developed relatively strict rules of unavailability, admitting examinations only if the witness was demonstrably unable to testify in person. Several authorities also stated that a suspect's confession could be admitted only against himself, and not against others he implicated.

One recurring question was whether the admissibility of an unavailable witness's pretrial examination depended on whether the defendant had had an opportunity to cross-examine him. In 1696, the Court of King's Bench answered this question in the affirmative, in the widely reported misdemeanor libel case of King v. Paine, 87 Eng. Rep. 584. The court ruled that, even though a witness was dead, his examination was not admissible where "the defendant not being present when [it was] taken before the mayor . . . had lost the benefit of a cross-examination." . . .

Controversial examination practices were also used in the Colonies. . . . A decade before the Revolution, England gave jurisdiction over Stamp Act offenses to the admiralty courts, which followed civil-law rather than common-law procedures and thus routinely took testimony by deposition or private judicial examination. Colonial representatives protested that the Act subverted their rights "by extending the jurisdiction of the courts of admiralty beyond its ancient limits." John Adams, defending a merchant in a high-profile admiralty case, argued: "Examinations of witnesses upon Interrogatories, are only by the Civil Law. Interrogatories are unknown at common Law, and Englishmen and common Lawyers have an aversion to them if not an Abhorrence of them."

Many declarations of rights adopted around the time of the Revolution guaranteed a right of confrontation. The proposed Federal Constitution, however, did not. At the Massachusetts ratifying convention, Abraham Holmes objected to this omission precisely on the ground that it would lead to civil-law practices: "The mode of trial is altogether indetermined; . . . whether [the defendant] is to be allowed to confront the witnesses, and have the advantage of cross-examination, we are not yet told. [We] shall find Congress possessed of powers enabling them to institute judicatories little less inauspicious than a certain tribunal in Spain, . . . the *Inquisition.*" 2 Debates on the Federal Constitution 110-111 (J. Elliot 2d ed. 1863). . . . The First Congress responded by including the Confrontation Clause in the proposal that became the Sixth Amendment. Early state decisions shed light upon the original understanding of the common-law right. State v. Webb, 2 N.C. 103 (1794) (per curiam), decided a mere three years after the adoption of the Sixth Amendment, held that depositions could be read against an accused only if they were taken in his presence. . . .

III.

This history supports two inferences about the meaning of the Sixth Amendment. . . . First, the principal evil at which the Confrontation Clause was directed was the civil-law mode of criminal procedure, and particularly its use of *ex parte* examinations as evidence against the accused. It was these practices that the Crown deployed in notorious treason cases like Raleigh's; . . . that English law's assertion of a right to confrontation was meant to prohibit; and that the founding-era rhetoric decried. The Sixth Amendment must be interpreted with this focus in mind.

Accordingly, we once again reject the view that the Confrontation Clause applies of its own force only to in-court testimony, and that its application to out-of-court statements introduced at trial depends upon "the law of Evidence for the time being." Leaving the regulation of out-of-court statements to the law of evidence would render the Confrontation Clause powerless to prevent even the most flagrant inquisitorial practices. Raleigh was, after all, perfectly free to confront those who read Cobham's confession in court.

This focus also suggests that not all hearsay implicates the Sixth Amendment's core concerns. An off-hand, overheard remark might be unreliable evidence and thus a good candidate for exclusion under hearsay rules, but it bears little resemblance to the civil-law abuses the Confrontation Clause targeted. On the other hand, *ex parte* examinations might sometimes be admissible under modern hearsay rules, but the Framers certainly would not have condoned them.

The text of the Confrontation Clause reflects this focus. It applies to "witnesses" against the accused—in other words, those who "bear testimony." 1 N. Webster, An American Dictionary of the English Language (1828). "Testimony," in turn, is typically "[a] solemn declaration or affirmation made for the purpose of establishing or proving some fact." An accuser who makes a formal statement to government officers bears testimony in a sense that a person who makes a casual remark to an acquaintance does not. The constitutional text, like the history underlying the common-law right of confrontation, thus reflects an especially acute concern with a specific type of out-of-court statement. . . .

Regardless of the precise [definition of testimonial statements], some statements qualify under any definition — for example, *ex parte* testimony at a preliminary hearing. Statements taken by police officers in the course of interrogations are also testimonial under even a narrow standard. Police interrogations bear a striking resemblance to examinations by justices of the peace in England. . . . In sum, even if the Sixth Amendment is not solely concerned with testimonial hearsay, that is its primary object, and interrogations by law enforcement officers fall squarely within that class.[4] . . .

The historical record also supports a second proposition: that the Framers would not have allowed admission of testimonial statements of a witness who did not appear at trial unless he was unavailable to testify, and the defendant had had a prior opportunity for cross-examination. The text of the Sixth Amendment does not suggest any open-ended exceptions from the confrontation requirement to be developed by the courts. Rather, the "right . . . to be confronted with the witnesses against him," is most naturally read as a reference to the right of confrontation at common law, admitting only those exceptions established at the time of the founding. As the English authorities above reveal, the common law in 1791 conditioned admissibility of an absent witness's examination on unavailability and a prior opportunity to cross-examine. The Sixth Amendment therefore incorporates those limitations. . . .

This is not to deny . . . that "[there] were always exceptions to the general rule of exclusion" of hearsay evidence. Several had become well established by 1791. But there is scant evidence that exceptions were invoked to admit *testimonial* statements against the accused in a *criminal* case.[6] Most of the hearsay exceptions covered statements that by their nature were not testimonial — for example, business records or statements in furtherance of a conspiracy. . . .

V.

Roberts conditions the admissibility of all hearsay evidence on whether it falls under a "firmly rooted hearsay exception" or bears "particularized guarantees of trustworthiness." This test departs from the historical principles identified above in two respects. First, it is too broad: It applies the same mode of analysis whether or not the hearsay consists of *ex parte* testimony. This often results in close constitutional scrutiny in cases that are far removed from the core concerns of the Clause. At the

---

4. We use the term "interrogation" in its colloquial, rather than any technical legal, sense. Cf. Rhode Island v. Innis, 446 U.S. 291 (1980). Just as various definitions of "testimonial" exist, one can imagine various definitions of "interrogation," and we need not select among them in this case. Sylvia's recorded statement, knowingly given in response to structured police questioning, qualifies under any conceivable definition.

6. The one deviation we have found involves dying declarations. . . . Although many dying declarations may not be testimonial, there is authority for admitting even those that clearly are. We need not decide in this case whether the Sixth Amendment incorporates an exception for testimonial dying declarations. If this exception must be accepted on historical grounds, it is *sui generis*.

same time, however, the test is too narrow: It admits statements that *do* consist of *ex parte* testimony upon a mere finding of reliability. This malleable standard often fails to protect against paradigmatic confrontation violations. . . .

Where testimonial statements are involved, we do not think the Framers meant to leave the Sixth Amendment's protection to the vagaries of the rules of evidence, much less to amorphous notions of "reliability." . . . To be sure, the Clause's ultimate goal is to ensure reliability of evidence, but it is a procedural rather than a substantive guarantee. It commands, not that evidence be reliable, but that reliability be assessed in a particular manner: by testing in the crucible of cross-examination. . . .

The Raleigh trial itself involved the very sorts of reliability determinations that *Roberts* authorizes. In the face of Raleigh's repeated demands for confrontation, the prosecution responded with many of the arguments a court applying *Roberts* might invoke today: that Cobham's statements were self-inculpatory, that they were not made in the heat of passion, and that they were not "extracted from [him] upon any hopes or promise of Pardon." It is not plausible that the Framers' only objection to the trial was that Raleigh's judges did not properly weigh these factors before sentencing him to death. Rather, the problem was that the judges refused to allow Raleigh to confront Cobham in court, where he could cross-examine him and try to expose his accusation as a lie.

Dispensing with confrontation because testimony is obviously reliable is akin to dispensing with jury trial because a defendant is obviously guilty. This is not what the Sixth Amendment prescribes. . . .

The legacy of *Roberts* in other courts vindicates the Framers' wisdom in rejecting a general reliability exception. . . . Reliability is an amorphous, if not entirely subjective, concept. There are countless factors bearing on whether a statement is reliable; the nine-factor balancing test applied by the Court of Appeals below is representative. See, e.g., People v. Farrell, 34 P.3d 401 (Colo. 2001) (eight-factor test). Whether a statement is deemed reliable depends heavily on which factors the judge considers and how much weight he accords each of them. Some courts wind up attaching the same significance to opposite facts. . . .

Roberts' failings were on full display in the proceedings below. Sylvia Crawford made her statement while in police custody, herself a potential suspect in the case. Indeed, she had been told that whether she would be released "depend[ed] on how the investigation continues." In response to often leading questions from police detectives, she implicated her husband in Lee's stabbing and at least arguably undermined his self-defense claim. Despite all this, the trial court admitted her statement, listing several reasons why it was reliable. In its opinion reversing, the Court of Appeals listed several *other* reasons why the statement was *not* reliable. Finally, the State Supreme Court relied exclusively on the interlocking character of the statement and disregarded every other factor the lower courts had considered. The case is thus a self-contained demonstration of *Roberts'* unpredictable and inconsistent application. . . .

We have no doubt that the courts below were acting in utmost good faith when they found reliability. The Framers, however, would not have been content to indulge this assumption. They knew that judges, like other government officers, could not always be trusted to safeguard the rights of the people. . . . By replacing categorical constitutional guarantees with open-ended balancing tests, we do violence to their design. . . .

Where nontestimonial hearsay is at issue, it is wholly consistent with the Framers' design to afford the States flexibility in their development of hearsay law — as does *Roberts*, and as would an approach that exempted such statements from Confrontation Clause scrutiny altogether. Where testimonial evidence is at issue, however, the Sixth Amendment demands what the common law required: unavailability and a prior opportunity for cross-examination. We leave for another day any effort to spell out a comprehensive definition of "testimonial." Whatever else the term covers, it applies at a minimum to prior testimony at a preliminary hearing, before a grand jury, or at a former trial; and to police interrogations. These are the modern practices with closest kinship to the abuses at which the Confrontation Clause was directed. . . .

REHNQUIST, C.J., concurring in the judgment.

I dissent from the Court's decision to overrule Ohio v. Roberts, 448 U.S. 56 (1980). I believe that the Court's adoption of a new interpretation of the Confrontation Clause is not backed by sufficiently persuasive reasoning to overrule long-established precedent. . . .

The Court's distinction between testimonial and nontestimonial statements, contrary to its claim, is no better rooted in history than our current doctrine. Under the common law, although the courts were far from consistent, out-of-court statements made by someone other than the accused and not taken under oath, unlike *ex parte* depositions or affidavits, were generally not considered substantive evidence upon which a conviction could be based. Testimonial statements such as accusatory statements to police officers likely would have been disapproved of in the 18th century, not necessarily because they resembled *ex parte* affidavits or depositions as the Court reasons, but more likely than not because they were not made under oath. Without an oath, one usually did not get to the second step of whether confrontation was required. Thus, while I agree that the Framers were mainly concerned about sworn affidavits and depositions, it does not follow that they were similarly concerned about the Court's broader category of testimonial statements. . . .

With respect to unsworn testimonial statements, there is no indication that once the hearsay rule was developed courts ever excluded these statements if they otherwise fell within a firmly rooted exception. Dying declarations are one example. . . . It is an odd conclusion indeed to think that the Framers created a cut-and-dried rule with respect to the admissibility of testimonial statements when the law during their own time was not fully settled. . . .

Exceptions to confrontation have always been derived from the experience that some out-of-court statements are just as reliable as cross-examined in-court testimony due to the circumstances under which they were made. . . . That a statement might be testimonial does nothing to undermine the wisdom of one of these exceptions. [C]ross-examination is a tool used to flesh out the truth, not an empty procedure. "[I]n a given instance [cross-examination may] be superfluous. . . ." 5 [J. Wigmore, Evidence] §1420, at 251 [(J. Chadbourn rev. 1974)].

[The] thousands of federal prosecutors and the tens of thousands of state prosecutors need answers as to what beyond the specific kinds of "testimony" the Court lists is covered by the new rule. They need them now, not months or years from now. Rules of criminal evidence are applied every day in courts throughout the country, and parties should not be left in the dark in this manner. . . .

■ KEVIN GRAY v. MARYLAND
523 U.S. 185 (1998)

BREYER, J.

The issue in this case concerns the application of Bruton v. United States, 391 U.S. 123 (1968). *Bruton* involved two defendants accused of participating in the same crime and tried jointly before the same jury. One of the defendants had confessed. His confession named and incriminated the other defendant. The trial judge issued a limiting instruction, telling the jury that it should consider the confession as evidence only against the codefendant who had confessed and not against the defendant named in the confession. *Bruton* held that, despite the limiting instruction, the Constitution forbids the use of such a confession in the joint trial.

The case before us differs from *Bruton* in that the prosecution here redacted the codefendant's confession by substituting for the defendant's name in the confession a blank space or the word "deleted." We must decide whether these substitutions make a significant legal difference. We hold that they do not and that *Bruton*'s protective rule applies.

In 1993, Stacy Williams died after a severe beating. Anthony Bell gave a confession, to the Baltimore City police, in which he said that he (Bell), Kevin Gray, and Jacquin "Tank" Vanlandingham had participated in the beating that resulted in Williams' death. Vanlandingham later died. A Maryland grand jury indicted Bell and Gray for murder. The State of Maryland tried them jointly.

The trial judge, after denying Gray's motion for a separate trial, permitted the State to introduce Bell's confession into evidence at trial. But the judge ordered the confession redacted. Consequently, the police detective who read the confession into evidence said the word "deleted" or "deletion" whenever Gray's name or Vanlandingham's name appeared. Immediately after the police detective read the redacted confession to the jury, the prosecutor asked, "after he gave you that information, you subsequently were able to arrest Mr. Kevin Gray; is that correct?" The officer responded, "That's correct." The State also introduced into evidence a written copy of the confession with those two names omitted, leaving in their place blank white spaces separated by commas. The State produced other witnesses, who said that six persons (including Bell, Gray, and Vanlandingham) participated in the beating. Gray testified and denied his participation. Bell did not testify.

When instructing the jury, the trial judge specified that the confession was evidence only against Bell; the instructions said that the jury should not use the confession as evidence against Gray. The jury convicted both Bell and Gray. Gray appealed. . . .

Bruton, as we have said, involved two defendants—Evans and Bruton—tried jointly for robbery. Evans did not testify, but the Government introduced into evidence Evans' confession, which stated that both he (Evans) and Bruton together had committed the robbery. The trial judge told the jury it could consider the confession as evidence only against Evans, not against Bruton.

This Court held that, despite the limiting instruction, the introduction of Evans' out-of-court confession at Bruton's trial had violated Bruton's right, protected by the Sixth Amendment, to cross-examine witnesses. The Court recognized that in many circumstances a limiting instruction will adequately protect one defendant from the prejudicial effects of the introduction at a joint trial of evidence intended for use only against a different defendant. But it said that

> there are some contexts in which the risk that the jury will not, or cannot, follow instructions is so great, and the consequences of failure so vital to the defendant, that the practical and human limitations of the jury system cannot be ignored. Such a context is presented here, where the powerfully incriminating extrajudicial statements of a codefendant, who stands accused side-by-side with the defendant, are deliberately spread before the jury in a joint trial. Not only are the incriminations devastating to the defendant but their credibility is inevitably suspect. . . . The unreliability of such evidence is intolerably compounded when the alleged accomplice, as here, does not testify and cannot be tested by cross-examination. [391 U.S. at 135-136.]

In Richardson v. Marsh, 481 U.S. 200 (1987), the Court considered a redacted confession. The case involved a joint murder trial of Marsh and Williams. The State had redacted the confession of one defendant, Williams, so as to "omit all reference" to his codefendant, Marsh — indeed, to omit all indication that anyone other than Williams and a third person had participated in the crime. The trial court also instructed the jury not to consider the confession against Marsh. As redacted, the confession indicated that Williams and the third person had discussed the murder in the front seat of a car while they traveled to the victim's house. The redacted confession contained no indication that Marsh — or any other person — was in the car. Later in the trial, however, Marsh testified that she was in the back seat of the car. For that reason, in context, the confession still could have helped convince the jury that Marsh knew about the murder in advance and therefore had participated knowingly in the crime.

The Court held that this redacted confession fell outside *Bruton*'s scope and was admissible (with appropriate limiting instructions) at the joint trial. The Court distinguished Evans' confession in *Bruton* as a confession that was "incriminating on its face," and which had "expressly implicat[ed]" *Bruton*. By contrast, Williams' confession amounted to "evidence requiring linkage" in that it became incriminating in respect to Marsh "only when linked with evidence introduced later at trial." The Court held that "the Confrontation Clause is not violated by the admission of a nontestifying codefendant's confession with a proper limiting instruction when, as here, the confession is redacted to eliminate not only the defendant's name, but any reference to his or her existence." The Court added: "We express no opinion on the admissibility of a confession in which the defendant's name has been replaced with a symbol or neutral pronoun."

Originally, the codefendant's confession in the case before us, like that in *Bruton*, referred to, and directly implicated another defendant. The State, however, redacted that confession by removing the nonconfessing defendant's name. Nonetheless, unlike *Richardson*'s redacted confession, this confession refers directly to the "existence" of the nonconfessing defendant. The State has simply replaced the nonconfessing defendant's name with a kind of symbol, namely the word "deleted" or a blank space set off by commas. The redacted confession, for example, responded to the question "Who was in the group that beat Stacey," with the phrase, "Me, _____, and a few other guys." And when the police witness read the confession in court, he said the word "deleted" or "deletion" where the blank spaces appear. . . .

Bruton, as interpreted by *Richardson*, holds that certain "powerfully incriminating extrajudicial statements of a codefendant" — those naming another defendant—considered as a class, are so prejudicial that limiting instructions cannot work. Unless the prosecutor wishes to hold separate trials or to use separate juries or to abandon use of the confession, he must redact the confession to reduce significantly or to eliminate the special prejudice that the *Bruton* Court found. Redactions that simply replace a name with an obvious blank space or a word such as "deleted" or a symbol or other similarly obvious indications of alteration, however, leave statements that, considered as a class, so closely resemble *Bruton*'s unredacted statements that, in our view, the law must require the same result.

For one thing, a jury will often react similarly to an unredacted confession and a confession redacted in this way, for the jury will often realize that the confession refers specifically to the defendant. This is true even when the State does not blatantly link the defendant to the deleted name, as it did in this case by asking whether Gray was arrested on the basis of information in Bell's confession as soon as the officer had finished reading the redacted statement. Consider a simplified but typical example, a confession that reads "I, Bob Smith, along with Sam Jones, robbed the bank." To replace the words "Sam Jones" with an obvious blank will not likely fool anyone. A juror somewhat familiar with criminal law would know immediately that the blank, in the phrase "I, Bob Smith, along with _____, robbed the bank," refers to defendant Jones. A juror who does not know the law and who therefore wonders to whom the blank might refer need only lift his eyes to Jones, sitting at counsel table, to find what will seem the obvious answer, at least if the juror hears the judge's instruction not to consider the confession as evidence against Jones, for that instruction will provide an obvious reason for the blank. A more sophisticated juror, wondering if the blank refers to someone else, might also wonder how, if it did, the prosecutor could argue the confession is reliable, for the prosecutor, after all, has been arguing that Jones, not someone else, helped Smith commit the crime. For another thing, the obvious deletion may well call the jurors' attention specially to the removed name. By encouraging the jury to speculate about the reference, the redaction may overemphasize the importance of the confession's accusation— once the jurors work out the reference. . . .

Finally, *Bruton*'s protected statements and statements redacted to leave a blank or some other similarly obvious alteration, function the same way grammatically. They are directly accusatory. Evans' statement in *Bruton* used a proper name to point explicitly to an accused defendant. And *Bruton* held that the "powerfully incriminating" effect of . . . an out-of-court accusation creates a special, and vital, need for cross-examination—a need that would be immediately obvious had the codefendant pointed directly to the defendant in the courtroom itself. The blank space in an obviously redacted confession also points directly to the defendant, and it accuses the defendant in a manner similar to Evans' use of Bruton's name or to a testifying codefendant's accusatory finger. By way of contrast, the factual statement at issue in *Richardson*—a statement about what others said in the front seat of a car—differs from directly accusatory evidence in this respect, for it does not point directly to a defendant at all.

We concede certain differences between *Bruton* and this case. A confession that uses a blank or the word "delete" (or, for that matter, a first name or a nickname) less obviously refers to the defendant than a confession that uses the defendant's full and proper name. Moreover, in some instances the person to whom the blank refers may not be clear: Although the follow-up question asked by the State in this case eliminated all doubt, the reference might not be transparent in other cases in which a confession, like the present confession, uses two (or more) blanks, even though only one other defendant appears at trial, and in which the trial indicates that there are more participants than the confession has named. . . . We also concede that the jury must use inference to connect the statement in this redacted confession with the defendant. But inference pure and simple cannot make the critical difference, for if it did, then *Richardson* would also place outside *Bruton*'s scope confessions that use shortened first names, nicknames, descriptions as unique as the "red-haired, bearded, one-eyed man-with-a-limp," and perhaps even full names of defendants who are always known by a nickname. This Court has assumed, however, that nicknames and specific descriptions fall inside, not outside, *Bruton*'s protection. . . .

That being so, *Richardson* must depend in significant part upon the kind of, not the simple fact of, inference. *Richardson*'s inferences involved statements that did not refer directly to the defendant himself and which became incriminating "only when linked with evidence introduced later at trial." The inferences at issue here involve statements that, despite redaction, obviously refer directly to someone, often obviously the defendant, and which involve inferences that a jury ordinarily could make immediately, even were the confession the very first item introduced at trial. Moreover, the redacted confession with the blank prominent on its face, in *Richardson*'s words, "facially incriminat[es]" the codefendant. . . .

Nor are the policy reasons that *Richardson* provided in support of its conclusion applicable here. *Richardson* expressed concern lest application of *Bruton*'s rule apply where "redaction" of confessions, particularly "confessions incriminating by connection," would often not be possible, thereby forcing prosecutors too often to abandon use either of the confession or of a joint trial. Additional redaction of a confession that uses a blank space, the word "delete," or a symbol, however, normally is possible. Consider as an example a portion of the confession before us: The witness who read the confession told the jury that the confession (among other things) said, "Question: Who was in the group that beat Stacey? Answer: Me, deleted, deleted, and a few other guys." Why could the witness not, instead, have said: "Question: Who was in the group that beat Stacey? Answer: Me and a few other guys." . . .

The *Richardson* Court also feared that the inclusion, within *Bruton*'s protective rule, of confessions that incriminated "by connection" too often would provoke mistrials, or would unnecessarily lead prosecutors to abandon the confession or joint trial, because neither the prosecutors nor the judge could easily predict, until after the introduction of all the evidence, whether or not *Bruton* had barred use of the confession. To include the use of blanks, the word "delete," symbols, or other indications of redaction, within *Bruton*'s protections, however, runs no such risk. Their use is easily identified prior to trial and does not depend, in any special way, upon the other evidence introduced in the case. . . .

For these reasons, we hold that the confession here at issue, which substituted blanks and the word "delete" for the respondent's proper name, falls within the class of statements to which *Bruton*'s protections apply. . . .

SCALIA, J., dissenting.

. . . The almost invariable assumption of the law is that jurors follow their instructions. This rule "is a pragmatic one, rooted less in the absolute certitude that the presumption is true than in the belief that it represents a reasonable practical accommodation of the interests of the state and the defendant in the criminal justice process." *Richardson*. . . . In *Bruton*, we recognized a "narrow exception" to this rule. . . .

We declined in *Richardson*, however, to extend *Bruton* to confessions that incriminate only by inference from other evidence. When incrimination is inferential, "it is a less valid generalization that the jury will not likely obey the instruction to disregard the evidence." Today the Court struggles to decide whether a confession redacted to omit the defendant's name is incriminating on its face or by inference. [T]he statement "Me, deleted, deleted, and a few other guys" does not facially incriminate anyone but the speaker. The Court's analogizing of "deleted" to a physical description that clearly identifies the defendant does not survive scrutiny. By "facially incriminating," we have meant incriminating independent of other evidence introduced at trial. Since the defendant's appearance at counsel table is not evidence, the description "red-haired, bearded, one-eyed man-with-a-limp" would be facially incriminating — unless, of course, the defendant had dyed his hair black and shaved his beard before trial, and the prosecution introduced evidence concerning his former appearance. . . . By contrast, the person to whom "deleted" refers in "Me, deleted, deleted, and a few other guys" is not apparent from anything the jury knows independent of the evidence at trial. Though the jury may speculate, the statement expressly implicates no one but the speaker.

Of course the Court is correct that confessions redacted to omit the defendant's name are more likely to incriminate than confessions redacted to omit any reference to his existence. But it is also true — and more relevant here — that confessions redacted to omit the defendant's name are less likely to incriminate than confessions that expressly state it. The latter are "powerfully incriminating" as a class; the former are not so. Here, for instance, there were two names deleted, five or more participants in the crime, and only one other defendant on trial. The jury no doubt may "speculate about the reference" as it speculates when evidence connects a defendant to a confession that does not refer to his existence. The issue, however, is not whether the confession incriminated petitioner, but whether the incrimination is so "powerful" that we must depart from the normal presumption that the jury follows its instructions. I think it is not — and I am certain that drawing the line for departing from the ordinary rule at the facial identification of the defendant makes more sense than drawing it anywhere else.

We explained in *Richardson* that forgoing use of codefendant confessions or joint trials was too high a price to insure that juries never disregard their instructions. The Court minimizes the damage that it does by suggesting that additional redaction of a confession that uses a blank space . . . normally is possible. In the present case, it asks, why could the police officer not have testified that Bell's answer was "Me and a few other guys"? The answer, it seems obvious to me, is because that is not what Bell said. Bell's answer was "Me, Tank, Kevin and a few other guys." Introducing the statement with full disclosure of deletions is one thing; introducing as the complete statement what was in fact only a part is something else. . . . The risk to the integrity of our system (not to mention the increase in its complexity) posed by the approval of such freelance editing seems to me infinitely greater than the risk posed by the entirely honest reproduction that the Court disapproves.

The United States Constitution guarantees, not a perfect system of criminal justice (as to which there can be considerable disagreement), but a minimum standard of fairness. Lest we lose sight of the forest for the trees, it should be borne in mind that federal and state rules of criminal procedure — which can afford to seek perfection because they can be more readily changed — exclude nontestifying-codefendant confessions even where the Sixth Amendment does not. Under the Federal Rules of Criminal Procedure (and Maryland's), a trial court may order separate trials if joinder will prejudice a defendant. . . . Federal and most state trial courts (including Maryland's) also have the discretion to exclude unfairly prejudicial (albeit probative) evidence. Fed. Rule Evid. 403; Md. Rule Evid. 5-403. Here, petitioner moved for a severance on the ground that the admission of Bell's confession would be unfairly prejudicial. The trial court denied the motion, explaining that where a confession names two others, and the evidence is that five or six others participated, redaction of petitioner's name would not leave the jury with the "unavoidable inference" that Bell implicated Gray.

I do not understand the Court to disagree that the redaction itself left unclear to whom the blank referred. That being so, the rule set forth in *Richardson* applies, and the statement could constitutionally be admitted with limiting instruction. . . .

Notes

1. *Hearsay exceptions and confrontation.* Rules of evidence in all jurisdictions exclude out-of-court hearsay statements (that is, statements made out of court by someone other than the witness, offered to prove the truth of the matter addressed in the statement) but then make exceptions to allow into evidence some of the more reliable statements. Before the Supreme Court decided *Crawford*, federal and state law allowed the government to use hearsay statements of a person who would not testify at trial so long as the evidence fell within a "firmly rooted" exception to the bar on hearsay. When no such exception was available, the confrontation clause prevented use of the evidence unless the judge found some "particularized guarantees of trustworthiness." Ohio v. Roberts, 448 U.S. 56 (1980). Did these cases reflect a practical judgment that cross-examination would not test the accuracy of evidence falling under one of the firmly rooted hearsay exceptions? See Lilly v. Virginia, 527 U.S. 116 (1999) (right to confrontation prevented prosecutors from using a statement made to police by an alleged accomplice who admitted some criminal activity but blamed the defendant for the most serious criminal acts; although the statement was against the speaker's penal interest, it was not "so trustworthy that adversarial testing can be expected to add little to [the statement's] reliability").

Does the older "reliability" test or *Crawford's* "testimonial" test better capture the modern-day meaning of the Sixth Amendment's text, embodying a right for a defendant "to be confronted with the witnesses against him"? In a world that relies so much on guilty pleas and so little on trials to adjudicate criminal cases, is the right to confront witnesses in the courtroom only one means to an end — reliable evidence to support a conviction?

2. *The role of timing and motives.* What sorts of prosecutions depend most heavily on "testimonial" statements and are thus most affected by *Crawford*? The timing of the statement is part of the equation, along with the purposes of the questioner. In Davis v. Washington, 126 S. Ct. 2266 (2006), the Supreme Court evaluated, under *Crawford*, statements made to police officers during an investigation. Statements made in the course of police interrogations are not "testimonial," and hence not subject to the Confrontation Clause, if they were

made under circumstances "objectively indicating" that the primary purpose of the interrogation was to enable police assistance to meet an "ongoing emergency." It is fair to assume that the motives of the police for obtaining witness statements, along with the witness's motives for providing the statements, are often mixed: they hope for immediate help to prevent an ongoing harm, and to collect evidence for prosecution of the alleged offender. Does this *Davis* test weaken the *Crawford* holding?

In domestic violence cases, the government traditionally introduces into evidence a recording of the alleged victim's emergency call to the police. This happens even when the victim does not testify at trial. Consider this description of the evidence in an Ohio prosecution against Jerry Lee for domestic violence:

> In the tape recording, the victim, Lee's wife Kathy, says that her husband stabbed her door, hit her, and tried to throw her out the door. When police officers arrived at the scene, two minutes after receiving a dispatch, the couple's eighteen-year-old son told them, "I think my father is killing my mother." Within five more minutes, Kathy made additional statements to one of the officers, including one that Jerry had tried to stab her. The trial court admitted all these statements. . . . Neither Kathy Lee nor the son testified, and the State made no attempt to account for their absence.

Richard D. Friedman & Bridget McCormack, Dial-in Testimony, 150 U. Pa. L. Rev. 1171, 1173-74 (2002). How would you prosecute such a case after *Crawford?* Will the Court's ruling in *Davis* change police investigative practices in domestic violence cases?

How will courts classify statements made by a child abuse complainant to a social worker or to medical staff facilitating a police investigation? See People v. Vigil, 127 P.3d 916 (Colo. 2006). How about crime scene statements made by an assault victim to a field officer? The victim's identification of the defendant from a photographic array? State v. Lewis, 619 S.E.2d 830 (N.C. 2005), vacated 126 S. Ct. 2983 (2006).

3. *Out-of-court statements by co-defendants: majority position.* A co-defendant who has confessed and implicated the defendant may be unavailable for testimony or cross-examination at trial because of the co-defendant's privilege against self-incrimination. In Bruton v. United States, 391 U.S. 123 (1968), the Court prevented the use of the co-defendant's statement in a joint jury trial, even if the judge cautions the jury to consider the confession as evidence only against the co-defendant. When the co-defendant takes the stand at trial (and is therefore available for cross-examination), or when the defendant has also confessed and offered enough similar details to make the two confessions "interlocking," the co-defendant's confession may come into evidence. Cruz v. New York, 481 U.S. 186 (1987) (similarities in interlocking confessions provide enough indicia of reliability to satisfy confrontation clause); Nelson v. O'Neil, 402 U.S. 622 (1971) (testimony of co-defendant). Virtually all state courts allow the government to introduce co-defendant confessions under circumstances such as these.

4. *Redacted statements.* The decision in Gray v. Maryland considered the types of redactions to a co-defendant confession that would make the statement admissible against the co-defendant in a joint trial. See also Commonwealth v. Travers, 768 A.2d 845 (Pa. 2001) (*Bruton* not violated by admission of nontestifying co-defendant confession redacted by replacement of the defendant's name with the phrase

"the other man"). Before the Supreme Court announced its decision in *Gray*, state courts divided on the question of whether to admit co-defendant confessions when the defendant's name is simply replaced with a neutral pronoun or a word such as "deleted." One group of courts (describing themselves as "facial incrimination" jurisdictions) concluded that replacement of the defendant's name in the confession is enough to prevent the jury from using the evidence improperly. The *Bruton* bar, they said, applies only to co-defendant confessions that facially incriminate the defendant by naming him or making some equivalent identification. Another group of courts (the "contextual" jurisdictions) looked to the other evidence in the case to determine the probability that the jury would use the other evidence to identify the defendant as the unnamed person mentioned in the co-defendant's confession. See Ex parte Sneed, 783 So. 2d 863 (Ala. 2000) (statement edited to cure *Bruton* problem was irreconcilably inconsistent with theory of defense); Jefferson v. State, 359 Ark. 454 (2004) (in a case involving a small cast of characters, replacing defendant's name in co-defendant's confession did not solve *Bruton* problem). Did the U.S. Supreme Court in *Gray* side with one of these groups of state courts, or did it create a new method of analysis?

Justice Scalia's dissent in *Gray* points out that joinder and severance rules give trial judges discretion to order separate trials for co-defendants if a joint trial would be prejudicial. Would the need to edit a co-defendant's confession convince you, as a trial judge, to adopt a strong presumption in favor of separate trials? Does the operation of the *Bruton* rule call for any changes in joinder and severance rules? See Judith L. Ritter, The X Files: Joint Trials, Redacted Confessions and Thirty Years of Sidestepping *Bruton*, 42 Vill. L. Rev. 855 (1997).

3. Unavailable Topics

Rules of evidence limit the sorts of inquiries a party may pursue at trial. Clearly this has an effect on the defendant's ability to confront and cross-examine prosecution witnesses. Perhaps the most striking of these rules are those that limit the questions the defense may ask about past and current criminal charges against the prosecution's witness. These evidentiary rules are based on the assumption that prior convictions or other wrongdoing could lead the jury to conclude too hastily that the witness is not credible. The following case explores the outer reach of such evidentiary limits on the power to cross-examine.

■ JOHNNY CARROLL v. STATE
916 S.W.2d 494 (Tex. Crim. App. 1996)

Baird, J.

Appellant was convicted of murder and sentenced to 30 years confinement. . . . We granted review to determine whether [a State's witness may] be cross-examined concerning pending criminal charges. We will reverse and remand.

The right of confrontation has ancient roots. Over 2,000 years ago the Roman Governor Porcius Festus reported to King Agrippa: "It is not the manner of the Romans to deliver any man up to die before the accused has met his accusers face to face, and has been given a chance to defend himself against the charges." The right of confrontation was also recognized in English common law. Initially, the right of the accused to confront witnesses was recognized in trials for treason. Arguably, the most notorious treason trial in England was that of the Sir Walter Raleigh, accused of conspiring to overthrow the King of England. Raleigh was charged with treason after a third party, Cobham, confessed under torture, to conspiring with Raleigh. At trial, Raleigh was denied the opportunity to confront Cobham and Cobham's statement was used to convict and ultimately execute Raleigh. . . .

Cross-examination serves three general purposes: cross-examination may serve to identify the witness with his community so that independent testimony may be sought and offered concerning the witness' reputation for veracity in that community; cross-examination allows the jury to assess the credibility of the witness; and, cross-examination allows facts to be brought out tending to discredit the witness by showing that his testimony in chief was untrue or biased. Alford v. United States, 282 U.S. 687 (1931). Cross-examination is by nature exploratory and there is no general requirement that the defendant indicate the purpose of his inquiry. Indeed, the defendant should be granted a wide latitude even though he is unable to state what facts he expects to prove through his cross-examination.

The Constitutional right of confrontation is violated when appropriate cross-examination is limited. The scope of appropriate cross-examination is necessarily broad. A defendant is entitled to pursue all avenues of cross-examination reasonably calculated to expose a motive, bias or interest for the witness to testify. . . . This broad scope necessarily includes cross-examination concerning criminal charges pending against a witness and over which those in need of the witness' testimony might be empowered to exercise control. A witness' pecuniary interest in the outcome of the trial is also an appropriate area of cross-examination.

Nevertheless, there are several areas where cross-examination may be inappropriate and, in those situations the trial judge has the discretion to limit cross-examination. Specifically, a trial judge may limit cross-examination when a subject is exhausted, or when the cross-examination is designed to annoy, harass, or humiliate, or when the cross-examination might endanger the personal safety of the witness. See generally Delaware v. Van Arsdall, 475 U.S. 673 (trial judge may exercise discretion to prevent harassment, prejudice, confusion of the issues, the witness' safety, and repetitive or marginally relevant interrogation.); Tex. R. Crim. Evid. 608, 609, 404 and 405.

In the instant case, the State presented two witnesses who testified they were present at the time of the murder. Charles Fitzgerald testified he and the victim were at a bar when they saw appellant. Appellant showed Fitzgerald a pistol and shortly thereafter got into an argument with the victim. Fitzgerald and the victim moved to a table and appellant followed. Appellant shot the victim with the pistol, and continued shooting as the victim moved toward the back of the bar. Although Fitzgerald testified he only consumed two beers, the officers who interviewed him the night of the murder testified Fitzgerald was intoxicated. Appellant impeached Fitzgerald's testimony with proof of his intoxication at the time of the killing.

Herman Russell testified appellant and the victim argued over a mutual girlfriend. When the victim indicated the girlfriend had moved in with him, appellant pulled a pistol and told the victim he should not talk to the girl. Appellant then put the pistol into his waistband and Russell went to a back room. In less than a minute

Russell heard a gunshot and saw the victim running while holding his arm. Russell testified appellant continued to shoot the victim.[7]

Appellant sought to impeach Russell's testimony with evidence that Russell was currently incarcerated and awaiting trial on an aggravated robbery charge and that he had several prior felony convictions. The State asked the trial judge to prohibit appellant from conducting such cross-examination, contending such evidence was not relevant. Appellant contended Russell's testimony had a potential for bias because Russell's testimony in the instant case might favorably affect the outcome in the aggravated robbery case. Appellant further contended Russell's previous convictions could be used to enhance the felony charge, thus increasing the punishment range and creating a greater likelihood for bias. The trial judge agreed with the State and prohibited the testimony. The Court of Appeals affirmed, holding that Tex. R. Crim. Evid. 608(b) specifically prohibited the use of the pending aggravated robbery charge for impeachment.[9]

There exists a long line of federal and state authority holding a pending criminal charge is an appropriate area of cross-examination. Davis v. Alaska, 415 U.S. 308 (1974); Carmona v. State, 698 S.W.2d 100 (Tex. Crim. App. 1985). Indeed, the instant situation differs little from that confronted by the Supreme Court in Alford v. United States, 282 U.S. 687 (1931), where a prosecution witness testified to Alford's actions and incriminating statements. On cross-examination, Alford sought to elicit testimony that the witness was in federal custody "for the purpose of showing whatever bias or prejudice he may have." However, the trial judge refused to allow such evidence because it was not based upon a final conviction.

The Supreme Court reversed, holding cross-examination is a matter of right. Although the extent of cross-examination is subject to the sound discretion of the trial judge, the trial judge abuses that discretion when he prevents appropriate cross-examination. And inquiry into a witness' potential bias arising from incarceration was appropriate. Indeed, the Supreme Court held Alford should have been allowed to cross-examine the witness to demonstrate the "testimony was biased because given under a promise or expectation of immunity, or under the coercive effect of his detention by officers [who were] conducting the present prosecution." . . .

In Harris v. State, 642 S.W.2d 471 (Tex. Crim. App. 1982), the defendant sought to question the State's witness concerning her pending juvenile charges. The trial judge sustained the State's objections to such cross-examination. On appeal the defendant contended he was entitled to cross-examine the witness concerning any probable bias or interest in her testimony. [W]e reversed stating the defendant "had an unqualified right to ask . . . the only witness linking him with the offense, whether she too had been 'accused' of the offense on trial, and to receive her answer. . . ." The jury was entitled to the "whole picture" in order to evaluate and judge the witness' credibility.

Alford and *Harris* control our resolution of the instant case. Appellant's cross-examination was clearly an attempt to demonstrate that Russell held a possible motive, bias or interest in testifying for the State. Appellant's inquiry into Russell's

---

7. [Carroll] testified he did not display his weapon. Instead, he and the victim were discussing the mutual girlfriend when the victim used profanity and reached into his pants as if to retrieve a weapon. Appellant shot the victim because the girlfriend had informed him that the victim "had something that would take care of [him]."

9. Tex. R. Crim. Evid. 608(b) provides: "Specific instances of the conduct of a witness, for the purpose of attacking or supporting his credibility, other than conviction of crime as provided in Rule 609, may not be inquired into on cross-examination of the witness nor proved by extrinsic evidence."

incarceration, his pending charge and possible punishment as a habitual criminal, was appropriate to demonstrate Russell's potential motive, bias or interest to testify for the State. A defendant is permitted to elicit any fact from a witness intended to demonstrate that witness' vulnerable relationship with the state.

The State contends appellant's cross-examination was impermissible because no agreement existed between the State and Russell which might affect Russell's motive to testify for the State. However, the existence of such an agreement is not determinative. [It] is possible, even absent an agreement, that Russell believed his testimony in this case would be of later benefit. . . .

Finally, the Court of Appeals' holding that appellant was unable to impeach Russell under Rule 608(b) is erroneous for at least two reasons. First, appellant's cross-examination concerning Russell's incarceration was not an inquiry into a specific instance of conduct. Instead, appellant's cross-examination focused on Russell's possible motive, bias or interest in testifying for the State. To understand this distinction we draw upon . . . Ramirez v. State, 802 S.W.2d 674 (Tex. Crim. App. 1990), which involved the interpretation and application of Rule 608(b). In *Ramirez*, the mother of an eight-year-old victim testified she did not believe appellant sexually assaulted the victim. The State cross-examined the mother regarding her prior use of heroin suggesting that, at the time of the offense, she was under its influence and unaware of what happened to her child. The State offered no evidence to show the mother either previously used heroin, or was under its influence at the time of the incident. Relying on Rule 608(b), we held the State was improperly allowed to question the mother about a specific instance of conduct.

In the instant case the Court of Appeals improperly relied upon Rule 608(b) because appellant . . . did not seek to cross-examine Russell about the underlying facts which gave rise to the aggravated robbery charge. Rather, appellant attempted to inform the jury that Russell had a vulnerable relationship with the State at the time of his testimony. . . . Consequently, the Court of Appeals erred in relying on Rule 608(b) to uphold the trial judge's limitation on appellant's cross-examination of Russell.

Second, although we see no conflict between the right to cross-examine a witness about a pending charge and Rule 608(b), if such a conflict existed, the constitutional right of confrontation would prevail. . . . Accordingly, the judgment of the Court of Appeals is reversed and the case is remanded to that Court. . . .

MEYERS, J., concurring.

In this case the charges pending against the State's witness originated in the same jurisdiction and were brought by the identical authorities as those for which the appellant stands accused. I therefore agree with the decision of our lead opinion to allow the defendant to use these charges for impeachment on cross-examination of this witness. However, in future contexts, should these charges emanate from another jurisdiction or authority, I would hold that release of the information to the jury is subject to a discretionary ruling of the trial court under Rule 403 of the Texas Rules of Criminal Evidence. With these additional comments, I join the opinion of the Court.

MANSFIELD, J., dissenting.

The State presented two witnesses who testified they were in the bar at the time the murder was committed. Charles Fitzgerald testified appellant showed him a pistol and observed him arguing with Robert Brzowski, the victim. Fitzgerald testified further appellant followed him and Mr. Brzowski to another table, shot Mr. Brzowski with the pistol and continued shooting at Mr. Brzowski as he fled toward the back of the bar. Appellant introduced evidence, including the testimony of two police officers who interviewed Fitzgerald after the shooting, that Fitzgerald was intoxicated at the time of the shooting.

The second witness, Herman Russell, the bartender, testified and gave essentially the same version of what occurred as Fitzgerald. Russell testified appellant and Mr. Brzowski argued over a mutual female acquaintance and things went down hill from there, concluding with appellant shooting and killing Mr. Brzowski.

At trial, appellant sought to impeach Russell with evidence of prior felony convictions, i.e., two convictions for cattle theft from 1962 and 1965. Though conceding Texas Rule of Criminal Evidence 609(b)* would ordinarily bar use of the convictions for impeachment as the convictions were too remote (over ten years old), appellant claimed they were relevant as they could be used to enhance punishment if Russell were convicted of his pending charge. Additionally, appellant sought to impeach Russell with evidence of a pending aggravated robbery charge and that he was currently incarcerated awaiting trial on that charge. Appellant alleged Russell was potentially biased because his testimony in the present case might affect the outcome in his pending aggravated robbery case, and he was entitled to show the jury Russell's testimony might be influenced by the charge pending against him.

At the hearing, Russell testified there had been no deals made with the State concerning the pending aggravated robbery charge in relation to his testimony in the present case. He testified he had already given a statement regarding the present case (the killing occurred on April 11, 1992) prior to being arrested on the aggravated robbery charge (the robbery allegedly was committed in 1988). Finally, he testified his testimony in the present case would not be affected by the case pending against him, which was scheduled to be prosecuted in a different court. The trial court denied appellant's motion, and Russell testified without being impeached by evidence of his prior convictions or of the pending aggravated robbery charge. . . .

Texas Criminal Evidence Rule 608(b) does not allow a witness to be impeached, for purposes of attacking his credibility, by proof of specific instances of conduct, other than conviction of crimes as provided by Rule 609, either on cross-examination or by extrinsic evidence. . . . Rule 608(b) is much more restrictive as to impeachment of witnesses by instances of conduct other than convictions than its federal counterpart. . . .

Appellant cites Davis v. Alaska, 415 U.S. 308 (1974), in support of his claim that the Confrontation Clause of the U.S. Constitution requires that he be permitted to show any fact, including a pending charge, which would tend to establish bias or motive of a witness (i.e. Russell) testifying against him. The majority, I respectfully assert, reads Davis in a too-broad manner. In Davis, counsel for petitioner was denied the opportunity to cross-examine a State's witness as to his status as a probationer, which counsel alleged would tend to show possible motive or bias on the part of the witness. The Supreme Court held "petitioner was thus denied the right of

---

*Rule 609 enables the court to admit into evidence the prior conviction of a witness for impeachment purposes, if the crime was a felony or involved moral turpitude and the court determines that the probative value of admitting this evidence outweighs its prejudicial effect. Evidence of a conviction is not admissible if more than 10 years have elapsed since the date of conviction or release from prison, whichever is later. — EDS.

effective cross-examination which would be constitutional error of the first magnitude and no amount of showing or want of prejudice would cure it."

The present case differs markedly from the facts of *Davis*. First, the witness in *Davis* was on probation resulting from a recent adjudication of delinquency in a juvenile court and likely could have been impeached with that adjudication under Rule 609(d) had this been a Texas case. Second, unlike in *Davis*, appellant in the present case had available to him, under Rule 612, for impeachment purposes, Russell's statement taken at the time of the killing and before he was arrested on the aggravated robbery charge. Third, in the present case, a hearing was held at which the witness (Russell) testified that he would testify truthfully, he would not be affected by his pending charge as to his testimony and no "deal" had been made with the State concerning his testimony. No such examination of the witness (Green) for bias or motive took place in *Davis*. Fourth, a juvenile adjudication is a final determination by a court and is analogous to a conviction. In the present case the witness had merely been charged with a crime and had not been even tried, much less been convicted. Given these differences, appellant's right to an effective cross-examination was not denied.

There is little doubt — notwithstanding Rule 608(b) — *Davis* mandates that a criminal defendant be permitted to impeach a State witness on cross-examination with evidence of a pending charge against the witness where a deal concerning the witness' testimony with the State existed or was under discussion. Similarly, *Davis* would be implicated where, unlike in the present case, the defendant had no other reasonable means to impeach the witness (e.g. by a prior statement if inconsistent with his testimony) or had not been afforded a hearing by the court at which he could support his claim of bias or motive of the witness which could be shown only by allowing him to cross-examine the witness — before the jury — as to a pending charge. . . . I respectfully dissent.

KELLER, J., dissenting.

. . . Under the majority's analysis the failure to allow cross-examination regarding a pending charge is always error. I agree that, ordinarily, the mere existence of a pending charge gives rise to an inference that the witness may have been influenced. But in some cases, additional facts in the record may show that such an inference is not warranted. . . . When a witness' testimony corresponds with his statement given prior to the point at which the motive for bias arose, and the defendant does not otherwise show that the pending charge may have influenced the witness' testimony at trial, I believe that it is not an abuse of discretion to disallow cross-examination regarding an unrelated pending criminal charge that is alleged to be the motive for bias. Such are the facts in this case. Accordingly, I dissent.

Problem 8-6. Evidence Off Limits

James Egelhoff spent an evening drinking with two friends. Some time after 9 P.M., Egelhoff and his friends left a party in a station wagon. Egelhoff bought beer at 9:20 P.M.. At about midnight, the sheriff's department received reports of a possible drunken driver. The deputies who responded to the call discovered the station wagon stuck in a ditch along a U.S. highway. In the front seat were Egelhoff's two friends, each dead from a single gunshot to the head. Egelhoff lay in the rear of the station wagon, yelling obscenities. His blood-alcohol level measured .36, more than one hour later. On the floor of the car, near the brake pedal, lay Egelhoff's .38 caliber handgun, with four loaded rounds and two empty casings. He had gunshot residue on his hands.

At his trial for deliberate homicide, Egelhoff testified that his intoxication made it impossible for him to commit the crime. Although he remembered "sitting on a hill passing a bottle of Black Velvet back and forth" with his friends, he recalled nothing further because of his extreme intoxication. Because he was physically incapable of carrying out the killing and could not remember the events of the evening, Egelhoff concluded that some fourth party had killed his friends.

Deliberate homicide, under state law, occurs when a person "purposely" or "knowingly" causes the death of another human being. Although the trial court allowed Egelhoff to testify about his intoxication, the judge also instructed the jury, consistent with a state statute, that it could not consider Egelhoff's "intoxicated condition in determining the existence of a mental state which is an element of the offense." The jury found Egelhoff guilty as charged.

The defendant argues on appeal that the state statute violated his due process right to present to the jury all relevant evidence to rebut the state's evidence on all elements of the offense charged. Evidence of his intoxication was relevant to deciding whether he had killed the victims "knowingly" or "purposely." The exclusion of this evidence, he says, lessened the government's burden of proof in establishing the mens rea for the crime. How would you rule on the defendant's appeal? Compare Montana v. Egelhoff, 518 U.S. 37 (1996).

Notes

1. *Cross-examination about pending charges: majority position.* As mentioned earlier, rules of evidence control the scope of questions that can be asked during cross-examination. For instance, the rules restrict the cross-examining lawyer to questions related to the subjects covered during direct examination. They also limit questions about prior convictions or pending criminal charges against the witness. However, the constitutional right to confrontation sometimes allows a defendant to go beyond these usual restrictions on cross-examination to ask questions that the prosecuting attorney could not ask. In Delaware v. Van Arsdall, 475 U.S. 673 (1986), the Court held that a defendant's rights secured by the confrontation clause were violated when the trial court prohibited "all inquiry" into the possibility that a witness would be biased after agreeing to testify in exchange for favorable treatment in a different criminal matter. The Court noted that the witness's agreement about the pending charges could show a "prototypical form of bias." The jury "might have received a significantly different impression" of the witness's credibility if defense counsel had been permitted to pursue the proposed line of cross-examination. See also Davis v. Alaska, 415 U.S. 308 (1974) (refusal to allow defendant to cross-examine key prosecution witness to show his probation status for juvenile offense denied defendant his constitutional right to confront witnesses, notwithstanding state policy protecting anonymity of juvenile offenders).

State courts have also concluded that their constitutions allow defendants to pursue lines of cross-examination that the rules of evidence would not allow for other litigants. About 30 states have endorsed the federal position. Like the

Supreme Court in *Van Arsdall,* these courts ask if the proposed questions would explore a "prototypical form of bias." They most often conclude that defense counsel may ask questions about criminal charges pending against the witness. See State v. Mizzell, 563 S.E.2d 315 (S.C. 2002) (trial court violated confrontation rights by forbidding defense counsel to elicit from prosecution witness, charged with same crime as defendant "Tootie" Mizzell, the punishment he could receive if convicted). However, state courts will sometimes uphold a trial court that restricts defense cross-examination on this subject, if the witness asserts that she expects no benefit to flow from testifying. See Marshall v. State, 695 A.2d 184 (Md. 1997). Can an appellate court develop sound rules on this question, or is the issue better left to the discretion of the trial court?

2. *Prior criminal record of prosecution witnesses.* On topics of cross-examination other than pending criminal charges against the witness, trial courts tend to have more discretion to limit cross-examination. This is true, for instance, when defense counsel tries to explore the prior criminal record of prosecution witnesses. Although trial judges often allow at least some cross-examination on this subject, appellate courts uphold most efforts to limit questioning on the topic. Many state courts conclude that the prior convictions of a witness do not demonstrate a "prototypical form" of bias against the defendant, but are simply a generalized attack on the witness's credibility that might confuse the jury. Trial judges can impose reasonable limits on cross-examination to guard against harassment, prejudice, confusion of the issues, or waste of time. See State v. Lanz-Terry, 535 N.W.2d 635 (Minn. 1995). Why do courts treat prior convictions differently from pending criminal charges against a prosecution witness?

3. *Ethics of cross-examination.* Sometimes a judge's evidentiary ruling arrives too late. An attorney's leading question on cross-examination might suggest an answer to the jury, even if the witness never has to answer the question. In response to this problem, rules of legal ethics typically instruct attorneys not to ask a question on cross-examination if there is no reasonable factual basis for the question. See ABA Model Rule of Professional Conduct 3.4(e) (lawyer at trial shall not "allude to any matter that the lawyer does not reasonably believe is relevant or that will not be supported by admissible evidence"). If you were a staff attorney working within the disciplinary body of the state bar, how would you expect to enforce this rule?

4. *Limits on defense evidence.* Our discussion has focused on the defendant's power to "confront" adverse witnesses and test the prosecution's case, mostly through cross-examination of witnesses. Defendants will also answer the prosecution's case by presenting their own evidence. As with cross-examination, a range of legal rules can restrict the evidence a defendant might present. Rules of evidence require generally that any evidence be relevant to an issue in controversy and that its probative value outweigh its prejudicial impact. See Fed. R. Evid. 403 ("Although relevant, evidence may be excluded if its probative value is substantially outweighed by the danger of unfair prejudice, confusion of the issues, or misleading the jury, or by considerations of undue delay, waste of time, or needless presentation of cumulative evidence"). States sometimes enact rules or statutes for a particular subject matter that defendants might try to raise at trial. For instance, most jurisdictions have "rape shield" laws, which limit the power of a defendant in a sexual assault case from inquiring into certain aspects of the sexual history of the victim of the alleged crime.

Statutes and rules of evidence in some jurisdictions also limit the defendant's ability to introduce evidence of voluntary intoxication. In Montana v. Egelhoff,

518 U.S. 37 (1996), the basis for Problem 8-6 above, the Court upheld the constitutionality of a statute that precluded the jury from considering evidence of intoxication when it determined whether the defendant had the mens rea to commit the crime. The Court indicated that 10 states had enacted similar statutes or rules; since the *Egelhoff* decision appeared, the number has grown. The statute in *Egelhoff* appears to place a new type of limit on defense efforts to present evidence. The Montana legislature did not justify its rule by arguing that intoxication evidence is unreliable, cumulative, privileged, or irrelevant. The state instead adopted the rule to deter irresponsible behavior, to incapacitate those who cannot control violent impulses while drunk, and to express society's moral judgment that persons who voluntarily become intoxicated should remain responsible for their actions. After *Egelhoff*, is there any legal or practical limit on the legislature's power to prevent the defendant from presenting evidence that many juries might find convincing? See Holmes v. South Carolina, 126 S. Ct. 1727 (2006) (defendant's federal constitutional rights violated by an evidence rule precluding defense from introducing proof that third party committed the crime charged, even if the prosecution has introduced forensic evidence that strongly supports a guilty verdict against the defendant); Clark v. Arizona, 126 S. Ct. 2709 (2006) (upholding state statute limiting defense uses of evidence of defendant's mental illness; statute required defendant to assert affirmative defense of insanity rather than using evidence of paranoid schizophrenia to deny specific intent to shoot a police officer).

5. *Commentary on evidence.* Although judges constantly evaluate evidence and rule on its admissibility, many states have constitutional or statutory provisions that prohibit the judge from "commenting" on the evidence or the credibility of witnesses. See Wash. Const. art. IV, §16; Ga. Code §17-8-57. There is, however, no federal constitutional bar to judicial commentary on evidence, and some states do not impose such a bar. See Quercia v. United States, 289 U.S. 466 (1933) (no error for judge to comment on evidence so long as the comment does not "excite [in the jury] a prejudice which would preclude a fair and dispassionate consideration of the evidence"; court here committed error by saying that witness displayed mannerisms of a person who is lying).

C. SELF-INCRIMINATION PRIVILEGE AT TRIAL

Once the prosecution has presented its case in chief, the defendant may present evidence as well. The central strategic question for the defendant at this point is whether to testify. While the defendant might present testimony from other witnesses, that evidence is not likely to carry the same weight as a defendant's personal denial of the crime and personal explanation of the prosecution's key evidence. At the same time, a defendant might not feel capable of making a convincing denial at trial, because of nervousness, concern about charges of perjury, or for some other reason.

In the United States, as in most Western legal systems, the law allows the defendant alone to choose whether to testify at trial. The privilege against self-incrimination allows the defendant to refuse to cooperate during certain phases of an investigation, but the privilege provides the clearest protections during a criminal trial. Professor John Langbein has traced the origins of the privilege to the emergence in the eighteenth century of adversary criminal procedure and a prominent role for defense counsel who could speak for the defendant and challenge the government's evidence. See John Langbein, The Historical Origins of the Privilege Against Self-Incrimination at Common Law, 92 Mich. L. Rev. 1047 (1994).

Because of the privilege against self-incrimination, a criminal defendant may refuse to cooperate in some investigative efforts and may refuse to testify at trial. Is there any price for such refusals? As a practical matter, some disadvantages do flow from invoking the privilege. A jury or judge might infer from a defendant's silence that she is guilty or at least that she has no answer to the government's evidence. But can the prosecutor urge the factfinder to draw such inferences? Should the judge do or say anything to prevent the jury from drawing such conclusions? The *Griffin* case reprinted below announced the bright-line constitutional rule that all American courts follow on this question; the following *Murray* opinion from the European Court of Human Rights describes a position encountered in other Western legal systems.

■ EDDIE DEAN GRIFFIN v. CALIFORNIA
380 U.S. 609 (1965)

Douglas, J.

Petitioner was convicted of murder in the first degree after a jury trial in a California court. He did not testify at the trial on the issue of guilt, though he did testify at the separate trial on the issue of penalty. The trial court instructed the jury on the issue of guilt, stating that a defendant has a constitutional right not to testify. But it told the jury:

> As to any evidence or facts against him which the defendant can reasonably be expected to deny or explain because of facts within his knowledge, if he does not testify or if, though he does testify, he fails to deny or explain such evidence, the jury may take that failure into consideration as tending to indicate the truth of such evidence and as indicating that among the inferences that may be reasonably drawn therefrom those unfavorable to the defendant are the more probable.

It added, however, that no such inference could be drawn as to evidence respecting which he had no knowledge. It stated that failure of a defendant to deny or explain the evidence of which he had knowledge does not create a presumption of guilt nor by itself warrant an inference of guilt nor relieve the prosecution of any of its burden of proof.

Petitioner had been seen with the deceased the evening of her death, the evidence placing him with her in the alley where her body was found. The prosecutor made much of the failure of petitioner to testify:

> The defendant certainly knows whether Essie Mae had this beat up appearance at the time he left her apartment and went down the alley with her. . . . He would know that. He would know how she got down the alley. He would know how the blood got on the bottom of the concrete steps. He would know how long he was with her in that box. He would know how her wig got off. He would know whether he beat her or mistreated her. He would know whether he walked away from that place cool as a cucumber when he saw Mr. Villasenor because he was conscious of his own guilt and wanted to get away from that damaged or injured woman. These things he has not seen fit

to take the stand and deny or explain. And in the whole world, if anybody would know, this defendant would know. Essie Mae is dead, she can't tell you her side of the story. The defendant won't.

The death penalty was imposed and the California Supreme Court affirmed. The case is here on a writ of certiorari which we granted to consider whether comment on the failure to testify violated the Self-Incrimination Clause of the Fifth Amendment which we made applicable to the States by the Fourteenth in Malloy v. Hogan, 378 U.S. 1 (1964). . . . [3]

If this were a federal trial, reversible error would have been committed. Wilson v. United States, 149 U.S. 60 (1893), so holds. It is said, however, that the *Wilson* decision rested not on the Fifth Amendment, but on an Act of Congress, now 18 U.S.C. §3481.[4] That indeed is the fact. . . . But that is the beginning, not the end, of our inquiry. The question remains whether, statute or not, the comment rule, approved by California, violates the Fifth Amendment.

We think it does. It is in substance a rule of evidence that allows the State the privilege of tendering to the jury for its consideration the failure of the accused to testify. No formal offer of proof is made as in other situations; but the prosecutor's comment and the court's acquiescence are the equivalent of an offer of evidence and its acceptance. The Court in the *Wilson* case stated:

> . . . It is not every one who can safely venture on the witness stand though entirely innocent of the charge against him. Excessive timidity, nervousness when facing others and attempting to explain transactions of a suspicious character, and offences charged against him, will often confuse and embarrass him to such a degree as to increase rather than remove prejudices against him. It is not every one, however honest, who would, therefore, willingly be placed on the witness stand. The statute, in tenderness to the weakness of those who . . . may have been in some degree compromised by their association with others, declares that the failure of the defendant in a criminal action to request to be a witness shall not create any presumption against him.

[C]omment on the refusal to testify is a remnant of the inquisitorial system of criminal justice, which the Fifth Amendment outlaws. It is a penalty imposed by courts for exercising a constitutional privilege. It cuts down on the privilege by making its assertion costly. It is said, however, that the inference of guilt for failure to testify as to facts peculiarly within the accused's knowledge is in any event natural and irresistible, and that comment on the failure does not magnify that inference into a penalty for asserting a constitutional privilege. What the jury may infer, given no help from the court, is one thing. What it may infer when the court solemnizes the silence of the accused into evidence against him is quite another. [We] hold that the Fifth Amendment, in its direct application to the Federal Government, and in its bearing on the States by reason of the Fourteenth Amendment, forbids either comment by the prosecution on the accused's silence or instructions by the court that such silence is evidence of guilt. Reversed.

3. [Most states do not allow] comment on the defendant's failure to testify. The legislatures or courts of 44 States have recognized that such comment is, in light of the privilege against self-incrimination, "an unwarrantable line of argument."

4. Section 3481 reads as follows: "In [a federal criminal trial] the person charged shall, at his own request, be a competent witness. His failure to make such request shall not create any presumption against him."

STEWART, J., dissenting.

... Article I, §13, of the California Constitution establishes a defendant's privilege against self-incrimination and further provides: "... whether the defendant testifies or not, his failure to explain or to deny by his testimony any evidence or facts in the case against him may be commented upon by the court and by counsel, and may be considered by the court or the jury." In conformity with this provision, the prosecutor in his argument to the jury emphasized that a person accused of crime in a public forum would ordinarily deny or explain the evidence against him if he truthfully could do so. Also in conformity with this California constitutional provision, the judge instructed the jury [that they could draw a negative inference from the defendant's failure to deny to explain evidence or facts if he had the knowledge to make such an explanation].

We must determine whether the petitioner has been "compelled ... to be a witness against himself." Compulsion is the focus of the inquiry. Certainly, if any compulsion be detected in the California procedure, it is of a dramatically different and less palpable nature than that involved in the procedures which historically gave rise to the Fifth Amendment guarantee. When a suspect was brought before the Court of High Commission or the Star Chamber, he was commanded to answer whatever was asked of him, and subjected to a far-reaching and deeply probing inquiry in an effort to ferret out some unknown and frequently unsuspected crime. He declined to answer on pain of incarceration, banishment, or mutilation. And if he spoke falsely, he was subject to further punishment. Faced with this formidable array of alternatives, his decision to speak was unquestionably coerced.

Those were the lurid realities which lay behind enactment of the Fifth Amendment, a far cry from the subject matter of the case before us. I think that the Court in this case stretches the concept of compulsion beyond all reasonable bounds, and that whatever compulsion may exist derives from the defendant's choice not to testify, not from any comment by court or counsel. ...

It is not at all apparent to me, on any realistic view of the trial process, that a defendant will be at more of a disadvantage under the California practice than he would be in a court which permitted no comment at all on his failure to take the witness stand. How can it be said that the inferences drawn by a jury will be more detrimental to a defendant under the limiting and carefully controlling language of the instruction here involved than would result if the jury were left to roam at large with only its untutored instincts to guide it, to draw from the defendant's silence broad inferences of guilt? The instructions in this case expressly cautioned the jury that the defendant's failure to testify "does not create a presumption of guilt or by itself warrant an inference of guilt"; it was further admonished that such failure does not "relieve the prosecution of its burden of proving every essential element of the crime." ...

I think the California comment rule is not a coercive device which impairs the right against self-incrimination, but rather a means of articulating and bringing into the light of rational discussion a fact inescapably impressed on the jury's consciousness. The California procedure is not only designed to protect the defendant against unwarranted inferences which might be drawn by an uninformed jury; it is also an attempt by the State to recognize and articulate what it believes to be the natural probative force of certain facts. ...

No constitution can prevent the operation of the human mind. Without limiting instructions, the danger exists that the inferences drawn by the jury may be unfairly broad. Some States have permitted this danger to go unchecked, by forbidding any comment at all upon the defendant's failure to take the witness stand. Other States have dealt with this danger in a variety of ways, as the Court's opinion indicates. Some might differ, as a matter of policy, with the way California has chosen to deal with the problem, or even disapprove of the judge's specific instructions in this case. But, so long as the constitutional command is obeyed, such matters of state policy are not for this Court to decide. I would affirm the judgment.

■ **KEVIN SEAN MURRAY v. UNITED KINGDOM**
  22 Eur. Ct. H.R. 29 (1996)

    . . . The applicant was arrested by police officers at 17.40 on 7 January 1990. . . . Pursuant to Article 3 of the Criminal Evidence (Northern Ireland) Order 1988, he was cautioned by the police in the following terms:

> You do not have to say anything unless you wish to do so but I must warn you that if you fail to mention any fact which you rely on in your defence in court, your failure to take this opportunity to mention it may be treated in court as supporting any relevant evidence against you. If you do wish to say anything, what you say may be given in evidence.

In response to the police caution the applicant stated that he had nothing to say. . . .

    13. At 21.27 on 7 January a police constable cautioned the applicant pursuant to Article 6 of the Order, inter alia, requesting him to account for his presence at the house where he was arrested. He was warned that if he failed or refused to do so, a court, judge or jury might draw such inference from his failure or refusal as appears proper. He was also served with a written copy of Article 6 of the Order. In reply to this caution the applicant stated: "nothing to say." . . .

    15. The applicant was interviewed by police detectives at Castlereagh Police Office on 12 occasions during 8 and 9 January. In total he was interviewed for 21 hours and 39 minutes. At the commencement of these interviews he was either cautioned pursuant to Article 3 of the Order or reminded of the terms of the caution.

    16. During the first 10 interviews on 8 and 9 January the applicant made no reply to any questions put to him. He was able to see his solicitor for the first time at 18.33 on 9 January. At 19.10 he was interviewed again and reminded of the Article 3 caution. He replied: "I have been advised by my solicitor not to answer any of your questions." A final interview, during which the applicant said nothing, took place between 21.40 and 23.45 on 9 January. His solicitor was not permitted to be present at any of these interviews.

    17. In May 1991 the applicant was tried by a single judge, the Lord Chief Justice of Northern Ireland, sitting without a jury, for the offences of conspiracy to murder, the unlawful imprisonment, with seven other people, of a certain Mr. L and of belonging to a proscribed organisation, the Provisional Irish Republican Army (IRA).

    18. According to the Crown, Mr. L had been a member of the IRA who had been providing information about their activities to the Royal Ulster Constabulary. On

discovering that Mr. L was an informer, the IRA tricked him into visiting a house in Belfast on 5 January 1990. He was falsely imprisoned in one of the rear bedrooms of the house and interrogated by the IRA until the arrival of the police and the army at the house on 7 January 1990. It was also alleged by the Crown that there was a conspiracy to murder Mr. L as punishment for being a police informer.

19. In the course of the trial, evidence was given that when the police entered the house on 7 January the applicant was seen by a police constable coming down a flight of stairs wearing a raincoat over his clothes and was arrested in the hall of the house. Mr. L testified that he was forced under threat of being killed to make a taped confession to his captors that he was an informer. He further said that on the evening of 7 January he had heard scurrying and had been told to take off his blindfold. . . . The applicant had told him that the police were at the door and to go downstairs and watch television. While he was talking to him the applicant was pulling tape out of a cassette. On a search of the house by the police . . . a tangled tape was discovered in the upstairs bedroom. The salvaged portions of the tape revealed a confession by Mr. L that he had agreed to work for the police. . . . At no time, either on his arrest or during the trial proceedings, did the applicant give any explanation for his presence in the house.

20. At the close of the prosecution case the trial judge, acting in accordance with Article 4 of the Order, called upon [Murray to give evidence in his own defense]:

> I am also required by law to tell you that if you refuse to come into the witness box to be sworn or if, after having been sworn, you refuse, without good reason, to answer any question, then the court in deciding whether you are guilty or not guilty may take into account against you to the extent that it considers proper your refusal to give evidence or to answer any questions.

21. Acting on the advice of his solicitor and counsel, the applicant chose not to give any evidence. No witnesses were called on his behalf. Counsel . . . submitted, inter alia, that the applicant's presence in the house just before the police arrived was recent and innocent.

22. On 8 May 1991 the applicant was found guilty of the offence of aiding and abetting the unlawful imprisonment of Mr. L and sentenced to eight years' imprisonment. He was acquitted of the remaining charges. . . .

25. In concluding that the applicant was guilty of the offence of aiding and abetting false imprisonment, the trial judge drew adverse inferences against the applicant under both Articles 4 and 6 of the Order. The judge stated that in the particular circumstances of the case he did not propose to draw inferences against the applicant under Article 3 of the Order. . . .

27. Criminal Evidence (Northern Ireland) Order 1988 includes the following provisions:

> Article 3: Circumstances in which inferences may be drawn from accused's failure to mention particular facts when questioned, charged, etc.
>
> (1) Where, in any proceedings against a person for an offence, evidence is given that the accused
>
> (a) at any time before he was charged with the offence, on being questioned by a constable trying to discover whether or by whom the offence had been committed, failed to mention any fact relied on in his defence in those proceedings; or

(b) on being charged with the offence or officially informed that he might be prosecuted for it, failed to mention any such fact, being a fact which in the circumstances existing at the time the accused could reasonably have been expected to mention when so questioned, charged or informed, as the case may be, paragraph (2) applies.

(2) [The] court or jury, in determining whether the accused is guilty of the offence charged, may . . . draw such inferences from the failure as appear proper [and] on the basis of such inferences treat the failure as, or as capable of amounting to, corroboration of any evidence given against the accused in relation to which the failure is material. . . .

Article 4: Accused to be called upon to give evidence at trial . . .

(2) Before any evidence is called for the defence, the court . . . shall tell the accused that he will be called upon by the court to give evidence in his own defence, and . . . shall tell him in ordinary language what the effect of this Article will be if . . . when so called upon, he refuses . . . to answer any question. . . .

(3) If the accused . . . refuses to be sworn, . . . paragraph (4) applies.

(4) The court or jury, in determining whether the accused is guilty of the offence charged, may . . . draw such inferences from the refusal as appear proper [and] treat the refusal as, or as capable of amounting to, corroboration of any evidence given against the accused in relation to which the refusal is material. . . .

Article 6: Inferences from failure or refusal to account for presence at a particular place

(1) Where (a) a person arrested by a constable was found by him at a place or about the time the offence for which he was arrested is alleged to have been committed, and (b) the constable reasonably believes that the presence of the person at that place and at that time may be attributable to his participation in the commission of the offence, and (c) the constable informs the person that he so believes, and requests him to account for that presence, and (d) the person fails or refuses to do so, then if, in any proceedings against the person for the offence, evidence of those matters is given, paragraph (2) applies.

(2) [The] court or jury, in determining whether the accused is guilty of the offence charged, may . . . draw such inferences from the failure or refusal as appear proper [and] treat the failure or refusal as, or as capable of amounting to, corroboration of any evidence given against the accused in relation to which the failure or refusal is material.

(3) Paragraphs (1) and (2) do not apply unless the accused was told in ordinary language by the constable when making the request mentioned in paragraph (1)(c) what the effect of this Article would be if he failed or refused to do so. . . .

40. The applicant alleged that there had been a violation of the right to silence and the right not to incriminate oneself contrary to Article 6(1) and (2) of the Convention. . . . The relevant provisions provide as follows:

1. In the determination of . . . any criminal charge against him, everyone is entitled to a fair and public hearing within a reasonable time by an independent and impartial tribunal. . . .

2. Everyone charged with a criminal offence shall be presumed innocent until proved guilty according to law. . . .

41. In the submission of the applicant, the drawing of incriminating inferences against him under the Criminal Justice (Northern Ireland) Order 1988 violated Article 6(1) and (2) of the Convention. It amounted to an infringement of the right to silence, the right not to incriminate oneself and the principle that the prosecution bear the burden of proving the case without assistance from the accused.

He contended that a first, and most obvious element of the right to silence is the right to remain silent in the face of police questioning and not to have to testify against oneself at trial. In his submission, these have always been essential and fundamental elements of the British criminal justice system. Moreover the Commission in Saunders v. United Kingdom, No. 19187/91, Comm. Rep. 10.5.94 (1994) and the Court in Funke v. France, 1 C.M.L.R. 897 (1993) have accepted that they are an inherent part of the right to a fair hearing under Article 6. In his view these are absolute rights which an accused is entitled to enjoy without restriction.

A second, equally essential element of the right to silence was that the exercise of the right by an accused would not be used as evidence against him in his trial. However, the trial judge drew very strong inferences, under Articles 4 and 6 of the Order, from his decision to remain silent under police questioning and during the trial. Indeed, it was clear from the trial judge's remarks . . . that the inferences were an integral part of his decision to find him guilty.

Accordingly, he was severely and doubly penalised for choosing to remain silent: once for his silence under police interrogation and once for his failure to testify during the trial. To use against him silence under police questioning and his refusal to testify during trial amounted to subverting the presumption of innocence and the onus of proof resulting from that presumption: it is for the prosecution to prove the accused's guilt without any assistance from the latter being required. . . .

43. The Government . . . emphasised that the Order did not detract from the right to remain silent in the face of police questioning and explicitly confirmed the right not to have to testify at trial. They further noted that the Order in no way changed either the burden or the standard of proof: it remained for the prosecution to prove an accused's guilt beyond reasonable doubt. What the Order did was to confer a discretionary power to draw inferences from the silence of an accused in carefully defined circumstances. [The] Order merely allows the trier of fact to draw such inferences as common sense dictates. The question in each case is whether the evidence adduced by the prosecution is sufficiently strong to call for an answer. . . .

45. Although not specifically mentioned in Article 6 of the Convention, there can be no doubt that the right to remain silent under police questioning and the privilege against self-incrimination are generally recognised international standards which lie at the heart of the notion of a fair procedure under Article 6. By providing the accused with protection against improper compulsion by the authorities these immunities contribute to avoiding miscarriages of justice and to securing the aim of Article 6.

46. The Court does not consider that it is called upon to give an abstract analysis of the scope of these immunities and, in particular, of what constitutes in this context "improper compulsion." What is at stake in the present case is whether these immunities are absolute in the sense that the exercise by an accused of the right to silence cannot under any circumstances be used against him at trial or, alternatively, whether informing him in advance that, under certain conditions, his silence may be used, is always to be regarded as "improper compulsion."

47. On the one hand, it is self-evident that [it] is incompatible with the immunities under consideration to base a conviction solely or mainly on the accused's silence or on a refusal to answer questions or to give evidence himself. On the other hand, the Court deems it equally obvious that these immunities cannot and should not prevent that the accused's silence, in situations which clearly call for an explanation from him, be taken into account in assessing the persuasiveness of the evidence adduced by the prosecution. Wherever the line between these two

extremes is to be drawn, it follows from this understanding of "the right to silence" that the question whether the right is absolute must be answered in the negative. . . .

48. As regards the degree of compulsion involved in the present case, it is recalled that the applicant was in fact able to remain silent. Notwithstanding the repeated warnings as to the possibility that inferences might be drawn from his silence, he did not make any statements to the police and did not give evidence during his trial. [H]is insistence in maintaining silence throughout the proceedings did not amount to a criminal offence or contempt of court. . . .

50. Admittedly a system which warns the accused — who is possibly without legal assistance (as in the applicant's case) — that adverse inferences may be drawn from a refusal to provide an explanation to the police . . . involves a certain level of indirect compulsion. However, since the applicant could not be compelled to speak or to testify, as indicated above, this factor on its own cannot be decisive. The Court must rather concentrate its attention on the role played by the inferences in the proceedings against the applicant and especially in his conviction.

51. In this context, it is recalled that these were proceedings without a jury, the trier of fact being an experienced judge. Furthermore, the drawing of inferences under the Order is subject to an important series of safeguards designed to respect the rights of the defence and to limit the extent to which reliance can be placed on inferences.

In the first place, before inferences can be drawn under Article 4 and 6 of the Order appropriate warnings must have been given to the accused as to the legal effects of maintaining silence. Moreover, . . . the prosecutor must first establish a prima facie case against the accused, i.e. a case consisting of direct evidence which, if believed and combined with legitimate inferences based upon it, could lead a properly directed jury to be satisfied beyond reasonable doubt that each of the essential elements of the offence is proved.

The question in each particular case is whether the evidence adduced by the prosecution is sufficiently strong to require an answer. The national court cannot conclude that the accused is guilty merely because he chooses to remain silent. It is only if the evidence against the accused "calls" for an explanation which the accused ought to be in a position to give that a failure to give an explanation "may as a matter of common sense allow the drawing of an inference that there is no explanation and that the accused is guilty." Conversely if the case presented by the prosecution had so little evidential value that it called for no answer, a failure to provide one could not justify an inference of guilt. In sum, it is only common sense inferences which the judge considers proper, in the light of the evidence against the accused, that can be drawn under the Order.

In addition, the trial judge has a discretion whether, on the facts of the particular case, an inference should be drawn. [T]he judge must explain the reasons for the decision to draw inferences and the weight attached to them. The exercise of discretion in this regard is subject to review by the appellate courts.

52. In the present case, the evidence presented against the applicant by the prosecution was considered by the Court of Appeal to constitute a "formidable" case against him. It is recalled that when the police entered the house some appreciable time after they knocked on the door, they found the applicant coming down the flight of stairs in the house where Mr. L had been held captive by the IRA. [Soon after the police arrived, the] applicant was pulling a tape out of a cassette. The tangled tape and cassette recorder were later found on the premises. Evidence by the applicant's co-accused that he had recently arrived at the house was discounted as not being credible. . . .

54. In the Court's view, having regard to the weight of the evidence against the applicant, as outlined above, the drawing of inferences from his refusal, at arrest, during police questioning and at trial, to provide an explanation for his presence in the house was a matter of common sense and cannot be regarded as unfair or unreasonable in the circumstances. [T]he courts in a considerable number of countries where evidence is freely assessed may have regard to all relevant circumstances, including the manner in which the accused has behaved or has conducted his defence, when evaluating the evidence in the case. [W]hat distinguishes the drawing of inferences under the Order is that, in addition to the existence of the specific safeguards mentioned above, it constitutes, as described by the Commission, "a formalised system which aims at allowing common sense implications to play an open role in the assessment of evidence." . . .

55. The applicant submitted that it was unfair to draw inferences under Article 6 of the Order from his silence at a time when he had not had the benefit of legal advice. . . . In this context he emphasised that under the Order once an accused has remained silent a trap is set from which he cannot escape: if an accused chooses to give evidence or to call witnesses, he is, by reason of his prior silence, exposed to the risk of an Article 3 inference sufficient to bring about a conviction; on the other hand, if he maintains his silence inferences may be drawn against him under other provisions of the Order.

56. The Court [will not] speculate on the question whether inferences would have been drawn under the Order had the applicant, at any moment after his first interrogation, chosen to speak to the police or to give evidence at his trial or call witnesses. Nor should it speculate on the question whether it was the possibility of such inferences being drawn that explains why the applicant was advised by his solicitor to remain silent.

Immediately after arrest the applicant was warned in accordance with the provisions of the Order but chose to remain silent. [T]here is no indication that the applicant failed to understand the significance of the warning given to him by the police prior to seeing his solicitor. Under these circumstances the fact that during the first 48 hours of his detention the applicant had been refused access to a lawyer does not detract from the above conclusion that the drawing of inferences was not unfair or unreasonable. . . .

57. [T]he Court does not consider that the criminal proceedings were unfair or that there had been an infringement of the presumption of innocence. . . . For these reasons, the Court [h]olds by 14 votes to 5 that there has been no violation of Article 6(1) and (2) of the Convention arising out of the drawing of adverse inferences on account of the applicant's silence. . . .

WALSH, partly dissenting.

1. In my opinion there have been violations of Article 6(1) and (2) of the Convention. The applicant was by Article 6(2) guaranteed a presumption of innocence in the criminal trial of which he complains. Prior to the introduction of the Criminal Evidence (Northern Ireland) Order 1988 a judge trying a case without a jury could not lawfully draw an inference of guilt from the fact that an accused person did not proclaim his innocence. Equally in a trial with a jury it would have been contrary to law to instruct the jurymen that they could do so. [T]he object and effect of the 1988 Order was to reverse that position. . . .

3. . . . To permit such a procedure is to permit a penalty to be imposed by a criminal court on an accused because he relies upon a procedural right guaranteed

by the Convention. I draw attention to the decision of the Supreme Court of the United States in Griffin v. California, 380 U.S. 609 (1965), which dealt with a similar point in relation to the Fifth Amendment of the Constitution by striking down a Californian law which permitted a court to make adverse comment on the accused's decision not to testify. . . .

Problem 8-7. Telling the Jury

Two police officers on patrol learned of an activated security alarm around 2:25 A.M. at Pleasants Hardware Store in the Pinewood Shopping Center. As they approached the plaza, the officers observed a car parked about 100 yards from the shopping center facing away from the hardware store. The store was not lit, and the parking lot was empty. When the officers got out of their car and inspected the premises, they noticed a large hole in the concrete block wall at the rear of the building.

After this initial investigation, the officers drove to the location of the car they had seen earlier to obtain license tag numbers but discovered that it was gone. Within two minutes, they observed the car traveling north on Highway 321 at a high speed with its headlights off. After a brief pursuit, the driver of the car pulled over. The driver, Joseph Reid, told the officers he had stopped in the area of the shopping center because his car had run out of gas. When the officers asked why the car was running at that time, Reid said it had started unexpectedly. The officers found a sledgehammer near the location where Reid stopped his car.

Reid was tried in superior court on the charge of breaking and entering with intent to commit the felony of larceny. During the prosecution's closing argument to the jury, the following exchange took place:

The State: Now defendant hasn't taken the stand in this case —
Defense Counsel: Objection to his remarks about that, Your Honor.
The Court: Overruled.
Defense Counsel: Exception.
The State: The defendant hasn't taken the stand in this case. He has that right. You're not to hold that against him. But we have to look at the other evidence to look at intent in this case.

The prosecutor's remark that the defendant had not testified mirrored the North Carolina Pattern Jury Instructions regarding a criminal defendant's right not to testify. Did the prosecutor commit reversible error by quoting to the jury from the pattern jury instructions? Compare State v. Reid, 434 S.E.2d 193 (N.C. 1993).

Problem 8-8. Pre-arrest Silence

At 2:30 A.M., Patrick Easter's Isuzu Trooper collided with a yellow taxicab. Easter was returning from a wedding reception to his home near the accident site. The cab was carrying six university students. Easter suffered injuries in the accident, and four of the students were seriously injured. A test administered shortly after the accident showed Easter's blood alcohol content was approximately .11. Several days later, Easter was arrested and charged with four counts of vehicular assault.

Easter did not testify at trial. The state and the defense presented evidence supporting different versions of how the accident happened. Officer Fitzgerald's testimony occupied much of the trial, although he did not observe the accident or take a statement from a witness. He testified that he arrived within minutes of the accident and found Easter in the bathroom of a gas station at the intersection, with torn clothes, a cut forehead, and blood on his elbows and knees. He testified that Easter then "totally ignored" him when he asked what happened. He also testified that when he continued to ask questions, Easter looked down, "once again ignoring me, ignoring my questions."

Fitzgerald said that he "felt the defendant was being smart drunk." The officer explained that when he used the term "smart drunk," he meant to say that Easter "was evasive, wouldn't talk to me, wouldn't look at me, wouldn't get close enough for me to get good observations of his breath and eyes, I felt that he was trying to hide or cloak."

Fitzgerald testified he took Easter back to the intersection and told him he would be placed under arrest or he could submit to a voluntary blood-alcohol test at a hospital. Fitzgerald suspected Easter was intoxicated because of Easter's slightly slurred speech, bloodshot eyes, and the odor of alcohol on his breath, although Easter had no coordination problems, walked without difficulty, and produced his license without fumbling or stumbling. After learning that he would be arrested, Easter's attitude changed. He asked for business papers in the truck and for a friend to be telephoned. Easter answered questions about his driver's license and said his home was a mile north of the accident scene.

In closing, the prosecutor argued that the trial testimony was best summed up with the words "smart drunk." He referred several times to testimony that Easter was a "smart drunk" who had ignored Officer Fitzgerald, except when asking about his papers and friend, and concluded, "Easter is a smart drunk." He closed his final argument with these words: "I urge you to find Mr. Easter, the smart drunk in this case, guilty." Did the prosecutor and the prosecution witness improperly comment on the defendant's invocation of his right to silence? See State v. Easter, 922 P.2d 1285 (Wash. 1996).

Notes

1. *Commenting on silence: majority position.* The Supreme Court's broad holding in *Griffin* that a prosecutor may not comment on a defendant's silence at trial has taken an even broader form over time in the state and federal courts. The *Griffin* rule applies not only to a prosecutor's statements literally pointing out that a defendant has not testified. It also prevents the prosecutor from calling the defendant to the witness stand to allow the jury to see the defendant invoke the privilege. The principle also covers veiled references to a defendant's failure to testify. See State v. McLamb, 69 S.E.2d 537 (N.C. 1952) (argument that defendant was "hiding behind his wife's coattail" was equivalent to comment on defendant's failure to testify on his own behalf). Most state courts say that the constitutional rule bars any comments "manifestly intended" to note a defendant's silence, or statements that are reasonably likely to draw a jury's attention to the fact that the defendant did not testify. See Knowles v. United States, 224 F.2d 168 (10th Cir. 1955); People v. Arman, 545 N.E.2d 658 (Ill. 1989). While the prosecutor may usually comment on a

defendant's failure to produce *other* witnesses or exculpatory evidence to contradict the government's evidence, even a statement that the government's proof is "uncontradicted" could run afoul of the *Griffin* rule when it is highly unlikely that anyone other than the defendant could rebut the evidence. See Smith v. State, 787 A.2d 152 (Md. 2001) (prosecutor in closing argument improperly commented that the defendant had given "zero" answer to key piece of incriminating evidence; proper test is whether the prosecutor's comment is "susceptible of the inference" by the jurors that they were to consider silence); but cf. United States v. Robinson, 485 U.S. 25 (1988) (prosecutor may refer to defendant's failure to testify when defense counsel claims in closing argument that government did not allow defendant to explain defendant's side of story). If a prosecutor makes an improper statement and the defense counsel objects, most states require the trial court to give a curative instruction to the jury immediately. Does this vigorous enforcement amount to any real benefit for defendants? Do juries act differently when none of the attorneys mention the defendant's silence, or is that something a jury will consider regardless of what the attorneys say?

2. *Jury instructions about silence.* The constitutional right to silence at trial encompasses a right to have the judge instruct the jury not to draw any inferences from the defendant's decision not to testify. As the court said in Carter v. Kentucky, 450 U.S. 288, 303 (1981), "No judge can prevent jurors from speculating about why a defendant stands mute in the face of a criminal accusation, but a judge can, and must, if requested to do so, use the unique power of the jury instruction to reduce that speculation to a minimum." Most jurisdictions rely on pattern jury instructions about a defendant's silence, along these lines: "The defendant has an absolute right not to testify. The fact that the defendant did not testify should not be considered by you in any way in arriving at your verdict." As defense counsel, would you rather have the judge deliver this jury instruction, or would you rather not call attention to the defendant's silence?

3. *Inferences based on silence at trial: other legal systems.* The European Court of Human Rights, as indicated by the *Murray* opinion, reflects a common position in foreign legal systems. Not all systems allow the defendant to remain silent at trial; even among those allowing silence, most empower the judge to draw inferences against the defendant based on this silence. See Criminal Procedure Act of Norway, ch. 9, §93 ("If the person charged refuses to answer, or states that he reserves his answer, the president of the court may inform him that this may be considered to tell against him"); Myron Moskovitz, The O.J. Inquisition: A United States Encounter with Continental Criminal Justice, 28 Vand. J. Transnat'l L. 1121 (1995) (setting the O. J. Simpson murder trial in a typical European civil law courtroom; the presiding judge calls the first witness as follows: "Bailiffs, please bring the Accused forward"). In the United States, the federal and state constitutions as well as some statutes and rules of evidence prevent the factfinder from drawing inferences based on the defendant's silence at trial. See Conn. Gen. Stat. §54-84(b). Is there any value in preventing comments on silence if the factfinder is a judge rather than a jury? Would it be more consistent with truth-seeking if the judge (but not the prosecutor) could tell the jury it may draw inferences from silence?

4. *Incentives to remain silent.* Even if a defendant is convinced that the jury looks unfavorably on a decision not to testify, there are some powerful reasons to remain silent at trial. Once a defendant chooses to take the stand at trial, he may not selectively invoke the privilege to avoid answering the most difficult questions.

The defendant is subject to the ordinary scope of cross-examination. For many defendants, this means that the prosecutor can introduce evidence of some prior convictions as a method of impeaching the defendant's credibility as a witness. What remedy is appropriate if a defendant takes the stand but refuses to answer some questions on cross-examination?

5. *Use at trial of pretrial silence.* Although it is clear that a prosecutor cannot make even an indirect reference to the defendant's silence at trial, there is more leeway to comment at trial on some forms of *pretrial* silence by the defendant. The Supreme Court has drawn fine distinctions under the federal constitution. The prosecutor may not use any pretrial silence of the defendant *after* arrest and the delivery of *Miranda* warnings. Doyle v. Ohio, 426 U.S. 610 (1976). However, the government can use a defendant's *pre-arrest* silence as a basis for impeachment during the defendant's testimony at trial. The same is true for post-arrest silence when there is no indication that *Miranda* warnings were delivered, or even post-arrest silence after a defendant has waived the right to silence after receiving proper warnings. Fletcher v. Weir, 455 U.S. 603 (1982) (post-arrest, pre-*Miranda* silence); Jenkins v. Anderson, 447 U.S. 231 (1980) (pre-arrest silence); Anderson v. Charles, 447 U.S. 404 (1980) (selective silence after waiver of right to silence). Is there any real difference in the evidentiary value of these various forms of silence?

State courts are about evenly divided between those that follow this cluster of federal rulings and those that depart from one or more of the components. It is most common to find state courts ruling that post-arrest unwarned silence cannot be used as impeachment material at trial. These courts base such rulings both on state constitutional provisions and on rules of evidence. See Weitzel v. State, 863 A.2d 999 (Md. 2004) (pre-arrest silence despite allegations of guilt from other witnesses is not probative enough to qualify as substantive evidence of guilt; right to silence is widely known even without *Miranda* warnings); State v. Leach, 807 N.E.2d 335 (Ohio 2004) (allowing use of pre-arrest silence for impeachment, but not as substantive evidence of guilt). Note that the prosecutor in Problem 8-8 above used the defendant's pre-arrest silence not for impeachment purposes but during direct examination of a prosecution witness and during closing arguments. Should the use of such evidence depend on the defendant's choice to take the stand at trial?

In 1994 the British Parliament changed the rule regarding silence before trial. A 1984 statute required the police to inform suspects in custody that they have a right to consult an attorney before any interrogation. Under §34 of the Criminal Justice and Public Order Act of 1994, a court may draw inferences from the fact that a person is questioned and fails to mention a fact that an innocent person could reasonably be expected to mention during questioning, so long as the constable warns the accused of this fact at the time of questioning.

6. *Comments on presence at trial.* In Portuondo v. Agard, 529 U.S. 61 (2000), the prosecutor pointed out to the jury that the defendant, who was present in the courtroom, had the opportunity to hear all other witnesses and to tailor his testimony accordingly. Agard claimed that the prosecutor's comments violated his Fifth Amendment right to be present at trial and his Sixth Amendment right to confront his accusers. He drew an analogy to Griffin v. California, suggesting that in his case, just as in *Griffin*, the prosecutor was making the exercise of these constitutional trial rights more costly. Are there meaningful differences between this prosecutor's comment and a comment about a defendant's refusal to testify? The Supreme Court found no constitutional violation.

7. *Compulsory process for defense witnesses.* The defendant who hopes to call witnesses and collect evidence to undermine the prosecution's case receives some significant help from the government. Provisions in the federal constitution and in virtually all state constitutions give the defendant the power of "compulsory process," that is, the power to subpoena witnesses who must inform the court of what they know about the events in question. For instance, the Sixth Amendment to the federal constitution grants to the accused the right "to have compulsory process for obtaining witnesses in his favor." Statutes and rules of procedure also confirm the defendant's power to obtain government support in presenting witnesses.

8. *Threats of perjury charges against defense witnesses.* While it is surely true that the law makes it easier for defendants to obtain favorable testimony, there are also some legal obstacles to finding defense witnesses. To begin with, the defense witnesses might invoke the privilege against self-incrimination. Further, the potential witnesses might fear that if they testify, they will create a risk of perjury charges if the prosecutor believes that the testimony is not truthful. To what extent can government agents, such as judges or prosecutors, use these incentives to make it more difficult for the defendant to obtain witnesses?

The due process clause of the federal constitution controls the statements of prosecutors and judges about possible criminal charges to be filed against defense witnesses. In the leading Supreme Court decision, Webb v. Texas, 409 U.S. 95 (1972), a trial judge warned the defendant's only witness against committing perjury and explained the consequences of a perjury conviction. The Court held that the judge's statements violated due process. See also State v. Finley, 998 P.2d 95 (Kan. 2000) (right to present defense infringed when prosecutor suggests state will charge potential defense witness with felony murder based on her testimony); State v. Goad, 355 S.E.2d 371 (W. Va. 1987).

High state courts have read *Webb* flexibly to mean that the judge or prosecutor can sometimes mention possible criminal charges to a defense witness. Applying federal due process principles rather than state constitutional provisions, the courts often condemn a prosecutor for saying that she "will" bring criminal charges against the defense witness if the witness testifies. See Mills v. State, 733 P.2d 880 (Okla. Crim. App. 1985). However, when a prosecutor tells a defense witness that testimony "could" expose the witness to criminal charges, courts are less likely to find a due process violation. The same distinction applies to a trial judge who informs the witness about possible criminal charges which could result from testifying. See Jones v. State, 655 N.E.2d 49 (Ind. 1995). Should it matter whether the prosecutor speaks directly to the defense witness or instead sends a message by way of the defense attorney or some other third party?

Defendants have much less success when they complain that the government has deported aliens whom the defendant planned to call as defense witnesses. United States v. Valenzuela-Bernal, 458 U.S. 858 (1982) (no due process violation in prosecution for illegal transportation of aliens when government deports all aliens who would have testified for defendant). Can you explain why these claims are more difficult to sustain than those dealing with threats of criminal charges against witnesses?

9. *Defense grants of immunity.* If a prosecution witness invokes her privilege against self-incrimination, the prosecutor has the option of "immunizing" the witness from later prosecution based on the testimony, and the court will compel the witness to testify despite the privilege. However, the defense does not have a comparable

power to immunize defense witnesses who invoke the privilege. Defendants sometimes ask the court to order the prosecution to grant immunity to a defense witness, but courts routinely deny the requests. See State v. Roy, 668 A.2d 41 (N.H. 1995). Why have defendants been so unsuccessful in obtaining grants of immunity, even for their most crucial witnesses? When a defendant requests a grant of immunity for a witness and does not receive it, should the judge explain to the jury that the defendant had hoped to call a witness who is now "missing" because of the privilege against self-incrimination?

D. ETHICS AND LIES AT TRIAL

Ethical issues arise at all stages in the prosecution and defense of criminal defendants. Issues before trial include the conduct of interrogations, the grounds for filing charges, and the statements made while negotiating plea bargains. During trial preparation, ethical obligations may require discovery disclosures beyond those required by constitutional doctrine, statutes, or rules of procedure. Throughout the criminal process, ethical dilemmas for defense counsel arise from the tension between the search for truth and the zealous representation of the defendant. For the prosecutor, ethical dilemmas arise from the conflict between the obligation to seek justice on behalf of the public as a whole and the need to consult and defer to the wishes of crime victims.

Some of the most difficult ethical questions in all of legal practice arise when the lawyer believes the client is acting illegally or is lying. Related problems arise when a lawyer believes that a friendly witness is lying. Consider the extent to which the ethical obligations of defense lawyers and prosecutors at trial are — or should be — different.

■ PEOPLE v. DEREK ANDRADES
828 N.E.2d 599 (N.Y. 2005)

G.B. SMITH, J.

In People v. DePallo, 96 N.Y.2d 437 (N.Y. 2001), we held that defense counsel properly balanced the duties he owed to his client and the duties he owed to the court and to the criminal justice system when, during a jury trial, counsel notified the court that his client had offered perjured testimony and refused to use that testimony in his closing argument to the jury. We left open the question of the propriety of a similar disclosure under circumstances where the court sits as the factfinder. We address that issue in the case now before us and hold that counsel's disclosure to the court, which was open to the inference that his client intended to perjure himself upon taking the stand, did not deprive defendant of a fair hearing or of the effective assistance of counsel.

Defendant became enraged when he heard rumors that Magalie Nieves, a woman with whom he had had a sexual relationship, was infected with the HIV virus. Defendant, with the aid of 14-year-old Ericka Cruz, confronted Nieves and a fight ensued. Subsequently, defendant and Cruz lured Nieves to an isolated area where defendant choked her with a bandana, and he and Cruz stabbed her in the ear and in the breast, killing her. Days later, the police arrested Cruz, who offered a confession of the killing. The next day, defendant was arrested and charged, inter alia, with second degree murder and first degree manslaughter. Upon his arrest, defendant was read his *Miranda* rights and gave both written and videotaped statements in which he admitted to acting in concert with Cruz in killing Nieves.

Defendant moved to suppress his confessions. . . . Prior to the hearing, defendant's attorney asked to be relieved as counsel, stating, "There is an ethical conflict with my continuing to represent [defendant] and I can't go any further than that." The prosecutor opposed the application, citing the age of the case. The court asked defense counsel to state the nature of the ethical dilemma without disclosing privileged information so that the court could make an effective ruling. Counsel stated, however, that he could not elaborate. The court then presumed that counsel's ethical dilemma concerned defendant's right to testify. The court denied counsel's application and told him that if the problem arose, he would have to offer more specific information to the court.

After the People presented their case at the . . . hearing, defense counsel informed the court that defendant intended to testify. Outside defendant's presence, counsel stated:

> As part and parcel of my request to be relieved in this matter, I think I should tell the Court and place on the record that I did tell [defendant] and advise [defendant] that he should not testify at the hearing and as a result of the problem that I'm having, the ethical problem I'm having. What I'm going to do is just basically direct his attention to date, time and location of the statement and let him run with the ball.

The court, recognizing that defense counsel was not permitted to divulge privileged matters to the court, concluded that counsel's conduct complied with his ethical obligations under the disciplinary rules given his anticipation that defendant "could possibly, could commit perjury on the witness stand." The court further concluded that counsel could still afford defendant the effective assistance of counsel. [The court also concluded that it was not necessary for defendant to be present during the conference because it did not constitute a critical stage of his trial.]

Defendant thereafter testified on his own behalf, largely in narrative form, with the court and counsel asking clarifying questions. Defendant testified that at the time he provided his statements to the police, he did not remember the events leading to Nieves's death and specifically did not recall stabbing her. He stated that during his interrogation, the police informed him of Cruz's version of the events, and he believed what she said because he did not think that Cruz would lie about him. Defendant stated that he initially refused to sign the written confession drafted by the police officers because its contents were not true, but that later he signed it only after one of the officers took him into a private room. Defendant further testified that when he gave his videotaped statement, he simply restated Cruz's rendition of the killing as described to him by the officers. Thus, he claimed that this confession was not a recounting of events from his own memory. Finally, defendant stated that by the time he had provided the videotaped confession at approximately 10:00 P.M., he was hungry because he had not eaten all day, and was not permitted food until after he had given that statement.

Defense counsel offered no closing argument, choosing instead to rest on the record and the papers submitted. Following the People's closing statement, the court denied defendant's motion to suppress his confessions. In a subsequent written decision, the court noted that it "did not find the defendant's testimony credible or worthy of belief." The court held that defendant made his written and videotaped statements after voluntarily waiving his constitutional rights. Upon a jury trial, at which defendant largely defended himself, defendant was convicted of second degree murder and sentenced to a prison term of 25 years to life. . . .

In *DePallo*, we recognized that a defense attorney's duty to zealously represent a client must be circumscribed by his or her duty as an officer of the court to serve the truth-seeking function of the justice system. Moreover, as perjury is a criminal offense, defense counsel has a duty to refrain from participating in the client's commission of it. Thus, we stated that while counsel must pursue all reasonable means to reach the objectives of the client, counsel must not in any way assist a client in presenting false evidence to the court. See Nix v. Whiteside, 475 U.S. 157 (1986).

Indeed, New York's Code of Professional Responsibility specifically addresses an attorney's ethical obligations in providing lawful representation. Disciplinary Rule 7-102 expressly states that an attorney may not "knowingly use perjured testimony or false evidence," DR 7-102(a)(4); "knowingly make a false statement of law or fact," DR 7-102(a)(5); "participate in the creation or preservation of evidence when the lawyer knows or it is obvious that the evidence is false," DR 7-102(a)(6); "counsel or assist the client in conduct that the lawyer knows to be illegal or fraudulent," DR 7-102(a)(7); or "knowingly engage in other illegal conduct," DR 7-102(a)(8).

In light of the ethical obligations of an attorney in this state, and in accordance with United States Supreme Court jurisprudence, an attorney faced with a client who intends to commit perjury has the initial responsibility to attempt to dissuade the client from pursuing the unlawful course of action. Nix v. Whiteside, 475 U.S. at 169-170. Should the client insist on perjuring himself, counsel may seek to withdraw from the case. If counsel's request is denied, defense counsel, bound to honor defendant's right to testify on his own behalf, should refrain from eliciting the testimony in traditional question-and-answer form and permit defendant to present his testimony in narrative form. However, in accordance with DR 7-102(a)(4), counsel may not use the perjured testimony in making argument to the court.

Here, defense counsel properly discharged his ethical obligations under the circumstances presented. Counsel clearly advised defendant against lying on the witness stand; indeed, counsel encouraged defendant not to take the stand at all. Yet defendant insisted on testifying at the hearing, and his attorney believed that the evidence he intended to present was false. Thus, it was entirely proper for counsel to seek to withdraw as defendant's attorney prior to the hearing based on his perceived ethical dilemma.

While defendant does not argue the propriety of his attorney's actions up to that point, he does take issue with his attorney's telling the court that the ethical dilemma he faced concerned defendant's right to testify at the hearing. Defendant argues that such a disclosure signifies defendant's intention to commit perjury to the court which sits as the factfinder for the hearing. He contends that such a disclosure inevitably affected the court's ability to assess his credibility in determining the outcome of the hearing.[3] In that same vein, defendant argues that his attorney should not have told the court of his intent to question defendant in

---

3. In support of his position, defendant relies on Lowery v. Cardwell, 575 F.2d 727 (9th Cir. 1978). In that case, defendant testified at her bench trial and perjured herself, to the surprise of her attorney. Counsel requested a recess, at which time he unsuccessfully attempted to withdraw from the case. Counsel then ended the defendant's testimony and made no reference to the defendant's perjured testimony

the narrative before having done so. Defendant asserts that his attorney should have said nothing, proceeded to question defendant in the narrative, and if counsel's suspicions about defendant's testimony ripened into a reality, counsel could simply refrain from using the perjured testimony in his closing argument.

We disagree. As an initial matter, we note that at no time did counsel ever disclose to the court that defendant intended to commit perjury or otherwise disclose any client secrets. Rather, the court inferred defendant's perjurious intent based upon the nature of counsel's application. However, counsel could have properly made such a disclosure since a client's intent to commit a crime is not a protected confidence or secret. See Nix v. Whiteside, 475 U.S. at 174; Code of Professional Responsibility DR 4-101(c)(3). Moreover, counsel's ethical obligations do not change simply because a judge rather than a jury is sitting as the factfinder. Moreover, as a practical matter, defendant's suggestion would solve nothing because counsel would likely find it difficult to allow defendant to testify in the narrative without prior explanation. Like the direct examination of any witness, defendant's examination must be guided by proper questioning. Had counsel attempted to offer defendant's testimony in the narrative, it would have been subject to objection either by the prosecutor or the court. Even if counsel were permitted to present defendant's testimony in narrative form without objection, the very fact of defendant testifying in such a manner would signify to the court that counsel believes that his client is perjuring himself.

We therefore conclude that defense counsel properly balanced his duties to his client with his duties to the court and the criminal justice system and that in doing so, defendant was not denied his right to a fair hearing. Furthermore, absent a breach of any recognized professional duty, defendant's claim that he was denied the effective assistance of counsel must also fail.

Finally, we reject defendant's contention that he was denied his right to be present during a material stage of the trial because he was absent during the colloquy between the court and the attorneys regarding defense counsel's intent to present defendant's testimony in the narrative. [A] colloquy of this nature involves procedural matters at which a defendant can offer no meaningful input. Therefore, defendant had no right to be present. . . .

■ PEOPLE v. VICTOR REICHMAN

819 P.2d 1035 (Colo. 1991)

Per Curiam.

This is an attorney discipline case. A hearing panel approved the findings and recommendation of a majority of the hearing board that the respondent receive a public censure for conduct involving dishonesty, fraud, deceit or misrepresentation,

during his closing arguments. The United States Court of Appeals for the Ninth Circuit held that counsel's actions denied the defendant a fair trial because counsel's actions gave the judge the impression that counsel believed that the defendant had testified falsely. The court stated that by his actions, counsel placed himself in opposition to his client's interests. The court suggested that it would have been the better practice for the attorney to have made a record for his own protection in the event that he was ever questioned about his professional conduct. We expressly reject this approach because it requires an attorney to remain silent while the client commits perjury, which is wholly incompatible with counsel's role as an officer of the court and, more specifically, counsel's obligation to reveal fraud perpetrated by a client upon the court.

and conduct prejudicial to the administration of justice. We accept the recommen-dation of the hearing panel and publicly censure the respondent and order that he be assessed the costs of these proceedings.

[T]he respondent was the duly appointed or elected District Attorney of the Sixth Judicial District, which includes La Plata County. . . . In the spring of 1987, the respondent and other members of law enforcement in the Sixth Judicial District formed a de facto task force, or "LEADS committee," to conduct undercover opera-tions to investigate and prosecute drug trafficking in the district. A police officer from outside the judicial district was retained to conduct the undercover investiga-tions, and the officer chose the fictitious identity of one "Colton Young," an unemployed biker. The respondent served as the head of the task force.

After several months undercover, "Young" had developed a list of names of suspected drug traffickers in the judicial district. In addition, two individuals had told "Young" that an attorney, Robin Auld, accepted drugs in lieu of fees.[2] Then, in September 1987, "Young" called an emergency meeting of the task force to announce that he believed his undercover identity may have been compromised. The task force decided to rehabilitate "Young's" identity. With the respondent's approval, "Young" was "arrested" for a traffic violation on the main street of Durango outside of the business establishment of a significant target of the task force. Auld was not this target. A search of "Young" was then conducted in such a way that the fruits of the search could be easily suppressed and the charges dismissed. "Young" was instructed to contact Robin Auld and retain him as defense counsel.[3]

As part of the plan, fictitious charges were lodged against "Young" with the respondent's knowledge and approval. The respondent, either personally or through his agents, filed a false criminal complaint against "Young," charging him with the illegal possession of a firearm and of marihuana in the County Court of La Plata County. Other documents filed by or on behalf of the respondent in the "Young" case included a surety bond and an offense report, falsely stating "Young's" name and address, and falsely stating that "Young" had committed certain criminal offenses. In addition, with the respondent's knowledge and approval, "Young" appeared in county court and made false statements to the county judge, who was unaware of the deception.

A majority of the hearing board concluded that the respondent's conduct in filing the false documents and the fictitious criminal complaint, and otherwise creating and maintaining the deception of the county court, violated DR 1-102(A)(4) (conduct involving dishonesty or misrepresentation), and DR 1-102(A)(5) (conduct prejudicial to the administration of justice).

The respondent argues that his conduct was not unethical and he points to a number of cases in which prosecutors engaged in deception during "sting" oper-ations. . . . United States v. Murphy, 768 F.2d 1518 (7th Cir. 1985), discussed the participation of the FBI and federal prosecutors in Operation Greylord. The defendant in Murphy, a former associate judge of the Circuit Court of Cook County, Illinois, was convicted of accepting bribes to fix the outcomes of hundreds of

---

2. On March 19, 1990, this court suspended Robin Auld from the practice of law for six months for his involvement in the occurrences which form the basis for this proceeding.

3. The actual objective of the "arrest" and the filing of the fictitious charges against "Young" was hotly disputed. The special assistant disciplinary counsel sought to establish that the respondent's inten-tion was to coerce Auld into betraying Auld's client or clients. The hearing board did not find that this was the respondent's design by clear and convincing evidence. For the purpose of this opinion, we assume that the respondent's intention was to rehabilitate "Young's" undercover identity.

criminal cases that came before him. As part of Operation Greylord, FBI agents posed as corrupt lawyers, and other agents testified in made-up criminal cases heard by Judge Murphy. Murphy argued that his convictions were invalid because the Operation Greylord "cases" were frauds on the court, and the undercover agents committed perjury. The court of appeals disagreed, finding that while the agents' acts appeared criminal, the acts were not crimes because they were performed without the requisite criminal intent. Further, *Murphy* held:

> The FBI and prosecutors behaved honorably in establishing and running Operation Greylord. They assure us that they notified the Presiding Judge of the Circuit Court's Criminal Division, the State's Attorney of Cook County, the Attorney General of Illinois, and the Governor of Illinois. Such notice may not be necessary, and certainly a criminal defendant is in no position to complain of the absence of such notice (for he has no personal right to protect the dignity of the Cook County courts), but the notice dispels any argument that the federal Government has offended some principle requiring respect of the internal operations of the state courts. [768 F.2d at 1529.]

Prosecutorial deception may not always constitute prosecutorial misconduct for purposes of determining whether a criminal complaint or indictment must be dismissed. It does not necessarily follow, however, that prosecutorial deception of a type which results in directly misleading a court should be exempted from the proscriptions of the Code of Professional Responsibility simply because the deception is not such as to warrant the dismissal of a criminal case.

In the case of In re Friedman, 392 N.E.2d 1333 (Ill. 1979), the attorney-respondent, Friedman, was a state prosecutor. In two separate investigations involving bribery of two police officers, Friedman instructed the police officers to testify falsely in court hearings. [Defense attorneys had attempted to bribe the officers to testify falsely in favor of their clients, and the prosecutor instructed the officers to do so as part of a bribery investigation directed at the defense attorneys.] Four justices of the Supreme Court of Illinois found that Friedman's conduct violated the Code of Professional Responsibility notwithstanding his motives. Two justices found that Friedman's conduct was unethical but did not merit discipline because he "acted without the guidance of precedent or settled opinion and because there is apparently considerable belief . . . that the respondent acted properly in conducting the investigation. . . ." Two justices concurred in the decision of the court not to impose discipline because they determined that Friedman did not violate the Code of Professional Responsibility. Two justices concluded that Friedman's conduct was unethical and warranted censure.

[The *Friedman* court rejected the argument that the attorney's] conduct was not unethical because he was motivated by . . . his public responsibilities. This argument is the equivalent of the contention that the end justifies the means, and "that pernicious doctrine," Olmstead v. United States, 277 U.S. 438 (1928) (Brandeis, J., dissenting),[5] is unacceptable in the administration of the criminal law.

---

5. As Justice Brandeis said in dissent in *Olmstead:*

Crime is contagious. If the Government becomes a lawbreaker, it breeds contempt for law; it invites every man to become a law unto himself; it invites anarchy. To declare that in the administration of the criminal law the end justifies the means — to declare that the Government may commit crimes in order to secure the conviction of a private criminal — would bring terrible retribution. Against that pernicious doctrine this Court should resolutely set its face.

[W]e conclude, as did the hearing panel and the majority of the hearing board, that the respondent's conduct violated DR 1-102(A)(1), and DR 1-102(A)(5). District attorneys in Colorado owe a very high duty to the public because they are governmental officials holding constitutionally created offices. This court has spoken out strongly against misconduct by public officials who are lawyers. The respondent's responsibility to enforce the laws in his judicial district grants him no license to ignore those laws or the Code of Professional Responsibility. While the respondent's motives and the erroneous belief of other public prosecutors that the respondent's conduct was ethical do not excuse these violations of the Code of Professional Responsibility, they are mitigating factors to be taken into account in assessing the appropriate discipline. The respondent has no prior discipline. We find, therefore, that the respondent's misconduct warrants discipline consistent with our duties to protect the public and maintain the integrity of the legal profession.

Accordingly, we accept the recommendation of the hearing panel and publicly censure the respondent Victor Reichman. While the surrounding circumstances may tend to explain and mitigate the misconduct, they do not excuse the deception imposed on the court. We therefore publicly reprimand Reichman and assess him the costs of these proceedings in the amount of $4,851.28. . . .

Notes

1. *Lying clients: majority view.* As the U.S. Supreme Court made clear in Nix v. Whiteside, 475 U.S. 157 (1986), the federal constitutional right to effective counsel does not compel an attorney to remain silent when a client plans to commit perjury during testimony. Nor does the Constitution require the attorney to take any other particular action, such as withdrawing from the case or informing the court of the client's plans. The same can be said for state constitutional rulings: They leave the attorney with several acceptable options. The most pertinent legal requirements in this situation come not from constitutions, but from the rules of legal ethics, often embodied in state statutes. The first ethical duty of the defense attorney who learns that a client might commit perjury at trial is to convince the client not to commit perjury. What exactly does an attorney tell a client accused of a crime who apparently plans to lie during testimony?

Before taking any further steps, the attorney must have sufficient reason to believe that her client plans to lie during testimony, despite her best efforts to convince him otherwise. ABA Model Rule of Professional Conduct 3.3(a)(4) phrases it this way: "A lawyer shall not knowingly offer evidence that the lawyer knows to be false." How will an attorney "know" that a client's testimony will be false? State courts sometimes require the attorney to be convinced "beyond a reasonable doubt" that the client plans to commit perjury. Other formulations include "good cause to believe the defendant's proposed testimony would be deliberately untruthful," "compelling support," a "firm factual basis," a "good-faith determination," and "actual knowledge." See Commonwealth v. Mitchell, 781 N.E.2d 1237 (Mass. 2003) (reviewing standards and adopting "firm basis in fact" because standard of beyond reasonable doubt would "eviscerate" attorney's ethical obligation of candor to tribunal).

2. *Defense counsel responses to perjury.* If the attorney knows that a client plans to commit perjury, or has already committed perjury at trial, several options are open

to her under the rules of ethics. One possibility is to withdraw from the case. Ethics rules allow (or even require) the attorney in most pretrial situations to make the motion, although courts often will deny the motion. ABA Model Rule of Professional Conduct 1.16(a)(1) (a lawyer "shall withdraw from the representation of a client if . . . the representation will result in violation of the rules of professional conduct or other law"). What should the attorney say in the motion to withdraw? Suppose the case is set for a bench trial. Does withdrawal prevent any harm from befalling the client or the tribunal? See Norman Lefstein, Client Perjury in Criminal Cases: Still in Search of an Answer, 1 Geo. J. Legal Ethics 521 (1988).

The attorney who does not withdraw must deal with a "trilemma — that is, the lawyer is required to know everything, to keep it in confidence, and to reveal it to the court." Monroe Freedman, Lawyers' Ethics in an Adversary System 28 (1975). The traditional resolution of these conflicting ethical duties was to emphasize the duties to investigate and to hold confidences, and to compromise the duty to reveal matters to the court. However, since the appearance of the ABA's Model Rules of Professional Conduct in 1983 (now adopted in about 40 jurisdictions), the states have moved toward rules requiring counsel to reveal the potential perjury to the court. In the words of Rule 3.3(a)(2), a lawyer "shall not knowingly . . . fail to disclose a material fact to a tribunal when disclosure is necessary to avoid assisting a criminal or fraudulent act by the client."

The defense attorney might allow the client to testify but use a "narrative" form of testimony, in which the attorney asks an open-ended question, such as "tell us what happened," and the defendant relates his story without further questions from defense counsel. See People v. Guzman, 755 P.2d 917 (Cal. 1988) (no violation of California constitution or ethics rules). Does this response strike the right balance among the defense lawyer's ethical obligations? Is this an appropriate response to perjury by a defense witness other than the defendant?

3. *Lying prosecution witnesses.* The *Reichman* case from Colorado dealt with perjury by prosecution witnesses in the context of a disciplinary proceeding against a prosecutor. The same issue also comes up when defendants challenge the validity of a conviction based on false testimony by prosecution witnesses. A prosecutor who knowingly allows prosecution witnesses to present false testimony about a material fact violates the federal due process clause. This is true even if the government attorney who knows about the false testimony is not the same as the trial attorney. Once the prosecution witness has delivered the false testimony, the prosecutor must inform the court of the falsehood. See Giglio v. United States, 405 U.S. 150 (1972); Mooney v. Holohan, 294 U.S. 103 (1935); Ex parte Frazier, 562 So. 2d 560 (Ala. 1989) (establishing standard for obtaining new trial when alleging false testimony by prosecution witnesses; prosecution witnesses were "not the prom queen, the Archbishop, or the Mayor of Mobile"); Stephen A. Saltzburg, Perjury and False Testimony: Should the Difference Matter So Much? 68 Fordham L. Rev. 1537 (2000) (*Brady* disclosure obligations have weakened earlier line of cases such as *Mooney*, concerned with presenting false testimony).

What inquiries would you expect prosecutors to make about the truthfulness of the testimony from government witnesses? What if the local police department has developed a reputation for "testilying" (providing false testimony to strengthen the prosecution's case)? See Samuel R. Gross, Kristen Jacoby, Daniel J. Matheson, Nicholas Montgomery & Sujata Patil, Exonerations in the United States, 1989 through 2003, 95 J. Crim. L. & Criminology 523 (2005) (study of 340 individual exonerations; for murder cases, the leading cause of false convictions was perjury, including perjury by police officers, by jailhouse snitches, by the real killers, and by supposed participants and eyewitnesses to the crime who knew the innocent defendants in advance); Jim Dwyer, "Videos Challenge Accounts of Convention Unrest," N.Y. Times, April 12, 2005 (video footage made possible by inexpensive cameras in the hands of private citizens and the police themselves, shifted debate over what happened on city streets during the Republican National Convention in 2004; defendant discovered that the police tape used as evidence in his trial had been edited at two spots, removing images that showed him behaving peacefully; when volunteer film archivist found a more complete version of the tape and gave it to defense lawyer, prosecutors dropped charges and said that a technician had cut the material by mistake).

Prosecuting attorneys and defense attorneys apparently have different obligations to the court when it comes to false testimony from their witnesses. Is this simply an outgrowth of the burden of proof and the beyond-a-reasonable-doubt standard in criminal cases?

PART THREE

MEASURING PUNISHMENT AND REASSESSING GUILT

IX

Sentencing

Criminal adjudication points toward sentencing. At sentencing, the system finally announces a "bottom line" outcome for those defendants who have proceeded all the way through the criminal process. Along the way, defense counsel, prosecutors, judges, and police make choices with one eye on the possible sentence. This anticipation of sentencing is perhaps most evident in plea bargaining.

Just as much of criminal procedure looks ahead to sentencing, the sentencing phase offers a chance to look back on the earlier steps in the process. At sentencing, the criminal justice system surveys once again all the major decisions it has reached regarding an offender, from investigation through conviction. It also takes a broader view of the offender's past and future, the victim's past and future, and the community's present attitude toward the crime. After this panoramic survey is complete, the sentencing authority selects a sanction.

One major puzzle for modern sentencing procedures can be summed up in this question: Why go to all the trouble of following intricate procedures for police and prosecutors, before and during trial, if the last step in the system ignores those procedural protections? This question, however, raises another: If the sentencing authority had to be bound by all determinations made prior to conviction, would convicted offenders receive undue protection, as if they were still presumed innocent?

A. WHO SENTENCES?

In most criminal justice systems, several institutions share the decision about the proper sentence to impose: Legislatures and judges always have a say in the sentence, and juries, parole commissions, or sentencing commissions may participate. But the precise division of labor in deciding on sentencing policy and sentences in particular cases varies a great deal from place to place. This division of labor in turn shapes the procedures that a court follows as it selects the sanction to impose on a convicted offender.

1. Indeterminate Sentencing

Until recently, sentencing in the United States was an area characterized more by discretion than procedure. In 1950 every state and the federal system had an "indeterminate" sentencing system. Under this type of system, the legislature prescribed broad potential sentencing ranges, and the trial judge sentenced without meaningful legal guidance and typically without offering any detailed explanation for the sentence. An executive branch agency (usually a parole board) ultimately determined the actual sentence each defendant would serve. There were virtually no judicial opinions explaining or reviewing a sentence, and legal counsel ordinarily made oral arguments at sentencing hearings without any written submissions to the court. The unwritten nature of the arguments and the decisions, together with the unavailability of pre-sentence investigation reports, made it difficult to get a handle on sentencing law and practice in an indeterminate system. Perhaps that reveals the most important point about such a system: Sentencing happened without much law.

The following materials offer a glimpse of indeterminate sentencing systems at work. The U.S. Supreme Court decision in Williams v. New York, which came at the high water mark for indeterminate sentencing, captures not only the huge discretion given to trial judges but also some of the principles underlying that discretion. The documents related to the 1989 sentencing of Col. Oliver North were filed after his conviction for obstruction of a congressional investigation into a secret (and illegal) use of funds, derived from a sale of weapons to Iran, to support insurgents in Nicaragua known as "Contras" (hence the name "Iran-Contra Affair"). The specific charges involved in North's case are less important for our purposes than the style of argument at work. The documents present, in an unusually visible and systematic form, the types of arguments and reasoning that operate in the many cases still sentenced today in indeterminate sentencing systems.

■ SAMUEL WILLIAMS v. NEW YORK
337 U.S. 961 (1949)

BLACK, J.

A jury in a New York state court found appellant guilty of murder in the first degree. The jury recommended life imprisonment, but the trial judge imposed sentence of death. In giving his reasons for imposing the death sentence the judge discussed in open court the evidence upon which the jury had convicted stating that this evidence had been considered in the light of additional information obtained through the court's "Probation Department, and through other sources." [A New York statute authorized the court to consider "any information that will aid the court in determining the proper treatment of such defendant." Williams claimed that the sentence, which was based on information supplied by witnesses, violated due process because the defendant had no chance to confront or cross-examine the witnesses or to rebut the evidence.]

The record shows a carefully conducted trial lasting more than two weeks in which appellant was represented by three appointed lawyers who conducted his defense with fidelity and zeal. The evidence proved a wholly indefensible murder committed by a person engaged in a burglary. . . .

About five weeks after the verdict of guilty with recommendation of life imprisonment, and after a statutory pre-sentence investigation report to the judge, the defendant was brought to court to be sentenced. [T]he judge gave reasons why he felt that the death sentence should be imposed. . . . He stated that the pre-sentence investigation revealed many material facts concerning appellant's background which though relevant to the question of punishment could not properly have been brought to the attention of the jury in its consideration of the question of guilt. He referred to the experience appellant "had had on 30 other burglaries in and about the same vicinity" where the murder had been committed. The appellant had not been convicted of these burglaries although the judge had information that he had confessed to some and had been identified as the perpetrator of some of the others. The judge also referred to certain activities of appellant as shown by the probation report that indicated appellant possessed "a morbid sexuality" and classified him as a "menace to society." The accuracy of the statements made by the judge as to appellant's background and past practices were not challenged by appellant or his counsel, nor was the judge asked to disregard any of them or to afford appellant a chance to refute or discredit any of them by cross-examination or otherwise.

The case presents a serious and difficult question. The question relates to the rules of evidence applicable to the manner in which a judge may obtain information to guide him in the imposition of sentence upon an already convicted defendant. . . . To aid a judge in exercising this discretion intelligently the New York procedural policy encourages him to consider information about the convicted person's past life, health, habits, conduct, and mental and moral propensities. The sentencing judge may consider such information even though obtained outside the courtroom from persons whom a defendant has not been permitted to confront or cross-examine. . . .

Tribunals passing on the guilt of a defendant always have been hedged in by strict evidentiary procedural limitations. But both before and since the American colonies became a nation, courts in this country and in England practiced a policy under which a sentencing judge could exercise a wide discretion in the sources and types of evidence used to assist him in determining the kind and the extent of punishment to be imposed within limits fixed by law. Out-of-court affidavits have been used frequently, and of course in the smaller communities sentencing judges naturally have in mind their knowledge of the personalities and backgrounds of convicted offenders. . . .

In addition to the historical basis for different evidentiary rules governing trial and sentencing procedures there are sound practical reasons for the distinction. In a trial before verdict the issue is whether a defendant is guilty of having engaged in certain criminal conduct of which he has been specifically accused. Rules of evidence have been fashioned for criminal trials which narrowly confine the trial contest to evidence that is strictly relevant to the particular offense charged. These rules rest in part on a necessity to prevent a time consuming and confusing trial of collateral issues. They were also designed to prevent tribunals concerned solely with the issue of guilt of a particular offense from being influenced to convict for that offense by evidence that the defendant had habitually engaged in other misconduct. A sentencing judge, however, is not confined to the narrow issue of guilt. His task within fixed statutory or constitutional limits is to determine the type and extent of punishment after the issue of guilt has been determined. Highly relevant — if not essential — to his selection of an appropriate sentence is the possession of the fullest information possible concerning the defendant's life and characteristics. And modern concepts individualizing punishment have made it all the more necessary that a sentencing judge not be denied an opportunity to obtain pertinent information by a requirement of rigid adherence to restrictive rules of evidence properly applicable to the trial.

Undoubtedly the New York statutes emphasize a prevalent modern philosophy of penology that the punishment should fit the offender and not merely the crime. The belief no longer prevails that every offense in a like legal category calls for an identical punishment without regard to the past life and habits of a particular offender. This whole country has traveled far from the period in which the death sentence was an automatic and commonplace result of convictions — even for offenses today deemed trivial. . . . Indeterminate sentences, the ultimate termination of which are sometimes decided by nonjudicial agencies, have to a large extent taken the place of the old rigidly fixed punishments. . . . Retribution is no longer the dominant objective of the criminal law. Reformation and rehabilitation of offenders have become important goals of criminal jurisprudence. . . .

Under the practice of individualizing punishments, investigation techniques have been given an important role. Probation workers making reports of their investigations have not been trained to prosecute but to aid offenders. Their reports have been given a high value by conscientious judges who want to sentence persons on the best available information rather than on guesswork and inadequate information. To deprive sentencing judges of this kind of information would undermine modern penological procedural policies that have been cautiously adopted throughout the nation after careful consideration and experimentation. We must recognize that most of the information now relied upon by judges to guide them in the intelligent imposition of sentences would be unavailable if information were restricted to that given in open court by witnesses subject to cross-examination. And the modern probation report draws on information concerning every aspect of a defendant's life. The type and extent of this information make totally impractical if not impossible open court testimony with cross-examination. Such a procedure could endlessly delay criminal administration in a retrial of collateral issues.

The considerations we have set out admonish us against treating the due-process clause as a uniform command that courts throughout the Nation abandon their age-old practice of seeking information from out-of-court sources to guide their judgment toward a more enlightened and just sentence. . . . So to treat the due-process clause would hinder if not preclude all courts — state and federal — from making progressive efforts to improve the administration of criminal justice. We hold that appellant was not denied due process of law. Affirmed.

MURPHY, J., dissenting.

[Williams] was convicted of murder by a jury, and sentenced to death by the judge. . . . In our criminal courts the jury sits as the representative of the community; its voice is that of the society against which the crime was committed. A judge even though vested with statutory authority to do so, should hesitate indeed to increase the severity of such a community expression.

He should be willing to increase it, moreover, only with the most scrupulous regard for the rights of the defendant. The [evidence here] would have been inadmissible at the trial. Some, such as allegations of prior crimes, was irrelevant. Much was incompetent as hearsay. All was damaging, and none was subject to scrutiny by the defendant.

Due process of law includes at least the idea that a person accused of crime shall be accorded a fair hearing through all the stages of the proceedings against him. I agree with the Court as to the value and humaneness of liberal use of probation reports as developed by modern penologists, but, in a capital case, against the unanimous recommendation of a jury, where the report would concededly not have been admissible at the trial, and was not subject to examination by the defendant, I am forced to conclude that the high commands of due process were not obeyed.

■ UNITED STATES v. OLIVER NORTH
Government's Sentencing Memorandum (June 19, 1989)

The Government respectfully submits this memorandum in connection with the sentencing of Oliver L. North, scheduled for June 23, 1989. [We] focus on those matters we believe are appropriate for the Court to consider in imposing sentence.

The most striking thing about North's posture on the eve of sentencing is his insistence that he has done nothing wrong. Instead, on the day of the verdict, he declared that his "vindication" was not "complete," and promised to "continue the fight" until it is. At the same time, he continues to profit from his notoriety, even while he decries the wastefulness and injustice of his prosecution.

The Government recognizes that sentencing North presents difficult issues. The defendant was a public official who worked tirelessly on programs he and his superiors believed should be pursued. But the crimes of which he was convicted, involving a cover-up even after those programs became known to the public, were crimes designed to protect himself and his associates, not the national security. [North] apparently sees nothing wrong with alteration and destruction of official national security records. His participation in the preparation of a false and misleading chronology [to present during a congressional hearing on the Iran-Contra affair] has not led to any acknowledgment of wrongdoing. Certainly, he sees nothing wrong with lying to Congress, when in the view of himself and his superiors lying is necessary.

His contempt for Congress and the public is accompanied by venality in financial matters. The jury found him guilty of accepting a $13,800 security system from Richard Secord, a man with whom he had been doing business in his official capacity for two years. North does not appear to question the propriety of his other financial relationships with Secord and Hakim, including the use of large amounts of cash without accountability. . . .

In fashioning a just sentence in this case, we urge the Court to consider the seriousness of North's abuse of the public trust, the need for deterrence, North's failure to accept personal responsibility for his actions, his lack of remorse and his perjury on the witness stand. Taking all of these factors into account . . . the Government submits that a term of incarceration is appropriate and necessary.

The conduct of North in this case constituted a serious breach of the public trust. . . . North seems to believe that such activities are business as usual in government or necessary tactics in a "political firestorm." But after a non-political trial and a non-political verdict, the Court, in its sentence, should alert all government officials that such activities are indeed unlawful, and that if officials engaging in such conduct are caught and convicted, the punishment will be severe. Further, the private citizens of this country, who continue to follow this case closely, are entitled to the reassurance only this Court can give that these are serious crimes and that powerful government officials are not accorded special treatment.

Deterrence is particularly important in a case involving not only obstruction, lying and cover-up, but also personal venality. While it is understandable that a person under threat of danger might seek to protect his family, this concern arises frequently for some officials engaged in the areas of intelligence, covert action or, for that matter, law enforcement. They cannot accept private gifts from those doing business with the government. Where, as here, a public official receives a substantial gratuity from an individual with whom he has conducted official business, and proceeds to create fraudulent, back-dated letters to cover it up, the Court must respond.

A sentence in this case that included no period of incarceration would send exactly the wrong message to government officials and to the public. It would be a statement that 15 years after Watergate, government officials can participate in a brazen cover-up, lie to Congress and collect a substantial gratuity and still receive only a slap on the wrist.

[A]cting in his position at the National Security Council, North wielded enormous power in the government. By his own description, he met with presidents and kings. He was the primary official responsible for the coordination of counterterrorism, the release of American hostages and relations with the Contras. . . . Thus, North held a position of substantial public trust that far exceeded his military rank. . . .

North's disregard for this basic precept of a democratic society was graphically demonstrated during his trial testimony. At one point, the Court asked the defendant whether at any time he considered in his own mind not drafting false answers to Congress but, instead, simply saying "no." In a revealing moment, the defendant stated that he never considered the possibility of not doing it. This society cannot tolerate government officials unwilling and unable to exercise independent judgment and responsibility in refusing to perform illegal acts. . . .

Although he calls himself a "scapegoat," he invited this role. He joked about the danger that he would be jailed and bragged that he would be protected because "the old man love[s] my ass." Similarly, his decision to stand trial and gamble on acquittal, a right granted by the Constitution, was also undertaken as a challenge to the capability of our system of justice to respond to crimes with political overtones, given the expressed sympathy and support of this country's then President and Vice President. . . .

North was not content merely to exercise his constitutional right to put the Government to its proof at trial. Instead, he sought to pervert the processes of justice much as he had corrupted the processes of government. With supreme faith in his ability to deceive, North took the stand and perjured himself. For example, his unsupported claim that he had a $15,000 fund in a steel box in his closet echoed the flimsy lies offered by corrupt municipal officials in the days of Tammany Hall. North's attempt to use the steel box to explain his cash purchase of a car in two installments graphically demonstrated North's penchant for weaving a tale that by its conclusion is preposterous. . . .

North's lack of remorse is particularly troubling in view of the fact that he continues to travel throughout the country, like a politician on the stump, giving speeches and discoursing on his defiance of Congress. Apparently, North has become a wealthy man in the process. The fact that this defendant is cultivating a popular following, which reinforces his lack of remorse, makes it all the more important for the Court to underscore the gravity of North's offenses by imposing a term of incarceration.

Oliver North's sentence will be known to, and closely evaluated by, all who view the perversion of government as a permissible means to the attainment of their goals. The sentence will also be carefully considered by those officials who may now be weighing the advantages of deception, obstruction and personal greed against the risks of punishment. It will also be noted by those serving substantial prison sentences for more personal crimes far less damaging to the nation. Most importantly, the sentence will be closely scrutinized by a citizenry whose confidence in government and the political system has been seriously undermined by the activities of this defendant. . . . Under all these circumstances, we respectfully submit that a term of incarceration is appropriate and necessary.

■ SENTENCING MEMORANDUM ON BEHALF OF OLIVER NORTH

Lt. Col. Oliver L. North is before the court for sentencing upon being found guilty of 3 of the 16 charges brought against him by the IC.[*] . . .

The IC's memorandum demonstrates that it will stop at nothing in its effort to crush Oliver North. The Supreme Court declared more than 50 years ago that the prosecutor "may strike hard blows, but he is not at liberty to strike foul ones." [Berger v. United States, 295 U.S. 78 (1935).] The IC has ignored the court's command; the blows that it strikes in its memorandum are as foul as any we have seen. It attacks Lt. Col. North for asserting his constitutional right to assert his innocence and stand trial; it ignores his 20 years of loyal and courageous service to this country; it takes him to task for asserting a simple truth — that most of the conduct with which he was charged was authorized by his superiors; and it blasts him for failing to show remorse, when his trial testimony makes clear that he deeply regrets many of his actions.

But the IC does not stop there. Unable to accept the jury's verdict of not guilty on 9 of 12 counts, the IC asks this Court to punish Lt. Col. North for charges on which the jury acquitted him. And not only does the IC ask the Court to disregard the jury's verdict of acquittal; it actually levels new charges, accusing Oliver North of having "supreme faith in his ability to deceive" and claiming without a shred of support that Lt. Col. North committed perjury at trial.

Just as the IC likened Lt. Col. North to Adolf Hitler at trial, it now attacks him for "arrogance"; for "personal venality"; for being "defian[t] of Congress"; and for possessing a "continuing callous attitude toward the judicial process and our democratic institutions." The IC does not offer evidence to support these charges; it plainly assumes that if it throws enough mud, some will stick. . . .

We submit that Lt. Col. North has already been punished sufficiently for the three offenses of which he was found guilty. He was fired from his job at the NSC. He has lost his career as a Marine Corps officer. He may lose his Marine Corps pension

---

[*] North was prosecuted by a specially-appointed "independent counsel," or IC. — EDS.

after 20 years of service. He remains under threat of assassination by a dangerous terrorist organization as a direct result of his service to this country. He has been subjected to unrelenting and often hostile press scrutiny for the past two-and-a-half years. Every detail of his life has been probed, first in nationally televised hearings conducted by the joint Iran/Contra committee and then by the IC. He has heard himself likened to Hitler by a prosecutor who appears to lack any sense of fairness and rumors in the press, before Congress, in court, in a nationally televised "docudrama," and now in the IC's memorandum. His children have been tormented. By any standard, the toll that this ordeal has already taken on Lt. Col. North and his family fulfills every legitimate purpose of punishment.

If the Court accepts the IC's view that this punishment is not enough — that Oliver North must be punished further for the three offenses of which he was found guilty — then that punishment should take the form of probation conditioned on community service. As the testimony at trial and letters to the Court demonstrate, Lt. Col. North is a man of extraordinary energy and talents, with remarkable compassion for his fellow man. We urge the Court to permit him to continue using those talents on behalf of the country that he has served with such devotion. A sentence of imprisonment would be cruel and unjust. . . .

In determining the proper sentence for Oliver North, the Court should consider the man as an individual, not — as the IC would have it — merely as a vehicle through which to send a "public message." The Court should weigh carefully Lt. Col. North's service to this country and to society, the devastating impact that imprisonment would have on his family, and the unique confluence of circumstances that gave rise to his conduct. This careful, individualized sentencing is essential to ensure that "the punishment should fit the offender and not merely the crime." Williams v. New York, 337 U.S. 241 (1949).

Oliver North devoted 20 years to the service of this country, from Vietnam to Tehran to Beirut. He has risked his own life and saved the lives of others. We submit that the Court should weigh this service in Lt. Col. North's favor at sentencing.

Upon graduation from the Naval Academy in 1968, Oliver North was commissioned in the United States Marine Corps and served as a platoon commander in Vietnam. His courage protected the lives of many young Marines, including Bill Haskell. In his letter to the Court, Mr. Haskell describes how Oliver North rescued him in the face of hostile fire as he lay wounded:

> . . . Early in the combat I was severely wounded so we needed help quickly. Ollie came to the rescue. In the face of an almost unbelievable barrage of enemy fire, he led a counterattack with his platoon driving the enemy back so that the Marines could medivac their wounded. I think I know Ollie well enough to say that his primary motivation for such heroic action was the desire to save his fellow Marines rather than just to achieve victory over the enemy. Ollie saved my life that day.

Oliver North received the Silver Star Medal for his heroism in saving Bill Haskell and his platoon. He received other medals as well for his service in Vietnam, including two Purple Hearts; a Bronze Star Medal with Combat "V"; and a Navy Commendation Medal with Combat "V." . . .

Following his service in Vietnam, Oliver North became an instructor for other Marines. He devoted himself to ensuring that other young men would be prepared if they were thrust into combat as he had been in Vietnam. . . .

In 1981, Oliver North was assigned to the National Security Council staff. At the NSC, he quickly established himself as a dedicated and hard-working staff officer. . . . Oliver North served initially with distinction on a highly sensitive national security project under the direct supervision of then-Vice President Bush. Lt. Gen. Ben Lewis [says that the project] "put in place, in record time, key mechanisms that were essential to meaningful negotiations with our Allies and the Soviet Union on reducing the size of nuclear forces." . . . As National Intelligence Officer Charles Allen writes, "[I]n a dangerous world, Lt. Col. North has helped make the world safer for every American" through his work on this sensitive project.

By 1984, Oliver North was responsible for two principal areas: counterterrorism and Central America. He worked tirelessly to fulfill these responsibilities. . . .

As a direct result of his critical work to protect Americans from the terrorist threat, Oliver North was targeted for assassination by the Abu Nidal terrorist group — described by Mr. Allen, a counterterrorism expert, as "the most dangerous and capable terrorist group in the Middle East and one of the most dangerous terrorist groups in the world." . . .

A further example demonstrates Lt. Col. North's courageous service to this country. In May 1986, at the President's direction, he and a handful of others undertook a dangerous mission to Tehran in an effort to achieve an opening to Iran and free the American hostages held in Lebanon. This trip entailed great personal danger to Lt. Col. North and his companions; they were the first American officials to travel to Iran since the revolution, and radical Iranians posed a significant threat of death or torture. The danger was particularly great because the trip was absolutely secret. But Lt. Col. North left his family behind — unable even to tell them where he was going — and risked his life for his country and for those held hostage. We ask that the Court give this record of service great weight in choosing the appropriate sentence for Oliver North.

Oliver North . . . has worked to improve society in other ways as well. Since the Congressional hearings of 1987, he has put his unsought and unwanted notoriety to use in service of his fellow citizens, particularly America's youth. Two examples illustrate Lt. Col. North's compassion and concern — and put the lie to the IC's claim that Lt. Col. North displays "contempt for the public."

First, shortly after his Congressional testimony, Lt. Col. North learned that it was the dream of a terminally ill boy to see him before the boy died. Lt. Col. North agreed to meet the boy to give him courage in his final days. The woman who arranged the meeting describes what happened in her letter to the Court:

> [The boy] told me he wanted to meet Lt. Col. North because this was the strongest person that he could ever know. [The boy] said that he needed this man to teach him how to become stronger mentally so that he could deal with his fast-approaching death. . . .
>
> To my amazement and delight, Lt. Col. North brought with him a large Bible with certain scriptures marked throughout the Bible that he said he lives by, that his strength comes from his faith in God. He sat down and read with the child from the Bible and they prayed together that [the boy] would find his answers. Lt. Col. North spent one and a half hours alone with [the boy] helping him to find the strength that the child was very much in need of. . . .

Lt. Col. North placed the following inscription on a photograph for the dying boy: "Courageous Hero, Inspiration, Fighter — Semper Fidelis. 18 September '87, Oliver L. North."

Second, Lt. Col. North has spoken out throughout America against drug use and in favor of improved drug prevention and rehabilitation. As but one example, he delivered a speech on behalf of the drug-prevention organization Reach Out America. . . .

Oliver and Betsy North have been married for almost 21 years. They have three daughters and one son. In sentencing Oliver North, the Court should consider both the devastation that this matter has already inflicted on the North family, and the further damage that any term of imprisonment would cause. . . . Two of Oliver North's daughters have been cruelly mocked at school. The family has been portrayed in grossly unfair ways in a nationally televised "docudrama." And the press has forced Oliver North and his family into an inescapable limelight—sometimes cruel, sometimes favorable, but always present.

The Court should also consider the damage that any period of incarceration would cause the North family in the future, particularly the children. . . . It would be wrong to take Oliver North away from his family at this most vulnerable time.

Criminal punishment serves four legitimate purposes: it incapacitates the offender, to prevent him from harming society; it rehabilitates him; it deters him and others from committing further offenses; and it reflects the seriousness of the offenses. The punishment that Oliver North and his family have suffered to date more than adequately fulfills each of these purposes.

1. *Incapacitation.* There is no need to incapacitate Oliver North. Far from representing a threat to society, Lt. Col. North devoted his professional life to ensuring the safety of Americans at home and abroad. . . .

2. *Rehabilitation.* No one can seriously contend that Oliver North needs rehabilitation, and it would be preposterous to suggest that, if rehabilitation *were* necessary, it would occur in prison. . . .

3. *Deterrence.* The punishment that Oliver North has suffered to date fully satisfied any need for deterrence; no additional sentence is necessary.

First, there is no need for a harsh punishment to achieve *specific* deterrence—deterrence of Lt. Col. North from future unlawful acts. In light of his record of service to this country and the excruciating ordeal that he and his family have endured, there is no chance that he will commit offenses in the future.

Second, *general* deterrence—deterrence of those other than Lt. Col. North—provides no basis for harsh punishment. The punishment that Lt. Col. North has suffered to date—including the loss of his position at the NSC, the loss of his career in the Marine Corps, and the minute and public scrutiny of his most private affairs by Congress, the IC, and frequently the media—should amply deter others.

Moreover, a prison sentence for Lt. Col. North would *not* deter high government officials from using their subordinates to carry out actions that are legally or politically risky. It would not escape the notice of such officials if Oliver North were to go to prison while others remain in government in positions of power or return to private-sector sinecures. . . .

4. *The Seriousness of the Offense.* The punishment that Lt. Col. North has suffered to date more than adequately reflects the gravity of the offenses of which he was found guilty. The three offenses—aiding and abetting an obstruction of Congress, destroying, altering, and/or removing official NSC documents, and accepting an unlawful gratuity—are serious. Each is a felony; each has a maximum prison term of between two and five years; and each carries a maximum fine of $250,000. But the

seriousness of these offenses is significantly reduced by the unique circumstances of this case.

Lt. Col. North's conduct with respect to the security system is particularly understandable. His life had been threatened and his family placed at risk by one of the world's most dangerous terrorists. He had compelling evidence that Abu Nidal had the ability to carry out the threat in the United States. . . . Oliver North permitted a security system to be installed at his home for the protection of his family. That conduct may have represented poor judgment, but there are powerful mitigating factors, and no one could argue that it was seriously culpable. . . .

■ UNITED STATES v. OLIVER NORTH
Transcript (D.D.C. July 5, 1989)

GESELL, J.

I can assure you, Colonel North, that I'm going to take into full consideration the important fact that before you came to the White House you had served your country with distinction in the highest traditions of the Marine Corps. And the court is not going to overlook that there were major matters of military and quasi-military nature which you performed, again with the highest distinction at great personal risk to yourself after you came to the White House. But I'm sure you realize that this case has little to do with your military behavior, commitment or expertise.

The indictment involves your participation in particular covert events. I do not think that in this area you were a leader at all, but really a low ranking subordinate working to carry out initiatives of a few cynical superiors. You came to be the point man in a very complex power play developed by higher-ups. Whether it was because of the excitement and the challenge or because of conviction, you responded certainly willingly and sometimes even excessively to their requirements. And along the way you came to accept, it seems to me, the mistaken view that Congress couldn't be trusted and that the fate of the country was better left to a small inside group, not elected by the people, who were free to act as they chose while publicly professing to act differently. Thus you became . . . part of a scheme that reflected a total distrust in some constitutional values. . . .

As you stand there now you're not the fall guy for this tragic breach of the public trust. . . . You're here now because of your own conduct when the truth was coming out. Apparently you could not face disclosure and decided to protect yourself and others. You destroyed evidence, altered and removed official documents, created false papers after the events to keep Congress and others from finding out what was happening.

Now, I believe that you knew this was morally wrong. It was against your bringing up. It was against your faith. It was against all of your training. Under the stress of the moment it was easier to choose the role of a martyr but that wasn't a heroic, patriotic act nor was it in the public interest.

You have had great remorse for your family and understandably so. It is often the tragic part of what happens when mistakes are made. I believe you still lack full understanding, however, of how the public service has been tarnished. Nonetheless, what you believe is your own business and jail would only harden your misconceptions. Given the many highly commendable aspects of your life your punishment will not include jail. Indeed, community service may in the end make you more conscious of certain values which at times you and your associates appear to have overlooked in the elite isolation of the White House. . . .

I fashioned a sentence that punishes you. It is my duty to do that. But it leaves the future up to you. This is the sentence of the court. On count six where you are found guilty of aiding and abetting [an] obstruction of Congress, I'm going to impose a sentence of three years and suspend the execution of the sentence, place you on probation for two years, fine you $100,000 and I have to impose a special assessment of $50.

Under count nine, altering, removing and destroying the permanent historical records of the National Security Council I impose a sentence of two years, suspend the execution of sentence, place you on probation for two years, fine you $35,000 and impose a special assessment of $50 and I am required by the statute to impose another mandatory penalty. You are hereby disqualified from holding any office under the United States.

Under count ten, receiving an illegal gratuity, I'll impose a sentence of one year, suspend the execution of that sentence, place you on probation for two years, fine you $15,000 and impose a special assessment again of $50. These sentences and the probation are to run concurrently. The fines are to run consecutively.

Your probation shall consist in addition to the normal requirements of community service in a total amount of 1200, 800 the first year, and 400 the second year and you will remain under the supervision of the District of Columbia probation officer who is familiar with your situation and who has prepared the pre-sentence report. . . .

Notes

1. *Informal procedure at sentencing: majority position.* The New York statute discussed in *Williams,* which allowed the sentencing judge to consider evidence inadmissible under the rules of evidence, typifies sentencing practices in most states. See also Tex. Crim. Proc. Code Ann. §37.07(3). The informal presentation of evidence supposedly supports an effort to obtain the most information possible about the offender and the offense and to make an individualized (perhaps even clinical) decision. Many different actors participate over time in the decision about how best to respond to an individual offender. Thus, the indeterminate sentencing system is one of "multiple discretions." Professor Franklin Zimring describes the system as follows:

> The best single phrase to describe the allocation of sentencing power in state and federal criminal justice is multiple discretion. Putting aside the enormous power of the police to decide whether to arrest, and to select initial charges, there are four separate institutions that have the power to determine criminal sentences — the legislature, the prosecutor, the judge, and the parole board or its equivalent. . . . With all our emphasis on due process in the determination of guilt, our machinery for setting punishment lacks any principle except unguided discretion. Plea bargaining, disparity of treatment and uncertainty are all symptoms of a larger malaise — the absence of rules or even guidelines in determining the distribution of punishments. . . .

Zimring, Making the Punishment Fit the Crime: A Consumer's Guide to Sentencing Reform, 12 Occasional Papers of the University of Chicago Law School (1977). More than half of the states use such an indeterminate sentencing system for large groups of cases, although many of these same states might use more narrowly circumscribed sentencing rules for some crimes.

2. *Williams revisited.* Samuel Titto Williams, a black man, was 18 years old at the time he killed 15-year-old Selma Graff, who surprised him during a burglary. He had no record of prior convictions, but he had been accused of burglary at age 11. The judgment in juvenile court was suspended. The probation report—a report prepared by probation officers prior to sentencing, also called a pre-sentence investigation report—informed the judge that Williams was suspected of (but not charged with) committing 30 burglaries during the two months before the murder. A seven-year-old girl who was present during one of those burglaries told the probation department that Williams had molested her sexually. She identified Williams as the perpetrator two weeks after the incident. The probation report also stated that Williams was living with two women, and had brought different men into the apartment for the purpose of having sexual relations with the women. It alleged that he had once gone to a local school to photograph "private parts of young children." Finally, the sentencing judge relied on injuries inflicted on the murder victim's brother during the burglary. The prosecutor had not brought any charges based on the assault. See Kevin Reitz, Sentencing Facts: Travesties of Real-Offense Sentencing, 45 Stan. L. Rev. 523 (1993). Is the problem in *Williams* the new offender information at sentencing or the lack of access to that information?

3. *Capital punishment and informal procedure.* Although the *Williams* Court empha-sized that rehabilitative purposes of sentencing required far-reaching information about an offender, the proposed "treatment" for Williams was execution. It brings to mind the statement attributed to the comedian W. C. Fields, who quoted a con-demned prisoner on his way to the electric chair, saying, "This will certainly be a lesson to me." *Williams* is still cited with approval in support of informal sentencing procedures generally. However, it has been partially overruled in the context of capital sentencing. In Gardner v. Florida, 430 U.S. 349 (1977), the trial judge sen-tenced a defendant to death after consulting confidential and unrebutted informa-tion in the pre-sentence investigation report. A plurality of the Supreme Court found that due process required, at least in capital cases, that the defendant have access to information that will influence the sentencing judge and have an oppor-tunity to test its reliability.

4. *Discretion in different institutions.* When judges describe the factors they con-sider in sentencing under an indeterminate system, they often list the types of considerations that the lawyers and the judge discussed in the Oliver North case. One study of sentences in white-collar crime cases in federal court concluded that judges considered three common principles during sentencing: (1) the harm the offense produced; (2) the blameworthiness of the defendant, judged both from the defendant's criminal intent and from other details of the crime and defendant's earlier life; and (3) the consequences of the punishment, both for deterring future wrongdoing and for the well-being of the defendant's family and community. Despite the presence of these common principles for sentencing, judges selected very different sentences because they did not agree on how to measure each of the principles or the relative weight to place on each. See Stanton Wheeler, Kenneth Mann & Austin Sarat, Sitting in Judgment: The Sentencing of White-Collar Criminals (1988).

Observers in higher-volume courts, such as state misdemeanor courts, have described a very different reality. During plea bargaining the parties settle quickly on a proper sentence, hinging largely on the charges finally filed and on the parties' interpretation of the facts as reflected in the police reports. These negotiations do not often involve individualized haggling, as in a Middle Eastern bazaar. Rather, they are "more akin to modern supermarkets in which prices for various commodities have been clearly established and labeled." Malcolm Feeley, The Process Is the Punishment: Handling Cases in a Lower Criminal Court 187 (1979). What determines whether a given case will receive the "supermarket" form of sentencing or a more individualized assessment? Is it the presence or absence of a plea agreement?

5. *Sentencing juries.* In some states, juries not only rule on guilt or innocence but also decide the sentence to impose, even in noncapital cases. In about six of these states, the jury's choice is binding; in a few others, the jury only recommends a sentence to the judge. See Fla. Stat. §921.141 (jury recommends sentence); Tex. Crim. Proc. Code Ann. §37.07 (judge can assess punishment if defendant does not request probation or jury sentence; jury must be instructed about parole and other devices for reducing actual amount of prison time offender must serve). Sentencing juries tend to impose longer prison terms than sentencing judges would impose in comparable cases. See Nancy J. King & Rosevelt L. Noble, Felony Jury Sentencing in Practice: A Three-State Study, 57 Vand. L. Rev. 885 (2004). Even in a system that gives no formal sentencing power to juries, the jury might consider likely punishments as it deliberates on the verdict in the case. The jury might acquit if it believes the sanction is too severe.

The ABA Standards for Criminal Justice: Sentencing 18-1.4 (3d ed. 1994) call for the abolition of jury sentencing. Why do the ABA standards, along with the strong majority of the states, give sentencing responsibilities to the judge and not the jury, the representatives of the community? For proposals to expand the use of jury sentencing, see Jenia Iontcheva, Jury Sentencing as Democratic Practice, 88 Va. L. Rev. 311 (2003); Adriaan Lanni, Note, Jury Sentencing in Noncapital Cases: An Idea Whose Time Has Come (Again)? 108 Yale L.J. 1775 (1999).

Should the sentencing jury be required to vote unanimously for a particular sentence? Should its voting rules be the same as the rules for its vote on guilt and innocence? See Manual for Courts-Martial, Rule 1006(d) (Exec. Order No. 12,473) (members of court martial may propose sentences; panel must consider each proposed sentence from least severe to most severe; unanimous vote needed for death penalty; three-fourths of members must recommend confinement for more than 10 years; two-thirds of members must recommend other sentences).

2. Legislative Sentencing

Although indeterminate sentencing has been the norm in this country for most of the twentieth century, new arrangements have emerged over the past generation. Some of those alternative approaches have put the legislature more firmly in control of sentencing. Legislators have decided for themselves the precise sentence that will attach to various types of offenses; other sentencing institutions such as courts are supposed to carry out the choices of the legislature without adding any meaningful choices of their own.

Sentences dominated by legislative choices go back to some of the earliest recorded sources of law. American legislatures during the eighteenth and nineteenth centuries often set specific sentences for designated crimes. Only in the late nineteenth and early twentieth centuries did the state and federal legislatures routinely create more "indeterminate" sentences, authorizing a range of sentences from which a sentencing judge could select a sentence to impose on a particular offender. When legislatures began once again, in the middle of the twentieth century, to designate the specific punishments for certain crimes, they were returning to earlier practices.

■ CODE OF HAMMURABI
(C. H. W. Johns Trans., 1911)

§1: If a man weave a spell and put a ban upon a man, and has not justified himself, he that wove the spell upon him shall be put to death.

§8: If a man has stolen ox or sheep or ass, or pig, or ship, whether from the temple or the palace, he shall pay thirtyfold. If he be a poor man, he shall render tenfold. If the thief has naught to pay, he shall be put to death.

§15: If a man has caused either a palace slave or palace maid, or a slave of a poor man or a poor man's maid, to go out of the gate, he shall be put to death.

§195: If a man has struck his father, his hands one shall cut off.

§196: If a man has caused the loss of a gentleman's eye, his eye one shall cause to be lost.

§197: If he has shattered a gentleman's limb, one shall shatter his limb.

§198: If he has caused a poor man to lose his eye or shattered a poor man's limb, he shall pay one mina of silver.

§209: If a man has struck a gentleman's daughter and caused her to drop what is in her womb, he shall pay ten shekels of silver for what was in her womb.

§210: If that woman has died, one shall put to death his daughter.

§211: If the daughter of a poor man through his blows he has caused to drop that which is in her womb, he shall pay five shekels of silver.

§212: If that woman has died, he shall pay half a mina of silver.

■ U.S. SENTENCING COMMISSION, MANDATORY MINIMUM PENALTIES IN THE FEDERAL CRIMINAL JUSTICE SYSTEM
i-ix, 5-15, 27-32 (1991)

Mandatory minimum sentences are not new to the federal criminal justice system. As early as 1790, mandatory penalties had been established for capital offenses. In addition, at subsequent intervals throughout the 19th Century, Congress enacted provisions that required definite prison terms, typically quite short, for a variety of other crimes. Until recently, however, the enactment of mandatory minimum provisions was generally an occasional phenomenon that was not comprehensively aimed at whole classes of offenses.

A change in practice occurred with the passage of the Narcotic Control Act of 1956, which mandated minimum sentences of considerable length for most drug importation and distribution offenses. . . . In 1970, Congress drew back from the comprehensive application of mandatory minimum provisions to drug crimes enacted 14 years earlier. Finding that increases in sentence length "had not shown the expected overall reduction in drug law violations," Congress passed [legislation] that repealed virtually all mandatory penalties for drug violations.

[Growing criticism of efforts to rehabilitate inmates led lawmakers] to renew support for mandatory minimum penalties. On the state level this trend began in New York in 1973, with California and Massachusetts following soon thereafter. While the trend toward mandatory minimums in the states was gradual, by 1983, 49 of the 50 states had passed such provisions. . . . On the federal level, a comparable but more comprehensive trend was under way. Beginning in 1984, and every two years thereafter, Congress enacted an array of mandatory minimum penalties specifically targeted at drugs and violent crime. . . . Today there are approximately 100 separate federal mandatory minimum penalty provisions located in 60 different criminal statutes. . . . Of the 59,780 cases sentenced under mandatory minimum statutes [between 1984 and 1990], four statutes account for approximately 94 percent of the cases. These four statutes . . . all involve drugs and weapons violations. . . .

Reasons Cited in Support of Mandatory Minimums

[Field interviews with] judges, assistant United States attorneys, defense attorneys, and probation officers . . . identified six commonly offered rationales for mandatory minimum sentencing provisions.

Retribution or "Just Deserts." Perhaps the most commonly voiced goal of mandatory minimum penalties is the "justness" of long prison terms for particularly serious offenses. Proponents generally agree that longer sentences are deserved and that, absent mandatory penalties, judges would impose sentences more lenient than would be appropriate.

Deterrence. . . . Those supporting mandatory minimums on deterrence grounds point not only to the strong deterrent value of the certainty of substantial punishment these penalties are intended to provide, but also to the deterrent value of sentence severity that these penalties are intended to ensure in the war against crime.

Incapacitation, Especially of the Serious Offender. Mandating increased sentence severity aims to protect the public by incapacitating offenders convicted of serious crimes for definite, and generally substantial, periods of time. Proponents argue that one way to increase public safety, particularly with respect to guns and drugs, is to remove drug dealers and violent offenders from the streets for extended periods of time.

Disparity. Indeterminate sentencing systems permit substantial latitude in setting the sentence, which in turn can mean that defendants convicted of the same offense are sentenced to widely disparate sentences. Supporters of mandatory minimum penalties contend that they greatly reduce judicial discretion and are therefore more fair. Mandatory minimums are meant to ensure that defendants convicted of similar offenses receive penalties that at least begin at the same minimal point.

Inducement of Cooperation. Because they provide specific lengthy sentences, mandatory minimums encourage offenders to assist in the investigation of criminal conduct by others. This is because cooperation — that is, supplying information concerning the activities of other criminally involved individuals — is the only statutorily recognized way to permit the court to impose a sentence below the length of imprisonment required by the mandatory minimum sentence.

Inducement of Pleas. Although infrequently cited by policymakers, prosecutors express the view that mandatory minimum sentences can be valuable tools in obtaining guilty pleas, saving scarce enforcement resources and increasing the certainty of at least some measure of punishment. In this context, the value of a mandatory minimum sentence lies not in its imposition, but in its value as a bargaining chip to be given away in return for the resource-saving plea from the defendant to a more leniently sanctioned charge.

[Now we turn to some of the criticisms of mandatory minimum sentences.]

The "Tariff" Effect of Mandatory Minimums

Years ago, Congress used tariff sentences in sanctioning broad categories of offenses, ranging from quite serious crimes (e.g., homicide) to fairly minor property theft. This tariff approach has been rejected historically primarily because there were too many defendants whose important distinctions were obscured by this single, flat approach to sentencing. A more sophisticated, calibrated approach that takes into account gradations of offense seriousness, criminal record, and level of culpability has long since been recognized as a more appropriate and equitable method of sentencing. . . .

The mandatory minimums set forth in 21 U.S.C. §841(b), applicable to defendants convicted of trafficking in the more common street drugs, are illustrative. For those convicted of drug trafficking under this section, one offense-related factor, and only one, is determinative of whether the mandatory minimum applies: the weight of the drug or drug mixture. Any other sentence-individualizing factors that might pertain in a case are irrelevant as far as the statute is concerned. Thus, for example, whether the defendant was a peripheral participant or the drug ring's kingpin, whether the defendant used a weapon, whether the defendant accepted responsibility or, on the other hand, obstructed justice, have no bearing on the mandatory minimum to which each defendant is exposed. . . .

The "Cliff" Effect of Mandatory Minimums

Related to the proportionality problems posed in mandatory minimums already described are the sharp differences in sentence between defendants who fall just below the threshold of a mandatory minimum compared with those whose criminal conduct just meets the criteria of the mandatory minimum penalty. Just as mandatory minimums fail to distinguish among defendants whose conduct and prior records in fact differ markedly, they distinguish far too greatly among defendants who have committed offense conduct of highly comparable seriousness.

[A] lack of coordination between statutory maximum and mandatory minimum penalties for the same or similar offenses can create dramatic sentencing cliffs among similarly situated defendants. For example, 21 U.S.C. §884 mandates a minimum five-year term of imprisonment for a defendant convicted of first-offense, simple possession of 5.01 or more grams of "crack." . . . However, a first-offender convicted of simple possession of 5.0 grams of crack is subjected to a *maximum* statutory penalty of one year imprisonment. . . .

The "Charge-Specific" Nature of Mandatory Minimums

. . . In general, a mandatory minimum becomes applicable only when the prosecutor elects to *charge* and the defendant is *convicted* of the specific offense carrying the mandatory sentence. . . . Mandatory minimums employ a structure that allows a shifting of discretion and control over the implementation of sentencing policies from courts to prosecutors. [There] is substantial reason to believe that mandatory minimums are not in fact pursued by prosecutors in all instances that the underlying statutes otherwise would require. . . .

Problem 9-1. The Shopaholic

Gary Ewing walked into the pro shop of the El Segundo Golf Course in Los Angeles County on March 12, 2000. He walked out with three golf clubs, priced at $399 apiece, concealed in his pants leg. A shop employee, whose became suspicious when he saw Ewing limp out of the pro shop, telephoned the police. The police apprehended Ewing in the parking lot.

This was not Ewing's first contact with the criminal justice system. In 1984, at the age of 22, he pleaded guilty to theft. The court sentenced him to six months in jail (a suspended term), three years' probation, and a $300 fine. In 1988 he was convicted of felony grand theft auto and sentenced to one year in jail and three years' probation. After Ewing completed probation, however, the sentencing court reduced the crime to a misdemeanor, permitted Ewing to withdraw his guilty plea, and dismissed the case. In 1990 he was convicted of petty theft with a prior conviction, and sentenced to 60 days in the county jail and three years' probation. In 1992 Ewing was convicted of battery and sentenced to 30 days in the county jail and two years' summary probation. One month later, he was convicted of theft and sentenced to 10 days in the county jail and 12 months' probation. In January 1993 Ewing was convicted of burglary and sentenced to 60 days in the county jail and one year's summary probation. In February 1993 he was convicted of possessing drug paraphernalia and sentenced to six months in the county jail and three years' probation. In July 1993 he was convicted of appropriating lost property and sentenced to 10 days in the county jail and two years' summary probation. In September 1993 he was convicted of unlawfully possessing a firearm and trespassing, and was sentenced to 30 days in the county jail and one year's probation.

In October and November 1993 Ewing committed three burglaries and one robbery at a Long Beach, California, apartment complex over a five-week period. During the robbery, Ewing accosted a victim in the mailroom of the apartment complex. Ewing claimed to have a gun and ordered the victim to hand over his wallet. When the victim resisted, Ewing produced a knife and forced the victim back to the apartment itself. While Ewing rifled through the bedroom, the victim fled the apartment screaming for help. Ewing absconded with the victim's money and credit cards. A jury convicted Ewing of first-degree robbery and three counts of residential burglary. The court sentenced him to nine years and eight months in prison, and Ewing was paroled in 1999.

Only 10 months later, while he was still on parole status, Ewing stole the golf clubs at issue in this case. He was convicted of one count of felony grand theft of personal property in excess of $400.

California has a "three strikes and you're out" law that was designed "to ensure longer prison sentences and greater punishment for those who commit a felony and have been previously convicted of serious and/or violent felony offenses." Cal. Penal Code §667(b). When a defendant is convicted of a felony, and has previously been convicted of one or more prior felonies defined as "serious" or "violent" in

Cal. Penal Code Ann. §§667.5 and 1192.7, sentencing is conducted pursuant to the three-strikes law. If the defendant has one prior "serious" or "violent" felony conviction, he must be sentenced to twice the term otherwise provided as punishment for the current felony conviction. If the defendant has two or more prior "serious" or "violent" felony convictions, he must receive an indeterminate term of life imprisonment. Defendants sentenced to life under the three-strikes law become eligible for parole on a date calculated by reference to a "minimum term," which is the greater of (a) three times the term otherwise provided for the current conviction, (b) 25 years, or (c) the term determined by the court pursuant to §1170 for the underlying conviction, including any enhancements.

Under California law, certain offenses may be classified as either felonies or misdemeanors. These crimes are known as "wobblers." Some crimes that would otherwise be misdemeanors become "wobblers" because of the defendant's prior record. For example, petty theft, a misdemeanor, becomes a "wobbler" when the defendant has previously served a prison term for committing specified theft-related crimes. Other crimes, such as grand theft, are "wobblers" regardless of the defendant's prior record. Both types of "wobblers" are triggering offenses under the three strikes law only when they are treated as felonies.

In California, prosecutors may exercise their discretion to charge a "wobbler" as either a felony or a misdemeanor. Trial courts may avoid imposing a three-strikes sentence in two ways: first, by reducing "wobblers" to misdemeanors (which do not qualify as triggering offenses), and second, by vacating allegations of prior "serious" or "violent" felony convictions.

In Ewing's case, the prosecutor formally alleged, and the trial court later found, that Ewing had been convicted previously of four serious or violent felonies for the three burglaries and the robbery in the Long Beach apartment complex.

Before sentencing Ewing, the trial court took note of his entire criminal history, including the fact that he was on parole when he committed his latest offense. The judge determined that the grand theft should remain a felony. The court also ruled that the four prior strikes for the three burglaries and the robbery in Long Beach should stand. As a newly convicted felon with two or more "serious" or "violent" felony convictions in his past, Ewing was sentenced under the three strikes law to 25 years to life.

Does this sentence qualify as "cruel and unusual punishment" for purposes of the Eighth Amendment, when the court imposes such a prison term on a repeat offender who stole $1,197 worth of gold clubs? Cf. Ewing v. California, 538 U.S. 11 (2003).

Notes

1. *Federal constitutional limits on legislative choice of sanctions: majority position.* Courts by and large allow legislatures to choose any punishment for a given crime (with the exception of the death penalty) and turn aside most claims that a punishment is "cruel and unusual" or "disproportionate" to the crime. According to the Supreme Court in Ewing v. California, 538 U.S. 11 (2003), the Eighth Amendment does not require strict proportionality between crime and sentence. Instead, it forbids only extreme sentences that are "grossly disproportionate" to the crime. Courts applying this proportionality test engage in three related inquiries. First, the court weighs the crime committed against the sentence imposed. If this "threshold"

inquiry leads to an inference of gross disproportionality, the court then compares sentences imposed on other criminals in the same jurisdiction (the "intrajurisdictional analysis") and sentences imposed for commission of the same crime in other jurisdictions (the "interjurisdictional analysis"). In a companion case to *Ewing*, Lockyer v. Andrade, 538 U.S. 63 (2003), the defendant stole videotapes worth $154 from two Kmart stores. Andrade also had a criminal record, with several convictions for misdemeanor theft, residential burglary, and transportation of marijuana. Although Andrade was sentenced under California's three-strikes law to a life term lasting at least 50 years, the Court upheld the sentence. How can the Court assess the first prong of its test — the gravity of the offense and the harshness of the penalty — other than by relying on the second and third prongs to provide an answer?

Does the decision in *Ewing* reflect merely the predilections of the majority of the Court rather than a principled assessment of the sentence? Would it have been more honest for the Court to decline proportionality review in imprisonment cases generally? See also Harmelin v. Michigan, 501 U.S. 957 (1991) (because of the severe social harms flowing from illegal drugs, the Court decided that there was no gross disparity between the crime of possession of 650 grams of cocaine and the sentence of life imprisonment); Solem v. Helm, 463 U.S. 277 (1983) (cruel and unusual punishment to impose life imprisonment without possibility of parole on defendant for uttering no-account check for $100; defendant had three prior convictions for third-degree burglary, one prior conviction for obtaining money under false pretenses, one prior conviction of grand larceny, and one prior conviction of third-offense driving while intoxicated).

2. *Proportionality in the state courts.* State courts have applied the *Ewing* test under the Eighth Amendment to bar some disproportionate sentences. See Crosby v. State, 824 A.2d 894 (Del. 2003) (life sentence of 45 years for second-degree forgery was excessive, even for defendant with prior felony convictions). It is more common for state courts to uphold a legislative choice of sanctions in the case at hand, even if they recognize that a proportionality challenge might succeed in theory. State v. Moss-Dwyer, 686 N.E.2d 109 (Ind. 1997) (recognizing possible proportionality challenges under state constitution, but refusing to declare a sentence disproportionate where statute made misinformation on a handgun permit application a greater crime than carrying a handgun without a license). A few state courts have been willing to insist, under various provisions of their state constitutions, that the legislature select a punishment that is proportionate to the crime. See People v. Miller, 781 N.E.2d 300 (Ill. 2002). Whose standards — those of the state, the nation, or the local community — should apply in determining what shocks the conscience?

Nonconstitutional limitations on imprisonment provide more meaningful day-to-day controls than do constitutional limitations. Sentencing guidelines, for example, set out presumptive sentencing ranges for specific offenses. While guideline regimes allow for departures, they require detailed justifications and are open to appellate challenges. Another statutory limitation on imprisonment is the federal safety valve program, which allows for the sentencing of low-level, nonviolent drug offenders to prison terms below the mandatory minimum. Other limitations may be imposed by state statutes mandating that certain offenders not be sentenced to prison. Among such legislation is the 2002 California referendum requiring drug treatment rather than imprisonment for first-time, nonviolent drug offenders. For discussion of a similar statute, see State v. DePiano, 926 P.2d 494 (Ariz. 1996) (despondent mother's unsuccessful attempt to commit suicide and infanticide by asphyxiation was punished by 34-year prison term; court reduced sentence under statute allowing reduction if "the punishment imposed is greater than under the circumstances of the case ought to be inflicted").

3. *Internal consistency: similar statutes, similar safety threats.* In State v. Walden, 769 N.E.2d 928 (Ill. 2002), the court struck down a 15-year sentencing enhancement for the carrying of a firearm during an armed robbery as violating the proportionate penalties clause of the Illinois constitution. That clause, found at Article I, section 11, says, "All penalties shall be determined both according to the seriousness of the offense and with the objective of restoring the offender to useful citizenship."

David Walden was charged with one count of armed robbery while in possession of a firearm. He challenged his sentence as disproportionate under the state constitution, because it punished him more severely than a related crime in the state code, armed violence predicated upon aggravated robbery. The appellate court reviewed the legislative history of the two provisions and concluded that they share a statutory purpose—the more severe punishment of violent crimes when committed with firearms:

> Having concluded that the two offenses share an identical statutory purpose, we next must determine whether one offense is more serious than the other. This is not a difficult inquiry, as armed violence predicated upon aggravated robbery is clearly the more serious offense. [Armed] violence predicated upon aggravated robbery . . . requires that the offender, while using or threatening the imminent use of force, inform the victim that he or she is presently armed with a firearm. Thus, armed robbery while in possession of a firearm may be committed while carrying a concealed firearm that is neither revealed nor even mentioned to the victim. . . .
>
> Our final inquiry, then, is whether armed robbery while in possession of a firearm is punished more or less severely than armed violence predicated upon aggravated robbery. [Armed] robbery while in possession of a firearm is punishable by 21 to 45 years in prison. Armed violence predicated upon aggravated robbery is a Class X felony punishable by either 10 to 30 or 15 to 30 years in prison, depending upon the type of firearm used in the offense. Thus, it is the less serious offense—armed robbery while in possession of a firearm—that is punished more severely. The 15-year enhancement for armed robbery while in possession of a firearm therefore violates the proportionate penalties clause of the Illinois Constitution and is unenforceable. [769 N.E.2d at 931-32.]

Should courts engage in a proportionality review of the internal consistency of state sentencing laws? How would a state legislator react to *Walden*?

4. *Judicial discretion and mandatory penalties.* Many criticisms of mandatory minimum statutes focus on the loss of judicial discretion in sentencing. Consider, for example, the 1970 statement of then-Representative George Bush:

> Federal judges are almost unanimously opposed to mandatory minimums, because they remove a great deal of the court's discretion. In the vast majority of cases which reach the sanctioning stage today, the bare minimum sentence is levied—and in some cases, less than the minimum mandatory is given. . . . Probations and outright dismissals often result. Philosophical differences aside, practicality requires a sentence structure which is generally acceptable to the courts, to prosecutors, and to the general public.

116 Cong. Rec. H33314, Sept. 23, 1970. These criticisms and others have led some state and federal judges to believe that mandatory minimum statutes too often force them to impose a fundamentally unjust sentence. A 1993 survey of judicial opinion found that 90 percent of federal judges and 75 percent of state judges believe that mandatory minimum sentences for drug cases were "a bad idea." More than half of the federal judges believed that mandatory minimums were "too harsh" on first-time offenders. A.B.A. J., October 1993, at 78. Are all mandatory minimums subject to the criticisms about uneven enforcement and loss of judicial discretion? Could a legislature address these problems by using only narrow definitions of offenses and offenders eligible for a mandatory sentence?

Can any decisionmaker other than a judge — who decides many individual cases — appreciate the facts about an offender's past that should lead to a lighter sentence? Why do judges sentence below what the legislature might choose as a minimum sentence? Do judges generally share a different political view on crime control? Do they see too many individual cases?

5. *Mandatory mandatories.* Most mandatory minimum statutes instruct the judge to impose a particular sentence for a particular charge, but they do not require the prosecutor to file a given charge when adequate facts are present. Thus, typical mandatory sentencing statutes give prosecutors considerable bargaining power during plea negotiations; they also offer prosecutors opportunities to avoid mandatory minimum sentences when they believe that such sentences would be unjust or a poor use of resources. Legislatures sometimes constrain this prosecutorial power by passing statutes that require the prosecutor to file charges and that prevent plea bargaining. For instance, in 1973 New York passed a "Rockefeller drug law" imposing severe mandatory minimums and restricting plea bargaining. After passage of this law, there were fewer arrests, indictments, and convictions for drug offenses, but those convicted served longer terms. Jacqueline Cohen & Michael Tonry, Sentencing Reforms and the Impacts, in Research on Sentencing: The Search for Reform 348-49 (Alfred Blumstein et al. eds., 1983). This sort of "mandatory mandatory" statute is rare. Why do legislators hesitate to pass statutes that remove the prosecutor's discretion to decline charges or to select a charge not subject to the minimum penalty?

6. *Net effects of mandatory minimum penalties.* Studies of mandatory minimum penalties have reached different conclusions about the effect of these laws on the crime rates for the targeted offenses. Some studies have found a deterrent effect for gun crimes and homicides, but other studies have found no such effect on the commission of drug crimes or violent crimes generally. The effects of mandatory minimum penalties on the criminal justice system are clearer. These laws consistently lead to fewer arrests for the designated crimes, fewer charges filed, more dismissals of charges, more trials rather than guilty pleas, and longer sentences imposed and served. See Dale Parent, Terence Dunworth, Douglas McDonald & William Rhodes, Key Legislative Issues in Criminal Justice: Mandatory Sentencing (National Institute of Justice, Research in Action) (January 1997, NCJ 161839).

7. *Self-correcting democratic process.* If mandatory minimum sentences truly produce the ill effects described by critics, won't the democratically elected legislature recognize these flaws after a time and abandon the experiment? There are a few examples of this happening. In Connecticut in 2001, the legislature granted judges authority to depart from mandatory minimum sentences for certain drug crimes, such as first-time sales or possession within 1,500 feet of a school. A 2001 Indiana law eliminated mandatory 20-year sentences for cocaine dealers (anyone caught with more than

3 grams of cocaine), and Louisiana repealed mandatory sentences for some simple possession and other nonviolent drug offenses. On the other hand, other jurisdictions, such as New York, have debated for years about changing mandatory minimum drug sentences, without ever taking action. See Ronald F. Wright, Are the Drug Wars De-Escalating? Where to Look for Evidence, 14 Fed. Sentencing Reporter 141 (2002). What might prevent the legislature from rethinking self-destructive legislation? Is it a lack of information, a lack of time, or something else?

3. Sentencing Commissions

While the legislature always sets the upper and lower boundaries on the permissible punishments for a crime, those boundaries can still leave open many choices about the sentence in particular cases. Rather than leaving the remaining sentencing choices to the discretion of judges and parole authorities, some state legislatures have empowered permanent "sentencing commissions" to create additional rules to guide judges as they select sentences within the statutory range. These guidelines (some embodied in statutes and others in administrative rules) are different from statutory maximum and minimum punishments because they allow judges, under some circumstances, to go above or below the recommended range so long as the final sentence remains within the statutorily authorized range. Sentencing guidelines can be binding or merely advisory for the sentencing judge depending on the judge's statutory authority to "depart" from the guidelines without risking reversal on appeal.

What are the effects of creating a sentencing commission and asking it to formulate sentencing rules more specific than the outer bounds of the statutory maximum and minimum sentence? Will sentencing commissions produce rules that look systematically different from the sentencing rules a legislature would adopt on its own? Will those sentencing guidelines produce a different pattern of sentences in individual cases than judges would impose, if left to their own devices? Whatever other effects a sentencing commission may have, it is certainly true that commissions (and the guidelines they create) give sentencing courts a more refined vocabulary for discussing sentencing choices and make more explicit the types of considerations that matter to a sentencing court. Indeed, without sentencing guidelines and the judicial decisions applying them, it would be difficult to study sentencing at all as a topic in a criminal procedure course.

Sentencing commissions have created sentencing rules in almost half of the states. The materials below introduce the basic structure and functions of such commissions, with particular attention paid to the sentencing commission in Minnesota, one of the earliest and most influential of these bodies.

■ ABA STANDARDS FOR CRIMINAL JUSTICE SENTENCING STANDARD 18-1.3(a)
(3d ed. 1994)

The legislature should create or empower a governmental agency to transform legislative policy choices into more particularized sentencing provisions that guide sentencing courts. The agency should also be charged with responsibility to collect, evaluate and disseminate information regarding sentences imposed and carried out within the jurisdiction.

■ DALE PARENT,
STRUCTURING CRIMINAL SENTENCING
2-5, 28, 51-53, 57-60 (1988)

For centuries, legislative control over the sentencing process fluctuated between two statutory models of how to formulate punishments for crimes. One model prescribed mandatory penalties, such as capital punishment in nineteenth century England for every theft of fifty shillings or more, or a minimum of two years in prison in twentieth century Michigan for anyone convicted of possessing a gun. The second model prescribed discretionary penalty ranges. [A] person convicted of robbery, for example, could receive probation in the community, or as much as 25 years in prison, or any sanction in between depending on how the facts of the case were assessed in the discretion of the individual judge.

Under the mandatory model, legislatures ousted judges from control over sentencing by stipulating sentences in advance. Every sentencing was required to impose either a stated penalty, or a mandatory minimum sentence, on every offender convicted of the crime, without regard to mitigating circumstances. The judge was permitted no discretion for downward adjustments to reflect either the offender's reduced culpability for the past crime, or his high promise to avoid crime in the future.

The discretionary model exemplified an entirely different approach to the setting of punishment. Under this model, the legislature deferred to the sentencing court's closer opportunity to learn the facts of each crime, to see each offender in person, and to fashion a sentence to fit the particular case. This model left it to the judgment of a single judge to determine how high, or how low, to set the penalty within the authorized sentencing range. The experience or inexperience of the judge, his or her subjective appraisal of the crime's seriousness and the offender's blameworthiness, the decisionmaker's prediction or hunch regarding the offender's likely future conduct — these and similar factors could all influence the discretion to set a severe, moderate, or lenient sentence. . . .

The advantages of each model reflected the disadvantages of the other. By removing all discretion from judges, mandatory sentences sometimes produced punishment that was too severe and disproportionate to the crime. Discretionary sentencing, on the other hand, conferred unguided discretion on judges and inevitably produced unjustifiable discrepancies — unduly lenient sentences for some, undue harshness for others. Whereas mandatory sentences reflected legislative arbitrariness and coerced uniformity, discretionary sentencing power allowed anarchy among judges and produced both arbitrariness and unwarranted disparity.

In at least three major respects, Minnesota's venture altered traditional institutions and concepts in the realm of criminal sentencing:

- It substituted a new system — guided discretion — for the more extreme methods of dividing authority over the punishment process between legislatures and courts.

- It inserted a new governmental entity—the sentencing commission—between the legislature and the judiciary, and authorized the commission to monitor and continuously adjust criminal sentences.
- And it established an unprecedented conceptual connection—known as capacity constraint—between the degree of severity with which guidelines could specify prison sentences and the extent to which state prison resources were available to carry such sentences into effect. . . .

The former system of indeterminate prison sentences set by a judge, subject to the possibility of early release in the discretion of a parole board, was abolished. In its place came a system of determinate sentences, set by the judge under guidance from the sentencing commission, with review by an appellate court. Five key elements were incorporated into this plan:

- First, sentences would be scaled to take account of differences both in the gravity of crimes and the prior records of offenders. Guidance would be specified in the form of sentencing ranges, rather than precise sentences.
- Second, factors relevant to the individualization process would be standardized and weighted in advance. Clear rules would encourage similar outcomes in similar cases. Proportionality among different cases would be facilitated by a carefully constructed hierarchy of offense seriousness.
- Third, a set of departure principles would define the circumstances under which judges could deviate from the guideline sentencing range with good reasons. Judges would thus retain discretion to set the actual sentence, to do justice on a case-by-case basis.
- Fourth, sentencing judges would be required to state reasons for each sentence that differed from the applicable guideline, to assure accountability and reviewability.
- Fifth, all sentences would be subject to review by an appellate court whose written opinions could, over time, evolve finely tuned principles to guide future sentencers. . . .

The [1988 Minnesota] law created a nine-member Sentencing Guidelines Commission, consisting of the chief justice or his designee, two district court judges appointed by the chief justice, the Commission of Corrections, the chairman of the Minnesota Corrections Board, and four gubernatorial appointees—a prosecutor, a public defender, and two citizens. Commission members would serve four-year terms and be eligible for reappointment. The Commission was authorized to hire a director and other staff. . . .

The guidelines . . . were to recommend when state imprisonment was appropriate and to recommend presumptive sentencing durations. The Commission could set ranges of permissible deviation about the fixed sentence of plus or minus 15 percent, which would not constitute departures. The guidelines were to be based on reasonable combinations of offender and offense characteristics. . . . Judges had to give written reasons for sentences that departed from the guidelines recommendation. The state or the defense could appeal any sentence. On appeal, the Supreme Court was to determine if the sentence was illegal, inappropriate, unjustifiably disparate, or not supported by findings of fact. . . .

The Commission sought to assure that guideline punishments would be proportional to the seriousness of offenders' crimes. To achieve that proportionality, it was necessary for the Commission to rank crimes in the order of their seriousness. The seriousness of a crime varies according to the gravity of the offense and the blameworthiness of the offender. Gravity is determined by the harm caused, directly or as a consequence, by the crime. Blameworthiness is determined by the offender's motivation, intent, and behavior in the crime and is enhanced if the offender previously has been convicted of and sentenced for criminal acts. . . .

In devising an offense seriousness ranking, the Commission had to make . . . relatively broad decisions about elements of behavior and intent as they relate to offense seriousness. For example, most would agree that crimes that involve or threaten physical injury generally are more serious than those that involve the loss of property. Case-level judgments involve finer distinctions and are used to distinguish among offenders convicted of similar crimes who have similar prior records.

Although most of us have an intuitive sense of offense seriousness, the concept is highly complex. Most criminal events consist of an offender and a victim linked by an act defined by law as a crime. Thus, judgments about the seriousness of criminal events may involve facts about offenders, victims, and criminal acts.

Some factors can be dismissed because all would agree they are irrelevant to assessing gravity or ascribing blame — for example, that the victim was a Mason or the offender was a Methodist. Some facts are both irrelevant and invidious — such as that the offender and the victim were of the same or different races. But there is a long list of factors that some would consider relevant to assessing harm or ascribing blame.

Most Frequent Offenses in Seriousness Scale

Seriousness Level	Most Frequent Offenses
1	Aggravated forgery, less than $100
	Possession of marijuana (more than 1.5 ounces)
	Unauthorized use of a motor vehicle
2	Aggravated forgery, $150 to $2,500
	Sale of marijuana . . .
3	Aggravated forgery, over $2,500
	Arson, third-degree . . .
	Theft crimes, $150 to $2,500
	Sale of cocaine
	Possession of LSD, PCP
4	Burglary, nondwellings and unoccupied dwellings
	Theft crimes, over $2,500
	Receiving stolen goods, $150 to $2,500
	Criminal sexual conduct, fourth-degree
	Assault, third-degree (injury)
5	Criminal negligence (resulting in death)
	Criminal sexual conduct, third-degree
	Manslaughter, second-degree . . .
	Witness tampering
	Simple (unarmed) robbery . . .

Seriousness Level	Most Frequent Offenses
6	Assault, second-degree (weapon)
	Burglary (occupied dwelling) . . .
	Criminal sexual conduct, fourth-degree . . .
	Kidnapping (released in a safe place)
	Sale, LSD or PCP
	Sale, heroin and remaining hard narcotics
	Receiving stolen goods, over $2,500
7	Aggravated (armed) robbery
	Arson, first-degree
	Burglary (victim injured)
	Criminal sexual conduct, second-degree
	Criminal sexual conduct, third-degree
	Kidnapping (not released in a safe place)
	Manslaughter, first-degree
	Manslaughter, second-degree
8	Assault, first-degree (great bodily harm)
	Kidnapping (great bodily harm)
	Criminal sexual conduct, first-degree
	Manslaughter, first-degree
9	Murder, third-degree
10	Murder, second-degree

The victim may be a normal healthy adult or a person who may be especially vulnerable due to age or infirmity. In violent crimes the extent of physical injury may vary from a scratch to death. Some victims may recover fully from physical injuries, while others suffer permanent damage or impairment. In property crimes, the victim's loss could range from a small amount to a fortune. The consequences of property loss may vary greatly with the economic status of the victim. The crime may involve one victim or many. A crime might involve an offender acting alone or in concert with others. The offender might have been immature or mentally impaired and easily induced to participate in a crime. He or she might have been the ringleader who induced others. . . .

The list of factors relevant, or arguably relevant, to assessing offense seriousness is large, and the above variations are a mere sample. Their potential combinations are virtually infinite. Given events as complex and diverse as criminal acts, how was the Commission to go about judging their seriousness?

In the initial unsatisfactory effort [to rank offenses,] each member received a randomly arranged deck of sixty offense cards. Each card listed one offense [and] its statutory maximum sentence. . . . Each member arranged his or her deck in decreasing order of seriousness. [For] the most serious person offenses — homicides — the members' individual ranks clustered together, reflecting a high level of consensus. For less serious person offenses — robberies, sexual assaults, and so forth — consensus declined.

[The] Commission expressed concern about the initial ranking exercise [because it] had overloaded members with information. [The Commission created a subcommittee to divide the task into more manageable components. The subcommittee grouped] crimes into 6 categories — violent, arson, sex, drug, property, and miscellaneous — 5 of which contained 20 or fewer crimes. . . .

The subcommittee instructed the Commission to focus on the usual or typical case in [a] ranking exercise. . . . In phase one individual Commission members ranked crimes within each of the six categories. . . . Phases two, three, and four relied on identification of differences among members, on the articulation of reasons for those differences, and on debate about those reasons. . . . When differences existed it assured that the basis of the differences would be discovered and scrutinized and that the final rankings would reflect a majority opinion.

[T]he Commission divided the overall ranking into ten seriousness levels. . . . [The table on pp. 654-655 shows the most common types of offenses within each of the ten seriousness levels.

■ MICHAEL TONRY, SENTENCING GUIDELINES AND
THEIR EFFECTS
17-20 (1987)

The "sentencing commission model" incorporates three main elements — the sentencing commission, presumptive sentencing guidelines, and appellate sentencing review. . . . The *sentencing commission* was indispensable because it possessed the institutional capacity to develop sentencing standards of greater subtlety and specificity than a legislature could. *Presumptive sentencing guidelines* provided a mechanism for expressing sentencing standards in a form that has more legal authority than voluntary guidelines, is less rigid than mandatory sentencing laws, and is much more specific than the maximum and minimum sentences specified by criminal-law statutes. *Appellate sentence review* provided a mechanism for assuring that trial judges either imposed sentences that were consistent with the applicable guidelines or had adequate and acceptable reasons for imposing sentences that were different. The attraction of the sentencing commission model is its merger of the three elements. . . .

When the sentencing commission model was first proposed by Marvin Frankel in 1972, his basic argument was that sentencing was "lawless": no substantive criteria existed to guide either the trial judge's sentence or the appellate judge's review of that sentence. Judge Frankel observed that legislatures are unlikely to be very good at developing detailed sentencing standards. Instead he urged creation of a special-purpose administrative agency that had the institutional capacity, and might develop the institutional competence, to establish substantive sentencing rules.

Minnesota . . . became the first jurisdiction to establish a sentencing commission. . . . The Minnesota commission made a number of bold policy decisions. First, it decided to be "prescriptive" and to establish its own explicit sentencing priorities [rather than] to be "descriptive," to attempt to replicate existing sentencing patterns. Second, the commission decided to de-emphasize imprisonment as a punishment for property offenders and to emphasize imprisonment for violent offenders; this was a major sentencing policy decision, because research on past Minnesota sentencing patterns showed that repeat property offenders tended to go to prison and that first-time violent offenders tended not to. Third, in order to attack sentencing disparities, the commission established narrow sentencing ranges (for example, 30 to 34 months, or 50 to 58 months) and to authorize departures from guideline ranges only when "substantial and compelling" reasons were present. Fourth, the commission elected to adopt "just deserts" as the governing premise of its policies concerning who receives prison sentences. Fifth, the commission chose to interpret an ambiguous statutory injunction that it take correctional resources into "substantial consideration" as a mandate that its guidelines not increase prison populations beyond existing capacity constraints. This meant the commission had to make deliberate trade-offs in imprisonment policies. If the commission decided to increase the lengths of prison terms for one group of offenders, it had also either to decrease prison terms for another group or to shift the in/out line and divert some group of prisoners from prison altogether. Sixth, the commission forbade consideration at sentencing of many personal factors — such as education, employment, marital status, living arrangements — that many judges believed to be legitimate. This decision resulted from a policy that sentencing decisions not be based on factors that might directly or indirectly discriminate against minorities, women, or low-income groups. . . .

Minnesota's guidelines initially proved more successful than even the commission anticipated. Rates of compliance with the guidelines were high. More violent offenders and fewer property offenders went to prison. Disparities in prison sentences diminished. Prison populations remained under control.

Later there was backsliding; as time passed, sentencing patterns came to resemble those that existed before the guidelines were implemented. Few would deny, however, that the Minnesota guideline system has been an impressive effort with important long-term consequences.

Notes

1. *Sentencing commissions and guidelines: majority position.* Almost half the states use sentencing guidelines created by sentencing commissions. The federal system also operates under sentencing guidelines, created in 1987 by the U.S. Sentencing Commission. A state sentencing commission typically drafts the initial set of guidelines on behalf of the legislature, which then enacts it as an integrated package of sentencing reforms. In other states, the state judiciary adopts a package of guidelines as procedural rules or as informal guidance to judges. Some guidelines are truly "voluntary": There is no practical consequence for a judge who decides to sentence outside the range recommended in the guidelines, so long as the judge remains within the statutory maximum and minimum for the crime. Other guidelines, to some degree or another, are "presumptive." That is, a judge who sentences outside the presumed range for sentences encounters more risk of reversal. Perhaps a reviewing court will reverse the sentence if the sentencing judge did not write an explanation for the unusual sentence; in other states, a sentence could be reversed if the judge's reason does not satisfy some legal standard (in Minnesota, a "substantial and compelling" reason is necessary). Why would a legislature ask a commission to create a set of sentencing guidelines? Does a commission have any advantages over a legislature in setting specific sentencing ranges for particular types of offenses and offenders? Does it have any advantages over a sentencing court with complete discretion to sentence offenders within statutory boundaries?

2. *Amending the rules.* The states that have adopted sentencing guidelines have recognized a need to amend the guidelines over time, and they typically give the leading role in the amendment process to a permanent sentencing commission. However, the extent of the commission's power to amend the guidelines varies.

In the largest group of states, the commission only recommends changes to the guidelines, and the legislature (and sometimes the state supreme court) must approve the changes before they become law. Elsewhere, amendments to the guidelines take effect at the end of the commission's administrative rulemaking process or after a waiting period that allows the legislature a chance to pass a statute disapproving of the changes. Do these procedural variations make any difference in the content of sentencing guidelines?

3. *Departures from the rules.* Most guidelines allow the judge to depart from the narrow sentence range designated in the guidelines. The departure could affect either the "disposition" of the sentence (active prison term or non-prison sanctions) or the "duration" of the sentence (the number of months to serve). The departure statutes generally require the judge to explain any departure, and an inadequate explanation can lead to reversal on appeal. Appellate courts in these jurisdictions have developed an extensive case law approving or disapproving of various grounds for departure. However, in theory the sentencing court still retains substantial discretion in deciding whether to depart from the guidelines.

In virtually all the guideline systems, the number of departures have remained well below the number of cases sentenced within the guidelines. For instance, in Minnesota "dispositional" departures have occurred in around 10 percent of the total cases sentenced, while "durational" departures have occurred in about 25 percent of the cases involving an active prison term. See Richard Frase, Implementing Commission-Based Sentencing Guidelines: The Lessons of the First Ten Years in Minnesota, 2 Cornell J.L. & Pub. Pol'y 279 (1993). By what criteria could a sentencing commission decide how many departures are "too many"?

4. *Appellate courts as the source of sentencing guidelines.* Most sentencing statutes provide only the most general guidance to the sentencing court and do not provide for appellate review of any sentence imposed within the broad statutory limits. Indeed, statutes in about half of the states limit appellate courts to the simple task of determining whether the sentence of the trial court fell within the statutory minimum and maximum for the charged crimes. A second, large group of states create a more searching appellate review of sentences, in which the appellate court confirms both the legality and the "reasonableness" or "proportionality" of the sentence. Minn. Stat. §244.11. Given that judges see so many individual cases and develop such expertise in sentencing, shouldn't judges develop sentencing rules rather than just apply rules that others create? Statutes establishing sentencing commissions often reserve some commission posts for judges. Are there other ways to involve judges in the creation of general sentencing rules? For two thoughtful proposals to increase the role of federal judges in the creation of federal sentencing rules, see Douglas A. Berman, A Common Law for this Age of Federal Sentencing: The Opportunity and Need for Judicial Lawmaking, 11 Stan. L. & Pol'y Rev. 93 (1999); Joseph W. Luby, Reining in the "Junior Varsity Congress": A Call for Meaningful Judicial Review of the Federal Sentencing Guidelines, 77 Wash. U. L.Q. 1199 (1999).

The law in Great Britain enables the appellate courts themselves to develop more specific guidelines for sentencing, announced in decisions of particular cases. Appellate courts in Great Britain have become one of the main institutions for developing sentencing policy. See R. v. Aramah, 76 Crim. App. Rep. 190 (1982) (conviction for importation of herbal cannabis; court establishes benchmark sentences for importation of various drugs in different amounts); Andrew Ashworth,

Three Techniques for Reducing Sentencing Disparity, in Principled Sentencing (Andrew von Hirsch & Andrew Ashworth eds., 1992). What might constitute a proper or persuasive reason for an appellate court to change its own sentencing guidelines? R. v. Bilinski, 86 Crim. App. Rep. 146 (1987) (amending the *Aramah* guidelines to reflect new increased statutory maximum sentences). See also State v. Wentz, 805 P.2d 962 (Alaska 1991) (limiting use of judicially created "benchmark" sentence for assault).

5. *Research instead of rules.* Are presumptive sentencing rules, created by commissions and approved by legislatures, subject to the same criticisms leveled against legislatively determined sentences? Would sentencing commissions be more valuable if they limited their recommendations to the most commonly encountered "paradigm" cases for sentencing and conducted research into the effects of various types of sanctions? Is lack of knowledge a more pressing concern than lack of uniformity among sentencing judges? See Albert Alschuler, The Failure of Sentencing Guidelines: A Plea for Less Aggregation, 58 U. Chi. L. Rev. 901 (1991).

6. *Parole and parole guidelines.* Wherever judges or juries exercise great discretion in selecting criminal sentences, states have found it necessary to give parole or corrections authorities the power to review those decisions at some later date. This later review imposes a centralized perspective on the decisions of judges or juries from all over the state, and it coordinates the sentences with the amount of correctional resources actually available. In that way, a parole board performs some of the same functions as a sentencing commission. However, parole boards decide on the actual time an offender will serve *after* the judge has already announced a sentence. Some parole boards decide cases according to formal parole guidelines, while others make more ad hoc decisions, depending on prison capacity and other factors. What are the advantages and disadvantages of selecting the release date later in the process through a parole board rather than through a judge applying up-front sentencing rules?

Prison officials also have some influence over the amount of a prison sentence served. In most states, prison officials have the power to reduce the sentence by up to one-third or one-half of the maximum sentence set by the judge or the parole authority. Prison authorities use this discretion to reward good behavior by inmates: The reductions are known as "good time." Jim Jacobs has pointed out the anomaly of placing legal controls on other sentencing decisions, while leaving good time decisions unregulated. Jacobs, Sentencing by Prison Personnel: Good Time, 30 UCLA L. Rev. 217 (1982). Which institutions would be best suited to create legal constraints on good time decisions?

B. REVISITING INVESTIGATIONS AND CHARGES

All sentencing systems must address a few foundational issues. In an indeterminate sentencing system, each sentencing judge addresses these core issues implicitly in individual cases. Sentencing guidelines and other forms of structured sentencing have brought these issues into the open for debate and have given names to practices that have long gone unnoticed or unexamined.

One important facet of the sentencing process is that it involves a reconsideration of earlier decisions, from investigation to adjudication. Sentencing courts never explicitly reverse earlier decisions in the same case, but a sentencing court might allow a close or difficult question decided one way at an earlier stage (for or against the defendant) to influence the sentence. This section evaluates the extent to which courts should reconsider investigative and charging decisions in determining a proper sentence.

1. Revisiting Investigations

Should offenders be punished based on their own choices and behavior or based on choices and behavior by government agents? If some of the defendant's bad acts or statements during investigations are excluded from consideration at a suppression hearing — say because of a *Miranda* violation — should the sentencing judge consider that information after conviction? If some of the government's bad acts during investigations (for example, when government agents propose multiple drug transactions simply to increase the total amount of drugs at issue) do not affect the guilty verdict, should that information nevertheless affect the sentence?

When government agents behave in an outrageous fashion or encourage a person who would not otherwise have committed a crime to do so, the defendant may have a complete defense to the charges, based on entrapment or a due process "outrageous misconduct" claim. But entrapment defenses rarely succeed, even when the government agents can control the severity of the defendant's crimes. Entrapment, like other complete defenses, is an all-or-nothing doctrine, allowing no subtlety or gradation in the analysis of government behavior or its effect. Sentencing, defendants claim, is a proper time to make more carefully graded judgments about both the relative culpability of the offender (compared to offenders not subject to government encouragement) and harms more properly attributed to government actions. Claims of "sentencing entrapment" or "sentencing manipulation" often arise in drug cases where the amount of drugs in a transaction can have a major impact on the likely sentence.

■ PEOPLE v. DEON LAMONT CLAYPOOL
684 N.W.2d 278 (Mich. 2004)

TAYLOR, J.

The issue in this case is whether it is permissible for Michigan trial judges, sentencing under the legislative sentencing guidelines pursuant to M.C.L. §769.34, to consider, for the purpose of a downward departure from the guidelines range, police conduct that is described as sentencing manipulation, sentencing entrapment, or sentencing escalation. These doctrines are based on police misconduct, which, alone, is not an appropriate factor to consider at sentencing. Rather, we hold that, pursuant to People v. Babcock, 666 N.W.2d 231 (Mich. 2003), if it can be objectively and verifiably shown that police conduct or some other precipitating cause altered a defendant's intent, that altered intent can be considered by the sentencing judge as a ground for a downward sentence departure. . . .

This case arose from a series of sales of crack cocaine by defendant to an undercover police officer. An acquaintance of defendant's in the drug trade introduced him to an undercover officer as a potential customer. On March 8, 2001, the officer bought 28.35 grams of crack cocaine for $1,100. On March 12, 2001, he bought 49.2 grams for $2,000. Finally, on March 14, 2001, he bought 127.575 grams for $4,000. Defendant was arrested and charged with delivery of 50 or more, but less than 225, grams of cocaine, reflecting the third sale.

Defendant pleaded guilty to this charge.[1] The offense carries a statutorily mandated minimum sentence of ten years of imprisonment. However, according to the legislative sentencing guidelines and the former M.C.L. §333.7401(4), the statutorily mandated minimum ten-year sentence for this offense can be reduced or "departed from," as it is described, if certain conditions set forth in M.C.L. §769.34(3) are met.[3] [The statute provides as follows:

> A court may depart from the appropriate sentence range established under the sentencing guidelines if the court has a substantial and compelling reason for that departure and states on the record the reasons for departure. . . . (b) The court shall not base a departure on an offense characteristic or offender characteristic already taken into account in determining the appropriate sentence range unless the court finds from the facts contained in the court record, including the presentence investigation report, that the characteristic has been given inadequate or disproportionate weight.]

At the sentencing hearing, the defense requested a downward departure from the statutorily mandated ten-year minimum sentence on the bases that defendant has a limited criminal history (only one criminal conviction for misdemeanor retail fraud) for his age of twenty-six and that he has an addiction to cocaine, which was costly and jeopardized his ability to pay for his home. In this case, defense counsel also argued that the police had manipulated defendant by making repeated purchases for increasing quantities of cocaine and that, by doing so, they "escalated" the sentence to which defendant would be subjected. In particular, defense counsel argued that the undercover police officer did not arrest defendant after either of the initial buys, but went back to him repeatedly to purchase cocaine. The defense argued that the officer even paid defendant at least $500 more than the going rate to persuade him to sell a larger quantity of crack cocaine than he otherwise would have sold.

The prosecutor countered that the officer had legitimate law enforcement reasons for the repeated purchases. Those reasons were that many usual sellers of large amounts only will sell small amounts to new buyers, and, thus, it is only by working up to larger amounts that law enforcement can in fact determine what type of seller the suspect is. The prosecutor, however, did not address the defense's distinct claim that no matter what the police motivation may have been, the fact that the police paid defendant $500 over the market price was the sole reason defendant's intent to sell changed from selling a lesser amount to selling a greater amount.

---

1. Defendant also pleaded guilty to charges concerning the first and second buys in the series and various other offenses that he committed during the time surrounding the series of buys. However, the present appeal involves only defendant's sentence for the third offense. . . .

3. When the trial court imposes a mandatory minimum sentence that exceeds the statutory sentencing guidelines range, it is not departing from the statutory sentencing guidelines. Thus, in this case, although the sentence imposed exceeds the recommended sentence range, the trial court does not have to articulate "substantial and compelling" reasons to justify its upward departure *from the guidelines*. However, because the trial court departed downward from the mandatory minimum, it must articulate such reasons to justify *this* downward departure from the mandatory minimum.

At the conclusion of these arguments, the trial court found substantial and compelling reasons to depart from the mandatory minimum sentence on the basis of defendant's age, minimal criminal history, and stable employment history of approximately two years, and, finally, on the basis of the fact that, in the court's view, defendant had been "escalated" and precluded from getting substance abuse treatment earlier. The trial court did not indicate if the compelling nature of this escalation factor was the view that the police conduct itself was somehow offensive or that the police had overcome the will of a small dealer by the lure of more money and created a greater criminal out of someone who otherwise would have remained a lesser criminal. The court then departed downward two years from the statutorily mandated minimum sentence of ten years and sentenced defendant to eight to twenty years of imprisonment. . . .

To decide whether sentencing manipulation, sentencing entrapment, or sentencing escalation could ever be a substantial and compelling reason for a departure as a matter of law, we must interpret the former M.C.L. §333.7401(4) and the general legislative sentencing guidelines provision in M.C.L. §769.34(3). Statutory interpretation is subject to review de novo. A trial court's decision that a particular factor is sufficiently substantial and compelling for a departure is reviewed for an abuse of discretion.

In Michigan, the Legislature has established sentencing guidelines. The underlying approach of the guidelines is that the person to be sentenced is first placed in a narrow sentencing compartment based on rigid factors surrounding the offense and offender variable statuses. Then the individual is eligible to be removed from such "default" compartments on the basis of individualized factors. In cases involving controlled substances, however, the Legislature has also established statutorily mandated minimum sentences. See the former M.C.L. §333.7401. Under both provisions, M.C.L. §769.34(3) and the former M.C.L. §333.7401(4), departure from a guidelines range or mandatory sentence is permissible. All these provisions allow a downward departure if the court has a "substantial and compelling reason" for the departure. This Court has determined that this statutory language means that there must be an "objective and verifiable" reason that "keenly or irresistibly grabs our attention"; is of "considerable worth" in determining the appropriate sentence; and "exists only in exceptional cases."

It is clear from the legislative sentencing guidelines that the focus of the guidelines is that the court is to consider *this* criminal and *this* offense. As People v. Babcock, 666 N.W.2d 231 (Mich. 2003), said after discussing the roots of our nation's attachment to the concept of proportionality in criminal sentencing: "The premise of our system of criminal justice is that, everything else being equal, the more egregious the offense, and the more recidivist the criminal, the greater the punishment."

Because of this approach, police misconduct, on which the doctrines of sentencing manipulation, sentencing entrapment, and sentencing escalation are based,[10] is not an appropriate factor to consider at sentencing. Police misconduct,

---

10. The federal definition of sentencing manipulation can be found in United States v. Shephard, 4 F.3d 647, 649 (8th Cir. 1993), [where the court] held that sentencing manipulation occurs when "the government stretches out the investigation merely to increase the sentence" a defendant would receive. Although Michigan has not defined sentencing manipulation by case law, a majority of state courts addressing the issue has adopted similar language as the functioning definition of the term. See, e.g., People v. Smith, 80 P.3d 662 (Calif. 2003). Sentencing entrapment has been discussed by our Court of Appeals in People v. Ealy, 564 N.W.2d 168 (Mich. App. 1997). There, the Court of Appeals referred to the

standing alone, tells us nothing about the defendant. However, if the defendant has an enhanced intent that was the product of police conduct or any other precipitating factor, and the enhanced intent can be shown in a manner that satisfies the requirements for a sentencing departure as outlined in *Babcock*, it is permissible for a court to consider that enhanced intent in making a departure.

The trial court in this case concluded, without more, that the defendant was "escalated." It is not clear whether the court was thinking about defendant's intent or the police conduct. Thus, resentencing or rearticulation of the court's reasons for departure on this factor is required because, under M.C.L. §769.34(3), "it is not enough that there *exists* some potentially substantial and compelling reason to depart from the guidelines range. Rather, this reason must be articulated by the trial court on the record." *Babcock*, 666 N.W.2d 231. Moreover, a trial court must articulate on the record a substantial and compelling reason why its *particular* departure was warranted. The trial court is instructed to do this on remand.

Further, we hold that two of the other reasons for departure that the trial court articulated are not substantial and compelling: (1) defendant's employment for two years, and (2) that at defendant's age of twenty-six years he had only one previous criminal conviction. With regard to the employment factor, . . . defendant's employment as a taxi cab driver [for a period of less than two years] does not "keenly" or "irresistibly" grab one's attention and, therefore, does not warrant a downward departure. . . . Nor does the fact that defendant only had one previous criminal conviction (misdemeanor retail fraud) until he reached the age of twenty-six "keenly" or "irresistibly grab" our attention. The trial judge stated that he was "impressed" that defendant had made it to the advanced age of twenty-six with only one previous criminal conviction of a minor nature. We are not. We do not believe that the age of twenty-six is particularly old to not yet have a more lengthy criminal record. Thus, the trial court abused its discretion in this regard.

If a trial court articulates multiple reasons for departure, some of which are substantial and compelling and some of which are not, and the appellate court cannot determine if the sentence departure is sustainable without the offending factors, remand is appropriate. Accordingly, we remand this case for resentencing or rearticulation on the record of the trial court's reasons for departure. On remand, defendant may argue any factor left unaddressed by our decision today, and, under the standards of *Babcock*, that his intent in committing the crime was also a proper factor for consideration.

The Chief Justice . . . contends that we are employing the subjective factor of intent to determine whether a sentencing departure is warranted in a particular case. That is, she believes that because intent is subjective, it can never be shown to have been altered in an objective and verifiable way. We disagree. For example, if under surveillance a defendant is importuned to sell more of an illegal substance than he wished and it is clear that he would not have sold it absent the buyer's pleas

---

definition from the United States Court of Appeals for the Ninth Circuit: Sentencing entrapment occurs when a defendant, "although predisposed to commit a minor or lesser offense, is entrapped in committing a greater offense subject to greater punishment." United States v. Staufer, 38 F.3d 1103, 1106 (9th Cir. 1994). [Sentencing] escalation can mean either sentencing manipulation or sentencing entrapment, as defined above.

The Chief Justice states that the substantive defense of entrapment is akin to the sentencing entrapment doctrine. This is not the case. The substantive defense of entrapment in Michigan is a complete bar to prosecution. See People v. Johnson, 647 N.W.2d 480 (Mich. 2002). The doctrine of sentencing entrapment, as defined in the federal courts, merely allows a downward departure from a sentence. . . .

to do so, the tape of their conversations could well establish in an objective and verifiable fashion the change in the defendant's intent. . . . This is all to say that the trial court cannot depart from the mandatory minimum sentence or guidelines sentence without basing its decision on some actual facts external to the representations of the defendant himself. While objectively and verifiably showing an altered intent will not be easy, nevertheless, we do not believe that the Legislature's statutory sentencing scheme forecloses outright the consideration of a defendant's altered intent at sentencing.

Moreover, we do not consider the intent element of this crime to be "nullified" by allowing a trial judge to consider altered intent as a factor for sentence departure, as the Chief Justice states. The crime of delivery of a controlled substance of a particular amount is a general intent crime. Thus, the only intent required to be convicted of the offense is the intent to deliver a controlled substance. The accused need not have the intent to sell a particular amount of the substance. . . .

The Chief Justice asserts that by considering the defendant's intent at the time of sentencing we are evading the Legislature's determination that the specific intent of the individual not be considered for the purpose of conviction. Yet, we are not doing that. We are considering the defendant's intent for the purpose of sentencing. It seems obvious that the sentencing stage is different from the trial stage. Indeed, the latitude for the trial court in sentencing to consider things inadmissible at trial can be found in the Legislature's requirements of what a presentence report can contain. A presentence report . . . can include hearsay, character evidence, prior convictions, and alleged criminal activity for which the defendant was not charged or convicted. Moreover, the sentencing guidelines themselves use this approach by empowering the trial court to consider virtually *any* factor that meets the substantial and compelling standard. . . .

In light of the applicable sentencing statutes and our recent decision in *Babcock*, we . . . remand this case to the trial court for resentencing or rearticulation of the court's reasons for departure, consistent with this opinion.

Corrigan, C.J., concurring in part and dissenting in part.

Although I agree with the result of the majority's decision, I cannot agree with its analysis. Any sentencing departure that endorses an inherently subjective factor such as the defendant's intent cannot satisfy our Legislature's requirement that any sentencing departures be based on objective and verifiable factors. I continue to believe that sentencing escalation or entrapment is merely the entrapment defense asserted at sentencing rather than before trial and that these related concepts have no valid legal foundation.

[The] entrapment defense and the concept of sentencing entrapment or escalation are two sides of the same coin. The effect of the entrapment defense is to absolve of responsibility those whose conduct the Legislature has deemed criminal, and the effect of sentencing entrapment or escalation is to partially absolve of responsibility those whose conduct the Legislature has determined warrants a specific minimum penalty. . . .

Indeed, sentencing entrapment or escalation is often used to effectively nullify an element of a crime for which the defendant was convicted by purporting to lessen or eliminate the defendant's intent. This is no different than the application of the entrapment defense before trial. Evidence regarding the nature and extent of defendant's intent is only a proper subject for the case-in-chief, when determining whether the elements of a crime have been established. Reviewing a defendant's subjective intent at sentencing can amount to a nullification of a conviction, or at least an element of a crime, without procedural protections.

In cases in which only a general intent is required, the Legislature has already determined that the specific intent of the individual defendant is irrelevant for the purpose of a conviction. If the intent is irrelevant at the initial stage for the purpose of the conviction, it cannot be used at sentencing as an end-run around the Legislature's decision. Here, the Legislature determined that those who intend to distribute drugs assume the risk of punishment according to the amount distributed. It is not for this Court to make a different policy decision upon sentencing.

[Under the Michigan sentencing guidelines, the trial court is required to choose a sentence within the guidelines range, unless there is a "substantial and compelling" reason for departing from this range.] For a reason to be "substantial and compelling," it must be "objective and verifiable."

Although the majority attempts to conform to the legislative requirements by requiring objective and verifiable proof that police conduct (or any other general cause) influenced the defendant's intent, the fact remains that the departure is, in fact, based on the defendant's intent, which is an inherently *subjective* factor. I cannot fathom how a person's subjective intent can ever be considered objective or verifiable.

"Intent" is defined as "the state of a person's mind that directs his or her actions toward an objective." Random House Webster's College Dictionary (1997). The state of a defendant's mind is an inherently subjective factor and cannot suffice as an objective and verifiable factor for a sentencing departure. Subjective intent or motivation cannot satisfy *Babcock*, no matter how "objectively" the defendant presents his version of the state of his mind. Therefore, the concept of sentencing entrapment or escalation is at odds with our legislatively mandated sentencing scheme.[3]

CAVANAGH, J., concurring in part and dissenting in part.

[Some courts and scholars] distinguish between sentencing factor manipulation and sentencing entrapment. . . . Under this approach, sentencing factor manipulation may exist regardless of the defendant's predisposition. The doctrine focuses exclusively on the motives of law enforcement authorities in manipulating the sentence, as when an agent delays an arrest with the purpose of increasing the defendant's sentence. . . . One commentator illustrated the distinction:

> An example of "sentencing entrapment" would be when a government agent offers a kilogram of cocaine to a person who has previously purchased only gram or "user" amounts, for the purpose of increasing the amount of drugs for which he ultimately will be held accountable. On the other hand, an example of "sentencing manipulation" would be when an undercover agent continues to engage in undercover drug purchases with a defendant, thereby stretching out an investigation which could have concluded earlier, for the sole purpose of increasing the defendant's sentencing exposure, or

---

3. To the extent that the majority is actually talking about a defendant's motive, and not intent, there may be situations in which objective and verifiable evidence of motive will keenly and irresistibly grab the court's attention and justify a sentencing departure. Under the facts of this case, however, I question how defendant's subjective decision to sell drugs of varying amounts from his employer's vehicle on company time can be considered an objective and verifiable factor that keenly or irresistibly grabs the court's interest.

when an undercover agent insists that a defendant "cook" powder cocaine into "crack," well knowing that sentences for dealing in crack are significantly higher than sentences for dealing in powder cocaine.

Amy Levin Weil, In Partial Defense of Sentencing Entrapment, 7 Fed. Sentencing Rep. 172, 174 (1995). [The] sentencing entrapment and manipulation doctrines both require a finding of improper motive on the part of the government before a departure is warranted.

Rather than vacating and remanding, I would simply affirm the decision of the Court of Appeals. The trial court stated on the record that the downward departure was based on substantial and compelling reasons that were objective and verifiable. On appeal, the Court of Appeals [noted], "it objectively appears that the police made additional purchases that resulted in escalating the seriousness of the offenses of which defendant was convicted." . . . Because I believe such determinations to have been proper, . . . I would affirm the decision of the Court of Appeals.

WEAVER, J., dissenting in part and concurring in part.

I respectfully dissent from the majority's decision to . . . remand this case for resentencing. . . . I would consider all relevant factors, including police conduct, when determining whether there is a substantial and compelling reason to depart from the sentencing guidelines ranges, and I would not limit how the factor of police conduct may be considered.[3] [The] trial court did not abuse its discretion in departing downward from the sentencing guidelines range because the trial court's sentence in this case was within the principled range of outcomes. . . .

YOUNG, J., concurring in part and dissenting in part.

. . . Although the majority states that police misconduct, standing alone, is not an appropriate factor to consider at sentencing, it nevertheless allows consideration of any police conduct that can be "objectively and verifiably shown" to have "altered a defendant's intent." I believe that this is an internally inconsistent holding and that it constitutes an expansion of the substantive defense of entrapment, a judicially created defense that I believe is violative of the doctrine of separation of powers. . . . Not only does the majority's holding permit the inappropriate extrapolation of the substantive entrapment defense into the sentencing context, it *broadens* the defense in that (1) it permits (indeed, it *requires*) application of a subjective, rather than objective, assessment of the defendant's response to police conduct, and (2) it does not even require *impermissible* or *reprehensible* police conduct, the hallmark of the traditional entrapment defense.

[The examples proffered by the majority aptly illustrate the inconsistency of its holding.] Consider the first example, in which there is evidence that a defendant sells more of an illegal substance than he was initially prone to sell because the buyer has pleaded for more. It is entirely beyond me how such evidence demonstrates that the defendant's intent was "altered" by external factors. Rather, the defendant, at the time he committed the offense, *intended* to sell whatever amount of the illegal

---

3. The majority holds that while police misconduct may not be considered, an "enhanced intent" that results from police misconduct may be considered when determining whether to depart from the guidelines ranges. The majority opinion does not explain how sentencing courts are to distinguish practically between police misconduct, which is an impermissible consideration under its analysis, and the "enhanced intent" that results from police misconduct, which is a permissible consideration under its analysis.

substance he, in fact, sold; the buyer's pleas simply provided a *motivation* for the defendant's decision to commit the crime of selling a larger amount. Under the majority's view, the defendant's presentation of a videotape depicting him reluctantly pulling the trigger of a gun and killing a victim in response to an accomplice's urgings would presumably support a downward departure from a mandatory sentence or from the sentencing guidelines range. . . .

A subjective factor such as intent is not somehow transformed into an objective factor simply because it can be supported by evidence other than the defendant's own representations. Although the existence of such external evidence might well render a particular factor *verifiable,* an otherwise subjective factor will remain subjective, even in the face of a mountain of proof. [For example, much like intent, a defendant's *remorse* is a subjective state-of-mind factor that may not be properly considered at sentencing. Remorse would not be somehow transformed into a proper sentencing factor by virtue of tangible or otherwise external evidence, such as testimony that the defendant cries himself to sleep every night or that he wrote apologetic letters to the victim's family. In such a case, the remorse would be *verifiable,* but it would not be *objective.*]

Accordingly, on remand, I would preclude the trial court from considering as a proper sentencing factor defendant's intent.

Problem 9-2. Learning a Lesson

Barbara Graham sold a small amount of cocaine to an undercover police officer. The officer selected the location for this sale, an apartment complex that happened to be approximately 650 feet from a private school. The transaction took place on a Friday night at 11:30 P.M. Graham had no prior drug arrests or convictions. A Florida statute requires a mandatory minimum term of three years' imprisonment for any offender who sells illicit drugs within 1,000 feet of a school. If you were the court, would you nevertheless sentence the defendant to less than three years? How would you explain such a decision? Would you reduce the sentence whenever the government provides the defendant with an opportunity to commit an act (such as selling a larger amount of drugs) that will enhance the punishment under sentencing statutes or guidelines? Compare Graham v. State, 608 So. 2d 123 (Fla. Dist. Ct. App. 1992).

Problem 9-3. Reversing the Exclusion

Juan Guzon Valera shot and killed his wife and another man after he discovered them engaging in sexual activity in a car. After inadequate *Miranda* warnings, Valera told a Hawaii County Police Officer about the events leading up to the killings, and where he had illegally obtained the gun. The statement indicated that Valera did not discover his wife's activities by chance, but followed her car to a parking lot expecting to witness her meeting with another man. The statement also showed that he chased the victims on foot a considerable distance away from their car before shooting them. The jury convicted him of manslaughter (but not second-degree murder) and firearms violations. Although the trial judge suppressed these statements during the jury trial, he relied on them during sentencing to enhance the sentence.

The sentencing judge refused to strike from the pre-sentence investigation report several references to Valera's statement to the police. The judge stated: "I think if the jury had heard the evidence which had to be barred because of the way the police questioned Mr. Valera, a different result would have occurred. I think in sentencing, the Court can consider those items which had to be barred. I think in this case, Mr. Valera acted as an executioner. He stalked his victims and shot them one after the other." He sentenced Valera to serve two 10-year consecutive terms of imprisonment for manslaughter, and lesser, concurrent terms of imprisonment for the firearms violations.

Valera argues on appeal that the sentencing judge violated his constitutional rights to due process and to counsel, and his privilege against self-incrimination as guaranteed by article I, sections 5, 14, and 10 of the Hawaii Constitution, by relying almost exclusively upon his suppressed statements in determining his sentence. How would you rule? Compare State v. Valera, 848 P.2d 376 (Haw. 1993).

Notes

1. *Sentence entrapment and manipulation: majority position.* Indeterminate sentencing statutes do not tell a judge whether to take corrective action if she believes that government agents have attempted to manipulate a sentence. Likewise, most structured sentencing systems have not addressed the issue of "sentencing entrapment" or "manipulation." A few courts have refused to recognize government behavior as a factor at sentencing. More courts have recognized the possibility of taking account of the behavior of government agents but have not found facts that support a departure in a particular case. A few lower state courts in structured sentencing systems have altered sentences because of investigators' choices. For instance, in State v. Sanchez, 848 P.2d 208 (Wash. Ct. App. 1993), the government arranged a series of three drug transactions between the defendant and one confidential informant, and the trial court departed downward to a sentence greater than the norm for one buy but less than the norm for three independent buys.

> In this case, the difference between the first buy, viewed alone, and all three buys, viewed cumulatively, was trivial or trifling. All three buys were initiated and controlled by the police. All three involved the same buyer, the same seller, and no one else. All three occurred inside a residence within a 9-day span of time. All three involved small amounts of drugs. The second and third buys had no apparent purpose other than to increase Sanchez's presumptive sentence. We conclude, as the sentencing court apparently did, that the second and third buys added little or nothing to the first. Nothing in our holding necessarily applies to drug transactions that are not police-initiated controlled buys, or that involve different sellers or purchasers, or that involve large quantities of drugs, or that have a law enforcement purpose other than to generate an increase in the offender's standard range.

"Reverse buys" — in which the government agent sells to the target of the investigation and can choose the amount and price to offer — highlight claims about sentencing manipulation. The federal sentencing guidelines have a specific instruction for judges facing this situation: "If, in a reverse sting operation . . . , the court finds that the government agent set a price for the controlled substance that was substantially below the market value of the controlled substance, thereby leading to the defendant's purchase of a significantly greater quantity of the controlled substance than his available resources would have allowed him to purchase . . . , a downward departure may be warranted." U.S.S.G. §2D1.1 (Application Note 17). Is this policy an adequate response to potential government manipulation of the sentence?

2. *Developing rules for sentence manipulation.* How might structured sentencing systems take account of manipulative behavior by government agents? Perhaps government agents could be required to arrest a suspect whenever they have enough proof to make conviction at trial likely. What if government agents wish to continue an undercover operation to obtain information about other suspects? For a year? Two hundred additional transactions? A court might require the government to state its reasons for continuing its investigation after obtaining enough evidence for a conviction. Would a detailed set of rules measuring the contribution of government choices to a defendant's presumptive sentence undermine confidence in the behavior of the government? In the idea of guilt?

3. *Inadequate self-defense and other "partial" substantive criminal law defenses.* Should courts develop refined or modified versions of substantive criminal law defenses other than entrapment, such as self-defense or duress? For instance, a defendant's self-defense argument may not result in an acquittal, but the court may nevertheless rely on the argument to reduce a sentence. Some state sentencing statutes explicitly recognize "partial" or "near-miss" defenses at sentencing: In Tennessee, the court may reduce a sentence if "substantial grounds exist tending to excuse or justify the defendant's criminal conduct, though failing to establish a defense." Tenn. Code §40-35-113(3); see also United States v. Whitetail, 956 F.2d 857 (8th Cir. 1992) (battered woman defense); United States v. Cheape, 889 F.2d 477 (3d Cir. 1989) (duress, defendant participated in robbery at gunpoint). Discussions of criminal law defenses often postpone until sentencing any effort to refine the determination of blameworthiness beyond what is necessary to conclude that a defendant is guilty or not guilty. Does the lack of a more refined set of "partial" defenses undermine the basic principles of liability? The purposes of punishment?

4. *Exclusionary rule at the sentencing hearing: majority position.* Most jurisdictions allow sentencing judges to consider evidence obtained in violation of a defendant's constitutional rights, even when that evidence is suppressed at trial. See Elson v. State, 659 P.2d 1195 (Alaska 1983) (evidence obtained illegally may be used at sentencing unless violation was for purpose of obtaining facts to enhance sentencing); Smith v. State, 517 A.2d 1081 (Md. 1986). The U.S. Supreme Court held in Estelle v. Smith, 451 U.S. 454 (1981), that a sentencing judge in a capital case could not consider a statement obtained in violation of the Fifth Amendment, but it has never addressed whether the exclusionary rule applies generally in sentencing proceedings. Some state statutes and cases allow the introduction of illegally obtained evidence in capital cases, at least within the boundaries of Estelle v. Smith. See, e.g., Utah Code §76-3-207(2) ("Any evidence the court deems to have probative force may be received regardless of its admissibility under the exclusionary rules of evidence"); Stewart v. State, 549 So. 2d 171 (Fla. 1989). Most lower federal courts have decided that the exclusionary rule does not apply at sentencing in noncapital proceedings, concluding that (1) exclusion would not deter police misconduct because the evidence is already excluded at trial, and (2) the sentencing court needs as much information as possible about the offense and offender to select a proper sanction. See, e.g., United States v. Torres, 926 F.2d 321 (3d Cir. 1991).

A smaller group applies the exclusionary rule at sentencing. See Pens v. Bail, 902 F.2d 1464 (9th Cir. 1990). If the application of the exclusionary rule to sentencing depends on whether procedural rules at sentencing can truly influence law enforcement officers, do the "sentencing manipulation" cases throw any light on this question? Perhaps the acceptability of illegally obtained evidence should depend on the impact of admitting it in different systems. Where the sentencing judge has only to consult the statutory maximum and minimum sentences, and a list of other factors listed in the statute, exclusion might have little measurable effect on sentences. Would the importance of an exclusionary rule be different in a more highly structured sentencing system, one that instructed the judge to attach a precise weight to specific facts?

2. Revisiting Charging Decisions: Relevant Conduct

It might seem obvious that defendants can be punished only for the crimes of which they have been convicted. Obvious, perhaps, but that is not the law in most jurisdictions. To varying degrees, sentencing laws allow defendants to be punished for the "real offense" and not just for the offense of conviction. When a judge considers a defendant's behavior beyond the facts necessary to prove the offense of conviction, the judge is said to be considering "relevant conduct."

How can defendants be punished for acts that are not the basis for a conviction? Under an unstructured sentencing system, the sentencing court can consider any evidence of the offender's wrongdoing, whether or not the conduct formed the basis of the criminal charges. The statutory floor and ceiling for punishing the crime of conviction leave the sentencing judge with plenty of latitude to set a punishment, even if it is based in part on uncharged conduct. It is difficult and perhaps impossible to define offenses with all of the detail necessary to capture facts that affect the assessment of culpability or harm. Even structured sentencing systems tend to allow a *range* of presumptive sentences, and when choosing a sentence within that range, a judge may account for circumstances that the bare bones elements of the crime cannot capture.

Judges receive information about conduct beyond the offense itself from several sources: during trial, from prosecutors, and in pre-sentence investigation reports. Some of this information, although not strictly necessary to establish the elements of the crime of conviction, nonetheless relates directly to the charged offense. The "relevant conduct" might be an element of an offense other than the crime charged, either more or less serious. For instance, the defendant may have used a gun during the robbery, even though the charge was robbery and not armed robbery. Other facts about the offense, such as the defendant's role in a multiparty offense, may receive no mention in the statutory framework.

The extra information could relate to other uncharged offenses committed during the same time period as the charged crime or as part of the same overarching criminal scheme. A court may also consider all suspected criminal conduct in the past, whether or not it led to a conviction. If a prosecutor ignores some wrongdoing, the judge may nevertheless take it into account. Finally, the court might rely on past noncriminal conduct that is nevertheless blameworthy. The sentencing laws allowing the judge to consider uncharged conduct are sometimes called "real offense" systems (as opposed to "charge offense" systems) because the judge sentences based on the "real" criminal behavior, independent of the prosecutor's charging decisions.

Under indeterminate sentencing, it was possible for a judge to consider all of this information, though some judges would reject some or all of it as irrelevant. Structured sentencing has brought the issue of relevant conduct to a more formal and visible level. Legislatures, sentencing commissions, and judges must now decide explicitly which additional facts a sentencing judge may or may not consider and how much impact the uncharged "relevant conduct" should have.

■ U.S. SENTENCING GUIDELINES §1B1.3(a)

[The seriousness of the offense] shall be determined on the basis of the following:

(1)(A) all acts and omissions committed, aided, abetted, counseled, commanded, induced, procured, or willfully caused by the defendant; and

(B) in the case of a jointly undertaken criminal activity (a criminal plan . . . undertaken by the defendant in concert with others, whether or not charged as a conspiracy), all reasonably foreseeable acts and omissions of others in furtherance of the jointly undertaken criminal activity, that occurred during the commission of the offense of conviction, in preparation for that offense, or in the course of attempting to avoid detection or responsibility for that offense. . . .

(3) all harm that resulted from the acts and omissions specified in [subsection (a)(1)], and all harm that was the object of such acts and omissions. . . .

ILLUSTRATION OF CONDUCT FOR WHICH THE DEFENDANT
IS ACCOUNTABLE . . .

Defendants F and G, working together, design and execute a scheme to sell fraudulent stocks by telephone. Defendant F fraudulently obtains $20,000. Defendant G fraudulently obtains $35,000. Each is convicted of mail fraud. Defendants F and G each are accountable for the amount he personally obtained under subsection (a)(1)(A). Each defendant is accountable for the amount obtained by his accomplice under subsection (a)(1)(B) because the conduct of each was in furtherance of the jointly undertaken criminal activity and was reasonably foreseeable in connection with that criminal activity.

■ FLORIDA RULE OF CRIMINAL PROCEDURE 3.701(d)(11)

Departures from the recommended or permitted guideline sentence should be avoided unless there are circumstances or factors that reasonably justify aggravating or mitigating the sentence. Any sentence outside the permitted guideline range must be accompanied by a written statement delineating the reasons for the departure. Reasons for deviating from the guidelines shall not include factors relating to prior arrests without conviction or the instant offenses for which convictions have not been obtained.

■ **STATE v. DOUGLAS McALPIN**
740 P.2d 824 (Wash. 1987)

CALLOW, J.

Douglas McAlpin received a sentence of 90 months following his plea of guilty to a charge of first degree robbery. [This sentence] exceeded the presumptive sentence range established under the Sentencing Reform Act of 1981 (SRA). The defendant appealed. . . .

Under the SRA the defendant's presumptive sentence range for first degree robbery was 46 to 61 months. This range, which is based on the seriousness of the crime committed and the offender's "criminal history," accounted for: (1) the defendant's two other current convictions for conspiracy and burglary; and (2) two prior juvenile convictions for second degree theft, both crimes being committed while the defendant was between 15 and 18 years of age and both convictions being entered on the same date.

At the defendant's sentencing hearing, it was revealed that his actual record of juvenile crime far exceeded that which was accounted for in determining the standard sentence range. The presentence report confirmed that the defendant had, in fact, amassed a juvenile record of "three files comprising hundreds of pages." The prosecutor supplemented this report with additional information obtained from juvenile court authorities.

The defendant's juvenile record included the following: (1) prior to reaching his 15th birthday he was convicted four times for second degree burglary, and once for taking a motor vehicle without permission (all felonies); (2) between the ages of 15 and 18, he had been found guilty of false reporting and third degree malicious mischief (both misdemeanors); (3) he had been committed to juvenile institutions on four occasions; and (4) he had had "various additional felony arrests which were handled informally."

The presentence report described the defendant as a "textbook sociopath" who had no remorse for his crimes, a long history of drug abuse as a youth, and two episodes in which he had tortured animals. While in the Kitsap County Corrections Center, sharpened toothbrushes were taken away from him. The report aptly characterized the defendant as an "exceedingly dangerous young man." The defendant's counsel did not object to the introduction of the above record at any time prior to the trial court's oral pronouncement of sentence. . . .

In addition to the juvenile record, it was disclosed that the defendant, in entering his guilty plea to the first degree robbery charge, had also signed a plea bargaining agreement. The prosecutor had agreed not to file charges regarding additional crimes to which the defendant had confessed, and for which he had agreed to make restitution.

The prosecutor recommended a sentence of 61 months, the top of the presumptive range. The trial court, however, imposed a 90-month exceptional sentence. The court cited the following reasons for imposing this sentence:

> That the defendant has an extensive criminal history, as set forth in the presentence report. . . . That such criminal history includes at least five felony convictions as a juvenile prior to the defendant's 15th birthday, four commitments to juvenile institutions and various additional felony arrests which were handled informally. That in the course of the police investigations of the instant offenses the defendant also confessed

to his involvement in additional burglaries or criminal trespasses with which he was not charged but for which he agreed to make restitution. That such convictions were not computed as prior criminal history and thus the defendant is not being penalized twice for his behavior. . . .

[According to the statute governing appellate review of exceptional sentences,] we must independently determine, as a matter of law, whether the trial court's reasons justify an exceptional sentence. There must be "substantial and compelling" reasons for imposing such a sentence. RCW 9.94A.120(2). . . .

We turn first to the trial court's consideration of the defendant's lengthy record of juvenile felonies. Generally, "criminal history" may not be used to justify an exceptional sentence, because it is one of two factors (the other being the "seriousness level" of the current offense committed) which is used to compute the presumptive sentence range for a particular crime. A factor used in establishing the presumptive range may not be considered a second time as an "aggravating circumstance" to justify departure from the range.

The term "criminal history" as used in the SRA for purposes of the presumptive range calculation includes only certain types of juvenile crimes. Specifically, it is limited to juvenile felonies committed while the defendant was between 15 and 18 years of age. The trial court, recognizing this limitation, did not rely on the defendant's two prior juvenile convictions for second degree theft, both committed while he was between 15 and 18 years of age, as reasons to impose an exceptional sentence. These crimes had already been considered when computing the presumptive sentence range.

On the other hand, the trial court did cite the defendant's five prior pre-age-15 felony convictions as aggravating factors justifying an exceptional sentence. The defendant asserts that this constituted error; he argues that the Legislature, by excluding such crimes from the presumptive range calculation, intended to exclude consideration of them entirely. We disagree.

One of the overriding purposes of the sentencing reform act is to ensure that sentences are proportionate to the seriousness of the crime committed and the defendant's criminal history. This purpose would be frustrated if a court were required to blind itself to a significant portion of a defendant's juvenile criminal record. . . . The trial court here did not err in concluding that a defendant who has amassed an extensive and recent record of pre-age-15 felonies is significantly different from a defendant who has no record at all. . . .

The trial court cited the following two findings as additional aggravating factors:

[1] That [the defendant's] criminal history includes . . . various additional [juvenile] felony arrests which were handled informally.

[2] That in the course of the police investigations of the instant offenses the defendant also confessed to his involvement in additional burglaries or criminal trespasses with which he was not charged but for which he agreed to make restitution.

We agree with the defendant that the trial court improperly relied on the above findings. The sentencing reform act bars the court from considering unproven or uncharged crimes as a reason for imposing an exceptional sentence. RCW 9.94A.370, at the time of sentencing, provided inter alia: "Real facts that establish elements of a higher crime, a more serious crime, or additional crimes cannot be used to go outside the presumptive sentence range except upon stipulation." In David Boerner, Sentencing in Washington §9.16, at 9-49 to 9-50 (1985), the author states:

> The policy reasons behind this provision are obvious, and sound. To consider charges that have been dismissed pursuant to plea agreements will inevitably deny defendants the benefit of their bargains. If the state desires to have additional crimes considered in sentencing, it can insure their consideration by refusing to dismiss them and proving their existence. . . .

It is not sufficient that the defendant has a record of arrests which were "handled informally." Nor is it sufficient that the defendant confessed to additional uncharged "burglaries or criminal trespasses." Since these arrests and confessions have not resulted in convictions, they may not be considered at all.

We conclude that some of the trial court's reasons for imposing the exceptional sentence could not be considered as aggravating factors. However, the defendant's lengthy record of pre-age-15 felonies, standing alone, is a substantial and compelling reason and justification for imposing the exceptional sentence. The trial court did not err in deciding to impose a sentence outside the standard range. . . .

Notes

1. *Relevant conduct in state sentencing: majority position.* Sentencing judges in indeterminate sentencing systems have always had the power (but not an obligation) to consider any conduct of the defendant, whether charged or uncharged. This conduct might influence the judge's choice of a maximum or minimum sentence from within the broad statutory range. See People v. Lee, 218 N.W.2d 655 (Mich. 1974) (pending charges mentioned in PSI); Anderson v. People, 337 P.2d 10 (Colo. 1959) (conviction for forgery; evidence at sentencing of forgeries submitted to six additional victims); People v. Grabowski, 147 N.E.2d 49 (Ill. 1958) (indictments pending for other crimes in same series of events); see also Williams v. New York, 337 U.S. 961 (1949) (death sentence imposed by judge based on pre-sentence report suggesting defendant had been involved in "30 other burglaries" in area of murder).

States with more structured sentencing systems place more restrictions on the use of the defendant's uncharged conduct. Formally, the structured state systems adopt "charge offense" rather than "real offense" sentencing. The charged offense determines a fairly small range of options available to the judge in the normal case. But "real" and "charge" offense concepts define the ends of a spectrum, and all systems allow varying degrees of real offense conduct to affect the sentencing determination. At a minimum, the uncharged conduct is available to influence the judge's selection of a sentence *within* the narrow range that the guidelines designate for typical cases. Some states go further, and allow judges to use uncharged conduct as a basis for a "departure" from the designated normal range of sentences. Other structured sentencing states (like Florida) prevent the judge from using uncharged conduct to depart from the guideline sentence. Commentary to the Minnesota sentencing guidelines states that "departures from the guidelines should not be permitted for elements of alleged offender behavior not within the definition of the offense of conviction." Minn. Stat. Ann. §244 cmt. II.D.103. The ABA Standards for

Criminal Justice: Sentencing 18-3.6 (3d ed. 1994) opt for an offense-of-conviction model.

2. *Relevant conduct in federal sentencing.* In contrast to the states, the federal guidelines create a "modified real offense" system. In a 1995 self-study report, the federal sentencing commission described the tradeoffs at stake in framing a relevant conduct provision:

> If uncharged misconduct is considered, punishment is based on facts proven outside procedural protections constitutionally defined for proving criminal charges, introducing an argument of unfairness. . . . The scope of conduct considered at sentencing will also affect, at least to some extent, the complexity of a sentencing system. The scope can be as limited as the conduct defined by the elements of the offense or as broad as any wrongdoing ever committed by the defendant or the defendant's partners in crime. All things being equal, a large scope of considered conduct will require more fact-finding than a more limited scope. . . . Besides fairness and complexity, the scope of conduct considered at sentencing may have serious implications for the balance between prosecutorial and judicial power in sentencing. For example, if the scope of considered conduct is confined to the offense of conviction, many argue that the sentencing system will provide relatively more power to prosecutors to control sentences. . . . Finding the right balance among fairness, complexity, and the role of the prosecutor has been a struggle for sentencing commissions generally. . . .

Discussion Paper, Relevant Conduct and Real Offense Sentencing (1995) (available at *http://www.ussc.gov/simple/relevant.htm*). The federal system uses the offense of conviction as a starting point for guidelines calculations, but then calls for adjustments to the "offense level" based on other relevant conduct. The commission explained its support for "real offense" factors on several grounds. First, such a system mirrored prior practices in the indeterminate system. It also gave judges a means to refine and rationalize the chaotic federal criminal code. Finally, the real offense features of the system gave judges a way to check the power of the prosecutor to dictate a sentence based upon the selection of charges. See Julie R. O'sullivan, In Defense of the U.S. Sentencing Guidelines' Modified Real-Offense System, 91 Nw. U. L. Rev. 1342 (1997).

The use of relevant conduct to enhance sentences in the federal system has come under sharp attack from scholars. See Kate Stith & Jose A. Cabranes, Fear of Judging: Sentencing Guidelines in the Federal Courts 66-77 (1998); Elizabeth Lear, Is Conviction Irrelevant? 40 UCLA L. Rev. 1179 (1993); Kevin Reitz, Sentencing Facts: Travesties of Real-Offense Sentencing, 45 Stan. L. Rev. 523 (1993); David Yellen, Illusion, Illogic and Injustice: Real-Offense Sentencing and the Federal Sentencing Guidelines, 78 Minn. L. Rev. 403 (1993). Critics have attacked the uses of uncharged or dismissed conduct as bad policy, because of the uncertain proof of the uncharged conduct, and the difficulty of achieving uniform practices in deciding how much uncharged conduct is "relevant." They have also raised constitutional questions about whether reliance on such information violates due process (by punishing a person for conduct without proving it beyond a reasonable doubt) or undermines the investigative and charging functions of the grand jury. Does real offense sentencing shift power back toward judges? Are there other ways for courts, legislatures, or commissions to respond to potential prosecutorial abuse?

3. *Varieties of uncharged conduct.* In *McAlpin,* what difference is there, if any, between the aspects of the juvenile record that were proper for the sentencing

judge to consider and those aspects of McAlpin's prior conduct that were improper for the court to consider? Some wrongdoing by defendants could form the basis for additional criminal charges, or more serious criminal charges. Other conduct, while blameworthy, does not affect the charging options available to the prosecutor. For example, under the federal criminal code, a mail fraud that nets $10,000 is eligible for the same punishment as a mail fraud that nets $100,000. Should it matter to a sentencing judge (or to a sentencing commission creating sentencing guidelines) whether the conduct in question is an element of some crime for which the defendant was not charged? Consider this approach to the problem in Kansas Statutes §21-4716(b)(3): "If a factual aspect of a crime is a statutory element of the crime . . . , that aspect of the current crime of conviction may be used as an aggravating or mitigating factor only if [it] is significantly different from the usual criminal conduct captured by the aspect of the crime."

4. *Sentencing for multiple counts.* Defendants are often convicted of multiple offenses arising out of the same transaction or course of conduct. The sentencing judge in an indeterminate system has the discretion to impose separate sentences for the multiple convictions and to decide whether those sentences will be served concurrently (all the terms begin at the same time) or consecutively (a second sentence starts after the first one ends). This gives the judge power to limit the effect of a prosecutor's decision to file multiple charges based on the same conduct. Judges with complete power over the concurrent or consecutive nature of sentences have tended to give what might be termed a "volume discount." Additional convictions will increase the total sentence served, but in decreasing amounts for each additional conviction. Some structured systems limit the judge's ability to adjust a sentence based on multiple convictions. The federal sentencing guidelines have intricate rules for the "grouping" of offenses. See U.S. Sentencing Guidelines ch. 3D. More typical is this provision from the Kansas guidelines, codified in Kan. Stat. §21-4720(b):

> When the sentencing judge imposes multiple sentences consecutively, [t]he sentencing judge must establish a base sentence for the primary crime. The primary crime is the crime with the highest crime severity ranking. . . . The total prison sentence imposed in a case involving multiple convictions arising from multiple counts within an information, complaint or indictment cannot exceed twice the base sentence. . . .

For instance, if a defendant is convicted of aggravated assault and three counts of burglary in one proceeding, the sentence would be limited to twice the guideline sentence for aggravated assault (the more serious charge).

Problem 9-4. Double Counting and Double Jeopardy

In June 1990, Steven Kurt Witte and several co-conspirators arranged with Roger Norman, an undercover agent of the Drug Enforcement Administration, to import large amounts of marijuana from Mexico and cocaine from Guatemala. Norman had the task of flying the contraband into the United States, with Witte providing the ground transportation for the drugs once they arrived. The agreement called for delivery of 4,400 pounds of marijuana, plus some cocaine if there was room on the plane. Federal authorities arrested some of the participants in the scheme at an airstrip in Mexico and seized 591 kilograms of cocaine. While still undercover, Norman met Witte the following day to explain that the pilots had been unable to land in Mexico because police had raided the airstrip. Witte was not taken into custody at that time, and the activities of the conspiracy lapsed for several months.

Norman next spoke with Witte five months later, in January 1991, and asked if Witte would be interested in purchasing 1,000 pounds of marijuana. Witte agreed to give Norman $50,000 for the marijuana. When Witte and Norman met in Houston on February 7, Witte delivered half of the cash to Norman and asked that he load the marijuana into a motor home. Undercover agents took the motor home away to load the marijuana; they returned it the next morning loaded with approximately 375 pounds of marijuana, and they arrested Witte when he took possession of the contraband.

In March 1991, a federal grand jury in Texas indicted Witte and Kelly for conspiring and attempting to possess marijuana with intent to distribute it. The indictment was limited on its face to conduct occurring on or about January 25 through February 8, 1991, thus covering only the later marijuana transaction. On February 21, 1992, Witte pleaded guilty to the attempted possession count and agreed to cooperate with the government "by providing truthful and complete information concerning this and all other offenses." In exchange, the government agreed to dismiss the conspiracy count and to file a motion for a downward departure under the sentencing guidelines.

In calculating Witte's base offense level under the federal sentencing guidelines, the pre-sentence report prepared by the U.S. probation office considered the total quantity of drugs involved in all the transactions contemplated by the conspirators, including the planned 1990 shipments of both marijuana and cocaine. The pre-sentence report suggested that Witte was accountable for the 1,000 pounds of marijuana involved in the attempted possession offense to which he pleaded guilty, 4,400 pounds of marijuana that Witte and others had planned to import from Mexico in 1990, and the 591 kilograms of cocaine seized at the Mexican airstrip in August 1990.

At the sentencing hearing, both the defendant and the government urged the court to hold that the 1990 activities concerning importation of cocaine and marijuana were not part of the same course of conduct as the 1991 marijuana offense to which Witte had pleaded guilty, and therefore should not be considered in sentencing for the 1991 offense. The district court concluded, however, that because the 1990 importation offenses were part of the same continuing conspiracy, they were "relevant conduct" under the guidelines and should be taken into account. The court therefore aggregated the quantities of drugs involved in the 1990 and 1991 episodes, resulting in a more severe sentence.

In September 1992, another grand jury in the same district returned a two-count indictment against Witte for conspiring and attempting to import cocaine. The indictment alleged that, between August 1989 and August 1990, Witte tried to import about 591 kilograms of cocaine from Central America. Witte moved to dismiss, arguing that he had already been punished for the cocaine offenses because the cocaine involved in the 1990 transaction had been considered as "relevant conduct" at sentencing for the 1991 marijuana offense. Thus, he said, the court should dismiss the indictment because punishment for these offenses would violate the prohibition against multiple punishments contained in the double jeopardy clause of the Fifth Amendment. Should the court grant the motion? Compare Witte v. United States, 515 U.S. 389 (1995).

Notes

1. *Double jeopardy for enhancing sentences based on prior crimes: majority position.* When criminal conduct gives a sentencing judge the basis for increasing a sentence against a defendant charged with some separate crime, would a later sentence for the original crime constitute a "multiple punishment" for double jeopardy purposes? In Witte v. United States, 515 U.S. 389, 397 (1995), the Supreme Court rejected a double jeopardy challenge based on the facts described in Problem 9-4:

> Traditionally, sentencing courts have not only taken into consideration a defendant's prior convictions, but have also considered a defendant's past criminal behavior, even if no conviction resulted from that behavior. . . . That history, combined with a recognition of the need for individualized sentencing, [leads us to conclude that] a sentencing judge may appropriately conduct an inquiry broad in scope, largely unlimited either as to the kind of information he may consider, or the source from which it may come. [T]he uncharged criminal conduct was used to enhance petitioner's sentence within the range authorized by statute. . . .
>
> We are not persuaded by petitioner's suggestion that the Sentencing Guidelines somehow change the constitutional analysis. A defendant has not been "punished" any more for double jeopardy purposes when relevant conduct is included in the calculation of his offense level under the Guidelines than when a pre-Guidelines court, in its discretion, took similar uncharged conduct into account. . . . Regardless of whether particular conduct is taken into account by rule or as an act of discretion, the defendant is still being punished only for the offense of conviction.

Can you reconstruct how Witte might have argued that the sentencing guidelines made enhancements based on prior criminal record more like "punishment"? The handful of state high courts that have addressed a double jeopardy challenge on similar facts have reached the same result, holding that there is no constitutional violation in enhancing a sentence based on relevant conduct that is subsequently the basis for a separate indictment, conviction, and punishment. See, e.g., Traylor v. State, 801 S.W.2d 267 (Ark. 1990).

In Monge v. California, 524 U.S. 721 (1998), the Supreme Court decided that the double jeopardy clause does not apply at all to noncapital sentencing proceedings. When Monge was convicted of narcotics crimes, the trial court doubled his sentence based on a previous assault conviction. After a state appeals court overturned the sentence because there was insufficient proof of the details of the assault, Monge argued that a retrial on the sentence enhancement would violate double jeopardy principles. The U.S. Supreme Court disagreed, because double jeopardy protections are inapplicable to sentencing proceedings: The determinations at a sentencing hearing do not place a defendant in jeopardy for an "offense."

2. *Prosecutorial motives and control.* Do rules allowing higher punishment for multiple counts than for a single count give too much power to prosecutors? It is often said that structured sentencing systems shift power from judges to prosecutors. Are there avenues other than "real offense" sentencing to limit these types of

prosecutorial control over sentences? In this regard, consider the federal "*Petite* policy" governing successive prosecutions in federal court. See Chapter 4.

When sentencing rules place great weight on the charges and criminal history, the prosecutor has greater influence over the sentence to be imposed. Despite the power of prosecutors to influence sentences in structured sentencing states, research suggests they do not tend to change their charging or plea bargaining practices. Structured systems have not produced dramatically longer sentences or changed rates of guilty pleas. See Dale Parent, Structuring Criminal Sentences (1988); Terance Miethe, Charging and Plea Bargaining Practices Under Determinate Sentencing: An Investigation of the Hydraulic Displacement of Discretion, 78 J. Crim. L. & Criminology 155 (1987). This is not to say that plea bargains have no effect on the viability or uniformity of sentencing rules. Sometimes the prosecutor and defendant agree to charges and to factual and guideline stipulations that place the sentence outside the range that would ordinarily be prescribed by the guidelines — without asking the judge to depart from the guidelines. See Ilene Nagel & Stephen Schulhofer, A Tale of Three Cities: An Empirical Study of Charging and Bargaining Practice Under the Federal Sentencing Guidelines, 66 S. Cal. L. Rev. 501 (1992).

C. REVISITING PLEAS AND TRIALS

Just as sentencing provides an opportunity to reconsider the significance of events during investigations and charge selection, it also provides an opportunity to reconsider choices made during the resolution of charges. This section reviews the interaction between the sentence, guilty pleas, and decisions made at trial.

1. Revisiting Proof at Trial

The prosecution carries the burden of proving all the elements of an offense at trial beyond a reasonable doubt or establishing a factual basis in a guilty plea hearing to show that the government *could have* satisfied this burden. But once the government obtains a conviction, the burden of proving new facts relevant to sentencing becomes easier. Generally, the government need only demonstrate the facts at sentencing by a preponderance of the evidence; there are some sentencing facts for which the *defendant* bears the burden of proof, usually also by a preponderance, such as the facts necessary to justify a downward departure from a presumptive sentence. Hence, it is critical to know which facts must be proven at trial and which can wait until the sentencing hearing.

If the question of which facts are elements of an offense and which are "mere" sentencing facts were left entirely to judgment of the legislature, then the role of courts would be simply to determine legislative intent for each crime. The U.S. Supreme Court and state supreme courts have held that due process requires the government to prove each element of every offense beyond a reasonable doubt. Sullivan v. Louisiana, 508 U.S. 275 (1993); In re Winship, 397 U.S. 358 (1970). See Chapter 8, section A. The courts have also decided that legislatures are not completely free to shift facts from "element" status to "sentencing" status.

In McMillan v. Pennsylvania, 477 U.S. 79 (1986), the Court held that the government did not violate due process by proving facts supporting a "sentencing enhancement" for visibly possessing a firearm using the lower preponderance standard of proof. The Court recognized, however, that legislatures could not freely convert offense elements into sentencing facts, and that in some situations sentencing facts would have to be treated as if they were elements and would have to be proved to the jury beyond a reasonable doubt. The following case develops further the idea that some factfinding must happen at trial rather than at sentencing, regardless of the label the legislature uses.

■ RALPH BLAKELY v. WASHINGTON
542 U.S. 296 (2004)

SCALIA, J.
Petitioner Ralph Howard Blakely, Jr., pleaded guilty to the kidnaping of his estranged wife. The facts admitted in his plea, standing alone, supported a maximum sentence of 53 months. Pursuant to state law, the court imposed an "exceptional" sentence of 90 months after making a judicial determination that he had acted with "deliberate cruelty." We consider whether this violated petitioner's Sixth Amendment right to trial by jury.

I

Petitioner married his wife Yolanda in 1973. He was evidently a difficult man to live with, having been diagnosed at various times with psychological and personality disorders including paranoid schizophrenia. His wife ultimately filed for divorce. In 1998, he abducted her from their orchard home in Grant County, Washington, binding her with duct tape and forcing her at knifepoint into a wooden box in the bed of his pickup truck. In the process, he implored her to dismiss the divorce suit and related trust proceedings.

When the couple's 13-year-old son Ralphy returned home from school, petitioner ordered him to follow in another car, threatening to harm Yolanda with a shotgun if he did not do so. Ralphy escaped and sought help when they stopped at a gas station, but petitioner continued on with Yolanda to a friend's house in Montana. He was finally arrested after the friend called the police.

The State charged petitioner with first-degree kidnaping. Upon reaching a plea agreement, however, it reduced the charge to second-degree kidnaping involving domestic violence and use of a firearm. Petitioner entered a guilty plea admitting the elements of second-degree kidnaping and the domestic-violence and firearm allegations, but no other relevant facts.

The case then proceeded to sentencing. In Washington, second-degree kidnaping is a class B felony. State law provides that [a person convicted of a class B felony faces a maximum punishment of ten years confinement]. Other provisions of state law, however, further limit the range of sentences a judge may impose. Washington's Sentencing Reform Act specifies, for petitioner's offense of second-degree kidnaping with a firearm, a "standard range" of 49 to 53 months. A judge may impose a sentence above the standard range if he finds "substantial and compelling reasons justifying an exceptional sentence." The Act lists aggravating factors that justify such a departure, which it recites to be illustrative rather than exhaustive. . . . When a judge imposes an exceptional sentence, he must set forth findings of fact and conclusions of law supporting it. A reviewing court will reverse the sentence if it finds that under a clearly erroneous standard there is insufficient evidence in the record to support the reasons for imposing an exceptional sentence.

Pursuant to the plea agreement, the State recommended a sentence within the standard range of 49 to 53 months. After hearing Yolanda's description of the kidnaping, however, the judge rejected the State's recommendation and imposed an exceptional sentence of 90 months—37 months beyond the standard maximum. He justified the sentence on the ground that petitioner had acted with "deliberate cruelty," a statutorily enumerated ground for departure in domestic-violence cases.

Faced with an unexpected increase of more than three years in his sentence, petitioner objected. The judge accordingly conducted a 3-day bench hearing featuring testimony from petitioner, Yolanda, Ralphy, a police officer, and medical experts. After the hearing, he issued 32 findings of fact, [and] adhered to his initial determination of deliberate cruelty. Petitioner appealed, arguing that this sentencing procedure deprived him of his federal constitutional right to have a jury determine beyond a reasonable doubt all facts legally essential to his sentence.

II

This case requires us to apply the rule we expressed in Apprendi v. New Jersey, 530 U.S. 466, 490 (2000): "Other than the fact of a prior conviction, any fact that increases the penalty for a crime beyond the prescribed statutory maximum must be submitted to a jury, and proved beyond a reasonable doubt." This rule reflects two longstanding tenets of common-law criminal jurisprudence: that the "truth of every accusation" against a defendant "should afterwards be confirmed by the unanimous suffrage of twelve of his equals and neighbours," 4 W. Blackstone, Commentaries on the Laws of England 343 (1769), and that "an accusation which lacks any particular fact which the law makes essential to the punishment is . . . no accusation within the requirements of the common law, and it is no accusation in reason," 1 J. Bishop, Criminal Procedure §87, p. 55 (2d ed. 1872). These principles have been acknowledged by courts and treatises since the earliest days of graduated sentencing. . . .

Apprendi involved a New Jersey hate-crime statute that authorized a 20-year sentence, despite the usual 10-year maximum, if the judge found the crime to have been committed "with a purpose to intimidate . . . because of race, color, gender, handicap, religion, sexual orientation or ethnicity." . . .

In this case, petitioner was sentenced to more than three years above the 53-month statutory maximum of the standard range because he had acted with "deliberate cruelty." The facts supporting that finding were neither admitted by petitioner nor found by a jury. The State nevertheless contends that there was no Apprendi violation because the relevant "statutory maximum" is not 53 months, but the 10-year maximum for class B felonies in §9A.20.021(1)(b). . . . Our precedents make clear, however, that the "statutory maximum" for Apprendi purposes is the maximum sentence a judge may impose solely on the basis of the facts reflected in the jury verdict or admitted by the defendant. In other words, the relevant "statutory maximum" is not the maximum sentence a judge may impose after finding additional facts, but the maximum he may impose without any additional findings. When a judge inflicts punishment that the jury's verdict alone does not allow, the jury has not found all the facts "which the law makes essential to the punishment," Bishop, supra, §87, at 55, and the judge exceeds his proper authority.

The judge in this case could not have imposed the exceptional 90-month sentence solely on the basis of the facts admitted in the guilty plea. Those facts alone were insufficient because, as the Washington Supreme Court has explained, "[a] reason offered to justify an exceptional sentence can be considered only if it takes into account factors other than those which are used in computing the standard range sentence for the offense," State v. Gore, 21 P.3d 262, 277 (Wash. 2001), which in this case included the elements of second-degree kidnaping and the use of a firearm. Had the judge imposed the 90-month sentence solely on the basis of the plea, he would have been reversed. . . .

The State defends the sentence by drawing an analogy to those we upheld in McMillan v. Pennsylvania, 477 U.S. 79 (1986), and Williams v. New York, 337 U.S. 241 (1949). Neither case is on point. *McMillan* involved a sentencing scheme that imposed a statutory minimum if a judge found a particular fact. We specifically noted that the statute "does not authorize a sentence in excess of that otherwise allowed for [the underlying] offense." *Williams* involved an indeterminate-sentencing regime that allowed a judge (but did not compel him) to rely on facts outside the trial record in determining whether to sentence a defendant to death. The judge could have sentenced the defendant to death giving no reason at all. Thus, neither case involved a sentence greater than what state law authorized on the basis of the verdict alone. . . .

III

Our commitment to *Apprendi* in this context reflects not just respect for long-standing precedent, but the need to give intelligible content to the right of jury trial. That right is no mere procedural formality, but a fundamental reservation of power in our constitutional structure. Just as suffrage ensures the people's ultimate control in the legislative and executive branches, jury trial is meant to ensure their control in the judiciary. *Apprendi* carries out this design by ensuring that the judge's authority to sentence derives wholly from the jury's verdict. Without that restriction, the jury would not exercise the control that the Framers intended.

Those who would reject *Apprendi* are resigned to one of two alternatives. The first is that the jury need only find whatever facts the legislature chooses to label elements of the crime, and that those it labels sentencing factors — no matter how much they may increase the punishment — may be found by the judge. This would mean, for example, that a judge could sentence a man for committing murder even if the jury convicted him only of illegally possessing the firearm used to commit it — or of making an illegal lane change while fleeing the death scene. Not even *Apprendi*'s critics would advocate this absurd result. The jury could not function as circuit-breaker in the State's machinery of justice if it were relegated to making a determination that the defendant at some point did something wrong, a mere preliminary to a judicial inquisition into the facts of the crime the State actually seeks to punish.

The second alternative is that legislatures may establish legally essential sentencing factors within limits — limits crossed when, perhaps, the sentencing factor is a "tail which wags the dog of the substantive offense." *McMillan*, 477 U.S., at 88.

What this means in operation is that the law must not go too far—it must not exceed the judicial estimation of the proper role of the judge.

The subjectivity of this standard is obvious. Petitioner argued below that second-degree kidnaping with deliberate cruelty was essentially the same as first-degree kidnaping, the very charge he had avoided by pleading to a lesser offense. . . . Petitioner's 90-month sentence exceeded the 53-month standard maximum by almost 70 percent; the Washington Supreme Court in other cases has upheld exceptional sentences 15 times the standard maximum. Did the court go too far in any of these cases? There is no answer that legal analysis can provide. . . .

Whether the Sixth Amendment incorporates this manipulable standard rather than *Apprendi*'s bright-line rule depends on the plausibility of the claim that the Framers would have left definition of the scope of jury power up to judges' intuitive sense of how far is too far. We think that claim not plausible at all, because the very reason the Framers put a jury-trial guarantee in the Constitution is that they were unwilling to trust government to mark out the role of the jury.

IV

. . . This case is not about whether determinate sentencing is constitutional, only about how it can be implemented in a way that respects the Sixth Amendment. . . .

Justice O'Connor argues that, because determinate sentencing schemes involving judicial factfinding entail less judicial discretion than indeterminate schemes, the constitutionality of the latter implies the constitutionality of the former. This argument is flawed on a number of levels. First, the Sixth Amendment by its terms is not a limitation on judicial power, but a reservation of jury power. It limits judicial power only to the extent that the claimed judicial power infringes on the province of the jury. Indeterminate sentencing does not do so. It increases judicial discretion, to be sure, but not at the expense of the jury's traditional function of finding the facts essential to lawful imposition of the penalty. . . . In a system that says the judge may punish burglary with 10 to 40 years, every burglar knows he is risking 40 years in jail. In a system that punishes burglary with a 10-year sentence, with another 30 added for use of a gun, the burglar who enters a home unarmed is entitled to no more than a 10-year sentence—and by reason of the Sixth Amendment the facts bearing upon that entitlement must be found by a jury.

But even assuming that restraint of judicial power unrelated to the jury's role is a Sixth Amendment objective, it is far from clear that *Apprendi* disserves that goal. Determinate judicial-factfinding schemes entail less judicial power than indeterminate schemes, but more judicial power than determinate jury-factfinding schemes. Whether *Apprendi* increases judicial power overall depends on what States with determinate judicial-factfinding schemes would do, given the choice between the two alternatives. Justice O'Connor simply assumes that the net effect will favor judges, but she has no empirical basis for that prediction. Indeed, what evidence we have points exactly the other way: When the Kansas Supreme Court found *Apprendi* infirmities in that State's determinate-sentencing regime in State v. Gould, 23 P.3d 801, 809-814 (Kan. 2001), the legislature responded not by reestablishing indeterminate sentencing but by applying *Apprendi*'s requirements to its current regime. The result was less, not more, judicial power.

Justice Breyer argues that *Apprendi* works to the detriment of criminal defendants who plead guilty by depriving them of the opportunity to argue sentencing factors to a judge. But nothing prevents a defendant from waiving his *Apprendi* rights. When a defendant pleads guilty, the State is free to seek judicial sentence enhancements so long as the defendant either stipulates to the relevant facts or consents to judicial factfinding. . . . Even a defendant who stands trial may consent to judicial factfinding as to sentence enhancements, which may well be in his interest if relevant evidence would prejudice him at trial. We do not understand how *Apprendi* can possibly work to the detriment of those who are free, if they think its costs outweigh its benefits, to render it inapplicable.

Nor do we see any merit to Justice Breyer's contention that *Apprendi* is unfair to criminal defendants because, if States respond by enacting "17-element robbery crimes," prosecutors will have more elements with which to bargain. Bargaining already exists with regard to sentencing factors because defendants can either stipulate or contest the facts that make them applicable. If there is any difference between bargaining over sentencing factors and bargaining over elements, the latter probably favors the defendant. Every new element that a prosecutor can threaten to charge is also an element that a defendant can threaten to contest at trial and make the prosecutor prove beyond a reasonable doubt. Moreover, given the sprawling scope of most criminal codes, and the power to affect sentences by making (even nonbinding) sentencing recommendations, there is already no shortage of in terrorem tools at prosecutors' disposal.

Any evaluation of *Apprendi*'s "fairness" to criminal defendants must compare it with the regime it replaced, in which a defendant, with no warning in either his indictment or plea, would routinely see his maximum potential sentence balloon from as little as five years to as much as life imprisonment . . . based not on facts proved to his peers beyond a reasonable doubt, but on facts extracted after trial from a report compiled by a probation officer who the judge thinks more likely got it right than got it wrong. . . .

Justice Breyer's more general argument — that *Apprendi* undermines alternatives to adversarial factfinding — is not so much a criticism of *Apprendi* as an assault on jury trial generally. . . . Ultimately, our decision cannot turn on whether or to what degree trial by jury impairs the efficiency or fairness of criminal justice. One can certainly argue that both these values would be better served by leaving justice entirely in the hands of professionals; many nations of the world, particularly those following civil-law traditions, take just that course. There is not one shred of doubt, however, about the Framers' paradigm for criminal justice: not the civil-law ideal of administrative perfection, but the common-law ideal of limited state power accomplished by strict division of authority between judge and jury. . . .

Petitioner was sentenced to prison for more than three years beyond what the law allowed for the crime to which he confessed, on the basis of a disputed finding that he had acted with "deliberate cruelty." The Framers would not have thought it too much to demand that, before depriving a man of three more years of his liberty, the State should suffer the modest inconvenience of submitting its accusation to "the unanimous suffrage of twelve of his equals and neighbours," 4 Blackstone, Commentaries, at 343, rather than a lone employee of the State. . . .

O'CONNOR, J., dissenting.

The legacy of today's opinion, whether intended or not, will be the consolidation of sentencing power in the State and Federal Judiciaries. The Court says to Congress and state legislatures: If you want to constrain the sentencing discretion of judges and bring some uniformity to sentencing, it will cost you — dearly. Congress and States, faced with the burdens imposed by the extension of *Apprendi* to the present context, will either trim or eliminate altogether their sentencing guidelines schemes and, with them, 20 years of sentencing reform. . . .

I

. . . Prior to 1981, Washington, like most other States and the Federal Government, employed an indeterminate sentencing scheme. . . . This system of unguided discretion inevitably resulted in severe disparities in sentences received and served by defendants committing the same offense and having similar criminal histories. . . . To counteract these trends, the state legislature passed the Sentencing Reform Act of 1981. The Act had the laudable purposes of making the criminal justice system "accountable to the public," and ensuring that "the punishment for a criminal offense is proportionate to the seriousness of the offense [and] commensurate with the punishment imposed on others committing similar offenses." Wash. Rev. Code Ann. §9.94A.010. The Act neither increased any of the statutory sentencing ranges for the three types of felonies . . . nor reclassified any substantive offenses. It merely placed meaningful constraints on discretion to sentence offenders within the statutory ranges, and eliminated parole. There is thus no evidence that the legislature was attempting to manipulate the statutory elements of criminal offenses or to circumvent the procedural protections of the Bill of Rights. . . .

II

Far from disregarding principles of due process and the jury trial right, as the majority today suggests, Washington's reform has served them. Before passage of the Act, a defendant charged with second degree kidnaping, like petitioner, had no idea whether he would receive a 10-year sentence or probation. The ultimate sentencing determination could turn as much on the idiosyncrasies of a particular judge as on the specifics of the defendant's crime or background. A defendant did not know what facts, if any, about his offense or his history would be considered relevant by the sentencing judge or by the parole board. After passage of the Act, a defendant charged with second degree kidnaping knows what his presumptive sentence will be; he has a good idea of the types of factors that a sentencing judge can and will consider when deciding whether to sentence him outside that range; he is guaranteed meaningful appellate review to protect against an arbitrary sentence. . . .

While not a constitutional prohibition on guidelines schemes, the majority's decision today exacts a substantial constitutional tax. [Facts] that historically have been taken into account by sentencing judges to assess a sentence within a broad range — such as drug quantity, role in the offense, risk of bodily harm — all must now be charged in an indictment and submitted to a jury simply because it is the legislature, rather than the judge, that constrains the extent to which such facts may be used to impose a sentence within a pre-existing statutory range. . . . The majority may be correct that States and the Federal Government will be willing to bear some of these costs. But simple economics dictate that they will not, and cannot, bear them all. To the extent that they do not, there will be an inevitable increase in judicial discretion with all of its attendant failings.

[The] guidelines served due process by providing notice to petitioner of the consequences of his acts; they vindicated his jury trial right by informing him of the stakes of risking trial; they served equal protection by ensuring petitioner that invidious characteristics such as race would not impact his sentence. Given these observations, it is difficult for me to discern what principle besides doctrinaire formalism actually motivates today's decision. . . .

The consequences of today's decision will be as far reaching as they are disturbing. Washington's sentencing system is by no means unique. Numerous other States have enacted guidelines systems, as has the Federal Government. Today's decision casts constitutional doubt over them all and, in so doing, threatens an untold number of criminal judgments. Every sentence imposed under such guidelines in cases currently pending on direct appeal is in jeopardy. . . . What I have feared most has now come to pass: Over 20 years of sentencing reform are all but lost, and tens of thousands of criminal judgments are in jeopardy. I respectfully dissent.

KENNEDY, J., dissenting.

. . . The Court, in my respectful submission, disregards the fundamental principle under our constitutional system that different branches of government converse with each other on matters of vital common interest. . . . Case-by-case judicial determinations often yield intelligible patterns that can be refined by legislatures and codified into statutes or rules as general standards. As these legislative enactments are followed by incremental judicial interpretation, the legislatures may respond again, and the cycle repeats. This recurring dialogue, an essential source for the elaboration and the evolution of the law, is basic constitutional theory in action.

Sentencing guidelines are a prime example of this collaborative process. Dissatisfied with the wide disparity in sentencing, participants in the criminal justice system, including judges, pressed for legislative reforms. In response, legislators drew from these participants' shared experiences and enacted measures to correct the problems. [Because] the Constitution does not prohibit the dynamic and fruitful dialogue between the judicial and legislative branches of government that has marked sentencing reform on both the state and the federal levels for more than 20 years, I dissent.

BREYER, J., dissenting.

[The] difference between a traditional sentencing factor and an element of a greater offense often comes down to a legislative choice about which label to affix. [One might ask why it should matter for jury trial purposes whether the statute (or guideline) labels a fact as a sentencing factor or a crime element. But] the conclusion that the Sixth Amendment always requires identical treatment of the two scenarios [carries] consequences that threaten the fairness of our traditional criminal justice system; it distorts historical sentencing or criminal trial practices; and it upsets settled law on which legislatures have relied in designing punishment systems. . . .

As a result of the majority's rule, sentencing must now take one of three forms, each of which risks either impracticality, unfairness, or harm to the jury trial right the majority purports to strengthen. This circumstance shows that the majority's Sixth Amendment interpretation cannot be right. . . .

A

A first option for legislators is to create a simple, pure or nearly pure "charge offense" or "determinate" sentencing system. In such a system, an indictment would charge a few facts which, taken together, constitute a crime, such as robbery. Robbery would carry a single sentence, say, five years' imprisonment. . . .

Such a system assures uniformity, but at intolerable costs. First, simple determinate sentencing systems impose identical punishments on people who committed their crimes in very different ways. When dramatically different conduct ends up being punished the same way, an injustice has taken place. Simple determinate sentencing has the virtue of treating like cases alike, but it simultaneously fails to treat different cases differently. . . .

Second, in a world of statutorily fixed mandatory sentences for many crimes, determinate sentencing gives tremendous power to prosecutors to manipulate sentences through their choice of charges. Prosecutors can simply charge, or threaten to charge, defendants with crimes bearing higher mandatory sentences. Defendants, knowing that they will not have a chance to argue for a lower sentence in front of a judge, may plead to charges that they might otherwise contest. . . .

B

A second option for legislators is to return to a system of indeterminate sentencing. . . . When such systems were in vogue, they were criticized, and rightly so, for producing unfair disparities, including race-based disparities, in the punishment of similarly situated defendants. [Under] such a system, the judge could vary the sentence greatly based upon his findings about how the defendant had committed the crime — findings that might not have been made by a "preponderance of the evidence," much less "beyond a reasonable doubt." Returning to such a system would . . . do little to ensure the control of what the majority calls "the people," i.e., the jury, "in the judiciary," since "the people" would only decide the defendant's guilt, a finding with no effect on the duration of the sentence. . . .

C

A third option is that which the Court seems to believe legislators will in fact take. That is the option of retaining structured schemes that attempt to punish similar conduct similarly and different conduct differently, but modifying them to conform to *Apprendi*'s dictates. Judges would be able to depart downward from presumptive sentences upon finding that mitigating factors were present, but would not be able to depart upward unless the prosecutor charged the aggravating fact to a jury and proved it beyond a reasonable doubt. . . .

This option can be implemented in one of two ways. The first way would be for legislatures to subdivide each crime into a list of complex crimes, each of which would be defined to include commonly found sentencing factors such as drug quantity, type of victim, presence of violence, degree of injury, use of gun, and so on. A legislature, for example, might enact a robbery statute, modeled on robbery sentencing guidelines, that increases punishment depending upon (1) the nature of the institution robbed, (2) the (a) presence of, (b) brandishing of, (c) other use of, a firearm, (3) making of a death threat, (4) presence of (a) ordinary, (b) serious, (c) permanent or life threatening, bodily injury, (5) abduction, (6) physical restraint, (7) taking of a firearm, (8) taking of drugs, (9) value of property loss, etc.

[Under this option, the] prosecutor, through control of the precise charge, controls the punishment, thereby marching the sentencing system directly away from, not toward, one important guideline goal: rough uniformity of punishment for those who engage in roughly the same real criminal conduct. . . .

This "complex charge offense" system . . . prejudices defendants who seek trial, for it can put them in the untenable position of contesting material aggravating facts in the guilt phases of their trials. Consider a defendant who is charged, not with mere possession of cocaine, but with the specific offense of possession of more than 500 grams of cocaine. Or consider a defendant charged, not with murder, but with the new crime of murder using a machete. Or consider a defendant whom the prosecution wants to claim was a "supervisor," rather than an ordinary gang member. How can a Constitution that guarantees due process put these defendants, as a matter of course, in the position of arguing, "I did not sell drugs, and if I did, I did not sell more than 500 grams" or, "I did not kill him, and if I did, I did not use a machete," or "I did not engage in gang activity, and certainly not as a supervisor" to a single jury? . . .

The majority announces that there really is no problem here because "States may continue to offer judicial factfinding as a matter of course to all defendants who plead guilty" and defendants may stipulate to the relevant facts or consent to judicial factfinding. [The] fairness problem arises because States may very well decide that they will not permit defendants to carve subsets of facts out of the new, *Apprendi*-required 17-element robbery crime, seeking a judicial determination as to some of those facts and a jury determination as to others. . . .

The second way to make sentencing guidelines *Apprendi*-compliant would be to require at least two juries for each defendant whenever aggravating facts are present: one jury to determine guilt of the crime charged, and an additional jury to try the disputed facts that, if found, would aggravate the sentence. Our experience with bifurcated trials in the capital punishment context suggests that requiring them for run-of-the-mill sentences would be costly, both in money and in judicial time and resources. . . . The Court can announce that the Constitution requires at least two jury trials for each criminal defendant — one for guilt, another for sentencing — but only because it knows full well that more than 90% of defendants will not go to trial even once, much less insist on two or more trials.

What will be the consequences of the Court's holding for the 90% of defendants who do not go to trial? The truthful answer is that we do not know. . . . At the least, the greater expense attached to trials and their greater complexity, taken together in the context of an overworked criminal justice system, will likely mean, other things being equal, fewer trials and a greater reliance upon plea bargaining — a system in which punishment is set not by judges or juries but by advocates acting under bargaining constraints. At the same time, the greater power of the prosecutor to control the punishment through the charge would likely weaken the relation between real conduct and real punishment as well. . . .

For more than a century, questions of punishment (not those of guilt or innocence) have reflected determinations made, not only by juries, but also by judges, probation officers, and executive parole boards. Such truth-seeking determinations have rested upon both adversarial and non-adversarial processes. The Court's holding undermines efforts to reform these processes, for it means that legislatures cannot both permit judges to base sentencing upon real conduct and seek, through guidelines, to make the results more uniform. . . .

Now, let us return to the question I posed at the outset. Why does the Sixth Amendment permit a jury trial right (in respect to a particular fact) to depend upon a legislative labeling decision, namely, the legislative decision to label the fact a sentencing fact, instead of an element of the crime? The answer is that the fairness and effectiveness of a sentencing system, and the related fairness and effectiveness of the criminal justice system itself, depends upon the legislature's possessing the constitutional authority (within due process limits) to make that labeling decision. To restrict radically the legislature's power in this respect, as the majority interprets the Sixth Amendment to do, prevents the legislature from seeking sentencing systems that are consistent with, and indeed may help to advance, the Constitution's greater fairness goals. . . . Whatever the faults of guidelines systems — and there are many — they are more likely to find their cure in legislation emerging from the experience of, and discussion among, all elements of the criminal justice community, than in a virtually unchangeable constitutional decision of this Court. . . .

Notes

1. *Juries and determinate sentencing laws.* The decision in *Blakely* created a great deal of upheaval in the state and federal courts. Defendants could now insist that juries rather than judges find any facts that authorize an increase in the legally available range of sentences. The key appears to be appellate review: if a judge could be overturned on appeal for selecting a given sentence without establishing the existence of a given fact, the jury trial right attaches to that fact. This dynamic affects any "upward departures" from sentences designated in guidelines, if those guidelines have "presumptive" authority and are not simply voluntary for judges.

Within a few months, the Supreme Court ruled in United States v. Booker, 543 U.S. 220 (2005), that the federal sentencing guidelines were unconstitutional because they authorized judges to increase the available range of guideline sentences only after finding various facts about the offense, factual findings that a jury must make. The Court fashioned an unexpected remedy for this Sixth Amendment problem: It severed portions of the statute making the guidelines binding on judges, and thus declared the federal guidelines advisory. In so doing, the Court tried to ensure that the guidelines would continue to operate in a manner as close to the old system as possible: "district courts, while not bound to apply the Guidelines, must consult those Guidelines and take them into account when sentencing." Federal courts of appeals were still authorized by statute to review sentences, overturning any sentences that were not "reasonable."

2. *Other factfinding that affects sentences served.* The effects of *Blakely* might not be limited to determinate sentencing structures. Justice Scalia's bold assertion that "every defendant has the *right* to insist that the prosecutor prove to a jury all facts legally essential to the punishment" could ultimately prove to be far reaching. Restitution orders, revocation of probation and parole, and a host of other punishment decisions that rest on nonjury factfinding may be subject to constitutional

challenge. The *Apprendi* ruling also has implications for capital sentencing, which requires that "aggravating factors" be found before a court may impose the death penalty. See Ring v. Arizona, 536 U.S. 584 (2002) (jury rather than judge must find an aggravating circumstance necessary for imposing death penalty).

3. *Translation of jury functions to a new context.* For a judge who interprets the Constitution in light of the historical meaning of the text and historical practices, the right to a jury trial in criminal cases presents several challenges. The criminal system has changed enormously in the past few centuries, most recently in the increased role of guilty pleas and the enormous innovations in sentencing rules. How can courts in the twenty-first century give meaning to the constitutional vision of a criminal adjudication process that is bounded by the views of juries about reasonable application of the criminal law?

Consider some of the ways that juries' involvement in sentencing might go beyond *Blakely*'s mandate. First, a legislature might require juries to be the finders of all (or at least all significant) sentencing facts. Second, a legislature might want juries not only to find facts but also to advise judges about appropriate punishments or even to impose specific punishments. In this context, it is worth remembering that jury participation in death penalty sentencing is the norm; juries typically find and weigh aggravating and mitigating facts and also recommend or impose the ultimate sentence. Suppose you are advising a sentencing commission in a jurisdiction with sentencing guidelines affected by *Apprendi* and *Blakely*. What changes would you advise the commission to make to comply with these cases?

4. *Minimum sentences, discretionary sentencing, and mitigating adjustments.* Despite the breadth of *Blakely*'s holding and dicta, the ruling still allows judicial factfinding in an array of sentencing settings. *Blakely* formally distinguished United States v. Harris, 536 U.S. 545 (2002), which permits judges to find facts that increase *minimum* sentences, and Williams v. New York, 337 U.S. 241 (1949), which permits judges to find facts in the course of making discretionary sentencing determinations. In addition, the *Apprendi* and *Blakely* rulings apply only to facts that increase sentences; judges may still find facts that the law provides as the basis for *decreasing* sentences. Could a jurisdiction, drawing on these gaps in the reach of the *Blakely* rule, construct a sound sentencing system that is still administered principally through judicial factfinding? Should a jurisdiction aspire to do so?

5. *Prior criminal record exception.* As a result of the decision in Almendarez-Torres v. United States, 523 U.S. 224 (1998), a "prior conviction" exception has been built into the Sixth Amendment's application in *Apprendi* and *Blakely*. Both *Apprendi* and *Blakely* state that its rule requiring sentence-enhancing facts to be proven to a jury beyond a reasonable doubt or admitted by the defendant applies only to facts "other than the fact of a prior conviction." The theoretical soundness of this exception has been widely questioned, and there may no longer be five votes on the Court to support it. State and federal courts have split over the scope and application of the prior conviction exception, debating whether only the fact of a prior conviction or other related facts (such as a defendant's status on probation) fall within the exception.

6. *Standard of proof at sentencing: majority position.* In McMillan v. Pennsylvania, 477 U.S. 79 (1986), the Court declared that the federal due process clause allows states to prove some facts affecting the sentence by a preponderance of the evidence. Although *Blakely* changed which facts could be found by a judge at the sentencing

hearing rather than by a jury at trial, the Court did not overturn the standard of proof to be used in the sentencing hearing.

Nearly all states have adopted by statute the preponderance standard for facts to be proven at sentencing. Structured sentencing systems in the states typically provide for a presumptive guideline sentence that is set by reference to the facts underlying a conviction, either proven beyond a reasonable doubt at trial or admitted by the defendant in a guilty plea. Yet these guidelines also allow judges, in varying degrees, to depart from the sentence indicated in the guidelines. The departure might be based on facts proven at the sentencing hearing, and most require the prosecution to show these facts only by a preponderance.

7. *Rules of evidence at sentencing.* Williams v. New York established that the rules of evidence for criminal trials need not apply in sentencing hearings. This is true both for indeterminate sentencing systems and for most structured sentencing systems. The Federal Rules of Evidence state this explicitly: "The rules (other than with respect to privileges) do not apply in . . . sentencing." Fed. R. Evid. 1101(d)(3). The federal sentencing guidelines also adopt this position: "any information may be considered, so long as it has sufficient indicia of reliability to support its probable accuracy." U.S. Sentencing Guidelines §6A1.3(a). The rules do not apply because of the perceived burden they would place on sentencing judges, converting the sentencing hearing into a second trial. Should Congress or the U.S. Sentencing Commission change positions and apply the rules of evidence to sentencing hearings? Professor Deborah Young favors the rules of evidence over other methods of increasing the reliability of factfinding at sentencing because use of the rules of evidence corrects potential errors whether they benefit the prosecution or the defense. She argues that evenhanded factfinding rules make sense at sentencing precisely because an offender has already been convicted and should no longer be given the benefit of the presumption of innocence. Deborah Young, Fact-Finding at Federal Sentencing: Why the Guidelines Should Meet the Rules, 79 Cornell L. Rev. 299 (1994).

8. *Confrontation of witnesses.* Although the evidentiary rules governing hearsay do not apply to sentencing hearings in federal or state courts, the overlapping protections of the Sixth Amendment's confrontation clause (and the equivalent provisions of the state constitution) still might require that a defendant be allowed to cross-examine witnesses at the sentencing hearing. The small group of courts addressing this question, however, have mostly concluded that the confrontation clause does not apply to the evidence presented during a sentencing hearing. For example, in United States v. Wise, 976 F.2d 393 (8th Cir. 1992), the sentencing court relied on hearsay testimony by a probation officer regarding facts contained in the presentence investigation report. The judge allowed the defendant to cross-examine the probation officer and to introduce witnesses of his own but did not prevent the probation officer from introducing hearsay statements into evidence. The appellate court upheld the sentence and concluded that confrontation of witnesses at sentencing was unnecessary. See also State v. DeSalvo, 903 P.2d 202 (Mont. 1995). Different rules apply to capital sentencing proceedings: The imposition of a death sentence based on information that a defendant does not have the opportunity to deny or explain may run afoul of the confrontation clause. See Gardner v. Florida, 430 U.S. 349 (1977). The Supreme Court has held that the sentencing hearing is part of the "criminal proceedings" and that the right to counsel applies at that stage as well. Mempa v. Rhay, 389 U.S. 128 (1967) (establishing right to

counsel at sentencing). If the Sixth Amendment's right to counsel (granted to "the accused") applies at sentencing, why doesn't the Sixth Amendment's right to confront witnesses also apply?

2. Revisiting Jury Verdicts and Guilty Pleas

Because the judge decides the defendant's sentence independently, an opportunity exists to revisit questions that were already answered in the jury's verdict after trial or in the defendant's plea of guilty. To what extent should a sentencing judge fashion a sentence to reward a plea of guilty or to punish a decision to go to trial? What should the sentencing judge do when the jury acquits on some counts and convicts on at least one other count, yet the judge believes that the defendant probably committed all the crimes as charged?

■ UNITED STATES SENTENCING GUIDELINES §3E1.1

(a) If the defendant clearly demonstrates acceptance of responsibility for his offense, decrease the offense level by 2 levels.

(b) If the defendant qualifies for a decrease under subsection (a), the offense [is serious enough to qualify for a level 16 or greater], and the defendant has assisted authorities in the investigation or prosecution of his own misconduct by taking one or more of the following steps:

(1) timely providing complete information to the government concerning his own involvement in the offense; or

(2) timely notifying authorities of his intention to enter a plea of guilty, thereby permitting the government to avoid preparing for trial and permitting the court to allocate its resources efficiently,

decrease the offense level by 1 additional level.

Problem 9-5. Trial Penalty or Reward for Plea?

An experienced police officer watched Milton Coles speak with another person and give that person currency in exchange for a ziplock plastic bag, which the latter retrieved from a hiding place in a nearby tree. A jury found Coles guilty of one count of possessing marijuana. At sentencing, the trial judge made the following statement:

> I never understood why you went to trial in this case, Mr. Coles. Your lawyer did the best he could with no defense at all. I was amazed how successfully he was able to even come up with something plausible. If you had come before the Court and said, "Look, I had a little stuff on me and I needed a little extra money," I would have had some sympathy for you. As it is, though, I don't have any sympathy for you at all. So the Court sentences you to one year.

One year was the maximum available sentence for this offense. Coles has challenged the validity of this sentence, because he claims that the judge penalized him for exercising his constitutional right to stand trial. How would you rule on appeal? Compare Coles v. United States, 682 A.2d 167 (D.C. 1996).

Notes

1. *Sentencing after refusal to plead guilty: majority position.* In a plea agreement a defendant agrees to waive trial, normally in exchange for some perceived advantage at the time of sentencing. In unstructured sentencing systems, judges almost always accept a plea bargain if offered by the parties, but it is not clear what effect the defendant's willingness to plead guilty has on the sentence. Research has shown that defendants pleading guilty tend to receive substantially lower sentences than defendants who go to trial (in some studies the "plea discount" has been one-third or more off post-trial sentences) but that judges tend to sentence based on the original charges filed rather than the charges forming the basis of the guilty plea.

Almost all high state courts say that a sentencing court cannot punish a refusal to plead guilty but can enhance a punishment based on "lack of remorse" or failure to "accept responsibility" for a crime. Jennings v. State, 664 A.2d 903 (Md. 1995). Courts routinely treat an agreement to plead guilty as an appropriate reason for imposing a less severe sentence. State v. Balfour, 637 A.2d 1249 (N.J. 1994) (defendant's agreement to plead guilty can appropriately be weighed in the decision to downgrade an offense to a lower degree at sentencing). In practice, is there a difference between "punishing the exercise of trial rights" and "rewarding acceptance of responsibility"? Do these rules encourage judges to do anything more than choose their words carefully?

2. *Plea bargaining and structured sentencing rules.* Section 3E1.1 of the federal sentencing guidelines, reprinted above, allows the sentencing judge to reduce a sentence for "acceptance of responsibility," while commentary to that guideline provision insists that courts should not equate acceptance of responsibility with a decision to plead guilty. Rules in various structured sentencing systems give sentencing judges different instructions about the impact of a plea agreement. The possibilities range from rules saying that plea agreements should not change the sentence at all to rules that allow the judge to accept the sentencing recommendations of the parties within certain broad limits. For instance, under the Minnesota sentencing guidelines, judges must impose the sentence indicated in the guideline grid unless there is a valid ground for departure. A plea agreement, standing alone, is not a sufficient reason to depart from the guidelines. In Washington state, statutory guidelines tell the judge to "determine if the agreement is consistent with the interests of justice and with the [statutory] prosecuting standards" and to reject the agreement if it is not. Wash. Rev. Code §9.94A.090(1). The federal sentencing guidelines also advise judges to limit the impact of a guilty plea at sentencing. The court may accept sentencing recommendations offered in a plea agreement "if the court is satisfied either that: (1) the recommended sentence is within the applicable guideline range; or (2) the recommended sentence departs from the applicable guideline range for justifiable reasons." U.S. Sentencing Guidelines §6B1.2(b) (reprinted in Chapter 6, section B).

3. *Sentence enhancements for perjury and obstruction of justice at trial.* Judges who preside at trial also typically impose the sentence on the same defendant after conviction. In United States v. Dunnigan, 507 U.S. 87 (1993), the Court concluded

that a sentencing court can enhance a defendant's sentence by a designated amount under the federal guidelines if the court finds that the defendant committed perjury at trial. A defendant's right to testify "does not include a right to commit perjury." To reduce the risk that a court will wrongfully punish a truthful defendant, the court must make "findings to support all the elements of a perjury violation in the specific case." Does the sentencing judge's power to punish perjury without a perjury conviction punish the right to trial?

If perjury at trial can enhance a sentence, this adds to the long list of incentives for defendants not to testify at trial. As we saw in the previous chapter, the Fifth Amendment declares that a factfinder may not draw adverse inferences from this silence at trial. Does the same protection apply to silence at sentencing? In Mitchell v. United States, 526 U.S. 314 (1999), the Supreme Court decided that a guilty plea in federal court does not extinguish the defendant's Fifth Amendment right to remain silent at sentencing. The government in this narcotics case presented testimony from co-defendants at Mitchell's sentencing hearing; the co-defendants claimed that she had sold 1.5 to 2 ounces of cocaine twice a week for 18 months. The sentencing judge found that this testimony established the 5-kilogram threshold for a mandatory 10-year minimum, and noted that Mitchell's failure to testify was a factor in persuading the court to rely on the co-defendants' testimony. The Supreme Court declared that a sentencing judge may not draw adverse inferences from the defendant's silence at the sentencing hearing in selecting a sentence for the defendant.

4. *Acquitted conduct at sentencing.* Although indeterminate sentencing systems typically allow judges to consider prior misconduct when setting a sentence, many states make an exception for acquitted conduct — conduct that formed the basis for a charge resulting in an acquittal at trial. Judges in many states have developed common law rules preventing the use of acquitted conduct at sentencing. See Bishop v. State, 486 S.E.2d 887 (Ga. 1997); Anderson v. State, 448 N.E.2d 1180 (Ind. 1983); State v. Cobb, 732 A.2d 425 (N.H. 1999). On the other hand, a roughly equal number of states approve the use of acquitted conduct. State v. Huey, 505 A.2d 1242 (Conn. 1986); State v. Woodlief, 90 S.E. 137 (N.C. 1916); State v. Leiter, 646 N.W.2d 341 (Wis. 2002). Why do so many states limit the use of acquitted conduct but permit sentencing judges to consider prior convictions and prior uncharged conduct more generally?

The Supreme Court in United States v. Watts, 519 U.S. 148 (1997), ruled that neither the Constitution nor the federal sentencing statutes or guidelines bar a judge from considering acquitted conduct at sentencing. In that case, police discovered cocaine in a kitchen cabinet and two loaded guns in a bedroom closet of Watts's house. The jury acquitted Watts of the firearms charge but convicted him of drug possession. The judge increased Watts's sentence on the drug charges after finding by a preponderance of the evidence that Watts had possessed the weapons illegally. The Court explained the use of information underlying acquittals in terms of the different standards of proof at trial and sentencing: Evidence that was insufficient to establish guilt beyond a reasonable doubt might nevertheless be enough to convince the judge to enhance a sentence. In effect, this allows the sentencing judge to ignore the verdict of the jury. See also Edwards v. United States, 523 U.S. 511 (1998) (sentencing judge can determine that defendants were trafficking in both crack and powder, even if jury believed defendants were trafficking only in powder). Do the rulings in *Watts* and *Edwards* survive the later decisions in *Apprendi* and *Blakely*?

5. *"Vindictive" sentencing after retrial.* Just as courts insist that a sentence may not be increased to punish a defendant for exercising the right to trial, federal and state

courts say that a trial judge may not punish a defendant for exercising the statutory right to appeal. If a defendant successfully appeals a conviction and is convicted again after retrial, a sentence higher than the original sentence imposed is presumed to be a product of "vindictiveness" by the sentencing judge. A sentence motivated by such vindictiveness violates federal due process. The judge must rebut this presumption by placing on the record his reasons for increasing the sentence after the second conviction. See North Carolina v. Pearce, 395 U.S. 711 (1969). According to *Pearce,* those reasons could be based on "objective information concerning identifiable conduct on the part of the defendant occurring after the time of the original sentence proceeding." Later, the Court said that a court could rebut the presumption of vindictiveness by pointing to any "objective information" that the court did not consider during the first sentencing proceeding. Texas v. McCullough, 475 U.S. 134 (1986).

6. *Probation officers.* Judges who sentence a defendant after a guilty plea have not heard an extensive presentation of the evidence at trial and thus depend heavily on the pre-sentence investigation (PSI) report to inform them about the offender and the offense. Especially in structured sentencing systems in which particular facts have an identifiable impact on the sentence, probation officers (who create the PSI reports) are critical players in the sentencing process. See Charlie Varnon, The Role of the Probation Officer in the Guideline System, 4 Fed. Sentencing Rep. 63 (1991). How might a prosecutor or a defense attorney influence the recommendations of the probation officer? What institutional or individual biases might the probation officer bring to her assessment (and recommendation) of proper sentences?

D. NEW INFORMATION ABOUT THE OFFENDER AND THE VICTIM

We have seen how sentencing courts revisit and refine the choices made prior to conviction. But the sentencing judge does more than this; the judge goes on to consider a broader range of information about the offender's past and future, the broader context of the offense, and the viewpoint of the victim.

1. Offender Information

Although the offender's involvement in the crime of conviction is critical to a sentence, judges also consider other aspects of the offender's character and past conduct. In this section, we consider the use at sentencing of the offender's prior criminal record, cooperation with the government in other investigations, and other aspects of an offender's personal history and prospects.

a. Criminal History

At sentencing, the court learns about the defendant's life before the crime of conviction took place. Probation officers collect some of this information; attorneys for either the prosecution or the defense present facts, as well. Often the offender's past will include prior convictions or other encounters with the criminal justice system. Under an unstructured sentencing system, the judge gives the prior criminal record whatever weight she thinks appropriate. Sentencing statutes and guidelines, however, instruct judges in some systems more precisely about the effect that a prior criminal record must have on a sentence.

■ MELVIN TUNSTILL v. STATE
568 N.E.2d 539 (Ind. 1991)

DeBruler, J.

Appellant was tried to a jury on a charge of murder and was found guilty of voluntary manslaughter, a Class B felony. . . . He received an executed sentence of 20 years [and brought this appeal].

The evidence produced at trial most favorable to the verdict shows that the victim, Jerry Wayne Haggard, died of a single stab wound inflicted by appellant during a scuffle which occurred at a little after 2:00 A.M. on July 19, 1987, in the parking lot of B & B Liquors in Indianapolis. Appellant and Haggard had been acquainted for six or seven years and often socialized and drank together. . . . At approximately 1:45 A.M. on July 19, appellant walked from his house to B & B Liquors to buy some wine before closing time. [S]everal people were congregated in the parking lot, [and] appellant brushed into Haggard. Appellant turned and said to Haggard, "Hey, what's happening?," whereupon Haggard kicked appellant in the groin. Appellant backed away, repeating, "Hey, man, what's going on? What's wrong with you?" and Haggard kicked him again. Haggard kicked appellant a third time, this time in the shins, and appellant pushed Haggard backward. Haggard stumbled, and appellant pulled out a knife and, still backing up but swinging the knife from side to side in front of him, said, "What's wrong with you? You must want to die." [T]he two "clenched," according to one witness, then Haggard staggered back with his hands pressed against his body and fell onto a parked car. He died shortly thereafter. . . .

The trial court enhanced the standard 10-year sentence for a Class B felony by an additional 10 years and imposed a 20-year executed sentence. At the sentencing hearing, the trial court stated that the imposition of an enhanced sentence was warranted by the presence of two aggravating circumstances: 1) appellant was on probation at the time of the instant crime and 2) appellant's criminal history, consisting of three prior arrests. . . .

Appellant first argues that the trial court erred in considering him to have been a probationer at the time the instant offense was committed. Prior to the events at issue here, appellant was convicted of possession of heroin and methadone. He received a suspended sentence, was ordered to pay a $320 fine and court costs, and was placed on a year's probation which was to run from March 7, 1986, to March 7, 1987. In March of 1987, four months before the instant crime, a petition was filed charging that appellant was in violation of his probation because he had not paid the fine and costs. [T]he record indicates that the final hearing on the probation violation was held approximately a week before the sentencing hearing on the instant charge. . . . Appellant's probation period was tolled until the time that a final determination on the violation petition was made, which occurred well after the commission of the charged crime. While not entitled to much weight, appellant's continuing status as a probationer could properly be considered by the trial court as an aggravating circumstance.

Appellant next contends that the trial court committed error by citing three prior arrests as the basis for its finding that his criminal history constituted an aggravating circumstance and in failing to consider evidence of mitigating circumstances apparent on the record. The statement setting out the trial court's rationale for imposing an enhanced sentence read in its entirety as follows:

> The Court does find the following aggravating circumstances: That the defendant was on probation at the time the offense was committed. That the defendant's prior criminal history, consisting of an arrest on February 3, 1970, of carrying a concealed weapon, an arrest on May 18, 1971, for assault and battery with intent to kill, an arrest on March 13, 1983 for battery with injury, and other arrests indicating that the defendant's conduct was in fact escalated from carrying a concealed weapon, to in fact, voluntary manslaughter.

At the time of appellant's sentencing hearing, I.C. 35-38-1-7 . . . identified the factors which the court was to take into consideration in imposing sentence. Subsections (b) and (c) set out circumstances which the court was allowed to consider in aggravation and mitigation; subsection (d) stated that "the criteria listed in subsections (b) and (c) do not limit the matters that the court may consider in determining the sentence."

If the sentencing court found that appellant "ha[d] a history of criminal or delinquent activity," the court was authorized to consider that fact as an aggravating circumstance under I.C. 35-38-1-7(b)(2), and it is clear from the court's sentencing statement that it considered appellant's prior arrests to be instances of criminal behavior establishing such a history. In this, the court was in error. A record of arrest, without more, does not establish the historical fact that the defendant committed a criminal offense on a previous occasion such that it may be properly considered as evidence that the defendant has a history of criminal activity. In order to enhance a criminal sentence based, in whole or in part, on the defendant's history of criminal activity, a sentencing court must find instances of specific criminal conduct shown by probative evidence to be attributable to the defendant. A bare record of arrest will not suffice to meet this standard.

An arrest is "the taking of a person into custody, that he may be held to answer for a crime." I.C. 35-33-1-5. An arrest is permissible without a warrant if the arresting officer had, at the time of the arrest, probable cause to believe that the person had committed a felony. An arrest may also be made pursuant to a warrant, which is itself based upon either the return of an indictment or upon probable cause. Probable cause exists when, at the time the warrant is sought or the arrest is made, the arresting officer has knowledge of facts and circumstances which would warrant a man of reasonable caution to believe that the person committed the criminal act in question. The act of placing a person under arrest indicates only a belief, albeit strong, that the arrested person is guilty of a crime, but does not itself constitute a determination of the historical fact of that person's guilt.

The historical fact that a defendant has committed a crime, such that it may then be properly found to constitute the aggravator of a criminal history, may be established upon evidence that the defendant has been convicted of another crime, upon his own admission of guilt of another crime, or upon evidence that the defendant committed another crime which is properly admitted at trial under an exception to the general prohibition against evidence of prior bad acts. Once a defendant's guilt of the other crime is established by conviction, admission, or properly admitted trial evidence, whether or not he was ever placed under arrest is irrelevant. The substance of the aggravator, "history of criminal activity," is the fact that the defendant committed the other crime, not that he was arrested for it.

This is not to say that a record of arrests, particularly a lengthy one, should carry no aggravating weight or that it may not be considered by a sentencing court. A long line of cases from this Court holds that allegations of prior criminal activity need not be reduced to conviction before they may be properly considered as aggravating circumstances by a sentencing court. The court must, however, place this type of information in the proper context when considering it and determining its relative weight. A record of arrests cannot be considered as an aggravator under I.C. 35-38-1-7(b)(2) because it does not reveal to the sentencing court that the defendant has engaged in the kind of behavior which the legislature identified as an aggravator in that subsection. I.C. 35-38-1-7(d), however, gives a sentencing court the flexibility to consider any factor which reflects on the defendant's character, good or bad, in addition to those expressly set out in the rest of the statute when determining the appropriate sentence to impose on that defendant. It is in this category that a record of arrests is properly considered. While a record of arrests does not establish the historical fact of prior criminal behavior, such a record does reveal to the court that subsequent antisocial behavior on the part of the defendant has not been deterred even after having been subject to the police authority of the State and made aware of its oversight of the activities of its citizens. This information is relevant to the court's assessment of the defendant's character and the risk that he will commit another crime and is therefore properly considered by a court in determining sentence.

This Court has also held that criminal charges which are pending at the time of a defendant's sentencing hearing may properly be considered as an aggravating circumstance. Pending charges, like arrests, do not establish the historical fact that the defendant committed the crime alleged, but, like arrests, are relevant and may be considered by a sentencing court as being reflective of the defendant's character and as indicative of the risk that he will commit other crimes in the future.

As noted above, the sentencing statement at issue here makes it clear that the court inferred that appellant actually committed the crimes for which he was arrested, and this inference constitutes error. [A] remand is necessary for the court to conduct a new sentencing hearing and then to issue an order which reflects that the nature of the aggravators and their relative weights were correctly assessed and found to merit an enhanced sentence or to impose a standard sentence. . . .

■ WASHINGTON STATE SENTENCING GUIDELINES
Implementation Manual

The offender score is measured on the horizontal axis of the sentencing guidelines grid. An offender can receive anywhere from 0 to 9+ points on that axis. In general terms, the number of points an offender receives depends on four factors: 1) the number of prior felony criminal convictions; 2) the relationship between any prior offenses(s) and the current offense of conviction; 3) the presence of multiple prior or current convictions; and 4) whether the crime was committed while the offender was on community placement. [A higher number of points translates into a longer prison term or a change from nonprison to prison disposition.] RCW 9.94A.030(12) defines criminal history to include the defendant's prior adult convictions in this state, federal court, and elsewhere, as well as [felonies adjudicated] in juvenile court if [they did not result in a diversion].

"Washout" of Certain Prior Felonies

In certain instances, prior felony convictions are not calculated into the offender score. . . . Prior Class A and sex offense felony convictions are always included in the offender score. Prior Class B felony convictions are not included if 1) the offender has spent ten years in the community; and 2) has not been convicted of any felonies since the most recent of either the last date of release from confinement . . . or the day the sentence was entered. Prior Class C felonies are not included if the offender has spent five years in the community and has not been convicted of any felonies since the most recent of either the last date of release from confinement . . . or the day the sentence was entered.

■ CALIFORNIA PENAL CODE §667 ("THREE STRIKES")

(e)(2)(A) If a defendant has two or more prior [serious or violent] felony convictions as defined [elsewhere in the code] that have been pled and proved, the term for the current felony conviction shall be an indeterminate term of life imprisonment with a minimum term of the indeterminate sentence calculated as the greater of:

> (i) Three times the term otherwise provided as punishment for each current felony conviction subsequent to the two or more prior felony convictions.
>
> (ii) Imprisonment in the state prison for 25 years. . . .

(f)(1) Notwithstanding any other law, [the sentence enhancement described in subdivision (e)] shall be applied in every case in which a defendant has a prior felony conviction as defined [by this statute]. The prosecuting attorney shall plead and prove each prior felony conviction except as provided in paragraph (2).

> (2) The prosecuting attorney may move to dismiss or strike a prior felony conviction allegation in the furtherance of justice . . . or if there is insufficient evidence to prove the prior conviction. If upon the satisfaction of the court that there is insufficient evidence to prove the prior felony conviction, the court may dismiss or strike the allegation.

(g) Prior felony convictions shall not be used in plea bargaining. . . . The prosecution shall plead and prove all known prior felony convictions and shall not enter into any agreement to strike or seek the dismissal of any prior felony conviction allegation except as provided in paragraph (2) of subdivision (f).

Problem 9-6. Striking Out

John Saenz, whose criminal record began in 1959, is 58 years old. He has five felony convictions, including two robberies, assault with a deadly weapon, and auto theft. In a 1985 robbery, Saenz pointed a gun at a San Diego police officer. In 1995 (while still on parole from a prior offense, and while misdemeanor drug charges were still pending against him), Saenz stole $75 worth of clothing, sunglasses, a mustache trimmer, and a birthday card from a discount store in California.

Saenz has admitted stealing the merchandise. His conduct qualifies as petty theft, which is a felony. There is also a provision in the state code for misdemeanor theft. If you were the prosecuting attorney in this case, would you file felony charges against Saenz? If you were the judge, would you grant the defendant's motion to dismiss the felony charge and to accept a proposed guilty plea for misdemeanor theft (which could result in a prison sentence of up to one year)?

Problem 9-7. Personal History and Prospects

Kelley Grady began a love affair with Brenda Croslin while she was living with her husband, Michael, and their two children. Eventually, Brenda left Michael and began renting a home owned by Kelley's mother.

Michael and Brenda had a violent relationship. On more than one occasion Michael choked and beat Brenda in the presence of their children, and threatened to kill her. On March 7, 1993, Michael and Brenda argued on the telephone, and Michael went to Brenda's house, where Kelley and the children were also present. Michael began yelling for Kelley to come out of the house and threatened to kill him. Kelley telephoned the police, and Michael left after the police arrived.

On July 20, 1993, Brenda went to Michael's house after work to pick up their children. When Brenda arrived, Michael began yelling at her, poking her in the chest, slapping her with his hand, and telling her that she was moving back in with him. Brenda told Michael she was not moving back in with him, and Michael became enraged. Michael called Kelley on the telephone and told him Brenda was moving out of the rental house. Kelley heard Brenda crying in the background. Michael began punching, kicking, and choking Brenda.

After his conversation with Michael, Kelley drove his truck to Brenda's house. Finding nobody there, he drove to Michael's house, parked in front, and honked the horn. Kelley had a cellular telephone, a knife, and a semiautomatic handgun in his car. Brenda went onto the porch and told Kelley to leave. But Kelley began yelling "wife beater" and told Michael to come out of the house and pick on someone his own size. Michael took a butcher knife from the kitchen and jumped off the porch into the yard. Kelley saw Michael come out of the house with what he thought was a gun. Kelley reached into his vehicle, retrieved his gun, and began shooting at Michael and running. There were three initial gunshots, a pause, and then another series of shots. Michael fell to the ground face first. Kelley threw the gun down, told Brenda to call 911, and went to his truck.

The police arrested Kelley when they arrived. Michael was pronounced dead immediately after arriving at the hospital, and an autopsy revealed 11 separate bullet wounds. A toxicology report showed a blood alcohol concentration of .164.

Kelley was charged with one count of first-degree premeditated murder in Michael's death. He claimed self-defense, but the jury found him guilty of voluntary manslaughter. At the sentencing hearing, various witnesses testified that Kelley had a reputation as a peaceful, nonaggressive, nonviolent person who sought to avoid conflict. He had no prior criminal history.

Prior to sentencing, the defendant filed a motion for a "downward departure" sentence. Based on the offense of conviction and the defendant's lack of criminal history, the presumptive sentence under the state sentencing guidelines was a term of incarceration of 46-51 months. The defendant requested a nonprison sentence of 36 months, including up to 30 days in jail, up to 180 days in community corrections, a period of probation, and public and monetary restitution. The trial court sentenced the defendant to 30 days in jail, 180 days in residential Community Corrections, 1 year on electronic surveillance, and 1,000 hours of public restitution. The judge also ordered the defendant to make no contact with the Croslin children until later review by the Court, and to pay for a psychological evaluation of the Croslin children.

Under the relevant statute, an appellate court may review a "departure" sentence only to determine whether the findings of fact are "supported by evidence in the record" and whether the reasons justifying the departure are "substantial and compelling." As an appellate judge, would you uphold this sentence? Compare State v. Grady, 900 P.2d 227 (Kan. 1995).

Notes

1. *Prior convictions, prior arrests, and pending charges: majority position.* In all U.S. sentencing systems, the prior convictions of an offender are among the most important determinants of the sentence imposed. In jurisdictions with detailed sentencing rules, prior convictions for more serious offenses typically increase the sentence more than prior convictions for less serious offenses. In some systems (such as the Washington system, illustrated above), prior convictions that occurred long ago have less impact on the current sentence. Prior convictions for the same type of crime as the current offense can increase a sentence more than prior convictions for unrelated wrongdoing. What purposes do these provisions serve? Are they designed to deter the offender, or other offenders, from committing future crimes? Are they designed to select a sentence "proportionate" to the crime committed (that is, to give the offender her "just deserts")? Some sentencing judges are more reluctant to increase a sentence based on a prior arrest or a pending unadjudicated criminal charge. Nevertheless, it is highly unusual for sentencing rules to prevent judges from relying on a prior arrest or a pending charge in setting the current sentence. Under the federal sentencing guidelines, a court may depart from the designated range of sentences if the guidelines' calculation of prior criminal record does not adequately account for "similar adult criminal conduct not resulting in a criminal conviction." U.S. Sentencing Guidelines §4A1.3.

2. *Guidelines versus statutes.* The California code section reprinted above provides an example of a "habitual offender" law popularly known as "three strikes and you're out." Almost all states have habitual felon statutes, which increase sentences by designated amounts for offenders with the necessary prior felony record. The "three strikes" variety is distinctive for the type of prior record necessary and the amount of increase in the sentence; about half the states have statutes of this type.

Both the California statute and the Washington guidelines provisions instruct a sentencing judge on the amount to increase a sentence in light of a prior criminal record. Nonetheless, they function quite differently. Under the Washington guidelines, the amount of increase moves up gradually as the prior record becomes more serious. The judge can depart from the guidelines in exceptional cases. Guidelines also do not allow *prosecutors* to choose whether to use the prior record to increase a sentence; many "habitual offender" laws do allow prosecutors to choose whether to charge a defendant as a "habitual offender." Why would a legislature choose a statute (like California's) rather than guidelines (like the Washington provisions) to control the impact of prior criminal record?

3. *Unreliable prior convictions.* The use of prior convictions to enhance the sentence for the current offense becomes more controversial when there are reasons to question the accuracy of the earlier charges. This is true especially when the earlier conviction occurred without the involvement of defense counsel. The federal constitution bars the use at sentencing of uncounseled prior convictions, but only if the government obtained the prior conviction by violating the defendant's constitutional right to counsel. See Nichols v. United States, 511 U.S. 738 (1994) (sentencing court may consider defendant's previous uncounseled misdemeanor conviction in sentencing him for subsequent offense); United States v. Tucker, 404 U.S. 443 (1972) (conviction obtained in violation of Sixth Amendment rights cannot enhance later sentence). These questions often arise when the prior conviction took place in the juvenile system or when the earlier case dealt with charges of driving while intoxicated. See State v. LaMunyon, 911 P.2d 151 (Kan. 1996) (juvenile); State v. Brown, 676 A.2d 350 (Vt. 1996) (DWI).

4. *Offender characteristics at sentencing: majority rule.* A criminal defendant is more than the sum of his contacts with the criminal justice system. The sentencing judge in most cases adjusts the sentence in light of the offender's overall character, including the facts known about his family, physical or mental health, and prospects for rehabilitation. In an unstructured sentencing system, it is difficult to say which personal characteristics of an offender tend to influence the sentence. Most structured systems do not consider such personal characteristics at all in setting the presumptive guideline sentence. Nevertheless, most do allow (and even encourage) the sentencing judge to depart from the guidelines on the basis of personal characteristics. Consider the various grounds the defendant in Problem 9-7 might assert as reasons to reduce his sentence. How could a sentencing court in this system best insulate a departure sentence from reversal on appeal?

5. *Family and community.* Sentencing judges also consider the impact of a proposed sentence on the defendant's family and community. The federal sentencing guidelines attempt to limit this practice by declaring that many personal characteristics of the defendant (including the defendant's "family ties and responsibilities") are "not ordinarily relevant" to a sentence. Appellate courts have upheld departure sentences based on such circumstances only when they are present to an "extraordinary" degree. See United States v. Johnson, 964 F.2d 124 (2d Cir. 1992) (upholding downward departure for payroll clerk at VA hospital convicted for defrauding government; defendant was sole support for three children under 7 years of age, institutionalized adult daughter, 17-year-old son, and 6-year-old granddaughter). What are "extraordinary" family circumstances? According to a 1991 survey, 61.6 percent of all federal prisoners and 56.7 percent of all state prisoners had children under age 18. Among female prisoners, the comparable numbers are 61.4 percent and 66.6 percent. In the state systems, 42.9 percent of the prisoners with children under 18 had only one child below that age, 28.9 percent had two, 15.4 percent had three, and 12.8 percent had four or more. Bureau of Justice Statistics, Comparing Federal and State Prison Inmates (1994, NCJ 145864). See Jack

Weinstein, The Effect of Sentencing on Women, Men, the Family, and the Community, 5 Colum. J. Gender & L. 169 (1996).

As a staff attorney for a sentencing commission, how would you draft guidance for sentencing courts in identifying the sorts of family circumstances that should lead to a departure up or down from the ordinary sentence? Would one circumstance be the number of children? The likely home for those children if the parent is incarcerated? Would you follow the ABA approach or would you leave these questions entirely to the discretion of the sentencing courts? See United States v. Monaco, 23 F.3d 793 (3d Cir. 1994) (decreasing sentence because of father's remorse and mental anguish over involving his adult son in a scheme to defraud government during execution of defense contract); United States v. Ledesma, 979 F.2d 816 (11th Cir. 1992) (enhancing sentence because defendant involved her adult daughter in drug trafficking).

b. Cooperation in Other Investigations

Just as a defendant's past conduct can influence the sentence, so can the defendant's future conduct. Perhaps the most important future conduct for sentencing purposes is the defendant's ability and willingness to help the government investigate other suspects. The defendant can tell investigators about past events or can agree to take part in future "sting" operations. In the federal system, "substantial assistance" to the government is by far the most common reason judges give for "departing" downward to give a sentence lower than the range specified in the guidelines. Substantial assistance accounted for more than 70 percent of the downward departures in 1992 (the next most frequent reason appeared in only 7.9 percent of the departures). It is clear that all sentencing systems allow trial judges to reduce a defendant's sentence based on cooperation. What is less clear is exactly who can determine whether the defendant should benefit from an effort to cooperate, and how much the benefit should be.

■ TAGGART PARRISH v. STATE
12 P.3d 953 (Nev. 2000)

Agosti, J.

... On March 9, 1998, police stopped a vehicle in which the appellant, Taggart Parrish, was riding as a passenger. Parrish attempted to flee on foot from the officers. Immediately, several officers gave chase. During the foot pursuit, Parrish attempted to aim a handgun in one officer's direction. Fortunately, the officer knocked the handgun out of Parrish's hand. A lengthy struggle ensued, during which Parrish attempted to reach the handgun numerous times. Finally, the police subdued and arrested Parrish. The police subsequently discovered methamphetamine in the vehicle in which Parrish had been riding.

After Parrish's arrest, detectives assigned to the Consolidated Narcotics Unit ("CNU") met with Parrish at the jail to discuss the possibility that Parrish would provide "substantial assistance" pursuant to NRS 453.3405(2), [which empowers the sentencing judge to reduce sentences for defendants who qualify under the statutory terms]. The detectives testified that Parrish was very cooperative during this meeting. Parrish, in conjunction with his fiancée, provided information concerning fourteen individuals allegedly involved in drug trafficking. The information was detailed and particular, including names and telephone numbers, maps of areas where police could find drug traffickers, information about surveillance, and how the police could protect themselves during later investigations.

The CNU detectives admitted that it was a "large list" and conceded that Parrish had supplied more information than would normally be provided by others attempting to render substantial assistance. Furthermore, the detectives testified that they recognized three names on the list Parrish provided. One person on the list had already been arrested in California. At the time of Parrish's sentencing hearing, two other individuals on the list had been arrested through means unrelated to the information provided by Parrish. When asked whether he would have liked to have followed up on the information Parrish had provided, one of the CNU detectives responded that he was "definitely interested" in doing so.

However, CNU detectives never investigated the information Parrish gave them. When asked during the sentencing hearing why they had not followed up on these leads, a CNU detective explained:

> Caseload and priorities. Priorities of the unit in the last couple of months have not been to respond to these types of leads. I mean, we have been responding to citizens' complaints, and there's an operation that we have been involved with over the last couple of months that has taken all of our time.

Besides a lack of time and other "priorities," CNU detectives testified that because of the events surrounding Parrish's arrest, they would not work with Parrish because Parrish would present a danger to officers. The detectives testified that normally the CNU works with defendants who are attempting to provide substantial assistance by having the defendant participate in a "controlled buy," that is, the police would fit the defendants with a wire, give them money and have them "do a buy for us." However, the detectives admitted that it was possible to investigate the information without involving Parrish and that they were willing to try that approach. Nevertheless, the information Parrish had provided was never investigated in this, or any other, manner.

The detectives also testified that it is the CNU's opinion that lists, like the one provided by Parrish, do not constitute substantial assistance unless "we fully follow it up and it results in arrest." Furthermore, the detectives stated that their supervisors do not like officers testifying at a defendant's sentencing hearing that the defendant provided substantial assistance unless the information provided resulted in "actual bodies and product. That's their policy." [NRS 453.3405(2) requires that the arresting law enforcement agency be given an opportunity to be heard concerning whether the defendant has rendered substantial assistance.]

In addition to a fine of not more than $500,000, the punishment for trafficking in twenty-eight or more grams of a controlled substance is either: (1) life imprisonment, with the possibility of parole after a minimum of ten years has been served; or (2) a definite term of twenty-five years imprisonment, with the possibility of parole after a minimum of ten years has been served. NRS 453.3385(3). Additionally, NRS 453.3405(1) mandates that a defendant convicted of trafficking in a controlled substance is not eligible for a reduced or suspended sentence. . . .

At the sentencing hearing, Parrish moved for a suspended sentence on the trafficking count pursuant to NRS 453.3405(2). Parrish was informed by the written plea memorandum, his attorney and the district court at the time he entered his plea of guilty that he was not eligible for probation on the trafficking count unless the district court determined that he had [rendered] substantial assistance to law enforcement officials. The district court heard evidence on Parrish's motion at the sentencing hearing. However, the district court made no finding concerning whether Parrish had or had not provided substantial assistance. Instead, the district court sentenced Parrish to [life imprisonment], the maximum prison sentence allowed for the crime of trafficking in a controlled substance, [and a fine of $25,000. The district court sentenced Parrish to a consecutive term of twelve to forty-eight months in prison for obstructing and resisting a public officer with the use of a dangerous weapon.] On appeal, Parrish claims that the district court abused its discretion by failing to find that he rendered substantial assistance. . . .

NRS 453.3405(2) allows the district court, upon proper motion, to reduce or suspend the sentence of the defendant when the district court finds the defendant rendered substantial assistance in the identification or apprehension of other drug traffickers. NRS 453.3405(2) reads:

> The judge, upon an appropriate motion, may reduce or suspend the sentence of any person convicted of violating any of the provisions of NRS 453.3385 [or two other drug statutes] if he finds that the convicted person rendered substantial assistance in the identification, arrest or conviction of any of his accomplices, accessories, coconspirators or principals or of any other person involved in trafficking in a controlled substance in violation of NRS 453.3385 [or two other drug statutes]. The arresting agency must be given an opportunity to be heard before the motion is granted. Upon good cause shown, the motion may be heard in camera.

We note that several other states, as well as the federal system, have similar provisions. See, e.g., U.S. Sentencing Commission, Guidelines Manual §5K1.1; Fla. Stat. Ann. §893.135(4); Ga. Code Ann. §16-13-31(f)(2). Such statutes are obviously intended to provide an incentive to drug-trafficking offenders to cooperate with law enforcement in the investigation of other drug traffickers.

Parrish contends that the nature and amount of information he provided to the detectives, information which did identify other drug traffickers, constituted substantial assistance. . . . Parrish further argues that the detectives' failure to follow up on the information he gave them, choosing instead to prioritize other investigations over following up on Parrish's information, should not result in a finding that Parrish had not rendered substantial assistance. Therefore, Parrish contends the district court abused its discretion by failing to find that he rendered substantial assistance. . . .

We begin by noting that the district court is afforded wide discretion when sentencing a defendant. As we have acknowledged, "judges spend much of their professional lives separating the wheat from the chaff and have extensive experience in sentencing, along with the legal training necessary to determine an appropriate sentence." We are also cognizant that in this case the legislature has clearly vested the district court with discretion, by stating that the judge "*may* reduce or suspend the sentence . . . *if* he finds that the convicted person rendered substantial assistance." NRS 453.3405(2) (emphasis added).

Nevertheless, this discretion is not limitless. When imposing a sentence, a district court may not abuse its discretion. Therefore, on appeal, in the absence of a showing of abuse of such discretion, we will not disturb the sentence.

In addition to the "abuse of discretion" standard, we are also mindful of our holding in Matos v. State, 878 P.2d 288 (Nev. 1994). In *Matos,* the defendant, in an effort to reduce his sentence, offered to assist the police pursuant to NRS 453.3405(2). However, because Matos had threatened to kill several members of the Consolidated Narcotics Unit, and had gone so far as to have a "contract" put out on a former police informant, law enforcement officers refused to accept his assistance. Under the facts of *Matos,* we concluded that since the defendant clearly posed a danger to law enforcement officers, those officers could legitimately reject his offer to render substantial assistance. Furthermore, we observed that on appeal this court would imply findings of fact and conclusions of law if the record clearly supports the district court's ruling. Therefore, we held in *Matos* that even if the district court erred in its technical interpretation of the statute, the district court did not err in concluding the defendant had not rendered substantial assistance.

Today's case does not overrule these sound principles. Rather, Parrish's situation does not present the case where law enforcement officers legitimately rejected his offer to assist drug agents. On the contrary, Parrish was approached by CNU officers after he was arrested and was asked if he was willing to provide substantial assistance. . . . Therefore, unlike *Matos,* this is not a case where detectives legitimately refused to work with the defendant. In contrast to *Matos,* detectives in this case seemed quite willing to extract information from Parrish; they simply did not want to work personally with and in close proximity to Parrish.

Parrish correctly argues that nowhere in NRS 453.3405(2) is there a requirement that the police personally work with a defendant who is attempting to provide substantial assistance. While police may legitimately refuse to work closely with a defendant who, in the view of police officers, poses a danger to themselves or the public, substantial assistance, pursuant to the terms of the statute, may be rendered in other ways. We understand the detectives' unwillingness to utilize Parrish in a controlled buy operation after he engaged in a prolonged physical struggle with law enforcement officers during his arrest and had, during the same incident, drawn a weapon on those officers. However, it is clear in this case that the information Parrish provided could have been investigated in a manner that did not personally involve Parrish. The officers themselves evaluated the information positively and thought it was sound enough to warrant further investigation. Therefore, the district court could have found that Parrish rendered substantial assistance even though the detectives refused to work closely with Parrish.[7]

What is so troubling about this case is the district court's apparent acceptance of CNU's "policy" concerning substantial assistance. The CNU detectives testified that in their opinion only arrests, or as they put it, information resulting in "actual bodies and product," constituted substantial assistance. Because the district court did not specifically address this interpretation and sentenced Parrish to the maximum sentence allowed, it seems that the district court may have implicitly accepted CNU's "policy" as a correct statement of the law.

---

7. From the record, it is unclear whether the police refused to work with Parrish due to the circumstances surrounding his arrest, or whether a lack of time and resources simply prevented the officers from fully investigating the information provided by Parrish. In any event, it is clear that Parrish did provide the police with a large amount of apparently valuable information.

CNU's policy clearly constitutes a misinterpretation of the statute. NRS 453.3405(2) plainly states that the district court may find that the defendant rendered "substantial assistance in the identification, arrest *or* conviction" of other drug traffickers. (Emphasis added.) A plain reading of the statute reveals that an arrest is not a necessary prerequisite to a determination that a defendant has rendered substantial assistance. While CNU is free to develop its own internal policy concerning when the agency, in exercising its opportunity to be heard pursuant to NRS 453.3405(2), will recommend that the court reduce or suspend the sentence of an offender, CNU is not free to represent to the court that substantial assistance has not been rendered simply because their internal requirements have not been met.

Furthermore, we take this opportunity to elaborate on the discretion with which district courts are vested under NRS 453.3405(2). Under this statute, once an appropriate motion is made, the district court may permissibly exercise its discretion in one of two ways. First, the district court may find that a defendant has not rendered substantial assistance under the statute, and therefore is not eligible for a sentence reduction or suspension. Second, even if the district court finds that a defendant has rendered substantial assistance in accordance with NRS 453.3405(2), the district court is still free in its discretion to reduce or suspend the sentence. The difficulty in this case is that we are unable to ascertain from the record why the district court sentenced Parrish to the maximum sentence allowed.

Our holding today does not require law enforcement to work with every defendant who wishes to render substantial assistance. Neither is law enforcement required to act on every piece of information provided to them by a defendant attempting to render substantial assistance in an attempt to avoid an otherwise harsh, mandatory sentence. Nor do we hold that substantial assistance is rendered as a matter of law whenever a defendant provides law enforcement officers with information. The trial judge is always in the best position to evaluate the sincerity, reliability, quality and value of a defendant's efforts to provide substantial assistance. However, a judicial determination of whether or not substantial assistance has been rendered must be made by application of the statutory requirements to the defendant's efforts. If the district court sets a higher standard than is statutorily required for a finding of substantial assistance, the purpose of the statute is defeated. What is more, offenders who might otherwise be willing to trade information for the possibility of leniency will not do so if the carrot of leniency is illusory.

Those responsible for enforcing the laws of this state, and in turn the public, are benefited when defendants choose to provide the police with information that leads to the "identification, arrest or conviction" of others involved in the drug trade. When offenders perform substantial assistance, it would be unfair to provide no relief under the statute to them unless an articulable reason exists not to reduce or suspend the sentence.

In this case, Parrish provided CNU with a considerable amount of information. The detectives were able to independently corroborate some of that information. It is clear that this information did identify drug traffickers known to law enforcement through its own resources. This enhances the possibility that the rest of the information, if investigated, would have led to the "identification, arrest or conviction" of other drug traffickers. While we are unwilling to hold as a matter of law that Parrish rendered substantial assistance, it is clear to us, based on the nature and amount of information Parrish provided to law enforcement, that the district court could have found that Parrish provided substantial assistance. As we stated in *Matos,* this court may imply factual findings if the record clearly supports the lower court's ruling. Here, we cannot say that the record clearly supports the district court's decision.

Accordingly, we hold that when evidence is presented to the district court concerning whether or not a defendant has rendered substantial assistance pursuant to NRS 453.3405(2), the district court is required to expressly state its finding concerning whether or not substantial assistance has been provided. Because the district court in this case made no such finding, and because the record does not clearly support a finding that there had been no substantial assistance provided to law enforcement, we vacate Parrish's sentence. We cannot determine from the record in this case whether the district court misinterpreted NRS 453.3405(2) since evidence was presented which could support a finding that Parrish had provided substantial assistance. Based on the foregoing, we affirm Parrish's judgment of conviction but vacate his sentence and remand this case for a new sentencing hearing before a different district judge.

■ U.S. SENTENCING GUIDELINES §5K1.1

Upon motion of the government stating that the defendant has provided substantial assistance in the investigation or prosecution of another person who has committed an offense, the court may depart from the guidelines.

The appropriate reduction shall be determined by the court for reasons stated that may include, but are not limited to, consideration of the following: (1) the court's evaluation of the significance and usefulness of the defendant's assistance, taking into consideration the government's evaluation of the assistance rendered; (2) the truthfulness, completeness, and reliability of any information or testimony provided by the defendant; (3) the nature and extent of the defendant's assistance; (4) any injury suffered, or any danger or risk of injury to the defendant or his family resulting from his assistance; (5) the timeliness of the defendant's assistance.

Notes

1. *Assisting in other investigations.* In the unstructured sentencing states, cooperation with the government in investigating and trying other criminal cases is generally believed to have some positive effect both on the sentencing court's disposition of the case and on the duration of the sentence imposed. State v. Johnson, 630 N.W.2d 583 (Iowa 2001). Even in highly discretionary sentencing systems, statutes commonly address the sentencing discount a court must give to a defendant who provides assistance to the government. See Brugman v. State, 339 S.E.2d 244 (Ga. 1986) (discussing statute). The more structured sentencing states have followed the same route, instructing the judge that cooperation with the government can serve as a basis for departing from the guideline sentence and imposing some lesser sentence. See Or. Admin. R. 253-08-002(1)(F).

2. *Substantial in whose eyes?* There is some variation in the amount of control the prosecution has over the use of the "substantial assistance" sentencing

factor. If the prosecution refuses to accept a defendant's offer of cooperation, then the sentence usually will not be affected. But what happens if the government accepts the cooperation and later determines that it was not valuable or complete? Section 5K1.1 of the federal guidelines requires a government motion before the court can reduce the sentence based on the defendant's cooperation, while 18 U.S.C. §3553(e) requires the same before a court can reduce a sentence below a statutory mandatory minimum. Should the court have an independent power to reduce a sentence on these grounds, even in the absence of a government motion? State legislatures and courts have been debating this issue for years, although the state debate has not figured at all in the later federal discussions of this question. See La. Rev. Stat. §40:967(G)(2) (allowing reduction or suspension of sentence if district attorney requests reduction for person providing substantial assistance); State v. Sarabia, 875 P.2d 227 (Idaho 1994) (declaring unconstitutional a statute allowing sentence below mandatory minimum only when prosecutor moves for reduction based on substantial assistance).

In Wade v. United States, 504 U.S. 181 (1992), the Supreme Court held that the Constitution does not preserve for federal judges the power to depart for "substantial assistance" without permission of the government. Only when the defendant makes a "substantial threshold showing" of an unconstitutional motive can the court adjust the sentence without a government motion: "Thus, a defendant would be entitled to relief if a prosecutor refused to file a substantial-assistance motion, say, because of the defendant's race or religion." What else might qualify as a constitutionally improper reason for a prosecutor to withhold a motion?

3. *Nonconstitutional controls on assistance discounts.* The real debate over limiting prosecutorial power in this sphere takes place at the non-constitutional level. Legislatures and sentencing commissions must decide whether to make a prosecutor's motion a necessary precondition to this sort of sentence reduction. The concern, of course, is that an unsupervised prosecutor will make the recommendations on arbitrary or inconsistent grounds. In the federal system, prosecutors have attempted to regulate themselves, by creating written policies about which defendants should receive a reduced sentence for substantial assistance. About 80 percent of the federal districts have adopted written guidelines on the subject, and their content is fairly consistent. However, a study sponsored by the U.S. Sentencing Commission (known as the "Maxfield-Kramer Study") found great variety among the 94 federal districts in their granting of substantial assistance motions. Linda Drazga Maxfield & John Kramer, Substantial Assistance: Empirical Yardstick Gauging Equity in Federal Policy and Practice (1998). The study found that demographic characteristics of defendants had some influence on whether they received a motion: defendants who were male, black, Hispanic, noncitizens, and older were all less likely to receive a motion. As a chief prosecutor, how would you react to this news? Could you create guidelines within your office that would promote more consistent decisions about sentence discounts for cooperating defendants? See Frank Bowman, Substantial Assistance: An Old Prosecutor's Meditation on *Singleton, Sealed Case,* and the Maxfield-Kramer Report, 12 Fed. Sentencing Rep. 45 (1999); Cynthia Y. K. Lee, From Gatekeeper to Concierge: Reining in the Federal Prosecutor's Expanding Power over Substantial Assistance Departures, 50 Rutgers L. Rev. 199 (1997).

2. New Information About the Victim and the Community

What information not related to the offender or the offense may affect the sentence? This section considers two kinds of information beyond the offense and offender: information about the victim and information about the community.

In a traditional indeterminate sentencing system, victims do not formally address the sentencing court. The trial is seen as a process through which the state prosecutes and punishes individuals for violations of collective norms; individuals are compensated through private law (tort) remedies. Of course, the prosecutor attempts in many cases to bring the victim's concerns or information to the court's attention, and the judge may account for this in imposing a sentence. But until recently, the victim has had little opportunity to speak directly to the sentencing court.

In recent decades, through statutes, state constitutional provisions, and procedural rules, most jurisdictions have created a formal role for victims. Many jurisdictions give victims an opportunity to address the court, both to provide information about the harm caused by the crime and to express an opinion about the proper sentence to impose. But what impact should victims have on individual sentences? Should the personal or family circumstances of the victim matter? Will these factors, if considered, become a cover for invidious factors such as wealth and race?

■ TERRY NICHOLS v. COMMONWEALTH

839 S.W.2d 263 (Ky. 1992)

WINTERSHEIMER, J.

. . . Nichols, while in jail in Ohio, volunteered information regarding a series of unsolved burglaries in Boyd and Greenup Counties, Kentucky. Nichols reached a plea agreement with the prosecution in all cases and the prosecutor recommended a sentence of five years on each of the 11 counts to run concurrently. Nichols appeared in Greenup Circuit Court on January 25, 1989, and pled guilty to 11 counts of burglary in the second degree. . . . He waived formal sentencing and requested to be sentenced immediately. The trial judge indicated that he was inclined to follow the recommendation of the prosecution.

However, before rendering sentence, the judge inquired of the prosecutor if the victims of the burglaries had been consulted in regard to the recommendation, and the prosecutor responded that he did not know. Upon learning that at least one of the victims had not been informed of the proceedings, the trial judge withdrew sentence and set the matter for trial. He advised the prosecution to contact the victims. Three of the 11 victims did not agree with the prosecutor's recommendation. The Greenup County Jailer was one of the victims dissatisfied. These three cases were then sent to a jury only for the purpose of recommending sentence and not for any fact finding of guilt. The jury recommended five year concurrent sentences on the three offenses and indicated that the sentences were to run concurrently with the other eight charges. At final sentencing on May 24, 1989, the trial judge ordered that the three counts run concurrently with each other but further ordered that those terms be served consecutively to the others for a total of ten years in prison. Nichols appealed the ten year sentence, [and] argues that the trial judge should have recused himself because the sentence was motivated by the desire to please the local jailer. . . .

The record indicates that the trial judge directed the prosecution to contact all the victims of the burglaries and not just the jailer. . . . The expression of the concern by the trial judge that the victims of the crimes be informed of the prosecution recommendation does not provide a basis for reversible error based on bias, prejudice or personal knowledge. . . . Clearly the record does indicate that the trial judge was concerned about the views of the victims, including the County Jailer. The trial judge said, "Well, I certainly don't want Mr. Salmons to be mad at the judge. If he, the jailer, thinks he ought to have more . . . I'm not going to give him more. I'm going to give him a fair trial."

K.R.S. 421.500 provides that victims of crimes have a right to make an impact statement for consideration by the court at the time of the defendant's sentencing. The county jailer, who is a victim of crime, has as much right as anyone to make such an impact statement regardless of his official position. The language of the trial judge does not provide a basis for personal bias. The comments of the trial judge were a proper expression of the requirement for notification to all crime victims of their right to express an opinion on a sentencing proceeding. The statement, "I don't want him mad at me," should not be unduly expanded in such a context. [The sentence] is affirmed.

COMBS, J., dissenting.

The Commonwealth recommended a 5-year effective sentence; the trial judge was initially disposed to accept the recommendation; but, to accommodate Jailer Salmons, the court resolved to impose a harsher penalty; the jury fixed the sentence for the Salmons burglary at 5 years; bound by the verdict as to the term, the court nevertheless sentenced Nichols to 10 years by ordering consecutive service. That is what appears from this proceeding, making it one not distinguished for an appearance of integrity. . . .

The majority would have it that the judge's concern for Mr. Salmons was no more than that due any burglary victim pursuant to KRS 421.500, dealing with victim-impact information as a factor in sentencing. I do not fault a trial court for its concern for a victim, as a victim. Here, however, it is evident that the trial court's solicitude toward Jailer Salmons was due not to the impact of the crime upon the victim, but due to the personal relationship between the victim and the court: "Well, I certainly don't want Mr. Salmons mad at the Judge." While there are a number of salutary reasons for considering genuine victim-impact information, not counted among them, because not relevant to tailoring the penalty to the crime, is the preservation of an individual's personal esteem for the judge.

Moreover, no genuine victim-impact information is to be found in this record. KRS 421.500(3)(c) requires law enforcement personnel to inform the victim as to the "criminal justice process as it involves the participation of the victim"; and subsection (5)(b) requires the prosecutor, "[i]f the victims so desire," to notify a victim of his/her "right to make an impact statement for consideration by the court at the time of sentencing." This right to make an impact statement is more fully discussed in KRS 421.520. . . . Section .520 implies that "the victim has the right to submit a written victim impact statement," which "may contain, but need not be limited to, a description of the nature and extent of any physical, psychological or financial harm suffered by the victim . . . and the victim's recommendation for an appropriate sentence." The statute purports to compel the court to consider the statement prior to making its sentencing decision.

First, deaf to cries of nitpicking, I observe that the present record is devoid of written victim-impact statements. One may also, as I have, search in vain for even an oral statement by any victim. Where does the statute provide for, and why should we (or a trial court) countenance, the prosecutor's hearsay reports of victims' statements?

Second, what the prosecutor did report was that the three victims' objections "boil down to they do not believe in concurrent sentencing for someone who has committed so many offenses." Where in this is any "recommendation for an appropriate sentence"? Where is any information as to impact of a crime upon a victim? I venture that the statute intends that a victim may recommend a "sentence" (that is, a term of years . . .) appropriate for the crime committed against him/her, but not consecutive sentencing for crimes committed against others. This view is neatly supported by the definition of "victim" found in KRS 421.500(1): " 'victim' means an individual who suffers direct or threatened physical, financial, or emotional harm as the result of the commission of a crime. . . ." A victim-impact statement is not a committee report. Perhaps the court would have had to consider victim A's (written!) opinion that Nichols should draw 999 years for burglarizing A's home; but the court's consideration of (indeed, deference to) A's opinion that Nichols should be sentenced more harshly (or consecutively) for other crimes, of which A was not a victim, went far beyond the intent of the statute.

Furthermore, it went far beyond the bounds of due process. Concede that the impact upon an individual victim ought to be considered in fixing a sentence for a crime. Concede even that the impact upon each victim is relevant to determining whether multiple sentences should run concurrently or consecutively. But do not concede, I say, that the discretion to assess the effect of accumulated offenses rests elsewhere than in an impartial jury and/or an impartial judge; do not concede that it may be delegated, even in part, to a (justifiably) biased victim. . . .

■ MICHIGAN CONSTITUTION §24

(1) Crime victims, as defined by law, shall have the following rights, as provided by law:
— The right to be treated with fairness and respect for their dignity and privacy throughout the criminal justice process. . . .
— The right to be reasonably protected from the accused throughout the criminal justice process.
— The right to notification of court proceedings.
— The right to attend trial and all other court proceedings the accused has the right to attend.
— The right to confer with the prosecution.
— The right to make a statement to the court at sentencing.
— The right to restitution.
— The right to information about the conviction, sentence, imprisonment, and release of the accused.
(2) The legislature may provide by law for the enforcement of this section.

Problem 9-8. Vulnerable Victim

Billy Creech obtained from a local newspaper a list of recently married men. From that list, he selected a victim to whom he sent a letter threatening to "torture your family members while you watch, or kill one in front of you," unless the victim periodically sent Creech a money order for $100. The letter ended by saying that "Failure to do this will end in bodily harm to your wife!" Creech was convicted for mailing a letter containing a threat to injure the addressee, a federal crime. Can the court consider this newlywed to be a "vulnerable victim"? Compare United States v. Creech, 913 F.2d 780 (10th Cir. 1990).

Notes

1. *Victims' rights at sentencing: majority view.* Over the past 20 years, nearly every state has decided to allow victim involvement at sentencing. See generally National Victim Center, The 1996 Victims' Rights Sourcebook: A Compilation and Comparison of Victims' Rights Laws (1996). It is difficult to capture the depth, range, and impact of this dramatic change in sentencing practice. Almost all states allow victim input through the PSI report. Many allow victims a separate opportunity to make a written or oral statement regarding sentencing, often detailing the kinds of information victims may offer. A few states have retained sharper limits: Several allow judges to choose whether to admit or refuse victim impact information; Texas allows a victim to make a statement only after sentencing, Tex. Code Crim. Proc. art. 42.03. The Victim and Witness Protection Act of 1982 amended the Federal Rules of Criminal Procedure to require the inclusion of a victim impact statement as a part of the PSI report in federal court. Fed. R. Crim. P. 32 ("The presentence report must contain . . . verified information, stated in a nonargumentative style, containing an assessment of the financial, social, psychological, and medical impact on any individual against whom the offense has been committed"). Federal legislation and constitutional amendments have been proposed that would increase victim participation at sentencing.

The *Nichols* case from Kentucky might at first seem to stress an odd and unlikely event: The jailer was a victim who, being acquainted with the judge, was likely to influence his views at sentencing. But victim impact information is supposed to influence the judge; indeed, many statutes require the judge to take account of victim information. The rich variety of statutes has not produced a substantial case law regarding victim impact statements in the noncapital context. When the impact of such statements is challenged, it often takes the form of the claim in *Nichols*—that the judge was biased, or unduly influenced, by the information. For example, in People v. Vecchio, 819 P.2d 533, 534-35 (Colo. Ct. App. 1991), the court rejected a claim that the trial judge should have recused himself after the prosecutor filed more than 100 victim impact statements.

> The theory behind the collection of these victim impact statements evidently was that all residents of the community were victims of the theft of public property and might properly express their views about the effect of the offenses on them and the community as well as their views of the appropriate sentence which should be imposed upon the defendant. In addition, a considerable number of these statements expressed

dissatisfaction with sentences which had previously been imposed by the trial judge's predecessor in office in two unrelated cases involving public figures which, according to the motion and affidavits, had resulted in the removal from office at the retention election of the prior judge. From these facts [the defendant argues that] the "Court is at the mercy of an angry community," and "it must be presumed that this Court is 'interested' in the outcome of this case." . . .

In ruling the allegations here legally insufficient to require disqualification, the trial judge observed, among other things: "Cases which come before this Court are often of such nature as to arouse public passion. . . . If a Court were to find that the grounds in a motion such as this one were sufficient, [judges] would virtually be unable to serve in communities where they lived." We agree with these statements. Moreover, every sitting judge faces a future retention election and is aware that his conduct in office will have a direct impact upon the outcome thereof. There can be no legal presumption that a judge is intimidated by the outrage of the community in which he serves; retribution at the polls is a risk undertaken by every judicial candidate upon acceptance of appointment in a judicial position. To put it in general parlance, "it goes with the territory."

When 100 people submit impact statements, is that a statement of victims or of the community? Should judges rely on their own sense of the unique nature of harm imposed in particular cases? Does victim impact information differ in kind from other types of new information, such as information about the offender?

2. *Victim impact statements in capital cases.* Courts and legislatures have wrestled with the special problems of integrating victim impact statements with the complex law of capital sentencing. The U.S. Supreme Court limited introduction of victim evidence in capital cases in Booth v. Maryland, 482 U.S. 496 (1987) (victim impact statement in capital cases leads to arbitrary and capricious decisions because sentencing jury's focus would shift away from the defendant and onto the victim and the victim's family), and South Carolina v. Gathers, 490 U.S. 805 (1989) (rejecting prosecutorial argument about victim impact). The Court reversed itself in Payne v. Tennessee, 501 U.S. 1277 (1991), holding that the jury could hear victim impact information. In *Payne* the Court upheld admission of testimony from a murder victim's mother, describing the impact of the killing on the victim's three-year-old son. The Court held that the victim impact statements "illustrated quite poignantly some of the harm that Payne's killing had caused." State courts and state legislatures have overwhelmingly followed the invitation in *Payne* to allow victim impact evidence in capital cases. See State v. Muhammad, 678 A.2d 164 (N.J. 1996). A few states still ban victim evidence in capital cases or limit the topics that victims can address. See Bivins v. State, 642 N.E.2d 928 (Ind. 1994); Mack v. State, 650 So. 2d 1289 (Miss. 1994).

3. *Implementing victims' rights at sentencing.* As a Michigan legislator, how would you draft legislation to enforce section 24 of the Michigan constitution? Would you provide for victim statements prior to the sentencing hearing, along with any statement at the hearing? If the victim is unwilling to testify, would your statute nevertheless allow the defense or prosecution to subpoena the victim and obtain his evidence under oath? Compare ABA Standards for Criminal Justice: Sentencing §§18-5.9 to 18-5.12.

4. *Vulnerable victims.* Structured sentencing rules often instruct a judge to enhance a sentence if the victim of the crimes was "vulnerable" or otherwise worthy of exceptional protection. The Minnesota Sentencing Guidelines authorize the

judge to decrease a sentence if "the victim was an aggressor in the incident," and to increase the sentence if the "victim was particularly vulnerable due to age, infirmity, or reduced physical or mental capacity, which was known or should have been known to the offender" or if the "victim was treated with particular cruelty for which the individual offender should be held responsible." Minn. Sentencing Guidelines II.D.2.a.1, II.D.2.b.1-2. The federal guidelines contain a similar provision for enhancement of the sentence by a designated amount if "the defendant knew or should have known that a victim of the offense was unusually vulnerable due to age, physical or mental condition, or that a victim was otherwise particularly susceptible to criminal conduct." U.S. Sentencing Guidelines §3A1.1. A specified increase is also required when the victim is "a government officer or employee" or a law enforcement officer.

Problem 9-9. Community as Victim

Marvin Jones and Taifi Griffith were members of the "Crips" gang in Seattle. They were on "Black Gangster Disciples" (BGD) turf on Horton Street near John Muir Elementary School talking to some girls, when four members of the BGD gang saw them. Everyone "flashed" their respective gang signs, then one of the BGDs ran away from the group to retrieve a gun. The Crips got into two automobiles and started to drive away. Antwon Johnson, a BGD member who lived across the street from John Muir Elementary School, jumped from some bushes and fired a handgun at the two cars as they passed in front of the school building. The incident occurred while school was in session.

The prosecutor charged Johnson with assault in the first degree. At trial, the prosecution presented testimony from the BGD members, and from several other eyewitnesses. They included William Robbins, a parent picking up his child from school at the time of the shooting, and Roy Dunn, a crossing guard who observed the shooting and collected from the street several spent cartridges following the shooting. The jury found Johnson guilty of assault in the first degree.

At sentencing, Judge Eberharter found that a defendant with Johnson's criminal history, convicted of assault in the first degree, would normally receive a sentence between 85 and 113 months. However, Judge Eberharter found that "substantial and compelling reasons exist which justify a sentence above the Standard range," and he imposed on Johnson an exceptional sentence of 170 months' incarceration. The statutory maximum for the crime is a life term. As the primary reason justifying the exceptional sentence, the judge pointed to the community impact of the shootings. The judge had received several letters from residents of the Mount Baker community near John Muir Elementary School expressing fear and anxiety caused by the shooting. The court's factual findings were as follows: (1) the impact of Johnson's assaults went far beyond the intended victims; (2) as a result of Johnson's actions, children became frightened to attend school and parents fearful that their children are not safe while at the school; and (3) Johnson invaded the community's zone of safety.

Is the impact of this crime on the community different enough from the typical first-degree assault to justify an exceptional sentence? Is the community impact here a "substantial and compelling" reason to justify a sentence higher than the norm for this crime? Compare State v. Johnson, 873 P.2d 514 (Wash. 1994).

Problem 9-10. Local Conditions

An international flight made a scheduled stop at Puerto Rico's airport en route from Colombia to Frankfurt, West Germany. Jorge Armando Aguilar-Pena was aboard. Customs officials conducted an inspection of in-transit passengers and discovered that he was carrying cocaine. After conviction, the probation officer consulted the sentencing guidelines and fixed the sentencing range at 21-27 months. The court accepted the computational conclusions contained in the PSI report, but it departed from the guidelines and sentenced Aguilar to a prison term of 48 months. The court gave the following reasons for its upward departure:

> First, it is a well-known fact that Puerto Rico is being utilized by South American drug traffickers as a convenient stopover point for the distribution of narcotics into the Continental United States and other places in the world via commercial, scheduled airline flights. Second, departure from the guidelines is warranted in order to discourage the utilization of the Puerto Rico International Airport, an airport with lesser law-enforcement capabilities than those in the mainland, as a connecting point for international narcotics trafficking and/or for introduction of narcotics into the Continental United States. Puerto Rico's airport is less secure than airports in cities such as Miami and New York. Third, a sentence within the guidelines in a case of this nature would also be in violation of the Puerto Rico public sentiment, feelings, and mores regarding this type of crime.

Under the federal sentencing guidelines, a sentencing court can depart in a case that presents aggravating or mitigating factors of a kind or to a degree "not adequately considered" by the sentencing commission when formulating guidelines. The federal guidelines make no provision for "local conditions." The authorizing federal legislation directed the federal sentencing commission to "take into account only to the extent that they do have relevance the community view of the gravity of the offense; . . . the public concern generated by the offense; . . . the current incidence of the offense in the community and in the Nation as a whole." 28 U.S.C. §§994(c)(4), (5), (7). Was this a proper upward departure? Compare United States v. Aguilar-Pena, 887 F.2d 347 (1st Cir. 1989).

Notes

1. *Community views at sentencing: majority position.* Judges do not hand down sentences in a vacuum. Judges may respond implicitly to changing societal conceptions of the seriousness of the offense, or to changes in the prevalence of an offense, or to the particular "message" that a sentence may send to the community. But can judges do so openly? Information about community impact is available much less often than information about the impact on specific victims. One problem with considering community impact is identifying the relevant community. Who should express the community's view? Some courts have allowed victims to offer information about broader community impact. For example, the Pennsylvania Supreme Court in Commonwealth v. Penrod, 578 A.2d 486 (Pa. 1990), allowed victims, family members, and friends to testify at sentencing for drunken-driving defendants "regarding the impact of the offense on the victim, the impact on the community generally, and/or the impact on the family members or friends as members of the

community." Should representatives of victims' rights organizations be allowed to speak at every sentencing? Should equal time be given to representatives of those who believe sentences are too severe or that imprisonment harms communities by removing vital members?

2. *Judicial experience and community priorities.* Is it appropriate for judges in the same jurisdiction to weigh community impact differently? Federal judge Reena Raggi argues that federal guidelines should allow local variation among federal districts because particular crimes may create special harms in some localities and because the judges in that area develop special expertise on certain topics:

> I first began to question [the nationally uniform approach of the sentencing guidelines] when I had to impose sentences on a number of defendants who had unlawfully transported firearms into New York from other states. Almost daily my fellow New Yorkers and I would read in the press of the senseless shooting of young children, on the streets, even in their own homes, all victims of random gun fire. Indeed, 16 children were shot in this manner in New York City over approximately 10 weeks [in 1990]; 5 of them died. Almost invariably the guns used in these crimes, as well as most others unlawfully possessed in this area, had come from out of state.
>
> This sort of interstate transportation of guns into the New York area is big business. In the two years between 1990 and 1992, a joint federal-state task force operating in New York arrested 260 people for such trafficking. And yet, when it came time for me to impose sentences in my cases that summer of 1990, I was confronted by a guideline range that rarely exceeded six months' incarceration. . . .
>
> The insight judges have about crimes in their particular districts goes beyond simply recognizing which conduct is more destructive to a community. It also reaches the question of how different levels of conduct contribute to an area's crime problems. For example, despite the fact that no part of the United States is immune from the problem of drugs, few judges have as broad an experience dealing with drug importation and large-scale distribution as my colleagues in the Eastern District of New York. The piers and airports of the district make it, for all intents and purposes, the port of New York and, thus, the entry point for a large percentage of the contraband entering this country. Within the district reside the leaders of most of the distribution networks operating in the northeast. . . . District judges should enjoy more discretion — indeed they should be encouraged — to depart from the guidelines to reflect specific local concerns.

Raggi, Local Concerns, Local Insights, 5 Fed. Sentencing Rep. 306 (1993).

3. *Prosecutorial experience and community priorities.* If judges can adjust sentences to take account of local priorities, should prosecutors also be able to make charging decisions on the basis of local needs? Should prosecutorial needs and resources then be allowed to affect sentences? For instance, the U.S. Attorney's Office in San Diego receives far more immigration cases than it can prosecute. Of the 565,581 illegal aliens apprehended in fiscal year 1992, the U.S. Attorney prosecuted 245 felony immigration cases and another 5,000 misdemeanors. Because the San Diego district attorney, as a matter of policy, will not prosecute any cases related to the border, these cases must be prosecuted in federal court or not at all. William Braniff, Local Discretion, Prosecutorial Choices and the Sentencing Guidelines, 5 Fed. Sentencing Rep. 309 (1993). Should the judge enhance a sentence when she knows that an unusually large number of offenders are going unpunished? Should the judge reduce the sentence out of concern for selective and discriminatory treatment or ignore prosecutorial priorities entirely?

E. RACE AND SENTENCING

Race is an unavoidable part of modern American criminal procedure. Difficult questions arise at all stages of the criminal process: What is the role of race in stops and investigations? Can race be an element in the determination of reasonable suspicion or probable cause? When are racial disparities sufficient to justify challenges to charging practices? What role should race play in jury selection? In arguments at trial?

Previous chapters have explored some of these questions about the role that race plays in decisions throughout the criminal process. But perhaps the most common and visible questions about race arise at the end of the process, in the form of claims that black Americans and other minorities are punished more severely than whites. This section considers the charge that racism is an inherent part of the criminal justice process and that its end product is unequal punishment. In some situations, the responsible decisionmakers may be identifiable; in other situations, the source of racial disparities may be hard to specify even when disparity clearly exists.

Discussion of race and punishment must start with some disquieting facts about prison and jail populations. In June 2001, 44.5 percent of the inmates in state and federal prisons and local jails were African American, although African Americans constitute only about 13 percent of the population. The rate of imprisonment for black males aged 25-29 is about 13.4 percent, while the rate for Hispanic males of the same age group is 4.1 percent, and the comparable rate for white males is 1.8 percent. Bureau of Justice Statistics, Prison and Jail Inmates at Midyear 2001, at table 15 (2002, NCJ 191702). After combining the number of young men on probation or parole with the number in prison or jail, almost a third of young black men are under criminal justice supervision on any given day. African American women remain the fastest growing group in prisons and jails. Drug policies have contributed more than any other crimes to the fast growth in the imprisonment rate for African Americans. As Marc Mauer and Tracy Huling have noted,

> While African American arrest rates for violent crime — 45% of arrests nationally — are disproportionate to their share of the population, this proportion has not changed significantly for twenty years. For drug offenses, though, the African American proportion of arrests increased from 24% in 1980 to 39% in 1993, well above the African American proportion of drug users nationally.

Mauer & Huling, Young Black Americans and the Criminal Justice System (1995).

These materials provoke a recurring question: Does the criminal justice system exacerbate or mediate larger social problems? Can criminal justice systems respond to intentional or unintentional racial bias in society? If so, what is the proper role for courts, police, prosecutors, and legislators in crafting such a response?

1. Race and the Victims of Crime

The influence of race on punishment has received the most sustained attention in the context of capital punishment. Many facets of the story of race in American capital punishment emerge in the story of Warren McCleskey and his extraordinary trip through the criminal justice system.

On the morning of May 13, 1978, McCleskey drove to pick up Ben Wright, Bernard Dupree, and David Burney. The four men planned to commit a robbery; they drove from Marietta, Georgia, into Atlanta and decided on the Dixie Furniture Store as a target. McCleskey had a .38 caliber Rossi nickel-plated revolver, which he had stolen in an armed robbery of a grocery store a month earlier. Ben Wright carried a sawed-off shotgun, and the two others had blue steel pistols. McCleskey, who was black, entered the front of the store, and the other three came through the rear by the loading dock. He secured the front of the store by forcing all the customers and employees there to lie on the floor while the other robbers rounded up the employees in the rear and began to bind them with tape. A pistol was taken from George Malcom, an employee, at gunpoint. Before all the employees were tied up, Officer Frank Schlatt, answering a silent alarm, stopped his patrol car in front of the building. Officer Schlatt, who was white, entered the front door and proceeded about 15 feet down the center aisle, where he was shot twice, once in the face and once in the chest. The head wound was fatal. The robbers fled. Sometime later, McCleskey was arrested in Cobb County in connection with another armed robbery. He confessed to the Dixie Furniture Store robbery but denied the shooting. Ballistics showed that Schlatt had been shot by a .38 caliber Rossi revolver. The weapon was never recovered.

McCleskey was convicted in 1978. The jury found two aggravating circumstances that authorized the use of the death penalty: (1) the murder was committed while the offender was committing another capital felony (armed robbery), and (2) the murder was committed against a police officer engaged in the performance of his official duties. The jury sentenced McCleskey to death for murder. Co-defendant Burney was sentenced to life imprisonment, while another co-defendant received a 20-year sentence.

On direct appeal in the Georgia courts, McCleskey first raised the claim that the death penalty violates the due process and equal protection provisions of the federal and state constitutions because prosecutorial discretion permits the government to apply the penalty in a racially discriminatory way. The Georgia Supreme Court rejected this claim as follows: "Appellant's argument is without merit. Gregg v. Georgia, 428 U.S. 153 (1976); Moore v. State, 243 S.E.2d 1 (Ga. 1978)." McCleskey v. State, 263 S.E.2d 146 (Ga. 1980).

Eventually, McCleskey took his claims to federal court: The U.S. district court had the power, under the venerable Habeas Corpus Act of 1867, 28 U.S.C. §2254, to invalidate state convictions obtained in violation of the federal constitution. In federal district court, McCleskey presented the findings of a massive statistical study, dubbed the "Baldus" study (named after its principal author, Professor David Baldus of the University of Iowa). The study analyzed almost 2,500 murder and voluntary manslaughter convictions for crimes committed (or for defendants arrested) between 1973 and 1978 in Georgia. For a random sample of these cases, researchers answered more than 500 questions about each case, such as the defendant's mental and physical condition, the defendant's race and other demographic information, the defendant's prior criminal record, the method of killing, the victim's role in the offense, and so forth. Due to the large number of variables, the researchers could not match many cases that differed in only one respect (for instance, cases that were identical in every respect, except one defendant shot the victim twice while the other defendant shot the victim only once). Thus, they used a statistical technique known as "multivariate regression analysis" to estimate the amount of influence each feature of the case had on the ultimate decision of whether the defendant received the death penalty.

The study concluded that the race of the defendant was not a "statistically significant" factor in the outcome, after "controlling" for all the other factors that could influence the outcome. However, the race of the *victim* remained one of the most important influences on the outcome, even after controlling for other factors.

The district court decided that the study did not establish the intentional discrimination necessary to show a violation of equal protection because the study was flawed. For instance, the court pointed to several errors in the collection of data and noted that "the questionnaire could not capture every nuance of every case." The court also suggested that the study had not successfully isolated the effects of race but instead measured the effects of other permissible factors that were "correlated" with race. McCleskey v. Zant, 580 F. Supp. 338 (N.D. Ga. 1984).

The federal court of appeals took a different approach to the question. It was willing to assume that the study successfully demonstrated "what it purports to prove": Defendants who kill a white victim have a greater chance of receiving the death penalty, and part of that increased risk is based on the race of the victim. Nevertheless, the court of appeals said that this statistical evidence was not enough for McCleskey to prove intentional racial discrimination in his case. When a party relies on statistical patterns of discrimination, the court said, it must show such large racial disparities that the evidence "compels a conclusion that . . . purposeful discrimination . . . can be presumed to permeate the system." The estimated effects of the race of the victim on the death penalty decision were not enough to compel such a conclusion. Indeed, the court said, any statistical study would have difficulty making such a showing about a complex process involving many different decisionmakers. McCleskey v. Kemp, 753 F.2d 877 (11th Cir. 1985). McCleskey then appealed to the U.S. Supreme Court.

■ WARREN McCLESKEY v. RALPH KEMP
481 U.S. 279 (1987)

POWELL, J.

This case presents the question whether a complex statistical study that indicates a risk that racial considerations enter into capital sentencing determinations proves that petitioner McCleskey's capital sentence is unconstitutional under the Eighth or Fourteenth Amendment.

[In support of his habeas claim], McCleskey proffered a statistical study performed by Professors David Baldus, Charles Pulaski, and George Woodworth (the Baldus study) that purports to show a disparity in the imposition of the death sentence in Georgia based on the race of the murder victim and, to a lesser extent, the race of the defendant. The Baldus study is actually two sophisticated statistical studies that examine over 2,000 murder cases that occurred in Georgia during the 1970's. The raw numbers collected by Professor Baldus indicate that defendants charged with killing white persons received the death penalty in 11% of the cases, but defendants charged with killing blacks received the death penalty in only 1% of the cases. . . . Baldus also divided the cases according to the combination of the race of the defendant and the race of the victim. He found that the death penalty was assessed in 22% of the cases involving black defendants and white victims; 8% of the cases involving white defendants and white victims; 1% of the cases involving black defendants and black victims; and 3% of the cases involving white defendants and black victims. . . .

Baldus subjected his data to an extensive analysis, taking account of 230 variables that could have explained the disparities on nonracial grounds. One of his models concludes that, even after taking account of 39 nonracial variables, defendants charged with killing white victims were 4.3 times as likely to receive a death sentence as defendants charged with killing blacks. . . . Thus, the Baldus study indicates that black defendants, such as McCleskey, who kill white victims have the greatest likelihood of receiving the death penalty. . . .

McCleskey's first claim is that the Georgia capital punishment statute violates the Equal Protection Clause of the Fourteenth Amendment.[7] He argues that race has infected the administration of Georgia's statute. . . . McCleskey's claim of discrimination extends to every actor in the Georgia capital sentencing process, from the prosecutor who sought the death penalty and the jury that imposed the sentence, to the State itself that enacted the capital punishment statute and allows it to remain in effect despite its allegedly discriminatory application. [T]his claim must fail.

[To] prevail under the Equal Protection Clause, McCleskey must prove that the decisionmakers in his case acted with discriminatory purpose. He offers no evidence specific to his own case that would support an inference that racial considerations played a part in his sentence. Instead, he . . . argues that the Baldus study compels an inference that his sentence rests on purposeful discrimination. McCleskey's claim that these statistics are sufficient proof of discrimination, without regard to the facts of a particular case, would extend to all capital cases in Georgia, at least where the victim was white and the defendant is black.

The Court has accepted statistics as proof of intent to discriminate in certain limited contexts. First, this Court has accepted statistical disparities as proof of an equal protection violation in the selection of the jury venire in a particular district. Although statistical proof normally must present a "stark" pattern to be accepted as the sole proof of discriminatory intent under the Constitution, because of the nature of the jury-selection task, we have permitted a finding of constitutional violation even when the statistical pattern does not approach such extremes. Second, this Court has accepted statistics in the form of multiple-regression analysis to prove statutory violations under Title VII of the Civil Rights Act of 1964.

But the nature of the capital sentencing decision, and the relationship of the statistics to that decision, are fundamentally different from the corresponding elements in the venire-selection or Title VII cases. Most importantly, each particular decision to impose the death penalty is made by a petit jury selected from a properly constituted venire. Each jury is unique in its composition, and the Constitution requires that its decision rest on consideration of innumerable factors that vary according to the characteristics of the individual defendant and the facts of the particular capital offense. Thus, the application of an inference drawn from the general statistics to a specific decision in a trial and sentencing simply is not comparable to the application of an inference drawn from general statistics to a specific

---

7. [We] assume the study is valid statistically without reviewing the factual findings of the District Court. Our assumption that the Baldus study is statistically valid does not include the assumption that the study shows that racial considerations actually enter into any sentencing decisions in Georgia. Even a sophisticated multiple-regression analysis such as the Baldus study can only demonstrate a risk that the factor of race entered into some capital sentencing decisions and a necessarily lesser risk that race entered into any particular sentencing decision.

venire-selection or Title VII case. In those cases, the statistics relate to fewer entities, and fewer variables are relevant to the challenged decisions.

Another important difference between the cases in which we have accepted statistics as proof of discriminatory intent and this case is that, in the venire-selection and Title VII contexts, the decisionmaker has an opportunity to explain the statistical disparity. Here, the State has no practical opportunity to rebut the Baldus study. Controlling considerations of public policy dictate that jurors cannot be called to testify to the motives and influences that led to their verdict. Similarly, the policy considerations behind a prosecutor's traditionally wide discretion suggest the impropriety of our requiring prosecutors to defend their decisions to seek death penalties, often years after they were made.[17] Moreover, absent far stronger proof, it is unnecessary to seek such a rebuttal, because a legitimate and unchallenged explanation for the decision is apparent from the record: McCleskey committed an act for which the United States Constitution and Georgia laws permit imposition of the death penalty.

Finally, McCleskey's statistical proffer must be viewed in the context of his challenge. McCleskey challenges decisions at the heart of the State's criminal justice system. One of society's most basic tasks is that of protecting the lives of its citizens and one of the most basic ways in which it achieves the task is through criminal laws against murder. Implementation of these laws necessarily requires discretionary judgments. Because discretion is essential to the criminal justice process, we would demand exceptionally clear proof before we would infer that the discretion has been abused. . . . Accordingly, we hold that the Baldus study is clearly insufficient to support an inference that any of the decisionmakers in McCleskey's case acted with discriminatory purpose.

[McCleskey also] contends that the Georgia capital punishment system is arbitrary and capricious in application, and therefore his sentence is excessive [and contrary to the Eighth Amendment], because racial considerations may influence capital sentencing decisions in Georgia. . . . To evaluate McCleskey's challenge, we must examine exactly what the Baldus study may show. Even Professor Baldus does not contend that his statistics prove that race enters into any capital sentencing decisions or that race was a factor in McCleskey's particular case. Statistics at most may show only a likelihood that a particular factor entered into some decisions. There is, of course, some risk of racial prejudice influencing a jury's decision in a criminal case. There are similar risks that other kinds of prejudice will influence other criminal trials. The question is at what point that risk becomes constitutionally unacceptable. McCleskey asks us to accept the likelihood allegedly shown by the Baldus study as the constitutional measure of an unacceptable risk of racial prejudice influencing capital sentencing decisions. This we decline to do.

Because of the risk that the factor of race may enter the criminal justice process, we have engaged in "unceasing efforts" to eradicate racial prejudice from our criminal justice system.[30] [However,] McCleskey's argument that the Constitution

17. Requiring a prosecutor to rebut a study that analyzes the past conduct of scores of prosecutors is quite different from requiring a prosecutor to rebut a contemporaneous challenge to his own acts. See Batson v. Kentucky, 476 U.S. 79 (1986).

30. This Court has repeatedly stated that prosecutorial discretion cannot be exercised on the basis of race. Nor can a prosecutor exercise peremptory challenges on the basis of race. More generally, this Court has condemned state efforts to exclude blacks from grand and petit juries. Other protections apply to the trial and jury deliberation process. Widespread bias in the community can make a change of venue constitutionally required. The Constitution prohibits racially biased prosecutorial arguments. If the circumstances of a particular case indicate a significant likelihood that racial bias may influence a jury,

condemns the discretion allowed decisionmakers in the Georgia capital sentencing system is antithetical to the fundamental role of discretion in our criminal justice system. Discretion in the criminal justice system offers substantial benefits to the criminal defendant. Not only can a jury decline to impose the death sentence, it can decline to convict or choose to convict of a lesser offense. Whereas decisions against a defendant's interest may be reversed by the trial judge or on appeal, these discretionary exercises of leniency are final and unreviewable. Similarly, the capacity of prosecutorial discretion to provide individualized justice is firmly entrenched in American law. As we have noted, a prosecutor can decline to charge, offer a plea bargain, or decline to seek a death sentence in any particular case. Of course, the power to be lenient also is the power to discriminate, but a capital punishment system that did not allow for discretionary acts of leniency would be totally alien to our notions of criminal justice. . . .

At most, the Baldus study indicates a discrepancy that appears to correlate with race. Apparent disparities in sentencing are an inevitable part of our criminal justice system. [There] can be no perfect procedure for deciding in which cases governmental authority should be used to impose death. Despite these imperfections, our consistent rule has been that constitutional guarantees are met when the mode for determining guilt or punishment itself has been surrounded with safeguards to make it as fair as possible. Where the discretion that is fundamental to our criminal process is involved, we decline to assume that what is unexplained is invidious. In light of the safeguards designed to minimize racial bias in the process, the fundamental value of jury trial in our criminal justice system, and the benefits that discretion provides to criminal defendants, we hold that the Baldus study does not demonstrate a constitutionally significant risk of racial bias affecting the Georgia capital sentencing process.

Two additional concerns inform our decision in this case. First, McCleskey's claim, taken to its logical conclusion, throws into serious question the principles that underlie our entire criminal justice system. The Eighth Amendment is not limited in application to capital punishment, but applies to all penalties. Thus, if we accepted McCleskey's claim that racial bias has impermissibly tainted the capital sentencing decision, we could soon be faced with similar claims as to other types of penalty. Moreover, the claim that his sentence rests on the irrelevant factor of race easily could be extended to apply to claims based on unexplained discrepancies that correlate to membership in other minority groups, and even to gender. Similarly, since McCleskey's claim relates to the race of his victim, other claims could apply with equally logical force to statistical disparities that correlate with the race or sex of other actors in the criminal justice system, such as defense attorneys or judges. Also, there is no logical reason that such a claim need be limited to racial or sexual bias. If arbitrary and capricious punishment is the touchstone under the Eighth Amendment, such a claim could — at least in theory — be based upon any arbitrary variable, such as the defendant's facial characteristics, or the physical attractiveness of the defendant or the victim, that some statistical study indicates may be influential in jury decisionmaking. As these examples illustrate, there is no limiting principle to the type of challenge brought by McCleskey. . . .

---

the Constitution requires questioning as to such bias. Finally, in a capital sentencing hearing, a defendant convicted of an interracial murder is entitled to such questioning without regard to the circumstances of the particular case.

Second, McCleskey's arguments are best presented to the legislative bodies. It is not the responsibility — or indeed even the right — of this Court to determine the appropriate punishment for particular crimes. It is the legislatures, the elected representatives of the people, that are constituted to respond to the will and consequently the moral values of the people. Legislatures also are better qualified to weigh and evaluate the results of statistical studies in terms of their own local conditions and with a flexibility of approach that is not available to the courts. Capital punishment is now the law in more than two-thirds of our States. It is the ultimate duty of courts to determine on a case-by-case basis whether these laws are applied consistently with the Constitution. Despite McCleskey's wide-ranging arguments that basically challenge the validity of capital punishment in our multiracial society, the only question before us is whether in his case the law of Georgia was properly applied. [This] was carefully and correctly done in this case. . . .

BRENNAN, J., dissenting.

At some point in this case, Warren McCleskey doubtless asked his lawyer whether a jury was likely to sentence him to die. A candid reply to this question would have been disturbing. First, counsel would have to tell McCleskey that few of the details of the crime or of McCleskey's past criminal conduct were more important than the fact that his victim was white. Furthermore, counsel would feel bound to tell McCleskey that defendants charged with killing white victims in Georgia are 4.3 times as likely to be sentenced to death as defendants charged with killing blacks. In addition, frankness would compel the disclosure that it was more likely than not that the race of McCleskey's victim would determine whether he received a death sentence: 6 of every 11 defendants convicted of killing a white person would not have received the death penalty if their victims had been black, while, among defendants with aggravating and mitigating factors comparable to McCleskey's, 20 of every 34 would not have been sentenced to die if their victims had been black. Finally, the assessment would not be complete without the information that cases involving black defendants and white victims are more likely to result in a death sentence than cases featuring any other racial combination of defendant and victim. The story could be told in a variety of ways, but McCleskey could not fail to grasp its essential narrative line: there was a significant chance that race would play a prominent role in determining if he lived or died. . . .

Evaluation of McCleskey's evidence cannot rest solely on the numbers themselves. We must also ask whether the conclusion suggested by those numbers is consonant with our understanding of history and human experience. Georgia's legacy of a race-conscious criminal justice system, as well as this Court's own recognition of the persistent danger that racial attitudes may affect criminal proceedings, indicates that McCleskey's claim is not a fanciful product of mere statistical artifice.

For many years, Georgia operated openly and formally precisely the type of dual system the evidence shows is still effectively in place. The criminal law expressly differentiated between crimes committed by and against blacks and whites, distinctions whose lineage traced back to the time of slavery. During the colonial period, black slaves who killed whites in Georgia, regardless of whether in self-defense or in defense of another, were automatically executed. A. Higginbotham, In the Matter of Color: Race in the American Legal Process 256 (1978). By the time of the Civil War, a dual system of crime and punishment was well established in

Georgia. See Ga. Penal Code (1861). The state criminal code contained separate sections for "Slaves and Free Persons of Color," and for all other persons. . . .

The Court . . . states that its unwillingness to regard petitioner's evidence as sufficient is based in part on the fear that recognition of McCleskey's claim would open the door to widespread challenges to all aspects of criminal sentencing. Taken on its face, such a statement seems to suggest a fear of too much justice. Yet surely the majority would acknowledge that if striking evidence indicated that other minority groups, or women, or even persons with blond hair, were disproportionately sentenced to death, such a state of affairs would be repugnant to deeply rooted conceptions of fairness. The prospect that there may be more widespread abuse than McCleskey documents may be dismaying, but it does not justify complete abdication of our judicial role. . . .

In fairness, the Court's fear that McCleskey's claim is an invitation to descend a slippery slope also rests on the realization that any humanly imposed system of penalties will exhibit some imperfection. Yet to reject McCleskey's powerful evidence on this basis is to ignore both the qualitatively different character of the death penalty and the particular repugnance of racial discrimination, considerations which may properly be taken into account in determining whether various punishments are "cruel and unusual." Furthermore, it fails to take account of the unprecedented refinement and strength of the Baldus study.

In more recent times, we have sought to free ourselves from the burden of [our history of racial discrimination]. Yet it has been scarcely a generation since this Court's first decision striking down racial segregation, and barely two decades since the legislative prohibition of racial discrimination in major domains of national life. These have been honorable steps, but we cannot pretend that in three decades we have completely escaped the grip of a historical legacy spanning centuries. Warren McCleskey's evidence confronts us with the subtle and persistent influence of the past. His message is a disturbing one to a society that has formally repudiated racism, and a frustrating one to a Nation accustomed to regarding its destiny as the product of its own will. Nonetheless, we ignore him at our peril, for we remain imprisoned by the past as long as we deny its influence in the present. . . .

Notes

1. *Compelling evidence of intent.* What sort of statistical study might provide the circumstantial evidence necessary to convince a court that arbitrary racial discrimination plays enough of a role in a sentencing system to invalidate the outcome in one case? Is such a statistical study possible? If racial discrimination does influence some decisionmakers, to some degree, in some cases, how might one demonstrate that fact in a court of law? Both the court of appeals and the Supreme Court concluded that a stronger statistical showing would be necessary before racial influences in sentencing would amount to a constitutional problem. What sort of evidence did the courts have in mind?

2. *Whose race, victim's or defendant's?* Note that the Baldus study found that the race of the *defendant* had no statistically significant effect on the use of capital punishment. In Furman v. Georgia, 408 U.S. 238 (1972), the Supreme Court struck down several capital punishment statutes, declaring that the death penalty (as administered at that time) was "cruel and unusual punishment" and a violation of the

Eighth Amendment. Among the many reasons for this decision discussed in the various concurring opinions, several of the justices argued that capital punishment could not stand because it was imposed disproportionately against the poor and racial minorities. Would the Supreme Court have reached a different outcome in *McCleskey* if the Baldus study had pointed to racial discrimination based on the race of the defendant rather than the race of the victim? Can a punishment be racially discriminatory if the government imposes it equally on defendants of all races?

3. *Other venues.* Suppose that on the day after the district court issued its order, the NAACP sends a copy of the Baldus study to a member of the Georgia legislature, and that member distributes copies. As the chair of the senate's committee on criminal justice matters, would you hold hearings? If so, what would be the topic of the hearings — the validity of the study or the most appropriate response to the study? If the Supreme Court had concluded instead that the influence of race in Georgia's capital punishment system rendered McCleskey's sentence unconstitutional, how would you advise Georgia legislators and prosecutors to respond? Would a victory for McCleskey mean abolition of the death penalty in Georgia?

4. *Statistical studies of capital punishment after* McCleskey. The "race of the victim" effect that appeared in the Baldus study in Georgia has also appeared in statistical studies of other states. These claims have gotten very little serious attention from courts; many simply cite *McCleskey* with no further discussion in refusing to consider the studies as relevant evidence of racial discrimination in the use of capital punishment. See People v. Davis, 518 N.E.2d 78 (Ill. 1987). The Supreme Court of New Jersey has indicated that evidence along the lines of that presented in *McCleskey* could be sufficient to establish a prima facie case of a violation of the state constitution. However, the court has also indicated that New Jersey has not yet executed enough people to form the basis for a convincing statistical study. See State v. Bey, 645 A.2d 685 (N.J. 1994) ("The statistics do not support his contention. Our abiding problem with analyzing the effect of race is that the case universe still contains too few cases to prove that the race of a defendant improperly influences death sentencing.").

2. Race and Discretionary Decisions Affecting Punishment

Racial disparities at sentencing can result from decisions made by actors at early stages of the criminal justice process. A strong bias in investigations or arrests may be passed through and perhaps even validated by studies showing unbiased decision making at a later stage of the process. For example, if whites and blacks who are convicted of a particular offense are punished identically, but members of one race are disproportionately investigated, then the sanction will appear neutral but will in fact be highly disparate, because the investigatory practices do not accurately reflect actual underlying behavior. It is not only police decisions that can generate sharp disparities that are passed through the system: Prosecutors may disproportionately direct cases involving members of one race to state court and identical cases by another race to federal court, where very different punishments attach to analogous state and federal charges. Or prosecutors may offer pleas in a racially disproportionate fashion. Indeed, the impact from an early police or prosecutorial decision can be so strong that the initial decision is in effect also a decision to punish.

This section highlights the difficulty of proving the source of discriminatory effects in large, complicated systems with many participants. Discrimination may be especially hard to unearth when it is the product of repeated, low-level behavior of a large group of individuals, and perhaps the result of unconscious influences on decision making. This section also raises questions about the capacity of the law to change group behavior. A fundamental challenge throughout the law is to design rules and remedies that deter bad conduct. It is hard enough to alter the behavior of individuals; the challenge of developing effective rules is multiplied when disfavored outcomes reflect complex decisions by large groups of people.

■ FREDDIE STEPHENS v. STATE
456 S.E.2d 560 (Ga. 1995)

FLETCHER, J.

Freddie Stephens challenges the constitutionality of OCGA §16-13-30(d), which provides for life imprisonment on the second conviction of the sale or possession with intent to distribute a controlled substance. He contends that the provision as applied is irrational and racially discriminatory in violation of the United States and Georgia Constitutions. . . . The challenged statute states:

> [A]ny person who violates subsection (b) of this Code section . . . shall be guilty of a felony and, upon conviction thereof, shall be punished by imprisonment for not less than five years nor more than 30 years. Upon conviction of a second or subsequent offense, he shall be imprisoned for life.

Subsection (b) makes it unlawful to "manufacture, deliver, distribute, dispense, administer, sell, or possess with intent to distribute any controlled substance." For a defendant to receive a life sentence for a second conviction, the state must notify the defendant prior to trial that it intends to seek the enhanced punishment based on past convictions.

Stephens contends that the statute as applied discriminates on the basis of race. He argues that this court should infer discriminatory intent from statewide and county-wide statistical data on sentences for drug offenders. In Hall County, where Stephens was convicted, the trial court found that one hundred percent (14 of 14) of the persons serving a life sentence under OCGA §16-13-30(d) are African-American, although African-Americans make up less than ten percent of the county population and approximately fifty to sixty percent of the persons arrested in drug investigations. Relying on evidence provided by the State Board of Pardons and Paroles, the trial court also found that 98.4 percent (369 of 375) of the persons serving life sentences for drug offenses as of May 1, 1994 were African-American, although African-Americans comprise only 27 percent of the state's population. Finally, a 1994 Georgia Department of Corrections study on the persons eligible for a life sentence under subsection (d) shows that less than one percent (1 of 168) of the whites sentenced for two or more convictions for drug sales are serving a life sentence, compared to 16.6 percent (202 of 1219) of the blacks.

In an earlier challenge to death penalty sentencing in Georgia based on statistics showing that persons who murder whites are more likely to be sentenced to death than persons who murder blacks, the United States Supreme Court held that the defendant had the burden of proving the existence of purposeful discrimination and that the purposeful discrimination had a discriminatory effect on him. McCleskey v. Kemp, 481 U.S. 279 (1987). . . .

Stephens concedes that he cannot prove any discriminatory intent by the Georgia General Assembly in enacting the law or by the Hall County district attorney in choosing to seek life imprisonment in this case. His attorney stated at the sentencing hearing: "I cannot prove and I do not feel there is any evidence to show that the district attorney's office is exercising their prosecutorial discretion in a discriminatory manner [and] I don't think I can demonstrate the legislature acted with discriminatory intent in enacting this code section." These concessions preclude this court from finding an equal protection violation under the United States Constitution.

We also conclude that the statistical evidence Stephens presents is insufficient evidence to support his claim of an equal protection violation under the Georgia Constitution. Stephens fails to present the critical evidence by race concerning the number of persons eligible for life sentences under OCGA §16-13-30(d) in Hall County, but against whom the district attorney has failed to seek the aggravated sentence. Because the district attorney in each judicial circuit exercises discretion in determining when to seek a sentence of life imprisonment, a defendant must present some evidence addressing whether the prosecutor handling a particular case engaged in selective prosecution to prove a state equal protection violation. . . .

Stephen's argument about inferring intent from the statistical evidence also ignores that other factors besides race may explain the sentencing disparity. Absent from the statistical analysis is a consideration of relevant factors such as the charges brought, concurrent offenses, prior offenses and sentences, representation by retained or appointed counsel, existence of a guilty plea, circuit where convicted, and the defendant's legal status on probation, in prison, or on parole. Without more adequate information about what is happening both statewide and in Hall County, we defer deciding whether statistical evidence alone can ever be sufficient to prove an allegation of discriminatory intent in sentencing under the Georgia Constitution.

The dissent argues that McCleskey v. Kemp is not the controlling precedent, instead relying on the United States Supreme Court decision on peremptory challenges in jury selections in Batson v. Kentucky, 476 U.S. 79 (1986). We must look to *McCleskey* for a proper analysis of the substantive issue before us, rather than *Batson,* because *McCleskey* dealt with the use of statistical evidence to challenge racial disparity in sentencing, as does this case.

The Supreme Court in *McCleskey* pointed out several problems in requiring a prosecutor to explain the reasons for the statistical disparity in capital sentencing decisions. Many of these same problems exist in requiring district attorneys to justify their decisions in seeking a life sentence for drug offenses based on statewide, and even county-wide, statistics of persons serving life sentences in state prisons for drug offenses.

First, "requiring a prosecutor to rebut a study that analyzes the past conduct of scores of prosecutors is quite different from requiring a prosecutor to rebut a contemporaneous challenge to his own acts. See Batson v. Kentucky, 476 U.S. 79 (1986)." *McCleskey,* 481 U.S. at 296. Second, statewide statistics are not reliable in determining the policy of a particular district attorney. [Even the statistics from Hall County do not accurately reflect the record of the district attorney in this case since she did not assume office until 1993.] Finally, the Court stated that the policy considerations behind a prosecutor's discretion argue against requiring district attorneys to defend their decisions to seek the death penalty. Since district attorneys are elected to represent the state in all criminal cases, it is important that they be able to exercise their discretion in determining who to prosecute, what charges to bring, which sentence to seek, and when to appeal without having to account for each decision in every case. [There] is a rational basis for the sentencing scheme in OCGA §16-13-30(d) and that it does not deprive persons of due process or equal protection under the law.

THOMPSON, J., concurring specially.

[W]e are presented once again with the claim that OCGA §16-13-30(d) is being used in a discriminatory fashion. This time, we are introduced to statewide statistical information which must give us pause: From 1990 to 1994, OCGA §16-13-30(d) was used to put 202 out of 1,107 eligible African-Americans in prison for life. During that same period, the statute was used to put 1 out of 167 eligible whites in prison for life. A life eligible African-American had a 1 in 6 chance of receiving a life sentence. A life eligible white had a 1 in 167 chance of receiving a life sentence. An African-American was 2,700 percent more likely to receive a life sentence than a white. . . . These statistics are no doubt as much a surprise to those who work and practice within the judicial system as to those who do not.

Statistical information can inform, not explain. It can tell what has happened, not why. However, only a true cynic can look at these statistics and not be impressed that something is amiss. That something lies in the fact that OCGA §16-13-30(d) has been converted from a mandatory life sentence statute into a statute which imposes a life sentence only in those cases in which a district attorney, in the exercise of his or her discretion, informs a defendant that the State is seeking enhanced punishment.

McCleskey v. Kemp, 481 U.S. 279 (1987), provides a workable test for determining whether the death penalty statute is being applied discriminatorily. *McCleskey* should continue to be applied in death penalty cases where there is a system of checks and balances to ensure that death sentences are not sought and imposed autocratically. Likewise *McCleskey* should be applied in other cases where the courts have discretion to determine the length of time to be served. However, *McCleskey* probably should not be applied where a district attorney has the power to decide whether a defendant is sentenced to life, or a term of years. . . .

I am persuaded that Batson v. Kentucky, 476 U.S. 79 (1986), could be used to supply a general framework in analyzing cases of this kind. . . . Nevertheless, it is my considered view that the judgment in this case must be affirmed because the defendant has failed to meet his burden even under a *Batson*-type analysis.

In order to establish a prima facie case under *Batson,* a defendant must prove systematic discrimination in his particular jurisdiction. Although the statistics presented by defendant are indicative of a statewide pattern of discrimination in the use of OCGA §16-13-30(d), the Hall County statistics are insufficient to make such a case. They simply show that all the persons in Hall County serving a life sentence under OCGA §16-13-30(d) are African-Americans. They do not show how many African-Americans were eligible to receive a life sentence under the statute; nor do they show how many whites were eligible. Moreover, they offer no information concerning the record of the district attorney in this case. Thus, upon careful review,

I must conclude that this defendant, in this case and on this record, failed to prove a pattern of systematic discrimination in his jurisdiction. . . .

Statewide, approximately 15 percent of eligible offenders receive a life sentence under OCGA §16-13-30(d). The statistical evidence presented in this case serves as notice to the General Assembly of Georgia that the mandatory life sentence provision of OCGA §16-13-30(d) has been repealed *de facto*. With such notice, there are at least three courses of action the legislature might now choose to pursue.

One. The General Assembly could choose to leave the mandatory life sentence on the books realizing that it is being used in a small percentage of the eligible cases. Militating against this course of action is the fact that all laws passed by the legislature should be followed. Contempt for and failure to follow any law breeds contempt for and failure to follow other laws.

Two. The General Assembly could reaffirm its commitment to a mandatory life sentence by requiring district attorneys to inform all defendants of prior convictions and thus enforce OCGA §16-13-30(d) with respect to all life eligible offenders. Militating against this course of action is the fact that mandatory life sentences are not favored by the prosecuting bar or by the defense bar. That is evidenced by the fact that from 1990 to 1994 only 203 out of 1,274 life eligible defendants actually received a life sentence under OCGA §16-13-30(d). . . .

Three. The General Assembly could choose to change the mandatory life sentence penalty to one of several sentencing options which the court could impose. For example, the penalty for a second or subsequent sale could be imprisonment for not less than 5 nor more than 30 years, or life. . . . It is my concern that these problems be resolved in whatever way the General Assembly deems best and that, thereafter, the prosecutors and the courts carry out that legislative will.

BENHAM, P.J., dissenting.

Of those persons from Hall County serving life sentences pursuant to OCGA §16-13-30(d), which mandates a life sentence for the second conviction for sale of or possession with intent to distribute certain narcotics, 100 percent are African-American, although African-Americans comprise only approximately 10 percent of Hall County's population. In our state prison system, African-Americans represent 98.4 percent of the 375 persons serving life sentences for violating OCGA §16-13-30(d). These statistics were part of the finding of the trial court in this case. In the face of such numbing and paralyzing statistics, the majority say there is no need for inquiry. It is with this determination that I take issue.

[In Batson v. Kentucky, 476 U.S. 79 (1986), the Supreme Court] installed a system that shifted the burden to the prosecutor to give race-neutral reasons for the peremptory challenges once the defendant established facts supporting an inference that the prosecutor's use of peremptory challenges was racially motivated. [The] court in *Batson* stated that an inference of discriminatory intent could be drawn from certain conduct or statistical data. Beyond its effect on peremptory challenges, the importance of *Batson* was that it significantly reduced the burden on one claiming discrimination, recognizing that under certain circumstances, the crucial information about an allegedly discriminatory decision could only come from the one who made the decision.

This is the course of reasoning we need to follow in analyzing the issue in this case rather than the more restrictive course taken in McCleskey v. Kemp and applied by the majority. . . . I am not unmindful or unappreciative of the vital and taxing role district attorneys are called upon to undertake in the ongoing battle against the blight of illicit drug trafficking. Throughout this state, they shoulder an enormous burden of responsibility for advancing the fight against drugs, and to do so successfully, they must be invested with considerable discretion in making decisions about ongoing prosecutions. However, it is the very breadth of that discretion, concentrated in a single decision-maker, which makes it necessary that the one exercising the discretion be the one, when confronted with facts supporting an inference of discriminatory application, to bear the burden of establishing that the discretion was exercised without racial influence. This case is more like *Batson* than *McCleskey* because all the discretion in the sentencing scheme involved in this case resides in the district attorney, to the exclusion of the trial court, whereas in death penalty cases such as *McCleskey,* the spread of discretion among the prosecutor, the trial court, and the jurors introduces variables which call for more rigorous statistical analysis. In addition, the complexity of the death penalty procedure, with its many safeguards and the recurring necessity of specific findings at every stage from the grand jury to the sentencing jury, differentiates it from the relative simplicity of the sentencing scheme applicable to this case.

[The] U.S. Supreme Court recognized in *McCleskey* itself that statistical proof which presents a "stark pattern" may be accepted as the sole proof of discriminatory intent. In distinguishing *McCleskey* from such a case, the Supreme Court mentioned in a footnote two cases in which "a statistical pattern of discriminatory impact demonstrated a constitutional violation." One was Gomillion v. Lightfoot, 364 U.S. 339 (1960), where a city's boundaries were altered so as to exclude 395 of 400 black voters without excluding a single white voter, and the other was Yick Wo v. Hopkins, 118 U.S. 356 (1886), in which an ordinance requiring permits for the operation of laundries was applied so as to exclude all of the over 200 Chinese applicants and only one white applicant. The statistics in those cases presented a "stark pattern," but no more stark than the pattern presented in this case. In the present case, based on evidence from law enforcement officers who testified as to arrest rates and other relevant statistics,[2] the trial court found that 100% of the people from that county who were serving life sentences pursuant to OCGA §16-13-30(d) were African-Americans and that statewide, 98.4% of all the persons serving life sentences pursuant to OCGA §16-13-30(d) were African-Americans. . . .

In some instances we must lead the way. [T]his is the time for this Court to draw from our historical strength and our determination that the citizens of this state be treated fairly before the law, and declare that Georgia's constitutional guarantee of equal protection requires that OCGA §16-13-30(d) be applied evenly, in a race-neutral fashion. . . . I would hold, therefore, as a matter purely of state constitutional law, that equal protection of the law in the context of OCGA §16-13-30(d) requires that the prosecution be required, when a defendant has made a prima facie showing sufficient to raise an inference of unequal application

---

2. Agent David McIlwraith testified that 50% of the drug investigations involved black males. Investigator Shelly Manny testified that of the 60 drug investigations she conducted in Hall County, only 9 involved blacks and that only 50% of her undercover buys involved black males. Another narcotics investigator testified that since 1989, he had made over 300 cocaine distribution cases in Hall County and only 60% involved black males.

of the statute, to "demonstrate that permissible racially neutral selection criteria and procedures have produced the monochromatic result." *Batson.* . . .

Because appellant has made a sufficient showing of discriminatory application of OCGA §16-13-30(d) that the State should be required to give race-neutral reasons for the "monochromatic" application of that statute in Hall County, this court should vacate the life sentences and remand this case to the trial court for a hearing. At such a hearing, should the trial court find that the prosecution could not provide race-neutral reasons for the "monochromatic result" of the application of OCGA §16-13-30(d) in Hall County, sentencing for the offenses involved would still be permissible, but not with the aggravation of punishment authorized by OCGA §16-13-30(d). On the other hand, should the trial court find that the State has provided appropriate race-neutral reasons, the life sentences would be reimposed, whereupon appellant would be entitled to a new appeal. . . .

The statistics offered in this case show an enormous potential for injustice, and those statistics are just like the tip of an iceberg, with the bulk lying below the surface, yet to be realized. And unless we reveal or expose this massive obstacle that lies in the shipping lanes of justice, it will . . . tear a gaping hole in the ship of state, just as a gaping hole was ripped in the Titanic. . . .

Notes

1. *Who discriminates against whom?* What discrimination does Freddie Stephens claim? Who did Warren McCleskey claim had discriminated against him? Other than the fact that both McCleskey and Stephens asserted that race was the basis for discrimination, were these similar claims?

The racial impact of charges under the Georgia statute described above is not the only example of punishment differences that flow from stark racial differences in charging decisions. In a study of charging for crack cocaine offenses in Los Angeles, Richard Berk and Alex Campbell found that black defendants are more likely than white or Latino defendants to be charged in federal court with sale of crack cocaine (which translates into more severe punishments than for comparable charges in state court). While black defendants represented 58 percent of those arrested by the Sheriff's Department for sale of crack cocaine in Los Angeles between 1990 and 1992, they made up 83 percent of the defendants charged with that crime in federal court. White and Latino defendants arrested for this crime were more likely to be prosecuted in state court. Berk & Campbell, Preliminary Data on Race and Crack Charging Practices in Los Angeles, 6 Fed. Sentencing Rep. 36 (1993). What might be the sources of the racially disparate federal crack prosecutions reported in the Berk and Campbell study?

2. *Competing analogies.* Did the majority in Stephens v. State think that Stephens's claim was the same as McCleskey's? Were you convinced by the competing analogy to discriminatory jury selection in Batson v. Kentucky? Justice Robert Benham, dissenting in *Stephens,* argued that sentencing under the Georgia drug statute was different from capital punishment because it concentrates the decision in the hands of the district attorney. Do you agree? Are there ways a police officer might influence who receives a life sentence under the statute? Do the voters in the county or in the state have some control over this question?

Problem 9-11. The Crack-Powder Differential

In 1986 the United States Congress passed the Anti-Drug Abuse Act to increase the penalties for various drug crimes. The new law imposed heavier penalties on cocaine base (or "crack") than on cocaine powder, a relationship now called the "100 to 1 ratio." An offense involving mixtures weighing 5 grams or more containing cocaine base was subject to the same punishment as an offense involving mixtures weighing 500 grams or more containing cocaine powder. Congress considered crack cocaine to be more dangerous than cocaine powder because of crack's potency, its more highly addictive nature, and its greater accessibility because of its relatively low cost.

Some of the impetus for the federal law came from the news media. Stories associated the use of crack cocaine with social maladies such as gang violence and parental neglect among user groups. Critics of the federal law, however, argued that these social problems did not result from the drug itself, but instead from the disadvantaged social and economic environment in places where the drug often is used.

In practice, the increased penalties for crack meant that African American defendants received heavier penalties than whites for possession and sale of cocaine. Over 90 percent of all people arrested for sale or possession of crack were African American; roughly 80 percent of all people arrested for sale or possession of powder cocaine were white.

By 1989 the Minnesota legislature was debating the same issue. The legislators considered a bill that would make a person guilty of a third-degree offense if he or she possessed 3 or more grams of crack cocaine. Under the same statute, a person who possessed 10 or more grams of cocaine powder would be guilty of the same offense; someone who possesses less than 10 grams of cocaine powder would be guilty of a fifth-degree offense. The bill became known as the "10 to 3 ratio" law.

The sponsors of the bill argued that this structure facilitated prosecution of "street level" drug dealers. Law enforcement officers who testified at legislative hearings suggested that 3 grams of crack and 10 grams of powder indicated a level at which dealing, not merely using, took place. A person convicted of selling 100 grams of crack may often be characterized as a mid-level dealer (someone who provides the drug to street-level retailers). By comparison, 100 grams of powder usually typifies a low-level retailer; 500 grams is more indicative of a mid-level dealer. However, witnesses from the Department of Public Safety Office of Drug Policy contradicted these estimates for the typical amount of drugs carried by dealers, suggesting that most cocaine powder users are dealers as well.

The customary unit of sales for the two drugs were also different. The normal sales unit of crack was a "rock" weighing .1 gram and selling on the street for $20 or $25. On the other hand, the customary unit of sale for powder was the "8-ball," 1/8 ounce or about 3.5 grams, which sold for about $350. Ten grams of powder cocaine could be easily converted into more than 3 grams of crack.

Sponsors of the bill also argued that crack is more addictive and dangerous than cocaine powder. Witnesses at the hearings testified that crack cocaine had a more severe effect on the central nervous system and is more addictive than powder cocaine. Other witnesses pointed out, however, that crack and powder cocaine have the same active ingredient, and both produce the same type of pharmacological effects. The differences in effect between the two drugs were based on the fact that cocaine powder is sniffed through the nostrils, while crack cocaine is smoked. If powder cocaine is dissolved and injected, it is just as addictive as crack.

As a member of the Minnesota legislature, would you support the "10 to 3 ratio" bill? What else would you like to know before you vote? Compare State v. Russell, 477 N.W.2d 886 (Minn. 1991).

Notes

1. *Constitutional challenges to punishment differentials: majority position.* Racial disparities in the application of death penalty laws highlight several distinct forms of discrimination. A law could be discriminatory in intent, either at the point of creation or when it is applied. A criminal sanction could also be discriminatory in effect because of uneven (though not intentionally skewed) application of the law. But these are not the only dynamics that create racial differences in criminal punishments. Some laws have racially discriminatory effects, even though the people who create and enforce the law do not intend to burden one racial group more than another and even though they apply the law with complete evenhandedness. These effects occur when the criminal sanctions apply to behavior that people of one race engage in more often than people of other races. Would it ever be unconstitutional for a legislature to criminalize conduct when one racial group is more likely to engage in it?

A number of defendants convicted of trafficking in crack cocaine have argued for a downward departure from the guideline sentence (or an invalidation of the relevant guidelines and statutes) based on an equal protection claim. Federal courts have uniformly rejected this assertion, reasoning that any racial impact of the crack cocaine statutes and guidelines was unintentional. See, e.g., United States v. Reece, 994 F.2d 277 (6th Cir. 1993) (per curiam); United States v. Thomas, 900 F.2d 37 (4th Cir. 1990). While not often addressing such claims, high state courts have usually rejected the constitutional challenges.

2. *Legislative response.* The Minnesota Supreme Court struck down the legislation described in Problem 9-11 on state constitutional grounds in State v. Russell, 477 N.W.2d 886 (Minn. 1991). The legislature responded to the *Russell* decision by increasing the penalties for powder to equal the former penalties for crack. Minn. Stat. §152.021-023. Minnesota's cocaine penalties are now among the toughest in the country, stiffer in some ways than in the federal system.

The federal penalty structure punishes cocaine power and cocaine crack offenders the same for amounts that differ 100 times — the so-called 100-to-1 ratio. Note that this is not a ratio of penalties but of the amounts of drugs that spur similar penalties. In 1994 Congress ordered the U.S. Sentencing Commission, the administrative agency that sets sentencing rules for the federal system, to report on cocaine punishment policies in the federal system. In 1995 the commission issued a report attacking the 100-to-1 ratio, and recommended to Congress a 1-to-1 crack-powder ratio, along with other proposed changes in the federal system that would punish behavior *associated* with crack offenses more severely.

The U.S. Sentencing Commission's recommendation to move to a 1-to-1 quantity ratio came under attack from legislators across the political spectrum. Congress passed legislation to overturn the commission's proposal on October 18, 1995, by a vote of 332 to 83, and President Clinton signed the measure. This was the first time in the history of the commission that Congress voted to override a proposed amendment to the sentencing guidelines. The 100-to-1 quantity ratio remains in effect in the federal system.

As a matter of political reality, how could the U.S. Sentencing Commission recommend the rejection of a policy (the 100-to-1 quantity ratio) that had already received the overwhelming endorsement of the legislative branch when the cocaine penalties were originally enacted? Would Congress have reacted differently to a proposal to reduce, but not eliminate, the differences between crack and powder? Is this equivalent to arguing that a small amount of racial discrimination is acceptable?

3. *Race and crack.* Are you persuaded that racial differentials are the central issue in the crack-cocaine punishment debate? Do different parts of the criminal world just happen to be controlled by groups of a particular race or ethnicity, as an analogy to the use of racketeering laws against the Mafia suggests? Or do you find convincing the argument that racially disproportionate effects (but not intent) justify reworking the system to start with a 1-to-1 quantity ratio?

Michael Tonry surveyed the various causes of the increasing racial divide in criminal punishments in the United States during the 1980s and 1990s. After tracking the steady increase in the proportion of blacks in the nation's prison population during those years, Tonry notes that the increase did not occur because of increased black participation in serious violent crimes: "The proportions of serious violent crimes committed by blacks have been level for more than a decade. Since the mid-1970s, approximately 45 percent of those arrested for murder, rape, robbery, and aggravated assault have been black (the trend is slightly downward)." Instead, most of the changing racial impact of criminal sentences during this time can be traced to drug law enforcement. According to Tonry, politicians pursued the "War on Drugs" with full knowledge of its likely racial impact. Those policies caused

the ever harsher treatment of blacks by the criminal justice system, and it was foreseeable that they would do so. Just as the tripling of the American prison population between 1980 and 1993 was the result of conscious policy decisions, so also was the greater burden of punishment borne by blacks. Crime control politicians wanted more people in prison and knew that a larger proportion of them would be black.

Michael Tonry, Malign Neglect: Race, Crime and Punishment in America 52 (1995). Is this the sort of "discriminatory intent" that could form the basis for an equal protection challenge? Does this argument create a politically viable basis for revising penalties for violation of the drug laws?

X

Appeals

Errors happen in virtually every felony criminal trial, and in many misdemeanor cases. Appellate courts cannot correct every mistake that occurs at the trial level, but they do try to identify and correct the errors that matter most. Depending on the pertinent double jeopardy rules, an appellate court might respond to a trial error by ordering a new trial or a new sentencing proceeding, by remanding the case for further factual findings by the judge (after a bench trial), or by dismissing the charges.

In this chapter, we explore limits on the power or willingness of appellate courts to correct errors in criminal proceedings. The chapter addresses deceptively simple questions: Who should be able to appeal, and when? How much deference should an appellate court show to findings of fact by the trier of fact? When, if ever, should an appellate court allow a judgment to stand even when it believes that an error occurred? What could be more important than getting the right answer in criminal proceedings?

A. WHO APPEALS?

With rare exceptions (notably in capital cases), appeals are not automatic. Cases can be heard on appeal only when at least one of the parties has the legal authority to request an appeal. This section explores the typical legal limits on the power of parties to file an appeal and the circumstances under which parties are willing to do so.

1. Right to Appeal

Most federal and state constitutions do not guarantee criminal defendants any "right to appeal." Instead, statutes and rules of appellate procedure determine who can file an appeal and what issues the parties can raise. What limits do legislatures tend to place on the parties' authority to appeal?

■ ARKANSAS STATUTES §16-91-101

(a) Any person convicted of a misdemeanor or a felony by virtue of a trial in any circuit court of this state has the right of appeal to the Supreme Court of Arkansas. . . .

(c) There shall be no appeal from a plea of guilty or nolo contendere.

■ ARKANSAS RULE OF CRIMINAL PROCEDURE 24.3(b)

With the approval of the court and the consent of the prosecuting attorney, a defendant may enter a conditional plea of guilty or nolo contendere, reserving in writing the right, on appeal from the judgment, to review of an adverse determination of a pretrial motion to suppress evidence. If the defendant prevails on appeal, he shall be allowed to withdraw his plea.

■ CALIFORNIA PENAL CODE §1237.5

No appeal shall be taken by the defendant from a judgment of conviction upon a plea of guilty or nolo contendere, or a revocation of probation following an admission of violation, except where both of the following are met:

(a) The defendant has filed with the trial court a written statement, executed under oath or penalty of perjury showing reasonable constitutional, jurisdictional, or other grounds going to the legality of the proceedings.

(b) The trial court has executed and filed a certificate of probable cause for such appeal with the clerk of the court.

■ CALIFORNIA RULE OF COURT 31(d)

. . . If the appeal from a judgment of conviction entered upon a plea of guilty or nolo contendere is based solely upon grounds (1) occurring after entry of the plea which do not challenge its validity or (2) involving a search or seizure, the validity of which was contested . . . , the provisions of section 1237.5 of the Penal Code requiring a statement by the defendant and a certificate of probable cause by the trial court are inapplicable, but the appeal shall not be operative unless the notice of appeal states that it is based upon such grounds.

Notes

1. Nonconstitutional basis for right to appeal. The Supreme Court held long ago in McKane v. Durston, 153 U.S. 684 (1894), that there is no federal constitutional basis for the right to appeal. That holding still accurately describes the law. State constitutions also do not typically provide for a right to appeal, although there are some exceptions. See Mich. Const. art. I, §20; Wash. Const. art. 1, §22. This is an area dominated by statutes, which address in some detail the types of cases and claims where appeal is available. All states do provide for at least some appellate review of criminal convictions. If one could demonstrate that appellate review is far more common and important today than it was in 1894, might that convince a court to find a new constitutional basis for appeal? How might you demonstrate that appellate review is more common or important today than a century ago?

2. *Appeal after guilty plea: majority position.* Some states (such as Arkansas) allow appeals after guilty pleas only for those issues expressly reserved for appeal in a conditional plea agreement. Others give either the trial court or the appellate court the power to allow the appeal as a completely discretionary matter. Still others (such as California) give the court discretion to allow the appeal only when the defendant meets certain preconditions specified in statute or rule. What variables would be most important in convincing a court to allow an appeal after a plea of guilty? In light of the numbers of appeals and trials occurring each year, how often do you imagine that discretionary appeals after pleas are allowed?

3. *Number of appeals.* The number of defendants who file appeals each year tends to exceed the number of defendants who are convicted at trial. Consider the following statistics for the federal system:

Year	Criminal Appeals	Total Convictions	Guilty or Nolo Pleas	Convictions After Trial
1991	9,949	46,768	41,213	5,555
2000	9,162	68,156	64,939	3,217

Bureau of Justice Statistics, Federal Case Processing 2000, with Trends 1982-2000 at table 5, table 7 (2001, NCJ 189737). To the extent that these numbers are typical of other jurisdictions, they suggest that appeal rights may be important to more defendants than trial rights and that a crucial dimension of appeal rights is the availability of appeals after guilty pleas.

4. *Bail pending appeal.* Most felony defendants, in most places, are released at some point prior to their trials or guilty pleas. See Chapter 2. After conviction, however, statutes and court rules make it far less likely that a trial court will release an offender while the appeal is pending. See 18 U.S.C. §§3143(b)(2), 3145(c); Ex parte Anderer, 61 S.W.3d 398 (Tex. 2001) (condition placed on post-conviction bail — prohibition on operating automobile — was aimed at protecting public and "reasonable" under applicable statute). A convicted person who escapes is ineligible to appeal in most systems, although it may be possible to file an appeal upon recapture. See Ortega-Rodriguez v. United States, 507 U.S. 234 (1993) (non-constitutional federal law creates no absolute bar to escapee's filing of appeal upon recapture); State v. Troupe, 891 S.W.2d 808 (Mo. 1995) ("escape" rule bars appeal, even for those recaptured).

5. *Motions for new trial.* A defendant may convince a trial judge to reconsider a judgment before taking an appeal to another court. A motion for a new trial is, in effect, an "appeal" to the trial court. The motion is made routinely after convictions at trial, and trial judges deny the motion in the overwhelming majority of cases. If

you were drafting rules of appellate procedure, would you require such a motion before allowing a party to file an appeal with the appellate court? Would you require it for some issues but not for others?

2. Appeals by Indigent Defendants

Although defendants have no federal constitutional right to an appeal, the federal equal protection clause does require states to make its chosen appeals process available to all defendants, even those without the financial resources to pay for an appeal. According to Griffin v. Illinois, 351 U.S. 12 (1956), the state must provide a defendant with a free transcript of a trial record, if such a transcript is necessary to file an appeal. In Douglas v. California, 372 U.S. 353 (1963), the Court extended *Griffin* to require the government to provide indigent appellants with an attorney for an initial "appeal as of right." Even when appellate counsel for an indigent defendant believes the defendant could raise only frivolous issues on appeal, she must advise the appellate court of any colorable issue. Anders v. California, 386 U.S. 738 (1967). Consider the following effort by the state of California to structure the work of appointed defense counsel on appeal.

■ GEORGE SMITH v. LEE ROBBINS
528 U.S. 259 (2000)

Thomas, J.

Not infrequently, an attorney appointed to represent an indigent defendant on appeal concludes that an appeal would be frivolous and requests that the appellate court allow him to withdraw or that the court dispose of the case without the filing of merits briefs. In Anders v. California, 386 U.S. 738 (1967), we held that, in order to protect indigent defendants' constitutional right to appellate counsel, courts must safeguard against the risk of granting such requests in cases where the appeal is not actually frivolous. We found inadequate California's procedure — which permitted appellate counsel to withdraw upon filing a conclusory letter stating that the appeal had "no merit" and permitted the appellate court to affirm the conviction upon reaching the same conclusion following a review of the record. We went on to set forth an acceptable procedure. California has since adopted a new procedure, which departs in some respects from the one that we delineated in *Anders*. The question is whether that departure is fatal. We hold that it is not. The procedure we sketched in *Anders* is a prophylactic one; the States are free to adopt different procedures, so long as those procedures adequately safeguard a defendant's right to appellate counsel.

Under California's new procedure, established in People v. Wende, 600 P.2d 1071 (Calif. 1979) . . . counsel, upon concluding that an appeal would be frivolous, files a brief with the appellate court that summarizes the procedural and factual history of the case, with citations of the record. He also attests that he has reviewed the record, explained his evaluation of the case to his client, provided the client with a copy of the brief, and informed the client of his right to file a pro se supplemental brief. He further requests that the court independently examine the record for arguable issues. Unlike under the *Anders* procedure, counsel following *Wende* neither explicitly states that his review has led him to conclude that an appeal would be frivolous . . . nor requests leave to withdraw. Instead, he is silent on the merits of the case and expresses his availability to brief any issues on which the court might desire briefing.

The appellate court, upon receiving a "*Wende* brief," must conduct a review of the entire record, regardless of whether the defendant has filed a pro se brief. . . . If the appellate court, after its review of the record pursuant to *Wende*, also finds the appeal to be frivolous, it may affirm. If, however, it finds an arguable (i.e., non-frivolous) issue, it orders briefing on that issue.

In 1990, a California state-court jury convicted respondent Lee Robbins of second-degree murder (for fatally shooting his former roommate) and of grand theft of an automobile (for stealing a truck that he used to flee the State after committing the murder). Robbins was sentenced to 17 years to life. He elected to represent himself at trial, but on appeal he received appointed counsel. His appointed counsel, concluding that an appeal would be frivolous, filed with the California Court of Appeal a brief that complied with the *Wende* procedure. Robbins also availed himself of his right under *Wende* to file a pro se supplemental brief, filing a brief in which he contended that there was insufficient evidence to support his conviction and that the prosecutor violated Brady v. Maryland, 373 U.S. 83 (1963), by failing to disclose exculpatory evidence. The California Court of Appeal, agreeing with counsel's assessment of the case, affirmed. The court explained that it had "examined the entire record" and [found no support for the two issues that Robbins raised]. After exhausting state postconviction remedies, Robbins filed in [federal district court] for a writ of habeas corpus. . . .

The District Court [concluded] that there were at least two issues that, pursuant to *Anders*, counsel should have raised in his brief (in a *Wende* brief, as noted above, counsel is not required to raise issues): first, whether the prison law library was adequate for Robbins's needs in preparing his defense after he elected to dismiss his appointed counsel and proceed pro se at trial, and, second, whether the trial court erred in refusing to allow him to withdraw his waiver of counsel. . . .

In *Anders*, we reviewed an earlier California procedure for handling appeals by convicted indigents. Pursuant to that procedure, *Anders*'s appointed appellate counsel had filed a letter stating that he had concluded that there was "no merit to the appeal." *Anders*, in response, sought new counsel; the State Court of Appeal denied the request, and *Anders* filed a pro se appellate brief. That court then issued an opinion that reviewed the four claims in his pro se brief and affirmed, finding no error (or no prejudicial error). . . .

We held that "California's action does not comport with fair procedure and lacks that equality that is required by the Fourteenth Amendment." We placed the case within a line of precedent beginning with Griffin v. Illinois, 351 U.S. 12 (1956), and continuing with Douglas v. California, 372 U.S. 353 (1963), that imposed constitutional constraints on States when they choose to create appellate review. [A] finding that the appeal had "no merit" was not adequate, because it did not mean that the appeal was so lacking in prospects as to be "frivolous." [We] set out what would be an acceptable procedure for treating frivolous appeals:

> [I]f counsel finds his case to be wholly frivolous, after a conscientious examination of it, he should so advise the court and request permission to withdraw. That request must, however, be accompanied by a brief referring to anything in the record that might arguably support the appeal. A copy of counsel's brief should be furnished the indigent

and time allowed him to raise any points that he chooses; the court — not counsel — then proceeds, after a full examination of all the proceedings, to decide whether the case is wholly frivolous. If it so finds it may grant counsel's request to withdraw and dismiss the appeal insofar as federal requirements are concerned, or proceed to a decision on the merits, if state law so requires. On the other hand, if it finds any of the legal points arguable on their merits (and therefore not frivolous) it must, prior to decision, afford the indigent the assistance of counsel to argue the appeal.

We then concluded by explaining how this procedure would be better than the California one that we had found deficient. Among other things, we thought that it would "induce the court to pursue all the more vigorously its own review because of the ready references not only to the record but also to the legal authorities as furnished it by counsel."

The Ninth Circuit ruled that this final section of *Anders,* even though unnecessary to our holding in that case, was obligatory upon the States. We disagree. [This] view runs contrary to our established practice of permitting the States, within the broad bounds of the Constitution, to experiment with solutions to difficult questions of policy.

In McCoy v. Court of Appeals of Wisconsin, Dist. 1, 486 U.S. 429 (1988), we rejected a challenge to Wisconsin's variation on the *Anders* procedure. Wisconsin had departed from *Anders* by requiring *Anders* briefs to discuss why each issue raised lacked merit. The defendant argued that this rule was contrary to *Anders* and forced counsel to violate his ethical obligations to his client. We, however, emphasized that the right to appellate representation does not include a right to present frivolous arguments to the court. [The Wisconsin procedure], by providing for one-sided briefing by counsel against his own client's best claims, probably made a court more likely to rule against the indigent than if the court had simply received an *Anders* brief.

[It] is more in keeping with our status as a court, and particularly with our status as a court in a federal system, to avoid imposing a single solution on the States from the top down. . . . Accordingly, we hold that the *Anders* procedure is merely one method of satisfying the requirements of the Constitution for indigent criminal appeals. States may — and, we are confident, will — craft procedures that, in terms of policy, are superior to, or at least as good as, that in *Anders.* The Constitution erects no barrier to their doing so. . . .

A State's procedure provides [adequate and effective] review so long as it reasonably ensures that an indigent's appeal will be resolved in a way that is related to the merit of that appeal. . . . In determining whether a particular state procedure satisfies this standard, it is important to focus on the underlying goals that the procedure should serve — to ensure that those indigents whose appeals are not frivolous receive the counsel and merits brief required by *Douglas,* and also to enable the State to protect itself so that frivolous appeals are not subsidized and public moneys not needlessly spent. For although, under Douglas, indigents generally have a right to counsel on a first appeal as of right, it is equally true that this right does not include the right to bring a frivolous appeal and, concomitantly, does not include the right to counsel for bringing a frivolous appeal. . . . The obvious goal of *Anders* was to prevent this limitation on the right to appellate counsel from swallowing the right itself, and we do not retreat from that goal today.

We think the *Wende* procedure reasonably ensures that an indigent's appeal will be resolved in a way that is related to the merit of that appeal. . . . Although we did not, in *Anders*, explain in detail why the California procedure was inadequate . . . a significant factor was that the old California procedure did not require either counsel or the court to determine that the appeal was frivolous; instead, the procedure required only that they determine that the defendant was unlikely to prevail on appeal. . . . *Wende*, by contrast, requires both counsel and the court to find the appeal to be lacking in arguable issues, which is to say, frivolous.

An additional problem with the old California procedure was that it apparently permitted an appellate court to allow counsel to withdraw and thereafter to decide the appeal without appointing new counsel. . . . Under *Wende*, by contrast, . . . counsel does not move to withdraw and . . . the court orders briefing if it finds arguable issues.

In *Anders*, we also disapproved the old California procedure because we thought that a one paragraph letter from counsel stating only his "bare conclusion" that the appeal had no merit was insufficient. [T]he *Wende* brief provides more than a one-paragraph "bare conclusion." Counsel's summary of the case's procedural and factual history, with citations of the record, both ensures that a trained legal eye has searched the record for arguable issues and assists the reviewing court in its own evaluation of the case.

[The *Anders* procedure] has, from the beginning, faced consistent and severe criticism. One of the most consistent criticisms . . . is that *Anders* is in some tension both with counsel's ethical duty as an officer of the court (which requires him not to present frivolous arguments) and also with his duty to further his client's interests (which might not permit counsel to characterize his client's claims as frivolous). California, through the *Wende* procedure, has made a good-faith effort to mitigate this problem by not requiring the *Wende* brief to raise legal issues and by not requiring counsel to explicitly describe the case as frivolous.

Another criticism of the *Anders* procedure has been that it is incoherent and thus impossible to follow. Those making this criticism point to our language in *Anders* suggesting that an appeal could be both "wholly frivolous" and at the same time contain arguable issues, even though we also said that an issue that was arguable was "therefore not frivolous." In other words, the *Anders* procedure appears to adopt gradations of frivolity and to use two different meanings for the phrase "arguable issue." The *Wende* procedure attempts to resolve this problem as well, by drawing the line at frivolity and by defining arguable issues as those that are not frivolous.[13] . . .

Our purpose is not to resolve any of these arguments. The Constitution does not resolve them, nor does it require us to do so. . . . It is enough to say that the *Wende* procedure . . . affords adequate and effective appellate review for criminal indigents.

[It] may be, as Robbins argues, that his appeal was not frivolous and that he was thus entitled to a merits brief rather than to a *Wende* brief. Indeed, both the District Court and the Ninth Circuit found that there were two arguable issues on direct appeal. The meaning of "arguable issue" as used in the opinions below,

---

13. A further criticism of *Anders* has been that it is unjust. More particularly, critics have claimed that, in setting out the *Anders* procedure, we were oblivious to the problem of scarce resources (with regard to both counsel and courts) and, as a result, crafted a rule that diverts attention from meritorious appeals of indigents and ensures poor representation for all indigents.

however, is far from clear. The courts below most likely used the phrase in the unusual way that we used it in *Anders*— an issue arguably supporting the appeal even though the appeal was wholly frivolous. Such an issue does not warrant a merits brief. But the courts below may have used the term to signify issues that were "arguable" in the more normal sense of being nonfrivolous and thus warranting a merits brief.

[The] proper standard for evaluating Robbins's claim that appellate counsel was ineffective in neglecting to file a merits brief is that enunciated in Strickland v. Washington, 466 U.S. 668 (1984). Respondent must first show that his counsel was objectively unreasonable in failing to find arguable issues to appeal— that is, that counsel unreasonably failed to discover nonfrivolous issues and to file a merits brief raising them. If Robbins succeeds in such a showing, he then has the burden of demonstrating prejudice. That is, he must show a reasonable probability that, but for his counsel's unreasonable failure to file a merits brief, he would have prevailed on his appeal. . . .

SOUTER, J., dissenting.

In a line of cases beginning with Griffin v. Illinois, this Court examined appellate procedural schemes under the principle that justice may not be conditioned on ability to pay. Even though absolute equality is not required, we held in Douglas v. California that when state criminal defendants are free to retain counsel for a first appeal as of right, the Fourteenth Amendment requires that indigent appellants be placed on a substantially equal footing through the appointment of counsel at the State's expense.

Two services of appellate counsel are on point here. Appellate counsel examines the trial record with an advocate's eye, identifying and weighing potential issues for appeal. This is review not by a dispassionate legal mind but by a committed representative, pledged to his client's interests, primed to attack the conviction on any ground the record may reveal. If counsel's review reveals arguable trial error, he prepares and submits a brief on the merits and argues the appeal. The right to the first of these services, a partisan scrutiny of the record and assessment of potential issues, goes to the irreducible core of the lawyer's obligation to a litigant in an adversary system. . . .

The right is unqualified when a defendant has retained counsel, and I can imagine no reason that it should not be so when counsel has been appointed. Because the right to the second service, merits briefing, is not similarly unqualified, however, the issue we address today arises. The limitation on the right to a merits brief is that no one has a right to a wholly frivolous appeal, against which the judicial system's first line of defense is its lawyers. Being officers of the court, members of the bar are bound not to clog the courts with frivolous motions or appeals. . . .

The rub is that although counsel may properly refuse to brief a frivolous issue and a court may just as properly deny leave to take a frivolous appeal, there needs to be some reasonable assurance that the lawyer has not relaxed his partisan instinct prior to refusing, in which case the court's review could never compensate for the lawyer's failure of advocacy. A simple statement by counsel that an appeal has no merit, coupled with an appellate court's endorsement of counsel's conclusion, gives no affirmative indication that anyone has sought out the appellant's best arguments or championed his cause to the degree contemplated by the adversary system. [T]here must be some prod to find any reclusive merit in an ostensibly unpromising case and some process to assess the lawyer's efforts after the fact. A judicial process that renders constitutional error invisible is, after all, itself an affront to the Constitution.

In *Anders,* we devised such a mechanism to ensure respect for an appellant's rights. . . . *Anders* thus contemplates two reviews of the record, each of a markedly different character. First comes review by the advocate, the defendant's interested representative. His job is to identify the best issues the partisan eye can spot. Then comes judicial review from a disinterested judge, who asks two questions: whether the lawyer really did function as a committed advocate, and whether he misjudged the legitimate appealability of any issue. In reviewing the advocate's work, the court is responsible for assuring that counsel has gone as far as advocacy will take him with the best issues undiscounted. . . .

Without the assurance that assigned counsel has done his best as a partisan, his substantial equality to a lawyer retained at a defendant's expense cannot be assumed. And without the benefit of the lawyer's statement of strongest claims, the appellate panel cannot act as a reviewing court, but is relegated to an inquisitorial role. It is owing to the importance of assuring that an adversarial, not an inquisitorial, system is at work that I disagree with the Court's statement today that our cases approve of any state procedure that "reasonably ensures that an indigent's appeal will be resolved in a way that is related to the merit of that appeal." . . .

California's *Wende* procedure fails to measure up. Its primary failing is in permitting counsel to refrain as a matter of course from mentioning possibly arguable issues in a no-merit brief; its second deficiency is a correlative of the first, in obliging an appellate court to search the record for arguable issues without benefit of an issue-spotting, no-merit brief to review. . . .

The *Wende* procedure does not assure even the most minimal assistance of counsel in an adversarial role. The Constitution demands such assurances, and I would hold Robbins entitled to an appeal that provides them.

Notes

1. Counsel for indigent appellants. The Supreme Court has read the equal protection clause to require equal access to some aspects of the appeals process for both indigent appellants and those who can afford an attorney and various fees. Under Griffin v. Illinois, 351 U.S. 12 (1956), the state must provide an indigent defendant with a free transcript of a trial record, if the rules of appellate procedure require parties to use such a transcript when filing an appeal. In Douglas v. California, 372 U.S. 353 (1963), the Court extended *Griffin* to require the government to provide indigent appellants with an attorney for an initial "appeal as of right." The Supreme Court has now expanded the constitutional bases for the right to counsel on appeal. In Halbert v. Michigan, 545 U.S. 605 (2005), the Court declared that the due process and equal protection clauses require appointment of counsel for indigent defendants who pursue first-tier appellate review, even if they were convicted on the basis of a guilty plea. As with the right to appointed counsel at trial, many states use their own constitutions, statutes, or rules of procedure to expand the availability of counsel on appeal beyond what the federal constitution requires.

But not every aspect of the appeals process is available on equal terms to indigent defendants. Under Ross v. Moffitt, 417 U.S. 600 (1974), there is no constitutional requirement to provide counsel for preparation of petitions for discretionary appellate review. As the Supreme Court explained in Smith v. Robbins, when appellate counsel for an indigent defendant believes the defendant could raise only frivolous issues on appeal, states still must have some mechanism for bringing potential issues to the court's attention. See Turner v. State, 818 So. 2d 1186 (Miss. 2001) (counsel who views a defendant's appeal as lacking merit must determine that the defendant is unlikely to prevail on appeal, file a brief referring to anything in record that might arguably support appeal, and advise client of his right to file a pro se supplemental brief). Do the mechanisms described in *Anders* and in the *Wende* case from California give indigent defendants the functional equivalent of retained appellate counsel?

2. *Self-representation on appeal.* In Martinez v. Court of Appeal of California, 528 U.S. 152 (2000), the Supreme Court refused to extend the right of self-representation at trial — established in Faretta v. California, 422 U.S. 806 (1975) — to a direct appeal. The appellate courts may properly appoint counsel for the appellant, even if the appellant objects. One of the Court's reasons to embrace the right of self-representation at trial was "respect for individual autonomy." Are there any differences between the interests of a defendant at trial and the interests of an appellant when it comes to self-representation?

3. Interlocutory Appeals

Appeals usually take place after a final judgment, but on occasion the rules allow for an "interlocutory" appeal of an issue before the proceedings below have reached an end. These interlocutory appeals are especially important to the government. In general, prosecutors have less access to appellate review than defendants. The U.S. Supreme Court noted the state of the common law on prosecutorial appeals in 1892:

> In a few States, decisions denying a writ of error to the State after judgment for the defendant on a verdict of acquittal have proceeded upon the ground that to grant it would be to put him twice in jeopardy, in violation of a constitutional provision. But the courts of many States, including some of great authority, have denied, upon broader grounds, the right of the State to bring a writ of error in any criminal case whatever, even when the discharge of the defendant was upon the decision of an issue of law by the court, as on demurrer to the indictment, motion to quash, special verdict, or motion in arrest of judgment.

United States v. Sanges, 144 U.S. 310, 312-13 (1892). As the Court suggested in *Sanges,* the double jeopardy clauses of the federal and state constitutions have some bearing on when the prosecutor can appeal: They limit the power of the prosecution to request an appeal after jeopardy "attaches," and they bar virtually any prosecutorial appeal after an acquittal. Against this common law presumption against appeals by the state (bolstered by the constitutional limits on double jeopardy), consider the following statute and judicial decision interpreting a rule of appellate procedure.

■ DELAWARE CODE TIT. 10, §§9902, 9903

§9902

(a) The State shall have an absolute right to appeal to an appellate court a final order of a lower court where the order constitutes a dismissal of an indictment or information or any count thereof, or the granting of any motion vacating any verdict or judgment of conviction where the order of the lower court is based upon the invalidity or construction of the statute upon which the indictment or information is founded or the lack of jurisdiction of the lower court over the person or subject matter.

(b) When any order is entered before trial in any court suppressing or excluding substantial and material evidence, the court, upon certification by the Attorney General that the evidence is essential to the prosecution of the case, shall dismiss the complaint, indictment or information or any count thereof to the proof of which the evidence suppressed or excluded is essential. [The] reasons of the dismissal shall be set forth in the order entered upon the record.

(c) The State shall have an absolute right of appeal to an appellate court from an order entered pursuant to subsection (b) of this section and if the appellate court upon review of the order suppressing evidence shall reverse the dismissal, the defendant may be subjected to trial.

§9903

The State may apply to the appellate court to permit an appeal to determine a substantial question of law or procedure, and the appellate court may permit the appeal in its absolute discretion. The appellate court shall have the power to adopt rules governing the allowance of the appeal; but, in no event of such appeals shall the decision or result of the appeal affect the rights of the defendant and he or she shall not be obligated to defend the appeal, but the court may require the Public Defender of this State to defend the appeal and to argue the cause.

■ STATE v. MATTHEW MEDRANO
67 S.W.3d 892 (Tex. Crim. App. 2002)

COCHRAN, J.

The issue in this case is whether article 44.01(a)(5) of the Texas Code of Criminal Procedure[1] permits the State to bring a pretrial appeal of an adverse ruling on a motion to suppress evidence when the trial court does not conclude that the evidence was "illegally obtained." Although this Court, in State v. Roberts, 940 S.W.2d 655 (Tex. Crim. App. 1996), held that the State cannot appeal a pretrial evidentiary ruling unless the defendant claims that the evidence was "illegally obtained," neither the language of the statute nor legislative intent supports this limitation. It is not consistent with the interpretation other state or federal courts have given to the same or similar language in their government-appeal statutes. Moreover, the rule in *Roberts* has proved unworkable in practice. Therefore, we overrule *Roberts* and hold that under article 44.01(a)(5), the State is entitled to appeal any adverse pre-trial ruling which suppresses evidence, a confession, or an

---

1. Article 44.01(a), in pertinent part, provides:

The State is entitled to appeal an order of a court in a criminal case if the order: . . . (5) grants a motion to suppress evidence, a confession, or an admission, if jeopardy has not attached in the case and if the prosecuting attorney certifies to the trial court that the appeal is not taken for the purpose of delay and that the evidence, confession, or admission is of substantial importance to the case.

admission, regardless of whether the defendant alleges, or the trial court holds, that the evidence was "illegally obtained."

Appellee, Matthew Medrano, was charged with capital murder for the robbery-murder of Benton Smith, a pizza delivery man. The State's only witness to the robbery-murder was Jennifer Erivez, a fourteen-year-old girl, who was standing in the driveway of her home at about 10:00 p.m. waiting for her boyfriend. Jennifer testified that she saw the pizza delivery man drive by and park down the street. Then she saw a maroon car, like a Chrysler LeBaron, drive past slowly and stop under a street light. A man got out of the front passenger side and did something like take the license plate off of the car. Jennifer saw the man's face clearly, but could not recall the car's license plate number. The car then drove further down the street and parked behind the pizza delivery man's truck. The same man got out of the car and walked up to the pizza delivery man. Jennifer heard a gunshot and then saw the man run back to the car. He got in, and the driver sped away.

A few hours later, Jennifer gave police a written description of the person she had seen get out of the car and approach the pizza delivery man. . . . Jennifer also stated that the maroon car contained a total of four people. Because she was unable to recall the car's license plate number, an El Paso police officer, trained in hypnosis, conducted a videotaped hypnotic session the next day. She was still unable to recall the license plate number. About a week later, the police conducted two photo lineups for Jennifer. She did not identify anyone in those lineups, [although Medrano's photo was not in either of those lineups]. After she identified Mr. Medrano as the shooter in a third photo lineup two days later, he was arrested and charged with capital murder.

Defense counsel filed a "Motion to Suppress In Court Identification." . . . After a pretrial suppression hearing, the trial judge orally granted the defense motion. Her written order stated that she granted the motion "for the reasons stated on the record" at the hearing and that she "also f[ound] said identification was obtained in violation of the 4th, 5th, 6th and 14th Amendments of the United States Constitution and Article I, sections 9, 10, 13, and 19 of the Texas Constitution." The State certified that it could not prosecute the case without Jennifer's testimony and filed an appeal. . . .

Article 44.01 was enacted as a vehicle for the State to challenge "questionable legal rulings excluding what may be legally admissible evidence."[5] The purpose of the statute is to permit the pretrial appeal of erroneous legal rulings which eviscerate the State's ability to prove its case. The Texas legislature, in passing Senate Bill 762 in 1987, clearly intended to provide Texas prosecutors with the same vehicle of appeal for pretrial evidentiary rulings as federal prosecutors. . . . There is no question that under 18 U.S.C. §3731, federal prosecutors may appeal a wide variety of pretrial evidentiary rulings — not just those tied to motions to suppress illegally obtained evidence. . . .

5. Bill Analysis, S.B. 762, Acts 1987, 70th Leg., ch. 382, §1. The "Background" Section of the bill analysis begins:

The Texas Constitution provides that the State has no right to appeal in a criminal case, making Texas the only state that bans all prosecution appeals. This prohibition is viewed as a serious problem in the administration of justice for several reasons: (1) On occasion, defendants are released because of questionable legal rulings excluding what may be legally admissible evidence; (2) Legal issues that have been wrongly decided by trial courts nevertheless stand as precedent, albeit unbinding, for police, prosecutors, and courts; and (3) Trial judges may have a tendency to resolve doubtful legal questions in favor of the defendant because such a ruling cannot harm the judge's reversal rate.

All fifty states, as well as the District of Columbia, have provisions permitting the government to appeal adverse rulings of a question of law. Many of those states [at least eighteen of them] use the same or very similar language as that contained in art. 44.01(a)(5), and they permit the State to appeal any pretrial ruling suppressing evidence if that evidence is likely to be outcome determinative. [At least thirteen other] states explicitly grant the prosecution a broad right to appeal *any* pretrial suppression, evidentiary or other legal ruling which is likely to determine the outcome of the case. A few states explicitly permit the State to appeal only orders excluding "seized evidence," "evidence illegally obtained," or "evidence seized in violation of the Constitution." A handful of state courts [four of them] have construed their government-appeal statutes to permit only appeals of constitutionally based pretrial rulings excluding evidence. State v. Shade, 867 P.2d 393 (Nev. 1994); State v. Counts, 472 N.W.2d 756 (N.D. 1991). At least one state, Ohio, has judicially broadened its government-appeal statute to permit pretrial appeals of nonconstitutional trial rulings excluding evidence, despite language to the contrary. O.R.C. §2945.67; Ohio Crim. R. 12. Although a few states apply their government-appeal statutes narrowly, the vast majority of courts and legislatures across the nation broadly construe their state's-right-to-appeal statutes. They focus upon the same major themes: 1) Does this pretrial ruling effectively prevent the government from presenting its case to a jury? And 2) Is the ruling based upon an erroneous interpretation or application of law?

In *Roberts,* this Court followed that handful of states which have very narrowly construed their state's right-to-appeal statutes. This Court ruled that it lacked jurisdiction to consider a State's appeal from a trial court's ruling that civil deposition testimony was inadmissible. We held that the phrase "motion to suppress evidence," as used in article 44.01(a)(5), was limited to motions which sought to suppress evidence on the basis that such evidence was "illegally obtained." The defendant in *Roberts* contended that a videotaped deposition from a civil case was inadmissible hearsay; he did not claim that the deposition testimony was illegally obtained. Because the defendant's motion was not a "motion to suppress evidence" contemplated under art. 44.01(a)(5), went the logic, the order granting the motion was not appealable. [The *Roberts* Court] relied on the fact that the corresponding federal statute authorizes an appeal by the Government, under 18 U.S.C. §3731, "from a decision or order of a district court suppressing or excluding evidence. . . ." Texas article 44.01(a)(5) authorizes an appeal from a motion to suppress evidence, but it does not explicitly authorize an appeal from a motion to *exclude* evidence. In *Roberts,* this Court reasoned, "[B]y using the term 'suppress' alone, not in conjunction with the broader term 'exclude,' the Legislature meant to limit the State's appeal to those instances where evidence is suppressed in the technical sense, not merely excluded."

The legislative history of article 44.01 shows otherwise. The legislative intent, explicitly stated in the Bill Analysis, was to permit the State to appeal any "questionable legal rulings excluding what may be legally admissible evidence." Period.

[The] Texas Legislature was already familiar with the use of the term "motion to suppress evidence" in the context of pretrial hearings. The Texas Legislature apparently chose the term "motion to suppress evidence" in article 44.01(a)(5) because pretrial "motions to suppress evidence" can be heard under article 28.01. . . . Because the only type of pretrial evidentiary motion mentioned in article 28.01 is a "motion to suppress evidence," it follows that the only type of pretrial evidentiary motion that the State can appeal is the same type that the defendant may file. They are both called a "motion to suppress evidence." Under article 28.01, a motion to suppress evidence is one in which the defendant (or the State) claims that certain evidence should not be admitted at trial for a constitutional, statutory, evidentiary or procedural reason. There is no logical, legal, or linguistic reason that a single phrase concerning the same pretrial evidentiary motion, should bear one meaning for purposes of which pretrial motions a court may consider, but bear a totally different meaning when the State appeals an adverse ruling on that motion. The rule is simple: If the trial court can rule upon a pretrial motion to suppress evidence, the State can appeal it. A motion for the goose is a motion for the gander.

Finally, the rule in *Roberts* is, as this case demonstrates, unworkable. Who decides whether a pretrial motion to suppress evidence is one that seeks to exclude "illegally obtained" evidence? If the defendant labels his motion as one to suppress illegally obtained evidence, is that determinative? If the defendant cites constitutional provisions, is that determinative? If the trial court, in ruling, cites constitutional provisions, is that determinative? Or, as in this case, if the court of appeals determines that, even though both the defendant and trial judge cited constitutional provisions, the motion (and ruling) was not really a motion to suppress illegally obtained evidence? This is a linguistic puzzle that only Humpty Dumpty or a rejection of *Roberts* can resolve. . . .

The trial court's ruling in this case does not involve evidence which would normally be considered "illegally obtained." Still, the ruling excluding Jennifer's identification testimony — which was a legal ruling excluding evidence — is appealable under article 44.01 (a) (5) if it could be determined pretrial under article 28.01, §1 (6). Relying on the standards concerning the admissibility of post-hypnotic testimony set out in Zani v. State, 758 S.W.2d 233 (Tex. Crim. App. 1988), the trial court orally ruled that Jennifer's identification of Mr. Medrano was inadmissible. After hearing arguments from the prosecutor, the trial court affirmed her oral order with a written ruling that specifically held that the identifications were obtained in violation of the United States and Texas Constitutions. The trial court's written ruling falls squarely within the rulings intended to be appealable under Article 44.01. . . .

WOMACK, J., dissenting

. . . Today the Court says [our holding in *Roberts*] was wrong because the legislature modeled art. 44.01 after the corresponding federal provision generally, a statute that permits an appeal by the government from suppression or exclusion of evidence. I want to point out four things. First, drafting a statute to apply only to "suppressing" is an odd way of modeling on the federal statute that specifies both "suppressing" and "excluding." Second, our 1996 decision was based on the language of the statute, which is more important than the intentions and interpretations of witnesses who supported the act, which are the primary support for today's decision. "It is the law that governs, not the intent of the lawgiver," Antonin Scalia, A Matter of Interpretation 17 (1997), much less the intent of the lawgiver's committee witnesses. But this is only to rehash the 1996 decision of the Court.

In 2002 the more important points are my third and fourth: Today's construction of the ambiguous word increases the scope of the statute, applying it to "excluding" evidence as well as to "suppressing" it. And if that is the correct scope of the statute, the legislature had but to amend the statute by inserting the words "or excluding." Three sessions of the legislature have intervened since our decision, with no action. In this case, that is significant.

If this case were the opposite (if the statute had read "suppressing or excluding evidence," and we had held that it did not apply to the excluding of evidence) legislative inaction might mean little or nothing. What could the legislature do to express more clearly that the statute applied to the excluding of evidence? But when the statute says it applies only to "suppressing" evidence and this Court held that "suppressing" does not mean every "excluding" of evidence, the remedy is quick and easy. If we have misconstrued a statute that is stated clearly, what can the legislature do? Reenact the statute with the additional phrase, "and we really mean it"? When we have misconstrued a criminal-procedure statute that is unambiguous, *stare decisis* has its least force. In such a case we should be more free to overrule our earlier decision. . . .

The Court's other argument that "suppress evidence" means "suppress or exclude evidence" is by reference to Code of Criminal Procedure article 28.01, which provides the procedure for a pretrial hearing like the one that was held in this case. . . . The Court reasons thus: pretrial hearings are to determine motions to suppress evidence; the motion that was filed in this case was decided at a pretrial hearing; therefore it must have been a motion to suppress evidence. . . .

Although pretrial hearings are for motions to suppress evidence (and the other matters that are listed in Article 28.01, section 1), they are not for only those matters. There are two reasons. On its face, the statutory list is not exclusive, so the pretrial hearing is not limited to the eleven items on the list. Even if it were exclusive, one item on the list is "(2) Pleadings of the defendant," which include "any other motions or pleadings permitted by law to be filed." Tex. Code Crim. Proc. art. 27.02. It was, therefore, proper for the appellee to file and the court to decide a motion to exclude, not suppress, evidence. So the Court's conclusion that the pretrial motion must be a motion to suppress is invalid.

[There are] strong arguments why the State should be allowed to appeal pretrial rulings excluding evidence. But the statute that was enacted did not allow it, and it still does not. We have no authority to change the statute. I respectfully dissent.

Notes

1. Appeal of pretrial issues by the government: majority position. Statutes and procedural rules in most states have now expanded beyond the common law bar on government appeals, granting the government power to appeal certain pretrial rulings. Most of these rules cover a trial judge's decision to dismiss charges before trial or a decision during a suppression hearing to exclude key evidence. The federal statute, 18 U.S.C. §3731, allows the government to appeal the dismissal of an indictment or information as well as a decision "suppressing or excluding evidence . . . not made after the defendant has been put in jeopardy." Under this statute, the government may also appeal a decision to release a person from pretrial detention. Appeals of pretrial rulings do not create double jeopardy problems because double jeopardy does not "attach" in the lower court until the start of a trial.

2. Appeal after jeopardy attaches. Once a trial has begun, the government will have more difficulty obtaining appellate review for any errors of the trial judge. If the judge's error leads to an acquittal or a dismissal of the charges, double jeopardy clearly would prevent a second trial for the same offense. But can the government suspend the proceedings at trial once a major error has occurred and obtain appellate review before an acquittal or dismissal? Most criminal procedure rules and statutes block such appeals; there is, however, a small and growing number of states willing to allow the government to bring an appeal after trial has begun but before an acquittal or a dismissal takes place. See, e.g., State v. Malinovsky, 573 N.E.2d 22 (Ohio 1991) (allowing prosecutorial appeal of midtrial evidentiary ruling, based on procedural rule allowing appeal of "motion to suppress evidence").

Double jeopardy clearly bars government appeals after an acquittal. Ball v. United States, 163 U.S. 662 (1896). However, that limit does not matter in the great majority of cases: Acquittals occur in 1 percent of all felony cases filed. Felony Defendants in Large Urban Counties, 1998 (November 2001, NCJ 187232). Dismissals of charges after jeopardy attaches are more common than acquittals, and government appeals after dismissals present more complex legal issues. If a dismissal on a legal question occurs after a conviction, an appellate court can reverse the legal ruling and reinstate the fact finder's verdict without requiring a second trial. For dismissals taking place before a verdict, the government may not appeal if the ruling amounts to a resolution, "correct or not, of some or all of the factual elements of the offense charged." United States v. Scott, 437 U.S. 82, 97 (1978); Smith v. Massachusetts, 543 U.S. 462 (2005) (after trial judge granted motion to dismiss one among several charges based on insufficiency of government's evidence, double jeopardy barred any reconsideration by judge on this count). However, if the pre-verdict dismissal is based on some legal issue not going to the defendant's guilt or innocence (such as pretrial delay), then a reprosecution after a government appeal is consistent with double jeopardy limits.

When *defendants* appeal after conviction and convince the court to overturn the judgment, the government may ordinarily retry the case without violating double jeopardy. One exception occurs when the fact finder at trial is presented with both a greater and lesser included offense and convicts the defendant only of the lesser offense. In that setting, the "implied acquittal" of the defendant prevents the government from retrying the greater charges if the defendant succeeds on appeal. Green v. United States, 355 U.S. 184 (1957). The government also cannot retry a case after a defendant wins an appeal if the error was the government's failure to present legally sufficient facts to support a conviction.

Do "asymmetric" appeal rights actually hurt defendants? If the prosecutor has only one shot at obtaining a conviction, does that mean the government spends more than it otherwise would on the initial trial? If so, then asymmetric appeal rights might increase the number of false convictions and increase litigation costs for defendants. See Vikramaditya S. Khanna, Double Jeopardy's Asymmetric Appeal Rights: What Purpose Do They Serve? 82 B.U. L. Rev. 241 (2002).

3. Prosecutorial and appellate court screening of appeals. Most state statutes leave the chief prosecutor with some control over which issues the government may appeal. The chief prosecutor (or some statewide representative of the government, such as the attorney general) must certify to the appellate court that the trial court's ruling dealt with evidence or some other claim critical to the prosecution of the case and that the appeal is not taken "merely" for purposes of delay. Under what circumstances might the chief prosecutor refuse to certify an issue for appeal? Is this a meaningful limitation on the scope of the government's appeal rights? Should appellate courts themselves sort the important claims from the less important ones? Appellate rules of procedure often give courts the discretion to decline to hear government claims that otherwise qualify for appeal. See State v. Doucette, 544 A.2d 1290, 1293 (Me. 1988).

4. *"Moot" appeals by the prosecution.* A few states, such as Kansas, permit the ernment to appeal from an acquittal to the state supreme court if the legal issu statewide interest and vital to the administration of justice. The appellate deci only advisory; even if the appellate court sustains the government's position, the trial court acquittal remains final. See Kan. Stat. §3602(b)(1)-(3); State v. Martin, 658 P.2d 1024 (Kan. 1983); State v. Viers, 469 P.2d 53 (Nev. 1970) (striking down a provision similar to Kansas statute on the ground that an advisory appeal presents no case or controversy under the state constitution). In Canada, the appellate court has discretionary power to hear government claims of legal error leading to an acquittal. See Alan Mewett, An Introduction to the Criminal Process in Canada 209-12 (1988). Will the defense point of view receive adequate representation in such "moot" appeals?

5. *Interlocutory appeals by the defense.* Defendants may also bring interlocutory appeals, although they can do so for fewer issues than the government. Denials of motions for pretrial release and the trial judge's setting of a bail amount are common grounds for defense interlocutory appeals. See Ill. Supreme Ct. R. 604(c). Why do these decisions receive exceptional treatment? What other choices might a defendant most desire to appeal on an interlocutory basis?

B. APPELLATE REVIEW OF FACTUAL FINDINGS

Appellate courts could take a wide range of approaches in selecting which judgments made at trial to review. They could conceivably engage in complete and new ("de novo") review for all issues of fact and law. But this approach would engender huge administrative costs; in effect, the appellate court would retry the entire case. Alternatively, appellate courts might play an extremely limited role in reviewing verdicts, presuming that all judgments of fact and law are correct and reversing only for fundamental failures in process that would undermine confidence in the fairness of the decisionmakers or the ability of the defendant to put on a case (such as a failure to provide counsel, evident bias on the part of the judge, or jury tampering). An even more extreme system might abolish appellate courts altogether, trusting completely in the trial process.

Appellate courts operate under standards that lie somewhere between these conceivable boundaries. Courts distinguish between review of factual findings and legal judgments at trial. The standards of review for factual findings tend to be more deferential because the factfinder at trial (whether a jury or judge) is in a better position to view and weigh evidence. The standard of review on questions of law is different: Appellate courts often assert the same (or greater) competence in assessing legal issues and tend to review questions of law de novo.

Most cases that go to trial (as opposed to those settled through a plea bargain) involve factual disputes. Perhaps the defendant claims she did not do the alleged act at all, or she claims that the facts point to a different crime from the one the prosecution charged (for example, voluntary manslaughter instead of second-degree murder). Whichever side loses at trial will often believe that the factfinder made the wrong decision. Of course, if the defendant is acquitted at trial, then double jeopardy will bar a prosecutorial appeal to reassess her innocence. When should the defendant be able to challenge the factfinder's judgments?

The Supreme Court in Jackson v. Virginia, 443 U.S. 307 (1979), announced the standard that most appellate courts now apply when reviewing the sufficiency of the evidence to support a guilty verdict. James Jackson had been convicted at trial of murdering Mary Cole.

> That the petitioner had shot and killed Mrs. Cole was not in dispute at the trial. The State's evidence established that she had been a member of the staff at the local county jail, that she had befriended him while he was imprisoned there on a disorderly conduct charge, and that when he was released she had arranged for him to live in the home of her son and daughter-in-law. Testimony by her relatives indicated that on the day of the killing the petitioner had been drinking and had spent a great deal of time shooting at targets with his revolver. [That evening, Cole drove Jackson] to a local diner. There the two were observed by several police officers, who testified that both the petitioner and the victim had been drinking. The two were observed by a deputy sheriff as they were preparing to leave the diner in her car. The petitioner was then in possession of his revolver, and the sheriff also observed a kitchen knife in the automobile. The sheriff testified that he had offered to keep the revolver until the petitioner sobered up, but that the latter had indicated that this would be unnecessary since he and the victim were about to engage in sexual activity.
>
> Her body was found in a secluded church parking lot a day and a half later, naked from the waist down, her slacks beneath her body. Uncontradicted medical and expert evidence established that she had been shot twice at close range with the petitioner's gun. She appeared not to have been sexually molested. Six cartridge cases identified as having been fired from the petitioner's gun were found near the body.

443 U.S. at 309-10. Following the common law formula, Virginia defined murder as "the unlawful killing of another with malice aforethought." Premeditation distinguished murder in the first degree from murder in the second degree, and the prosecution bore the burden of proof on this element. Jackson admitted shooting Cole but contended that the shooting had been accidental and that the gun had gone off while he was resisting her sexual advances, and that in any case he had been too intoxicated to support a finding of premeditation.

The trial judge found Jackson guilty of first-degree murder. Jackson challenged the conviction in both state and federal court on the grounds that the evidence was constitutionally insufficient. Although the Supreme Court announced in its opinion the standard of review for factual judgments on federal collateral review of state convictions, the constitutional standard in *Jackson* has been applied in state and federal courts for almost all review of factual findings, including on direct appeal. The Court held:

> After *Winship* the critical inquiry on review of the sufficiency of the evidence to support a criminal conviction must be not simply to determine whether the jury was properly instructed, but to determine whether the record evidence could reasonably support a finding of guilt beyond a reasonable doubt. But this inquiry does not require a court to "ask itself whether it believes that the evidence at the trial established guilt beyond a reasonable doubt." Instead, the relevant question is whether, after viewing the evidence in the light most favorable to the prosecution, any rational trier of fact could have found the essential elements of the crime beyond a reasonable doubt. This familiar standard gives full play to the responsibility of the trier of fact fairly to resolve conflicts in the testimony, to weigh the evidence, and to draw reasonable inferences from basic facts to ultimate facts. Once a defendant has been found guilty of the crime charged, the

factfinder's role as weigher of the evidence is preserved through a legal conclusion that upon judicial review all of the evidence is to be considered in the light most favorable to the prosecution. The criterion thus impinges upon "jury" discretion only to the extent necessary to guarantee the fundamental protection of due process of law.

443 U.S. at 317-20. Applying this new standard, the Court concluded that "a rational factfinder could readily have found the petitioner guilty beyond a reasonable doubt of first-degree murder under Virginia law."

States modify the *Jackson* standards in two ways. First, as with many other broad standards applied throughout the criminal process, different legal cultures and groups of judges will apply similar standards differently and will reach consistently different outcomes. Thus, the flexibility of the *Jackson* standard allows for more aggressive or more deferential review. Second, some states have supplemented the *Jackson* standard to require from appellate courts an additional task when reviewing the factual support for the guilty verdict. Consider whether Texas has improved on *Jackson* in the following case.

■ ELBERT CLEWIS v. STATE
922 S.W.2d 126 (Tex. Crim. App. 1996)

Maloney, J.

[In anticipation of a burglary, seven Dallas police officers participated in a covert surveillance operation at Fashionworks, a Dallas business. This location had been burglarized on three previous Monday nights. On Monday, November 11, 1991, at approximately 10:00 p.m., Officers Robert Baird and Mark Sears saw three individuals approach the front of the building. Two of the people pried the front door open with a tire tool and entered the building. The third person, later identified as Elbert Clewis, stood on the porch looking around in all directions, watched the first two suspects open the doors, and then followed them into the building. Baird and Sears saw the three individuals exit the business carrying clothing. Upon seeing the police, they dropped the clothing and fled. The police then apprehended all three suspects. Sears and Baird saw no evidence that Clewis was intoxicated on the night of the offense. Another officer on the scene, Michael Beatty, first saw Clewis that night when he ran around the corner of the Fashionworks building. Beatty noticed that Clewis seemed to be "in a state of shock," and appeared "real nervous and was just real jittery, unsure of what to do" when the police apprehended him. However, Beatty did not believe that Clewis was intoxicated.

After each of the officers testified at trial, defense counsel called Peggy Shivers, mother of one of the suspects. She testified that she had seen Clewis at her house earlier that evening. Mrs. Shivers stated that Clewis was intoxicated at that time: "He was staggering, so I would say on a scale from one to ten, I would give him ten." Clewis argued that his intoxication prevented him from forming the mens rea necessary to establish the elements of burglary. Clewis was convicted of burglary of a building, and the Fifth Court of Appeals affirmed his conviction.]

In his sole ground for review, appellant contends that the court of appeals erred in refusing to review the evidence to determine whether it was factually sufficient to sustain his conviction. Specifically, appellant avers that the evidence was factually insufficient to show that he knowingly and intentionally entered the building. . . .

We hold that the proper standard of review for factual sufficiency of the elements of the offense is [as follows: an appellate court considers] all the evidence without [viewing it] "in the light most favorable to the prosecution" and sets aside the verdict only if it is so contrary to the overwhelming weight of the evidence as to be clearly wrong and unjust.

. . . The Texas Constitution confers appellate jurisdiction upon the courts of appeals, Tex. Const. art. V, §§5 & 6, that includes the power to review questions of fact in criminal cases.[4] [T]he Legislature has consistently recognized the ability of courts with criminal appellate jurisdiction to review the facts of a case and . . . Article 44.25 of the Texas Code of Criminal Procedure[7] has remained nearly identical since 1857 with each subsequent code revision. When their jurisdiction to review fact questions is properly invoked, the courts of appeals cannot ignore constitutional and statutory mandates.

[T]he United States Supreme Court in Jackson v. Virginia, 443 U.S. 307 (1979), set . . . the minimum standard for sustaining a conviction under the Due Process Clause of the Fourteenth Amendment. [Under *Jackson*, an appellate court must ask "whether, after viewing the evidence in the light most favorable to the prosecution, any rational trier of fact could have found the essential elements of the crime beyond a reasonable doubt."] Although Texas courts have adopted the *Jackson* standard as the legal sufficiency standard in direct appeals, we have never held that its application precluded any other type of review. As we explicitly noted in Griffin v. State, 614 S.W.2d 155 (Tex. Crim. App. 1981), "States are free to set higher standards of review than *Jackson*."

[If] the evidence is insufficient under the *Jackson* standard, it is "legally insufficient." A determination that the evidence is "legally insufficient" means that the case should never have been submitted to the jury. In contrast, the issue of factual sufficiency is a question of fact. A *Jackson* review, "viewing the evidence in the light most favorable to the prosecution," is not a factual sufficiency review; rather, it is an analytical tool used to determine whether there is a fact issue at all.[12] The *Jackson* standard "gives full play to the responsibility of the trier of fact fairly to resolve conflicts in the testimony, to weigh the evidence, and to draw reasonable inferences from basic facts to ultimate facts." *Jackson*, 443 U.S. at 319.

In conducting a factual sufficiency review, an appellate court reviews the factfinder's weighing of the evidence and is authorized to disagree with the factfinder's determination. This review, however, must be appropriately deferential so as to

---

4. Art. V, §6 of the Texas Constitution provides in relevant part:

Said Courts of Appeals shall have appellate jurisdiction . . . under such restrictions and regulations as may be prescribed by law. Provided, that the decisions of said courts [courts of appeals] shall be conclusive on all questions of fact brought before them on appeal or error.

The last sentence above is referred to as the "factual conclusivity" clause. [This] clause is a limit on the jurisdiction of the Supreme Court and the Court of Criminal Appeals in discretionary matters.

7. Tex. Code Crim. Proc. Ann. art. 44.25 provides: "The courts of appeals or the Court of Criminal Appeals may reverse the judgment in a criminal action, as well upon the law as upon the facts."

12. [The following example illustrates] the distinction between legal and factual sufficiency: The prosecution's sole witness, a paid informant, testifies that he saw the defendant commit a crime. Twenty nuns testify that the defendant was with them at the time, far from the scene of the crime. Twenty more nuns testify that they saw the informant commit the crime. If the defendant is convicted, he has no remedy under *Jackson* because the informant's testimony, however incredible, is legally sufficient evidence.

avoid an appellate court's substituting its judgment for that of the jury. . . . If a reviewing court determines that the evidence is insufficient under the *Jackson* standard, it must render a judgment of acquittal. . . . However, when conducting a factual sufficiency review, an appellate court cannot substitute its judgment for that of the factfinder since this would violate the defendant's right to trial by jury. Accordingly, courts of appeals should vacate a conviction based on factually insufficient evidence and remand the cause for a new trial. . . .

Appellant urges us to hold that when the factual sufficiency of an element of the offense is challenged, courts of appeals should apply the Stone standard of review, articulated by the Third Court of Appeals. Stone v. State, 823 S.W.2d 375 (Tex. Ct. App. 1992). [The] *Stone* court observed that a factual sufficiency review begins with the presumption that the evidence supporting the jury's verdict was legally sufficient, that is, sufficient under the *Jackson* test. In conducting a factual sufficiency review, the court of appeals "views all the evidence without the prism of 'in the light most favorable to the prosecution' . . . and sets aside the verdict only if it is so contrary to the overwhelming weight of the evidence as to be clearly wrong and unjust." . . .

The Code of Criminal Procedure contains two provisions establishing that the jury is the judge of the facts. Tex. Code Crim. Proc. Ann. art. 36.13[17] & 38.04.[18] Notably, Chapter 36, "Trial Before the Jury," and Chapter 38, "Evidence in Criminal Actions," do not reference the appellate process, and no similar provision appears in the Rules of Appellate Procedure. The import of the provisions in the Code is, in part, to distinguish the role of the jury from the role of the judge at trial. [An interpretation of these statutes that precludes] any appellate review of the jury's determination of the facts and the weight to be given the evidence . . . conflicts with appellate courts' jurisdiction and obligation to review criminal convictions "as well upon the law as upon the facts." Tex. Code Crim. Proc. Ann. art. 44.25. The appropriate balance between the jury's role as the judge of the facts and the reviewing court's duty to review criminal convictions is struck by not allowing the appellate court to "find" facts, or substitute its judgment for that of the jury; rather, when it determines that the verdict is against the great weight of the evidence presented at trial so as to be clearly wrong and unjust, it must reverse the verdict and remand for a new trial.

[When] the courts of appeals exercise their fact jurisdiction, they [might] substitute their judgment for that of the jury. However, . . . sufficient safeguards can be imposed by this Court to guarantee that the mental processes of the scrivener are reflected in the opinion so that we may ascertain whether the process resulted in a usurpation of the jury function. [In the civil context, the reviewing court in its written opinion must] "detail the evidence relevant to the issue in consideration and clearly state why the jury's finding is factually insufficient . . . as to be manifestly unjust; why it shocks the conscience; or clearly demonstrates bias. . . ." Pool v. Ford Motor Co., 715 S.W.2d 629, 635 (Tex. 1986). [These] safeguards help ensure that the factfinder is given the appropriate deference and that the defendant's right to trial by jury remains inviolate.

---

17. "Unless otherwise provided in this Code, the jury is the exclusive judge of the facts, but it is bound to receive the law from the court and be governed thereby."

18. "The jury, in all cases, is the exclusive judge of the facts proved, and of the weight to be given to the testimony. . . ."

Neither the federal nor the Texas prohibition against double jeopardy, U.S. Const. amend. V; Tex. Const. art. I, §14, preclude defendants from seeking an acquittal through a new trial. As the United States Supreme Court held, the Double Jeopardy Clause does not prohibit a retrial if the reversal is based on factual insufficiency of the evidence. Tibbs v. Florida, 457 U.S. 31 (1982). However, retrial is prohibited where the reviewing court determines that the evidence is insufficient under *Jackson.* That is, as a practical matter, the State has only one opportunity to present evidence legally sufficient to convict a defendant. [We] hold that the Stone standard correctly imports the beyond-a-reasonable-doubt burden of proof and successfully adapts the factual sufficiency standard to the burden of proof at a criminal trial. . . .

MEYERS, J., concurring.
. . . Appellant is not contending . . . that there was no evidence to support the verdict (legal insufficiency) or that he was conclusively shown to be not guilty (innocence as a matter of law), either of which argument would present a legal, not a factual, question. [He] is not specifically contending that the evidence supporting conviction was insufficient in itself to prove his guilt. He is only claiming that the contrary evidence was so great that it overwhelmed the evidence of guilt. Under such circumstances, he argues, a guilty verdict is clearly wrong, manifestly unjust, or irrational.

This distinction between the contention that evidence is insufficient to prove a fact and the somewhat different contention that other evidence overwhelmingly disproves that fact is important in the present context because the kind of evidentiary review performed by appellate courts under the rubric established by the United States Supreme Court in Jackson v. Virginia, 443 U.S. 307 (1979), plainly does not contemplate that a reviewing court consider the probative weight of exculpatory evidence when evaluating the sufficiency of inculpatory evidence to sustain a criminal conviction. . . .

Whether it is a good idea for appellate courts to engage in this kind of factual review is a serious question, and one which has sparked intense debate from time to time in the Texas Supreme Court. That debate invariably focuses on the question whether such review effectively denies one or more of the litigants his constitutional right to a jury trial. But, it has been well-established in our civil jurisprudence for many years that the Texas courts of appeals do have the constitutional authority to perform such a review and to reverse judgments upon the facts either because the evidence was factually insufficient to support an affirmative factfinding or because the evidence militating against such factfinding was overwhelmingly greater. It is generally thought that such reversals do not violate the right to a jury trial so long as the appellate court does not render judgment for one of the parties, but rather the cause for another jury determination of the question. Thus, in such circumstances, the appellate court is said not to find facts, as a jury does, but merely to unfind them.

[Our] opinion today only validates a long-standing truth of Texas constitutional law, that the courts of appeals in this state have authority to require a new trial whenever a verdict of guilty is so clearly against the evidence as to be manifestly unjust. The public can be assured that the reversal of criminal convictions on this basis will be most uncommon in practice and that, with few exceptions, there will be no good reason to resent the ones that do occur.

That is why the dissenters' position in this case is so disappointing. Their main complaint seems to be that well-founded convictions will routinely be set aside by appellate judges who are more interested in coddling criminals than in seeing justice done. This attitude toward the courts of appeals is not only unjustified, but it is disrespectful as well. . . . Just because we acknowledge the authority of appellate courts to review jury verdicts on their facts does not mean, therefore, that those courts will perform factual evaluations in an unreasonable, insensitive, or unjust manner. Those who are inclined to be alarmed by our lead opinion should withhold judgment at least until they see how it actually works in practice. . . .

McCormick, P.J., dissenting.

What this case boils down to is whether in criminal cases the appellate courts can substitute their judgment for the jury's on questions of credibility and weight of the evidence. Because the majority does not leave these matters to be resolved at the local level by a jury, I dissent.

A civil "factual sufficiency" standard, which I assume the majority intends to adapt to the criminal side, requires the reviewing court to consider and weigh all the evidence; i.e., the reviewing court considers the evidence without the prism of "in the light most favorable to the verdict." See Pool v. Ford Motor Co., 715 S.W.2d 629 (Tex. 1986). The main difference between the Jackson v. Virginia standard and a "factual sufficiency" standard is the Jackson v. Virginia standard requires the reviewing court to defer to the jury on questions of credibility and weight of the evidence while the "factual sufficiency" standard allows the reviewing court to second-guess the jury on these questions. See Tibbs v. Florida, 457 U.S. 31 (1982) (when a reviewing court reverses the verdict based on the weight of the evidence, the reviewing court sits as a "thirteenth juror" and disagrees with the jury's resolution of conflicting testimony).

The issue here largely involves a question of statutory construction since the grant of appellate jurisdiction is subject to such exceptions and regulations as may be "prescribed by law." See Article V, Sections 5 & 6. The statutory scheme of things on the criminal side shows the Legislature undertook to insure a "factual sufficiency" standard would not be applicable in criminal cases.

The majority relies on Tex. Code Crim. Proc. Ann. Article 44.25, to support its conclusion the courts of appeals have the power to apply a "factual sufficiency" standard. However, the Legislature made significant changes to Article 44.25 in 1981 when the courts of appeals received criminal jurisdiction in noncapital direct appeal cases. The 1981 amendments modified Article 44.25 to its current form: "The courts of appeals or the Court of Criminal Appeals may reverse the judgment in a criminal action, as well upon the law as upon the facts." Prior to this, Article 44.25 and its statutory predecessors provided: "The Court of Criminal Appeals may reverse the judgment in a criminal action, as well upon the law as upon the facts. A cause reversed because the verdict is contrary to the evidence shall be remanded for a new trial." . . .

Therefore, any questions about this Court's and the courts of appeals' power to apply a "factual sufficiency" standard were resolved in 1981 when the Legislature deleted the . . . portions of Article 44.25 which allowed the remedy of a new trial when the verdict was contrary to the weight of the evidence. The legislative changes to Article 44.25 indicate a legislative intent to limit the power of this Court and the courts of appeals to reverse the judgment and remand the case for a new trial when they subjectively believe the verdict is contrary to the weight of the evidence. Any other construction would render the legislative changes to Article 44.25 meaningless. . . .

The majority apparently concludes the 1981 legislative changes to Article 44.25 were [passed simply in an effort to avoid a violation of double jeopardy. Under Burks v. United States, 437 U.S. 1 (1978), and Greene v. Massey, 437 U.S. 19 (1978), an acquittal is necessary when a reviewing court has determined the evidence to be "legally insufficient." However, in Tibbs v. Florida, 457 U.S. 31 (1982), the Supreme Court held that double jeopardy does not bar a retrial when an appellate court reverses a conviction because it was contrary to the weight of the evidence. Thus, the majority argues, the 1981 changes to the statute were a response to a perceived double jeopardy problem that no longer exists.]

More importantly, Article 38.04, Tex. Code Crim. Proc., also shows a legislative intent that a "factual sufficiency" standard is not applicable in criminal cases. Article 38.04, in relevant part, says the jury in all criminal cases "is the exclusive judge of the facts proved and of the weight to be given to the testimony." . . . The majority decides Article 38.04 does not apply to appellate review of sufficiency issues because Article 38.04 is meant "to distinguish the role of the jury from the role of the judge at trial." The majority's interpretation of Article 38.04 is contrary to its "plain language" and exceeds the scope of this Court's power by legislating an "exception" to Article 38.04. Also, it makes no sense to hold the trial judge, who has observed the witnesses testify and their demeanor, has no power to weigh the evidence, while the reviewing court has the power to weigh the evidence on a cold record. . . .

The majority also implicitly explains its holding is necessary to prevent an "unjust" conviction. However, the majority does not explain how this question is relevant to the issue before the Court or how a verdict that meets the Jackson v. Virginia standard can be considered "unjust."[7] Properly applied, the Jackson v. Virginia standard is about as exacting a standard as a "factual sufficiency" standard because both standards require the reviewing court to consider all the evidence. After a reviewing court determines the evidence is sufficient to support the verdict under the Jackson v. Virginia standard, it is practically impossible to say, under a proper application of a "factual sufficiency" standard, the verdict is so contrary to the overwhelming weight of the evidence as to be manifestly unjust. . . .

Law-abiding citizens, who are unconcerned with the legal niceties discussed in these pages, should understand the majority opinion increases the likelihood they will become a victim of violent crime because, according to the majority, this is the only protection a criminal defendant has from an "unjust" conviction. The majority opinion does not cite one instance of an "unjust conviction" under *Jackson*, and, in light of the foregoing discussion, a guilty verdict that meets the Jackson v. Virginia standard can never be considered an "unjust" conviction. The Jackson v. Virginia standard strikes a proper balance between granting defendants a fair evidentiary review of their convictions and protecting society from dangerous criminals. . . .

WHITE, J., dissenting.

Law-abiding Texans, hold on to your hats. We have another "run-away train" and it is again driven by a reckless, careless, and mischievous driver, Judge

---

7. The majority presents a hypothetical in footnote twelve of its opinion to illustrate an "unjust" conviction under the Jackson v. Virginia standard; i.e., the 40 nuns hypothetical. This hypothetical makes two assumptions neither of which [is] very practical. It assumes a prosecutor would choose to prosecute under that fact situation and a jury would actually convict under that fact situation. However, if such a conviction was ever had, the reviewing court in applying Jackson v. Virginia should not have too much trouble concluding that no rational trier of fact could have found beyond a reasonable doubt the essential elements of the offense. Therefore, the 40 nuns hypothetical would not result in an "unjust" conviction under Jackson v. Virginia.

Maloney. . . . The majority has not provided this Court with a sufficient reason to abandon Jackson v. Virginia's standard for reviewing evidentiary sufficiency as the sole standard for reviewing sufficiency of the evidence and, instead, add the civil standard for reviewing factual sufficiency of the evidence to the review of the appeals in criminal cases.

This holding by the majority represents more than a decision to usurp the role of the jury in our criminal courts; it is no less than a breach of faith by a majority of this Court by which it has abrogated its traditional duty of respecting the abilities of the juries and trial courts of this State to fulfill their responsibility to evaluate and assess the weight and credibility of the evidence presented to them. [There] are mechanisms within place in our criminal justice system which already serve more than adequately to correct manifestly unjust verdicts. [A] defendant can pursue relief from an unjust verdict under the authority of Tex. Code Crim. Proc. art. 11.07. [This provision, dealing with post-conviction challenges to the validity of a conviction,] provides an avenue for relief for a defendant who is asserting a claim of factual innocence. . . . A defendant can also pursue relief through the executive clemency process. . . . Lastly, if a defendant is able to show that the verdict rendered against him at trial is so contrary to the overwhelming weight of the evidence as to be clearly wrong and unjust, then he or she would be eligible to pursue federal habeas relief. . . .

Problem 10-1. Wrong Place, Wrong Time?

An undercover police officer approached an apartment on Sixth Avenue in Saginaw, Michigan, at about 8:30 p.m. on a December evening. He asked a man inside the apartment for a "$10 rock" of crack cocaine and passed two marked $5 bills through an open window. He heard some conversation inside the apartment, then received a small plastic bag containing crack cocaine. Within two hours, the undercover officer returned with a search warrant and several other officers. They found four men inside the apartment: Lemiel Wolfe, Darren Rogers, Alan Wise, and Leonard James.

When the officers entered the apartment, all four of the men in the apartment ran to the back bedroom. The officers found a loaded twelve-gauge shotgun on the floor in the front room. When the police officers entered the back bedroom of the apartment they saw Wise standing over an open vent in the floor, with the grate removed. The officers recovered 27 plastic baggies of crack cocaine from the vent, amounting to less than 50 grams of cocaine. They found no glass pipes or other paraphernalia typically used to smoke cocaine. It appeared to the officers that no one was living in the apartment. The front room contained only a couch, a refrigerator, and a broken television set. The apartment had no running water and the toilet was not in working condition. The bath tub was being used as a toilet.

The officers arrested and searched all four of the men in the apartment. Wolfe was holding $265 in cash, including the two marked $5 bills. In addition, he had a beeper and a key to the back door of the apartment. The search of Rogers revealed a piece of paper with the number of Wolfe's beeper written on it and a shotgun shell of the same type as the shotgun they found in the front room.

The government charged Wolfe and Rogers with possession with intent to deliver less than 50 grams of cocaine, and possession of a firearm during the commission of a felony. Police officers testified at trial to establish the events as described above.

Wolfe testified at trial that he went to Saginaw to visit a friend. He arrived around 6:00 p.m. that evening and went to the Sixth Avenue apartments to visit Sharon Johnson, whose relatives lived in the apartment next to the apartment where the arrest took place. Wolfe visited with her for about five minutes.

Wolfe said that he had invited several friends from Detroit (Rogers, James, and Wise) to visit Johnson. Around 8:00 p.m., he saw his Detroit friends approaching on the street outside the apartments, and he called out to them from the front porch because they were not familiar with the location. Wolfe testified that he left after a few minutes to visit another friend's house. When he returned to Sixth Avenue around 10:00 p.m., Wolfe spoke briefly with the next-door residents, then joined his friends for a party. He went to the local store for food and beer, after collecting money from the others. When Wolfe returned from the store, Leonard James repaid a prior $20 debt with four $5 bills, two of which were the marked bills that James had received earlier that night from the undercover police officer. As the group sat and watched television, Wolfe saw James smoking cocaine, but testified that he saw no other drugs in the apartment. Shortly after his return from the convenience store, the police raided the apartment and arrested Wolfe, along with several others.

Rogers testified as follows:

Q. Wolfe testified that it was about eight o'clock when he saw you. Is he correct?
A. I don't really know what time it was, but when we got there, it was about six when we saw him standing outside. . . .
Q. And how long after Wolfe came back up did he stay upstairs with you?
A. A good little while.
Q. How long is a "good little while"?
A. I'd say an hour, two hours.

Rogers also testified that Leonard James gave Wolfe the marked $5 bills before Wolfe left the Sixth Avenue apartment to visit his other friend.

Wolfe and Rogers were both convicted on both counts; Wolfe appealed. He argues that the government's evidence did not support either of the two charges, because the evidence did not prove that he possessed the cocaine with intent to distribute it, nor did it prove that he possessed a firearm. Under the case law of Michigan, the government can establish possession of cocaine by showing that the defendant physically possessed the cocaine, or that the defendant "had the right to exercise control of the cocaine and knew that it was present." A person's presence, by itself, at a location where drugs are found is insufficient to prove possession. Just as proof of actual possession of narcotics is not necessary to prove possession, actual delivery of narcotics is not required to prove intent to deliver. Intent to deliver has been inferred from the quantity of narcotics in a defendant's possession, from the way in which those narcotics are packaged, and from other circumstances surrounding the arrest.

How would you rule on appeal? Was the evidence sufficient to sustain one or both of the convictions? Was either of the convictions contrary to the weight of the evidence? Would you reach the same outcomes if the police had not found any key on Wolfe when they searched him? Compare People v. Wolfe, 489 N.W.2d 748 (Mich. 1992).

Notes

1. *Sufficiency of the evidence and weight of the evidence.* The federal due process clause, as we have seen, requires a minimum level of evidentiary support for a conviction. Prior to Jackson v. Virginia, 443 U.S. 307 (1979), appellate courts could affirm a conviction so long as there was "some evidence" to support the judgment. In *Jackson,* the Supreme Court decided that a federal court, when reviewing a state court conviction during postconviction habeas corpus proceedings, must confirm that there was sufficient evidence to support a "reasonable trier of fact" in concluding that the government had proven guilt beyond a reasonable doubt. Does this due process standard for the "sufficiency" of the evidence require the appellate court to consider the inculpatory evidence alone, or to consider it in light of the exculpatory evidence?

Texas is not the only state to create an additional form of appellate review for factual findings. The "weight of the evidence" inquiry was more common years ago than it is today, but some states still grant their appellate courts this authority. Is it necessary, now that the *Jackson* test has replaced the "some evidence" test? Why did the choice among types of appellate factual review generate such strong feelings in the *Clewis* case? Whose right to a jury was at stake?

2. *Evidentiary review and double jeopardy.* The precise type of factual review that an appellate court uses can have double jeopardy consequences. According to Tibbs v. Florida, 457 U.S. 31 (1982), a retrial is possible after an appellate court reverses a conviction because it is contrary to the "weight of the evidence." The prosecution, in such a case, has met the constitutional minimum burden of proof during the first trial, and the defendant's appeal therefore does not bar a second trial. If the prosecution fails to present evidence sufficient to meet the *Jackson* standard in the first trial, it will not receive a second chance. Given this more favorable outcome for the state under the double jeopardy clause, should prosecutors generally favor giving to appellate courts the option of a "weight of the evidence" review?

3. *Videotape and retrial after reversal.* Suppose all the testimony in a trial were presented to the jury in videotaped format:

> [The] case would initially be tried as if the jury has been waived. The prosecution and defense would present their cases in open court with the defendant present, but without a jury. All of the proceedings would be taped. At the conclusion of the case, questions leading to sustained objections would be deleted from a copy of the tape as would any statements ruled improper in opening or closing arguments. Testimony could even be taken out of order to meet the convenience of witnesses or attorneys and edited into the tape at the correct place. Sidebars and time intensive nontestimonial activities such as legal arguments and the marking of exhibits would also be eliminated from the final tape. [A jury is impaneled] only at the end of the process to watch the taped trial and deliberate on the verdict.

Ronald Goldstock & James B. Jacobs, A Blockbuster Trial: Catch It All on Tape, Crim. Just. (Spring 1998). How might this innovation at the trial level change practices in the appellate courts? Would appellate judges, after viewing the tapes for themselves, become more willing to question factual findings? Would they become more willing to find reversible error, knowing that an error-free retrial becomes cheaper if the tape is corrected and shown to a new jury?

C. HARMLESS ERROR

"For every wrong there should be a remedy." This notion entered U.S. legal culture through the words of William Blackstone, conveyed by Chief Justice John Marshall. Marbury v. Madison, 5 U.S. (1 Cranch) 137, 163 (1803) ("it is a settled and invariable principle . . . that every right, when withheld, must have a remedy, and every injury its proper redress") (quoting 3 William Blackstone, Commentaries *109). Indeed, this principle has crystallized in many state constitutions, which include language such as Illinois Constitution article I, section 12: "Every person shall find a certain remedy in the laws for all injuries and wrongs which he receives to his person, privacy, property or reputation. He shall obtain justice by law, freely, completely, and promptly." Surely if this principle applies anywhere, it should apply to the operation of the justice system itself. If a defendant's rights are violated during trial on criminal charges, the error should be correctable on appeal.

Yet criminal trials are complex events, and few long trials occur without some error. If the remedy for every error at trial were a new trial, no major trial would ever end. But in cases where the proof is overwhelming, won't the outcome at the retrial be inevitable? Even for substantial errors, if the outcome is inevitable, why drag witnesses, jurors, and judges through a mere charade? Indeed, can there ever be reversible error in obvious cases?

The doctrine of harmless error aims to sort out the tension between a desire to be fair to a wronged defendant and the need to have an efficient system that focuses on errors that may have produced a wrong outcome. If stated too broadly, harmless error rules have the capacity to undermine whatever other procedural rules the system has created.

The U.S. Supreme Court took up this challenge in Fahy v. Connecticut, 375 U.S. 85 (1963), where the defendant was charged with willfully injuring a public building by painting swastikas on a synagogue. The Court found that the erroneous admission of an illegally seized can of paint and paintbrush was not harmless because there was "a reasonable possibility that the evidence complained of might have contributed to the conviction."

In Chapman v. California, 386 U.S. 18 (1967), the Court squarely addressed the issue of whether constitutional errors can be considered harmless. Ruth Chapman and Thomas Teale were convicted in a California state court upon a charge that they robbed, kidnapped, and murdered a bartender. At the trial, the prosecutor commented extensively on the decision by both defendants to remain silent; these comments were in keeping with a provision of the California constitution, which stated that a defendant's "failure to explain or to deny by his testimony any evidence or facts in the case against him may be commented upon by the court and by counsel." The U.S. Supreme Court struck down the California provision in Griffin v. California, 380 U.S. 609 (1965). In concluding that the denial of the federal rights recognized in *Griffin* amounted to harmless error in Chapman's case, the Court wrote:

> In fashioning a harmless-constitutional-error rule, we must recognize that harmless-error rules can work very unfair and mischievous results when, for example, highly important and persuasive evidence, or argument, though legally forbidden, finds its way into a trial in which the question of guilt or innocence is a close one. What harmless-error rules all aim at is a rule that will save the good in harmless-error practices while avoiding the bad, so far as possible.

[We] do no more than adhere to the meaning of our *Fahy* case when we hold, as we now do, that before a federal constitutional error can be held harmless, the court must be able to declare a belief that it was harmless beyond a reasonable doubt. While appellate courts do not ordinarily have the original task of applying such a test, it is a familiar standard to all courts, and we believe its adoption will provide a more workable standard, although achieving the same result as that aimed at in our *Fahy* case. [386 U.S. at 22-24.]

While allowing harmless error analysis to apply to some constitutional errors, the *Chapman* Court recognized that other constitutional errors are "so basic to a fair trial that their violation can never be treated as harmless error," and cited Gideon v. Wainwright, 372 U.S. 335 (1963) (right to counsel); Payne v. Arkansas, 356 U.S. 560 (1958) (coerced confession); and Tumey v. Ohio, 273 U.S. 510 (1927) (impartial judge).

In Arizona v. Fulminante, 499 U.S. 279 (1991), the Court reconsidered whether a coerced confession was one of the errors "so basic to a fair trial" that harmless error analysis could not apply. *Fulminante* created a new conceptual divide between "trial errors," which are subject to harmless error analysis, and "structural defects," which are not.

The admission of an involuntary confession—a classic "trial error"—is markedly different from the other two constitutional violations referred to in the *Chapman* footnote as not being subject to harmless-error analysis. One of those violations, involved in Gideon v. Wainwright, was the total deprivation of the right to counsel at trial. The other violation, involved in Tumey v. Ohio, was a judge who was not impartial. These are structural defects in the constitution of the trial mechanism, which defy analysis by "harmless-error" standards. The entire conduct of the trial from beginning to end is obviously affected by the absence of counsel for a criminal defendant, just as it is by the presence on the bench of a judge who is not impartial. Since our decision in *Chapman,* other cases have added to the category of constitutional errors which are not subject to harmless error the following: unlawful exclusion of members of the defendant's race from a grand jury, see Vasquez v. Hillery, 474 U.S. 254 (1986); the right to self-representation at trial, see McKaskle v. Wiggins, 465 U.S. 168 (1984); and the right to public trial, see Waller v. Georgia, 467 U.S. 39 (1993). Each of these constitutional deprivations is a similar structural defect affecting the framework within which the trial proceeds, rather than simply an error in the trial process itself. Without these basic protections, a criminal trial cannot reliably serve its function as a vehicle for determination of guilt or innocence, and no criminal punishment may be regarded as fundamentally fair.

It is evident from a comparison of the constitutional violations which we have held subject to harmless error, and those which we have held not, that involuntary statements or confessions belong in the former category. The admission of an involuntary confession is a "trial error," similar in both degree and kind to the erroneous admission of other types of evidence. . . . When reviewing the erroneous admission of an involuntary confession, the appellate court, as it does with the admission of other forms of improperly admitted evidence, simply reviews the remainder of the evidence against the defendant to determine whether the admission of the confession was harmless beyond a reasonable doubt.

Another example of a "structural error" is the right to a jury verdict of guilt beyond a reasonable doubt, based on a proper instruction to the jury about the meaning of reasonable doubt. See Sullivan v. Louisiana, 508 U.S. 275 (1993). A typical example of a "trial error" that can be ignored if "harmless" is the improper admission of "other crimes" evidence at trial. See State v. Johnson, 664 So. 2d 94 (La. 1995).

States have wrestled with their own harmless error standards, which apply to any errors based in state law. Some apply a unitary rule for constitutional and nonconstitutional errors, while others apply a different standard — usually one that makes it harder to find reversible error — for nonconstitutional errors. Most states have procedural rules that limit reversible error to those errors that affect the outcome or the "substantial rights" of the defendant. The case law on harmless error is often difficult to harmonize even within individual states. Courts still differ on some of the most fundamental questions about this doctrine, such as the burden of proof for establishing the harmlessness of the error.

Harmless error analysis now applies to most kinds of error at trial, but that is only the start of the analysis. In each case courts must also assess whether the error subject to analysis was in fact "harmless." The Supreme Court elaborated on the precise question to ask in the harmless error analysis in Sullivan v. Louisiana, 508 U.S. 275 (1993). The *Sullivan* inquiry "is not whether, in a trial that occurred without the error, a guilty verdict would surely have been rendered, but whether the guilty verdict actually rendered in this trial was surely unattributable to the error."

Few cases in state or federal court spend much time analyzing the legal standard for harmless error, yet the courts apply the doctrine in a huge number of cases. In the end, the rules do not give much guidance. Harmless error analysis is often applied in a single paragraph at the end of opinions, without detailed explanation of the facts. Does harmless error doctrine quietly overwhelm all the meaningful procedural choices made earlier in the case?

■ FEDERAL RULE OF CRIMINAL PROCEDURE 52(a) HARMLESS ERROR

Any error, defect, irregularity, or variance that does not affect substantial rights must be disregarded.(b) Plain Error. A plain error that affects substantial rights may be considered even though it was not brought to the court's attention.

■ TENNESSEE CRIMINAL PROCEDURE RULE 52(a) HARMLESS ERROR

No judgment of conviction shall be reversed on appeal except for errors which affirmatively appear to have affected the result of the trial on the merits.(b) Plain Error. An error which has affected the substantial rights of an accused may be noticed at any time, even though not raised in the motion for a new trial or assigned as error on appeal, in the discretion of the appellate court where necessary to do substantial justice.

■ PEOPLE v. WALTER BUDZYN
566 N.W.2d 229 (Mich. 1997)

RILEY, J.

In this appeal, we are asked to review the fairness of the trial for two police officers who were convicted of second-degree murder for killing a suspected drug user while attempting to arrest him while the suspect was holding contraband. We conclude that defendants have demonstrated that their juries were exposed to extrinsic influences that created a real and substantial possibility of prejudice, depriving them of their constitutional rights under the Sixth Amendment. These errors, however, were harmless beyond a reasonable doubt with regard to defendant Larry Nevers. Therefore, we affirm defendant Nevers' conviction. With regard to defendant Walter Budzyn, we conclude that the extrinsic influences were not harmless beyond a reasonable doubt. Accordingly, we vacate defendant Budzyn's conviction and remand for a new trial.

Defendants Budzyn and Nevers were police officers with the Detroit Police Department. They were on duty when the incident occurred that resulted in Malice Green's death. Both were tried at a single criminal proceeding with two different juries.[1]

On November 5, 1992, at approximately 10:15 p.m., defendants were patrolling in the City of Detroit in plain clothes in an unmarked vehicle. They apparently observed a Topaz, driven by Malice Green, with bullet holes in its front passenger door. Defendant Nevers, who only gave testimony before his own jury, testified that he observed the car pull up in front of a house known for its drug activity. Budzyn and Nevers stopped behind the Topaz to investigate. The home, with a storefront attached to it, was occupied by Ralph Fletcher. . . . Robert Hollins and Teresa Pace, witnesses to the event, were present at Fletcher's house and had been smoking cocaine that evening.

Defendant Budzyn, who only testified before his own jury, said that he witnessed Robert Knox running along the building and explained that he chased Knox because, apparently by mistake, he believed that Knox had been in the vehicle with Green. Budzyn caught Knox, brought him around to the front of Fletcher's place, and patted him down for weapons. He also patted down Fletcher, who had been in the car with Green. Manuel Brown, who had been smoking cocaine at Fletcher's place, was walking away from the house, but stopped to watch this activity. Nevers asked Malice Green for his driver's license. Green did not respond to Nevers' request, but walked around to the passenger side of his vehicle and got in. Green was sitting in the passenger seat, with his legs hanging out the open doorway. Budzyn came around to the passenger side, shined his flashlight on him, and asked for his license. Green began to look in the glove compartment, grasped at something that was on the floor, apparently cocaine, and Budzyn asked him to let go of what was in his hand.

At this point, there is substantial disagreement in the testimony given by defendants Budzyn and Nevers and the witnesses to the incident, Brown, Fletcher, Hollins, Knox, and Pace regarding what happened.

---

1. There were charges that their crime was racially motivated. Consequently, we note that Budzyn and Nevers are white and Malice Green is black.

The five civilian witnesses testified that after Green refused to open his hand, Budzyn began to hit him repeatedly on the hand with the police flashlight, telling him to open his hand. Budzyn then climbed onto Green, who did not resist but did not comply, straddling him. Brown testified that Budzyn struck Green about ten times on his head with the flashlight. Fletcher, who was only three to five feet away, testified that Budzyn repeatedly hit Green on the hand. Hollins said that he heard Budzyn hit Green six or seven times, and, although he did not see the blows land, that these blows must have landed on Green's head. Knox said that he saw Budzyn hit Green in the hand because Green did not open it when Budzyn asked. Pace testified that from the position on which Budzyn sat on Green, he must have been hitting him on the head.

These five witnesses also said that, while Budzyn was struggling with Green in the Topaz, Nevers struck Green on his knee several times. Brown and Fletcher said that Nevers then went around to the other side of the car, the driver's side, opened the door, and struck Green, who was now lying on the front seat, on the head with his flashlight. Nevers instructed these people to leave the scene.

In contrast to this testimony, Budzyn explained to his jury that while Green was sitting in the passenger side of the vehicle, he suspected that Green was holding narcotics in his fist. He said that he grabbed Green's right arm and that Green kicked him with both his legs. He produced evidence of a small injury to his knee. Budzyn said that he turned and fell backward into the vehicle, dropping his flashlight. Budzyn denied that he ever hit Green at all. Budzyn also said that he only held Green's hands because he suspected that he was holding narcotics. Budzyn called for backup assistance. Budzyn explained that he heard "two hits" after Nevers went around to the driver's door and said that he later was "shocked" to find so much blood on the scene. Budzyn said he retrieved four rocks of cocaine from inside the vehicle.

Like Budzyn, Nevers testified to his jury that he assisted Budzyn when Green resisted Budzyn's efforts to open his hand. Nevers explained that he only hit Green on his knees when Green brought his knees up to stop Nevers from prying open his hand. Nevers then went to the other side of the vehicle because Budzyn told him that Green was attempting to get out of the other side of the car. Nevers then told the people from Fletcher's place to leave. Nevers explained that he hit Green in the head with his flashlight because Green was grabbing for his gun. Nevers said that after he struck him, "[Green] finally let go of my gun and I did not hit him [again]" at that time. Nevers flagged down the EMS medical technicians who had been called to the scene. Green continued to struggle with the officers and Nevers said he saw something "shiny" in Green's right hand and he struck him again, the blow landing on Green's head, because Nevers feared he might be carrying a razor blade or knife. Nevers admitted that, during the course of the incident he hit Green five or six times on the head with his flashlight.

The EMS medical technicians arrived in two vehicles. The first to arrive were Albino Martinez and Mithyim Lewis. The other EMS vehicle soon arrived with two other medical technicians, Lee Hardy and Scott Walsh. Several marked police cars arrived soon after the EMS vehicles. Martinez, Lewis, Hardy, and Walsh all testified that Green was covered with blood and was hanging from the driver's side door when they arrived. There was a pool of blood under his head on the street. These witnesses said that Nevers struck Green in the head with his heavy police flashlight repeatedly even though Green was not offering any significant resistance. Martinez and Walsh said that Nevers told Green to open his hands and hold still, and that, when he did not, Nevers hit him with the flashlight. Martinez and Lewis said that Nevers hit Green four times in the head with the flashlight, while Hardy said he saw Nevers hit Green approximately ten times in the head. Martinez explained that Green was "dazed," and Hardy described him as "stuporous," relating that Green was uttering only a few words like "wait" while Nevers was striking him.

Officer Robert Lessnau, who arrived on the scene in one of the marked police vehicles, pulled Green from the vehicle. The EMS medical technicians testified that Lessnau hit Green with his fists. Martinez and Walsh said that while Lessnau was striking Green, Nevers also hit Green twice in the ribs. Green finally released the car keys he held in one hand and a piece of white paper, apparently for rolling rock cocaine, he held in the other. The uniformed officers, including Sergeant Freddie Douglas, then cuffed Green's hands behind his back as Green struggled. The EMS medical technicians began rendering care to Green. Green suffered a seizure and, soon after, died.

The people presented Dr. Kalil Jiraki, an assistant Wayne County Medical Examiner, as a medical expert to testify regarding the nature of Green's wounds and the cause of his death. Dr. Jiraki testified that Green died from "[b]lunt force trauma to [his] head" and that he suffered at least fourteen blows to the head. Dr. Jiraki also explained that Green had 0.5 micrograms of cocaine in his body, indicating that he was under the influence of cocaine at the time of his death. He concluded, however, that it had "no bearing on the cause of his death." In response, defendants presented three pathologists, one of whom, Dr. L. G. Dragovic, testified that he identified eleven blunt-force injuries to Green's head.

Budzyn and Nevers were charged with second-degree murder. Beginning with the first reports of Green's death, the case produced a firestorm of media publicity in the Detroit metropolitan area. The incident occurred soon after the California state courts acquitted four white Los Angeles police officers who had been videotaped beating black motorist Rodney King. The acquittal in the King case resulted in a terrible riot in Los Angeles that drew the attention of the national media. The media reports in Detroit of Green's death included a comparison of the two incidents. Before the trial began, the Detroit Police Department fired defendants. The City of Detroit also agreed to a multimillion dollar settlement with Green's estate. In response to some criticisms of the settlement, a city attorney stated that a generous settlement might spare the city the riotous violence that racked Los Angeles after the acquittal of the police officers. These events occurred during the interval between Green's death in November 1992 and the start of defendants' trial in June 1993, seven months later.

Defendants moved to sever the trials, and the trial court refused to separate the proceedings, but did grant defendants separate juries. Nevers asked for a change of venue because of the extensive pretrial publicity, but the trial court denied this motion. The trial court began the voir dire on June 2, 1993. The people began presenting their case on June 18, 1993. During a recess near the end of trial, on August 5 and 6, 1993, the trial court provided the juries with several film videos to watch to entertain themselves, including a copy of *Malcolm X*. The film begins with a video of the Los Angeles police officers beating Rodney King. Defendants moved for a mistrial on this basis, but this motion was denied.[7]

---

7. The trial judge did not select the movies or approve the selections himself, but he took responsibility for the action taken by the employees of the court. The trial judge disqualified himself on ruling on defendants' motion. The Chief Judge of Recorder's Court referred the motion to a third judge who heard the motion and denied it.

After approximately seven weeks of trial, the juries began deliberating on August 13, 1993. Budzyn and Nevers were convicted of second-degree murder. The jury in Budzyn's trial deliberated for eight days, and, in Nevers' trial, the jury deliberated for nine days. . . .

[The supreme court held that defendants had been denied their right to a fair and impartial jury because they considered extraneous facts not introduced into evidence. It was undisputed that the jurors watched the film *Malcolm X*; it was also alleged that jurors were made aware of city plans to handle riots after the verdict and that defendants had been involved in a special police anti-drug unit. The film begins with the voice of *Malcolm X*'s character giving a provocative speech charging "the white man with being the greatest murderer on earth" while the viewer is shown footage of Rodney King being beaten by Los Angeles police officers, interspersed with a picture of an American flag. The Rodney King videotape is shown in slow motion, in eight segments, as the American flag begins to burn. The voiceover makes an explicit reference to Detroit, the location of the incident in the instant case, by stating that the black community has been deprived of democracy in the "streets of Detroit." At another point in the film Malcolm X confronts the police, who finally relent and allow him to call an ambulance and take a bleeding man from the police station to the hospital; Malcolm X says "A hundred years ago, they used to put on white sheets and sic bloodhounds on us. Well, nowadays they've traded in the sheets — well, some of them traded in sheets — . . . they have traded in those white sheets for police uniforms. They've traded in the bloodhounds for the police dogs. . . . You've got these Uncle Tom Negro leaders today that are telling us we ought to pray for our enemy. We ought to love our enemy. We ought to integrate with an enemy who bombs us, who kills and shoots us, who lynches us, who rapes our women and children. No!"]

[W]e must decide whether any error was harmless beyond a reasonable doubt. There is no dispute that the extrinsic evidence was not duplicative of other properly admitted evidence for either defendant. Hence, we must determine whether the evidence against defendants was overwhelming. We believe that these extraneous influences were harmless for defendant Nevers in light of the overwhelming evidence of his guilt, but that the errors do require reversal for defendant Budzyn because the evidence against him was not overwhelming.

In the Nevers trial, the four EMS witnesses, who had no apparent motive to lie, provided interlocking testimony that Nevers repeatedly bludgeoned Malice Green in the head with his heavy police flashlight while Green was dazed and not offering significant resistance. The medical testimony of the injuries to Green's head also substantiated this testimony. The people have proven that there was unimpeachable, compelling evidence that defendant Nevers harbored, at the very least, an unjustified intent to commit great bodily harm against Green. Thus, . . . the extraneous influences were harmless. . . . In Budzyn's trial, however, we believe that the evidence against defendant Budzyn, particularly considering he was convicted of second-degree murder, was not overwhelming. The evidence against him was fundamentally weaker than the evidence against Nevers for three reasons.

First, of the three civilian witnesses who testified that defendant Budzyn hit Green in the head with his flashlight (Manuel Brown, Robert Hollins, and Teresa Pace), none was able to see the flashlight actually make contact with Green's head. Unlike the EMS witnesses, they did not have a direct view of the blows. Instead, the three witnesses each inferred the fact that the flashlight hit Green in the head from the positions of the two men in the vehicle and from Budzyn's use of the flashlight to strike Green. Brown, who arguably gave the most damaging testimony of any witness, was the farthest witness away, standing fifteen feet from Fletcher, Hollins, Knox, and Pace.

This testimony also contained some inconsistencies. The three key witnesses who testified that Budzyn hit Green on the head with his flashlight gave conflicting testimony on the nature of the blows that Budzyn administered: Pace and Hollins testified that Budzyn lifted the flashlight above his head or shoulders and brought the flashlight down, while Brown insisted that the blows were horizontal, across his body, and that Budzyn did not lift the flashlight above his head. Also, Fletcher, who was only three to five feet away and was the closest of the witnesses to the incident, testified that Budzyn hit Green's clenched fist with the flashlight, but that he did not see Budzyn hit Green anywhere else on his body.

Second, the civilian witnesses admitted that the altercation occurred after Green refused Budzyn's request that he turn over the incriminating evidence he held in his hand. The civilian witnesses all agreed that Green never complied and that he struggled with Budzyn, although they said he never struck him or kicked him. In fact, Fletcher testified that during the entire episode, Budzyn held onto Green's closed fist, attempting to retrieve the contraband. This is a very different setting from the description the EMS medical technicians gave of the situation in which defendant Nevers was striking Green in the head. Because the exchange occurred in the confined context of the car with the car obscuring the witnesses' view, their testimony that Green did not kick Budzyn does not directly rebut his claim that Green did. The medical evidence also does not necessarily contradict Budzyn's claims, because Nevers hit Green with significant force in the head and these blows may have been the cause of Green's extensive head injuries.

Third, in this credibility contest between Budzyn and these witnesses, the civilian witnesses all had either consumed alcohol or cocaine sometime before witnessing the exchange, three of them were friends with Green (Fletcher, Hollins, and Pace), and there was some suggestion from their testimony that they had reason to dislike these officers. This fact is relevant because an inquiry into whether an error was harmless requires a focus on the nature of the error in light of the weight and strength of the other evidence. People v. Mateo, 551 N.W.2d 891 (Mich. 1996). Defendant Budzyn had searched Fletcher and Knox for weapons before defendant Nevers asked to see Malice Green's driver's license. Defendant Budzyn had also broken into Fletcher's home while Fletcher and Hollins among others were there, a week and a half before this incident, searching the house without warrant, and, on another occasion, had arrested two people outside the house. Thus, these witnesses were not in the same objective position as the EMS medical technicians, who, incidentally, did not offer any testimony regarding Budzyn's actions against Green because they had not yet arrived on the scene.

Even if the jury reasonably believed the testimony of the civilian witnesses, they still might not have concluded that Budzyn was guilty of second-degree murder. The question whether Budzyn's unnecessary use of force as described by the civilian witnesses would be second-degree murder or manslaughter is an issue for the jury. We do not believe that the only, possible reasonable conclusion to draw from this evidence is that it established beyond a reasonable doubt that he harbored an intent to kill, an intent to do great bodily harm, or to commit an act in wanton and wilful disregard that the likelihood that the natural tendency of his conduct was to cause death or great bodily harm. In contrast, the testimony from the EMS medical technicians against Nevers made the conclusion inescapable that he was guilty of second-degree murder. We cannot say that the extraneous factors may not have affected the Budzyn jury's verdict. We, therefore, reverse his conviction and remand for a new trial. . . .

BOYLE, J., concurring in part and dissenting in part.

I agree with the majority's result and rationale with regard to defendant Nevers, and its result in respect to defendant Budzyn. I write separately to explain my disagreement with certain aspects of the rationale in Budzyn.

First, despite differences of origin, history, class, education, race, ethnicity, sex, economic status, or educational level, it is a fundamental presumption of the judicial system that all Americans are equally capable of fairly discharging their public responsibilities. Batson v. Kentucky, 476 U.S. 79 (1986). Therefore, I disagree with the analysis of the opinions of both Chief Justice Mallett and Justice Riley regarding the showing of the movie, *Malcolm X*, to the extent that each employs assumptions about the predispositions of jurors. The system addresses the mind-set of jurors through voir dire, challenges for cause, and motions for change of venue, all of which require a demonstration of reasons why a prospective juror or a given community may be suspect. The approach is both aspirational and pragmatic. The judiciary has no competence to assess the cultural or psychological mind-set of a given jury and assess its reactions in light of its own assumptions. I also agree with the prosecution that the movie was not an extraneous communication, and find no error in this regard. . . .

However, I agree with the majority that the communication of incorrect information to the jurors during deliberations that defendant Budzyn was a member of STRESS [the special police anti-drug unit] was error requiring reversal. . . . Evaluated in the context of the evidence as a whole, the prejudicial significance is that Budzyn's membership in STRESS indicated a propensity for abuse of young black males. By all accounts, Green had what turned out to be cocaine in his hands and refused to surrender it. Thus, Budzyn's initiation of force against Green was lawful, whichever version of the testimony is believed. The issue in Nevers' trial turned on whether the jury believed Nevers' testimony that the deceased was trying to take his gun, thus justifying the life-threatening response. The issue in Budzyn's trial, by contrast, was whether, and at what point, the lawful use of force became unreasonable.

In substance, the jurors were told that Budzyn was a bad actor with a propensity for violence against young black men. Coupled with other evidence admitted at trial, this information could have persuaded the jurors that Budzyn had a man-endangering state of mind. Thus, it is not only the fact, as the majority observes, that this evidence was relevant to besmirching the defendant's character, but the fact that this information supported the prosecution's theory that defendant was guilty of second-degree murder, that is prejudicial.

Our responsibility is not to decide what we would have done or what we think the jury should have done. It is to hypothesize what the jury would have done had it not been exposed to the extrinsic information. Because there was substantial and real prejudice, I cannot conclude that the error was harmless beyond a reasonable doubt. I join in the opinion for reversal of defendant Budzyn's conviction of second-degree murder. I would affirm the conviction of defendant Nevers.

MALLETT, C.J., concurring in part and dissenting in part.

. . . The issues of greatest concern to both the majority and to myself relate to whether defendants were denied their right to a fair trial as a result of exposure to certain extraneous influences. In particular, I am most concerned with the jurors' exposure to the movie *Malcolm X* and to media accounts of contingency plans of suburban law enforcement in case of a riot. . . . Extensive media coverage continued through the trial, including reports speculating on contingency plans in place in the event of postverdict rioting. Jurors on both Budzyn's and Nevers' panels were exposed to portions of these reports.

[B]eyond showing exposure to an extraneous influence, the defendants. . . . must make a showing of prejudice reverberating from the extraneous information. The test for determining whether the threshold level of prejudice is met is whether defendants have established a real and substantial possibility that the extraneous matter could have affected the verdict.

The first factor in this threshold inquiry is the nature and source of the extraneous material. The defendants focus their claim of prejudice resulting from the showing of *Malcolm X* on the opening footage of the movie. In an attempt to make his movie more provocative, producer-director Spike Lee presents opening footage of the beating of motorist Rodney King by Los Angeles police officers against the backdrop of a burning American flag. Along with these images, the viewer hears words from a speech by Malcolm X. Virtually every person in America had been exposed to the footage detailing the brutal beating given Mr. King by members of the Los Angeles Police Department. While it was unfortunate that the jurors were perhaps once again confronted with this footage, is it the defendants' position that the jurors became inflamed and were engulfed by emotion and thus rendered incapable of rendering a fair verdict? The possibility that a few police officers will absolutely violate department rules and procedures is never far from the minds of African-Americans, no matter their station in life. The presence of racism in any community can, and sometimes does, cause American citizens to react emotionally and render less than clear judgment. But there is no reasonable probability that the Rodney King footage affected the jurors in this case.

Racism has not and will not quell the desire of African-Americans to fully exercise all the rights and responsibilities associated with democracy. If this were not true, then the four-hundred-year-old struggle for freedom and economic opportunity would have been abandoned long ago. The defendants have not established that the picture of one black man being beaten by police officers could reasonably have prevented the jurors from rendering a fair verdict.

The words of Malcolm X in the opening sequence are indeed provocative.[12] But when these words are taken in the context of the effect of the overall message of the movie, their effect is greatly lessened. Please be clear, I do not dismiss the power of words. I do dismiss the conclusion that there is a real and substantial possibility that conscientious jurors watching this movie, shown during a recess purely for entertainment purposes, would have allowed it to affect their verdict. . . .

Regarding the nature and source of this extraneous influence, the defendants emphasize that the movie was supplied by the court; this factor alone is not

12. For example: "Brothers and Sisters, I am here to tell you that I charge the white man, I charge the white man with being the greatest murderer on earth. . . . I charge him with being the greatest kidnapper on earth. . . . We didn't see any democracy on the streets of Harlem . . . on the streets of Detroit. . . . We've experienced only the American nightmare."

determinative. While this fact does tend to bolster the movie's potential prejudicial effect, the nature of this particular extraneous influence weighs heavily against a finding of prejudice. The movie was chosen by the jurors from three others made available to them purely for purposes of entertainment. The jurors should be credited with enough sophistication to separate entertainment from evidence. . . .

I would further find that, even if the defendants had met their initial burden, a reversal is not required here because it can be said, beyond a reasonable doubt, that the other evidence adduced at trial was so overwhelming that there is no real and substantial possibility that viewing the movie might have contributed to the convictions. I respectfully disagree with the majority's conclusion that the evidence supporting second-degree murder against defendant Budzyn was not overwhelming. [A]ll five of the eyewitnesses, Fletcher, Pace, Hollins, Brown, and Knox, testified that Budzyn initiated the beating by repeatedly striking Green on the hands. Witnesses Pace and Hollins, who observed the scene from essentially the same vantage point, saw Budzyn swinging his flashlight over his shoulder down toward Green in the direction of Green's head. They both testified that on the basis of the positioning of Budzyn and Green, and the sound of impact, it appeared that Budzyn was repeatedly hitting Green on the head with his flashlight. Further, eyewitness Brown, who observed the scene from a different vantage point, standing on the curb at a slight elevation and to the rear of the car, testified that he actually saw Budzyn strike Green on the head with the flashlight several times. Witness Fletcher's testimony, which did not indicate that Budzyn's blows appeared to land on Green's head, was not necessarily inconsistent with the conclusion of the other witnesses. Fletcher explained that he did not see everything that transpired after observing the blows to Green's hand and after Budzyn positioned himself further into the car on top of Green because Officer Budzyn was positioned in a way that obstructed his view for a period.

I cannot help but conclude that the evidence concerning Budzyn's actions was overwhelming to support the verdict of second-degree murder. This conclusion would not be different even if, as the majority suggests, the injuries actually causing Green's death could have been inflicted solely by Nevers. While Budzyn's actions were perhaps less brutal than Nevers', he initiated the encounter with Green that ultimately resulted in Green's death. His actions went far beyond the level of force necessary in the situation. Rather than calling his partner to assist him in pulling Mr. Green out of the car and handcuffing him, Officer Budzyn exerted excessive force in attempting to get Green to open his clenched fist. Further, Budzyn did not step in to stop Nevers' beating of Green when Nevers continued the beating with actions that were clearly an unjustified and brutal show of force.

The majority attempts to discount the evidence against Budzyn by questioning the credibility of the eyewitnesses. It may or may not be true that because each of these witnesses had been implicated in criminal activity, or because they may have smoked cocaine or consumed alcohol before witnessing the events leading up to Green's death, they were less credible than the EMS witnesses who testified against defendant Nevers. This Court, however, is not in a position to judge the relative credibility of the witnesses against the two officers. The jurors heard the testimony from eyewitnesses Pace, Hollins, Brown, and Fletcher, all of whom were subjected to thorough cross-examination, and evidently found it to be credible. . . .

I recognize that the great majority of police officers conscientiously perform their duties with the utmost regard for the rights of those they seek to protect.

However, when police officers cross over the line from keepers of the peace and protectors of lives to aggressors, exerting force far beyond that required in the given situation, the law must treat them no differently than other defendants.

The right to a fair trial by an impartial jury is of paramount importance in securing our liberty. Consequently, this Court has properly taken very seriously the defendants' claims that their juries' exposure to extraneous influences denied them this right. After careful review however, I am left with the distinct and firm impression that the defendants received a fair trial. The potential prejudice from the asserted influences is real. However, it does not rise to a level sufficient to persuade me of a real and substantial possibility that the verdicts were affected. Additionally, given the overwhelming evidence supporting the verdicts, it can be said, beyond a reasonable doubt, that these influences did not contribute to the verdicts.

Problem 10-2. Preserving Error

On an October afternoon, two men wearing dark jeans and hooded pullover sweatshirts entered the lobby of a hotel on South Lake Shore Drive in Chicago. According to Angela Eiland, the hotel's front desk supervisor, one man was around six feet tall, and the other man was shorter, "probably around five-five." Though the hoods covered their foreheads, Eiland observed that the taller man had a missing tooth; the shorter man had a darker complexion and an unshaven face. Eiland asked if she could help them, and the shorter man replied, "Give me the money." He jumped over the counter with a gray cotton bag, while the taller man pointed a gun at her. Eiland opened the register, and the shorter man grabbed the money and turned toward the back office just as Lisa Brooks, hostess of the hotel restaurant, was leaving the office. The shorter man grabbed Brooks and pulled her back into the office. The taller man kept the gun pointed at Eiland.

Robert Comanse, the hotel's front office manager, heard a commotion and left his office, which was adjacent to the back office, to investigate. When he entered the back office, he saw the shorter man holding Brooks' arm. Comanse later described the shorter man as 5-feet-10 or 5-feet-11-inches tall with spotty facial hair. As Comanse walked by Brooks on his way to the lobby, Brooks told Comanse that the man was a robber. Comanse, close enough to the man to smell his breath, laughed. The man put a gun in his face and said, "This is real. It's a real gun." He ordered Comanse and Brooks to lie face down on the floor. The shorter man demanded, "Where's the money?" Comanse answered that there was no money in the office; the rest of the hotel's money was locked in a safe downstairs.

Outside the lobby Robert Priester, the hotel's director of security, was waiting to accompany Brooks with her "bank" money to open the restaurant. Priester entered the lobby and approached Eiland to determine why Brooks was delayed. The taller man backed away from the desk, and Eiland mouthed the words to Priester that the hotel was being robbed. Priester turned toward the taller man and asked what he was doing. A struggle ensued. The taller man shouted, "They got me, G," and a gunshot rang through the lobby. Priester slumped down, bleeding from his neck. The two men fled. Priester died within hours at Northwestern Memorial Hospital.

Comanse told the police that he had never seen the robbers before, but described the man in the back office as 5-feet-10-inches or 5-feet-11-inches tall, wearing a black hooded sweatshirt covering his hair but not his face. Comanse said that he viewed the man's face for approximately 20 to 25 seconds before he laid face down on the floor. He viewed a photo lineup that day, but did not identify anyone.

Fifteen months later, the police investigation of the shooting led to James Brisbon. After interviewing Brisbon, the police started looking for two additional suspects, Nakia Herron and Kenneth Durant. Herron voluntarily came to the police station to participate in several lineups. Although Brooks could not identify anyone, the police still arrested Herron. The next day, Herron spoke with a Chicago police detective on the way to the lockup, saying that he had gone to the hotel with Brisbon and another person, but that he stayed outside while Brisbon and the other person went inside. Two weeks later, in another lineup, Eiland identified Durant as the taller man, but she did not identify Herron as one of the robbers. Comanse identified Herron as the shorter man in the hotel.

After the close of evidence at Herron's trial, the parties discussed jury instructions. The following exchange occurred:

Assistant State's Attorney: No. 10 is IPI Criminal No. 3.15.
The Court: That has all the points in it?
Assistant State's Attorney: Yes.
Defense Counsel: Okay. No objection, judge.

The bulk of the State and defense closing arguments centered around the reliability of eyewitness identifications. In instructing the jury, the trial court recited Illinois Pattern Instruction, Criminal, No. 3.15, as follows:

When you weigh the identification testimony of a witness, you should consider all the facts and circumstances in evidence, including, but not limited to, the following: The opportunity the witness had to view the offender at the time of the offense or the witness's degree of attention at the time of the offense or the witness's earlier description of the offender or the level of certainty shown by the witness when confronting the defendant or the length of time between the offense and the identification confrontation.

The jury found the defendant guilty of first-degree murder and armed robbery. The trial court denied the defendant's motion for a new trial, amended motion for a new trial, and motion to reconsider sentence.

The defendant appealed, arguing that the trial court erred in its reading of the pattern instruction. Specifically, the defendant charged that the trial court's use of the word "or" between the listed factors signaled that the jury could find an eyewitness's testimony reliable based on a single factor. The defendant acknowledged that he did not object to the instruction at trial or in a post-trial motion. Instead, he argued that the appellate court should consider this forfeited issue under the plain-error doctrine.

Will the appellate court hear the argument on the merits? Assuming the legal argument about the jury instruction is correct, will the appellate court reverse the conviction? Cf. People v. Herron, 830 N.E.2d 467 (Ill. 2005).

Notes

1. *Harmless error standards: majority position.* State and federal courts vary widely in the details of their harmless error standards, but most courts apply variations on the standards enunciated by the Supreme Court in *Fahy*, *Chapman*, and *Sullivan*. Was the U.S. Supreme Court correct when it asserted that the *Chapman* standard assessing whether the errors were harmless "beyond a reasonable doubt" was the same as in *Fahy*, where the test of harmless error was "whether there is a reasonable possibility that the evidence complained of might have contributed to the conviction"? Compare the *Chapman* standard to the newer formulation in *Sullivan*, in which the Court explained that the test "is not whether, in a trial that occurred without the error, a guilty verdict would surely have been rendered, but whether the guilty verdict actually rendered in this trial was surely unattributable to the error." What other standards might courts use? What factors might argue for a standard even more restrictive than "harmless beyond a reasonable doubt"? See State v. Van Kirk, 32 P.3d 735 (Mont. 2001) (applies "cumulative evidence" approach rather than "overwhelming" weight of evidence approach; question is whether fact-finder was presented with admissible evidence that proved same facts as tainted evidence proved).

According to Kotteakos v. United States, 328 U.S. 750 (1946), the "harmless error" standard that applies to nonconstitutional errors is slightly different. Non-constitutional error is harmless only when "the error did not influence the jury, or had but very slight effect." Some states create separate standards for reviewing constitutional and nonconstitutional errors; most apply a single standard to both types of error, following the unitary direction of rules like the federal and Tennessee procedure rules printed above.

2. *Applying the standard.* One striking feature of harmless error review is how often appellate courts apply the concept, without explanation, to affirm judgments after even substantial errors. Even when harmless error is the central question and there is detailed analysis of the facts, as in Budzyn, courts treat the standard of review as so well established that it does not require restating.

But we can learn as much from what courts do as from what they say. A study by Landes and Posner, based on a sample of over 1,000 federal appeals, identifies patterns in the outcomes of harmless error cases even if the court opinions do not themselves offer much analysis. Intentional prosecutor and judge errors are more likely than inadvertent errors to be found harmful. Appellate courts are more likely to ignore prosecutor errors than judge errors, possibly because judge errors have a greater influence on jurors. William M. Landes & Richard A. Posner, Harmless Error, 30 J. Legal Stud. 161 (2001).

Another study noted that some courts apply the harmless error test as if it were a "but for" causation test from tort law, while others use the equivalent of the "substantial factor" test for factual causation in tort. The "but for" courts find harmless error nearly twice as often as the "substantial factor" courts. Jason M. Solomon, Causing Constitutional Harm: How Tort Law Can Help Determine Harmless Error in Criminal Trials, 99 Nw. U. L. Rev. 1053 (2005).

3. *Structural and trial error.* As we have seen, courts classify errors under two headings: "trial" errors, which are subject to harmless error analysis, and "structural" errors, which call for automatic reversal. See Gonzalez-Lopez v. United States, 126 S. Ct. 2557 (2006) (trial court's violation of a defendant's Sixth

Amendment right to be represented by paid counsel of choice amounts to structural error; remedy is reversal of conviction without a showing of prejudice). The admission at trial of unconstitutional confessions — the issue reconsidered in *Fulminante* — is an uncommon issue compared to errors such as faulty jury instructions, since most coerced confessions will be suppressed before trial. Why did most courts, before the U.S. Supreme Court decision in *Fulminante*, place unconstitutional confessions in the automatic reversal category? Only a few courts since *Fulminante* have considered whether state law will allow harmless error analysis for unconstitutional confessions used at trial in state cases, and none so far has rejected the Supreme Court's lead in *Fulminante*. See People v. Cahill, 853 P.2d 1037 (Cal. 1993). Given the willingness of state supreme courts to adopt their own procedural rules in many areas, why might state courts not wish to reject *Fulminante*? Is *Fulminante* a case that gives state courts more or less power relative to other branches of government? Is it a case that gives state courts more or less power over their own dockets?

One of the most common and difficult harmless error problems arises in assessing the impact of improper jury instructions. The U.S. Supreme Court has wrestled for at least a decade with whether different kinds of instructional error should be subject to harmless error analysis. Is the distinction in *Fulminante* between "trial" and "structural" errors useful in assessing the impact of erroneous jury instructions? Should courts assess whether the outcome (guilt and sentence) would have been the same in the absence of the erroneous instruction, or whether the defendant was clearly guilty of the crime charged? What difference might a proper instruction have made to the jury in determining the proper offense? The proper punishment? In Sullivan v. Louisiana, 508 U.S. 275 (1993), a unanimous Court held that a constitutionally defective reasonable-doubt instruction was a "structural error" not subject to harmless error analysis. Most states, however, continue to apply harmless error analysis to most instructional errors. Compare People v. Harris, 886 P.2d 1193 (Cal. 1994) (misinstruction on elements of robbery harmless error) with Commonwealth v. Conefrey, 650 N.E.2d 1268 (Mass. 1995) (harmless error does not apply to failure to give "unanimity" instruction to jury).

Other deviations from the usual procedure for empanelling and instructing a jury are very often deemed to be structural errors in the trial. See State v. LaMere, 2000 Mt. 45 (2000) (summoning jurors by telephone rather than by mail in violation of statute governing juror summonses requires automatic reversal); State v. Cleveland, 959 S.W.2d 948 (Tenn. 1997) (absence of juror during part of closing argument cannot ever be harmless error).

4. *The capacity of harmless error to make procedure irrelevant.* If a harmless error standard allows many cases with clear trial error to be immune from appellate review, then the justice system may lose the shaping function of appellate courts. See Sam Kamin, Harmless Error and the Rights/Remedies Split, 88 Va. L. Rev. 1 (2002). Are not cases that are obvious most likely to be subject to guilty pleas? Are trials — at least difficult or long ones — ever so obvious that the outcome would be the same regardless of how the evidence was presented or the approach taken by the lawyers?

5. *Procedural forfeiture of error.* The defendant typically must object to an error at trial or raise the objection in a post-trial motion for a new trial. If defense counsel fails to take the proper steps at trial (or during pretrial proceedings) to "preserve"

the error for appellate review, the appellate courts might never hear the issue. This failure to follow proper procedures at trial can block the appellate court from hearing some errors that could have survived a harmless error test. What purposes could such a limit on appellate review serve? It is commonly justified as a way to give trial judges the chance to correct errors before they become too costly, and to prevent defense counsel from remaining silent about the errors they observe, creating an insurance policy if the jury happens to convict (a strategy known as "sandbagging"). The rules are also said to encourage the creation of complete appellate records. Is this rule about the scope of appellate review too remote from events at trial to have these desired effects?

6. *Plain error.* As we have seen, an error not brought to the attention of the trial judge for immediate correction usually cannot form the basis for a later appeal. However, appellate courts make an exception for "plain error," as described in the Rules of Criminal Procedure reprinted above. If the error is plain, the appellate court will ignore the procedural failure of the defense counsel to preserve the error at trial. While the "harmless error" doctrine often involves constitutional arguments, "plain error" is treated as a matter of common law interpretation of the procedural rules. See United States v. Cotton, 525 U.S. 625 (2002) (omission from federal indictment of a fact that enhances the statutory maximum sentence does not amount to plain error); United States v. Vonn, 535 U.S. 55 (2002) (federal defendant who allows Rule 11 error to pass without objections in trial court must satisfy Rule 52(b) plain error rule).

D. RETROACTIVITY

Legal questions are typically subject to de novo review. But not every erroneous legal decision by the trial court will lead to a reversal of the judgment. There are several categories of legal errors that will not undermine the judgment below. When lower courts violate rules of law announced in later appellate decisions, appellate courts are sometimes willing to ignore those errors by saying that the new rule of law will not receive "retroactive" application.

The question of which appellate decisions should receive retroactive application seems simple — and until the middle of this century, it was. Common law systems operated on the assumption that courts "found" the law, and therefore each decision reflected law already in existence. Since the law existed before, during, and after a court's decision, it applied "retroactively" to other active cases, and perhaps (through postconviction review such as habeas corpus) even to defendants who have concluded their direct appeals (sometimes many years ago).

We no longer live in such innocent times. Since the middle of the twentieth century, legal realism has led lawyers and judges to recognize that courts make law, at least interstitially. In light of this honest assessment, some courts have declared that their own rulings will have only prospective application (like statutes) or only limited retroactive effect. When appellate courts say that a decision should receive only prospective application, what conception of judicial powers do they reveal?

The common law, in contrast, recognized legislatures as law "makers" rather than law "finders," and thus statutes were presumed to apply only prospectively. Constitutional doctrine bolstered this assumption: The "ex post facto clause" barred legislation that enhanced the punishment for a prior act.

Like courts reshaping the concept of judicial power by issuing prospective rulings, legislatures have increasingly enacted laws that apply not only to future but to present and past cases. What limits does the ex post facto principle place on such statutes? Compare the two cases below and the retroactivity limits they place on judges and legislatures. Do legislatures think differently about laws if they are limited to prospective application? Do courts think differently about their rulings if decisions are generally applied retroactively?

■ STATE v. CURTIS KNIGHT
678 A.2d 642 (N.J. 1996)

STEIN, J.

After a jury trial, defendant, Curtis Knight, was convicted of first-degree murder, third-degree possession of a weapon for an unlawful purpose, and fourth-degree unlawful possession of a weapon. The Appellate Division reversed defendant's convictions [because] the admission into evidence of defendant's statement to his arresting officer violated defendant's state constitutional right to counsel as construed in State v. Sanchez, 609 A.2d 400 (N.J. 1992). In *Sanchez,* we held that mere recitation of the *Miranda* warnings does not provide an indicted defendant with information sufficient to make a knowing and intelligent waiver of the right to counsel. Recognizing that *Sanchez* was decided after Knight's trial had concluded, the Appellate Division nevertheless determined that the *Sanchez* rule applies retroactively and requires the reversal of Knight's convictions. . . . We affirm.

In March 1990, defendant was tried along with Cesar Glenn for the murder of Glenn Brown, who was also known as Hassan. The State contended that Cesar Glenn held Brown while defendant beat him to death with a pipe. [B]ecause defendant and his girlfriend, Kathy Capella, had moved to California in October of 1988, New Jersey law enforcement authorities had been unable to find defendant prior to or after his indictment. On October 25, 1989, F.B.I. Agent Mark Wilson and local police officers located and apprehended defendant in Palmdale, California. . . . According to Wilson, defendant waived his *Miranda* rights and stated that while he was living in New Jersey he had been robbed by Brown. After the robbery, defendant learned that someone named Rahaem or Knight had beaten up Brown and inflicted serious injuries in the process. Brown's friends apparently believed that defendant was the culprit, and were looking for defendant to exact revenge for the beating. Defendant thus explained to Wilson that he left New Jersey because he feared for his life and that he did not know that the police were looking for him. Although defendant's explanation was not directly inculpatory, at trial the State used defendant's story to connect him to Brown and to argue that defendant killed Brown to get revenge for the robbery. . . . The jury found defendant guilty of all charged offenses: first-degree murder, fourth-degree unlawful possession of a weapon, and third-degree possession of a weapon for an unlawful purpose.

[Knight] contends that his statement to F.B.I. Agent Wilson should not have been admitted into evidence at trial because defendant had not validly waived his right to counsel before speaking with Wilson. The resolution of that issue turns on whether State v. Sanchez, 609 A.2d 400 (N.J. 1992), which we decided after Knight's trial had concluded but before the Appellate Division had ruled on his appeal, applies retroactively to this case. . . .

This Court has four options in any case in which it must determine the retroactive effect of a new rule of criminal procedure. The Court may decide to apply the new rule purely prospectively, applying it only to cases in which the operative facts arise after the new rule has been announced. Alternatively, the Court may apply the new rule in future cases and in the case in which the rule is announced, but not in any other litigation that is pending or has reached final judgment at the time the new rule is set forth. A third option is to give the new rule "pipeline retroactivity," rendering it applicable in all future cases, the case in which the rule is announced, and any cases still on direct appeal. Finally, the Court may give the new rule complete retroactive effect, applying it to all cases, including those in which final judgments have been entered and all other avenues of appeal have been exhausted.

However, before a court chooses from among those four options, it customarily engages in the threshold inquiry of whether the rule at issue is a "new rule of law" for purposes of retroactivity analysis. Our cases have recognized that if a ruling does not involve a "departure from existing law," the retroactivity question never arises and our power to limit the retroactive effect of a decision is not implicated. That approach apparently stems from the concept, prevalent at common law, that the duty of courts was not to pronounce new law but rather to "maintain and expound" extant judicial rulings. See Linkletter v. Walker, 381 U.S. 618, 622 (1965) (quoting 1 William Blackstone, Commentaries 69 (15th ed. 1809)). A court could "discover" what the law had always been, but it could not create new law. The recognition that the retrospective effect of a judicial ruling could be restricted was unknown to the common-law courts and incompatible with the common-law view that an overruled holding was not bad law, it was simply never the law. In time, however, courts came to accept that some decisions represent a break from prior jurisprudence, and that to apply such new rules retroactively could inflict unjustified burdens on the courts and law enforcement personnel.

In State v. Lark, 567 A.2d 197 (N.J. 1989), we discouraged undue emphasis on the old rule/new rule distinction, and noted our reluctance to decide retroactivity questions on the basis of the now-discredited common-law view of law as "perpetual and immutable." [We] cited approvingly the federal Supreme Court's broad definition of "new rule" that provides that a "case announces a new rule when it breaks new ground or imposes a new obligation on the States or the Federal Government [or] if the result was not dictated by precedent existing at the time the defendant's conviction became final." Teague v. Lane, 489 U.S. 288, 301 (1989). Moreover, we held that a decision involving an "accepted legal principle" announces a new rule for retroactivity purposes so long as the decision's application of that general principle is "sufficiently novel and unanticipated."

If a decision indeed sets forth a "new rule," three factors generally are considered to determine whether the rule is to be applied retroactively: "(1) the purpose of the rule and whether it would be furthered by a retroactive application, (2) the degree of reliance placed on the old rule by those who administered it, and (3) the effect a retroactive application would have on the administration of justice." State v. Nash, 317 A.2d 689 (N.J. 1974). Although those three factors have received detailed attention in our retroactivity case law, our cases also indicate that the retroactivity determination often turns more generally on the court's view of what is just and consonant with public policy in the particular situation presented.

The first factor, the purpose of the new rule, is often the pivotal consideration. For example, if the newly announced rule is an exclusionary rule intended solely to discourage police misconduct, then the rule's purpose would not be served by applying the rule to conduct occurring before the rule was announced. For that reason, exclusionary rules are rarely given retroactive effect. On the other hand, if the old rule was altered because it substantially impaired the reliability of the truth-finding process, the interest in obtaining accurate verdicts may suggest that the new rule be given complete retroactive effect.

The second and third factors come to the forefront of the retroactivity analysis when the inquiry into the purpose of the new rule does not, by itself, reveal whether retroactive application of the new rule would be appropriate. The second factor inquires whether law enforcement agents justifiably relied on the old rule in performing their professional responsibilities. The reasoning underlying this inquiry is that state agents should not be penalized for complying in good faith with prevailing constitutional norms when carrying out their duties. In instances where prior judicial decisions gave state officials reason to question the continued validity of the old rule, the significance of the reliance factor correspondingly decreases.

The third factor in the retroactivity analysis, the effect a retroactive application would have on the administration of justice, recognizes that courts must not impose unjustified burdens on our criminal justice system. Thus, we generally have avoided applying new rules retroactively when such an application would undermine the validity of large numbers of convictions. We have noted our concern about over-whelming courts with retrials, and our awareness of the difficulty in re-prosecuting cases in which the offense took place years in the past.

Our three-pronged retroactivity analysis stems from the test set forth by the United States Supreme Court in Linkletter v. Walker, 381 U.S. 618 (1965). Over the years, however, the federal jurisprudence shifted course, and the federal Supreme Court eventually abandoned the *Linkletter* factors in favor of a more mechanical approach. Under current federal law, new rules based on interpretation of the federal Constitution are to be applied to all cases still on direct appeal, see Griffith v. Kentucky, 479 U.S. 314 (1987), but only in rare circumstances to cases in which all avenues of direct review have been exhausted. Teague v. Lane, 489 U.S. 288 (1989). Although we have noted our agreement with some of the principles underlying *Teague*, we have continued to determine the retroactivity of state rules of law under the *Linkletter* test. See State v. Lark. . . .

The threshold retroactivity issue in this case, whether *Sanchez* announced a new rule of law, is a close question. Our analysis begins with Patterson v. Illinois, 487 U.S. 285 (1988), which was decided four years before *Sanchez*. In *Patterson*, the United States Supreme Court held that reading the *Miranda* rights to an indicted defendant enables that defendant to make an informed and valid waiver of the Sixth Amendment right to counsel. The Court rejected the contention that the Sixth Amendment right to counsel is "more difficult to waive than the Fifth Amendment counterpart." . . .

Four years later, in *Sanchez*, we held that after a defendant has been indicted, administration of Miranda warnings during police-initiated interrogation is not adequate to elicit a knowing and voluntary waiver of the right to counsel guaranteed by the State Constitution. We saw *Patterson* as a "change of direction" in the

Supreme Court's Sixth Amendment jurisprudence, and found the basis for our decision in "our traditional commitment to the right to counsel." Those observations might imply that the rule set forth in *Sanchez* was not "new," but rather . . . a continuation of traditional adherence to a heightened importance of the right to counsel once the criminal adversarial process has begun. On the other hand, focusing on the period before *Sanchez* was decided, *Patterson* represented the United States Supreme Court's resolution of the question under the federal Constitution, and the *Patterson* Court squarely had rejected the right-to-counsel argument later accepted in *Sanchez*. . . . We therefore conclude that the *Sanchez* rule is "sufficiently novel and unanticipated" to implicate this Court's power to limit the retroactive effect of its decisions. Accordingly, we consider whether retroactive application of the *Sanchez* rule would be appropriate.

To guide us in the inquiry into the purpose of the *Sanchez* rule, we look to the rationale for that rule set forth in *Sanchez* itself:

> The return of an indictment transforms the relationship between the State and the defendant. By obtaining the indictment, the State represents that it has sufficient evidence to establish a prima facie case. Once the indictment is returned, the State is committed to prosecute the defendant. From that moment, if not before, the prosecutor and the defendant are adversaries. . . . Under those circumstances, the perfunctory recitation of the right to counsel and to remain silent may not provide the defendant with sufficient information to make a knowing and intelligent waiver. Such a recitation does not tell the defendant the nature of the charges, the dangers of self-representation, or the steps counsel might take to protect the defendant's interests. [609 A.2d at 408.]

In this case, the inquiry into the purpose of the new rule does not, by itself, reveal whether retroactive application of the rule would be appropriate. Although the *Sanchez* rule is intended, in part, to discourage police interrogation of indicted, unrepresented defendants, it is not solely an exclusionary rule. Similarly, although the rule aims to enhance the reliability of confessions by reducing the inherent coercion of custodial interrogation, it does not replace a rule that substantially impaired the truth-finding function of the criminal trial. Accordingly, we must add to our analysis a consideration of the "reliance" and "administration of justice" factors. Those factors are, to an extent, interrelated in this case.

We fail to discern any appreciable reliance by law enforcement officials on pre-*Sanchez* law. [Only] in exceptional situations would a New Jersey law enforcement officer attempt to interrogate an indicted defendant outside the presence of a defense attorney. We note that in urban counties the first appearance by criminal defendants occurs in Central Judicial Processing (CJP) courts, and in those courts, forms requesting assigned counsel generally are completed by defendants prior to their initial court appearance, and at that court appearance counsel from the public defender's office are generally available to provide representation. . . . Thus, the prevailing practice across much of the State is to provide counsel to defendants immediately after the criminal complaint is filed—even before the grand jury has returned an indictment. . . . Thus, the *Sanchez* rule, which concerns waiver of the right to counsel by indicted yet unrepresented defendants, is implicated only in those unusual cases in which indicted defendants deliberately forgo the right to counsel or absent themselves from their initial court appearance and miss the opportunity to be assigned an attorney. Our assumption is that police do not customarily interrogate indicted and uncounseled defendants.

The third retroactivity factor, the effect retroactive application would have on the administration of justice, militates in favor of limited retroactive application of the *Sanchez* rule. As noted, cases in which the *Sanchez* rule is implicated arise relatively infrequently. Thus, applying *Sanchez* retroactively to cases on direct appeal would neither be chaotic nor overwhelm our courts. However, administration-of-justice considerations counsel against affording *Sanchez* more than "pipeline retroactivity." To accord *Sanchez* complete retroactive effect would impose on the State the burden of reprosecuting some cases in which the offense took place years in the past. Because of failing memories and unavailable witnesses, the problems encountered in prosecuting such cases often are insurmountable.

Based on the three retroactivity factors, we conclude that it would be just and consonant with public policy to apply the *Sanchez* rule in this case. Neither the purpose of the *Sanchez* rule, reliance on pre-*Sanchez* law, nor administration-of-justice considerations justify limiting application of the *Sanchez* rule to cases arising after that decision was announced. Because the pre-*Sanchez* rule did not substantially impair the reliability of the truth-finding process, we will not burden the criminal justice system with the post-conviction-relief applications and retrials that would result from a fully retroactive application of the *Sanchez* decision. *Sanchez* will therefore not apply to those defendants who had exhausted all avenues of direct relief at the time *Sanchez* was decided. . . .

COLEMAN, J., dissenting.

I dissent from the Court's holding that State v. Sanchez should apply retroactively to pipeline cases. The effect of that holding is to require the suppression of an otherwise reliable inculpatory statement by defendant because an F.B.I. Agent in California did not predict that New Jersey would not follow a sixteen-month-old decision of the United States Supreme Court. . . .

As the majority points out, Patterson v. Illinois was consistent with our law and New Jersey did not announce a different rule until nearly four years later when *Sanchez* was decided. Thus, *Sanchez* represented a new rule that could not have been predicted. I fail to see why a rule that served New Jersey well in assuring the reliability of confessions for thirty years under its existing constitution after Miranda was decided in 1966 should overnight be found so unreliable as to justify retroactive application of a new rule. The Court rationalizes its conclusion by conjecturing that law enforcement did not rely on *Patterson*. I disagree. It is hard to imagine a rule more deeply etched in the minds of law enforcement agents than the *Miranda* warnings and its progeny, of which *Patterson* is a part. . . . Agent Wilson had every right to rely on the United States Supreme Court's *Patterson* rule when he interrogated defendant only sixteen months after *Patterson* was decided. . . .

■ MARION REYNOLDS STOGNER v. CALIFORNIA
539 U.S. 607 (2003)

BREYER, J.

California has brought a criminal prosecution after expiration of the time periods set forth in previously applicable statutes of limitations. California has done so under the authority of a new law that (1) permits resurrection of otherwise time-barred criminal prosecutions, and (2) was itself enacted *after* pre-existing limitations periods had expired. We conclude that the Constitution's Ex Post Facto Clause, Art. I, §10, cl. 1, bars application of this new law to the present case.

In 1993, California enacted a new criminal statute of limitations governing sex-related child abuse crimes. The new statute permits prosecution for those crimes where "the limitation period specified in [a prior statute of limitations] has expired"—provided that (1) a victim has reported an allegation of abuse to the police, (2) "there is independent evidence that clearly and convincingly corroborates the victim's allegation," and (3) the prosecution is begun within one year of the victim's report. Cal. Penal Code §803(g). A related provision, added to the statute in 1996, makes clear that a prosecution satisfying these three conditions "shall revive any cause of action barred by [prior statutes of limitations]." The statute thus authorizes prosecution for criminal acts committed many years beforehand—and where the original limitations period has expired—as long as prosecution begins within a year of a victim's first complaint to the police.

In 1998, a California grand jury indicted Marion Stogner, the petitioner, charging him with sex-related child abuse committed decades earlier—between 1955 and 1973. Without the new statute allowing revival of the State's cause of action, California could not have prosecuted Stogner. The statute of limitations governing prosecutions at the time the crimes were allegedly committed had set forth a 3-year limitations period. And that period had run 22 years or more before the present prosecution was brought. Stogner moved for the complaint's dismissal. He argued that the Federal Constitution's Ex Post Facto Clause, Art. I, §10, cl. 1, forbids revival of a previously time-barred prosecution.

[The] new statute threatens the kinds of harm that, in this Court's view, the Ex Post Facto Clause seeks to avoid. Long ago the Court pointed out that the Clause protects liberty by preventing governments from enacting statutes with "manifestly *unjust and oppressive*" retroactive effects. Calder v. Bull, 3 Dall. 386 (1798). [The] kind of statute at issue falls literally within the categorical descriptions of ex post facto laws set forth by Justice Chase more than 200 years ago in Calder v. Bull. . . . Drawing substantially on Richard Wooddeson's 18th-century commentary on the nature of ex post facto laws and past parliamentary abuses, Chase divided ex post facto laws into categories [as follows]:

> I will state what laws I consider ex post facto laws, within the words and the intent of the prohibition. 1st. Every law that makes an action done before the passing of the law, and which was innocent when done, criminal; and punishes such action. *2d. Every law that aggravates a crime, or makes it greater than it was, when committed.* 3d. Every law that changes the punishment, and inflicts a greater punishment, than the law annexed to the crime, when committed. *4th. Every law that alters the legal rules of evidence, and receives less, or different, testimony, than the law required at the time of the commission of the offence, in order to convict the offender.* All these, and similar laws, are manifestly unjust and oppressive. . . . (Emphasis altered from original.)

The second category—including any "law that *aggravates a crime,* or makes it greater than it was, when committed"—describes California's statute as long as those words are understood as Justice Chase understood them—i.e., as referring to a statute that "inflicts *punishments,* where the party was not, by *law,* liable to any punishment." After (but not before) the original statute of limitations had expired, a party such as Stogner was not "liable to any *punishment.*" California's new statute therefore "aggravated" Stogner's alleged crime, or made it "greater than it was, when committed," in the sense that, and to the extent that, it "inflicted punishment" for past criminal conduct that (when the new law was enacted) did not trigger any such liability. . . .

So to understand the second category (as applying where a new law inflicts a punishment upon a person not then subject to that punishment, to any degree) explains why and how that category differs from both the first category (making criminal noncriminal behavior) and the third category (aggravating the punishment). . . .

[Numerous] legislators, courts, and commentators have long believed it well settled that the Ex Post Facto Clause forbids resurrection of a time-barred prosecution. Such sentiments appear already to have been widespread when the Reconstruction Congress of 1867—the Congress that drafted the Fourteenth Amendment—rejected a bill that would have revived time-barred prosecutions for treason that various Congressmen wanted brought against Jefferson Davis and "his coconspirators," Cong. Globe, 39th Cong., 2d Sess., 279 (1866-1867) (comments of Rep. Lawrence). Radical Republicans such as Roscoe Conkling and Thaddeus Stevens, no friends of the South, opposed the bill because, in their minds, it proposed an ex post facto law, and threatened an injustice tantamount to "judicial murder." In this instance, Congress ultimately passed a law extending unexpired limitations periods, ch. 236, 15 Stat. 183—a tailored approach to extending limitations periods that has also been taken in modern statutes. . . .

The dissent . . . emphasizes the harm that child molestation causes, a harm that "will plague the victim for a lifetime," and stresses the need to convict those who abuse children. [We] agree that the State's interest in prosecuting child abuse cases is an important one. But there is also a predominating constitutional interest in forbidding the State to revive a long-forbidden prosecution. And to hold that such a law is ex post facto does not prevent the State from extending time limits for the prosecution of future offenses, or for prosecutions not yet time barred. . . .

KENNEDY, J., dissenting.

California has enacted a retroactive extension of statutes of limitations for serious sexual offenses committed against minors. The new period includes cases where the limitations period has expired before the effective date of the legislation. To invalidate the statute in the latter circumstance, the Court tries to force it into the second category of Calder v. Bull, which prohibits a retroactive law "that *aggravates a crime,* or makes it *greater* than it was, when committed." These words, in my view, do not permit the Court's holding, but indeed foreclose it. A law which does not alter the definition of the crime but only revives prosecution does not make the crime "greater than it was, when committed." Until today, a plea in bar has not been thought to form any part of the definition of the offense. . . .

The California statute can be explained as motivated by legitimate concerns about the continuing suffering endured by the victims of childhood abuse. The California Legislature noted that young victims often delay reporting sexual abuse because they are easily manipulated by offenders in positions of authority and trust, and because children have difficulty remembering the crime or facing the trauma it can cause. The concern is amply supported by empirical studies.

The problem the legislature sought to address is illustrated well by this case. Petitioner's older daughter testified she did not report the abuse because she was afraid of her father and did not believe anyone would help her. After she left petitioner's home, she tried to forget the abuse. Petitioner's younger daughter did not report the abuse because she was scared. He tried to convince her it was a normal way of life. Even after she moved out of petitioner's house, she was afraid to speak for fear she would not be believed. She tried to pretend she had a normal childhood. It was only her realization that the father continued to abuse other children in the family that led her to disclose the abuse, in order to protect them. . . .

There are two rationales to explain the proposed dichotomy between unexpired and expired statutes, and neither works. The first rationale must be the assumption that if an expired statute is extended, the crime becomes more serious, thereby violating category two; but if an unexpired statute is extended, the crime does not increase in seriousness. . . .

This leaves the second rationale, which must be that an extension of the expired statute destroys a reliance interest. We should consider whether it is warranted to presume that criminals keep calendars so they can mark the day to discard their records or to place a gloating phone call to the victim. The first expectation is minor and likely imaginary; the second is not, but there is no conceivable reason the law should honor it. And either expectation assumes, of course, the very result the Court reaches; for if the law were otherwise, there would be no legitimate expectation. The reliance exists, if at all, because of the circular reason that the Court today says so; it does not exist as part of our traditions or social understanding.

In contrast to the designation of the crime, which carries a certain measure of social opprobrium and presupposes a certain punishment, the statute of limitations has little or no deterrent effect. The Court does not claim a sex offender would desist if he knew he would be liable to prosecution when his offenses were disclosed. . . .

The gravity of the crime was known, and is being measured, by its wrongfulness when committed. It is a common policy for States to suspend statutes of limitations for civil harms against minors, in order to protect minors during the period when they are unable to protect themselves. Some States toll the limitations periods for minors even where a guardian is appointed, and even when the tolling conflicts with statutes of repose. The difference between suspension and reactivation is so slight that it is fictional for the Court to say, in the given context, the new policy somehow alters the magnitude of the crime. The wrong was made clear by the law at the time of the crime's commission. The criminal actor knew it, even reveled in it. It is the commission of the then-unlawful act that the State now seeks to punish. The gravity of the crime is left unchanged by altering a statute of limitations of which the actor was likely not at all aware. . . .

Notes

1. *Retroactivity of appellate decisions: majority position.* Historically, appellate courts applied their precedents to all litigants bringing appeals to them, even if the precedents were announced after the proceedings in the trial court were completed. The Warren Court altered the historical approach to retroactivity in Linkletter v. Walker, 381 U.S. 618 (1965), and Stovall v. Denno, 388 U.S. 293 (1967). *Linkletter*

dealt with the retroactivity of Mapp v. Ohio, 367 U.S. 643 (1961), which applied the exclusionary rule in state court proceedings for evidence obtained through unconstitutional searches or seizures. Under the new retroactivity doctrine, the appellate court could refuse to give some appellants the benefit of a new constitutional ruling. The defendant in the original appeal would always receive the benefit of the ruling, but other appellants who were complaining on direct appeal about government conduct taking place before the announcement of the new rule might or might not receive the benefit. The answer would depend on the three factors described in the *Knight* decision from New Jersey.

These changes in retroactivity doctrine appeared at a time when the Supreme Court was expanding the influence of the federal constitution in state criminal proceedings. What part did the retroactivity doctrine play in the "activism" of the Warren Court? Imagine yourself as one of the justices who routinely opposed the Court's expansive reading of the constitution. What would be your views about the new retroactivity doctrine? Did it limit the "damage" of wrongheaded decisions, or did it make them possible? See John C. Jeffries, Jr., The Right-Remedy Gap in Constitutional Law, 109 Yale L.J. 87 (1999).

In Griffith v. Kentucky, 479 U.S. 314 (1987), the Supreme Court abandoned the flexible *Linkletter* approach to retroactivity and announced that it would apply its decisions to all cases on direct appeal, even if the new rule of law did not exist at the time of the defendant's trial. In the wake of the *Griffith* case, some state courts have followed suit and have altered their own "retroactivity" standards (which govern the application of state law rulings). See State v. Waters, 987 P.2d 1142 (Mont. 1999) (follows *Griffith*; new rules of criminal procedure are applicable to cases still subject to direct review regardless of whether those rules represent "clear breaks" with the past). It is still common, however, to find decisions such as the New Jersey opinion in *Knight* that retain some discretion on the retroactivity question. When courts insist on some flexibility in deciding retroactivity, are they proclaiming an "activist" posture toward constitutional criminal procedure? Are they suggesting that their decisions in this field are more legislative than judicial, in the traditional senses of those terms?

2. *Retroactivity and plain error.* Recall that appellate courts will normally not hear a claim about legal error at trial if defense counsel failed to preserve that error in the trial court; the only exceptions occur when the legal challenge involves a "plain error." How should courts apply this rule when the legal doctrine involved was not explicitly announced until the time interval between the end of trial and the resolution of the appeal? Won't defendants virtually always fail to object at trial to a failure to observe legal requirements that had not been established at the time of trial? Will defendants actually benefit more if the courts ignore the plain error rule in the context of retroactive changes to the law, but apply the more flexible *Linkletter* approach to retroactivity on direct appeal? Consider this endorsement of limited retroactivity over the plain error rule:

[One prominent criticism of flexible retroactivity] can be avoided entirely once it is recalled that there is no freestanding constitutional right to a criminal appeal, much less an absolute entitlement to appellate reversal in any situation in which, according to a reviewing court's best current understanding of the law, a constitutional error occurred at the defendant's trial. . . . In addition to being less objectionable than is often supposed, the nonretroactivity approach has a number of advantages. Nonretroactivity analysis represents an honest effort to confront directly the problems posed by legal change, as well as the real costs of efforts to limit such change's disruptive effects. Not only is this candor a virtue in and of itself, but it also means that the nonretroactivity approach leads us to ask the right sorts of questions. See Toby Heytens, Managing Transitional Moments in Criminal Cases, 115 Yale L.J. 922 (2006).

3. *Retroactivity and collateral review.* Courts usually treat retroactivity questions differently when they arise during post-conviction challenges. Federal courts apply decisions retroactively to cases on direct appeal but not to most defendants who have completed their direct appeals and are bringing a post-conviction collateral attack on the judgment. Teague v. Lane, 489 U.S. 288 (1989). If new legal rules were available for post-conviction challenges, would new claims flood the court whenever it announced a new procedural rule? Could this problem be solved by allowing retroactive application of a new rule only for prisoners who have pending collateral attacks at the time of the decision? Are there reasons other than sheer numbers of claims to treat those on direct appeal differently from those who have filed (or might file) a collateral attack? See Taylor v. State, 10 S.W.3d 673 (Tex. Crim. App. 2000) (rejects federal retroactivity doctrine and adopts a multifactor approach to determine whether new rules of nonconstitutional state law should be retroactively applied in state post-conviction proceedings).

4. *Ex post facto laws and retroactive statutes.* The ex post facto clause of the federal constitution provides that "[n]o state shall . . . pass any . . . ex post facto law." U.S. Const. art. I, §10, cl. 1. In Calder v. Bull, 3 U.S. (3 Dall.) 386, 390 (1798), the Supreme Court explained that the ex post facto clause prohibited the following kinds of laws:

(1) Every law that makes an action done before the passing of the law, and which was innocent when done, criminal, and punishes such action.
(2) Every law that aggravates a crime, or makes it greater than it was when committed.
(3) Every law that changes the punishment, and inflicts a greater punishment than the law annexed to the crime when committed.
(4) Every law that alters the legal rules of evidence, and receives less, or different, testimony than the law required at the time of the commission of the offense in order to convict the offender.

In Thompson v. Utah, 170 U.S. 343 (1898), the Court held that a Utah law reducing the size of a criminal jury from 12 to 8 deprived a defendant of "a substantial right involved in his liberty" and thus violated the ex post facto clause. The Court overruled *Thompson* in Collins v. Youngblood, 497 U.S. 37 (1990), concluding that the ex post facto clause does not apply to every change of procedure that "alters the situation of a party to his disadvantage." It upheld a statute allowing an appellate court to reform an unauthorized verdict without having to remand for retrial, even for crimes committed before the passage of the statute. Does *Collins* give a legislature flexibility on the retroactivity question comparable to that of the *Link-letter* rule? Most courts limit application of the ex post facto principle to laws that enhance punishment or are found to be "substantive" rather than "procedural." See also Rogers v. Tennessee, 532 U.S. 451 (2001) (state supreme court abolished common law defense in criminal case and applied new rule retroactively to defendant; due process clause rather than the ex post facto clause controls this situation because it involves judicial rather than legislative action).

5. *Ex post facto and revivification statutes.* In Stogner v. California, 539 U.S. 607 (2003), the Court addressed for the first time the constitutionality of state "revivification" statutes that revive the possibility of prosecution by creating a new and extended statute of limitations after the original time bar has run. Statutes like the one at issue in *Stogner* have been enacted expressly to deal with the psychology that keeps some young offenders from reporting domestic sexual abuse. Both the majority and dissent treat the issue as an easy one under established ex post facto jurisprudence. Do you agree? The majority distinguishes statutes that merely "extend" a prior statute of limitations that has not yet run, saying in dicta that such statutes are constitutional. Can the principles that limit revivification be distinguished from those that allow extension? Does the ex post facto clause have anything to say about how long statutes of limitation can be in the first place?

XI

Habeas Corpus

A conviction and appeal are not the end of the line for the criminal defendant. Even after the direct appeal is complete, the offender can still challenge the validity of the conviction in court. These post-conviction review procedures take a variety of names with somewhat different historical roots; the best-known form, used in both federal and state constitutions, is the writ of habeas corpus. Some states structure their post-conviction processes around a different historical writ — error coram nobis — which focuses more on new evidence. Others have supplanted the traditional (and quite limited) post-conviction remedies with broader statutes, often simply labeled "post-conviction review" acts. These various post-conviction review procedures are referred to under the general heading of "collateral" review, and they are nominally civil proceedings. If the judge in a collateral proceeding becomes convinced that the government obtained the conviction illegally, she sometimes has the power to grant relief to the "petitioner" and overturn the conviction. In this chapter, we study the conditions under which judges will engage in this collateral review of convictions.

This chapter emphasizes the foundations and future of *judicial* post-conviction review. (There are also executive post-conviction review procedures in most states, including parole and pardon.) The first section of this chapter considers the history and theory behind the common law writ of habeas corpus. The second section considers some of the basic features of collateral review in the states. Two central questions arise here: What distinguishes collateral review procedures from appeals, and to what extent are such procedures necessary at all? The third section considers the particular and highly political debate about federalism that arises when federal courts review and invalidate convictions obtained in state court.

A. HISTORY AND THEORY OF HABEAS CORPUS

Debates today over post-conviction judicial review in the United States focus on what may be a 33-year legal quirk — the expansion of habeas corpus review in federal court of state court convictions. Expanded federal habeas review began around 1963, and has been sharply restricted by judicial decisions and by federal legislation in 1996. But the history of habeas corpus is much older than these recent battles, and is built on concerns about separation of powers and protection of individuals by the judiciary against abuses of power by the executive branch. The future of habeas corpus and other forms of judicial post-conviction review will almost certainly transcend whatever restrictions remain on the special case of federal post-conviction review of state convictions.

The many forms of post-conviction judicial review now available in state courts derive from several historical common law writs; the writ of habeas corpus was the most important of them. In England, even before the time of Magna Carta, courts issued writs of habeas corpus to a government official (usually a jailer or warden) who was detaining a person. The writ, issued after a petitioner established a prima facie case, required the official to appear before the court (along with the prisoner himself — his "corpus") and to present proper justification for detaining the person. The habeas corpus writ became one tool that the English law courts used to release persons held by order of other courts (such as the Chancery and the prerogative courts) and thus to protect the jurisdiction of the law courts. Over time, the habeas corpus writ also became the primary method for challenging royal power to detain a person. Daniel Meador, Habeas Corpus and Magna Carta: Dualism of Power and Liberty 3-9 (1966). In an era of growing distrust of royal power, habeas corpus offered the hope that the rule of law could control executive branch tyranny.

By the early seventeenth century, courts would still refuse to inquire into the validity of a detention in many cases. For instance, in Chamber's Case, 79 Eng. Rep. 746 (K.B. 1629), the petitioner had been detained "by virtue of a decree in the Star Chamber, by reason of certain words he used at the council table, viz. that the merchants of England were screwed up here in England more than in Turkey." He was imprisoned until he agreed to pay a fine of two thousand pounds. When the petitioner asked the royal courts for a writ of habeas corpus to challenge the legality of this confinement, the court refused to grant any relief: "to deliver one who was committed by the decree of one of the Courts of justice, was not the usage of this Court."

However, Parliament strengthened the emerging view of habeas corpus as a writ generally available to challenge illegal detentions in the Habeas Corpus Act of 1679. William Blackstone, in his treatise on English common law, described the terms and significance of this statute:

> [The] glory of the English law consists in clearly defining the times, the causes, and the extent, when, wherefore, and to what degree, the imprisonment of the subject may be lawful. This induces an absolute necessity of expressing upon every commitment the reason for which it is made; that the court upon an *habeas corpus* may examine into its validity; and according to the circumstances of the case may discharge, admit to bail, or remand the prisoner. . . .
>
> [The Habeas Corpus Act of 1679] enacts, 1. That the writ shall be returned and the prisoner brought up within a limited time according to the distance, not exceeding in

any case twenty days. . . . 3. That on complaint and request in writing by or on behalf of any person committed and charged with any crime (unless committed for treason or felony expressed in the warrant, or for suspicion of the same, or as accessory thereto before the fact, or convicted or charged in execution by legal process) the lord chancellor or any of the twelve judges, in vacation, upon viewing a copy of the warrant or affidavit that a copy is denied, shall . . . award a *habeas corpus* for such prisoner, returnable immediately before himself or any other of the judges; and upon the return made shall discharge the party, if bailable, upon giving security to appear and answer to the accusation in the proper court of judicature. . . . 6. That every person committed for treason or felony shall, if he requires it the first week of the next term or the first day of the next session of *oyer* and *terminer*, be indicted in that term or session, or else admitted to bail; unless the king's witnesses cannot be produced at that time: and if acquitted, or if not indicted and tried in the second term of session, he shall be discharged from his imprisonment for such imputed offence.

[By these] admirable regulations, judicial as well as parliamentary, the remedy is now complete for removing the injury of unjust and illegal confinement. A remedy the more necessary, because the oppression does not always arise from the ill-nature, but sometimes from the mere inattention, of government.

Blackstone, 3 Commentaries on the Laws of England 129-38 (1768).

The American colonists of the eighteenth century were acquainted with the English writ of habeas corpus as it had developed in the seventeenth century. It was often used to challenge custody pending trial, and less often to challenge detention based on a conviction issued by a court without proper jurisdiction, or (later) a conviction obtained through improper procedures. See Dallin Oaks, Habeas Corpus in the States — 1776-1865, 32 U. Chi. L. Rev. 243, 258-62 (1965). Despite (or because of) the common use of the writ, most of the earliest state constitutions did not mention habeas corpus or guarantee its availability. One exception was the Massachusetts Constitution of 1780, pt. 2, ch. 6, art. 7, which provided: "The privilege and benefit of the writ of *habeas corpus* shall be enjoyed in this commonwealth, in the most free, easy, cheap, expeditious, and ample manner; and shall not be suspended by the legislature, except upon the most urgent and pressing occasions, and for a limited time, not exceeding twelve months." The federal Constitution, in Article I, section 9, clause 2, declares that "The Privilege of the Writ of Habeas Corpus shall not be suspended, unless when in Cases of Rebellion or Invasion, the public Safety may require it." During the ratification debates, some argued that the guarantee of habeas corpus in Article I did not go far enough. In the end, none of the first ten amendments to the federal constitution mentioned habeas corpus. Apparently, the Article I guarantee was thought to be sufficient.

The legislative debate reprinted below deals with an incident early in our nation's history that revealed the purposes and importance of the habeas corpus writ. In 1804 Vice President Aaron Burr, after losing in his bid to win the governorship of New York and killing Alexander Hamilton in a duel, went to Philadelphia, where he hatched with others a scheme to create a new empire in the West, including parts of Mexico. By 1807 Burr had purchased 1 million acres in Orleans Territory; had gathered supplies, boats, and men; and had sent coded messages to fellow schemers to be ready to attack Mexico.

One of the conspirators, General James Wilkinson (the governor of the Louisiana Territory) revealed the plot. Wilkinson said he had received a coded message from Burr, which indicated that Burr planned to move 500 to 1,000 men in light boats to Natchez by mid-December. In the message, Burr guaranteed the success of the plan with "the lives, the honour, and fortunes of hundreds, the best blood of our country." The people of the region, said Burr, "are prepared to receive us" and he anticipated that "in three weeks all will be settled."

Wilkinson's revelation led President Jefferson to order Burr's arrest. After Burr learned of the proclamation for his arrest from a newspaper story, he surrendered at Natchez, was released on bail, and tried to leave the area. He was captured and taken to Richmond to be arraigned before Chief Justice John Marshall. Burr was later indicted for treason, along with several of his coconspirators. Burr was acquitted on September 1, 1807, when Marshall found a failure of proof of "levying War" against the United States as required by the federal Constitution. See Thomas Abernathy, The Burr Conspiracy (1954). In the midst of this threat to national security, the House of Representatives debated the possibility of suspending the availability of a writ of habeas corpus.

■ SUSPENSION OF THE HABEAS CORPUS
U.S. HOUSE OF REPRESENTATIVES
Annals vol. 16, 26 Jan. 1807

A message was received from the Senate, by Mr. SAMUEL SMITH, as follows . . .

Gentlemen of the House of Representatives: The Senate have passed a bill suspending for three months the privilege of the writ of habeas corpus, in certain cases, which they think expedient to communicate to you in confidence, and to request your concurrence therein, as speedily as the emergency of the case shall in your judgment require.

Mr. SMITH also delivered in the bill referred to in the said communication, and then withdrew. The bill was read as follows:

A Bill suspending the writ of Habeas Corpus for three months, in certain cases. *Be it enacted, by the Senate and House of Representatives of the United States of America, in Congress assembled,* That in all cases, where any person or persons, charged on oath with treason, misprision of treason, or other high crime or misdemeanor, endangering the peace, safety, or neutrality of the United States, have been or shall be arrested or imprisoned, by virtue of any warrant or authority of the President of the United States, or from the Chief Executive Magistrate of any State or Territorial Government, or from any person acting under the direction or authority of the President of the United States, the privilege of the writ of *habeas corpus* shall be, and the same hereby is suspended, for and during the term of three months from and after the passage of this act, and no longer. . . .

Mr. BURWELL [noted that the] President, in his Message of the 22d, says, "on the whole the fugitives from Ohio and their associates from Cumberland, or other places in that quarter, cannot threaten serious danger to the city of New Orleans." If that be the case, upon what ground shall we suspend the writ of habeas corpus? Can any person imagine the United States are in danger, after this declaration of the President, who unquestionably possesses more correct information than any other person can be supposed to have.

[The] correct and proper mode of proceeding can be had under the existing laws of the United States. These persons may be transferred from the military to the civil authority, and be proceeded against according to law. Those, therefore, who fear the escape of the traitors already apprehended, and would, by this measure, obviate the difficulty, must perceive that consequence would not ensue. [Is] the danger sufficiently great to justify the suspension of this most important right of the citizen, to proclaim the country in peril, and to adopt a measure so pregnant with mischief, by which the innocent and guilty will be involved in one common destruction? [This] was not the first instance of the kind since the formation of the Federal Government; there had been already two insurrections in the United States, both of which had defied the authority of Congress, and menaced the Union with dissolution. Notwithstanding one of them justified the calling out of fifteen thousand men, and the expenditure of one million of dollars, he had not heard of a proposition to suspend the writ of habeas corpus. . . .

What . . . would be the effect of passing such a law? Would it not establish a dangerous precedent? A corrupt and vicious Administration, under the sanction and example of this law, might harass and destroy the best men of the country. It would only be necessary to excite artificial commotions, circulate exaggerated rumors of danger, and then follows the repetition of this law, by which every obnoxious person, however honest, is surrendered to the vindictive resentment of the Government. It will not be a sufficient answer, that this power will not be abused by the President of the United States. He, Mr. Burwell believed, would not abuse it, but it would be impossible to restrain all those who are under him. Besides, he would not consent to advocate a principle, bad, in itself, because it will not, probably, be abused. For these reasons, Mr. Burwell said, he should vote to reject the bill.

Mr. ELLIOT: [Objectionable] as the bill upon the table is in point of principle, it is, if possible, still more objectionable in point of detail. It invests with the power of violating the first principles of civil and political liberty, not only the supreme Executive, and the Executives of individual States and Territories, but all civil and military officers who may derive any authority whatever from the Chief Magistrate. And it extends the operation of the suspension of the privileges of the habeas corpus, not only to persons guilty or suspected of treason, or misprision of treason, but, to those who may be accused of any other crime or misdemeanor, tending to endanger the "peace, safety, or neutrality," of the United States! What a vast and almost illimitable field of power is here opened, in which Executive discretion may wander at large and uncontrolled! A vast and dangerous scene of power, indeed! It gives the power of dispensing with the ordinary operation of the laws to a host of those *little great men*, who are attached to every Government under heaven. . . .

Mr. VARNUM [asked, Will gentlemen] deny that the conspiracy has been formed with deliberation, and has existed for a long time? Is it not evident that it has become very extensive? If, then, this is the case, and the head of the conspiracy has said that he is aided by a foreign Power; if this is true, are we justified in considering the country in a perfect state of safety, until it is brought to a close? I conceive not. I consider the country, in a degree, in a state of insecurity; and if so, the power is vested in the Congress of the United States, under the Constitution, to suspend the writ of habeas corpus. I am also apprehensive that we shall not be able to trace the conspiracy to its source without such a suspension. We have had an instance in which the head of the conspiracy has been brought before a court of justice, and where nothing has been brought against him. It is not my wish to insinuate that any court or public functionary is contemplated by this conspiracy; yet it is possible that this may be the case, and the very existence of the country may depend on tracing it to its source. . . .

Will gentlemen say that any innocent man will have a finger laid upon him, should this law pass? No; there is no probability of it; it is scarcely possible. But, even if it be possible, if the public good requires the suspension of the privilege, every man attached to the Government and to the liberty he enjoys, will be surely willing to submit to this inconvenience for a time, in order to secure the public happiness. The suspension only applies to particular crimes, the liberties of the people will not therefore be touched. . . . I shall, therefore, vote for this bill, under the impression that it will not have the injurious effects that some gentlemen seem to apprehend; and that it will only more effectually consign the guilty into the hands of justice.

. . . The yeas and nays were then taken on the question, "Shall the bill be rejected?" — yeas 113, nays 19.

■ YASER ESAM HAMDI v. DONALD RUMSFELD
542 U.S. 507 (2004)

O'CONNOR, J.

At this difficult time in our Nation's history, we are called upon to consider the legality of the Government's detention of a United States citizen on United States soil as an "enemy combatant" and to address the process that is constitutionally owed to one who seeks to challenge his classification as such. . . . We hold that although Congress authorized the detention of combatants in the narrow circumstances alleged here, due process demands that a citizen held in the United States as an enemy combatant be given a meaningful opportunity to contest the factual basis for that detention before a neutral decisionmaker.

I.

On September 11, 2001, the al Qaeda terrorist network used hijacked commercial airliners to attack prominent targets in the United States. Approximately 3,000 people were killed in those attacks. One week later, in response to these "acts of treacherous violence," Congress passed a resolution authorizing the President to "use all necessary and appropriate force against those nations, organizations, or persons he determines planned, authorized, committed, or aided the terrorist attacks" or "harbored such organizations or persons, in order to prevent any future acts of international terrorism against the United States by such nations, organizations or persons." Authorization for Use of Military Force ("the AUMF"), 115 Stat. 224. Soon thereafter, the President ordered United States Armed Forces to Afghanistan, with a mission to subdue al Qaeda and quell the Taliban regime that was known to support it.

This case arises out of the detention of a man whom the Government alleges took up arms with the Taliban during this conflict. His name is Yaser Esam Hamdi. Born an American citizen in Louisiana in 1980, Hamdi moved with his family to Saudi Arabia as a child. By 2001, the parties agree, he resided in Afghanistan. At some point that year, he was seized by members of the Northern Alliance, a coalition of military groups opposed to the Taliban government, and eventually was turned over to the United States military. The Government asserts that it initially detained and interrogated Hamdi in Afghanistan before transferring him to the United States Naval Base in Guantanamo Bay in January 2002. In April 2002, upon learning that Hamdi is an American citizen, authorities transferred him to a naval brig in Norfolk, Virginia, where he remained until a recent transfer to a brig in Charleston, South Carolina. The Government contends that Hamdi is an "enemy combatant," and that this status justifies holding him in the United States indefinitely—without formal charges or proceedings—unless and until it makes the determination that access to counsel or further process is warranted.

In June 2002, Hamdi's father, Esam Fouad Hamdi, filed the present petition for a writ of habeas corpus under 28 U.S.C. §2241 in the Eastern District of Virginia, naming as petitioners his son and himself as next friend. The elder Hamdi alleges in the petition that he has had no contact with his son since the Government took custody of him in 2001, and that the Government has held his son "without access to legal counsel or notice of any charges pending against him." The petition contends that Hamdi's detention was not legally authorized. . . . Although his habeas petition provides no details with regard to the factual circumstances surrounding his son's capture and detention, Hamdi's father has asserted in documents found elsewhere in the record that his son went to Afghanistan to do "relief work," and that he had been in that country less than two months before September 11, 2001, and could not have received military training. The 20-year-old was traveling on his own for the first time, his father says, and "because of his lack of experience, he was trapped in Afghanistan once that military campaign began."

[The] Government filed a response and a motion to dismiss the petition. It attached to its response a declaration from one Michael Mobbs (hereinafter "Mobbs Declaration"), who identified himself as Special Advisor to the Under Secretary of Defense for Policy. . . . The declaration states that Hamdi "traveled to Afghanistan" in July or August 2001, and that he thereafter "affiliated with a Taliban military unit and received weapons training." It asserts that Hamdi "remained with his Taliban unit following the attacks of September 11" and that, during the time when Northern Alliance forces were "engaged in battle with the Taliban," Hamdi's Taliban unit surrendered to those forces, after which he "surrendered his Kalishnikov assault rifle" to them. . . . Mobbs states that Hamdi was labeled an enemy combatant "based upon his interviews and in light of his association with the Taliban." According to the declaration, a series of "U.S. military screening teams" determined that Hamdi met the criteria for enemy combatants, and "a subsequent interview of Hamdi has confirmed that he surrendered and gave his firearm to Northern Alliance forces, which supports his classification as an enemy combatant." . . .

II.

. . . There can be no doubt that individuals who fought against the United States in Afghanistan as part of the Taliban, an organization known to have supported the al Qaeda terrorist network responsible for those attacks, are individuals Congress sought to target in passing the AUMF. We conclude that detention of individuals falling into the limited category we are considering, for the duration of the particular conflict in which they were captured, is so fundamental and accepted an incident to war as to be an exercise of the "necessary and appropriate force" Congress has authorized the President to use. . . .

Hamdi objects, nevertheless, that Congress has not authorized the indefinite detention to which he is now subject. . . . We recognize that the national security underpinnings of the "war on terror," although crucially important, are broad and malleable. . . . If the Government does not consider this unconventional war won for two generations, and if it maintains during that time that Hamdi might, if released, rejoin forces fighting against the United States, then the position it has taken throughout the litigation of this case suggests that Hamdi's detention could last for the rest of his life.

It is a clearly established principle of the law of war that detention may last no longer than active hostilities. . . . Active combat operations against Taliban fighters apparently are ongoing in Afghanistan. The United States may detain, for the duration of these hostilities, individuals legitimately determined to be Taliban combatants who engaged in an armed conflict against the United States. If the record establishes that United States troops are still involved in active combat in Afghanistan, those detentions are part of the exercise of "necessary and appropriate force," and therefore are authorized by the AUMF. . . .

III.

Even in cases in which the detention of enemy combatants is legally authorized, there remains the question of what process is constitutionally due to a citizen who disputes his enemy-combatant status. Hamdi argues that he is owed a meaningful and timely hearing and that "extra-judicial detention [that] begins and ends with the submission of an affidavit based on third-hand hearsay" does not comport with the Fifth and Fourteenth Amendments. The Government counters that any more process than was provided below would be both unworkable and "constitutionally intolerable." Our resolution of this dispute requires a careful examination both of the writ of habeas corpus, which Hamdi now seeks to employ as a mechanism of judicial review, and of the Due Process Clause, which informs the procedural contours of that mechanism in this instance.

[It] is undisputed that Hamdi was properly before an Article III court to challenge his detention under 28 U.S.C. §2241. Further, all agree that §2241 and its companion provisions provide at least a skeletal outline of the procedures to be afforded a petitioner in federal habeas review. Most notably, §2243 provides that "the person detained may, under oath, deny any of the facts set forth in the return or allege any other material facts," and §2246 allows the taking of evidence in habeas proceedings by deposition, affidavit, or interrogatories. . . . The Government recognizes the basic procedural protections required by the habeas statute, but asks us to hold that, given both the flexibility of the habeas mechanism and the circumstances presented in this case, . . . no further process is due.

[The Government argues] that further factual exploration is unwarranted and inappropriate in light of the extraordinary constitutional interests at stake. . . . At most, the Government argues, courts should review its determination that a citizen is an enemy combatant under a very deferential "some evidence" standard. Under this review, a court would assume the accuracy of the Government's articulated basis for Hamdi's detention, as set forth in the Mobbs Declaration, and assess only whether that articulated basis was a legitimate one. In response, Hamdi emphasizes that this Court consistently has recognized that an individual challenging his detention may not be held at the will of the Executive without recourse to some proceeding before a neutral tribunal to determine whether the Executive's asserted justifications for that detention have basis in fact and warrant in law. . . .

Both of these positions highlight legitimate concerns. And both emphasize the tension that often exists between the autonomy that the Government asserts is necessary in order to pursue effectively a particular goal and the process that a citizen contends he is due before he is deprived of a constitutional right. The ordinary mechanism that we use for balancing such serious competing interests, and for determining the procedures that are necessary to ensure that a citizen is not "deprived of life, liberty, or property, without due process of law," U.S. Const., Amdt. 5, is the test that we articulated in Mathews v. Eldridge, 424 U.S. 319 (1976). *Mathews* dictates that the process due in any given instance is determined by weighing "the private interest that will be affected by the official action" against the Government's asserted interest, "including the function involved" and the burdens the Government would face in providing greater process. The *Mathews* calculus then contemplates a judicious balancing of these concerns, through an analysis of "the risk of an erroneous deprivation" of the private interest if the process were reduced and the "probable value, if any, of additional or substitute safeguards." We take each of these steps in turn.

It is beyond question that substantial interests lie on both sides of the scale in this case. Hamdi's "private interest . . . affected by the official action," is the most elemental of liberty interests — the interest in being free from physical detention by one's own government. . . . On the other side of the scale are the weighty and sensitive governmental interests in ensuring that those who have in fact fought with the enemy during a war do not return to battle against the United States. [The] law of war and the realities of combat may render such detentions both necessary and appropriate, and our due process analysis need not blink at those realities. Without doubt, our Constitution recognizes that core strategic matters of warmaking belong in the hands of those who are best positioned and most politically accountable for making them.

The Government also argues at some length that its interests in reducing the process available to alleged enemy combatants are heightened by the practical difficulties that would accompany a system of trial-like process. In its view, military officers who are engaged in the serious work of waging battle would be unnecessarily and dangerously distracted by litigation half a world away, and discovery into military operations would both intrude on the sensitive secrets of national defense and result in a futile search for evidence buried under the rubble of war. To the extent that these burdens are triggered by heightened procedures, they are properly taken into account in our due process analysis.

Striking the proper constitutional balance here is of great importance to the Nation during this period of ongoing combat. But it is equally vital that our calculus not give short shrift to the values that this country holds dear or to the privilege that is American citizenship. It is during our most challenging and uncertain moments that our Nation's commitment to due process is most severely tested; and it is in those times that we must preserve our commitment at home to the principles for which we fight abroad.

With due recognition of these competing concerns, we . . . hold that a citizen-detainee seeking to challenge his classification as an enemy combatant must receive notice of the factual basis for his classification, and a fair opportunity to rebut the Government's factual assertions before a neutral decisionmaker. . . . It is equally fundamental that the right to notice and an opportunity to be heard must be granted at a meaningful time and in a meaningful manner. These essential constitutional promises may not be eroded.

At the same time, the exigencies of the circumstances may demand that, aside from these core elements, enemy combatant proceedings may be tailored to alleviate their uncommon potential to burden the Executive at a time of ongoing military conflict. Hearsay, for example, may need to be accepted as the most reliable available evidence from the Government in such a proceeding. Likewise, the Constitution would not be offended by a presumption in favor of the Government's evidence, so long as that presumption remained a rebuttable one and fair opportunity for rebuttal were provided. . . .

We think it unlikely that this basic process will have the dire impact on the central functions of warmaking that the Government forecasts. The parties agree that initial captures on the battlefield need not receive the process we have discussed here; that process is due only when the determination is made to continue to hold those who have been seized. The Government has made clear in its briefing that documentation regarding battlefield detainees already is kept in the ordinary course of military affairs. Any factfinding imposition created by requiring a knowledgeable affiant to summarize these records to an independent tribunal is a minimal one. Likewise, arguments that military officers ought not have to wage war under the threat of litigation lose much of their steam when factual disputes at enemy-combatant hearings are limited to the alleged combatant's acts. This focus meddles little, if at all, in the strategy or conduct of war, inquiring only into the appropriateness of continuing to detain an individual claimed to have taken up arms against the United States. . . .

In so holding, we necessarily reject the Government's assertion that separation of powers principles mandate a heavily circumscribed role for the courts in such circumstances. . . . We have long since made clear that a state of war is not a blank check for the President when it comes to the rights of the Nation's citizens. Whatever power the United States Constitution envisions for the Executive in its exchanges with other nations or with enemy organizations in times of conflict, it most assuredly envisions a role for all three branches when individual liberties are at stake. . . .

Today we are faced only with such a case. Aside from unspecified "screening" processes and military interrogations in which the Government suggests Hamdi could have contested his classification, Hamdi has received no process. An interrogation by one's captor, however effective an intelligence-gathering tool, hardly constitutes a constitutionally adequate factfinding before a neutral decisionmaker. That even purportedly fair adjudicators are disqualified by their interest in the controversy to be decided is, of course, the general rule. Tumey v. Ohio, 273 U.S. 510 (1927). Plainly, the "process" Hamdi has received is not that to which he is entitled under the Due Process Clause. . . .

SOUTER, J., concurring.

[Because Congress adopted the Authorization for Use of Military Force] one week after the attacks of September 11, 2001, it naturally speaks with some generality, but its focus is clear, and that is on the use of military power. It is fairly read to authorize the use of armies and weapons, whether against other armies or individual terrorists. But . . . it never so much as uses the word detention, and there is no reason to think Congress might have perceived any need to augment Executive power to deal with dangerous citizens within the United States, given the well-stocked statutory arsenal of defined criminal offenses covering the gamut of actions that a citizen sympathetic to terrorists might commit. See, e.g., 18 U.S.C. §2339A (material support for various terrorist acts); §2339B (material support to a foreign terrorist organization); §2332a (use of a weapon of mass destruction, including conspiracy and attempt); §2332b(a)(1) (acts of terrorism "transcending national boundaries," including threats, conspiracy, and attempt); §2339C (financing of certain terrorist acts); §3142(e) (pretrial detention). . . .

It is worth adding a further reason for requiring the Government to bear the burden of clearly justifying its claim to be exercising recognized war powers before declaring §4001(a) satisfied. Thirty-eight days after adopting the Force Resolution, Congress passed the statute entitled Uniting and Strengthening America by Providing Appropriate Tools Required to Intercept and Obstruct Terrorism Act of 2001 (USA PATRIOT ACT), 115 Stat. 272; that Act authorized the detention of alien terrorists for no more than seven days in the absence of criminal charges or deportation proceedings, 8 U.S.C. §1226a(a)(5). It is very difficult to believe that the same Congress that carefully circumscribed Executive power over alien terrorists on home soil would not have meant to require the Government to justify clearly its detention of an American citizen held on home soil incommunicado. . . .

Because I find Hamdi's detention forbidden by §4001(a) and unauthorized by the Force Resolution, I would not reach any questions of what process he may be due in litigating disputed issues in a proceeding under the habeas statute or prior to the habeas enquiry itself. . . .

SCALIA, J., dissenting.

. . . Where the Government accuses a citizen of waging war against it, our constitutional tradition has been to prosecute him in federal court for treason or some other crime. Where the exigencies of war prevent that, the Constitution's Suspension Clause, Art. I, §9, cl. 2, allows Congress to relax the usual protections temporarily. Absent suspension, however, the Executive's assertion of military exigency has not been thought sufficient to permit detention without charge. . . .

The very core of liberty secured by our Anglo-Saxon system of separated powers has been freedom from indefinite imprisonment at the will of the Executive. Blackstone stated this principle clearly:

> Of great importance to the public is the preservation of this personal liberty: for if once it were left in the power of any, the highest, magistrate to imprison arbitrarily whomever he or his officers thought proper . . . there would soon be an end of all other rights and immunities. . . . To bereave a man of life, or by violence to confiscate his estate, without accusation or trial, would be so gross and notorious an act of despotism, as must at once convey the alarm of tyranny throughout the whole kingdom. But confinement of the person, by secretly hurrying him to gaol, where his sufferings are unknown or forgotten; is a less public, a less striking, and therefore a more dangerous engine of arbitrary government. . . . To make imprisonment lawful, it must either be, by process from the courts of judicature, or by warrant from some legal officer, having authority to commit to prison; which warrant must be in writing, under the hand and seal of the magistrate, and express the causes of the commitment, in order to be examined into (if necessary) upon a habeas corpus. . . . 1 W. Blackstone, Commentaries on the Laws of England 132-133 (1765).

802 XI ■ Habeas Corpus

These words were well known to the Founders. Hamilton quoted from this very passage in The Federalist No. 84. The two ideas central to Blackstone's understanding — due process as the right secured, and habeas corpus as the instrument by which due process could be insisted upon by a citizen illegally imprisoned — found expression in the Constitution's Due Process and Suspension Clauses.

The gist of the Due Process Clause, as understood at the founding and since, was to force the Government to follow those common-law procedures traditionally deemed necessary before depriving a person of life, liberty, or property. When a citizen was deprived of liberty because of alleged criminal conduct, those procedures typically required committal by a magistrate followed by indictment and trial. . . .

These due process rights have historically been vindicated by the writ of habeas corpus. In England before the founding, the writ developed into a tool for challenging executive confinement. [Under the Habeas Corpus Act of 1679], imprisonment without indictment or trial for felony or high treason under §7 would not exceed approximately three to six months. The writ of habeas corpus was preserved in the Constitution — the only common-law writ to be explicitly mentioned. See Art. I, §9, cl. 2.

The allegations here, of course, are no ordinary accusations of criminal activity. Yaser Esam Hamdi has been imprisoned because the Government believes he participated in the waging of war against the United States. The relevant question, then, is whether there is a different, special procedure for imprisonment of a citizen accused of wrongdoing by aiding the enemy in wartime.

Justice O'Connor, writing for a plurality of this Court, asserts that captured enemy combatants (other than those suspected of war crimes) have traditionally been detained until the cessation of hostilities and then released. That is probably an accurate description of wartime practice with respect to enemy aliens. The tradition with respect to American citizens, however, has been quite different. Citizens aiding the enemy have been treated as traitors subject to the criminal process. . . .

The Founders inherited the understanding that a citizen's levying war against the Government was to be punished criminally. The Constitution provides: "Treason against the United States, shall consist only in levying War against them, or in adhering to their Enemies, giving them Aid and Comfort"; and establishes a heightened proof requirement (two witnesses) in order to "convict" of that offense. Art. III, §3, cl. 1. In more recent times, too, citizens have been charged and tried in Article III courts for acts of war against the United States, even when their noncitizen co-conspirators were not. For example, two American citizens alleged to have participated during World War I in a spying conspiracy on behalf of Germany were tried in federal court. See United States v. Fricke, 259 F. 673 (S.D.N.Y. 1919). . . .

Where the Executive has not pursued the usual course of charge, committal, and conviction, it has historically secured the Legislature's explicit approval of a suspension [of habeas corpus]. Our Federal Constitution contains a provision explicitly permitting suspension, but limiting the situations in which it may be invoked: "The privilege of the Writ of Habeas Corpus shall not be suspended, unless when in Cases of Rebellion or Invasion the public Safety may require it." Art. I, §9, cl. 2. . . .

The Suspension Clause was by design a safety valve, the Constitution's only express provision for exercise of extraordinary authority because of a crisis.

Very early in the Nation's history, President Jefferson unsuccessfully sought a suspension of habeas corpus to deal with Aaron Burr's conspiracy to overthrow the Government. During the Civil War, Congress passed its first Act authorizing Executive suspension of the writ of habeas corpus, to the relief of those many who thought President Lincoln's unauthorized proclamations of suspension unconstitutional. . . . During Reconstruction, Congress passed the Ku Klux Klan Act, which included a provision authorizing suspension of the writ, invoked by President Grant in quelling a rebellion in nine South Carolina counties.

[The] text of the 1679 Habeas Corpus Act makes clear that indefinite imprisonment on reasonable suspicion is not an available option of treatment for those accused of aiding the enemy, absent a suspension of the writ. In the United States, this Act was read as enforcing the common law, and shaped the early understanding of the scope of the writ. . . . Section 7 of the Act specifically addressed those committed for high treason, and provided a remedy if they were not indicted and tried by the second succeeding court term. That remedy was not a bobtailed judicial inquiry into whether there were reasonable grounds to believe the prisoner had taken up arms against the King. Rather, if the prisoner was not indicted and tried within the prescribed time, "he shall be discharged from his Imprisonment." The Act does not contain any exception for wartime. . . .

The proposition that the Executive lacks indefinite wartime detention authority over citizens is consistent with the Founders' general mistrust of military power permanently at the Executive's disposal. In the Founders' view, the "blessings of liberty" were threatened by "those military establishments which must gradually poison its very fountain." The Federalist No. 45 (J. Madison). No fewer than 10 issues of the Federalist were devoted in whole or part to allaying fears of oppression from the proposed Constitution's authorization of standing armies in peacetime. Many safeguards in the Constitution reflect these concerns. Congress's authority "to raise and support Armies" was hedged with the proviso that "no Appropriation of Money to that Use shall be for a longer Term than two Years." U.S. Const., Art. 1, §8, cl. 12. . . . A view of the Constitution that gives the Executive authority to use military force rather than the force of law against citizens on American soil flies in the face of the mistrust that engendered these provisions.

It follows from what I have said that Hamdi is entitled to a habeas decree requiring his release unless (1) criminal proceedings are promptly brought, or (2) Congress has suspended the writ of habeas corpus. . . .

If Hamdi is being imprisoned in violation of the Constitution (because without due process of law), then his habeas petition should be granted; the Executive may then hand him over to the criminal authorities, whose detention for the purpose of prosecution will be lawful, or else must release him. . . .

If civil rights are to be curtailed during wartime, it must be done openly and democratically, as the Constitution requires, rather than by silent erosion through an opinion of this Court. . . .

THOMAS, J., dissenting.

The Executive Branch, acting pursuant to the powers vested in the President by the Constitution and with explicit congressional approval, has determined that Yaser Hamdi is an enemy combatant and should be detained. This detention falls squarely within the Federal Government's war powers, and we lack the expertise and capacity to second-guess that decision. As such, petitioners' habeas challenge should fail. . . .

[In] United States v. Salerno, 481 U.S. 739 (1987), the Court explained that the Due Process Clause "lays down [no] categorical imperative." The Court continued: "We have repeatedly held that the Government's regulatory interest in community safety can, in appropriate circumstances, outweigh an individual's liberty interest. For example, in times of war or insurrection, when society's interest is at its peak, the Government may detain individuals whom the Government believes to be dangerous." Cf. Kansas v. Hendricks, 521 U.S. 346 (1997). The Government's asserted authority to detain an individual that the President has determined to be an enemy combatant, at least while hostilities continue, comports with the Due Process Clause. . . .

Problem 11-1. Citizen and Designated Enemy

The United States government took Jose Padilla, a United States citizen, into custody in May 2002. When Padilla filed in federal court for a writ of habeas corpus, the government offered the following account of events to explain why the court should not hear his claim on the merits.

According to the government, al Qaeda operatives recruited Jose Padilla to train for jihad in Afghanistan in February 2000, while Padilla was on a religious pilgrimage to Saudi Arabia. Subsequently, Padilla met with al Qaeda operatives in Afghanistan, received explosives training in an al Qaeda–affiliated camp, and served as an armed guard at what he understood to be a Taliban outpost. When United States military operations began in Afghanistan, Padilla and other al Qaeda operatives moved from safehouse to safehouse to evade bombing or capture. Padilla was, according to the government, "armed and present in a combat zone during armed conflict between al Qaeda/Taliban forces and the armed forces of the United States."

Padilla eventually escaped to Pakistan, armed with an assault rifle. Once in Pakistan, Padilla met with Khalid Sheikh Mohammad, a senior al Qaeda operations planner, who directed Padilla to travel to the United States for the purpose of blowing up apartment buildings, in continued prosecution of al Qaeda's war of terror against the United States. After receiving further training, as well as cash, travel documents, and communication devices, Padilla flew to the United States to carry out his accepted assignment.

Upon arrival at Chicago's O'Hare International Airport on May 8, 2002, Padilla was detained by FBI agents, who interviewed and eventually arrested him pursuant to a material witness warrant issued by the district court for the Southern District of New York in conjunction with a grand jury investigation of the September 11 attacks. Padilla was transported to New York, where he was held at a civilian correctional facility until, on June 9, 2002, the president designated him an "enemy combatant" against the United States and directed the secretary of defense to take him into military custody. The text of the president's memorandum appears below:

> Based on the information available to me from all sources,
>   In accordance with the Constitution and consistent with the laws of the United States, including the Authorization for Use of Military Force Joint Resolution;

I, George W. Bush, as President of the United States and Commander in Chief of the U.S. armed forces, hereby determine for the United States of America that:

(1) Jose Padilla, who is under the control of the Department of Justice and who is a U.S. citizen, is, and at the time he entered the United States in May 2002 was, an enemy combatant;

(2) Mr. Padilla is closely associated with al Qaeda, an international terrorist organization with which the United States is at war;

(3) Mr. Padilla engaged in conduct that constituted hostile and war-like acts, including conduct in preparation for acts of international terrorism that had the aim to cause injury to or adverse effects on the United States;

(4) Mr. Padilla possesses intelligence, including intelligence about personnel and activities of al Qaeda, that, if communicated to the U.S., would aid U.S. efforts to prevent attacks by al Qaeda on the United States or its armed forces, other governmental personnel, or citizens;

(5) Mr. Padilla represents a continuing, present and grave danger to the national security of the United States, and detention of Mr. Padilla is necessary to prevent him from aiding al Qaeda in its efforts to attack the United States or its armed forces, other governmental personnel, or citizens;

(6) it is in the interest of the United States that the Secretary of Defense detain Mr. Padilla as an enemy combatant; and

(7) it is consistent with U.S. law and the laws of war for the Secretary of Defense to detain Mr. Padilla as enemy combatant.

Accordingly, you are directed to receive Mr. Padilla from the Department of Justice and to detain him as an enemy combatant.

After his delivery into the custody of military authorities, Padilla was detained at a naval brig in South Carolina. In his petition for a writ of habeas corpus, Padilla claimed that his detention violated the Constitution. Based on the opinions in Hamdi v. Rumsfeld, do you believe a federal court would hear the merits of Padilla's claim? What constitutional arguments do you anticipate he would make? Cf. Padilla v. Hanft, 423 F.3d 386 (4th Cir. 2005).

Notes

1. *Habeas corpus, error coram nobis, and statutory forms of the writs.* In the common law tradition, habeas corpus is the writ allowing a judge to inquire into the lawfulness of detention. The person petitioning for the writ asks a judge with jurisdiction over the detaining official (such as a prison warden) to issue the writ and to require this official to justify the detention. The petitioner could be a criminal defendant awaiting trial, an immigrant in a detention facility, or a convicted person who questions the legal validity of the criminal conviction. The writ of error coram nobis has a different emphasis. It allows the court that entered judgment on a criminal conviction to reopen proceedings when presented with new *facts* not available during the earlier proceedings. Every state has statutes or rules to codify and extend the reach of the common law writs, under generic titles such as "post-conviction relief."

2. *Habeas corpus as a post-conviction remedy.* Historians disagree sharply about the types of petitioners who could obtain a writ of habeas corpus. According to one view, the traditional habeas corpus writ in England and the United States was available only to challenge pretrial detention, or in rare instances for persons convicted of a crime by a court lacking jurisdiction. See Ex parte Watkins, 28 U.S. (3 Pet.) 193

(1830) (convicted person sought habeas relief because federal indictment failed to state an offense; court declined, saying that "the judgment of a court of general criminal jurisdiction justifies his imprisonment, and . . . the writ of habeas corpus ought not to be awarded"); Paul Bator, Finality in Criminal Law and Federal Habeas Corpus for State Prisoners, 76 Harv. L. Rev. 441 (1963) (habeas corpus extended to convictions in courts lacking jurisdiction or to convictions in states which provided no reasonable opportunity to raise claims). Is it relevant that the 1807 debate over suspension of habeas corpus focused on the power of the executive to arrest and detain persons before trial, rather than any unjust detention after conviction?

Other historians contend that habeas corpus was available in the nineteenth century to challenge the validity of criminal convictions obtained through some fundamental injustice, such as a procedural error at trial that violated the due process clause. Gary Peller, In Defense of Federal Habeas Corpus Relitigation, 16 Harv. C.R.-C.L. L. Rev. 579 (1982); see also Ann Woolhandler, Demodeling Habeas, 45 Stan. L. Rev. 575 (1993); James Liebman, Apocalypse Next Time? The Anachronistic Attack on Habeas Corpus/Direct Review Parity, 92 Colum. L. Rev. 1997 (1992). According to this view, whatever limits may have applied at one time to the common law writ of habeas corpus, courts in the nineteenth century evolved toward using the habeas writ as a method to challenge final convictions on grounds other than jurisdictional defects. Some support for the expansive view comes from Ex parte Lange, 85 U.S. (18 Wall.) 163 (1873). Lange was convicted in federal court of the theft of postal equipment, and he challenged the conviction in habeas corpus on double jeopardy grounds. The Supreme Court declared that a constitutional error in the proceedings, such as a double jeopardy error at sentencing, could deprive a court of jurisdiction. See also Whitten v. Tomlinson, 160 U.S. 231 (1895).

The historical debate over the scope of habeas corpus is important when deciding the type of review that legislators intended when they codified habeas corpus practice in statutes such as the federal Habeas Corpus Act of 1867. In the end, it will prove very difficult to resolve all historical doubts, because the evidence of habeas corpus practice in American and English courts is limited to a handful of arguably atypical appellate decisions.

3. *The federal constitutional guarantee of habeas.* Article I, section 9, clause 2 of the federal Constitution says that habeas corpus "shall not be suspended, unless when in Cases of Rebellion or Invasion the public Safety may require it." The purpose of this constitutional language, like the scope of traditional habeas corpus relief, is not entirely clear today. Perhaps it was designed to prevent the Congress from limiting federal judicial review of federal convictions. See Ex Parte Bollman and Swartout, 8 U.S. (4 Cranch) 75 (1807) (declaring that habeas corpus must be available in federal court for federal prisoners, including those accused of participation in the Burr conspiracy). If so, the Judiciary Act of 1789 avoided any constitutional problems by giving federal judges the power to grant writs of habeas corpus to prisoners in custody under federal law. On the other hand, perhaps the Article I guarantee was meant to prevent Congress from interfering in *state* court review of those held in federal custody. See William Duker, A Constitutional History of Habeas Corpus 8, 126-80 (1980); but see Tarble's Case, 80 U.S. (13 Wall.) 397 (1871) (rejecting this reading of Article I guarantee).

It is quite clear that the drafters of the federal Constitution did not intend in Article I to guarantee the availability of federal habeas corpus for those convicted in state court. The Judiciary Act of 1789 explicitly barred such federal review, and created no controversy at the time. Nevertheless, it is entirely possible that constitutional change of various sorts (including the process of "incorporation" under the Fourteenth Amendment) may have converted the Article I guarantee into a constitutional protection for federal habeas review of state convictions. See Jordan Steiker, Incorporating the Suspension Clause: Is There a Constitutional Right to Federal Habeas Corpus for State Prisoners?, 92 Mich. L. Rev. 862, 871-74 (1994).

In Felker v. Turpin, 518 U.S. 651 (1996), the Supreme Court considered the constitutionality of a federal statute placing limits on "successive" federal habeas corpus petitions (petitions after the first one). It held that these statutory limits did not repeal the Supreme Court's authority to entertain original habeas petitions, and were not comprehensive enough to constitute a "suspension" of habeas corpus. Throughout its discussion, the Court assumed that the federal constitution *does* require that state prisoners have some form of habeas corpus writ in federal court: "[W]e assume, for purposes of decision here, that the Suspension Clause of the Constitution refers to the writ as it exists today, rather than as it existed in 1789."

B. THE AVAILABILITY OF POST-CONVICTION REVIEW

Post-conviction review is available to correct some errors in the criminal process even after that process has reached its final conclusion at the close of a direct appeal. Every state currently has a post-conviction review process that has been substantially modernized and restructured in the last 50 years. The major state reforms of post-conviction process took place in the 1960s through the 1980s, though many states have continued to adjust their post-conviction machinery. The post-conviction legal terrain is convoluted, since in a majority of states more than one form of post-conviction remedy applies. For example, in around a dozen states, the writ of habeas corpus is the principal post-conviction remedy, while in almost 40 states the principal form of collateral review is modeled on error coram nobis. The legislature has rewritten the law in the majority of states, but in a few states the modernization of the habeas corpus procedures have come through case law or judicially promulgated court rules. Changes in the past decade or so have tended to make post-conviction review more difficult to obtain. See generally Donald Wilkes, Federal and State Postconviction Remedies and Relief §9-2 (1992) (Appendix A).

Regardless of the form of collateral review allowed in each state, a few central questions define the essential function and scope of such review. For example, post-conviction review is not able to correct every error and every shortcoming of the earlier proceedings. First, there are some *subjects* that are not "cognizable" on post-conviction review: even though the trial court or appellate court may have decided the question wrongly, post-conviction relief is not available for questions dealing with that subject matter and the mistake will go uncorrected for the sake of "finality" in the criminal justice process. Second, there may be some claims that do raise a subject that is cognizable, and yet the claim cannot be heard because the defendant (or the "petitioner" in post-conviction proceedings) failed to follow the proper *procedures* to keep the issue alive, such as objecting to the error at trial, or raising the issue on direct appeal. The following materials consider these two types of limitations on all claims for post-conviction relief. The third part of this chapter considers what has become an especially frequent and compelling claim on collateral review: whether trial or appellate counsel provided adequate assistance.

1. Cognizable Subject Matter

There are some subjects that no court will consider in any post-conviction proceeding as a basis for overturning a conviction. States draw different lines to mark the subjects that are off limits for post-conviction review. Sometimes the statutes distinguish between constitutional and nonconstitutional claims, with only the former qualifying as a proper subject for post-conviction review. Other statutes reserve collateral review for violations of a criminal defendant's "fundamental" rights. Still others allow challenges based on any "illegal" action. One recurring question deals with claims of actual innocence. When a petitioner claims that there is new evidence to show that she did not commit the crime, will a court ever refuse to hear the claim because of subject matter limits?

■ 42 PENNSYLVANIA CONSOLIDATED STATUTES §9543(a)

To be eligible for relief under this subchapter, the petitioner must plead and prove by a preponderance of the evidence all of the following:
(1) That the petitioner has been convicted of a crime under the laws of this Commonwealth and is at the time relief is granted . . . serving a sentence of imprisonment, probation or parole for the crime . . . .
(2) That the conviction or sentence resulted from one or more of the following:
(i) A violation of the Constitution of this Commonwealth or the Constitution or laws of the United States which, in the circumstances of the particular case, so undermined the truth-determining process that no reliable adjudication of guilt or innocence could have taken place. . . .
(iii) A plea of guilty unlawfully induced where the circumstances make it likely that the inducement caused the petitioner to plead guilty and the petitioner is innocent.
(iv) The improper obstruction by government officials of the petitioner's right of appeal where a meritorious appealable issue existed and was properly preserved in the trial court. . . .
(vi) The unavailability at the time of trial of exculpatory evidence that has subsequently become available and would have changed the outcome of the trial if it had been introduced.
(vii) The imposition of a sentence greater than the lawful maximum.
(viii) A proceeding in a tribunal without jurisdiction.
(3) That the allegation of error has not been previously litigated or waived.
(4) That the failure to litigate the issue prior to or during trial, during unitary review or on direct appeal could not have been the result of any rational, strategic or tactical decision by counsel.

■ OKLAHOMA STATUTES, TIT. 22, §1089(c)

The only issues that may be raised in an application for post-conviction relief [by a petitioner sentenced to death] are those that:

1. Were not and could not have been raised in a direct appeal; and
2. Support a conclusion either that the outcome of the trial would have been different but for the errors or that the defendant is factually innocent.

The applicant shall state in the application specific facts explaining as to each claim why it was not or could not have been raised in a direct appeal and how it supports a conclusion that the outcome of the trial would have been different but for the errors or that the defendant is factually innocent. . . .

■ PEOPLE v. KURTIS WASHINGTON
665 N.E.2d 1330 (Ill. 1995)

FREEMAN, J.

The question in this case is whether due process is implicated in a claim of innocence based upon new evidence so as to permit the claim to be raised in a petition under the Post-Conviction Hearing Act (725 ILCS 5/122-1 et seq.). We hold that it is.

In 1982, Kurtis Washington was sentenced to 25 years in prison for murdering Tony Hightie. Hightie had been murdered outside his home in Chicago shortly after 9 P.M. on May 9, 1980. Washington was implicated in the crime by Donna McClure, Hightie's girlfriend, and Ronald Tapes.

McClure and Tapes witnessed the murder. At trial, they said that they had been sitting in a parked car near Hightie's home when they were approached by a man. The man said that he was looking for someone named Will. When McClure and Tapes proved no help, the man approached Hightie just as he left his home. Hightie had been wearing a jacket and hat that belonged to Tapes' brother, who was named William. McClure and Tapes said that after a few words with Hightie, the man shot him. The man, McClure and Tapes said, was Washington. Washington's defense was that he had been at a grocery store at the time of Hightie's murder. The store cashier, a person who had accompanied Washington, and Washington's mother all testified to that fact.

The [intermediate] appellate court affirmed the conviction and sentence on direct review. In 1990, Washington filed a post-conviction petition [including a claim that new evidence cast doubt on the accuracy of the verdict. The claim was supported with an affidavit and in camera testimony of Jacqueline Martin]. Martin, who was 16 years old at the time, told how she had been present when Marcus Halsey, then her boyfriend, and Frank Caston had left Halsey's house to revenge an earlier beating of Halsey's brother. She, Halsey, Caston, and Caston's girlfriend drove in a car to an alley in a neighborhood in Chicago. She later learned that it happened to be the neighborhood where Hightie lived. Martin told how, after Halsey and Caston left the car, she had heard two gunshots, and, when the two returned, she had heard Halsey say "it was the wrong guy." . . .

Halsey was questioned by police the next morning. . . . Martin said that after the police questioning, Halsey had threatened to kill her if she told anyone what had happened. Halsey's threats continued, Martin said, and so she eventually stopped going to Halsey's house. Some months later, Halsey's brother confronted her as she was walking near a park and forcibly took her to Halsey. She said that she was kept against her will at Halsey's house for three weeks to a month. She eventually escaped [and] went immediately to her mother's house. That same day she left for Mississippi. She stayed there for six years. Martin told how at the time of the hearing she still feared Halsey. [T]he trial judge granted a new trial on the ground that Martin's testimony was new evidence which, if believed, would have "had some significant impact" upon the jury. The State appealed. . . .

The claim Washington raised is a "free-standing" claim of innocence; the newly discovered evidence is not being used to supplement an assertion of a constitutional violation with respect to his trial [such as a claim that counsel was ineffective in failing to investigate and uncover the new evidence]. The issue is not whether the evidence at trial was insufficient to convict Washington beyond a reasonable doubt. The appellate court rejected that challenge on direct appeal. The issue is whether Washington's claim of newly discovered evidence can be raised in a petition under the Post-Conviction Hearing Act to entitle Washington to a new trial. Post-conviction relief is Washington's remaining hope for a judicial remedy, the time limitations of other avenues offering relief for such a claim having lapsed. See 735 ILCS 5/2-1202(c) (allowing such claims to be made in a motion for a new trial within 30 days); 735 ILCS 5/2-1401(c) (permitting such claims up to two years after a final judgment, the period being excused in certain limited situations, including "fraudulent" concealment of evidence). Executive clemency, of course, would remain available to Washington.

To decide the issue, we must see if either a federal or Illinois constitutional right is implicated in such a free-standing claim of innocence, since Post-Conviction Hearing Act relief is limited to constitutional claims. 725 ILCS 5/122-1. Washington argues that his claim implicates due process protections. The beginning point for addressing that argument is Herrera v. Collins, 506 U.S. 390 (1993), where the Supreme Court rejected the contention as a federal constitutional matter. In light of our own constitution's due process guaranty, we must also assess Washington's argument as a matter of Illinois constitutional jurisprudence.

The issue in *Herrera* was whether a free-standing claim of innocence following a Texas capital conviction could be raised in a habeas corpus petition in view of either the eighth amendment protection against cruel and unusual punishment or the fourteenth amendment due process clause. Ten years after his conviction, Herrera claimed that his brother, who had since died, committed the crimes. The claim was supported by two affidavits. . . .

Looking first to the eighth amendment, the Court admitted an "elemental appeal" in the notion that the Constitution should be construed to prohibit the execution or imprisonment of the innocent. But constitutionally, a newly discovered evidence claim had to "be evaluated in the light of the previous proceedings" in which guilt or innocence was determined. The Court explained that once the usual constitutional safeguards for ensuring against the risk of convicting the innocent in trial proceedings were met, a conviction must mean that the person convicted is no longer "innocent" but is one "who has been convicted by due process of law." Recognizing a free-standing claim of innocence would amount to according "additional process." . . . A claim of innocence itself simply was not, the Court concluded, cognizable under the eighth amendment [or the due process clause].

In the last portion of the opinion, the Court nevertheless addressed "for the sake of argument" the petitioner's claim—rejecting it—as if it were constitutionally cognizable. To do so, the Court proceeded under an assumption that "a truly persuasive demonstration of actual innocence" in a capital case where there was "no state avenue open to process such a claim" would be unconstitutional. . . . On one hand *Herrera* underscores the unkind reality that, though the Constitution offers unparalleled protections against convicting the innocent, it cannot guaranty that result. Then again, the last portion of the opinion suggests that the Constitution must somehow be made to do so, at least in a capital case. . . .

Conflicted or not, at least for noncapital cases, *Herrera* clearly states . . . that a free-standing claim of innocence is not cognizable as a fourteenth amendment due process claim. And so Washington's effort to state a federal constitutional due process claim under the Post-Conviction Hearing Act must fail.

The possibility remains that Washington's claim may be cognizable under the Illinois Constitution's due process protection. . . . Perhaps the closest this court has come to determining that our constitution's due process clause could be a means to recognize a newly discovered evidence claim for post-conviction purposes was in People v. Cornille, 448 N.E.2d 857 (Ill. 1983). There, the court held that a post-conviction claim based upon the discovery that an expert testifying in an arson prosecution lied about his expertise was cognizable under the due process clauses of both the United States and Illinois Constitutions. However, the decision did not turn on a differentiation of the clauses. The State's failure to prevent the perjury by verifying the expert's credentials was sufficient "indicia of State action" which, linked to the "adjudicatory process," made the expert's conduct a due process violation under both. *Cornille* finds its place among a long line of related cases holding that the use of false testimony underlying a conviction is a due process violation.

Those kinds of claims are fundamentally different from ones such as Washington has raised. Washington can claim no state action with regard to the evidence he now relies upon for post-conviction relief. And the "adjudicatory process" by which he was convicted did not otherwise lack due process. Essentially, then, the issue is the time relativeness of due process as a matter of this State's constitutional jurisprudence; that is, should additional process be afforded in Illinois when newly discovered evidence indicates that a convicted person is actually innocent?

We believe so as a matter of both procedural and substantive due process. In terms of procedural due process, we believe that to ignore such a claim would be fundamentally unfair. Imprisonment of the innocent would also be so conscience shocking as to trigger operation of substantive due process. The conflicted analysis in *Herrera* is some proof of that. . . . The Supreme Court rejected substantive due process as means to recognize free-standing innocence claims because of the idea that a person convicted in a constitutionally fair trial must be viewed as guilty. That made it impossible for such a person to claim that he, an innocent person, was unfairly convicted.

We think that the Court overlooked that a "truly persuasive demonstration of innocence" would, in hindsight, undermine the legal construct precluding a substantive due process analysis. The stronger the claim—the more likely it is that a convicted person is actually innocent—the weaker is the legal construct dictating that the person be viewed as guilty. A "truly persuasive demonstration of innocence" would effectively reduce the idea to legal fiction. . . .

We therefore hold as a matter of Illinois constitutional jurisprudence that a claim of newly discovered evidence showing a defendant to be actually innocent of the crime for which he was convicted is cognizable as a matter of due process. That holding aligns Illinois with other jurisdictions likewise recognizing, primarily as a matter of state habeas corpus jurisprudence, a basis to raise such claims under the rubric of due process. [The court cited cases from Texas, Connecticut, and Florida.]

That only means, of course, that there is footing in the Illinois Constitution for asserting free-standing innocence claims based upon newly discovered evidence under the Post-Conviction Hearing Act. Procedurally, such claims should be resolved as any other brought under the Act. Substantively, relief has been held to require that the supporting evidence be new, material, noncumulative and, most importantly, of such conclusive character as would probably change the result on retrial. As for this case, we find neither reason to disagree with the appellate court that those concerns were satisfied nor need to elaborate upon that conclusion. The judgment of the appellate court is affirmed.

McMorrow, J., specially concurring.

. . . The State asks this court to overrule the holding in State v. Molstad, 461 N.E.2d 398 (Ill. 1984), that the defendant's evidence must be "of such conclusive character that it will probably change the result on retrial." The State argues that this court should adopt a more stringent standard by which to gauge a post-conviction petitioner's claim of newly discovered evidence of actual innocence. The State proposes that the defendant should be required to prove that, based upon the newly discovered evidence as well as the other evidence produced at trial, no rational trier of fact could find beyond a reasonable doubt that the defendant was guilty of the crime charged. However, this standard applies to a review of the evidence where the defendant claims that the State's evidence was insufficient to prove him guilty beyond a reasonable doubt. Moreover, where a reviewing court determines that no rational trier of fact could find the defendant guilty beyond a reasonable doubt, the proper remedy is not a new trial but an acquittal on the charges for which there was insufficient evidence to convict the defendant. In light of these considerations, the more stringent standard suggested by the State is not properly applicable to a post-conviction request for a new trial based on newly discovered evidence of actual innocence. . . .

Requests for a new trial based on newly discovered evidence of actual innocence are to be viewed with great caution and are not lightly granted. The trial court's determination is a discretionary one that will be overturned only upon a clear abuse of discretion. There is no basis in the present record to find an abuse of discretion in the trial court's granting of the defendant's request for post-conviction relief because of newly discovered evidence of actual innocence.

The record shows that the defendant could not have discovered Jacqueline Martin or the substance of her testimony while he was standing trial for the Hightie murder. At the time defendant was being prosecuted, Jacqueline had fled to Mississippi and virtually no one knew of her whereabouts. . . .

The record also demonstrates that Jacqueline's testimony was critical to a determination of defendant's guilt. . . . Jacqueline's testimony established that Marcus and Frank went to Tony Hightie's neighborhood on the night of the shooting, that they had a gun with them, and that they went there in order to retaliate for the beating that Marcus' brother had sustained earlier that day. Jacqueline stated that

Marcus and Frank left the car and walked to a nearby location. Jacqueline then heard two gunshots and the boys came running back to the vehicle. Jacqueline heard Marcus tell Frank that they had shot the wrong person. . . .

In light of this evidence, I find no error in the trial court's allowance of the defendant's post-conviction petition. . . . I note that defendant's post-conviction petition included photographs of both the defendant and Frank Caston, an alleged friend of Marcus, and that these photographs show a remarkable facial resemblance between defendant and Frank Caston. For these reasons, I concur in the majority's conclusion that the defendant in the instant cause should receive a new trial.

MILLER, J., dissenting.

. . . Illinois law affords convicted defendants a number of opportunities to raise allegations of newly discovered evidence of innocence; the availability of these forms of relief refutes the majority's conclusion that procedural due process compels a post-conviction remedy for the same claim. First, a defendant may present such evidence in a motion for a new trial, filed within 30 days of the verdict or finding of guilty. If the defendant discovers the evidence too late to satisfy the preceding time limit, relief may be available under section 2-1401 of the Code of Civil Procedure. While at one time it was the rule that claims of newly discovered evidence could not be raised in a petition under [this section], more recent cases have recognized that such claims may be prosecuted under section 2-1401. Notably, the two-year time limit for bringing actions under section 2-1401 corresponds to the two-year limit imposed by Rule 33 of the Federal Rules of Criminal Procedure, which provides the sole means for bringing claims of newly discovered evidence of innocence by convicted defendants in the federal system. . . . Because Illinois law provides convicted defendants with sufficient means by which to raise claims of actual innocence, I do not agree with the majority that considerations of procedural due process mandate an additional remedy under the Post-Conviction Hearing Act.

As an alternative basis for today's holding, the majority concludes that principles of substantive due process also compel recognition of the defendant's claim. This further rationale is equally unpersuasive, however. A defendant seeking to assert a claim of actual innocence in a post-conviction petition has, by definition, been convicted of the charge following a trial or a guilty plea. [T]he majority asserts that the "legal construct" of a convicted defendant's guilt becomes weaker as the showing of actual innocence grows stronger. Although that observation has some theoretical appeal, it slights the role of the trial in our system of criminal justice. At the time a person files a post-conviction petition, he stands before the court, and society, as a convicted defendant, having been found guilty following a trial or guilty plea at which, presumably, all constitutional rights were honored. I do not believe that the legal significance of that event waxes or wanes depending on the strength of a subsequent showing of actual innocence. Given the passage of time, and the fading of memories, there can certainly he no assurance that an adjudication made following a new trial would be any more reliable than the adjudication of the original proceeding, which produced the defendant's conviction. . . .

Finally, I would note that the out-of-state authorities cited by the majority in support of today's decision are fundamentally different from the case at bar. . . . The cases cited by the majority either involve capital defendants or were maintained under statutes that do not expressly require a constitutional violation as a predicate for relief.

BILANDIC, C.J., dissenting.

. . . What standard for relief should apply to a post-conviction petitioner raising a free-standing claim of actual innocence based on newly discovered evidence? Without any analysis, the majority applies the standard applicable to a defendant's post-trial motion for a new trial: i.e., the newly discovered evidence must be "new, material, noncumulative" and of such conclusive character as would "probably change the result on retrial." The majority then awards the defendant a new trial in which he can present his newly discovered evidence, the testimony of Jacqueline Martin.

This standard is not appropriate for analyzing post-conviction petitioners' claims of actual innocence for many reasons. The standard (1) does not comport with the rationale underlying the majority's recognition of this due process right; (2) wrongly cloaks the already-convicted defendant with a new presumption of innocence; (3) gives no consideration to the need for finality in criminal proceedings; and (4) inappropriately requires a new trial, which may take place decades after the crime and original trial. Also, the standard is not consistent with that applied in other jurisdictions.

The . . . problem with the majority's standard is that it allows the presumption of innocence to survive a constitutionally valid conviction. This happens because the defendant is awarded a new trial in which the State will again bear the burden of proving the defendant's guilt beyond a reasonable doubt. This result is not acceptable. An appropriate standard would recognize that a valid conviction strips the defendant of the presumption of innocence. Accordingly, the defendant should bear the burden of proving his actual innocence.

[T]he majority's standard [also] fails to give due consideration to society's interests in the finality of criminal proceedings. An appropriate standard would take into account the passage of time and would recognize that it becomes substantially more difficult for the State to obtain convictions once memories have faded and evidence has disappeared. . . .

Given the many serious problems with the majority's standard, it is not surprising that other jurisdictions have explicitly rejected it. [The dissenting opinion cited cases from California, Connecticut, and Texas.] This court should not have adopted it either. I urge my fellow justices to rectify this grave error as quickly as possible.

Notes

1. *New facts establishing innocence in post-conviction proceedings: majority position.* Most states have several statutory routes for convicted persons to submit new evidence to demonstrate their innocence. Motions for new trials may be granted on the basis of newly available evidence, although the time limit for such motions is often brief. The ancient writ of error coram nobis focused on the presentation of new evidence, and that practice is now reflected in the post-conviction remedy statutes and case law of most states. See In re Clark, 855 P.2d 729 (Cal. 1993) (habeas corpus available for claims of new evidence, jurisdictional defects, or constitutional claims carrying risk of convicting an innocent person).

The difficult questions arise when the available post-conviction remedy statute limits coverage (as in the Illinois statute at issue in *Washington*) to constitutional questions. Is there a constitutional violation when the state holds a convicted person in custody in the face of convincing evidence of innocence? As we saw, the U.S. Supreme Court declared in Herrera v. Collins, 506 U.S. 390 (1993), that claims of new evidence of innocence do not ordinarily raise due process questions that a federal court must hear on habeas corpus. Only a few state courts have confronted this question, because statutes often provide for methods of considering such evidence regardless of its constitutional status. Those state courts addressing the question have usually agreed with the position of the Illinois court. See Miller v. Commissioner, 700 A.2d 1108 (Conn. 1997).

2. *Constitutional claims on post-conviction.* As we have seen, some state post-conviction remedies are available only to correct state or federal *constitutional* errors in the criminal proceedings: violations of state statutes or procedural rules would not qualify for relief. Federal habeas corpus relief is available for violations of the federal constitution, see Brown v. Allen, 344 U.S. 443 (1953). The federal statute also allows habeas relief for those whose custody violates the "law or treaties" of the United States, see 28 U.S.C. §2241, although it would be rare for a state criminal trial to violate a federal statutory requirement.

Not all constitutional claims are available for post-conviction review in state or federal court. To begin with, the harmless error doctrine applies to post-conviction review. See Milton v. Wainwright, 407 U.S. 371 (1972). Many habeas corpus regimes also block courts from hearing constitutional claims if the constitutional error does not undermine the reliability of the factfinding process. For instance, claims of failure to exclude evidence obtained through an unconstitutional search or seizure are not available in federal court. This was the holding in the famous case of Stone v. Powell, 428 U.S. 465 (1976). The same is true in some state courts. See In re Sterling, 407 P.2d 5 (Cal. 1965).

Note that the Pennsylvania statute reprinted above covers constitutional claims only when the error "so undermined the truth-determining process that no reliable adjudication of guilt or innocence could have taken place." The Oklahoma statute reaches both constitutional and nonconstitutional claims, but only when the error supports a conclusion that "the outcome of the trial would have been different but for the errors or that the defendant is factually innocent." Does the public have any legitimate interest in correcting legal errors that occur in criminal proceedings, even when those errors do not undermine the reliability of the guilty verdict?

3. *Jurisdictional and nonconstitutional claims on post-conviction.* Some state collateral review statutes adhere to the traditional limit on habeas corpus as a method for correcting only jurisdictional errors. See State ex rel. Dotson v. Roger, 607 N.E.2d 453 (Ohio 1993). Other nonconstitutional bases for collateral review appear commonly in the state statutes, such as a challenge to a sentence in excess of the maximum authorized by law. See Florida Rule of Criminal Procedure 3.850.

2. Procedural Bars

In addition to subject matter bars, state and federal laws governing post-conviction review place "procedural bars" on the power of the court to hear the merits of a petitioner's claim. State law requires a criminal defendant to take a variety of procedural steps to preserve a claim of error for later review. These steps often include raising an objection at trial or raising a claim on direct appeal — though sometimes having previously raised a claim is itself a reason to bar later review. It is becoming common for statutes of limitations to require petitioners to bring claims promptly — sometimes with periods measured in days rather than months or years. If the defendant fails to take these steps, any later effort to get judicial review of the alleged legal error will be "procedurally barred" because of the petitioner's "procedural default," and the court will refuse to consider the merits of the claim.

Most systems do allow petitioners to raise some claims on collateral review that they did not raise at trial or on direct review, but only if the petitioner provides an adequate reason for that failure. The more extensive the procedural requirements, the more likely a petitioner will fail to preserve some claim and will need to explain the failure to follow those procedures: thus, the bypass standard and its application are critical elements of any system of post-conviction review. As you read the following materials, continue to ask what the role of post-conviction collateral review ought to be. Does a particular view about the role of post-conviction review help to determine the best doctrinal boundaries on procedural defaults? Consider, as well, the relationship of procedural bars to the subject matter bars covered in the previous subsection. Is there a clear distinction between "subject matter" and "procedural" bars?

■ IDAHO CODE §19-4901

(a) Any person who has been convicted of, or sentenced for, a crime and who claims:

(1) That the conviction or the sentence was in violation of the constitution of the United States or the constitution or laws of this state;

(2) That the court was without jurisdiction to impose sentence;

(3) That the sentence exceeds the maximum authorized by law;

(4) That there exists evidence of material facts, not previously presented and heard, that requires vacation of the conviction or sentence in the interest of justice; . . .

(6) [That] the petitioner is innocent of the offense; or

(7) That the conviction or sentence is otherwise subject to collateral attack upon any ground of alleged error heretofore available under any common law, statutory or other writ, motion, petition, proceeding, or remedy:

may institute, without paying a filing fee, a proceeding under this act to secure relief.

(b) This remedy is not a substitute for nor does it affect any remedy incident to the proceedings in the trial court, or of an appeal from the sentence or conviction. Any issue which could have been raised on direct appeal, but was not, is forfeited and may not be considered in post conviction proceedings, unless it appears to the court, on the basis of a substantial factual showing by affidavit, deposition or otherwise, that the asserted basis for relief raises a substantial doubt about the reliability of the finding of guilt and could not, in the exercise of due diligence, have been presented earlier. . . .

■ DENNIS JACKSON v. COMMISSIONER
629 A.2d 413 (Conn. 1993)

BORDEN, J.

The petitioner, Dennis Jackson, appeals from the judgment of the habeas court dismissing his petition for a writ of habeas corpus. The habeas court concluded that the petitioner had failed to demonstrate good cause for his failure to pursue on direct appeal his claim of unconstitutional jury composition that was the basis of his habeas petition. We affirm the judgment of the habeas court.

The record sets forth the facts and lengthy procedural history of this case. At his criminal trial, conducted in May, 1982, the petitioner was represented by Attorney John Buckley. Prior to the trial, Buckley had reached an agreement with assistant state's attorney Patrick Clifford, who Buckley understood would be prosecuting the petitioner's case. Buckley had agreed with Clifford that, in challenging the jury array in the petitioner's case, the petitioner could rely on evidence presented in another case that Buckley and Clifford had tried together and in which a jury array challenge had been brought.

Clifford, however, did not try the petitioner's case, but instead was replaced by assistant state's attorney Robert Devlin. Devlin, unlike Clifford, was unwilling to stipulate to the jury array evidence that had been presented in the case that Buckley and Clifford had tried together. Devlin also argued to the trial court that the petitioner's motion challenging the array was untimely.

In response, the trial court asked Buckley whether he was ready to present evidence necessary to challenge the array. Buckley stated to the court that he would need additional time to subpoena the appropriate witnesses and that he was not prepared to present evidence at that time.[2] Although Buckley informed the trial court that he needed additional time because he had relied on his prior agreement with Clifford, the trial court denied his request for a continuance. The petitioner, therefore, was unable to introduce evidence to support his challenge to the jury array.

The petitioner was subsequently convicted, after a jury trial, of first degree sexual assault, second degree kidnapping and first degree robbery. The petitioner appealed his conviction to this court and we affirmed the judgment of the trial court. In his direct appeal, the defendant did not raise a claim that the trial court had abused its discretion by denying his request for a continuance so that he could produce evidence to challenge the jury array.

In 1987, the petitioner filed a petition for a writ of habeas corpus claiming that the jury array from which his petit jury had been selected had been summoned in violation of his federal and state constitutional rights.[3] The habeas court denied the petition for habeas corpus and the petitioner subsequently appealed. His appeal was consolidated with the appeals of thirty-three other habeas petitioners. [The commissioner of correction] asserted that the proper standard by which to analyze the petitioners' failure to raise their jury array challenges at trial was the cause and prejudice standard as articulated in Wainwright v. Sykes, 433 U.S. 72 (1977), as

---

2. The petitioner had previously been granted a two-week continuance that began after the jury had been selected but prior to trial.

3. The petitioner, a black male, claimed that members of his race were underrepresented on his jury array in violation of his equal protection rights guaranteed by the fourteenth amendment to the United States constitution and article first, §20, of the Connecticut constitution.

opposed to the deliberate bypass rule; see Fay v. Noia, 372 U.S. 391 (1963); upon which the habeas court had relied. We affirmed the judgment of the habeas court. In so doing, we concluded that the appropriate standard by which to analyze procedural defaults at trial was the *Wainwright* standard of cause and prejudice. . . . Johnson v. Commissioner of Correction, 589 A.2d 1214 (Conn. 1991). [We] remanded "the case [to the habeas court] for further proceedings relating to whether there was good cause for [the petitioner's] failure to raise before trial the claim of unconstitutional jury composition that is the basis for his habeas petition." On the remand, the habeas court concluded that there was not adequate cause to excuse the petitioner's failure to pursue the jury array challenge on direct appeal. . . . This appeal followed. . . .

Prior to 1991, we employed the deliberate bypass rule, as articulated in Fay v. Noia, in order to determine the reviewability of constitutional claims in habeas corpus proceedings that had not been properly raised at trial or pursued on direct appeal. In Fay v. Noia (1963), the United States Supreme Court held that federal habeas corpus jurisdiction was not affected by the procedural default, specifically a failure to appeal, of a petitioner during state court proceedings resulting in his conviction. The court recognized, however, a limited discretion in the federal habeas judge to deny relief to an applicant who has deliberately by-passed the orderly procedure of the state courts and in so doing has forfeited his state court remedies. . . . This deliberate bypass standard for waiver required an intentional relinquishment or abandonment of a known right or privilege by the petitioner personally and depended on his considered choice. . . . A choice made by counsel not participated in by the petitioner does not automatically bar relief.

In Wainwright v. Sykes, however, the United States Supreme Court subsequently rejected the sweeping language of *Fay*, which would make federal habeas review generally available to state convicts absent a knowing and deliberate waiver of the federal constitutional contention. The court upheld a state court's refusal to decide the merits of a claimed *Miranda* violation first raised in a posttrial motion and in state habeas corpus proceedings, contrary to a state contemporaneous objection rule. The court adopted as a new standard for federal habeas review . . . that in a collateral attack upon a conviction, the petitioner must make not only a showing of cause for the defendant's failure to challenge the composition of the grand jury before trial, but also a showing of actual prejudice. Thus was born the *Wainwright* cause and prejudice standard for habeas review.

In *Johnson*, the petitioner's original appeal from the judgment of the habeas court, we reconsidered, in light of *Wainwright*, whether the deliberate bypass was the appropriate standard by which to analyze the reviewability of habeas claims that were procedurally defaulted at trial. We decided, after a full review of the relevant considerations, to abandon the deliberate bypass standard of Fay v. Noia, and to adopt the *Wainwright* cause and prejudice standard as the proper standard to determine the reviewability of such claims. In *Johnson*, however, we expressly did not reach the related issue of whether the cause and prejudice standard should replace the deliberate bypass rule for claims procedurally defaulted on appeal.

We now conclude that the *Wainwright* cause and prejudice standard should be employed to determine the reviewability of habeas claims that were not properly pursued on direct appeal. In Johnson v. Commissioner of Correction, we outlined the significant policy reasons for abandoning the deliberate bypass rule and adopting the cause and prejudice standard for claims procedurally defaulted at trial. First, as a general matter, we noted that

> special problems . . . are likely to arise relating to the feasibility of a second trial when a conviction is set aside by a habeas court rather than by an appellate court. These problems are related mainly to the more extended delay of the second trial that frequently results from a reversal of a conviction by a habeas court. There is no statute of limitation or other time limit that would bar a habeas petition. Ordinarily the petition may not be filed until appellate remedies have been exhausted. . . . The greater time lapse that results when a second trial is ordered by a habeas court has a serious impact on the availability of witnesses and other evidence for the second trial. Memories fade with the passage of time, exhibits are lost, and other evidence is less likely to be available. Appellate counsel would have less incentive to raise on appeal all arguable constitutional claims of the defendant if another opportunity to raise such claims were available in the habeas court. . . .
>
> If deliberate bypass were the sole barrier to such review, it could seldom be invoked for a default at trial. It is not common practice and would be unduly cumbersome to establish a record in the trial court showing that the defendant had personally made a knowledgeable waiver of his constitutional procedural rights on each of the myriad occasions that arise during a criminal trial when such rights are involved. Most of these choices during trial, such as whether to move for suppression of evidence or to cross-examine a particular witness, must necessarily be left to counsel, subject to the requirement that his performance satisfy reasonable standards of competency. . . .

The "special problems" regarding procedural defaults at trial that we noted in *Johnson* apply equally to procedural defaults on direct appeal, and militate in favor of our adoption of one standard by which to measure procedural defaults occurring at trial or on direct appeal. As the United States Supreme Court has noted in specifically adopting the cause and prejudice standard to analyze procedural defaults on direct appeal: "A State's procedural rules serve vital purposes at trial, on appeal, and on state collateral attack. [Such rules afford] the opportunity to resolve the issue shortly after trial, while evidence is still available both to assess the defendant's claim and to retry the defendant effectively if he prevails in his appeal. . . . This type of rule promotes not only the accuracy and efficiency of judicial decisions, but also the finality of those decisions, by forcing the defendant to litigate all of his claims together, as quickly after trial as the docket will allow, and while the attention of the appellate court is focused on his case." Murray v. Carrier, 477 U.S. 478 (1986).

We also recognize that the judicial system's legitimate interest in procedural rules is undermined regardless of whether the breach results from counsel's ignorance or inadvertence rather than a deliberate decision, tactical or not, to abstain from raising the claim.[8] Just as with procedural defaults occurring at trial, the costs

---

8. In adopting the cause and prejudice standard for procedural defaults occurring at trial, we recognized that, particularly in jury array challenges, the deliberate bypass rule would encourage astute counsel to "sandbag" the court by saving their claims until habeas review. Johnson v. Commissioner of Correction, 589 A.2d 1214 (Ct. 1991). This possibility exists because if the time limitations for bringing a challenge at trial were followed, any constitutional defect in the array could be cured, and the trial could be continued. Consequently, "[s]trong tactical considerations would militate in favor of delaying the raising of the claim in hopes of an acquittal, with the thought that if those hopes did not materialize, the claim could be used to upset an otherwise valid conviction at a time when reprosecution might well be difficult."

The same danger of "sandbagging" would exist, albeit to a lesser extent, if we were to continue to apply the deliberate bypass rule to procedural defaults on appeal. The defendant's counsel on appeal might well conclude that the best strategy is to raise a few promising claims on appeal, while reserving others for later habeas review should the direct appeal be unsuccessful.

of violation of our procedural rules are incurred regardless of the kind of attorney error that led to the failure of counsel to pursue a claim on appeal. . . .

One of the underlying rationales for preferring the cause and prejudice standard to the deliberate bypass rule, regarding trial court defaults, is that it is unrealistic and inconsistent with the proper role of trial counsel to require consultation with the client regarding every legal or tactical consideration. The same is true of appellate counsel. It is unrealistic and inconsistent with the proper role of appellate counsel to require consultation with the client, and presumably to secure the client's consent, with respect to the decision of whether to raise or forego particular legal claims on appeal. Indeed, applying the deliberate bypass rule to such decisions of appellate advocacy would create the incentive for counsel to remain silent, rather than to confer with the client because ultimately the client would be better served in a habeas action by remaining ignorant of potential claims on direct appeal. . . .

The petitioner next claims that, even if the cause and prejudice standard is the appropriate standard by which to analyze his failure to pursue his claim on direct appeal, the habeas court improperly concluded that there was insufficient cause for the petitioner's failure to pursue on direct appeal his claim that the composition of the jury array violated his constitutional rights. We are unpersuaded.

[The] denial of a request for a continuance is appealable. Consequently, the petitioner was free to challenge the denial of the continuance on direct appeal if he believed that the denial had been improper under the circumstances of the case. If he then convinced the reviewing court that the denial was reversible error, he would have been entitled, on remand to the trial court, to present the evidence regarding the jury array that he had originally intended to present. Under that scenario, however, if his jury array challenge were successful, a new trial would have ensued shortly after the direct appeal, rather than now, eleven years later.

BERDON, J., dissenting.

At the very least, we should continue to employ the deliberate bypass standard to determine the reviewability of habeas claims that were not properly pursued on direct appeal. The majority's decision closes the door to petitioners who may have meritorious claims to challenge their confinement and who may, in fact, be innocent, but who, through no fault of their own, are precluded from pursuing their claims.

I must confess that the scales weigh heavily, at least for me, in favor of granting a new trial to persons whose claims cast a substantial cloud on the validity of their convictions. The rules established today have equal application for those who are incarcerated for life as well as those who are awaiting the death penalty. The majority, emulating the United States Supreme Court, restricts habeas corpus in the name of finality of decisions. Lest we forget, there is nothing more final than the imposition of the death penalty.

Furthermore, as in the present case, the vast majority of criminal defendants are represented either by public defenders or by special public defenders assigned by the state. These competent and dedicated attorneys carry heavy caseloads, which often play a role in procedural defaults. . . . The state, therefore, must take its share of the blame for the procedural defaults.

[T]he majority notes the problems associated with granting a new trial years after the alleged crime. I too recognize the difficulty of conducting a second trial when memories have faded and evidence is not easily available. In many cases, however, these problems are ameliorated by the rules of evidence permitting admission of a witness' testimony at a prior proceeding under certain circumstances. In addition, a witness' prior inconsistent statement could be introduced into evidence for substantive purposes under certain circumstances.

[T]he majority claims that under the deliberate bypass standard there must be a showing that "the defendant had personally made a knowledgeable waiver of his constitutional procedural rights" and uses this extreme interpretation to reject the deliberate bypass rule. Whether there has been a "deliberate bypass" on appeal should not depend on whether the defendant made a personal, deliberate choice not to pursue a certain claim, but rather, on whether the choice was made by appellate counsel. . . .

Even if the "cause and prejudice" standard is applied, I would get to the merits of the petition in this case. . . . This court has granted the trial court such broad discretion in determining whether to grant or deny a continuance that an appeal on that issue is for all practical purposes frivolous. When the trial court's discretion is so great that it is virtually impossible to obtain reasonable review, the omission of that claim, especially when there is no proof that it was a deliberate omission, should satisfy the "cause" standard.

In addition, the defendant's substantive claim goes to the core of our judicial process. . . . Neither the accused in this case nor the African-American community can possibly believe that the defendant was justly convicted when his jury was not selected from a pool of persons representing a fair cross section of the population. Accordingly, I would find that the "prejudice" has been established. . . .

Notes

1. *Standard for assessing procedural default: majority view.* The trend among the states for assessing a failure to raise a claim prior to a challenge on collateral review has been away from more generous standards such as the "deliberate bypass" standard of Fay v. Noia, 372 U.S. 391 (1963), or simply a general (and sympathetic) "cause" standard. States have moved instead towards the more restrictive requirements of "cause and prejudice" articulated by the U.S. Supreme Court in Wainwright v. Sykes, 433 U.S. 72 (1977), or functional equivalents. Is the Idaho "due diligence" standard more or less exacting than "cause"? Is the Idaho "substantial doubt" standard more or less exacting than the requirement of "prejudice"? Connecticut appears to have been the last state to abandon the "deliberate bypass" standard. However, many states continue to apply a standard different from the "cause and prejudice" standard used in the federal courts and adopted by Connecticut. Utah, for example, requires a showing of "unusual circumstances" to explain any procedural default. See, e.g., Hurst v. Cook, 777 P.2d 1029 (Utah 1989) ("[While] habeas corpus is not a substitute for appeal, a conviction may nevertheless be challenged by collateral attack in "unusual circumstances," that is, where an obvious injustice or a substantial and prejudicial denial of a constitutional right has occurred, irrespective of whether an appeal has been taken."). Colorado Rev. Stat. §16-12-206(1)(c) provides:

> A motion for postconviction review may raise only the following issues: (I) Whether there exists evidence of material facts, not previously presented and heard, which by the exercise of reasonable diligence could not have been known or learned by the defendant or trial counsel prior to the imposition of the sentence and which require that the conviction or the death sentence be vacated in the interests of justice. . . .

The Connecticut court in *Jackson* applies the same standard to assess failure to raise a claim at trial and on appeal. Should the standard be the same?

Not every procedural default is evaluated under the "cause and prejudice" standard. Some procedural failures in state court are considered unimportant enough to ignore in federal habeas corpus. See Lee v. Kemna, 534 U.S. 362 (2002) (defendant's witnesses did not arrive at courthouse on trial date and defendant moved for continuance but did not file written motion as required by state law; procedural default inadequate to prevent federal habeas review because properly filed motion would not have changed outcome in state court and defendant substantially complied with state rules). In addition, a state might waive its procedural rule requirements. If a state court speaks to the merits of the defendant's claim despite the procedural default, the federal courts are also allowed to address the merits. See Stewart v. Smith, 536 U.S. 856 (2002).

2. *The standard for reassessing facts on habeas.* Often petitioners on collateral review request evidentiary hearings to develop a record supporting their claims. Should courts apply the same standards in deciding whether to hold an evidentiary hearing, and whether to grant relief? In Keeney v. Tamayo-Reyes, 504 U.S. 1 (1992), the Supreme Court directed federal courts to apply the "cause and prejudice" standard in deciding whether to hold evidentiary hearings. *Tamayo-Reyes* overruled Townsend v. Sain, 372 U.S. 293, 313 (1963), one of the linchpin decisions in the expansion of federal collateral review of state convictions. *Townsend* held that a federal court must hold an evidentiary hearing "if the habeas applicant did not receive a full and fair evidentiary hearing in a state court."

Most states, in contrast, apply a lower standard to determine whether a court should hold an evidentiary hearing. Consider the two different standards that Illinois courts use to consider an evidentiary hearing under Ill. Stat. ch. 725, para. 5/122-2.1:

> (a) Within 90 days after the filing and docketing of each petition the court shall examine such petition and enter an order thereon pursuant to this Section.
>
> (1) If the petitioner is under sentence of death and is without counsel and alleges that he is without means to procure counsel, he shall state whether or not he wishes counsel to be appointed to represent him. If appointment of counsel is so requested, the court shall appoint counsel if satisfied that the petitioner has no means to procure counsel.
>
> (2) If the petitioner is sentenced to imprisonment and the court determines the petition is frivolous or is patently without merit, it shall dismiss the petition in a written order, specifying the findings of fact and conclusions of law it made in reaching its decision. Such order of dismissal is a final judgment and shall be served upon the petitioner by certified mail within 10 days of its entry.
>
> (b) If the petition is not dismissed pursuant to this Section, the court shall order the petition to be docketed for further consideration. . . .

3. *What is sufficient "cause"?* The *Jackson* case raises sharply the question of what is an adequate "cause" for failing to raise a claim. When the U.S. Supreme Court announced the "cause and prejudice" standard in *Sykes,* it chose not to define either term, "leav[ing] open for resolution in future decisions the precise definition of the cause-and-prejudice standard," emphasizing "only that it is narrower than the [knowing and deliberate waiver] standard" in Fay v. Noia. In Murray v. Carrier,

477 U.S. 478 (1986), the Supreme Court confronted the question whether attorney error in failing to raise a claim that fell short of "ineffective assistance" could nonetheless satisfy the "cause" requirement and thus open the door for habeas review. The Court answered "No," and explained that

> the existence of cause for a procedural default must ordinarily turn on whether the prisoner can show that some objective factor external to the defense impeded counsel's efforts to comply with the State's procedural rule. [A] showing that the factual or legal basis for a claim was not reasonably available to counsel or that "some interference by officials" made compliance impracticable, would constitute cause under this standard. [477 U.S. at 488.]

State courts that apply the "cause and prejudice" standard have generally followed federal law in defining these concepts. See Younger v. State, 580 A.2d 552 (Del. 1990); but cf. People v. Reed, 535 N.W.2d 496 (Mich. 1995) (dividing over whether state habeas law should or must follow federal law). Consider the special definition of "cause" used in §99-39-21(4) of the Mississippi Code: "The term 'cause' as used in this section shall be defined and limited to those cases where the legal foundation upon which the claim for relief is based could not have been discovered with reasonable diligence at the time of trial or direct appeal." Under this statute, the burden is on the prisoner to allege any facts necessary to demonstrate that the claims are not procedurally barred.

Remarkable foresight is necessary to assert some claims of "cause" in the federal system. According to Edwards v. Carpenter, 529 U.S. 446 (2000), when a habeas petitioner points to ineffective assistance of counsel as the reason for her failure to raise some challenge within the state system, the ineffective assistance claim itself is also subject to procedural default rules. That is, the petitioner must either follow all state procedural rules when raising the ineffective assistance argument, or show some "cause and prejudice" for failing to raise this "cause" argument in the proper way.

4. *What is "prejudice"?* In United States v. Frady, 456 U.S. 152, 170 (1982), a case involving an erroneous jury instruction on malice murder, the Supreme Court held that a petitioner must show "not merely that the errors at his trial created a possibility of prejudice, but that they worked to his actual and substantial disadvantage, infecting his entire trial with error of constitutional dimensions." State courts applying the "cause and prejudice" default standard have tended to follow federal law. E.g., Turpin v. Todd, 493 S.E.2d 900 (Ga. 1997). However, some legislatures have retained more generous standards. In State v. Bush, 297 S.E.2d 563 (N.C. 1982), the North Carolina Supreme Court applied a statute that employs ordinary harmless error standard for constitutional claims on collateral review, and a standard assessing the "reasonable possibility that . . . a different result would have been reached" for nonconstitutional claims.

5. *Procedural bar and statute of limitations.* One of the strongest complaints about habeas corpus and other forms of collateral review is that they undermine finality. Proponents of narrow collateral review standards point to cases — especially capital cases — that have wandered back and forth through state and federal courts for years. One response has been to require that all issues be raised in a single collateral petition, subject to extremely narrow exceptions. A second response has been to

incorporate statutes of limitations where none previously existed. Consider Nev. Stat. §34.726:

> 1. Unless there is good cause shown for delay, a petition that challenges the validity of a judgment or sentence must be filed within 1 year after entry of the judgment of conviction or, if an appeal has been taken from the judgment, within 1 year after the supreme court issues its remittitur. For the purposes of this subsection, good cause for delay exists if the petitioner demonstrates to the satisfaction of the court: (a) That the delay is not the fault of the petitioner; and (b) That dismissal of the petition as untimely will unduly prejudice the petitioner.
>
> 2. The execution of a sentence must not be stayed for the period provided in subsection 1 solely because a petition may be filed within that period. A stay of sentence must not be granted unless: (a) A petition is actually filed; and (b) The petitioner establishes a compelling basis for the stay.

After a long history without any statute of limitations on claims to federal courts in habeas, Congress in 1996 passed the Antiterrorism and Effective Death Penalty Act of 1996. Despite the title, this statute largely focused on adding new limitations to federal review of state convictions. Congress amended 28 U.S.C. §2244(d) to provide:

> (1) A one-year period of limitation shall apply to an application for a writ of habeas corpus by a person in custody pursuant to the judgment of a State court. The limitation period shall run from the latest of (A) the date on which the judgment became final by the conclusion of direct review or the expiration of the time for seeking such review; (B) the date on which the impediment to filing an application created by State action in violation of the Constitution or laws of the United States is removed, if the applicant was prevented from filing by such State action; (C) the date on which the constitutional right asserted was initially recognized by the Supreme Court, if the right has been newly recognized by the Supreme Court and made retroactively applicable to cases on collateral review; or (D) the date on which the factual predicate of the claim or claims presented could have been discovered through the exercise of due diligence.
>
> (2) The time during which a properly filed application for State post-conviction or other collateral review with respect to the pertinent judgment or claim is pending shall not be counted toward any period of limitation under this subsection.

Senator Orrin Hatch (R-Utah) said the law would "stop the frivolous appeals that have been driving people nuts throughout this country and subjecting victims and families of victims to unnecessary pain for year after year after year." See Duncan v. Walker, 533 U.S. 167 (2001) (petitioner filed first federal habeas petition four days before state conviction became final, petition dismissed three months later for failure to exhaust remedies; petitioner filed second federal petition eleven months later; the first petition did not toll the running of limitations period).

The Supreme Court has resolved several disputes over the meaning of the federal statute of limitations in favor of petitioners. In Carey v. Saffold, 536 U.S. 214 (2002), the Court interpreted the word "pending" in the tolling provision of the statute of limitations broadly, to include periods between a state court's decision on an application for collateral review and the filing of a notice of appeal to a higher state court. And in Clay v. United States, 537 U.S. 522 (2003), the Supreme Court ruled that a federal conviction becomes "final," and starts the one-year period for seeking collateral relief, when the time period for seeking certiorari runs out.

Problem 11-2. Successive Petitions

William Andrews was convicted of three counts of first-degree murder and two counts of aggravated robbery for the killings of three people in the course of a robbery at the Hi-Fi Shop in Ogden, Utah, and was sentenced to death. The Utah Supreme Court affirmed the conviction in 1977, and the U.S. Supreme Court denied certiorari in 1978. The following month, Andrews filed a petition for post-conviction relief in the district court of Salt Lake County. That court dismissed the petition on the ground that all of the issues raised had been or could have been raised on direct appeal and thus Andrews was barred from any post-conviction review. On appeal, the Utah Supreme Court affirmed this ruling in 1980. Again the U.S. Supreme Court denied certiorari.

Andrews then filed for federal habeas corpus relief in the United States District Court for the District of Utah, Central Division. That court stayed the proceedings and ordered Andrews to return to the state courts to seek possible relief under a decision in another capital case just decided by the Utah Supreme Court. In 1983 the Utah Supreme Court again denied Andrews relief, holding that the decision in the other, newly decided case was not retroactive. Andrews resumed pursuit of his federal habeas corpus petition, but the federal district court denied all requested relief in 1984. The U.S. Court of Appeals for the Tenth Circuit affirmed that decision in 1986, and the U.S. Supreme Court again denied certiorari in 1988.

In October 1987, approximately four months before the United States Supreme Court denied certiorari, Andrews filed a new petition for post-conviction relief in the district court of Salt Lake County. He argued that the court should overturn his death sentence because the trial court committed constitutional error when it did not give the jury a lesser included offense instruction on second degree felony murder. He also alleged that the Utah Supreme Court committed constitutional error when it failed on direct appeal to address sua sponte the trial court's failure to give such an instruction. Andrews pointed out that he was indigent and unable to retain counsel of his choice at trial or on direct appeal, and his court-appointed counsel had failed to effectively research and present these arguments.

The district court denied the petition, because Andrews could or should have raised the issues presented either on appeal or in prior post-conviction petitions. The district judge concluded that the petition was "an abuse of post-conviction relief and procedurally defective." Andrews appeals from the denial of his petition, which he filed pursuant to Utah Rule of Civil Procedure 65B(i)(2):

> The complaint shall further state that the legality or constitutionality of his commitment or confinement has not already been adjudged in a prior habeas corpus or other similar proceeding; and if the complainant shall have instituted prior similar proceedings in any court, state or federal, within the state of Utah, he shall so state in his complaint, . . . and shall set forth the reasons for the denial of relief in such other court. In such case, if it is apparent to the court in which the proceeding under this rule is instituted that the legality or constitutionality of his confinement has already been adjudged in such prior proceedings, the court shall forthwith dismiss such complaint, giving written notice thereof by mail to the complainant, and no further proceedings shall be had on such complaint.

Subsection (4) of that rule states that "All claims of the denial of any of complainant's constitutional rights shall be raised in the postconviction proceeding brought under this rule and may not be raised in another subsequent proceeding except for good cause shown therein."

Andrews explains his decision to present this claim in a successive petition for post-conviction relief on these grounds: (1) the case law regarding his right to a lesser included offense instruction at his trial was in an unsettled and evolutionary state during at least part of the period between his conviction and this petition, (2) there is a strong possibility that he was entitled to a lesser included offense instruction and may have been mistakenly sentenced to death as a result of its absence, and (3) his counsel erred in not making the lesser included offense claim. How would you rule? Compare Andrews v. Schulsen, 773 P.2d 832 (Utah 1989).

Notes

1. *Successive petitions and abuse of the writ: majority view.* Should the procedural hurdles for a second or third petition collaterally attacking a conviction or sentence be the same or higher than for an initial petition? Rules governing review of successive collateral challenges are often referred to under the label "abuse of the writ." The general trend in both federal and state systems has been to severely restrict successive collateral attacks. In the federal system the "cause and prejudice" standard is applied to determine whether a petitioner has abused the writ. See McCleskey v. Zant, 499 U.S. 467 (1991). How much guidance does the "cause" standard provide in the context of successive petitions? States often apply different and more restrictive standards to successive petitions. Under §9-14-51 of the Georgia Code, any grounds for relief not raised by a petitioner in his original or amended petition "are waived unless the Constitution of the United States or of this state otherwise requires or unless [the judge] finds grounds for relief asserted therein which could not reasonably have been raised in the original or amended petition."

In the federal system, the Antiterrorism and Effective Death Penalty Act of 1996 makes it difficult for a federal court to hear claims for a second time. Under the statute, the merits of concluded criminal proceedings should not be revisited in federal court unless the petitioner makes a strong showing of "actual" or "factual" innocence. The Supreme Court has interpreted the federal statute to allow for at least one hearing on the merits in federal court, even if the issue is raised but not resolved in an initial federal petition. See Slack v. McDaniel, 529 U.S. 473 (2000) (federal habeas petition filed after an initial federal petition was dismissed without adjudication on the merits for failure to exhaust state remedies is not a "second or successive" petition; petitioner is not limited in refiled petition to the claims made in the original dismissed petition); Stewart v. Martinez-Villareal, 523 U.S. 637 (1998) (prisoner whose habeas petition was dismissed for failure to exhaust state remedies, and who then did exhaust those remedies and returned to federal court, is not filing a "successive" petition barred by statute; similarly, claim raised in federal court and dismissed as premature can be heard when raised in timely manner in later federal petition).

2. *Successive petitions: Court burden in noncapital and capital cases.* Problem 11-2 is typical for capital cases in terms of the number of successive reviews after conviction, both on direct appeal and collaterally, and in both state and federal systems.

However, prisoners in noncapital cases (who are, of course, far more numerous than defendants sentenced to death) are much less likely to file successive petitions.

3. Collateral Review of Ineffective Assistance Claims

How many defendants file collateral attacks on their conviction or sentence? What claims do they typically make? How often do courts grant relief? While reading the following excerpts from a major empirical study of habeas corpus in both state and federal courts, consider whether consistent patterns in collateral review cases throw light on the proper choice of legal doctrines.

■ VICTOR FLANGO, HABEAS CORPUS IN STATE AND FEDERAL COURTS
State Justice Institute, 1994

Many of the important points of contention in the current debate about habeas corpus are empirical questions, yet the amount of data brought to bear on these issues is slight. . . . Only a few states report the number of habeas corpus petitions filed or disposed as a separate case category. Data from the California Administrative Office of Courts showed 9,415 petitions were filed in California Superior Court in 1990, while the same year 1,070 habeas petitions were filed in all U.S. District Courts in California. Habeas corpus filings in California have been declining steadily from a high of approximately 15,000 in 1980. In smaller states, the habeas filings in U.S. District Court and state courts of general jurisdiction are roughly equivalent, but small. Examples from 1990 include Connecticut Superior Court 246, U.S. District Court 75; Nebraska District Court 59, U.S. District Court 63; Utah District Court 129, U.S. District Court 24; and Washington Superior Court 114; U.S. District Court 195.*

[This] research was designed to cover all habeas petitions disposed in state and federal court at two separate time periods and so is a snapshot of petitions rather than an historical picture of habeas corpus. [The] four states chosen for the study were: California, New York, Texas and Alabama. . . .

What types of prisoners file habeas corpus petitions? [Only] prisoners sentenced to a fairly long term have time to complete the rather lengthy procedures prerequisite to filing a habeas corpus petition. [The] length of the sentences of habeas petitioners is relatively long, with median times ranging from a minimum sentence of 24 years to a maximum of 30 years in state courts, and 16 to 24 years for petitioners in federal courts.

[Habeas petitioners] are much more likely to have been convicted at trial. Research in 26 urban areas reveals that the jury trial rate for felonies averages 6 percent, yet the majority of habeas petitioners were convicted by a jury trial (62 percent of the state court sample and 66 percent of the federal court sample). [While] guilty pleas do not prevent filing of a habeas petition, they may reduce the number of issues over which the petitioner may complain. [It] is clear that habeas

---

*This paragraph appeared as a footnote. — EDS.

Type of Claims Raised

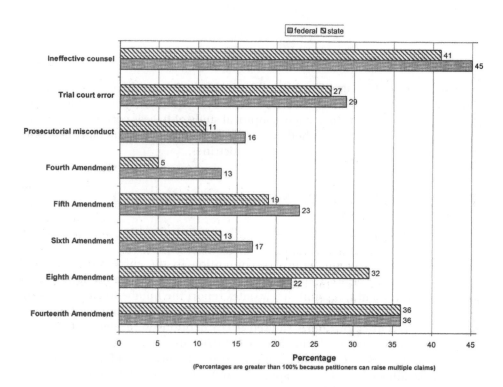

□ federal ☒ state

Ineffective counsel	41 / 45
Trial court error	27 / 29
Prosecutorial misconduct	11 / 16
Fourth Amendment	5 / 13
Fifth Amendment	19 / 23
Sixth Amendment	13 / 17
Eighth Amendment	32 / 22
Fourteenth Amendment	36 / 36

Percentage
(Percentages are greater than 100% because petitioners can raise multiple claims)

petitions are *not* used by a representative sample of all convicted state prisoners, but rather by the smaller proportion in custody as a result of a jury trial conviction for a serious offense.

Perhaps also as a consequence of the seriousness of the offense, petitioners were likely to have been represented in state court during the original trial. . . . Although the overwhelming number of petitioners were represented by counsel for their initial offense, most were *not* represented by counsel in filing the habeas corpus petitions. . . . Three quarters (75 percent) of the petitioners in state court and 91 percent of the petitioners in federal court represented themselves. . . .

Of the state petitioners, 35 percent were filing their first petition, 15 percent had filed one previous petition, 17 percent had filed two prior petitions, and the remainder [33 percent] filed three or more prior habeas petitions. Of the federal petitioners, 46 percent were filing their first petition, 18 percent their second, 17 percent their third, while the remainder [19 percent] had previously filed three or more petitions. . . .

Which claims are raised by petitioners? . . . Do petitioners primarily question the practices and procedures of attorneys, the police, the prosecutor, or the courts? . . . Challenges to the competency of the attorney representation were the most common claims in both state and federal court. . . . In one sense, this claim is a precondition for all others because ineffective assistance of counsel is a reason given for not raising related claims previously. . . .

Of the 1,835 petitions in the state sample, 755 (41 percent) raised the claim [of ineffective assistance of counsel] either generally or specifically. . . . Of the 1,626 petitioners in the federal sample, 736 (45 percent) claimed ineffective assistance of counsel. . . . General claims included such allegations as the attorney lacked trial experience, violated the attorney-client privilege, or failed to file a claim or discovery motion, meet with the defendant on a regular basis, or otherwise failed to prepare adequately. . . .

[Many] petitions do not indicate the type of ineffective assistance of counsel received. . . . In both state and federal courts, failure to investigate and failure to object to admissibility or the insufficiency of evidence were not only the claims most likely to be raised, but also the two claims most likely to be raised together. The claim that attorneys misled the defendant was often raised in the context where the attorney failed to explain adequately the plea agreement and its consequences to the defendant. Forty-three percent (66) of the 152 petitioners in the state sample and 50 percent of the 128 petitioners in the federal sample who claimed a coerced guilty plea, also claimed ineffective assistance of counsel. . . .

Nearly 30 percent of both state and federal court petitioners claimed trial court error. . . . Many of the general claims of trial court error included the claim that the judge failed to explain the charges to the defendant. Detrimental procedural error was the single most frequent trial court error claim specified in state court, whereas failure to suppress improper evidence was the single trial court error most often specified in federal court. . . .

Prosecutorial misconduct was claimed by 11 percent of the state petitioners and 16 percent of the federal petitioners. . . . The specific claim made most frequently by both state and federal prisoners was the failure to disclose. [The second most common specific claim, made by around two percent of state petitioners, was use of perjured testimony, followed by improper comments (one percent), and inflammatory summation (one percent)].

Which claims raised tend to be granted? [B]ecause so few petitions in either the state or federal courts were granted, conclusions drawn from success rates of petitions must be regarded with care. Of the 1,626 federal petitions in the sample, only 17 were granted. Of the petitions filed in state courts, only 1 was granted in California, and only 3 were granted in Alabama. In New York, 48 petitions were granted. [The record-keeping system in Texas made it hard for the researchers to find a comparable number: they noted that in 1992, the Texas Court of Criminal Appeals disposed of 2,244 habeas corpus petitions, sending 116 back to trial courts for additional hearings, setting 152 for hearings before the appellate court, and granting 8 with specific orders.]

	State Courts		Federal Courts	
Claims Raised	Number of Claims	% Granted	Number of Claims	% Granted
Ineffective assistance	732	8	584	<1
Trial court error	528	6	378	2
Prosecutorial misconduct	199	3	206	<1
Fourth Amendment	79	1	172	<1
Fifth Amendment	414	2	380	<1
Sixth Amendment	220	1	224	<1
Eighth Amendment	463	11	261	<1
Fourteenth Amendment	728	7	426	1

[F]ederal courts grant a very small proportion of habeas petitions, typically less than one in a hundred in state court and . . . the claims raised do not affect the petitioner's success rate. The picture in state courts is somewhat different. For prosecutorial misconduct and Fourth, Fifth and Sixth Amendment claims, petitioner's success rates in state courts is comparable to the low success rate in federal courts. The success rate for Eighth Amendment claims was markedly different. Further analysis revealed that 41 of the 149 petitions granted involved questions of excessive bail in New York. Eleven of the 41 granted petitions involved coerced guilty pleas. Ineffective assistance of counsel, trial court error and Fourteenth Amendment concerns were also granted at a higher rate. . . .

The Flango study reveals the practical importance of ineffective assistance of counsel claims on collateral challenges made in both state and federal courts. Are there stronger arguments, in general, for using collateral review primarily to assess ineffective assistance claims as opposed to directly addressing the underlying substantive claims (e.g. an issue that an attorney failed to raise, or the impact of facts the attorney failed to develop)? Do the following statutes and case explain the focus on effective assistance issues?

■ 42 PENNSYLVANIA CONSOLIDATED STATUTES §9543

(a) General rule.—To be eligible for relief under this subchapter, the petitioner must plead and prove by a preponderance of the evidence . . .
  (2) That the conviction or sentence resulted from one or more of the following: . . .
    (ii) Ineffective assistance of counsel which, in the circumstances of the particular case, so undermined the truth-determining process that no reliable adjudication of guilt or innocence could have taken place.
  (3) That the allegation of error has not been previously litigated or waived.
  (4) That the failure to litigate the issue prior to or during trial, during unitary review or on direct appeal could not have been the result of any rational, strategic or tactical decision by counsel.

■ COMMONWEALTH v. TAIBU MODAMU GRANT
813 A.2d 726 (Pa. 2002)

Cappy, J.
  . . . The facts surrounding the case are as follows. The victim, Keith Gilliam, and his wife were leaving the Where's It At Bar when gunshots were heard. The victim was killed. Shortly thereafter, a maroon car drove by and a second round of shots rang out, wounding two other people. Various witnesses testified to the details of the shooting, the police response, and the forensic evidence. The Commonwealth presented one witness who identified Appellant, Taibu Grant, as the shooter.
  At trial a public defender represented Appellant. Following the conclusion of trial, a jury convicted Appellant of first-degree murder and sentenced him to life imprisonment. An appeal was filed by another member of the public defender's

office. The trial court found the existence of a conflict of interest and appointed new counsel to represent Appellant on appeal. On appeal, . . . we directed the parties to present argument on whether this court should reconsider the practice first announced in Commonwealth v. Hubbard, 372 A.2d 687 (Pa. 1977), requiring that claims related to counsel ineffectiveness be raised at the earliest stage of the proceedings at which the allegedly ineffective counsel no longer represents the defendant. . . .

On appeal to the Superior Court, . . . Appellant argued that trial counsel was ineffective for failing to uncover impeachment evidence regarding [prosecution witness] Christopher Moore. Additionally, Appellant argued that trial counsel was ineffective for failing to call two Commonwealth witnesses. The Superior Court dismissed both of these claims for lack of adequate development. Appellant argues that the Superior Court's action was improper. According to Appellant, the procedural rules prescribed by this court require an appellant to confine his issues raised on appeal to those contained in the record. Thus, the rules prevented Appellant from supplementing the record on appeal and rendered him incapable of providing concrete evidence, through reports or documents, regarding the alleged ineffectiveness. Thus, Appellant concludes that rather than dismissing the claims for inadequate development, the Superior Court should have remanded the claims to the trial court in order to give him the opportunity to fully develop his claims.

[Our holding in Commonwealth v. Hubbard, 372 A.2d 687 (Pa. 1977)] provides that claims of ineffectiveness must be raised at the time a defendant gets new counsel. In the event that the claims are not raised at that time, they are waived. As Appellant's argument in this case highlights, the *Hubbard* rule is often difficult to reconcile with traditionally accepted rules of procedure, which normally do not allow issues to be raised for the first time on appeal and do not allow an appellant to supplement the record on appeal. . . .

[In Commonwealth v. Dancer, 331 A.2d 435 (Pa. 1975)], this court considered "whether a [petitioner] represented on direct appeal by an attorney other than his trial counsel waives his claim of ineffective assistance of trial counsel by failing to raise that issue on direct appeal." The court first looked at the language of the Post-Conviction Hearing Act ("PCHA"), which created a rebuttable presumption that the failure to raise an issue was "knowing and understanding."[9] Due to this presumption, the court determined that the failure to raise an issue on direct appeal will only be justified where extraordinary circumstances exist. Furthermore, the court concluded that ineffectiveness of trial counsel may only be raised in collateral proceedings under the following circumstances:

> 1) where petitioner is represented on appeal by his trial counsel, for it is unrealistic to expect trial counsel on direct appeal to argue his own ineffectiveness, 2) where the petitioner is represented on appeal by new counsel, but the grounds upon which the claim of ineffective assistance are based do not appear in the trial record, 3) where the petitioner is able to prove the existence of other "extraordinary circumstances" justifying his failure to raise the issue or 4) where the petitioner rebuts the presumption of "knowing and understanding failure."

---

9. The PCHA provided that an issue was waived if a petitioner "knowingly and understandingly" failed to raise it on direct appeal. 19 P.S. §1180-3(d). The equivalent section of the [current] Post Conviction Relief Act, §9544(b), no longer has the "knowing and understanding" language.

Thus, the general rule was that claims of ineffectiveness were to be presented at the time a petitioner obtained new counsel. However, this general rule implicitly recognized that all claims were not suited for direct appeal by preserving a few well-defined exceptions to the general rule.

Nevertheless, when this rule was restated in *Hubbard*, the requirement that the claim must be raised at the time a petitioner had new counsel was made absolute. In the aftermath of *Hubbard*, there was no flexibility to the rule. The rule became that claims of trial counsel ineffectiveness must be raised at the time that the petitioner obtained new counsel regardless of the myriad of impracticalities associated with such an unbending pronouncement.[10] Most recently, as a result of this absolute declaration, the necessity of "layering" arose. In the aftermath of *Hubbard*, the only way to consider claims related to trial counsel's ineffectiveness that were not raised on direct appeal by new counsel was to plead and prove the additional claim of appellate counsel's ineffectiveness, i.e., a layered claim of ineffectiveness. . . .

Appellate courts in Pennsylvania routinely decline to entertain issues raised on appeal for the first time. Indeed, the Pennsylvania Appellate Rules of Procedure specifically proscribe such review. See Pa. R.A.P. 302(a). The Rules and case law indicate that such a prohibition is preferred because the absence of a trial court opinion can pose a substantial impediment to meaningful and effective appellate review. Further, appellate courts normally do not consider matters outside the record or matters that involve a consideration of facts not in evidence. Most importantly, appellate courts do not act as fact finders, since to do so would require an assessment of the credibility of the testimony. . . .

Yet, in the arena of ineffectiveness claims, appellate courts are routinely called upon to perform each of these tasks. In ruling on an ineffectiveness claim, it is rare that a trial court opinion exists which will aid the appellate court in examining the claim. Appellate courts are frequently called upon to consider matters outside the record. Moreover, appellate courts often engage in some fact finding by being required to speculate as to the trial strategy of trial counsel in order to rule upon these claims. It seems anomalous that where the issues involve claims of ineffectiveness, we employ the exact opposite appellate review process that we require in almost all other appeals. In fact, we require the defendant to raise a new claim for the first time on appeal. When an appellant has not raised this new claim on appeal, he is subject to the waiver provision of the PCRA, 42 Pa. C.S. §9544(b). . . . However, the mere fact that our current process to review ineffectiveness claims does not square with the rules of appellate procedure employed in most cases cannot conclude our discussion of this matter, since these rules of appellate procedure existed at the time we announced the *Hubbard* rule. Thus, we will also consider the decisions of other jurisdictions on the matter of presenting ineffectiveness claims within a collateral proceeding.

A handful of jurisdictions impose an absolute rule, similar to the rule announced in Hubbard. See, e.g., Hooks v. Ward, 184 F.3d 1206, 1213 (10th Cir.1999); White v. Kelso, 401 S.E.2d 733 (Ga. 1991); Tachibana v. State, 900 P.2d 1293 (Haw. 1995); State v. Litherland, 12 P.3d 92 (Utah 2000). Most jurisdictions considering this issue, however, express a clear preference that ineffectiveness claims be raised in collateral review proceedings.

10. The only exception to this rule that is currently recognized by this court is in capital cases on direct appeal, where this court "relaxes" the waiver rules and reviews the issue as one of trial court error, even where there is intervening counsel and the issue was not preserved in the court below.

For example, the federal courts have generally recognized that ineffectiveness claims are not appropriate for direct appeal, but should be raised in a collateral action. See, e.g., United States v. McIntosh, 280 F.3d 479, 481 (5th Cir. 2002) ("A claim of ineffective assistance of counsel generally cannot be reviewed on direct appeal unless it has been presented to the district court."). These courts recognize that exceptional circumstances may exist where the ineffectiveness is patent on the record and therefore, can be addressed on direct appeal. See, e.g., United States v. Cronic, 466 U.S. 648, 659 (1984) (recognizing that counsel's conduct may be so egregious that "no amount of showing of want of prejudice would cure it"). However, as a general rule, the federal courts defer review of ineffectiveness claims until collateral review. Similarly, an overwhelming majority of states indicate a general reluctance to entertain ineffectiveness claims on direct appeal. People v. Mendoza Tello, 933 P.2d 1134 (Cal. 1997) (claims should be raised on collateral review, unless they are obvious on the record); Downey v. People, 25 P.3d 1200 (Colo. 2001); State v. Lucas, 323 N.W.2d 228 (Iowa 1982); State v. Seiss, 428 So. 2d 444 (La.1983); Ware v. State, 759 A.2d 764 (Md. 2000); State v. Henry, 898 P.2d 1195 (Mont. 1995); State v. Preciose, 609 A.2d 1280 (N.J. 1992); Duncan v. Kerby, 851 P.2d 466 (N.M. 1993); People v. Alvarado, 683 N.Y.S.2d 501 (N.Y.A.D.1998); Robinson v. State, 16 S.W.3d 808 (Tex. Crim. App. 2000). These states will only review those claims on direct appeal that can be adequately reviewed on the existing record. Even among the states expressing a preference that ineffectiveness claims be raised on direct appeal, those states limit that requirement to claims of ineffectiveness that "were known or apparent from the record." State v. Suggs, 613 N.W.2d 8, 11 (Neb. 2000). Thus, similar to the federal jurisdictions, most states express a preference to review ineffectiveness claims in collateral proceedings.

[There are] sound rationales behind the general preference expressed by the overwhelming majority of jurisdictions that ineffectiveness claims be deferred until the collateral review stage. . . . First, ineffectiveness claims, by their very nature, often involve claims that are not apparent on the record. Thus, appellate counsel must not only scour the existing record for any issues, but also has the additional burden of raising any extra-record claims that may exist by interviewing the client, family members, and any other people who may shed light on claims that could have been pursued before or during trial and at sentencing. Importantly, appellate counsel must perform this Herculean task in the limited amount of time that is available for filing an appeal from the judgment of sentence — 30 days. Pa. R. Crim. P. 720. Further, . . . it is not even clear if appellate counsel's duty extends to finding extra-record claims or whether appellate counsel would be ineffective for failing to uncover extra-record claims.

Second, even presuming the merit of the claim is apparent on the existing record, oftentimes demonstrating trial counsel's ineffectiveness will involve facts that are not available on the record. For example, the prejudicial effect of trial counsel's chosen course of action is determined more accurately after the trial and appellate courts have had the opportunity to review the alleged claims of error and if necessary, correct any trial court errors. It is only after this review that the full effect of counsel's conduct can be placed in the context of the case. Third, . . . the trial court is in the best position to review claims related to trial counsel's error in the first instance as that is the court that observed firsthand counsel's allegedly deficient performance.

What is apparent from the above discussion of other jurisdictions' review of ineffectiveness claims is that the same concerns that animated our general approach to appellate review should apply with equal vigor in the ineffectiveness arena. . . . Deferring review of trial counsel ineffectiveness claims until the collateral review stage of the proceedings offers a petitioner the best avenue to effect his Sixth Amendment right to counsel. Accordingly, for the reasons stated herein, we over-rule *Hubbard* to the extent that it requires that trial counsel's ineffectiveness be raised at that time when a petitioner obtains new counsel or those claims will be deemed waived.

We now hold that, as a general rule, a petitioner should wait to raise claims of ineffective assistance of trial counsel until collateral review.[14] Thus, any ineffective-ness claim will be waived only after a petitioner has had the opportunity to raise that claim on collateral review and has failed to avail himself of that opportunity. Our holding today does not alter the waiver provision of the PCRA, 42 Pa. C.S. §9544(b); it merely alters that time when a claim will be considered waived. Simply stated, a claim raising trial counsel ineffectiveness will no longer be considered waived because new counsel on direct appeal did not raise a claim related to prior counsel's ineffectiveness. . . .

Applying the new rule to the instant case, the claims regarding trial counsel's ineffectiveness will be dismissed without prejudice. Appellant can raise these claims in addition to other claims of ineffectiveness in a first PCRA petition and at that time the PCRA court will be in a position to ensure that Appellant receives an evidentiary hearing on his claims, if necessary. Accordingly, consistent with our holding today, the order of the Superior Court, affirming Appellant's judgment of sentence, is affirmed.

SAYLOR, J., concurring.

As a general proposition, I see benefit in the majority's preference to channel claims of ineffective assistance of counsel into the collateral review process, and I have no quarrel with its effort to treat such claims in a more systematic fashion. On balance, however, I would not eliminate the requirements of Commonwealth v. Hubbard, 372 A.2d 687 (Pa. 1977), at this juncture. . . . First, I do not regard the *Hubbard* rule, in and of itself, as being as inflexible as the majority portrays. The majority fails to mention that *Hubbard* allows for remand by an appellate court to the trial court for an evidentiary hearing concerning the merits of a claim of ineffective assistance of trial counsel raised for the first time on appeal. . . .

CASTILLE, J., concurring and dissenting.

Although I join in the majority opinion's abrogation of the procedural rule first announced by this Court in *Hubbard*, I respectfully dissent from . . . the majority's formulation of the new rule which would replace *Hubbard*. . . .

The majority holds that, as a "general rule," criminal defendants on direct appeal "should" wait until collateral review to raise new claims of trial counsel ineffectiveness. In addition to employing the equivocal word "should" in the actual

---

14. The general rule announced today is limited by the issues raised in this case. Appellant does not raise an allegation that there has been a complete or constructive denial of counsel or that counsel has breached his or her duty of loyalty. Under those limited circumstances, this court may choose to create an exception to the general rule and review those claims on direct appeal. However, as there is no issue raising such a question in this case, such a consideration is more appropriately left to another day.

standard, the majority also appends a footnote in which it suggests, in dicta, an exception to the new rule. . . .

The potential for uncertainty and equivocation is particularly acute in light of the exception to the general rule suggested by the majority. The majority suggests that the Court might create an exception if the appellant merely alleged "that there has been a complete or constructive denial of counsel or that counsel has breached his or her duty of loyalty." This particular sub-class of claims involving the steward-ship of counsel has indeed been afforded distinctive Sixth Amendment treatment by the U.S. Supreme Court—but not on the procedural ground that there is something in the nature of such claims that requires that they be entertained for the first time on direct appeal. Instead, the Court has afforded such claims different substantive treatment. Specifically, it has held that in situations where assistance of counsel in fact has been denied entirely or during a critical stage of the proceeding, or where counsel in fact actively represented conflicting interests, the defendant does not need to demonstrate the *Strickland* prejudice that would otherwise be required for a showing of ineffectiveness, i.e., he need not show that, but for counsel's errors, the outcome of the proceeding would probably have been different.

Of course, it is easy in the extreme to allege that an ineffectiveness claim involves an instance where prejudice should be deemed presumed; we see such allegations in almost all the capital cases. But the allegation is far more difficult to prove under the prevailing Sixth Amendment standard. . . .

Consistently with the general standards of issue preservation that govern all appeals, and to avoid the confusion the majority's new rule will engender, I would formulate the new "general rule" as holding that claims sounding in the ineffectiveness of trial counsel, which were not properly raised and preserved in the trial court, are unavailable for review upon direct appeal and must, instead, be pursued under the PCRA. . . .

Notes

1. *Ineffective assistance claims on collateral review: majority position.* The Pennsylvania court in *Grant* explains that the capacity for additional factfinding, especially of matters occurring outside of the trial courtroom, makes collateral review especially appropriate for reviewing claims of ineffective assistance of counsel. Federal courts may grant relief on habeas corpus for an attorney's failure to raise a Fourth Amendment claim at trial or on appeal, even though under the doctrine of Stone v. Powell, 428 U.S. 465 (1976), the federal habeas court could not address the merits of the Fourth Amendment claim itself. See Kimmelman v. Morrison, 477 U.S. 365 (1986).

The Flango study confirms that ineffective assistance of counsel is the most common claim in both state and federal systems. In state systems, claims of ineffective assistance are among the most *successful*, while this does not appear to be true in the federal system. What might be the source of this difference? Is the Pennsylvania statute consistent with or in tension with the generally more sympathetic legal posture toward ineffective assistance claims?

In Massaro v. United States, 538 U.S. 500 (2003), the defendant in a federal criminal case waited until a collateral proceeding to raise his claim of ineffective assistance of trial counsel. The Supreme Court held that the defendant did not lose this claim even though he could have raised it on direct appeal and even though the trial record was sufficiently developed to raise the claim. The Court reasoned that it is more efficient to allow defendants to raise the claim in collateral proceedings, because ineffectiveness claims often require evidentiary hearings on whether there was some strategic reason for the lawyer's act or omission. Appellate courts are not capable of taking testimony or other evidence, so judicial economy is best served by allowing defendants to raise the claim initially in collateral proceedings. Even when the necessary facts already appear in the trial record, counsel on direct appeal must rely on trial counsel to become familiar with the case on a short deadline, making it awkward for the appellate lawyer to raise a claim of ineffective assistance.

2. *Ineffective assistance by collateral review counsel.* Some states provide appointed counsel for collateral review, at least in cases where courts have determined that a petition raises a substantial claim. For example, Tex. Code Crim. Proc. art. 1.051(d)(3) authorizes a trial court to appoint counsel to indigent capital defendants in state habeas corpus proceedings "if the court concludes that the interests of justice require representation." See Tex. Op. Atty. Gen. 1995, No. DM-354. When habeas counsel is appointed by a court, the performance of that counsel can typically be challenged as ineffective in later proceedings. See Crump v. Demosthenes, 934 P.2d 247 (Nev. 1997). However, where there is no statutory or constitutional basis for appointing counsel on habeas corpus review, some courts refuse to consider later ineffective assistance claims regarding representation in prior habeas corpus proceedings. See McKague v. Whitely, 912 P.2d 255 (Nev. 1996). How might you explain this different treatment?

3. *Empirical analysis of collateral review.* The Flango study is one of only a handful of empirical studies of habeas corpus and other forms of collateral review. The years since the Flango study have seen major changes in both federal and state law, and further empirical work is needed. The centrality of ineffective assistance claims to collateral attacks may have become even more pronounced.

The Flango study noted that a majority of habeas petitioners were convicted after trial rather than a plea. Consider the effect and wisdom of Nev. Rev. Stat. §34.810(1): "The court shall dismiss a petition if the court determines that [the] petitioner's conviction was upon a plea of guilty or guilty but mentally ill and the petition is not based upon an allegation that the plea was involuntarily or unknowingly entered or that the plea was entered without effective assistance of counsel."

The Flango study indicates a very low rate of success for habeas petitioners in both state and federal systems. Why, then, has habeas corpus remained so controversial? First, the tension between finality and continuing claims of denial of justice is a real tension, however a particular court resolves it. This tension is heightened for some classes of cases, especially cases where there is a claim of "true innocence" and in capital cases, where the consequences of finality are obviously more "final" than for other cases. Second, a small handful of habeas corpus petitions are truly silly, but sometimes these cases receive a fair amount of publicity, and therefore help to shape legislative and popular concerns. Under the heading of "ridiculous cases make bad law" are claims by prisoners that the substitution of smooth for chunky peanut butter or nutra loaf for actual meat loaf constitutes "cruel and unusual" punishment. Third, even as collateral review doctrines have tended to restrict access to collateral review in both state and federal courts, the number of cases remains substantial (though the success rate and the grounds for disposition may be changing, along with the time burden on the courts).

4. *Ineffective assistance of counsel in death cases.* Claims of ineffective assistance of counsel take on a special power and poignancy in death penalty cases, where the person responsible for the error and the person suffering the consequences are different. Capital appellate advocate Stephen Bright has noted:

> Poor people accused of capital crimes are often defended by lawyers who lack the skills, resources, and commitment to handle such serious matters. This fact is confirmed in case after case. It is not the facts of the crime, but the quality of legal representation, that distinguishes this case, where the death penalty was imposed, from many similar cases, where it was not. . . .
>
> A poor person facing the death penalty may be assigned an attorney who has little or no experience in the defense of capital or even serious criminal cases, one reluctant or unwilling to defend him, one with little or no empathy or understanding of the accused or his particular plight, one with little or no knowledge of criminal or capital punishment law, or one with no understanding of the need to document and present mitigating circumstances. Although it is widely acknowledged that at least two lawyers, supported by investigative and expert assistance, are required to defend a capital case, some of the jurisdictions with the largest number of death sentences still assign only one lawyer to defend a capital case. . . . Lawyers can make more money doing almost anything else. Even many lawyers who have an interest in criminal defense work simply cannot afford to continue to represent indigents while also repaying their student loans and meeting their familial obligations.

Stephen Bright, Counsel for the Poor: The Death Sentence Not for the Worst Crime but for the Worst Lawyer, 103 Yale L.J. 1835, 1836, 1845-46, 1850 (1994).

C. FEDERAL HABEAS CORPUS REVIEW OF STATE CONVICTIONS

The modern debate in the United States over habeas corpus has not primarily been a debate about the division of labor between appeals and later collateral reviews of convictions — the topic considered in the prior sections. Instead, the debate has centered on whether and to what extent federal courts (and especially federal district courts) should review final state convictions. This is as much a debate about federalism as about habeas corpus. One reason this topic has generated so much heat in the last few decades may be suggested by the number of habeas corpus petitions filed by state prisoners in federal court (technically petitions under the federal habeas corpus statute, 28 U.S.C. §2254). State prisoners filed 1,020 federal petitions in 1961, 8,372 petitions in 1971, 7,786 petitions in 1981, 10,325 petitions in 1991, and 21,345 petitions in 2000. See Bureau of Justice Statistics: Prisoner Petitions Filed in U.S. District Courts, 2000, with Trends, 1980-2000 (2002, NCJ 189430).

The absolute number of federal habeas petitions by state prisoners is higher than ever, and reveals that habeas corpus petitions occupy a noticeable portion of the workload for the federal courts. Nevertheless, the absolute number of petitions may overstate the impact of federal review on state criminal justice, because the number of state prisoners has increased far more quickly than the number of federal petitions. This data does not describe the rate of federal habeas petitions (i.e., what proportion of state inmates file a federal petition in any given year) or the number of petitions where a federal court actually grants relief. Consider the chart above,

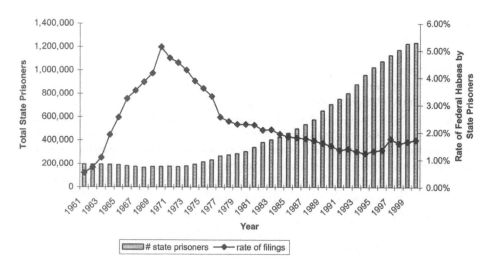

illustrating the rate of federal petitions filed by state prisoners between 1961 and 2000.

This chart suggests a dramatic change in federal habeas corpus in the early 1960s. The most important development was the 1963 U.S. Supreme Court decision in Fay v. Noia. The chart also suggests that the rate of federal habeas petitions by state prisoners had returned by 1994 to about what it was in 1963, when *Fay* was decided. This section considers the expansion and contraction of federal review of state convictions through habeas corpus over the past three decades.

1. *Expansion*

Habeas corpus was available in state courts from the earliest days of the nation, but the Judiciary Act of 1789 provided habeas corpus in federal court only for federal prisoners. After the Civil War, the Reconstruction Congress authorized federal courts to review convictions obtained in state courts as part of its general effort to strengthen the national government. However, the Habeas Corpus Act of 1867 did not lead to many challenges of state convictions until the middle of the twentieth century. At about the same time that the U.S. Supreme Court began to expand the influence of the federal constitution in state criminal justice systems (by "incorporating" various parts of the Bill of Rights against the states under the fourteenth amendment), the Court also started to read the habeas corpus statute more broadly. Habeas corpus became the leading procedural mechanism for the federal courts to enforce the new dictates of federal law. As you read the following case, ask whether the Supreme Court had other viable options for enforcing newly announced constitutional requirements.

■ EDWARD FAY v. CHARLES NOIA
372 U.S. 391 (1963)

Brennan, J.

This case presents important questions touching the federal habeas corpus jurisdiction in its relation to state criminal justice. The narrow question is whether

the respondent Noia may be granted federal habeas corpus relief from imprisonment under a New York conviction now admitted by the State to rest upon a confession obtained from him in violation of the Fourteenth Amendment, after he was
denied state post-conviction relief because the coerced confession claim had been
decided against him at the trial and Noia had allowed the time for a direct appeal to
lapse without seeking review by a state appellate court.

Noia was convicted in 1942 with Santo Caminito and Frank Bonino in the
County Court of Kings County, New York, of a felony murder in the shooting and
killing of one Hammeroff during the commission of a robbery. The sole evidence
against each defendant was his signed confession. Caminito and Bonino, but not
Noia, appealed their convictions to the Appellate Division of the New York
Supreme Court. These appeals were unsuccessful, but subsequent legal proceedings resulted in the releases of Caminito and Bonino on findings that their confessions had been coerced and their convictions therefore procured in violation
of the Fourteenth Amendment. Although it has been stipulated that the coercive
nature of Noia's confession was also established, the United States District Court
for the Southern District of New York held in Noia's federal habeas corpus proceeding that because of his failure to appeal he must be denied relief. [We hold
that federal] courts have power under the federal habeas statute to grant relief
despite the applicant's failure to have pursued a state remedy not available to him
at the time he applies; the doctrine under which state procedural defaults are
held to constitute an adequate and independent state law ground barring direct
Supreme Court review is not to be extended to limit the power granted the
federal courts under the federal habeas statute. . . . Noia's failure to appeal cannot under the circumstances be deemed an intelligent and understanding waiver
of his right to appeal such as to justify the withholding of federal habeas corpus
relief. . . .

We do well to bear in mind the extraordinary prestige of the Great Writ, habeas
corpus ad subjiciendum, in Anglo-American jurisprudence. [Its] function has been
to provide a prompt and efficacious remedy for whatever society deems to be intolerable restraints. Its root principle is that in a civilized society, government must
always be accountable to the judiciary for a man's imprisonment. . . . There is nothing novel in the fact that today habeas corpus in the federal courts provides a mode
for the redress of denials of due process of law. Vindication of due process is precisely its historic office.

[The] nature and purpose of habeas corpus have remained remarkably
constant. . . . The principle that judicial as well as executive restraints may be intolerable received dramatic expression in Bushell's Case, 124 Eng. Rep. 1006 (1670).
Bushell was one of the jurors in the trial, held before the Court of Oyer and Terminer at the Old Bailey, of William Penn and William Mead on charges of tumultuous
assembly and other crimes. When the jury brought in a verdict of not guilty, the
court ordered the jurors committed for contempt. Bushell sought habeas corpus,
and the Court of Common Pleas, in a memorable opinion by Chief Justice Vaughan,
ordered him discharged from custody. The case is by no means isolated, and when
habeas corpus practice was codified in the Habeas Corpus Act of 1679, 31 Car. II, c.
2, no distinction was made between executive and judicial detentions.

Nor is it true that at common law habeas corpus was available only to inquire
into the jurisdiction, in a narrow sense, of the committing court. Bushell's Case is
again in point. Chief Justice Vaughan did not base his decision on the theory that
the Court of Oyer and Terminer had no jurisdiction to commit persons for

contempt, but on the plain denial of due process, violative of Magna Charta, of a court's imprisoning the jury because it disagreed with the verdict. . . .

Thus, at the time that the Suspension Clause was written into our Federal Constitution and the first Judiciary Act was passed conferring habeas corpus jurisdiction upon the federal judiciary, there was respectable common-law authority for the proposition that habeas was available to remedy any kind of governmental restraint contrary to fundamental law.

[Although the Habeas Corpus Act] of 1867, like its English and American predecessors, nowhere defines habeas corpus, its expansive language and imperative tone, viewed against the background of post-Civil War efforts in Congress to deal severely with the States of the former Confederacy, would seem to make inescapable the conclusion that Congress was enlarging the habeas remedy as previously understood, not only in extending its coverage to state prisoners, but also in making its procedures more efficacious. In 1867, Congress was anticipating resistance to its Reconstruction measures and planning the implementation of the post-war constitutional Amendments. Debated and enacted at the very peak of the Radical Republicans' power, the measure that became the Act of 1867 seems plainly to have been designed to furnish a method additional to and independent of direct Supreme Court review of state court decisions for the vindication of the new constitutional guarantees. Congress seems to have had no thought, thus, that a state prisoner should abide state court determination of his constitutional defense — the necessary predicate of direct review by this Court — before resorting to federal habeas corpus. Rather, a remedy almost in the nature of removal from the state to the federal courts of state prisoners' constitutional contentions seems to have been envisaged. . . .

The breadth of the federal courts' power of independent adjudication on habeas corpus stems from the very nature of the writ. . . . It is of the historical essence of habeas corpus that it lies to test proceedings so fundamentally lawless that imprisonment pursuant to them is not merely erroneous but void. [T]he traditional characterization of the writ of habeas corpus as an original . . . civil remedy for the enforcement of the right to personal liberty, rather than as a stage of the state criminal proceedings or as an appeal therefrom, emphasizes the independence of the federal habeas proceedings from what has gone before. This is not to say that a state criminal judgment resting on a constitutional error is void for all purposes. But conventional notions of finality in criminal litigation cannot be permitted to defeat the manifest federal policy that federal constitutional rights of personal liberty shall not be denied without the fullest opportunity for plenary federal judicial review.

[T]he question of the instant case has obvious importance to the proper accommodation of a great constitutional privilege and the requirements of the federal system. [W]e have consistently held that federal court jurisdiction is conferred by the allegation of an unconstitutional restraint and is not defeated by anything that may occur in the state court proceedings. State procedural rules plainly must yield to this overriding federal policy.

A number of arguments are advanced against this conclusion. One, which concedes the breadth of federal habeas power, is that a state prisoner who forfeits his opportunity to vindicate federal defenses in the state court has been given all the process that is constitutionally due him, and hence is not restrained contrary to the Constitution. . . . But this ignores the important difference between rights and particular remedies. A defendant by committing a procedural default may be debarred from challenging his conviction in the state courts even on federal constitutional grounds. But a forfeiture of remedies does not legitimize the uncon-stitutional conduct by which his conviction was procured. . . . In what sense is Noia's custody not in violation of federal law simply because New York will not allow him to challenge it? . . .

Although we hold that the jurisdiction of the federal courts on habeas corpus is not affected by procedural defaults incurred by the applicant during the state court proceedings, we recognize a limited discretion in the federal judge to deny relief to an applicant under certain circumstances. [The] federal habeas judge may in his discretion deny relief to an applicant who has deliberately by-passed the orderly procedure of the state courts and in so doing has forfeited his state court remedies. But we wish to make very clear that this grant of discretion is not to be interpreted as a permission to introduce legal fictions into federal habeas corpus. The classic definition of waiver enunciated in Johnson v. Zerbst, 304 U.S. 458 (1938) — "an intentional relinquishment or abandonment of a known right or privilege" — furnishes the controlling standard. If a habeas applicant, after consultation with competent counsel or otherwise, understandingly and knowingly forewent the privilege of seeking to vindicate his federal claims in the state courts, whether for strategic, tactical, or any other reasons that can fairly be described as the deliberate by-passing of state procedures, then it is open to the federal court on habeas to deny him all relief if the state courts refused to entertain his federal claims on the merits — though of course only after the federal court has satisfied itself, by holding a hearing or by some other means, of the facts bearing upon the applicant's default. At all events we wish it clearly understood that the standard here put forth depends on the considered choice of the petitioner. A choice made by counsel not partic-ipated in by the petitioner does not automatically bar relief. Nor does a state court's finding of waiver bar independent determination of the question by the federal courts on habeas, for waiver affecting federal rights is a federal question.

The application of the standard we have adumbrated to the facts of the instant case is not difficult. Under no reasonable view can the State's version of Noia's reason for not appealing support an inference of deliberate by-passing of the state court system. For Noia to have appealed in 1942 would have been to run a substantial risk of electrocution. His was the grisly choice whether to sit content with life imprisonment or to travel the uncertain avenue of appeal which, if successful, might well have led to a retrial and death sentence. He declined to play Russian roulette in this fashion. . . . Surely no fair-minded person will contend that those who have been deprived of their liberty without due process of law ought neverthe-less to languish in prison. . . . If the States withhold effective remedy, the federal courts have the power and the duty to provide it. Habeas corpus is one of the precious heritages of Anglo-American civilization. We do no more today than confirm its continuing efficacy. . . .

CLARK, J., dissenting.

[There] can be no question but that a rash of new applications from state prisoners will pour into the federal courts, and 98% of them will be frivolous, if history is any guide.[1] This influx will necessarily have an adverse effect upon the disposition of meritorious applications, for, as my Brother Jackson said, they will "be buried in a flood of worthless ones. He who must search a haystack for a needle is

---

1. In the 12-year period from 1946 to 1957 the petitioners were successful in 1.4% of the cases.

likely to end up with the attitude that the needle is not worth the search." Brown v. Allen, 344 U.S. 443 (1953) (concurring opinion). In fact, the courts are already swamped with applications which cannot, because of sheer numbers, be given more than cursory attention.[2] . . .

Essential to the administration of justice is the prompt enforcement of judicial decrees. After today state judgments will be relegated to a judicial limbo, subject to federal collateral attack — as here — a score of years later despite a defendant's willful failure to appeal. . . .

HARLAN, J. dissenting.

This decision, both in its abrupt break with the past and in its consequences for the future, is one of the most disquieting that the Court has rendered in a long time. . . .

The formative stage of the development of habeas corpus jurisdiction may be said to have ended in 1915, the year in which Frank v. Mangum, 237 U.S. 309, was decided. During this period the federal courts, on applications for habeas corpus complaining of detention pursuant to a judgment of conviction and sentence, purported to examine only the jurisdiction of the sentencing tribunal. In the leading case of Ex parte Watkins, 3 Pet. 193 (1830), the Court stated: "An imprisonment under a judgment cannot be unlawful, unless that judgment be an absolute nullity; and it is not a nullity if the court has general jurisdiction of the subject, although it should be erroneous." Many subsequent decisions . . . reaffirmed the limitation of the writ to consideration of the sentencing court's jurisdiction over the person of the defendant and the subject matter of the suit.

The concept of jurisdiction, however, was subjected to considerable strain during this period, and the strain was not lessened by the fact that until the latter part of the last century, federal criminal convictions were not generally reviewable by the Supreme Court. The expansion of the definition of jurisdiction occurred primarily in two classes of cases: (1) those in which the conviction was for violation of an allegedly unconstitutional statute, and (2) those in which the Court viewed the detention as based on some claimed illegality in the sentence imposed, as distinguished from the judgment of conviction. . . .

The next stage of development may be described as beginning in 1915 with Frank v. Mangum, 237 U.S. 309, and ending in 1953 with Brown v. Allen, 344 U.S. 443. In *Frank*, the prisoner had claimed before the state courts that the proceedings in which he had been convicted for murder had been dominated by a mob, and the State Supreme Court, after consideration not only of the record but of extensive affidavits, had concluded that mob domination had not been established. Frank then sought federal habeas, and this Court affirmed the denial of relief. But in doing so the Court recognized that Frank's allegation of mob domination raised a constitutional question which he was entitled to have considered by a competent tribunal uncoerced by popular pressures. Such "corrective process" had been afforded by the State Supreme Court, however, and since Frank had received "notice, and a hearing, or an opportunity to be heard" on his constitutional claims his detention was not in violation of federal law and habeas corpus would not lie.

---

2. The increase in number of habeas corpus applications filed in Federal District Courts by state prisoners is illustrated by the following figures: 127 in 1941; 536 in 1945; 560 in 1950; 660 in 1955; 872 in 1960; 906 in 1961; 1,232 in 1962.

It is clear that a new dimension was added to habeas corpus in this case, for in addition to questions previously thought of as "jurisdictional," the federal courts were now to consider whether the applicant had been given an adequate opportunity to raise his constitutional claims before the state courts. And if no such opportunity had been afforded in the state courts, the federal claim would be heard on its merits. . . . But habeas would not lie to reconsider constitutional questions that had been fairly determined. And a fortiori it would not lie to consider a question when the state court's refusal to do so rested on an adequate and independent state ground. . . .

In 1953, this Court rendered its landmark decisions in Brown v. Allen and Daniels v. Allen, 344 U.S. 443, 482-87 (1953). Both cases involved applications for federal habeas corpus by prisoners who were awaiting execution pursuant to state convictions. In both cases, the constitutional contentions made were that the trial court had erred in ruling confessions admissible and in overruling motions to quash the indictment on the basis of alleged discrimination in the selection of jurors.

In *Brown,* these contentions had been presented to the highest court of the State, on direct appeal from the conviction, and had been rejected by that court on the merits, after which this Court had denied certiorari. At this point, the Court held, Brown was entitled to full reconsideration of these constitutional claims, with a hearing if appropriate, in an application to a Federal District Court for habeas corpus. It is manifest that this decision substantially expanded the scope of inquiry on an application for federal habeas corpus. . . .

But what if the validity of the state decision to detain rested not on the determination of a federal claim but rather on an adequate nonfederal ground which would have barred direct review by this Court? That was the question in *Daniels.* The attorney for the petitioners in that case had failed to mail the appeal papers on the last day for filing, and although he delivered them by hand the next day, the State Supreme Court refused to entertain the appeal, ruling that it had not been filed on time. This ruling, this Court held, barred federal habeas corpus consideration of the claims that the state appellate court had refused to consider. [Habeas] corpus would not lie for a prisoner who was detained pursuant to a state judgment which, in the view of the majority in *Daniels,* rested on a reasonable application of the State's own procedural requirements. . . .

The true significance of today's decision can perhaps best be laid bare in terms of a hypothetical case presenting questions of the powers of this Court on direct review, and of a Federal District Court on habeas corpus. Assume that a man is indicted, and held for trial in a state court, by a grand jury from which members of his race have been systematically excluded. Assume further that the State requires any objection to the composition of the grand jury to be raised prior to the verdict, that no such objection is made, and that the defendant seeks to raise the point for the first time on appeal from his conviction. If the state appellate court refuses to consider the claim because it was raised too late, and if certiorari is sought and granted, the initial question before this Court will be whether there was an adequate state ground for the judgment below. If the petitioner was represented by counsel not shown to be incompetent, and if the necessary information to make the objection is not shown to have been unavailable at the time of trial, it is certain that the judgment of conviction will stand, despite the fact the indictment was obtained in violation of the petitioner's constitutional rights. . . .

For this Court to go beyond the adequacy of the state ground and to review and determine the correctness of that ground on its merits would, in our hypothetical case, be to assume full control over a State's procedures for the administration of its own criminal justice. This is and must be beyond our power if the federal system is to exist in substance as well as form. The right of the State to regulate its own procedures governing the conduct of litigants in its courts, and its interest in supervision of those procedures, stand on the same constitutional plane as its right and interest in framing "substantive" laws governing other aspects of the conduct of those within its borders.

The adequate state ground doctrine thus finds its source in basic constitutional principles, and the question before us is whether this is as true in a collateral attack in habeas corpus as on direct review. Assume, then, that after dismissal of the writ of certiorari in our hypothetical case, the prisoner seeks habeas corpus in a Federal District Court, again complaining of the composition of the grand jury that indicted him. Is that federal court constitutionally more free than the Supreme Court on direct review to "ignore" the adequate state ground, proceed to the federal question, and order the prisoner's release?

The answer must be that it is not. . . . In habeas as on direct review, ordering the prisoner's release invalidates the judgment of conviction and renders ineffective the state rule relied upon to sustain that judgment. Try as the majority does to turn habeas corpus into a roving commission of inquiry into every possible invasion of the applicant's civil rights that may ever have occurred, it cannot divorce the writ from a judgment of conviction if that judgment is the basis of the detention. . . . The effect of the approach adopted by the Court is, indeed, to do away with the adequate state ground rule entirely in every state case, involving a federal question, in which detention follows from a judgment.

[The substitute that the Court] has fashioned — that of "conscious waiver" or "deliberate bypassing" of state procedures — is . . . wholly unsatisfactory. [It] amounts to no limitation at all. [The] Court states . . . that "[a] choice made by counsel not participated in by the petitioner does not automatically bar relief." It is true that there are cases in which the adequacy of the state ground necessarily turns on the question whether the defendant himself expressly and intelligently waived a constitutional right. Foremost among these are the cases involving right to counsel, for the Court has made it clear that this right cannot be foregone without deliberate choice by the defendant. See Johnson v. Zerbst, 304 U.S. 458 (1938). But to carry this principle over in full force to cases in which a defendant is represented by counsel not shown to be incompetent is to undermine the entire representational system.

[When] it comes to apply the "waiver" test in this case, the Court . . . seems to be saying . . . that no waiver of a right can be effective if some adverse consequence might reasonably be expected to follow from exercise of that right. Under this approach, of course, there could never be a binding waiver, since only an incompetent would give up a right without any good reason, and an incompetent cannot make an intelligent waiver. . . .

It is the adequacy, or fairness, of the state ground that should be the controlling question in this case. This controlling question the Court does not discuss. . . . Certainly the State has a vital interest in requiring that appeals be taken on the basis of facts known at the time, since the first assertion of a claim many years later might otherwise require release long after it was feasible to hold a new trial. . . .

I recognize that Noia's predicament may well be thought one that strongly calls for correction. But the proper course to that end lies with the New York Governor's powers of executive clemency, not with the federal courts. Since Noia is detained pursuant to a state judgment whose validity rests on an adequate and independent state ground, the judgment below should be reversed.

Notes

1. *Legal revolutions.* How does Justice Brennan cast the majority decision in *Fay* as an extension of tradition rather than a legal revolution? Do the dissents make a compelling case that *Fay* was a revolution? Could both be correct? Arguments about the historical scope of the federal habeas corpus writ must deal with many seemingly inconsistent Supreme Court cases, describing the writ in both broad and narrow terms. Some of the broader pronouncements about the scope of habeas corpus could be explained away (just as Justice Harlan did in his dissent) as aberrations, or as modest extensions of the traditional idea that a habeas court may review the "jurisdiction" of the criminal court or the legality of the sentence. On the other hand, the narrower pronouncements could be explained (as in Justice Brennan's opinion) as the result of the historically narrow scope of Supreme Court criminal appeals jurisdiction, or the narrow scope of the due process concept, rather than the narrow scope of the habeas remedy itself.

Whatever its exact relationship to past developments, the decision in Fay v. Noia marked the beginning of a high-water period of federal habeas corpus review. See Sanders v. United States, 373 U.S. 1 (1963) (expanding availability of successive federal petitions); Townsend v. Sain, 372 U.S. 293 (1963) (expanding availability of factfinding hearing in federal habeas proceedings). At a time when the Court was expanding the reach of the federal constitution, it gave lower federal courts broader authority than ever before to review state convictions. See Robert Cover & Alexander Aleinikoff, Dialectical Federalism: Habeas Corpus and the Court, 86 Yale L.J. 1035 (1977).

The high water of federal habeas corpus started to recede only a decade after the decision in Fay v. Noia. We have already seen that *Fay* itself has been overruled in the federal system. In Wainwright v. Sykes, 433 U.S. 72 (1977), the Court gave renewed importance to the procedural requirements that state courts place on criminal defendants, and replaced the "deliberate bypass" standard with the "cause and prejudice" standard. See also Coleman v. Thompson, 501 U.S. 722 (1991) (rejecting deliberate bypass standard for failure to raise issue on state appeal). Does the relationship between federal and state courts influence the sort of "procedural default" doctrine that should apply on federal habeas corpus, or would the same doctrine be relevant whenever *any* court in collateral proceedings is evaluating earlier criminal proceedings?

2. *Federal factfinding and presumptions.* A federal court ruling on a habeas corpus petition will need to draw some conclusions about facts, that is, historical facts that happened during the investigation and prosecution. What is the impact of the state courts' earlier rulings on questions of fact? For the most part, the federal habeas court must accept the facts as found in the state court proceedings. The federal statute attaches a "presumption of correctness" to the factual findings of state courts. The party objecting to the state court's factual finding must ordinarily demonstrate to the federal court by "clear and convincing evidence" that the state court's finding was erroneous. The petitioner can avoid this presumption of correctness for state factfinding (and the resulting heavy burden of proof) by showing

at the threshold that the state court engaged in a procedurally "unreasonable determination" of the facts "in light of the evidence presented in the State court proceeding." 28 U.S.C. §§2254(d)(2), (e)(1). The federal court reviews "mixed questions" of law and fact (as opposed to pure questions of basic, historical facts) under the same standards as issues of federal law. See Moore v. Dempsey, 261 U.S. 86 (1923) (Holmes, J.). Is the rationale for federal courts deferring to the factual findings of state courts different from the rationale for appellate courts deferring to trial courts on fact questions?

If the state courts have made no finding of facts on a relevant issue, the federal habeas court can conduct its own factfinding hearing only under very limited circumstances. Before 1996, judicial decisions defined the circumstances when a federal court could hold a factfinding hearing. See Townsend v. Sain, 372 U.S. 293 (1963) (creating broad powers for federal courts to hold evidentiary hearings on collateral review); Keeney v. Tamayo-Reyes, 504 U.S. 1 (1992) (applying cause and prejudice standard to determine when to hold evidentiary hearings). Under a 1996 revision to the federal habeas corpus statute, federal courts may conduct a hearing to determine facts that the petitioner "failed to develop" in the state courts only when (1) the petitioner had adequate "cause" for the failure to develop the facts — such as the appearance of a new rule of constitutional law made retroactive to habeas corpus petitions, or the need to determine facts that could not have been developed in state court despite the "due diligence" of the petitioner — *and* (2) the facts in question would establish a constitutional error that resulted in the conviction of an innocent defendant (in other words, "but for" the constitutional error, "no reasonable factfinder" would have found the petitioner guilty). 28 U.S.C. §2254(e)(2).

In Williams v. Taylor, 529 U.S. 420 (2000), the Supreme Court read the statute's "fails to develop" standard to require some showing of "fault" by the petitioner. A failure to develop a claim's factual basis "is not established unless there is lack of diligence, or some greater fault, attributable to the prisoner or his counsel." The necessary "diligence" under the statute requires a petitioner to make "a reasonable attempt, in light of the information available at the time, to investigate and pursue claims in state court." The fact that a particular investigation would have been *successful* is not enough to show that it was a *necessary* part of any reasonable investigation.

3. *Exhaustion of state remedies.* The federal habeas statute requires state prisoners to "exhaust" the remedies available to them in the state court system. The Supreme Court created the exhaustion requirement in Ex parte Royall, 117 U.S. 241 (1886), and Congress codified it in 1948. 28 U.S.C. §§2254(b), (c). To meet this requirement, a petitioner must present a claim of error to the available state courts to hear the claim before including that claim in a federal habeas petition. If a federal petition is "mixed," (that is, if it contains both exhausted and unexhausted claims), the federal court must dismiss the entire petition. Rose v. Lundy, 455 U.S.509 (1982). A federal petition dismissed on exhaustion grounds may be refiled after the petitioner has sought the available remedies from the state courts. See Rhines v. Weber, 544 U.S. 269 (2005) (district court has discretion to stay a "mixed" habeas corpus petition containing both exhausted and unexhausted claims while the petitioner returns to state court; stay in federal court tolls statute of limitations; court must find good cause for the failure to exhaust, unexhausted claims must be potentially meritorious, and there is no suggestion of intentional delay).

Note the interaction between the exhaustion rule described here and the statutes of limitations and limits on "successive petitions" described in section B of this chapter. As legal counsel for a state prisoner during post-conviction proceedings, would the exhaustion rule influence the specificity of your claims of legal error during state court proceedings?

2. *Contraction*

Over time, the Supreme Court became more skeptical of the value of federal habeas corpus review of state convictions. In a series of cases interpreting the (still essentially unchanged) federal statute, the Court declared that claims relating to improper searches and seizures would not be "cognizable" in federal habeas corpus, Stone v. Powell, 428 U.S. 465 (1976); and that a federal court would ordinarily not hear the merits of a claim if a petitioner committed "procedural default" by failing to preserve the claim for review in the state system, Wainwright v. Sykes, 433 U.S. 72 (1977). The following case announced what many considered to be the most important limitation on the availability of federal habeas corpus.

■ FRANK DEAN TEAGUE v. MICHAEL LANE
489 U.S. 288 (1989)

O'CONNOR, J.

In Taylor v. Louisiana, 419 U.S. 522 (1975), this Court held that the Sixth Amendment required that the jury venire be drawn from a fair cross section of the community. . . . The principal question presented in this case is whether the Sixth Amendment's fair cross section requirement should now be extended to the petit jury. Because we adopt Justice Harlan's approach to retroactivity for cases on collateral review, we leave the resolution of that question for another day.

Petitioner, a black man, was convicted by an all-white Illinois jury of three counts of attempted murder, two counts of armed robbery, and one count of aggravated battery. During jury selection for petitioner's trial, the prosecutor used all 10 of his peremptory challenges to exclude blacks. Petitioner's counsel used one of his 10 peremptory challenges to exclude a black woman who was married to a police officer. On appeal, petitioner argued that the prosecutor's use of peremptory challenges denied him the right to be tried by a jury that was representative of the community. The Illinois Appellate Court rejected petitioner's fair cross section claim. The Illinois Supreme Court denied leave to appeal, and we denied certiorari. Petitioner then filed a petition for a writ of habeas corpus in the United States District Court for the Northern District of Illinois. [The District Court declined to grant any relief and the Court of Appeals rejected Teague's fair cross section claim, holding that the fair cross section requirement was limited to the jury venire.]

In the past, the Court has, without discussion, often applied a new constitutional rule of criminal procedure to the defendant in the case announcing the new rule, and has confronted the question of retroactivity later when a different defendant sought the benefit of that rule. [However, we believe that retroactivity] is properly treated as a threshold question, for, once a new rule is applied to the defendant in the case announcing the rule, evenhanded justice requires that it be applied retroactively to all who are similarly situated. Thus, before deciding whether the fair cross section requirement should be extended to the petit jury, we should ask whether such a rule would be applied retroactively to the case at issue. . . .

It is admittedly often difficult to determine when a case announces a new rule, and we do not attempt to define the spectrum of what may or may not constitute a new rule for retroactivity purposes. In general, however, a case announces a new rule when it breaks new ground or imposes a new obligation on the States or the Federal Government. To put it differently, a case announces a new rule if the result was not dictated by precedent existing at the time the defendant's conviction became final. Given the strong language in *Taylor,* application of the fair cross section requirement to the petit jury would be a new rule.

Not all new rules have been uniformly treated for retroactivity purposes. Nearly a quarter of a century ago, in Linkletter v. Walker, 381 U.S. 618 (1965), the Court attempted to set some standards by which to determine the retroactivity of new rules. The question in *Linkletter* was whether Mapp v. Ohio, 367 U.S. 643 (1961), which made the exclusionary rule applicable to the States, should be applied retroactively to cases on collateral review. The Court determined that the retroactivity of *Mapp* should be determined by examining [1] the purpose of the exclusionary rule, [2] the reliance of the States on prior law, and [3] the effect on the administration of justice of a retroactive application of the exclusionary rule. Using that standard, the Court held that *Mapp* would only apply to trials commencing after that case was decided.

The *Linkletter* retroactivity standard has not led to consistent results. Instead, it has been used to limit application of certain new rules to cases on direct review, other new rules only to the defendants in the cases announcing such rules, and still other new rules to cases in which trials have not yet commenced. . . . Dissatisfied with the *Linkletter* standard, Justice Harlan advocated a different approach to retroactivity. He argued that new rules should always be applied retroactively to cases on direct review, but that generally they should not be applied retroactively to criminal cases on collateral review.

In Griffith v. Kentucky, 479 U.S. 314 (1987), [this Court] adopted the first part of the retroactivity approach advocated by Justice Harlan. . . . We gave two reasons for our decision. First, because we can only promulgate new rules in specific cases and cannot possibly decide all cases in which review is sought, "the integrity of judicial review" requires the application of the new rule to "all similar cases pending on direct review." . . . Second, because selective application of new rules violates the principle of treating similarly situated defendants the same, we refused to continue to tolerate the inequity that resulted from not applying new rules retroactively to defendants whose cases had not yet become final. [Thus, under *Griffith,*] a new rule for the conduct of criminal prosecutions is to be applied retroactively to all cases, state or federal, pending on direct review or not yet final, with no exception for cases in which the new rule constitutes a "clear break" with the past. . . .

Justice Harlan believed that new rules generally should not be applied retroactively to cases on collateral review. He argued that retroactivity for cases on collateral review could "be responsibly [determined] only by focusing, in the first instance, on the nature, function, and scope of the adjudicatory process in which such cases arise. The relevant frame of reference, in other words, is not the purpose of the new rule whose benefit the [defendant] seeks, but instead the purposes for which the writ of habeas corpus is made available." Mackey v. United States, 401 U.S. 667, 682 (1971). With regard to the nature of habeas corpus, Justice Harlan wrote:

> Habeas corpus always has been a collateral remedy, providing an avenue for upsetting judgments that have become otherwise final. It is not designed as a substitute for direct review. The interest in leaving concluded litigation in a state of repose, that is, reducing the controversy to a final judgment not subject to further judicial revision, may quite legitimately be found by those responsible for defining the scope of the writ to outweigh in some, many, or most instances the competing interest in readjudicating convictions according to all legal standards in effect when a habeas petition is filed. . . .

Justice Harlan identified only two exceptions to his general rule of nonretroactivity for cases on collateral review. First, a new rule should be applied retroactively if it places "certain kinds of primary, private individual conduct beyond the power of the criminal law-making authority to proscribe." Second, a new rule should be applied retroactively if it requires the observance of "those procedures that . . . are implicit in the concept of ordered liberty." Mackey, 401 U.S. at 693 (quoting Palko v. Connecticut, 302 U.S. 319 (1937) (Cardozo, J.)).

We agree with Justice Harlan's description of the function of habeas corpus. The Court never has defined the scope of the writ simply by reference to a perceived need to assure that an individual accused of crime is afforded a trial free of constitutional error. Rather, we have recognized that interests of comity and finality must also be considered in determining the proper scope of habeas review. Thus, if a defendant fails to comply with state procedural rules and is barred from litigating a particular constitutional claim in state court, the claim can be considered on federal habeas only if the defendant shows cause for the default and actual prejudice resulting therefrom. See Wainwright v. Sykes, 433 U.S. 72 (1977). We have declined to make the application of the procedural default rule dependent on the magnitude of the constitutional claim at issue, or on the State's interest in the enforcement of its procedural rule. . . .

Application of constitutional rules not in existence at the time a conviction became final seriously undermines the principle of finality which is essential to the operation of our criminal justice system. Without finality, the criminal law is deprived of much of its deterrent effect. The fact that life and liberty are at stake in criminal prosecutions "shows only that conventional notions of finality should not have as much place in criminal as in civil litigation, not that they should have none." Friendly, Is Innocence Irrelevant? Collateral Attacks on Criminal Judgments, 38 U. Chi. L. Rev. 142, 150 (1970).

The costs imposed upon the States by retroactive application of new rules of constitutional law on habeas corpus generally far outweigh the benefits of this application. [State] courts are understandably frustrated when they faithfully apply existing constitutional law only to have a federal court discover, during a habeas proceeding, new constitutional commands.

We find these criticisms to be persuasive, and we now adopt Justice Harlan's view of retroactivity for cases on collateral review. Unless they fall within an exception to the general rule, new constitutional rules of criminal procedure will not be applicable to those cases which have become final before the new rules are announced.

Petitioner's conviction became final in 1983. As a result, the rule petitioner urges would not be applicable to this case, which is on collateral review, unless it would fall within an exception. The first exception suggested by Justice Harlan . . . is not relevant here. Application of the fair cross section requirement to the petit jury would not accord constitutional protection to any primary activity whatsoever. The second exception suggested by Justice Harlan — that a new rule should be applied retroactively if it requires the observance of "those procedures that . . . are implicit in the concept of ordered liberty" — we apply with a modification.

[Our] cases have moved in the direction of reaffirming the relevance of the likely accuracy of convictions in determining the available scope of habeas review. See, e.g., Kuhlmann v. Wilson, 477 U.S. 436 (1986) (a successive habeas petition may be entertained only if the defendant makes a "colorable claim of factual innocence"); Murray v. Carrier, 477 U.S. 478 (1986) ("[W]here a constitutional violation has probably resulted in the conviction of one who is actually innocent, a federal habeas court may grant the writ even in the absence of a showing of cause for the procedural default"); Stone v. Powell, 428 U.S. 465 (1976) (removing Fourth Amendment claims from the scope of federal habeas review if the State has provided a full and fair opportunity for litigation creates no danger of denying a "safeguard against compelling an innocent man to suffer an unconstitutional loss of liberty"). [Concerns] about the difficulty in identifying both the existence and the value of accuracy-enhancing procedural rules can be addressed by limiting the scope of the second exception to those new procedures without which the likelihood of an accurate conviction is seriously diminished.

Because we operate from the premise that such procedures would be so central to an accurate determination of innocence or guilt, we believe it unlikely that many such components of basic due process have yet to emerge. We are also of the view that such rules are best illustrated by recalling the classic grounds for the issuance of a writ of habeas corpus — that the proceeding was dominated by mob violence; that the prosecutor knowingly made use of perjured testimony; or that the conviction was based on a confession extorted from the defendant by brutal methods.

An examination of our decision in *Taylor* applying the fair cross section requirement to the jury venire leads inexorably to the conclusion that adoption of the rule petitioner urges would be a far cry from the kind of absolute prerequisite to fundamental fairness that is "implicit in the concept of ordered liberty." [The] fair cross section requirement does not rest on the premise that every criminal trial, or any particular trial, is necessarily unfair because it is not conducted in accordance with what we determined to be the requirements of the Sixth Amendment. Because the absence of a fair cross section on the jury venire does not undermine the fundamental fairness that must underlie a conviction or seriously diminish the likelihood of obtaining an accurate conviction, we conclude that a rule requiring that petit juries be composed of a fair cross section of the community would not be a "bedrock procedural element" that would be retroactively applied under the second exception we have articulated.

Were we to recognize the new rule urged by petitioner in this case, we would have to give petitioner the benefit of that new rule even though it would not be applied retroactively to others similarly situated. . . . But the harm caused by the failure to treat similarly situated defendants alike cannot be exaggerated: such inequitable treatment hardly comports with the ideal of administration of justice with an even hand. . . .

If there were no other way to avoid rendering advisory opinions, we might well agree that the inequitable treatment described above is an insignificant cost for adherence to sound principles of decision-making. But there is a more principled way of dealing with the problem. We can simply refuse to announce a new rule in a given case unless the rule would be applied retroactively to the defendant in the case and to all others similarly situated. We think this approach is a sound one. Not only does it eliminate any problems of rendering advisory opinions, it also avoids the inequity resulting from the uneven application of new rules to similarly situated defendants. We therefore hold that, implicit in the retroactivity approach we adopt today, is the principle that habeas corpus cannot be used as a vehicle to create new constitutional rules of criminal procedure unless those rules would be applied retroactively to all defendants on collateral review through one of the two exceptions we have articulated. Because a decision extending the fair cross section requirement to the petit jury would not be applied retroactively to cases on collateral review under the approach we adopt today, we do not address petitioner's claim.

STEVENS, J., concurring in part and concurring in the judgment.
. . . I am persuaded this petitioner has alleged a violation of the Sixth Amendment. I also believe the Court should decide that question in his favor. I do not agree with Justice O'Connor's assumption that a ruling in petitioner's favor on the merits of the Sixth Amendment issue would require that his conviction be set aside.
When a criminal defendant claims that a procedural error tainted his conviction, an appellate court often decides whether error occurred before deciding whether that error requires reversal or should be classified as harmless. I would follow a parallel approach in cases raising novel questions of constitutional law on collateral review, first determining whether the trial process violated any of the petitioner's constitutional rights and then deciding whether the petitioner is entitled to relief. If error occurred, factors relating to retroactivity — most importantly, the magnitude of unfairness — should be examined before granting the petitioner relief. Proceeding in reverse, a plurality of the Court today declares that a new rule should not apply retroactively without ever deciding whether there is such a rule. . . .
I am persuaded that the Court should adopt Justice Harlan's analysis of retroactivity for habeas corpus cases as well for cases still on direct review. I do not agree, however, with the plurality's dicta proposing a "modification" of Justice Harlan's fundamental fairness exception. [Justice Harlan stated the exception this way]: "[In] some situations it might be that time and growth in social capacity, as well as judicial perceptions of what we can rightly demand of the adjudicatory process, will properly alter our understanding of the bedrock procedural elements that must be found to vitiate the fairness of a particular conviction." [Justice Harlan did not link] the fundamental fairness exception to factual innocence. [A] touchstone of factual innocence would provide little guidance in certain important types of cases, such as those challenging the constitutionality of capital sentencing hearings. Even when assessing errors at the guilt phase of a trial, factual innocence is too capricious a factor by which to determine if a procedural change is sufficiently "bedrock" or "watershed" to justify application of the fundamental fairness exception. In contrast, given our century-old proclamation that the Constitution does not allow exclusion of jurors because of race, Strauder v. West

Virginia, 100 U.S. 303 (1880), a rule promoting selection of juries free from racial bias clearly implicates concerns of fundamental fairness. . . .

BRENNAN, J., dissenting.

Today a plurality of this Court, without benefit of briefing and oral argument, adopts a novel threshold test for federal review of state criminal convictions on habeas corpus. It does so without regard for — indeed, without even mentioning — our contrary decisions over the past 35 years delineating the broad scope of habeas relief. . . .

For well over a century, we have read [the Habeas Corpus Act of 1867] to authorize federal courts to grant writs of habeas corpus whenever a person's liberty is unconstitutionally restrained. Nothing has happened since to persuade us to alter that judgment. . . . In particular, our decisions have made plain that the federal courts may collaterally review claims such as Teague's once state remedies have been exhausted. In Brown v. Allen, 344 U.S. 443 (1953), for example, we held that state prisoners alleging discrimination in the selection of members of the grand jury that indicted them and the petit jury that tried them were entitled to reconsideration of those allegations in federal court. . . .

Few decisions on appeal or collateral review are "dictated" by what came before. Most such cases involve a question of law that is at least debatable, permitting a rational judge to resolve the case in more than one way. Virtually no case that prompts a dissent on the relevant legal point, for example, could be said to be "dictated" by prior decisions. By the plurality's test, therefore, a great many cases could only be heard on habeas if the rule urged by the petitioner fell within one of the two exceptions the plurality has sketched. Those exceptions, however, are narrow. . . . The plurality's approach today can thus be expected to contract substantially the Great Writ's sweep.

Its impact is perhaps best illustrated by noting the abundance and variety of habeas cases we have decided in recent years that could never have been adjudicated had the plurality's new rule been in effect. [This observation applies to] numerous right-to-counsel and representation claims we have decided where the wrong alleged by the habeas petitioner was unlikely to have produced an erroneous conviction. See, e. g., Moran v. Burbine, 475 U.S. 412 (1986) (failure of police to inform defendant that attorney retained for him by somebody else sought to reach him does not violate Sixth Amendment); Morris v. Slappy, 461 U.S. 1 (1983) (state court's denial of continuance until public defender initially assigned to represent defendant became available does not violate Sixth Amendment); Ross v. Moffitt, 417 U.S. 600 (1974) (States need not provide indigent defendants with counsel on discretionary appeals).

Likewise, because the Fifth Amendment's privilege against self-incrimination is not an adjunct to the ascertainment of truth, claims that a petitioner's right to remain silent was violated would, if not dictated by earlier decisions, ordinarily fail to qualify under the plurality's second exception. . . . Habeas claims under the Double Jeopardy Clause will also be barred under the plurality's approach . . . , because they bear no relation to the petitioner's guilt or innocence. So, too, will miscellaneous due process and Sixth Amendment claims that relate only tangentially to a defendant's guilt or innocence. See, e.g., Bordenkircher v. Hayes, 434 U.S. 357 (1978) (no due process violation when prosecutor carries out threat to reindict on stiffer charge); Barker v. Wingo, 407 U.S. 514 (1972) (5-year delay does not violate right to speedy trial). . . .

These are massive changes, unsupported by precedent. They also lack a reasonable foundation. By exaggerating the importance of treating like cases alike and granting relief to all identically positioned habeas petitioners or none, the Court acts as if it has no choice but to follow a mechanical notion of fairness without pausing to consider sound principles of decisionmaking. Certainly it is desirable, in the interest of fairness, to accord the same treatment to all habeas petitioners with the same claims. . . . Other things being equal, our concern for fairness and finality ought to . . . lead us to render our decision in a case that comes to us on direct review.

Other things are not always equal, however. Sometimes a claim which, if successful, would create a new rule not appropriate for retroactive application on collateral review is better presented by a habeas case than by one on direct review. In fact, sometimes the claim is only presented on collateral review. In that case, while we could forgo deciding the issue in the hope that it would eventually be presented squarely on direct review, that hope might be misplaced, and even if it were in time fulfilled, the opportunity to check constitutional violations and to further the evolution of our thinking in some area of the law would in the meanwhile have been lost. In addition, by preserving our right and that of the lower federal courts to hear such claims on collateral review, we would not discourage their litigation on federal habeas corpus and thus not deprive ourselves and society of the benefit of decisions by the lower federal courts when we must resolve these issues ourselves. . . .

Notes

1. *New claims on habeas corpus.* Portions of the decision in Teague v. Lane were adopted by a plurality rather than a majority of the court, but later decisions confirmed the basic outlines of that case. See Butler v. McKellar, 494 U.S. 407 (1990). What qualifies as a "new" claim that is now unavailable to state prisoners seeking federal habeas corpus relief? The *Teague* court said that a new claim "breaks new ground or imposes a new obligation" on the government; a rule is new if "the result was not dictated by precedent." This latter formulation suggests that the class of new rules will be very large, for most litigated claims are not "dictated" by precedent. In later cases, the Supreme Court has declared that a decision is new if it rejects any "reasonable, good faith interpretations" of past cases. See O'Dell v. Netherland, 521 U.S. 151 (1997).

2. *Subconstitutional claims.* Federal habeas corpus still extends to all claims alleging violations of previously established constitutional law. It also reaches some, but not all, nonconstitutional claims based on federal law. In Stone v. Powell, 428 U.S. 465 (1976), the Court declared that claims based on the use of evidence obtained through illegal searches and seizures are not available on federal habeas. The exclusionary rule remedy, the Court concluded, is not itself a constitutional requirement and does not contribute to the accuracy of the guilt-innocence determination. On the other hand, in Withrow v. Williams, 507 U.S. 680 (1993), the Court decided that *Miranda* claims are available on federal habeas corpus, despite the fact that the "prophylactic" *Miranda* warnings are not themselves constitutional requirements.

Because the *Miranda* rule is a "fundamental" requirement of federal law that protects individual constitutional rights and effectively prevents some violations of those rights, violations of the rule can be presented in a federal habeas claim. See also Reed v. Farley, 512 U.S. 339 (1994) (violations of federal statutes applicable to state criminal proceedings are cognizable on federal habeas corpus if the violation shows a "fundamental" defect that results in a "miscarriage of justice," or if the violation presents "special circumstances"). Are habeas corpus cases the proper forum for the Supreme Court to signal its retreat from earlier constitutional rulings that it now considers ill advised or less than "fundamental"? What are the alternatives?

3. *Cognizable issues under the 1996 statute.* The Congress made major changes to the federal habeas corpus statutes in 1996. These changes are probably the most important since the passage of the 1867 Act. A key provision of the new statute, §2254(d), says:

> An application for a writ of habeas corpus on behalf of a person in custody pursuant to the judgment of a State court shall not be granted with respect to any claim that was adjudicated on the merits in State proceedings unless the adjudication of the claim —
> (1) resulted in a decision that was contrary to, or involved an unreasonable application of, clearly established Federal law as determined by the Supreme Court of the United States; or (2) resulted in a decision that was based on an unreasonable determination of the facts in light of the evidence presented in the State proceeding.

Readers of the revised statute have acknowledged that protracted debate over the statutory language, along with the rich case law at work in the background, makes this an exceptionally difficult statute to interpret. It is clear that the Congress wanted to amend the existing statute to require federal habeas courts to give greater weight to the legal decisions of state courts that have considered a petitioner's claims; it is equally clear that Congress did not intend to give state court decisions binding *res judicata* effect. What would make a state court's application of established federal law "unreasonable"? Does the new statute codify *Teague,* or does it do something more or less than that decision? See Horn v. Banks, 536 U.S. 266 (2002) (*Teague* retroactivity limit is distinct from AEDPA analysis). What has become of *Teague*'s two exceptions?

Other sections of the 1996 statute create filing deadlines for federal petitions: Roughly speaking, federal petitions must be filed within one year of the end of the relevant state proceedings. The statute also limits evidentiary hearings in federal court, limits successive federal petitions, and creates special habeas corpus rules for capital cases in those states that "opt in" to the special rules by appointing counsel for indigent petitioners.

The Supreme Court has begun to answer some of the questions about the meaning of the key statutory language: "a decision that was contrary to, or involved an unreasonable application of, clearly established Federal law." In Williams v. Taylor, 529 U.S. 362 (2000), the Court declared that the 1996 statute placed a "new constraint" on the power of federal courts to hear challenges to state convictions. Under the first clause (the "contrary to" clause), a federal habeas court may grant relief if the state court "arrives at a conclusion opposite to that reached by this Court on a question of law" or "confronts facts that are materially indistinguishable from a relevant Supreme Court precedent and arrives at a result opposite to ours."

A routine application of the federal rule to different facts would not qualify for relief under the "contrary to" clause, even if a federal court might have applied the federal rule differently to those facts.

As for the second, "unreasonable application" clause, a federal habeas court should ask whether the state court's application of federal law was "objectively unreasonable." The federal habeas court should not simply ask whether any "reasonable jurist" would apply the federal rule in the same way as the state court did in the case at hand. On the other hand, "unreasonable" is not the same as "incorrect." A federal court might believe that the state court applied federal law incorrectly, and yet decide that the application was reasonable (and therefore unreviewable in habeas corpus).

4. *Harmless error.* When a court declares on direct appeal that some error took place at trial, it will nevertheless uphold the conviction if the error was "harmless beyond a reasonable doubt." Chapman v. California, 386 U.S. 18 (1967). Until recently the same harmless error standard applied to federal habeas corpus proceedings: A cognizable constitutional error would lead the federal court to grant habeas corpus relief (typically ordering a new trial) unless the error was harmless beyond a reasonable doubt. However, in Brecht v. Abrahamson, 507 U.S. 619 (1993), the Court changed the harmless error standard for federal courts to use in habeas corpus proceedings. Now the standard for determining whether habeas relief must be granted is whether the error "had substantial and injurious effect or influence in determining the jury's verdict." Does this change in the harmless error standard further the interest in finality of judgments? Does a federal court respect the comity of state courts by finding that constitutional errors occurred and then leaving the judgment undisturbed unless the error had a "substantial and injurious effect" on the verdict?

5. *Habeas and federal appellate review.* Views about the wisdom of the *Teague* case and the statutory amendments of 1996 depend on what one considers to be the proper function of federal habeas corpus. For those who contend that the basic purpose of habeas corpus is to prevent injustice in individual cases, what would be the best reaction to *Teague* and to the 1996 amendments? Another potential view emphasizes the distinctive abilities of federal courts, and looks to habeas corpus to assure a federal adjudication of every federal claim. This point of view is difficult to square with the reality that state courts often adjudicate federal claims. Professor Barry Friedman has sketched out a third position: Federal habeas corpus is best suited as a proxy for federal direct appellate review. To the extent that a state prisoner could at one time expect the U.S. Supreme Court to exercise direct appellate review in an era when caseload and certiorari practice made that review meaningful, federal habeas corpus could provide state prisoners with an alternative federal appellate court in an era when the U.S. Supreme Court is no longer practically available. See Barry Friedman, Pas de Deux: The Supreme Court and the Habeas Courts, 66 S. Cal. L. Rev. 2467 (1993); Barry Friedman, A Tale of Two Habeas, 73 Minn. L. Rev. 247 (1988). If this is indeed a proper function of federal habeas review, what does it imply about *Teague* and the 1996 amendments?

6. *Appellate courts as gatekeepers.* The Antiterrorism and Effective Death Penalty Act of 1996 gives federal appeals courts the power to block some habeas petitions from reaching the appeals court. The statute says that a party cannot appeal the final order in a post-conviction proceeding to a court of appeals, unless a circuit judge

issues a "certificate of appealability," or "COA." The petitioner may obtain such a certificate only by making a substantial showing of the denial of a constitutional right. 28 U.S.C. §2253(c). The federal courts reading this provision broadly to allow appeals in a wide range of claims. See Hohn v. United States, 524 U.S. 236 (1998) (petitioner was complaining about sufficiency of evidence, a constitutional claim covered by COA statute). Petitioners may show a denial of a "constitutional right" even if the district court refused to hear the merits of the claim. According to Slack v. McDaniel, 529 U.S. 473 (2000), when the district court dismisses a petition on procedural grounds, the "substantial showing necessary to obtain a COA has two components. One component deals with the underlying constitutional claim, while another deals with the district court's procedural holding. A COA should issue if the petitioner shows that "jurists of reason" would find it "debatable" whether (1) the person was denied a constitutional right, and (2) the district court was correct in its procedural ruling.

7. *Judicial attitudes toward habeas corpus.* Do federal and state judges have different attitudes about the importance of federal habeas corpus review of state convictions? In a 1996 survey, federal and state judges were asked if elected state judges have "sufficient independence to make difficult decisions that may favor the rights of convicted offenders." Among federal judges, 74 percent replied "yes," while 81 percent of the state judges replied "yes." When asked if there is a "need for continued existence and availability" of federal habeas review of state convictions, 29 percent of the state judges answered "no," while only 7 percent of the federal judges gave the same answer. Most of the state and federal judges approved of the restrictions on federal habeas review created by Rehnquist Court decisions. See Christopher E. Smith & Darwin L. Burke, Judges' Views on Habeas Corpus: A Comparison of State and Federal Judges, 22 Okla. City U. L. Rev. 1125 (1997). Should legislators consider the views of judges about habeas corpus when debating changes in the statutes governing post-conviction review? If so, for what specific purpose?

Problem 11-3. New Law

The definition of new claims under *Teague* creates a bind for petitioners. They might want to establish that a claim is "new" as a way to explain "cause" for a failure to avoid state procedural default or to obtain a successive federal petition. At the same time, they will need to establish that the claim is not new within the meaning of the retroactivity bar established in *Teague*. Can a claim be considered new for some purposes and not for others? Consider the following facts:

> Henry Griggs and Henry Crawford were accused of murdering James Bush, an enforcer for the then-notorious Phenix City Gang. Griggs and Crawford were tried separately and were defended by lawyers hired by Crawford; both were convicted of murder and sentenced to life imprisonment in 1954. Counsel for Griggs filed a motion for a new trial but evidently did not pursue the appeal. His motion was dismissed for want of prosecution.
>
> In 1990, Griggs petitioned for a writ of habeas corpus, arguing that the trial court erred in not setting aside his conviction because then-Code §38-416, which precluded an accused from testifying under oath on his own behalf, effectively impaired his ability to mount a defense and violated his rights under the Sixth and Fourteenth

Amendments. Although the statute did declare an accused incompetent to testify under oath in his own behalf at his trial, §38-415 allowed the accused to make an unsworn statement to the jury, a statement unguided by the accused's counsel and not subject to cross-examination.

If Griggs had filed a federal habeas petition in 1960, before Fay v. Noia, should the court grant relief on a claim that he was denied his Fourteenth Amendment right to due process? (Remember that the Sixth Amendment right to counsel was not incorporated until Gideon v. Wainwright, in 1963, and the Fifth Amendment privilege against self-incrimination was not incorporated until Malloy v. Hogan, in 1964.) How should the court rule if Griggs filed his claim in 1966, after the decision in Fay v. Noia? What result in 1995, post-*Teague*? What result in 1999, after the appearance of new statutory federal standards under the Effective Death Penalty Act of 1996?

In Ferguson v. Georgia, 365 U.S. 570 (1961), the Supreme Court ruled this provision of the Georgia Code unconstitutional, holding: "Georgia, consistently with the Fourteenth Amendment, could not, in the context of §38-416, deny appellant the right to have his counsel question him to elicit his statement." The Georgia statute was unusual at the time. Indeed, Georgia was the only state (and the only jurisdiction in the common-law world) to retain the common-law rule that a criminal defendant is incompetent to testify under oath in his own behalf at his trial. Every other state had abolished the disqualification by the turn of the century. Does this change your analysis in 1960 (pre-*Fay*)? In 1966 (after *Fay*)? In 1995 (after *Teague*)? In 1999 (after the 1996 amendments)? Compare Griggs v. State, 425 S.E.2d 644 (Ga. 1993).

Does this case suggest that Justice Harlan was right to keep a "fundamental fairness" exception to the retroactivity bar, and that *Teague* was wrong to reject that element of Harlan's position? What does this case indicate about the interrelationship between the doctrines of bypass and retroactivity?

Notes

1. *New enough, but not too new.* Before *Teague*, a claim based on "new" law was a strong foundation for a habeas petition. A habeas petitioner who had failed to raise a claim earlier could explain this "procedural default" by saying that the newness of the legal theory was the "cause" of the default. Furthermore, the retroactivity rules on direct appeal and on habeas corpus allowed for a greater "backward" impact from important new decisions. Following *Teague*—which is as much a retroactivity decision as it is a revision of the scope of federal habeas — a claim based on new law has become far more difficult and subtle. The attorney must now demonstrate that the desired outcome would be new enough to meet the "cause and prejudice" standard to avoid a procedural default, but not so new that the claim is barred from federal habeas corpus under *Teague*.

2. *The inevitability of new law claims.* Retroactivity rules respond to a major reality of our legal system: Laws change, and convictions obtained properly under one set of procedural rules would not stand if a newer set of rules were to apply. Persons convicted under the old rules will ask, in any available forum, whether courts (and society at large) can tolerate punishing a person based on procedural rules that are

now considered inadequate and unjust. Sometimes these claims will be compelling. A legal culture that aspires to equal treatment of litigants and to the idea of progress (that is, today's understanding of justice is an improvement upon yesterday's understanding of justice) will seek a way to respond to such claims. How would you expect federal habeas corpus to accommodate claims based on new law, even after *Teague* and the 1996 statutory amendments? How would you expect retroactivity rules on appeal and on collateral attack in state courts to change in light of these federal developments? What kind of pressures might restrictive collateral review place on the executive branch in considering requests that it exercise its power to pardon convicted offenders?

Table of Cases

Index